W9-BKB-334

© AVALON TRAVEL

HANDBOOKS

MAINE

HILARY NANGLE

MAINE

Contents

Discover Maine

Tipping the northeasternmost corner of the United States and comprising 33,215 square miles, Maine boldly promotes itself as "The Way Life Should Be." Not to say that everything's perfect, mind you, but Maine is an extraordinarily special place, where the air is clear, the water is pure, and the traditional traits of honesty, thrift, and ruggedness remain refreshingly appealing.

From the glacier-scoured beaches of the Southern Coast, around spruce-studded islands and Acadia's granite shores to the craggy cliffs Down East, Maine's coastline follows a zigzagging route that would measure about 5,500 miles if you stretched it taut. Eons ago, glaciers came crushing down from the north, squeezing Maine's coastline into a wrinkled landscape with countless bony fingers reaching toward the sea. Each peninsula has its own character, as does each island, each city, and each village.

But don't stop at the coast; venture inland to Maine's playground: 6,000 lakes and ponds, 32,000 miles of rivers, and 17 million acres of timberlands for hiking and biking, skiing and snowmobiling, paddling and fishing. Intrepid Appalachian Trail hikers finish at the summit of Katahdin, Maine's tallest peak; determined canoeists spend a week on the Allagash, a water lifeline through the wilderness.

Pair natural highs with human pleasures: fine and quirky museums, theatrical and musical performances, artisan studios and art galleries, designer boutiques and specialty shops.

Lobster, of course, is king, but don't overlook luscious wild blueberries, sweet Maine maple syrup, delicious farmstead cheeses, and the homemade pies and preserves sold at roadside stands and farmers markets. Access to this bounty is why talented chefs are drawn here. But balance a fancy meal with a beanhole or chowder *suppah,* where you can share a table with locals, the umpteenth-generation Mainers who add character to this special place: the fishermen who make their living from the bone-chilling waters, the lumbermen who know every nook and cranny of the forested wilderness, the farmers who tame the rocky fields. If you're lucky, you might hear a genuine Maine accent (hint: *Ayuh* isn't so much a word as a sharp two-part intake of breath).

A student of Maine-born author Mary Ellen Chase once mused, "Maine is different from all other states, isn't it? I suppose that's because God never quite finished it." Maine may indeed be a work in progress, but it's a masterwork.

Planning Your Trip

▶ WHERE TO GO

Southern Coast

Sandy beaches occasionally punctuated by rocky headlands are the jewels of Maine's Southern Coast, but this region also oozes history. Colonial roots are preserved in historical buildings; fishing traditions echo in fish shacks turned trendy boutiques; the arts legacy is preserved in museums and galleries. Complementing (or detracting) from these are Route 1's endless shopping opportunities: antiques, boutiques, and factory outlets.

Greater Portland

In this compact region are rocky coastline and sandy beaches, lighthouses and lobster shacks, coastal islands and L. L. Bean. Brine-scented air, cackling gulls, lobster boats, and fishing trawlers give notice that this is a seafaring town, but it's also Maine's cultural center, rich in museums and performing-arts centers, and the state's shopping hub. Increasingly,

Portland is earning national repute as a destination for culinary travelers.

Mid-Coast Region

No region of Maine has more lobster shacks or as rich a maritime history as this peninsula-rich stretch of coastline. Shaped by powerful freshwater rivers, the Mid-Coast is dotted with traditional fishing villages as well as towns that were once thriving ports, mill towns, or shipbuilding centers. The Maine Maritime Museum preserves that heritage; Bath Iron Works continues it; and the grand homes, brick townscapes, renovated mills, and plentiful shops brimming with maritime treasures and worldly antiques keep it alive.

Penobscot Bay

With the Camden hills as a backdrop, island-studded Penobscot Bay delivers the Maine coast in microcosm. Boat-filled harbors, sandy pocket beaches, soaring spruce trees,

Postcard-perfect harbors await those who mosey down Mid-Coast peninsulas.

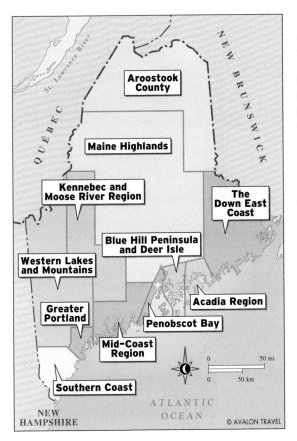

villages. Locals, a blend of summer rusticators, genteel retirees, artists, boatbuilders, and back-to-the-landers, have worked diligently to preserve not only the landscape but also the heritage. It's a fine place to kick back, relax, and savor the good life.

Acadia Region

Mountains tumbling to the sea, ocean waves crashing upon granite ledges, serene lakes and soaring cliffs—Acadia has it all in spades. Watch the sun rise out of the Atlantic from Cadillac Mountain's summit, mosey along Acadia National Park's icon-rich Park Loop Road, hike through forests and up coastal peaks, pedal the famed carriage roads, and paddle coastal nooks and crannies. Intimate yet expansive, wild yet civilized, Acadia is as accessible or as remote as you desire.

and lighthouses illuminating treacherous ledges pepper the shoreline. Gentrifying fishing villages neighbor cosmopolitan towns; traditional seafarers share driveways with summer rusticators. Antiques shops, art galleries, artisans' studios, and museums are as plentiful as lobster boats.

Blue Hill Peninsula and Deer Isle

Water, water everywhere. Around nearly every bend is a river or stream, a cove, a boat-filled harbor, or a serene pond. It's an inspired and inspiring landscape dotted with historic homes and forts and classic fishing

The Down East Coast

Remote, rural, and sparsely populated, this is what many folks picture when they envision Maine. Here the pace slows, traffic subsides, and fast-food joints and traffic lights all but disappear. Blueberry barrens color the landscape; huge tides rule daily life. Two national wildlife reserves and numerous preserves lure hikers and bird-watchers, but the main attraction is the rugged and wild expanse of coastline.

Aroostook County

When you really want to leave the tourists behind, Aroostook awaits. It's vast, rural,

The dock at Twin Pine Camps, near Millinocket, is well situated for taking in the grandeur of Katahdin.

undeveloped, and few folks make the effort to discover Maine's largest county. This is Maine's original melting pot, home to Acadian heritage sites, Maine's Swedish Colony, and Amish settlements. Remnants of the bloodless Aroostook War with Canada dot the border, including the original 1839 Fort Kent Blockhouse. In winter, world-class trails and training centers lure cross-country skiers, and 1,600 miles of groomed snowmobile trails connect to an international network.

Maine Highlands

Here's where tar gives way to dirt, where it's possible to hike, paddle, and play undisturbed. The Maine Highlands are Maine's wilderness playground, home to Baxter State Park, with miles of hiking trails, including those on mile-high Katahdin, the official terminus of the Appalachian Trail; the Allagash Wilderness Waterway, a paddling route through the wilderness; the Penobscot River, a favorite for white-water fans and anglers; and Moosehead Lake, where you can cruise in historical fashion aboard the *Kate*.

Kennebec and Moose River Region

Route 201, which follows the Kennebec River, is the major thoroughfare between Québec City and the coast. "Benedict Arnold Slept Here" signs are posted all along the Old Canada Road National Scenic Byway, which follows his famous march on Québec.

IF YOU HAVE . . .

If you truly want to see all of Maine, you'll need three weeks to a month, especially if you're someone who would rather do than just look. If your plans don't permit getting away for that long, the best strategy is to focus on a region or two and immerse yourself.

- **ONE WEEK:** Explore Kennebunkport, Greater Portland, and Acadia National Park.

- **TWO WEEKS:** Add Bath, Camden, and Rockland, Deer Isle, and Greenville or Rangeley.

- **THREE WEEKS:** Add Monhegan Island, the Down East Coast, Millinocket, Baxter State Park, Bethel, Sebago, and Poland Springs.

In Augusta, Maine's capital, the Maine State Museum is an excellent introduction to the state, and Old Fort Western is the nation's oldest stockade fort. Discover the real Golden Pond with a cruise on the Great Pond Mail Boat. Of course, a white-water rafting trip down the Kennebec is a must.

Western Lakes and Mountains

Generations of rusticators and summer campers have long favored the lakes pocketed in the mountains of western Maine. Cruise Long Lake on the *Songo River Queen II*, cast a line in the Rangeley Lakes, hike through Grafton Notch State Park, or spend a leisurely afternoon splashing in Sebago and you'll understand why. Poke around Poland Spring, now famed for bottled water but also the site of a few intriguing museums; visit the last inhabited Shaker community; or shop for antiques in Cornish. In winter, major alpine resorts keep things hopping.

▶ WHEN TO GO

Late May-mid-October is prime season, with July and August, the warmest months, being the busiest. Recreation options seem unlimited, and festivals and special events crowd the calendar. Of course, that means peak-season rates, congested roads, and difficulty getting reservations at the best restaurants and accommodations. Late June and late August tend to be a bit quieter, and everything is still in full swing.

September-mid-October is arguably the best season to travel in Maine. Days are warm and mostly dry, nights are cool, fog is rare, the bugs are gone, and the crowds are few. Foliage is turning by early October, usually reaching its peak by mid-month.

In winter, especially inland, skiing, snowshoeing, and ice-skating replace hiking, biking, and boating. On the coast, choices in lodging, dining, and activities are fewer, but rates are generally far lower. In areas with solid year-round populations, life goes on full tilt.

Farmers markets pepper Maine's rural roads.

Explore Maine

▶ THE BEST OF MAINE

It's a tough job to single out Maine's sightseeing icons. It offers so many. Unless you have years to spend, such a big chunk of real estate needs some whittling to be made explorable. This itinerary exposes you to a good part of Maine while taking in many of the state's icons in 20 days.

The downside: You'll be doing a fair bit of driving, primarily on two-lane roads where speeds through towns are often 25 mph or lower, and during the season when road construction is a fact of life. While this itinerary is planned as 20 days, if your schedule permits, you'll be rewarded if you spend longer in any of the locations.

Book your first two nights' lodging in Portland, then book nights 3 and 4 in Rockland or vicinity; 5 and 6 on Mount Desert Island; 7 and 8 in the Millinocket area; 9 and 10 in the Moosehead region; 11 and 12 in The Forks; 13 and 14 in Rangeley; 15 and 16 in Bethel; and 17–19 in the Sebago area.

Day 1

Stretch your legs after your journey to Maine with a refreshing walk on Ogunquit Beach, one of Maine's prettiest and proof that there's plenty of sand along Maine's fabled rockbound coast. Afterward, head to Kennebunkport and indulge your passions: shopping in the boutiques and galleries that crowd Dock Square, taking a walking tour to view the historic homes, or enjoying a leisurely drive along the waterfront.

Day 2

Begin the day with a visit to Portland Head Light, a Cape Elizabeth landmark and Maine's oldest lighthouse (1791) at the edge of 94-acre Fort Williams Park. Spend the afternoon in the Portland Museum of Art, Maine's premier art museum, smack in the heart of the state's largest city. End the day with a sunset cruise on Casco Bay.

Day 3

Make a pilgrimage to giant sports retailer and outfitter L. L. Bean, hub of the hubbub in Freeport, Maine's outlet bonanza. Either spend the morning shopping or taking a Walk-on Adventure class. In the afternoon, visit the Maine Maritime Museum in Bath, 10 acres of indoor and outdoor exhibits celebrating the state's nautical heritage.

MAINE COLLEGE TOUR

If you have children or relatives thinking about college, plan a vacation around visiting Maine's college campuses.

BRUNSWICK: BOWDOIN COLLEGE

Bowdoin's campus is in downtown Brunswick and hosts many of the Mid-Coast town's cultural institutions, including the **Bowdoin College Museum of Art** and the **Peary-MacMillan Arctic Museum.** During summer months, the **Bowdoin International Music Festival** presents concerts in various campus locales and Pickard Theater is home to the **Maine State Music Theatre.** Steps off campus are the **Joshua L. Chamberlain Museum,** which honors the Union Army hero, a Bowdoin grad, and **First Paris Church,** where Harriet Beecher Stowe was inspired to write *Uncle Tom's Cabin.* Browse downtown Brunswick's shops and mosey down the Harpswell peninsula.

LEWISTON: BATES COLLEGE

Just outside downtown Lewiston, the Bates College campus is home to the **Bates College Museum of Art** and the **Olin Arts Center.** Free lakeside concerts are held during the summer months.

The **Bates Mill** and **Museum L-A** in town explain the city's industrial heritage. There is a bird sanctuary on the outskirts of town and within an easy day-trip are the **Shaker Museum** and **Poland Spring** museums.

WATERVILLE: COLBY COLLEGE

You can spy the Georgian-style buildings on the Colby campus from I-95. The **Colby College Museum of Art** is a destination unto itself, with major holdings in American and contemporary art, including a wing dedicated to works by Alex Katz. If the weather's fine, pack a picnic and take to the trails of **Perkins Arboretum and Bird Sanctuary.**

Plan a visit during the warmer months, when

Colby College is a private, liberal arts institution in Waterville with a gorgeous campus.

you can spend a day playing in the **Belgrade Lakes area,** perhaps paddling one of the lakes or taking a cruise on the **Great Pond Mail Boat,** the inspiration for the movie *On Golden Pond.*

ORONO: UNIVERSITY OF MAINE

The sprawling flagship campus of the University of Maine is home to the **Hudson Museum, Maynard F. Jordan Planetarium, Lyle E. Littlefield Ornamental Trail Garden,** and the **Page Farm and Home Museum,** as well as the **Collins Center for the Arts,** a renowned performing arts center. The **University of Maine Museum of Art** is in nearby Bangor.

BAR HARBOR: COLLEGE OF THE ATLANTIC

The oceanfront campus of the environmentally oriented College of the Atlantic is home to the kid-friendly **George B. Dorr Natural History Museum** and the **Dive-In Theater Boat Cruise,** a must for youngsters, but quite enthralling for adults, too.

The campus is within walking distance of downtown Bar Harbor, the site of the **Bar Harbor Whale Museum** and the **Abbe Museum. Acadia National Park** is also nearby.

Day 4

Take a day trip to Monhegan Island from Port Clyde. This car-free, carefree gem, about a dozen miles off the coast, is laced with hiking trails and has earned a place in art history books as the Artists' Island.

Day 5

Drive or hike to the top of Mount Battie, in Camden Hills State Park on the northern fringe of Camden. The vistas are magnificent, with the broad sweep of Penobscot Bay for a backdrop. Then continue up the coast to Mount Desert Island and begin your explorations of Acadia National Park. If you've arrived on the island before noon, pick up a picnic lunch and then drive the Park Loop Road, a perfect introduction to Acadia that covers many of the highlights.

Day 6

Welcome the day by watching the sunrise from the summit of Cadillac Mountain. Afterward, if you haven't either driven or bicycled the Park Loop, do so. If you have,

then explore the park: Go hiking, bicycling, or sea kayaking, take a carriage ride, or book an excursion boat to Islesford or for whale-watching.

Day 7

Depart Mount Desert Island and head inland to Millinocket, perhaps detouring to see Katahdin Iron Works but arriving in time for a late-afternoon moose safari.

Day 8

Venture into Baxter State Park for a day of hiking or rent a canoe and paddle one of the many lakes and rivers.

Day 9

Drive across the Golden Road to Greenville and Moosehead Lake. If time permits, continue to Rockwood and take the shuttle over to Kineo for a hike.

Day 10

Take a cruise on the *Kate* and prowl around the area, perhaps driving to Pittston Farm or hiking.

The lawns in front of the Island Inn on Monhegan Island deliver views of the harbor and barren Manana Island.

Keep an eye out for moose while traveling in the Maine Highlands region.

Day 11

Drive to The Forks via the Old Canada Road National Scenic Byway and stretch your legs on a hike into Moxie Falls.

Day 12

Go white-water rafting on the Kennebec River.

Day 13

Take the scenic drive to Rangeley via Route 16, keeping an eye out for moose along the way. Work out the driving kinks with either an afternoon paddle or a hike.

Day 14

Take a lazy—or not—day: Hike, swim, paddle, explore, or simply sit and enjoy the environment.

Day 15

Head south on Route 17 over Height of Land, perhaps stopping in Coos Canyon to try your hand at panning for gold. Continue to Grafton Notch State Park.

Day 16

Prowl around Bethel's historic district and explore the Mahoosuc section of the White Mountains.

Day 17

Snake southward through the White Mountain foothills, perhaps exploring Waterford Flats or Lovell.

Day 18

Poke around Bridgton and Naples, and perhaps take a cruise on the *Songo River Queen II*.

Day 19

Visit the Shaker Museum, the world's last inhabited Shaker colony, and tour Poland Spring; there's a lot more here than bottled water.

Day 20

Head home after a dip in Sebago Lake.

Mountain-ringed Rangeley Lake is a favored spot for boating.

FOLIAGE FAVORITES

Maine tends to get fewer leaf peepers than other New England states, which means roads are less congested and it's usually easier to get lodging and dining reservations, especially if you follow one of these suggested itineraries. But do plan in advance, and *sh*, don't tell too many people. For help in planning, consult www.mainefoliage.com.

MOOSEHEAD AND THE KENNEBEC RIVER

Few leaf peepers make it as far north as Greenville, but those who make the effort are well rewarded. Plan a minimum of two nights, ideally three or longer, and spend one full day driving one of the state's most spectacular foliage routes.

The Route: Loop from Greenville over to the Kennebec River and back on Routes 5 to Jackman, 201 south to Bingham, 16 east to Abbott, then 5 north to return to Greenville. You'll parallel the shoreline of Moosehead Lake before arriving in Rockwood. As you head south the views are spectacular along the Old Canada Road Scenic Byway. Dip into the Attean View rest area for views extending over the lakes and peaks toward Canada. Need to stretch the legs? Consider the relatively easy hike to Moxie Falls. From here to Bingham, Route 201 can be really spectacular, as it snakes along the Kennebec River.

Pleasant diversions: Cruise Moosehead Lake aboard the *Kate*, take a flightseeing tour or a moose safari, or drive to a remote sporting camp for lunch.

BETHEL AND RANGELEY

Combine New England's trees with lakes and mountains and you have the best of all worlds when it comes to viewing autumn's palette. Divide your lodging between Bethel and Rangeley.

The Route: From Bethel, take Route 26 north to Errol, New Hampshire, then Route 16 north to Rangeley. Return via Route 17 south to Route 2 west. Heading north, you'll cut through Grafton Notch State Park; the rest of the drive is mostly through undeveloped lands speckled with mountains, lakes, and streams. Returning south from Rangeley, the Rangeley Lakes National Scenic Byway passes over Height of Land. The entire route is through prime moose country, so keep alert.

Pleasant diversions: Hike in Grafton Notch or Rangeley, paddle the Rangeley Lakes, or pan for gold in Coos Canyon.

ACADIA AND DOWN EAST

To the magic foliage mix of lakes and mountains, add the ocean and top it off with wild blueberry barrens, which turn crimson in foliage season. Book lodging in the Schoodic region.

The Route: From Hancock, mosey inland on Route 182 along the Blackwoods Scenic Byway to Cherryfield. Then head south on Route 1A to Milbridge, continuing south on Route 1. In Steuben, dip down Pigeon Hill Road to the Petit Manan section of the Maine Coastal Islands National Wildlife Reserve before continuing south on Route 1 to Route 186, which loops around the Schoodic Peninsula.

Pleasant diversions: Bike the Schoodic Loop, hike Black or Schoodic Mountains, detour north from Cherryfield to Deblois to see the blueberry barrens, or browse art galleries.

The fall color in Maine's Western Mountains is spectacular.

► LIGHTHOUSES, LOBSTER, AND L. L. BEAN

Maine's biggest draws are the three L's: lighthouses, lobster, and L. L. Bean. Maine's 64 lighthouses stretch from York's Nubble to candy-striped West Quoddy Head in Lubec. Lobster, of course, can be found practically everywhere along the coast, but the best way to enjoy it is at a no-fuss lobster shack. L. L. Bean's ever-expanding campus in Freeport is the massive outdoor retailer's mother ship, but it also has an outlet in Ellsworth.

This six-day tour concentrates on the Greater Portland, Mid-Coast, and Penobscot Bay regions. Book your first night's lodging in Portland, the second two in Damariscotta or Newcastle, and the last two in the Thomaston-Rockland area. If you're arriving by air, use Portland International Jetport.

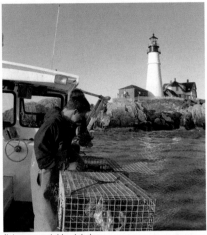

fisherman catching lobster

Day 1

Try to arrive in Portland in time to enjoy an afternoon cruise with Lucky Catch Lobster Tours; perhaps you'll catch your dinner. If not, you can still enjoy a lobster on the waterfront.

Day 2

Loop out to South Portland and Cape Elizabeth to visit Spring Point Ledge Light and Portland Head Light, a Maine icon. You won't find a better setting for lunch than The Lobster Shack, with views of crashing surf and Cape Elizabeth Light. In the afternoon, consider visiting the Portland Museum of Art to view masterworks by Maine-related artists or book a sail amid the islands of Casco Bay. Still craving lobster? Try an inspired version by one of Maine's nationally recognized chefs (reservations required).

Day 3

Get an early start and begin at famed outlet store L. L. Bean in Freeport. You might even take a Walk-on Adventure with Bean's Discovery School. In the afternoon, visit the Maine Maritime Museum in Bath, and if time permits, take a lighthouse cruise on the Kennebec River. Perhaps mosey down

Outdoor retailer and outfitter L. L. Bean put Freeport on America's shopping map.

to Georgetown for dinner at Five Islands or stop in Wiscasset for a lobster roll.

Day 4

Spend the morning in Boothbay Harbor, stepping back in time for a visit with light keeper Joseph Muise and his family on a Burnt Island Tour. In the late afternoon, drive down to Pemaquid Point to view Pemaquid Point Lighthouse, perhaps climbing to the top. Be sure to visit the Fisherman's Museum in the keeper's house. End the day with lobster in the rough in Round Pond.

Day 5

Begin the day with a visit to Marshall Point Lighthouse Museum in Port Clyde, and then board the mail boat to Monhegan Island. Be sure to visit the museum in the lighthouse keeper's house. Lunch? Lobster at Fish House Fish, of course.

Day 6

Greet the day with a sunrise walk out on the breakwater to Rockland Breakwater Lighthouse. Afterward, tour the Maine Lighthouse Museum and Farnsworth Art Museum. In the afternoon, take a lighthouse-themed cruise or sea kayak tour out of Rockport or Rockland. End the day and your lobster-infused vacation at the James Beard Award–winning lobster shack Waterman's Beach Lobster in South Thomaston. En route, take the short side jaunt out to Owls Head Light in Owls Head.

Few settings can compare with that of the Marshall Point Lighthouse Museum in Port Clyde.

MAINE OFF THE BEATEN TRACK

West Branch Pond Camps, a traditional Maine sporting camp surrounded by conservation lands near Greenville

You've been there, done that, and seen all the icons. If you have a sense of adventure, consider poking around some of the state's nooks and crannies.

AROOSTOOK LOOP

Few visitors make it to **Aroostook County,** and that's a pity, because it is a rural gem with great outdoor resources, including **Aroostook State Park** and intriguing heritage sites, such as the **Acadian Village.** Because of the sheer immensity of the county, you'll want to plan at least a full week.

Be sure to explore the back roads for big views and surprises. Along Route 2 between Sherman Mills and Houlton is **Golden Ridge** with panoramic views, a railroad museum, and an Amish colony. Route 164 loops out to the **Salmon Brook Historical Society** and **Woodland Bog Preserve.** And tucked just off Route 161 is **Maine's Swedish Colony.**

WAY DOWN EAST

Few folks travel northeast of the Acadia region, but those who do are rewarded with a more authentic Maine experience. From **Milbridge** through **Calais,** the Maine Coast has a much different feel than points south. Fishing villages have yet to be gussied up or gentrified, and harbors are filled with working boats, not yachts. Museums, such as the **Sardine History Museum** and **Maine Central Model Railroad** in Jonesport, the **Ruggles House** in Columbia Falls, and the **Tides Institute and Museum of Art** in Eastport, are small in size but rich in local heritage.

Coastal hiking trails and wildlife preserves attract birders, and if you continue inland to **Grand Lake Stream,** you'll stumble upon an anglers' paradise.

SPORTING CAMP ADVENTURE

There's no finer way to experience Maine's forested wilderness than to immerse yourself in it at a traditional sporting camp. Created more than a century ago to cater to the needs of hunters and anglers, today most are wonderful family destinations during the summer. You can hike, fish, paddle, swim, search for moose or other wildlife, or simply relax and enjoy the away-from-it-all experience.

Sporting camps dot Maine's North Country, with concentrations around the **Rangeley Lakes** and along the waterways surrounding **Baxter State Park** and **Moosehead Lake.**

▶ QUIRKY MAINE

While Maine is rich in classic museums and heritage sites, it's also home to quite a few quirky sites. For a different take on Maine, plan a vacation around this eight-day itinerary.

Book your first two nights in Portland, the next two in the Pemaquid Peninsula area, nights 4 and 5 in Millinocket, and the last two in Jonesport.

Days 1 and 2: Greater Portland

Begin in Portland, home to two of Maine's most unusual museums, The International Cryptozoology Museum, filled with artifacts and kitsch highlighting hidden animals such as Bigfoot, and the Umbrella Cover Museum on Peaks Island, which pays homage to the lowly umbrella cover.

Also in Portland is the Museum of African Culture, a not-so-quirky gem devoted to sub-Saharan African arts and culture, including spectacular Nigerian tribal masks dating back to A.D. 1600 and Beninese lost-wax bronzes.

Days 3 and 4: Mid-Coast

Follow Route 1 north to Wiscasset, home to the Musical Wonder House, with more than 5,000 restored music boxes, player grand pianos and organs, musical birds, and, well, just about anything that emanates music.

Continue on to the Maine Antique Toy and Art Museum in Waldoboro, where you can rekindle memories of favorite childhood toys, including cereal-box and radio premiums as well as original Disney *Fantasia* animation art.

Next, head inland on Route 220 to Thorndike. The Bryant Stove and Music Museum is a four-part find. Inside are a doll circus, exhibits of working steam and electric engines, all manner of antique musical instruments, and antique stoves.

Paddle or cruise to the Ambajejus Boom House near Millinocket for a better understanding of Maine's logging era.

MAINE DECATHLON

Maine is a vast playground for outdoor enthusiasts. While you can work one or perhaps more of these adventures into a vacation, completing all 10 will require either moving here or returning again and again. Many aren't for the faint of heart or weak of muscle; almost all require planning well ahead.

DOGSLEDDING

Mush a team of huskies across the frozen **Lake Umbagog** wilderness north of Bethel. Sample the sport with a day trip, or immerse yourself in winter with a multiple-day winter wilderness dogsledding trek.

Mahoosuc Guide Service offers winter dogsledding trips across frozen Umbagog Lake.

ALPINE SKIING AND SNOWBOARDING

Crowning the summit of **Sugarloaf** are the **Snowfields,** the only lift-serviced skiing in the East above the tree line. This is backcountry, experts-only, out-of-bounds terrain, but when the gate's open these fields are worth braving the natural obstacles.

MOUNTAIN BIKING

Pedal between **Carrabassett Valley** and **The Forks** via the **Maine Huts and Trails** system, a 12-foot-wide corridor through the wilderness. Connecting the points are three full-service huts, each roughly 12 miles apart.

RAFTING

Maine is blessed with three dam-controlled white-water roller coasters: the **Kennebec River,** the **Penobscot River,** and the **Dead River.**

HIKING

Mile-high **Katahdin,** terminus of the **Appalachian Trail,** is Maine's tallest peak. Although it tops out on Baxter Peak, it also comprises several neighboring ones. The infamous and appropriately named **Knife Edge** provides the 1.1-mile connection between **Baxter Peak** and **Pamola Peak.**

CANOEING

The biggie of wilderness paddles, the **Allagash Wilderness Waterway** stretches 92 miles from Telos Lake to East Twin Brook through pristine lakes, rapids, and a portage around **Allagash Falls.** The biggest challenges are the distance and the weather.

CROSS-COUNTRY SKIING

Ski a groomed trail through the forested wilderness between four trail-linked traditional sporting camps in the conservation lands edging the Appalachian Trail's famed **100-Mile Wilderness.** In winter the cabins are primitive, but meals are provided and a gear shuttle is available.

SEA KAYAKING

Escape the crowds and paddle along Maine's coast from Kittery to Machias Bay on the **Maine Island Trail,** a 375-mile-long waterway past more than 180 island and mainland sites available for backcountry camping.

WALKING

For those not up for hiking, **Acadia National Park's carriage roads** are just the ticket. These 57 miles of crushed gravel roadways lace the park and are accented with 17 handsome roughstone bridges.

SAILING

No exercise or experience is required to sail the Maine coast aboard a **Maine windjammer**. All-inclusive sails ranging from three days to a week are possible on vessels both historic and new.

South Solon Meetinghouse

Days 5 and 6: Kennebec River and Maine Highlands

Stay north on Route 220 to Newport, take Route 2 west to Skowhegan, then Route 201 north to Solon. The South Solon Meetinghouse is a traditional New England meetinghouse on the exterior, but inside practically every surface is covered with frescoes depicting interdenominational religious scenes.

Choose your route and segue northwest to Millinocket. Here's where it gets a bit tricky; you'll either need to rent a boat or book a cruise to visit Ambajejus Boom House, but if you make the effort, you'll be rewarded with a brief immersion in the heyday of Maine's logging era.

Days 7 and 8: Acadia and Down East

Zip down I-95 to Bangor—check out the Paul Bunyan statue—then follow Route 1A. About 10 miles north of Ellsworth is The New England Museum of Telephony, where you can hand-crank a phone and make and receive calls through a switchboard.

From Ellsworth, drive on Route 1 north to Columbia Falls, then dip down on Route 187 to Jonesport to find the Maine Coast Sardine

History Museum, where Ronnie and Mary Peabody share their collection of artifacts and memorabilia from the days when there were more than 400 canneries along the coast. Just up the road is the Maine Central Model Railroad, Buz and Helen Beal's amazing model railway detailed with familiar Maine places.

Legendary lumberjack Paul Bunyan is allegedly a Bangor native.

SOUTHERN COAST

Drive over the I-95 bridge from New Hampshire into Maine's Southern Coast region on a bright summer day and you'll swear the air is cleaner, the sky bluer, the trees greener, the roadside signs more upbeat—"Welcome to Maine: The Way Life Should Be." (Or is it the way life *used* to be?)

Most visitors come to this region for the spectacular attractions of the justly world-famous Maine coast—the inlets, islands, and especially the beaches—but it's also rich in history. Southernmost York County, part of the Province of Maine, was incorporated in 1636, only 16 years after the *Mayflower* pilgrims reached Plymouth, Massachusetts, and reeks of history: ancient cemeteries, musty archives, and architecturally stunning homes and public buildings. Probably the best places to dive into that history are the sites of the Old York Historical Society in York Harbor.

Geological fortune smiled on this 50-mile ribbon, endowing it with a string of sandy beaches—nirvana for sun worshippers but less enchanting to swimmers, who need to steel themselves to be able to spend much time in the ocean, especially in early summer before the water temperature has reached a tolerable level.

Complementing those beaches are amusement parks and arcades, fishing shacks turned chic boutiques, a surprising number of good restaurants given the region's seasonality, and some of the state's prettiest parks and preserves. Spend some time poking around the small villages that give the region so much character. Many have been gussied up and

HIGHLIGHTS

◖ Old York Historical Society: York dates from the 1640s, and on this campus of historic buildings you can peek into early life in the area (page 31).

◖ Nubble Light and Sohier Park: You'll likely recognize this often-photographed Maine Coast icon, which is the easiest lighthouse to see in the region (page 31).

◖ Ogunquit Museum of American Art: It's hard to say which is more jaw-dropping, the art or the view (page 41).

◖ Marginal Way: Escape the hustle and bustle of Ogunquit with a stroll on this paved shorefront path (page 42).

◖ Wells Reserve at Laudholm Farm: Orient yourself at the visitors center, where you can learn about the history, flora, and fauna, and then take a leisurely walk to the seashore, passing through a variety of habitats (page 42).

◖ Seashore Trolley Museum: Ring-ring-ring goes the bell, and zing-zing-zing go your heartstrings, especially if you're a trolley fan (page 51).

◖ Dock Square: Brave the shopping crowds and browse the dozens of fish shacks–turned-boutiques in the heart of Kennebunkport (page 54).

◖ St. Anthony's Monastery: It's hard to believe this oasis of calm is just a short stroll from busy-busy Dock Square (page 54).

◖ Wood Island Lighthouse: Tour Maine's second-oldest lighthouse and perhaps even climb the tower (page 68).

LOOK FOR ◖ TO FIND RECOMMENDED SIGHTS, ACTIVITIES, DINING, AND LODGING.

gentrified quite a bit yet retain their seafaring or farming bones.

Some Mainers refer to the Southern Coast as northern Massachusetts. Sometimes it can seem that way, not only for the numbers of Massachusetts plates in evidence but also because many former Massachusetts residents have moved here for the quality of life but continue to commute to jobs in the Boston area. The resulting downside is escalating real-estate prices that have forced families off land that

has been in their families for generations and pushed those in traditional seafaring occupations inland. Still, if you nose around and get off the beaten path, you'll find that real Maine is still here.

PLANNING YOUR TIME

The good news is that Maine's Southern Coast is a rather compact region. The bad news is that it's heavily congested, especially in summer. Still, with a minimum of four days, you should

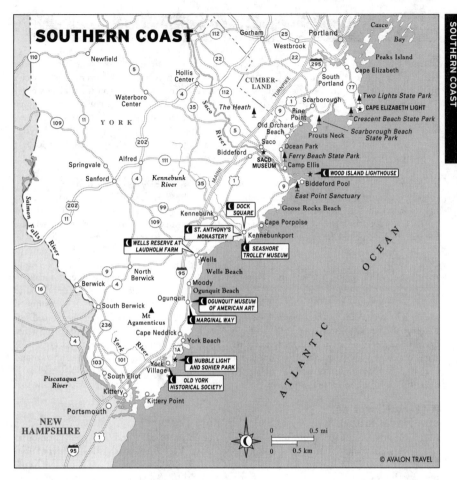

SOUTHERN COAST

be able to take in most of the key sights, including beaches to museums, as long as you don't spend too many hours basking in the sun.

Route 1, the region's primary artery, often has bumper-to-bumper traffic. If you're hopscotching towns, consider using I-95, which has exits for York, Kennebunk, and Saco–Biddeford–Old Orchard Beach. Parking can also be a challenge and expensive, but a trolley system operates in summer and connects most towns, making it easy to avoid the hassles and help the environment.

July and August are the busiest months. If you can avoid them, do. Spring and fall are lovely times to visit, and most attractions are open. In winter, you can walk the beaches without running into another soul, it's easy to get dinner reservations, and lodging prices plummet; the trade-off is that fewer businesses are open.

Kittery

Maine is home to a lot of well-kept secrets, Kittery being one of them. Shoppers rarely get beyond the 120-plus outlets along Route 1, but there's equal value in exploring the back roads of Maine's oldest town, settled in 1623 and chartered in 1647. Parks, a small nautical museum, historic architecture, and foodie finds are only a few of the attractions in Kittery and its "suburb," Kittery Point. It was also on Kittery's Badger Island where the sloop *Ranger* was launched in 1777. The shipbuilding continues at Portsmouth Naval Shipyard on Kittery's Dennet's Island, the first government shipyard in the United States.

SIGHTS

Avoid the outlet sprawl and see the prettiest part of the area by driving along squiggly Route 103 from the Route 1 traffic circle in Kittery through Kittery Point (administratively part of Kittery) and on to Route 1A in York. You can even make a day of it, stopping at the sights mentioned here. Be very careful to watch for cyclists and pedestrians, as there are no shoulders and lots of blind corners and hills.

Kittery Historical and Naval Museum

Maritime history buffs shouldn't miss the small but well-stocked Kittery Historical and Naval Museum (200 Rogers Rd. Ext., near the junction of Rte. 1 and Rte. 236, Kittery, 207/439-3080, www.kitterymuseum.com, 10 A.M.–4 P.M. Tues.–Sat. June–mid-Oct., $3 adults, $1.50 ages 7–15, $6 family). A large exhibit hall and a small back room contain ship models, fishing gear, old photos and paintings, and an astonishing collection of scrimshaw (carved whale ivory).

Lady Pepperrell House

The 1760 Georgian Lady Pepperrell House (Pepperrell Rd./Rte. 103, just before the Fort McClary turnoff) is privately owned and no longer open to the public, but it's worth admiring from afar. Nearby, across from the First Congregational Church, is the area's most-visited burying ground. Old-cemetery buffs should bring rubbing gear here for some interesting grave markers. The tomb of Levi Thaxter (husband of poet Celia Thaxter) bears an epitaph written for him by Robert Browning.

Fort McClary Historic Site

Since the early 18th century, fortifications have stood on this 27-acre headland protecting Portsmouth Harbor from seaborne foes. Contemporary remnants at Fort McClary (Rte. 103, Kittery Point, 207/439-2845, $3 nonresident adults, $2 Maine adults, $1 ages 5–11 and nonresident seniors) include several outbuildings, an 1846 blockhouse, granite walls, and earthworks—all with a view of Portsmouth Harbor. Opposite are the sprawling buildings of the Portsmouth Naval Shipyard. Bring a picnic (covered tables and a lily pond are across the street) and turn the kids loose to run and play. It's officially open May 30–October 1, but the site is accessible in off-season. The fort is 2.5 miles east of Route 1.

Fort Foster

The only problem with Fort Foster (Pocahontas Rd., off Rte. 103, Gerrish Island, Kittery Point, 207/439-3800, 10 A.M.–8 P.M. daily late May–early Sept., 10 A.M.–8 P.M. Sat.–Sun. May and Sept., $10 vehicle pass, $5 adult walk-in, $1 child walk-in) is that it's no secret, so parking can be scarce at this 90-acre municipal park at the entrance to Portsmouth Harbor. On a hot day, arrive early. You can swim, hike the nature trails, fish off the pier (no license needed), picnic, and investigate the tide pools. Bring your sailboard and a kite; there's almost always a breeze. From nearby **Seapoint Beach** (residents parking only May 15–Sept. 30; no facilities) on a clear day there's a wide-open view of the offshore Isles of Shoals, owned jointly by Maine and New Hampshire.

ENTERTAINMENT
Summer Concert Series
Kittery Recreation (207/439-3800, www.kittery.org) presents a summer concert series, which varies year to year; most of the concerts are free.

SHOPPING
There is no question that you'll find bargains at Kittery's 120-plus factory outlets (www.thekitteryoutlets.com), which are actually a bunch of mini-malls clustered along Route 1. All the household names are here: Bass, Calvin Klein, Eddie Bauer, J. Crew, Mikasa, Esprit, Lenox, Timberland, Tommy Hilfiger, Gap, Villeroy & Boch, and plenty more (all open daily). Anchoring it all is the **Kittery Trading Post** (301 Rte. 1, 207/439-2700 or 888/587-6246, www.kitterytradingpost.com), a humongous sporting-goods and clothing emporium. Try to avoid the outlets on weekends, when you might need to take a number for the fitting rooms.

RECREATION
Brave Boat Harbor
One of the Rachel Carson National Wildlife Refuge's 11 Maine coastal segments is Brave Boat Harbor (207/646-9226), a beautifully unspoiled 560-acre wetlands preserve in Kittery Point. There are hiking trails, but the habitat is particularly sensitive here, so be kind to the environment. Take Route 103 to Chauncey Creek Road and continue past the Gerrish Island bridge to Cutts Island Lane. Just beyond it and across a small bridge is a pullout on the left. You have a couple of options for hikes: a 1.8-mile loop trail, including a spur, or a half-mile loop. Bring binoculars to spot waterfowl in the marshlands.

Captain and Patty's Piscataqua River Tours
Take a spin around the Piscataqua River Basin with Captain and Patty's Piscataqua River Tours (Town Dock, Pepperrell Rd., Kittery Point, 207/451-8156 or 207/439-8976, www.capandpatty.com, $12 adults, $8 under age 10). The 80-minute historical tour aboard an open launch departs six times daily. En route, Captain Neil Odams points out historic forts, lighthouses, and the Naval Shipyard.

ACCOMMODATIONS
Rates reflect peak season.

Put a little ooh and aah into your touring with a visit to the **Portsmouth Harbor Inn and Spa** (6 Water St., Kittery, 207/439-4040, www.innatportsmouth.com, $185–215). The handsome brick inn, built in 1889, looks out over the Piscataqua River, Portsmouth, and the Portsmouth Naval Shipyard. Five attractive Victorian-style guest rooms, most with water views, are furnished with antiques and have air-conditioning, TVs, and phones. There's an outdoor hot tub, and beach chairs are available. Breakfasts are multicourse feasts. Request a back room if you're noise sensitive, although air-conditioning camouflages traffic noise in summer. Rooms on the third floor have the best views, but these also have handheld showers. Now for the "aah" part: The inn also has a full-service spa.

After a day of power shopping, retreat to **Ocean's Edge Bed & Breakfast** (11 Trafton Lane, Kittery, 207/439-3350, www.oceansedgebnb.com, $160–275), a newish gabled gambrel fronting on tidal Spruce Creek. Three guest rooms, one with a shared bath, vary in size and amenities, but all have air-conditioning, Wi-Fi, and CD-DVD players. Guests have access to a home theater and an exercise room. Rates include a full breakfast prepared from organic ingredients. Guests can rent canoes and kayaks, a motorboat, and bicycles for explorations.

FOOD
Local Flavors
Kittery has an abundance of excellent specialty food stores that are perfect for stocking up for a picnic lunch or dinner. Most are along the section of Route 1 between the Portsmouth bridge and the traffic circle, and three are within steps of each other. At **Beach Pea Baking Co.** (53 Rte. 1, 207/439-3555, www.beachpeabaking.com, 7:30 A.M.–6 P.M. Mon.–Sat.) you can buy fabulous breads and pastries. Sandwiches and

salads are made to order 11 A.M.–3 P.M. daily. There's pleasant seating indoors and on a patio. Next door is **Golden Harvest** (47 State Rd./Rte. 1, 207/439-2113, 7 A.M.–6:30 P.M. Mon.–Sat., 9 A.M.–6 P.M. Sun.), where you can load up on luscious produce. Across the street is **Terracotta Pasta Co.** (52 Rte. 1, 207/475-3025, www.terracottapastacompany.com, 10 A.M.–6 P.M. Mon., 9 A.M.–6:30 P.M. Tues.–Sat., 10:30 A.M.–4 P.M. Sun.), where in addition to handmade pastas you'll find salads, soups, sandwiches, prepared foods, and lots of other goodies.

Old World artisanal breads made from organic ingredients are available at the company store for **When Pigs Fly** (447 Rte. 1, 207/439-3114, www.sendbread.com).

Craving a down-home breakfast or lunch? The **Sunrise Grill** (182 State Rd./Rte. 1, Kittery traffic circle, Kittery, 207/439-5748, www.sunrisegrillinc.com, 6:30 A.M.–2 P.M. daily) delivers with waffles, granola, omelets, Diana's Benedict, salads, sandwiches, and burgers.

Casual Dining

Executive Chef Charlie Cicero's commitment to using fresh and local foods and his flair for bringing big flavors out of simple ingredients have earned ◖ **Anneke Jans** (60 Wallingford Sq., Kittery, 207/439-0001, www.annekejans.net, 5–10 P.M. daily) kudos far beyond Kittery. Signature dishes include the Bangs Island mussels prepared with bacon, shallots, and blue cheese, available as an appetizer or entrée. Charcoal walls, white tablecloths with moss centerpieces, a wine bar, and windows that open to the street create an especially hip and stylin' atmosphere. The French-American bistro menu has prices ranging $17–33. The extensive wine list has more than 30 available by the glass. This is a local hot spot with a lively crowd; reservations are recommended.

Ethnic Fare

Craving Cal-Mex? Some of the recipes in Luis Valdez's **Loco Coco's Tacos** (36 Walker St., Kittery, 207/438-9322, www.lococos.com, 11 A.M.–9 P.M. daily) have been passed down for generations, and the homemade salsas have flavor and kick. If you're feeling really decadent, go for the artery-busting California fries. There's a kids menu too. Most choices are less than $10. Choose from self-serve, dining room, or bar seating.

After years of operating a prepared-foods operation, chefs Janet Howe and Rajesh Mandekar opened **Tulsi** (2 Government St., Kittery, 207/451-9511, www.tulsiindianrestaurant.com, 5–10 P.M. Tues.–Sat., 5–9 P.M. Sun., $9–20). Mandekar, from Mumbai, has cooked at venues ranging from five-star restaurants to a cruise line, and he blends techniques drawn from Indian, French, and Italian cuisines to create rave-worthy Indian fare. It's a tiny spot; reservations are recommended.

Lobster and Clams

If you came to Maine to eat lobster, **Chauncey Creek Lobster Pier** (16 Chauncey Creek Rd., off Rte. 103, Kittery Point, 207/439-1030, www.chaunceycreek.com, 11 A.M.–8 P.M. daily mid-May–early Sept., 11 A.M.–7 P.M. daily early Sept.–Columbus Day) is the real deal. Step up to the window, place your order, take a number, and grab a table (you may need to share) overlooking tidal Chauncey Creek and the woods on the close-in opposite shore. It's a particularly picturesque—and extremely popular—place; parking is a nightmare. BYOB and anything else that's not on the menu.

If clams are high on your must-have list, pay a visit to **Bob's Clam Hut** (315 Rte. 1, Kittery, 207/439-4233, www.bobsclamhut.com, 11 A.M.–9 P.M. Mon.–Thurs., 11 A.M.–9:30 P.M. Fri.–Sat., 11 A.M.–8 P.M. Sun. year-round), next to the Kittery Trading Post. Using vegetable oil for frying, Bob's turns out scallops, shrimp, calamari, and, of course, clams; the tartar sauce is the secret weapon. Expect to pay market rates, but nothing is too pricey.

The Yorks

Four villages with distinct personalities—upscale **York Harbor,** historic **York Village,** casual **York Beach,** and semirural **Cape Neddick**—make up the Town of York. First inhabited by Native Americans, who named it Agamenticus, the area was settled as early as 1624, so history is serious business here. Town high points were its founding by Sir Ferdinando Gorges and the arrival of well-to-do vacationers in the 19th century. In between were Indian massacres, economic woes, and population shuffles. The town's population explodes in summer, which is pretty obvious in July–August when you're searching for a free patch of York Beach sand or a parking place. York Beach, with its seasonal surf and souvenir shops and amusements, has long been the counterpoint to genteel York Village, but that's changing with the restoration and rebirth of York Beach's downtown buildings and the arrival of tony restaurants, shops, and condos.

History and genealogy buffs can study the headstones in the Old Burying Ground or comb the archives of the Old York Historical Society. For lighthouse fans, there are Cape Neddick Light Station ("Nubble Light") and Boon Island, six miles offshore. You can rent horses or mountain bikes on Mount Agamenticus, board a deep-sea fishing boat in York Harbor, or spend an hour hiking the Cliff Path in York Harbor. For the kids there's a zoo, a lobster-boat cruise, a taffy maker, and, of course, the beach.

SIGHTS
◖ Old York Historical Society
Based in York Village, the Old York Historical Society (207 York St., York Village, 207/363-4974, www.oldyork.org, museum buildings 10 a.m.–5 p.m. Mon.–Sat. early June–mid-Oct., $12 adults or $6 one building, $10 seniors or $5 one building, $5 ages 4–16 or $3 one building, $25 family or $15 one building) is the driving force behind a collection of eight colonial and postcolonial buildings plus a research library

open throughout the summer. Start at the Jefferds' Tavern Visitor Center (5 Lindsay Rd., York Village), where you'll need to buy tickets. Don't miss the Old Burying Ground, dating from 1735, across the street (rubbings are not allowed). Nearby are the Old Gaol and the School House (both fun for kids), Ramsdell House, and the Emerson-Wilcox House. About 0.5 miles down Lindsay Road on the York River are the John Hancock Warehouse and the George Marshall Store Gallery (140 Lindsay Rd.), operated in the summer as a respected contemporary-art gallery; across the river is the Elizabeth Perkins House. Antiques buffs shouldn't miss the Wilcox and Perkins Houses. These two and the Ramsdell House are open by guided tour; other buildings are self-guided. Visit some or all of the buildings at your own pace; no one leads you from one to another. You can walk to some of the sites from the tavern; to reach others you'll need a car, and parking may be limited.

◖ Nubble Light and Sohier Park
The best-known photo op in York is the distinctive 1879 lighthouse known formally as Cape Neddick Light Station, familiarly "The Nubble." Although there's no access to the lighthouse's island, the Sohier Park Welcome Center (Nubble Rd., off Rte. 1A, between Long and Short Sands Beaches, York Beach, 207/363-7608, 9 a.m.–7 p.m. daily mid-May–mid-Oct.) provides the perfect viewpoint (and has restrooms). Parking is limited, but the turnover is fairly good. It's not a bad idea, however, to walk from the Long Sands parking area or come by bike, even though the road has inadequate shoulders. Weekdays this is also a popular spot for scuba divers.

Sayward-Wheeler House
Owned by the Boston-based Historic New England, the 1718 Sayward-Wheeler House (9 Barrell Lane Ext., York Harbor, 207/384-2454, www.historicnewengland.org, $5) occupies a prime site at the edge of York Harbor. It's open

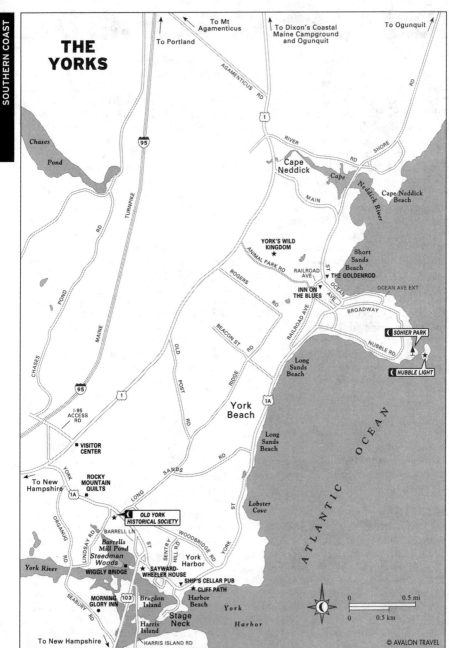

THE YORKS

To Mt Agamenticus

To Dixon's Coastal Maine Campground and Ogunquit

To Ogunquit

To Portland

AGAMENTICUS RD

RD

Chases Pond

95

RIVER RD

SHORE RD

Cape Neddick

MAIN

Cape

Neddick River

Cape Neddick Beach

POND RD

TURNPIKE

MAINE

YORK'S WILD KINGDOM ★

ANIMAL PARK RD

ROGERS RD

RAILROAD AVE

Short Sands Beach

ST

THE GOLDENROD ▼

INN ON THE BLUES ▼

OCEAN AVE

OCEAN AVE EXT

BROADWAY

CHASES

95

1

BEACON ST RD

RIDGE RD

RAILROAD AVE

SOHIER PARK ☾ ★

NUBBLE RD

NUBBLE LIGHT ☾ ★

Long Sands Beach

OLD POST RD

I-95 ACCESS RD

VISITOR CENTER ■

York Beach

1A

Long Sands Beach

ATLANTIC OCEAN

To New Hampshire →

YORK ST

ROCKY MOUNTAIN QUILTS ■

LONG SANDS RD

1A

Lobster Cove

OLD YORK HISTORICAL SOCIETY ☾ ★

BARRELL LN

ORANUG

LINDSAY RD

Barrells Mill Pond

Steedman Woods

ST

SENTRY HILL RD

WOODBRIDGE RD

YORK ST

York River

WIGGLY BRIDGE

★ **SAYWARD-WHEELER HOUSE**

York Harbor

RD

SEABURY RD

103

MORNING GLORY INN ■

Bragdon Island

SHIP'S CELLAR PUB ★

★ **CLIFF PATH**

Harbor Beach

Harris Island

Stage Neck

York Harbor

To New Hampshire ↓

HARRIS ISLAND RD

0   0.5 mi

0   0.5 km

© AVALON TRAVEL

© HILARY NANGLE

The Sayward-Wheeler House is one of York's architectural treasures.

with tours on the hour 11 A.M.–4 P.M. the second and fourth Saturday of the month June–mid-October. In the house are original period furnishings, all in excellent condition. Take Route 1A to Lilac Lane (Rte. 103) to Barrell Lane and then to Barrell Lane Extension, or access it from the Fisherman's Walk.

York's Wild Kingdom

More than 250 creatures—including tigers, zebras, llamas, deer, lions, elephants, and monkeys—find a home at York's Wild Kingdom (102 Railroad Ave., off Rte. 1, York Beach, 207/363-4911 or 800/456-4911, www.york-zoo.com). It's not what you'd call a state-of-the-art zoo, but it keeps the kids entertained. Elephant shows and other animal "events" occur three times daily in July–August. Between the zoo and the amusement-park rides, it's easy to spend a day here. Admission (covering the zoo and some of the rides) is in the neighborhood of $20 adults, $15 ages 4–10, $5 under age 4; an unlimited-rides day pass is $10. Zoo-only admission is $15 adults,

$9 ages 4–10, $1 under age 4. The zoo is open 10 A.M.–5 P.M. Monday–Friday late May–June and September, 10 A.M.–5 P.M. Monday–Friday and 10 A.M.–6 P.M. Saturday–Sunday July–August; amusement park hours are noon–9:30 P.M. daily late June–early September.

ENTERTAINMENT AND EVENTS
Live Music

Inn on the Blues (7 Ocean Ave., York Beach, 207/351-3221, www.innontheblues.com) has live music or a DJ (acoustic, blues, reggae) every night during the summer. The **Ship's Cellar Pub** (480 York St., York Harbor, 800/343-3869) in the York Harbor Inn frequently has live entertainment too. Free concerts are often held at the **Ellis Park Gazebo,** by Short Sands Beach, usually 7–9 P.M. early July–early September; check local papers for schedule.

Festivals and Events

Each year, the Old York Historical Society invites decorators to transform a local house for

RAMBLE THROUGH THE BERWICKS

Probably the best known of the area's present-day inland communities is the riverside town of South Berwick, thanks to a historical and literary tradition dating to the 17th century, with antique cemeteries to prove it. The 19th- and 20th-century novels of Sarah Orne Jewett and Gladys Hasty Carroll have lured many a contemporary visitor to explore their rural settings, an area aptly described by Carroll as "a small patch of earth continually occupied but never crowded for more than three hundred years."

A ramble through the Berwicks – South Berwick and its siblings – makes a nice diversion from the coast, and because it's off most visitors' radar screens, it's a good alternative for lodging and dining too. For an easy day trip, loop northwest on Route 236 from Kittery or Route 91 from York to South Berwick, on the New Hampshire border; continue northeast on Route 236 to Berwick, then head northeast on Route 9 to North Berwick. Continue on Route 9 to return to Wells and the coast.

Don't blink or you might miss the tiny sign outside the 1774 **Sarah Orne Jewett House** (5 Portland St./Rte. 4, South Berwick, 207/384-2454, www.historicnewengland.org, 11 A.M.–5 P.M. Fri.–Sun. June 1-Oct. 15, $5) smack in the center of town. Park on the street and join one of the tours to learn details of the Jewett family and its star, Sarah (1849-1909), author of *The Country of the Pointed Firs*, a New England classic. Books by and about her are available in the gift shop. House tours are at 11 A.M. and 1, 2, 3, and 4 P.M. The house is one of two local Historic New England properties.

The other property is the 18th-century **Hamilton House** (40 Vaughan's Lane, South Berwick, 207/384-2454, www.historicnewengland.org, 11 A.M.–5 P.M. Wed.–Sun. June 1-Oct. 15, $8), which crowns a bluff overlooking the Salmon Falls River and is flanked by handsome colonial revival garden. Knowledgeable guides relate the house's fascinating history. Tours begin only on the hour, the last at 4 P.M. In July the **Sunday in the Garden** concert series takes place on the lawn ($8, includes a free pass to

come back and see the house). Pray for sun; the concert is moved indoors on rainy days. From Route 236 at the southern edge of South Berwick (watch for a signpost), turn left onto Brattle Street and take the second right onto Vaughan's Lane.

Also here is the 150-acre hilltop campus of **Berwick Academy,** Maine's oldest prep school, chartered in 1791 with John Hancock's signature. The coed school's handsome gray-stone William H. Fogg Memorial Library ("The Fogg") is named for the same family connected with Harvard's Fogg Art Museum. The building's highlight is an incredible collection of dozens of 19th-century stained-glass windows, most designed by Victorian artist Sarah Wyman Whitman, who also designed jackets for Sarah Orne Jewett's books. Thanks to a diligent fund-raising effort, the windows have been restored to their former glory.

When you're ready to stretch your legs, head to **Vaughan Woods State Park** (28 Oldfields Rd., South Berwick, 207/384-5160, 9 A.M.–8 P.M. daily late May-early Sept., accessible all year, $3 adults, $1 ages 5-11, free over age 65 or under age 5) and wander along the three miles of trails in the 250-acre riverside preserve. It adjoins Hamilton House and is connected via a path, but there's far more parking at the park itself.

Another reason to venture inland is to catch a production at the **Hackmatack Playhouse** (538 School St./Rte. 9, Berwick, 207/698-1807, www.hackmatack.org), midway between North Berwick and Berwick. The popular summer theater, operating since 1972, is based in a renovated barn reminiscent of a past era and has 8 P.M. performances Wednesday-Saturday, a 2 P.M. matinee Thursday, and children's shows. Tickets are $22 adults, $20 seniors, $10 students under 20; matinees are $2 less.

ACCOMMODATIONS

These two inns are sleepers (sorry, couldn't resist). Both are within easy striking distance of the coast yet provide far more value than similar properties in the name communities.

© HILARY NANGLE

Slumber in architectural splendor at bed-and-breakfast Angel of the Berwicks.

Once the headmaster's residence for nearby Berwick Academy, the elegant turn-of-the-20th-century **Academy Street Inn Bed and Breakfast** (15 Academy St., South Berwick, 207/384-5633, year-round, $99-109 d) has crystal chandeliers, leaded-glass windows, working fireplaces, and high-ceilinged rooms full of antiques. Paul and Lee Fopeano's handsome home has five guest rooms with private baths. Full breakfast or afternoon lemonade on the 60-foot screened porch is a real treat.

Innkeepers Ben Gumm and Sally McLaren have turned the outstanding 25-room Queen Anne-style Hurd mansion into the **Angel of the Berwicks** (2 Elm St., North Berwick, 207/676-2133, www.angeloftheberwicks.com, $99-179), an elegant antiques-filled inn. The property, listed on the National Register of Historic Places, has 11-foot ceilings, stained-glass windows, hand-carved friezes, and ornate mantelpieces. There's even a baby grand piano in the music room.

Rates include a full breakfast and afternoon refreshments.

FOOD

A local institution since 1960, **Fogarty's** (471 Main St., South Berwick, 207/384-8361, www.fogartysrestaurant.net, 11 A.M.-8 P.M. daily) has expanded through the years from a simple takeout place to a local favorite for inexpensive family-friendly dining. Ask for a river-view table in the back room.

Far jazzier is **Pepperland Café** (279 Main St., South Berwick, 207/384-5535, noon-11:30 P.M. Tues.-Sat., 9 A.M.-3 P.M. Sun.), a family-friendly pub-meets-bistro serving comfort food with pizzazz. Make a meal from smaller plates and salads ($5-10) or go big with the entrées ($17-24).

Relish (404 Main St., South Berwick, 207/384-8249, 5:30-9 P.M. Tues.-Sat.), previously known as Margaux, is an intimate, low-key neighborhood bistro where Linda Robinson and Christine Prunier serve well-crafted dinners, with most entrées less than $20.

the **Decorator Show House,** culminating in an open house mid-July–mid-August.

Late July–early August, the **York Days** festivities enliven the town for 10 days with concerts, dances, walking tours, a road race, sandcastle contests, antiques and art shows, a dog show, fireworks, a parade, and public suppers.

York Village's **Annual Harvestfest** takes place in October and combines colonial crafts and cooking demonstrations, hayrides, museum tours, entertainment for adults and kids, and an ox roast with beanhole beans. This is one of the town's most popular events; most activities are free.

The annual **Lighting of the Nubble** in late November includes cookies, hot chocolate, music, and an appearance by Santa Claus. The best part, though, is seeing the lighthouse glowing for the holidays.

SHOPPING

Expect to wash your hands before examining any of the 400-plus museum-quality antique quilts at Betsy Telford's **Rocky Mountain Quilts** (130 York St., York Village, 207/363-6800 or 800/762-5940, www.rockymountainquilts.com); this isn't a place for browsers.

RECREATION
Walks

Next to Harbor Beach, near the Stage Neck Inn, a sign marks the beginning of the **Cliff Path,** a walkway worth taking for its dramatic harbor views in the shadow of elegant summer cottages. On the one-hour round-trip, you'll pass the York Harbor Reading Room, an exclusive club. The path is on private property, traditionally open to the public courtesy of the owners, but controversy surfaces periodically about property rights, vandalism, and the condition of some sections of the walk. Note that it's called the Cliff Path for a reason; it's not a good choice for little ones.

A less strenuous route is known variously as the **Shore Path, Harbor Walk,** or **Fisherman's Walk,** running west along the harbor and river from Stage Neck Road (next to Edwards' Harborside Inn) and passing the

Sayward-Wheeler House before crossing the tiny green-painted Wiggly Bridge leading into the **Steedman Woods** preserve. Carry binoculars for good boat watching and birding in the 16-acre preserve, owned by the Old York Historical Society. A one-mile double-loop trail takes less than an hour of easy strolling.

Mount Agamenticus

Drive to the summit of Mount Agamenticus ("The Big A") and you're at York County's highest point. It's only 692 feet, but on a clear day you'll have panoramic views of ocean, lakes, woods, and sometimes the White Mountains. The 10,000-acre preserve (www.agamenticus .org), one of the largest remaining expanses of undeveloped forest in coastal New England, is considered among the most biologically diverse wilderness in Maine. It includes vernal pools and ponds and is home to rare and endangered species. At the summit are a billboard map of the 40-mile trail network and a curious memorial to Saint Aspinquid, a 17th-century Algonquian Indian leader. Mountain biking is also hugely popular on Agamenticus. Take a picnic, a kite, and binoculars. In the fall, if the wind is from the northwest, watch for migrating hawks; in winter, bring a sled for the best downhill run in southern Maine. From Route 1 in Cape Neddick, take Mountain Road (also called Agamenticus Rd.) 4.2 miles west to the access road.

Golf

The **Ledges Golf Club** (1 Ledges Dr., off Rte. 91, York, 207/351-9999, www.ledgesgolf .com) is an 18-hole course with daily public tee times.

Swimming

Sunbathing and swimming are big draws in York, with four beaches of varying sizes and accessibility. Bear in mind that traffic can be gridlocked along the beachfront (Rte. 1A) in midsummer, so it may take longer than you expect to get anywhere. **Lifeguards** are usually on duty 9:30 A.M.–4 P.M. mid-June–Labor Day at Short Sands Beach, Long Beach, and Harbor

Beach. Bathhouses at Long Sands and Short Sands are open 9 A.M.–7 P.M. daily in mid-summer. The biggest parking area (metered) is at Long Sands, but that 1.5-mile beach also draws the most visitors. The scarcest parking is at Harbor Beach near the Stage Neck Inn and at Cape Neddick (Passaconaway) Beach near the Ogunquit town line.

Sea Kayaking

Kayak rentals begin at $55 per day single, $75 double, from **Excursions: Coastal Maine Outfitting Company** (1740 Rte. 1, Cape Neddick, 207/363-0181, www.excursionsin maine.com). Or sign up for a half-day tour ($60 ages 14 and older, $50 children). A four-hour basics clinic for ages 16 and older is $85. Excursions is based at Dixon's Campground on Route 1, four miles north of the I-95 York exit.

Harbor Adventures (Harris Island Rd., York Harbor, 207/363-8466, www.harborad ventures.com) offers instruction and guided sea-kayaking trips from Kittery through Kennebunkport. Prices begin around $45 for a two-hour harbor tour.

Surfing

Want to catch a wave? For surfing informa-tion, lessons, or rentals, call **Liquid Dreams Surf Shop** (171 Long Beach Ave., York, 207/351-2545, www.liquiddreamssurf.com, 10 A.M.–5 P.M. daily). It's right across from Long Sands Beach.

Bicycling

The **Daily Spin** (Rte. 1A, York Beach, 207/363-5040) rents beach-cruiser bicycles ($10 per hour, $20 full-day). It's located at the Daily Grind coffee shop near the zoo.

Fishing

A local expert on fly-fishing, spin fishing, and conventional tackle is **Eldredge Bros. Guide Service** (1480 Rte. 1, Cape Neddick, 207/373-9269, www.eldredgeflyshop.com). Four-hour guided trips for one or two anglers begin at $250 in freshwater or saltwater.

ACCOMMODATIONS
York Harbor
BED-AND-BREAKFASTS

Hosts Donna and Paul Archibald have turned Fannie Chapman's 1889 summer cottage into the elegant and romantic **Chapman Cottage** (370 York St., York Harbor, 207/363-2059 or 877/363-2059, www.chapmancottagebandb .com, $175–250), a truly special retreat. Rooms are huge and plush, with air-conditioning, Wi-Fi, TVs, and spacious baths; most have whirlpool baths and fireplaces (some in the bathrooms), and a few have private decks and river views. The pampering includes bathrobes, sherry and truffles, and fine linens. Dinner is available weekends off-season.

Inviting Adirondack-style chairs accent the green lawn rolling down to the harbor at **Edwards' Harborside Inn** (7 Stage Neck Rd., York Harbor, 207/363-3037 or 800/273-2686, www.edwardsharborside.com, $200–300). Many of the 10 guest rooms can be combined into suites, and most have water views. All have TVs, phones, Wi-Fi, and air-conditioning. One suite has a party-size whirlpool tub facing the harbor; another has a grand piano. Watch the sunset from the inn's 210-foot pier, stroll the ad-jacent shorefront paths, wander over to the beach, or just settle into one of those shorefront chairs and watch the world go by. A lovely full buffet breakfast is served in the water-view sunporch.

Bill and Bonnie Alstrom, former innkeep-ers at Tanglewood Hall, weren't looking to downsize, but on a lark they stumbled upon this woodland cottage and they were smitten. After more than a year of renovations, they opened ◖ **Morning Glory Inn** (120 Seabury Rd., York Harbor, 207/363-2062, www.morn-inggloryinnmaine.com, $175–245). A boutique bed-and-breakfast catering to romantics, the Morning Glory has just three guest rooms, all very spacious and private and all with doors to private patios or yards, air-conditioning, TVs with DVD players, fridges, Wi-Fi, and plenti-ful other little amenities. The living room, in the original section of the house, was a 17th-century cottage, barged over from the Isles of Shoals; the newer post-and-beam great room doubles as a dining area, where a hot breakfast buffet is served. The property is ultraquiet—listen to the birds singing in the gardens; it's truly a magical setting, far removed yet convenient to everything York offers.

FULL-SERVICE INNS

York Harbor Inn (Rte. 1A, York Harbor, 207/363-5119 or 800/343-3869, www.yorkharborinn.com, $99–349 d) is an accommodating spot with a country-inn flavor and a wide variety of guest-room and package-plan options throughout the year. The oldest section of the inn is a 17th-century cabin from the Isles of Shoals. Accommodations are spread out in the inn, the adjacent Yorkshire building, and two elegantly restored houses, both with resident innkeepers: neighboring Harbor Hill and pet-friendly 1730 Harbor Crest, about a half mile away. All have TVs, phones, free Wi-Fi, and air-conditioning; some have four-poster beds, fireplaces, and whirlpools; many have water views. Rates include a generous continental breakfast.

You can't miss the **Stage Neck Inn** (100 Stage Neck Rd., York Harbor, 207/363-3850 or 800/340-9901, www.stageneck.com, year-round, $255–405), occupying its own private peninsula overlooking York Harbor. Modern resort-style facilities include an indoor and an outdoor pool, tennis courts, golf privileges, a spa, a fitness center, and spectacular views from balconies and terraces. The formal Harbor Porches restaurant (no jeans, entrées $21–30) and the casual Sandpiper Bar and Grille are open to nonguests.

York Beach

HOTEL AND MOTEL

For more than 150 years, **The Union Bluff** (8 Beach St., York Beach, 207/363-1333 or 800/833-0721, www.unionbluff.com, $179–379) has stood sentry like a fortress overlooking Short Sands Beach. Many of the guest rooms have ocean views. All have TVs, air-conditioning, and phones; some have fireplaces, whirlpool baths, or ocean-view decks. Furnishings are modern motel-style. Also on the premises are the Beach Street Grill dining room and a pub serving lighter fare. The best deals are the packages, which include breakfast and dinner. The hotel and pub are open year-round; the restaurant is seasonal. It's probably best to avoid dates when there's a wedding in-house.

Art deco fans take note: The **Nevada Motel** (Rte. 1A, York Beach, 207/363-4504, $135–190) is a classic. Built in 1951 and with few, if any, updates since, the white two-story motel with aqua trim faces Long Sands Beach. It's well maintained, but the rooms are small and the bathrooms tiny. It has no frills, period.

BED-AND-BREAKFASTS

Everything's casual and flowers are everywhere at the brightly painted **Katahdin Inn** (11 Ocean Ave., York Beach, 207/363-1824, www.thekatahdininn.com, year-round, $95–145), overlooking the breakers of Short Sands Beach. Longtime owners Rae and Paul LeBlanc appropriately refer to it as a "bed and beach." It was built in 1863 and has always been a guesthouse. Nine smallish guest rooms on three floors, eight of them with water views, have four-poster beds and mostly shared baths. Breakfast is not included, but coffee is always available, the rooms have refrigerators, and several eateries are nearby.

Not oceanfront but offering ocean views from many rooms and just a short walk from Short Sands Beach is Barbara and Michael Sheff's **Candleshop Inn** (44 Freeman St., York Beach, 207/363-4087 or 888/363-4087, www.candleshopinn.com, $120–185). The 10 guest rooms with private and shared baths are decorated in country cottage style, with area rugs, painted furniture, and florals; many are set up for families. The day begins with a vegetarian breakfast and a yoga class. Spa services, including massage and Reiki, are available on-site by appointment.

CONDOMINIUM SUITES

Fabulously sited on the oceanfront and overlooking the Nubble Light, the high-end **ViewPoint** (229 Nubble Rd., York Beach, 207/363-2661 or 888/363-4087, www.viewpointhotel.com, $375 one-bedroom–$625 three-bedroom, $2,700–4,200 per week) comprises luxuriously appointed 1–3-bedroom suites. All have gas fireplaces; fully equipped kitchens; washer-dryers; TVs; phones; private patios, porches, or decks; Wi-Fi; and daily maid service. On the premises are an outdoor heated pool, a grilling area, gardens, and a playground.

CAMPING
Dixon's Coastal Maine Campground (1740 Rte. 1, Cape Neddick, 207/363-3626, www .dixonscampground.com, $34–40) has more than 100 well-spaced sites on 26 wooded and open acres. It can accommodate tents and small RVs. Electric and water hookups are available. Facilities include a playground and a good-size outdoor heated pool. It's also the base for Excursions sea kayaking.

FOOD
Local Flavors
Both *Gourmet* and *Saveur* magazines know where to get dogs here. Sometimes the line runs right out the door of the low-ceilinged, reddish-brown roadside shack that houses local institution **Flo's Steamed Dogs** (Rte. 1, opposite the Mountain Rd. turnoff, Cape Neddick, no phone, www.floshotdogs.com). Founder Flo Stacy died in 2000 at age 92, but her legend and her family live on. There is no menu—just steamed Schultz wieners, buns, chips, beverages, and an attitude. The secret? The spicy, sweet-sour hot-dog sauce, allegedly once sought by the H. J. Heinz corporation, but the Stacy family isn't telling or selling. The cognoscenti know to order their dogs only with mayonnaise and the special sauce, nothing heretical such as ketchup or mustard. It's open 11 A.M.–3 P.M., and not a minute later, Thursday–Tuesday year-round.

See those people with their faces pressed to the glass? They're all watching the taffy makers inside **The Goldenrod** (2 Railroad Ave., York Beach, 207/363-2621, www.thegoldenrod.com), where machines spew out 180 Goldenrod Kisses a minute, 65 tons a year, and have been at it since 1896. The Goldenrod is an old-fashioned place with a tearoom, a gift shop, an old-fashioned soda fountain with 135 ice cream flavors, and a rustic dining room as well as equally old-fashioned prices. It's open for breakfast at 8 A.M., lunch, and dinner daily late May–Columbus Day.

After viewing The Nubble, head across the road to **Brown's Ice Cream** (232 Nubble Rd., York Beach, 207/363-1277), where unusual flavors complement the standards.

Prepared foods by the pound are sold at **Lucia's Kitchen** (1151A Rte. 1, Cape Neddick, 207/363-5557, www.luciaskitchen.net, 11:30 A.M.–7 P.M. Mon.–Fri., 11:30 A.M.–6 P.M. Sat.), but sandwiches, cookies, and burritos are always available too.

Craving jerk chicken or curried goat? Stop by **Jamaican Jerk Center** (1400 Rte. 1, Cape Neddick, 207/351-3033, www.jamaicanjerk-center.com, 11 A.M.–9 P.M. daily), a seasonal takeout with tables under a tent and on the lawn. There's live reggae music on weekends beginning at 4 P.M.

Stop in at the **Gateway Farmers Market** (York Chamber of Commerce Visitor Center, Rte. 1, York, 9 A.M.–1 P.M. Sat. mid-June–mid-Oct.) and stock up for a picnic. If you still need more, head next door to Stonewall Kitchen.

Family Favorites
The York Harbor Inn's **Ship's Cellar Pub** (11:30 A.M.–11:30 P.M. Mon.–Thurs., 11:30 A.M.–midnight Fri.–Sat., 3–11:30 P.M. Sun.) attracts even the locals. The menu is the same as in the main dining room (burgers to lobster, $8–32), but the setting is far more casual. The space is designed to resemble in the interior of a yacht. The pub doubles as a favorite local watering hole, with live music Wednesday–Sunday. Happy hour, with free munchies, is 4–6 P.M. weekdays and sometimes draws a raucous crowd.

Wild Willy's (765 Rte. 1, York, 207/363-9924, www.wildwillysburgers.com, 11 A.M.–8 P.M. Mon.–Sat., $6–8, cash only) has turned burgers into an art form. More than a dozen hefty mouthwatering burgers, all made from certified Angus beef, are available, from the classic Willy burger to the Rio Grande, with roasted green chilies from New Mexico and cheddar cheese. Don't miss the hand-cut fries. Chicken sandwiches, steak chili, and frappés are also served, as are beer and wine. Order at the counter before grabbing a seat in the dining area or out on the back deck; the servers will find you when it's ready.

Locals swear by **Rick's All Seasons Café** (240 York St., York, 207/363-5584, breakfast and lunch 5 A.M.–2 P.M. Tues.–Sat., 5 A.M.–12:15 P.M. Sun., dinner 4–7 P.M. Wed.–Thurs.), where the prices are low, the food is good, and the gossip is even better. Go for breakfast or lunch; the fried clams earn raves. Have patience: Almost everything is cooked to order.

Casual and Fine Dining

It's hard to know whether *Food* or *Shopping* is the right category for **Stonewall Kitchen** (Stonewall Lane, York, 207/351-2712 or 800/207-5267, www.stonewallkitchen.com), a phenomenally successful company that concocts imaginative condiments and other food products, many of which have received national awards. The headquarters building, home to a handsome shop with tasting areas and a "viewing gallery" where you can watch it all happen, is next to the York Chamber of Commerce building on Route 1. Go hungry: There are an espresso bar and an excellent café on the premises. Stonewall is open daily for breakfast and lunch and light fare in the late afternoon.

Don't let the forlorn and faded exterior deter you. Serving "food that loves you back," **Frankie and Johnny's Natural Foods** (1594 Rte. 1 N., Cape Neddick, 207/363-1909, www.frankie-johnnys.com, from 5 P.M. Wed.–Sun. Feb.–Dec., $18–30) is vibrant inside. Chef-owner John Shaw's eclectic menu includes vegan and vegetarian choices in addition to creative treatments of steak, chicken, and fish; the house-made pastas are excellent. Reservations are recommended for summer weekends. Be forewarned: Portions are more than generous. They do not take credit cards ("plastic is not natural"). BYOB.

I'm not sure what to tell you about **Blue Sky on York Beach** (Rte. 1A, York Beach, 207/363-0050, www.blueskyonyorkbeach.com, lunch 11:30 A.M.–3 P.M. Sun.–Fri., dinner 5:30–10 P.M. daily), located on the second floor of the Atlantic House. Opened by celebrity chef Lydia Shire, it never hit its stride, and she's no longer associated with it. The space is elegant yet welcoming, with gleaming wood floors and a wood-burning fireplace. In summer there's also seating on the porch. Food quality has been uneven and the service can be abysmal; ask locally about its current reputation, and call for menu details.

INFORMATION AND SERVICES

The Maine Tourism Association operates a **Maine State Visitor Information Center** (1 Rte. 95, Kittery, 207/439-1319) in Kittery between Route 1 and I-95, with access from either road. It's chock-full of brochures and has restrooms and a picnic area.

For York area information, head for the shingle-style palace of the **York Chamber of Commerce** (1 Stonewall Lane, off Rte. 1, York, 207/363-4422, www.gatewaytomaine.org), at I-95's York exit. Inside are restrooms. It's open daily in summer.

GETTING AROUND

The Maine Turnpike, a toll road, is generally the fastest route if you're trying to get between two towns. Route 1 parallels the turnpike on the ocean side. It's mostly two lanes and is lined with shops, restaurants, motels, and other visitor-oriented sites, which means stop-and-go traffic that often slows to a crawl. If you're traveling locally, it's best to walk or use the local trolley systems, which have the bonus of saving you the agony of finding a parking spot.

The **York Trolley** (207/748-3030, www.yorktrolley.com) operates a **York Beach Shuttle** late June–early September. The service between Long and Short Sands Beaches ($1.50 one-way) runs every 30 minutes 10 A.M.–10:15 P.M.

The **Shore Road Shuttle** (207/324-5762, www.shorelineexplorer.com) operates hourly between York's Short Sands Beach and Ogunquit's Perkins Cove late June–Labor Day; check for an exact schedule. The fare is $1 each way; a 12-ride pass is $10; age 18 and younger ride free.

Ogunquit and Wells

Ogunquit has been a holiday destination since the indigenous residents named it "beautiful place by the sea." What's the appeal? An unparalleled, unspoiled beach, several top-flight albeit pricey restaurants, a dozen art galleries, and a respected art museum with a view second to none. The town has been home to an art colony attracting the glitterati of the painting world starting with Charles Woodbury in the late 1880s. The summertime crowds continue, multiplying the minuscule year-round population. These days it's an especially gay-friendly community too. Besides the beach, the most powerful magnet is Perkins Cove, a working fishing enclave that looks more like a movie set. The best way to approach the cove is via trolley-bus or on foot, along the shoreline Marginal Way from downtown Ogunquit; midsummer parking in the cove ($3 per hour) is madness.

Wells, once the parent of Ogunquit and since 1980 its immediate neighbor to the north, was settled in 1640. Nowadays it's best known as a long, skinny, family-oriented community, seven miles of splendid beachfront, and heavy-duty commercial activity with lots of antiques and used-book shops. It also claims two spectacular nature preserves worth a drive from anywhere. At the southern end of Wells, abutting Ogunquit, is **Moody,** an enclave named after 18th-century settler Samuel Moody.

SIGHTS
◖ Ogunquit Museum of American Art (OMAA)

Not many museums can boast a view as stunning as the one at the Ogunquit Museum of American Art (543 Shore Rd., Ogunquit, 207/646-4909, www.ogunquitmuseum.org, 10 A.M.–5 P.M. Mon.–Sat., 1–5 P.M. Sun. late

© HILARY NANGLE

A wall of windows frame sculpture gardens and crashing surf at the Ogunquit Museum of American Art.

May–Oct. 31, $8 adults, $7 seniors and students, free under age 12), nor can many communities boast such renown as a summer art colony. Overlooking Narrow Cove 1.4 miles south of downtown Ogunquit, the museum prides itself on its distinguished permanent 1,600-piece American art collection. Works by Marsden Hartley, Rockwell Kent, Walt Kuhn, Henry Strater, and Thomas Hart Benton, among others, are displayed in five galleries. Special exhibits are mounted each summer, when there is an extensive series of lectures, concerts, and other programs, including the annual "Almost Labor Day Auction," a social season must. OMAA has a well-stocked gift shop, wheelchair access, and landscaped grounds with sculptures, a pond, and manicured lawns.

(Marginal Way

No visit to Ogunquit is complete without a leisurely stroll along Marginal Way, the mile-long foot path edging the ocean from Shore Road (by the Sparhawk Resort) to Perkins Cove. It has been a must-walk since Josiah Chase gave the right-of-way to the town in the 1920s. The best times to appreciate this shrub-lined shorefront walkway are early morning or when everyone's at the beach. En route are tide pools, intriguing rock formations, crashing surf, pocket beaches, benches (although the walk's a cinch and is even partially wheelchair-accessible), and a marker listing the day's high and low tides. When the surf's up, keep a close eye on the kids—the sea has no mercy. A midpoint access is at Israel's Head (behind a sewage plant masquerading as a tiny lighthouse), but getting a parking space is pure luck.

Perkins Cove

Turn-of-the-20th-century photos show Ogunquit's Perkins Cove lined with gray-shingled shacks used by a hardy colony of local fishermen, fellows who headed offshore to make a tough living in little boats. They'd hardly recognize it today. Although the cove remains a working lobster-fishing harbor, several old shacks have been reincarnated as boutiques

and restaurants, and photographers go crazy shooting the quaint inlet spanned by a little pedestrian drawbridge. In the cove are galleries, gift shops, a range of eateries (fast food to lobster to high-end dining), boat excursions, and public restrooms.

(Wells Reserve at Laudholm Farm

Known locally as Laudholm Farm (the name of the restored 19th-century visitors center), Wells National Estuarine Research Reserve (342 Laudholm Farm Rd., Wells, 207/646-1555, www.wellsreserve.org) occupies 1,690 acres of woods, beach, and coastal salt marsh on the southern boundary of the Rachel Carson National Wildlife Refuge, just 0.5 miles east of Route 1. Seven miles of trails wind through the property. The best trail is the Salt Marsh Loop, with a boardwalk section leading to an overlook with panoramic views of the marsh and Little River inlet. Another winner is the Barrier Beach Walk, a 1.3-mile round-trip that goes through multiple habitats all the way to beautiful Laudholm Beach. Allow 1.5 hours for either; you can combine the two. Some trails are wheelchair-accessible. The informative exhibits in the visitors center (10 A.M.–4 P.M. Mon.–Sat., noon–4 P.M. Sun. late May–mid-Oct., 10 A.M.–4 P.M. Mon.–Fri. Oct.–Mar., closed mid-Dec.–mid-Jan.) make a valuable prelude for enjoying the reserve. An extensive program schedule (Apr.–Nov.) includes lectures, nature walks, and children's programs. Reservations are required for some programs. Trails are accessible 7 A.M.–dusk. Late May–mid-October, admission is charged: $3 adults, $1 ages 6–16, maximum $10 per car.

Rachel Carson National Wildlife Refuge

Eleven chunks of coastal Maine real estate between Kittery Point and Cape Elizabeth make up this refuge (321 Port Rd./Rte. 9, Wells, 207/646-9226, http://rachelcarson.fws.gov) headquartered at the northern edge of Wells near the Kennebunkport town line. Pick up a *Carson Trail Guide* at the refuge office (parking is very limited) and follow the mile-long wheelchair-accessible walkway past tidal creeks, salt pans, and salt marshes. It's a bird-watcher's paradise during migration seasons. Office hours are 8 A.M.–4:30 P.M. Monday–Friday year-round; trail access is sunrise–sunset daily year-round. Leashed pets are allowed.

Ogunquit Arts Collaborative Gallery

Closer to downtown Ogunquit is the Ogunquit Arts Collaborative Gallery (Shore Rd. and Bourne Lane, Ogunquit, 207/646-8400, www.barngallery.org, 11 A.M.–5 P.M. Mon.–Sat., 1–5 P.M. Sun. late May–early Oct., free), also known as the Barn Gallery, featuring the works of member artists, an impressive group. The OAC is the showcase for the Ogunquit Art Association, established by Charles Woodbury, who was inspired to open an art school in Perkins Cove in the late 19th century. Special programs throughout the season include concerts, workshops, gallery talks, and an art auction.

Wells Auto Museum

The late Glenn Gould's collection of more than 80 vintage vehicles, some restored, others not, plus a collection of old-fashioned nickelodeons (bring nickels and dimes; they work), are jam-packed into the Wells Auto Museum (Rte. 1, Wells, 207/646-9064, www.wellsautomuseum.com, 10 A.M.–5 P.M. daily late June–late Sept., $7 adults, $4 ages 6–12). From the outside it looks like a big warehouse; inside its treasures include an original 1918 Stutz Bearcat, four Pierce Arrows, a Stanley Steamer, and an emphasis on Brass Era vehicles.

Local History Museum

Ogunquit's history is preserved in the **Ogunquit Heritage Museum** (86 Obeds Lane, Dorothea Jacobs Grant Common, Ogunquit, 207/646-0296, www.ogunquitheritagemuseum.org, 1–5 P.M. Tues.–Sat. June–Sept., donation), which opened in 2001 in the restored Captain James Winn House, a 1785 cape house listed on the National Register of Historic Places. Exhibits here and in a new ell focus on Ogunquit's role as an art colony, its maritime heritage, town history, and local architecture.

ENTERTAINMENT
Theater

Having showcased top-notch professional theater since the 1930s, the 750-seat **Ogunquit Playhouse** (Rte. 1, Ogunquit, 207/646-5511, www.ogunquitplayhouse.org), a summer classic, knows how to do it right: It presents comedies and musicals daily in summer with big-name stars. The air-conditioned building is wheelchair accessible. The box office is open daily in season, beginning in early May; tickets range $49–67. The playhouse also presents a children's series. Parking can be a hassle; consider walking the short distance from the Bourne Lane trolley-bus stop.

Live Music

Ogunquit has several nightspots with good reputations for food and live entertainment. Best known is **Jonathan's** (2 Bourne Lane, Ogunquit, 207/646-4777 or 800/464-9934 in Maine), where national headliners often are on the schedule upstairs. Advance tickets are cheaper than at the door, and dinner guests (entrées $19–32) get preference for seats; all show seats are reserved.

Ogunquit Performing Arts (207/646-6170) presents a full slate of programs, including classical concerts, ballet, and theater. The **Wells Summer Concert Series** runs most Saturday evenings early July–early September at the Hope Hobbs Gazebo in Wells Harbor Park. A wide variety of music is represented, from sing-alongs to swing.

FESTIVALS AND EVENTS

Harbor Fest takes place the second weekend of July in Harbor Park in Wells and includes a concert, a craft fair, a parade, a chicken barbecue, and children's activities.

In mid-August Ogunquit Beach hosts a **Sandcastle-Building Contest,** and in late August is the annual **Sidewalk Art Show and Sale.**

Capriccio is a performing arts festival with daytime and evening events as well as a kite festival held during the first week of September. The second weekend that month, Wells National Estuarine Research Reserve (Laudholm Farm) hosts the **Laudholm Nature Crafts Festival,** a two-day juried crafts fair with children's activities and guided nature walks. This is an especially fine event. The third weekend of September, the **Annual Ogunquit Antiques Show** benefits the Historical Society of Wells and Ogunquit.

SHOPPING
Antiques and Antiquarian Books
Antiques are a Wells specialty. You'll find more than 50 shops with a huge range of prices. The majority are on Route 1. **R. Jorgensen Antiques** (502 Post Rd./Rte. 1, Wells, 207/646-9444) is a phenomenon in itself, filling 11 showrooms in two buildings with European and American 18th- and 19th-century furniture and accessories. **MacDougall-Gionet Antiques and Associates** (2104 Post Rd./Rte. 1, Wells, 207/646-3531) has been in business since 1959, and its reputation is stellar. The 65-dealer shop, in an 18th-century barn, carries American and European country and formal furniture and accessories.

If you've been scouring antiquarian bookshops for a long-wanted title, chances are you'll find it at **Douglas N. Harding Rare Books** (2152 Post Rd./Rte. 1, Wells, 207/646-8785 or 800/228-1398). Well cataloged and organized, the sprawling bookshop at any given time stocks upward of 100,000 books, prints, and maps, plus a hefty selection of Maine and New England histories.

Lighthouse Depot
Several mini-lighthouses stand watch over the Lighthouse Depot (Post Rd./Rte. 1, Wells, 207/646-0608 or 800/758-1444, www.lighthousedepot.com), a must-stop for lighthouse aficionados. Imagine this: two floors of lighthouse books, sculptures, videos, banners, Christmas ornaments, lawn ornaments, paintings, and replicas running the gamut from pure kitsch to attractive collectibles. Depot owners Tim Harrison and Kathy Finnegan also publish the *Lighthouse Digest,* a monthly magazine focusing on North American lighthouses (annual subscription $35).

Craft
Fans of fine craft shouldn't miss **Panache** (Rte. 1, Ogunquit, 207/646-4878). It boasts of having New England's largest selection of fine contemporary art glass, but there's so much more; it's a visual treat.

RECREATION
Water Sports
BEACHES
One of Maine's most scenic and unspoiled sandy beachfronts, Ogunquit's 3.5-mile stretch of sand fringed with sea grass is a magnet for hordes of sunbathers, spectators, swimmers, surfers, and sandcastle builders. Getting there means crossing the Ogunquit River via one of three access points. For Ogunquit's **Main Beach**—with a spanking new bathhouse and big crowds—take Beach Street. To reach **Footbridge Beach,** marginally less crowded, either take Ocean Street and the footbridge or take Bourne Avenue to Ocean Avenue in adjacent Wells and walk back toward Ogunquit. **Moody Beach,** at Wells's southern end, is technically private property, a subject of considerable legal dispute. Lifeguards are on duty all summer at the public beaches, and there are restrooms in all three areas. The beach is free, but parking is not. Main Beach parking is $25 per day; the others are $15–20 per day and fill up early on warm midsummer days. After 3:30 P.M. some parking is free. It's far more sensible to opt for the frequent trolley-buses.

Wells beaches continue where Ogunquit's leave off. **Crescent Beach** (Webhannet Dr. between Eldredge Rd. and Mile Rd.) is the tiniest, with tide pools, no facilities, and limited parking. **Wells Beach** (Mile Rd. to Atlantic Ave.) is the major (and most crowded) beach, with lifeguards, restrooms, and parking. Around the other side of Wells Harbor is **Drakes Island Beach** (take Drakes Island Rd. at the blinking light), a less crowded spot with restrooms and lifeguards. Walk northeast from Drakes Island Beach and you'll eventually reach Laudholm Beach, with great birding along the way. Summer beach-parking fees are $15 per day for nonresidents ($5 for a motorcycle, $25 for an RV); if you're staying longer, a 10-visit pass ($75) is a better bargain.

EXCURSION BOATS

Depending on your interests, you can go deep-sea fishing, whale-watching, or just gawking out of Perkins Cove in Ogunquit.

Between April and early November, Captain Tim Tower runs half-day (departing 4 P.M., $45 pp) and full-day (departing 7 A.M., $75 pp) **deep-sea fishing trips** aboard the 40-foot *Bunny Clark* (207/646-2214, www .bunnyclark.com), moored in Perkins Cove. Reservations are necessary. Tim has a science degree, so he's a wealth of marine biology information. All gear is provided, and the crew will fillet your catch for you; dress warmly and wear sunblock.

Barnacle Billy's Dock at Perkins Cove is home port for the Hubbard family's **Finestkind Cruises** (207/646-5227, www .finestkindcruises.com). Motorboat options include: 1.5-hour 14-mile Nubble Lighthouse cruises; one-hour cocktail cruises; a 75-minute breakfast cruise, complete with coffee, juice, and a muffin; and 50-minute lobster-boat trips. Rates run $15–22 adults, $8–12 children. Also available are 1.75-hour sails ($30 pp) aboard *The Cricket,* a locally built wooden sailboat. Reservations are advisable but usually unnecessary midweek. Finestkind does not accept credit cards.

SEA KAYAKING

World Within Sea Kayaking (746 Ocean Ave., Wells, 207/646-0455, www.worldwithin.com) has both tours and rentals. Rentals are available on the tidal Ogunquit River to experienced kayakers for $15 per hour single, $25 per hour double.

Bike, Kayak, and Surfboard Rentals

At **Wheels and Waves** (579 Post Rd./Rte. 1, Wells, 207/646-5774, www.wheelsnwaves .com), bike rentals begin at $25 per day, including delivery to some hotels. Surfboards are $25. A single kayak is $55 per day, double $65.

Put in right at the harbor and explore the estuary from **Webhannet River Kayak and Canoe Rentals** (345 Harbor Rd., Wells, 207/646-9649, www.webhannetriver.com). Rates begin at $25 solo, $40 tandem for two hours.

Golf

The 18-hole Donald Ross–designed **Cape Neddick Country Club** (650 Shore Rd., 207/361-2011, www.capeneddickgolf.com) is a semiprivate 18-hole course with a restaurant and a driving range.

ACCOMMODATIONS

Rates are for peak season; most charge less in spring and fall. Most properties are open only seasonally.

Ogunquit
MOTELS

You're almost within spitting distance of Perkins Cove at the 37-room **Riverside Motel** (159 Shore Rd., 207/646-2741, www.riverside-motel.com, $189–219), where you can perch on your balcony and watch the action or, for that matter, join it. Guest rooms have phones, air-conditioning, refrigerators, Wi-Fi, cable TV, and fabulous views. Rates include continental breakfast. The entire 3.5-acre property is smoke-free.

Juniper Hill Inn (336 Main St., 207/646-4501 or 800/646-4544, www.ogunquit.com, year-round, $139–234) is a particularly well-run motel-style lodging on five acres close to downtown Ogunquit, with a footpath to the beach. Amenities include refrigerators, cable TV, coin-operated laundry, a fitness center, indoor and outdoor pools and hot tubs, and golf privileges. Rooms have all the amenities, including free Wi-Fi.

You can't get much closer to the water than the **Above Tide Inn** (66 Beach St., 207/646-7454, www.abovetideinn.com, $190–250), built on a wharf over the tidal Ogunquit River with views to the open Atlantic. It is steps from the beach and downtown Ogunquit. Each of the nine guest rooms has air-conditioning, a TV, and a mini-fridge, but no phone; a light breakfast is provided.

COTTAGES

It's nearly impossible to land a peak-season cottage at **The Dunes** (518 Main St., 207/646-2612, www.dunesonthewaterfront.com), but it's worth trying. The property is under its third generation of ownership and guests practically will their weeks to their descendants. Nineteen tidy, well-equipped 1–2-bedroom housekeeping cottages with screened porches and wood-burning fireplaces as well as 17 guest rooms are generously spaced on shady, grassy lawns that roll down to the river, with the dunes just beyond. Facilities include a dock with rowboats, a pool, and lawn games. Amenities include Wi-Fi, TVs, phones, and refrigerators. It's all meticulously maintained. In peak season, the 1–2-bedroom cottages require a 1–2-week minimum stay; guest rooms require three nights. Rooms begin around $140, cottages at $235 per night or $1,540 weekly.

ECLECTIC PROPERTIES

It's not easy to describe the **Sparhawk Oceanfront Resort** (41 Shore Rd., 207/646-5562, www.thesparhawk.com, $195–315), a sprawling one-of-a-kind place popular with honeymooners, sedate families, and seniors. There's lots of tradition in this thriving six-acre complex—it has had various incarnations since the turn of the 20th century—and the "Happily Filled" sign regularly hangs out front. Out back is the Atlantic Ocean with forever views, and the Marginal Way starts right here. It offers a tennis court, gardens, and a heated pool; breakfast is included. The 87 guest rooms in four buildings vary from motel-type (best views) rooms and suites to inn-type

suites. There's a seven-night minimum during July–August.

The Beachmere Inn (62 Beachmere Pl., 207/646-2021 or 800/336-3983, www.beachmereinn.com, year-round, $160–380) is another unique property. The private family-owned and operated oceanfront property comprises an updated Victorian inn, a new seaside motel, and other buildings, all meticulously maintained and often updated, along with its own beaches. All rooms have air-conditioning, TVs, and phones; many rooms have kitchenettes; most have balconies, decks, or terraces; some have fireplaces. There's also a small spa with a hot tub, a steam sauna, and a fitness room. Morning coffee and pastries are provided.

BED-AND-BREAKFASTS

Built in 1899 for a prominent Maine lumbering family, **C Rockmere Lodge** (40 Stearns Rd., 207/646-2985, www.rockmere.com, year-round, $185–235) underwent a meticulous six-month restoration in the early 1990s thanks to preservationists Andy Antoniuk and Bob Brown, and in 2006 the duo, along with Doug Flint, gave the inn and grounds a complete rejuvenation, lightening the decor a bit. Near the Marginal Way on a peaceful street, the handsome home has eight very comfortable Victorian guest rooms, all with CD players and cable TV (a 1,000-title library of films and CDs is available) and most with ocean views. Rates include a generous breakfast. A wrap-around veranda, a gazebo, and "The Lookout," a third-floor windowed nook with comfy chairs, make it easy to settle in and just watch the passersby on the Marginal Way. The woodwork throughout is gorgeous, and the grounds double as a public garden. Beach towels, chairs, and umbrellas are provided for guests. Pets are not allowed; there are four dogs in residence.

Jacqui Grant's warm welcome, gracious hospitality, and stellar breakfasts combined with a quiet residential location within walking distance of both the village and Footbridge Beach have earned **Almost Home** (27 King's Lane, 207/641-1754, www.almosthomeinnogunquit

.com, $169–199) a stellar reputation. She often serves afternoon cheese with wine from her son's California winery. Rooms are spacious and have nice seating areas, and the backyard makes a quiet retreat.

RESORTS

Founded in 1872, **The Cliff House Resort and Spa** (Shore Rd., 207/361-1000, www .cliffhousemaine.com, late Mar.–early Dec., $265–360), a self-contained complex, sprawls over 70 acres topping the edge of Bald Head Cliff midway between the centers of York and Ogunquit. Third-generation innkeeper Kathryn Weare keeps updating and modernizing the facilities. Among the most recent additions is a spa building with oversize rooms with king beds, gas fireplaces, and balconies as well as a full-service spa, an indoor pool, an outdoor infinity pool, and a glass-walled fitness center overlooking the Atlantic. A central check-in building with an indoor amphitheater connects the main building to the spa building. The 150 guest rooms and suites vary widely in decor, from old-fashioned to contemporary; all have cable TV and phones, some have gas fireplaces, and most have a spectacular ocean view. Other facilities include a dining room, a lounge, family indoor and outdoor pools, a games room, and tennis courts. Eight pet-friendly rooms ($25) have a bowl, a bed, and treats, and there's a fenced-in exercise area. Packages offer the best bang for the buck.

Wells

Once part of a giant 19th-century dairy farm, the **Beach Farm Inn** (97 Eldredge Rd., 207/646-8493, www.beachfarminn.com, year-round, $100–135) is a 2.5-acre oasis in a rather congested area 0.2 miles off Route 1. Guests can swim in the pool, relax in the library, or walk 0.25 miles down the road to the beach. Five of the eight guest rooms have private baths (two are detached); third-floor rooms have air-conditioning. Rates include a full breakfast; two cottages go for $695 and $975 per week.

Even closer to the beach is **Haven by the Sea** (59 Church St., Wells Beach, 207/646-

4194, www.havenbythesea.com, $209–269), a heavenly bed-and-breakfast in a former church. Innkeepers John and Susan Jarvis have kept the original floor plan, which allows for some surprises. Inside are hardwood floors, cathedral ceilings, and stained-glass windows. The confessional is now a full bar, and the altar has been converted to a dining area that opens to a marsh-view terrace—the bird-watching is superb. Guest rooms have sitting areas, and the suite has a whirlpool tub and a fireplace. Guests have plenty of room to relax, including a living area with a fireplace. Rates include a full breakfast and afternoon hors d'oeuvres.

FOOD
Ogunquit
LOCAL FLAVORS

The Egg and I (501 Maine St./Rte. 1, 207/646-8777, www.eggandibreakfast.com, 6 A.M.–2 P.M. daily, no credit cards) has more than 200 menu choices and earns high marks for its omelets and waffles. You can't miss it; there's always a crowd. Lunch choices are served after 11 A.M.

Equally popular is **Amore Breakfast** (309 Shore Rd., 207/646-6661, www.amorebreakfast.com, 7 A.M.–1 P.M. daily). Choose from 14 omelets, eight versions of eggs Benedict (including lobster and a spirited rancheros version topped with salsa and served with guacamole), as well as French toast, waffles, and all the regulars and irregulars.

Eat in or take out from **Village Food Market** (Main St., Ogunquit Center, 207/646-2122, www.villagefoodmarket.com). A breakfast sandwich is less than $3, subs and sandwiches are available in three sizes, and there's even a children's menu. The Pick Three prepared dinner special includes an entrée, two side dishes, and bread for $9.95.

Scrumptious baked goods, tantalizing salads, and vegetarian lunch items are available to go at Mary Breen's fabulous **Bread and Roses** (246 Main St., 207/646-4227, www.breadandrosesbakery.com, 7 A.M.–11 P.M. daily), a small bakery right downtown with a few tables outside.

Harbor Candy Shop (26 Main St., 207/646-8078 or 800/331-5856) is packed with the most outrageous chocolate imaginable. Fudge, truffles, and turtles are all made on-site.

ETHNIC FARE

The closest thing to an upscale rustic French country inn is the dining room at **(Provence** (262 Shore Rd., 207/646-9898, www.98provence.com, 5:30 p.m.–close Wed.–Mon.), also referred to as 98 Provence. Chef-owner Pierre Gignac turns out appetizers and superb entrées in the $22–35 range, but there are also three fixed menus ($30–45). Possibilities may include foie gras, escargot, rabbit, cassoulet, and always a fish of the day. Service is attentive and well paced. Don't miss it, and be sure to make reservations.

The best and most authentic Italian dining is at **Angelina's Ristorante** (655 Main St./Rte. 1, 207/646-0445, www.angelinasogunquit.com, 4:30–10 p.m. daily year-round, $15–27). Chef-owner David Giarusso uses recipes handed down from his great grandmother, Angelina Peluso. Dine in the dining room, wine room, lounge, or out on the terrace, choosing from pastas, risottos (the house specialty), and other classics.

Angelina's sister restaurant, actually a martini bar and lounge, is **Tapas and Tini's** (125 Main St./Rte. 1, 207/646-9700, www.angelinasogunquit.com, 4:30–10 p.m. daily). It's perfect for making a meal out of small plates but also has salads, sandwiches, and entrées, all with a worldly flair.

CASUAL DINING

Gypsy Sweethearts (10 Shore Rd., 207/646-7021, www.gypsysweethearts.com, 5:30–9 p.m. Tues.–Sun., entrées $18–30) serves in four rooms on the ground floor of a restored house and a garden. It's one of the region's most reliable restaurants, and the creative menu is infused with ethnic accents and includes vegetarian choices. Seating is both inside and out. Reservations are advised in midsummer.

Equally reliable and just to the south is **Five-O** (50 Shore Rd., 207/646-6365, www.five-oshoreroad.com, dinner 5–10 p.m. daily, breakfast 8–11:30 a.m. Sat.–Sun.), which turns out classics with flair complemented by well-conceived inspirations. The menus changes frequently, but entrées usually run $25–33. Lighter fare ($12–24) is available until 11 p.m. in the lounge, where martinis are a specialty. In the off-season, multicourse regional dinners are held about once a month ($70). Valet parking is available. There are also a piano bar and a lounge with seating and food service.

Boisterous and lively, **The Front Porch** (9 Shore Rd., 207/646-4005, www.thefrontporch.net, dinner from 4 p.m. Wed.–Sat., from 1 p.m. Sun., $13–29) is not for those looking for romantic dining, but it is a good choice for families with divergent tastes. The menu ranges from flatbread pizzas to filet mignon.

DINING WITH A VIEW

There's not much between you and Spain when you get a window seat at **(MC** (Oarweed Lane, Perkins Cove, Ogunquit, 207/646-6263, www.mcperkinscove.com, 11:30 a.m.–3:30 p.m. and 5–11 p.m. daily late May–mid-Oct., 11:30 a.m.–3:30 p.m. and 5–11 p.m. Wed.–Sun. mid-Oct.–Dec. and Feb.–late May, dinner entrées $24–34), sister restaurant of the mega-high-end Arrows Restaurant. Almost every table on both floors has a view. Service is attentive, and the food is fab, creative, and in keeping with James Beard Award–winning chefs Mark Gaier and Clark Frasier, ultra fresh. If you can't justify the splurge for Arrows, get a taste of their cuisine here. The bar menu, also served in the dining room by request, is served until 11 p.m. Keep it light with a burger or fish tacos, or opt for the dinner menu, where choices might include sesame-crusted deep-fried rainbow trout or lobster "mac and cheese." There's often live music on Wednesday nights. A jazz brunch is served beginning at 11 a.m. Sunday September–June. Reservations are essential for dinner.

Equally if not more impressive are the views from the dining room at **The Cliff**

© HILARY NANGLE

You can't get much closer to crashing surf than at The Cliff House in Ogunquit.

House (Shore Rd., Ogunquit, 207/361-1000, entrées $23–35). Go for the breakfast buffet 7:30 A.M.–1 P.M. Sunday. Service can be so-so. Before or after dining, wander the grounds.

DESTINATION DINING

Restrain yourself for a couple of days and then splurge on an elegant dinner at **Arrows** (Berwick Rd., about 1.5 miles west of Rte. 1, 207/361-1100, www.arrowsrestaurant.com, dinner from 6 P.M. Wed.–Sun. June–mid-Oct.; Thurs.–Sun. late Apr.–May, late Oct., and Dec.; Fri.–Sun. Nov.), one of Maine's finest—and priciest—restaurants. In a beautifully restored 18th-century farmhouse overlooking well-tended gardens (including a one-acre kitchen garden that supplies about 90 percent of the produce), co-owners Mark Gaier and Clark Frasier, the 2010 James Beard Best Chefs Northeast Award winners, do everything right. Plan on spending at least $250 per couple. Appetizers run $18–25, entrées cost close to $50, or consider the six-course tasting menu ($95); serious foodies might

splurge on the indulgence tasting menu (10 courses for $135). On Friday nights a three-course bistro menu is offered ($39). A credit card is required for reservations—essential in midsummer and on weekends. Jackets are preferred for men, and shorts are not allowed. Off-season, ask about winemaker, regional, and bistro nights as well as specialty dinners and cooking classes.

LOBSTER

Creative marketing, a knockout view, and efficient service help explain why more than 1,000 pounds of lobster bite the dust every summer day at **Barnacle Billy's** (Perkins Cove, 207/646-5575 or 800/866-5575, www.barn-billy.com, 11 A.M.–9 P.M. daily seasonally). Billy's has a full liquor license; try for the deck, with a front-row seat on Perkins Cove.

Less flashy and less pricey is **The Lobster Shack** (Perkins Cove, 207/646-2941, www.lobster-shack.com, 11 A.M.–9 P.M. daily), serving lobsters, stews, chowders, and some landlubber choices too.

Wells

LOCAL FLAVORS

Bean suppers are held 5–7 P.M. on the first Saturday of the month May–October at the Masonic Hall on Sanford Road.

For scrumptious baked goods and made-to-order sandwiches, head to **Borealis Bread** (Rte. 1, Wells, 8:30 A.M.–5:30 P.M. Mon.–Sat., 9 A.M.–4 P.M. Sun.), in the Aubuchon Hardware plaza adjacent to the Wells Auto Museum.

Pick up all sorts of fresh goodies at the **Wells Farmers Market** (1–5:30 P.M. Wed.) in the Town Hall parking lot (208 Sanford Rd.).

FAMILY FAVORITES

No eatery in this category qualifies as heart-healthy; don't say you weren't forewarned.

For fresh lobster, lobster rolls, fish-and-chips, chowders, and homemade desserts, you can't go wrong at the Cardinali family's ◖ **Fisherman's Catch** (Harbor Rd./Rte. 1, 207/646-8780, www.fishermanscatchwells.com, 11:30 A.M.–9 P.M. daily early May–mid-Oct., $7–21). Big windows in the rustic dining room frame the marsh; some even have binoculars for wildlife spotting. It might seem out of the way, but trust me, the locals all know this little gem.

SURF AND TURF

A good steak in the land of lobster? You betcha: **The Steakhouse** (1205 Post Rd./Rte. 1, 207/646-4200, www.the-steakhouse.com, 4–9:30 P.M. Tues.–Sun., entrées $14–26) is a great big barn of a place where steaks are hand cut from USDA prime and choice corn-fed Western beef that has never been frozen. Chicken, seafood, lobster (great stew), and even a vegetarian stir-fry are also on the menu; a children's menu is also available. Service is efficient but they don't take reservations, so be prepared for a wait; this place is very popular.

FINE DINING

Chef Joshua W. Mather of ◖ **Joshua's** (1637 Rte. 1, 207/646-3355, www.joshuas.biz, 5–10 P.M. Mon.–Sat., entrées $20–31) grew up on his family's nearby organic farm, and produce from that farm highlights the menu. In a true family operation, his parents not only still work the farm, they also work in the restaurant, a converted 1774 home with many of its original architectural elements. Everything is made on the premises, from the fabulous bread to the hand-churned ice cream. The Atlantic haddock, with caramelized onion crust, chive oil, and wild mushroom risotto, is a signature dish, and it alone is worth coming for. A vegetarian pasta entrée is offered nightly. Save room for the maple walnut pie with maple ice cream. Yes, it's gilding the lily, but you can always walk the beach afterward. Reservations are essential for the dining rooms, but the full menu is also served in the bar.

INFORMATION AND SERVICES

At the southern edge of Ogunquit, right next to the Ogunquit Playhouse, the **Ogunquit Chamber of Commerce's Welcome Center** (Rte. 1, Ogunquit, 207/646-2939, www.ogunquit.org) provides all the usual visitor information and has public restrooms. Ask for the Touring and Trolley Route Map, showing the Marginal Way, beach locations, and public restrooms. The chamber of commerce's annual visitor booklet thoughtfully carries a high-tide calendar for the summer.

Just over the Ogunquit border in Wells (actually in Moody) is the **Wells Information Center** (Rte. 1 at Bourne Ave., 207/646-2451, www.wellschamber.org).

The handsome fieldstone **Ogunquit Memorial Library** (74 Shore Rd., Ogunquit, 207/646-9024) is downtown's only building on the National Register of Historic Places. Or visit the **Wells Public Library** (1434 Post Rd./Rte. 1, 207/646-8181, www.wells.lib.me.us).

GETTING THERE

Amtrak's *Downeaster* (800/872-7245, www.thedowneaster.com), which connects Boston's North Station with Portland, Maine, stops in Wells. The Shoreline Explorer trolley connects in season.

GETTING AROUND

The Maine Turnpike, a toll road, is generally the fastest route if you're trying to get between two towns. Route 1 parallels the turnpike on the ocean side. It's mostly two lanes and is lined with shops, restaurants, motels, and other tourist-oriented sites, which means stop-and-go traffic that often slows to a crawl. If you're traveling locally, it's best to walk or use the local trolley systems, which have the bonus of saving you the agony of finding a parking spot.

Trolleys

The **Shoreline Explorer** (207/324-5762, www.shorelineexplorer.com) trolley system makes it possible to connect from York to Kennebunkport without your car. Each town's system is operated separately and has its own fees. The **Shoreline Trolley Route 4,** operating late June–early September, serves Wells; one-way fare is $1, a day pass is $3, and those age 18 and younger ride free.

The Kennebunks

The world may have first learned of Kennebunkport when George Herbert Walker Bush was president, but Walkers and Bushes have owned their summer estate here for three generations. Visitors continue to come to the Kennebunks (the collective name for **Kennebunk, Kennebunkport, Cape Porpoise,** and **Goose Rocks Beach**) hoping to catch a glimpse of the former first family, but they also come for the terrific ambience, bed-and-breakfasts, boutiques, boats, biking, and beaches.

The Kennebunks' earliest European settlers arrived in the mid-1600s. By the mid-1700s, shipbuilding had become big business in the area. Two ancient local cemeteries—North Street and Evergreen—provide glimpses of the area's heritage. Its Historic District reveals Kennebunk's moneyed past—the homes where wealthy ship owners and shipbuilders once lived, sending their vessels to the Caribbean and around the globe. Today, unusual shrubs and a dozen varieties of rare maples still line Summer Street—the legacy of ship captains in the global trade. Another legacy is the shiplap construction in many houses—a throwback to a time when labor was cheap and lumber plentiful. Closer to the beach in Lower Village stood the workshops of sailmakers, carpenters, and mast makers whose output drove the booming trade to success.

While Kennebunkport draws most of the sightseers and summer traffic, Kennebunk feels more like a year-round community. Its old-fashioned downtown has a mix of shops, restaurants, and attractions. Yes, its beaches are also well known, but many visitors drive right through the middle of Kennebunk without stopping to enjoy its assets.

SIGHTS
◖ Seashore Trolley Museum

There's nothing quite like an antique electric trolley to dredge up nostalgia for bygone days. With a collection of more than 250 transit vehicles (more than two dozen trolleys on display), the Seashore Trolley Museum (195 Log Cabin Rd., Kennebunkport, 207/967-2800, www.trolleymuseum.org, $8 adults, $6 seniors, $5.50 ages 6–16) verges on trolley mania. Whistles blowing and bells clanging, restored streetcars do frequent trips (10:05 A.M.–4:15 P.M.) on a 3.5-mile loop through the nearby woods. Ride as often as you wish, then check out the activity in the streetcar workshop and go wild in the trolley-oriented gift shop. Bring a picnic lunch and enjoy it here. Special events are held throughout the summer, including Ice Cream and Sunset Trolley Rides ($5, includes ice cream) at 7 P.M. every Wednesday–Friday in July–August. And here's an interesting wrinkle: Make a reservation, plunk down $60, and you can have a one-hour "Motorman" experience driving your own trolley (with help, of

THE KENNEBUNKS

- SEASHORE TROLLEY MUSEUM
- ARUNDEL BARN PLAYHOUSE
- THE BRICK STORE MUSEUM
- KENNEBUNK POLICE
- WEDDING CAKE HOUSE
- INFORMATION CENTER
- DOCK SQUARE
- GRISSINI
- ALL DAY BREAKFAST
- THE WHITE BARN INN
- ST. ANTHONY'S MONASTERY
- KENNEBUNKPORT POLICE
- THE NOTT HOUSE
- CAPTAIN LORD MANSION
- LUCAS ON 9
- NUNAN'S LOBSTER HUT
- GOAT ISLAND LIGHT
- THE BUSH ESTATE
- CAPE ARUNDEL INN
- RACHEL CARSON NATIONAL WILDLIFE REFUGE
- WELLS RESERVE AT LAUDHOLM FARM

Cape Porpoise

Kennebunkport

Kennebunk

West Kennebunk

Arundel

Goose Rocks Beach

Lower Village

Mother's Beach

Colony Beach

Gooch's Beach

Walker's Point

Spouting Rock

Turbat's Creek

Cape Porpoise Harbor

Stage Island

Trott Island

Vaughn's Island

ATLANTIC OCEAN

To Biddeford

To Wells

© AVALON TRAVEL

course). The museum is 1.7 miles southeast of Route 1. It's open 10 A.M.–5 P.M. daily late May–mid-October and on weekends in May, late October, and Christmas Prelude.

Walker's Point: The Bush Estate

There's no public access to Walker's Point, but you can join the sidewalk gawkers on Ocean Avenue overlooking George and Barbara Bush's summer compound. The 41st president and his wife lead a low-key laid-back life when they're here, so if you don't spot them through binoculars, you may well run into them at a shop or restaurant in town. Intown Trolley's regular narrated tours go right past the house—or it's an easy, scenic family walk from Kennebunkport's Dock Square. On the way, you'll pass **St. Ann's Church,** whose stones came from the ocean floor, and the paths to **Spouting Rock** and **Blowing Cave,** two natural phenomena that create spectacular water fountains if you manage to be there midway between high and low tides.

Wedding Cake House

The Wedding Cake House (104 Summer St., Kennebunk) is a private residence, so you can't go inside, but it's one of Maine's most-photographed buildings. Driving down Summer Street (Rte. 35), midway between the downtowns of Kennebunk and Kennebunkport, it's hard to miss the yellow and white Federal mansion with gobs of gingerbread and Gothic Revival spires and arches. Built in 1826 by shipbuilder George Bourne as a wedding gift for his wife, the Kennebunk landmark remained in the family until 1983.

Cape Porpoise

When your mind's eye conjures an idyllic lobster-fishing village, it probably looks a lot like Cape Porpoise, only 2.5 miles from busy Dock Square. Follow Route 9 eastward from Kennebunkport; when Route 9 turns north, continue straight and take Pier Road to its end. From the small parking area, you'll see lobster boats at anchor, a slew of working wharves,

© HILARY NANGLE

Cape Porpoise's harbor is crowded with lobster boats.

and 19th-century **Goat Island Light,** now automated, directly offshore.

Local History Museums

Occupying four restored 19th-century buildings in downtown Kennebunk, including the 1825 William Lord store, **The Brick Store Museum** (117 Main St., Kennebunk, 207/985-4802, www.brickstoremuseum.org, 10 A.M.–4:30 P.M. Tues.–Fri., 10 A.M.–1 P.M. Sat., $5 suggested donation) has garnered a reputation for unusual exhibits: a century of wedding dresses, a two-century history of volunteer firefighting, and life in southern Maine during the Civil War. The museum encourages appreciation for the surrounding Kennebunk Historic District with 50–90-minute **architectural walking tours** ($5), usually May–mid-October but call for a current schedule. If the schedule doesn't suit, the museum sells a walk-it-yourself booklet ($5).

Owned and maintained by the Kennebunkport Historical Society, **The Nott House** (8 Maine St., Kennebunkport, 207/967-2751, www.kporthistory.org, guided tours 10 A.M.–4 P.M. Thurs., 1–4 P.M. Fri., 10 A.M.–1 P.M. Sat. early July–late Aug., reduced hours spring and fall, donation) is a mid-19th-century Greek Revival mansion filled with Victorian furnishings. Be sure to visit the restored gardens. Hour-long architectural walking tours ($7 adults, free under age 18) of the Kennebunkport Historic District depart from the Nott House at 11 A.M. Thursday in July–August and Saturday September–mid-October. At the house, you can buy a guidebook ($4) for a do-it-yourself tour.

(Dock Square

Even if you're not a shopper, make it a point to meander through the heart of Kennebunkport's shopping district, where one-time fishing shacks have been restored and renovated into upscale shops, boutiques, galleries, and dining spots. Some shops, especially those on upper floors, offer fine harbor views. If you're willing to poke around a bit, you'll find some unusual items that make distinctive souvenirs or

gifts—pottery, vintage clothing, books, specialty foods, and yes, T-shirts.

(St. Anthony's Monastery

Long ago, 35,000 Native Americans used this part of town as a summer camp. So did a group of Lithuanian Franciscan monks who in 1947 fled war-ravaged Europe and acquired the 200-acre St. Anthony's Franciscan Monastery (Beach St., Kennebunk, 207/967-2011, www.framon.net). They ran a high school here 1956–1969, and the monks still occupy the handsome Tudor great house, but the well-tended grounds (sprinkled with shrines and a recently restored sculpture created by Vytautas Jonynas for the Vatican Pavilion at the 1964 World's Fair) are open to the public sunrise–sunset daily. A short path leads from the monastery area to a peaceful gazebo overlooking the Kennebunk River. Pets and bikes are not allowed; public restrooms are available.

ENTERTAINMENT AND EVENTS

Kennebunk Parks and Recreation sponsors **Concerts in the Park,** a weekly series of free concerts 6:30–7:30 P.M. Wednesday late June–mid-August in Rotary Park on Water Street. The Breakwater Inn screens free **Movies on the Lawn** at 8 P.M. Thursday.

Live professional summer theater is on tap at the **Arundel Barn Playhouse** (53 Old Post Rd., Arundel, 207/985-5552, www.arundelbarnplayhouse.com, $28–39), with productions staged in a renovated 1888 barn June–September.

River Tree Arts (RTA)

The area's cultural spearhead is River Tree Arts (35 Western Ave., Kennebunk, 207/967-9120, www.rivertreearts.org), an incredibly energetic volunteer-driven organization that sponsors concerts, classes, workshops, exhibits, and educational programs throughout the year.

Festivals and Events

The **Fine Living Festival** in early June celebrates art and food with exhibits, social

© HILARY NANGLE

The walking trails at St. Anthony's Monastery provide nice views of the Kennebunk River.

events, food and wine tastings, celebrity chef dinners, and live music. The first two weekends of December mark the festive **Christmas Prelude,** during which spectacular decorations adorn historic homes, candle-toting carolers stroll through the Kennebunks, stores have special sales, and Santa Claus shows up in a lobster boat.

SHOPPING

Lots of small attractive boutiques surround **Dock Square,** the hub of Kennebunkport, so gridlock often develops in midsummer. Avoid driving through here at the height of the season. Take your time and walk, bike, or ride the local trolley-bus. This is just a sampling of the shopping opportunities.

Antiques and Art

English, European, and American furniture and architectural elements and garden accessories are just a sampling of what you'll find at **Antiques on Nine** (Rte. 9, Lower Village, Kennebunk, 207/967-0626). Another good place

for browsing high-end antiques as well as home accents is **Hurlburt Designs** (Rte. 9, Lower Village, Kennebunk, 207/967-4110). More than 30 artists are represented at **Wright Gallery** (Pier Rd., Cape Porpoise, 207/967-5053).

Jean Briggs represents nearly 100 artists at her topflight **Mast Cove Galleries** (Maine St. and Mast Cove Lane, Kennebunkport, 207/967-3453, www.mastcove.com), in a handsome Greek Revival house near the Graves Memorial Library. Prices vary widely, so don't be surprised if you spot something affordable. The gallery often sponsors 2.5-hour evening jazz concerts in July–August ($15 donation includes light refreshments). Call for a schedule.

The Gallery on Chase Hill (10 Chase Hill Rd., Kennebunkport, 207/967-0049), in the stunningly restored Captain Chase House, mounts rotating exhibits and represents a wide variety of Maine and New England artists. It's a sibling of the **Maine Art Gallery** (14 Western Ave., Kennebunkport, 207/967-0049, www.maine-art.com), which is right

© HILARY NANGLE

Dock Square is the heart of Kennebunkport's shopping district.

down the street. **Compliments** (Dock Sq., Kennebunkport, 207/967-2269) has a truly unique and fun collection of contemporary fine American crafts, with an emphasis on glass and ceramic wear.

Specialty Shops

Since 1968, **Port Canvas** (9 Ocean Ave., Kennebunkport, 207/985-9765 or 800/333-6788) has been turning out the best in durable cotton-canvas products. Need a new double-bottomed tote bag? It's here. Also available are golf-bag covers, belts, computer cases, day packs, and, of course, duffel bags.

Quilt fans should make time to visit **Mainely Quilts** (108 Summer St./Rte. 35, Kennebunk, 207/985-4250), behind the Waldo Emerson Inn. The shop has a nice selection of contemporary and antique quilts.

Most of the clothing shops clustered around Dock Square are rather pricey. Not so **Arbitrage** (28 Dock Sq., Kennebunkport, 207/967-9989), which combines designer consignment clothing with new fashions,

vintage designer costume jewelry, shoes, and handbags.

All-natural beeswax bowls can be filled with sand, rocks, plants, and other natural objects at **Presence of Nature** (24 Ocean Ave., Kennebunkport, 207/604-4779).

Irresistible eye-dazzling costume jewelry, hair ornaments, handbags, lotions, cards, and other delightful finds fill every possible space at **Dannah** (123 Ocean Ave., Kennebunkport, 207/967-8640), in the Breakwater Spa building, with free customer-only parking in the rear.

Tom's of Maine Natural Living Store (Storer St., just off Main St., Kennebunk, 207/985-3874) is an eco-sensitive local-turned-global firm that makes soaps, toothpaste, oils, and other products. The "factory seconds" are real bargains.

For a good read, stop by **Kennebooks** (149 Port Rd., Lower Village, Kennebunk, 207/967-6136), which carries books and a whole lot more.

RECREATION
Parks and Preserves

Thanks to a dedicated coterie of year-round and summer residents, the foresighted **Kennebunkport Conservation Trust** (KCT, kporttrust.org), founded in 1974, has become a nationwide model for land-trust organizations. The KCT has managed to preserve from development several hundred acres of land, including 11 small islands off Cape Porpoise Harbor, and most of this acreage is accessible to the public, especially with a sea kayak. The trust has even assumed ownership of 7.7-acre Goat Island, with its distinctive lighthouse visible from Cape Porpoise, and other coastal vantage points.

VAUGHN'S ISLAND PRESERVE

To visit Vaughn's Island you'll need to do a little planning, tide-wise, since the 96-acre island is about 600 feet offshore. Consult a tide calendar and aim for low tide close to the new moon or full moon, when the most water drains away. Allow yourself an hour or so before and after low tide, but no longer, or you may need a boat rescue. Wear treaded rubber boots, since the crossing is muddy and slippery with rockweed. Keep an eye on your watch and explore the ocean (east) side of the island, along the beach. It's worth the effort, and there's a great view of Goat Island Light off to the east. From downtown Kennebunkport, take Maine Street to Wildes District Road. Continue to Shore Road (also called Turbat's Creek Rd.), go 0.6 miles, jog left 0.2 miles more, and park in the tiny lot at the end.

EMMONS PRESERVE
Also under Kennebunkport Conservation Trust's stewardship, the Emmons Preserve has three trails (blazed blue, yellow, and pink) meandering through 146 acres of woods and fields on the edge of Batson's River (also called Gravelly Brook). The yellow trail gives best access to the water. Fall colors here are brilliant, birdlife is abundant, and you can do a loop in half an hour. But why rush? This is a wonderful oasis in the heart of Kennebunkport. From Dock Square, take North Street to Beachwood Avenue (right turn) to Gravelly Brook Road (left turn). The trailhead is on the left.

PICNIC ROCK
About 1.5 miles up the Kennebunk River from the ocean, Picnic Rock is the centerpiece of the **Butler Preserve,** a 14-acre enclave managed by the Nature Conservancy. Well named, the rock is a great place for a picnic and a swim, but don't count on being alone. A short trail loops through the preserve. Consider bringing a canoe or kayak (or renting one) and paddling with the tide past beautiful homes and the Cape Arundel Golf Club. From Lower Village Kennebunk, take Route 35 west and hang a right onto Old Port Road. When the road gets close to the Kennebunk River, watch for a Nature Conservancy oak-leaf sign on the right. Parking is along Old Port Road; walk down through the preserve to Picnic Rock, right on the river.

Water Sports
BEACHES
Ah, the beaches. The Kennebunks are well endowed with sand but not with parking spaces.

Parking permits are required, and you need a separate pass for each town. Many lodgings provide free permits for their guests—be sure to ask when making room reservations. You can avoid the parking nightmare altogether by hopping aboard the Intown Trolley, which goes right by the major beaches.

The main beaches in **Kennebunk** (east to west, stretching about 2 miles) are 3,346-foot-long Gooch's (the most popular), Kennebunk (locally called Middle Beach or Rocks Beach), and Mother's (a smallish beach next to Lords Point, where there's also a playground). Lifeguards are on duty at Gooch's and Mother's Beaches July–Labor Day. Ask locally about a couple of other beach options. Mid-June–mid-September you'll need to buy a parking permit ($15 per day, $25 per week, $50 for the season) from the Kennebunk Town Hall (4 Summer St., 207/985-3675).

Kennebunkport's claim to beach fame is three-mile-long Goose Rocks Beach, one of the loveliest in the area. Parking spaces are scarce, and a permit is required. Permits ($12 per day, $50 per week, $100 for the season) are available from the Kennebunkport Police Station (101 Main St., 207/967-4243, 24 hours daily) and Kennebunkport Town Hall (6 Elm St.). To reach the beach, take Route 9 from Dock Square east and north to Dyke Road (Clock Farm Corner). Turn right and continue to the end (King's Hwy.).

The prize for tiniest beach goes to Colony (officially Arundel) Beach, near The Colony resort complex. It's close to many Kennebunkport lodgings and an easy walk from Dock Square; no permit is necessary.

EXCURSION BOATS
Join Captain Gary aboard the 87-foot **Nick's Chance** (4 Western Ave., Lower Village, Kennebunk, 207/967-5507 or 800/767-2628, www.firstchancewhalewatch.com, $48 adults, $28 ages 3–12, $10 under age 3, cash only) for 4.5-hour whale-watching trip to Jeffrey's Ledge, weather permitting. The destination is the summer feeding grounds for finbacks, humpbacks, minkes, the rare blue whale,

and the endangered right whale. The boat departs once or twice daily late June–early September, weekends only spring and fall, from Performance Marine, behind Bartley's Restaurant, in Kennebunk Lower Village.

Under the same ownership and departing from the same location is the 65-foot open lobster boat *Kylie's Chance,* which departs four times daily in July–August for 1.5-hour scenic lobster cruises ($20 adults, $15 ages 3–12, cash only); the schedule is reduced in spring and fall. A lobstering demonstration is given on most trips but never on the evening one.

For day sailing, the 37-foot one-ton former racing yacht *Bellatrix* (95 Ocean Ave., Kennebunkport, 207/590-1125, www.sailing trips.com) charges $300 for a three-hour sail for up to six people. The handsome 55-foot gaff-rigged schooner *Eleanor* (Arundel Wharf, 43 Ocean Ave., Kennebunkport, 207/967-8809, www.gwi.net/schoonersails) heads out for two-hour sails ($40 pp), weather and tides willing, 1–3 times daily during the summer.

CANOEING AND KAYAKING

Explore the Kennebunk River by canoe or kayak. **Kennebunkport Marina** (67 Ocean Ave., Kennebunkport, 207/967-3411, www .kennebunkportmarina.com) rents canoes and single kayaks ($25 for 2 hours, $45 per half-day) and double kayaks ($45 for 2 hours, $60 per half-day). Check the tide before you depart, and plan your trip to paddle with it rather than against it.

Coastal Maine Kayak (8 Western Ave., Lower Village, Kennebunk, 207/967-6065, www.coastalmainekayak.com) offers daylong guided kayak tours to Cape Porpoise ($80), including instruction and equipment but not lunch. Rental kayaks are $35 half-day, $60 full day, and $300 per week; doubles are $60, $80, and $500.

SPORTFISHING

Saltwater, light tackle, and fly sportfishing are the specialties of **Lady J Sportfishing Charters** (207/985-7304, www.ladyjcharters .com). Two-hour Discover Fishing trips for

Rent a canoe or kayak and paddle the Kennebunk River, but be wary of the tide.

families ($200) include hauling lobster traps. Inshore trips for stripers and bluefish begin at $200 for two hours. Trips leave from behind Performance Marine (Rte. 9, Lower Village, Kennebunk).

SURFING

If you want to catch a wave, stop by **Aquaholics Surf Shop** (166 Port Rd., Kennebunk, 207/967-8650, www.aquaholicsurf.com). The shop has boards, wetsuits, and related gear both for sale and rental, and it offers lessons and surf camps.

Bicycling

Cape-Able Bike Shop (83 Arundel Rd., Town House Corners, Kennebunkport, 207/967-4382, www.capeablebikes.com), a local institution since 1974, has all kinds of rentals and accessories, repairs your wounded gear, sponsors Saturday-morning group rides, and provides a free area bike map and the best insider information. (The bike map is also available at the chamber of commerce.) Rentals begin around $23 per day. Delivery service is available, but the shop operates a seasonal outpost in Lower Village, next to the chamber of commerce. Also available are guided tours. The 10–15 mile Comfort Beach Tour lasts 2.5–3 hours and costs $59 adults, $29 under age 16, including a snack. A Singletrack Adventure two-hour mountain bike ride for experienced cyclists covers about eight miles and costs $59 adults with bike rental, $40 without, and includes a snack.

Golf

Three 18-hole golf courses make the sport a big deal in the area. **Cape Arundel Golf Club** (19 River Rd., Kennebunkport, 207/967-3494), established in 1897, and **Webhannet Golf Club** (8 Central Ave., Kennebunk, 207/967-2061), established in 1902, are semiprivate and open to nonmembers; call for tee times at least 24 hours ahead. At Cape Arundel, where George Bush plays, no jeans or sweatpants are allowed. In nearby Arundel, **Dutch Elm Golf Course** (5 Brimstone Rd., Arundel, 207/282-9850) is a

© HILARY NANGLE

Lobster boats crowd Cape Porpoise's harbor, and anglers often cast a line off the dock.

public course with rentals, pro shop, and putting greens.

ACCOMMODATIONS

Rates listed are for peak season; most stay open through Christmas Prelude.

Inns and Hotels

Graciously dominating its 11-acre spread at the mouth of the Kennebunk River, **The Colony Hotel** (140 Ocean Ave. at King's Hwy., Kennebunkport, 207/967-3331 or 800/552-2363, www.thecolonyhotel.com/maine) springs right out of a bygone era, and its distinctive cupola is an area landmark. It has had a longtime commitment to the environment, with recycling, waste-reduction, and educational programs. There's a special feeling here, with cozy corners for reading, lawns and gardens for strolling, an ocean-view swimming pool, room service, tennis privileges at the exclusive River Club, bike rentals, massage therapy, and lawn games. Peak doubles begin at $269, including breakfast, plus a $5 pp daily service charge. Pets are $30 per night.

© HILARY NANGLE

The Colony Hotel is a Kennebunkport landmark.

The White Barn Inn and its siblings have cornered the ultrahigh-end boutique inn market, with four in this category. Most renowned is the ultraexclusive **White Barn Inn** (37 Beach Ave., Kennebunk, 207/967-2321, www.whitebarninn.com), where peak season doubles begin around $450. Also part of the empire are **The Beach House Inn** (211 Beach Ave., Kennebunk, 207/967-3850, www.beachhseinn.com), with peak season doubles from around $300; **The Breakwater Inn, Hotel, and Spa** (127 Ocean Ave., Kennebunkport, 207/967-3118, www.thebreakwaterinn.com), with peak season doubles from around $275; **The Yachtsman Lodge and Marina** (Ocean Ave., Kennebunkport, 207/967-2511, www.yachtsmanlodge.com), where peak season doubles begin around $350; along with three restaurants. Guest rooms in all properties have air-conditioning, phones, satellite TV, and video and CD players; bikes and canoes are available for guests. Rates include bountiful continental breakfasts and afternoon tea, but check out the off-season packages, especially if you want to dine at one of the restaurants. All but the Beach House are within walking distance of Dock Square.

The White Barn Inn is the most exclusive, with Relais & Châteaux status. It's home to one of the best restaurants in the *country*. Many rooms have fireplaces and marble baths with separate steam showers and whirlpool tubs (you can even arrange for a butler-drawn bath). Service is impeccable, and nothing has been overlooked in terms of amenities. There's an outdoor heated European-style infinity pool, where lunch is available, weather permitting, as well as a full-service spa. The inn also has a Hinckley Talaria-44 yacht available for charter.

The Beach House Inn faces Middle Beach and is less formal than the White Barn (splurge on upper-floor guest rooms with views and avoid the first-floor back ones). The Breakwater, at the mouth of the Kennebunk River, comprises a beautifully renovated historical inn with wraparound porches and an adjacent, more modern, newly renovated building with guest rooms and a full-service spa. The complex is also home to Stripers Restaurant. Finally, there's the Yachtsman, an innovative blend of a motel and bed-and-breakfast, with all rooms opening onto patios facing the river and the marina where George H. W. Bush keeps his boat. Pets are allowed here by advance reservation for $25 per night.

All but two guest rooms at the **(Cape Arundel Inn** (208 Ocean Ave., Kennebunkport, 207/967-2125, www.capearundelinn.com, Mar.–Jan. 1, $335–395) overlook crashing surf and the Bush estate. The compound comprises the shingle-style main inn building, the Rockbound motel-style building, and the Carriage House Loft, a large suite on the upper floor of the carriage house; an expanded continental breakfast buffet is included. Most guest rooms have fireplaces; Rockbound and Carriage House have TVs. The inn's restaurant (entrées $27–40), where every table has an ocean view, earns raves for its intriguingly creative cuisine.

The sprawling riverfront **Nonantum Resort** (95 Ocean Ave., Kennebunkport, 207/967-4050 or 800/552-5651, www.nonantumresort.com, $249–449) complex, which dates from 1884, includes a bit of everything, from small rooms with old-fashioned Victorian decor in the main building to modern family suites with kitchenettes in the newer Portside building. Facilities include a dining room, a small outdoor heated pool, and docking facilities; lobster boat and sailing tours, fishing charters, and kayak rentals are available. A slew of activities are offered daily. All 115 guest rooms have air-conditioning, Wi-Fi, and TVs; some have refrigerators. Some could use a facelift. Rates include a full breakfast. The water-view dining room is also open for dinner and, in July–August, lunch. Packages, many of which include dinner, are a good choice. Note that weddings take place here almost every weekend.

Bed-and-Breakfasts

Three of Kennebunkport's loveliest inns are rumored to have been owned by brothers-in-law, all of whom were sea captains. Rivaling the White Barn Inn for service, decor, amenities, and overall luxury is the three-story **(Captain Lord Mansion** (Pleasant St., Kennebunkport, 207/967-3141 or 800/522-3141, www.captainlord.com, $259–499), which is one of the finest bed-and-breakfasts anywhere. And no wonder: Innkeepers Rick and Bev Litchfield have been at it since 1978, and they're never content to rest on their laurels. Each year the inn improves upon seeming perfection. If you want to be pampered and stay in a meticulously decorated and historical bed-and-breakfast with marble bathrooms (heated floors, many with double whirlpool tubs), fireplaces, original artwork, phones, TVs, Wi-Fi, air-conditioning in all guest rooms, and even a few cedar closets, look no further. A multicourse breakfast is served to shared tables. Bicycles as well as beach towels and chairs are available. Afternoon treats are provided.

The elegant Federal-style **Captain Jefferds Inn** (5 Pearl St., Kennebunkport, 207/967-2311 or 800/839-6844, www.captainjefferdsinn.com, $179–369), in the historic district, provides the ambience of a real captain's house. Each of the 15 guest rooms and suites (11 in the main house and four more in the carriage house) has plush linens, fresh flowers, down comforters, TVs and DVD players, CD players, Wi-Fi, and air-conditioning; some have fireplaces, whirlpool tubs, and other luxuries. A three-course breakfast and afternoon tea are included. Five rooms are dog friendly, at $30 per day per dog; pet sitting is available.

The Captain Fairfield Inn (8 Pleasant St., Kennebunkport, www.captainfairfield.com, $275–385) is perhaps the most modest architecturally of the three, but it doesn't scrimp on amenities. Guest rooms are divided between traditional and contemporary decor, but all have flat-screen TVs, air-conditioning, and Wi-Fi; some have gas fireplaces, double whirlpools, and rainfall showers. The lovely grounds are a fine place to retreat for a snooze in the hammock or a game of croquet. Rates include a four-course breakfast and afternoon cookies.

The inspiration for the **English Meadows Inn** (141 Port Rd., Lower Village, Kennebunk, 207/967-5766, www.englishmeadowsinn.com, $219–389) came from those lovely English manor homes, elegant yet comfortable. The 1860s original Greek Revival architecture was married to the Victorian Queen Anne style later in the century. New owners Liz and Eric Brodar are updating and redecorating, adding fireplaces, flat-screen TVs, Wi-Fi, and other contemporary touches. Books fill the inn's many nooks and crannies. Guest rooms are split between the main house; the carriage house, where children are welcome; and a pet-friendly two-bedroom cottage, a good choice for young families.

The low-key turn-of-the-20th-century **Green Heron Inn** (126 Ocean Ave., Kennebunkport, 207/967-3315, www.greenheroninn.com, $180–215) sees many repeat guests thanks to a primo cove-side location, welcoming hosts, and to-die-for breakfasts. Ten guest rooms and a two-story cottage ($325–350) have TVs, phones, and air-conditioning; some have fireplaces, microwaves, and refrigerators; and most have cove views. Children are welcome; some pets are accepted ($15 per night).

Slip away from the crowds at the Gott family's antiques-filled **Bufflehead Cove Inn** (B18 Bufflehead Cove Lane, Kennebunkport, 207/967-3879, www.buffleheadcove.com, $165–375), a secluded riverfront home in the woods, less than one mile from K'port's action. Really, with a location like this and pampering service, you just might not want to stray from the front porch or dock. Rooms have Wi-Fi, TVs, and air-conditioning; some have fireplaces and whirlpool tubs; rates include a full breakfast and afternoon treats.

Neighboring the Wedding Cake House, **The Waldo Emerson Inn** (108 Summer St./Rte. 35, Kennebunk, 207/985-4250, www.waldoemersoninn.com, $155–175) has a charming colonial feel, as it should, since the main section was built in 1784. Poet Ralph Waldo Emerson spent many a summer here; it

was his great-uncle's home. Three of the six attractive guest rooms have working fireplaces. Rates include a full breakfast. Quilters, take note: In the barn is Mainely Quilts, a well-stocked quilt shop; ask about retreats and workshops.

Traveling with a pooch? **The Hounds Tooth Inn** (82 Summer St., Kennebunk, 207/985-0117, www.houndstoothinn.biz, $155–185, plus $10 per pet) extends a welcome paw, allowing dogs in public rooms (but not the kitchen) and providing a fenced-in play area. Rates include a full breakfast.

Motels

Patricia Mason is the ninth-generation innkeeper at **The Seaside Motor Inn** (80 Beach Ave., Kennebunk, 207/967-4461 or 800/967-4461, www.kennebunkbeach.com, $229–289), a property that has been in her family since 1667. What a location! The 22-room motel is the only truly beachfront property in the area, with a private beach for guests. Rooms are spacious, with TVs, Wi-Fi, air-conditioning, and refrigerators. Guests have use of an ocean-view hot tub and bicycles. A continental breakfast is included in the rates. Kids age 12 and younger stay free.

Second-generation innkeepers David and Paula Reid keep the **Fontenay Terrace Motel** (128 Ocean Ave., Kennebunkport, 207/967-3556, www.fontenaymotel.com, $140–175) spotless. It borders a tidal inlet and has a private grassy and shaded lawn, perfect for retreating from the hubbub of busy Kennebunkport. Each of the eight guest rooms has air-conditioning, a mini-fridge, a microwave, Wi-Fi, cable TV, and a phone; some have water views. A small beach is 300 yards away, and it's a pleasant one-mile walk to Dock Square.

The clean and simple **Cape Porpoise Motel** (12 Mills Rd./Rte. 9, Cape Porpoise, 207/967-3370, www.capeporpoisemotel.com, $129–150) is a short walk from the harbor. All rooms have TV and air-conditioning, and some have kitchenettes; rates include a continental breakfast, with homemade baked goods, fresh fruit, cereals, and bagels. Also available by the week or month are efficiencies with full kitchens, phones, and one or more bedrooms.

Here's a bargain: The nonprofit **Franciscan Guest House** (28 Beach Ave., Kennebunk, 207/967-4865, www.franciscanguesthouse .com), on the grounds of the monastery, has accommodations spread among two buildings and three other Tudor-style cottages. Decor is vintage 1970s, frills are few, and yes, its in need of updating, but there are some nice amenities, including TVs, air-conditioning, a saltwater pool, Wi-Fi, and beach passes. The location is walking distance to the beach and Dock Square. A buffet breakfast is included in the rates, and a buffet dinner is often available (around $17). There is no daily maid service, but fresh towels are provided daily. Rooms are $89–159, and 1–3-bedroom suites are $129–289. They do not accept credit cards.

FOOD

Hours are for peak season, when reservations are advised. Call ahead September–June.

Local Flavors

All Day Breakfast (55 Western Ave./Rte. 9, Lower Village, Kennebunk, 207/967-5132, 7 A.M.–1:30 P.M. Mon.–Fri., 7 A.M.–2 P.M. Sat.–Sun. mid-Jan.–mid-Dec.) is a favorite meeting spot, offering such specialties as invent-your-own omelets and crepes, Texas French toast, and the ADB sandwich.

Conveniently near the Kennebunk and Kennebunkport Chamber of Commerce, **H. B. Provisions** (15 Western Ave., Lower Village, Kennebunk, 207/967-5762, www.hbprovisions .com, 6 A.M.–10 P.M. daily year-round) has an excellent wine selection, along with plenty of picnic supplies, newspapers, and all the typical general-store inventory. It also serves breakfast and prepares hot and cold sandwiches, salads, and wraps.

Equal parts fancy food and wine store and gourmet café, **Cape Porpoise Kitchen** (Rte. 9, Cape Porpoise, 207/967-1150, 7 A.M.–6 P.M.

daily) sells sandwiches, salads, prepared foods, desserts, and everything to go with.

Pair a fine wine with light fare at **Old Vines** (141 Port Rd., Lower Village, Kennebunk, 207/967-5766, 4 P.M.–midnight Mon. and Wed.–Thurs., noon–midnight Fri.–Sat., noon–10:30 P.M. Sun.), an Old World–meets–New World European-style wine bar housed in a renovated barn.

The **Kennebunk Farmers Market** sets up shop 8 A.M.–1 P.M. Saturday mid-May–mid-October in the Grove Street municipal parking lot off Route 1 (adjacent to Village Pharmacy).

Grab a stool at the counter, slip into a booth, or wait for a table at the **Wayfarer** (Pier Rd., Cape Porpoise, 207/967-8961, 7 A.M.–2 P.M. Tues.–Sat., 7 A.M.–noon Sun., dinner entrées $10–19, no credit cards), a casual restaurant that serves breakfast, lunch, and dinner to locals and in-the-know visitors; the lobster stew is good.

Family Favorites

A bit off the beaten track is **Lucas on 9** (62 Mills Rd./Rte. 9, Cape Porpoise, 207/967-0039, www.lucason9.com, noon–9 P.M. Wed.–Mon., $9–22), a family-friendly, family-operated restaurant. The Lane family knows food: Chef Jonathan Lane makes everything from scratch and delivers on his mother Deborah's mission of "Good American food at affordable prices." Jonathan's travels have infused his preparations with more than a bow toward his work on Southern riverboats (Louisiana spicy crab soup, bread pudding with whiskey). There are at least six specials nightly in addition to plenty of other choices.

Burgers, pizza, sandwiches, even a turkey dinner with the trimmings—almost everything on the menu is less than $10 at **Duffy's Tavern & Grill** (4 Main St., Kennebunk, 207/985-0050, www.duffyskennebunk.com, lunch and dinner from 11 A.M. daily, breakfast from 8 A.M. Sun.). Extremely popular with locals, Duffy's is located inside a renovated mill in Lafayette Center. It's an inviting space with exposed beams, gleaming woodwork, brick walls, and big windows framing the Mousam River. And if you want to catch the game while you eat, big-screen high-def TVs make it easy.

Opened in 2010 and immediately earning raves from locals, **Brandy's on the Rocks** (278 Mills Rd., Kennebunkport, 207/967-8388, 11 A.M.–9 P.M. Sun.–Thurs., 11 A.M.–10 P.M. Fri.–Sat., dinner entrées $14–24), a sibling of the Wayfarer, is favored for its nightly home-style specials, although its wide-ranging menu covers burgers to lobster; the lobster stew is legendary.

Casual Dining

Just west of the junction of Routes 9 and 35 is **Grissini** (27 Western Ave., Kennebunk, 207/967-2211, www.restaurantgrissini.com, 5:30–8:30 P.M. Sun.–Thurs., 5:30–9 P.M. Fri.–Sat. year-round, entrées $15–34), a sibling of the White Barn Inn. Attentive service, a wood-burning oven, an inspired Tuscan menu, and a bright open-beamed space anchored by a walk-in fireplace make it an appealing spot. Pizzas are a specialty, but don't miss the *capesante* (pan-seared scallops). In nice weather, try for the sunken patio. Downstairs, **Grotta** serves lighter fare ($9–15).

The views complement the food at **Hurricane Restaurant** (29 Dock Sq., Kennebunkport, 207/967-9111, www.hurricanerestaurant.com, 11:30 A.M.–3:30 P.M. and 5–9:30 P.M. daily, entrées $19–45). Thanks to a Dock Square location and a dining room that literally hangs over the river, it reels in the crowds for both lunch and dinner, but a three-course fixed price menu ($30) is served 5–6:30 P.M. nightly.

Eat well and feel good about it at **Bandaloop** (2 Dock Sq., Kennebunkport, 207/967-4994, www.bandaloop.biz, lunch 11:30 A.M.–2 P.M. Wed.–Sun. mid-June–mid-Oct., dinner 5–10 P.M. Sun.–Thurs., 5–11 P.M. Fri.–Sat. year-round, $17–29), a hip, vibrant restaurant where chef-owner W. Scott Lee likes to push boundaries. Lee named the restaurant for author Tom Robbins's fictional tribe that knew the secret to eternal life. Lee believes the secret is fresh, local, organic, and cruelty free. Selections vary from meats and fish to vegetarian and vegan prepared with creativity.

Floor-to-ceiling windows frame the Kennebunk River breakwater, providing perfect views for those indulging at **Stripers** (Breakwater Inn, 127 Ocean Ave., Kennebunkport, 207/967-5333, noon–9 P.M. Mon.–Thurs., noon–9:30 P.M. Fri.–Sat., 11 A.M.–9 P.M. Sun.), another White Barn Inn sibling, where fish and seafood are the specialties. The emphasis on fish is also accented by a saltwater tank with coral reef and exotic fish. Most entrées range $18–30. On Sunday, a three-course meal is available for $25. A lighter menu is served in the bar. Dress is casual; valet parking is available.

Chef Peter and his wife, Kate, operate **Pier 77** (77 Pier Rd., Cape Porpoise, 207/967-8500, www.pier77restaurant.com, 11:30 A.M.–2:30 P.M. and 5–9 P.M. daily, entrées $17–32), which overlooks Cape Porpoise Harbor with lobster boats hustling to and fro. The menu varies from paella to seafood mixed grill. There's frequent live entertainment, which can make conversation difficult. Reservations are advisable. Practically hidden downstairs is **The Ramp Bar and Grille** (11:30 A.M.–9 P.M. daily), with lighter fare as well as the full menu and a sports-pub decor.

Local is the key word at **50 Local** (50 Main St., Kennebunk, 207/985-0850, www.localkennebunk.com, 5–10 P.M. Mon.–Sat.), a bright spot in downtown Kennebunk opened by Merrilee Paul and David Ross in 2010. The menu changes daily, but it's easy to cobble together a meal here that fits your appetite and budget. Perhaps a mix and match of starters, soups, sandwiches, or salads, or opt for the heftier entrées ($18–28).

Fine Dining

Every table at the **Cape Arundel Inn** (208 Ocean Ave., Kennebunkport, 207/967-2125, www.capearundelinn.com, dinner daily in season, dinner Tues.–Sun. off-season,

$27–40) has a knockout view of crashing surf, and the food matches the view. White-clothed tables topped with cobalt blue glassware add to the inn's casual yet elegant feel; local artwork covers the walls. Chef Rich Lemoine's menu emphasizes fish and seafood in classic preparations, all prepared and served with care.

Fusion cuisine reigns at **On the Marsh** (46 Western Ave./Rte. 9, Lower Village, Kennebunk, 207/967-2299, www.onthemarsh .com, 5:30–9:30 P.M. daily Feb.–Dec., entrées $25–35), a restored barn overlooking marshlands leading to Kennebunk Beach. A three-course fixed-price menu is served Wednesday for $30. The space is infused with arts and antiques and European touches courtesy of owner Denise Rubin, an interior designer with a passion for the continent. Dining locations include the two-level dining area and an "owner's table" in the kitchen; there's also a bar menu. Quiet piano music adds to the elegant but unstuffy ambience on weekends; service is attentive. Reservations are essential in midsummer.

Destination Dining

One of Maine's biggest splurges and worth every penny is **The White Barn Inn** (37 Beach Ave., Kennebunkport, 207/967-2321, www .whitebarninn.com, 6–9 P.M. Mon.–Thurs., 5:30–9:15 P.M. Fri.–Sun. Feb.–Dec.), with haute cuisine and haute prices in a haute-rustic barn. In summer, don't be surprised to run into members of the senior George Bush clan (probably at the back window table). Soft piano music accompanies impeccable service, and chef Jonathan Cartwright's outstanding four-course (plus extras) fixed-price menu (about $100 pp, add $48 or $85 for wine pairings). Reservations are essential—well ahead during July–August—and you'll need a credit card (cancel 24 hours ahead or you'll be charged). Jackets are required, and no jeans or sneakers are allowed. It's New England's only five-star, five-diamond, Relais Gourmands restaurant.

Lobster and Clams

Nunan's Lobster Hut (9 Mills Rd., Cape Porpoise, 207/967-4362, www.nunanslobster hut.com, 5 P.M.–close daily) is an institution.

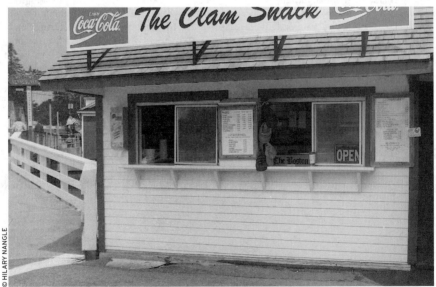

Try the best fried clams in the Kennebunks from The Clam Shack, just off Dock Square.

Sure, other places might have better views, but this casual dockside eatery with indoor and outdoor seating has been serving lobsters since 1953.

Adjacent to the bridge connecting Kennebunkport's Dock Square to Kennebunk's Lower Village is another time-tested classic, **The Clam Shack** (Rte. 9, Kennebunkport, 207/967-2560, www.theclamshack.net, lunch and dinner from 11 A.M. daily May–Oct.). The tiny takeout stand serves perhaps the state's best lobster rolls, jam-packed with meat and available with either butter or mayo, and dee-lish fried clams.

Lobster and crab rolls are the specialties at **Port Lobster** (122 Ocean Ave., Kennebunkport, 207/967-2081, www.portlobster.com), a fresh-fish store located just northeast of Dock Square.

INFORMATION AND SERVICES
Information
The **Kennebunk and Kennebunkport Chamber of Commerce** (17 Western Ave./Rte. 9, Lower Village, Kennebunk, 207/967-0857, www.visitthekennebunks.com) produces an excellent area guide to accommodations, restaurants, area maps, bike maps, tide calendars, recreation, and beach parking permits.

Check out **Louis T. Graves Memorial Public Library** (18 Maine St., Kennebunkport, 207/967-2778, www.graves.lib.me.us) or **Kennebunk Free Library** (112 Main St., 207/985-2173, www.kennebunklibrary.org), which has a café serving light fare.

Public Restrooms
Public toilets are at Gooch's and Mother's Beaches and at St. Anthony's Monastery, the chamber of commerce building (17 Western Ave.), and at the chamber's Dock Square Hospitality Center.

GETTING THERE AND AROUND
Amtrak's *Downeaster* (800/872-7245, www.thedowneaster.com) connects Boston's North Station with Portland, Maine, with stops in Wells, Saco, and Old Orchard Beach (seasonal).

Late May–mid-October the **Intown Trolley** (207/967-3686, www.intowntrolley.com) operates a narrated sightseeing tour throughout Kennebunk and Kennebunkport, originating in Dock Square and making regular stops at beaches and other attractions. The entire route takes about 45 minutes, with the driver providing a hefty dose of local history and gossip. Seats are park bench–style. An all-day ticket is $15 adults, $5 children 3–17. You can get on or off at any stop. The trolley operates hourly 10 A.M.–5 P.M. daily in July–August, 10 A.M.–4 P.M. daily in spring and fall.

The **Shoreline Explorer Kennebunk Shuttle** (www.shorelineexplorer.com, 10 A.M.–9:30 P.M. daily late June–Labor Day) circulates hourly between Grove Street parking lot, Stop and Shop, Landing Store, Lower Village, and the beaches. It connects with the Shoreline and Intown trolleys. Fare is $1 one-way or $10 for a 12-ride pass; those age 18 and younger ride free.

Old Orchard Beach Area

Seven continuous miles of white sand beach have been drawing vacation-oriented folks for generations to the area stretching from Camp Ellis in Saco to Pine Point in Scarborough. Cottage colonies and condo complexes dominate at the extremities, but the center of activity has always been and remains Old Orchard Beach.

In its heyday, **Old Orchard Beach's pier** reached far out into the sea, huge resort hotels lined the sands, and wealthy Victorian folk (including Rose Fitzgerald and Joe Kennedy, who met on these sands in the days when men strolled around in dress suits and women toted parasols) came each summer to see and be seen.

Storms and fires have taken their toll through the years, and the grand resorts have been replaced by endless motels, many of which display "Nous parlons français" signs to welcome the masses of French Canadians who arrive each summer. They're joined by young families who come for the sand and surf along with T-shirted and body-pierced young pleasure seekers who come for the nightlife.

Although some residents are pushing for gentrification and a few projects are moving things in that direction, Old Orchard Beach remains somewhat honky-tonk, and most of its visitors would have it no other way. French fries, cotton candy, and beach-accessories shops line the downtown, and as you get closer to the pier you pass arcades and amusement parks. There's not a kid on earth who wouldn't have fun in Old Orchard—even if some parents might find it all a bit much.

Much more sedate are the villages on the fringes. The **Ocean Park** section of Old Orchard, at the southwestern end of town, was established in 1881 as a religious summer-cottage community. It still offers interdenominational services and vacation Bible school, but it also has an active cultural association that sponsors concerts, Chautauqua-type lectures, films, and other events throughout the summer. All are open to the public.

South of that is **Camp Ellis.** Begun as a small fishing village named after early settler Thomas Ellis, it is crowded with longtime summer homes that are in a constant battle with the sea. A nearly mile-long granite jetty—designed to keep silt from clogging the Saco River—has taken the blame for massive beach erosion since it was constructed. But the jetty is a favorite spot for wetting a line (no fishing license needed) and for panoramic views off toward Wood Island Light (built in 1808) and Biddeford Pool. Camp Ellis Beach is open to the public, with lifeguards on duty in midsummer. Parking—scarce on hot days—is $10 per day.

As you head north from Old Orchard you'll pass **Pine Point,** another longtime community of vacation homes. Services are few and parking is $10 per day.

Old Orchard Beach's pier, although not as long as it once was, still stretches over the beach toward the sea.

© HILARY NANGLE

Most folks get to Old Orchard by passing through **Saco** and **Biddeford,** which have long been upstairs-downstairs sister cities, with wealthy mill owners living in Saco and their workers and workplaces in Biddeford. But even those personalities have always been split—congested commercial Route 1 is part of Saco, and the exclusive enclave of Biddeford Pool is, of course, in below-stairs Biddeford. Saco still has an attractive downtown, with boutiques and stunning homes on Main Street and beyond.

Blue-collar Biddeford is working hard to change its mill-town image. It's home to the magnificent Biddeford City Theater and the University of New England, and as a Main Street community it's getting a much-needed sprucing up. New shops and restaurants are balancing the numerous thrift shops downtown, and artisans and woodworkers are filling vacant mills. Another Biddeford hallmark is its Franco-American tradition, thanks to the French-speaking workers who sustained the textile and shoemaking industries in the 19th century.

SIGHTS
Saco Museum
Founded in 1866, the Saco Museum (371 Main St., Saco, 207/283-3861, www.dyerlibrarysacomuseum.org, noon–4 P.M. Tues.–Thurs. and Sun., noon–8 P.M. Fri., 10 A.M.–4 P.M. Sat. June–Dec., $4 adults, $3 seniors, $2 students and children age 6 and older) rotates selections from its outstanding collection, including 18th- and 19th-century paintings, furniture, and other household treasures. Lectures, workshops, and concerts are also part of the annual schedule. Admission is free after 4 P.M. Friday.

◖ Wood Island Lighthouse
The all-volunteer Friends of Wood Island Light (207/286-3229, www.woodislandlighthouse.org) is restoring Maine's second-oldest lighthouse, which was commissioned by president Thomas Jefferson, built in 1808 (reconstructed in 1858) on 35-acre Wood Island, and abandoned in 1986. In July–August the Friends offer 1.5-hour guided tours ($10 pp recommended donation) of the two-story keeper's house and 42-foot-tall stone tower, relating tales of former keepers and their families to bring the site to life. You can even climb the 60 stairs to the tower's lantern room for splendid views. The tour departs from Vine's Landing in Biddeford Pool. Once on the island, it's about a half-mile walk to the site. Reservations are accepted within one week of the tour date; see the website or call for a current schedule.

ENTERTAINMENT
At 6 P.M. every Thursday late June–Labor Day **free concerts** are staged in Old Orchard's Memorial Park, followed by **fireworks** set off by the pier at 9:45 P.M.

Family concerts and other performances are staged at the outdoor **Seaside Pavilion** (Union Ave. and 6th St., Old Orchard Beach, 207/934-2024, www.oobpavilion.org).

Live music, concerts by nationally recognized performers, dance parties, and comedy nights are all staged at **The Landing at Pine Point** (353 Point Rd., Scarborough, 207/774-4527, www.thelandingatpinepoint.com).

Ocean Park's **Temple,** a 19th-century octagon that seats over 800, is the venue for Sunday-night concerts (7:30 P.M., $10 adults) and many other programs throughout the summer.

Designed by noted architect John Calvin Stevens in 1896, the 500-seat **City Theater** (205 Main St., Biddeford, 207/282-0849, www.citytheater.org) in Biddeford, on the National Register of Historic Places, has been superbly restored, and the acoustics are excellent even when Eva Gray, the resident ghost, mixes it up backstage. A respected community theater group mounts a winter drama season and showcases other talent throughout the year.

A rainy-day godsend, Saco's new in 2009 **IMAX Theater** (779 Portland Rd./Rte. 1, Saco, 207/282-6234, www.cinemagicmovies.com) has digital sound, stadium seating, a restaurant, and online ticketing.

Pair burritos and other Tex-Mex faves with live music at **Bebe's Burritos** (140 Main St., Biddeford, 207/283-4222, www.bebesburritos.com, 6–10 P.M. Thurs.–Sun.), with trivia on Sunday nights.

EVENTS

La Kermesse (meaning "the fair" or "the festival") is Biddeford's summer highlight, when nearly 50,000 visitors pour into town Thursday–Sunday on the last full weekend in June to celebrate the town's Franco-American heritage. Local volunteers go all-out to plan block parties, a parade, games, a carnival, live entertainment, and traditional dancing. Then there's *la cuisine franco-américaine;* you can fill up on *boudin, creton, poutine, tourtière, tarte au saumon,* and crepes (although your arteries may rebel).

The **Biddeford Art Walk** (www.biddefordartwalk.com) takes place the last Friday of the month March–December.

In July the parishioners of St. Demetrios Greek Orthodox Church (186 Bradley St., Saco, 207/284-5651) go all out to mount the annual **Greek Heritage Festival,** a three-day extravaganza of homemade Greek food, traditional Greek music and dancing, and a craft fair. Be sure to tour the impressive $1.5 million domed church building.

The beaches come to life in July with the annual **parade and Sandcastle Contest** in Ocean Park.

One weekend in mid-August, Old Orchard Beach's **Beach Olympics** is a family festival of games, exhibitions, and music benefiting Maine's Special Olympics program.

RECREATION
Parks and Preserves

Saco Bay Trails (www.sacobaytrails.org), a local land trust, has produced a very helpful trail guide ($10) that includes the Saco Heath, the East Point Sanctuary, and more than a dozen other local trails. The Cascade Falls trail, for example, is a half-mile stroll ending at a waterfall. Copies are available at a number of Biddeford and Saco locations, including the Dyer Library, or from Saco Bay Trails. Trail information is also on the organization's website.

EAST POINT SANCTUARY

Owned by Maine Audubon (207/781-2330, www.maineaudubon.org), the 30-acre East Point Sanctuary is a splendid preserve at the eastern end of Biddeford Pool. Crashing surf, beach roses, bayberry bushes, and offshore Wood Island Light are all features of the two-part perimeter trail, which skirts the exclusive Abenakee Club's golf course. Allow at least an hour; even in fog, the setting is dramatic. During spring and fall migrations it's one of southern Maine's prime birding locales, so you'll have plenty of company at those times, and the usual street-side parking may be scarce. It's poorly signposted (perhaps deliberately), so the directions: From Route 9 (Main St.) in downtown Biddeford, take Route 9/208 (Pool Rd.) southeast about five miles to the Route 208 turnoff to Biddeford Pool. Go 0.6 miles on Route 208 (Bridge Rd.) and then turn left onto Mile Stretch Road. Continue to Lester B. Orcutt Boulevard, turn left, and go to the end. Be careful: There's poison ivy on the point.

THE HEATH

Owned by the Nature Conservancy, 870-acre Saco Heath Preserve is the nation's southernmost "raised coalesced bog," where peat accumulated through eons into two above-water dome shapes that eventually merged into a single natural feature. A bit of esoterica: It's the home of the rare Hessel's hairstreak butterfly. Pick up a map at the parking area and follow the mile-long self-guided trail through the woods and then into the heath via a boardwalk. The best time to visit is early–mid-October, when the heath and woodland colors are positively brilliant and insects are on the wane. You're likely to see deer and perhaps even spot a moose. The preserve entrance is on Route 112 (Buxton Rd.), two miles west of I-95. Pets are not allowed in the preserve.

FERRY BEACH STATE PARK

When the weather's hot, arrive early at Ferry Beach State Park (Bay View Rd., off Rte. 9, Saco, 207/283-0067, $6 nonresident adult, $4 Maine resident adult, $2 nonresident seniors, $1 ages 5–11), a pristine beach backed by dune grass on Saco Bay. In the 117-acre park are changing rooms, restrooms, a lifeguard, picnic tables, and five easy interconnected nature

AMUSEMENT PARKS AND AMUSING PLACES

If you've got kids or just love amusement parks, you'll find Maine's best in the Old Orchard area, where sand and sun just seem to complement arcades and rides perfectly.

The biggie is **Funtown/Splashtown USA** (774 Portland Rd./Rte. 1, Saco, 207/284-5139 or 800/878-2900, www.funtownsplashtownusa.com). Ride Maine's only wooden roller coaster; fly down New England's longest and tallest log flume ride; free fall 200 feet on Dragon's Descent; get wet and go wild riding speed slides, tunnel slides, raft slides, and river slides or splashing in the pool. Add a huge

Palace Playland has been keeping kids happy for generations.

© HILARY NANGLE

kiddie ride section as well as games, food, and other activities for a full day of family fun. Funtown opens weekends in early May, Splashtown in mid-June; everything's up and running daily late June–Labor Day, when Funtown is open 10 A.M.–9 P.M. Sunday–Friday, 10 A.M.–10 P.M. Saturday, and Splashtown is open 10 A.M.–6 P.M. daily. Ticketing options vary by the activities included and height, ranging $22-35 for "Big" (48 inches and taller), $18-26 for "Little" (38-48 inches tall) and "Senior" (over age 60), and free for kids under 38 inches tall.

Three miles north of Funtown/Splashtown USA, **Aquaboggan Water Park** (980 Portland Rd./Rte. 1, Saco, 207/282-3112, www.aquabogganwaterpark.com, 10 A.M.–6 P.M. daily late June–Labor Day) is wet and wild, with such stomach turners as the Yankee Ripper, the Suislide, and the Stealth, with an almost-vertical drop of 45 feet – enough to accelerate to 30 mph on the descent. Wear a bathing suit that won't abandon you in the rough-and-tumble. Also, if you wear glasses, safety straps and plastic lenses are required. Besides all the water stuff, there are mini-golf, an arcade, go-karts, and bumper boats. A day pass for all pools, slides, and mini-golf is $20 (48 inches and taller), $16 (under 48 inches tall), and $5 (under 38 inches tall). Mondays

are $12 general admission days. A $30 super-pass also includes two go-kart rides and unlimited bumper-boat rides.

The biggest beachfront amusement park, **Palace Playland** (1 Old Orchard St., Old Orchard, 207/934-2001, www.palaceplayland.com, Memorial Day–Labor Day) has more than 25 rides and attractions packed into four acres, including a giant water slide, a fun house, bumper cars, a Ferris wheel, a roller coaster, and a 24,000-square-foot arcade with more than 200 games. For a bird's-eye view of the area, ride the 75-foot-high gondola Sunwheel. Rev up the action on two roller coasters, one with a five-story drop, both with high-speed twisting turns. Kiddie Land has more than a dozen rides, including a fun house and a splashing whale. An unlimited pass is $29 per day; a kiddie pass good for all two-ticket rides is $22; two-day, season, and single tickets are available.

The **Old Orchard Beach's pier,** jutting 475 feet into the ocean from downtown, is a mini-mall of shops, arcades, and fast-food outlets. Far longer when it was built in 1898, it has been lopped off gradually by fires and storms. The current incarnation has been here since the late 1970s.

trails winding through woodlands, marsh-lands, and dunes. Later in the day, keep the insect repellent handy. It's open daily late May–late September but accessible all year; trail markers are removed in winter.

Golf

Opened in 1922 as a nine-hole course, the **Biddeford-Saco Country Club** (101 Old Orchard Rd., Saco, 207/282-5883) added a back nine in 1987 (the toughest hole on the par-71 course is the 11th). Tee times are not usually needed, and fees are moderate.

Covering more than 300 acres is the challenging 18-hole par-71 **Dunegrass Golf Club** (200 Wild Dunes Way, Old Orchard Beach, 207/934-4513 or 800/521-1029). Booking a tee time is essential; greens fees are a bit steep.

Water Sports
SEA KAYAKING
Gone with the Wind (Yates St., Biddeford Pool, 207/283-8446, www.gwtwonline.com) offers two tours, afternoon and sunset, with prices varying with the number of people on the tour (for 2 people it's about $85 pp). Wetsuits are supplied. The most popular trip is to Beach Island. Also available are rentals ($40 half-day, $65 full day).

SURFING
A seasonal branch of **Aquaholics Surf Shop** (www.aquaholicsurf.com) rents surfboards, bodyboards, wetsuits, and related gear from a shop at Old Orchard Beach.

ACCOMMODATIONS

The area has hundreds of beds—mostly in mo-tel-style lodgings. The chamber of commerce is the best resource for motels, cottages, and the area's more than 3,000 campsites. The rates noted are for peak season.

The Old Orchard Beach Inn (6 Portland Ave., Old Orchard Beach, 207/934-5834 or 877/700-6624, www.oldorchardbeachinn .com, year-round, $135–200) was rescued from ruin by owner Steve Cecchetti and opened in 2000. Built in 1730, and most recently known

as the Staples Inn, the building, on the National Register of Historic Places, has 18 antiques-filled guest rooms with air-conditioning, phones, and TVs. Continental breakfast is included in the rates; a two-bedroom suite is $425–450.

Practically next door is **The Atlantic Birches Inn** (20 Portland Ave./Rte. 98, Old Orchard Beach, 207/934-5295 or 888/934-5295, www.atlanticbirches.com, $121–141), with 10 air-conditioned guest rooms in a Victorian house and a separate cottage. Decor leans toward froufrou, breakfast is hearty continental, and there's a swimming pool. The beach is an easy walk. It's open all year, but call ahead off-season.

FOOD
Old Orchard Beach
Dining is not Old Orchard's strong point. The nicest place (although service and quality are inconsistent) is **Joseph's by the Sea** (55 W. Grand Ave., Old Orchard Beach, 207/934-5044, www.josephsbythesea.com, 7–11 A.M. and 5–9 P.M. daily, entrées $18–33), a quiet shorefront restaurant amid all the hoopla. Request a table on the screened patio. The menu is French with a dash of Maine. Reservations are advisable in midsummer.

Camp Ellis
At **Huot's Seafood Restaurant** (Camp Ellis Beach, Saco, 207/282-1642, www.huotssea-foodrestaurant.com, 11:30 A.M.–9 P.M. Tues.–Sun.), under third-generation management, the menu is huge, portions are large, and prices are reasonable. It's a good value for fresh seafood.

Saco
Craving fast-ish food? The Camire family operates Maine's best home-grown option, **Rapid Ray's** (189 Main St., 207/283-4222, www .rapidrays.biz, 11 A.M.–12:30 A.M. Mon.–Thurs., 11 A.M.–1 A.M. Fri.–Sat., 11 A.M.–11 P.M. Sun.). Burgers, dogs, and fried foods are the specialty at the standing-room-only joint.

Super soups and sandwiches come from **Vic & Whits** (206 Main St., Saco, 207/284-6710, 8 A.M.–8 P.M. Mon.–Sat., 8 A.M.–1 P.M. Sun.), which also has a nice selection of retail wine, beer, and Maine cheeses.

For more leisurely dining, book a reservation at **Mia's** (17 Pepperell Sq., Saco, 207/284-6427, www.miasatpepperellsquare.com, lunch 11:30 A.M.–2 P.M. Wed.–Sat., dinner 5–9 P.M. Mon.–Sat., $17–25), where chef-owner Steve Rogers excels at creating classic fare without fuss. Dinner entrées include butter-poached lobster and beef stroganoff.

Biddeford and Biddeford Pool

For a town grounded in Franco-American culture, Biddeford has an expanding array of inexpensive ethnic choices, including a few that garner praise far beyond city limits: For well-prepared Indian cuisine, seek out **Jewel of India** (26 Alfred St., 207/282-5600, www.thejewelofindia.com, 11 A.M.–10 P.M. Mon.–Sat., 4–10 P.M. Sun., entrées $10–16). If you're longing for pho and Vietnamese coffee, head into **Que Huong** (49 Main St., 207/571-8050, 11 A.M.–8 P.M. Mon.–Sat.), a tiny and very inexpensive Vietnamese restaurant.

Buffleheads (122 Hills Beach Rd., 207/284-6000, www.buffleheadsrestaurant.com, 11:30 A.M.–2 P.M. and 5–8:30 P.M. daily, closed Mon. off-season, $11–26) is a family dining find with spectacular ocean views. Ray and Karen Wieczoreck opened the restaurant in 1994 and have built a strong local following through the years. The kids can munch on pizza, burgers, spaghetti, and other favorites while adults savor well-prepared seafood with a home-style spin or landlubber classics. Lobster pie and a turkey dinner with all the trimmings are both perennial favorites. Hills Beach Road branches off Route 9 at the University of New England campus.

Take your lobster or fried seafood dinner to an oceanfront picnic table on the grassy lawn behind **F. O. Goldthwaite's** (3 Lester B. Orcott Blvd., Biddeford Pool, 207/284-8872, 11 A.M.–7:30 P.M. daily, $4–market rates), an old-fashioned general store. Salads, fried seafood, sandwiches, and kid-friendly fare round out the menu.

INFORMATION AND SERVICES

Sources of visitor information are **Biddeford-Saco Chamber of Commerce and Industry** (110 Main St., Saco, 207/282-1567, www.biddefordsacochamber.org), **Old Orchard Beach Chamber of Commerce** (1st St., Old Orchard Beach, 207/934-2500 or 800/365-9386, www.oldorchardbeachmaine.com), and **Ocean Park Association** (207/934-9068, www.oceanpark.org).

The **Dyer Library** (371 Main St., Saco, 207/282-3031, www.sacomuseum.org), next door to the Saco Museum, attracts scads of genealogists to its vast Maine history collection. Also check out **Libby Memorial Library** (Staples St., Old Orchard Beach, 207/934-4351, www.ooblibrary.org).

GETTING THERE

Amtrak's *Downeaster* (800/872-7245, www.thedowneaster.com) connects Boston's North Station with Portland, Maine, with stops in Wells, Saco, and Old Orchard Beach (seasonal).

GETTING AROUND
Bus and Trolley

The **Biddeford-Saco-Old Orchard Beach Transit Committee** (207/282-5408, www.shuttlebus-zoom.com) operates three systems that make getting around simple. The **Old Orchard Beach Trolley** (10 A.M.–midnight daily late June–Labor Day) operates two routes on a regular schedule that connects restaurants and campgrounds. You can flag it down anywhere en route. Fare is $1 per ride; children under age 5 ride free. **ShuttleBus Local Service** provides frequent weekday and less-frequent weekend service (except on national holidays) between Biddeford, Saco, and Old Orchard Beach. One-way fare is $1.25 ages 5 and older, exact change required. **ShuttleBus InterCity Service** connects Biddeford, Saco, and Old Orchard with Portland, South Portland, and Scarborough. Fares vary by zones, topping out at $5 for anyone over age 5.

GREATER PORTLAND

Whenever national magazines highlight the 10 best places to live, Greater Portland often makes the list. The very things that make the area so popular with residents make it equally attractive to visitors. Small in size but big in heart, Greater Portland entices visitors with the staples—lighthouses, lobster, and L. L. Bean—but wows them with everything else it offers. It is the state's cultural hub, with performing-arts centers, numerous festivals, and varied museums; it's also a dining destination, with nationally recognized chefs as well as an amazing assortment and variety of everyday restaurants; and despite its urban environment it has a mind-boggling amount of recreational opportunities. No wonder the National Heritage Trust named it a Distinctive Destination.

Portland's population hovers around 65,000, but when the suburbs are included it climbs to nearly 250,000, making it Maine's largest city by far. Take a swing through the bedroom communities of Scarborough, Cape Elizabeth, and South Portland, and you'll better understand the area's popularity: easily accessible parks, beaches, rocky ledges, and lighthouses all minutes from downtown along with a slew of ferry-connected islands dotting Casco Bay. Head north through suburban Falmouth and Yarmouth, and you'll arrive in Freeport, home of mega-retailer L. L. Bean. En route you'll still see the vestiges of the region's heritage: sailboats and lobster boats, traps and buoys piled on lawns or along driveways, and tucked here and there, farms with farm stands brimming with fresh produce.

Greater Portland also marks a transitional

© GREATER PORTLAND CVB

HIGHLIGHTS

◖ **The Old Port and the Waterfront:** Plan to spend at least a couple of hours browsing the shops, dining, and enjoying the energy of this restored historic district (page 77).

◖ **Portland Museum of Art:** This museum houses works by masters such as Winslow Homer, John Marin, Andrew Wyeth, Edward Hopper, and Marsden Hartley as well as works by Monet, Picasso, and Renoir (page 82).

◖ **Victoria Mansion:** This house is considered one of the most richly decorated dwellings of its period remaining in the country (page 83).

◖ **Portland Observatory:** Climb the 103 steps to the orb deck of the only remaining maritime signal tower on the Eastern Seaboard, and you'll be rewarded with views from the White Mountains to Casco Bay's islands (page 84).

◖ **Portland Head Light:** This lighthouse, commissioned by President George Washington, is fabulously sited on the rocky ledges of Cape Elizabeth (page 86).

◖ **Casco Bay Tour:** Take a three-hour tour on the mail boat, which stops briefly at five islands en route (page 92).

◖ **Lobstering Cruise:** Go out on a working lobster boat in Portland Harbor, see the sights, and perhaps return with a lobster for dinner (page 94).

◖ **L. L. Bean:** The empire's flagship store is in Freeport, and no trip to this shopping mecca is complete without a visit (page 107).

◖ **L. L. Bean Outdoor Discovery Schools:** Don't miss the opportunity for an inexpensive introduction to a new sport (page 110).

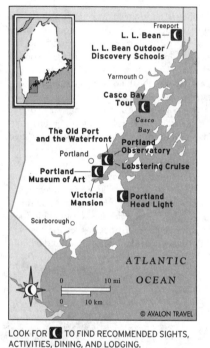

LOOK FOR ◖ TO FIND RECOMMENDED SIGHTS, ACTIVITIES, DINING, AND LODGING.

point on Maine's coastline. The long sand beaches of the Southern Coast begin to give way to islands and a coastline edged with a jumble of rocks and ledges interrupted by rivers and coves.

While it's tempting to dismiss Portland in favor of seeking the "real Maine" elsewhere along the coast, the truth is, the real Maine is here. And while Portland alone provides plenty to keep a visitor busy, it's also an excellent base for day trips to places such as the Kennebunks, Freeport, Brunswick, and Bath, where more of that real Maine flavor awaits.

PLANNING YOUR TIME

July and August are the most popular times to visit, but Greater Portland is a year-round destination. Spring truly arrives by mid-May, when most summer outfitters begin operations at least on weekends. September is perhaps the

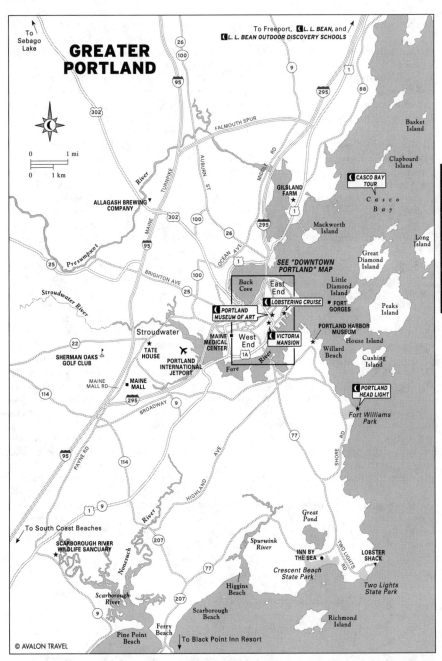

GREATER PORTLAND

To Sebago Lake

GREATER PORTLAND

To Freeport, **L. L. BEAN**, and **L. L. BEAN OUTDOOR DISCOVERY SCHOOLS**

0   1 mi
0   1 km

FALMOUTH SPUR

ALLAGASH BREWING COMPANY

GILSLAND FARM

CASCO BAY TOUR

Casco Bay

Basket Island

Clapboard Island

Mackworth Island

Long Island

Presumpscot River

Stroudwater River

Great Diamond Island

SEE "DOWNTOWN PORTLAND" MAP

Back Cove

East End

Little Diamond Island

Peaks Island

Stroudwater

LOBSTERING CRUISE

PORTLAND MUSEUM OF ART

FORT GORGES

SHERMAN OAKS GOLF CLUB

TATE HOUSE

MAINE MEDICAL CENTER

West End

VICTORIA MANSION

PORTLAND HARBOR MUSEUM

House Island

Willard Beach

Cushing Island

MAINE MALL RD

MAINE MALL

PORTLAND INTERNATIONAL JETPORT

Fore River

BROADWAY

PORTLAND HEAD LIGHT

Fort Williams Park

HIGHLAND AVE

SHORE RD

To South Coast Beaches

SCARBOROUGH RIVER WILDLIFE SANCUARY

Great Pond

INN BY THE SEA

LOBSTER SHACK

PAYNE RD

Nonesuch River

Spurwink River

Crescent Beach State Park

TWO LIGHTS RD

Two Lights State Park

Scarborough River

Higgins Beach

Scarborough Beach

Richmond Island

Pine Point Beach

Ferry Beach

To Black Point Inn Resort

© AVALON TRAVEL

loveliest month of the year weather-wise, and by mid-October those fabled New England maples are turning crimson.

To do the region justice, you'll want to spend at least three or four days, more if your plans call for using Greater Portland as a base for day trips to more distant points. You can easily kill two days in downtown Portland alone, what with all the shops, museums, historical sites, waterfront, and neighborhoods to explore. If you're staying in town and are an avid walker, you won't need a car to get to the in-town must-see sights.

You will need a car to reach beyond the city. Allow a full day for a leisurely tour through South Portland and Cape Elizabeth and on to Prouts Neck in Scarborough.

Rabid shoppers should either stay in Freeport or allow at least a day for L. L. Bean and the 100 or so outlets in its shadow. If you're traveling with a supershopper, don't despair. Freeport has parks and preserves that are light-years removed from the frenzy of its downtown, and the fishing village of South Freeport offers seaworthy pleasures.

HISTORY

Portland's downtown, a crooked-finger peninsula projecting into Casco Bay and today defined vaguely by I-295 at its "knuckle," was named Machigonne (Great Neck) by the Wabanaki, the Native Americans who held sway when English settlers first arrived in 1632. Characteristically, the Brits renamed the region Falmouth (it included present-day Falmouth, Portland, South Portland, Westbrook, and Cape Elizabeth) and the peninsula Falmouth Neck, but it was 130 years before they secured real control of the area. Anglo-French squabbles spurred by the governments' conflicts in Europe drew in the Wabanaki from Massachusetts to Nova Scotia. Falmouth was only one of the battlegrounds, and it was a fairly minor one. Relative calm resumed in the 1760s only to be broken by the stirrings of rebellion centered on Boston. When Falmouth's citizens expressed support for the incipient revolution, the punishment was a 1775 naval onslaught that wiped out 75 percent of the houses, which created a decade-long setback. In 1786, Falmouth Neck became Portland, a thriving trading community where shipping flourished until the 1807 imposition of the Embargo Act. Severing trade and effectively shutting down Portland Harbor for a year and a half, the legislation did more harm to the fledgling colonies of the United States than to the French and British it was designed to punish.

In 1820, when Maine became a state, Portland was named its capital. The city became a crucial transportation hub with the arrival of the railroad. The Civil War was barely a blip in Portland's history, but the year after it ended, the city suffered a devastating blow: Exuberant Fourth of July festivities in 1866 sparked a conflagration that virtually leveled the city. The Great Fire spared only the Portland Observatory and a chunk of the West End. Evidence of the city's Victorian rebirth remains today in many downtown neighborhoods.

After World War II, Portland slipped into decline for several years, but that is over. The city's waterfront revival began in the 1970s and continues today, despite commercial competition from South Portland's Maine Mall; Congress Street has blossomed as an arts and retail district; public green space is increasing; and an influx of immigrants is changing the city's cultural makeup. With the new century, Portland is on a roll.

Portland

Often compared to San Francisco (an oft-cited but never verified statistic boasts that it vies with San Francisco for the title of most restaurants per capita), Portland is small, friendly, and easily explored on foot, although at times it may seem that no matter which direction you head, it's uphill. The heart of Portland is the peninsula jutting into Casco Bay. It's bordered by the Eastern and Western Promenades, Back Cove, and the working waterfront. Salty sea breezes cool summer days and make winter ones seem even chillier. Unlike that other city by the bay, snow frequently blankets Portland December–March.

Portland is Maine's most ethnically diverse city, with active refugee resettlement programs and dozens of languages spoken in the schools. Although salty sailors can still be found along the waterfront, Portland is increasingly a professional community with young, upwardly mobile residents spiffing up Victorian houses and infusing new energy and money into the city's neighborhoods.

The region's cultural hub, Portland has world-class museums and performing-arts centers, active historical and preservation groups, an art school and a university, a symphony orchestra, numerous galleries and coffeehouses, and enough activities to keep culture vultures busy well into the night, especially in the thriving, handsomely restored Old Port and the up-and-coming Arts District.

Portland is also a playground for sports- and outdoor-lovers, with trails for running, biking, skating, and cross-country skiing, water sports aplenty, and a beloved minor league baseball team, the Sea Dogs. When city folks want to escape, they often hop a ferry for one of the islands of Casco Bay or head to one of the parks, preserves, or beaches in the suburbs.

Still, Portland remains a major seaport. Lobster boats, commercial fishing vessels, long-distance passenger boats, cruise ships, and local ferries dominate the working waterfront, and the briny scent of the sea—or bait—seasons the air.

PORTLAND NEIGHBORHOODS

The best way to appreciate the character of Portland's neighborhoods is on foot. So much of Portland can (and should) be covered on foot that it would take a whole book to list all the possibilities, but several dedicated volunteer groups have produced guides to facilitate the process.

Greater Portland Landmarks (207/774-5561, www.portlandlandmarks.org) is the doyenne, founded in 1964 to preserve Portland's historic architecture and promote responsible construction. The organization has published more than a dozen books and booklets, including *Discover Historic Portland on Foot,* a packet of four well-researched walking-tour guides to architecturally historic sections of Portland's peninsula: Old Port, Western Promenade, State Street, and Congress Street. It's available online or for $6 at local bookstores, some gift shops, and the Visitor Information Center (14 Ocean Gateway Pier, 207/772-5800).

◖ The Old Port and the Waterfront

Tony shops, cobblestone sidewalks, replica streetlights, and a casual upmarket crowd (most of the time) set the scene for a district once filled with derelict buildings. Scores of boutiques, enticing restaurants, and spontaneous street-corner music make it a fun area to visit year-round. Nightlife centers on the Old Port, and a few dozen bars keep everyone hopping until after midnight. Police keep a close eye on the district, but it can get a bit dicey after 11 P.M. on weekends.

At 10:30 A.M. daily July–early October, knowledgeable guides from Greater Portland Landmarks (207/774-5561, www.portland landmarks.org) lead fascinating 90-minute **Old Port walking tours** ($10, free for kids under age 16 with an adult) in downtown Portland. No reservations are needed, and tours are first-come, first served. Purchase tickets at the walk meeting place; locations vary, so check online or call first.

GREATER PORTLAND

GREATER PORTLAND

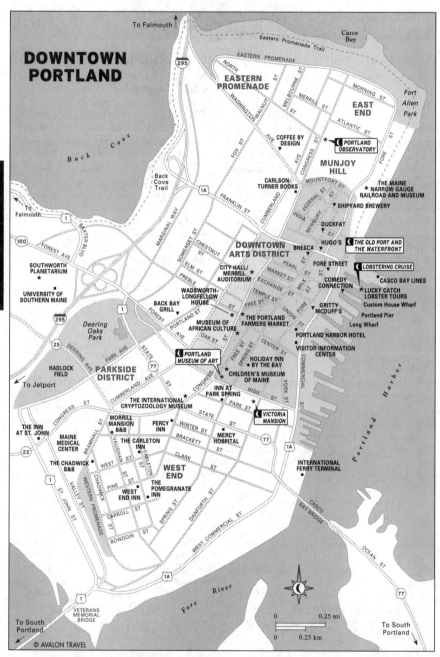

DOWNTOWN PORTLAND

To Falmouth ↑

Casco Bay

Eastern Promenade Trail

EASTERN PROMENADE

Back Cove

Back Cove Trail

EAST END

Fort Allen Park

COFFEE BY DESIGN

★ ◖ PORTLAND OBSERVATORY

MUNJOY HILL

CARLSON-TURNER BOOKS

★ THE MAINE NARROW GAUGE RAILROAD AND MUSEUM

♦ SHIPYARD BREWERY

DUCKFAT

DOWNTOWN ARTS DISTRICT

BRESCA

HUGO'S

◖ THE OLD PORT AND THE WATERFRONT

SOUTHWORTH PLANETARIUM

CITY HALL/ MERRILL AUDITORIUM

FORE STREET

◖ LOBSTERING CRUISE

UNIVERSITY OF SOUTHERN MAINE

WADSWORTH-LONGFELLOW HOUSE

COMEDY CONNECTION

● CASCO BAY LINES

★ LUCKY CATCH LOBSTER TOURS

BACK BAY GRILL

THE PORTLAND FARMERS MARKET

Custom House Wharf

GRITTY McDUFF'S

Portland Pier

Deering Oaks Park

MUSEUM OF AFRICAN CULTURE

Long Wharf

● PORTLAND HARBOR HOTEL

PARKSIDE DISTRICT

◖ PORTLAND MUSEUM OF ART

VISITOR INFORMATION CENTER

HADLOCK FIELD

HOLIDAY INN ● BY THE BAY

Portland Harbor

To Jetport

★ CHILDREN'S MUSEUM OF MAINE

INN AT PARK SPRING

THE INTERNATIONAL CRYPTOZOOLOGY MUSEUM

★ ▪ VICTORIA MANSION

THE INN AT ST. JOHN

MORRILL MANSION B&B

PERCY INN

MAINE MEDICAL CENTER

THE CARLETON INN

MERCY HOSPITAL

THE CHADWICK B&B

WEST END

THE POMEGRANATE INN

INTERNATIONAL FERRY TERMINAL

WEST END INN

To South Portland

VETERANS MEMORIAL BRIDGE

Fore River

To South Portland

CASCO BAY BRIDGE

OCEAN ST

0   0.25 mi

0   0.25 km

© AVALON TRAVEL

corner of Fore and Exchange Streets in the Old Port

Congress Street and the Downtown Arts District

Bit by bit, once-declining Congress Street is becoming revitalized, showcasing the best of the city's culture. Artists, starving and otherwise, spend much of their time here thanks largely to encouragement from the energetic grassroots Downtown Arts District Association (DADA). Galleries, artists' studios, coffeehouses, cafés, and bistros as well as libraries, museums, and performing-arts centers are all part of the ongoing renaissance.

West End

Probably the most diverse of the city's downtown neighborhoods, and one that largely escaped the Great Fire of 1866, the West End includes the historically and architecturally splendid Western Promenade, Maine Medical Center (the state's largest hospital), the city's best bed-and-breakfasts, a gay-friendly community with a laissez-faire attitude, and a host of cafés and restaurants as well as a few niches harboring the homeless and forlorn.

Munjoy Hill and the East End

A once slightly down-at-the-heels neighborhood enclave with a pull-'em-up-by-the-bootstraps attitude, Portland's East End is rapidly gentrifying. Munjoy Hill is probably best known for the distinctive wooden tower that adorns its summit.

Named for George Munjoy, a wealthy 17th-century resident, this district has a host of architectural and historic landmarks, making it well worth a walking tour. Fortunately, Greater Portland Landmarks (207/774-5561, www .portlandlandmarks.org) has produced a 24-page booklet, *Munjoy Hill Historic Guide* ($3), which documents more than 60 notable sites, including the Eastern Cemetery, which is on the National Register of Historic Places, and the Eastern Promenade and Fort Allen Park, with spectacular harbor views. Early June–early October, the group also offers guided walking tours of the East End and Munjoy Hill as well as the historic Eastern Cemetery, the oldest burial ground on the peninsula; call for current schedules and fees.

CASCO BAY ISLANDS

© HILARY NANGLE

ferry dock on Peaks Island

Casco Bay is dotted with so many islands that an early explorer thought there must be at least one for every day of the year and so dubbed them the Calendar Islands. Truthfully, there aren't quite that many, even if you count all the ledges that appear at low tide. No matter; the islands are as much a part of Portland life as the Old Port.

Casco Bay Lines (207/774-7871, www.cascobaylines.com) is the islands' lifeline, providing car and passenger service daily in summer. For an island taster, take the daily mail-boat run. Indeed, on hot days it may seem as if half the city's population is hopping a ferry to enjoy the cool breezes and calming views.

PEAKS ISLAND

Peaks Island is a mere 20-minute ferry ride from downtown Portland, so it's no surprise that it has the largest year-round population. Historically a popular vacation spot — two lodges were built for Civil War veterans — it's now an increasingly popular suburb.

Although you can walk the island's perimeter in 3-4 hours, the best way to see it is via bike (extra ferry cost $6.50 adults, $3.25 children), pedaling around clockwise. It can take less than an hour to do the five-mile island circuit, but plan on relaxing on the beach, savoring the views, and visiting the museums. Rental bikes are available on the island from Brad Burkholder at **Brad and Wyatt's Bike Shop** (115 Island Ave., Peaks Island, 207/766-5631, 10 A.M.-6 P.M. daily, $15 per day, hourly rentals available).

Another way to see the island is on a golf-cart tour with **Island Tours** (207/653-2549, www.peaksislandtours.com, $15 adults, $12 seniors, $8 children), which offers a variety of 90-minute island tours.

Civil War buffs have two museums worth visiting. The **Fifth Maine Regiment Center** (45 Seashore Ave., Peaks Island, 207/766-3330, www.fifthmainemuseum.org, noon-4 P.M. Mon.-Thurs., 11 A.M.-4 P.M. Sat.-Sun. July 1-early Sept., 11 A.M.-4 P.M. Sat.-Sun. late May-July 1 and early Sept.-mid Oct., $5 requested donation) is a Queen Anne-style cottage built by Civil War veterans in 1888 that now houses exhibits on the war and island history. Just a few steps away is the **Eighth Maine Regimental Memorial** (13 Eighth Maine Ave., Peaks Island, 207/766-5086, http://eighthmaine.com, 11 A.M.-4 P.M. Tues.-Sat. July 1-early Sept., $5 requested donation). Tours detail the building's fascinating history and its collection of artifacts pertaining to the Eighth Maine as well as material on the island, World War II, and more. Rustic lodging is available.

Another museum perhaps worthy of a visit just for its quirkiness is the **Umbrella Cover Museum** (207/766-4496, www.umbrellacovermuseum.org, call for hours, donation), where owner Nancy 3. Hoffman (yes, 3) displays her collection.

Food
Both **The Cockeyed Gull** (78 Island Ave., 207/766-2880, www.cockeyedgull.com, 11:30 A.M.-9 P.M. daily, entrées $7-25) and the **Shipyard Brewhaus** (33 Island Ave., www.innonpeaks.com, entrées $8-18) have inside dining as well as outdoor tables with water views.

Lodging
The **Inn on Peaks Island** (33 Island Ave., www.innonpeaks.com, $250-300) overlooks the ferry dock and has jaw-dropping sunset views over the Portland skyline; no island roughing it here. The spacious cottage-style suites have fireplaces, sitting areas, whirlpool baths, TVs and video players, and refrigerators; rates include a continental breakfast.

On the other end of the Peaks Island luxury scale is the extremely informal and communal **Eighth Maine Living Museum and Lodge** (13 Eighth Maine Ave., 207/766-5086 mid-

May-mid-Sept., 914/237-3165 off-season, www.eighthmaine.com, $99-139 d), a rustic shorefront living-history lodge overlooking White Head Passage. Shared baths and a huge shared kitchen allow you to rusticate in much the same manner as the Civil War vets who built this place in 1891 with a gift from a veteran who had won the Louisiana Lottery. It has no housekeeping – you're responsible for stripping the linens and cleaning the room and your kitchen space before departing.

GREAT CHEBEAGUE

Everyone calls Great Chebeague just "Chebeague" (shuh-BIG). Yes, there's a Little Chebeague, but it's a state-owned park and no one lives there. Chebeague is the largest of the bay's islands – 4.5 miles long by 1.5 miles wide – and the relatively level terrain makes it easy to get around. Don't plan to bring a car; it's too complicated to arrange. You can bike the leisurely 10-mile circuit of the island in a couple of hours, but unless you're in a hurry, allow time to relax and enjoy your visit.

If the tide is right, cross the sand spit from The Hook and explore **Little Chebeague.** Start out about two hours before low tide (preferably around new moon or full moon, when the most water drains away) and plan to be back on Chebeague no later than two hours after low tide.

Back on Great Chebeague, when you're ready for a swim, head for **Hamilton Beach,** a beautiful small stretch of sand lined with dune grass and not far from the Chebeague Island Inn. Also on this part of the island is **East End Point,** with a spectacular panoramic view of Halfway Rock and the bay.

Chebeague Transportation Company, from Cousins Island, Yarmouth, also serves the island.

Food

Visitors to Chebeague Island have two food choices. For simple home-cooked fare, head to **Calder's Clam Shack** (108 North Rd., Chebeague Island, 207/846-5046, www.caldersclamshack.com, 11:30 A.M.-8 P.M. Tues.-Sun.), a takeout serving burgers, pizza, chowders, salad, sandwiches, and of course, fried seafood. On the fancier side is **Chebeague Island Inn** (61 South Rd., Chebeague Island, 207/846-5155, www.chebeagueislandinn.com, 7 A.M.-9 P.M.). Dinner entrées, such as Maine farm cheeseburger and butter-poached lobster, run $16-38.

Lodging

Get that old-timey island experience at the **Chebeague Island Inn** (61 South Rd., Chebeague Island, 207/846-5155, www.chebeagueislandinn.com, $220-380), a nicely updated historical inn that charms guests with an artsy spirit and comforts them with down duvets and fancy sheets. The inn's dining room serves all meals.

EAGLE ISLAND

Seventeen-acre Eagle Island (207/624-6080, www.peareyeagleisland.org, 10 A.M.-5 P.M. mid-June-early Sept.) juts out of Casco Bay, rising to a rocky promontory 40 feet above the crashing surf. On the bluff's crest, Robert Edwin Peary, the first man to lead a party to the north pole without the use of mechanical or electrical devices, built his dream home. It's now a state historic site that's accessible via excursion boats from Portland or Freeport. The half-day trip usually includes a narrated cruise to the island and time to tour the house, filled with Peary family artifacts, and wander the nature trails. Trails are usually closed until approximately mid-July to protect nesting eider ducks.

Peary envisioned the island's rocky bluff as a ship's prow and built his house to resemble a pilot house. Wherever possible, he used indigenous materials from the island in the construction, including timber drift, fallen trees, beach rocks, and cement mixed with screened beach sand and small pebbles. From the library, Peary corresponded with world leaders, adventurers, and explorers such as Teddy Roosevelt, the Wright Brothers, Roald Amundsen, and Ernest Shackleton, and planned his expeditions. Peary reached the north pole on April 6, 1909, and his wife, Josephine, was on Eagle Island when she received word via telegraph of her husband's accomplishment. After Peary's death in 1920, the family continued to spend summers on Eagle until Josephine's death in 1955. The family then decided to donate the island to the state of Maine.

GREATER PORTLAND

Eastern Promenade in Munjoy Hill

Bayside and Parkside

A Babel of languages reverberates in these districts just below Portland City Hall. Bayside experienced the arrival of refugees—Cambodian, Laotian, Vietnamese, Central European, and Afghan families—from war-torn lands during the 1980s and 1990s. Nowadays you'll hear references to Somali Town, an area named for all the resettled refugees from that shattered country. Others have come from Sudan and Ethiopia. Portland's active Refugee Resettlement Program has assisted all of them, and many newcomers have become entrepreneurs, opening restaurants and small markets catering to their compatriots but increasingly gaining customers among other residents.

Stroudwater

Off the downtown peninsula at the western edge of Portland, close to the Portland Jetport, is the historic area known as Stroudwater, once an essential link in Maine water transport. The 20-mile-long **Cumberland and Oxford Canal,**

hand-dug in 1828, ran through here as part of the timber-shipping route linking Portland Harbor, the Fore and Presumpscot Rivers, and Sebago Lake. Twenty-eight wooden locks allowed vessels to rise the 265 feet between sea level and the lake. By 1870 trains took over the route, condemning the canal to oblivion. The centerpiece of the Stroudwater area today is the historic 18th-century Tate House.

SIGHTS
⟪ Portland Museum of Art (PMA)

Three centuries of art and architecture can be discovered at Maine's oldest (since 1882) and finest art museum, the Portland Museum of Art (7 Congress Sq., 207/775-6148, recorded info 207/773-2787 or 800/639-4067, www .portlandmuseum.org, 10 A.M.–5 P.M. Sat.–Sun. and Tues.–Thurs., 10 A.M.–9 P.M. Fri., closed Mon. mid-Oct.–late May, $10 adults, $8 seniors and students, $4 ages 6–17, free ages 5–9 P.M. every Fri.). The museum's top-flight collection of American and impressionist masters and fine and decorative arts

LIGHTHOUSES AND PARKS TOUR

Whether in a car or on a bike, it's easy to loop through South Portland and Cape Elizabeth on a route that takes in lighthouses, forts, beaches, and parks.

Begin just over the Casco Bay Bridge from downtown Portland on Route 77, take Broadway, and continue to the end at **Southern Maine Community College (SMCC),** overlooking the bay. The best time to come here is evenings and weekends, when there's ample parking. Unless it's foggy (when the signal is deafening) or thundering (when you'll expose yourself to lightning), walk out along the 1,000-foot granite breakwater to the **Spring Point Ledge Light** (207/699-2676, www.spring-pointlight.org), with fabulous views in every direction; call or check the website for current hours. Also here are picnic benches, the remains of Fort Preble, and the **Spring Point Shoreline Walkway,** a scenic three-mile path with views to House, Peaks, and Cushings Islands. At the end of the path you'll reach crescent-shaped **Willard Beach,** a neighborhood place with lifeguards, a changing building, a snack bar, and those same marvelous views.

From the SMCC campus, return on Broadway to the major intersection with Cottage Road and bear left. Cottage Road becomes Shore Road at the Cape Elizabeth town line. Loop into Fort Williams Park and make a pilgrimage to **Portland Head Light** before continuing on Shore Road to its intersection with Route 77. Bear left, follow it to Two Lights Road, and follow the signs to 40-acre **Two Lights State Park.** Almost a pocket park, it has picnicking and restroom facilities, but its biggest asset is the panoramic ocean view from atop a one-time gun battery. Summer admission is $4.50 nonresident adults, $3 Maine resident adults, $1.50 nonresident seniors, $1 ages 5-11.

Before or after visiting the park, take a left just before the park entrance, a continuation of Two Lights Road; the sign says "Lighthouses." Continue to the parking lot at the end, where you'll see the signal towers for which Two Lights is named. There's no access to either one, and only one still works. If you haven't brought a picnic for the state park, there are few places finer to enjoy the view and a lobster than at **The Lobster Shack.**

To get some beach time, return to Route 77 and continue to **Crescent Beach State Park,** a 243-acre park with changing rooms, a lifeguard, restrooms, picnic tables, and a snack bar. Admission is $6.50 nonresident adults, $4.50 Maine resident adults, $1.50 senior nonresidents, $1 ages 5-11. Directly offshore is Saco Bay's **Richmond Island,** a 200-acre private preserve with a checkered past dating to the 17th century.

is displayed in three architecturally stunning connected buildings: the award-winning Charles Shipman Payson building, designed by I. M. Pei and opened in 1983; the newly restored Federal-era McLellan House; and the beaux arts L. D. M. Sweat Memorial Galleries, designed by noted Maine architect John Calvin Stevens. The museum also has a well-stocked gift shop and a pleasant café that's open for lunch daily (11 A.M.–4 P.M.) and dinner Friday until 7:30 P.M. Check the website for current family activities, lectures, and other events, including **Movies at the Museum** ($7), showcasing foreign, classical, and art films.

🄲 Victoria Mansion

The jaws of first-time visitors literally drop when they enter the Italianate Victoria Mansion (109 Danforth St., 207/772-4841, www.victoriamansion.org, 10 A.M.–4 P.M. Mon.–Sat., 1–5 P.M. Sun. May–Oct., special hours in Dec., $15 adults, $13.50 seniors, $5 children 6–17, $35 family, no senior discount in holiday season), also called the Morse-Libby Mansion. It's widely considered the most magnificently ornamented dwelling of its period remaining in the country. The National Historic Landmark is rife with Victoriana: carved marble fireplaces, elaborate porcelain and paneling, a freestanding mahogany staircase, gilded glass chandeliers, a restored 6- by 25-foot stained-glass ceiling window, and unbelievable trompe l'oeil touches. It's even more spectacular at Christmas, with yards of roping, festooned trees, and carolers; this is the best time to bring kids, as the house itself may not particularly intrigue them. The mansion was built in the late 1850s by Ruggles Sylvester Morse, a Maine-born entrepreneur whose New Orleans–based fortune enabled him to hire 93 craftspeople to complete the house. The interior, designed by Gustave Herter, still boasts 90 percent of the original furnishings. Guided 45-minute tours begin every half hour on the quarter hour in season; tours are self-guided during the holidays.

◖ Portland Observatory

Providing a head-swiveling view of Portland (and the White Mountains on a clear day), the octagonal red-painted Portland Observatory (138 Congress St., 207/774-5561, www.portlandlandmarks.org, 10 A.M.–5 P.M. daily late May–Columbus Day, last tour at 4:30 P.M., sunset tours 5–8 P.M. Thurs. July–Aug., $8 adults, $5 children 6–16 with a paid adult) is the only remaining marine signal tower on the Eastern Seaboard. Built in 1807 at a cost of $5,000 by Captain Lemuel Moody to keep track of the port's shipping activity, the tower has 122 tons of rock ballast in its base. Admission in those days (only men were allowed to climb the 103 interior steps) was 12.5 cents. Today, admission includes the small museum at the tower's base and a guided tour to the top.

The Longfellow Connection

A few blocks down Congress Street from the PMA you can step back in time to the era of Portland-born poet Henry Wadsworth Longfellow, who lived in the accurately restored **Wadsworth-Longfellow House** (485 Congress St., 207/774-1822, www.mainehistory.org, 10:30 A.M.–4 P.M. Mon.–Sat., noon–4 P.M. Sun. May 1–Oct. 31, special holiday hours Nov.–Dec., $8 adults, $7 seniors and students, $3 ages 5–17) as a child in the early 1800s, long before the brick mansion was dwarfed by surrounding

WINSLOW HOMER

Discovering Maine in his early 40s, Winslow Homer (1836-1910) was smitten – enough to spend the last 27 years of his life in Prouts Neck (Scarborough, south of Portland), a small fishing village that is now gradually morphing into an exclusive summer enclave. In a cluttered, rustic studio converted from a stable, he produced his finest works: the seascapes that have become so familiar. The Portland Museum of Art recently acquired his studio and plans to open it to the public on a limited basis. He painted the sea in every mood, the rocks in every light, the snow in all its bleakness, and the hardy trees bent to the wind. Occasional forays to the Bahamas, the Adirondacks, and the Canadian wilderness inspired other themes, but Prouts Neck always lured him back. Homer's last work, an oil titled *Driftwood*, painted in 1909 when his health was in major decline, depicts once again the struggle against the roiling surf that Homer knew so intimately from his life on the coast of Maine.

high-rises. Wadsworth and Longfellow family furnishings fill the three-story house, owned by the Maine Historical Society, and savvy guides provide insight into Portland's 19th-century life. Don't miss the urban oasis—a wonderfully peaceful garden—behind the house (same hours, free). Buy tickets at the adjacent Center for Maine History, which also houses the **Maine History Gallery** (489 Congress St., 207/774-1822, www.mainehistory.org, 10 A.M.–5 P.M. Mon.–Sat., noon–5 P.M. Sun., $5 adults, $4 seniors, $2 children), where you can take in the Maine Historical Society's current exhibits and find an extensive collection of Maine history books in the gift shop.

Maine Narrow Gauge Railroad and Museum

A three-mile ride along Portland's waterfront is the highlight of a visit to the Maine Narrow

Gauge Railroad Company and Museum (58 Fore St., 207/828-0814, www.mngrr.org). The museum (10 A.M.–4 P.M. daily late May–late Oct., 10 A.M.–4 P.M. Mon.–Fri. off-season, $2 adults, $1 seniors and ages 3–12, free with train ticket) owns more than three dozen train cars and has others on long-term loan, most from Maine's five historic narrow-gauge railroads, the last of which closed in 1943. You can board a number of the cars and see others undergoing restoration. For a fee you can ride the two-foot rails aboard a multicar train. The schedule roughly follows museum hours, with rides on the hour ($10 adults, $9 seniors, $6 ages 3–12). The track edges Casco Bay along the Eastern Promenade; it's a short but enjoyable excursion that's a real kid pleaser.

Museum of African Culture

Here's a little treasure: Founded in 1998, the Museum of African Culture (13 Brown St., 207/871-7188, www.museumafricanculture .org, 10:30 A.M.–4 P.M. Tues.–Fri., noon–4 P.M. Sat., $5 suggested donation) is the brainchild of Nigerian-born Oscar Mokeme (the director) and Arthur Aleshire. It's devoted to sub-Saharan African arts and culture. Among the museum's 2,500 or so treasures—not all on display at once—are Nigerian tribal masks and Beninese lost-wax bronzes.

Children's Museum of Maine

Here's the answer to parents' prayers: a whole museum in downtown Portland catering to kids. At the Children's Museum of Maine (142 Free St., 207/828-1234, www.kitetails.com, 10 A.M.–5 P.M. Mon.–Sat., noon–5 P.M. Sun. late May–early Sept., 10 A.M.–5 P.M. Tues.–Sat., noon–5 P.M. Sun. early Sept.–late May, $9, free for children under age 2, $1 admission 5–8 P.M. first Fri. of each month) lots of hands-on displays encourage interaction and guarantee involvement for a couple of hours.

The International Cryptozoology Museum

An eight-foot-tall likeness of a bigfoot greets visitors at the door to former university professor and author Loren Coleman's cryptozoology museum (661 Congress St., 207/518-9496, www .cryptozoologymuseum.com, 11 A.M.–6 P.M. Wed.–Sat., noon–5 P.M. Sun., call to confirm hours, $5). Coleman is a renowned expert in cryptozoology, the story of hidden animals such as bigfoot, the Loch Ness monster, and the abominable snowman. He has amassed a collection of artifacts such as skulls and footprint castings that lend credence to the existence of these rumored beasts, as well as kitsch that includes movie props and souvenir memorabilia. The last tour departs 30 minutes before closing.

Breweries

Look for the keg topping the flagpole at **Shipyard Brewery** (86 Newbury St., 207/761-0807, www.shipyard.com). Video tours of the award-winning microbrewery are offered on the hour 11 A.M.–4 P.M. Monday–Saturday, noon–4 P.M. Sunday. Full brewery tours are offered on Tuesday evenings; advance reservations are a good idea.

Other Portland breweries offering tours are **Allagash Brewing Company** (50 Industrial Way, 207/878-5385, www.allagash.com), three times daily on weekdays; and **Geary's Brewing Company** (38 Evergreen Dr., 207/878-2337, www.gearybrewing.com), by appointment.

Southworth Planetarium

Under a 30-foot dome with comfy theater seats and a state-of-the-art laser system, the Southworth Planetarium (Science Building, lower level, University of Southern Maine, 96 Falmouth St., 207/780-4249, www.usm.maine. edu/~planet, 7 and 8:30 P.M. Fri.–Sat., $6–9 adults, $5–8 seniors and children) presents astronomy shows. Computer-savvy kids will head for the interactive computers in the exhibit area; the gift shop stocks astronaut ice cream and other science stuff. For recorded information on moon and planet positions, eclipses, and other astronomical happenings, call the **Skywatch Hotline** (207/780-4719). Take exit 6B off I-295 and go west on Forest Avenue to Falmouth Street (a left turn). The Science Building is on the left past the parking lot.

Tate House

Just down the street from the Portland International Jetport, in the Stroudwater district, is the 1755 Tate House (1270 Westbrook St., 207/774-6177, www.tatehouse.org, 10 A.M.–4 P.M. Wed.–Sat., 1–4 P.M. Sun., last tour 3 P.M., mid-June–mid-Oct., $8 adults, $6 seniors, $3 ages 6–12), a National Historic Landmark owned by the Colonial Dames of America. Built by Captain George Tate, who was prominent in shipbuilding, the house overlooks the Stroudwater River and has superb period furnishings and a lovely 18th-century herb garden with more than 70 species. Tours last 40 minutes. Wednesdays mid-June–mid-September are "summer garden days," when tea and goodies follow tours of the garden (for an extra charge).

◖ Portland Head Light

Just four miles from downtown Portland in Cape Elizabeth, Fort Williams feels a world away. This oceanfront town park, a former military base, is home to Portland Head Light

(1000 Shore Rd., Cape Elizabeth, 207/799-2661, www.portlandheadlight.com, dawn–dusk daily). Commissioned by President George Washington and first lit in 1791, it has been immortalized in poetry, photography, and philately. The surf here is awesome—perhaps too awesome, as the *Annie C. Maguire* was shipwrecked below the lighthouse on Christmas Eve 1886. There's no access to the 58-foot automated light tower, but the superbly restored keeper's house has become **The Museum at Portland Head Light** (10 A.M.–4 P.M. daily late May–mid-Oct., 10 A.M.–4 P.M. Sat.–Sun. late spring and late fall, call to confirm dates, $2 adults, $1 ages 6–18). It's filled with local history and lighthouse memorabilia. The 90-acre oceanfront park offers much more to explore, including ruins of the fort and the Goddard mansion. Walk the trails, play a game of tennis, dip your toes in the surf at the rocky beach, but be careful, as there's a strong undertow here. You might even catch the Portland Symphony Orchestra, which occasionally performs here in summer. The grassy headlands

Portland Head Light

are great places to watch the boat traffic going in and out of Portland Harbor. Bring a picnic lunch, and don't forget a kite. From downtown Portland, take Route 77 and then Broadway, Cottage Road, and Shore Road; the route is marked.

ENTERTAINMENT AND EVENTS

The best places to find out what's playing at area theaters, cinemas, concert halls, and nightclubs are the *Portland Phoenix* (www.portland-phoenix.com) and the *Go* supplement in the Thursday edition of the *Portland Press Herald* (www.mainetoday.com). Both have online listings; hard copies are available at bookstores and supermarkets. The *Phoenix* is free.

Nightlife
LIVE MUSIC
The Portland Conservatory of Music presents free weekly **Noonday Concerts** at First Parish Church (425 Congress St., 207/773-5747, www.portlandconservatory.net) at 12:15 P.M. Thursday October–early April (excluding late Nov.). The music varies widely and includes saxophone, Scottish fiddle and dance, a string quartet, and Irish baroque.

Portland Parks and Recreation sponsors **Summer in the Parks** (207/756-8275, www.portlandmaine.gov/rec/summer.htm, July–Aug., free), a number of evening concert series and a midday kids performance series in downtown parks.

In summer, take the ferry to Peaks Island for Reggae Sundays on the deck at **Jones Landing** (at the ferry landing, Peaks Island, 207/766-4400); doors open at 11:30 A.M.

BREWPUBS AND BARS
Portland is a beer town, with an ever-increasing number of microbreweries and brewpubs. It's also vigilant about enforcing alcohol laws, so even if you're well older than 21, be sure to bring identification to prove it.

Not only is **Gritty McDuff's** (396 Fore St., Old Port, 207/772-2739, 11:30 A.M.–1 A.M. daily) one of Maine's most popular breweries,

its brewpub was the state's first—opened in 1988. The menu includes pub classics such as fish-and-chips and shepherd's pie as well as burgers, salads, and sandwiches. Among the Gritty's beers and ales on tap are Sebago Light and Black Fly Stout. Gritty's also books live entertainment fairly regularly. Tours are available by appointment. Gritty's also has a branch in Freeport.

A longtime favorite pub, **$3 Dewey's** (241 Commercial St., Old Port, 207/772-3310, www.threedollardeweys.com) is so authentic that visiting Brits, Kiwis, and Aussies often head here to assuage their homesickness. Inexpensive fare, 36 brews on tap, free popcorn, and frequent live music make it a very popular spot.

Especially popular in the late afternoon and early evening is **J's Oyster** (5 Portland Pier, 207/772-4828, 11:30 A.M.–1 A.M. daily), a longtime fixture (some might call it a dive) on the waterfront known for its raw bar and for pouring a good drink.

Of all Portland's neighborhood hangouts, **Ruski's** (212 Danforth St., 207/774-7604, 7 A.M.–12:45 A.M. Mon.–Sat., 9 A.M.–12:45 A.M. Sun., no credit cards) is the most authentic—a small, usually crowded onetime speakeasy that rates just as highly for breakfast as for nighttime schmoozing. Expect basic homemade fare for well under $10, plus darts and a big-screen TV. Dress down or you'll feel out of place.

That said, it's **Rosie's** (330 Fore St., 207/772-5656) that *Esquire* magazine named as one of the country's best bars. **Blackstones** (6 Pine St., 207/775-2885, www.blackstones.com) claims to be Portland's oldest neighborhood gay bar.

Novare Res Bier Cafe (4 Canal Plaza, 207/761-2437, www.novareresbiercafe.com, 4 P.M.–1 A.M. Mon.–Thurs., 3 P.M.–1 A.M. Fri., noon–1 A.M. Sat.–Sun.) carries more than 300 bottled beers from around the world. Pair them with selections from the meat and cheese bar, sandwiches, or small plates.

West of I-295, **The Great Lost Bear** (540 Forest Ave., 207/772-0300, www.greatlost-bear.com, 11:30 A.M.–11:30 P.M. Mon.–Sat., noon–11 P.M. Sun.) has 65 brews on tap, representing 15 Maine microbreweries and others from New England. The bear motif and the punny menus are a bit much, but the 15 or so varieties of burgers are not bad. It's a kid pleaser.

For more upscale tippling, head for **Top of the East** (157 High St., near Congress Sq., 207/775-5411), the lounge at the top of the Eastland Park Hotel, where all of Portland is at your feet.

BARS WITH ENTERTAINMENT

There are so many possibilities in this category that the best advice is to scope out the scene when you arrive; the *Portland Phoenix* has the best listings. Most clubs have cover charges. The coolest venue with the hottest acts is **Port City Music Hall** (504 Congress St., 207/899-4990, www.portcitymusichall .com), a three-floor entertainment emporium. **Asylum** (121 Center St., 207/772-8274, www .portlandasylum.com) caters to a young crowd with dance jams, CD release parties, DJ nights, and live bands. **Geno's** (13 Brown St., 207/772-7891) has been at it for years—an old reliable for rock music with an emphasis on local bands. Ever popular for Wednesday hip-hop and weekend bands is **The Big Easy** (55 Market St., 207/871-8817, www.bigeasy-portland.com). **Blue** (650A Congress St., 207/774-4111, www.portcityblue.com) presents local artists and musicians in a small space and serves beer, wine, tea, and light fare; traditional Irish music is always featured on Wednesday evening, and jazz on Saturday. Wanna rock? See what's on the calendar at **Empire Dine and Dance** (575 Congress St., 207/879-8988, www.portlandempire.com), where the entertainment includes live music and CD release parties upstairs as well as daily entertainment ranging from bluegrass to jazz downstairs.

Performing Arts

MERRILL AUDITORIUM

The magnificently restored Merrill Auditorium (20 Myrtle St., box office 207/874-8200, www .portlandevents.com) is a 1,900-seat theater inside Portland City Hall on Congress Street with two balconies and one of the country's only municipally owned pipe organs, the **Kotzschmar Organ** (207/553-4363, www .foko.org). A summer classical organ concert series with guest artists is held at 7:30 P.M. most Tuesdays mid-June–August ($10 donation), with a preconcert talk at 6:30 P.M.

Special events and concerts are common at Merrill, and the auditorium is also home to a number of the city's arts organizations. The **Portland Symphony Orchestra** (207/842-0800, www.portlandsymphony.org) and **PCA Great Performances** (207/773-3150, www .pcagreatperformances.org) have extensive, well-patronized fall and winter schedules; the PSO presents three summer Independence Pops concerts as well. The **Portland Opera Repertory Theatre** (437 Congress St., 207/879-7678, www.portopera.org) performs a major opera each summer. In addition there are films, lectures, and other related events throughout July. Tickets for the symphony, PCA, and opera are available through PortTix (207/942-0800, www.porttix.com).

1 LONGFELLOW SQUARE

Diverse programming is the hallmark of 1 Longfellow Square (207/761-1757, www.one-longfellowsquare.com), an intimate venue for performances and lectures at the corner of Congress and State Streets.

STATE THEATER

The State (690 Congress St., 207/956-6000, www.statetheatreportland.com), which opened in 1929, has had an up-and-down history. It reopened again in late 2010 with plans for up to 80 performances annually.

PORTLAND STAGE COMPANY

Innovative staging and controversial contemporary dramas are typical of the Portland Stage Company (Portland Performing Arts Center, 25A Forest Ave., 207/774-0465, www.port-landstage.com), established in 1974 and going strong ever since. Equity pros present a half-dozen plays each winter season in a 290-seat performance space.

Comedy

Portland's forum for stand-up comedy is the **Comedy Connection** (16 Custom House Wharf, 207/774-5554, www.mainecomedy .com, Thurs.–Sun. evenings), a crowded space that draws nationally known pros. Avoid the front tables unless you enjoy being the fall guy or guinea pig, and don't bring anyone squeamish about the F-word. Be sure to catch Bob Marley if he's got a show.

Events

Pick up a free copy of the *Portland Area Arts and Events Calendar* at Portland shops and cafés, the Visitor Information Center, or City Hall (389 Congress St.).

Summer brings a host of events, including the **Old Port Festival,** one of the city's largest festivals, usually the first weekend of June. It has entertainment, food and craft booths, and impromptu fun in Portland's Old Port. The **Greek Heritage Festival,** usually the last weekend of June, features Greek food, dancing, and crafts at Holy Trinity Church (133 Pleasant St.).

Some of the world's top runners join upward of 500 racers in the **Beach to Beacon Race,** held in late July–early August. The 10K course goes from Crescent Beach State Park to Portland Head Light in Cape Elizabeth.

In mid-August the **Italian Street Festival** showcases music, Italian food, and games at St. Peter's Catholic Church (72 Federal St.). Artists from all over the country set up in 350 booths along Congress Street for the annual **Sidewalk Arts Festival** in late August.

The big October wing-ding is the **Harvest on the Harbor,** a celebration of all things food-and wine-related with tastings, dinners, exhibits, and special events.

The **Maine Brewers' Festival,** the first weekend in November at the Portland Exposition Building, is a big event that expands every year thanks to the explosion of Maine microbreweries; there are samples galore. From Thanksgiving weekend to Christmas Eve, **Victorian Holiday** in downtown Portland harks back with caroling, special sales, concerts, tree lighting, horse-drawn wagons, and Victoria Mansion tours and festivities.

SHOPPING

The Portland peninsula—primarily Congress Street and the Old Port waterfront district—is thick with non–cookie-cutter shops and galleries. These listings offer just a taste to spur your explorations.

Bookstores

Carlson-Turner Books (241 Congress St., 207/773-4200 or 800/540-7323), based on Munjoy Hill, seems to have Portland's largest used-book inventory. Look for unusual titles and travel narratives.

Cookbook mavens will drool over the collection at **Rabelais Books** (86 Market St., 207/774-1044, www.rabelaisbooks.com), ideally situated in Portland's foodie neighborhood. Don and Samantha Hoyt Lindgren specialize in food and wine, carrying a delicious blend of thousands of current, rare, and out-of-print books covering culinary history, food lit, cookbooks, wine, and related topics.

Art Galleries

In-town Portland's galleries host a **First Friday Artwalk** (www.firstfridayartwalk.com) on the first Friday evening of each month, with exhibition openings, open houses, meet-the-artist gatherings, and other such artsy activities.

Galleries specializing in contemporary art are clustered in the Arts District. These include **June Fitzpatrick Gallery** (112 High St., 207/879-5742, www.junefitzpatrickgallery.com) and **Institute for Contemporary Art** (Maine College of Art, 522 Congress St., 207/879-5742, www.meca.edu). Another gallery hotbed is the Old Port, where you can visit **Aucocisco** (89 Exchange St., 207/553-2222, www.aucocisco.com), specializing in contemporary fine art, and **Greenhut Galleries** (146 Middle St., 207/772-2693, www.greenhut-galleries.com), specializing in contemporary

Maine art and sculpture. More than 15 Maine potters—with a wide variety of styles and items—market their wares at the **Maine Potters Market** (376 Fore St., 207/774-1633, www.mainepottersmarket.com).

Specialty Shops

Check out the latest clothing and home accessories from Maine-based designers with national reputations: **Angela Adams** (273 Congress St., 207/774-3523), Alex Carleton's **Rogues Gallery** (41 Wharf St., 207/553-1999), and Nicola Manganello's **Nicola Homes** (215 Commercial St., 207/899-3218).

Bring home a nautical treasure from **Shipwreck and Cargo** (207 Commercial St., Old Port, 207/775-3057, www.shipwreckand-cargo.com), which stocks a wide assortment of marine-related items—boat models, barometers, Navy surplus stuff, and more.

Woof: The company outlet **Planet Dog** (211 Marginal Way, 207/347-8606, www.planetdog .com) is a howling good time for dogs and their owners. You'll find all sorts of wonderful products, and Planet Dog, committed to "think globally and act doggedly," has established a foundation to promote and serve causes such as dog therapy, service, search and rescue, bomb sniffing, and police dogs.

RECREATION
Parks, Preserves, and Beaches

Greater Portland is blessed with green space, thanks largely to the efforts of 19th-century mayor James Phinney Baxter, who had the foresight to hire the famed Olmsted Brothers to develop an ambitious plan to ring the city with public parks and promenades. Not all the elements fell into place, but the result is what makes Portland such a livable city.

DOWNTOWN PENINSULA

Probably the most visible of the city's parks, 51-acre **Deering Oaks** (Park Ave. between Forest Ave. and Deering Ave.) may be best known for the quaint little duck condo in the middle of the pond. Other facilities and highlights here are tennis courts, a playground, horseshoes,

rental paddleboats, a snack bar, the award-winning Rose Circle, a farmers market (7 A.M.–noon Sat.), and, in winter, ice-skating. After dark, steer clear of the park.

At one end of the Eastern Promenade, where it meets Fore Street, **Fort Allen Park** overlooks offshore Fort Gorges (coin-operated telescopes bring it closer). A central gazebo is flanked by an assortment of military souvenirs dating as far back as the War of 1812. All along the Eastern Prom are walking paths, benches, play areas, and even an ill-maintained fitness trail—all with that terrific view. Down by the water is **East End Beach,** with parking, token sand, and the area's best launching ramp for sea kayaks or powerboats.

WEST OF THE DOWNTOWN PENINSULA

Just beyond I-295 along Baxter Boulevard (Rte. 1) and tidal **Back Cove** is a skinny green strip with a 3.5-mile trail for walking, jogging, or just watching the sailboards and the skyline. Along the way, you can cross Baxter Boulevard and spend time picnicking, playing tennis, or flying a kite in 48-acre **Payson Park.**

Talk about an urban oasis. The 85-acre **Fore River Sanctuary** (sunrise to sunset daily), owned by Maine Audubon, has two miles of blue-blazed trails that wind through a salt marsh, link with the historic Cumberland and Oxford Canal towpath, and pass near **Jewell Falls,** Portland's only waterfall, protected by Portland Trails. From downtown Portland, take Congress Street West (Rte. 22) past I-295. There are two access routes from here: Either turn right onto Stevens Avenue (Rte. 9), continue to Brighton Avenue (Rte. 25), turn left, and go about 1.25 miles to Rowe Avenue, and then turn left and park at the end of the road; or continue past Stevens Avenue about 0.5 miles to Frost Avenue, take a hard right, and then left into the Maine Orthopedic Center parking lot. Portland Trails raised the funds for the handsome 90-foot pedestrian bridge at this entrance to the sanctuary. Pets are not allowed in the sanctuary.

Bird-watchers flock to 239-acre **Evergreen Cemetery** (Stevens Ave.) in May to see warblers, thrushes, and other migratory birds that gather in the ponds and meadows. During peak periods it's possible to see as many as 20 warbler species in a morning, including the Cape May, bay breasted, mourning, and Tennessee. Naturalists from Maine Audubon often are on-site helping to identify birds. For more info, check the events calendar at www.mainebirding.net.

SCARBOROUGH
Scarborough Beach Park (Black Point Rd./ Rte. 207, 207/883-2416, www.scarborough beachstatepark.com, $6.50 nonresident adults, $4.50 Maine resident adults, $2 children), a long stretch of sand, is the best beach for big waves. Between the parking area and the lovely stretch of beach you'll pass Massacre Pond, named for a 1703 skirmish between resident Native Americans and wannabe residents (score: Indians 19, wannabes 0). The park is open all year for swimming, surfing (permit required), beachcombing, and ice-skating, but on weekends in summer the parking lot fills early.

At 3,100 acres, **Scarborough Marsh** (Pine Point Rd./Rte. 9, 207/883-5100, www.maine-audubon.org, 9:30 A.M.–5:30 P.M. daily mid-June–early Sept., 9:30 A.M.–5:30 P.M. Sat.–Sun. late May and Sept.), Maine's largest salt marsh, is prime territory for bird-watching and canoeing. Rent a canoe ($16 for 1 hour, $23 for 1.5 hours, $30 for 2 hours) at the small nature center operated by Maine Audubon and explore on your own. Or join one of the daily 90-minute guided tours (call for the schedule, $11 adults, $9 children, subtract $1.50 pp if you have your own canoe). Guided full-moon tours ($12 adults, $10 children) June–September are particularly exciting; dress warmly and bring a flashlight. Other special programs, some geared primarily for children, include wildflower walks, art classes, and dawn bird-watching trips; all require reservations and very reasonable fees. Also here is a walking-tour trail of less than one mile. Pick up a map at the center.

Overlooking the marsh is 52-acre **Scarborough River Wildlife Sanctuary** (Pine Point Rd./Rte. 9), with 1.5 miles of walking trails that loop to the Scarborough River and past two ponds.

FALMOUTH
Nearly a dozen of Falmouth's parks, trails, and preserves, official and unofficial, are described and mapped in the *Falmouth Trail Guide,* a handy little booklet published by the Falmouth Conservation Commission. Copies are available at Gilsland Farm, Falmouth Town Hall, and local bookstores. Two of the best options are described below.

A 65-acre wildlife sanctuary and environmental center on the banks of the Presumpscot River, **Gilsland Farm** (20 Gilsland Farm Rd., 207/781-2330, www.maineaudubon.org, dawn–dusk daily) is state headquarters for Maine Audubon. More than two miles of easy well-marked trails wind through the grounds, taking in salt marshes, rolling meadows, woodlands, and views of the estuary. Observation blinds allow inconspicuous spying during bird-migration season. In the education center (9 A.M.–5 P.M. Mon.–Sat., noon–4 P.M. Sun.) are hands-on exhibits, a nature store, and classrooms and offices. Fees are charged for special events, but otherwise it's all free. The visitors center is 0.25 miles off Route 1.

Once the summer compound of the prominent Baxter family, Falmouth's 100-acre **Mackworth Island** (sunrise–sunset daily year-round), reached via a causeway, is now the site of the Governor Baxter School for the Deaf. Limited parking is just beyond the security booth on the island. On the 1.5-mile vehicle-free perimeter path, which has great Portland Harbor views, you'll meet bikers, hikers, and dog walkers. Just off the trail on the north side of the island is the late governor Percival Baxter's stone-circled pet cemetery, maintained by the state at the behest of Baxter, who donated this island as well as Baxter State Park to the people of Maine. From downtown Portland, take Route 1 across the Presumpscot River to Falmouth Foreside. Andrews Avenue (third street on the right) leads to the island.

Trail Network
Portland Trails (305 Commercial St., 207/775-2411, www.trails.org), a dynamic membership conservation organization

incorporated in 1991, is dedicated to creating and maintaining a 50-mile network of hiking and biking trails in Greater Portland. It already has 30 mapped trails to its credit, including the 2.1-mile Eastern Promenade Trail, a landscaped bay-front dual pathway circling the base of Munjoy Hill and linking East End Beach to the Old Port, and a continuing trail connecting the Eastern Prom with the 3.5-mile Back Cove Trail, on the other side of I-295. Trail maps are available on the website. The group also holds organized walks ($5 nonmembers)—a great way to meet some locals. Better still, join Portland Trails ($35 per year) and support its ambitious efforts.

Walking Tours
PORTLAND FREEDOM TRAIL
Pick up a copy of this free map and brochure (also available online) detailing a self-guided walking tour of 16 marked sights related to Portland's role in Maine's Underground Railway (www.portlandfreedomtrail.org). Among the highlights are the Abyssinian Meeting House, the third-oldest African American Meeting House still standing in the United States (currently undergoing restoration); the First Parish Unitarian Universalist Church, where abolitionist William Lloyd Garrison spoke in 1832; and Mariners' Church, location of an antislavery bookstore and print shop that printed the first Afrocentric history of the world.

PORTLAND WOMEN'S HISTORY TRAIL
Another self-guided walking tour, this one details four loops—Congress Street, Munjoy Hill, State Street, and the West End—with about 20 stops on each. Among the sites: a long-gone chewing-gum factory where teenage girls worked 10-hour shifts. The trail guide is available online (www.usm.maine.edu/~history/newtrail.html) or for $8.50 in selected bookstores and at the Maine History Gallery gift shop (489 Congress St., 207/879-0427).

GREATER PORTLAND LANDMARKS
Greater Portland Landmarks (207/774-5561,

www.portlandlandmarks.org) sponsors neighborhood walking tours as well as an annual **summer tour program** that features four or five walking trips and excursions to offshore islands, historic churches, revamped buildings, and gardens. Many of the destinations are private or otherwise inaccessible, so these are special opportunities. Registration is limited, and there's only one trip to each site. Tours run mid-July–mid-October, primarily on weekends.

MAINE FOODIE TOURS
Just as the name promises, Maine Foodie Tours (10 Moulton St., 207/233-7485, www.mainefoodietours.com) delivers a taste of Maine. The Old Port Culinary Walking Tour ($39) visits seven vendors selling everything from cheese to lobster to chocolate; Culinary Delights Trolley Tour ($39) includes both onboard and in-shop tastings; Port City Beer Tour ($27) is a 0.25-mile walk focused on Portland's brewing heritage with three stops en route.

C Casco Bay Tour
Casco Bay Lines (Commercial St. and Franklin St., Old Port, 207/774-7871, www.cascobaylines.com), the nation's oldest continuously operating ferry system (since the 1920s), is the lifeline between Portland and six inhabited Casco Bay islands. What better way to sample the islands than to take the three-hour ride along with mail, groceries, and island residents? The Casco Bay Lines mail boat stops—briefly—at **Long Island, Chebeague, Cliff,** and **Little Diamond** and **Great Diamond Islands.** Departures are 10 A.M. and 2:15 P.M. daily mid-June–Labor Day (plus 7:45 A.M. weekdays), 10 A.M. and 2:45 P.M. in other months. Fares are $14.50 adults, $12.50 seniors, and $7.25 ages 5–9. The longest cruise on the Casco Bay Lines schedule is the nearly six-hour narrated summertime trip (late June–early Sept., $24 adults, $21.25 seniors, $11 ages 5–9) with a two-hour stopover on **Bailey Island,** departing from Portland at 10 A.M. daily. Dogs ($3.75) on leashes and bicycles ($6) need separate tickets.

Land and Sea Tours

Various commercial operators offer area land-and-sea tours, but frankly, none is first-rate. Guides on each often present incorrect information. Still, such tours are a good way to get the city's general layout.

The best of the lot is the 1.5-hour narrated sightseeing tour of Portland in a trolley-bus by **Portland Discovery Land and Sea Tours** (3 Moulton St., Old Port, 207/774-0808, www.portlanddiscovery.com, $18 adults, $12 children). You can combine this tour with a 90-minute Lighthouse Lover's cruise on Casco Bay. The combined price is $33 adults, $21 children.

An alternative, especially if you're traveling with kids, is the 60–70-minute **Downeast Duck Adventures** (207/774-3825, www.downeastducktours.com, early May–early Oct., $24 adults, $20 seniors, $17 ages 6–12, $5 under age 6). Call for departure point, then purchase tickets aboard or online. Prepare to do a lot of quacking on the tour and to hear a lot of quackery regarding local history.

Bicycling

The **Bicycle Coalition of Maine** (207/623-4511, www.bikemaine.org) has an excellent website that lists nearly two dozen trails in Greater Portland. You'll also find info on events, organized rides, bike shops, and more. Another good resource is **Casco Bay Bicycle Club** (www.cascobaybicycleclub.org), a recreational cycling club with rides several times weekly. Check the website for details.

For rentals (hybrids $25 per day) and repairs, visit **Cycle Mania** (59 Federal St., 207/774-2933, www.cyclemania1.com).

The best locales for island bicycling—fun for families and beginners but not especially challenging for diehards—are Peaks and Great Chebeague Islands, but do remember to follow the rules of the road.

Golf

You'll have no problem finding a place to tee off in Greater Portland. Some of the best courses are private, so if you have an "in," so much the better—but there are still plenty of public and semiprivate courses for every skill level. Free advice on helping you choose a course is offered by Maine's Golf Concierge (info@golfme.com).

Kids of all ages find plenty to quack about on Downeast Duck Adventures.

Consider just Greater Portland's 18-hole courses. **Sable Oaks Golf Club** (505 Country Club Dr., South Portland, 207/775-6257, www.sableoaks.com) is considered one of the toughest and best of Maine's public courses. Since 1998, **Nonesuch River Golf Club** (304 Gorham Rd./Rte. 114, Scarborough, 207/883-0007 or 888/256-2717, www.nonesuchgolf .com) has been drawing raves for the challenges of its par-70 championship course and praise from environmentalists for preserving wildlife habitat; there's also a full-size practice range and green. The City of Portland's **Riverside Municipal Golf Course** (1158 Riverside St., 207/797-3524, www.playriverside.com) has an 18-hole par-72 course (Riverside North) and a nine-hole par-35 course (Riverside South). Opt for the 18-hole course.

Sea Kayaking

With all the islands scattered through Casco Bay, Greater Portland has become a hotbed of sea-kayaking activity. The best place to start is out on Peaks Island, 15 minutes offshore via Casco Bay Lines ferry. **Maine Island Kayak Company** (MIKCO, 70 Luther St., Peaks Island, 207/766-2373 or 800/796-2373, www .maineislandkayak.com) is a successful tour operation that organizes half-day, all-day, and multiday local kayaking trips as well as national and international adventures. An introductory half-day tour in Casco Bay is $65 pp; a full day is $110 pp and includes lunch. Reservations are essential. MIKCO also does private lessons and group courses and clinics (some require previous experience). MIKCO's owner, Tom Bergh, has a flawless reputation for safety and skill.

Lobstering Cruise

Learn all kinds of lobster lore and maybe even catch your own dinner with **Lucky Catch Lobster Tours** (170 Commercial St., 207/233-2026 or 888/624-6321, www.luckycatch.com, $25 adults, $22 seniors, $20 ages 13–18, $15 ages 2–12). Captain Tom Martin offers three different 80–90-minute cruises on his 37-foot lobster boat. On each cruise (except late

Cruise ships and freighters dock side-by-side in Portland's busy harbor.

Saturday and all day Sunday, when state law prohibits it), usually 10 traps are hauled and the process and gear explained. You can even help if you want. Any lobsters caught are available for purchase after the cruise for wholesale boat price (and you can have them cooked nearby for a reasonable rate). Wouldn't that make a nice story to tell the folks back home?

Excursion Boats

Down on the Old Port wharves are several excursion-boat businesses. Each has carved out a niche, so choose according to your interest and your schedule. Dress warmly and wear rubber-soled shoes. Remember that all cruises are weather-dependent.

Portland Discover–Land & Sea Tours (Long Wharf, 207/774-0808, www.portland-discovery.com) comprises **Mainely Tours, Eagle Island Tours** and **Bay View Cruises.** Options include a Lighthouse Lover's Cruise ($18 adults, $12 children), departing 2–3 times daily; a 90-minute Sunset Lighthouse Cruise ($20 adults, $14 children); and a four-hour cruise to Eagle Island ($33 adults, $20 children), departing five days weekly late June–August, weekends only in September. The Eagle Island cruise visits the island where Arctic explorer Admiral Robert Peary built his summer home, allowing time on the island to visit the house and wander the grounds. Pack a picnic.

Cruise up to 20 miles offshore seeking whales with **Odyssey Whale Watch** (Long Wharf, 170 Commercial St., 207/775-0727, www.odysseywhalewatch.com, $47 adults, $38 under age 12). Four–five-hour whale watches aboard the *Odyssey* depart daily June–early September as well as on spring and fall weekends. (Don't overload on breakfast that day, and take preventive measures if you're motion-sensitive.)

Sail quietly across the waters of Casco Bay aboard a windjammer with **Portland Schooner Company** (Maine State Pier, 56 Commercial St., 207/766-2500, www.portlandschooner .com, late May–Oct., $35 adults, $10 under age 13). Three–four two-hour sails are offered

© HILARY NANGLE

The Portland Schooner Company's historic sailing vessels dock near the city's whaling wall.

daily on two schooners, the 72-foot *Bagheera* and the 88-foot *Wendameen,* both historical vessels designed by John G. Alden and built in East Boothbay. Overnight windjammer trips also are available for $240 pp, including dinner and breakfast.

Spectator Sports

A pseudo-fierce mascot named Slugger stirs up the crowds at baseball games played by the **Portland Sea Dogs** (Hadlock Field, 271 Park Ave., 207/879-9500 or 800/936-3647, www.portlandseadogs.com, less than $10), a AA Boston Red Sox farm team. Ever since the team arrived in 1994, loyal local fans have made tickets scarce, so it's wise to reserve well ahead (you'll pay a minimal reservation surcharge). The season schedule (early Apr.–Aug.) is available after January 1.

For ice hockey action, the **Portland Pirates** (207/775-3458, www.portlandpirates.com, $13–19), a farm team for the American Hockey League's Buffalo Sabres, plays winter and spring home games at the 8,700-seat Cumberland County Civic Center (1 Civic Center Sq.).

The newest entry among Portland's professional teams is the **Red Claws** (207/210-6655, www.maineredclaws.com, $10–30), an NBA development team for the Boston Celtics. Home court is the Portland Expo (239 Park Ave.).

ACCOMMODATIONS
Downtown Portland

Portland's peninsula doesn't have an overwhelming amount of sleeping space, but it does have good variety in all price ranges. Rates reflect peak season.

INNS AND BED-AND-BREAKFASTS

All of these are in older buildings without elevators; stairs may be steep.

Railroad tycoon John Deering built **The Inn at St. John** (939 Congress St., 207/773-6481 or 800/636-9127, www.innatstjohn .com, $100–225) in 1897. The comfortable (if somewhat tired) moderately priced 37-room

hostelry welcomes children and pets and even has bicycle storage. Cable TV, air-conditioning, free local calls, free parking, free airport pickup, and a meager continental breakfast are provided. Most guest rooms have private baths (some are detached); some have fridges and microwaves. The downside is the lackluster neighborhood—in the evening you'll want drive or take a taxi when going out. It's about a 30-minute walk to the Old Port or an $8 taxi fare.

Staying at **The Pomegranate Inn** (49 Neal St. at Carroll St., 207/772-1006 or 800/356-0408, www.pomegranateinn.com, $185–295) is an adventure in itself, with faux paintings, classical statuary, art, antiques, and whimsical touches everywhere—you'll either love it or find it a bit much. The elegant 1884 Italianate mansion has seven guest rooms and a suite, all with air-conditioning, TV, and phones, some with fireplaces. Afternoon refreshments are served.

Take a carefully renovated 1830s town house, add contemporary amenities and a service-oriented innkeeper, and the result is the **Morrill Mansion Bed and Breakfast** (249 Vaughan St., 207/774-6900 or 888/566-7745, www.morrillmansion.com, $149–239), on the West End. Six guest rooms and one suite are spread out on the 2nd and 3rd floors. No frilly Victorian accents here—the decor is understated yet tasteful, taking advantage of hardwood floors and high ceilings. You'll find free Wi-Fi and local calls and a TV with a DVD player in each room. A continental breakfast is included; off-street parking is free. It's near the hospital, so you might hear a siren or two.

In the same neighborhood is **(The Chadwick Bed & Breakfast** (140 Chadwick St., 207/774-5141 or 800/774-2137, www.thechadwick.com, $160–185), where innkeeper Buddy Marcum welcomes guests warmly and treats them like royalty with plush linens, cozy robes, and memorable breakfasts. All rooms have flat-screen TVs with DVD players and Wi-Fi; a movie library is available.

In 2010, Marcum purchased **The Carleton Inn** (46 Carlton St., 207/775-1910 or 800/639-

1779, www.innoncarleton.com, $160–185), an 1869 Victorian with a convenient location in the city's West End. He's adding his blend of comforts and perks. While all guest rooms have private baths, some are detached.

Former travel writer Dale Northrup put his experience to work in opening the **Percy Inn** (15 Pine St., 207/871-7638 or 888/417-3729, www.percyinn.com, $129–209), just off Longfellow Square. You can easily hole up in the air-conditioned guest rooms, which are furnished with phones, fax machines, CD players, TVs with video players, wet bars, and stocked refrigerators. It's best suited for independent-minded travelers who don't desire much contact with the host or other guests, as public rooms are few and the innkeeper is rarely on-site. Breakfast is a continental buffet.

Built in 1835, **The Inn at Park Spring** (135 Spring St., 207/774-1059 or 800/427-8511, www.innatparkspring.com, $149–205) is one of Portland's longest-running bed-and-breakfasts. Current innkeepers Nancy and John Gonsalves are adding their own touches to make guests feel right at home. The location is excellent, just steps from most Arts District attractions. Six somewhat quirky guest rooms are spread out on three floors. All have air-conditioning and phones, and some have Internet access; one has a private patio and entrance. There's a guest fridge on each floor. Rates include a full breakfast served around a common table.

Built in 1877, the handsome Georgian-style **West End Inn** (146 Pine St. at Neal St., 207/772-1377 or 800/338-1377, www.westendbb.com, $195–240) has six nicely decorated 2nd- and 3rd-floor guest rooms. A full breakfast and afternoon refreshments are served. Pack light if you're on the 3rd floor.

FULL-SERVICE HOTELS

You might have trouble finding the **Portland Regency** (20 Milk St., 207/774-4200 or 800/727-3436, www.theregency.com, $250–300): This hotel, registered with the National Trust for Historic Preservation as a historic property, is secreted in a renovated armory in the heart of the Old Port. The rooms are a bit tired, but local calls, Wi-Fi, and shuttles to all major Portland transportation facilities are free, and service is excellent. Be forewarned: Room configurations vary widely—some provide little natural window light or are strangely shaped. All have 27-inch TVs, minibars, and air-conditioning. A restaurant, spa, and fitness center are on-site.

Newest and most luxurious is the **Portland Harbor Hotel** (468 Fore St., 207/775-9090 or 888/798-9090, www.portlandharborhotel.com, $269–379), an upscale boutique hotel in the Old Port built around a garden courtyard. Rooms are plush, with chic linens, duvets, down pillows on the beds, Wi-Fi and digital cable TV, and bathrooms with separate soaking tubs and showers. Bike rentals are available ($15 per day), and the hotel offers a free local car service. The restaurant is excellent. The downside is that the neighborhood can be noisy at night, so request a room facing the interior courtyard, preferably on the upper floors. Best splurge are the suites, added in 2009.

Yes, it's a chain, and yes, it's downright ugly, but the **Holiday Inn by the Bay** (88 Spring St., 207/775-2311 or 800/345-5050, www.innbythebay.com, $166–266) provides a lot of bang for the buck. It's conveniently situated between the waterfront and the Arts District; rooms on upper floors have views either over Back Cove or Portland Harbor; Wi-Fi and parking are free, as is a shuttle service. It also has an indoor pool, a sauna, a fitness room, on-site laundry facilities, a restaurant, and a lounge.

The Burbs

South of Portland are two upscale beachfront inns. In 2007 the **Black Point Inn Resort** (510 Black Point Rd., Prouts Neck, Scarborough, 207/883-2500 or 800/258-0003, www.blackpointinn.com, $250–310 pp includes breakfast, afternoon tea, and dinner) reopened after being dramatically downsized and upscaled. The historic shingle-style hotel opened in 1878 at the tip of Prouts Neck, overlooking Casco

Bay from one side and down to Old Orchard from the other; it has beaches out the front and back doors. Now owned by a local partnership, the inn has returned to its roots, catering to wealthy rusticators. The Point Restaurant is open to nonguests by reservation (6–8:30 P.M. daily, $28–38), and the less-fussy Chart Room (11:30 A.M.–9 P.M. daily, $10–18) serves lighter fare—but first, have cocktails on the porch at sunset. Guests have access to a private 18-hole golf course and tennis courts. Staying here is splurge-worthy.

Equally splurge-worthy and especially suited for families is the oceanfront **C Inn by the Sea** (40 Bowery Beach Rd./Rte. 77, Cape Elizabeth, 207/799-3134 or 800/888-4287, www.innbythesea.com, from around $400), just seven miles south of downtown Portland. Guests stay in handsome suites and cottages, most with kitchens or expanded wet bars, comfy living rooms, and big views. A major renovation and expansion in 2008 added a cozy lounge, a full-service spa, and a small cardio room. Big windows frame ocean views at **Sea Glass** (207/299-3134, entrées $23–34), where chef Mitchell Kaldrovich favors Maine ingredients in his creative breakfasts, lunches, and dinners. Other facilities include an outdoor pool, a *boules* court, wildlife habitats, and a private boardwalk winding through a salt marsh to the southern end of Crescent Beach State Park. By reservation, pets are honored guests; they even have their own room-service menu.

FOOD

Named "America's Foodiest Small Town" by *Bon Appétit* magazine in 2009, downtown Portland alone has more than 100 restaurants, so it's impossible to list even all the great ones— and there are many. The city's proximity to fresh foods from both farms and the sea makes it popular with chefs, and its Italian roots and growing immigrant population mean a good choice of ethnic dining too. Here is a choice selection, by neighborhood, with open days and hours provided for peak season. Some restaurants don't list a closing time; that's because they shut the doors when the crowd thins, so

to be safe call ahead if you're heading out much after 8 P.M. Do make reservations, whenever possible, and as far in advance as you can, especially in July–August. If you're especially into the food scene, check www.portlandfoodmap.com for a breakdown by cuisine of Portland restaurants with links to recent reviews.

In addition to the many restaurant options listed here, check the "Community News" listings in each Wednesday's *Portland Press Herald.* Under "Potluck," you'll find listings of **public meals,** usually benefiting nonprofit organizations. Prices are always quite low (under $10 for adults, $2–4 for children), mealtimes quite early (5 or 6 P.M.), and the flavor quite local.

When you need a java fix, **Coffee by Design** (620 Congress St.; 67 India St.; 43 Washington Ave., 207/879-2233) is the local choice, not only for its fine brews but also for its support of local artists and community causes.

The Portland Farmers Market sets up on Wednesday on Monument Square and on Saturday in Deering Oaks Park.

The Old Port and the Waterfront
LOCAL FLAVORS
All of these venues are east of the Franklin Street Arterial between Congress and Commercial Streets.

Best known for the earliest and most filling breakfast, **Becky's Diner** (Hobson's Wharf, 390 Commercial St., Old Port, 207/773-7070, www.beckysdiner.com, 7 A.M.–9 P.M. Mon.–Sat., 8 A.M.–8 P.M. Sun.) has more than a dozen omelet choices, just for a start. It also serves lunch and dinner, all at downright cheap prices.

Enjoy pizza with a view at **Flatbread Company** (72 Commercial St., 207/772-8777, www.flatbreadcompany.com, 11:30 A.M.– 10 P.M. daily), part of a small New England chain. The all-natural pizza is baked in a primitive wood-fired clay oven and served in a dining room with a wall of windows overlooking the ferry terminal and Portland Harbor. Vegan options are available.

For gourmet goodies, don't miss **Browne Trading Market** (Merrill's Wharf, 262

Commercial St., 207/775-7560, www.brownetrading.com). Owner Rod Mitchell became the Caviar King of Portland by wholesaling Caspian caviar, and now he's letting the rest of us in on it. Fresh fish and shellfish fill the cases next to the caviar and cheeses. The mezzanine is literally wall-to-wall wine, specializing in French.

When you're craving carbs, want pastries for breakfast, or need to boost your energy with a sweet, follow your nose to **Standard Baking Company** (75 Commercial St., 207/773-2112), deservedly famous for its handcrafted breads and pastries.

CASUAL DINING

Walter's (2 Portland Sq., 207/871-9258, www.walterscafe.com, 11 A.M.–2:30 P.M. and 5–9 P.M. daily, no lunch Sun., $16–26) has been serving creative fusion fare since the 1990s (although in a new location as of late 2009). Despite the longevity, it's never tiresome and retains well-earned status as a favored go-to among the city's foodie set.

Chef-entrepreneur Harding Lee Smith's **The Grill Room** (84 Exchange St., 207/774-2333, www.thefrontroomrestaurant.com, lunch 11:30 A.M.–2:30 P.M. Mon.–Sat., dinner 5:30–9 P.M. Sun.–Wed., 5:30–10 P.M. Thurs.–Sat., $8–37) turns out excellent steaks, seafood, and pizzas from its wood-fired grill and oven.

Small plates and big flavors come from the open kitchen of **The Salt Exchange** (245 Commercial St., 207/347-5687, www.thesaltexchange.net, lunch 11:30 A.M.–3 P.M. Tues.–Sat., dinner 5:30–9 P.M. Tues.–Thurs., 5:30–10 P.M. Fri.–Sat.), a contemporary restaurant and lounge decorated with local artwork that changes quarterly. You'll probably want to order at least three plates ($9–18 each) to make a meal.

SEAFOOD

Ask around and everyone will tell you the best seafood in town is at **Street and Company** (33 Wharf St., Old Port, 207/775-0887, www.streetandcompany.net, 5–9:30 P.M.

© GREATER PORTLAND CVB

culinary creation at Street and Company

Sun.–Thurs., 5–10 P.M. Fri.–Sat., entrées from $18). Fresh, beautifully prepared fish is what you get, often with a Mediterranean flair. Tables are tight, and it's often noisy in the informal brick-walled rooms.

For a broader seafood menu and more landlubber options, consider **Old Port Sea Grille and Raw Bar** (93 Commercial St., 207/879-6100, www.theoldportseagrill.com, from 11:30 A.M. daily, entrées $20–33), a sleek modern spot near the waterfront with a fabulous raw bar and a 500-gallon aquarium inside.

For lobster in the rough, head to **Portland Lobster Company** (180 Commercial St., 207/775-2112, www.portlandlobstercompany.com, 11 A.M.–10 P.M. daily). There's a small inside seating area, but it's much more pleasant to sit out on the wharf and watch the excursion boats come and go. Expect to pay in the low $20 range for a one-pound lobster with fries and slaw. Other choices ($8–23) and a kids menu are available.

ETHNIC FARE

Be forewarned: Your first foray into ◖ **Bresca** (111 Middle St., 207/772-1004, www.restaurantbresca.com, from 5:30 P.M. Tues.–Sat., $22–28) won't be your last. Chef Krista Kerns delivers big flavor in this tiny Mediterranean-flavored space next to Portland's police station. She shops each morning, buying just enough for that night's meal (yes, items do sell out). You'll need a reservation to land one of the 20 seats. Service is personal, the meal is leisurely, and the food is divine. Save room for dessert: Krista initially made her name as a pastry chef.

Top-notch for northern Italian is **Cinque Terre Ristorante** (36 Wharf St., 207/347-6154, www.cinqueterremaine.com, 5–9 P.M. Sun.–Thurs., 5–10 P.M. Fri.–Sat., $12–28). Chef Lee Skawinski is committed to sustainable farming, and much of the seasonal and organic produce used comes from the restaurant owners' Laughing Stock Farm and other Maine farms. Choose from half- or full-size portions.

The Corner Room Kitchen and Bar (110 Exchange St., 207/879-4747, www

.thefrontroomrestaurant.com, 11:30 A.M.–10 P.M. Mon.–Fri., 5–10 P.M. Sat., 4–9 P.M. Sun., $8–15), another of popular local chef Harding Lee Smith's restaurants, takes its cue from rustic Italian fare, with hearty and delicious pizzas, pastas, and paninis.

Pasta doesn't get much more authentic than that served at **Paciarino** (468 Fore St., 207/774-3500, www.paciarino.com, 11:30 A.M.–2:30 P.M. and 6–9 P.M. daily, $15–20). Owners Fabiana De Savino and Enrico Barbiero moved here from Milan in 2008, and they make their pastas and sauces fresh daily using recipes from De Savino's *nonna*.

Vegan and vegetarian cuisine comes with an Asian accent at **Green Elephant** (608 Congress St., 207/347-3111, www.greenelephantmaine.com, 11:30 A.M.–2:30 P.M. and 5–9:30 P.M. Tues.–Sat., $9–14). There's not one shred of meat on the creative menu, but you won't miss it.

You might think you've landed in Paris at Jean Claude Vassalle's **Merry Table Creperie** (43 Wharf St., 207/899-4494, 11:30 A.M.–3:30 P.M. and 5–9:30 P.M. Mon.–Sat., 11 A.M.–3 P.M. Sun.), a charming French country bistro specializing in savory and sweet crepes ($9–13).

Irish fare with a Maine accent fills the menu at **Ri-Ra** (72 Commercial St., Old Port, 207/761-4446, www.rira.com, 11:30 A.M.–10 P.M. daily). Entrées in the glass-walled second-floor dining room, overlooking the Casco Bay Lines ferry terminal, are $12–25. The ground-floor pub, elegantly woody with an enormous bar, is inevitably stuffed to the gills on weekends—a great spot for such traditional fare as corned beef and cabbage (pub entrées $8–16) as long as you can stand the din. They don't take reservations, so be prepared to wait, especially on weekends.

For New World flavors in an Old World setting, dine at **Sonny's** (83 Exchange St., 207/772-7774, www.sonnysportland.com, lunch 11:30 A.M.–2 P.M. Mon.–Fri., dinner 5:30–10 P.M. Sun.–Thurs., 5:30–10:30 P.M. Fri.–Sat.), in a former bank, serving Southwestern and South American foods such as jerk-spiced mushroom manchego burger with yam fries or Bahia-spiced seared local whitefish.

DESTINATION DINING

Plan well in advance to land a reservation at ❰❰ **Fore Street** (288 Fore St., Old Port, 207/775-2717, www.forestreet.biz, 5:30–10 P.M. Sun.–Thurs., 5:30–10:30 P.M. Fri.–Sat., entrées from $20). Chef Sam Hayward, renowned for his passionate and creative use of Maine-sourced ingredients, won the James Beard Award for Best Chef in the Northeast in 2004 and has been featured in most of the foodie publications. The renovated former warehouse has copper-topped tables, an open kitchen, and industrial decor chic—quiet it's not. The restaurant is a joint project with Street and Company owner Dana Street.

Arts District

These restaurants are clustered around Danforth Street and along Congress Street.

LOCAL FLAVORS

Can't make up your mind? Peruse the choices available at **Public Market House** (28 Monument Sq., 207/228-2056, www.public-markethouse.com, 8 A.M.–7 P.M. Mon.–Sat., 10 A.M.–5 P.M. Sun.), a growing space with vendors selling meats, cheeses, breads, sandwiches, baked goods, soups, and other fresh fare.

Be sure to have a reservation if you're going before the theater to **BiBo's Madd Apple Café** (23 Forest Ave., 207/774-9698, www.bibosportland.com, 11:30 A.M.–2 P.M. and 5:30–9 P.M. Wed.–Fri., 11 A.M.–2 P.M. and 5:30–9 P.M. Sat., 11 A.M.–2 P.M. Sun., dinner entrées from $17)—it's right next to the Portland Performing Arts Center. On the other hand, it's popular anytime thanks to chef Bill Boutwell ("BiBo"). There's no way of predicting what will be on the bistro-fusion menu.

Well off most visitors' radar screens is **Artemisia Café** (61 Pleasant St., 207/761-0135, 11 A.M.–3 P.M. Mon.–Fri., 9 A.M.–2 P.M. Sat.–Sun.), a cheery neighborhood café with a creative menu drawing on international influences.

Nosh (551 Congress St., 207/553-2227, www.noshkitchenbar.com, 11:30 A.M.–2 P.M. and 4 P.M.–1 A.M. Mon.–Thurs., 11:30 A.M.–1 A.M. Sat., 4 P.M.–1 A.M. Sun.) updates the concept of New York–style deli fare with a fresh-and-local twist. The setting is sleek, with a granite bar on one side, copper-tables on the other, and comfy lounge-like seating at the entry. Nosh serves inspired salads, sandwiches, and burgers by day ($6–11). At night, the menu expands to include create-your-own tasting plates, allowing you to choose from charcuterie, artisanal cheeses, seafood, and vegetables. Be sure to order the fries, offered in flavors including bacon-dusted and salt-and-vinegar and accompanied by a choice from a tempting array of mayos, cheese sauces, and even *sriracha* sauce.

ETHNIC FARE

Slip into sleek **Emilitsa** (547 Congress St., 207/221-0245, www.emilitsa.com, 5–9 P.M. Mon.–Thurs., 5–10 P.M. Fri.–Sat., $18–35) for finely crafted authentic Greek food paired with Greek wines.

Duck into chef-owner Asmeret Teklu's **Asmara** (51 Oak St., 207/253-5122, 11:30 A.M.–2 P.M. and 5–9 P.M. Tues.–Fri., 5–9 P.M. Sat., entrées $9–14) to be transported to eastern Africa. Traditional Eritrean and Ethiopian dishes, a mix of mild to spicy curried stews, and vegetarian plates are served on *injera,* spongy flat bread made from teff flour that doubles as an eating utensil (silverware is available, if you ask). Entrées are generous and come with a salad and choice of vegetable. Service is leisurely; this is a one-woman show.

Sushi approaches an art form at **Miyake** (129 Spring St., 207/871-9170, www.restaurantmiyake.com, 11:45 A.M.–1:45 P.M. and 5–9 P.M. Mon.–Thurs., 11:45 A.M.–1:45 P.M. and 5–9:30 P.M. Fri., 5–9:30 P.M. Sat.). Chef Masa Miyake's tiny, ultrainformal neighborhood joint is considered a must-go among discerning sushi lovers, who think nothing of $35–50 for dinner; BYOB (you can purchase sake at the neighboring market).

Masa Miyake is also the chef-owner of **Pai**

Men Miyake (188 State St., 207/541-9204, entrées $7–12), a traditional Japanese noodle bar serving miso and ramen soup along with amazing pork gyoza and pork buns. It's open for lunch and dinner, but call for details.

Ever-popular **Local 188** (685 Congress St., 207/761-7909, www.local188.com, 5:30–10 P.M. Mon.–Fri., 9 A.M.–2 P.M. and 5:30–10 P.M. Sat.–Sun.) serves fabulous Mediterranean-inspired food with a tapas-heavy menu. It doubles as an art gallery with rotating exhibits. Most tapas selections are under $10, most heartier choices and entrées run $16–20. There is free parking behind the building.

Authentic Thai—not the Americanized version but the kind of food you might purchase from a street vendor in Bangkok—is served in a very non-Thai, cool-yet-sophisticated space at **Boda** (671 Congress St., 207/347-7557, www.bodamaine.com, 5 P.M.–1 A.M. Tues.–Sun.). Make a meal out of small plates, or opt for an entrée ($5–19); vegetarian and gluten-free dishes are available.

Just outside the Arts District, **El Rayo Taqueria** (101 York St., 207/780-8226, www.elrayotaqueria.com, 11 A.M.–9 P.M. daily), in a former gas station, delivers Cal-Mex flavors, with almost everything costing less (often far less) than $10.

DESTINATION DINING

Fun, whimsical, and artsy describes most restaurants in the Arts District, but not **Five Fifty-Five** (555 Congress St., 207/761-0555, www.fivefifty-five.com, 5–9:30 P.M. Mon.–Thurs., 5–10:30 P.M. Fri.–Sat., 9:30 A.M.–2 P.M. and 5–9:30 P.M. Sun., $8–32), where chef Steve Corry was named by *Food & Wine* magazine as one of the top 10 Best New Chefs in the country. Fresh, local, and seasonal are blended in creative ways on his ever-changing menu, which is divided into small plates, green plates, savory plates, cheese plates, and sweet plates. A five-course tasting menu is around $60. If you can't afford to splurge in the main restaurant, Corry serves lighter fare in the lounge.

West End

Chef Abby Harmon's **Caiola's Restaurant** (58 Pine St., 207/772-1111, www.caiolas.com, 5:30–9:30 P.M. Tues.–Thurs., 5:30–10 P.M. Fri.–Sat., 9 A.M.–2 P.M. Sun., entrées from $14) delivers comfort food with pizzazz in a cozy neighborhood bistro. This little gem is off most visitors' radar screens, but locals fill it nightly.

Superb thin-crust pizzas in usual and unusual flavor combos emerge from the wood-fired oven at chef Oliver Outerbridge's **Bonobo** (46 Pine St., 207/347-8267, www.bonobopizza.com, lunch 11:30 A.M.–2:30 P.M. Wed.–Fri., noon–4 P.M. Sat., dinner 4–10 P.M. Sun.–Thurs., 4–11 P.M. Fri.–Sat., $9–16). After the pizza, head to the ice cream window, serving Maple's Organics gelato.

Have breakfast or lunch or pick up prepared foods at **Aurora Provisions** (64 Pine St., 207/871-9061, www.auroraprovisions.com, 8 A.M.–6:30 P.M. Mon.–Sat.), a combination market and café with irresistible goodies, most made on the premises.

Tiny **Dogfish Cafe** (953 Congress St., 207/253-5400, www.thedogfishcafe.com, 11:30 A.M.–9:30 P.M. Mon.–Wed., 11:30 A.M.–10 P.M. Thurs.–Sat., 10 A.M.–2 P.M. Sun., $8–12) packs 'em in for salads, sandwiches, and grilled goodies. It's just a couple of doors down from the Inn on St. John.

Bayside

Portlanders have long favored **Bintliff's American Café** (98 Portland St., 207/774-0005, www.bintliffscafe.com, 7 A.M.–2 P.M. daily) for its breakfasts and brunches ($7–12); the menu is humongous. They don't take reservations, so expect to wait in line on weekends.

Breakfast is served all day at the **Miss Portland Diner** (140 Marginal Way, 207/210-6673, www.missportlanddiner.com, 7 A.M.–3 P.M. Mon.–Tues., 7 A.M.–9 P.M. Wed.–Sat.), a 1949 Worcester Diner (car no. 818) that was rescued, restored, and reopened in 2007. Snag a counter stool or a booth in the original dining car, not the addition, then treat yourself to breakfast for dinner. Sure, there are more traditional choices—soups, sandwiches, wraps, burgers, dogs, comfort foods, seafood plates and platters, or nightly dinner specials (most choices range $7–12), but breakfast and diners go together like bacon and eggs. An added bonus: Parking is plentiful and free.

For an elegant meal in a true fine-dining setting, reserve a table at the **(Back Bay Grill** (65 Portland St., near the main post office, 207/772-8833, www.backbaygrill.com, 5–9 P.M. Tues.–Thurs., 5–9:30 P.M. Fri.–Sat.). The serene dining room is accented by a colorful mural; arts and crafts wall sconces cast a soft glow on the white linen-draped tables. The menu, which highlights fresh seasonal ingredients, ranks among the best in the city, and the wine list is long and well chosen. Service is professional. Entrées are $19–35 and worth every penny.

East End

These dining spots are all east of the Franklin Street Arterial. Poke around this end of the city and you'll find quite a few ethnic hole-in-the-wall places on and around Washington Avenue. It's an ever-changing array, but if you're adventurous or budget confined, give one a try.

LOCAL FLAVORS

Chocoholics take note: When a craving strikes, head to **Dean's Sweets** (82 Middle St., 207/899-3664) for adult-flavored dark-chocolate truffles made without nuts.

If you're a tea fan, don't miss **Homegrown Herb & Tea** (195 Congress St., 207/774-3484, www.homegrownherbandtea.com), an ayurvedic shop that blends black, green, and herbal teas and serves light fare, including a delightful lavender shortbread.

The most incredible fries come from **(Duckfat** (43 Middle St., 207/774-8080, www.duckfat.com, 11 A.M.–9 P.M. Sun.–Wed., 11 A.M.–10 P.M. Thurs.–Sat., $8–14), an ultracasual joint owned by chef Rob Evans of Hugo's fame—so you know it's not only good but it has that spark too. Fries—fried in duck fat, of course—are served in a paper

cone and accompanied by your choice of six sauces; the truffle ketchup is heavenly. Want to really harden those arteries? Order the *poutine,* Belgian fries topped with Maine cheese curd and homemade duck gravy. In addition, Duckfat serves paninis, soups, salads, and really good milk shakes; wine and beer are available.

Mainers love their Italian sandwiches, and **Amato's** (71 India St., 207/773-1682, www.amatos.com, 6:30 A.M.–11 P.M. daily, entrées $10–16) is credited with creating this drool-worthy sub, usually made with ham, cheese, tomatoes, green peppers, black olives, and onions wrapped in a doughy roll and drizzled with olive oil. Also available are calzones, salads, and other Italian-inspired foods. Amato's has outlets throughout southern Maine; this one has outdoor patio seating.

Micucci's Grocery Store (45 India St., 207/775-1854) has been serving Portland's Italian community since 1949. It's a great stop for picnic fixings and a nice selection of inexpensive wines. It's also home to baker Stephen Lanzalotta's to-die-for breads, pastries, and pizzas.

Huge portions at rock-bottom prices make **Silly's** (40 Washington Ave., 207/772-0360, www.sillys.com, 11 A.M.–9 P.M. Tues.–Fri., 9 A.M.–9 P.M. Sat.–Sun.) an ever-popular choice among the young and budget-minded. The huge menu has lots of international flair along with veggie, vegan, gluten-free, and dairy-free options. A separate menu lists milk shakes in dozens of wacky flavors. The decor? Vintage 1950s Formica and chrome.

Traditional Salvadorian foods (think Mexican with attitude) have turned hole-in-the-wall **Tu Casa** (70 Washington Ave., 207/828-4971, www.tucasaportland.com, 11 A.M.–9 P.M. Sun.–Fri.) into a must-visit for in-the-know foodies. It's also a budget find, with almost everything on the menu going for less than $10.

Just try *not* to walk out with something from **Two Fat Cats Bakery** (47 India St., 207/347-5144)—oh, the cookies! The breads! The pies!

CASUAL DINING

Blue Spoon (89 Congress St., 207/773-1116, 11:30 A.M.–3 P.M. and 5–9 P.M. Mon.–Sat., entrées $12–18) was one of the first upscale eateries on Portland's gentrifying East End. Chef-owner David Iovino, who studied at the French Culinary Institute, has created a warm, welcoming, and inexpensive neighborhood bistro where one of the best sellers is roast chicken that's pan seared and then roasted beneath a hot brick. Vegetarian and vegan selections are available.

Big flavors come out of the small plates served at **Bar Lola** (100 Congress St., 207/775-5652, www.barlola.net, 5–10 P.M. Wed.–Sat., $8–18), an intimate and cozy neighborhood bistro serving a tapas-oriented menu. You can opt for a five-course prix fixe ($39) or the Just Say "Feed Me" ($44).

Primo rustic Italian fare is the rule at **Ribollita** (41 Middle St., 207/774-2972, www.ribollitamaine.com, 5–9 P.M. Tues.–Thurs., 5–10 P.M. Fri.–Sat., $13–20). You'll want reservations at this small, casual trattoria that's justly popular for delivering fabulous food at fair prices; just be in the mood for a leisurely meal.

You never know what'll be on the menu (Indonesian chicken, North African stuffed peppers, maybe Caribbean shrimp cakes) at funky **Pepperclub** (78 Middle St., 207/772-0531, www.pepperclubrestaurant.com, 5–9 P.M. Sun.–Thurs., 5–10 P.M. Fri.–Sat., entrées $12–18), but take the risk. Vegetarian and vegan specials are always available, as are local and organic meats and seafood. If your kids are even vaguely adventuresome, they'll find food to like—and the prices are reasonable. In the morning, it morphs into **The Good Egg** (7–11 A.M. Tues.–Fri., 8 A.M.–1 P.M. Sat.–Sun.), serving breakfast, including gluten-free foods.

DESTINATION DINING

Accolades and honors keep accruing for Rob Evans, chef-owner of ◖ **Hugo's** (88 Middle St. at Franklin St., 207/774-8538, www.hugos.net, 5:30–9 P.M. Tues.–Thurs., 5:30–9:30 P.M.

Sat.–Sun.). In 2009 he won the James Beard award for Best Chef in the Northeast; in 2004, *Food & Wine* magazine named him one of America's 10 Best New Chefs, making Hugo's a destination unto itself—not that savvy Portlanders hadn't already been beating a path to his door for his outstanding New American cuisine. Evans and partner Nancy Pugh offer a menu of small plates ($12–28), making it easy and fun to taste the inspired cuisine. Bar seating is available; reservations are essential for the dining room.

Beyond the Downtown Peninsula

Craving pho? **Thanh Thanh** (782 Forest Ave., 207/828-1114, 10 A.M.–9:30 P.M. daily, entrées $8–12) is the go-to for Vietnamese cuisine.

A garage-turned-fish shack, **Susan's Fish-N-Chips** (1135 Forest Ave., 207/878-3240, www.susansfishandchips.com, 11 A.M.–8 P.M. Sun.–Thurs., 11 A.M.–9 P.M. Fri.–Sat.) evokes the sea, from the mermaids and fish painted on the exterior to the netting hanging over the counter inside. But don't expect a fishy odor; Susan's is clean, efficient, and dishes out some of Portland's best and cheapest fried seafood. Expect big portions, low prices, crispy flavorful fish, and daily specials.

The Burbs

Gorgeous presentation, rare cheeses, a ripening room, and a knowledgeable staff all add up to making **The Cheese Iron** (200 Rte. 1, 207/883-4057, www.thecheeseiron.com) a major destination for cheeseheads. Add wine, sandwiches, and a handful of other gourmet goodies and you've got a first-class picnic or party.

Great sunset views over Portland's skyline, a casual atmosphere, and excellent fare have earned **Saltwater Grille** (231 Front St., South Portland, 207/799-5400, www.saltwatergrille.com, 11 A.M.–3 P.M. and 5–9 P.M. daily, dinner entrées $18–27) an excellent reputation. Dine inside or on the waterfront deck.

If you're venturing out to Cape Elizabeth, detour into **The Good Table** (527 Ocean House Rd./Rte. 77, Cape Elizabeth, 207/799-

© HILARY NANGLE

The Lobster Shack at Two Lights in Cape Elizabeth is the ideal setting for a lobster dinner.

4663, www.thegoodtablerestaurant.net, 8 A.M.–9 P.M. Tues.–Sun., entrées $11–20). Lisa Kostopoulos's popular local restaurant serves home-style favorites as well as Greek specialties.

Every Mainer has a favorite lobster eatery (besides home), but **The Lobster Shack** (222 Two Lights Rd., Cape Elizabeth, 207/799-1677, www.lobstershack-twolights.com, 11 A.M.–8 P.M. daily late Mar.–mid-Oct.) tops an awful lot of lists. Seniority helps—it has been here since the 1920s. There is scenery as well: a panoramic vista in the shadow of Cape Elizabeth Light. The menu has seafood galore along with burgers and hot dogs for those who'd rather not have lobster. Opt for a sunny day; the lighthouse's foghorn can kill your conversation when the fog rolls in.

INFORMATION AND SERVICES
Information
The **Visitor Information Center of the Convention and Visitors Bureau of Greater Portland** (14 Ocean Gateway Pier, 207/772-5800, www.visitportland.com) has tons of brochures, plenty of restaurant menus, and public restrooms. The **Portland Downtown District** (94 Free St., 207/772-6828, www.portland-maine.com) has a useful website.

Check out the **Portland Public Library** (5 Monument Sq., 207/871-1700, www.portlan-dlibrary.com).

Public Restrooms
In the Old Port area, you'll find restrooms at the Visitor Information Center (14 Ocean Gateway Pier), Spring Street parking garage (45 Spring St.), Fore Street Parking Garage (419 Fore St.), and Casco Bay Lines ferry terminal (Commercial St. and Franklin St.).

On Congress Street, find restrooms at Portland City Hall (389 Congress St.) and the Portland Public Library (5 Monument Sq.). In Midtown, head for the Cumberland County Civic Center (1 Civic Center Sq.). In the West End, use Maine Medical Center (22 Bramhall St.).

© HILARY NANGLE

Ferries are the lifeline between Portland and the islands of Casco Bay.

GETTING THERE AND AROUND

The best overall resource for transportation planning is www.transportme.org. It lists schedules, fares, and other information for airlines, buses, ferries, and trains.

The ultraclean and comfortable **Portland Transportation Center** (100 Thompson Point Rd., 207/828-3939) is the base for **Concord Coachlines** (800/639-3317, www.concordtcoachlines.com) and **Amtrak**'s *Downeaster* (800/872-7245, www.thedowneaster.com). Parking is $3 per day, and the terminal has free coffee, free newspapers (while they last), and vending machines. The **Metro** (114 Valley St., 207/774-0351, $1.50, exact change) and the Zoom buses, with service from Biddeford and Saco, stop here and connect with **Portland International Jetport** (207/774-7301, www .portlandjetport.org), **Vermont Transit Lines** (950 Congress St., 207/772-6587 or 800/552-

8737), and **Casco Bay Lines ferry service** (www.cascobaylines.com). If you show your Trailways or Amtrak ticket stub to the Metro bus driver, you'll get a free ride downtown. Taxis charge $1.90 for the first 0.1 miles plus $0.30 for each additional 0.1 miles; minimum fare is $5; airport fares add $1.50 surcharge.

Parking

Metered street parking is $1 per hour. Parking garages and lots are strategically situated all over downtown Portland, particularly in the Old Port and near the civic center. Some lots accept Park and Shop stickers, each valid for one free hour, from participating merchants. A day of parking generally runs $8–16. The Casco Bay Lines website (www.cascobaylines .com) has a very useful parking map listing parking lots and garages and their fees.

For winter parking-ban information, call 207/879-0300.

Freeport

Freeport has a special claim to historic fame—it's the place where Maine parted company from Massachusetts in 1820. The documents were signed on March 15, making Maine its own state.

At the height of the local mackerel-packing industry, countless tons of the bony fish were shipped out of South Freeport, often in ships built on the shores of the Harraseeket River. Splendid relics of the shipbuilders' era still line the streets of South Freeport, and no architecture buff should miss a walk, cycle, or drive through the village. Even downtown Freeport still reflects the shipbuilders' craft, with contemporary shops tucked in and around handsome historic houses. Some have been converted to bed-and-breakfasts, others are boutiques, and one even disguises the local McDonald's franchise.

Today, Freeport is best known as the mecca for the shop-till-you-drop set. The hub, of course, is sporting giant L. L. Bean, which has been here since 1912 when founder Leon Leonwood Bean began making his trademark hunting boots (and also unselfishly handed out hot tips on where the fish were biting). More than 120 retail operations now fan out from that epicenter, and you can find almost anything in Freeport, except maybe a convenient parking spot in midsummer.

When you tire of shopping, you can always find quiet refuge in the town's preserves and parks along with plenty of local color at the Town Wharf in the still honest-to-goodness fishing village of South Freeport.

An orientation note: Don't be surprised to receive directions (particularly for South Freeport) relative to "the Big Indian"—a 40-foot-tall landmark at the junction of Route 1 and South Freeport Road. If you stop at the Maine Visitor Information Center in Yarmouth and continue on Route 1 toward Freeport, you can't miss it.

SHOPPING

Logically, this category must come first in any discussion of Freeport, since shopping is the biggest game in town. It's pretty much a given that anyone who visits Freeport intends to darken the door of at least one shop.

◖ L. L. Bean

If you visit only one store in Freeport, it's likely to be "Bean's." The whole world beats a path to L. L. Bean (95 Main St./Rte. 1, 207/865-4761 or 800/341-4341, www.llbean.com)—or so it seems in July–August and December. Established as a hunting and fishing supply shop, this giant sports outfitter now sells everything from kids clothing to cookware on its ever-expanding downtown campus. Look for the outlet store—a great source for deals on equipment and clothing—in the Village Square Shops across Main Street.

Until the 1970s, Bean's remained a rustic store with a creaky staircase and a closet-size women's department. Then a few other

Giant outdoor retailer and outfitter L. L. Bean put Freeport on America's shopping map.

merchants began arriving, Bean's expanded, and a feeding frenzy followed. The Bean reputation rests on a savvy staff, high quality, an admirable environmental consciousness, and a no-questions-asked return policy. Bring the kids—for the indoor trout pond, the clean restrooms, and the "real deal" outlet store. The store's open-round-the-clock policy has become its signature; if you show up at 2 A.M. you'll have much of the store to yourself, and you may even spy vacationing celebrities or the rock stars who often visit after Portland shows.

Outlets and Specialty Stores

After Bean's, it's up to your whims and your wallet. The stores stretch for several miles up and down Main Street and along many side streets. Pick up a copy of the *Official Map and Visitor Guide* at any of the shops or restaurants, at one of the visitor kiosks, or at the Hose Tower Information Center (23 Depot St., two blocks east of L. L. Bean). All the big names are here, as are plenty of little ones. Don't overlook the small shops tucked on the side streets, such as **Earrings and Company, Wilbur's of Maine Chocolate Confections,** and **Edgecomb Potters.**

SIGHTS
Desert of Maine

OK, so maybe it's a bit hokey, but talk about sands of time: More than 10,000 years ago, glaciers covered the region surrounding the Desert of Maine (95 Desert Rd., 207/865-6962, www.desertofmaine.com, early May–mid-Oct., $9.75 adults, $6.75 ages 13–16, $5.75 ages 5–12). When they receded they scoured the landscape, pulverizing rocks and leaving behind a sandy residue that was covered by a thin layer of topsoil. Jump forward to 1797, when William Tuttle bought 300 acres and moved his family here along with his house and barn and cleared the land. Now jump forward again to the present and tour where a once-promising farmland has become a desert wasteland. The 30-minute guided safari-style tram tours combine history, geology, and environmental science and an opportunity for children to hunt

for "gems" in the sand. Decide for yourself: Is the desert a natural phenomenon? A human-made disaster? Or does the truth lie somewhere in the middle?

Harrington House and Pettengill Farm

A block south of L. L. Bean is the Harrington House (45 Main St./Rte. 1, 207/865-3170, www.freeporthistoricalsociety.org, free), home base of the Freeport Historical Society. You can pick up walking maps detailing Freeport's architecture for a small fee and tour the house (call for current hours). Displays pertaining to Freeport's history and occasionally exhibits by local artists are presented in two rooms in the restored 1830 Enoch Harrington House, a property on the National Register of Historic Places.

Also listed on the register is the society's Pettengill Farm, a 19th-century saltwater farm comprising a circa-1810 saltbox-style house, woods, orchards, a salt marsh, and lovely perennial gardens. The farmhouse is open only during the annual Pettengill Farm Days in the fall, but the grounds are open at all times. From Main Street, take Bow Street 1.5 miles and turn right onto Pettengill Road. Park at the gate, and then walk along the dirt road for about 15 minutes to the farmhouse.

Maine Potato Vodka

Find out how many Maine-grown potatoes it takes to make a bottle of Cold River Vodka (Rte. 1, 207/865-4828, www.coldrivervodka.com). Free tours of the distillery cover the process from farm to vodka: cooking, distilling, blending, and bottling. Tours are offered Tuesday–Saturday afternoon, but call in advance to be sure a guide is available.

Eartha

She's a worldly woman, that Eartha. The **DeLorme Mapping Co.** (Rte. 1, Yarmouth, 207/846-7000, www.delorme.com/about/eartha.aspx) is home to the world's largest rotating and revolving globe, a three-story tall spherical scale model of earth. Eartha, as she's known, is quite robust: She measures 41 feet in diameter with a 130-foot waist and weighs nearly three tons. Eartha spins in DeLorme's glass-walled lobby, making her visible to passersby, but she's best appreciated up close and, well, as personal as you can get with a monstrous globe. Each continent is detailed with mountains and landforms, vegetation and civilization. Better yet, she spins. She can be viewed 9:30 A.M.–5 P.M. Monday–Friday. Take Route 1 south from downtown Freeport to the I-295 exit 17 interchange; DeLorme is on the left.

ENTERTAINMENT

Shopping seems to be more than enough entertainment for most of Freeport's visitors, but don't miss the **L. L. Bean Summer Concert Series** (800/341-4341, ext. 37222). At 7:30 P.M. most Saturdays early July–Labor Day weekend, Bean's hosts free big-name family-oriented events in Discovery Park, in the Bean's complex (95 Main St./Rte. 1). Arrive early—these concerts are *very* popular—and bring a blanket or a folding chair.

Almost every night's a party at **Venue** (5 Depot St., 207/865-1780, www.venuemusicbar .com), with live music varying from open mike to jazz nights. A light menu is available.

RECREATION
Parks, Preserves, and Other Attractions
MAST LANDING SANCTUARY

Just one mile from downtown Freeport, Mast Landing Audubon Sanctuary (Upper Mast Landing Rd., 207/781-2330, www.maine-audubon.org, free) is a reprieve from the crowds. Situated at the head of the tide on the Harraseeket River estuary, the 140-acre preserve has 3.5 miles of signed trails weaving through an apple orchard, across fields, and through pines and hemlocks. The name? Ages ago it was the source of masts for the Royal Navy. To find it, take Bow Street (across from L. L. Bean) one mile to Upper Mast Landing Road and turn left. The sanctuary is 0.25 miles along on the left.

WOLFE'S NECK WOODS STATE PARK

Five miles of easy to moderate trails meander through 233-acre Wolfe's Neck Woods State Park (Wolfe's Neck Rd., 207/865-4465, $4.50 nonresident adults, $3 Maine resident adults, $1 ages 5–11), just a few minutes' cycle or drive from downtown Freeport. You'll need a trail map, available near the parking area. The easiest route (partly wheelchair-accessible) is the Shoreline Walk, about 0.75 miles, starting near the salt marsh and skirting Casco Bay. Sprinkled along the trails are helpful interpretive panels explaining various points of natural history—bog life, osprey nesting, glaciation, erosion, and tree decay. Guided tours are offered at 2 P.M. daily mid-July–late August, weather permitting. Leashed pets are allowed. Adjacent **Googins Island,** an osprey sanctuary, is off-limits. From downtown Freeport, follow Bow Street (across from L. L. Bean) for 2.25 miles; turn right onto Wolfe's Neck Road (also called Wolf Neck Rd.) and go another 2.25 miles.

WOLFE'S NECK FARM

Kids love Wolfe's Neck Farm (10 Burnett Rd., 207/865-4469, www.wolfesneckfarm.org), a 626-acre saltwater farm dedicated to sustainable agriculture and environmental education. Visit with farm animals and enjoy the farm's trails and varied habitats—fields, forests, seashore, and gardens—at no charge.

WINSLOW MEMORIAL PARK

Bring a kite. Bring a beach blanket. Bring a picnic. Bring a boat. Bring binoculars. Heck, bring a tent. Freeport's 90-acre oceanfront town-owned playground, Winslow Memorial Park (207/865-4198, www.freeportmaine.com, $2 nonresidents) has a spectacular setting on a peninsula extending into island-studded Casco Bay. Facilities include a boat launch ($3–15), a campground ($21–28, no hookups), a fishing pier, a volleyball court, scenic trails, a playground, restrooms, picnic facilities, and a sandy beach—the best swimming is at high tide, and there is no lifeguard. On Thursday evenings in July–August, local bands play. The park is 5.5 miles from downtown. Head south on Route 1 to the Big Indian (you'll know it when you see it), go left on the South Freeport Road for one mile to Staples Point Road, and follow it to the end.

BRADBURY MOUNTAIN STATE PARK

Six miles from the hubbub of Freeport you're in tranquil, wooded 590-acre Bradbury Mountain State Park (Rte. 9, Pownal, 207/688-4712, $4.50 nonresident adults, $3 Maine resident adults, $1 ages 5–11), with facilities for picnicking, hiking, mountain biking, and rustic camping, but no swimming. Pick up a trail map at the gate and take the easy 0.4-mile round-trip Mountain Trail to the 485-foot summit, with superb views east to the ocean and southeast to Portland. It's gorgeous in fall. Or take the Tote Road Trail, on the western side of the park, where the ghost of Samuel Bradbury allegedly occasionally brings a chill to hikers in a hemlock grove. A playground keeps the littlest tykes happy. The camping fee is $19 per site nonresidents, $11 for residents. The park season is May 15–October 15, but there's winter access for cross-country skiing. From Route 1, cross over I-95 at exit 20 and continue west on Pownal Road to Route 9 and head south.

PINELAND FARMS

Once a home for Maine's mentally disabled citizens, the 1,600-acre Pineland (15 Farm View Dr., New Gloucester, 207/688-4539, www.pinelandfarms.org) campus was closed in 1996. In 2000 the Libra Foundation bought it; the property now comprises 19 buildings and 5,000 acres of farmland, and much of it is open for recreation. Walk or ski the trails, sight birds in the fields and woods, watch cheese being made, stroll through the garden, fish the pond or skate on it in winter, play tennis, go mountain biking or orienteering, or even take a horseback-riding lesson. It's a vast outdoor playground, but your first stop should be the market and visitors center (8 A.M.–7 P.M. daily) to see a list of any events (frequent ones include guided farm tours and family experiences), pick up maps, pay any necessary fees, shop for farm-fresh products, or

even grab lunch or snacks. Some activities, such as cross-country and mountain-biking trail access and horseback-riding lessons, require fees. Dogs are not allowed.

◖ L. L. Bean Outdoor Discovery Schools

Since the early 1980s, the sports outfitter's Outdoor Discovery Schools (888/552-3261, www.llbean.com) have trained thousands of outdoors enthusiasts to improve their skills in fly-fishing, archery, hiking, canoeing, sea kayaking, winter camping, cross-country skiing, orienteering, and even outdoor photography. Here's a deal that requires no planning. **Walk-on Adventures** ($15, includes equipment) provide 1.5–2.5-hour lessons in sports such as kayak touring, fly casting, archery, clay shooting, snowshoeing, and cross-country skiing. All of the longer fee programs, plus canoeing and camping trips, require preregistration well in advance because of their popularity. Some of the lectures, seminars, and demonstrations held in Freeport are free, and a regular catalog lists the schedule. Bean's waterfront **Flying Point Paddling Center** hosts many of the kayaking, saltwater fly-fishing, and guiding programs and is home to the annual **PaddleSports Festival** in June, with free demonstrations, seminars, vendors, lessons, and more.

Excursion Boats

Atlantic Seal Cruises (Town Wharf, South Freeport, 207/865-6112 or 877/285-7325, www.atlanticsealcruises.com), owned and operated by Captain Tom Ring, makes two 2.5-hour cruises ($35 adults, $25 ages 5–12, $20 ages 1–4) daily to 17-acre **Eagle Island** (www.pearyeagleisland.org), a State Historic Site once owned by Admiral Robert Peary, the north pole explorer. The trip includes a lobstering demonstration (except Sunday, when lobstering is banned). Once a week he offers a daylong excursion to **Seguin Island** ($55 ages 10 and older, $40 kids), off the Phippsburg Peninsula, where you can climb the light tower and see Maine's only first-order Fresnel lens, the largest on the coast.

© HILARY NANGLE

Admiral Robert Peary's Eagle Island home is open to visitors who arrive via Atlantic Seal Cruises.

Sail the waters of Casco Bay from South Freeport Harbor aboard **Nimbus** (207/232-1751, www.sailfreeport.com), a 37-foot classic wooden sloop designed by John G. Alden and built in 1938. Captain Troy Scott offers two-hour or three-hour sails (from $35 pp) from Stout's Point Wharf Co.

Kayak and Canoe Rentals

Ring's Marine Service (Smelt Brook Rd., South Freeport, 207/865-6143 or 866/865-6143, www.ringsmarineservice.com) rents single kayaks for $38, tandems for $60, and canoes for $28 per day, with longer-term rentals and delivery available.

ACCOMMODATIONS

If you'd prefer to drop where you shop, Freeport has plentiful accommodations. Rates listed are for peak season.

Downtown

One of Freeport's pioneering bed-and-breakfasts is on the main drag but away from much of the traffic in a restored house where Arctic explorer Admiral Donald MacMillan once lived. The 19th-century **White Cedar Inn** (178 Main St., 207/865-9099 or 800/853-1269, www.whitecedarinn.com, $150–290) has seven attractive guest rooms and a two-bedroom suite with antiques, air-conditioning, and Wi-Fi; some have gas fireplaces, and one has a TV and accepts dogs ($25). The full breakfast will power you through a day of shopping.

Two blocks north of L. L. Bean, the **(Harraseeket Inn** (162 Main St., 207/865-9377 or 800/342-6423, www.harraseeket-inn.com, $195–315) is a splendid 84-room country inn with an indoor pool, cable TV, air-conditioning, phones, and Wi-Fi; many rooms have fireplaces and hot tubs. One room is decorated with Thomas Moser furnishings; otherwise decor is colonial reproduction in the two antique buildings and a modern addition. Rates include a hot-and-cold buffet breakfast and afternoon tea with finger sandwiches and sweets—a refreshing break. Pets are permitted in some guest rooms for $25, which includes a dog bed, a small can of food, a treat, and dishes. Ask about packages, which offer excellent value. Children 12 and younger stay free. If you're traveling solo, the nightly Innkeeper's Table (207/865-1085, reservation required by 5:30 P.M. for 6:30 P.M. seating) is a communal table hosted by an innkeeper and a great way to meet other guests.

Three blocks south of L. L. Bean on a quiet side street shared with a couple of other bed-and-breakfasts is **The James Place Inn** (11 Holbrook St., 207/865-4486 or 800/964-9086, www.jamesplaceinn.com, $155–190). Innkeepers Robin and Tori Baron welcome guests to seven comfortable guest rooms, all with air-conditioning, Wi-Fi, TVs and DVD players; a few have double whirlpool tubs, and one has a fireplace and private deck. If the weather is fine, enjoy breakfast on the deck. After shopping, collapse on the hammock for two.

Beyond Downtown

Three miles north of downtown is the **Maine Idyll** (1411 Rte. 1, 207/865-4201, www.maineidyll.com, $70–110), a tidy cottage colony operated by the Marstaller family for three generations. It is a retro throwback and a find for budget-bound travelers. Twenty studio to three-bedroom pine-paneled cottages are tucked under the trees. The Ritz this is not, but all have refrigerators, fireplaces, and TVs, and most have limited cooking facilities. Wi-Fi is available near the office. A light breakfast is included. Well-behaved pets are welcome for $4.

The family-run **《 Casco Bay Inn** (107 Rte. 1, 207/865-4925 or 800/570-4970, www.cascobayinn.com, $99–129) is a bit fancier than most motels. It has a pine-paneled lounge with a fieldstone fireplace and a guest Internet station as well as Wi-Fi throughout. The spacious guest rooms have double sinks in the bath area, and some have a refrigerator and a microwave. A continental breakfast with a newspaper is included.

Here's a find, if you're lucky enough to snag it, given that there's only one guest room: **Wolf Neck Bed and Breakfast** (93 Birch Point Rd., 207/865-1725, www.wolfneckbb.com, $175) is Dianne Gaudet and Steve Norton's waterfront shingle-style home, built in 2002, where the sole guest suite comes complete with a sitting room and a private deck. Longtime area residents, Dianne and Steve are a great resource on the region. They also provide a full breakfast. Bring your own boat and launch it right here, or rent a canoe or kayaks from the hosts.

Camping

For anyone seeking peace, quiet, and low-tech camping in a spectacular setting, **Recompence Shore Campsites** (134 Burnett Rd., 207/865-9307, www.freeportcamping.com, $26–44) is it. Part of Wolfe's Neck Farm, the eco-sensitive campground has 175 wooded tent sites and a few hookups, many on the farm's three-mile-long Casco Bay shorefront. Kayak and canoe rentals are available; swimming depends on the tides. Facilities include a playground and snack bar with Wi-Fi. Take Bow Street (across from L. L. Bean) to Wolfe's Neck Road, turn right, go 1.6 miles, then turn left on Burnett Road.

FOOD

Freeport has an ever-increasing number of places to eat, but there are nowhere near enough to satisfy hungry crowds at peak dining hours on busy days. Go early or late for lunch, and make reservations for dinner. Days and hours are for peak season, but it's always wise to verify.

Local Flavors

South of downtown, **Royal River Natural Foods** (443 Rte. 1, 207/865-0046, www.rrnf.com) has a small selection of prepared foods, including soups, salads, and sandwiches, and there is a seating area.

Craving a proper British tea? **Jacqueline's Tea Room** (201 Main St., 207/865-2123, www.jacquelinestearoom.com) serves a four-course tea by reservation for about $25 pp in an elegant setting. Seatings for the two-hour indulgence are between 11 A.M. and 1 P.M. Tuesday–Friday and every other weekend.

At the Big Indian **Old World Gourmet Deli and Wine Shop** (117 Rte. 1, 207/865-4477, www.oldworldgourmet.com), the offerings are just as advertised, with sandwiches, soups, salads, and prepared foods. There are a few tables inside, but it's mostly a to-go place.

Casual Dining

The Harraseeket Inn's woodsy-themed 🄲 **Broad Arrow Tavern** (162 Main St., 207/865-9377 or 800/342-6423, 11:30 A.M.–10 P.M. daily, 11:30 A.M.–11 P.M. Fri.–Sat., $10–30), just two blocks north of L. L. Bean but seemingly a world away, is a perfect place to escape shopping crowds and madness. The food is terrific, with everything made from organic and naturally raised foods. Can't decide? Opt for the extensive all-you-can-eat lunch buffet ($17) that highlights a bit of everything.

Good wine and fine martinis are what reels them into **Conundrum** (117 Rte. 1, 207/865-0303, 4:30–10 P.M. Tues.–Sat., $7–27), near Freeport's Big Indian, but the food is worth noting too. Dozens of wines by the glass, more than 20 martinis, and 20 champagnes will keep most oenophiles happy. The food, varying from pâtés and cheese platters to cheeseburgers and maple-barbecued chicken, helps keep patrons sober.

Ethnic Fare

Dine indoors or out on the tree-shaded patio at **Azure Italian Café** (123 Main St., 207/865-1237, www.azurecafe.com, 11:30 A.M.–9 P.M. Sun.–Thurs., 11:30 A.M.–10 P.M. Fri.–Sat.). Go light, mixing selections from antipasto, *insalate,* and *zuppa* choices, or savor the heartier entrées ($18–32). The service is pleasant, and the indoor dining areas are accented by well-chosen contemporary Maine artwork. Live jazz is a highlight some evenings.

Down the side street across from Azure is **Mediterranean Grill** (10 School St., 207/865-1688, www.mediterraneangrill .biz, 11 A.M.–10 P.M. daily, entrées $16–25). Because it's off Main Street, the Cigri family's excellent Turkish-Mediterranean restaurant rarely gets the crowds. House specialties such as moussaka, lamb chops, and *tiropetes* augment a full range of kebab and vegetarian choices. Or simply make a meal of the appetizers—the platters are meals in themselves. Sandwiches and wraps are available at lunch.

Two surprisingly good, easy-on-the-budget Asian restaurants share a building on the south end of town. **China Rose** (23 Main St., 207/865-6886, 11 A.M.–9:30 P.M. Sun.–Thurs., 11 A.M.–10 P.M. Fri.–Sat., entrées $10–16) serves Szechuan, Mandarin, and Hunan specialties in a pleasant first-floor dining area. Upstairs is **Miyako** (207/865-6888, 11 A.M.–9:30 P.M. Sun.–Thurs., 11 A.M.–10 P.M. Fri.–Sat., $6–20), with an extensive sushi bar menu; it also serves other Japanese specialties, including tempura, teriyaki, *nabemono,* and noodle dishes. Luncheon specials are available at both.

Good food and attentive service has made **Thai Garden** (491 Rte. 1, 207/865-6005, 11 A.M.–9 P.M. daily, $8–15) an ever-popular choice.

Fine Dining

The Harraseeket Inn's **Maine Dining Room** (207/865-1085, 6–9 P.M. Sun.–Thurs., 6–9:30 P.M. Fri.–Sat., dinner entrées $24–38) is the finest in town, but it's not overly fancy or fussy. The service is excellent, and chef Theda Lyden's menu favors natural and organic foods. Tableside preparations (for 2–7 people), such as Caesar salad, chateaubriand, and flaming desserts, add an understated note of theater. Brunch (11:45 A.M.–2 P.M. Sun., $25) is a seemingly endless buffet, with whole poached salmon and Belgian waffles among the highlights.

Lobster

In South Freeport, order lobster in the rough at **Harraseeket Lunch and Lobster Company** (36 Main St., Town Wharf, South Freeport,

GREATER PORTLAND

Harraseeket Lunch and Lobster Company at the South Freeport harbor sells lobster in the rough.

lunch counter 207/865-4888, lobster pound 207/865-3535, 11 A.M.–8:45 P.M. daily summer, 11 A.M.–7:45 P.M. daily spring and fall, no credit cards). Grab a picnic table, place your order, and go at it. Be prepared for a wait in midsummer. Fried clams are particularly good here, and they're prepared either breaded or battered. Order both and decide for yourself which is better. BYOB.

Craving a crab or lobster roll? Pick up one to go at **Day's Seafood Takeout** (1269 Rte. 1, Yarmouth, 207/836-3436, 11 A.M.–8 P.M. daily), just south of the Freeport line. The fried clams are mighty tasty too. There are a few picnic tables out back on a tidal estuary.

INFORMATION AND SERVICES

Freeport Merchants Association (Hose Tower, 23 Depot St., 207/865-1212 or 800/865-1994, www.freeportusa.com) produces an invaluable foldout map-guide showing locations of all the shops, plus sites of lodgings, restaurants, visitor kiosks, pay phones, restrooms, and car and bike parking.

Just south of Freeport is the **Maine Visitor Information Center** (Rte. 1 at I-95 Exit 17, Yarmouth, 207/846-0833), part of the statewide tourism-information network. Also here are restrooms, phones, picnic tables, vending machines, and a dog-walking area.

MID-COAST REGION

In contrast to the Southern Coast's gorgeous sandy beaches, the Mid-Coast Region is characterized by a deeply indented shoreline with snug harbors and long gnarled fingers of land. Even though these fingers are inconvenient for driving and bicycling, this is where you'll find picture-book Maine in a panorama format. Mosey to the tips of the peninsulas and come upon lighthouses, fishing villages, country inns, and lobster wharves. The Mid-Coast, as defined in this chapter, stretches from Brunswick to Waldoboro.

The Bath-Brunswick area is one of the least touristy areas of the coast. Not that visitors don't come, but this area has a strong and varied economic base other than tourism, which means that no matter when you visit, you'll find shops, restaurants, and lodgings open and activities scheduled. Bowdoin College and Bath Iron Works also contribute to a population more ethnically diverse than in most of Maine, and there's an active retiree population. Still, as you drive down the peninsulas that reach seaward from Bath and Brunswick, the vibrancy gives way to traditional fishing villages pressed by the hard realities of maintaining such lifestyles in the modern world and hanging on to waterfront properties in the face of escalating real-estate values.

Wiscasset still clings to the nickname of prettiest village in Maine, but for many travelers heading through on Route 1, Wiscasset is nothing but a headache. Traffic often backs up for miles, inching forward through the bottleneck village. Although many are just glad to get through it, those who take time to explore

© TOM NANGLE

HIGHLIGHTS

◖ **Bowdoin College:** This beautiful shady campus is home to the Bowdoin College Museum of Art, the Peary-MacMillan Arctic Museum, and the Maine State Music Theater (page 118).

◖ **Maine Maritime Museum:** It's easy to while away half a day touring the exhibits in this museum's main and outer buildings and just enjoying the riverfront setting (page 130).

◖ **Burnt Island Tour:** Step back in history and visit with a lighthouse keeper's family circa 1952 on a living-history tour (page 151).

◖ **Coastal Maine Botanical Gardens:** This seaside garden comprises more than 240 acres of well-planned exhibits, trails, and art (page 155).

◖ **Pemaquid Point Lighthouse:** It's hard to say which is Maine's prettiest lighthouse, but Pemaquid's is right up there. It's also depicted on the Maine state quarter (page 165).

◖ **Colonial Pemaquid and Fort William Henry:** A beautiful setting overlooking John's Bay, a partially reconstructed fort, and remnants from archaeological digs researching one of the first English settlements in the New World make this site well worth a visit (page 166).

◖ **Lobster in the Rough:** Lobster wharves abound in Maine, but the Pemaquid Peninsula has a concentration of scenic spots for lobster lovers (page 177).

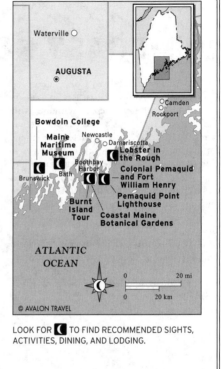

LOOK FOR ◖ TO FIND RECOMMENDED SIGHTS, ACTIVITIES, DINING, AND LODGING.

Wiscasset are rewarded with multitudes of antiques shops and lovely architecture.

The tempo changes northeast of Wiscasset. Traffic eases, and there's less roadside development. Detour down the Boothbay and Pemaquid Peninsulas, and you'll be rewarded with the Maine of postcards. These two peninsulas appear unchallenged as home to more lobster-in-the-rough spots than elsewhere on the coast, and Maine's creative economy is blossoming here, as evidenced by the artists' and artisans' studios that pepper these peninsulas.

PLANNING YOUR TIME

Route 1 is the primary artery connecting all the points in the Mid-Coast Region, and Wiscasset, a major bottleneck, is smack-dab in the middle. For this reason, it's best to split your lodging and explorations into two parts: south of Wiscasset and north of Wiscasset. Even then, driving down the long fingers of land requires patience. The towns south of Wiscasset are less touristy than those on the Boothbay or Pemaquid Peninsulas, with Orr's and Bailey's Islands and the Phippsburg

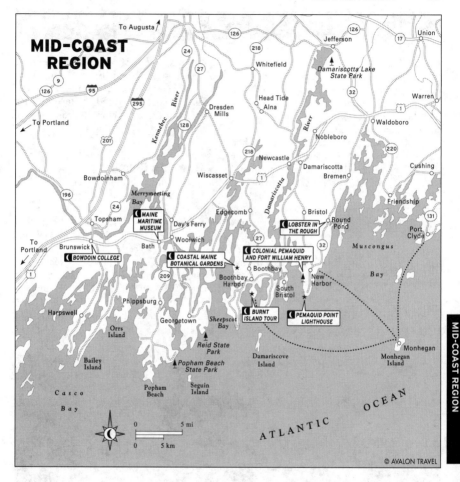

Peninsula being the best places to sprout roots for old-time summer flavor.

To cover the region, you'll need 4–5 days. Antiques mavens should concentrate their efforts in Bath, Wiscasset, and Damariscotta. Allow at least two days to appreciate the fine museums in Brunswick and Bath, and another day to tour Wiscasset's historical house museums and nearby fort. If you're an avid or even aspiring kayaker, you'll want time to puzzle through the nooks and crannies of the coastline in a boat, and if you value parks and preserves, this region offers plenty worth your time.

Brunswick Area

Brunswick, straddling Route 1, relies partly on modern defense dollars, but it was incorporated in 1738 and is steeped in history. It's home to prestigious Bowdoin College, classic homes and churches, several respected museums, and year-round cultural attractions.

Brunswick and **Topsham** face each other across roiling waterfalls on the Androscoggin River. The falls, which Native Americans knew by the tongue-twisting name of Ahmelahcogneturcook ("place abundant with fish, birds, and other animals"), were a source of hydropower for 18th-century sawmills and 19th–20th-century textile mills. Franco-Americans arrived in droves to beef up the textile industry in the late 19th century but eventually lost their jobs in the Great Depression. Those once-derelict mills now house shops, restaurants, and offices.

Brunswick is also the gateway to the **Harpswells,** a peninsula-archipelago complex linked by causeways, several bridges, and a unique granite cribstone bridge. Scenic back roads on Harpswell Neck inspire detours to the fishing hamlets of **Cundy's Harbor, Orr's Island,** and **Bailey Island,** and once you're here, it's easy to want to linger.

SIGHTS
◖ Bowdoin College

Bowdoin College (Brunswick, 207/725-3000, www.bowdoin.edu) got its start nearly 150 years before the Naval Air Station landed on the nearby Brunswick Plains. Founded in 1794 as a boys college with a handful of students, Bowdoin, coed since 1969, now has 1,550 students. The college has turned out such noted graduates as authors Nathaniel Hawthorne and Henry Wadsworth Longfellow, sex pioneer Alfred Kinsey, U.S. president Franklin Pierce, Arctic explorers Robert Peary and Donald MacMillan, U.S. senators George Mitchell

The Bowdoin College Museum of Art is an architectural gem designed by Charles McKim.

© TOM NANGLE

and William Cohen, and a dozen Maine governors. Massachusetts Hall, the oldest building on the 110-acre campus, dates from 1802. The stately Bowdoin pines, on the northeast boundary, are even older. The striking **David Saul Smith Union,** occupying 40,000 square feet in a former athletic building on the east side of the campus, has a café, a pub, a lounge, and a bookstore open to the public. Call for information on admissions and campus tours (207/725-3100) and on campus concerts, lectures, and performances open to the public (207/725-3375).

Photos and artifacts bring Arctic expeditions to life at the small but fascinating **Peary-MacMillan Arctic Museum** (Hubbard Hall, 207/725-3416, www.bowdoin.edu/ arctic-museum, 10 A.M.–5 P.M. Tues.–Sat., 2–5 P.M. Sun., free). Among the specimens are animal mounts, a skin kayak, fur clothing, snow goggles, and Inuit carvings—most collected by Arctic pioneers Robert E. Peary and Donald B. MacMillan, both Bowdoin grads. Permanent exhibits highlight the natural and cultural diversity of the Arctic. The small gift shop specializes in Inuit books and artifacts.

An astonishing array of Greek and Roman artifacts is only one of the high points at the **Bowdoin College Museum of Art** (Walker Art Building, 207/725-3275, www.bowdoin .edu/art-museum, 10 A.M.–5 P.M. Tues.–Sat., 2–5 P.M. Sun., free). Designed in the 1890s by Charles McKim of the famed McKim, Mead, and White firm, it's a stunning neoclassical edifice with an interior rotunda and stone lions flanking the entry. In 2007 the museum was expanded and modernized, adding a striking bronze-and-glass entry pavilion to preserve the facade while also achieving accessibility. The college's prized Assyrian reliefs, previously in the magnificent rotunda, were moved to a glass-walled addition facing Brunswick's Park Row. The renovated museum is far more user-friendly and a fitting setting for the impressive permanent collection of 19th- and 20th-century American art and other works.

Pejepscot Historical Society Museums

Side by side in an unusual cupola-topped duplex facing Brunswick's Mall (village green) are two museums operated by the Pejepscot Historical Society (159 and 160 Park Row, Brunswick, 207/729-6606, www.community.curtislibrary. com/pejepscot.htm), the **Pejepscot Museum** (159 Park Row, 10 A.M.–5 P.M. Mon.–Fri., free) and the **Skolfield-Whittier House** (161 Park Row, tours 11 A.M. and 3 P.M. Thurs.–Sat. late May–late Oct., $5 adults, $2.50 children). Focusing on local history, the museum has a collection of more than 50,000 artifacts and mounts an always interesting special exhibit each year. The 17-room Skolfield-Whittier House, on the right side of the building, looks as though the owners just stepped out for the afternoon. Unoccupied 1925–1982, the one-time sea captain's house has elegant Victorian furnishings and lots of exotic artifacts collected on global seafaring stints.

Also operated by the Pejepscot Historical Society, the **Joshua L. Chamberlain Museum** (226 Maine St., Brunswick, 207/729-6606, tours on the hour 10 A.M.–3 P.M. Tues.–Sat., $5 adults, $2.50 children), across from First Parish Church, commemorates the Union Army hero of the Civil War's Battle of Gettysburg, who's now gaining long-overdue respect. The partly restored house where Chamberlain lived in the late 19th century (and where Henry Wadsworth Longfellow had lived 30 years earlier) is a peculiar architectural hodgepodge with six rooms of exhibits of Chamberlain memorabilia, much of it Civil War–related. A gift shop stocks lots of Civil War publications, especially ones covering the Twentieth Maine Volunteers. A combination ticket for both historical houses is $8 adults, $4 children.

Uncle Tom's Church

Across the street from the Chamberlain museum is the historic 1846 **First Parish Church** (9 Cleaveland St. at Bath Rd., Brunswick, 207/729-7331), a Gothic Revival (or carpenter Gothic) board-and-batten structure crowning the rise at the head of Maine Street. Scores of celebrity preachers have ascended this pulpit, and Harriet Beecher Stowe was inspired to write *Uncle Tom's Cabin* while listening to her husband deliver an antislavery sermon here. Arrive here before noon any Tuesday early July–early August (or call ahead for details), when guest organists present 40-minute lunchtime concerts (12:10–12:50 P.M.) on the 1883 Hutchings-Plaisted tracker organ. A $5 donation is requested. At other times, the church is open by appointment.

Brunswick's Women's History Trail

With more than 20 points of interest, the Brunswick Women's History Trail covers such national notables as authors Harriet Beecher Stowe and Kate Douglas Wiggin along with lesser-known lights, including naturalist Kate Furbish, pioneering Maine pediatrician Dr. Alice Whittier, and the Franco-American women who slaved away in the textile mills at the turn of the 20th century. Buy the walking-tour booklet at the Pejepscot Museum gift shop ($2). The museum offers guided tours lasting about one hour once a month June–August (donation requested).

Brunswick Literary Art Walk

Cast your eyes downward while walking along Maine Street. Four bronze plaques recognize Brunswick's most famous writers: Henry Wadsworth Longfellow, Nathaniel Hawthorne,

JOSHUA L. CHAMBERLAIN, CIVIL WAR HERO

When the U.S. Civil War began in 1861, Joshua Chamberlain was a 33-year-old logic instructor at Bowdoin College in Brunswick; when it ended in 1865, Chamberlain earned the Congressional Medal of Honor for his "daring heroism and great tenacity in holding his position on the Little Round Top." He was designated by Ulysses S. Grant to formally accept the official surrender of Confederate General John Gordon (both men represented the infantry). He later became governor of Maine (1867-1871) and president of Bowdoin College, but Chamberlain's greatest renown, ironically, came more than a century later – in the 1990s, when PBS filmmakers focused on the Civil War and highlighted his strategic military role.

Joshua Lawrence Chamberlain was born in 1828 in Brewer, Maine, the son and grandson of soldiers. After graduating from Bowdoin in 1852, he studied for the ministry at Bangor Theological Seminary and then returned to his alma mater as an instructor.

With the nation in turmoil in the early 1860s, Chamberlain signed on to help, receiving a commission as a lieutenant colonel in the Twentieth Maine Volunteers in 1862. After surviving 24 encounters, six battle wounds, and having been promoted to brigadier general, then major general, Chamberlain was elected Republican governor of Maine in 1866 – by the largest margin in the state's history – only to suffer through four one-year terms of partisan politics. In 1871, Chamberlain became president of Bowdoin College, where he remained until 1883. He then dove into speechmaking and writing, his best-known work being *The Passing of the Armies*, a memoir of the Civil War's final campaigns. Chamberlain was surveyor of the Port of Portland 1900-1914, a presidential appointment that ended only when complications from a wartime abdominal wound finally did him in. He died at the grand old age of 86.

Brunswick's Joshua L. Chamberlain Museum, in his onetime home at 226 Maine Street, commemorates this illustrious Mainer, and thousands of Civil War buffs annually stream through the door in search of Chamberlain "stuff." To make it easier, the Pejepscot Historical Society has produced a helpful map titled *Joshua Chamberlain's Brunswick*, highlighting town and college ties to the man – his dorm rooms, his presidential office, his portraits, even his church pew (number 64 at First Parish Church). Chamberlain's gravesite, marked by a reddish granite stone, is in Brunswick's Pine Grove Cemetery, just east of the Bowdoin campus.

Harriet Beecher Stowe, and Robert P. T. Coffin. Each plaque bears a quote from the author commemorated.

Brunswick Hydro Generating Station

If you're in town mid-May–late June, plan to visit Central Maine Power's Brunswick Hydro generating station, straddling the falls on the Androscoggin River and the Brunswick-Topsham town line (Lower Maine St., next to Fort Andross, 207/729-7644 or 207/623-3521, ext. 2116, weekdays, or 800/872-9937). A glass-walled viewing room lets you play voyeur during the annual ritual of anadromous fish heading upstream to spawn. Amazingly undaunted by the obstacles, such species as alewives (herring), salmon, and smallmouth bass make their way from saltwater to fresh via a 40-foot-high, 570-foot-long artificial fish ladder. The viewing room, which maxes out at about 20 people, is open 1–5 P.M. Wednesday–Sunday during the brief spring spawning season.

ENTERTAINMENT

The region's extremely active arts organization, **Five Rivers Arts Alliance** (108 Main St., Brunswick, 207/798-6964, www.fiveriversartsalliance.org), maintains a calendar of area concerts, gallery openings, art shows, lectures, exhibits, and other arts-related events and also sponsors a few key events. Listings also appear on www.midcoastmaine.com/events.

The **Maine State Music Theatre** (Pickard Theater, Bowdoin College, box office 22 Elm St., Brunswick, 207/725-8769, www.msmt .org) has been a summer tradition since 1959. The renovated state-of-the-art air-conditioned theater brings real pros to its stage for four musicals (mid-June–late Aug., $30–52). Nonsubscription tickets go on sale in early May. Performances are at 8 P.M. Tuesday–Saturday; matinees are staged at 2 P.M. on an alternating schedule—each week has matinees on different days. No children under age four are admitted, but special family shows ($7–11) are performed during the season.

The **Bowdoin International Music Festival** (box office 12 Cleveland St., Brunswick, 207/725-3895, www.summermusic.org) is a showcase for an international array of classical talent of all kinds late June–early August. The six-week festival, part of an international music school, presents a variety of concert opportunities—enough that there's music almost every night of the week. Venues vary and tickets range free–$35. Call or check the website for the current schedule.

Second Friday Art Walks (207/725-4366) take place in downtown Brunswick 5–8 P.M. on the second Friday of the month May–November. Gallery openings, wine tastings, light refreshments, and other activities are usually part of the mix.

Music on the Mall presents family band concerts at 7 P.M. Wednesday (Thursday if it rains) in July–August on the Brunswick Mall, the lovely park in the center of town.

FESTIVALS AND EVENTS

The first full week of August, the **Topsham Fair** is a weeklong agricultural festival with exhibits, demonstrations, live music, ox pulls, contests, harness racing, and fireworks at the Topsham Fairgrounds.

The third Saturday of August, the **Maine Highland Games,** sponsored by the St. Andrew's Society of Maine, mark the annual wearing of the plaids—but you needn't be Scottish to join in the games, watch the Highland dancing, or browse the arts and crafts booths. (Only a Scot, however, can appreciate that unique concoction called haggis.)

September's **Annual Bluegrass Festival** is a four-day event with nonstop bluegrass, including big-name artists. Kickoff is at noon Thursday.

SHOPPING

Downtown Brunswick invites leisurely browsing, with most of the shops concentrated on Maine Street. Take special care when crossing the four-lane-wide street, and do so only at marked crosswalks.

MID-COAST REGION

© HILARY NANGLE

The Brunswick Mall, the town green, is a popular place to hang out, and on Fridays it's home to a farmers market.

Art, Craft, and Antiques Galleries

The **Bayview Gallery** (58 Maine St., Brunswick, 800/244-3007), mounts half a dozen superb shows annually, specializing in contemporary New England artists.

Facing the Mall, **Day's Antiques** (153 Park Row, Brunswick, 207/725-6959) occupies five rooms and the basement of the handsome historic building known as the Pumpkin House. Quality is high at David Day's shop, and prices are fair.

More than 140 dealers show and sell their wares at **Cabot Mill Antiques** (14 Maine St., 207/725-2855), in the renovated Fort Andross mill complex next to the Androscoggin River.

Part gallery, part resource center, **Maine Fiberarts** (13 Maine St., Topsham, 207/721-0678, www.mainefiberarts.org) is a must-stop for anyone interested in fiber-related artwork: knitting, quilting, spinning, and basketry. If you're really interested in finding artists and resources statewide, buy a copy of its resource book.

Nearly two dozen local artists exhibit their works in varied media at **Sebascodegan Artists Gallery** (Rte. 24, Great Island, Harpswell, 207/833-6260).

Bookstore

With an eclectic new-book inventory that includes lots of esoterica, **Gulf of Maine Books** (134 Maine St., Brunswick, 207/729-5083) has held the competition at bay since the early 1980s. The fiction selection is particularly good, as are the religion, health, and poetry sections. Poet, publisher, and renaissance man Gary Lawless oversees everything.

RECREATION
Excursion Train

Ride in restored vintage railcars on the scenic **Maine Eastern Railroad** (207/596-6725 or 800/637-2457, www.maineeasternrailroad.com), operating between Rockland and Brunswick with stops in Wiscasset and Bath. The train operates late May–early November, with special holiday trains in December. Adult fares are $42 round-trip, $27 one-way; ages

4–15 pay $21/$16; seniors are $37/$25; family rate is $109/$83, covering two adults and two kids. Packages with lodging, meals, and theater are available. Crated pets can travel for $20.

Hiking

In the village of Bailey Island, a well-maintained path edges the cliffs and passes the **Giant Stairs,** a waterfront stone stairway of mammoth proportions. To get there, take Route 24 from Cooks Corner toward Bailey Island and Land's End, keeping an eye out for Washington Avenue, on the left about 1.5 miles after the cribstone bridge. (Or drive to Land's End, park the car with the rest of the crowds, survey the panorama, and walk 0.8 miles back along Route 24 to Washington Avenue from there.) Turn onto Washington Avenue, go 0.1 miles, and park at the Episcopal Church (corner of Ocean St.). Walk along Ocean Street to the shorefront path. Watch for a tiny sign just before Spindrift Lane. Don't let small kids get close to the slippery rocks on the surf-tossed shoreline. The same advice holds for Land's End, where the rocks can be treacherous.

Thank the **Brunswick-Topsham Land Trust** (108 Maine St., Brunswick, 207/729-7694, www.btlt.org), founded in 1985, for access to the 11-acre **Skolfield Shores Preserve.** One of the two blue-blazed nature-trail loops skirts a salt marsh, where you're apt to see egrets, herons, and ospreys in summer. Adjacent to the preserve is an ancient Indian portage site that linked Middle Bay and Harpswell Coves when Native Americans spent their vacations here. Take Route 123 (Harpswell Rd.) south from Brunswick about three miles; when you reach the Middle Bay Road intersection (on the right), continue on Route 123 for 1.1 miles. Watch for a small sign and a small parking area on the right.

Tucked behind the Harpswell town office, off the Mountain Road linking Route 123 with Route 24, the **Cliff Trail** is a 1.5-mile loop that follows the shoreline along Strawberry Creek, passes through forests with fairy houses, and rises to 150-foot cliffs with dreamy views over Long Reach.

Nearly four miles of trails wind through fields and forests and edge cliffs on the 118-acre **Bowdoin College Coastal Studies Center,** which tips an Orr's Island peninsula dividing Harpswell. This is a spectacular chunk of oceanfront, and you'll likely have the seven trails practically to yourself. To find it, take Route 24 south and then turn right on Bayview Road, just after the Orr's Island Store (just under two miles beyond the bridge). Keep right at the fork. When the road turns to gravel, continue to a parking area with an info kiosk where you can pick up a trail map.

Swimming

Thomas Point Beach (29 Meadow Rd., Brunswick, 207/725-6009 or 877/872-4321, www.thomaspointbeach.com, 9 A.M.–sunset mid-May–Sept., $3.50 adults, $2 under age 12) is actually 85 acres of privately owned parkland with facilities for swimming (lifeguard on duty, bathhouses), fishing, field sports, picnicking (500 tables), and camping (75 tent and RV sites for $22; no water or sewer hookups, but electricity and a dump station is available). No pets, skateboards, or motorcycles are allowed. The sandy beach is tidal, so the swimming "window" is about two hours before high tide until two hours afterward; otherwise you're wallowing in mudflats. The same timing applies to kayakers and canoeists. Toddlers head for the big playground; teenagers gravitate to the arcade and the ice cream parlor. From Cooks Corner, take Route 24 south 1.5 miles, turn left, and follow signs for less than two miles to the park.

A terrific but nonsecret spot for freshwater swimming is **White's Beach** (Durham Rd., Brunswick, 207/729-0415, www.whitesbeachandcampground.com, $3.50 adults, $2.50 seniors and under age 13). The sandy-bottomed pond maxes out at nine feet. In mid-July the campground hosts a popular family bluegrass festival. Park facilities include a snack bar, a playground, hot showers, and campsites ($22–33). From Route 1 just south of the I-95 exit into Brunswick, take Durham Road 2.2 miles northwest.

Golf

Established in 1901 primarily for Bowdoin College students, the **Brunswick Golf Club** (River Rd., Brunswick, 207/725-8224) is now an especially popular 18-hole public course. Another possibility is the nine-hole **Brunswick Naval Air Station Golf Club** (Bath Rd., Brunswick, 207/921-2155).

Boating Excursions

Departing at noon from the Cook's Lobster House wharf (Cook's Landing) in Bailey Island (off Rte. 24), a large sturdy **Casco Bay Lines ferry** (207/774-7871, www.cascobaylines.com, $15.50 adults, $7.25 ages 5–9) does a 1.75-hour nature-watch circuit of nearby islands, including Eagle Island, the onetime home of Admiral Robert Peary (there are no stopovers on these circuits). Reservations aren't needed.

For a more intimate excursion in a smaller boat, Captain Les McNelly, owner of **Sea Escape Charters** (Bailey Island, 207/833-5531, www.seaescapecottages.com), operates two-hour on-demand sightseeing cruises throughout the summer (weather permitting) for $85 pp (two people) or $55 pp (four people). Or he'll take you out to Eagle Island for $160 per couple (cheaper if there are more passengers). He also offers fishing trips: $225 for four hours, including bait and tackle ($110 for each additional person); no fishing license is required, and bring your own lunch. Trips operate out of Sea Escape Cottages, 1–2-bedroom well-equipped cottages with full kitchens and ocean-side decks that rent for $150–175 per night or $920–1,105 per week, including linens and one change of towels.

Sea Kayaking

H2Outfitters (Orr's Island, 207/833-5257 or 800/205-2925, www.h2outfitters.com) has been a thriving operation since 1978. Based in a wooden building on the Orr's Island side of the famed cribstone bridge, this experienced company organizes guided trips, including island camping; all gear is included. A three-hour tour is $50.

Seaspray Kayaking (207/443-3646 or 888/349-7772, www.seaspraykayaking.com) has bases on the New Meadows River in Brunswick and Sebasco Harbor Resort in Phippsburg as well as rental centers in Bay Point, Georgetown, and Hermit Island Campground, Small Point. The New Meadows base is particularly good for those nervous about trying the sport. Rentals are $15–25 for the first hour, $5–10 for each additional hour, and $25–50 per day. Equipment options include solo and tandem kayaks, recreational kayaks, surf kayaks, and canoes. Tours, led by Registered Maine Guides, vary from sunset paddles to three-day expeditions and include moonlight paddles, island-to-island tours, and inn-to-inn tours. Rates begin at $40 adults. A striper-fishing kayak tour, including tackle and instruction, is $85.

If you're an experienced sea kayaker, consider exploring Harpswell Sound from the boat launch on the west side of the cribstone bridge; kayaks can also put in at Mackerel Cove, near Cook's Lobster House. A launch with plentiful parking is at Sawyer Park on the New Meadows River, on Route 1 just before you cross the river heading north.

ACCOMMODATIONS
Motels and Inns

The newly renovated **Capt. Daniel Stone Inn** (10 Water St., Brunswick, 877/373-2371, www.captaindanielstone.com, $169–209), the region's top full-service lodging, is an easy walk to downtown. Rooms are elegant, with amenities that include nightly turn-down service. There's a good restaurant on the premises as well as a fitness room, a spa, a hot tub, a sauna, and a business center. Ask for a room on the riverside (autumn–winter views) as opposed to the Route 1 side.

A dozen miles down Route 24 from Cooks Corner is the turnoff for Jo Atlass's **Little Island Motel** (44 Little Island Rd., Orr's Island, 207/833-2392, www.littleislandmotel.com, $125–145, no credit cards), a nine-unit complex on its own spit of land with deck views you won't believe. Basic guest rooms have cable TV and a small fridge. Rates include buffet breakfast and use of bikes, boats, and a little beach.

© HILARY NANGLE

The Brunswick Inn is within easy walking distance of all downtown Brunswick sights and attractions.

Continue another mile down Route 24, cross the cribstone bridge, and you'll come to Chip Black's **Bailey Island Motel** (Rte. 24, Bailey Island, 207/833-2886, www.baileyis-landmotel.com, mid-May–late Oct., $135), a congenial, clean, no-frills waterfront spot with 11 guest rooms and wowing views. Kids under 10 stay for free; age 10 and older are $15 extra. Continental breakfast is included, and guest rooms have cable TV and a small fridge. A dock is available for boat launching.

Looking rather like the film set of an old-fashioned tear-jerker, the family-run **Driftwood Inn** (81 Washington Ave., Bailey Island, 207/833-5461, www.thedriftwoodin-nmaine.com, mid-May–Oct., no credit cards) has 25 very rustic pine-paneled guest rooms in four buildings (some with a private toilet and sink; all with shared showers), six house-keeping cottages, a saltwater pool, a stunning view, a dining room, and a determinedly take-us-as-we-are ambience. There are no frills, period, but it has oceanfront porches, games, and an old-fashioned simplicity that you rarely

find anymore. You'll sleep at night listening to the waves crash on the rocky shore. It's all on three oceanfront acres near the Giant Stairs. The dining room, open to nonguests by reservation, serves a set home-cooked meal nightly (usually with a fish-of-the-day alternative), late June–early September, for $16–20; breakfast is $7.25. Meals aren't offered during spring and fall. Rooms are $85–130, and cottages rent by the week ($675–720). Dogs are allowed in the cottages.

Bed-and-Breakfasts

Right downtown, facing the tree-shaded Mall, is **❰ The Brunswick Inn** (165 Park Row, Brunswick, 207/729-4914 or 800/299-4914, www.brunswickbnb.com, year-round, $145–200), a stately 30-room Greek Revival mansion built in 1849. Fine art from a local gallery hangs throughout the inn, complementing the handsome decor. Fifteen comfortable guest rooms are split between the main house and the renovated Carriage House (with two fully accessible guest rooms); all have Wi-Fi and phones, and suites have TVs. There's also a pet-friendly ($20) small cottage with a kitchen. Inside the main inn is a laid-back lounge where there's occasional entertainment. The location puts all of downtown Brunswick within walking distance.

Within walking distance of downtown Brunswick, but across the bridge spanning the Androscoggin River, is the **Black Lantern B&B** (57 Elm St., Topsham, 207/725-4165 or 888/306-4165, www.blacklanternbandb.com, $110), Tom and Judy Connelie's lovely 1860s riverfront home. All guest rooms are decorated with an emphasis on comfort, and two have water views. Judy's quilts will warm you on a cool night.

On the outskirts of town, in a rural location smack-dab on Middle Bay, is **Middle Bay Farm Bed and Breakfast** (287 Pennellville Rd., Brunswick, 207/373-1375, www.middlebayfarm.com, year-round, $170–190), lovingly and beautifully restored by Phyllis Truesdell, who bought the property after it sat all but abandoned for a decade. Once the site of the Pennell Brothers Shipyard, the farmhouse and sail loft now house guests seeking an away-from-it-all yet convenient location. Four water-view guest rooms in the 1834 farmhouse are decorated with antiques and have TVs and video players. Also in the main house is a living room with fireplace and grand piano. Two suites in the sail loft each have a living room with a kitchenette and two tiny bedrooms, and they share an open porch. All guests receive a full breakfast in the water-view dining room. Bring a sea kayak to launch from the dock.

At the 1761 **Harpswell Inn** (108 Lookout Point Rd., South Harpswell, 207/833-5509 or 800/843-5509, www.harpswellinn.com, year-round), innkeepers Anne and Richard Moseley operate a comfortable, welcoming antiques-filled oasis on 2.5 secluded water-view acres. It's tough to break away from the glass-walled great room, but Middle Bay sunsets from the porch can do it. And just down the hill is Allen's Seafood, a takeout fish shack, where you can watch lobstermen unload their catches in a gorgeous cove and grab a lobster roll. In fall, the foliage on two little islets in the cove turns brilliant red. The bed-and-breakfast has

nine lovely guest rooms ($115–165), most with private baths; three suites ($245–259), and four cottages ($975–1,450 per week). Prices are slightly higher for one-night stays.

Thirteen miles south of Cooks Corner, **The Log Cabin** (Rte. 24, Bailey Island, 207/833-5546, www.logcabin-maine.com, $169–329) has nine nicely decorated guest rooms with phones, TVs and video players, private decks facing the bay, and, weather permitting, splendid sunset views to the White Mountains. Four guest rooms have kitchen facilities; some have gas fireplaces or whirlpool tubs. There's also an outdoor heated pool. Full breakfast is included; dinner ($18–33) is available.

FOOD

Brunswick and the Harpswells have an overabundance of dining options, from inexpensive cafés, delis, and coffeehouses to ethnic spots and seafood joints. Hours noted are for peak season but are subject to change. It's wise to call ahead, especially when traveling in the off-season.

Local Flavors

Wild O.A.T.S. Bakery and Café (149 Maine St., Tontine Mall, Brunswick, 207/725-6287, www.wildoatsbakery.com, 7 A.M.–5 P.M. Mon.–Fri., 8 A.M.–5 P.M. Sat., 8 A.M.–3 P.M. Sun.) turns out terrific made-from-scratch breads and pastries, especially the breakfast kind, in its cafeteria-style place. (Just so you know, the name stands for Original and Tasty Stuff.) It has inside and outside tables, moderate prices, good-for-you salads, and great sandwiches.

For food on the run—no-frills hot dogs straight from the cart—head for Brunswick's Mall, the village green where **Danny's on the Mall** (no phone) has been cooking dirt-cheap tube steaks since the early 1980s.

Fat Boy Drive-In (Bath Rd./Old Rte. 1, Brunswick, 207/729-9431, 11 A.M.–8:30 P.M. daily, no credit cards) is a genuine throwback—a landmark since 1955, boasting carhops, window trays, and a menu guaranteed to clog your arteries. Onion rings, frappés, and BLTs are specialties. Aim for the second Saturday in August, when the annual Sock Hop takes place.

Pizzas by the slice or pie in both the usual and specialty flavors and made from locally sourced ingredients emerge from the ovens at **Flipside** (111 Main St., Brunswick, 207/373-9448, 11 A.M.–9 P.M. Tues.–Sat.). Possible toppings include local greens, slow-roasted tomatoes, Maine shrimp, and maple-cured bacon.

Choose from up to 32 flavors of gelato and *sorbetto* at **The Gelato Fiasco** (74 Maine St., Brunswick, 207/607-4002, www.gelatofiasco .com, 11 A.M.–11 P.M. daily). You can find these to-die-for gelatos statewide, but this is ground zero.

A favorite for chowder is **Salt Cod Cafe** (1894 Harpswell Islands Rd., Orr's Island, 207/833-6210, 8 A.M.–5 P.M. daily), with a primo location overlooking the cribstone bridge. Sandwiches, wraps, rolls, and baked goods are also available.

The **Brunswick Farmers Market** sets up rain or shine on the Mall (village green) 8:30 A.M.–2 P.M. Tuesday and Friday May–November; Friday is the bigger day. On Saturday the market moves to Crystal Spring Farm, Pleasant Hill Road (8:30 A.M.–12:30 P.M.). You'll find produce, cheeses, crafts, condiments, live lobsters, and serendipitous surprises, depending on the season.

The chocolates, truffles, and bark made by Melinda Harris Richter are divine at **Island Candy Company** (Harpswell Islands Rd., Orr's Island, 207/833-6639, 11 A.M.–8 P.M. daily in season), and there are baked goods and ice cream too.

Family Favorites

Just over the bridge from Brunswick, in the renovated Bowdoin Mill complex overlooking the Androscoggin River, the **Sea Dog Brewery** (1 Main St., Topsham, 207/725-0162, www .seadogbrewing.com, 11:30 A.M.–1 A.M. daily, $11–18) has seating inside and on a deck overhanging the river. The menu ranges from burgers and sandwiches to full-plate entrées. It offers frequent acoustic entertainment, and there are games for kids and a games room with a video arcade and pool tables.

Casual Dining

A favorite destination before the theater or a concert, **Bacari** (212 Maine St., Brunswick, 207/725-2600, www. bacaribistro.com, 5–9 P.M. Tues.–Fri., 5–10 P.M. Sat.–Sun.) excels at crafting small plates ($10–23) of flavorful and fresh foods.

A local fave just enough off Maine Street to befuddle visitors, **Back Street Bistro & Wine Bar** (11 Town Hall Plaza, Brunswick, 207/725-4060, 5–8 P.M. Sun.–Mon., 5–9 P.M. Tues.–Sat., $17–28) is worth finding for well-prepared dishes, such as chicken piccata or strip steak.

Still casual but a bit fancier (it has tablecloths) is **【 Clementine** (44 Maine St., Brunswick, 207/721-9800, www.clementinemaine.com, 5–9 P.M. Tues.–Sat., entrées $18–29). The well-executed menu changes seasonally but usually includes fish, poultry, and meat prepared with a dash of creativity and artful presentation. A three-course menu is $25.

Ethnic and Eclectic Fare

Moussaka, braised goat, handmade organic pastas, and stuffed grape leaves are just a few of the Greek and Italian choices that might appear on the seasonally changing menu at **Trattoria Athena** (25 Mill St., Brunswick, 207/721-0700, www.trattoriaathena.com, 11:30 A.M.–1 P.M. and 5–9 P.M. Tues.–Thurs., 11:30 A.M.–1 P.M. and 5–10 P.M. Fri.–Sat., $16–22). The dining area is small, with a cozy rustic vibe that complements the cuisine. This gem, about a block off Maine Street, is worth finding.

Although the owners are Chinese, they do a decent job with the sushi and Japanese specialties at **Little Tokyo** (72 Maine St., Brunswick, 207/798-6888, www.littletokyomaine.com, 11:30 A.M.–9:30 P.M. daily, entrées $12–25).

Generous portions, moderate prices, efficient service, and narrow aisles are the story at **The Great Impasta** (42 Maine St., Brunswick, 207/729-5858, www.thegreatimpasta.com, 11 A.M.–9 P.M. Mon.–Thurs., 11 A.M.–10 P.M. Fri.–Sat., $13–22), a cheerful, informal eatery where the garlic meets you at the door. There are gluten-free choices and a "bambino menu" for the kids.

Hip, funky, and full of personality are words often used to describe **El Camino** (15 Cushing St., Brunswick, 207/725-8228, 5–9 P.M. Tues.–Sat.), which uses fresh, local, and often organic ingredients to create innovative Cal-Mex fare such as wild mushroom and spinach enchiladas. Prices top out around $15.

Eclectic doesn't begin to describe **Frontier Cafe** (Mill 3, Fort Andross, 14 Maine St. at Rte. 1 overpass, Brunswick, 207/725-5222, www.explorefrontier.com, 9 A.M.–9 P.M. Mon.–Thurs., 9 A.M.–10 P.M. Fri.–Sat., kitchen closes one hour earlier, entrées $9–15), a combination café, gallery, and cinema inspired by founder Michael Gilroy's world travels. The menu of soups, sandwiches, and salads changes weekly but usually includes wonderful market plates emphasizing the cuisine of a country or region—Maine, France, the Middle East, or Italy. Desserts are homemade, and there's also a kids menu. Wine and beer are served. Films are screened ($7 adults), and there are frequent events and entertainment.

World-class beer is the focus at **Lion's Pride** (112 Pleasant St., Brunswick, 207/373-1840, www.lionspridepub.com, 11:30 A.M.–10 P.M. Sun.–Thurs., 11:30 A.M.–11 P.M. Fri.–Sat.), where the expansive menu ($8–30) is geared around the brews. Some rather obscure pours (emphasis on Belgian) are drawn from the 35 hand-blown glass taps. The well-trained staff knows their brews and aims to educate their customers. Add tastings, frequent entertainment, beer classes, and special beer-oriented events.

Lobster and Seafood

In 2006 the Holbrook Community Foundation took ownership of Holbrook's Wharf, site of **Holbrook's Wharf and Grille** (984 Cundy's Harbor Rd., 207/729-0848, call for hours), along with Holbrook's General Store and the Trufant mansion, preserving this slice of Maine fishing-village life for future generations. The wharf lobster shack is a leased operation, and

The Dolphin Chowder House, in Harpswell, tops many a Mainer's list for the best chowder and views.

quality varies year to year; ask locally. When it's on, this is the real thing for authentic lobster in the rough, and the view is superb.

You want fresh? Fish doesn't get any fresher than that served at **Allen's Seafood** (119 Lookout Point Rd., Harpswell, 207/833-2828, 11 A.M.–7 P.M. Tues.–Sun.), a seasonal take-out trailer overlooking Middle Bay. Chowders, fried fish, lobster, and similar fare are prepared fresh from the bounty of the daily catch. Order and then grab a picnic table. Moorings and a dock are available if you arrive by boat.

Arguments rage endlessly about who makes the best chowder in Maine, but **❮ The Dolphin Chowder House** (Dolphin Marina, 515 Basin Point Rd., South Harpswell, 207/833-6000, www.dolphinmarinaandrestaurant.com, 11:30 A.M.–9 P.M. daily May 1–Oct. 31., $6–30) tops lots of lists for its fish chowder, accompanied by a blueberry muffin. Equally famed is its lobster stew, plus you can't beat the scenic 13-mile drive south from Brunswick and the spectacular water views through two walls of windows at the tip of Harpswell Neck.

Another good bet for lobster, along with chowders and fried seafood, is **Gurnet Trading Co.** (602 Gurnet Rd./Rte. 24, Brunswick, 207/729-7300, www.gurnettrading.com), serving lunch and dinner daily overlooking Buttermilk Cove.

INFORMATION AND SERVICES

The **Southern Midcoast Chamber of Commerce** (2 Main St., Topsham, 877/725-8797, www.midcoastmaine.com) publishes the *Guide to Southern Midcoast Maine.*

For information on Harpswell, visit the **Harpswell Business Association**'s website (www.harpswellmaine.org).

Check the website of **Curtis Memorial Library** (23 Pleasant St., Brunswick, 207/725-5242, www.curtislibrary.com) for excellent local resources and guides.

Bath Area

One of the smallest in area among Maine's cities, Bath packs a wallop in only nine square miles. Like Brunswick, it straddles Route 1, edges a river, and relies on modern military funding, but Bath's centuries of historical and architectural tradition and well-preserved Victorian downtown have earned it a prized designation: The National Trust for Historic Preservation named it a Distinctive Destination.

The defense part is impossible to ignore, since giant cranes dominate the riverfront cityscape at the huge Bath Iron Works complex, source of state-of-the-art warships—your tax dollars at work. Less evident (but not far away) is the link to the past: Just south of Bath, in Popham on the Phippsburg Peninsula, is the poorly marked site where a trouble-plagued English settlement, a sister colony to Jamestown, predated the Plymouth Colony by 13 years. (Of course, Champlain arrived before that, and Norsemen left calling cards even earlier.) In 1607–1608 settlers in the Popham Colony managed to build a 30-ton pinnace, *Virginia of Sagadahoc,* designed for transatlantic trade, but they lost heart during a bitter winter and abandoned the site. A replica is planned; for details, visit www.mainesfirstship.org.

Bath is the jumping-off point for two peninsulas to the south—**Phippsburg** (of Popham Colony fame) and **Georgetown.** Both are dramatically scenic, with glacier-carved farms and fishing villages. Drive (bicycling is best left to experienced pedalers) a dozen miles down any of these fingers and you're in different worlds.

Across the soaring Sagadahoc Bridge from Bath is Woolwich, from where you can continue northeastward along the coast or detour northward on Route 128 to the hamlet of Day's Ferry. Named after 18th-century resident Joseph Day, who shuttled back and forth in a gondola-type boat across the Kennebec River, the picturesque village has a cluster of 18th- and 19th-century homes and churches—all part of the Day's Ferry Historic District. The village's Old Stage Road saw many a stagecoach in its day; passengers would ferry from Bath and pick up the stage here to travel onward.

SIGHTS
Bath Iron Works
Known locally as BIW or The Yard, Bath Iron Works has been building ships on this 50-acre riverfront site since 1890. Currently its roughly 5,600 employees build destroyers for the U.S. Navy. BIW is open to the public for launchings, when it's a mob scene with hordes of politicos, townsfolk, and military pooh-bahs in their scrambled eggs and brass. The best way to get a peek at the workaday world behind the gates is on a Bath Iron Works Trolley Tour with the Maine Maritime Museum.

◖ Maine Maritime Museum
Spread over 25 acres on the Kennebec River is the state's premier marine museum, the Maine Maritime Museum (243 Washington St., Bath, 207/443-1316, www.mainemaritimemuseum .org, 9:30 A.M.–5 P.M. daily, $12 adults, $11 over age 65, $9 ages 4–16). On the grounds are five original 19th-century buildings from the Percy and Small Shipyard (1897–1920), a late-Victorian home, and hands-on exhibits, but the first thing you see is the architecturally dramatic Maritime History Building, locale for permanent and temporary displays of marine art and artifacts and a shop stocked with nautical books and gifts. Bring a picnic (or purchase lunch at the seasonal Even Keel Snack Bar) and let the toddlers loose in the children's pirate's play area. Then either wander the campus on your own or join one of the guided tours. Don't miss the boat shop, where volunteers build and restore small vessels. Shipyard demonstrations are held on a rotating schedule, and brown-bag lectures are often given. In summer, weather permitting, the museum sponsors a variety of special river cruises; call for information. May–mid-October the museum offers fascinating

MID-COAST REGION

© AVALON TRAVEL

© HILARY NANGLE

The Maine Maritime Museum's 25-acre campus is on the site of the former Percy and Small Shipyard. This sculpture gives visitors an idea of the size of the ships once constructed on the grounds.

one-hour **Bath Iron Works Trolley Tours** ($30 adults, $15 under age 17, includes two-day museum admission) conducted by former BIW employees. You'll need to reserve a week or longer in advance; it's well worth the effort. Pair it with a one-hour cruise to view the yard from the river. The museum is open year-round; the Percy and Small Shipyard is year-round but in winter only as conditions permit, with reduced-price admissions.

Bath Walking Tours

Sagadahoc Preservation (www.sagada-hocpreservation.org), founded in 1971 to rescue the city's architectural heritage, has produced podcasts of three different self-guided walking and driving architectural tours that accompany a foldout brochure (with maps). The podcasts can be downloaded from www .cityofbath.com: Click on "Visiting" and then "Walking Tours links." The free map and guide *The Historic Architecture of Downtown Bath, Maine* is available from Main Street Bath

(4 Centre St., Bath, 207/442-7291, www.main-stbath.com). Sagadahoc Preservation also offers an annual house tour, usually in June; check the website for details.

Phippsburg Peninsula

Thanks to a map-brochure (www.phipps-burghistorical.com) produced by the Phippsburg Historical Society and the Phippsburg Business Association, you can spend a whole day—or, better still, several days—exploring the peninsula that extends south from Bath. Along the way are campgrounds, bed-and-breakfasts, an updated traditional resort, restaurants, a unique state park, hiking trails, secluded coves, spectacular scenery, and tons of history.

About two miles south of Bath is a causeway known as **Winnegance,** a Wabanaki name usually translated as "short carry" or "little portage." Native Americans crossed here from the Kennebec River to the New Meadows River. Early settlers erected nearly a dozen tide-powered mills to serve the shipbuilding industry, but they're long gone. About 1.5 miles beyond the causeway is a left turn onto Fiddler's Reach Road, leading to the **Morse Cove Public Launching Facility,** one of the state's most scenic boat-launch sites. If you have a kayak, plan to go downriver on the ebb tide and return on the flow; otherwise you'll be battling the strong Kennebec River current. There's plenty of paved parking here plus a restroom.

Back on Route 209 it's another 1.3 miles to the **Dromore Burying Ground** (on the right), with great old headstones; the earliest is dated 1743. The next mile opens up with terrific easterly views of Dromore Bay. Right in the line of sight is 117-acre Lee Island, which the owners sold to the state in 1995. May–mid-July the island is off-limits to protect nesting eagles and waterfowl.

Next you're in **Phippsburg Center,** alive with shipbuilding from colonial days until the early 20th century. Hang a left onto Parker Head Road (but avoid this detour if you're on a bicycle; it's too narrow and winding). After the Phippsburg Historical Museum (2–4 P.M. Mon.–Fri. summer), in an 1859 schoolhouse, and the Alfred Totman Library, turn left onto Church Lane to see the **Phippsburg Congregational Church,** built in 1802. Out front is a "Constitution Tree," a huge English linden planted in 1774.

Parker Head Road continues southward and meets Route 209, which takes you to **Popham Beach State Park.** Continue to the end of Route 209 for **Fort Popham Historic Site,** where parking is woefully inadequate in summer (and costs an exorbitant $7 at nearby Percy's Store). The fort is accessible Memorial Day–September. Youngsters love this place—they can fish from the rocks, climb to the third level of the 1865 stone fortress, picnic on the seven-acre grounds, and create sand castles on the tiny beach next to the fort. Resist the urge to swim, though; the current is dangerous and there's no lifeguard. Across the river is Bay Point, a lobstering village at the tip of the Georgetown Peninsula. **Percy's Store**

(207/389-2010), by the way, with a handful of tables, is the best place down here for pizza, picnic fare, fried dough, and fishing tackle.

Across the cove from the fort is Fort Baldwin Road, a one-lane-wide winding road leading to the shorefront site of the 1607 Popham Colony. Climb the path up Sabino Hill to what's left of World War I–era **Fort Baldwin,** the best vantage point for panoramic photos.

Backtrack about four miles on Route 209, turn left onto Route 216, and head toward **Small Point.** Go about 0.9 miles to Morse Mountain Road, on the left, which leads to the parking area and trailhead for the **Bates-Morse Mountain Preserve.** Farther south are Head Beach and Hermit Island.

Returning northward on Route 216, you'll hook up with Route 209 and then see a left turn (Rte. 217) to Sebasco Harbor Resort. Take the time to go beyond the resort area. When the paved road goes left (to the Water's Edge Restaurant), turn right at a tiny cemetery and continue northward on the Old Meadowbrook Road, which meanders for about four miles along the west side of the peninsula. About midway along is **The Basin,** regarded by sailors as one of the Maine coast's best "hurricane holes" (refuges in high winds). As you skirt the Basin and come to a fork, bear right to return to Route 209; turn left and return northward to Bath.

ENTERTAINMENT AND EVENTS

Bath's most diversified entertainment setting is the **Center for the Arts at the Chocolate Church** (804 Washington St., Bath, 207/442-8455, www.chocolatechurch.com), a chocolate-brown board-and-batten structure built in 1846 as the Central Congregational Church. Year-round activities at the arts center include music and dance concerts, dramas, exhibits, and children's programs.

At 7 P.M. every Tuesday and Friday mid-June–August, the **Gazebo Concert Series** brings live entertainment to Bath's Library Park.

Five Rivers Arts Alliances holds **Third Friday Art Walk and Drive** (various locations,

Bath, 207/798-6964, 5–8 P.M.) on the third Friday of the month June–October.

Throughout the summer, the **Maine Maritime Museum** (207/443-1316) schedules special events, often hinging on visits by tall ships and other vessels. Some of the visiting boats are open to the public for an extra fee. Call the museum to check.

November–April 60 dealers show their wares at the monthly **Bath Antiques Shows** (207/443-8983, www.bathantiquesshows.com, $4) at the Bath Middle School.

SHOPPING

Front and Center Streets are lined with fun, independent shops, including a number of shops selling antiques and antiquarian books clustered on lower Front Street.

Bath is home to a good independent bookstore successfully bucking the megastore trend, the **Bath Book Shop** (96 Front St., Bath, 207/443-9338). For cheap beach reads and eclectic finds, visit **The Library Bookstore** (194 Front St., Bath, 207/443-1161).

Independent shops line downtown Bath's brick sidewalks.

© HILARY NANGLE

Right in the shadow of the Route 1 overpass is an incredible resource for knitters and weavers, **Halcyon Yarn** (12 School St., Bath, 207/442-7909 or 800/341-0282, www.halcyonyarn.com), a huge warehouse of a place that carries domestic and imported yarns, looms, spinning wheels, how-to videos, kits, and pattern books.

About nine miles down Route 127, you'll come to **Georgetown Pottery** (Rte. 127, Georgetown, 207/371-2801), a top-quality ceramics studio and shop.

Anyone who appreciates fine woodworking tools *must* visit the Shelter Institute's **Woodbutcher Tools** (873 Rte. 1, Woolwich, 207/442-7938), a retail shop and bookstore, five miles north of Bath.

Flea Market

One of Maine's biggest and most enduring flea markets is right on Route 1 north of Bath, often creating near-accidents as rubbernecking motorists slam to a halt. **Montsweag Flea Market** (Rte. 1 at Mountain Rd., Woolwich, 207/443-2809, www.montsweagfleamarket.com) is a genuine treasure trove about seven miles northeast of Bath's Sagadahoc bridge. It's open from 6:30 A.M. weekends May–mid-October, plus on Wednesday in summer (antiques and collectibles only from 5:30 A.M.).

RECREATION
Golf

The 18-hole **Bath Country Club** (Whiskeag Rd., Bath, 207/442-8411) has moderate greens fees, a pro shop, and a restaurant serving lunch and dinner.

The **Sebasco Harbor Resort** has a nine-hole course, open to nonguests on a space-available basis; call the resort's pro shop (207/389-9060) to inquire. Watch out for the infamous second hole, which gives new meaning to the term water hole, and be sure to say good morning to Sarah on the sixth tee: If you look nearby, you'll find a gravestone inscribed "Sarah Wallace—1862." A local rhyme goes:

Show respect to Sarah
You golfers passing by;
She's the only person on this course
Who can't improve her lie.

Bicycling

Bath-area headquarters for anything to do with bikes is **Bath Cycle and Ski** (Rte. 1, Woolwich, 207/442-7002 or 800/245-3626, www.bikeman.com). Rentals are $80 per week, route maps are available, and the shop sponsors weekly rides on Tuesday nights and Saturday and Sunday mornings.

Hiking

The Kennebec Estuary Land Trust (KELT, 207/442-8400, www.kennebecestuary.org) maintains two preserves worth a visit. In Bath at the end of High Street, at the tip of land where Whiskeag Creek meets the Kennebec River, is the **Thorn Head Preserve.** Allow a half hour for the easy walk to the headland and its stone "picnic" table with views toward Merrymeeting Bay. Allow longer if you want to explore any of the side trails. The **Whiskeag Trail,** a five-mile nonmotorized multiuse path, connects the preserve to the Bath YMCA; you can download map from KELT's website. For terrific views of this section of coast, hike the loop trail to the bedrock summit of Georgetown's **Higgins Mountain.** The Route 127 trailhead is on the right, 7.6 miles south of Route 1.

BATES-MORSE MOUNTAIN CONSERVATION AREA

Consider visiting Phippsburg's lovely 600-acre Bates-Morse Mountain Conservation Area only if you are willing to be extra conscientious about the rules for this private preserve. A relatively easy four-mile round-trip hike takes you through marshland (you'll need insect repellent) and to the top of 210-foot Morse Mountain, which has panoramic views, and then down to privately owned Seawall Beach. On a clear day you can see New Hampshire's Mount Washington from the summit. No pets or vehicles are allowed, and there are no recreational facilities; stay on the preserve road and the beach path at all times as the side roads are private. Least terns and piping plovers—both endangered species—nest in the dunes, so avoid this area, especially mid-May–mid-August. Bird-watching hint: Morse Mountain is a great locale for spotting hawks during their annual September migration southward. Pick up a map (and the rules) from the box in the parking area on Morse Mountain Road, off Route 216 just under a mile south of the intersection with Route 209.

PHIPPSBURG HIKING TRAILS

The town of Phippsburg and the Phippsburg Land Trust (207/443-6309, www.phippsburg-landtrust.org) have prepared a handy free brochure with a map that describes nine preserves that have trails. Three—Center Pond, Spirit Pond, and Ridgewell Preserve—have detailed maps and field guides available at trailhead boxes. The Land Trust also hosts guided walks mid-June–mid-September.

Preserves
HAMILTON SANCTUARY

Owned by Maine Audubon (207/781-2330, www.maineaudubon.org), Hamilton Sanctuary in West Bath is a peaceful site for walking and nature study on the New Meadows River, with 1.5 miles of trails winding through meadows and forests and along the Back Cove shoreline. From Route 1 between Bath and Brunswick, take the New Meadows Road exit. Head south on New Meadows. When it becomes Foster Point Road, go four miles to the sanctuary entrance.

JOSEPHINE NEWMAN SANCTUARY

A must-see for any nature lover, the 119-acre Josephine Newman Sanctuary (Rte. 127, Georgetown, no phone) has 2.5 miles of blazed loop trails winding through 110 wooded acres and along Robinhood Cove's tidal shoreline. Josephine Oliver Newman (1878–1968), a respected naturalist, bequeathed her family's splendid property to Maine Audubon (207/781-2330, www.maineaudubon.org), which maintains it today. The 0.6-mile self-guided trail is moderately difficult, but the rewards are 20 informative markers highlighting special features: glacial erratics, reversing falls, mosses, and marshes. The easiest route is the 0.75-mile Horseshoe Trail, which you can extend for another mile or so by linking into the Rocky End Trail. No pets or bikes are allowed. To find this hidden gem, take Route 127 from Route 1 in Woolwich (the road to Reid State Park) for 9.1 miles. Turn right at the sanctuary sign and continue up the narrow, rutted dirt road (hopefully no one's coming the other way) to the small parking lot. A map of the trail system is posted at the marsh's edge and available in the box.

ROBERT P. TRISTRAM COFFIN WILDFLOWER SANCTUARY

The New England Wildflower Society (www.newfs.org) owns this 177-acre trail-laced preserve bordering Merrymeeting Bay. It is home to more than 100 species of wildflowers. To find it, take Route 127 north for 2.2 miles, then Route 128 for 4.5 miles, and look for a small parking area on the left.

Swimming
POPHAM BEACH

On hot July and August weekends, the parking lot at Popham Beach State Park (Rte. 209, Phippsburg, 207/389-1335, $6 nonresident adults, $4 Maine resident adults, $2 nonresident seniors, free Maine resident seniors, $1 ages 5–11), 14 miles south of Bath, fills up by 10 A.M., so plan to arrive early at this huge crescent of sand backed by sea grass, beach roses, and dunes. Facilities include changing rooms, outside showers, restrooms, and seasonal lifeguards. It's officially open April 15–October 30, but the beach is accessible all year.

HEAD BEACH

Just off Route 216, about two miles south of the Route 209 turnoff to Popham Beach, is Head Beach, a sandy crescent that's open daily until 10 P.M. A day-use parking fee ($5) is payable at the small gatehouse; there's a restroom on the path to the beach and a store within walking distance.

Reid State Park

On the Georgetown Peninsula, Reid State Park (Seguinland Rd., Georgetown, 207/371-2303, $6.50 nonresident adults, $4.50 Maine resident adults, $2 nonresident seniors, free Maine resident seniors, $1 ages 5–11), is no secret, so plan to arrive early on summer weekends, when parking is woefully inadequate. Highlights of the 765-acre park are 1.5 miles of splendid beach in three distinct sections, marshlands, sand dunes, and tide pools. Kids love the tide pools, treasure troves left by the receding tide. Facilities include changing rooms with showers, picnic tables, restrooms, and snack bars. Test the water before racing in; even in midsummer it's breathtakingly cold. In winter, bring cross-country skis and glide along the shoreline. The park—14 miles south of Route 1 in Woolwich and two miles off Route 127—is open daily year-round.

Just 0.5 miles beyond the Reid State Park entrance is **Charles Pond,** where the setting is unsurpassed for freshwater swimming in the long, skinny pond. You'll wish this were a secret too, but it isn't. There are no facilities.

Excursion Boats

The 50-foot *Yankee* operates out of Small Point's Hermit Island Campground Monday–Saturday throughout the summer. You can go on nature cruises, enjoy the sunset, or visit Eagle Island; the schedule is different each day, and rates vary widely by trip. Call for information and reservations (207/389-1788).

The **MV *Ruth,*** a 38-foot excursion boat, runs cruises out of Sebasco Harbor Resort late June–Labor Day. You don't need to be a Sebasco guest to take the trips, but reservations are essential. The schedule changes weekly, but possible options are a nature cruise, a Cundy's Harbor lunch cruise, lobstering demos, a sunset cruise, and a trip to Pirate Island, with trips ranging 1–2 hours. Call the resort (207/389-1161) for the current week's schedule and rates.

Long Reach Cruises (207/442-0092 or 888/538-6785, www.longreachcruises.com) offers a variety of 1–3-plus-hour cruises departing from the Maine Maritime Museum. Options include narrated history, lighthouses, seal-watching, eagle-watching, and sunset cruises. Prices range $24–45 adults, $10–25 children and include two-day museum admission.

If you prefer a custom tour, call **River Run Tours** (207/504-2628, www.riverruntours .com). Whether you want to view lighthouses or wildlife or cruise up river to Swans Island, Captain Ed Rice will design an itinerary based on per-hour charges of $30 adults, $15 under age 13. His comfortable pontoon boat accommodates six; plan on at least two hours.

Canoeing and Kayaking

Close to civilization yet amazingly undeveloped, 392-acre **Nequasset Lake** is a great place to canoe. You'll see a few anglers, a handful of houses, and near-wilderness along the shoreline. Personal watercraft and motors over 10 hp are banned. Take Route 1 from Bath across the bridge to Woolwich. Continue to the flashing caution light at Nequasset Road; turn right and go 0.1 miles. Turn left, and left again, into the parking area for the Nequasset Stream Waterfront Park, a popular swimming hole. Launch your canoe and head upstream, under Route 1, to the lake.

Paddle the relatively calm and safe waters of Winnegance Creek with a rental canoe or kayak from **Paddle Up the Creak** (Rte. 209, Phippsburg, 207/443-4845, www.rentkayaks .com, $10 pp for 3 hours).

Seaspray Kayaking (888/349-7774, www .seaspraykayaking.com) operates from bases at the Sebasco Harbor Resort in Sebasco Estates, Hermit Island Campground on Small Point, and Bay Point Kayaking Center in Georgetown. Hourly rentals begin at $15–25 plus $5–10 for each additional hour, up to $25–50 daily, with longer-term rates and delivery available. A variety of guided tours are also offered, with half-day options for $50 adults, $25 children and specialty paddles, such as sunset or moonlight, for $40 pp.

Fishing Charters

Cast a line for stripers, bluefish, pike trout, and smallmouth bass with **Kennebec Tidewater Charters** (207/737-4695, www.kennebectide-water.com). Captain Robin Thayer, a Master Maine Guide, offers freshwater and saltwater cruises beginning at $300 for four hours. Tackle is provided, and instruction is available. Catch-and-release is encouraged.

ACCOMMODATIONS
Bath

Most of Bath's in-town bed-and-breakfasts and inns are in historic residences built by shipping magnates and their families, giving you a chance to appreciate the quality of craftsmanship they demanded in their ships and their homes alike. All are open year-round.

The flamboyant pink and plum Italianate **Galen Moses House** (1009 Washington St., Bath, 207/442-8771 or 888/442-8771, www .galenmoses.com, $119–259) is a standout in the city's Historic District. Original architectural features—soaring ceilings, friezes, chandeliers, elaborate woodwork, stained-glass windows—and period antiques make it equally appealing inside, as do hosts Jim Haught and Larry Kieft. All guest rooms have air-conditioning and Wi-Fi. It has plenty of common rooms for relaxing, including one with a TV and video player. A fancy full breakfast served at a communal table and afternoon refreshments are included. Pets are allowed in one guest room for $15 per night.

Innkeeper Elizabeth Knowlton blends elegance and comfort at the **Inn at Bath** (969 Washington St., Bath, 207/443-4294 or 800/423-0964, www.innatbath.com, $170–200). Her culinary skills, honed as chef and co-owner of a Montana fly-fishing lodge, have garnered national attention. Guest rooms in the 1810 Greek Revival–style inn are decorated with antiques, and each has air-conditioning, a TV and video player, Wi-Fi, and a phone. Two have wood-burning fireplaces, and two have two-person whirlpool tubs. Kids over age 4 and dogs are welcome. One room is wheelchair accessible.

MID-COAST REGION

When you want to be truly pampered, book a room at the ◖ **Kismet Inn** (44 Summer St., Bath, 207/443-3399, www.kismetinnmaine .com, $210–260), where innkeeper Shadi Towfighis offers five lovely guest rooms, each with either a Japanese soaking tub or a steam shower. The inn is decorated with a contemporary Old World style. The beds are covered with organic-cotton linens and were designed specifically for each guest room. Guests can arrange for in-room spa services. Be sure to reserve a private dinner; it's a treat. Shadi uses natural and organic ingredients to create meals that go beyond the usual B&B fare. Not only that, breakfast is served whenever you're ready; there are no set meal times. Guests must leave outdoor shoes in the entry to avoid bringing outside pollutants indoors. The inn faces Library Park and is just around the corner from Front Street's shops.

Just a few miles from downtown Bath yet feeling a world away is the **Fairhaven Inn** (118 North Bath Rd., Bath, 207/443-4391 or 888/443-4391, www.mainecoast.com/ fairhaveninn, $99–125). Antiques and country pieces furnish Dawn and Andrew Omo's truly rambling 1790 colonial, built on 16 quiet country acres with views over the Kennebec River. The six guest rooms have Wi-Fi and air-conditioning. The Omos grew up in Bath, so they know the area well. Pets are welcome for $10 per night.

Phippsburg Peninsula

The trouble with staying at the ◖ **Sebasco Harbor Resort** (Rte. 217, Sebasco Estates, 207/389-1161 or 800/225-3819, www.sebasco .com), a self-contained resort on 575 waterfront acres, is that between the beautiful setting and the bountiful offerings, you might not set foot off the premises during your entire vacation. Situated at the mouth of the saltwater New Meadows River, 12 miles south of Bath, Sebasco has attracted families who return year after year since 1930, when it opened. Sebasco changed hands in 1997, and owner Bob Smith has brought the resort up to 21st-century standards while keeping its old-style rusticity.

You'll have to look far and wide to find a better family resort. Scattered around the well-tended property are the main lodge and a variety of cottages (1–6 bedrooms; the two-bedroom units with a shared living room are a great choice for families), a main lodge, a four-story cupola-topped lighthouse building edging the harbor, and two new suites buildings, Harbor Village and the waterfront Fairwinds Spa, with more contemporary amenities. All have private baths, phones, and cable TV; many have water views; some have refrigerators or kitchenettes. Rates begin around $200; kids under age 11 are free. Rates that include breakfast and dinner are an additional $48 pp (no charge for children under age 11 when dining with an adult and from the kids menu). Weekly summer events include a Sunday-evening reception and grand buffet, lobster bakes, family barbecues, bingo, live entertainment, and the Camp Merrit children's program ($12 per day, includes lunch). Recreational facilities include two all-weather tennis courts, a nine-hole championship golf course and a three-hole regulation course for beginners and families, the state's largest outdoor saltwater pool, boat tours aboard the *Ruth,* sailing trips, sea kayak excursions, mountain-bike tours, candlepin bowling, horseshoes, a playground, a well-equipped fitness center, and as much or as little organized activity as you want.

Right on the beach between Popham Beach State Park and Fort Popham is the **Popham Beach Bed and Breakfast** (4 Ocean View Lane, Popham Beach, Phippsburg, 207/389-2409, www.pophambeachbandb.com, year-round, $185–235 d), a unique hostelry in a restored 1883 Coast Guard station. Innkeeper Peggy Johannessen takes guests to the rooftop lookout tower and shares the building's history as a maritime lifesaving center. Inside are three rooms and a suite, two with gas fireplaces. A full breakfast is served in the dining room each morning, and guests can hang out in the large oceanfront living room.

Magnificent gardens surround **Edgewater Farm Bed and Breakfast** (71 Small Point Rd./Rte. 216, Sebasco Estates, 207/389-1322

© HILARY NANGLE

Once a life-saving station, the Popham Beach Bed and Breakfast is ideal for those who want to work off hearty breakfasts with a stroll on the sand.

or 877/389-1322, www.ewfbb.com, $130–225), Carol and Bill Emerson's comfy, unfussy 19th-century farmhouse, just south of the turn-off to Popham Beach and close to the access for Morse Mountain. Families usually choose the carriage house, where kids can play in the huge recreation room. A brunch-size breakfast served in the many-windowed solarium benefits from lots of organic produce grown on the four-acre grounds. (The Emersons always plant extra to donate to the Bath food pantry each summer.) And then there's the four-foot-deep indoor lap pool, a hot tub outside on the deck, and the Benedictine labyrinth Bill created in a wooded grove. English, Spanish, a bit of French, and German are all spoken. Pets are welcome for $25.

Rock Gardens Inn (Rte. 218, Sebasco Estates, Phippsburg, 207/389-1339, www.rockgardensinn.com, from $140 pp d) hosts numerous artists' workshops, and no wonder: It sits on its own peninsula, and the pretty grounds are landscaped with wild and cultivated flowers. Guests stay in one of three inn rooms or 10 cottages and have use of an outdoor heated pool and sea kayaks. Rates include breakfast and dinner—and the weekly lobster cookout. After the minimum rate is reached per cottage, kids cost $55–115, depending on their age. Sebasco Harbor Resort is just steps away, and guests have access to its facilities as well. Ask about all-inclusive art retreats.

Step back in history at **The 1774 Inn** (44 Parker Head Rd., Phippsburg Center, 207/389-1774, www.1774inn.com, $140–205), a magnificently restored four-square Georgian colonial property, listed on the National Register of Historic Places, with an 1870 ell and barn. Many colonial details have been preserved, including shutters with peepholes and strong bars to defend against attack, paneled wainscoting, ceiling moldings, fluted columns, and wide pine floors. Most of the eight guest rooms (all but two with private baths) have views of the Kennebec River. All are spacious and furnished with antiques. Outside, the inn's four acres roll down to the river.

Georgetown Peninsula

It'll be hard to tear yourself away from the scenery and sanctuary at **The Mooring Bed and Breakfast** (132 Seguinland Rd., Georgetown, 207/371-2790 or 866/828-7348, www.themooringb-b.com, $150–200), the original home of Walter Reid, who donated Reid State Park to the state. His great-granddaughter Penny Barabe and her husband, Paul, have beautifully restored the house, situated on lovely oceanfront grounds with island-studded views. Each guest room has a water view and air-conditioning. There's plenty of room to spread out, including the appropriately named Spanish room. A full breakfast is served.

Even more secluded is **Coveside Bed & Breakfast** (6 Gott's Cove Lane, Georgetown, 207/371-2807 or 800/232-5490, www.covesidebandb.com, $135–200), a dreamy spot on five oceanfront acres near Five Islands. Tom and Carolyn Church have four guest rooms in the main house and three in the adjacent cottage. Some rooms have fireplaces; one has a whirlpool tub. Carolyn's pastry-chef skills are evident at breakfast. Wi-Fi is available, and a separate building has a TV and exercise room. Guests have use of bicycles and a canoe.

Campgrounds

Plan to book a site in January if you want a waterfront campsite in midsummer at the Phippsburg Peninsula's **Hermit Island Campground** (6 Hermit Island Rd., Phippsburg, 207/443-2101, www.hermitisland.com, no credit cards). With 275 campsites (no vehicles larger than pickup campers; no hookups) spread over a 255-acre causeway-linked island, this is oceanfront camping at its best. The well-managed operation has a store, a snack bar, a seasonal post office, boat rentals, boat excursions, trails, and seven private beaches. The hub of activity (and registration) is the Kelp Shed, next to the campsite entrance. Open and wooded sites run $35–57 (2 adults and 2 kids) mid-June–Labor Day, $33 early and late in the season. Reservations

for a week's stay or longer and for Memorial Day and Labor Day weekends can be made by mail beginning in early January and by phone in early February (call for the exact date). Reservations for stays of less than one week are accepted after March 1. It's open mid-May–Columbus Day, but full operation is really June–Labor Day. The campground is at the tip of the Phippsburg Peninsula. Pets are not allowed.

FOOD

Hours noted are for peak season but are subject to change. It's wise to call ahead, especially when traveling in the off-season.

Local Flavors

In Waterfront Park on Commercial Street, the **Bath Farmers Market** operates 8:30 A.M.–noon every Saturday May–October, featuring crafts, plants, condiments, baked goods, and cheeses in addition to seasonal produce.

For breakfast, lunch, or sweets, drop into the **Starlight Café** (15 Lambard St., 207/443-3005, 7 A.M.–2 P.M. Mon.–Fri.), a too-cute and too-tiny daylight-basement space across a side street from the Customs House. It's bright and cheerful, and the food is fab.

A wonderful multifaceted find is Susan Verrier's **North Creek Farm** (24 Sebasco Rd., Phippsburg, 207/389-1341, 9 A.M.–6:30 P.M. daily, lunch 11:30 A.M.–3:30 P.M. daily), an 1850s saltwater farm with fabulous organic gardens, including ornamental display gardens and lots of rugosa roses (a specialty—Susan has written two books on them). Visitors can meander down by a waterfall, creek, and salt marsh. Inside the barn is a small store stocked with garden and gourmet goodies and a small café, where Susan makes delicious soups and sandwiches to order. There are tables indoors, but there also are chairs and tables scattered in the gardens.

On the Georgetown Peninsula, **Five Islands Farm** (1375 Rte. 127, Five Islands, 297/371-9383, www.fiveislandsfarm.com) is a fine stop for picnic fixings, with an excellent assortment of Maine cheeses along with breads, meats, chips, salsa, and even wine.

Patty Mains retired early from Bath Iron Works to pursue her passion: chocolate. Her handcrafted chocolates are made from the best ingredients and from traditional recipes—try the Needhams, made with mashed potatoes. While chocolates are the centerpiece at **MainSweets** (Rte. 127, Georgetown, 207/371-2806), she also sells home-baked breads, cookies, brownies, fudge, and other sweet treats.

Some argue the state's best thin-crust pizza (and praiseworthy garlic knots) comes from the ovens at **The Cabin** (552 Washington St., Bath, 207/443-6224, 10 A.M.–10 P.M. Sun.–Thurs., 10 A.M.–11 P.M. Fri.–Sat., no credit cards), a somewhat rough-and-tumble working-class joint that's been a local fave since 1973. It's across from Bath Iron Works. Avoid it during BIW shift changes (3–5 P.M. Mon.–Fri.).

Barbecue
Finger-licking Memphis-style barbecue, along with other Southern specialties, is served in big quantities at **Beale Street Barbeque and Grill** (215 Water St., Bath, 207/442-9514, 11 A.M.–9 P.M. Sun.–Thurs., 11 A.M.–10 P.M. Fri.–Sat., $8–25). Everything's made on the premises. Find it next to the municipal parking lot.

Casual Dining
Kate and Andy Winglass operate **Mae's Café and Bakery** (160 Centre St. at High St., Bath, 207/442-8577, www.maescafeandbakery.com, 8 A.M.–3 P.M. daily), a longtime local favorite bakery and café with seating indoors and on a front deck. It's *the* place to go for brunch (reservations are essential on weekends). Most choices are in the $9–13 range. Rotating art shows enliven the open and airy dining rooms.

The cool and contemporary Danish decor matches the food at **Solo Bistro** (128 Front St., Bath, 207/443-3373, www.solobistro.com, from 5 P.M. daily, $13–28), a sophisticated storefront restaurant downtown where the choices might range from a bistro burger to pan-seared wild salmon. A nightly three-course fixed-price menu is usually around $23. The wine bar features jazz on Friday nights.

Dining With a View
All the places listed here are seasonal.

Even if you're not staying at **Sebasco Harbor Resort** (Rte. 217, Sebasco Estates, 207/389-1161 or 800/225-3819, www.sebasco.com), you can dine in either of its two waterfront restaurants, both with gasp-producing sunset views. Binoculars hang by windows in the **Pilot House** (5:30–9 P.M. Mon.–Sat., dinner entrées $17–27), the more formal of the two, so diners can get a better view of the boats or birds happening by. Below it is the casual **Ledges Pub** (11:30 A.M.–2 P.M. and 5–10 P.M. daily, $6–18), with indoor and outdoor seating and a menu varying from kid-friendly burgers and fried foods to salmon salad.

Gaze at seals playing in the Kennebec River, Fort Popham, and out to open ocean from **Spinney's Restaurant** (987 Rte. 209, Popham Beach, 207/389-2052, www.spinneysrestaurant.com, 8 A.M.–8:30 P.M. daily, entrées $10–30, sandwiches and hot dogs less). Food varies in quality from year to year. (Best advice: Keep it simple). You can't beat the view, and you can keep it budget-friendly by coming for breakfast.

Lobster in the Rough
PHIPPSBURG PENINSULA
The rustic buoy-draped **Lobster House** (395 Small Point Rd./Rte. 216, Small Point, 207/389-1596 or 207/389-2178, www.thelobsterhouse.net, 11:30 A.M.–9 P.M. Tues.–Sun. late May–early Sept.) overlooks a scenic tidal cove; the view is best when the tide is in. No surprise that lobster and seafood are featured, but sandwiches, soups, salads, pizza, and a few grilled items make the menu wallet-friendly for anyone.

GEORGETOWN PENINSULA
Just over a mile beyond the turnoff to Reid State Park, you'll reach the end of Route 127 at Five Islands. Here you'll find **Five Islands Lobster Company** (1447 Five Islands Rd., Five Islands, Georgetown, 207/371-2990, www.fiveislandslobster.com,

© HILARY NANGLE

Dreamy views of a boat-filled harbor await diners at Five Islands Lobster Company in Georgetown.

11:30 A.M.–8 P.M. daily mid-May–mid-Oct.), known for its slogan: "Eat on the dock with the fishermen, but best avoid the table by the bait-shack door." Here you can pig out on lobster rolls, better-than-usual onion rings, crab cakes, and if you must, burgers and hot dogs. It even takes credit cards, a rarity among lobster wharves. Dress down, BYOB, and enjoy the end-of-the-road ambience of this idyllic spot.

Destination Dining

The building alone is worth a visit to chef Michael Gagne's **Robinhood Free Meetinghouse** (210 Robinhood Rd., Georgetown, 207/371-2188, www.robin-hood-meetinghouse.com, 5:30–9 P.M. daily in peak season, entrées $24–28), in a beautifully restored 1855 building on the Georgetown Peninsula. Most tables are on the main floor; overflow diners go to the second floor, where many of the pews remain. The enormous (more than two dozen entrées and a dozen appetizers)

high-quality menu makes it even more enticing. If you're a chocoholic, save room for Gagne's swoon-worthy signature dessert: Obsession in Three Chocolates with chocolate sauce. Portions are large, and reservations are essential. In the off-season, ask about special "theme" nights. Gagne sells his famed 72-layer hand-cut cream cheese biscuits frozen, so take a half dozen or so home to enjoy with your leftovers. The restaurant is signed off Route 127. Open year-round.

INFORMATION AND SERVICES
Visitor Information

Information is available from the **Southern Midcoast Chamber of Commerce** (2 Main St., Topsham, 877/725-8797, www.mid-coastmaine.com). A visitors center is located in Bath's renovated train station (restrooms available), adjacent to the Bath Iron Works main yard. It's open year-round with brochure racks, and staffed by volunteers May–October.

Request copies of the *City of Bath Downtown Map and Guide* and the *Guide to Southern Midcoast Maine.*

Main Street Bath (4 Centre St., Bath, 207/442-7291, www.visitbath.com) produces a guide and has an informative website. More information is available on the city's website (www.cityofbath.com).

Check out **Patten Free Library** (33 Summer St., Bath, 207/443-5141, www.patten.lib.me.us).

Public Restrooms

Public restrooms are at Bath City Hall (55 Front St.), Patten Free Library (33 Summer St.), Sagadahoc County Courthouse (752 High St.), and in summer only at Waterfront Park (Commercial St.).

GETTING AROUND

The **Bath Trolley** circulates through the area, with each one-way trip costing $1. For a schedule, visit City Hall.

Wiscasset Area

Billing itself as "The Prettiest Village in Maine," Wiscasset works hard to live up to its slogan, with quaint street signs, well-maintained homes, and an air of attentive elegance.

Wiscasset ("meeting place of three rivers"), incorporated as part of Pownalborough in 1760, has had its current name since 1802. In the late 18th century it became the shire town of Lincoln County and the largest seaport north of Boston. Countless tall-masted ships sailed the 12 miles up the Sheepscot River to tie up here, and shipyards flourished, turning out vessels for domestic and foreign trade. The 1807 Embargo Act and the War of 1812 delivered a one-two punch that shut down trade and temporarily squelched the town's aspirations, but Wiscasset yards soon were back at it, producing vessels for the pre–Civil War clipper-ship era—only to face a more lasting decline with the arrival of the railroads and the onset of the industrial revolution.

The Davey Bridge, built in 1983, is the most recent span over the Sheepscot. The earliest, finished in 1847, was a toll bridge that charged a horse and wagon $0.15 to cross, pedestrians $0.03 each, and pigs $0.01 apiece. Before that, ferries carried passengers, animals, and vehicles between Wiscasset and Edgecomb's Davis Island (then named Folly Island).

Wiscasset is notorious for midsummer gridlock. Especially on weekends, traffic backs up on Route 1 for miles in both directions—to the frustration of drivers, passengers, and Wiscasset merchants. The state Department of Transportation has tested traffic medians, stoplights, and other devices, but nothing has solved the problem. A bypass has been under discussion for years, but not-in-my-backyard opposition to every route has halted progress. (When you stop in town, try to park pointed in the direction you're going; it's impossible to make turns across oncoming traffic.)

SIGHTS

In 1973 a large chunk of downtown Wiscasset was added to the National Register of Historic Places, and a walking tour is the best way to appreciate the Federal, Classical Revival, and even prerevolutionary homes and commercial buildings in the Historic District. Listed here are a few of the prime examples. If you do nothing else, be sure to swing by the homes on High Street. You can download a map of historical sights from the town's website (www.wiscasset.org).

Castle Tucker

Once known as the Lee-Tucker House, Castle Tucker (Lee St. and High St., Wiscasset, 207/882-7169, www.historicnewengland.org, tours on the hour 11 A.M.–4 P.M. Wed.–Sun. June–mid Oct., $5) is a must-see. Built in 1807 by Judge Silas Lee and bought by sea captain

MID-COAST REGION

© HILARY NANGLE

Wiscasset's Castle Tucker is a Victorian-era architectural masterpiece that's open for tours during the summer months.

Richard Tucker in 1858, the imposing mansion has Victorian wallpaper and furnishings, Palladian windows, an amazing elliptical staircase, and a dramatic view over the Sheepscot River. In 1997, Jane Tucker, Richard's granddaughter, magnanimously deeded the house to Historic New England.

Nickels-Sortwell House

Also owned by Historic New England, the three-story Nickels-Sortwell House (121 Main St., Wiscasset, 207/882-6218, www .historicnewengland.org, tours on the hour 11 A.M.–4 P.M. Fri.–Sun. June–mid Oct., $5) looms over Route 1, yet it's so close to the road that many motorists miss it. Don't make the same mistake. Sea captain William Nickels commissioned the mansion in 1807 but died soon after its completion. For 70 or so years it was the Belle Haven Hotel before Alvin and Frances Sortwell's meticulous Colonial Revival restoration in the early 20th century.

Lincoln County Jail and Museum

Wiscasset's Old Jail (133 Federal St., Wiscasset, 207/882-6817, 10 A.M.–4 P.M. Tues.–Sat., noon–4 P.M. Sun. July–Aug., Sat.–Sun. only June and Sept., $4 adults, $2 ages 7–17), completed in 1811, was the first prison in the District of Maine (then part of Massachusetts). Amazingly, it remained a jail—mostly for short-timers—until 1953. Two years after that the Lincoln County Historical Association took over, so each summer you can check out the 40-inch-thick granite walls, floors, and ceilings; the 12 tiny cells; and historic graffiti penned by the prisoners. Attached to the prison is the 1837 jailer's house, now the Lincoln County Museum, containing antique tools, the original kitchen, and various temporary exhibits. A Victorian gazebo overlooking the Sheepscot River is a great spot for a picnic. From Main Street (Rte. 1) in downtown Wiscasset, take Federal Street (Rte. 218) 1.2 miles.

RURAL RAMBLINGS

Surrounding Wiscasset are the lovely rural inland communities of Dresden, Sheepscot, and Alna, definitely worth a detour.

Begin in Dresden at the 1761 **Pownalborough Court House** (River Rd./Rte. 128, Dresden, 207/882-6817, 10 A.M.-4 P.M. Tues.-Sat. July-Aug., 10 A.M.-4 P.M. Sat. and noon 10-4 P.M. Sun. June and Sept., $4 adults, $2 ages 7-17), a pre-revolutionary riverfront courthouse listed on the National Register of Historic Places. President John Adams once handled a trial here — in a mid-18th-century frontier community (named Pownalborough) established by French and German settlers. During the 30-minute tour of the three-story courthouse, guides delight in pointing out the restored beams, paneling, and fireplaces as well as the on-site tavern that catered to judges, lawyers, and travelers. Walk a few hundred feet south and you'll find a cemetery with Revolution-era graves. Along the river is a nature trail developed by local Eagle Scouts. From Route 1 in Wiscasset, take Route 27 about nine miles north to the junction with Route 128. Turn left (south) and go 2.5 miles to the courthouse sign. The courthouse is also an easy drive from Bath.

Return to Wiscasset and follow Route 218 north for about eight miles to Head Tide Village, an eminently picturesque hamlet at the farthest reach of the Sheepscot River tides. From the late 18th century to the early 20th, Head Tide (now part of the town of Alna) was a thriving mill town, a source of hydropower for the textile and lumber industries. All that is long gone, but hints of that era come from the handful of well-maintained 18th- and 19th-century homes in the village center.

Up the hill, the stunning 1838 **Head Tide Church,** another fine example of local prosperity, is usually open 2-4 P.M. Saturday in July-August. Volunteer tour guides point out the original pulpit, a trompe l'oeil window, a kerosene chandelier, and walls lined with historic Alna photographs.

Head Tide's most famous citizen was the poet **Edwin Arlington Robinson,** born here in 1869. His family home, at the bend in Route 194 and marked by a plaque, is not open to the public. Perhaps his Maine roots inspired these lines in his poem "New England":

> Here where the wind is always north-north-east
> And children learn to walk on frozen toes.

Just upriver from the bend in the road is a favorite swimming hole, a millpond where you can join the locals on a hot summer day. Not much else goes on here, and there are no restaurants or lodgings, so Head Tide can't be termed a destination, but it's a village frozen in time — and an unbeatable opportunity for history buffs and shutterbugs.

Also historic but a bit more lively and fun for kids is the **Wiscasset, Waterville, and Farmington Railway** (97 Cross Rd., off Rte. 218, Sheepscot, 207/882-4193, www.wwfry.org, 9 A.M.-5 P.M. Sat. year-round, 9 A.M.-5 P.M. Sun. late May-mid-Oct.), a museum commemorating a two-foot-gauge common carrier railroad that operated in the early part of the 20th century from Wiscasset in the south to Albion and Winslow in the north. On the grounds are a museum in the old station (free) and train rides ($6 adults, $4 children 4-12) along the mainline track running north from Cross Road on the original roadbed. Trains depart Sheepscot hourly 10 A.M.-4 P.M. Saturday-Sunday. From Route 1 in Wiscasset, take Route 218 north 4.7 miles to a four-way intersection, and go left on Cross Road to the museum.

© HILARY NANGLE

Danilo Konvalinka shares his treasures at the Musical Wonder House in Wiscasset.

Musical Wonder House

The treasures in the Musical Wonder House (18 High St., Wiscasset, 207/882-7163, www .musicalwonderhouse.com), an 1852 sea captain's mansion, are indeed astonishing, and eccentric Austrian-born museum founder Danilo Konvalinka delights in sharing them—for a price. The best way to appreciate the collection of hundreds of 19th-century European music boxes, player pianos, and musical rarities is to take a guided tour (available 10 A.M.–5 P.M. Mon.–Sat., noon–5 P.M. Sun. late May–Oct. or by appointment, $10–40), which includes up to two-dozen player-piano and music-box demonstrations.

Fort Edgecomb

Built in 1808 to protect the Sheepscot River port of Wiscasset, the Fort Edgecomb State Historic Site (Eddy Rd., Edgecomb, 207/882-7777, 9 A.M.–5 P.M. daily late May–early Sept., $3 nonresident adults, $2 Maine resident adults, $1 ages 5–11) occupies a splendid three-acre riverfront spread ideal for picnicking and fishing

(no swimming). Many summer weekends, the encampments on the grounds of the octagonal blockhouse make history come alive with Revolutionary reenactments, period dress, craft demonstrations, and garrison drills. It's off Route 1; take Eddy Road just north of Wiscasset Bridge and go 0.5 miles to Fort Road.

FESTIVALS AND EVENTS

Wiscasset's daylong **Annual Strawberry Festival and Country Fair** (St. Philip's Episcopal Church, Hodge St., 207/882-7184) celebrates with tons of strawberries along with crafts and an auction on the last Saturday in June. The church is also the site of **Monday-night fish-chowder suppers,** mid-July–mid-August. Reservations are advised (207/882-7184) for these very popular 5:30 P.M. suppers.

A summer highlight at Watershed Center for the Ceramic Arts is its annual **Salad Days,** a fund-raising event held on a Saturday in July. For a $30 donation, you choose a handmade pottery plate, fill it from a piled-high buffet of fruit and veggie salads, and are part of an old-fashioned picnic social—and you even get to keep the plate. Afterward, there's plenty of time to explore the center's 32 acres. Call ahead to confirm the date (207/882-6075, www.watershedceramics.org).

SHOPPING

The oldest commercial building in town is **Wiscasset Hardware** (Water St., Wiscasset, 207/882-6622), built in 1797 as a ship chandlery on the east side of Water Street. These days the store sells more gifty items than hardware and dishes out homemade ice cream downstairs.

Natural beauty products and bamboo clothing fill Kelley Belanger's fun shop, **In the Clover** (85A Main St., Wiscasset, 207/882-9435, www.inthecloverbeauty.com).

Antiques and Art

It's certainly fitting that a town filled end-to-end with antique homes should have more than two dozen solo and group antiques shops.

Right downtown, **Blythe House Antiques** (161 Main St., Wiscasset, 207/882-1280) has multiple dealers exhibiting in room settings. French and English antiques are the specialty at **Daybreak Manor** (106 Rte. 1, Wiscasset, 207/882-9786). Both fine art and antiques are sold at **French and Vandyke** (8 Federal St., Wiscasset, 207/882-8302).

European and American 19th- and 20th-century painters are the broad focus at **Wiscasset Bay Gallery** (67 Main St./Rte. 1, Wiscasset, 207/882-7682 or 888/622-9445, www.wiscassetbaygallery.com), which schedules high-quality rotating shows throughout the season.

In the handsome open spaces of an early-19th-century brick schoolhouse, the **Maine Art Gallery** (Warren St., Wiscasset, 207/882-7511, www.maineartgallery.org) was founded in 1954 as a nonprofit organization to showcase contemporary Maine artists.

Two miles south of town is **Avalon Antiques Market** (563 Rte. 1, Wiscasset, 207/882-4239, www.avalonantiquesmarket.com), a huge red barn of a place filled with more than 100 dealers showing on three floors.

Folk-art fans must visit Lois and David Kwantz's **Butterstamp Workshop** (55 Middle St., Wiscasset, 207/882-7825), which creates and sells designs copied from antique molds. Sometimes you can watch the workshop operation, which produces butter and cookie molds, beeswax ornaments, and even magnets.

ACCOMMODATIONS

Rates listed are for peak season.

Bed-and-Breakfasts

Named after a famous Maine clipper ship, Paul and Melanie Harris's **Snow Squall Inn** (5 Bradford Rd. at Rte. 1, Wiscasset, 207/882-6892 or 800/775-7245, www.snowsquallinn.com, $100–170) is a renovated mid-19th-century house with four lovely guest rooms and three family suites, all with phones, air-conditioning, and Wi-Fi, and two with fireplaces. Ask Melanie, a licensed massage therapist and a *vinyasa* yoga instructor, about scheduling a massage or taking a class. It's open all year, but only by reservation November–April.

Then there's a major getaway—**The Squire Tarbox Inn** (1181 Main Rd./Rte. 144, Westport Island, 207/882-7693 or 800/818-0626, www.squiretarboxinn.com, mid-Apr.–Dec., $139–199), an elegantly casual bed-and-breakfast and inn that doubles as a working organic farm. Accomplished Swiss chef-owner Mario De Pietro and his wife, Roni, have continued the inn's reputation for dining excellence. Eleven lovely rooms, some with fireplaces, are divided between the late-18th-century main house and the early-19th-century carriage house; those in the main house are more formal. Rates include breakfast, and the dining room is open to nonguests by reservation for dinner. Also on the property are walking paths, a rowboat, mountain bikes, a working pottery, and a working farm, with organic vegetable gardens, chickens, and goats. A few guest rooms are pet friendly ($15 per night). From downtown Wiscasset, head southwest four miles on Route 1 to Route 144. Turn left and go about 8.5 scenic miles to the inn.

MID-COAST REGION

Motels

Fairly close to Route 1 but buffered a bit by century-old hemlocks, the **Wiscasset Motor Lodge** (Rte. 1, Wiscasset, 207/882-7137 or 800/732-8168, www.wiscassetmotorlodge .com, $72–108) is a comfortable, well-maintained motel. Guest rooms have phones, TVs, and air-conditioning, and a light breakfast is included in summer. Ask for a room in the back building if you're sensitive to noise.

FOOD

Hours noted are for peak season but are subject to change. It's wise to call ahead, especially when traveling in the off-season.

Across Federal Street from the Nickels-Sortwell House in downtown Wiscasset is the lovely **Sunken Garden,** an almost-unnoticed pocket park created around the cellar hole of a long-gone inn. It's a fine place for a picnic.

Local Flavors

Let's start with the obvious: **Red's Eats** (Main St. and Water St., Wiscasset, 207/882-6128, 11 A.M.–11 P.M. Mon.–Sat., noon–6 P.M. Sun., early May–mid-Oct.). This simple takeout stand has garnered national attention through the decades for its lobster rolls stuffed with the meat from a whole lobster. It's easy to spot because of the line. Expect to wait, perhaps for an hour or more. Is it worth it? I don't think so, but others rave about the cold lobster rolls, the fried fish, the hot dogs, and the wraps. If you're planning on one of Red's lobster rolls, ask someone who has just bought one the price before you get in line and make sure you have enough cash (no credit cards). Of course, you can skip the wait with a quick walk across Main Street to Town Wharf, where **Sprague Lobster** (22 Main St., Wiscasset, 207/882-2306) has set up a competing stand. Many locals prefer Sprague's. Lines are rare, and the lobster rolls also contain the meat from an entire crustacean.

Back up the street, across a side road from the post office, is **Treat's** (80 Main St., Wiscasset, 207/882-6192, www.treatsofmaine .com, 10 A.M.–6 P.M. Mon.–Sat., noon–5 P.M. Sun.), a superb source of gourmet picnic fixings: sandwiches, soups, wine, cheese, condiments, and artisanal breads.

Family Favorites

Two miles southwest of downtown Wiscasset, **The Sea Basket Restaurant** (303 Rte. 1, Wiscasset, 207/882-6581, www.seabasket.com, 11 A.M.–8 P.M. Wed.–Mon. Mar.–Dec., $4–22) has been serving hearty bowls of lobster stew and good-size baskets of eminently fresh seafood since 1981. There's always a crowd—locals eat here too—so expect to wait. The fried fish is almost healthful, thanks to convection-style frying using trans fat–free oil.

In a high-visibility location across Route 1 from Red's Eats, **Sarah's Cafe** (Main St./Rte. 1 and Water St., Wiscasset, 207/882-7504, www.sarahscafe.com, 11 A.M.–8 P.M. daily) is the home of huge "whaleboat" and "dory" sandwiches, homemade soups, pizza, vegetarian specials, and an ice cream fountain. Lobster meat shows up in salads, burritos, quesadillas, wraps, croissants, and more. The deck has front-row seats on the Sheepscot River. Food is reliably mundane; the service can be sluggish and indifferent, but crayons keep kids busy.

Casual Dining

Overlooking the Sheepscot River just two blocks off Route 1 is **Le Garage** (15 Water St., Wiscasset, 207/882-5409, www.legarageres-taurant.com, 11 A.M.–8:30 P.M. daily summer, 11 A.M.–8:30 P.M. Tues.–Sun. off-season, closed Jan., entrées $10–27), an enduringly popular spot serving traditional fare. The decor and the menu (and the clientele) are firmly rooted in the 1970s. Finnan haddie (smoked haddock) is a specialty. Light suppers are thrifty choices, and reservations are wise on weekends.

Well off the beaten path on an island connected to the mainland by a bridge is **◖ The Squire Tarbox Inn** (1181 Main Rd./Rte. 144, Westport Island, 207/882-7693 or 800/818-0626, www.squiretarboxinn.com, dinner Wed.–Mon. mid-June–mid-Oct., Thurs.–Sat. mid-Apr.–mid-June and mid-Oct.–Dec., entrées $25–30), a working organic farm where Swiss chef Mario De Pietro serves memorable meals.

Entrées, such as rack of lamb, Swiss-style veal, and a fish of the day, are served either on the porch or in an intimate dining room. Off-season, Thursday nights are Swiss night, with appropriate cuisine served. Ask about cooking classes.

INFORMATION AND SERVICES
Information
The best place to pick up Wiscasset info is the display rack at Big Al's Super Values, on Route 1, three miles southwest of downtown. Once you get into town, stop at Wiscasset Hardware (Water St.) for a free walking map of the downtown area.

Check out **Wiscasset Public Library** (21 High St., Wiscasset, 207/882-7161, www.wiscasset.lib.me.us).

Public Restrooms
The Town Wharf, Water Street, and the Lincoln County Court House, on Route 1 next to the sharp curve as you come down the hill from the south, have public restrooms.

Boothbay Peninsula

East of Wiscasset, en route to Damariscotta, only a flurry of signs along Route 1 in Edgecomb hints at what's down the peninsula bisected by Route 27 and framed by the Sheepscot and Damariscotta Rivers. Drive southward down the Boothbay Peninsula Memorial Day–Labor Day and you'll find yourself in one of Maine's longest-running summer playgrounds.

The four peninsula towns of **Boothbay, Boothbay Harbor, East Boothbay,** and, connected by a bridge, **Southport Island** are a maze of islands and peninsulas. When Route 27 arrives at the water, having passed

© HILARY NANGLE

MID-COAST REGION

Boats of all types can be seen in Boothbay Harbor.

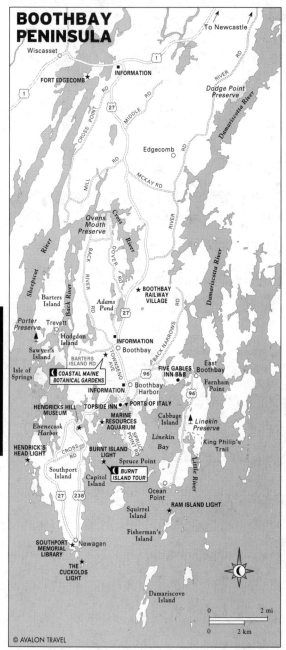

BOOTHBAY PENINSULA

Wiscasset

To Newcastle

INFORMATION

FORT EDGECOMB

Dodge Point Preserve

Edgecomb

Ovens Mouth Preserve

BOOTHBAY RAILWAY VILLAGE

Barters Island

Adams Pond

Porter Preserve

Trevett

Hodgdon Island

INFORMATION Boothbay

Sawyer's Island

BARTERS ISLAND RD

Isle of Springs

COASTAL MAINE BOTANICAL GARDENS

FIVE GABLES INN B&B

East Boothbay

INFORMATION

Boothbay Harbor

Farnham Point

HENDRICKS HILL MUSEUM

TOPSIDE INN

PORTS OF ITALY

MARINE RESOURCES AQUARIUM

Cabbage Island

Linekin Preserve

Ebenecook Harbor

Linekin Bay

King Philip's Trail

HENDRICK'S HEAD LIGHT

BURNT ISLAND LIGHT

Spruce Point

Southport Island

Capitol Island

BURNT ISLAND TOUR

Ocean Point

RAM ISLAND LIGHT

Squirrel Island

Fisherman's Island

SOUTHPORT MEMORIAL LIBRARY

Newagen

THE CUCKOLDS LIGHT

Damariscove Island

0   2 mi
0   2 km

© AVALON TRAVEL

through Boothbay Center, you're at Boothbay Harbor ("the Harbor"), scene of most of the action. The harbor itself is a boat fan's dream, loaded with working craft and pleasure yachts. Ashore are shops and galleries, restaurants and inns, and one-way streets, traffic congestion, and pedestrians everywhere. But don't despair; it's easy to escape the peak season crowds in one of the numerous parks and preserves, fine places for a hike or a picnic. Hop on an excursion boat to an offshore island, for a whale watch, or for an evening sail around the bay.

Try to save time for quieter spots: East Boothbay, Ocean Point, Southport Island, the Coastal Maine Botanical Gardens, or even just over the 1,000-foot-long footbridge stretching across one corner of the harbor. Cross the bridge and walk down Atlantic Avenue to the Fishermen's Memorial, a bronze fishing dory commemorating the loss of hardy souls who've earned a rugged living here by their wits and the sea. Across the street is Our Lady Queen of Peace Catholic Church, with shipwright-quality woodwork and its own fishing icon—a lobster trap next to the altar.

SIGHTS
Boothbay Railway Village

Boothbay Railway Village (Rte. 27, Boothbay, 207/633-4727, www.railwayvillage.org, 9:30 A.M.–5 P.M. daily early June–mid-Oct., $9 adults,

$5 ages 3–16) feels like a life-size train set. More than two dozen old and new buildings have been assembled here since the museum was founded in 1964, and a restored narrow-gauge steam train makes a 1.5-mile, 20-minute circuit throughout the day. You'll also find more than 50 antique cars and trucks. Train rides also operate on weekends from late May until daily opening in June and for a Halloween ride on the last weekend in October.

◖ Burnt Island Tour

Visit with a lighthouse keeper's family, climb the tower into the lantern room, and explore an island during a living- and natural-history program presented by the Maine Department of Marine Resources on Burnt Island (207/633-9580, www.maine.gov/dmr/education.htm, $22 adults, $12 under age 12). The tour is offered twice daily in July–August. Travel via excursion boat from 21st-century Boothbay Harbor to Burnt Island, circa 1950, where actors portray the family of lighthouse keeper Joseph Muise, who lived here 1936–1951. During the three-hour program, you'll spend time with the light keeper, his wife, and each of his children, learning about their lifestyles and views on island life. Historical documents, photographs, and lenses, from 1821 to the present, are displayed in the 45-foot covered walkway between the house and tower. You may climb the spiral stairway up to the lantern room and see how the lighthouse actually functions. On an easy hike, a naturalist explains the island's flora, fauna, and geology and recounts legends. During free time, you may hike other trails, listen to a program on present-day lobstering and Maine fisheries, go beachcombing, fish for mackerel off the dock, or just relax and enjoy it all.

Marine Resources Aquarium

A 20-foot touch tank, with slimy but pettable specimens, is a major kid magnet at the Marine Resources Aquarium (McKown Point Rd., West Boothbay Harbor, 207/633-9559, www.maine.gov/dmr/education.htm, 10 A.M.–5 P.M. daily late May–early Sept., 10 A.M.–5 P.M. Wed.–Sun. Sept., $5 adults, $3 seniors and ages 5–16), operated by the Maine Department of Marine Resources. Exhibits in the hexagonal aquarium include rare lobsters (oversize, albino, and blue) and other Gulf of Maine creatures; new residents arrive periodically. Self-guiding leaflets are available. Consider bringing a picnic—it's a great setting. At the height of summer, parking is limited, and it's a longish walk from downtown around the west side of the harbor, so plan to take the free local trolley-bus.

Southport Island

The nautical shortcut of Townsend Gut separates Boothbay Harbor from Southport Island. The island is ideal for a drive-about (or a pedal-about for experienced cyclists), following Route 27 south to the island's tip, then returning north on Route 238. En route are plentiful glimpses of island-salted ocean waters, especially if you explore some of the side roads. Here are a few other noteworthy sights.

A historic 1810 Cape-style building, carefully restored, is the 11-room home of the **Hendricks Hill Museum** (Rte. 27, West Southport, 207/633-4831, www.hendrickshill.org, 11 A.M.–3 P.M. Tues., Thurs., and Sat. July–Aug., donation), a community attic filled with all kinds of workaday tools and utensils and fascinating maritime memorabilia. The museum is about two miles south of the Southport Island bridge, on the right, in the center of West Southport.

From the Southport Village General Store, where you can pick up sandwiches for a picnic, decent lobster rolls, and baked goodies, among other treats, it's just a hop down Beach Road to **Hendricks Head,** with a nice sand beach and lighthouse views.

At the island's tip is the **Southport Memorial Library** (207/633-2741, 9 A.M.–4 P.M. and 7–9 P.M. Tues. and Thurs., 9 A.M.–4 P.M. Sat.). Displayed inside is a huge collection of mounted butterflies.

MID-COAST REGION

© HILARY NANGLE

Southport Island, near Hendrick's Head

ENTERTAINMENT

The renovated 1894 **Opera House** (86 Townsend Ave., Boothbay Harbor, 207/633-6855, www.boothbayoperahouse.org) hosts concerts, lectures, dramas, and special events. An upstairs bar, in the former Knights of Pythias Hall, is open to adults before performances and at intermission, and often for special events.

The **Boothbay Playhouse** (275 Rte. 27, Boothbay, 207/633-3379, www.boothbayplayhouse.com, $19 adults, $17 under age 13) is a vibrant family-oriented community theater with talent that will amaze you.

The **Lincoln Arts Festival** (207/633-3913, www.lincolnartsfestival.org) presents half a dozen or more concerts—classical, pops, choral, and jazz—and other arts-related events at various locations on the Boothbay Peninsula late June–late September.

Early July–August is a great time for music in Boothbay Harbor. Free **band concerts** at 8 P.M. Thursdays are performed on the Memorial Library lawn (4 Oak St.). Bring a blanket or folding chair.

Mid June–mid October there's live entertainment nightly at **McSeagulls** (14 Wharf St., Boothbay Harbor, 207/633-5900), which also serves decent food 11:30 A.M.–10 P.M. daily.

EVENTS

The **Fishermen's Festival** is a locally colorful early-season celebration, held the third weekend of April and beginning Friday with a Miss Shrimp Princess pageant. Saturday brings a lobster-crate race and afternoon contests such as trap hauling, scallop- and clam-shucking, fish-filleting, and net mending (plus a real steal—a lobster-eating contest you can enter for about $5). Saturday night, church suppers feature fish and shellfish, and on Sunday a chowder luncheon precedes the blessing of the fleet to ensure a successful summer season.

June is the month for **Windjammer Days,** two days of festivities centering on traditional windjammer schooners. Highlights are the Windjammer Parade, harbor-front concerts, plenty of food, and a fireworks extravaganza.

In early August the **Boat Builders Festival**

features shipyard and boat tours, food, and kids' activities.

Huge sailboats arrive in the harbor in early September for the **Shipyard Cup** (www.shipyardcup.com), with racing on two days. Hop aboard an excursion boat for a close-up view or drive out to Ocean Point.

RECREATION
Parks and Preserves
BOOTHBAY REGION LAND TRUST

Courtesy of the very active Boothbay Region Land Trust (137 Townsend Ave., Boothbay Harbor, 207/633-4818, www.bbrlt.org), more than 1,700 acres, including six islands, with more than 30 miles of trails available, have been preserved for wildlife, residents, and visitors. Individual preserve maps as well as a general brochure-map with driving directions are available at the information centers or at the trust office. Kiosks at the trailheads hold preserve maps. The trust also offers a free series of summertime guided walks and paddles in the various preserves along with talks. A free guide, available at local businesses and info centers, provides details and access points. Here's just a sampling of the possibilities.

Most popular is the **Porter Preserve,** a 19-acre property bordering the Sheepscot River. Follow the moderately easy 0.86-mile loop trail and be rewarded with spectacular views, especially at sunset. You might even spy some seals lolling in the ledges at low tide. To get there, take Route 27 south to the monument in Boothbay Center. Bear right on Cory Lane and go 0.3 miles, bearing right again on Barters Island Road. Follow it 12.2 miles (perhaps stopping at the Barters Island General Store for lobster rolls or subs to go), and then go left on Kimballtown Road. Go 0.5 miles and turn left at the fork onto Porter Point Road. Park in the small lot just beyond the cemetery.

The 146-acre **Ovens Mouth Preserve** has almost five miles of trails on two peninsulas linked by a 93-foot bridge (wear insect repellent). The 1.6-mile trail on the east peninsula is much easier than the 3.7 miles of trails on the west peninsula. To get there, from the

A pedestrian footbridge makes it easy to pass from one side of Boothbay Harbor to the other.

© HILARY NANGLE

MID-COAST REGION

DAMARISCOVE ISLAND

Summering Wabanakis knew it as Aquahega, but Damerill's Cove was the first European name attributed to the secure, fjord-like harbor at the southern tip of 210-acre Damariscove Island in 1614, when Captain John Smith of the Jamestown Colony explored the neighborhood. By 1622, Damerill's Cove fishermen were sharing their considerable codfish catch with starving Plimoth Plantation colonists desperate for food. Fishing and farming sustained resident Damariscovers during their up-and-down history, and archaeologists have found rich deposits for tracing the story of this early island settlement about seven miles south of Boothbay Harbor.

Rumors persist that the ghost of Captain Richard Pattishall, decapitated and tossed overboard by Indians in 1689, still roams the island, accompanied by the specter of his dog. The fog that often overhangs the bleak, almost-treeless low-slung island makes it easy to fall for the many ghost stories about Pattishall and other former residents. In summer, the island is awash with wildflowers, bayberries, raspberries, blackberries, and rugosa roses.

Since 2005, most of 1.7-mile-long Damariscove has been owned by **The Boothbay Region Land Trust** (1 Oak St., 2nd Fl., Boothbay Harbor, 207/633-4818, www.bbrlt.org). Day-use visitors are welcome on the island anytime, but the northern section (called Wood End) is to protect the state's largest nesting colony of eiders – nearly 700 nests. Damariscove Island became a National Historic Landmark in 1978. Dogs are not allowed.

Access to the island is most convenient if you have your own boat. Enter the narrow cove at the southern end of the island. You can disembark at the dock on the west side of the harbor, but don't tie-up here or at the adjacent stone pier. Two guest moorings and two courtesy dinghies are available. Summertime caretakers live in the small cabin above the dock, where a trail map is available. Stay on the trail (watch out for poison ivy) or on the shore and away from any abandoned structures; the former Coast Guard station is privately owned.

monument in Boothbay Center, travel 1.7 miles north and then go left on Adams Pond Road. Bear right at the fork and then continue 2.2 miles. To get to the east peninsula, bear right at the junction onto the Dover Road Extension. Proceed to the end of the tarred road to the parking lot on the left. To get to the west peninsula, bear left at the junction and continue 0.15 miles to the parking area on the right.

In East Boothbay, on the way to Ocean Point, is the 94.6-acre **Linekin Preserve,** stretching from Route 96 to the Damariscotta River. The 2.3-mile white-blazed River Loop (best done clockwise) takes in an old sawmill site, a beaver dam, and great riverfront views. You'll meet a couple of moderately steep sections on the eastern side, near the river, but otherwise it's relatively easy. To get there, take Route 96 for 3.8 miles and look for the parking area and trailhead on the left.

KNICKERCANE ISLAND

This gem is ideal for a picnic, perhaps with a lobster roll from the Trevett Country Store. The island is connected via a bridge, making it a pleasant place to stroll or, if you're brave, swim. Also here is an honest-to-God lobster pound (no, not the kind that serves the tasty crustaceans, but rather the impoundment area for them). The island is off the Barter's Island Road causeway. To find it, from Boothbay Center follow signs for the Coastal Maine Botanical Center, then continue until you come to open water on both sides of the road; the parking area is on the left.

BARRETT PARK

On the east side of the harbor, Barrett Park is an oceanfront park on Linekin Bay, with shade trees, picnic tables, swimming, and restrooms. To find it, take Atlantic Avenue and turn left on Lobster Cove Road (at the Catholic church).

☾ Coastal Maine Botanical Gardens

These shorefront gardens (Barters Island Rd., Boothbay, office Old Firehouse, Rte. 27, Boothbay, 207/633-4333, www.mainegardens.org, 9 A.M.–5 P.M. daily year-round, $10 adults, $8 seniors, $5 ages 5–17, $25 family of 4) are masterful and magical, yet still in their youth. The nonprofit project, designed to preserve more than 125 acres of woodlands with a trail network and landscaped pocket "theme" gardens, has grown to encompass 248 acres, with formal gardens, paths, herb and kitchen gardens, woods walks, a fairy village, a five-senses garden, and nearly a mile of waterfront. Artwork is placed throughout. A magical children's garden, new in 2010, encourages imagination, play, and discovery in a setting drawing from Maine-related children's literature such as *Blueberries for Sal* and *Miss Rumphius.* The visitors center has a café (10 A.M.–3 P.M. May 1–Oct. 15), a library, and a gift shop. Pick up a map and explore on your own, or ask whether a volunteer docent is available to provide a free tour. Allow at least two hours, although you could easily spend a full day here. Entrance to the preserve is on Barters Island Road, about 1.3 miles west of Boothbay Center.

Excursion Boats

Two major fleet operators provide practically every type of sea adventure imaginable. Boothbay Harbor's veteran excursion fleet is **Cap'n Fish's Cruises** (Pier 1, Wharf St., Boothbay Harbor, 207/633-3244, 207/633-2626, or 800/636-3244, www.boothbayboattrips.com, $19–30 adults, 10–15 children). Cap'n Fish's 150-passenger boats do nine varied, mostly 2–3-hour cruises. There is bound to be a tour length and itinerary (seal-watching, lobster-trap hauling, lighthouses, Damariscove, puffin cruises, and more) that piques your interest. Pick up a schedule at one of the information centers and call for reservations.

The harbor's other big fleet is **Balmy Days Cruises** (Pier 8, Commercial St., Boothbay

© HILARY NANGLE

It's easy to spend an entire day exploring the various gardens at the Coastal Maine Botanical Gardens.

Harbor, 207/633-2284 or 800/298-2284, www.balmydayscruises.com), operating three vessels on a variety of excursions. The *Novelty* does daily one-hour harbor tours (late June–Labor Day, $15 adults, $7.50 ages 3–11). Reservations usually are not necessary. The 31-foot Friendship sloop *Bay Lady* offers 90-minute sailing trips ($22 adults, $16 children) daily in summer. Reservations are wise for the *Bay Lady* as well as for the fleet's most popular cruise, a daylong trip to Monhegan Island ($32 adults, $18 children) on the *Balmy Days II,* departing at 9:30 A.M. and returning at 4:15 P.M. daily early June–late September, plus extended weekends in late May and early October. The three-hour round-trip allows about 3.5 hours ashore on idyllic Monhegan Island.

Sailing

A trip aboard *Schooner Eastwind,* a 65-foot traditional wooden schooner built in 2004, with **Appledore Cruises** (20 Commercial St., Boothbay Harbor, 207/633-6598, www.schoonereastwind.com, $28) is more than a day sail,

it's an adventure. Herb and Doris Smith not only built this schooner, they've sailed around the world in their previous boats through the years, providing fodder for many tales. They take passengers on 2.5-hour cruises to the outer islands and Seal Rocks up to four times daily. The boat departs from Fisherman's Wharf.

Whale- and Puffin-Watching

Variations in Gulf of Maine whale-migration patterns have added whale-watching to the list of Boothbay Harbor boating options as the massive mammals travel northeastward within reasonable boating distance. **Cap'n Fish's** (Pier 1, Wharf St., Boothbay Harbor, 207/633-3244, 207/633-2626, or 800/636-3244, www.mainewhales.com) is the best choice. Three–four-hour trips depart daily mid-June–mid-October. Tours cost $38 adults, $32 children 11–16, $25 ages 6–10, with a rain check if the whales don't show up. Reservations are advisable, especially early and late in the season and on summer weekends. No matter what the weather on shore, dress warmly and carry more clothing

Sail the waters around Boothbay Harbor aboard the 65-foot *Schooner Eastwind.*

than you think you'll need. Motion-sensitive children and adults need to plan ahead with appropriate medication.

Cap'n Fish's also runs 2.5-hour puffin-sighting tours to Easter Egg Rock, circling the island once or twice for the best views. Cruises are offered once weekly in June, then three times weekly in July–late August, for $27 adults, $15 children.

Sea Kayaking

From Memorial Day weekend through September, **Tidal Transit** (18 Granary Way, Chowder House Building, Boothbay Harbor, 207/633-7140, www.kayakboothbay.com), near the footbridge, will get you afloat with 2–3-hour guided lighthouse, wildlife, or sunset tours for around $50. No experience is necessary. Reservations are required. For do-it-yourselfers, Tidal Transit rents single kayaks ($20 per hour, $55 per day) and tandems ($30 per hour, $75 per day); other time options are available.

Outdoor Recreation Package

Here's a deal: For a full day of ocean-side play, book a **Play-for-the-Day** package at Linekin Bay Resort (92 Wall Point Rd., Boothbay Harbor, 207/633-2494 or 866/847-2103, www.linekinbayresort.com, $35 adults, $20 children), a campus of lodges and cabins with an enviable location on Linekin Bay. Day packages provide access to kayaks, canoes, rowboats, heated ocean-view saltwater pool, tennis, Wi-Fi, and common rooms with games and books.

SHOPPING

Artisans' galleries pepper the peninsula. Galleries, boutiques, and T-shirt and novelty shops crowd Boothbay Harbor, providing plenty of browsing for all budgets and tastes. Here are three worth seeking out.

A visit to the **Villard Gallery** (57 Campbell St., Boothbay Harbor, 207/633-3507, www.villardstudios.com) is a must for fans of fine-art crafts. Kim and Philippe Villard split their lives between Boothbay Harbor and southern

France, where they live in an abandoned village in the midst of a national park. Philippe is a talented sculptor, and Kim is an equally talented painter. They collaborate on woodcuts and handmade books, and the results are in collections and museums. Call in advance if you want a demonstration of the process. They have works in all price ranges, from poster prints to the actual woodblocks themselves.

Antiques store or museum, you decide. The **Palabra Shop** (53 Commercial St., Boothbay Harbor, 207/633-4225) has 10 rooms chock-full of antiques and collectibles. It's also home to the world's largest collection of Moses bottles, viewable by appointment.

One of the state's best fine art galleries, **Gleason Fine Art** (31 Townsend Ave., Boothbay Harbor, 207/633-6849, www.gleasonfineart.com) specializes in Maine art from the 19th–21st centuries. The gallery is light, bright, and a pleasure to browse. Even if you have no interest in buying, stop in to see works by some of Maine's top talents.

ACCOMMODATIONS

Here's a hint: If you want to concentrate your time in downtown Boothbay Harbor, shopping or taking boating excursions, stay in town and avoid the parking hassles.

Although the town practically rolls up the sidewalks in the winter, a few businesses do stay open year-round. Lodgings that usually do so are noted; others are seasonal, usually mid-May–mid-October. Rates noted are for peak season.

Classic Inns

To get away from it all, book in at the sigh-producing **Newagen Seaside Inn** (Rte. 27, Southport, 207/633-5242 or 800/654-5242 outside Maine, www.newagenseasideinn.com, mid-May–Sept., $165–285), an unstuffy full-service inn with casual fine dining and views that go on forever. Renovated guest rooms are split among the Main Inn; the Little Inn, where rooms have private decks, TVs, and kitchenettes; and five cottages ($1,620–6,000 per week). Plus there are a long rocky shore, a nature trail, a spa, tennis courts, a heated oceanfront saltwater pool and hot tub, guest rowboats, a game room, candlepin bowling, and porches just for relaxing. Rates include a generous buffet breakfast. The dining room is open to nonguests by reservation for dinner 5:30–9 P.M. daily; entrées run $16–28. There's also a pub serving lighter fare beginning at 4:30 P.M. The inn is six miles south of downtown Boothbay Harbor.

Over in East Boothbay, the **Ocean Point Inn** (Shore Rd., East Boothbay, 207/633-4200 or 800/552-5554, www.oceanpointinn.com, $99–230) wows guests with spectacular sunset views and an easygoing ambience that keeps guests returning generation after generation. The sprawling complex includes eclectic lodgings: an inn, a lodge, a motel, apartments, cottages, and others. Most guest rooms have ocean views; all have mini-fridges, phones, cable TV, and air-conditioning; some have kitchenettes. The property could use a facelift, but the rates, which include a light continental breakfast, reflect that. Also on the premises are a restaurant and tavern with fabulous ocean views, a pier, an outdoor heated pool, a hot tub, and Adirondack-style chairs set just so on the water's edge. The best deals are the packages.

Bed-and-Breakfasts

Topping an in-town hill with sigh-producing views over the inner and outer harbors and yet just a two-minute walk to shops and restaurants is ◖ **Topside Inn** (60 McKown St., Boothbay Harbor, 207/633-5404 or 877/486-7466, www.topsideinn.com, $145–245 d), a solid 19th-century sea captain's home with two annexes. Innkeepers Brian Lamb and Ed McDermott have completely renovated the three-building complex with an emphasis on comfort. Guest rooms in the three-story main inn are mostly spacious with nice views. Good books are everywhere, and the rockers on the wraparound porch and Adirondack chairs on the lawn are perfect places to read or relax. The annexes have motel-type guest rooms done in bed-and-breakfast style; all have decks and most have at least glimpses of the ocean. All guest rooms have phones and TVs, and there's Wi-Fi access in the main inn. Rates in all buildings include breakfast: a self-serve cold buffet with a hot entrée that's served to the table. Hot beverages are available all day; on some afternoons home-baked cookies magically appear in the living room or guest pantry.

Next door is **The Welch House** (56 McKown St., Boothbay Harbor, 207/633-3431 or 800/279-7313, www.welchhouseinn.com, year-round, $140–220), with stunning 180-degree views from the third-floor deck (and not-shabby ones from the lower deck). This 14-room bed-and-breakfast (all guest rooms have private baths, but some are down the hall) is an elegant getaway in a 19th-century shipbuilder's home. All of the guest rooms have air-conditioning, cable TV and video players, Wi-Fi, and phones; many have water views; some have fireplaces or whirlpool tubs. Breakfast in the solarium is a treat.

In town and on the water, the **Blue Heron Inn** (65 Townsend Ave., Boothbay Harbor, 207/633-7020 or 866/216-2300, www.blueheronseasideinn.com, year-round, $225–265) opened in 2003 and quickly made a name for itself. The clean, bright interior belies the Victorian vintage. Large guest rooms are accented with antiques and collectibles from Phil and Laura Chapman's years overseas. Each room has a waterfront deck, air-conditioning, a fridge, a microwave, an LCD HDTV, a microwave, Wi-Fi, and a phone; some also have a fireplace and a whirlpool tub. A dock with kayaks and a paddleboat is available. A full breakfast is elegantly served on Wedgwood china.

On the east side of the harbor, up a side street but within walking distance of in-town shops and restaurants, is Mary Huntington's **Pond House** (7 Bay St., Boothbay Harbor, 207/633-5842, www.pondhousemaine.com, $80–115). The 1920s barn-red home is just one block off the harbor, surrounded by beautiful gardens and edging a pond. The five guest rooms, some with shared or detached baths, have beautiful oak woodwork and are decorated with a mix of antiques and country pieces, including quilts topping most beds. Rotating artwork covers the walls, and studio space is available to visiting artists. Wi-Fi is available throughout the inn. Mary's breakfasts are legendary.

Escape the hustle and bustle of Boothbay Harbor at the ☖ **Five Gables Inn B&B** (107 Murray Hill Rd., East Boothbay, 207/633-4551 or 800/451-5048, www.fivegablesinn .com, $160–235), which began life as a no-frills summer hotel in the late 19th century. It's gone steadily upmarket since then, and well-traveled innkeepers De and Mike Kennedy, owners since 1995, have added their unique touches, including wonderful murals throughout and window seats in the gable rooms. All but one of the 16 light and airy guest rooms have Linekin Bay views, and some have fireplaces. The living room is congenial, the gardens are gorgeous, and the porch goes on forever. Rates include Mike's gourmet buffet breakfast. The inn, on a side road off Route 96 in the traditional boatbuilding hamlet of East Boothbay, is 3.5 miles from downtown Boothbay Harbor. Arriving by boat? One mooring is available for guests.

Quiet, private, and out of another era, **Sprucewold Lodge** (4 Nahanada Rd., Boothbay Harbor, 800/732-9778, www .sprucewoldlodge.com, $110–120) is reputed to be the largest existing log structure east of the Mississippi. The hand-hewn lodge with a covered porch was built in the 1920s. Inside are no-frills guest rooms along with a living room anchored by a huge stone fireplace. An expansive hot-and-cold buffet breakfast is served in the dining lodge (available to nonguests by reservation for $11) at large communal tables. Also here are a massive stone fireplace, games, and the property's only TV. General manager Richard Pizer goes all out to make guests welcome. One consideration: The lodge is popular with tour groups.

Motels and Hotels

A great location just 100 feet from the footbridge, a good dining room, a fun lounge, an indoor pool, and harbor views combine to make the **Rocktide Inn** (35 Atlantic Ave., Boothbay Harbor, 207/633-4455 or

© HILARY NANGLE

the Rocktide Inn, Boothbay Harbor's waterfront

800/762-8433, www.rocktideinn.com, $150–250) a popular spot. Rooms and suites are spread among four buildings, with rates varying according to the view. All have air-conditioning, cable TV, Wi-Fi, and phones, and a full buffet breakfast is included. Even if you don't stay here, pop over for a drink in the tastefully decorated tiki-style lounge (4–11 P.M. daily) or on the expansive decks overhanging the harbor. The dining room, open to nonguests for dinner (5:30–9 P.M. daily), has both casual and formal areas; men must wear jackets in the latter.

Since 1955 the Lewis family has owned and operated the **Mid-Town Motel** (96 McKown St., Boothbay Harbor, 207/633-2751, www.midtownmaine.com, $89), a spotless, no-frills vintage motel that's within steps of everything. It's a classic: clean, convenient, and relatively cheap, and the owners couldn't be nicer folks.

Every room at the lakefront **Beach Cove Hotel & Resort** (38 Lakeview Rd., Boothbay Harbor, 207/633-0353 or 866/851-0450, www.beachcovehotel.com, $99–199) has a water view, a balcony or deck, air-conditioning, a mini-fridge, and a microwave. The renovated property, about one mile from downtown, is extremely popular with families who appreciate its beach, dock, outdoor pool, and canoes and rowboats. A light continental breakfast is included.

Campgrounds
With 150 well-maintained wooded and open sites on 45 acres, **Shore Hills Campground** (Rte. 27, Boothbay, 207/633-4782, www.shorehills.com, $27–45) is a popular destination where reservations are essential in mid-summer. Be sure to request a wooded site away from the biggest RVs. Leashed pets are allowed. Facilities include a laundry and free use of canoes.

Much smaller and right on the ocean is the **Gray Homestead Oceanfront Camping** (21 Homestead Rd., Southport, 207/633-4612, www.graysoceancamping.com, $35–48), a family-run campground with 40 RV and tent-ing sites as well as cottages and apartments.

A stone beach, a pier, laundry facilities, kayak rentals, and lobsters—live or cooked—are available. There's even a small sandy beach.

FOOD
Local Flavors
It's worth the drive over to Trevett to indulge in a lobster roll from the **Trevett General Store** (207/633-1140), just before the bridge connecting Hodgdon and Barters Islands.

"Free beer tomorrow" proclaims the sign in front of **Bets Famous Fish Fry** (Village Common, Rte. 27, Boothbay), a takeout trailer that's renowned for its ultrafresh haddock fish-and-chips. Picnic tables are available.

On the east side, the **East Boothbay General Store** (255 Ocean Point Rd./Rte. 96, East Boothbay, 207/633-4503) has been serving locals since 1893. These days, it sells wine and specialty foods in addition to pizzas, sandwiches, and baked goods.

Lots of variety is the key at the seasonal **Boothbay Area Farmers Market** (Town Commons, Boothbay, 9 A.M.–noon Thurs.), with goat cheese, chicken, meats, preserves, breads, and fresh produce.

Baker's Way (90 Townsend Ave., Boothbay Harbor, 207/633-1119, 6 A.M.–9 P.M. daily), a hole-in-the-wall known locally as The Doughnut Shop, turns out the unusual combo of excellent baked goods and Vietnamese food. The breakfast sandwiches are good, and the sticky buns are renowned not only for their size but for their taste. After 11:30 A.M., Vietnamese dishes are available, most for less than $10. While the inside dining area is purely functional, there's also seating in a pleasant backyard garden. Everything is also available to go.

Tartans and terriers are the dominant motifs at **MacNab's Tea Room** (5 Lu Yu Tea Lane, off Back River Rd., Boothbay, 207/633-7222 or 800/884-7222, 10 A.M.–5 P.M. Tues.–Sat.), an informal, folksy place where Frances Browne serves lunch, high tea, afternoon tea, and royal tea, all by reservation only.

Reliably good and reasonably priced break-fasts and lunches are turned out by **D'Ellie's**

(Pier 1, Boothbay Harbor, 207/633-0277, 9 A.M.–3:30 P.M. daily). Sandwiches come in full and half sizes on a choice of homemade breads (the Anadama is fab).

Another locals' favorite serving breakfast, lunch, and dinner is the unassuming **Ebb Tide Restaurant** (43 Commercial St., Boothbay Harbor, 207/633-5692, 7 A.M.–9 P.M. daily). Booths line the tiny pine-paneled dining area where some mighty good home-style cooking is served. The chowders are renowned, and breakfast is served all day. Look for the red-and-white awning.

Don't tell too many people, but for lunch or a light dinner in an out-of-the-way spot, head to the Boothbay Country Club's **Grille Room** (33 Country Club Rd., Boothbay, 207/633-6085, 11:30 A.M.–7 P.M. daily).

Casual Dining

Real Northern Italian fare prepared by a real Italian chef is on the menu at **⬤ Ports of Italy** (47 Commercial St., Boothbay Harbor, 207/633-1011, www.portsofitaly.com, 4:30–10 P.M. daily), an upper-level restaurant with deck seating. New owner Sante Calandri hails from Perugia but more recently spent 23 years in New York City. This isn't a red-sauce place; expect well-prepared and in-novative fare, with especially good seafood. Most choices are in the $20 range, and a $20 three-course dinner is served 4:30–5:30 P.M. daily.

For spectacular sunset views and reliably good food, take a spin out to the **Ocean Point Inn** (Shore Rd., East Boothbay, 207/633-4200 or 800/552-5554, www.oceanpointinn.com, 7:30–10 A.M. and 6–9 P.M. daily, $16–25); lighter fare is served in the tavern. The lobster stew is rave-worthy, and a children's menu is available.

The tapas menu complements the views from the third-floor deck at **Boathouse Bistro** (12 The By-Way, Boothbay Harbor, 207/633-0400, www.theboathousebistro.com, 11:30 A.M.–11 P.M. daily). There are plenty of other options, but the tapas, pizzas, soups, and salads ($3–15) are the way to go.

One of the most reliable dining experiences in town is at **The Thistle Inn** (55 Oak St., Boothbay Harbor, 207/633-3541, www.theth-istleinn.com, from 5 P.M. daily). Everything from the salad dressings to the desserts is pre-pared on-site. It would be easy to make a meal from the appetizers alone—crab cakes, bran-died lobster, grilled Caesar salad—but then you wouldn't have room for the main event, perhaps lobster paella or Scottish salmon ($19–30). On a cold night, ask for a table by one of the fireplaces; on a warm evening, ask for one on the porch. Lighter fare from a far less pricey menu is served in the pub.

Lobster in the Rough

Boothbay Harbor and East Boothbay seem to have more eat-on-the-dock lobster shacks per square inch than almost anywhere else on the coast, but frankly they're all overcrowded, overpriced, and don't deliver an authentic experience.

Best of the in-town lot is **The Lobster Dock** (49 Atlantic Ave., Boothbay Harbor, 207/635-7120, www.thelobsterdock.com, 11:30 A.M.–8:30 P.M. daily), where lobsters are delivered twice daily; now, that's fresh. While there are a few choices for landlubbers—even PBJ for kids—lobster and fish are the prime attrac-tion. It's right on the harbor, so the views are superb.

Far more authentic and well worth the splurge is **Cabbage Island Clambakes** (Pier 6, Fisherman's Wharf, Boothbay Harbor, 207/633-7200, www.cabbageislandclambakes .com). Touristy, sure, but it's a delicious adven-ture. Board the excursion boat *Bennie Alice* at Pier 6 in Boothbay Harbor; cruise for about an hour past islands, boats, and lighthouses; and disembark at 5.5-acre Cabbage Island. Watch the clambake in progress, explore the island, or play volleyball. When the feast is ready, pick up your platter, find a picnic table, and dig in. A cash bar is available in the lodge, as are rest-rooms. When the weather's iffy, the lodge and covered patio have seats for 100 people. For about $60 (no credit cards), you'll get two lob-sters (or half a chicken), chowder, clams, corn,

© HILARY NANGLE

You can get to Boothbay Harbor's Lobster Dock restaurant by land or sea.

an egg, onions, potatoes, a blueberry cake, a beverage, and the boat ride. Clambake season is mid-June–mid-September. The 3.5-hour trips depart at 12:30 P.M. Monday–Friday, 12:30 and 5 P.M. Saturday, and 11 A.M. and 1:30 P.M. Sunday.

INFORMATION AND SERVICES
Information
Providing info about their members are the **Boothbay Harbor Region Chamber of Commerce** (207/633-2353, www.boothbay-harbor.com) and the **Boothbay Chamber of Commerce** (207/633-4743, www.boothbay.org).

Check out **Boothbay Harbor Memorial**

Library (4 Oak St., Boothbay Harbor, 207/633-3112, www.bmpl.lib.me.us). Thursday evenings in July–August there are band concerts on the lawn.

Public Restrooms
Public restrooms can be found at the municipal parking lot on Commercial Street (next to Pier 1) and at the municipal lot at the end of Granary Way. Saint Andrews Hospital, the town offices, the library, and the Marine Resources Aquarium also have restrooms.

GETTING AROUND
The Rocktide Inn operates free trolley-buses on continuous scheduled routes during the summer.

Pemaquid Region

At the head of the Pemaquid Peninsula, the riverfront towns of **Damariscotta** and her conjoined twin, **Newcastle,** anchor the western end of the Pemaquid Peninsula; **Waldoboro** anchors the eastern end. Along the peninsula are **New Harbor** (probably Maine's most photographed fishing village), **Pemaquid Point** (site of one of Maine's most photographed lighthouses), and historic ports reputedly used by Captain John Smith, Captain Kidd, and assorted less-notorious types. Here too are a restored fortress, Native American historic sites, antiques and craft shops galore, boat excursions to offshore Monhegan, and one of the best pocket-size sandy beaches in Mid-Coast Maine.

On Christmas Day 1614, famed explorer Captain John Smith anchored on Rutherford Island, at the tip of the peninsula, and promptly named the spot Christmas Cove. Today it is one of three villages that make up the town of South Bristol, the southwestern finger of the Pemaquid Peninsula. **South Bristol** and **Bristol** (covering eight villages on the bottom half of the peninsula) were named after the British port city.

As early as 1625, settler John Brown received title to some of this territory from the Wabanaki sachem (chief) Samoset, an agreeable fellow who learned snippets of English from English codfishermen. *Damariscotta* (dam-uh-riss-COT-ta), in fact, is a Wabanaki word for "plenty of alewives [herring]." The settlement here was named Walpole but was incorporated in 1847 under its current name.

Newcastle, incorporated in 1763, earned fame and fortune from shipbuilding and brick-making—which explains the extraordinary number of brick homes and office buildings throughout the town. In the 19th century,

New Harbor, on the Pemaquid Peninsula, is one of the Mid-Coast's numerous picturesque fishing harbors.

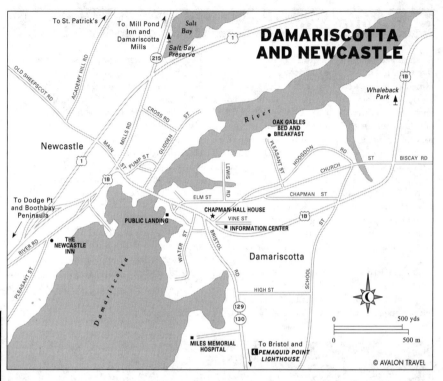

DAMARISCOTTA AND NEWCASTLE

© AVALON TRAVEL

Newcastle's shipyards sent clippers, down easters, and full-rigged ships down the ways and around the world.

Anchoring the northeastern end of the peninsula is Waldoboro. Route 1 cuts a commercial swath through the town without revealing the attractive downtown—or the lovely Friendship Peninsula, south of the highway. Duck into Waldoboro and then follow Route 220 south 10 miles to Friendship for an off-the-beaten-track drive.

Waldoboro's heritage is something of an anomaly in Maine. It's predominantly German, thanks to 18th-century Teutons who swallowed the blandishments of General Samuel Waldo, holder of a million-acre "patent" stretching as far as the Penobscot River. In the cemetery at the Old German Church, on Route 32, the inscription on a 19th-century marker sums up the town's early history:

This town was settled in 1748, by Germans who emigrated to this place with the promise and expectation of finding a populous city, instead of which they found nothing but a wilderness; for the first few years they suffered to a great extent by Indian wars and starvation. By perseverance and self-denial, they succeeded in clearing lands and erecting mills. At this time [1855] a large proportion of the inhabitants are descendants of the first settlers.

It sure makes you wonder why Waldo's name stuck to the town.

After the mill era, the settlers went into shipbuilding in a big way, establishing six shipyards and producing more than 300 wooden vessels, including the first five-masted schooner, the 265-foot *Governor Ames,* launched in 1888. Although the *Ames*'s ill-supported masts collapsed on her maiden voyage, repairs allowed her to serve as a coal hauler for more than 20 years, and many more five-masters followed in her wake. It's hard to believe today, but Waldoboro once was the sixth-busiest port in the United States. At the Town Landing, alongside the Medomak River, a marker describes the town's shipyards and shipbuilding heritage.

SIGHTS
Chapman-Hall House

Damariscotta's oldest surviving building is the Cape-style Chapman-Hall House (270 Main St., Damariscotta, noon–4 P.M. Sat.–Sun. late May–June and Sept.–mid-Oct., noon–4 P.M. Fri.–Sun. July–Aug., $4), built in 1754 by Nathaniel Chapman, whose family tree includes the legendary John Chapman, better known as Johnny Appleseed. Highlights are a 1754 kitchen and displays of local shipbuilding memorabilia. The house, on the National Register of Historic Places, was meticulously restored in the styles of three different eras. Don't miss the antique roses in the back garden. It's now cared for by the Lincoln County Historical Society (207/882-6817).

◖ Pemaquid Point Lighthouse

One of the icons of the Maine Coast, Pemaquid Point's lighthouse has been captured for posterity by gazillions of photographers and is depicted on the Maine state quarter. The lighthouse, adjacent keeper's house, and picnic grounds are a town park. Also on the premises is an art gallery. Admission to the grounds, payable at the gatehouse, is $2 age 12 and older. The lighthouse grounds are accessible all year, even after the museum closes for the season, when admission is free. The point is 15 miles south of Route 1 via winding two-lane Route 130.

Commissioned in 1827, Pemaquid Point Light (www.lighthousefoundation.org) stands sentinel over some of Maine's nastiest shoreline—rocks and surf that can reduce any wooden boat to kindling. Now automated, the light tower is licensed to the

RETURN OF THE ALEWIVES

If you're in the Damariscotta area in May and early June, don't miss a chance to go to Damariscotta Mills to see the annual **Alewife Run.** During this time more than 250,000 alewives (*Alosa pseudoharengus*, a kind of herring) make their way from Great Salt Bay to their spawning grounds in freshwater Damariscotta Lake, 42 feet higher. Waiting eagerly at the top are ospreys, gulls, cormorants, and sometimes eagles, ready to feast on the weary fish. Connecting the bay and the lake is an artificial stone-and-masonry "fish ladder" (www.damariscottamills. org), a zigzagging channel where you can watch the foot-long fish wriggle their way onward and upward. The ladder was built in 1807; restoration is ongoing. A walkway runs alongside the route, and informative display panels explain the event. It's a fascinating historical ecology lesson. To reach the fishway, take Route 215 for 1.6 miles west of Route 1. When you reach a small bridge, cross it and take a sharp left down a slight incline to a small parking area. Walk behind the fish house to follow the path to the fish ladder. Try to go on a sunny day – the fish are more active and their silvery sides glisten as they go.

American Lighthouse Foundation and is managed by the Friends of Pemaquid Point Lighthouse. Volunteers *aim* to open the tower 10:30 A.M.–5 P.M. daily late May–mid-October, weather permitting. There is no charge for the tower, but donations are appreciated. Still can't get enough? Newcastle Square Vacation Rentals (207/563-6500, www.mainecoastcottages.com) manages a one-bedroom apartment available for weekly rental ($1,150) in the keeper's house. Proceeds benefit preservation.

The adjacent **Fisherman's Museum** (207/677-2494, 9 A.M.–5 P.M. daily mid-May–mid-Oct., donation), in the former light keeper's house, points up the pleasures and perils of the lobstering industry and also has some lighthouse memorabilia.

While here, visit the **Pemaquid Art Gallery** (207/677-2752), displaying juried works by the Pemaquid Group of Artists since 1928.

Bring a picnic and lounge on the rocks below the light tower, but don't plan to snooze. You'll be busy protecting your food from the dive-bombing gulls and your kids from the treacherous surf.

⟨ Colonial Pemaquid and Fort William Henry

At the Colonial Pemaquid State Historic Site (end of Huddle Rd., 207/677-2423, www.friendsofcolonialpemaquid.org, 9 A.M.–6 P.M. daily late May–early Sept., $3 nonresident adults, $2 Maine resident adults, $1 ages 5–11), signed from Route 130 in New Harbor, visitors can gain a basic understanding of what life was like in an English frontier settlement. The 19-acre complex, listed on the National Register of Historic Places, comprises a museum–visitors

center, Fort William Henry, the Fort House, the remnants of a village, an 18th-century cemetery, a picnic area, a pier and boat ramp, and restrooms, all spread out on a grassy point sloping to John's Bay and bordered by McCaffrey's Brook, the Pemaquid River, and Pemaquid Harbor. Bring a picnic, bring a kite, bring a kayak, let the kids run—but do take time to visit the historic sites (a kids' activity book is available for $1). Demonstrations, tours, lectures, and reenactments are part of the site's summer schedule.

Three national flags fly over the ramparts of Fort William Henry, a reconstruction of a fort dating from 1692, the second of three that stood here between 1677 and the late 18th century. The forts were built to defend the English settlement of Pemaquid, settled between 1625 and 1628, from the French. From the rebuilt western tower, you'll have fantastic views of John's Bay and John's Island, named for none other than Captain John Smith; inside are artifacts retrieved from archaeological excavations of the 17th-century trading outpost.

© HILARY NANGLE

Climb to the roof of the rebuilt tower at Fort William Henry for fabulous views of John's Bay.

The square white Fort House, which dates to the late 1700s, houses a research library and archaeology lab as well as a gift shop.

Exhibits at the museum–visitors center focus on regional history, from early Native American life through the colonial period. Selections from the more than 100,000 artifacts uncovered during archaeological digs here are displayed along with a diorama of Pemaquid Village.

Take time to wander the village, 14 cellar holes of 17th- and 18th-century dwellings, a forge, a trading post, a jail, and other early buildings, all marked with interpretive signs. Also visit the burying ground. Note that rubbings are not permitted, as they could damage the fragile old stones.

Historic Houses of Worship

One of the oldest houses of worship in Maine that still holds services, **The Old Walpole Meeting House** (Rte. 129, Bristol Rd., Walpole), built in 1772, remains remarkably unchanged, with original hand-shaved shingles and handmade nails and hinges. The balcony—where African American servants were once relegated—is paneled with boards more than two feet wide. The meetinghouse is 3.5 miles south of Damariscotta and 0.25 miles south of where Routes 129 and 130 fork.

The **Harrington Meeting House** (Old Harrington Rd., off Rte. 130, 2–4:30 P.M. Mon., Wed., and Fri. July–Aug., donation), begun in 1772 and completed in 1775, now serves as Bristol's local-history museum— town-owned and run by the Pemaquid Historical Association. Behind it is an old cemetery that's fascinating to explore.

A remnant of Waldoboro's German connection is the **Old German Church** (Rte. 32, Waldoboro, 207/832-5369 or 207/832-7742, 1–3 P.M. daily July–Aug.) and its cemetery. The Lutheran church, built in 1772 on the opposite side of the Medomak River, was moved across the ice in the winter of 1794. Inside are box pews and a huge hanging pulpit. One of the three oldest churches in Maine, it lost its flock in the mid-19th century when new generations

no longer spoke German. An annual service is held at 3 P.M. the first Sunday of August.

Built in 1808, **St. Patrick's Catholic Church** (Academy Hill Rd., Damariscotta Mills, Newcastle, 207/563-3240, 9 A.M.–sunset daily), a solid brick structure with 1.5-foot-thick walls and a Paul Revere bell, is New England's oldest surviving Catholic church. Academy Hill Road starts at Newcastle Square in downtown Newcastle; the church is 2.25 miles from the square and one mile beyond Lincoln Academy.

St. Andrew's Episcopal Church (Glidden St., Newcastle, 207/563-3533), built in 1883, is nothing short of exquisite, with carved-oak beams, a stenciled ceiling, and, for the cognoscenti, a spectacular Hutchings organ.

The Thompson Ice House

On a Sunday morning in February (weather and ice permitting), several hundred helpers and onlookers gather at Thompson Pond, next to the Thompson Ice House (Rte. 129, South Bristol, 207/644-8551), for the annual ice harvest. Festivity prevails as a crew of robust fellows marks out a grid and saws out 12-inch-thick ice cakes, which are pushed up a ramp to the ice-storage house. More than 60 tons of ice is harvested each year. Sawdust-insulated 10-inch-thick walls keep the ice from melting in this building first used in 1826 and now listed on the National Register of Historic Places. In 1990 the house became part of a working museum (1–4 P.M. Wed. and Fri.–Sat. July–Aug., donation), with ice tools and a window view of the stored ice cakes. The grounds, including a photographic display board depicting a 1964 harvest, are accessible for free all year. The site is 12 miles south of Damariscotta on Route 129.

The Gut

At the foot of a hill on Route 129 is the tiny community of **South Bristol,** the heart of the town that stretches along the western edge of the Pemaquid Peninsula. In the village center is a green-painted swing bridge (it opens sideways) spanning a narrow waterway quaintly named The Gut. Separating the mainland from Rutherford Island, The Gut is a busy thoroughfare for local lobster-boat traffic, so the bridge opens and closes very often.

Waldoborough Historical Society Museum

The Waldoborough Historical Society Museum (1164 Main St., Waldoboro, 207/832-4713, www.waldoborohistory.us, 1–4:30 P.M. daily July–Labor Day, free) is a three-building roadside complex just 0.1 miles south of Route 1 at the eastern end of town. On the grounds are the 1857 one-room **Boggs Schoolhouse,** the 1819 **Town Pound** (to detain stray livestock), and two buildings filled with antique tools, toys, and utensils along with period costumes, antique fire engines, and artifacts from the shipbuilding era.

Maine Antique Toy and Art Museum

Indulge your inner child at the Maine Antique Toy and Art Museum (Rte. 1, Waldoboro, 207/832-7398, 10 A.M.–4 P.M. Thurs.–Mon. late May–mid-Oct., noon–4 P.M. Sat.–Sun. mid-Oct.–Christmas, $4). The museum houses an extensive collection of antique toys and original comic art. See how Mickey Mouse first appeared or browse a collection of Lone Ranger memorabilia. You'll find all the old favorites, including Popeye, Felix the Cat, Betty Boop, Snow White, Pogo, and Yoda. This museum is geared to nostalgic adults, not kids.

ENTERTAINMENT

Two struggling arts centers provide year-round concerts, plays, workshops, classes, and exhibits. **River Arts** (170 Business Rte. 1, Damariscotta, 207/563-1507, www.riverartsme.org) doubles as a gallery. Neoclassic on the outside, art deco within, the **Waldo Theatre** (916 Main St., Waldoboro, 207/832-6060, www.thewaldo.org) was built as a cinema in 1936. Restored in the mid-1980s, it now operates as a nonprofit organization and presents concerts, plays, films, lectures, and other year-round community events.

Lincoln County Community Theater (Theater St., Damariscotta, 207/563-3424, www.lcct.org) owns and operates the historic Lincoln Theater, dating from 1867. It also presents musicals and dramas, concerts, films, and more.

Salt Bay Chamberfest (207/522-3749, www.saltbaychamberfest.org) presents concerts in August.

The local **DaPonte String Quartet** (207/529-4555, www.daponte.org) frequently performs on the peninsula.

FESTIVALS AND EVENTS

July brings the annual **House and Garden Tour,** a peek into some lovely private homes and gardens, and the **St. Andrew's Lawn Party and Auction,** a fun event that always draws a crowd.

In mid-August, **Olde Bristol Days** features a craft show, a parade, road and boat races, live entertainment, and fireworks. At Fort William Henry in Pemaquid, it's a summer highlight on the peninsula.

SHOPPING

Downtown Damariscotta is the region's hub, and it has a nice selection of independent shops, galleries, and boutiques. Downtown parking in summer is a major headache; the municipal lot behind the storefronts has a three-hour limit, and it's almost always full. You'll usually find spots on some of the side streets.

Antiques and Antiquarian Books

Antiques shops are numerous along the Bristol Road (Rte. 130), where many barns have been turned into shops selling everything from fine antiques to old stuff. Serious antiques aficionados will find plenty to browse and buy along this stretch of road.

The multidealer **Nobleboro Antique Exchange** (104 Atlantic Hwy./Rte. 1, Nobleboro, 207/563-6800, www.nobleboroantiqueexchange.com) is housed in a light blue building that goes on and on, with more than 100 display areas on three levels. The selection is diverse, from period antiques to 20th-century collectibles.

Based in a screen-fronted antique carriage house just south of Round Pond Village, **Jean Gillespie Books** (1172 Rte. 32, Round Pond, 207/529-5555) has separate rooms and alcoves, all very user friendly. Specialties are cookbooks, nautical and Maine titles, and illustrated children's books; the "Royalty" category fills six shelves.

Art Galleries

Worth a visit for the building alone, the **Stable Gallery** (26 Water St., Damariscotta, 207/563-1991, www.stablegallerymaine.com), just off Main Street, was built in the 19th-century clipper-ship era and still has original black-walnut stalls—providing a great foil for the work of dozens of Maine craftspeople. Lining the walls are paintings and prints from the gallery's large stable of artists.

In his **River Gallery** (79 Main St., Damariscotta, 207/563-6330), dealer Geoff Robinson specializes in 19th- and early-20th-century European and American fine art—a connoisseur's inventory.

Betcha can't leave without buying something from **Pemaquid Craft Co-op** (Rte. 130, New Harbor, 207/277-2077), with 15 rooms filled with quality works by 50 Maine artisans.

Ronna Lugosch bases much of her **Peapod Jewelry** (1794 Rte. 32, Round Pond, 207/529-4411, www.peapodjewelry.com) on the natural peapod form, but instead of peas she uses pearls and gemstones. Also here is her little museum of all things peapod-inspired.

If you are especially interested in arts and crafts, make **Round Pond** part of your itinerary. The small village is home to about a dozen galleries and studios, many within walking distance of one another.

A delightful little off-the-beaten-path find is **Tidemark Gallery** (902 Main St., Waldoboro, 207/832-5109), showing fine arts and crafts from local artists.

Head south from Waldoboro down the Friendship Peninsula to find **Old Point Comfort** (28 Pitcher Rd./Rte. 220 S., Waldoboro, 207/832-8188), the gallery and showroom where weaver Sara Hotchkiss displays her tapestry-woven carpets.

Specialty and Eclectic Shops

The Pemaquid Peninsula is fertile ground for crafts and gifts, and many of the shop locations provide opportunities for exploring off the beaten path.

The inventory at the **Maine Coast Book Shop and Café** (158 Main St., Damariscotta, 207/563-3207) always seems to anticipate customers' wishes, so you're unlikely to walk out empty-handed. You'll find a superb children's section, helpful staff, and always something tempting in the café.

Just off Main Street (turn at Reny's) is **Weatherbird** (72 Courtyard St., Damariscotta, 207/563-8993), a terrifically eclectic shop with an inventory that defies description. Housewares, wines, toys, cards, and gourmet specialties are all part of the mix. Above it is **Tin Fish Etc.** (207/563-8204). Dana Moses's shop features brilliantly hand-painted tin objets d'art made from recycled roofing metal. She also accepts commissions.

All sorts of finds fill the **Walpole Barn** (Rte. 129, Walpole, 207/563-7050, www.walpolebarn.com), Warren and Deb Storch's retirement fun. Browse home and garden products, whimsies, gourmet foods, and even wines.

Eric and Sarah Herndon's **Granite Hall Store** (9 Backshore Rd., off Rte. 32, Round Pond, 207/529-5864) is an old-fashioned country store with merchandise ranging from toys to Irish imports. The "penny" candy, fudge, ice cream, and the old-fashioned peanut-roasting machine captivate the kids.

Bells reminiscent of lighthouses, buoys, and even wilderness sounds are crafted by **North Country Wind Bells** (544 Rte. 32, Round Pond, 207/677-2224, www.northcountrybells.com). Factory seconds are a bargain.

A well-chosen selection of silver jewelry fills **Purple Cactus** (107 Huddle Rd., New Harbor, 207/677-2262), Elizabeth Gamage's seasonal shop on the road to Colonial Pemaquid.

Puzzle fans come from all over the country to shop at **I'm Puzzled** (314 Rte. 1, Waldoboro, 207/832-4400), stocked with nearly 2,000 jigsaw puzzles.

Reny's

Whatever you do, don't leave downtown Damariscotta without visiting Reny's (207/563-5757 or 207/563-3011), with stores on each side of Main Street; one sells clothing, the other everything else. This is Reny's hometown, so the selection is huge in both. If you can recognize the edges of cutout labels, you'll find clothes from major retailers at very discounted prices. Stock up on housewares, munchies, puzzles, toiletries, shoes, and whatever else floats your boat; the prices can't be beat.

RECREATION
Parks and Preserves

Residents of the Pemaquid Peninsula region are incredibly fortunate to have several foresighted local conservation organizations, each with its own niche and mission: Damariscotta River Association, Pemaquid Watershed Association, Damariscotta Lake Watershed Association, and Medomak Valley Land Trust. In addition, the Nature Conservancy, Maine Audubon, and National Audubon all have holdings on the peninsula, a natural-resource bonanza. For good descriptions of trails throughout Lincoln County, buy a copy of Paula Roberts's *On the Trail in Lincoln County* ($15.75), which describes and provides directions to more than 60 area walking trails. It's available at Salt Bay Farm, which benefits from its sale.

SALT BAY FARM

Headquarters of the **Damariscotta River Association** (DRA, 110 Belvedere Rd., Damariscotta, 207/563-1393, www.draclt.org, 9 A.M.–5 P.M. Mon.–Fri.), founded in 1973, is the Salt Bay Farm Heritage Center, a late-18th-century farmhouse on a farm site. Here you can pick up maps, brochures, and other information on the more than 2,900 acres and 22 miles of shoreline protected and managed by the DRA. More than two miles of trails cover Salt Bay Farm's fields, salt marsh, and shore frontage and are open to the public sunrise–sunset daily year-round. DRA also has a healthy calendar of events, including bird-watching tours, natural-history trips, concerts,

and Trail Tamers, an opportunity to work on the trail system. To reach the farm from downtown Newcastle, take Mills Road (Rte. 215) to Route 1. Turn right (north) and go 1.4 miles to the blinking light (Belvedere Rd.). Turn left and go 0.4 miles.

SALT BAY PRESERVE HERITAGE TRAIL

Across Great Salt Bay from the DRA Salt Bay Farm is the trailhead for the Salt Bay Preserve Heritage Trail, a relatively easy three-mile loop around Newcastle's Glidden Point that touches on a variety of habitat and also includes remnants of oyster-shell middens (heaps) going back about 2,500 years. This part of the trail is protected by the federal government; do not disturb or remove anything. To reach the preserve from Newcastle Square, take Mills Road (Rte. 215) about two miles to the offices of the *Lincoln County News* (just after the post office). The newspaper allows parking in the northern end of its lot, but stay to the right, as far away from the buildings as possible, and be sure not to block any vehicles or access ways. Walk across Route 215 to the trailhead and pick up a brochure-map.

WHALEBACK PARK

How often do you get to see ancient shell heaps? Whaleback Park, an eight-acre public preserve designed to highlight what remains of the Glidden Midden, ancient oyster-shell heaps across the river from the park viewpoint. (The midden is also visible, but not as easily, from the Salt Bay Preserve Heritage Trail.) Informational signs explain the history of the midden, allegedly the largest such human artifact north of Florida. The "mini mountain" of castoffs was even vaster until the 1880s, when a factory harvested much of it to make lime. The trailhead and parking is on Business Route 1 opposite and between the Great Salt Bay School and the Central Lincoln County YMCA.

DODGE POINT PRESERVE

In 1989 the state of Maine acquired the 506-acre Dodge Point Preserve—one of the stars in its crown—as part of a $35 million bond issue. The Damariscotta River Association, which initiated its protection, helps manage and maintain the property. To sample what the Dodge Point Preserve has to offer, pick up a map at the entrance and follow the Old Farm Road loop trail, and then connect to the Shore Trail (Discovery Trail), heading clockwise, with several dozen highlighted sites. Consider stopping for a riverside picnic and swim at Sand Beach before continuing back to the parking lot. Hunting is permitted in the preserve, so November isn't the best time for hiking (unless you hike on Sunday, when hunting is banned). The Dodge Point parking area is on River Road, 2.6 miles southwest of Route 1 and 3.5 miles southwest of downtown Newcastle.

TRACY SHORE PRESERVE

Walk through a woodland wonderland that extends to ledgy shorefront along Jones Cove in South Bristol. Old cellars, moss-covered trails, lichen-covered rocks, a vernal pool, old pasture grounds, and spectacular views highlight this little-known gem, owned by the Nature Conservancy. It has cliffs and lots of slippery rocks, so be extra watchful of children. You can connect to another preserve, the Library Preserve, on a link crossing busy Route 129. The trailhead and parking are at the intersection of Route 129 and the S Road, 8.7 miles south of the split from Route 130.

RACHEL CARSON SALT POND AND LA VERNA PRESERVE

If you've never spent time studying the variety of sea life in a tidal pool, the Rachel Carson Salt Pond is a great place to start. Named after the famed author of *Silent Spring* and *The Edge of the Sea,* who summered in this part of Maine, the salt pond was one of her favorite haunts. The whole point of visiting a tide pool is to see what the tide leaves behind, so check the tide calendar (in local newspapers, or ask at your lodging) and head out a few hours after high tide. Wear rubber boots and beware of slippery rocks and rockweed. Among the many creatures you'll see in this

0.25-acre pond are mussels, green crabs, periwinkles, and starfish. Owned by the Nature Conservancy, the salt pond is on Route 32 in the village of Chamberlain, about a mile north of New Harbor. Parking is limited. Across the road is a trail into a 78-acre inland section of the preserve, most of it wooded. Brochures are available in the registration box.

Golf

The nine-hole **Wawenock Country Club** (Rte. 129, Walpole, 207/563-3938), established in the 1920s, is a challenging and popular public course.

Swimming

The best bet (but also the most crowded) on the peninsula for saltwater swimming is town-owned **Pemaquid Beach Park** (www.bristol-parks.org), a lovely tree-lined sandy crescent. There is no lifeguard, but there are cold-water showers and bathrooms, and the snack bar serves decent food. Admission is $4 for anyone over age 12. The gates close at 7 P.M. (restrooms close at 5 P.M.). The beach is just off Snowball Hill Road, west of Route 130.

A much smaller beach is the pocket-size sandy area in **Christmas Cove** on Rutherford Island. Take Route 129 around the cove and turn to the right, and then right again down the hill.

One of the area's most popular freshwater swimming holes is **Biscay Pond,** a long, skinny body of water in the peninsula's center. From Business Route 1 at the northern edge of Damariscotta, take Biscay Road (turn at McDonald's) three miles to the pond (on the right, heading east). On hot days, this area sees plenty of cars; pull off the road as far as possible.

Farther down the peninsula, on Route 130 in **Bristol Mills,** is another roadside swimming hole, between the dam and the bridge.

Boat Excursions

At 9 A.M. each day mid-May–early October, the 60-foot powerboat *Hardy III* departs for **Monhegan,** a Brigadoon-like island a dozen miles offshore where passengers can spend the day hiking the woods, picnicking on the rocks, bird-watching, and inhaling the salt air. At 3:15 P.M. everyone reboards, arriving in New Harbor just over an hour later. The cost is $32 adults, $18 ages 3–11, and reservations are required. Trips operate rain or shine, but heavy seas can affect the schedule. Early June–late September there's also a second Monhegan trip—used primarily for overnighters—departing New Harbor at 2 P.M. daily. Early and late in the season, Monhegan trips operate only Wednesday, Saturday, Sunday, and holidays. The *Hardy III* also operates daily 1.5-hour **puffin-watching tours** (5:30 P.M. mid-May–late Aug., $24 adults, $15 children), one-hour **seal-watching tours** (noon daily mid-June–early Sept. and Sept. weekends, $14 adults, $10 children), and one-hour evening **lighthouse cruises** (mid-June–early Sept., $14 adults, $10 children). **Hardy Boat Cruises** (Rte. 32, New Harbor, 207/677-2026 or 800/278-3346, www.hardyboat.com) is 19 miles south of Route 1, based at Shaw's Fish and Lobster Wharf. Parking is $3 per day at the baseball field near Shaw's.

Cruise Muscongus Bay aboard the Friendship sloop *Sarah Mead* with **Sail Muscongus** (207/380-5460, www.sailmuscongus.com) on its morning, island, or sunset cruises. Most last about three hours with rates ranging $30–50 pp; children under 12 are half price. Bring water and snacks. Muscongus Road is off Route 32, north of Round Pond. Parking is $5 per day.

Sea Kayaking and Canoeing

Pemaquid Paddlers, a local group, welcomes visitors to its weekly paddles, usually held beginning at 9 A.M. on Saturdays and lasting for about two hours. Check local papers or www .pemaquidwatershed.org for the schedule.

Midcoast Kayak (45 Main St., Damariscotta, 207/563-5732, www.midcoastkayak.com) has rentals and offers guided tours and lessons on Muscongus Bay and the Damariscotta River. Three-hour to full-day tours range $35–95 and include all sorts of options. If you would rather

do it yourself, recreational kayaks and sea kayaks are available at rates beginning at $22 for two hours. Instruction is also available.

Operating from a base near Colonial Pemaquid is **Maine Kayak** (113 Huddle Rd., New Harbor, 866/624-6351, www.mainekayak .com). Guided options include sunset paddles, wildlife paddles, puffin paddles, paddle-and-sail, half-day and full-day trips, and a variety of overnights. Rates begin at $40 for the shorter trips. Rentals begin at $25 single, $35 tandem for two hours, with free delivery in the New Harbor area.

If you have your own boat or just want to paddle the three-mile length of **Biscay Pond,** you can park at the beach area and put in. Another good launching site is a state ramp off Route 1 in **Nobleboro,** at the head of eight-mile-long **Lake Pemaquid.**

Two preserves are accessible if you have your own boat. Owned by the Damariscotta River Association, 30-acre **Menigawum Preserve (Stratton Island)** is also known locally as Hodgdon's Island. It's at the entrance to Seal Cove on the west side of the South Bristol peninsula. The closest public boat launch is at The Gut, about four miles downriver—a trip better done *with* (in the same direction as) the tide. The best place to land is Boat House Beach, in the northeast corner—also a great spot for shelling. Pick up a map from the small box at the north end of the island and follow the perimeter trail clockwise. At the northern end, you'll see osprey nests; at the southern tip are Native American shell middens—discards from hundreds of years of marathon summer lunches. (Needless to say, do not disturb or remove anything.) You can picnic in the pasture, but camping and fires are not allowed. Stay clear of the abandoned home site on the island's west side. The preserve is accessible sunrise–sunset.

Named for a 19th-century local woman dubbed "The Witch of Wall Street" for her financial wizardry, **Witch Island Preserve** is owned by Maine Audubon. The wooded 19-acre island has two beaches, a perimeter trail, and the ruins of the "witch's" house. A quarter of a mile offshore, it's accessible by canoe or kayak from the South Bristol town landing, just to the right after the swing bridge over The Gut. Put in, paddle under the swing bridge, and go north to the island.

ACCOMMODATIONS
Inns

Innkeeper Julie Bolthuis has breathed new life into **(The Newcastle Inn** (60 River Rd., Newcastle, 207/563-5685 or 800/832-8669, www.newcastleinn.com, $180–255), an 1860s sea captain's home with 14 guest rooms and suites (all with air-conditioning and Wi-Fi, some with fireplaces and whirlpool tubs) spread out between the main inn and carriage house. The lovely grounds descend to the edge of the Damariscotta River. Julie serves a full breakfast and stocks a pantry that includes a bottomless cookie jar. Two rooms are dog friendly.

Within easy walking distance of Pemaquid Light and 16 miles south of Route 1, **The Bradley Inn** (3063 Bristol Rd./Rte. 130, New Harbor, 207/677-2105 or 800/942-5560, www.bradleyinn.com, $175–375) is a restored late-19th-century three-story building with rooms and a suite (with a full kitchen and a fireplace) in the inn and carriage house, a separate cottage, and lovely gardens—a great location for a quiet weekend getaway. The inn's restaurant, overlooking the gardens and open to nonguests, has an ambitious and pricey menu (entrées $25–32). Room rates include full breakfast.

Almost on top of Pemaquid Light is the rambling and delightfully old-fashioned **Hotel Pemaquid** (3098 Bristol Rd./Rte. 130, New Harbor, 207/677-2312, www.hotelpemaquid .com, mid-May–mid-Oct., $85–160, no credit cards). Seventeen miles south of Route 1 but just 450 feet from the lighthouse (you can't see it from the inn, but you sure can hear the foghorn), the hotel has been welcoming guests since 1900; it's fun to peruse the old guest registers. Hang out in the large, comfortable parlor or on the wraparound veranda. The owners have gently renovated the property, updating and improving everything without losing the Victorian charm or quirks of an old seaside hotel. Don't expect fancy or fussy. The inn building has guest rooms with private and shared baths as well as suites. Other buildings have motel-style units with private baths. Apartments in the annex are $185–205. A beautiful second-floor suite in the carriage house, with a full kitchen and a deck, is $250, or $1,400 per week. For the Victorian flavor of the place, request an inn room or a suite. There is no restaurant, but The Bradley Inn and The Sea Gull Shop are nearby.

Bed-and-Breakfasts

Martha Scudder provides a warm welcome for her guests at **Oak Gables Bed and Breakfast** (Pleasant St., Damariscotta, 207/563-1476 or 800/335-7748, www.oakgablesbb.com, year-round, $120). At the end of a pretty lane, this 13-acre hilltop estate overlooks the Damariscotta River. Despite a rather imposing setting, everything's homey, informal, and hospitable. Four second-floor rooms, which can be joined in pairs, share a bath; a guest wing ($175 per night, $975 per week) has a full kitchen, a private bath, and a separate entrance. The heated swimming pool is a huge plus, as is the boathouse deck on the river. Guests can harvest blackberries from scads of bushes. Also on the grounds are a three-bedroom cottage ($1,400 per week), a river-view one-bedroom apartment ($185 per night, $1,100 per week), and a studio apartment ($175 per night, $975 per week), which is usually booked up well ahead.

Wake up with a dip after a restful sleep at the **(Mill Pond Inn** (50 Main St./Rte. 215, Damariscotta Mills, Nobleboro, 207/563-8014, www.millpondinn.com, $140, no credit cards). The 1780 colonial was restored and converted into an inn in 1986 by delightful owners Bobby and Sherry Whear. After a full breakfast, snooze in a hammock, watch for eagles and great blue herons, pedal a bicycle into nearby Damariscotta, or canoe the pond, which connects to 14-mile-long Damariscotta Lake. Bobby, a Registered Maine Guide, offers fishing trips and scenic tours of the lake in his restored antique

Lyman lapstrake (clinker-built) boat. Use of bicycles and a canoe is free for guests. The inn is just a five-minute drive from downtown Damariscotta, but a world away.

The mansard-roofed **Inn at Round Pond** (1442 Rte. 32, Round Pond, 207/529-2004, www.theinnatroundpond.com, year-round, $165–195) commands a sea captain's view of the harbor as it presides over the pretty village of Round Pond. It's an easy walk to a waterfront restaurant, two dueling lobster pounds, an old-timey country store, and a handful of galleries and shops. Each of three good-size rooms has harbor views and sitting areas. A full breakfast is included.

You can walk to Christmas Cove from **Sunset Bed and Breakfast** (16 Sunset Loop, South Bristol, 207/644-8849, www.sunsetbnb.com). Kay and Dick Miller have two small guest rooms under the eaves, one with a full-size bed, the other with twins, sharing one bath in their modest Cape-style house with to-die-for views. Various rates are available, from one room with a private bath ($130) to a family of four ($160); all include a hearty continental breakfast. Bring a kayak and launch it here.

About three miles south of town is **Blue Skye Farm** (1708 Friendship Rd., Waldoboro, 207/832-0300, www.blueskyefarm.com, $120–165), Jan and Peter Davidson's bed-and-breakfast in a gorgeous 18th-century farmhouse set amid 100 acres with trails, gardens, and lawns (but close to the road, so noise can be a problem for the sensitive). Original wall stencils by Moses Eaton decorate the entry. Breakfast is provided, and guests have full use of the country kitchen to prepare other meals. Other common rooms include the dining room, screened-in sun room, and a sitting room that's stocked with games and a fireplace. Five guest rooms, three with private baths, are meticulously decorated.

Motels and Cottage Colonies

You'll have to plan well in advance to snag one of the humble **Ye Olde Forte Cabins** (18 Old Fort Rd., Pemaquid Beach, 207/677-2261, www.yeoldefortecabins.com, $105–200 per day, $535–1,025 per week, no credit cards). These no-frills cabins have edged a grassy lawn dropping to John's Bay since 1922. Each has at least a toilet and a sink, but a shower house and a well-equipped cookhouse are part of the colony. Although guests are expected to clean up after themselves when using the kitchen, management keeps the place immaculate. The small private beach is a great place to launch a kayak. The cabins are less than 25 yards from Colonial Pemaquid and Fort William Henry.

Dan Thompson is the third-generation innkeeper at **The Thompson House and Cottages** (95 South Side Rd., New Harbor, 207/677-2317, www.thompsoncottages.net, $400–1,700 per week), a low-key, step-back-in-time complex of mostly waterfront rooms, apartments, and cottages split between two mini peninsulas. Most have fireplaces. Rowboats are available, and there's a library with games, books, and puzzles.

Now, here's a bargain. Up a long winding driveway behind Moody's Diner is **Moody's Motel** (Rte. 1, Waldoboro, 207/832-5362, www.moodysdiner.com, $54–74), in business since 1927; it's likely that little has changed in the meantime. Expect nothing more than a clean and well-run property, and you'll be pleased. The motel and tourist cabins all have screened porches, TVs, and Wi-Fi; a few have kitchenettes.

Campgrounds

A favorite with kayakers is **Sherwood Forest Camping** (Pemaquid Tr., New Harbor, 800/274-1593, www.sherwoodforestcampsite.com, $34–45). Facilities include a playground, a sundeck, and a pool, but the campground is just 800 feet from Pemaquid Beach. Two-bedroom rental cabins are $800 per week.

FOOD

Hours noted are for peak season, but are subject to change. It's wise to call ahead, especially when traveling in the off-season.

Local Flavors
DAMARISCOTTA
For a light breakfast, look no farther than **The Bakery** (85 Parking Lot Lane, 207/563-2867, 7 A.M.–2 P.M. Wed.–Sun.), a small place facing the municipal parking lot that turns out muffins, bagels, breads, and more.

For baked goods, sandwiches, soups, and gourmet goodies to go, head to **Weatherbird** (1168 Elm St., 207/563-8993, 8 A.M.–5:30 P.M. Mon.–Sat.). Eat at one of the handful of tables out front or take it to the waterfront.

The burgers, lobster rolls, and sweet-potato fries earn raves at **Larson's Lunch Box** (430 Main St., 207/563-5755), a no-frills takeout stand with a few picnic tables.

In a barn-style building at the northern edge of Damariscotta, **Round Top Ice Cream** (Business Rte. 1, 207/563-5307) has been dishing out homemade ice cream since 1924.

Rising Tide Natural Foods Market (323 Main St., 207/563-5556, www.risingtide.coop, 8 A.M.–7 P.M. daily), a thriving co-op organization since 1978, has all the natural and organic usuals, plus a self-service deli section with soups, sandwiches, salads, and entrées; indoor seating is available.

The **Damariscotta Area Farmers Market** sets up 9 A.M.–noon on Friday mid-May–October at Salt Bay Heritage Center (Belvedere Rd., just off Route 1) and 3–6 P.M. Monday at Rising Tide Market (323 Main St.). Condiments, baked goods, cheeses, local shellfish, and crafts are always available from about two dozen vendors, and you never know what else will turn up at this major market.

DOWN THE PENINSULA
You won't find a cozier, less expensive, or more welcoming home-based bakeshop than **Dot's Bakery** (1233 Rte. 32, Round Pond, 207/529-2514, 6 A.M.–8 P.M. Tues.–Sun.). Muffins, pies, doughnuts, soups, breads, and even buttermilk pancakes, sandwiches, and pizza are on the menu. Dine in on the central table or take it to go.

Homemade ice cream, delicious baked goods, prepared dishes, and sandwiches to go are just a few of the reasons to stop by the seasonal **Island Grocery** (12 West Side Rd., South Bristol, 207/644-8552, www.island-grocery.net). It also has breads, cheese, and all kinds of gourmet goodies—stock up for a picnic. To find it, take the first right after the swinging bridge.

Just around the corner from Colonial Pemaquid, **The Cupboard Cafe** (137 Huddle Rd., New Harbor, 207/677-3911, www.the-cupboardcafe.com, 8 A.M.–3 P.M. Tues.–Sat., 8 A.M.–noon Sun.) is a homey cabin serving fresh-baked goods, breakfasts, and a nice choice of fresh salads, burgers, sandwiches, and specials. Almost everything is made on the premises; the cinnamon and sticky buns are so popular they've spurred a mail-order business.

WALDOBORO
At the corner of Routes 1 and 220, opposite Moody's Diner, is the warehouse-y building that turns out superb **Borealis Breads** (1860 Atlantic Hwy./Rte. 1, 207/832-0655, www.borealisbreads.com, 8:30 A.M.–5:30 P.M. Mon.–Fri., 9 A.M.–4 P.M. Sun.). Using sourdough starters (and no oils, sweeteners, eggs, or dairy products), owner Jim Amaral and his crew produce baguettes, olive bread, lemon fig bread, rosemary focaccia, and about a dozen other inventive flavors; each day has its specialties. A refrigerated case holds a small selection of picnic fixings (sandwich spreads, juices). Great soups, salads, and excellent sandwiches are available to go.

Dine in or take out from **The Village Bakery & Cafe** (11 Friendship St., 207/832-2182, 6:30 A.M.–4:30 P.M. Mon.–Sat., 9 A.M.–2 P.M. Sun.), a casual downtown spot that has quickly earned favored status from locals seeking breakfast or lunch.

Pick up gourmet picnic fixings at **McKean and Charles** (1587 Rte. 1, 207/832-2221, www.mckeanandcharles.com, 10 A.M.–6 P.M. Mon.–Sat.), and while you're there, ask about any scheduled wine tastings. The store also sells more than 200 different beers and the state's largest selection of single malts.

MID-COAST REGION

Each fall around mid-September, a tiny, cryptic display ad appears in local newspapers: "Kraut's Ready." Savvy readers recognize this as the announcement of the latest batch of **Morse's sauerkraut**—an annual ritual since 1918. The homemade kraut is available in stores and by mail order, but it's more fun (and cheaper) to visit the shop, the **Kraut House** (3856 Washington Rd./ Rte. 220, 207/832-5569 or 800/486-1605, www.morsessauerkraut.com, 9 A.M.–6 P.M. Thurs.–Tues.), which also has a small restaurant (10:30 A.M.–4 P.M. Mon.–Tues., 8 A.M.–4 P.M. Thurs.–Sun.) serving traditional German fare, including sandwiches such as a classic Reuben, liverwurst, or Black Forest ham; homemade pierogies; sausages; and stuffed cabbage rolls, all less than $10. Big serve-yourself jars of Morse's pickles are on the tables. The red-painted farm store also carries Aunt Lydia's Beet Relish, baked beans, mustard, maple syrup, and other Maine foods as well as a mind-boggling selection of hard-to-find and unusual northern European specialties, cheeses, meats, and preserved fish. It's eight miles north of Route 1.

Truck drivers, tourists, locals, and notables have been flocking to **Moody's Diner** (Rte. 1 and Rte. 220, 207/832-7785, www.moodysdiner.com, 5 A.M.–10 P.M. Mon.–Sat., 6 A.M.–9 P.M. Sun., $5–15) since the early 1930s, when the Moody family established this classic diner on a Waldoboro hilltop. The antique neon sign has long been a Route 1 beacon, especially on a foggy night, and the crowds continue, with new generations of Moodys and considerable expansion of the premises. It has gone beyond dinerdom; expect hearty, no-frills fare and such calorific desserts as peanut butter or walnut pie. After eating, you can buy the cookbook.

An even humbler alternative to Moody's is **Deb's Diner** (1495 Rte. 1, 207/832-6144, 6 A.M.–2:30 P.M. Mon.–Sat., 7 A.M.–2 P.M. Sun.), a tiny spot where the portions are big and the prices are very low. You can easily get out of here for less than $5. In the off-season,

it sometimes serves dinner on Thursday and Friday nights.

Casual Dining
DAMARISCOTTA

A reliable standby in downtown Damariscotta, next to the Damariscotta Bank and Trust, the **Salt Bay Café** (88 Main St., 207/563-3302, www.saltbaycafe.com, 7:30 A.M.–8 P.M. Mon.–Thurs., 7:30 A.M.–9 P.M. Fri.–Sat., 8 A.M.–8 P.M. Sun.) has a loyal following thanks to its imaginative, reasonably priced cuisine and cheerful, plant-filled setting. Vegetarians have their own menu, with more than two-dozen choices. Most dinner entrées are $15–22, but hefty sandwiches are also available.

Chef Rick and Jean Kerrigan own **Damariscotta River Grill** (155 Main St., 207/563-2992, www.damariscottarivergrill.com, 11 A.M.–8:30 P.M. daily, bar menu until 9:30 P.M. Sat.–Sun., entrées $17–27), a reliable favorite where the open kitchen offers carefully prepared foods with an emphasis on ultrafresh seafood. The artichoke fondue is worth fighting over. Choose a table in the back with a river view, if available.

Bridging the gap between pub and restaurant is the **Newcastle Publick House** (Main St., Newcastle, 207/563-3434, 11 A.M.–11 P.M. Sun.–Thurs., 11 A.M.–midnight Fri.–Sat., $8–21). Emphasis is on local foods, including Pemaquid oysters, and pub favorites such as shepherd's pie or lamb shanks braised in Geary's London porter.

DOWN THE PENINSULA

The Kerrigans of the Damariscotta River Grill also own the **Anchor Inn** (Harbor Rd., Round Pond, 207/529-5584, www.anchorinnrestaurant.com, 11:30 A.M.–9 P.M. daily mid-May–mid-Oct., entrées $18–25), tucked away on the picturesque harbor in Round Pond, on the eastern side of the peninsula. Informal and rustic, with a menu that'll surprise you, the place always attracts a crowd. Reservations are advisable on summer weekends. After Labor Day, the schedule can be a bit erratic; call to confirm the hours.

The view is even better at **Coveside Restaurant** (105 Coveside Rd., Christmas Cove, South Bristol, 207/644-8282, www .covesiderestaurant.com, 11 A.M.–9 P.M. daily, $10–28), based at a marina on Rutherford Island, just off the end of the South Bristol peninsula. It's open for lunch and dinner as well as light meals. Grab a seat on the deck and watch a steady stream of boaters and summer vacationers during the cruising season.

Craving a bit o' Southern flavor? **The Samoset** (2477 Rte. 130, New Harbor, 207/677-6771, www.samosetrestaurant.com, 4–9 P.M. Tues.–Wed., 11:30 A.M.–9 P.M. Thurs.–Sun., $10–18) delivers with favorites such as Maine shrimp creole, low-country boil, and chicken-and-sausage gumbo as well as barbecue, other home-style classics, and the usual fried fare.

Location, location: Right next to Pemaquid Light is **The Sea Gull Shop** (3119 Bristol Rd., Pemaquid Point, 207/677-2374, www .seagullshop.com, 7:30 A.M.–8 P.M. daily mid-

May–mid-Oct., entrées $16–30), an oceanfront place with touristy prices but decent food—pancakes and muffins, for instance, overflowing with blueberries. BYOB, and call ahead for hours in spring and fall.

Lobster in the Rough

The Pemaquid Peninsula must have more eat-on-the-dock places per capita than any place in Maine. Some are basic no-frills operations; others are big-time commercial concerns. Each has a loyal following.

The biggest and best-known lobster wharf is **Shaw's Fish and Lobster Wharf** (Rte. 32, New Harbor, 207/677-2200 or 800/772-2209, 11 A.M.–9 P.M. daily mid-May–mid-Oct., 11 A.M.–8 P.M. mid-Oct.–mid-May). You can also order steak, margaritas, and oysters at the wharf raw bar. Fried seafood dinners run $8–17.

Facing each other across the dock in the hamlet of Round Pond are the **Round Pond Lobster Co-Op** (207/529-5725) and **Muscongus Bay Lobster** (207/529-5528). Both are good,

The oceanfront Sea Gull Shop restaurant is adjacent to Pemaquid Light.

and competition keeps prices low. Muscongus has enlarged in recent years, so it has a bigger menu and covered seating, but tiny Round Pond Lobster keeps it simple and oh-so-fresh. Both usually open around 10 A.M. daily for lunch and dinner and close around sunset.

Other seasonal lobster wharves salting the peninsula are the **New Harbor Co-op** (Rte. 32, New Harbor, 207/677-2791), **Pemaquid Fishermen's Co-Op** (Pemaquid Harbor Rd., Pemaquid Harbor, 207/677-2801), **South Bristol Fishermen's Co-op** (South Bristol, 207/644-8224), and **Broad Cove Marine Services** (off Rte. 32, Medomak, 207/529-5186), a low-key sleeper with a wowing view.

INFORMATION AND SERVICES

The **Damariscotta Region Chamber of Commerce** (15 Courtyard St., 207/563-8340, www.damariscottaregion.com) publishes a free annual information booklet about the area.

Skidompha Library (Main St., Damariscotta, 207/563-5513, www.skidompha.org) also operates a used-book shop. Incidentally, if you're puzzled by the name, it comes from the names of the members of a local literary society who founded the library at the turn of the 20th century. You can also check out **Waldoboro Public Library** (Main St., Waldoboro, 207/832-4484, www.waldoborolibrary.org).

PENOBSCOT BAY

The rugged and jagged shoreline edging island-studded Penobscot Bay is the image that has lured many a visitor to Maine. The coastline here ebbs and flows, rising to rocky headlands, dropping to protected harbors and linking fishing villages with comparatively cosmopolitan towns. Although the state considers this to be part of the Mid-Coast, this region has a different feel and view, one framed by coastal mountains in Camden and Lincolnville and accented by an abundance of islands.

From Thomaston through Searsport, no two towns are alike except that all are changing, as traditional industries give way to arts- and tourism-related businesses. Thomaston's Museum in the Streets, Rockland's art galleries, Camden's picturesque mountainside harbor, Lincolnville's pocket beach, Belfast's inviting downtown, Searsport's sea captains' homes, and Prospect's Fort Knox all invite exploration, as do offshore islands, many linked to the mainland by ferry.

From salty Port Clyde, take the mail boat to Monhegan, an offshore idyll known as the Artists' Island. From Rockland and Lincolnville Beach, car and passenger ferries depart to Vinalhaven, North Haven, Matinicus, and Islesboro. All are occupied year-round by hardy souls joined in summer by less-hardy ones. Except for Matinicus, they're great day-trip destinations.

If what appeals to you about a ferry trip is traveling on the water, you can get a taste of the great age of sail by booking a three-day or six-day cruise on one of the classic windjammer schooners berthed in Rockland, Rockport,

© TOM NANGLE

HIGHLIGHTS

LOOK FOR 🌙 TO FIND RECOMMENDED SIGHTS, ACTIVITIES, DINING, AND LODGING.

🌙 **Monhegan Historical and Cultural Museum:** View an impressive collection of masters at this museum adjacent to the lighthouse, then visit contemporary studios and find inspiration by hiking island trails (page 191).

🌙 **The Farnsworth Art Museum and the Wyeth Center:** Three generations of Wyeths are represented in this recently expanded museum, which also boasts an excellent collection of works by Maine and American masters (page 196).

🌙 **Owls Head Transportation Museum:** View a fabulous collection of vintage airplanes, automobiles, and even bicycles, many of which are flown, driven, or ridden during weekend special events (page 197).

🌙 **Rockland Breakwater:** Take a walk on this nearly mile-long breakwater to the lighthouse at the end (open on weekends). It's an especially fine place to watch the windjammers sail in or out of Rockland Harbor (page 198).

🌙 **Owls Head Light State Park:** The views of Penobscot Bay are spectacular, and it's a great place for a picnic lunch (page 201).

🌙 **Camden Hills State Park:** If you have time, hike the moderate trail to the summit for a gull's-eye view over Camden Harbor and Penobscot Bay. If not, take the easy route and drive (page 221).

🌙 **Penobscot Marine Museum:** Learn what life was *really* like during the Great Age of Sail in a town renowned for the number and quality of its sea captains (page 241).

🌙 **Fort Knox:** A good restoration, frequent events, and secret passages to explore make this late-19th-century fort one of Maine's best (page 241).

🌙 **Penobscot Narrows Bridge and Observatory:** On a clear day, the views from the 420-foot-high tower, one of only three in the world, extend from Katahdin to Cadillac Mountain (page 242).

© AVALON TRAVEL

and Camden. Or simply book a day sail or sea-kayak excursion.

While it's easy to focus on the water, this region is rich in museums and art galleries, antiques and specialty shops, some of the state's nicest inns, and many of its better restaurants.

Most folks arrive in July–August, but autumn, when turning leaves color the hills and reflect in the sea, the days remain warm, and nights are cool, is an ideal season to visit, especially for leaf peepers who want to get off the beaten track. And in winter, when snow blankets the Camden Hills, you can ski while gazing out to Camden Harbor.

PLANNING YOUR TIME

To hit just the highlights, you'll need at least three days. If you want to relax a bit and enjoy

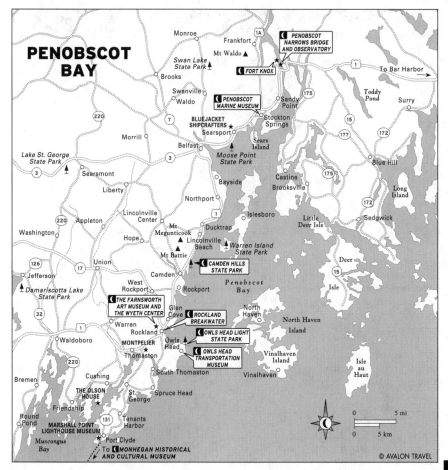

the area, plan on 4–5 days. Make it a full week if you plan on overnighting on any of the off-shore islands. In general, lodging is less expensive in Rockland, Belfast, and Searsport than it is in Camden. In any case, head for Monhegan or Vinalhaven on a fine day and save the museums for inclement ones.

Two-lane Route 1 is the region's central artery, with veins running down the peninsula limbs. Yes, traffic backs up, especially in Camden (and in Thomaston on the Fourth of July, when it's closed for a parade), but it rarely stops moving. If your destination is Rockland, take I-95 to Augusta and then Route 17 East; if it's Belfast or north, take I-95 to Augusta and then Route 3 East. Route 90 is a nifty bypass around Thomaston and Rockland, connecting Route 1 from Warren to Rockport. For a less direct route, the **Georges River Scenic Byway** is a 50-mile rural inland route, mostly along Route 131, between Port Clyde and Liberty. It parallels the coast, but it meanders through farmlands and tiny villages and by lakes and rivers, with antiques shops and farm stands along the way. It's simply gorgeous in autumn.

Thomaston Area

Thomaston is a little gem of a town and is becoming more so each year thanks to the razing of the old Maine State Prison. It's also the gateway to two lovely fingers of land bordering the St. George River and jutting into the Gulf of Maine—the Cushing and St. George Peninsulas.

In 1605, British adventurer Captain George Waymouth sailed up the river now named after him (the St. George River was originally called the Georges River). A way station for Plymouth traders as early as 1630, Thomaston was incorporated in 1777 and officially named after General John Thomas, a Revolutionary War hero.

Industry began with the production of lime, which was used for plaster. A growing demand for plaster, and the frequency with which the wooden boats were destroyed by fire while carrying loads of extremely flammable lime, spurred the growth of shipbuilding and its related infrastructure. Thomaston's slogan became "the town that went to sea."

Seeing the sleepy harbor-front today, it's hard to visualize the booming era when dozens of tall-masted wooden ships slid down the ways. But the town's architecture is a testament and tribute to the prosperous past. All those splendid homes on Main and Knox Streets were funded by wealthy ship owners and shipmasters who well understood how to occupy the idle hands of off-duty carpenters.

SIGHTS
Montpelier

As you head north out of Thomaston on Route 1, you'll come face-to-face with an imposing colonial hilltop mansion at the junction with Route 131 South. (Behind it, unfortunately, is the rather ugly outline of a huge cement plant.) Dedicated to the memory of General Henry Knox, president George Washington's secretary of war, Montpelier (Rte. 1 and Rte. 131, Thomaston, 207/354-8062, www.generalknox museum.org, 10 A.M.–3:30 P.M. Tues.–Sat. late

May–mid-Oct., $7 adults, $6 seniors, $4 ages 5–13, $18 family) is a 1930s replica of Knox's original Thomaston home. The mansion today contains Knox family furnishings and other period antiques—all described with great enthusiasm during the hour-long tours. A gift shop run by the Friends of Montpelier carries books and other relevant items. Concerts, lectures, and special events occur here periodically throughout the summer; General Knox's birthday is celebrated with considerable fanfare in July.

Museum in the Streets

Montpelier is the starting point for a three-mile walking, cycling, or, if you must, driving tour of nearly 70 sites in Thomaston's National Historic Landmark District. Pick up a copy of the tour brochure at one of the local businesses. Included are lots of stories behind the facades of the handsome 19th-century homes that line Main and Knox Streets; the architecture here is nothing short of spectacular. Much of this history is also recounted in the Museum in the Streets, a walking tour taking in 25 informative plaques illustrated with old photos throughout town.

EVENTS

Thomaston's **Fourth of July,** an old-fashioned hometown celebration reminiscent of a Norman Rockwell painting, draws huge crowds. A spiffy parade—with bands, veterans, kids, and pets—starts off the morning at 11 A.M., followed by races, craft and food booths, and lots more. If you need to get *through* Thomaston on the Fourth of July, do it well before the parade or well after noon; the marchers go right down Main Street (Rte. 1), and gridlock forces a detour.

SHOPPING

Thomaston has a block-long shopping street (on Rte. 1), with ample free parking out back behind the stores.

If you arrive at Marti Reed's **Personal Book Shop** (78 Main St., Thomaston, 207/354-8058) at the right time, you're likely to run into local writers' groups that gather frequently to swap tips and gossip. That's just the kind of place this is—an independent bookstore with a warm, nurturing feel, not to mention a dog and cat in residence.

The **Maine State Prison Showroom Outlet** (Main St./Rte. 1 at Wadsworth St., Thomaston, 207/354-3131) markets the handiwork of inmate craftsmen. Some of the souvenirs verge on kitsch; the bargains are wooden bar stools, toys (including dollhouses), and chopping boards. You'll need to carry your purchases with you; prison-made goods cannot be shipped.

At the southern end of Thomaston, in a renovated chicken barn, is **Thomaston Place Auction Gallery** (51 Atlantic Hwy./Rte. 1, Thomaston, 207/354-8141 or 888/834-5538, www.thomastonauction.com), the home of Kaja Veilleux, a longtime dealer, appraiser, and auctioneer. Auctions occur frequently with previews beforehand.

Just south of Thomaston is **Lie-Nielsen Toolworks** (Rte. 1, Warren, 800/327-2520, www.lie-nielsen.com), crafting heirloom-quality hand tools for connoisseurs; tours are available.

CAMPING

The best campground is on the Thomaston-Cushing town line at **Saltwater Farm Campground** (Wadsworth St./Cushing Rd., Cushing, 207/354-6735, www.saltwaterfarmcampground.com), a 35-acre Good Sam park 1.5 miles south of Route 1. Thirty-seven open and wooded tent and RV sites ($35–45) overlook the St. George River. Cabins go for $70. Facilities include a bathhouse, a pool, a hot tub, laundry facilities, a store, and a play area. The river is tidal, so swimming is best near high tide; otherwise you're dealing with mudflats.

FOOD

Often overlooked by visitors (but certainly not by locals) is casual **Thomaston Café and Bakery** (154 Main St./Rte. 1, Thomaston, 207/354-8589, www.thomastoncafe.com, 11 A.M.–2 P.M. Mon.–Thurs., 7:30 A.M.–2 P.M. and 5:30–8 P.M. Fri.–Sat., 8:30 A.M.–1:30 P.M. Sun., dinner entrées $16–24). German-born chef Herb Peters and his wife, Eleanor, produce superb pastries, breads, and desserts (eat here or take them out). Everything's homemade, there are children's options, and the café uses only organic poultry. Try the incredible wild-mushroom hash. Beer and wine only; reservations are essential. Call to verify days and hours of operation.

INFORMATION AND SERVICES

The **Rockland-Thomaston Area Chamber of Commerce** (Gateway Center, Rockland, 207/596-0376 or 800/562-2529, www.therealmaine.com) is the area's best resource.

The **Thomaston Public Library** (42 Main St., Thomaston, 207/354-2453) occupies part of the Greek Revival Thomaston Academy.

Cushing Peninsula

Cushing's recorded history goes back at least as far as 1605, when someone named "Abr [maybe Abraham] King"—presumably a member of explorer George Waymouth's crew—inscribed his name here on a ledge (now private property). Since 1789, settlers' saltwater farms have sustained many generations, and the active Cushing Historical Society keeps the memories and memorabilia from fading away. But the outside world knows little of this. Cushing is better known as "Wyeth country," the terrain depicted by the famous artistic dynasty of N. C., Andrew, and Jamie Wyeth and assorted other talented relatives.

If you're an Andrew Wyeth fan, visiting Cushing will give you the feeling of walking

BEANHOLE BEANS

"To be happy in New England," wrote one Joseph P. MacCarthy at the turn of the 20th century, "you must select the Puritans for your ancestors...[and] eat beans on Saturday night." There is no better way to confirm the latter requirement than to attend a beanhole bean supper – a real-live legacy of colonial times, with dinner baked in a hole in the ground.

Generally scheduled, appropriately, for a Saturday night (check local newspapers), a beanhole bean supper demands plenty of preparation from its hosts – and a secret ingredient or two. (Don't even think about trying to pry the recipe out of the cooks.) The supper always includes hot dogs, coleslaw, relishes, home-baked breads, and homemade desserts, but the beans are the star attraction. Typically, the suppers are also alcohol-free. Not only are they feasts; they're also bargains, never setting you back more than about $8.

The beans at the Broad Cove Church's annual mid-July beanhole bean supper, served family-style at long picnic tables, are legendary – attracting nearly 200 eager diners. Minus the secrets, here's what happens:

Early Friday morning: Church volunteers load 10 pounds of dry pea and soldier (yellow-eye) beans into each of four large kettles and add water to cover. The beans are left to soak and soften for 6-7 hours. Two or three volunteers uncover the churchyard's four rock-lined beanholes (each about three feet deep), fill the holes with hardwood kindling, ignite the wood,

and keep the fires burning until late afternoon, when the wood is reduced to red-hot coals.

Early Friday afternoon: The veteran chefs parboil the beans and stir in the seasonings. Typical additions are brown sugar, molasses, mustard, salt, pepper, and salt pork (much of the secret is in the exact proportions). When the beans are precooked to the cooks' satisfaction, the kettle lids are secured with wire and the pots are lugged outdoors.

Friday mid-afternoon: With the beans ready to go underground, some of the hot coals are quickly shoveled out of the pits. The kettles are lowered into the pits and the coals replaced around the sides of the kettles and atop their lids. The pits are covered with heavy sheet metal and topped with a thick layer of sand and a tarpaulin. The round-the-clock baking begins, and no one peeks before it's finished.

Saturday mid-afternoon: Even the veterans start getting nervous just before the pits are uncovered. Was the seasoning right? Did too much water cook away? Did the beans dry out? Not to worry, though – failures just don't happen here.

Saturday night: When a pot is excavated for the first of three seatings (about 5 P.M.), the line is already long. The chefs check their handiwork and the supper begins. No one seems to mind waiting for the second and third seatings – while others eat, a sing-along gets under way in the church, keeping everyone entertained.

---

through his paintings. The flavor of his Maine work is here—rolling fields, wildflower meadows, rocky tidal coves, broad vistas, character-filled farmhouses, and some well-hidden summer enclaves.

SIGHTS

Cushing's town boundary begins 1.3 miles south of Route 1 (take Wadsworth St. at the Maine State Prison Showroom Outlet). Two miles farther, you'll pass giant wooden sculptures in the yard of the late artist **Bernard Langlais,** who died in 1977.

Six miles from Route 1 is the **A. S. Fales and Son Store** (locally, just Fales's Store), Cushing's heart and soul and the source of fuel, film, gossip, and groceries. Built in 1889, the store has been in the Fales family ever since. You might want to pick up lunch while here. Just beyond the store, take the left fork, continuing down the peninsula toward the Broad Cove Church and the Olson House.

Broad Cove Church

Andrew Wyeth aficionados will recognize the Broad Cove Church as one of his subjects—alongside Cushing Road en route to the Olson House. It's open most days, so step inside and admire the classic New England architecture. The church is also well known as the site of one of the region's best beanhole bean suppers, held on a Saturday in mid-July and attracting several hundred appreciative diners. Bear left at the fork after Fales's Store; the church is 0.4 miles farther, on the right.

The Olson House

Many an art lover makes the pilgrimage to the Olson House (11 A.M.–4 P.M. daily late May–mid-Oct., $5), a famous icon near the end of Hathorn Point Road. The early-19th-century farmhouse appears in Andrew Wyeth's 1948 painting *Christina's World* (which hangs in New York's Museum of Modern Art), his best-known image of the disabled Christina Olson, who died in 1968. In 1991, two philanthropists donated the Olson House to the Farnsworth Art Museum in Rockland (a $12 combination ticket includes Farnsworth museum admission), which has retained the house's sparse, lonely, and almost mystical ambience. The clapboards outside remain unpainted, the interior walls bear only a few Wyeth prints (hung close to the settings they depict), and it is easy to sense Wyeth's inspiration for chronicling this place. From Route 1 in Thomaston, at the Maine State Prison Showroom Outlet, turn onto Wadsworth Street and go six miles to Fales's Store. Take the left fork after the store, go 1.5 miles, and turn left onto Hathorn Point Road. Go another 1.9 miles to the house.

St. George Peninsula

Even though the Cushing and St. George Peninsulas face each other across the St. George River, they differ dramatically. Cushing is far more rural, seemingly less approachable, and with little access to the surrounding waters; St. George has a slew of things to do and see, places to sleep and eat, and shore access in various spots along the peninsula.

The St. George Peninsula is actually better known by some of the villages scattered along its length: **Tenants Harbor, Port Clyde, Wiley's Corner, Spruce Head**—plus the smaller neighborhoods of Martinsville, Smalleytown, Glenmere, Long Cove, Hart's Neck, and Clark Island. Each has a distinct personality, determined partly by the different ethnic groups—primarily Brits, Swedes, and Finns—who arrived to work the granite quarries in the 19th century. Wander through the Seaview Cemetery in Tenants Harbor and you'll see the story: row after row of gravestones with names from across the sea.

A more famous former visitor was 19th-century novelist Sarah Orne Jewett, who holed up in an old schoolhouse in Martinsville, paid a weekly rental of $0.50, and wrote *The Country of the Pointed Firs*, a tale about "Dunnet's Landing" (Tenants Harbor).

Today the picturesque peninsula has saltwater farms, tidy hamlets, a striking lighthouse, spruce-edged tidal coves, an active yachting harbor, and at the tip, the tiny fishing village of Port Clyde, which serves as a springboard to offshore Monhegan Island.

Port Clyde is likely the best-known community here. (Fortunately, it's no longer called by its unappealing 18th-century name: Herring Gut.) George Waymouth explored Port Clyde's nearby islands in 1605, but you'd never suspect its long tradition. It's a sleepy place, with a general store, low-key inns, a few galleries, and pricey parking.

SIGHTS
Marshall Point Lighthouse Museum

Not many settings can compare with the spectacular locale of the Marshall Point Lighthouse Museum (Marshall Point Rd., Port Clyde, 207/372-6450, www.marshallpoint.org,

1–5 P.M. Sun.–Fri., 10 A.M.–5 P.M. Sat. late May–mid-Oct., free), a distinctive 1857 lighthouse and park overlooking Port Clyde, the harbor islands, and the passing lobster-boat fleet. Bring a picnic and let the kids run on the lawn (but keep them well back from the shoreline). The museum, in the 1895 keeper's house, displays lighthouse and local memorabilia. The grounds are accessible year-round. Take Route 131 to Port Clyde and watch for signs to the museum.

SHOPPING
Art
The St. George Peninsula has been attracting artists for decades, and galleries pepper the peninsula. Some have been here for years, others started up yesterday; most are worth a stop, so keep an eye out for their signs. In early August, a number of renowned artists usually coordinate an open-studio weekend.

Overlooking the reversing falls in downtown South Thomaston, **The Old Post Office Gallery** (Rte. 73, South Thomaston, 207/594-9396, www.artofthesea.com) has 11 rooms filled with marine art and antiques: ship models, prints, paintings, sculpture, scrimshaw, and jewelry.

Used Books
Drive up to the small parking area at **Lobster Lane Book Shop** (Island Rd., Spruce Head, 207/594-7520) and you'll see license plates from everywhere. The tiny shop, in a crammed but well-organized shed that has been here since the 1960s, has 50,000 or so treasures for used-book fans. For a few dollars, you can stock up on a summer's worth of reading. The shop is just under a mile east of Route 73, with eye-catching vistas in several directions (except, of course, when Spruce Head's infamous fog sets in).

General Store
Despite periodic ownership changes, **Port Clyde General Store** (Rte. 131, Port Clyde, 207/372-6543) remains a characterful destination, a two-century-old country store with ever-increasing upscale touches. Stock up on groceries, pick up a newspaper, order breakfast or a pizza, or buy a sweatshirt (you may need it on the Monhegan boat). The current owner Linda Bean has gussied it up even more and added a shop upstairs. She also operates the restaurant out back.

RECREATION
Swimming and Beachcombing
Drift Inn Beach, on Drift Inn Beach Road (also called Candy's Cove Road), isn't a big deal as beaches go, but it's the best public one on the peninsula, so it gets busy on hot days. The name comes from the Drift Inn, an early-20th-century summer hotel. Drift Inn Beach Road parallels Route 131, and the parking lot is accessible from both roads. Heading south on the peninsula, about 3.5 miles after the junction with Route 73, turn left at Drift Inn Beach Road. The sign frequently disappears; watch for an imposing square granite house and a red farmhouse on your left, turn, then continue 0.2 miles.

Sea Kayaking
The St. George Peninsula is especially popular for sea kayaking, with plenty of islands to add interest and shelter. **Port Clyde Kayaks** (Rte. 131, Port Clyde, 207/372-8128, www.port clydekayaks.com) offers 2.5-hour ($55) and four-hour ($79) guided tours around the tip of the peninsula, taking in Marshall Point lighthouse and the islands. Other options include full moon and sunset tours. Ask about multiday camping or bed-and-breakfast tours.

If you have kayaking experience, you can launch on the ramp just before the causeway that links the mainland with Spruce Head Island, in Spruce Head (Island Rd., off Rte. 73). Parking is limited. A great paddle goes clockwise around Spruce Head Island and nearby Whitehead (there's a lighthouse on its southeastern shore) and Norton Islands. Duck in for lunch at Waterman's Beach Lobster. Around new moon and full moon, plan your schedule to avoid low tide near the Spruce Head causeway, or you may become mired in mudflats.

Excursion Boats

The best boating experience on this peninsula is a passenger-ferry trip from Port Clyde to offshore **Monhegan Island**—for a day, overnight, or longer. Perhaps because the private ferry company has a monopoly on this harbor, the trip isn't cheap, and parking adds to the cost, but it's a "must" excursion, so try to factor it into the budget. Port Clyde is the nearest mainland harbor to Monhegan; this service operates all year. **Monhegan-Thomaston Boat Line** (Port Clyde, 207/372-8848, www.monheganboat.com) uses two boats, the *Laura B.* (70 minutes each way) and the newer *Elizabeth Ann* (50 minutes). Round-trip tickets are $32 adults, $18 ages 2–12. Leave your bicycle in Port Clyde; you won't need it on the island. Reservations are essential in summer, especially for the 10:30 A.M. boat; a $5 pp fee holds the reservation until 75 minutes before departure, so you have to get to the dock early. No deposit is needed for other boats, but show up 30 minutes before departure. Parking in Port Clyde is $4 per day. If a summer day trip is all you can manage, aim for the first or second boat and return on the last one; don't go just for the boat ride.

During the summer, the Monhegan–Thomaston Boat Line also offers 2.5-hour sightseeing cruises, on a varied schedule, including a Puffin and Nature Cruise and a Lighthouse Cruise. Each costs $25 adults, $10 children.

ACCOMMODATIONS

Rates noted are for peak season.

Inns

The dreamy island-dotted, oceanfront setting complements **The East Wind Inn** (Mechanic St., Tenants Harbor, 207/372-6366 or 800/241-8439, www.eastwindinn.com, year-round, $118–226), the perfect rendition of an old-fashioned country inn—some parts of it more old-fashioned than others. Built in 1860 and originally used as a sail loft, it has a huge veranda, a cozy parlor, harbor-view rooms, and a quiet dining room with a creditable New

England menu. Guest rooms are divided between the main inn, some with shared bath, and the spiffed-up 19th-century Meeting House, a former sea captain's home, which also has one apartment. All rates include a full breakfast. The water-view dining room is open to nonguests for breakfast (7:30–9:30 A.M. daily Apr.–June and Sept.–Nov., 7:30–10 A.M. daily July–Aug.) and dinner (5:30–8:30 P.M. daily Apr.–June and Sept.–Nov., 5:30–9:30 P.M. daily July–Aug.). Dinner entrées are $17–26, and reservations are advised. Lunch is available in summer at a dockside takeout. Children are welcome; pets are $15 per visit.

New owners in 2010 are breathing new life into the decidedly old-fashioned **Craignair Inn** (Clark Island Rd., off Rte. 71, Spruce Head, 207/594-7644, www.craignair.com, $80–160), built in 1928 to house granite workers. It's an unfussy, unpretentious spot with a killer oceanfront location overlooking the causeway connecting Spruce Head to Clark Island and beyond to open seas. Guest rooms are split between the main inn and the vestry annex; some share baths. Rates include breakfast. Craignair serves dinner (entrées $16–26) in its water-view dining room nightly beginning at 5:30 P.M. in season. Seafood is the specialty.

Bed-and-Breakfasts

In the center of South Thomaston village but overlooking the reversing falls on the tidal Wessaweskeag River, the 1830 **Weskeag at the Water** (14 Elm St./Rte. 73, South Thomaston, 207/596-6676 or 800/596-5576, www.weskeag.com, year-round, $125–150) has eight guest rooms, of which four have in-room private baths; one has a whirlpool tub. This place is especially relaxing, with games, puzzles, books, a huge video library, a great deck, and a lawn stretching to the river. Bring your sea kayaks and bicycles. It's 1.5 miles from the Owls Head Transportation Museum and a few more miles from the restaurants of downtown Rockland.

If you stay at the **Ocean House** (Rte. 131, Port Clyde, 207/372-6691 or 800/269-6691, www.oceanhousehotel.com, $110–145, no credit cards), you can plan to roll out of bed,

PENOBSCOT BAY

eat breakfast, and head down the hill to the Monhegan boat. Several of the 10 unpretentious guest rooms (seven with private baths) have great harbor views.

Smack-dab in the middle of Port Clyde, the **Seaside Inn** (5 Cold Storage Rd., Port Clyde, 207/372-0700 or 800/279-5041, www.seaside portclyde.com, $120–180) is an 1850s sea captain's home with both private and shared baths. A first-floor library has books, puzzles, a TV, and a fireplace. Rates include a full breakfast.

Every room has a view of Owl's Head Harbor at the **Trinity on the Ocean Bed and Breakfast** (20 Ocean Ave., Owl's Head, 207/596-0071, www.trinityontheocean.com, $180–220), an oceanfront bed-and-breakfast that's within walking distance of Primo restaurant. Hosts Steve and Donna Belyea are Rockland natives, so they know the area well, and they like to share their finds. Donna made the quilts topping the beds in the three guest rooms, each named after a Maine windjammer. A full breakfast is served either inside or on the ocean-view deck.

FOOD

Call to verify days and hours of operation.

Local Flavors

Don't be surprised to see the handful of tables occupied at the **Keag Store** (Rte. 73, Village Center, South Thomaston, 207/596-6810, 5 A.M.–9 P.M. Mon.–Sat., 6 A.M.–8 P.M. Sun.), one of the most popular lunch stops in the area. (Keag, by the way, is pronounced "gig"—short for "Wessaweskeag.") Roast-turkey sandwiches with stuffing are a big draw, as is the pizza, which verges on the greasy but compensates with its flavor—no designer toppings, just good pizza. Order it all to go and head across the street to the public wharf, where you can hang out and observe all the comings and goings.

Casual Dining

For a relaxing dinner with a gorgeous view, mosey on over to the **Craignair Inn Restaurant** (Clark Island Rd., off Rte. 71, Spruce Head, 207/594-7644, www.craignair .com, from 5:30 P.M. daily in season, entrées

Waterman's Beach Lobster provides amazing views of Penobscot Bay.

$16–24). Big windows in the dining room frame Clark Island and the ocean beyond, and the food complements the view.

Lobster in the Rough

These open-air lobster wharves are the best places in the area to get down and dirty and manhandle a steamed or boiled lobster.

Poking right into Wheeler's Bay, **Miller's Lobster Company** (Eagle Quarry Rd., off Rte. 73, Spruce Head, 207/594-7406, www .millerslobster.com, 11 A.M.–7 P.M. daily) is the quintessential lobster pound, a well-run operation that draws crowds all summer long. There are lobster rolls, steamed clams, crabmeat rolls, homemade pies, and even hot dogs if you need them. Several picnic tables are under cover for chilly or rainy weather. BYOB.

A broad view of islands in the Mussel Ridge Channel is the bonanza at **☾ Waterman's Beach Lobster** (343 Waterman's Beach Rd., South Thomaston, 207/596-7819, www .watermansbeachlobster.com, 11 A.M.–7 P.M. Wed.–Sun., no credit cards). This tiny operation has a big reputation: It won a James Beard Award. It turns out lobster, clam, and mussel dinners, fat lobster and crabmeat rolls, and superb pies as well as hot dogs and grilled cheese. Step up to the window and place your order. Service can be slow, but why rush with a view like this? Choose a good day; there's no real shelter from bad weather. BYOB. The wharf is on a side road off Route 73 between Spruce Head Village and South Thomaston; watch for signs on Route 73.

Monhegan Island

Eleven or so miles from the mainland lies a unique island community with gritty lobstermen, close-knit families, a longstanding summertime artists' colony, no cars, astonishingly beautiful scenery, and some of the best birdwatching on the Eastern Seaboard. Until the 1980s the island had only radiophones and generator power; with the arrival of electricity and real phones, the pace has quickened a bit—but not much. Welcome to Monhegan Island.

But first a cautionary note: Monhegan has remained idyllic largely because generations of residents, part-timers, and visitors have been ultrasensitive to its fragility. When you buy your ferry ticket, you'll receive a copy of the regulations, all very reasonable, and the captain of your ferry will repeat them. *Heed them, or don't go.*

Many of the regulations have been developed by The Monhegan Associates, an island land trust founded in the 1960s by Theodore Edison, son of inventor Thomas Edison. Firmly committed to preservation of the island in as natural a state as possible, the group maintains and marks the trails, sponsors natural-history

talks, and insists that no construction be allowed beyond the village limits.

The origin of the name Monhegan remains up in the air; it's either a Maliseet or Micmac name meaning "out-to-sea island" or an adaptation of the name of a French explorer's daughter. In any case, Monhegan caught the attention of Europeans after English explorer John Smith stopped by in 1614, but the island had already been noticed by earlier adventurers, including John Cabot, Giovanni da Verrazzano, and George Waymouth. Legend even has it that Monhegan fishermen sent dried fish to Plimoth Plantation during the Pilgrims' first winter on Cape Cod. Captain Smith returned home and carried on about Monhegan, catching the attention of intrepid souls who established a fishing and trading outpost here in 1625. Monhegan has been settled continuously since 1674, with fishing as the economic base.

In the 1880s, lured by the spectacular setting and artist Robert Henri's enthusiastic reports, gangs of artists began arriving, lugging their easels here and there to capture the surf, the light, the tidy cottages, the magnificent headlands, fishing boats, even the islanders' craggy features. American, German, French, and British artists have long come here, and they still do; well-known painters associated with Monhegan include Rockwell Kent, George Bellows, Edward Hopper, James Fitzgerald, Andrew Winter, Alice Kent Stoddard, Reuben Tam, William Kienbusch, and Jamie Wyeth.

Officially called Monhegan Plantation, the island has about 75 year-rounders. Several hundred others summer here. A handful of students attend the tiny school through eighth grade; high-schoolers have to pack up and move "inshore" to the mainland during the school year.

At the schoolhouse, the biggest social event of the year is the Christmas party, when everyone brings casseroles, salads, and desserts to complement a big beef roast. Kids perform their Christmas play, Santa shows up with presents, and dozens of adults look on approvingly. The islanders turn out en masse for almost every special event at the school, and the adults treat the island kids almost like common property, feeling free to praise or chastise them any time it seems appropriate—a phenomenon unique to isolated island communities.

For years, Monhegan's legislated lobster-fishing season perversely began on December 1 (locally known as Trap Day), but in 2007 it was moved forward to October 1, making it possible for visitors to view the action. An air of nervous anticipation surrounds the dozen or so lobstermen after midnight the day before as they prepare to steam out to set their traps on the ocean floor. Of course, with less competition from mainland fishermen that time of year, and a supply of lobsters fattening up since the previous June, there's a ready market for their catch. But success still depends on a smooth "setting." Meetings are held daily during the month beforehand to make sure everyone will be ready to "set" together. The season lasts into June.

March brings the annual town meeting, an important community event that draws every able-bodied soul and then some.

TEN RULES FOR MONHEGAN VISITORS

1. Smoking is banned everywhere except in the village.

2. Rock climbing is not allowed on the wild headlands on the back side of the island.

3. Preserve the island's wild state – do not remove flowers or lichens.

4. Bicycles and strollers are not allowed on island trails.

5. Camping and campfires are forbidden island-wide.

6. Swim only at Swim Beach, just south of the ferry landing – if your innards can stand the shock. Wait for the incoming tide, when the water is warmest (and this warmth is relative). It's wise not to swim alone.

7. Dogs must be leashed; carry a pooper-scooper to remove their waste.

8. Be respectful of private property; stay on the trails. (As the island visitors guide puts it, "Monhegan is a village, not a theme park.")

9. If you're staying overnight, bring a flashlight; the village paths are very dark.

10. Carry the island trail map when you go exploring; you'll need it.

A strong suggestion: Carry a trash bag, use it, and take it off the island when you leave.

Almost within spitting distance of Monhegan's dock (but you'll still need a boat) is whale-shaped **Manana Island,** once the home of a former New Yorker named Ray Phillips. Known as the Hermit of Manana, Phillips lived a solitary sheepherding existence on this barren island for more than half a century until his death in 1975. His story had spread so far afield that even the *New York Times* ran a front-page obituary when he died. (Photos and clippings are displayed in the Monhegan Museum.) In summer, youngsters with skiffs often hang around the harbor, particularly Fish Beach and Swim Beach, and you can usually talk one of them into taking you over for a fee. (Don't try to talk them down too much or they may not return to pick you up.) Some curious inscriptions on Manana (marked with a yellow X near the boat landing) have led archaeologists to claim that Vikings even made it here, but cooler heads attribute the markings to Mother Nature.

One last note: Monhegan isn't for the mobility impaired. There's no public transportation, and roads are rough and hilly.

When to Go

If a day trip is all your schedule will allow, visit Monhegan between Memorial Day weekend and mid-October, when ferries from Port Clyde, New Harbor, and Boothbay Harbor operate daily, allowing 5–8 hours on the island—time enough to do an extensive trail loop, visit the museum and handful of shops, and picnic on the rocks. Other months, there's only one ferry per day from Port Clyde, and only three per week November–April, so you'll need to spend the night—not a hardship, but it definitely requires planning.

Almost any time of year, but especially in spring, fog can blanket the island, curtailing photography and swimming (although usually not the ferries). A spectacular sunny day can't be beat, but don't be deterred by fog, which lends an air of mystery you won't forget. Rain, of course, is another matter; some island trails can be perilous even in a misty drizzle.

Other Points to Consider

Monhegan has no bank, but there are a couple of ATMs. Credit cards are not accepted everywhere. Personal checks, traveler's checks, or cash will do. The few public telephones in the village require phone credit cards.

The only public restroom unconnected to a restaurant or lodging is on Horn Hill, at the southern end of the village (near the Monhegan House), and it will cost you $1 to use it. Outrageous, perhaps, but the restroom was installed to protect the woods and trails and deter day-trippers from bothering innkeepers. Unfortunately, the fee inspires some people to spurn these facilities and head for the woods. Please spend the dollar and preserve the island.

SIGHTS

Monhegan is a getaway destination, a relaxing place for self-starters, so don't anticipate organized entertainment beyond the occasional lecture or narrated nature tour. Bring sturdy shoes (maybe even an extra pair in case trails are wet), a windbreaker, binoculars, a camera, and perhaps a sketchpad or a journal. If you're staying overnight, bring a flashlight for negotiating the unlighted island walkways, even in the village. For rainy days, bring a book. (If you forget, there's an amazingly good library.) In winter, bring ice skates for use on the Ice Pond.

◖ Monhegan Historical and Cultural Museum

The **Monhegan Lighthouse**—activated in July 1824, automated in 1959, and now on the National Register of Historic Places—stands at the island's highest point, Lighthouse Hill, an exposed summit that's also home to the Monhegan Historical and Cultural Museum (207/596-7003, www.monheganmuseum.org, 11:30 A.M.–3:30 P.M. daily July–Aug., hours vary June and Sept.) in the former keeper's house and adjacent buildings. Overseen by the Monhegan Historical and Cultural Museum Association, the museum contains an antique kitchen, lobstering exhibits, and a fine collection of paintings by noted and not-so-noted artists. Two outbuildings have tools and gear connected with fishing and ice-cutting, traditional island industries. The assistant light keeper's house, recently restored top to bottom as a handsome art gallery, provides a climate-controlled environment for the museum's impressive art collection. A volunteer is usually on hand to answer questions. The museum also owns two buildings designed and built by Rockwell Kent and later owned by James Fitzgerald. The house is maintained as a historic house museum; Fitzgerald's works are displayed in the studio. Both are open on a limited basis. Admission is technically free, but donations are encouraged.

Artists' Studios

Nearly 20 artists' studios are open to the public during the summer (usually July–August), but not all at once. At least five are open most days—most in the afternoon (Monday has the fewest choices). Sometimes it's tight time-wise for day-trippers who also want to hike the trails, but most of the studios are relatively close to the ferry landing. An annually updated map-schedule details locations, days, and times. It's posted on bulletin boards in the village and is available at lodgings and shops.

Two group galleries worth a visit are **Winter Works,** a craft co-op, and **Lupine Gallery**

(207/594-8131), with works by Monhegan artists and artists' supplies.

RECREATION
Hiking and Walking

Just over half a mile wide and 1.7 miles long, barely a square mile in area, Monhegan has 18 numbered hiking trails, most of them easy to moderate, covering about 11 miles. All are described in the *Monhegan Associates Trail Map* (www.monheganassociates.org), available at mainland ferry offices and island shops and lodgings or on the website. (The map is not to scale, so the hikes can take longer than they may appear.)

The footing is uneven everywhere, so Monhegan can present major obstacles to those with disabilities, even on the well-worn but unpaved village roads. Maintain an especially healthy respect for the ocean here, and don't venture too close; through the years, rogue waves on the island's back side have claimed victims young and old.

A relatively easy **day-tripper loop,** with a

The Monhegan Historical and Cultural Museum sits on the island's highest point.

© HILARY NANGLE

couple of moderate sections along the back side of the island, takes in several of Monhegan's finest features starting at the southern end of the village, opposite the church. To appreciate it, allow at least two hours. From the Main Road, go up Horn Hill, following signs for the **Burnthead Trail** (no. 4). Cross the island to the **Cliff Trail** (no. 1). Turn north on the Cliff Trail, following the dramatic headlands on the island's back side. There are lots of great picnic rocks in this area. Continue to Squeaker Cove, where the surf is the wildest, but be cautious. Then watch for signs to the **Cathedral Woods Trail** (no. 11), carpeted with pine needles and leading back to the village.

When you get back to Main Road, detour up the **Whitehead Trail** (no. 7) to the museum. If you're spending the night and feeling energetic, consider circumnavigating the island via the **Cliff Trail** (nos. 1 and 1-A). Allow at least 5–6 hours for this route; don't rush it.

Bird-Watching

One of the East Coast's best bird-watching sites during spring and fall migrations, Monhegan is a migrant trap for exhausted creatures winging their way north or south. Avid bird-watchers come here to add rare and unusual species to their life lists, and some devotees return year after year. No bird-watcher should arrive, however, without a copy of the superb *Birder's Guide to Maine*.

Predicting exact bird-migration dates can be dicey, since wind and weather aberrations can skew the schedule. Generally, the best times are mid–late May and most of September into early October. If you plan to spend a night (or more) on the island during migration seasons, don't try to wing it—reserve a room well in advance.

Around-the-Island Tour

On most days, the Balmy Days excursion boat makes a half-hour circuit around the island 2–2:30 P.M. for a nominal fee. Ask at the ferry dock.

ACCOMMODATIONS

The island has a variety of lodgings from rustic to comfortable, but none are luxurious. Pickup

There are more than a dozen miles of hiking trails on Monhegan Island.

© HILARY NANGLE

trucks of dubious vintage meet all the ferries and transport luggage to the lodgings. For cottage renters, Monhegan Trucking charges a small fee for each piece of luggage. Rates are quoted for peak season.

The best lodging is the **(Island Inn** (207/596-0371, www.islandinnmonhegan .com, $165–395), an imposing three-story hotel dating from 1816 that commands a prime chunk of real estate overlooking the harbor. Most guest rooms have been updated but retain the simplicity of another era, with painted floors, antique oak furnishings, and comfy beds covered with white down duvets. Just try to resist the siren song of the Adirondack chairs on the expansive veranda and lawns overlooking the ferry landing. Rates for the 32 harbor- and meadow-view guest rooms and suites (most with private baths) include full breakfast. Add $5 pp daily gratuity and $5 pp for a one-night stay.

In the heart of the village, **Monhegan House** (207/594-7983 or 800/599-7983, www .monheganhouse.com, late May–Columbus

PENOBSCOT BAY

Day, $86–90 s, $139–170), built in 1870, is a large four-story building with 33 guest rooms. All but one suite ($215) have shared baths, not always on the same floor as your room. Don't miss the loose-leaf notebook in the lobby. Labeled *A Monhegan Novel,* it's the ultimate in shaggy-dog sagas, created by a long string of guests since 1992. Rates include breakfast. There may be a $5 pp surcharge for one-night stays. Children are welcome; ages 4–12 are $18, ages 13 and older are $28.

A more modernized hostelry, **Shining Sails** (207/596-0041, www.shiningsails.com, $140–215) lacks the quaintness of the other inns, but the guest rooms and efficiencies are very comfortable, convenient to the dock, stay open all year, and have private baths. Breakfast (included only in season) is continental. "Well-supervised" children are welcome. An additional four apartments ($165–230) are in a separate building. Shining Sails also manages more than two dozen weekly-rental cottages and apartments, with rates beginning around $800 per week in season.

The funkiest lodging, and not for everyone, is **The Trailing Yew** (207/596-0440 or 800/592-2520, www.trailingyew.com, $190, no credit cards). Spread among five rustic buildings are 35 guest rooms, most with shared baths (averaging five rooms per bath and not always in the same building) and lighted with kerosene (about 12 have electricity). Rates include breakfast, dinner, taxes, and gratuities; kids are $55 and up, depending on age. The old-fashioned, low-key 50-seat dining room is open to nonguests by reservation for dinner at 5:45 P.M., served family-style, and for breakfast at 7:45 A.M. Bring a sleeping bag in spring or fall; rooms are unheated.

FOOD

Most visitors don't arrive on Monhegan expecting gourmet cuisine. Everything is quite casual, and food is hearty and ample. None of the eateries have liquor licenses, so buy beer or wine at one of the stores or the Barnacle Café, or bring it from the mainland. All of the restaurants and food sources are in or close to the village. In most cases hours change frequently, so call first.

Prepared foods, varying from pastries to sandwiches and salads, are available from **Barnacle Café** (207/596-0371), under the same ownership as the nearby Island Inn; **The Novelty,** behind and operated by The Monhegan House; **Black Duck Emporium** (207/596-7672); **Carina** (207/594-0837), a boutique grocery; and the **Monhegan Store.**

Casual Dining

The restaurant at the **Island Inn,** open to nonguests for breakfast and dinner from 6 P.M., has an excellent dinner menu with creative entrées ($15–27). It's also open for lunch Thursday–Sunday.

Islanders and visitors flock to the **Monhegan House Café,** overlooking the village, for breakfast and dinner (entrées $16–25).

Lobster in the Rough

You can't get much rougher for lobster in the rough than **Fish House Fish** (Fish Beach, www.fishbeachmonhegan.com, 11:30 A.M.–7 P.M. daily). Lobster and crabmeat rolls, locally smoked fish, and homemade stews and chowders are on the menu as well as fresh lobster. Take it to the picnic tables on the beach and enjoy.

INFORMATION AND SERVICES

Several free brochures and flyers, revised annually, will answer most questions about planning a day trip or overnight visit to Monhegan. Ferries supply visitors with the *Visitor's Guide to Monhegan Island* and sell the Monhegan Associates Trail Map ($1). Both are also available at island shops, galleries, and lodgings. Info is also available at www.monhegan.com, www.monheganwelcome.com, and www.monhegan.info.

Monhegan's pleasant little Jackie and Edward Library was named after two children who drowned in the surf in the 1920s. The fiction collection is especially extensive, and it's open to everyone.

© HILARY NANGLE

ferry ride to Monhegan Island

Also check the Rope Shed, the community bulletin board next to the meadow, right in the village. Monhegan's version of a bush telegraph, it's where everyone posts flyers and notices about nature walks, lectures, excursions, and other special events. You'll also see the current Monhegan Artists Studio Locations map.

GETTING THERE AND AROUND

Ferries travel year-round to Monhegan from Port Clyde at the end of the St. George Peninsula. Seasonal service to the island is provided from New Harbor by **Hardy Boat Cruises** and from Boothbay Harbor by **Balmy Days Cruises**.

Part of the daily routine for many islanders and summer folk is a stroll to the harbor when the ferry comes in, so don't be surprised to see a good-size welcoming party when you arrive. You're the live entertainment.

Monhegan's only vehicles are a handful of pickup trucks owned by local lobstermen and li'l ol' trucks used by **Monhegan Trucking**. If you're staying a night or longer and your luggage is too heavy to carry, they'll be waiting when you arrive at the island wharf.

Rockland

A "Share the Pride" campaign—kicked off in the 1980s to boost sagging civic self-esteem and the local economy—was the first step in the transformation of Rockland. Once a run-down county seat best known for the aroma of its fish-packing plants, the city has undergone a sea change and in 2010 was named a Distinctive Destination by the National Trust for Historic Preservation. The expansion of the Farnsworth Museum of American Art and the addition of its Wyeth Center was a catalyst. Benches and plants line Main Street (Rte. 1), stores offer appealing wares, coffeehouses and more than a dozen art galleries attract a diverse clientele, and Rockland Harbor is home to more windjammer cruise schooners than neighboring Camden (which had long claimed the title "Windjammer Capital"). If you haven't been to Rockland in the last decade, prepare to be astonished.

Foresighted entrepreneurs had seen the potential of the bayside location in the late 1700s and established a tiny settlement here called "Shore Village" (or "the Shore"). Today's commercial-fishing fleet is one of the few reminders of Rockland's past, when multimasted schooners lined the wharves, some to load volatile cargoes of lime destined to become building material for cities all along the eastern seaboard, others to head northeast—toward the storm-racked Grand Banks and the lucrative cod fishery there. Such hazardous pursuits meant an early demise for many a local seafarer, but Rockland's 5,000 or so residents were enjoying their prosperity in the late 1840s. The settlement was home to more than two dozen shipyards and dozens of lime kilns, was enjoying a construction boom, and boasted a newspaper and regular steamship service. By 1854, Rockland had become a city.

Today, Rockland remains a commercial hub—with Knox County's only shopping plazas (no malls, but the big-box stores have arrived), a fishing fleet that heads far offshore, and ferries that connect nearby islands.

Rockland also claims the title of "Lobster Capital of the World" thanks to Knox County's shipment nationally and internationally of 10 million pounds of lobster each year. The weathervane atop the police and fire department building is a giant copper lobster.

Rockland is more year-round community than tourist town, which adds to its appeal. But visitors pour in during two big summer festivals—the North Atlantic Blues Festival in mid-July and the Maine Lobster Festival in early August. A highlight of the Lobster Festival is King Neptune's coronation of the Maine Sea Goddess—carefully selected from a bevy of local young women—who then sails off with him to his water domain.

SIGHTS
◖ The Farnsworth Art Museum and the Wyeth Center

Anchoring downtown Rockland is the nationally respected Farnsworth Art Museum (16 Museum St., 207/596-6457, www.farnsworthmuseum.org), established in 1948 through a trust fund set up by Rocklander Lucy Farnsworth. With an ample checkbook, the first curator, Robert Bellows, toured the country, accumulating a splendid collection of 19th- and 20th-century Maine-related American art, the basis for the permanent "Maine in America" exhibition.

The 6,000-piece collection today includes work by Fitz Hugh Lane, Gilbert Stuart, Eastman Johnson, Childe Hassam, John Marin, Maurice Prendergast, Rockwell Kent, George Bellows, and Marsden Hartley. Best known are the paintings by three generations of the Wyeth family (local summer residents) and sculpture by Louise Nevelson, who grew up in Rockland. Sculpture, jewelry, and paintings by Nevelson form the core of the third-floor Nevelson-Berliawsky Gallery for 20th Century Art. (The only larger Nevelson collection is in New York's Whitney Museum of American Art.) The Wyeth Center, across

Union Street in a former church, contains the work of Andrew, N. C., and Jamie Wyeth. The 6,000-square-foot Jamien Morehouse Wing hosts rotating exhibits.

In the Farnsworth's library—a grand, high-ceilinged oasis akin to an English gentleman's reading room—browsers and researchers can explore an extensive collection of art books and magazines. The museum's education department annually sponsors hundreds of lectures, concerts, art classes for all ages, poetry readings, and field trips. Most are open to non-members; some require an extra fee. A glitzy gift shop stocks posters, prints, note cards, imported gift items, and art games for children.

Next door to the museum is the mid-19th-century Greek Revival **Farnsworth Homestead**, with original high-Victorian furnishings. Looking as though William Farnsworth's family just took off for the day, the house has been preserved rather than restored.

The Farnsworth also owns the **Olson House,** 14 miles away in nearby Cushing, where the whole landscape looks like a Wyeth diorama. Pick up a map at the museum to help you find the house; it's definitely worth the side trip.

The Farnsworth ($12 adults, $10 seniors and students age 17 and older, free under age 17 and Rockland residents) is open year-round, including summer holidays. Farnsworth hours are 10 A.M.–5 P.M. Thursday–Tuesday, 10 A.M.–8 P.M. Wednesday in summer; 10 A.M.–5 P.M. Wednesday–Sunday in winter. Call the museum for its current definition of summer and winter. The Homestead (10 A.M.–5 P.M. daily) and the Olson House (11 A.M.–4 P.M. daily) are open late May–mid-October. Admission is free after 5 P.M. on Wednesday.

(Owls Head Transportation Museum

Don't miss this place, even if you're not an old-vehicle buff. A generous endowment has made the Owls Head Transportation Museum (Rte. 73, Owls Head, 207/594-4418, www.ohtm.org, 10 A.M.–5 P.M. daily, $10 adults, $8 seniors,

© HILARY NANGLE

PENOBSCOT BAY

The Owls Head Transportation Museum is a must for fans of vintage wings and wheels and is often the site of air shows.

free under age 18, special events are extra) a premier facility for celebrating wings and wheels; it draws more than 75,000 visitors per year. Scads of eager volunteers help restore the vehicles and keep them running. On weekends May–October, the museum sponsors air shows (often including aerobatic displays) and car and truck meets for hundreds of enthusiasts. The season highlight is the annual rally and aerobatic show (early Aug.), when more than 300 vehicles gather for two days of festivities. Want your own vintage vehicle? Attend the antique, classic, and special-interest auto auction (third Sun. in Aug.). The gift shop carries transportation-related items. If the kids get bored (unlikely), there's a play area outside with picnic tables. In winter, groomed cross-country-skiing trails wind through the museum's 60-acre site; ask for a map at the information desk.

Maine Lighthouse Museum

The headliner at the Maine Discovery Center (1 Park Dr.) is the Maine Lighthouse Museum (207/594-3301, www.mainelighthousemuseum .com, 9 A.M.–5 P.M. Mon.–Fri., 10 A.M.–4 P.M. Sat.–Sun. June 1–Nov. 1 or by appointment, $5 adults, $4 seniors, free under age 12), home to the nation's largest collection of Fresnel lenses, along with a boatload-plus of artifacts related to lighthouses, the Coast Guard, and the sea. On view are foghorns, ships' bells, nautical books and photographs, marine instruments, ship models, scrimshaw, and so much more.

Project Puffin Visitor Center

If you can't manage a trip to see the puffins, Audubon's Project Puffin Visitor Center (311 Main St., 207/596-5566 or 877/478-3346, www.projectpuffin.org, 10 A.M.–5 P.M. Thurs.–Tues., 10 A.M.–7 P.M. Wed. June 1–Oct. 31, call for off-season hours) will bring them to you. Live videos of nesting puffins are just one of the highlights of the center, which also includes interactive exhibits, a gallery, and films, all highlighting successful efforts to restore and protect these clowns of the sea. On Wednesday evenings in July–August, there's a weekly lecture series.

(Rockland Breakwater

Protecting the harbor from wind-driven waves, the 4,346-foot-long Rockland Breakwater took 18 years to build with 697,000 tons of locally quarried granite. In the late 19th century it was piled up, chunk by chunk, from a base 175 feet wide on the harbor floor (60 feet below the surface) to the 43-foot-wide cap. The Breakwater Light—now automated—was built in 1902 and added to the National Register of Historic Places in 1981. The city of Rockland owns the keeper's house, but it is maintained by the Friends of the Rockland Breakwater Lighthouse (www .rocklandlighthouse.com). Member volunteers usually open the lighthouse to the public 10 A.M.–5 P.M. Saturday–Sunday late May–mid-October and for special events. The breakwater provides unique vantage points for photographers as well as a place to picnic or catch sea breezes or fish on a hot day, but it is extremely dangerous during storms. Anyone on the breakwater risks being washed into the sea or struck by lightning (ask the local hospital staff; it has happened). Do not take chances when the weather is iffy.

To reach the breakwater, take Route 1 North to Waldo Avenue and turn right. Take the next right onto Samoset Road and drive to the end to **Marie Reed Memorial Park** (with a tiny beach, benches, and limited parking). Or go to the Samoset Resort and take the path to the breakwater from there.

Sail Power & Steam Museum

Opened in 2009, the Sail Power & Steam Museum (Sharp's Point South, 75 Mechanic St., 207/701-7626, www.sailpowerandsteam museum.org, 11 A.M.–4 P.M. Wed.–Sun.) is Captain Jim Sharp's labor of love. Built on the grounds of the former Snow Shipyard, the museum displays highlight Rockland's maritime heritage and include half-models of boats used by shipbuilders in the 19th century, vintage photos, tools of the trade, and other artifacts. Docked nearby is the *Rekord,* a 1914 Norwegian freighter that is used by Sharp for harbor tours.

© HILARY NANGLE

A nearly mile-long breakwater connects the Samoset Resort to the Rockland Breakwater Lighthouse.

Main Street Historic District

Rocklanders are justly proud of their Main Street Historic District, lined with 19th- and early-20th-century Greek and Colonial Revival structures as well as examples of mansard and Italianate architecture. Most now house retail shops on the ground floor; upper floors have offices, artists' studios, and apartments. The chamber of commerce has a map and details.

Flightseeing

Soar and swoop on a glider ride with **Spirit Soaring** (207/319-9514, www.spiritsoaring .org). Rates begin at $120 for a half-hour ride over coastal Penobscot Bay. It operates from Knox County Regional Airport in Owls Head, just south of Rockland.

Excursion Train

Here's a different way to see the coast (and beat the traffic). Ride in restored vintage railcars on the scenic **Maine Eastern Railroad** (207/596-6725 or 800/637-2457, www.maineeastern railroad.com), operating between Rockland and Brunswick with stops in Wiscasset and Bath. The train operates late May–early November, with special holiday trains in December. Adult fares are $42 round-trip, $27 one-way; seniors $37/$27; ages 5–15 $21/$16; family rate $109/$83, covering two adults and two kids. Packages with lodging, meals, and theater are available.

ENTERTAINMENT AND EVENTS

Stop by the **Lincoln Street Center for Arts and Education** (24 Lincoln St., 207/594-6490, www.lincolnstreetcenter.org), a community arts center with exhibitions, performances, and classes, to see what's on the schedule.

The historic **Strand Theater** (339 Main St., 207/594-7266, www.rocklandstrand.com), opened in 1923, underwent an extensive restoration in 2005. Films as well as live entertainment are scheduled. It's also the venue for many **Bay Chamber Concerts** (207/236-2823 or 888/707-2770, www.baychamberconcerts .org) events.

PENOBSCOT BAY

WINDJAMMING

In 1936, Camden became the home of the "cruise schooner" (sometimes called "dude schooner") trade when Captain Frank Swift restored a creaky wooden vessel and offered sailing vacations to paying passengers. He kept at it for 25 years, gradually adding other boats to the fleet – and the rest, as they say, is history. Windjammers have become big business on the Maine coast, with Camden and Rockland sparring for the title of Windjammer Capital. Rockland wrested it from Camden in the mid-1990s and so far has held onto it.

Named for their ability to "jam" into the wind when they carried freight up and down the New England coast, windjammers trigger images of the Great Age of Sail. Most member vessels of the Maine Windjammer Association are

Members of the Maine Windjammer Association fleet sail by Rockland Breakwater Lighthouse.

rigged as schooners, with two or three soaring wooden masts; their lengths range 64-132 feet. Seven are National Historic Landmarks.

These windjammers head out for 3-6 days late May-mid-October, tucking into coves and harbors around Penobscot Bay and its islands. The mostly engineless craft set their itineraries by the wind, propelled by stiff breezes to Buck's Harbor, North Haven, and Deer Isle. Everything's totally informal, geared for relaxing.

You're aboard for the experience, not for luxury, so expect basic accommodations with few frills, although newer vessels were built with passenger trade in mind and tend to be a bit more comfy. Down below, cabins typically are small and basic, with paper-thin walls – sort of a campground afloat (earplugs are often available for light sleepers). It may not sound romantic, but be aware that the captains keep track of postcruise marriages. Most boats have shared showers and toilets. If you're Type A, given to pacing, don't inflict yourself on the cruising crowd; if you're flexible, ready for whatever, go ahead and sign on. You can help with the sails, eat, curl up with a book, inhale salt air, shoot photos, eat, sunbathe, bird-watch, eat, chat up fellow passengers, sleep, eat, or just settle back and enjoy spectacular sailing you'll never forget.

When you book a cruise, you'll receive all the details and directions, but for a typical six-day

trip, you arrive at the boat by 7 P.M. for the captain's call to meet your fellow passengers. You sleep aboard at the dock that night and then depart midmorning Monday and spend five nights and days cruising Penobscot Bay, following the wind, the weather, and the whims of the captain. (Many of the windjammers have no engines, only a motorized yawl boat used as a pusher and a water taxi.) You might anchor in a deserted cove and explore the shore, or you might pull into a harbor and hike, shop, and bar-hop. Then it's back to the boat for chow – windjammer cooks are legendary for creating three hearty all-you-can-eat meals daily, including at least one lobster feast. When the cruise ends, most passengers find it hard to leave.

On the summer cruising schedule, several weeks coincide with special windjammer events, so you'll need to book a berth far in advance for these: mid-June (Boothbay Harbor's Windjammer Days), Fourth of July week (Great Schooner Race), Labor Day weekend (Camden's Windjammer Weekend), and the second week in September (WoodenBoat Sail-in).

Most windjammers offering 3-6-day sails out of Camden, Rockland, and Rockport are members of the **Maine Windjammer Association** (800/807-9463, www.sailmainecoast.com), a one-stop resource for vessel and schedule information.

If you're a film buff, you might want to see what the **Saltwater Film Society** (www.saltwaterfilmsociety.org) has on its schedule.

The Historic Inns of Rockland coordinate the annual **January Pies on Parade**, when the inns and dozens of downtown businesses serve a variety of sweet and savory pies as a fundraiser for the local food pantry. It's always a sellout.

In mid-July the **North Atlantic Blues Festival** means a weekend of festivities featuring big names in blues. Thousands of fans jam Harbor Park for the nonstop music.

August's **Maine Lobster Festival** is a five-day lobster extravaganza with live entertainment, the Maine Sea Goddess pageant, a lobster-crate race, craft booths, boat rides, a parade, lobster dinners, and megacrowds (the hotels are full for miles in either direction). Tons of lobsters bite the dust during the weekend despite annual protests by People for the Ethical Treatment of Animals. (The protests, however, only seem to increase the crowds.)

SHOPPING
Galleries

Piggybacking on the fame of the Farnsworth Museum, or at least working symbiotically, art galleries line Rockland's main street and many side streets. Ask around and look around. During the summer, many of them coordinate monthly openings to coincide with **First Friday Art Walks** (www.artsinrockland.com), so you can meander, munch, and sip from one gallery to another.

Across from the Farnsworth's side entrance, the **Caldbeck Gallery** (12 Elm St., 207/594-5935, www.caldbeck.com) has gained a top-notch reputation as a must-see (and must-be-seen) space. Featuring the work of contemporary Maine artists, the gallery mounts more than half a dozen solo and group shows in May–September each year.

Eric Hopkins Gallery (21 Winter St., 207/594-1996, www.erichopkins.com) shows the North Haven artist's colorful aerial-view paintings.

Archipelago (386 Main St., 207/596-0701), on the ground floor of the Island Institute, a nonprofit steward of Maine's 4,617 offshore islands, is an attractive retail outlet for talented craftspeople from 14 year-round islands.

Other eminently browsable downtown Rockland galleries are **Harbor Square Gallery** (374 Main St., 207/594-8700 or 877/594-8700, www.harborsquaregallery.com), **Landing Gallery** (8 Elm St., 888/394-2787), **Playing with Fire! Glassworks & Gallery** (497 Main St., 207/594-7805, www.playingwithfireglassworks.com), and **Mulford Collectors Gallery** (313 Main St., 207/594-8481, www.mulfordgallery.com). All are within steps of each other.

Wineries

Head inland on Route 17 and then noodle off on the back roads to discover not one but two wineries. At **Sweetgrass Farm Winery and Distillery** (347 Carroll Rd., Union, 207/785-3024, www.sweetgrasswinery.com, 11 A.M.–5 P.M. daily late May–late Dec.), owner Keith Bodine uses Maine-grown fruits to produce both wines and spirits, and he is eager to show interested folks how. Bring a picnic to enjoy while hiking the winery's trails. Carroll Road is between Shepard Hill Road and North Union Road, both north of Route 17, west of Route 131.

Nearby is **Savage Oakes** (174 Barrett Hill Rd., Union, 207/785-5261, www.savageoakes.com, 11 A.M.–5 P.M. daily mid-May–late Oct.), where Elmer and Holly Savage and their sons have added winemaking to their second-generation Belted Galloway cattle farm. They grow nine varieties of grapes, both red and white, and produce more than half a dozen wines. Barrett Hill Road is off Route 17 directly opposite Route 131 South.

RECREATION
Parks
◖ OWLS HEAD LIGHT STATE PARK

On Route 73, about 1.5 miles past the junction of Routes 1 and 73, you'll reach North Shore Road in the town of Owls Head. Turn left toward Owls Head Light State Park. Standing 3.6 miles from this turn, Owls Head Light occupies a dramatic promontory with panoramic views over Rockland Harbor and Penobscot Bay. Don't miss it. The keeper's house and the light tower are off-limits, but the park surrounding the tower has easy walking paths, picnic tables, and a pebbly beach where you can sunbathe or check out Rockland Harbor's boating traffic. If it's foggy or rainy, don't climb the steps toward the light tower: The view evaporates in the fog, the access ramp can be slippery, and the fog-horn is dangerously deafening. Follow signs to reach the park. From North Shore Road, turn left onto Main Street, then left onto Lighthouse Road, and continue along Owls Head Harbor to the parking area. This is also a particularly pleasant bike route—about 10 miles round-trip from downtown Rockland—although, once again, the roadside shoulders are poor along the Owls Head stretch.

HARBOR PARK

If you're looking for a park with more commotion than quiet green space, spend some time at Harbor Park. Boats, cars, and delivery vehicles

© HILARY NANGLE

A lobster-trap Christmas tree adorned with buoys and topped with a lobster is a seasonal highlight in Rockland's Harbor Park.

come and go, and you can corner a picnic table, a bench, or a patch of grass and watch all the action. During the holidays, a lobster-trap Christmas tree presides over the park. Public restrooms (late May–mid-Oct.) are available. The park is just off Main Street.

Swimming

Lucia Beach is the local name for **Birch Point Beach State Park,** one of the best-kept secrets in the area. In Owls Head, just south of Rockland—and not far from Owls Head Light—the spruce-lined sand crescent (free) has rocks, shells, tide pools, and very chilly water. There are outhouses but no other facilities. There's ample room for a moderate-size crowd, although parking and turnaround space can get a bit tight on the access road. From downtown Rockland, take Route 73 one mile to North Shore Drive (on your left). Take the next right, Ash Point Drive, and continue past Knox County Regional Airport to Dublin Road. Turn right, go 0.8 miles, then turn left onto Ballyhac Road (opposite the airport landing lights). Go another 0.8 miles, fork left, and continue 0.4 miles to the parking area.

If frigid ocean water doesn't appeal, head for freshwater **Chickawaukee Lake,** on Route 17, two miles inland from downtown Rockland. Don't expect to be alone, though; on hot days, **Johnson Memorial Park**'s pocket-size sand patch is a major attraction. A lifeguard holds forth, and there are restrooms, picnic tables, a snack bar, and a boat-launch ramp. In winter, iceboats, snowmobiles, and ice-fishing shacks take over the lake. A signposted bicycle path runs alongside the busy highway, making the park an easy pedal from town.

Golf

The semiprivate **Rockland Golf Club** (606 Old County Rd., 207/594-9322, www.rocklandgolf.com, Apr.–Oct.) is an 18-hole course 0.2 miles northeast of Route 17.

For an 18-hole course in an unsurpassed waterfront setting (but with steep rental and greens fees), tee off at the **Samoset Resort**

(220 Warrenton St., Rockport, 207/594-2511 or 800/341-1650, www.samoset.com).

Sea Kayaking

Veteran Maine Guide and naturalist Mark DiGirolamo is the sparkplug behind **Breakwater Kayak** (Rockland Public Landing, 207/596-6895 or 877/559-8800, www.breakwaterkayak.com), which has a full range of tours, even multiday ones. A two-hour Rockland Harbor tour (usually offered twice daily at the height of summer) is $40, and the all-day Owls Head Lighthouse tour is $100, including lunch. Reservations are advisable. This outfit is particularly eco-sensitive—Mark has a degree in environmental science—and is definitely worth supporting. Maine Audubon often taps Mark to lead natural-history field trips. Dress warmly for these tours and be sure to bring a filled water bottle.

Excursion Boats

Marine biologist Captain Bob Pratt is the skipper of *A Morning in Maine* (207/594-1844 or 207/691-7245 seasonal boat phone, www.amorninginmaine.com), a classic 55-foot ketch designed by noted naval architect R. D. (Pete) Culler and built by Concordia Yachts. From June through October, *Morning* departs from the middle pier at the Rockland Public Landing three times daily for two-hour sails ($35), with plenty of knowledgeable commentary from Captain Pratt. A 6 P.M. sunset sail is available in July–August.

Watch Captain Steve Hale set and haul lobster traps during a 1.25-hour cruise ($25 adults, $15 under age 12) aboard the *Captain Jack* (Rockland Harbor, 207/594-1048, www.captainjacklobstertours.com), a 30-foot working lobster boat. Cruises depart up to six times daily Monday–Saturday May–October. Note that there are no toilets aboard. Captain Jack offers a lobster-roll lunch cruise for $45 pp. Reservations required; minimum two people for a trip.

Maine State Ferry Service

Car and passenger ferries service the islands of Vinalhaven, North Haven, and Matinicus.

The Vinalhaven and North Haven routes make fantastic day trips (especially with a bike), or you can spend the night; the Matinicus ferry is much less predictable, and island services are few.

Bicycling

Rentals ($20), sales, repair, and coffee are provided by **Bikesenjava** (481 Main St., 207/596-1004, www.haybikesenjava.com).

ACCOMMODATIONS

Rates noted are for peak season. If you're planning an overnight stay in the Rockland area the first weekend in August—during the Maine Lobster Festival—be sure to make reservations well in advance. Festival attendance runs close to 100,000, "No Vacancy" signs extend from Waldoboro to Belfast, and there just aren't enough beds or campsites to go around.

Samoset Resort

The 221-acre Samoset Resort (220 Warrenton St., Rockport, 207/594-2511 or 800/341-1650, www.samoset.com, from about $275) commands a spectacular oceanfront site straddling the boundary between Rockland and Rockport, the next town to the north. Built on the ashes of a classic 19th-century summer hotel, the Samoset is a full-service modern family-oriented resort. Most of its 178 guest rooms and suites, all refurbished since 2007, and four cottages have knockout ocean views and all the expected bells and whistles. Facilities include a fitness center with an indoor heated pool, an outdoor zero-entry heated pool with a bar and food service, lighted tennis courts, a children's day camp (ages 5–12, morning and evening sessions), daily planned activities, access to the adjacent famed Rockland Breakwater, and a fabulous 18-hole waterfront golf course. New additions planned for 2011 included a spa, a restaurant and lounge, and an outdoor terrace. For a real treat, book the Flume cottage.

Bed-and-Breakfasts

These bed-and-breakfasts are in Rockland's historic district, within easy walking distance of downtown attractions and restaurants, and are members of the **Historic Inns of Rockland Maine** (www.historicinnsofrockland.com), which coordinates the January Pies on Parade event—a blast.

Most elegant is ◖ **The Berry Manor Inn** (81 Talbot Ave., 207/596-7696 or 800/774-5692, www.berrymanorinn.com, $175–275), on a quiet side street a few blocks from downtown. Cheryl Michaelsen and Michael LaPosta have totally restored the manse built in 1898 by wealthy Rocklander Charles Berry as a wedding gift for his wife (thoughtful fellow). High ceilings and wonderful Victorian architectural touches are everywhere, especially in the enormous front hall and two parlors. Guest rooms and suites are spread between the main house and adjacent carriage house. Most have gas fireplaces and whirlpool tubs. All have air-conditioning, flat-screen TVs and video players, and Wi-Fi. A guest pantry is stocked with free soft drinks and juices and sweets—not that you'll be hungry after the extravagant breakfast.

Opened in 1996, the **Captain Lindsey House Inn** (5 Lindsey St., 207/596-7950 or 800/523-2145, www.lindseyhouse.com, $178–215) is more like a boutique hotel than a bed-and-breakfast. The Barnes family gutted the 1835 brick structure and restored it dramatically, adding such modernities as phones, air-conditioning, Wi-Fi, and TVs. The decor is strikingly handsome, not at all fussy or frilly. Don't miss the 1926 safe in the front hall or the hidden-from-the-street garden patio—not to mention the antiques from everywhere that fill the nine comfortable guest rooms. It's smack downtown, and a few rooms have glimpses of the water. Rates include an extensive hot-and-cold breakfast buffet and afternoon refreshments.

The Limerock Inn (96 Limerock St., 207/594-2257 or 800/546-3762, www.limerockinn.com, $159–239) is a lovely painted lady. The 1890s Queen Anne mansion, with wraparound porch and turret, is listed on the National Register of Historic Places. Each of the eight guest rooms has its own distinctive flavor—such as the Turret Room, with a wedding canopy bed, and the Island Cottage Room, with a private deck overlooking the back gardens. All are elegantly furnished with an emphasis on guest comfort. Three have whirlpool tubs, and one has a fireplace; there's Wi-Fi and air-conditioning throughout. The inviting decor blends family antiques with mid-century modern furnishings and original art.

Traveling with Fido and the kiddos? Check into the kid- and pet-friendly **Granite Inn** (546 Main St., Rockland, 800/386-9036, www.old-graniteinn.com, $95–215), where you can practically roll out of bed and onto an island ferry. Unlike most historical inns, the decor leans to contemporary and a bit artsy.

FOOD

Call to verify days and hours of operation.

Local Flavors

A winner for creative breakfasts and lunches is **The Brown Bag** (606 Main St., 207/596-6372 or 800/287-6372, bakery 207/596-6392, 7 A.M.–2:30 P.M. Mon.–Sat., bakery 7 A.M.–4 P.M. Mon.–Sat.). It's *the* place for breakfast, especially weekends, with fantastic baked goods and a full blackboard of other options. Order at the counter; there is no table service. Find it at the junction of Routes 1 and 17.

Holding down the other end of Main Street is the **Brass Compass Café** (305 Main St., 207/596-5960, 5 A.M.–3 P.M. Sun.–Thurs., 5 A.M.–9 P.M. Fri.–Sat.), a great choice for Maine fare. The portions are big, the prices are small, and most of the ingredients are locally sourced. In 2009 celebrity chef Bobby Flay challenged chef-owner Lynn Archer to a lobster club throw-down. Sit indoors or on the dog-friendly patio. If you go for breakfast, the fishcakes are a real taste of Maine.

Hot diggity dog! Backed up against an outside wall of The Brown Bag is a long-standing Rockland lunch landmark—**Wasses Hot Dogs** (2 N. Main St., 207/594-7472, 10:30 A.M.–6 P.M. Mon.–Sat., 11 A.M.–4 P.M. Sun. year-round), source of great chili dogs and creative ice cream in waffle cones. This one-time lunch wagon is now a permanent modular building—only for takeout, though.

Lots of Rockland-watchers credit Maine's first bookstore-café, **Rock City Books and Coffee** (328 Main St., 207/594-4123, www.rockcitycoffee.com, 6:30 A.M.–8 P.M. Mon.–Sat., 7 A.M.–8 P.M. Sun.), with sparking the designer-food renaissance in town. The menu has expanded greatly since the original coffee, tea, and treats to include frozen drinks, soups, salads, sandwiches, and wraps, including rockin' breakfast wraps, served until 11 A.M., and plenty of vegetarian choices. Order at the counter and then peruse the shelves of more than 10,000 carefully selected new and "gently used" books while you wait. There is frequently live entertainment on weekends.

Scratch-made bread, pastries, and grab-and-go sandwiches have made **Atlantic Baking Co.** (351 Main St., 207/596-0505, www.atlanticbakingco.com, 7 A.M.–6 P.M. Mon.–Sat., 8 A.M.–5 P.M. Sun.) a popular spot for a quick informal lunch. There are plenty of tables to enjoy your treats, or take it to the waterfront park.

Even closer to Harbor Park is **Sweets & Meats Market** (218 Main St., 207/594-2070, www.sweetsandmeatsmarket.com), with a nice selection of sandwiches, including a vegan option, as well as cheeses, meats, and baked goods; there's indoor seating and free Wi-Fi.

If you're craving a decent breakfast or lunch and are up for a little foray "down the peninsula," head for the **Owls Head General Store** (2 S. Shore Dr., Owls Head, 207/596-6038, 6 A.M.–7 P.M. Mon.–Sat., 7 A.M.–3 P.M. Sun.), where the atmosphere is friendly and definitely contagious. If you get lost, the helpful staff will steer you the right way, and they will even take your photograph in front of the store. Despite all the competition from lobster-in-the-rough places, the lobster roll here is among the best around, and more than one critic has proclaimed the burgers the state's best.

The **Rockland Farmers Market** gets under way 9 A.M.–1 P.M. every Thursday June–September at Harbor Park on Rockland's Public Landing. Wares from more than a dozen vendors include produce, chocolates, crafts, syrup, poultry, mushrooms, baked goods, and cheeses. Every week there's a special event—music, dancers, lectures, special giveaways, and occasionally a llama or goat for the kids to pet.

Fiore (503 Main St., 207/596-0276, www.fioreoliveoils.com), an artisan olive oil and vinegar tasting room and retail store, is a delicious addition to downtown Rockland.

Ethnic Fare

Ask local pooh-bah chefs where they go on their night off, and the answer often is Keiko Suzuki Steinberger's **Suzuki's Sushi Bar** (419 Main St., 207/596-7447, www.suzukisushi.com, 11 A.M.–2:30 P.M. and 5–8:30 P.M. Tues.–Sat.). The food matches the decor: simple yet sophisticated. Sashimi, *nigiri, maki,* and *temaki* choices range $6–10; hot entrées are $13–24. Both hot and cold sake are served, or try a saketume, made with gin or vodka, sake, and an *ume* plum. Reservations are essential.

Cassoulet! Moules Provençal! Steak tartare! Chefs Lynette Mosher and Robert Krajewski have created a delicious pocket of France in downtown Rockland at **Lily Bistro** (421 Main St., 207/594-4141, www.lilybistromaine.com, 5–9:30 P.M. daily, entrées $24–28).

A small dining area decorated in avocado and gold is the appropriate setting for the Cal-Mex food dished out at **Sunfire Mexican Grill** (488 Main St., 207/594-6196, lunch 11 A.M.–3 P.M. Tues.–Sat., dinner 5–8 P.M. Wed.–Sat.). You'll find all the usuals, from tacos ($3) to a chipotle shrimp tostada ($12). Everything is prepared fresh on-site.

When you're really famished, the place to go is **Conte's Fish Market and Restaurant** (148 S. Main St., no phone, dinner from 4 P.M. daily year-round, $10–20, no credit cards), where portions are humongous and prices are not. John Conte moved here from New York in 1995, bringing his family's century-old restaurant tradition. Specialties are pasta and seafood—Italian all the way, loaded with garlic. The decor is wildly funky, with fishnets, marine relics, old books, even stacks of canned plum tomatoes. Menus are handwritten on paper-towel rolls and in your face at the door (order before you sit down), table coverings are yesterday's newspapers, and Edith Piaf chansons or operatic arias sometimes play in the background. It's eccentric, unpredictable, not spotless, and definitely not for everyone. Bring your sense of humor, and don't be put off by the exterior or the attitude; there's life behind the doors. Beer and wine only.

Casual Dining

Big flavors come out of the tiny kitchen at **Café Miranda** (15 Oak St., 207/594-2034, www.cafemiranda.com, 5–9 P.M. daily). The menu is overwhelming in size and hard to read; it's even harder to digest the flavor contrasts, which will make your brain spin. When it works, it shines, but when it doesn't, it can be painful. Service is irregular. Entrées are $18–27, but many of the appetizers ($6.50–12.50) are enough for a meal. Fresh-from-the-brick-oven focaccia comes with everything. If you sit at the counter, you can watch chef Kerry Altiero's creations emerging from the oven. Beer and wine only. Reservations are essential throughout the summer and on weekends off-season; there is patio dining in season.

At the end of a day exploring Rockland, it's hard to beat **❰ In Good Company** (415 Main St., 207/593-9110, from 4:30 P.M. Tues.–Sun., $5–18), a chic and casual wine and tapas bar. Sit at the bar and watch chef-owner Melody Wolfertz, a Culinary Institute of America grad, concoct her creative tapas-style selection of small and large plates. It is always a pleasure, and the staff is accommodating and helpful.

Destination Dining

Arriving in Rockland trailing a James Beard Award–winning reputation, chef Melissa Kelly opened **Primo** (Rte. 73, 207/596-0770, www.primorestaurant.com, 5:30–10 P.M. Wed.–Mon. June–Dec.) in 2000 and hasn't had time to breathe since. She has gone on to open two other restaurants, and in 2007 expanded this one, in an air-conditioned Victorian home. Fresh local ingredients, many from the restaurant's gardens, are a high priority, and unusual fish specials appear every day. Appetizers are especially imaginative; entrées range $24–42, but a bar menu with lighter fare and a nightly special ($20) is also available. Kelly's partner, Price Kushner, produces an impressive range of breads and desserts. Reservations are essential, usually at least a week ahead on midsummer weekends—and you still may have to wait when you get there.

INFORMATION AND SERVICES
Information

For visitor information visit the **Penobscot Bay Regional Chamber of Commerce** (Gateway Center, 207/596-0376 or 800/562-2529, www.therealmaine.com), or **Rockland Public Library** (80 Union St., 207/594-0310, www.rocklandlibrary.org).

Public Restrooms

You'll find public restrooms at the Gateway Center; the Knox County Court House (Union St. and Masonic St.); the Rockland Recreation Center (Union St. and Limerock St.), across from the courthouse, next to the playground; the Rockland Public Library; and the Maine State Ferry Service terminal.

GETTING AROUND

All Aboard Trolley Co. (207/594-9300 or 866/594-9300, www.aatrolley.com) offers 40-minute narrated sightseeing tours of downtown Rockland ($8 adults, free under age 12), departing from the Penobscot Bay Regional Chamber of Commerce at the Gateway Center about six times daily.

Vinalhaven and North Haven Islands

Vinalhaven and neighboring North Haven have been known as the Fox Islands ever since 1603, when English explorer Martin Pring sailed these waters and allegedly spotted gray foxes in his search for sustenance. Nowadays, you'll find reference to that name only on nautical charts, identifying the passage between the two islands as the Fox Islands Thorofare—and there's nary a fox in sight.

Each island has its own distinct personality. To generalize, Vinalhaven is bustling, while North Haven is sedate and exclusive.

VINALHAVEN

Five miles wide, 7.5 miles long, and covering 10,000 acres, Vinalhaven is 13 miles off the coast of Rockland—a 75-minute ferry trip. The shoreline has so many zigs and zags that no place on the island is more than a mile from the water.

The island is famed for its granite. The first blocks headed for Boston around 1826, and within a few decades quarrymen arrived from as far away as Britain and Finland to wrestle out and shape the incredibly resistant stone. Schooners, barges, and "stone sloops" left **Carver's Harbor** carrying mighty cargoes of granite destined for government and commercial buildings in Boston, New York, and Washington, D.C. In the 1880s, nearly 4,000 people lived on Vinalhaven, North Haven, and Hurricane Island. After World War I, demand declined, granite gave way to concrete and steel, and the industry petered out and died. But Vinalhaven has left its mark in ornate columns, paving blocks, and curbstones in communities as far west as Kansas City.

Vinalhaven is a serious working community, not primarily a playground. Nearly 600 island residents depend on the lobster and fishing industry. Shopkeepers cater to locals as well as visitors, and increasing numbers of artists and

Working boats outnumber pleasure crafts in Vinalhaven's Carver's Harbor.

© HILARY NANGLE

PENOBSCOT BAY

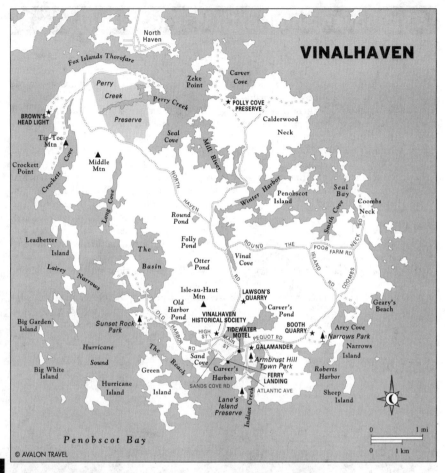

artisans work away in their studios. For day-trippers, there's plenty to do—shopping, picnicking, hiking, biking, swimming—but an overnight stay provides a chance to sense the unique rhythm of life on a year-round island.

Sights

One Main Street landmark that's hard to miss is the three-story cupola-topped **Odd Fellows Hall,** a Victorian behemoth with American flag motifs on the lower windows and assorted gewgaws in the upper ones. Artist Robert Indiana,

who first arrived as a visitor in 1969, owns the structure, built in 1885 for the Independent Order of Odd Fellows Star of Hope Lodge. It's not open to the public.

At the top of the hill just beyond Main Street (School St. and E. Main St.) is a greenish-blue replica **galamander,** a massive reminder of Vinalhaven's late-19th-century granite-quarrying era. Galamanders, hitched to oxen or horses, carried the stone from island quarries to the finishing shops. (By the way, the origin of the name remains unexplained.) Next to the galamander is a colorful wooden bandstand, site of very popular evening band concerts held sporadically during the summer.

The **Vinalhaven Historical Society** (207/863-4410, www.vinalhavenhistoricalsociety.org, noon–5 P.M. Tues.–Sat. July–Aug. or by appointment, free) operates a delightful museum in the onetime town hall on High Street, just east of Carver's Cemetery. The building itself has a tale, having been floated across the bay from Rockland, where it served as a Universalist church. The museum's documents and artifacts on the granite industry are particularly intriguing, and special summer exhibits add to the interest. Donations are welcome. At the museum, request a copy of *A Self-guided Walking Tour of the Town of Vinalhaven and Its Granite-quarrying History,* a handy little brochure that details 17 in-town locations related to the late-19th–early-20th-century industry.

Built in 1832 and now owned by the town of Vinalhaven, **Brown's Head Light** guards the southern entrance to the Fox Islands Thorofare. There is no access to the light itself, and the keeper's house is a private residence for the town manager, but to reach the grounds, take the North Haven Road about six miles, at which point you'll see a left-side view of the Camden Hills. Continue about another mile to the second road on the left, Crockett River Road. Turn and take the second road on the right, continuing past the Brown's Head Cemetery to the hill overlooking the lighthouse.

Entertainment

No one visits Vinalhaven for nightlife, but concerts (the Fox Island series and others), films, and lectures (most organized by the Vinalhaven Land Trust or the Vinalhaven Historical Society) are frequent. Check *The Wind* to see what's on the docket during your visit.

Shopping

Vinalhaven's shops change regularly, but here are a few that have withstood the test of time. **The Paper Store** (Vinal's News Stand, Main St., 207/863-4826) carries newspapers, gifts, film, maps, and odds and ends. **Five Elements**

© HILARY NANGLE

Brown's Head Light marks the entrance to the Fox Islands Thorofare.

PENOBSCOT BAY

Gallery + Studio (Main St., 207/863-2262) is filled with artist-owner Alison Thibault's jewelry creations and other finds. **New Era Gallery** (Main St., 207/863-9351, www.new-eragallery.com) has a well-chosen selection of art in varied media representing primarily island artisans. Don't miss the sculpture garden. A few doors away is **Second Hand Prose,** a used books store run by the Friends of the Vinalhaven Public Library.

The **Saturday-morning anything-goes flea markets** are an island must, as much for the browsing and buying as for the gossip.

Parks and Preserves

Vinalhaven is loaded with wonderful hikes and walks, some deliberately unpublicized. Since the mid-1980s, the foresighted **Vinalhaven Land Trust** (207/863-2543, www.vinalhaven-landtrust.org) has expanded the opportunities. When you reach the island, pick up maps at the land trust's office at **Skoog Memorial Park** (Sands Cove Road, west of the ferry terminal) or inquire at the town office or the Paper Store.

The trust also offers a seasonal series of educational walks and talks.

Some hiking options are the Perry Creek Preserve, which has a terrific loop trail; Middle Mountain Park; Tip-Toe Mountain; Polly Cove Preserve; Isle au Haut Mountain; Arey's Neck Woods; Huber Preserve; and Sunset Rock Park.

The Maine chapter of the **Nature Conservancy** (207/729-5181) owns or manages several islands and island clusters near Vinalhaven. **Big Garden** (formerly owned by Charles and Anne Morrow Lindbergh) and **Big White Islands** are easily accessible and great for shoreline picnics if you have your own boat. Other Nature Conservancy holdings in this area are fragile environments, mostly nesting islands off-limits mid-March–mid-August. Contact the Nature Conservancy for specifics.

No, you're not on the moors of Devon, but you could be fooled in the 45-acre **Lane's Island Preserve,** one of the Nature Conservancy's most-used island preserves.

Grimes Park, next to the ferry terminal on Vinalhaven, is a fine place for watching boats pass by.

Masses of low-lying ferns, rugosa roses, and berry bushes cover the granite outcrops of this sanctuary—and a foggy day makes it even more moor-like and mystical, like a setting for a Brontë novel. The best (albeit busiest) time to come is early August, when you can compete with the birds for blackberries, raspberries, and blueberries. Easy trails wind past old stone walls, an aged cemetery, and along the surf-pounded shore. The preserve is a 20-minute walk (or five-minute bike ride) from Vinalhaven's ferry landing. Set off to the right on Main Street, through the village. Turn right onto Water Street and then right on Atlantic Avenue. Continue across the causeway on Lane's Island Road and left over a salt marsh to the preserve. The large white house on the harbor side of Lane's Island is privately owned.

Next to the ferry landing in Carver's Harbor is **Grimes Park,** a wooded pocket retreat with a splendid view of the harbor. Owned by the American Legion, the 2.5-acre park is perfect for picnics or for hanging out between boats, especially in good weather.

Just behind the Island Community Medical Center, close to downtown, is 30-acre **Armbrust Hill Town Park,** once the site of granite-quarrying operations. Still pockmarked with quarry pits, the park has beautifully landscaped walking paths and native flowers, shrubs, and trees—much of it thanks to late island resident Betty Roberts, who made this a lifelong endeavor. From the back of the medical center, follow the trail to the summit for a southerly view of Matinicus and other offshore islands. If you're with children, be especially careful about straying onto side paths, which go perilously close to old quarry holes. Before the walk, lower the children's energy level at the large playground off to the left of the trail.

Recreation
SWIMMING
Abandoned quarries are all over the island, and most are on private property, but two town-owned ones are easy to reach from the ferry landing. **Lawson's Quarry** is one mile from downtown on the North Haven Road; **Booth Quarry** is 1.6 miles from downtown via East Main Street. Both are signposted. You'll see plenty of sunbathers on the rocks and swimmers on a hot day, but there are no lifeguards, so swimming is at your own risk. There are no restrooms or changing rooms. Note that pets and soap are not allowed in the water; camping, fires, and alcohol are not allowed in the quarry areas.

Down the side road beyond Booth Quarry is **Narrows Park,** a town-owned space looking out toward Narrows Island, Isle au Haut, and, on a clear day, Mount Desert Island.

For saltwater swimming, take East Main Street 2.4 miles from downtown to a crossroads, where you'll see a whimsical bit of local folk art—the Coke lady sculpture. Turn right (east) and go 0.5 miles to **Geary's Beach** (also called **State Beach**), where you can picnic and scour the shoreline for shells and sea glass.

BICYCLING
Even though Vinalhaven's 40 or so miles of public roads are narrow, winding, and poorly shouldered, they're relatively level, so a bicycle is a fine way to tour the island. Bring your own, preferably a hybrid or mountain bike, or rent one ($15 per day) at the **Tidewater Motel** (207/863-4618) on Main Street. A wide selection of rental bikes is available on the mainland in Rockport at **Maine Sport Outfitters** (Rte. 1, Rockport, 207/236-8797 or 888/236-8796), but you have to pay extra to bring a bike on the ferry.

A 10-mile, 2.5-hour bicycle route begins on Main Street and goes clockwise out on the North Haven Road (rough pavement), past Lawson's Quarry, to Round the Island Road (some sections are dirt), then Poor Farm Road to Geary's Beach and back to Main Street via Pequot Road and School Street. Carry a picnic and enjoy it on Lane's Island; stop for a swim in one of the quarries; or detour down to Brown's Head Light. If you're here for the day, keep track of the time so you don't miss the ferry.

© KATHRYN OSGOOD

If you're an experienced kayaker and have your own equipment, paddle over to White Island from Vinalhaven.

Far more rewarding view-wise, and far shorter, is the one-way-and-back pedal out along the Old Harbor Road to The Basin, which is rich in bird and wildlife and serves as a seal nursery. There's also a nice trail at the road's end to The Basin's shorefront and across to an island; ask Phil at the Tidewater Motel for directions.

SEA KAYAKING
Sea kayak rentals are available at the Tidewater Motel for $25 per day, including delivery. A guide can be arranged, but it's not necessary to have one to poke around the harbor or, even better, paddle through The Basin, which is especially popular with birders and wildlife-watchers.

BIRDING AND WILDLIFE-WATCHING
Expert bird guide **John Drury** (207/596-1841) takes birders and wildlife-watchers on 3.5-hour cruises ($280) to spy gannets, Arctic terns, puffins, eagles, and seals. Sightings have even included minke whales and albatross.

Accommodations
If you're planning on staying overnight, don't even consider arriving in summer without reservations. If you're coming for the day, pay attention to the ferry schedule and allow enough time to get back to the boat. The island has no campsites. Rates listed are for peak season.

Your feet practically touch the water when you spend the night at the (**Tidewater Motel and Gathering Space** (12 Main St., Carver's Harbor, 207/863-4618, www.tidewatermotel.com, year-round, $165–295), a well-maintained motel in two buildings cantilevered over the harbor. Owned by Phil and Elaine Crossman (she operates the New Era Gallery down the street), the 19-room motel was built by Phil's parents in 1970. It's the perfect place to sit on the deck and watch the lobster boats do their thing. Be aware, though, that commercial fishermen are early risers, and lobster-boat engines can rev up as early as 4:30 A.M. on a summer morning—all part of the pace of Vinalhaven. Phil is practically a one-man chamber of commerce. He can recommend hikes and other activities, and since he maintains the island's calendar of events, he always knows what's happening and when. A continental breakfast and use of bicycles are included in the rates; sea kayak rentals are available. Kids 10 and under are free; seven units are efficiencies. Also on the premises is **Island Spirits,** a small gourmet-foods store stocked with wines, beers, cheeses, breads, other goodies, and even picnic baskets to pack it all in. About once a month, the motel hosts a wine tasting in the second-floor Gathering Space, overlooking the harbor. If you want to get a better sense of island life, pick up a copy of Phil's book *Away Happens,* a collection of humorous essays about island living. You can see a sample from it on the motel's website.

Also convenient to downtown is **The Libby House** (Water St., 207/863-4696, www.libby-house1869.com, $75–140, no breakfast), with a two-bedroom apartment and five guest rooms, three sharing one bath.

Food

Hours listed are for peak season. Expect reduced hours and fewer days of operation at other times.

Baked bean suppers are regularly held at a couple of island locations. Check *The Wind* for details.

The island's best breakfast place is **Surfside** (Harbor Wharf, 207/863-2767, 4 A.M.–1:30 P.M. Mon.–Fri., 4–11 A.M. Sat.–Sun.). Eat inside or on the wharf. The fishcakes earn raves and are always available on Sunday. It may also be open for dinner.

Craving a cappuccino or a latte? Vinalhaven's student-run **ARCafé** (39 High St., 207/863-4191, 7 A.M.–5 P.M. Mon.–Sat.), next door to the historical society, is the island's best coffee source and provides free Internet access.

Good lunch options are the **Harbor Gawker** (Main St., 207/863-9365, 11 A.M.–8 P.M. Mon.–Sat.), a local landmark since 1975, but now with a nice indoor dining area; **Trickerville Sandwich Shop** (Atlantic St., 207/863-9344, 5 A.M.–4 P.M. Mon.–Sat., 11 A.M.–4 P.M. Sun.),

with a few tables inside and out, but no views. Lobster dinners are served some evenings; ask. **The Sand Bar** (Main St., 207/863-4500, 11 A.M.–9 P.M. Tues.–Sun.) has a full bar as well as a good menu of pub-style favorites, soups, salads, and pizza.

For casual dining, book a table at **The Haven Restaurant** (Main St., 207/863-4969), with two options: Harborside (Tues.–Sat., seatings at 6 and 8:15 P.M.) delivers on its name and serves a creative menu that changes nightly. Streetside (6:30–9 P.M., Wed.–Mon.) doesn't take reservations and serves pub-style fare. The restaurant is a one-woman show, and Torry Pratt doubles as a popular local caterer, so it's wise to call.

Information and Services

Vinalhaven Chamber of Commerce (www.vinalhaven.org) produces a useful little flyer-map showing locations in the Carver's Harbor area. Also helpful for trip planning is a guidebook published by Phil Crossman at the Tidewater Motel (207/863-4618, $3.50). On the island, pick up a copy of Vinalhaven's weekly newsletter, *The Wind,* named after the island's original newspaper, first published in 1884. It's loaded with island flavor: news items, public-supper announcements, editorials, and ads. A year's subscription is $50; free single copies are available at most downtown locales.

Check out the **Vinalhaven Public Library** (E. Main St. and Chestnut St., 207/863-4401).

Public restrooms are at the ferry landing and the town office (weekdays only).

Getting Around

I can't emphasize this enough: Don't bring a car unless it is absolutely necessary. If you're coming over for a day trip, you can get to parks and quarries, shops, restaurants, and the historical society museum on foot. If you want to explore farther, a bicycle is an excellent option, or you can rent a car or reserve a **taxi** through the Tidewater Motel (207/863-4618), or Phil will meet you at the ferry landing. Call well ahead to reserve.

PENOBSCOT BAY

NORTH HAVEN

Eight miles long by three miles wide, North Haven is 12 miles off the coast of Rockland—an hour by ferry. The island has sedate summer homes, open fields where hundreds of sheep once grazed, about 350 year-round residents, a yacht club called the Casino, and a village gift shop that has been here since 1954.

Originally called North Island, North Haven had much the same settlement history as Vinalhaven, but being smaller (about 5,280 acres) and more fertile, it has developed—or not developed—differently. In 1846, North Haven was incorporated and severed politically from Vinalhaven, and by the late 1800s, the Boston summer crowd began buying traditional island homes, building tastefully unpretentious new ones, and settling in for a whole season of sailing and socializing. Several generations later, "summer folk" now come for weeks rather than months, often rotating the schedules among slews of siblings. Informality remains the key, though—now more than ever.

The island has two distinct hamlets—North Haven Village, on the Fox Islands Thorofare, where the state ferry arrives; and Pulpit Harbor, particularly popular with the yachting set. The village is easily explored on foot in a morning.

North Haven doesn't offer a lot for the day visitor, and islanders tend not to welcome them with open arms.

Entertainment

Waterman's Community Center (Main St., 207/867-2100, www.watermans.org) provides a place for island residents and visitors to gather for entertainment, events, and even coffee and gossip. It's home to North Haven Arts & Enrichment. Check the schedule on the website to see what's planned.

Shopping

Fanning out from the ferry landing is a delightful cluster of substantial year-round clapboard homes—a marked contrast to the weathered-shingle cottages typical of so many island communities. It won't take long to stroll and shop Main Street.

Anchoring the handful of "downtown" shops and galleries is the **North Haven Gift Shop** (Main St., 207/867-4444), a rabbit warren of rooms that June Hopkins has been running since 1954. You'll have no problem spending money here—everything's tastefully selected, from the pottery to the note cards to the books, jewelry, and gourmet condiments. One room is a gallery with work by Maine artists.

Next door (connected via an elevated corridor) is the **Eric Hopkins Gallery** (Main St., 207/867-2229), owned by June Hopkins's son, a talented painter who has gained repute far beyond Maine. If you can't spring for an original (figure on several thousand dollars), his distinctive work—luminous bird's-eye views of island, sea, and forest—now appears also on note cards, postcards, T-shirts, and one-of-a-kind sweaters. It's open by chance or by appointment.

On the main floor of the four-story early-20th-century Calderwood Hall is **North Island Fiber Shop** (Main St.), a huge draw for knitters and hookers. It sells all-natural Maine-made yarns as well as wonderful creations, including quilts, throws, baskets, even candles and pottery, all crafted by Maine artists and artisans. Upstairs is **Herb Parsons Gallery.**

Recreation

North Haven has about 25 miles of paved roads that are conducive to **bicycling**, but, just as on most other islands, they are narrow, winding, and nearly shoulderless. Starting near the ferry landing in North Haven Village, take South Shore Road eastward, perhaps stopping en route for a picnic at town-owned Mullin's Head Park (also spelled Mullen Head) on the southeast corner of the island. Then follow the road around, counterclockwise, to North Shore Road and Pulpit Harbor.

Accommodations

Within walking distance of the ferry is **Nebo Lodge** (11 Mullins Lane, 207/867-2007, www.nebolodge.com, $125–250). Eight rooms (four year-round), some with shared baths, are decorated with island art, and many have rugs by Angela Adams. There's Wi-Fi throughout. Rates include a full breakfast and use of inn bikes.

Food

Stop into **Waterman's Coffee Shop** (Waterman Center, 207/867-2100, 7 A.M.–4 P.M. Mon.–Sat., 11:30 A.M.–4 P.M. Sun.) for coffee, sweets, and local news.

For a casual meal on the deck, inside, or takeout (if you've come for the morning, pick up a sandwich for the return ferry), slip into **Sip Ahoy** (207/867-2060, 11 A.M.–11 P.M. daily). For a sit-down meal with a view, head for the **Coal Wharf at H. P. Blake's** (Main St., 207/867-4739, 11 A.M.–11 P.M. daily July–Aug.); it's at Brown's Boatyard. Dinner is also available at **Nebo Lodge** (11 Mullins Lane, 207/867-2007, www.nebolodge.com, 6–8 P.M. Wed.–Sat., entrées $10–25).

Information

The best source of information about North Haven is the **North Haven Town Office**

(Upper Main St., 207/867-4433, www.north havenmaine.org).

GETTING THERE

The Maine State Ferry Service (207/596-2202, www.exploremaine.org) operates six round-trips daily between Rockland and Vinalhaven (75-minute crossing) in summer and three round-trips between Rockland and North Haven (70-minute crossing). Round-trip tickets are $17.50 adults, $8.50 children. Both ferries take cars ($49.50 round-trip, plus $14 reservation fee), but a bicycle ($16.50 round-trip per adult bike, $9.50 per child bike) will do fine unless you have the time or inclination to see every corner of the island. Getting car space on the ferry during midsummer can be a frustrating—and complicated—experience, so *avoid taking a car to the island.* Give yourself time to find a parking space and perhaps to walk from it to the terminal. If you leave a car at the Rockland lot (space is limited and availability varies), it's $10 per 24 hours or $50 per week. You can also park on some of Rockland's side streets and walk, or,

© HILARY NANGLE

North Haven's ferry dock is right in the middle of downtown.

PENOBSCOT BAY

for a day trip, in the city lot between Main Street and the water or Harbor Park.

No official ferry service travels between Vinalhaven and North Haven, even though the two islands are almost within spitting distance. Fortunately, the J. O. Brown and Sons boat shop on North Haven provides shuttles 7 A.M.–5 P.M. daily. Call the boat shop (207/867-4621) to arrange a pickup on the Vinalhaven side. The fee is $5 pp round-trip.

(A handy outdoor pay phone is at the north end of Vinalhaven—at the end of the North Haven Road.) Don't let anyone convince you to return to Rockland for the ferry to North Haven.

Penobscot Island Air (207/596-7500, www.penobscotislandair.net) flies twice daily to Vinalhaven and North Haven, weather permitting, from Knox County Regional Airport in Owls Head, just south of Rockland. Seat availability is dependent on mail volume.

Greater Camden

Camden, flanked by **Rockport** to the south and **Lincolnville** to the north, is one of the Mid-Coast's—even Maine's—prime destinations.

Camden is the better known of the three and typifies Maine nationwide, even worldwide, on calendars, postcards, and photo books. Much of its appeal is its drop-dead-gorgeous setting—a deeply indented harbor with parks, a waterfall, and a dramatic backdrop of low mountains. That harbor

is a summer-long madhouse, jammed with dinghies, kayaks, windjammers, mega-yachts, minor yachts, and a handful of fishing craft.

Driven apart by a local squabble in 1891, Camden and Rockport have been separate towns for more than a century, but they're inextricably linked. They share school and sewer systems and an often-hyphenated partnership. On Union Street, just off Route 1, a white

Camden Harbor Park was designed by Frederick Law Olmsted in 1931 and is now listed on the National Register of Historic Places.

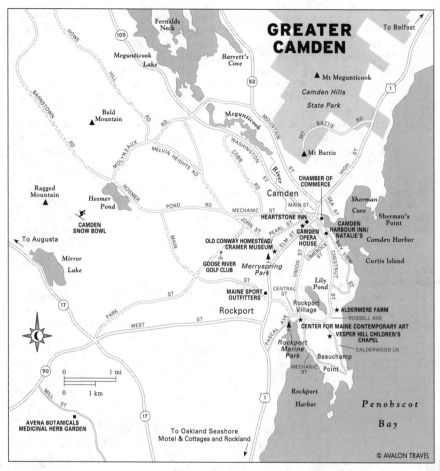

wooden arch reads Camden on one side and Rockport on the other. Rockport has a much lower profile, and its harbor is relatively peaceful—with yachts, lobster boats, and a single windjammer schooner.

Two distinct enclaves make up Lincolnville: oceanfront Lincolnville Beach ("the Beach") and, about five miles inland, Lincolnville Center ("the Center"). Lincolnville is laid-back and mostly rural; the major activity center is a short strip of shops and restaurants at the Beach, and few visitors realize there's anything else.

SIGHTS
Self-Guided Historical Tour

Historic Downtown Camden is an illustrated map and brochure detailing historical sites and businesses in and around downtown. To cover it all, you'll want a car or bike; to cover segments and really appreciate the architecture, don your walking shoes. Pick up a copy of the brochure at the chamber of commerce.

Old Conway Homestead and Cramer Museum

Just inside the Camden town line from

Rockport, the Old Conway Homestead and Cramer Museum (Conway Rd., Camden, 207/236-2257, www.crmuseum.org, 11 A.M.–3 P.M. Tues.–Fri. July–Aug., $5 adults, $2 children) is a six-building complex owned and run by the Camden-Rockport Historical Society. The 18th-century Cape-style Conway House, on the National Register of Historic Places, contains fascinating construction details and period furnishings; in the barn are carriages and farm tools. Two other buildings—a blacksmith shop and an 1820 maple sugarhouse used for making maple syrup—have been moved to the grounds and restored. In the contemporary Mary Meeker Cramer Museum (named for the prime benefactor) are displays from the historical society's collection of ship models, old documents, and period clothing. For local color, don't miss the Victorian outhouse. Also here is an education center for workshops and seminars. The museum and sap house are also open for maple-syrup demonstrations on Maine Maple Sunday (fourth Sunday in March).

Vesper Hill

Built and donated to the community by a local benefactor, the rustic open-air **Vesper Hill Children's Chapel** is dedicated to the world's children. Overlooking Penobscot Bay and surrounded by gardens and lawns, the nondenominational chapel is an almost mystical oasis in a busy tourist region. Except during weddings or memorial services, there's seldom a crowd, and if you're lucky, you might have the place to yourself. From Central Street in downtown Rockport, take Russell Avenue east to Calderwood Lane (the fourth street on right). On Calderwood, take the second right (Chapel St.) after the private golf course. If the sign is down, look for a boulder with "Vesper Hill" carved in it. From downtown Camden, take Chestnut Street to just past Aldermere Farm; turn left at Calderwood Lane and take the second right after the golf course.

Aldermere Farm (20 Russell Ave., Rockport, 207/236-2739, www.aldermere .org), by the way, is the home of the first U.S.

herd of Belted Galloway cattle—Angus-like beef cattle with a wide white midriff. First imported from Scotland in 1953, the breed now shows up in pastures all over the United States. The animals' startling "Oreo-cookie" hide pattern never fails to halt passersby—especially in spring and early summer, when the calves join their mothers in the pastures. Maine Coast Heritage Trust, a state conservation organization based in Brunswick, owns the 136-acre farm. Call for information on tours or other events.

Center for Maine Contemporary Art

Once a local firehouse, this attractive building has been totally rehabbed to provide display space for the work of Maine's best contemporary artists. The nonprofit Center for Maine Contemporary Art (62 Russell Ave., Rockport, 207/236-2875, www.artsmaine.org, 10 A.M.–5 P.M. Tues.–Sat., 1–5 P.M. Sun., donation) mounts as many as a dozen shows each summer, along with special lectures, a wildly popular art auction (early August), an annual juried art exhibition featuring more than 100 selections, and an annual juried craft show (mid-October) spotlighting several dozen artisans. An exceptional gift shop carries high-end crafts.

ENTERTAINMENT

At 8 P.M. Wednesday–Thursday in July–August, and once a month the rest of the year, **Bay Chamber Concerts** (207/236-2823 or 888/707-2770, www.baychamberconcerts .org) draw sell-out audiences to the beautifully restored (and air-conditioned) Rockport Opera House and Rockland's Strand Theatre. Founded in the 1960s as a classical series, the summer concerts feature a resident quartet, prominent guest artists, and outstanding programs. It has expanded to include world music, jazz, and dance. The first week in August ("Next Generation Week") is devoted to classes and concerts for and by talented teenagers. Seats are reserved for summer concerts ($30–40 adults, $8 under age 19, plus $5 processing fee per order, unless purchased online); open seating is the rule in winter, when tickets are less expensive and programs vary from classical to pops to jazz.

The beautifully renovated **Camden Opera House** (29 Elm St., Camden, 207/236-7963, box office 207/236-4884, www.camdenoperahouse.com) is the site of many performances by renowned performers.

The Lincolnville Band, one of the oldest town bands in the country, often plays in the park's Bicentennial Bandstand, built to commemorate the town's 200th birthday.

FESTIVALS AND EVENTS

One weekend in February is given over to the **Camden Conference,** an annual three-day foreign-affairs conference with nationally and internationally known speakers. Also in February, the **National Toboggan Championships** features two days of races and fun at the nation's only wooden toboggan chute at the Camden Snow Bowl.

The third Thursday of July is **House and Garden Day,** when you can take a self-guided tour (10 A.M.–4:30 P.M.) of significant homes and gardens in Camden and Rockport. Proceeds benefit the Camden Garden Club. **HarborArts,** on the third weekend in July, draws dozens of artists and craftspeople displaying and selling their wares at the Camden Amphitheatre, Harbor Park.

Labor Day weekend is also known as **Windjammer Weekend,** with cruises, windjammer open houses, fireworks, and all kinds of live entertainment in and around Camden Harbor. Twenty top artisans open their studios for the annual **Country Roads Artists and Artisans Tour** in September.

Dozens of artists and craftspeople display and sell their wares at the **Fall Festival and Arts and Crafts Show,** the first weekend in October at the Camden Amphitheatre in Harbor Park.

A who's who of entrepreneurs show up for the annual **PopTech** conference in late October.

Christmas by the Sea is a family-oriented early-December weekend featuring open houses, special sales, concerts, and a visit from Santa Claus.

SHOPPING
New and Old Books

The Owl and Turtle Bookshop (32 Washington St., Camden, 207/236-4769 or 800/876-4769), one of Maine's best independent new-books stores, has thousands of books and a wonderful children's room. It's just off Main Street in the Knox Mill Center.

Another source for books and a whole lot more is **Sherman's** (Main St., Camden, 207/236-2223), part of a small Maine chain.

If you want a good read at a great price, **Stone Soup Books** (33 Main St., Camden, no phone), a tiny second-floor shop across from the Lord Camden Inn, is Camden's best source for contemporary used fiction.

Dolls

Antique and hand-crafted museum-quality dolls and doll houses fill **Lucy's Doll House** (49 Bay View St., Camden, 207/236-4122).

Art, Crafts, and Gifts

You'll need to wander the streets to take in all the gift and craft shops, particularly in Camden. Some are obvious; others are tucked away on side streets and back alleys, so explore.

A downtown Camden landmark since 1940, **The Smiling Cow** (41 Main St., Camden, 207/236-3351 or 800/646-6169) is as good a place as any to pick up Maine souvenirs—a few slightly kitschy, but most reasonably tasteful. Before or after shopping here, head for the rear balcony for coffee and a knockout view of the harbor and the Megunticook River waterfall.

Also downtown is **Ducktrap Bay Trading Co.** (37 Bayview St., Camden, 207/236-9568), source of decoys, wildlife, and marine art and other fine crafts.

Just off Route 90, less than two miles from the Rockport intersection with Route 1, is **Carver Hill Gallery** (264 Meadow St., Rockport, 207/236-0745, www.carverhillgallery.com),

Many shops in downtown Camden remain open year-round.

© TOM NANGLE

exhibiting fine art and crafts in a center-chimney cape, barn, and gardens.

At **Danica Candleworks** (Rte. 90, West Rockport, 207/236-3060), owner Erik Laustsen learned the hand-dipping trade from his Danish relatives.

The **Messler Gallery** (25 Mill St., Rockport, 207/594-5611), just off Route 90 and on the campus of the Center for Furniture Craftsmanship, presents rotating shows that focus on woodworking.

Handsome dark wood buildings 0.2 miles north of the Beach are home to **Windsor Chairmakers** (Rte. 1, Lincolnville, 207/789-5188 or 800/789-5188). You can observe the operation, browse the display area, or order some of the well-made chairs, cabinets, and tables.

Professional boatbuilder Walt Simmons has branched out into decoys and wildlife carvings, and they're just as outstanding as his boats. Walt and his wife, Karen, run **Duck Trap Decoys** (Duck Trap Rd., Lincolnville, 207/789-5363, www.ducktrapdecoys.com), a gallery-shop that also features the work of more than 60 other woodcarvers.

It's a lot easier to get soft, wonderful hand-woven and hand-dyed **Swans Island Blankets** (231 Rte. 1, Northport, 297/338-9691) since the company moved its sales operation off the island near Mount Desert to the mainland, just 2.7 miles north of Lincolnville Beach. Such quality comes at a sky-high price.

Wine

Gaze out the backdoor of the **Cellardoor Vineyard** (367 Youngtown Rd., Lincolnville, 207/763-44778, www.mainewine.com) and it's possible to convince yourself you're in Sonoma Valley. Tucked in the folds of the rolling hills, just inland of Lincolnville Beach, Cellardoor occupies a farmhouse and barn overlooking six acres of grapes. Inside the barn, the retail shop offers free tastings, and you can pick up cheeses and other munchies for an impromptu picnic on the deck. The winery also has a retail shop at the intersection of Routes 1 and 90 in Rockport.

Discount Shopping

How could anyone resist a thrift shop with the name **Heavenly Threads** (57 Elm St./Rte. 1, Camden, 207/236-3203)? Established by Camden's community-oriented First Congregational Church (next door to the shop), Heavenly Threads carries high-quality pre-owned clothing, books, and jewelry. It's staffed by volunteers, with proceeds going to such local ecumenical causes as Meals on Wheels.

RECREATION
Parks and Preserves

For more than a century, the Camden-Rockport area has benefited from the providence of conscientious year-round and summertime conservationists. Thanks to their benevolence, countless acres of fragile habitat, woodlands, and scenic viewpoints have been preserved. Nowadays, the most active organization is the **Coastal Mountains Land Trust** (CMLT, 101 Mt. Battie St., Camden, 207/236-7091, www.coastalmountains.org), founded in 1986. It has protected more than 8,000 acres. Maps and information about trails open to the public are available from CMLT. Check the website for guided hikes and other events.

A Rockland-based group, **The Georges River Land Trust** (207/594-5166, www.grlt.org), whose territory covers the Georges (St. George) River watershed, is the steward for The Georges Highland Path, a 40-mile low-impact hiking trail that reaches Rockport and Camden from the back side of the surrounding hills.

◖ CAMDEN HILLS STATE PARK

A five-minute drive and a small fee gets you to the top of **Mount Battie,** centerpiece of 5,650-acre Camden Hills State Park (Belfast Rd./Rte. 1, 207/236-3109, www.parksandlands.com, $4.50 nonresident adults, $3 Maine resident adults, $1.50 nonresident seniors, free Maine resident seniors, $1 children 5–11) and the best place to understand why Camden is "where the mountains meet the sea." The summit panorama is breathtaking and reputedly

the inspiration for Edna St. Vincent Millay's poem "Renascence" (a bronze plaque marks the spot); information boards identify the offshore islands. Climb the summit's stone tower for an even better view. The 20 miles of hiking trails (some for every ability) include two popular routes up Mount Battie—an easy hour-long hike from the base parking lot (Nature Trail) and a more strenuous 45-minute hike from the top of Mount Battie Street in Camden (Mount Battie Trail). Or drive up the paved Mount Battie Auto Road. The park has plenty of space for picnics. In winter, ice climbers use a rock wall near the Maiden's Cliff Trail, reached via Route 52 (Mountain St.). The park entrance is two miles north of downtown Camden. Request a free trail map. The park is open mid-May–mid-October, but hiking trails are accessible all year, weather permitting.

MERRYSPRING PARK

Straddling the Camden-Rockport boundary, 66-acre Merryspring Park (Conway Rd., Camden, 207/236-2239, www.merryspring.org) is a magnet for nature lovers. More than a dozen well-marked trails wind through woodlands, berry thickets, and wildflowers; near the preserve's parking area are lily, rose, and herb gardens. Admission is free, but donations are welcome. Also free are family programs. Special programs (fee charged) include lectures, workshops, and demonstrations. The entrance is on Conway Road, 0.3 miles off Route 1, at the southern end of Camden. Trails are open dawn–dusk daily.

IN-TOWN PARKS

Just behind the Camden Public Library is the **Camden Amphitheatre** (also called the Bok Amphitheatre, after a local benefactor), a sylvan spot resembling a set for *A Midsummer Night's Dream* (which has been performed here). Concerts, weddings, and all kinds of other events take place in the park. Across Atlantic Avenue, sloping to the harbor, is **Camden Harbor Park,** with benches, a couple of monuments, and some of the best waterfront views in town. The noted landscape firm of Frederick Law Olmsted designed the park in 1931, and it is listed on the National Register of Historic Places. Both the park and the amphitheater were restored to their original splendor in 2004.

Rockport's in-town parks include **Marine Park,** off Pascal Avenue, at the head of the harbor; **Walker Park,** on Sea Street, on the west side of the harbor; **Mary-Lea Park,** overlooking the harbor next to the Rockport Opera House; and **Cramer Park,** alongside the Goose River just west of Pascal Avenue. At Marine Park are the remnants of 19th-century lime kilns, an antique steam engine, picnic tables, a boat-launching ramp, and a polished granite sculpture of André, a harbor seal adopted by a local family in the early 1960s. André had been honorary harbormaster, ring bearer at weddings, and the subject of several books and a film—and even did the honors at the unveiling of his statue—before he was fatally wounded in a mating skirmish in 1986 at the age of 25.

CURTIS ISLAND

Marking the entrance to Camden Harbor is town-owned Curtis Island, with a 26-foot automated light tower and adjoining keeper's house facing into the bay. Once known as Negro Island, it's a sight made for photo ops; the views are stunning in every direction. A kayak or dinghy will get you out to the island, where you can picnic (take water; there are no facilities), wander around, gather berries, or just watch the passing fleet. Land on the Camden (west) end of the island, allowing for the tide change when you beach your boat. Respect the privacy of the keeper's house in summer; it's occupied by volunteer caretakers.

FERNALD'S NECK

Three miles of Megunticook Lake shoreline, groves of conifers, and a large swamp ("the Great Bog") are features of 328-acre Fernald's Neck Preserve, on the Camden-Lincolnville line (and the Knox–Waldo County line). Shoreline and mountain views are stupendous, even more so during fall foliage season. The easiest trail is the 1.5-mile Blue Loop at

the northern end of the preserve; from it, you can access the 1-mile Orange Loop. From the Blue Loop, take the 0.2-mile Yellow Trail offshoot to Balance Rock for a great view of the lake and hills. Some sections can be wet; wear boots or rubberized shoes, and use insect repellent. From Route 1 in Camden, take Route 52 (Mountain St.) about 4.5 miles to Fernald's Neck Road, about 0.2 miles beyond the Youngtown Inn. Turn left and then bear left at the next fork and continue to the parking lot at the road's end. Pick up a map-brochure at the trailhead register. A map is also available at the chamber of commerce office. Dogs are not allowed, and the preserve closes and the gate is locked at 7:30 P.M.

AVENA BOTANICALS MEDICINAL HERB GARDEN

Visitors are welcome to visit Deb Soule's one-acre medicinal herb gardens (519 Mill St., Rockport, 207/594-2403, www.avenabotanicals.com, call for hours, free), part of an herbal and healing arts teaching center. Pick up a garden map and guide at the entrance, then stroll the paths. More than 125 species of common and medicinal herbs are planted, and everything is labeled. Mill Street is just shy of one mile south of the intersection of Routes 17 and 90 in West Rockport. Turn left on Mill Street and continue for almost one mile. Avena is on the right, down a long dirt driveway.

Recreation Centers

More than an alpine ski area, the **Camden Snow Bowl** (207/236-3438, www.camdensnowbowl.com) is a four-season recreation area with tennis courts, public swimming in Hosmer Pond, and hiking trails as well as alpine trails for day and night skiing and riding, a tubing park, and the only toboggan chute in Maine.

Maine Sport Outfitters

Local entrepreneurs Stuart and Marianne Smith have made Maine Sport Outfitters (Rte. 1, Rockport, 207/236-8797 or 888/236-8796, www.mainesport.com) a major destination for anyone interested in outdoor recreation. The knowledgeable staff can lend a hand and steer you in almost any direction, for almost any summer or winter sport. Nothing seems to stump them. The store sells and rents canoes, kayaks, bikes, skis, and tents, plus all the relevant clothing and accessories. A bicycle rents for $20 per day, calm-water canoes and kayaks are $30–40 per day. Sea kayaks are $50 per day single, $65 per day tandem.

Maine Sport Outdoor School (800/722-0826), a division of Maine Sport, has a full schedule of canoeing, kayaking, and camping trips. A two-hour guided Camden Harbor tour departs at least three times daily in summer and costs $35 adults, $30 ages 10–15. A four-hour guided harbor-to-harbor tour (Rockport to Camden) is offered once each day for $75 adults, $60 children, including a picnic lunch. Multiday instructional programs and tours are available. The store is 0.5 miles north of the junction of Routes 1 and 90.

Sea Kayaking

Ducktrap Kayak (2175 Rte. 1, Lincolnville Beach, 207/236-8608) runs guided coastal tours, with rates beginning at $30 pp. Rentals are also available, beginning at $20–30, depending on the type and size; delivery can be arranged.

If you have your own boat, good saltwater launch sites include Eaton Point, at the end of Sea Street in Camden, and Marine Park in Rockport; for freshwater paddling, put in at Megunticook Lake, west and east sides; Bog Bridge on Route 105, about 3.5 miles from downtown Camden; Barrett's Cove on Route 52, also about 3.5 miles from Camden; or in Lincolnville's Norton Pond and Megunticook Lake. You can even paddle all the way from the head of Norton Pond to the foot of Megunticook Lake, but use care navigating the drainage culvert between the two.

Hiking

There's enough hiking in **Camden Hills State Park** to fill any vacation, but many other options exist. For instance, there's **Bald Mountain,** northwest of downtown Camden, for magnificent views of Penobscot Bay. From Route 1 at the southern end of town, take John Street for 0.8 miles. Turn left and go 0.2 miles to a fork. Continue on the left fork (Hosmer Pond Rd.) for two miles. Bear left onto Barnestown Road (passing the Camden Snow Bowl) and go 1.4 miles to the trailhead on the right, signposted "Georges Highland Path Barnestown Access." Maps are available in the box; the parking lot holds half a dozen cars. The blue-blazed trail is relatively easy, requiring just over an hour round-trip; the summit views are spectacular, especially in fall. Carry a picnic and enjoy it at the top. Avoid this trail in late May–early June, however, when the blackflies take command. Depending on the season, you may encounter squishy areas, although trail stewards have installed some well-placed boardwalks.

The boundaries of both Camden Hills State Park and Fernald's Neck extend into Lincolnville, where the major state-park hike follows the **Ski Shelter Trail** to the **Bald Rock Trail.** From Route 1 in Lincolnville Beach, take Route 173 west about 2.5 miles to the marked parking area just beyond the junction of Youngtown Road. The 1,200-foot summit—with great views of Penobscot Bay (weather permitting)—is about two miles one-way of easy to moderate hiking. The route links with the rest of the state-park trail network, but unless you've arranged for a shuttle, it's best to do Bald Rock as a round-trip hike.

The Georges Highland Path will eventually wind through the Georges (St. George) River watershed from the source in Liberty to the outlet in Port Clyde. Spearheaded by members of the Georges River Land Trust (207/594-5166, www.grlt.org), the blue-blazed trail currently has 40 miles of connected trails in four main sections, including the Ragged Mountain Area. Contact the Rockland-based land trust for an up-to-date map, or pick it up from a trailhead box.

Swimming
FRESHWATER

The Camden area is blessed with several locales for freshwater swimming—a real boon, since Penobscot Bay can be mighty chilly, even at summer's peak. **Shirttail Point,** with limited parking, is a small sandy area on the Megunticook River. It's shallow enough for young kids and has picnic tables and a play area. From Route 1 in Camden, take Route 105 (Washington Street) 1.4 miles; watch for a small sign on the right. **Barrett's Cove,** on Megunticook Lake, has more parking spaces, usually more swimmers, and restrooms, picnic tables, and grills, as well as a play area. Diagonally opposite the Camden Public Library, take Route 52 (Mountain St.) about three miles; watch for the sign on the left. To cope with the parking crunch on hot summer days, bike to the beaches. You'll be ready for a swim after the uphill stretches, and it's all downhill on the way back.

Lincolnville has several ponds (some would call them lakes). On Route 52 in Lincolnville Center is Breezemere Park, a small town-owned swimming and picnic area on **Norton Pond.** Other Lincolnville options are **Coleman Pond, Pitcher Pond,** and **Knight's Pond.**

SALTWATER

The region's best ocean swimming is **Lincolnville Beach,** where Penobscot Bay flirts with Route 1 on a sandy stretch of shorefront in the congested hamlet of Lincolnville Beach. On a hot day, the sand is wall-to-wall people; during one of the coast's legendary northeasters, it's quite a wild place.

Another place for an ocean dip is **Laite Beach Park,** on Bay View Street about 1.5 miles from downtown Camden. It edges Camden Harbor and has a strip of sand, picnic tables, a playground, and children's musical events 1–3 P.M. every Wednesday in July–August. Check the local papers or contact Camden Parks and Recreation (207/236-3438) for the schedule.

In Rockport, dip your toes in the ocean at **Walker Park,** tucked away on the west side of the harbor. From Pascal Avenue, take Elm Street, which becomes Sea Street. Walker Park is on the left, with picnic tables, a play area, and a small pebbly beach.

Golf

On a back road straddling the Camden-Rockport line, the nine-hole **Goose River Golf Club** (50 Park St., Rockport, 207/236-8488) competes with the best for outstanding scenery.

Day Sails and Excursions

Most day sails and excursion boats operate late May–October, with fewer trips in the spring and fall than in July–August. You can't compare a two-hour day sail to a weeklong cruise on a Maine windjammer, but at least you get a hint of what could be—and it's a far better choice for kids, who aren't allowed on most windjammer cruises.

The classic wooden schooner *Olad* (207/236-2323, www.maineschooners.com, $35 adults, $22 under age 12) does several two-hour sails daily from Camden's Public Landing, weather permitting, late May–mid-October. Captain Aaron Lincoln is a Rockland native, so he's got the local scoop on the all the sights.

Another historic Camden day sailer is the 57-foot, 18-passenger schooner *Surprise* (207/236-4687, www.camdenmainesailing .com, $35) built in 1918 and skippered by congenial educator Jack Moore and his wife, Barbara. May–October they do daily two-hour sails departing from Camden's Public Landing; the minimum age is 12.

The 49-passenger *Appledore* (207/236-8353, www.appledore2.com), built in 1978 for round-the-world cruising, sails from Bay View Landing beginning around 10 A.M. 3–4 times daily June–October. Most cruises last two hours and cost $35 adults, $25 children. Cocktails, wine, and soft drinks are available.

Over in Rockport, the schooner *Heron* (207/236-8605 or 800/599-8605, www.wooden boatco.com) is a 65-foot John Alden–designed wooden yacht launched in 2003. Sailing options include a lobster-roll lunch sail, lighthouse sail, and sunset sails with hors d'oeuvres ($45–55 adults, $20–30 under age 12).

For a short cruise—but a great way to see Camden and Rockport and their lighthouses and shorelines—head down to the

Camden Public Landing and buy a ticket for the 30-passenger converted lobster boat *Betselma* (207/236-4446, www.betselma .com). Reservations usually aren't needed. Retired schooner captain Les Bex knows these waters, the wildlife, and the history. He does about eight hour-long trips daily, beginning at 10:30 A.M. June–September, for $10 adults, $5 under age 12. The last trip is at 7:30 P.M. He also does two two-hour trips—one in the morning, one in the afternoon—for $20 adults, $10 under age 12. A three-hour combo ($30 adults, $15 children) also is available. Pets are welcome.

If the kids are bombarding you with FAQs about lobsters, here's the solution. Take a two-hour trip aboard Captain Alan Philbrick's *Lively Lady Too* (207/236-6672, www.live-lyladytoo.com, $30 adults, $5 under age 15), berthed at Camden's Bay View Landing. He hauls in a trap, takes out a lobster, explains all its parts, and generally provides all the answers. As a former biology teacher, he's a whiz at natural history, so there's also information about seabirds, seals, and lots more. Trips depart Monday–Saturday.

ACCOMMODATIONS

The region is loaded with lodgings—from basic motels to cottage complexes to elegant inns and bed-and-breakfasts. Many of Camden's most attractive accommodations (especially bed-and-breakfasts) are on Route 1 (variously disguised as Elm St., Main St., and High St.), which is heavily trafficked in summer. If you're extra-sensitive to nighttime noises, request a room facing away from the street. Rates noted here are for peak season.

Camden
BED-AND-BREAKFASTS

A baker's dozen of Camden's finest bed-and-breakfasts have banded together in the **Camden Bed and Breakfast Association** (www.camdeninns.com), with an attractive brochure and website. Some of them are described here.

The 1874 **(Camden Harbour Inn** (83 Bayview St., 207/236-4200 or 800/236-4200,

Most of the rooms at the Camden Harbour Inn have at least a glimpse of Camden's harbor.

© HILARY NANGLE

www.camdenharbourinn.com, $350–700) underwent a masterful renovation and restoration by new Dutch owners, partners Raymond Brunyanszki and Oscar Verest, reopening in 2007 as a boutique bed-and-breakfast complete with 21st-century amenities. It retains the bones of a 19th-century summer hotel, but the decor is contemporary European, with worldly accent pieces and velour furnishings in purples, reds, and silvers. Guest rooms, some with fireplaces, patios, decks, or balconies, have at least a glimpse of Camden's harbor or Penobscot Bay. All have air-conditioning, Wi-Fi, flat-screen TVs, refrigerators, and king beds. Service is five-star, right down to chocolates and slippers at turndown. At breakfast, which is included, the menu includes choices such as lobster Benedict as well as a buffet with fresh baked items, smoked salmon, and other goodies. Snacks are always available. And their restaurant, Natalie's, is topnotch. The owners also speak Dutch, German, some French, and rudimentary Indonesian and Thai.

The **⟨ Hartstone Inn** (41 Elm St., 207/236-4259 or 800/788-4823, www.hartstoneinn.com, $125–285) is Michael and Mary Jo Salmon's imposing mansard-roofed Victorian close to the heart of downtown. Although some guest rooms face the street (and these are insulated with triple-pane windows), most do not, and all have air-conditioning. Once inside, you're away from it all. Even more removed are guest rooms in two other buildings under the Hartstone's umbrella. Suites in the Manor House, tucked behind the main inn, have contemporary decor. Guest rooms and suites in The Hideaway, in a residential neighborhood about a block away, have country French flair. All are elegant (Wi-Fi, air-conditioning); some have fireplaces and whirlpools. Be sure to make reservations for dinner. And then, there's the incredible breakfast. If you get hooked, the Salmons organize culinary classes during the winter, and you can even arrange for a one-on-one cooking experience with Michael.

Opened to guests in 1901, the **Whitehall Inn** (52 High St./Rte. 1, 207/236-3391 or 800/789-6565, www.whitehall-inn.com,

$149–199) retains its century-old genteel air. Lovely gardens, rockers on the veranda, a tennis court, and attentive service all add to the appeal of this historic country inn. Ask to see the Millay Room, commemorating famed poet Edna St. Vincent Millay, who graduated from Camden High School and first recited her poem "Renascence" to Whitehall guests in 1912. It also played a role in *Peyton Place,* and enlarged movie photos are displayed throughout. Spread between the main inn and the annex are 45 unpretentious guest rooms, all with flat-screen TVs, Internet access, and imported linens; a few share baths. Rates include a full-menu breakfast. The dining room, Vincent's, is open to nonguests for breakfast (7–10 A.M. daily) and dinner (6–9 P.M. Wed.–Mon., entrées $10–25). Also on the premises is Gossip, a bar serving pub fare; it's open mid-May–late October.

Claudio and Roberta Latanza, both natives of Italy, became the fourth innkeepers at the **Camden Maine Stay** (22 High St./Rte. 1, 207/236-9636, www.mainestay.com, $155–290) in 2009. Like their predecessors, they do everything right, from the comfortable yet elegant decor to the delicious breakfasts and afternoon snacks to the welcoming window candles and garden retreats. The stunning residence, built in 1802, faces busy Route 1 and is just a bit uphill from downtown, but inside and out back, behind the carriage house and barn, you'll feel worlds away.

In the heart of downtown Camden, **The Lord Camden Inn** (24 Main St./Rte. 1, 207/236-4325 or 800/336-4325, www.lordcamdeninn.com, $180–300) is a hotel alternative in a historic four-story downtown building (with an elevator). Top-floor rooms have harbor-view balconies. Rates include a breakfast buffet. Pooches are pampered in pet-friendly rooms for $25 per night, including a bed, biscuits, bowls, and local dog info.

ECLECTIC PROPERTIES
A hybrid of an inn, bed-and-breakfast, motel, and cottage, **The High Tide Inn on the Ocean** (Rte. 1, 207/236-3724 or 800/788-7068, www

.hightideinn.com, $75–230), three miles north of town, has enough variety for every budget—all in an outstanding seven-acre oceanfront setting with a private pebbly beach. Accommodations are a bit rustic, and some are dated. The two-story, eight-unit "Oceanfront" motel unit is closest to the water and farthest from Route 1. Rates include continental breakfast with fabulous popovers on the water-view porch. Pets can be accommodated in some rooms.

Step back in time at family-owned **Beloin's on the Maine Coast** (245 Belfast Rd./Rte. 1, 207/236-3262, www.beloins.com, $80–175). Don't judge this place from the roadside motel; down the road is another motel and cottages with spectacular oceanfront settings. Agnes Beloin keeps everything tidy, but it's all a bit dowdy (think 1950s). All guest rooms have TVs and phones, some have refrigerators or kitchenettes, and all guests have access to a private sand beach. A two-bedroom shorefront cottage is $160–240. Extra guests in rooms are $5 per night; pets are $10 per stay.

MOTEL
It's a short stroll into Merryspring Gardens from the **Cedar Crest Motel** (115 Elm St./Rte. 1, 207/236-4839, www.cedarcrestmotel .com, $129–144), a nicely maintained property on 3.5 wooded and landscaped acres on the southern edge of downtown. Each of the 37 guest rooms has air-conditioning, Wi-Fi, a phone, and a TV. Some have mini-fridges. On the premises are a guest computer, outdoor heated pool, playground, laundry, and restaurant serving all meals and live jazz on Friday evenings.

CAMPING
Camden Hills State Park (Belfast Rd./Rte. 1, 207/236-3109, $3 adults, $1 ages 5–11, camping $25 nonresidents, $15 Maine residents for basic site; $37.45 nonresidents, $26.75 Maine residents with water and electric) has a 112-site camping area and is wheelchair-accessible. Pets are allowed, showers are free, and the sites are large.

Rockport
MOTELS AND COTTAGE COLONIES
Step back in time at the oceanfront **◖ Oakland Seashore Motel & Cottages** (112 Dearborn Lane, 207/594-8104, www.oaklandseashore-cabins.com, $77–122), a low-key throwback on 70 mostly wooded acres that dates back more than a century. It was originally a recreational park operated by a trolley company, but its heyday passed with the arrival of the automobile. In the late 1940s shorefront cabins were added, and in the 1950s the dance pavilion was renovated into a motel. The rooms and cabins are simple, comfortable, clean, and right on the ocean's edge; some have kitchenettes, and a few have full kitchens. The bathrooms are tiny, and there are no phones or TVs. The grounds are gorgeous, with big shade trees, grassy lawns, and well-placed benches and chairs, and there's a rocky beach that's ideal for launching a kayak. This place isn't for those who need attentive service or fluffy accommodations, but it's a gem for those who appreciate quiet simplicity with a big view.

Clean rooms, a convenient location, lovely ocean views from most rooms, and reasonable prices have made the Beale family's **Ledges by the Bay** (930 Rte. 1, Glen Cove, 207/594-8944, www.ledgesbythebay.com, $89–189) a favorite among budget-conscious travelers. Guest rooms have air-conditioning, TVs, Wi-Fi, and phones; most have private balconies. Other pluses include a private shorefront, a small heated pool, and a light continental breakfast. Kids under 13 stay free in parents' room.

Family owned and operated, the all-suites **Country Inn** (8 Country Inn Way/Rte. 1, 207/236-2725 or 888/707-3945, www.countryinnmaine.com, $189–229 d) is an especially good choice for families, thanks to an indoor pool, play areas, guest laundry, and a fitness room. Rooms are divided between a main inn and cottage suites. Some units have fireplaces, whirlpool tubs, and microwaves; all have air-conditioning, phones, fridges, Wi-Fi, and TVs. A continental breakfast buffet and afternoon tea and cookies served in the library are included. Kids ages 6–16 are $5 per night; older kids are $10. On-site massage and yoga classes are available.

Lincolnville
INNS AND RESORTS
Private, secluded, and surrounded by 22 acres of woods and gardens, the oceanfront shingle-style **Inn at the Ocean's Edge** (Rte. 1, Lincolnville Beach, 207/236-0945, www.innatoceansedge.com, $280–425) is splurge-worthy. Every room has a king bed, a fireplace, and a whirlpool tub for two, as well as TV, air-conditioning, Wi-Fi, and superb ocean views. The grounds are lovely, with lounge chairs placed just so to take in the views. Facilities includes an outdoor heated pool that makes it seem as if you're almost in the ocean, an honor bar, a guest pantry, massage service, and a fitness room. Watch passing windjammers and lobster boats from the infinity pool or hot tub. There's an excellent restaurant on the premises. Rates include breakfast and afternoon snacks; packages with dinner are available.

Even more private and secluded is **The Inn at Sunrise Point** (Rte. 1, Lincolnville, Camden, 207/236-7716 or 800/435-6278, www.sunrisepoint.com, $345–575), an elegant retreat with all the whistles and bells you'd expect at these rates. The three handsome rooms in the main lodge, four separate cottages, two lofts, and two suites are all named after Maine authors or artists. Breakfast in the conservatory is divine.

The **Point Lookout Resort and Conference Center** (Rte. 1, Lincolnville, 800/515-3611, www.visitpointlookout.com, $200) is a former corporate retreat center with 106 well-equipped rooms on more than 100 wooded acres. All rooms have porches, Wi-Fi, TVs, cooking facilities, and some have fireplaces. The resort also features sporting facilities, an amazing fitness-wellness center, and a casual restaurant. The views over Penobscot Bay from the summit here are stupendous.

MOTEL AND COTTAGES
The family-run **Mount Battie Inn** (2158 Atlantic Hwy./Rte. 1, Lincolnville, 207/236-

The views from the Point Lookout Resort and Conference Center take in the panorama of Penobscot Bay.

© HILARY NANGLE

3870 or 800/224-3870, www.mountbattie
.com, $110–260) has 22 charming motel-
style guest rooms with air-conditioning, TVs,
phones, Wi-Fi, fridges, and continental breakfast, including home-baked treats.

Another family-run gem, the **Ducktrap
Motel** (12 Whitney Rd., Lincolnville, 207/789-
5400 or 877/977-5400, www.ducktrapmotel
.com, $92–115) is set back from Route 1 and
screened by trees. Both the grounds and the
rooms are meticulously maintained. All rooms
have TVs, fridges, coffeemakers, and air-conditioning; deluxe rooms have microwaves; the
cottage has an efficiency kitchen.

Completely renovated for 2010, with individual cottages designed by college interns, the **Bay
Leaf Cottages & Bistro** (2372 Rte. 1, 207/706-
7929 or 888/902-7929, www.bayleafcottages
.com, $100–200) welcomes families and pets
in a variety of cottages and motel rooms. A continental breakfast, with vegan and vegetarian
options, is served in the bistro; Saturday lobster
dinners are available for about $12 pp. Cooking
classes and other workshops and adventures are
offered, along with special programs for families
with children adopted from China.

FOOD
Call to verify days and hours of operation.

Local Flavors
ROCKPORT
The best source for health foods, homeopathic
remedies, and fresh seasonal produce is **Fresh
Off the Farm** (495 Rte. 1, 207/236-3260,
8 A.M.–7 P.M. Mon.–Sat., 9 A.M.–5:30 P.M.
Sun.), an inconspicuous red-painted roadside
place that looks like an overgrown farm stand
(which it is). Watch for one of those perma-
nent-temporary signs highlighting the latest
arrivals, which might include native blueberries
or native corn. The shop is 1.3 miles south of
the junction of Routes 1 and 90.

At the southern entrance to Rockport, a
sprawling red building is the home of **The
Rockport Marketplace and the State of
Maine Cheese Company** (461 Commercial
St./Rte. 1, 207/236-8895 or 800/762-8895,

9 A.M.–5 P.M. Mon.–Sat., noon–4 P.M. Sun.).
Inside are locally made varieties of cows' milk
hard cheeses, all named after Maine locations
(Aroostook Jack, Allagash Caraway, St. Croix
Black Pepper, and so on) as well as hundreds
of Maine-made products, from food to crafts.
Among the items are blueberry chutneys, maple
syrup, designer breads, great jams—it's a one-
stop shopping (and tasting) site.

At the junction of Routes 1 and 90, a colorfully painted barn is the home of **The Market
Basket** (Rte. 1, 207/236-4371, 7 A.M.–
6:30 P.M. Mon.–Sat., 9 A.M.–4 P.M. Sun.), the
best takeout source for creative sandwiches,
homemade soups, cheeses, exotic condiments,
pastries, wine (large selection), beer, and entrées to go. The market will also do boat provisioning. In winter, it sponsors weeklong
cooking classes.

CAMDEN
The **Camden Farmers Market** (3:30–6 P.M.
Wed. June–late Sept. and 9 A.M.–noon Sat.
early May–late Oct.), one of the best in the
state, holds forth at the Knox Mill Complex
on Washington Street. It continues through
the winter inside the Knox Mill.

The **Camden Bagel Cafe** (Brewster Mill, 26
Mechanic St., 207/236-2661, 6:30 A.M.–2 P.M.
Mon.–Sat., 7:30 A.M.–2 P.M. Sun., no credit
cards) has a hugely loyal clientele, drawn by
real coffee, fresh bagels, fast service, daily
newspapers, and a casual air.

Good coffee is a draw at the **Camden Deli**
(37 Main St., 207/236-8343, 7 A.M.–10 P.M.
daily), in the heart of downtown, but its biggest asset is the windowed seating overlooking the Megunticook River waterfall. The view
doesn't get much better than this (go upstairs
for the best angle). Made-to-order sandwiches
and wraps, homemade soups, veggie burgers,
and subs all add to the mix.

Since the early 1970s, **Scott's Place** (85 Elm
St./Rte. 1, 207/236-8751, 10:30 A.M.–4 P.M.
Mon.–Fri., 10:30 A.M.–3 P.M. Sat.), a road-
side lunch stand near Reny's at the Camden
Marketplace, has been dishing up inexpensive
($2–10) burgers and dogs, nowadays adding

veggie burgers and salads. Call ahead and it'll be ready.

Peek behind the old-fashioned facade at **Boynton-McKay Food Company** (30 Main St., 207/236-2465, 7 A.M.–5 P.M. Tues.–Sat., 8 A.M.–4 P.M. Sun., kitchen closes 3 P.M. daily) and you'll see an old-fashioned soda fountain, early-20th-century tables, antique pharmacy accessories, and a thoroughly modern café menu. Restored and rehabbed in 1997, Boynton-McKay had been *the* local drugstore for more than a century. The new incarnation features bagels, creative salads, homemade soups, superb wrap sandwiches, an espresso bar, and the whole works from the soda fountain. It's open for breakfast and lunch.

Facing downtown Camden's five-way intersection, **French and Brawn** (1 Elm St., 207/236-3361, 6 A.M.–8 P.M. Mon.–Sat., 8 A.M.–8 P.M. Sun.) is an independent market that earns the description *super*. Ready-made sandwiches, soups, and other goodies complement the oven-ready takeout meals, high-cal frozen desserts, esoteric meats, and staff with a can-do attitude.

LINCOLNVILLE
No question, **Nana's Kitchen** (Rte. 1, Northport, 207/338-1524, www.nanasgoodeats.com, 8 A.M.–9 P.M. daily, dinner entrées $10–24) looks a bit forlorn from the exterior, but this is the kind of home-cookin' gem chowhounds love to stumble on and devour. The breads, muffins, doughnuts, and biscuits are all homemade; the portions are generous and prices are reasonable.

Need a sandwich before heading for the hills or beach? **Dot's** (2457 Rte. 1, 207/706-7922, 7 A.M.–6 P.M. Mon.–Sat., 8 A.M.–3 P.M. Sun.) is the place. It also bakes breakfast goods and treats, makes salads and prepared meals, and sells cheeses and wines. There's seating inside.

Family Favorites
CAMDEN
Elm Street Grille (Cedar Crest Motel, 115 Elm St./Rte. 1, 207/236-4839, www.cedarcrestmotel.com) is a favorite for great breakfasts, lunch, and dinner Tuesday–Sunday. The pizzas get high marks. It's all very reasonably priced and served in a comfortable dining room, with a handful of seats on a deck. On Friday nights there's live jazz.

In the heart of Camden, **Cappy's** (1 Main St., 207/236-2254, www.cappyschowder.com, 11:30 A.M.–11 P.M. daily, $10–21) is small, a bit cramped, and very popular with locals and out-of-towners alike, despite being a bit pricey for food that's rather ordinary. In summer, request a table in the second-floor Crow's Nest, where you'll be less squished. It's a burger-and-sandwich menu with some heartier seafood choices; clam chowder is a specialty. During summer, Cappy's operates a bakery with takeout pastries, sandwiches, and other goodies underneath, facing on the alley that runs down to the public parking lot.

LINCOLNVILLE
Annamarie Ahern's oceanfront **Saltwater Farm** (25 Woodward Hill Rd., 207/230-0966, www.saltwaterfarm.com) is a haven for serious foodies. Five-course, communal Full Moon and Sunday Suppers ($65) are served by reservation only. Seating is very limited here, and the dinners are extremely popular, so advance planning is essential. Hands-on cooking classes (around $75 for a half-day class) and multi-day workshops are also offered.

Casual Dining
ROCKPORT
When **⬛ Shepherd's Pie** (18 Central St., 207/236-8500, 4–11:30 P.M. daily, $13–24) opened in spring 2010, it already had a cult following thanks to chef-owner Brian Hill's successful Francine Bistro in Camden. Here in a historical building with high tin ceilings and beautiful dark wood walls, Hill has created a delicious and inviting spot serving pub- and home-style favorites updated with verve; think duck hot dogs, pork belly sandwiches, fried clam tacos, and baked beans with candied bacon. No reservations; expect to wait for a table.

Food as art is the idea behind the **Gallery Café** (297 Commercial St./Rte. 1, Rockport,

207/230-0061, www.prismglassgallery-cafe
.com, 11 A.M.–3 P.M. and 5–9 P.M. Wed.–Sat.,
10 A.M.–3 P.M. and 4–8 P.M. Sun., $15–32,
brunch $10–16), a restaurant that's part of
Prismglass, a fine-art glass gallery and working
studio representing more than 50 glass artists.
The Italian-leaning menu changes seasonally.

CAMDEN

Chef-owner Brian Hill has created one of the
region's hottest restaurants with **Francine
Bistro** (55 Chestnut St., 207/230-0083, www
.francinebistro.com, 5:30–10 P.M. Tues.–Sat.,
entrées $24–30). The well-chosen menu is short
and focused on whatever's fresh and (usually) locally available that day. In addition to the dining
room, there's also seating at the bar and, when
the weather cooperates, on the front porch.

Down on the harbor is the informal, art-
filled **Atlantica** (1 Bay View Landing,
207/236-6011 or 888/507-8514, www.atlanti-
carestaurant.com, 5–9 P.M. daily, $22–29), two
floors of culinary creativity with an emphasis
on seafood. In summer, try for a table on the
deck hanging over the water.

The Waterfront Restaurant (Bay View
St., 207/236-3747, 11:30 A.M.–9:30 P.M. daily,
$13–28) has the biggest waterside dining deck
in town, but you'll need to arrive early to snag
one of the tables. Lunches are the most fun,
overlooking lots of harbor action; at high tide,
you're eye to eye with the boats. Most folks rave
about the place, but I've found it inconsistent.

LINCOLNVILLE

Appropriately named, **The Edge** (Inn at the
Ocean's Edge, Rte. 1, 207/236-4430, www
.innatoceansedge.com, 4–8:30 P.M. daily, $16–
30) provides a front-row seat on Penobscot Bay,
whether you're in the cozy dining room or on
the deck. The menu features familiar foods
with creative touches and an emphasis on fresh
and local. Sunday night is pizza night ($18)
with a family style Caesar salad and fancy pies
served to the table in rotation; keep sampling
until you're full.

Salt Water Farm (Salt Water Farm Rd.,
207/230-0966, www.saltwaterfarm.com) is

a hybrid: It's a farm, a hands-on recreational
cooking school, and a destination for special
multicourse suppers ($60 pp includes tip).
Advance reservations are essential, as these fill
quickly.

Fine Dining
CAMDEN

Reservations are a must for chef Michael
Salmon's five-course fixed-price extravaganzas
at the **Hartstone Inn** (41 Elm St., 207/236-
4259 or 800/788-4823, www.hartstoneinn
.com, $50). Michael, named Caribbean chef of
the year when they lived in Aruba, has cooked
at the Beard House by invitation. Even Julia
Child dined here. The menu changes weekly
to use the freshest ingredients. In the off-season, three-course bistro menus are offered some
nights.

Since opening in 2007 to rave reviews,
◖ **Natalie's at the Camden Harbour Inn**
(83 Bayview St., 207/236-4200, www.natalies
restaurant.com, 5–9:30 P.M. daily) has become
one of the state's top tables. The dining room
was designed to be reminiscent of the Left Bank
in Paris a century ago. The ambience is fancy
here, but casual attire is fine. Instead of looking out at the Seine, you're gazing over Camden
Harbor. Entrées begin in the high $20s, a five-
course tasting menu is $65, and a four-course
grand lobster menu reflects market prices.
Lighter fare is served in the bar and lounge.

LINCOLNVILLE

For a romantic, classic French experience,
head a bit inland to **Youngtown Inn and
Restaurant** (581 Youngtown Rd., 207/763-
4290 or 800/291-8438, www.youngtown-
inn.com, 6–9 P.M. Tues.–Sun., $22–30),
where chef-owner Manuel Mercier draws on
his Parisian heritage and European training.
Upstairs are six guest rooms ($160–175, in-
cludes breakfast).

Lobster in the Rough
LINCOLNVILLE

Lincolnville's best-known landmark is
The Lobster Pound Restaurant (Rte. 1,

The Lobster Pound Restaurant, Lincolnville Beach

© HILARY NANGLE

Lincolnville Beach, 207/789-5550, www.lobsterpoundmaine.com, 11:30 A.M.–8 P.M. daily Sept.–June, 11:30 A.M.–9 P.M. daily July–Aug., $12–35). About 300 people—some days, it looks like more than that—can pile into the restaurant and enclosed patio, so be sure to make reservations on summer weekends. Despite the crowds, food and service are reliably good. Lobster, of course, is king, but the huge menu will satisfy everyone.

INFORMATION AND SERVICES

Information

For planning, contact **Camden-Rockport-Lincolnville Chamber of Commerce** (207/236-4404 or 800/223-5459, www.visit-camden.com). Also handy is a directory published by the **Lincolnville Business Group** (www.lincolnville.org).

Check out **Camden Public Library** (Main St./Rte. 1, Camden, 207/236-3440, www.camden.lib.me.us) or **Rockport Public Library** (1 Limerock St., Rockport, 207/236-3642, www.rockport.lib.me.us).

Public Restrooms

Public restrooms are available at Camden's Public Landing, near the chamber of commerce, and at the Camden Public Library. In Rockport, there are restrooms at Marine Park. In Lincolnville, there are restrooms at the ferry terminal.

PENOBSCOT BAY

Belfast

Belfast is relatively small as cities go, but it's officially cool: *Budget Travel* magazine named it one of the top 10 coolest towns in the United States. Even before that, Belfast was one of those off-the-beaten-track destinations popular with tuned-in travelers. Chalk that up to its status as a magnet for leftover back-to-the-landers and enough artistic types to earn the city a nod for cultural cool. Belfast has a curling club, a food co-op and a green store, meditation centers, an increasing number of art galleries and boutiques, dance and theater companies, the oldest shoe store in the country, and half a dozen different 12-step self-help groups. It even has a poet laureate.

This eclectic city is a work in progress, a study in Maine-style diversity. It's also a gold mine of Federal, Greek Revival, Italianate, and Victorian architecture. Take the time to stroll the well-planned backstreets, explore the shops, and hang out at the gussied-up waterfront.

Separating Belfast from East Belfast, the Passagassawakeag River (puh-sag-gus-uh-WAH-keg) fortunately is known more familiarly as "the Passy." The Indian name has been translated as both "place of many ghosts" and the rather different "place for spearing sturgeon by torchlight." You choose. No matter, you can cross it via a pedestrian bridge.

Many travelers make Belfast a day stop on their way between Camden and Bar Harbor. Truly, Belfast is worth more time than that. Spend a full day or two here, and it's likely you'll be charmed, like many of the other urban refugees, into resettling here.

SIGHTS
Historic Walking Tour
No question, the best way to appreciate Belfast's fantastic architecture is to tour by ankle express. At the Belfast Area Chamber of Commerce, pick up the well-researched *Belfast*

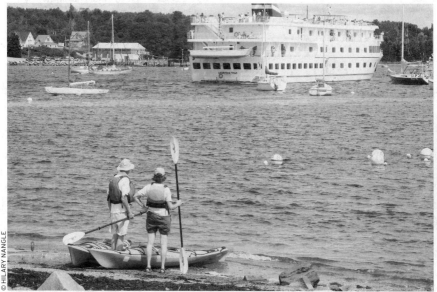

© HILARY NANGLE

Kayakers, sailboats, and cruiseships share Belfast's harbor.

ISLESBORO

Lying three miles offshore from Lincolnville Beach, 20 minutes via car ferry, is 12-mile-long Islesboro, a year-round community with a population of about 600 – beefed up annually by a sedate summer colony. Car ferries are frequent enough to make Islesboro an ideal day-trip destination – and that's the choice of most visitors, partly because food options are few and overnight lodging isn't available. The only camping is on nearby Warren Island State Park – and you have to have your own boat to get there.

The best way to get an island overview is to do an end-to-end auto or bike tour. Pick up an island map at the ferry terminal and explore, heading down to Dark Harbor and Town Beach at the island's bottom, then up to Pripet and Turtle Head at its top. You won't see all the huge "cottages" tucked down long driveways, and you won't absorb island life and its rhythms, but you'll scratch the surface of what Islesboro is about.

En route, you'll pass exclusive summer estates, workaday homes, spectacular seaside vistas, a smattering of shops, and the **Historical Society Museum** (388 Main St., 207/734-6744, www.islesborohistorical.org, 12:30-4:30 P.M. Sat.-Wed. July-Aug. or by appointment). On the up-island circuit, watch for a tiny marker on the west side of the road (0.8 miles north of the Islesboro Historical Society building). It commemorates the 1780 total eclipse witnessed here – the first recorded in North America. At the time, British loyalists still held Islesboro, but they temporarily suspended hostilities, allowing Harvard astronomers to lug their instruments to the island and document the eclipse.

Allow time before the return ferry to visit the **Sailors' Memorial Museum,** a town-owned museum filled with seafaring memorabilia and allegedly home to a benevolent ghost or two. It's in the keeper's house adjacent to **Grindle Point Light** (207/734-2253, http://lighthouse.cc/grindle), built in 1850, rebuilt in 1875, and now automated.

The car ferry *Margaret Chase Smith* (207/789-5611, Islesboro 207/734-6935, www.exploremaine.org) departs Lincolnville Beach almost every hour on the hour, 8 or 9 A.M.-5 P.M., and departs Islesboro on the half hour, 7:30 A.M.-4:30 P.M. Round-trip fares are $25 for a car, $8.50 adults, $3.25 kids, $7 adult bicycles, and $4 kids' bikes. Reservations are $5 extra. A slightly reduced schedule prevails late October–early May. The 20-minute trip crosses a stunning three-mile stretch of Penobscot Bay, with views of islands and the Camden Hills. In summer, avoid the biggest bottlenecks: Friday afternoon (to Islesboro), Sunday afternoon and Monday holiday afternoons (from Islesboro). The *Smith* remains on Islesboro overnight, so don't miss the last run to Lincolnville Beach.

Historic Walking Tour map-brochure. Among more than 40 highlights on the mile-long self-guided route are the 1818 Federal-style **First Church,** handsome residences on **High Street** and **Church Street,** and the 1840 **James P. White House** (Church St. and Northport Ave.), now an elegant bed-and-breakfast and New England's finest Greek Revival residence. Amazingly for a community of this size, the city actually has three distinct listed districts on the National Register of Historic Places: Belfast Commercial Historic District (47 downtown buildings), Church Street Historic District (residential), and Primrose Hill Historic District (also residential). Another walking tour is presented by the Belfast Historical Society's **Museum in the Streets,** comprising two large panels and 30 smaller ones highlighting historic buildings and people. Signs are in English and French.

Bayside

Continuing the focus on architecture, just south of Belfast in Northport is the Victorian enclave of Bayside, a neighborhoody sort of place with small, well-kept gingerbread-trimmed cottages cheek-by-jowl on pint-size lots. Formerly known as the Northport Wesleyan Grove Campground, the village took shape in the mid-1800s as a summer retreat for Methodists. In the 1930s the retreat was disbanded and the main meeting hall was razed, creating the waterfront park at the heart of the village. Today, many of the colorfully painted homes are rented by the week, month, or summer season, and their tenants are more likely to indulge in athletic rather than religious pursuits. The camaraderie remains, though, and a stroll (or cycle or drive) through Bayside is like a visit to another era. Bayside is four miles south of Belfast, just east of Route 1. If you want to join the fun, try **Bayside Cottage Rentals** (539 Bluff Rd., Northport, 207/338-5355, www.baysidecottagerentals.com).

Temple Heights

Continue south on Shore Road from Bayside to **Temple Heights Spiritualist Camp** (Shore Rd., Northport, 207/338-3029, www.templeheightscamp.org), yet another religious enclave—this one still ongoing. Founded in 1882, Temple Heights has become a shadow of its former self, reduced primarily to the funky 12-room Nikawa Lodge on Shore Road ($35 d, $25 s, shared bath, some with ocean views), but the summer program continues thanks to prominent mediums from all over the country. Even a temporary setback in 1996—when the camp president was suspended for allegedly putting a hex on Northport's town clerk—failed to derail the operation. Camp programs mid-June–Labor Day are open to the public; a schedule is published each spring. Spiritualist church services, séances, and group healing sessions are free; Saturday-morning workshops are $20. Better yet, sign up for a 1.5-hour or longer **group message circle,** when you'll sit with a medium and a dozen or so others and receive insights—often uncannily on target—from departed relatives or friends. Message circles are held at 7:30 P.M. Wednesday and Saturday (arrive a half-hour early). Suggested donation is $15 pp, and reservations are necessary. Private half-hour readings can be arranged for a donation of $40.

Bryant Stove and Music Museum

Sometimes you really do have to see it to believe it. That's the case with the Bryant Stove and Music Museum (27 Stovepipe Alley, Thorndike, 207/568-3665, www.bryantstove.com, $4), a labor of love collected, created, repaired, and assembled by Joe and Bea Bryant. Begin with the Doll Circus. Flip a switch and the room comes alive with dolls dancing, marching, swinging, turning, and twisting to music. Airplanes fly, a Ferris wheel turns, stuffed animals swing. There's a Barbie doll fashion show, a hula show, and a line of Barbies and Kens marching to the altar. No matter which you way look, dolls and stuffed animals are actively positioned in creative scenes. It's a jaw-dropping marriage of lights and music and movement. And that's just the first room. Beyond it are a small engine room with miniature working steam engines; a music section with player pianos, nickelodeons, juke boxes, organs, barrel pianos, hurdy-gurdies, and more. The museum is very hands-on, and visitors are encouraged to push buttons, play the instruments, and learn about the mechanisms. If that's not enough, there are also antique stoves and automobiles that Joe lovingly repaired. A separate part of the business specializes in antique stoves; quite a few celebrities have bought the restored beauties here. To find this gem, about 19 miles inland of Belfast, follow Route 137 northwest, then Route 220 north.

ENTERTAINMENT AND EVENTS

It's relatively easy to find nightlife in Belfast—not only are there theaters and a cinema, but there are usually a couple of bars open at least until midnight and sometimes later. Some spots also feature live music, particularly on weekends.

If you don't feel like searching out a newspaper to check the entertainment listings, just go to the **Belfast Co-op Store** (123 High St., 207/338-2532) and study the bulletin board. You'll find notices for more activities than you could ever squeeze into your schedule.

Open mike nights, jazz jams, classes, and

OFF THE BEATEN PATH IN LIBERTY

Seventeen miles west of Belfast, off Route 3, is Liberty (www.historicliberty.com), a tiny town with a funky tool store, a quirky museum, a bargain T-shirt shop, and a great state park. Everything is seasonal, running about mid-May–mid-October. Call before visiting if you want to be sure everything's open.

It's a store! It's a museum! It's amazing! More than 10,000 "useful" tools – plus used books and prints and other tidbits – fill the three-story **Liberty Tool Company** (Main St., Liberty, 207/589-4771). Drawn by nostalgia and a compulsion for handmade adzes and chisels, thousands of vintage-tool buffs arrive at this eclectic emporium each year; few leave empty-handed. Nor do the thousands of everyday home hobbyists looking to pick up a hammer or find a missing wrench to fill out a set. Nor do the antiques-seekers, who browse the trash and treasures on the upper floors. The collection is beyond amazing, especially in its organization. Owner Skip Brack brings back vanloads of finds almost every week, and after sorting and cleaning, many make it into this store.

The best-of-the-best make it into Brack's **Davistown Museum** (Main St., 207/589-4900, www.davistownmuseum.org), on the third floor of the building housing Liberty Graphics, across the street. The museum houses not only a history of Maine and New England hand tools but also local, regional, Native American, and environmental artifacts and information and an amazing collection of contemporary art, highlighted by works by artists such as Louise Nevelson (who used to buy tools across the street), Melitta Westerlund, and Phil Barter.

Downstairs is **Liberty Graphics Outlet Store** (1 Main St., 207/589-4035, www.lg-tees.com), selling the eco-sensitive company's overstocks, seconds, and discontinued-design T-shirts. Outstanding silkscreened designs are done with water-based inks, and many of the shirts are organic cotton; prices begin at $5.

Just down Main Street is the old **Liberty Post Office,** a unique octagonal structure that looks like an oversize box. It was built in 1867 as a harness-maker's shop and later used as the town's post office.

Two miles west of downtown, **Lake St. George State Park** (Rte. 3, 207/589-4255, $6 nonresident adults, $4 Maine resident adults, $1 ages 5–11) is a refreshing find. This 360-acre park has wooded picnic sites with grills along the lake, a beach, rental boats, a playground, volleyball and basketball courts, and five miles of hiking trails. Also available are campsites ($25 nonresidents, $15 Maine residents). Afterward, head to **John's Ice Cream** (Rte. 3, 207/589-3700) for amazing flavors handcrafted ("homemade" is too pedestrian to describe it) on the premises.

If you're up for more inland exploring, weave your way along the **Georges River Scenic Byway,** a 50-mile auto route along the St. George River (a.k.a. Georges River) from its inland headwaters to the sea in Port Clyde. It's lovely anytime but is especially pretty during foliage season. The official start is at the junction of Routes 3 and 220 in Liberty, but you can follow the trail in either direction, or pick it up anywhere along the way. Road signs are posted, but it's far better to obtain a map-brochure at a chamber of commerce or other information locale. Or contact the architects of the route, **The Georges River Land Trust** (207/594-5166, www.grlt.org).

lectures pepper the calendar for **Waterfall Arts** (265 High St., 207/338-2222, www.waterfallarts.org).

Just south of Belfast, the funky **Blue Goose Dance Hall** (Rte. 1, Northport, 207/338-3003) is the site for folk concerts, contra dances, auctions, and other events. Check local papers or the Belfast Co-op Store bulletin board.

About a dozen galleries participate in Belfast Arts' **Friday Gallery Walk** (www.artsbelfast.com), held every Friday night in July–August and every first Friday in June, September–October, and December.

Check local papers for the schedule of the **Belfast Maskers** (43 Front St., 207/338-9668, www.belfastmaskerstheater.com), a community theater group that never fails to win raves for its interpretations of contemporary and classical dramas. In winter wear an extra pair of socks; the floor is drafty.

Also worth checking out is the **Northport Music Theater** (851 Rte. 1, Northport, 207/338-8383, www.northportmusictheater .com, $20–25), a 128-seat summer theater.

The Belfast Garden Club sponsors **Open Garden Days** (www.belfastgardenclub.org) once a week mid-May–mid-September at the homes of club members and friends in and around Belfast. Gardens are open 10 A.M.–3 P.M. rain or shine; a $4 pp donation is requested to benefit local beautification projects. Check local newspapers or ask at the chamber of commerce for the schedule.

In early July, soon after the Fourth of July, the **Arts in the Park** festival gets under way at Heritage Park, on the Belfast waterfront. It's a weekend event with two days of music, juried arts and crafts, children's activities, and lots of food booths.

The **Belfast Bay Festival,** usually the third week of July, has music, carnival rides, fireworks, food, and more.

SHOPPING

It's easy and fun to shop in downtown Belfast, a town that has so far managed to keep the big boxes away, providing fertile ground for entrepreneurs. Downtown shops reflect the city's population, with galleries and boutiques, thrift and used-goods stores, and eclectic shops.

Books

Mr. Paperback (1 E. Belmont Ave., 207/338-2084), in the Reny's Plaza, is also home to an excellent café called **Bell the Cat** (207/338-2084, 9 A.M.–8 P.M. Mon.–Sat., 9 A.M.–6 P.M. Sun.).

Specialty Shops

Even if shoes aren't on your shopping list, stop in at "the oldest shoe store in America": Founded in the 1830s, **Colburn Shoe Store** (81 Main St., 207/338-1934 or 877/338-1934) may be old, but it isn't old-fashioned.

Brambles (69 Main St., 207/338-3448) is a gardener's delight, with fun, whimsical, and practical garden-themed merchandise.

Wooden toys are just one reason to visit **Out of the Woods** (48 Main St., 207/338-2692), which specializes in Maine-made wood products.

Just over the Belfast bridge is **Cherished Home** (31 Searsport Ave./Rte. 1, 207/338-4111), where Genie Francis (a.k.a. Laura of the famed Luke and Laura on the soap opera *General Hospital*) sells a nice selection of home-oriented merchandise.

About two miles east of Belfast's bridge, on the right, is the small roadside shop of **Mainely Pottery** (181 Searsport Ave./Rte. 1, 207/338-1108). Since 1988, Jeannette Faunce and Jamie Oates have been marketing the work of more than two dozen Maine potters, each with different techniques, glazes, and styles. It's the perfect place to select from a wide range of reasonably priced work.

The Green Store

Calling itself a "general store for the 21st century," The Green Store (71 Main St., 207/338-4045) carries a huge selection of environmentally friendly products. Whether you're thinking of going off the grid, need a composting toilet, or just want natural-fiber clothing or other natural-living products, this is the place. A very knowledgeable staff can answer nearly any question on environmentally sustainable lifestyles.

RECREATION
Parks

Belfast is rich in parks and picnic spots. One of the state's best municipal parks is just on the outskirts of downtown. Established in 1904, **Belfast City Park** (87 Northport Ave., 207/338-1661, free) has lighted tennis courts, an outdoor pool, a pebbly beach, plenty of picnic tables, an unusually creative playground, lots of green space for the kids, and fantastic views of Islesboro, Blue Hill, and Penobscot Bay. For more action right in the heart of Belfast, head for **Heritage Park,** at the bottom of Main Street, with front-row seats on waterfront happenings. Bring a picnic, grab a table, and watch the yachts, tugs, and lobster boats. Every street between the two parks that ends at the ocean is a public right of way.

Hiking

Here's an easy amble, with just enough rise and fall to make you think you got a bit of a workout: The blue-blazed **Little River Community Trail** parallels the east bank of the Little River, departing from a trailhead at the Water District complex on Route 1 and ebbing and flowing just shy of a mile to the Perkins Road. You can cross the road and continue for nearly another three miles to another trailhead near the YMCA on Route 52.

Golf

Just south of Belfast is the nine-hole **Northport Golf Club** (581 Bluff Rd., Northport, 207/338-2270), established in 1916.

Sailing

Sail aboard the Friendship sloop *Amity* (evenings 207/469-0849, daytime 207/323-1443, www.friendshipsloopamity.com), based at the Belfast Public Landing, for 90-minute morning ($20) or 2.5-hour afternoon ($30) sails; children under age 16 are half price. The classic Friendship sloop, built in 1901 in Friendship, was originally used for lobstering. Now beautifully restored, it carries up to six passengers. Home-baked cookies along with hot coffee and tea are served on all cruises. Captain Stephen O'Connell, a former journalist, explains the boat's history and its role in lobstering and regales passengers, when asked, with tales of his experiences living in exotic locations around the world.

Kayaking

If you don't have your own kayak, **Water Walker** (152 Lincolnville Ave., 207/338-6424, www.kayak-tour-maine.com) has a full range of options. Owner Ray Wirth, a Registered Maine Guide and ACA-certified open-water instructor, will arrange customized trips from a few hours to multiple days, as well as provide instruction. Two-hour Belfast Harbor tours are $35 pp; subtract $10 if you have your own boat.

Winter Sports

The Scottish national sport of curling has dozens of enthusiastic supporters at Maine's only curling rink, the **Belfast Curling Club** (Belmont Ave./Rte. 3, 207/338-9851, www .belfastcurlingclub.org), an institution here since the late 1950s. Leagues play regularly on weeknights, and the club holds bonspiels (tournaments) and open houses several times during the season, which runs early November–early April.

ACCOMMODATIONS
Bed-and-Breakfasts and Inns

On a quiet side street, **The Jeweled Turret** (40 Pearl St., 207/338-2304 or 800/696-2304, www.jeweledturret.com, $115–159) is one of Belfast's pioneer bed-and-breakfasts. Carl and Cathy Heffentrager understand the business and go out of their way to make guests comfortable. The 1898 Victorian inn is loaded with handsome woodwork and Victorian antiques—plus an astonishing stone fireplace. Carl can even fix your bike, if necessary, and he's up on all the local byways.

The White House (1 Church St., 207/338-1901 or 888/290-1901, www.mainebb.com, $175–250), the handsomest manse in Belfast, is the star of the Church Street Historic District. Built in 1840, the Greek Revival building is elegant inside and out—parlors, the library, and guest rooms are accented with plaster ceiling medallions, marble fireplaces, and chandeliers. Owners Diana and Santiago Rich have added fancy linens, Wi-Fi, plasma TVs, and other upscale touches. A giant copper beech tree dominates the parklike grounds and gardens.

Over three years, beginning in 2005, professional innkeepers Ed and Judy Hemmingsen renovated adjacent mid-19th-century row houses into an elegant boutique hotel, the ◖ **Belfast Bay Inn** (72 Main St., 207/338-5600, www.belfastbayinn.com, $268–375). The two guest rooms and six suites differ in size and design, some with fireplaces, others with balconies, but all have original art, expanded wet bars, and quality furnishings that invite relaxation. In-room spa services are available. A full breakfast is served to each room. The Hemmingsens delight in surprising guests with unexpected extras. Also here is **Molly Amber,** a little shop jam-packed with useful delights.

Motels

The 61 guest rooms at the oceanfront **Belfast Harbor Inn** (91 Searsport Ave., 207/338-2740 or 800/545-8576, www.belfastharborinn.com, $79–159) have TVs, air-conditioning, and free Wi-Fi and local calls; there's an outdoor heated pool—a real plus for families—as is the laundry. Pets are allowed in some guest rooms for $10 per night. Rates include a light continental breakfast buffet. If you can swing it, request an ocean-view room.

Camping

Every one of the 44 mostly open sites at the **Moorings Oceanfront RV Resort** (191 Searsport Ave./Rte. 1, 207/338-6860, www .mooringscamp.com) has an ocean view and hookups. Views are fabulous, and the rocky beach has a pocket of sand; swimming is only for the hardy. The downsides: Many sites feel crowded, and there's often a wait for showers. Sites in midsummer are $48–60 (two adults plus three kids under age 17). Facilities include laundry, a play area, a kayak launch, a game room, Wi-Fi, and an on-site restaurant.

FOOD

Call to verify days and hours of operation.

Local Flavors

Wraps are fast food at **Bay Wrap** (20 Beaver St., 207/338-9757, www.baywrap.com, 11 A.M.–7 P.M. Mon.–Fri., 11 A.M.–4 P.M. Sat.). There's no limit to what the staff can stuff into various flavors of tortillas. Eat here or get them to go. Another plus: **John's Ice Cream,** one of Maine's best homemade treats, is available here too.

Duck into **Belfast Soup & Sandwich Restaurant** (124 High St., Belfast, 207/338-6541, 10:30 A.M.–6 P.M. Mon.–Thurs.,

10:30 A.M.–2:30 P.M. Fri.–Sat.) for homemade soups, salads, and sandwiches served on an Old World Sicilian grilled bread.

The **Belfast Co-op Store** (123 High St., 207/338-2532, www.belfast.coop, 7:30 A.M.–8 P.M. daily) is an experience in itself. You'll have a good impression of Belfast after one glance at the clientele and the bulletin board. Open to members and nonmembers alike (with lower prices for members), the co-op is a full-service organic and natural foods grocery, with a deli-café serving lunches daily and weekend brunches.

The Belfast Farmers Market (Washington St. parking lot downtown, 9 A.M.–1 P.M. Fri.) provides the perfect opportunity for stocking up for a picnic.

Ethnic and Vegetarian Fare

Don't be put off by the lackluster exterior of **Seng Thai** (160 Searsport Ave./Rte. 1, 207/338-0010, 11 A.M.–9 P.M. Tues.–Sun., entrées $8–14), a small, low building across from the Comfort Inn. Inside the ambience is pleasant, the service is good, everything's available for takeout if you prefer, and best of all it's decent Thai food.

Fresh food prepared in creative ways has earned **Chase's Daily** (96 Main St., 207/338-0555, 7 A.M.–5 P.M. Tues.–Thurs. and Sat., 7 A.M.–8 P.M. Fri., 8 A.M.–2 P.M. Sun.) a devoted local following. The emphasis is on vegetarian fare, and most of the produce comes from the Chase family farm in nearby Freedom. Most choices are in the $7–12 range; dinner entrées range $15–22. The restaurant doubles as an art gallery, farmers market, and bakery. It's not the place for a quiet dinner, as the space is large and tends to be noisy.

Tina Del Santo and partner Anthony Jackovino opened **Delvino's Grill and Pasta House** (32 Main St., Belfast, 207/338-4565, 4–9 P.M. Mon., 11 A.M.–9 P.M. Tues.–Thurs. and Sun., 11 A.M.–11 P.M. Fri.–Sat., entrées $13–22) in 2010, satisfying the needs of locals who craved fresh pastas and appreciated the mussels marinara, haddock bruschetta, and gluten-free grilled vegetable medley.

© HILARY NANGLE

Marshall Wharf is home to both a lobster pound and a brewery, which are both adjacent to the Three Tides restaurant.

Casual Dining

A longtime standby for creative world cuisine, including vegetarian items, **Darby's Restaurant and Pub** (155 High St., 207/338-2339, www.darbysrestaurant.com, 11:30 A.M.–3:30 P.M. and 5–9 P.M. daily, entrées $11–20) served tofu before tofu was cool. This place has been providing food and drink since just after the Civil War; the tin ceilings and antique bar are reminders of that.

Industrial chic, casual, and laid-back best describe **Three Tides** (2 Pinchy Lane, on Marshall Wharf, 207/338-1707, www.3tides .com, 4–9 P.M. Tues.–Sat.). Grab a booth inside, a seat at the bar, or a table on the deck overlooking the working harbor, and then choose from the tapas-style menu ($3.50–12). You might even play a game of boccie while waiting. Beers and ales are brewed on the premises. Also part of the operation is **LB,** a lobster pound, so lobster is almost always on the menu.

It doesn't look like much from the outside, but **Papa J's and the Lobster Bar** (193 Searsport Ave., 207/338-6464, 4–10 P.M. Tues.–Sat., entrées $12–25) is warm and welcoming inside, with nice water views, a casual style, and—most important—well-prepared food complemented by a surprisingly good wine list. Order the lobster and feta pizza; you won't be disappointed.

INFORMATION AND SERVICES

Information

The **Belfast Area Chamber of Commerce** (16 Main St., 207/338-5900, www.belfast maine.org) produces a regional guide.

Check out **Belfast Free Library** (106 High St., 207/338-3884, www.belfast.lib.me.us).

Public Restrooms

Facilities are at the waterfront Public Landing, in the railroad station, at the Waldo County Court House, and at the Waldo County General Hospital.

Searsport Area

Five miles northeast of downtown Belfast, you're in the heart of Searsport, a name synonymous with the sea thanks to an enduring oceangoing tradition that's appropriately commemorated here in the state's oldest maritime museum. The seafaring heyday occurred in the mid-19th century, but settlers from the Massachusetts Colony had already made inroads here 200 years earlier. By the 1750s, Fort Pownall, in nearby **Stockton Springs,** was a strategic site during the French and Indian War (the North American phase of Europe's Seven Years' War).

Shipbuilding was under way by 1791, reaching a crescendo 1845–1866, with six year-round shipyards and nearly a dozen more seasonal ones. Ten percent of all full-rigged American-flag ships on the high seas were under the command of Searsport and Stockton Springs captains by 1885—a significant number of them bearing the names Pendleton, Nichols, or Carver. Many of these ships were involved in the perilous China trade, rounding notorious Cape Horn with great regularity.

All this global contact shaped Searsport's culture, adding a veneer of cosmopolitan sophistication. Imposing mansions of seafaring families were filled with fabulous Oriental treasures, many of which eventually made their way to the Penobscot Marine Museum. Brick-lined Main Street is more evidence of the mid-19th-century wealth, and local churches reaped the benefits of residents' generosity. The Second Congregational Church, known as the Safe Harbor Church and patronized by captains and shipbuilders (most ordinary seamen attended the Methodist church), boasts recently restored Tiffany-style windows and a Christopher Wren steeple.

Another inkling of this area's oceangoing superiority comes from visits to local burial grounds: Check out the headstones at Gordon, Bowditch, and Sandy Point cemeteries. Many have fascinating tales to tell.

Today the Searsport area's major draws are the Penobscot Marine Museum, the still-handsome brick Historic District, several bed-and-breakfasts, a couple of special state parks, and wall-to-wall antiques shops and flea markets. The Maine Historic Preservation Commission considers the buildings in Searsport's Main Street Historic District the best examples of their type outside Portland—a frozen-in-time mid-19th-century cluster of brick and granite structures. The ground floors of most of the buildings are shops or restaurants; make time to stop in and admire their interiors.

SIGHTS
Penobscot Marine Museum

Exquisite marine paintings, historical photographs, ship models, boats, and unusual China-trade objets d'art are just a few of the 10,000 treasures at the Penobscot Marine Museum (5 Church St. at Rte. 1, Searsport, 207/548-2529, www.penobscotmarinemuseum .org, 10 A.M.–5 P.M. Mon.–Sat., noon–5 P.M. Sun. late May–mid-Oct., $8 adults, $3 ages 7–15, $18 family), Maine's oldest maritime museum—founded in 1936. Allow several hours to explore the exhibits, housed in five separate buildings on the museum's downtown campus. For a start, you'll see one of the nation's largest collections of paintings by marine artists James and Thomas Buttersworth. And the 1830s Fowler-True-Ross House is filled with exotic artifacts from foreign lands. Call or check the website for the schedule of lectures, concerts, and temporary exhibits. This isn't a very sophisticated museum, but it is a treasure.

Fort Knox

Looming over Bucksport Harbor, the *other* Fort Knox (Rte. 174, Prospect, 207/469-7719, www .fortknox.maineguide.com, 9 A.M.–sunset May 1–Nov. 1, $4.50 nonresident adults, $3 Maine residents, $1 ages 5–11) is a 125-acre state historic site just off Route 1. Named for Major General Henry Knox, George Washington's first secretary of war, the sprawling granite fort was begun in 1844. Built to protect the upper Penobscot River from attack, it was never finished and never saw battle. Still, it was, as guide Kathy Williamson said, "very well thought out and planned, and that may have been its best defense." Begin your visit at the Visitor and Education Center, operated by the Friends of Fort Knox, a nonprofit group that has partnered with the state to preserve and interpret the fort. Guided tours are available Memorial Day–Labor Day, and well worth it, as guides point out some of the fort's distinguishing features, including two complete Rodman cannons. Wear rubberized shoes and bring a flashlight to explore the underground passages; you can set the kids loose. The fort hosts Civil War reenactments several times each summer as well as a Renaissance Fair, a paranormal-psychic fair, and other events (check the website).

PENOBSCOT BAY

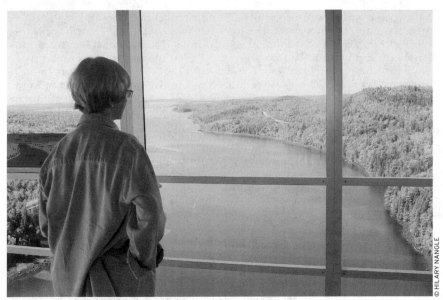

© HILARY NANGLE

view from the Penobscot Narrows Bridge and Observatory

The Halloween Fright at the Fort is a ghoulish event for the brave. The grounds are accessible all year. Bring a picnic; views over the river to Bucksport are fabulous.

🄲 Penobscot Narrows Bridge and Observatory

Do not miss the Penobscot Narrows Bridge and Observatory (9 A.M.–5 P.M. daily late May–June and Sept.–Nov. 1, 9 A.M.–6 P.M. daily July–Aug., $7 nonresident adults, $5 Maine resident adults, $3 ages 5–11, includes fort admission), accessible via Fort Knox. The observatory tops the 420-foot-high west tower of the new bridge spanning the Penobscot River. It's one of only three such structures in the world and the only one in the United States. You'll zip up in an elevator, and when the doors open, you're facing a wall of glass—it's a bit of a shocker, and downright terrifying for anyone with a serious fear of heights. Ascend two more flights (an elevator is available) and you're in the glass-walled observatory; the views on

a clear day extend from Katahdin to Mount Desert Island. Even when it's hazy, it's still a neat experience.

Museum in the Streets

Walk through Searsport's history by visiting a dozen placards detailing historic sites with text in both French and English. Pick up a brochure at the downtown info booth, the Penobscot Maritime Museum, or other local businesses.

BlueJacket Shipcrafters

Complementing the collections at the museum are the classic and contemporary models built by BlueJacket Shipcrafters (160 E. Main St./Rte. 1, Searsport, 800/448-5567, www.bluejacketinc.com), which boasts Maine's largest selection of ship models and nautical gifts. Even if you're not a hobbyist, stop in to see the incredibly detailed models on display. Shipcrafters is renowned for building one-of-a-kind museum-quality custom models—it's the official model-maker for the U.S. Navy—but don't despair, there are kits here for all abilities and budgets. It's easy to find: Just look for the inland lighthouse on Route 1.

SHOPPING

The word *shopping* in Searsport usually applies to antiques—from 25-cent flea-market collectibles to well-used tools to high-end china, furniture, and glassware. The town has more than a dozen separate businesses, some of them group shops with multiple dealers. Searsport vies with Wells and Wiscasset as Maine's "Antiques Capital."

More than two dozen dealers supply the juried inventory for Bob and Phyllis Sommer's **Pumpkin Patch** (15 W. Main St./Rte. 1, Searsport, 207/548-6047), with a heavy emphasis on Maine antiques. Specialties include quilts (at least 80 are always on hand), silver, paint-decorated furniture, Victoriana, and nautical and Native American items.

In excess of 70 dealers sell their antiques and collectibles at **Searsport Antique Mall** (149 E. Main St./Rte. 1, Searsport, 207/548-2640), making it another worthwhile stop for those seeking oldies but goodies.

The **Waldo County Craft Co-op** (307 E. Main St./Rte. 1, Searsport, 207/548-6686) features the work of about 30 Mainers: quilts, jams, bears, dolls, jewelry, baskets, pottery, floor cloths, and lots more.

Are you a hooker? Thirteen rooms full of hooked rugs and supplies fill **Searsport Rug Hooking** (396 E. Main St./Rte. 1, Searsport, 207/548-6100, www.searsportrughooking.com) in the midst of antiques shops and flea markets at the eastern end of town. The mother-daughter team of Christine Sherman and Julie Mattison, along with a talented staff, not only sell rugs, patterns, wool, and all the other supplies and necessities of the craft, they also design the patterns, dye the wools, teach, and demonstrate.

A local fixture in Stockton Springs since 1960, **The Book Barn** (E. Main St., Stockton Springs, 207/567-3351) is jam-packed with used and antiquarian books.

RECREATION
Parks
MOOSE POINT STATE PARK

Here's a smallish park with a biggish view—183 acres wedged between Route 1 and a dramatic Penobscot Bay panorama. Moose Point State Park (Rte. 1, Searsport, 207/548-2882, $3 nonresident adults, $2 Maine resident adults, $1 ages 5–11) is 1.5 miles south of downtown Searsport. Bring a picnic, let the kids hang out and play (there's no swimming, but good tide-pooling at low tide), or walk through the woods or along the meadow trail. It's officially open late May–October 1, but since it's alongside the highway the park is accessible, weather permitting, year-round.

MOSMAN PARK

Southeast of busy Route 1, the four-acre town-owned Mosman Park has picnic tables, a traditional playground, lots of grassy space, a pocket-size pebbly beach, seasonal toilets, and fabulous views of the bay. Turn off Route 1 at Water Street and continue to the end.

SEARS ISLAND

After almost two decades of heavy-duty squabbling over a proposed cargo port on Searsport's 936-acre Sears Island (www.protectsearsisland.org), the state bought the island for $4 million in 1997. The squabbling continued until 2009, when a conservation easement was created for posterity, protecting 601 acres on one of the largest uninhabited islands on the East Coast. The island is a fine place for bird-watching, picnicking, walking, fishing, and cross-country skiing; pick up a brochure at the kiosk. It's linked to the mainland by a causeway. From downtown Searsport, continue northeast on Route 1 two miles to Sears Island Road (on the right). Turn and go 1.2 miles to the beginning of the island, where you can pull off and park before a gate; cars aren't allowed on the island. An easy 1.5-mile walk will take you to the other side of the island, overlooking Mack Point (site of a rather unattractive cargo port) and hills off to the left. Bring a picnic and binoculars—and a swimsuit if you're hardy enough to brave the water.

FORT POINT STATE PARK

Continuing northeast on Route 1 from Sears Island will get you to the turnoff for Fort Point State Park (Fort Point Rd., Stockton Springs, 207/567-3356, $3 nonresident adults, $2 Maine resident adults, $1 ages 5–11) on Cape Jellison's eastern tip. Within the 154-acre park are the earthworks of 18th-century **Fort Pownall,** a British fortress built during the French and Indian War; **Fort Point Light,** a square 26-foot 19th-century tower guarding the mouth of the Penobscot River, with an adjacent bell tower; shoreline trails; and a 200-foot pier where you can fish or watch birds or boats. Bird-watchers can spot waterfowl—especially ruddy ducks but also eagles and ospreys. Bring picnic fixings, but stay clear of the keeper's house—it's private. At the Route 1 fork for Stockton Springs, bear right onto Main Street and continue to Mill Road, in the village center. Turn right and then left onto East Cape Road, then another left onto Fort Point Road, which leads to the parking area. Officially the park is open late May–Labor Day, but it's accessible year-round, weather permitting.

Bicycling

Birgfeld's Bicycle Shop (184 E. Main St./Rte. 1, Searsport, 207/548-2916 or 800/206-2916), in business since the 1970s, is a mandatory stop for any cyclist, novice or pro. Local information on about 15 biking loops, supplies, maps, weekly group rides, sales (also skateboards and scooters), and excellent repair services are all part of the Birgfeld's mix.

An especially good ride in this area is the **Cape Jellison** loop in Stockton Springs. Park at Stockton Springs Elementary School and do the loop from there. Including a detour to Fort Point, the ride totals less than 10 miles from downtown Stockton Springs.

ACCOMMODATIONS

Searsport's gorgeous and monstrous homes seem likely prospects as inns, and indeed many have tried, but few succeed. Most only last a season or two before reverting to private homes.

Bed-and-Breakfasts

The **1794 Watchtide** (190 W. Main St./Rte. 1, Searsport, 207/548-6575 or 800/698-6575, www.watchtide.com, $140–190) occupies a sprawling late-18th-century sea captain's home formerly known as The College Club Inn. Each of the four guest rooms and one suite has a historic-name connection; the Eleanor Roosevelt Suite acknowledges visits by former first ladies in decades past. All have air-conditioning, TVs, and mini-fridges. Two rooms have whirlpool tubs. Guest rooms in the back have the nicest views and are the most quiet. Breakfasts are fabulous. Collapse on the 60-foot sun porch overlooking the bay and you may never want to leave.

A budget find for vegetarians and vegans, **Elm Cottage** (5 Elm St., Searsport, 207/548-2941, www.elmcottageinsearsport.com, $85–90), an 1840 cape surrounded by colorful gardens, has two guest rooms, one with a water view, tucked under the eaves. The full vegetarian breakfast can be tailored to meet restrictive diets. Reiki is offered, and there's Wi-Fi.

Motels

The **Yardarm** (172 E. Main St./Rte. 1, Searsport, www.searsportmaine.com, May–late Oct., $75–125), a small motel set back from the road, is next door to BlueJacket Shipcrafters. Each of the 18 pine-paneled units has a TV, air-conditioning, Wi-Fi, and a phone; suites (perfect for families) have a dinette, a microwave, and a small fridge. A continental breakfast is served in a cheery breakfast room in the adjacent farmhouse. Two rooms are pet friendly.

Here's a find: **Bait's Motel** (215 E. Main St./Rte. 1, Searsport, 207/548-7299, www.baitsmotel.com, $79–119) doesn't look like much from the exterior, but inside the recently renovated guest rooms are outfitted with quality comfortable furniture, down duvets and pillows, and nice toiletries. Add fridges, cable TV, free local calls and Wi-Fi, and individually controlled heat and air-conditioning. Standard rooms are pet-friendly ($20). It's adjacent to Angler's Restaurant.

Camping

How can you beat 1,100 feet of tidal ocean-front and unobstructed views of Islesboro, Castine, and Penobscot Bay? **Searsport Shores Camping Resort** (216 W. Main St./Rte. 1, Searsport, 207/548-6059, www.campocean .com) gets high marks for its fabulous setting. About 100 good-size sites (including walk-in oceanfront tenting sites) go for $39–78. Facilities include a private beach, a small store, free show-ers, laundry, play areas, a recreation hall, nature trails, and a volleyball court. Request a site away from organized-activity areas. Bring a sea kayak and launch it here. Leashed pets are allowed. In early September, the campground hosts Fiber Arts College, a weekend of classes, demonstra-tions, and camaraderie for spinners, hookers, weavers, and the like.

FOOD

Call to verify days and hours of operation.

The ☾ **Anglers Restaurant** (215 E. Main St./Rte. 1, Searsport, 207/548-2405, www .anglersrestaurant.net, 11 A.M.–8 P.M. daily) is probably the least assuming and one of the most popular restaurants around. Expect hearty New England cooking, hefty portions, local color, no frills, and a bill that won't dent your wallet. Big favorites are the chowders, stews, and lobster rolls. Dinner entrées are $9–14, although lobsters are higher. The "min-now menu" for smaller appetites runs $6–13. Desserts are a specialty: The gingerbread with whipped cream is divine; kids love the "bucket

o' worms." If it's not too busy and you've or-dered a lobster, ask owner Buddy Hall if he'll demonstrate hypnotizing it. It's adjacent to the Bait's Motel, 1.5 miles northeast of downtown Searsport.

Good home cooking with an emphasis on fried food has made **Just Barb's** (Main St./Rte. 1, Stockton Springs, 207/567-3886, 6 A.M.–8 P.M. daily) a dandy place for an un-fussy meal at a low price. Fried clams and scal-lop stew are both winners; finish up with a slab of pie or shortcake. The $7.99 all-you-can-eat fish fry is available daily after 11 A.M.

Pick up sandwiches for a picnic at Fort Knox along with soups, wine, cheeses, prepared en-trées, baked goods, and homemade marma-lades and chutneys at **The Good Kettle** (247 Rte. 1, Stockton Springs, 207/567-2035, 10 A.M.–6 P.M. Wed.–Mon.).

INFORMATION AND SERVICES

The **Searsport Business and Visitors Guide** is online at www.searsportme.net.

The **Belfast Area Chamber of Commerce** (207/338-5900, www.belfastmaine.org) has in-formation about the Belfast area.

Searsport's small self-serve info center is in a shedlike building on Route 1 (at Norris St.), across from the Pumpkin Patch antiques shop.

Check out the **Carver Memorial Library** (Mortland Rd. and Union St., Searsport, 207/548-2303, www.carver.lib.me.us).

Bucksport Area

The new Penobscot Narrows Bridge pro-vides an elegant entry to the Bucksport area, a longtime rough-and-ready river port and papermaking town that's slowly gentrifying. Bucksport is no upstart. Native Americans first gravitated to these Penobscot River shores in summers, finding here a rich source of salmon for food and grasses for basket-mak-ing. In 1764 it was officially settled by Colonel

Jonathan Buck, a Massachusetts Bay Colony surveyor who modestly named it Buckstown and organized a booming shipping business here. His remains are interred in a local cem-etery, where his tombstone bears the distinct outline of a woman's leg; this is allegedly the result of a curse by a witch Buck ordered ex-ecuted, but in fact it's probably a flaw in the granite. (The monument is across Route 1 from the Hannaford supermarket, on the corner of Hinks Street.)

Just south of Bucksport, at the bend in the Penobscot River, Verona Island is best known as the mile-long link between Prospect and Bucksport. Just before you cross the bridge from Verona to Bucksport, hang a left and then a quick right to a small municipal park with a boat launch and broad views of Bucksport Harbor (and the paper mill). In the Buck Memorial Library is a scale model of Admiral Robert Peary's Arctic exploration vessel, the *Roosevelt*, built on this site.

Bucksport has a nice riverfront walkway, a historical theater, and the best views of Fort Knox. Route 1 east of Bucksport leads to **Orland,** with an idyllic setting on the banks of the Narramissic River. It's also the site of a unique service organization called H.O.M.E. (Homeworkers Organized for More Employment). East Orland (officially part of Orland) claims the Craig Brook National Fish Hatchery and Great Pond Mountain (you can't miss it, jutting from the landscape on the left as you drive east on Route 1).

SIGHTS
Alamo Theatre

Phoenixlike, the 1916 Alamo Theatre (85 Main St., Bucksport, 207/469-0924 or 800/639-1636, event line 207/469-6910, www.alamotheatre.org, 9 A.M.–4 P.M. Mon.–Fri. year-round) has been retrofitted for a new life—focusing on films about New England produced or revived by the unique Northeast Historic Film (NHF), which is headquartered here. Stop in, survey the restoration, visit the displays (donation requested), and browse the Alamo Theatre Store for antique postcards, T-shirts, toys, and reasonably priced videos on ice harvesting, lumberjacks, maple sugaring, and other traditional New England topics. A half mile west of Route 1, the Alamo has also become an active cinema, screening classic and current films regularly in the 120-seat theater, usually on weekends. Each summer there's also a silent film festival.

Bucksport Waterfront Walkway

Stroll the one-mile paved walkway from the Bucksport-Verona Bridge to Webber Docks. Along the way are historical markers, picnic tables, a gazebo, restrooms, and expansive views of the harbor and Fort Knox.

H.O.M.E.

Adjacent to the flashing light on Route 1 in Orland, H.O.M.E. (207/469-7961, www.homecoop.net) is tough to categorize. Linked with the international Emmaus Movement founded by a French priest, H.O.M.E. (Homeworkers Organized for More Employment) was started in 1970 by Lucy Poulin, still the guiding force, and two nuns at a nearby convent. The quasi-religious organization shelters refugees and the homeless, operates a soup kitchen and a car-repair service, runs a day-care center, and teaches work skills in a variety of hands-on cooperative programs. Seventy percent of its income comes from sales of crafts, produce, and services. At the Route 1 store (Rte. 1 and Upper Falls Rd., 9 A.M.–4:30 P.M. daily) you can buy handmade quilts, organic produce, maple syrup, and jams—and support a worthwhile effort. You can also tour the crafts workshops on the property.

SHOPPING

Locals come just as much for the coffee and conversation as the selection of new and used reads at **BookStacks** (71 Main St., Bucksport, 207/469-8992).

RECREATION
Craig Brook National Fish Hatchery

For a day of hiking, picnicking, swimming, canoeing, and a bit of natural history, pack a lunch and head for 135-acre Craig Brook National Fish Hatchery (306 Hatchery Rd., East Orland, 207/469-6701), on Alamoosook Lake. Turn off Route 1 six miles east of Bucksport and continue 1.4 miles north to the parking area just above the visitors center. The visitors center (8:30 A.M.–3:30 P.M. Mon.–Fri., 8 A.M.–3:30 P.M. Sat.–Sun. summer, free) offers interactive displays on Atlantic salmon (don't miss the downstairs viewing area), maps, and a restroom. The grounds are accessible 6 A.M.–sunset daily year-round. Established in 1889, the U.S. Fish and Wildlife Service hatchery raises sea-run Atlantic salmon for stocking six Maine rivers. The birch-lined shorefront has picnic tables, a boat-launching ramp, an Atlantic salmon display pool, additional parking, and a spectacular cross-lake view. Watch for eagles, ospreys, and loons. Also on the premises is the small **Atlantic Salmon Heritage Museum,** housed in a circa-1896 ice house and operated by the Friends of Craig Brook (call the hatchery for current hours). Inside are salmon and fly-fishing artifacts and memorabilia.

Great Pond Mountain Conservation

The Great Pond Mountain Conservation Trust (207/469-6772, www.greatpondtrust.org) acts as conscientious local steward for Great Pond Mountain and Great Pond Wildlands. It also hosts hikes and other activities.

Encompassing two parcels of land and nearly 4,300 acres, the Great Pond Wildlands is a jewel. The larger parcel totals 3,420 acres and surrounds Hothole Valley, including Hothole Brook, prized for its trout, and shoreline on Hothole Pond. The smaller 875-acre tract includes two miles of frontage on the Dead River (not to be confused with the Dead River of rafting fame in northwestern Maine) and reaches up Great Pond Mountain and down to the ominously named Hell Bottom Swamp. The land is rich with wildlife: black bears, moose, bobcats, and deer are just a few of the species, and the pond, swamp, and river make it ideal for bird-watching. With 14 miles of woods roads lacing the land, it's prime territory for walking, mountain biking, and snowshoeing, and the waterways invite fishing and paddling. Avoid the area during hunting season. Snowmobiling is permitted; ATVs are banned. Access to the Dead River tract is from the Craig Brook National Fish Hatchery; follow Don Fish Road to the Dead River Gate and Dead River Trail. The South Gate to Hothole Pond Tract is on Route 1, just southwest of Route 176. You can drive in along Valley Road about 2.5 miles to a parking area.

The biggest rewards for the 1.8-mile easy-to-moderate hike up 1,038-foot **Great Pond Mountain** are 360-degree views and lots of space for panoramic picnics. On a clear day, Baxter State Park's Katahdin is visible from the peak's north side. In fall, watch for migrating hawks. Access to the mountain is via gated private property beginning about a mile north of Craig Brook National Fish Hatchery on Hatchery Road in East Orland. Roadside parking is available near the trailhead, but during fall foliage season you may need to park at the hatchery. Pick up a brochure from the box at the trailhead, stay on the trail, and respect the surrounding private property.

Canoeing

If you've brought a canoe, **Silver Lake,** just two miles north of downtown Bucksport, is a beautiful place for a paddle. There's no development along its shores, and the bird-watching is excellent. Swimming is not allowed (there's a $500 fine); this is Bucksport's reservoir. To get to the public launch, take Route 15 north off Route 1 after crossing the Verona-Bucksport Bridge. Go 0.5 miles and turn right on McDonald Road, which becomes Silver Lake Road, and follow it 2.1 miles to the launch site.

Golf

Bucksport Golf Club (Duck Cove Rd./Rte. 46, 1.5 miles north of Rte. 1, 207/469-7612, mid-Apr.–Sept.), running 3,397 yards, prides itself on having Maine's longest nine-hole course.

ACCOMMODATIONS
Inns and Bed-and-Breakfasts

The **Orland House** (10 Narramissic Dr., Orland, 207/469-1144, www.orlandhousebb.com, $95–125), Alvion and Cindi Kimball's elegant yet comfortable 1820 Greek Revival home, overlooks the Narramissic River. It has been beautifully restored, preserving the architectural details but adding plenty of creature comforts.

Location, location, location: If only the six simple rooms at the old-timey **Alamoosook Lakeside Inn** (off Rte. 1, Orland, 207/469-6393 or 866/459-6393, www.alamoosooklakesideinn .com, year-round, $125) actually overlooked the lake, then it would be the perfect rustic lakeside lodge. The property is gorgeous, the location is well-suited for exploring the area, but the guest rooms are so-so, with tiny bathrooms. All have windows and doors opening onto a long sun porch overlooking the lake. The upside: The lodge has 0.25 miles of lakefront, and guests have access to canoes and kayaks. Paddle across the lake to the fish hatchery for a hike up Great Pond Mountain. A full breakfast is served, and there is free Wi-Fi.

Motels

In downtown Bucksport, the **Fort Knox Inn** (64 Main St., Bucksport, 207/469-3113, $115–199) is a four-story motel right at the harbor's edge. It's a bit tired, but the 40 guest rooms have phones, air-conditioning, free Wi-Fi, and satellite TV. Be sure to request a water view, or you'll be facing a parking lot.

Camping

The rivers, lakes, and ponds between Bucksport and Ellsworth make the area especially appealing for camping, and sites tend to be cheaper than in the Bar Harbor area. During July–August, especially on weekends, reservations are wise. Both of these campgrounds are on 10-mile-long Toddy Pond, which reaches 100 feet in depth in some places.

Six miles east of Bucksport, across from Craig Pond Road, is Back Ridge Road, leading to **Balsam Cove Campground** (286 Back Ridge Rd., East Orland, 207/469-7771 or 800/469-7771, www.balsamcove.com, late May–late Sept., $29–44). From Route 1, take Back Ridge Road 1.5 miles to the left turn for the campground on the shores of 10-mile-long Toddy Pond. Facilities on the 50 acres include 60 wooded waterfront or water-view tent and RV sites, a one-room rental cabin ($71), on-site rental trailers ($89), a dump station, a store, laundry, free showers and Wi-Fi, boat rentals,

and freshwater swimming. Dogs are welcome on camping sites for $2 per day.

The same season holds for 10-acre **Whispering Pines Campground** (Rte. 1, East Orland, 207/469-3443, www.whisperingpinesmaine.com, $36 for 2 people, $2 per child over age 7), also on Toddy Pond but with access directly from Route 1. Facilities include 50 tent and RV sites (request one close to the pond), free use of canoes and rowboats, freshwater swimming, a playground, free showers, and a recreation hall. Whispering Pines is 6.5 miles east of Bucksport.

FOOD

MacLeod's (Main St., Bucksport, 207/469-3963, 11 A.M.–8 P.M. Tues.–Sat., 4–8 P.M. Sun.) is Bucksport's most popular and enduring restaurant. Some tables in the pleasant dining room have glimpses of the river and Fort Knox. The wide-ranging menu has choices for all tastes and budgets. Reservations are wise for Saturday nights.

In what passes as downtown Orland (hint: don't blink), **Orland Market and Pizza** (91 Castine Rd./Rte. 175, Orland, 207/469-9999, www.orlandmarket.com, 7 A.M.–9 P.M. daily) is a delight. Established in 1860, the old-fashioned country store has a little of this and a bit of that along with breakfast sandwiches, hot and cold sandwiches, grilled foods, salad, and all kinds of pizza. Call or drop by to find out the day's homemade specials, perhaps lasagna or spaghetti and meatballs. Smoked ribs are the specialty every other Thursday, weather permitting.

INFORMATION AND SERVICES

The best source of local info is the **Bucksport Bay Area Chamber of Commerce** (52 Main St., Bucksport, 207/469-6818, www.bucksportchamber.org).

Public Restrooms

In Bucksport, public restrooms next to the town dock (behind the Bucksport Historical Society) are open spring–fall. Restrooms are open weekdays year-round in the Bucksport Municipal Office on Main Street.

BLUE HILL PENINSULA AND DEER ISLE

The Blue Hill Peninsula, once dubbed "The Fertile Crescent," is unique. Few other Maine locales harbor such a high concentration of artisans, musicians, and on-their-feet retirees juxtaposed with top-flight wooden-boat builders, lobstermen, and umpteenth-generation Mainers. Perhaps surprisingly, the mix seems to work.

Anchored by the towns of Bucksport to the east and Ellsworth to the west, the peninsula comprises several enclaves with markedly distinct personalities. Blue Hill, Castine, Orland, Brooklin, Brooksville, and Sedgwick are stitched together by a network of narrow, winding country roads. Thanks to the mapmaker-challenging coastline and a handful of freshwater ponds and rivers, there's a view of water around nearly every bend.

You can watch the sun set from atop Blue Hill Mountain; tour the home of the fascinating Jonathan Fisher; stroll through the village of Castine (charming verging on precious), whose streets are lined with dowager-like homes; visit *WoodenBoat* magazine's world headquarters in tiny Brooklin; and browse top-notch studios and galleries throughout the peninsula. Venture a bit inland of Route 1, and you find lovely lakes for paddling and swimming and another hill to hike.

After weaving your way down the Blue Hill Peninsula and crossing the soaring pray-as-you-go bridge to Little Deer Isle, you've entered the realm of island living. Sure, bridges and causeways connect the points, but the farther down you drive, the more removed from civilization you feel. The pace slows; the

© TOM NANGLE

HIGHLIGHTS

LOOK FOR ☾ TO FIND RECOMMENDED SIGHTS, ACTIVITIES, DINING, AND LODGING.

☾ **Parson Fisher House:** More than just another historic house, the Parson Fisher House is a remarkblwe testimony to one man's ingenuity (page 252).

☾ **Blue Hill Mountain:** It's a relatively easy hike for fabulous 360-degree views from the summit of this local landmark (page 255).

☾ **Flash! In the Pans Community Steel Band:** Close your eyes while listening to this phenomenal steel-pan band, and you just might think you're on a Caribbean island rather than in Maine (page 260).

☾ **Holbrook Island Sanctuary State Park:** Varied hiking trails and great bird-watching are the rewards for finding this off-the-beaten-path preserve (page 262).

☾ **Castine Historic Tour:** A turbulent history detailed on signs throughout town makes Castine an irresistible place to tour on foot or by bike (page 265).

☾ **Sea Kayaking:** Hook up with "Kayak Karen" to see Castine from the water (page 268).

☾ **Haystack Mountain School of Crafts:** Arrange your schedule to visit the spectacular architect-designed campus of this renowned oceanfront school (page 274).

☾ **Art and Craft Galleries:** The Haystack crafts school has inspired dozens of world-class artisans to set up shop on Deer Isle (page 277).

☾ **Guided Island Tours:** Join Captain Walter Reed for a boat tour amidst the islands, customized to your interests (page 283).

☾ **Acadia National Park:** Tipping sparsely populated **Isle au Haut** is a remote section of the national park, perfect for a day trip or longer (page 287).

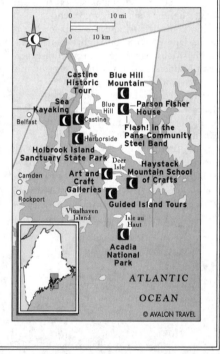

population dwindles. Fishing and lobstering are the mainstays; lobster boats rest near many homes, and trap fences edge properties. If your ultimate destination is the section of Acadia National Park on Isle au Haut, the drive down Deer Isle serves to help disconnect you from the mainland. To reach the park's acreage on Isle au Haut, you'll board the Isle au Haut ferryboat for the trip down Merchant Row to the island.

PLANNING YOUR TIME

To truly enjoy this region, you'll want to spend at least 3–4 days here, perhaps splitting your lodging between 2–3 locations. The region is designed for leisurely exploring; you won't be able to zip from one location to another. Traveling along the winding roads, discovering galleries and country stores, and lodging at traditional inns are all part of the experience.

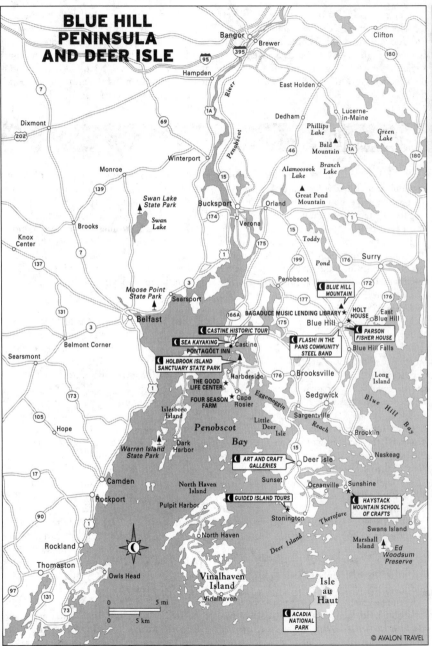

BLUE HILL PENINSULA AND DEER ISLE

Bangor
Brewer
Clifton
Hampden
East Holden
Lucerne-in-Maine
Dixmont
Dedham
Phillips Lake
Green Lake
Bald Mountain
Winterport
Alamoosook Lake
Branch Lake
Monroe
Great Pond Mountain
Swan Lake State Park
Bucksport
Orland
Verona
Brooks
Swan Lake
Toddy
Surry
Knox Center
Pond
Penobscot
BLUE HILL MOUNTAIN
Moose Point State Park
Searsport
BAGADUCE MUSIC LENDING LIBRARY
HOLT HOUSE
East Blue Hill
Belfast
CASTINE HISTORIC TOUR
Blue Hill
PARSON FISHER HOUSE
Belmont Corner
SEA KAYAKING
PONTAGÖET INN
Castine
FLASH! IN THE PANS COMMUNITY STEEL BAND
Blue Hill Falls
Searsmont
HOLBROOK ISLAND SANCTUARY STATE PARK
Harborside
Brooksville
Long Island
THE GOOD LIFE CENTER
FOUR SEASON FARM
Cape Rosier
Sedgwick
Blue Hill Bay
Islesboro Island
Penobscot Bay
Little Deer Isle
Sargentville
Brooklin
Hope
Warren Island State Park
Dark Harbor
ART AND CRAFT GALLERIES
Deer Isle
Naskeag
Camden
North Haven Island
Sunset
Oceanville
Sunshine
Rockport
Pulpit Harbor
GUIDED ISLAND TOURS
HAYSTACK MOUNTAIN SCHOOL OF CRAFTS
Stonington
Rockland
North Haven
Deer Island
Swans Island
Thomaston
Marshall Island
Ed Woodsum Preserve
Owls Head
Vinalhaven Island
Isle au Haut
0   5 mi
0   5 km
Vinalhaven
ACADIA NATIONAL PARK

© AVALON TRAVEL

Arts fans will want to concentrate their efforts in Blue Hill, Deer Isle, and Stonington. Outdoor-oriented folks should consider Deer Isle, Stonington, or Castine as a base for sea kayaking or exploring the area preserves. For architecture and history buffs, Castine is a must.

No visit to this region is complete without at least a cruise by if not a visit to Isle au Haut, an offshore island that's home to a remote section of Acadia National Park. Allow at least a few hours for a ride on the mail boat, but if you can afford the time, spend a full day hiking the park's trails. Don't forget to pack food and water.

Blue Hill

Twelve miles south of Route 1 is the hub of the peninsula, Blue Hill, exuding charm from its handsome old homes to its waterfront setting to the shops, restaurants, and galleries that boost its appeal.

Eons back, Native American summer folk gave the name Awanadjo ("small, hazy mountain") to the mini-mountain that looms over the town and draws the eye for miles around. The first permanent settlers arrived in the late 18th century, after the French and Indian War, and established mills and shipyards. More than 100 ships were built here between Blue Hill's incorporation in 1789 and 1882—bringing prosperity to the entire peninsula.

Critical to the town's early expansion was its first clergyman, Jonathan Fisher, a remarkable fellow who has been likened to Leonardo da Vinci. In 1803, Fisher founded Blue Hill Academy (predecessor of today's George Stevens Academy), then built his home (now a museum), and eventually left an immense legacy of inventions, paintings, engravings, and poetry.

Throughout the 19th century and into the 20th, Blue Hill's granite industry boomed, reaching its peak in the 1880s. Scratch the Brooklyn Bridge and the New York Stock Exchange and you'll find granite from Blue Hill's quarries. Around 1879, the discovery of gold and silver brought a flurry of interest, but little came of it. Copper was also found here, but quantities of it too were limited.

At the height of industrial prosperity, tourism took hold, attracting steamboat-borne summer boarders. Many succumbed to the scenery, bought land, and built waterfront

summer homes. Thank these summer folk and their offspring for the fact that music has long been a big deal in Blue Hill. The Kneisel Hall Chamber Music School, established in the late 19th century, continues to rank high among the nation's summer music colonies. New York City's Blue Hill Troupe, devoted to Gilbert and Sullivan operettas, was named for the longtime summer home of the troupe's founders.

SIGHTS
◖ Parson Fisher House
Named for a brilliant Renaissance man who arrived in Blue Hill in 1794, the Parson Fisher House (44 Mines Rd./Rte. 15/176, 207/374-2459, www.jonathanfisherhouse.org, 1–4 P.M. Thurs.–Sat. early July–mid-Oct., $5) immerses visitors in period furnishings and Jonathan Fisher lore. And Fisher's feats are breathtaking: He was a Harvard-educated preacher who also managed to be an accomplished painter, poet, mathematician, naturalist, linguist, inventor, cabinetmaker, farmer, architect, and printmaker. In his spare time, he fathered nine children. Fisher also pitched in to help build the yellow house on Tenney Hill, which served as the Congregational Church parsonage. Now it contains intriguing items created by Fisher, memorabilia that volunteer tour guides delight in explaining, including a camera obscura. Don't miss it.

Historic Houses
A few of Blue Hill's elegant houses have been converted to museums, inns, restaurants, and even some offices and shops, so you can see them from the inside out. To appreciate the

private residences, you'll want to walk, bike, or drive around town. Also ask at the Holt House about village walking tours.

In downtown Blue Hill, a few steps off Main Street, stands the **Holt House** (3 Water St., 207/326-8250, www.bluehillhistory.org, 1–4 P.M. Tues. and Fri., 11 A.M.–2 P.M. Sat. July–mid-Sept., $3 adults, free under age 13), home of the Blue Hill Historical Society. Built in 1815 by Jeremiah Holt, the Federal-style building contains restored stenciling, period decor, and masses of memorabilia contributed by local residents. In the carriage house are even more goodies, including old tools, a sleigh, carriages, and more.

Walk or drive up Union Street (Rte. 177), past George Stevens Academy, and wander **The Old Cemetery,** established in 1794. If gnarled trees and ancient headstones intrigue you, there aren't many good-sized Maine cemeteries older than this one.

Bagaduce Music Lending Library

At the foot of Greene's Hill in Blue Hill is one of Maine's more unusual institutions, a library where you can borrow from a collection of more than 1 million scores and pieces of sheet music (3 Music Library Lane/Rte. 172, 207/374-5454, www.bagaducemusic .org, 10 A.M.–4 P.M. Mon.–Fri. or by appointment). Somehow this seems so appropriate for a community that's a magnet for music lovers. Annual membership is $15 ($10 for students); fees range $1–4 per piece.

Scenic Routes

Parker Point Road (turn off Rte. 15 at the Blue Hill Library) takes you from Blue Hill to Blue Hill Falls the back way, with vistas en route toward Acadia National Park. For other great views, drive the length of **Newbury Neck** in nearby Surry, or head west on Route 15/176 toward Sedgwick, Brooksville, and beyond.

ENTERTAINMENT AND EVENTS

Variety and serendipity are the keys here. Check local calendar listings and tune in to radio station WERU (89.9 and 102.9 FM, www.weru.org), the peninsula's own community radio; there might be announcements of concerts by local resident pianist Paul Sullivan or the Bagaduce Chorale, or maybe a contra dance or a tropical treat from Flash! In the Pans Community Band (www.flashin thepans.org). The George Stevens Academy has a free Tuesday evening lecture series in July–August.

Live Music

Since 1922, chamber-music students have been spending summers perfecting their skills and demonstrating their prowess at the **Kneisel Hall Chamber Music School** (Pleasant St./ Rte. 15, 207/374-2811, www.kneisel.org). Faculty concerts run Friday evenings and Sunday afternoons late June–late August. The concert schedule is published in the spring, and reserved-seating tickets ($30 inside, $20 on the porch outside, nonrefundable) can be ordered online or by phone. Other opportunities to hear the students and faculty exist, including young artist concerts, children's concerts, open rehearsals, and more. Kneisel Hall is about 0.5 miles from the center of town.

The Blue Hill Congregational Church is the site for the **Vanderkay Summer Music Series** (207/374-2891), which ranges from choral music from the Middle Ages to bluegrass. Tickets are $15.

Chamber music continues in winter thanks to the volunteer **Blue Hill Concert Association** (207/326-4666, www.bluehillconcerts.org), which presents five concerts January–March at the Congregational Church. Recommended donation is $20.

Events

WERU's annual Full Circle Fair is usually held in mid-August at the Blue Hill Fairgrounds (Rte. 172, north of downtown Blue Hill). Expect world music, good food, crafts, and socially and environmentally progressive talks.

On Labor Day weekend, the **Blue Hill Fair** (Blue Hill Fairgrounds, Rte. 172, 207/374-9976) is one of the state's best agricultural fairs.

SHOPPING

Boutiques, antiques, galleries, and even two downtown bookstores make shopping a pleasure in Blue Hill.

Ever-helpful Bonnie Myers provides free advice on the region with a money-back guarantee at **North Light Books** (Main St., 207/374-5422). It's a delight to browse, the children's book selection is terrific, and out back is Blue Hill Hearth, with all sorts of treats.

Around the corner is **Blue Hill Books** (26 Pleasant St./Rte. 15, 207/374-5632, www .bluehillbooks.com), which organizes an "authors series" during the summer.

The **Blue Hill Wine Shop** (138 Main St., 207/374-2161), tucked into a converted horse barn, carries more than 1,000 wines, plus teas, coffees, breads, cheeses, sandwiches, and blended tobaccos and unusual pipes for diehard upscale smokers. Monthly wine tastings (usually 2:30–6 P.M. last Sat. of the month) are always an adventure.

A tasteful selection of this and that, from clothing to decorative items, fills **New Cargoes** (48 Main St., 207/374-3733).

GALLERY HOPPING IN BLUE HILL

Perhaps it's Blue Hill's location near the renowned Haystack Mountain School of Crafts. Perhaps it's the way the light plays off the rolling countryside and onto the twisting coastline. Perhaps it's the inspirational landscape. Whatever the reason, numerous artists and artisans call Blue Hill home, and top-notch galleries are abundant.

Judith Leighton knows contemporary art, and her **Leighton Gallery** (24 Parker Point Rd., 207/374-5001, www.leightongallery.com) is a real treat. The airy two-story-plus-basement space, in a converted barn on the Parker Point Road, is filled with a great selection. Be sure to visit the equally spectacular and extremely peaceful backyard sculpture garden. The **Liros Gallery** (14 Parker Point Rd., 207/374-5370 or 800/287-5370, www.lirosgallery.com) has been dealing in Russian icons since the mid-1960s. Prices are high, but the icons are fascinating. The gallery also carries Currier and Ives prints, antique maps, and 19th-century British and American paintings. From here, it's a short walk to **Blue Hill Bay Gallery** (Main St., 207/374-5773, www.bluehillbaygallery.com), which represents contemporary artists in various media and has a permanent collection of earlier works.

Don't miss the spacious, well-lit in-town gallery of **Jud Hartmann** (Main St. and Rte. 15, 207/359-2544, www.judhartmanngallery. com), who makes limited-edition bronze sculptures of the Woodland tribes of the Northeast. Hartmann often can be seen working on his next model in the gallery – a real treat. He's a wealth of information about his subjects, and he loves sharing the fascinating – even mesmerizing – stories he's uncovered during his meticulous research.

Also on Main Street are other fun artsy gallery-shops. **Handworks Gallery** (Main St., 207/374-5613, www.handworksgallery.org) sells a range of fun, funky, utilitarian and fine-art crafts by more than 50 Maine artists and craftspeople, including jewelry, furniture, rugs, wall hangings, and clothing. Browse **North Country Textiles** (Main St., 207/374-2715, www.northcountrytextiles.com) for fine handwoven throws, rugs, clothing, and table linens as well as other fine crafts.

Pottery is abundant in Blue Hill. **Rackliffe Pottery** (Rte. 172, 207/374-2297 or 888/631-3321, www.rackliffepottery.com), noted for its vivid blue wares, also makes its own glazes and has been producing lead-free pottery since 1969.

About two miles from downtown is another don't-miss. **Mark Bell Pottery** (Rte. 15, 207/374-5881), in a tiny building signaled only by a small roadside sign, is the home of exquisite award-winning porcelain by the eponymous potter. It's easy to understand why his wares were displayed at the Smithsonian Institution's Craft Fair as well as other juried shows across the country. The delicacy of each vase, bowl, or other item is astonishing, and the glazes are gorgeous. Twice each summer he has kiln openings – they're must-attend events for collectors and fans. Call for details.

Blue Hill Antiques (8 Water St., 207/374-2199 or 207/326-4973) specializes in 18th- and 19th-century French and American furniture. The same patrons seek out Brad Emerson's **Emerson Antiques** (100 Ellsworth Rd./Rte. 172, 207/374-5140), located just beyond downtown and concentrating on early Americana, such as hooked rugs and ship models.

RECREATION
◖ Blue Hill Mountain
"Mountain" seems a fancy label for a 943-footer, yet Blue Hill Mountain stands alone, visible from Camden and even beyond. On a clear day, head for the summit and take in the wraparound view encompassing Penobscot Bay, the hills of Mount Desert, and the Camden Hills. Climb the fire tower and you'll see even more. In mid-June the lupines along the way are breathtaking; in fall the colors are spectacular—with reddened blueberry barrens added to the variegated foliage. Go early in the day; it's a popular easy-to-moderate hike. A short loop on the lower slopes takes only half an hour. Take Route 15 (Pleasant St.) to Mountain Road. Turn right and go 0.8 miles to the trailhead (on the left) and the small parking area (on the right). You can also walk (uphill) the mile from the village.

Blue Hill Heritage Trust
A fine organization, the Blue Hill Heritage Trust (101 Union St., 207/374-5118, www .bluehillheritagetrust.org, 8 A.M.–5 P.M. Mon.–Fri.) works hard at preserving the region's landscape. It also presents a Walks and Talks series, with offerings such as kayaking by preservation land along Eggemoggin Reach, a full-moon hike up Blue Hill Mountain, and walks through other trust properties, such as 700-acre Kingdom Woods Conservation Preserve and Cooper Farm at Caterpillar Hill. Many include talks by knowledgeable folks on complementary topics.

Blue Hill Town Park
At the end of Water Street is a small park with a terrific view. It has a small pebble beach, picnic tables, a portable toilet, and a playground.

MERI Center
A great way to raise kids' environmental awareness is to enroll them in summer activities sponsored by the MERI Center for Marine Studies (55 Main St., 207/374-2135, www.meriresearch .org). MERI is the Marine Environmental Research Institute, a nonprofit marine-ecology organization, and schedules **island excursions** and **eco-cruises** ($20–60) geared to different age groups; cruises are limited to 12 passengers. It also offers kids programs on Thursday afternoons ($25, space limited). The MERI Center has a touch tank, a marine lending library, and exhibit space. The evening Ocean Environment lecture series is offered once or twice monthly. On Fridays during fall, winter, and spring, MERI offers a movie night, with refreshments, during which it screens marine-related films. It's free, but a $3 donation is appreciated. MERI is open Monday–Friday year-round and also Saturday in July and August.

Bike Rentals
The Activity Shop (61 Ellsworth Rd., 207/374-3600, www.theactivityshop.com) rents bicycles for $35 per week and Old Town canoes and kayaks at rates beginning at $25 per day, including delivery within a reasonable area.

ACCOMMODATIONS
Inns and Bed-and-Breakfasts
If you're trying to imagine a classic country inn, ◖ **The Blue Hill Inn** (Union St./Rte. 177, 207/374-2844 or 800/826-7415, www.bluehillinn.com, $175–245, mid-May–late Oct.) would be it. Sarah Pebworth graciously welcomes guests to her antiques-filled inn, open since 1840 and located steps from Main Street's shops and restaurants. Ten air-conditioned guest rooms and a suite have real chandeliers, four-poster beds, down comforters, fancy linens, and braided and Oriental rugs; three have wood-burning fireplaces. Rear rooms overlook the extensive cutting garden, with chairs and a hammock. A three-course breakfast is served in the elegant dining room (also available to nonguests, $15). Afternoon

refreshments with sweets appear in the living room daily, and superb hors d'oeuvres are served 6–7 P.M. in two elegant parlors or the garden. Also available are two year-round accommodations with cooking facilities in the elegant Cape House ($325).

Two miles north of town, at Marcia and Jim Schatz's **Blue Hill Farm Country Inn** (Rte. 15, 207/374-5126, www.bluehillfarminn.com, year-round, $95–115), a huge refurbished barn serves as the gathering spot for guests. If the weather is lousy, you can plop down in front of the oversize woodstove and start in on cribbage or other games. Antique sleigh-runner banisters lead to the barn's seven second-floor guest rooms—all with private baths, skylights, hooked rugs, and quilts. A wing of the farmhouse has seven more guest rooms with shared baths. Breakfast is generous continental. On the inn's 48 acres are well-cleared nature trails, an 18th-century cellar hole, and a duck pond.

FOOD

As always, hours are listed for peak season; call to verify days and hours of operation before making a special trip.

Local Flavors

Picnic fare and pizza are available at **Merrill & Hinckley** (11 Union St., 207/374-2821, 6 A.M.–9:30 P.M. Mon.–Fri., 7 A.M.–10 P.M. Sat., 8 A.M.–9 P.M. Sun.), a quirky 150-year-old family-owned grocery and general store.

The **Blue Hill Co-op and Cafe** (4 Ellsworth Rd./Rte. 172, 207/374-2165, café 207/374-8999, 7 A.M.–9 P.M. daily) sells organic and natural foods. Breakfast items, sandwiches, salads, and soups—many with ethnic flavors—are available in the café.

Tucked behind North Light Books is **Blue Hill Hearth** (58 Main St., 207/610-9090, 8 A.M.–7 P.M. Mon.–Fri., 9 A.M.–3 P.M. Sat.–Sun.). The breads are outstanding, but you can also pick up ready-made sandwiches, soups, and irresistible baked goods, including 15 different types of chocolate chip cookies. Vegan options are available, and these are made using completely separate utensils.

Local gardeners, farmers, and craftspeople peddle their wares at the **Blue Hill Farmers Market** (9–11:30 A.M. Sat. and 3–5 P.M. Wed. late May–mid-Oct.). It's a particularly enduring market, well worth a visit. Demonstrations by area chefs and artists are often on the agenda. Late May–late August the Saturday market is at the Blue Hill Fairgrounds; the Wednesday market is at the church.

Here's a double hit: **Bird Watcher's Store & Cafe** (37 Water St., 207/374-3740, 9 A.M.–5 P.M. Mon.–Fri., 9 A.M.–4 P.M. Sat.). Half of the building is a café serving baked goods, soups, salads, and sandwiches; the other half is a store catering to bird-watchers. Choose from tables inside on the water-view deck, or just take it down the street to the park.

The chowder earns raves at **The Pantry** (27 Water St., 207/374-2229, 8 A.M.–2 P.M. Mon.–Fri., 8 A.M.–2 P.M. Sat.–Sun.), a no-frills source of inexpensive meals.

Family Favorites

Very popular with local folks is **Marlintini's Grill** (83 Mines Rd., 207/374-2500, 11:30 A.M.–9 P.M. daily, bar until 1 A.M. daily, entrées $8–15). Inside, half is a sports bar, the other half a restaurant. You can sit in either, but the bar side can get raucous. Best bet: the screened-in porch. The menu includes soups, salads, burgers, fried seafood, rib eye, and nightly home-style specials; there's a kids menu too. The portions are big; the service is good; the food is OK.

Just south of town is **Barncastle** (125 South St., 207/374-2300, www.barncastlehotel.com, 3–8 P.M. daily, entrées $8–20), serving a creative selection of wood-fired pizzas in three sizes as well as sandwiches, subs, paninis, calzones, and salads in a lovely shingle-style cottage. There are vegetarian options. Expect to wait for a table; this is one popular spot, although service can be iffy.

Casual Dining

Here's a double header: **◖ Arborvine** and **The Vinery** (Main St., www.arborvine.com). For a light lunch or dinner, head to The Vinery (207/374-2441, 5:30–9 P.M. Wed.–Sun.,

$7–15), a piano and wine bar–bistro in a beautifully renovated barn, with live music. If you're up for something fancier, make reservations at the Arborvine (207/374-2119, 5:30–9 P.M. Tues.–Sun. summer, 5:30–9 P.M. Fri.–Sun. winter, entrées $26–35), a conscientiously renovated two-century-old Cape-style house with four dining areas, each with a different feel and understated decor. The wine list is small but select. Chef-owner John Hikade and his wife, Beth, operate both establishments.

Beard nominee Rich Hanson, chef-owner of the popular Cleonice in Ellsworth, is bringing new life to the historic old forge building that hangs over the river downtown. **Table: A Farmhouse Bistro** (66 Main St., 207/374-5677, www.farmkitchentable.com, 11:30 A.M.–9 P.M. daily) serves a mix of small plates such as pizzas and crab cakes ($10–12) and entrées ($18–35) that might include lobster mac and cheese or flatiron steak. Request a table on the porch, and you'll be serenaded by the water rushing (or, during dry spells, at least attempting to gurgle) underneath as you dine.

Seafood

For lobster, fried fish, and the area's best lobster roll, head to **The Fish Net** (163 Main St., 207/374-5240, 11 A.M.–8 P.M. Sun.–Thurs., 11 A.M.–9 P.M. Fri.–Sat.), an inexpensive mostly takeout joint on the eastern end of town.

It's not easy to find **Perry Long's Lobster Shack and Pier** (1076 Newbury Neck Rd., Surry, 207/667-1955, 10 A.M.–7 P.M. daily), but for a classic lobster-shack experience, make the effort. Expect lobster, rolls, corn, chips, mussels, and clams along with a few picnic tables on the water's edge. Call first. Oh, and save room for the homemade ice cream sandwiches.

INFORMATION AND SERVICES
Information

The **Blue Hill Peninsula Chamber of Commerce** (207/374-3242, www.bluehillpeninsula.org) has information on Blue Hill and the surrounding area. You can also find information (although some is outdated) at www.bluehillme.com. One interesting feature on this site is a section on wildlife sightings.

At the **Blue Hill Public Library** (5 Parker Point Rd., 207/374-5515, www.bluehill.lib.me.us), ask to see the armored vest, which *may* have belonged to Magellan. The library also sponsors a summer lecture series.

Public Restrooms

Public buildings with restrooms are the Blue Hill Town Hall (Main St.), Blue Hill Public Library (Main St.), and Blue Hill Memorial Hospital (Water St.).

Brooklin, Brooksville, and Sedgwick

Nestled near the bottom of the Blue Hill Peninsula and surrounded by Castine, Blue Hill, and Deer Isle, this often-missed area offers superb hiking, kayaking, and sailing, plus historic homes and unique shops, studios, lodgings, and personalities.

The best-known town is **Brooklin,** thanks to two magazines: *The New Yorker* and *WoodenBoat*. Wordsmiths extraordinaire E. B. and Katharine White "dropped out" to Brooklin in the 1930s and forever afterward dispatched their splendid material for *The*

New Yorker from here. (The Whites' former home, a handsome colonial not open to the public, is on Route 175 in North Brooklin, 6.5 miles from the Blue Hill Falls bridge.) In 1977, *WoodenBoat* magazine moved its headquarters to Brooklin, where its 60-acre shore-side estate attracts builders and dreamers from all over the globe. Nearby **Brooksville** drew the late Helen and Scott Nearing, whose book *Living the Good Life* made them role models for back-to-the-landers. Their compound now verges on must-see status. **Buck's Harbor,** a section of Brooksville, is the setting for *One Morning in Maine,* one of Robert McCloskey's beloved children's books. Incorporated in 1789, the oldest of the three towns is **Sedgwick,** which once included all of Brooklin and part of Brooksville. Now wedged between Brooklin and Brooksville, it includes the hamlet of Sargentville, the Caterpillar Hill scenic overlook, and a well-preserved complex of historic buildings. The influx of pilgrims—many of them artists bent on capturing the spirit that has proved so enticing to creative types—continues in this area.

SIGHTS
WoodenBoat Publications

On Naskeag Point Road, 1.2 miles from Route 175 in downtown Brooklin, a small sign marks the turn to the world headquarters of the *WoodenBoat* empire (Naskeag Point Rd., Brooklin, 207/359-4651, www.woodenboat.com). Buy magazines, books, clothing, and all manner of nautical merchandise at

Learn to build a wooden boat or other types of crafts at the *WoodenBoat* school.

© TOM NANGLE

the handsome new store, stroll the grounds, or sign up for one of the dozens of one- and two-week spring, summer, and fall courses in seamanship, navigation, boatbuilding, sailmaking, marine carving, and more. Special courses are geared to kids, women, pros, and all-thumbs neophytes; the camaraderie is legendary, and so is the cuisine. School visiting hours are 8 A.M.–5 P.M. Monday–Saturday June–October.

Historical Sights

Now used as the museum and headquarters of the Sedgwick-Brooklin Historical Society, the 1795 **Reverend Daniel Merrill House** (Rte. 172, Sedgwick, 207/359-8086, 2–4 P.M. Sun. July–Aug. or by appointment, donation) was the parsonage for Sedgwick's first permanent minister. Inside the house are period furnishings, old photos, toys, and tools; a few steps away are a restored 1874 schoolhouse, an 1821 cattle pound (for corralling wandering bovines), and a hearse barn. Pick up a brochure during open hours and guide yourself around the buildings and grounds. The **Sedgwick Historic District,** crowning Town House Hill, comprises the Merrill House and its outbuildings, plus the imposing 1794 Town House and the 23-acre Rural Cemetery (the oldest headstone dates from 1798) across Route 172.

The Good Life Center

Forest Farm, home of the late Helen and Scott Nearing, is now the site of The Good Life Center (372 Harborside Rd., Harborside, 207/326-8211, www.goodlife.org). Advocates of simple living and authors of 10 books on the subject, the Nearings created a trust to perpetuate their farm and philosophy. Resident stewards lead tours (usually 1–4 P.M. Thurs.–Mon. late June–early Sept., but call ahead, $5 donation suggested). Ask about the schedule for the traditional Monday-night meetings (7 P.M.), featuring free programs by gardeners, philosophers, musicians, and other guest speakers. Occasional work parties, workshops, and conferences are also on the docket. The farm is on Harborside Road, just before it

WRITER E. B. WHITE

Since the mid-1940s, every child has heard of E. B. White – author of the memorable *Stuart Little, Charlotte's Web,* and *Trumpet of the Swan* – and every college kid for decades has been reminded to consult his *Elements of Style* – but how many realize that White and his wife, Katharine, were living not in the Big City but in the hamlet of North Brooklin, Maine? It was Brooklin that inspired Charlotte and Wilbur and Stuart, and it was Brooklin where the Whites lived very full creative lives.

Abandoning their desks at *The New Yorker* in 1938, Elwyn Brooks White and Katharine S. White bought an idyllic saltwater farm on the Blue Hill Peninsula and moved here with their young son, Joel, who became a noted naval architect and yacht builder in Brooklin before his untimely death in 1997. Andy (as E. B. had been dubbed since his college days at Cornell University) produced 20 books, countless essays and letters to editors, and hundreds (maybe thousands) of "newsbreaks" – those wry clipping-and-commentary items sprinkled through each issue of *The New Yorker.* Katharine continued wielding her pencil as the magazine's standout children's-book editor, donating many of her review copies to Brooklin's Friend Memorial Library, one of her favorite "causes." (The library also has two original Garth Williams drawings from *Stuart Little,* courtesy of E. B., and a lovely garden dedicated to the Whites.) Katharine's book, *Onward and Upward in the Garden,* a collection of her *New Yorker* gardening pieces, was published in 1979, two years after her death.

Later in life, E. B. sagely addressed the young readers of his three award-winning children's books:

Are my stories true, you ask? No, they are imaginary tales, containing fantastic characters and events. In real life, a family doesn't have a child who looks like a mouse; in real life, a spider doesn't spin words in her web. In real life, a swan doesn't blow a trumpet. But real life is only one kind of life –there is also the life of the imagination. And although my stories are imaginary, I like to think that there is some truth in them, too –truth about the way people and animals feel and think and act.

E. B. White died on October 1, 1985, at the age of 86. He and Katharine and Joel left large footprints on this earth, but perhaps nowhere more so than in Brooklin.

---

turns to dirt. From Route 176 in Brooksville, take Cape Rosier Road, go eight miles, passing Holbrook Islands Sanctuary. At the Grange Hall, turn right and follow the road 1.9 miles to the end. Turn left onto Harborside Road and continue 1.8 miles to Forest Farm, across from Orrs Cove.

Four Season Farm

About a mile beyond the Nearings' place is Four Season Farm (609 Weir Cove Rd., Harborside, 207/326-4455, www.fourseasonfarm.com, 1–5 P.M. Mon.–Sat. June–Sept.), the lush organic farm owned and operated by internationally renowned gardeners Eliot Coleman and Barbara Damrosch. Both have written numerous books and articles and starred in TV gardening shows. Coleman is a driving force behind the use of the word "authentic" to mean "beyond organic," demonstrating a commitment to food that is local, fresh, ripe, clean, safe, and nourishing. He's successfully pioneered a "winter harvest," developing environmentally sound and economically viable systems for extending fresh vegetable production from October through May in cold-weather climates. The farm is a treat for the eyes as well as the taste buds—you've never seen such gorgeous produce. Ask about dinners on the farm and other events. Also here is the **Cape Rosier Artist Collective,** a gallery showing works by local artisans.

Scenic Routes

No one seems to know how **Caterpillar Hill** got its name, but its reputation comes from a panoramic vista of water, hills, and blueberry barrens—with a couple of convenient picnic tables where you can stop for lunch, photos, or a ringside view of sunset and fall foliage. From the 350-foot elevation, the views take in Walker Pond, Eggemoggin Reach, Deer Isle, Swans Island, and even the Camden Hills. The signposted rest area is on Route 175/15, between Brooksville and Sargentville, next to a gallery; watch out for the blind curve when you pull off the road. If you want to explore on foot, the one-mile Cooper Farm Trail loops through the blueberry barrens and woods. From the scenic overlook, walk down to and out Cooper Farm Road to the trailhead.

Between Sargentville and Sedgwick, Route 175 offers nonstop views of Eggemoggin Reach, with shore access to the Benjamin River just before you reach Sedgwick village.

Two other scenic routes are **Naskeag Point** in Brooklin and **Cape Rosier,** the western-most arm of the town of Brooksville. Naskeag Point Road begins off Route 175 in "down-town" Brooklin, heads down the peninsula for 3.7 miles past the entrance to WoodenBoat Publications, and ends at a small shingle beach (limited parking) on Eggemoggin Reach. Here you'll find picnic tables, a boat launch, a seasonal toilet, and a marker commemorating the 1778 Battle of Naskeag, when British sailors came ashore from the sloop *Gage,* burned several buildings, and were run off by a ragtag band of local settlers. Cape Rosier's roads are poorly marked, perhaps deliberately, so keep your DeLorme atlas handy. The Cape Rosier loop takes in Holbrook Island Sanctuary, Goose Falls, the hamlet of Harborside, and plenty of water and island views. Note that some roads are unpaved, but they usually are well maintained.

ENTERTAINMENT AND EVENTS

◖ Flash! In the Pans Community Steel Band

If you're a fan of steel-band music, the Flash! In the Pans Community Steel Band (207/374-2172, www.flashinthepans.org) usually performs somewhere on the peninsula 7:30–9 P.M. Monday mid-June–early September. Local papers carry the summer schedule for the nearly three-dozen-member band, which deserves its devoted following. Admission is usually a small donation to benefit a local cause. It's worth every penny to join the fun.

Brooksville Open Mike Nights

Meet locals, savor soup and bread, and share your talents at open mike nights at the **Tinder Hearth** (1452 Coastal Rd., Brooksville, 207/326-9266, www.tinderhearth.org), usually held in the barn 5–8 P.M. on the first and third Sunday during the warmer months. Check Tinder Hearth's website for other programs and workshops.

Eggemoggin Reach Regatta

Wooden boats are big attractions hereabouts, so when a huge fleet sails in for this regatta (usually the first Saturday in August, but the schedule can change), crowds gather. Don't miss the parade of wooden boats. The best locale for watching the regatta itself is on or near the bridge to Deer Isle or near the Eggemoggin Landing grounds on Little Deer Isle. For details, see www.erregatta.com.

SHOPPING

Most of these businesses are small owner-operated shops, which means they're often catch as catch can. If you want to be sure, call ahead.

Antiques

When you need a slate sink, a claw-foot tub, brass fixtures, or a Palladian window, **Architectural Antiquities** (52 Indian Point Lane, Harborside, 207/326-4938, www.archantiquities.com), on Cape Rosier, is just the ticket—a restorer's delight. Prices are reasonable for what you get, and they'll ship your purchases. Open all year by appointment; ask for directions when you call. Antiques dating from the Federal period through the turn of the 20th century are the specialties at **Sedgwick Antiques** (775 N. Sedgwick Rd./Rte. 172, Sedgwick, 207/359-

8834). Early furniture, handmade furniture, and a full range of country accessories and antiques can be found at **Thomas Hinchcliffe Antiques** (26 Cradle Knolls Lane, off Rte. 176, West Sedgwick, 207/326-9411). Painted country furniture, decoys, and unusual nautical items are specialties at Peg and Olney Grindall's **Old Cove Antiques** (106 Caterpillar Rd./Rte. 15, Sargentville, 207/359-2031 or 207/359-8585), a weathered-gray shop across from the Eggemoggin Country Store.

Artists' and Artisans' Galleries

Small studio-galleries pepper Route 175 (Reach Rd.) in Sedgwick and Brooklin; most are marked only by small signs, so watch carefully. First up is **Eggemoggin Textile Studio** (off Rte. 175/Reach Rd., Sedgwick, 207/359-5083, www.chrisleithstudio.com), where the incredibly gifted Christine Leith weaves scarves, wraps, hangings, and pillows with hand-dyed silk and wool; the colors are magnificent. You might catch her at work on the big loom in her studio shop, a real treat.

Continue along the road to find **Reach Road Gallery** (Reach Rd., Sedgwick, 207/359-8803, www.reachroadgallery.com), where Holly Meade sells her detailed woodblock prints as well as prints from the children's books she has illustrated.

Only a few doors down is **Mermaid Woolens** (Reach Rd., Sedgwick, 207/359-2747, www.mermaidwoolens.com), source of Elizabeth Coakley's wildly colorful hand knits—vests, socks, and sweaters. They're pricey but worth every nickel. She also does seascape paintings.

Continue over to Brooklin, where Virginia G. Sarsfield handcrafts paper products, including custom lamp shades, calligraphy papers, books, and lamps, at **Handmade Papers** (113 Reach Rd., Brooklin, 207/359-8345, www.handmadepapersonline.com).

Within easy walking distance of each other in what passes as downtown Brooklin are **Blossom Studio** (Naskeag Building, Brooklin, 207/359-8560), where glass artist Sihaya Hopkins sells handmade glass beads and jewelry, and Ken Carpenter's **Maine Hooked Rugs**

Pushcart Press Bookstore is the world's tiniest bookstore.

(6 Naskeag Rd., Brooklin, 207/359-9878, www .mainehookedrugs.com).

In Brooksville, more finds await on Route 176. You'll need to watch carefully for the sign marking the long drive to **Paul Heroux and Scott Goldberg Pottery** (2032 Coastal Rd./ Rte. 176, Brooksville, 207/326-9062). The small gallery is a treat for pottery fans.

Continue southwest on Route 176 and watch closely for signs for **Bagaduce Forge** (140 Ferry Rd., Brooksville, 207/326-9676); it isn't easy to find. Joseph Meltreder is both blacksmith and farrier, and his small forge, with big views, is the real thing. He turns out whimsical pieces. Especially fun are the nail people—you'll know them when you see them.

Wine, Books, and Gifts

Three varieties of English-style hard cider are specialties at **The Sow's Ear Winery** (Rte. 176 at Herrick Rd., Brooksville, 207/326-4649, no credit cards), a minuscule operation in a funky gray-shingled building. Winemaker Tom Hoey also produces sulfite-free blueberry, chokecherry, and rhubarb wines; he'll let you sample it all. Ask to see his cellar, where everything happens.

Betsy's Sunflower (12 Reach Rd., 207/359-5030), in Brooklin village, is filled with garden and kitchen must-haves and books.

Don't miss the "world's smallest bookstore," Bill Henderson's **Pushcart Press Bookstore** (Rte. 172, Sedgwick, 207/359-2427), located behind Sedgwick Antiques. It's a trove of literary fiction both used (paperbacks $2, hardbacks $5) and new, including edition of the *Pushcart Prize: Best of the Small Presses* annual series. Sales help support Pushcart fellowships.

RECREATION
◖ Holbrook Island Sanctuary State Park

In the early 1970s, foresighted benefactor Anita Harris donated to the state 1,230 acres in Brooksville that would become the Holbrook Island Sanctuary (207/326-4012, www.parksandlands.com, free). From Route 176, between West Brooksville and South Brooksville, head west on Cape Rosier Road, following brown-

and-white signs for the sanctuary. Trail maps and bird checklists are available in boxes at trailheads or at park headquarters. The easy Backshore Trail (about 30 minutes) starts here, or go back a mile and climb the steepish trail to **Backwoods Mountain** for the best vistas. Other attractions include shorefront picnic tables and grills, four old cemeteries, and super bird-watching during spring and fall migrations. Leashed pets are allowed, but no bikes are allowed on the trails, and camping is not permitted. The park is officially open May 15–October 15, but the access road and parking areas are plowed in winter for cross-country skiers.

Swimming

A small, relatively little-known beach is Brooklin's **Pooduck Beach.** From the Brooklin General Store (Rte. 175), take Naskeag Point Road about 0.5 miles, watching for the Pooduck Road sign on the right. Turn right and drive to the end; parking is very limited. You can also launch a sea kayak here into Eggemoggin Reach.

Bicycling

Bicycling in this area is for confident, experienced cyclists. The roads are particularly narrow and winding, with poor shoulders. Best bets for casual peddle pushers are the **Naskeag scenic route** or around **Cape Rosier,** where traffic is light.

Sailing

Captain LeCain Smith sails *Perelandra* (Buck's Harbor, 207/326-4279), a 44-foot steel-hulled ketch, in the waters of Penobscot Bay. Rates begin at $40 pp for a two-hour sail and increase to $100 pp for a full day. The boat holds a maximum of six passengers.

Ensign-class Antares day sailboats are available for rental at **Buck's Harbor Marine** (on the dock, South Brooksville, 207/326-8839, www.bucksharbor.com). The full-keel boats rent for $135 per day. Buck's Harbor also charters bareboat sail and power yachts to qualified skippers.

Picnicking

You can take a picnic to the **Bagaduce Ferry Landing,** in West Brooksville off Route 176, where there are picnic tables and cross-river vistas toward Castine.

ACCOMMODATIONS
Cottage Colony
The fourth generation manages the **Hiram Blake Camp** (220 Weir Cove Rd., Harborside, 207/326-4951, www.hiramblake.com, Memorial Day–late Sept., no credit cards), but other generations pitch in and help with gardening, lobstering, maintenance, and kibitzing. Thirteen cottages and a duplex line the shore of this 100-acre property, which has been in family hands since before the Revolutionary War. The camp itself dates from 1916. Don't bother bringing reading material: The dining room has ingenious ceiling niches lined with countless books. Guests also have the use of rowboats. Home-cooked breakfasts and dinners are served family style; lobster is always available at an additional charge. Much of the fare is grown in the expansive gardens. Other facilities include a dock, a recreation room, a pebble beach, and an outdoor chapel. There's a one-week minimum (beginning Sat. or Sun.) in July–August, when cottages go for $600–3,000 per week (including breakfast, dinner, and linens). Off-season rates (no meals or linens, but cottages have cooking facilities) are $660–940 per week. The best chances for getting a reservation are in June and September. Dogs are welcome.

Bed-and-Breakfast
Best known for its restaurant and pub, **The Brooklin Inn** (Rte. 175, Brooklin, 207/359-2777, www.brooklininn.com, year-round, $105–135 with breakfast; add $10 for a one-night stay) also has five comfortable bedrooms; two share a bath.

FOOD
As always, hours are listed for peak season; call to verify days and hours of operation.

Cooking Classes
In summer, chef Terence Janericco (617/426-7458, 207/359-2068 after July 1, www

.terencejanericcocookingclasses.com), author of a dozen cookbooks, moves his cooking school from Boston to Brooklin. The demonstration-only three-hour classes are $70 pp, which includes dining on the foods prepared.

Local Flavors
The **Brooklin General Store** (1 Reach Rd., junction of Rte. 175 and Naskeag Point Rd., Brooklin, 207/359-8817, 4:30 A.M.–8 P.M. Mon.–Sat., 6 A.M.–6 P.M. Sun.), vintage 1872, carries groceries, beer and wine, newspapers, takeout sandwiches, and local chatter.

In North Brooksville, where Route 175/176 crosses the Bagaduce River, stands the **Bagaduce Lunch** (11 A.M.–7 or 8 P.M. daily early May–mid-Sept.), named an "American Classic" by the James Beard Foundation in 2008. Owners Judy and Mike Astbury buy local fish and clams. Check the tide calendar and go when the tide is changing; order a clam roll or a hamburger, settle in at a picnic table, and watch the reversing falls. If you're lucky, you might sight an eagle, osprey, or seal. The food is so-so, but the setting is tops. The popular takeout stand has outdoor tables only.

Lunch is the specialty at **Buck's Harbor Market** (Rte. 176, South Brooksville, 207/326-8683, 7 A.M.–7 P.M. Mon.–Fri., 8 A.M.–7:30 P.M. Sat., 8 A.M.–6 P.M. Sun.), a low-key, marginally yuppified general store popular with yachties in summer. Pick up sandwiches, cheeses, breads, and treats for a Holbrook Island adventure.

Wine, cheese, and chocolate—what's not to like about **The Cave** (123 Reach Rd., Brooklin, 207/359-8008, www.thecavebrooklin.com)?

Ethnic Fare
El El Frijoles (41 Caterpillar Rd./Rte. 15, Sargentville, 207/359-2486, www.elelfrijoles.com, 11 A.M.–8 P.M. Wed.–Sun., $5–16) gets good marks for its made-from-scratch California-style empanadas, burritos, and tacos. It also serves local Millbrook's killer ice cream (alone worth a stop). There's outdoor seating only, with a play area for children.

Casual Dining

Behind the Buck's Harbor Market is **Buck's Restaurant** (6 Cornfield Hill Rd., Brooksville, 207/326-8688, 5:30–8:30 P.M. daily, $18–24), an outpost of fiery colors calmed down by white tablecloths. Respected chefs Jonathan Chase and Nancy McMillan create upscale comfort foods with a dash of creativity.

What's not organic is local, and what's not local is organic at **The Brooklin Inn** (Rte. 175, Brooklin, 207/359-2777, www.brooklininn.com, 5:30–9 P.M. daily, $19–40). In addition to à la carte selections, a three-course fixed-price menu usually is offered daily for about $25. Downstairs an **Irish pub** (5:30–10 P.M. daily) serves burgers, Guinness stew, and pizza in addition to the upstairs menu. Lunch might be available.

INFORMATION AND SERVICES

The best source of information about the region is the **Blue Hill Peninsula Chamber of Commerce** (207/374-2281, www.bluehill peninsula.org).

Libraries

Friends Memorial Library (Rte. 175, Brooklin, 207/359-2276) has a lovely Circle of Friends Garden, with benches and a brick patio. It's dedicated to the memory of longtime Brooklin residents E. B. and Katharine White. Also check out **Free Public Library** (1 Town House Rd./Rte. 176, Brooksville, 207/326-4560) and Sedgwick Village Library (Main St., Sedgwick, 207/359-2177).

Castine

Castine is a gem—a serene New England village with a tumultuous past. It tips a cape, surrounded by water on three sides, including the entrance to the Penobscot River, which made it a strategic defense point. Once beset by geopolitical squabbles, saluting the flags of three different nations (France, Britain, and Holland), its only crises now are local political skirmishes. This is an unusual community, a National Register of Historic Places enclave that many people never find. The town celebrated its bicentennial in 1996. Today a major presence is Maine Maritime Academy, yet Castine remains the quietest college town imaginable. Students in search of a party school won't find it here; naval engineering is serious business.

What visitors discover is a year-round community with a busy waterfront, an easy-to-conquer layout, a handful of traditional inns, wooded trails on the outskirts of town, an astonishing collection of splendid Georgian and Federalist architecture, and water views nearly every which way you turn. If you're staying in Blue Hill or even Bar Harbor, spend a day here. Or book a room in one of the town's lovely inns, and use Castine as a base for exploring here and beyond. Either way, you won't regret it.

HISTORY

Originally known as Fort Pentagouet, Castine received its current name courtesy of Jean-Vincent d'Abbadie, Baron de St-Castin. A young French nobleman manqué who married a Wabanaki princess named Pidiwamiska, d'Abbadie ran the town in the second half of the 17th century and eventually returned to France.

A century later, in 1779, occupying British troops and their reinforcements scared off potential American seaborne attackers (including Colonel Paul Revere), who turned tail up the Penobscot River and ended up scuttling their more than 40-vessel fleet—a humiliation known as the Penobscot Expedition and still regarded as one of the worst naval defeats for the United States.

When the boundaries for Maine were finally set in 1820, with the St. Croix River marking the east rather than the Penobscot River, the last British Loyalists departed, some floating their homes north to St. Andrews in New Brunswick, Canada, where they can still be seen today. For a while, peace and prosperity became the bywords for Castine—with lively commerce in fish and salt—but it all collapsed during the California

© TOM NANGLE

The John Perkins House, adjacent to The Wilson Museum, is open in summer for guided tours.

gold rush and the Civil War trade embargo, leaving the town down on its luck.

Of the many historical landmarks scattered around town, one of the most intriguing must be the sign on "Wind Mill Hill," at the junction of Route 166 and State Street:

> On Hatch's Hill there stands a mill. Old Higgins he doth tend it. And every time he grinds a grist, he has to stop and mend it.

In smaller print, just below the rhyme, comes the drama:

> Here two British soldiers were shot for desertion.

Castine has quite a history indeed.

SIGHTS
◖ Castine Historic Tour

To appreciate Castine fully, you need to arm yourself with the Castine Merchants Association's visitors brochure-map (all businesses and lodgings in town have copies) and follow the numbers on bike or on foot. With no stops, walking the route takes less than an hour, but you'll want to read dozens of historical plaques, peek into public buildings, shoot some photos, and perhaps even do some shopping.

Highlights of the tour include the late-18th-century **John Perkins House,** moved to Perkins Street from Court Street in 1969 and restored with period furnishings. It's open in July–August for guided tours (2–5 P.M. Sun. and Wed., $5).

Next door, **The Wilson Museum** (107 Perkins St., 207/326-8545, www.wilson museum.org, 10 A.M.–5 P.M. Mon.–Fri. and 2–5 P.M. Sat.–Sun. late May–late Sept., free), founded in 1921, contains an intriguingly eclectic two-story collection of prehistoric artifacts, ship models, dioramas, baskets, tools, and minerals assembled over a lifetime by John Howard Wilson, a geologist-anthropologist who first visited Castine in 1891 (and died in 1936). Among the exhibits are Balinese masks,

MAINE MARITIME ACADEMY

The state's only merchant-marine college, one of only seven in the nation, occupies 35 acres in the middle of Castine. Founded in 1941, the academy awards undergraduate and graduate degrees in such areas as marine engineering, ocean studies, and marina management, preparing a student body of about 750 men and women for careers as ship captains, Naval architects, and marine engineers.

The academy owns a fleet of 60 vessels, including the historic research schooner *Bowdoin*, flagship of Arctic explorer Admiral Donald MacMillan, and the 499-foot training vessel *State of Maine*, berthed down the hill at the waterfront. In 1996–1997 the *State of Maine*, formerly the U.S. Navy hydrographic survey ship *Tanner*, underwent a $12 million conversion for use by the academy. It is still subject to deployment, and in 2005 the school had to quickly find alternative beds for students using the ship as a dormitory when it was called into service in support of rescue and rebuilding efforts in New Orleans after Hurricane Katrina. Midshipmen conduct free 30-minute tours of the vessel on weekdays in summer (about mid-July–late August). The schedule is posted at the dock, or call 207/326-4311 to check; photo ID is required.

Weekday tours of the campus can be arranged through the **admissions office** (207/326-2206 or 800/227-8465 outside Maine, www.mainemaritime.edu). Campus highlights include the three-story Nutting Memorial Library in Platz Hall (open daily during the school year, weekdays in summer and during vacations); the Henry A. Scheel Room, a cozy oasis in Leavitt Hall containing memorabilia from late Naval architect Henry Scheel and his wife, Jeanne; and the well-stocked **bookstore** (Curtis Hall, 207/326-9333, 8 A.M.–3 P.M. Mon.–Fri.).

Maine Maritime Academy's training vessel is docked in Castine. Tours are available through the admissions office.

ancient oil lamps, cuneiform tablets, Zulu artifacts, pre-Inca pottery, and assorted local findings.

Open the same days and hours as the Perkins House are the **Blacksmith Shop,** where a smith does demonstrations, and the **Hearse House,** containing Castine's 19th-century winter and summer funeral vehicles. Both have free admission.

At the end of Battle Avenue stands the 19th-century **Dyce's Head Lighthouse,** no longer operating; the keeper's house is owned by the town. Alongside it is a public path (signposted; pass at your own risk) leading via a wooden staircase to a tiny patch of rocky shoreline and the beacon that has replaced the lighthouse.

The highest point in town is **Fort George State Park,** site of a 1779 British fortification. Nowadays, little remains except grassy earthworks, but there are interpretive displays and picnic tables.

Main Street, descending toward the water, is a feast for historic architecture fans. Artist Fitz Hugh Lane and author Mary McCarthy once lived in elegant houses along the elm-lined street (neither building is open to the public). On Court Street between Main and Green Streets stands turn-of-the-20th-century **Emerson Hall,** site of Castine's municipal offices. Since Castine has no official information booth, you may need to duck in here (it's open weekdays) for answers to questions.

Across Court Street, **Witherle Memorial Library,** a handsome early-19th-century building on the site of the 18th-century town jail, looks out on the Town Common. Also facing the Common are the Adams and Abbott Schools, the former still an elementary school. The **Abbott School** (10 A.M.–4 P.M. Tues.–Sat., 1–4 P.M. Sun. July–early Sept., reduced schedule spring and fall, donation), built in 1859, has been carefully restored for use as a museum and headquarters for the **Castine Historical Society** (207/326-4118, www.castinehistoricalsociety.org). A big draw at the volunteer-run museum is the 24-foot-long Bicentennial Quilt, assembled for Castine's 200th anniversary in 1996. The historical society, founded in 1966, organizes lectures, exhibits, and special events (some free) in various places around town.

On the outskirts of town, across the narrow neck between Wadsworth Cove and Hatch's Cove, stretches a rather overgrown canal (signposted "British Canal") scooped out by the occupying British during the War of 1812. Effectively severing land access to the town of Castine, the Brits thus raised havoc, collected local revenues for eight months, then departed for Halifax with enough funds to establish Dalhousie College, now Dalhousie University. Wear waterproof boots to walk the canal route; the best time to go is at low tide.

If a waterfront picnic sounds appealing, buy the fixings at Bah's Bakehouse and settle in on the grassy earthworks along the harbor-front at **Fort Madison,** site of an 1808 garrison (then Fort Porter) near the corner of Perkins and Madockawando Streets. The views from here are fabulous, and it's accessible all year. A set of stairs leads down to the rocky waterfront.

ENTERTAINMENT AND EVENTS

Possibilities for live music include **Dennett's Wharf** (15 Sea St., 207/326-9045), where some performances require a ticket, and **The Reef** (on the wharf, tucked underneath the bank facing the parking area and harbor).

The **Castine Town Band** often performs free concerts on the Common; check www.castine.org for its schedule.

The community-based **Castine Arts Association** (www.castinearts.org) presents concerts, exhibits, workshops, and other performances at various locations around town each summer.

The **Wilson Museum** (107 Perkins St., 207/326-8545, www.wilsonmuseum.org) frequently schedules concerts, lectures, and demonstrations.

The **Trinitarian Church** often brings in high-caliber musical entertainment.

Celebrate Castine (www.celebratecastine.com) is a town-wide event in mid-July.

SHOPPING
Antiques and Galleries

Tucked into the back of the 1796 Parson Mason House, one of Castine's oldest residences, **Leila Day Antiques** (53 Main St., 207/326-8786, www.leiladayantiques.com) is a must for anyone in the market for folk art, period furniture, and quilts.

Traditional American craftwork is sold at **Castine Historical Handworks** (9 Main St., 207/326-4460, www.castinehistoricalhand works.com).

Contemporary fine art is the focus at **Tarratine Gallery** (5 Main St.), a collaborative effort.

Oil paintings by local artists Joshua and Susan Adam are on view at **Adam Gallery** (140 Battle Ave., 207/326-8272, www.adam galleryonline.com).

Books

In downtown Castine, a block up from the waterfront, **The Compass Rose Bookstore and Café** (3 Main St., 207/326-9366 or 800/698-9366, www.compassrosebooks.com) carries new books, cards, games, and prints chosen by owner Sharon Biggie. In the back of the shop is a café serving hot and cold drinks (including espresso), soup, sandwiches, and tasty baked goods.

Furniture

Bench-made Windsor chairs are the specialty at **M&E Gummel Chairworks** (600 Shore Rd., 207/326-8122, www.gummelchairworks.com). The father-and-son team use 18th-century methods when handcrafting the chairs, colonial dining tables, and bowls one at a time in their late-19th-century barn workshop.

RECREATION
Witherle Woods

This 152-acre preserve, owned by Maine Coast Heritage Trust (maps available via email from info@mcht.org), is a popular walking area with a maze of trails and old woods roads leading to the water. Many Revolutionary War–era relics have been found here; if you see any, do not remove them. Access to the preserve is via an old woods road on Battle Avenue, located between the water district property (at the end of the wire fence) and the Manor's exit driveway and diagonally across from La Tour Street.

Sea Kayaking

Right near Dennett's Wharf is **Castine Kayak Adventures** (17 Sea St., 207/326-9045, www.castinekayak.com), spearheaded by Maine Guide Karen Francoeur. All skill levels are accommodated; "Kayak Karen," as she's known locally, is particularly adept with beginners, delivering wise advice from beginning to end. Three-hour half-day trips are $55; six-hour full-day tours are around $105 and include lunch. Two-hour sunset tours are $40; the sunrise tour includes a light breakfast for $55. Friday nights, there are special two-hour phosphorescence tours under the stars (weather permitting) for $55 pp. Longer trips are available for $150 per day. If you have your own boat, call Karen for advice; she knows these waters. She also offers instruction for all levels as well as a Maine Sea Kayak Guide course. Karen also rents bikes for $20 per day.

Swimming

Backshore Beach, a crescent of sand and gravel on Wadsworth Cove Road (turn off Battle Ave. at the Castine Golf Club), is a favorite saltwater swimming spot, with views across the bay to Stockton Springs. Be forewarned, though, that ocean swimming in this part of Maine is not for the timid. The best time to try it is on the incoming tide, after the sun has had time to heat up the mud. At mid- to high tide, it's also the best place to put in a sea kayak.

Golf

The nine-hole **Castine Golf Club** (200 Battle Ave., 207/326-8844, www.castinegolfclub .com) dates to 1897, when the first tee required a drive from a 30-step-high mound. It was redesigned in 1921 by Willie Park Jr.

kayaking Castine's harbor

© HILARY NANGLE

BLUE HILL PENINSULA

Excursion Boat

Glide over Penobscot Bay aboard the wooden motor sailer *Guildive* (207/701-1421, www .guildivecruises.com), captained by Kata Kana and Zander Parker. The two-hour sails cost $42–47; options and include day and sunset sails.

ACCOMMODATIONS
Inns

Castine is blessed with three fine traditional inns. This is not the place to come if you require in-room phones, air-conditioning, or fancy bathrooms. Rather, the pace is relaxed and the accommodations reflect the easy elegance of a bygone era.

The three-story Queen Anne–style **Pentagöet Inn** (26 Main St., 207/326-8616 or 800/845-1701, www.pentagoet.com, May–late Oct., $125–285) is the perfect Maine summer inn, right down to the lace curtains billowing in the breeze, the soft floral wallpapers, and the intriguing curiosities that accent but don't clutter the guest rooms. Congenial innkeepers Jack Burke, previously with the U.S.

Foreign Service, and Julie Van de Graaf, a pastry chef, took over the century-old inn in 2000 and have given it new life, upgrading rooms and furnishing them with Victorian antiques, adding handsome gardens, and carving out a niche as a dining destination. Their enthusiasm for the area is contagious. The inn's 16 guest rooms are spread between the main house (with Wi-Fi service) and the adjoining house (with in-room TVs). A hot buffet breakfast, afternoon refreshments, and evening hors d'oeuvres are provided. Jack holds court in Passports Pub (chock-full of vintage photos and prints as well as exotic antiques), advising guests on activities and opportunities. Borrow one of the inn's bikes and explore around town or simply walk—the Main Street location is convenient to everything Castine offers. Better yet, just sit on the wraparound porch and take it all in.

Once the summer "cottage" of Arthur Fuller, a South Boston Yacht Club commodore, **The Manor Inn** (Battle Ave., 207/326-4861 or 877/626-6746, www.manor-inn.com, mid-Feb.–late Dec., $115–275) overlooks the town and harbor from five mostly wooded acres elevated above Battle Avenue. Although the atmosphere is informal, there are lots of elegant architectural touches. Nancy Watson and Tom Ehrman, innkeepers here since 1998, continue to improve the inn each year. The 14 second- and third-floor guest rooms are an eclectic mix: Some have canopied beds and fireplaces, some are especially family-friendly. A separate guest building has a TV and games as well as Nancy's yoga studio; guests are welcome to join her morning Iyengar classes (Mon., Wed., Fri., $12 drop-ins). Wi-Fi is available. The trailhead for Witherle Woods is close by. The inn is often the site of weddings and receptions; ask before you book unless you don't mind being the odd man out. Well-behaved pets are $25 per stay.

In 2010 a group of local residents purchased the venerable **Castine Inn** (41 Main St., Castine, 207/326-4365, www.castineinn.com, $95–275), with 18 second- and third-floor guest rooms and suites, some with water views. Public space includes a formal living room, a TV room, and a pub as well as a wraparound porch overlooking the gardens. Breakfast is served in the dining room, which features a wraparound mural of Castine. Dinner may be served in the future.

FOOD

As always, hours are listed for peak season; call to verify days and hours of operation.

Local Flavors

Since 1920, locals have been buying lunch and ice cream at **Castine Variety** (1 Main St., 207/326-8625, 7 A.M.–8 P.M. daily). Go for the vintage feeling and the inexpensive breakfasts, lunches, and ice cream.

Another institution is **The Breeze** (Town Dock, 207/326-9200, 9 A.M.–7 P.M. daily), a waterfront takeout stand with reliably good basics like homemade doughnuts, burgers, fried clams, and ice cream. You can't beat the location or the view.

When everything else in town is closed, your best bet for late-night eats is **The Reef** (8 Sea St., on the wharf, tucked underneath the bank

facing the parking area and harbor, 207/326-4040, 11 A.M.–1 A.M. daily). The hand-tossed gourmet pizzas are available in three sizes. There are plenty of pub-style favorites too. The atmosphere is more bar than restaurant, with a pool table in the back and a small stage area for live entertainment.

Casual Dining

Here's a doubleheader: **Bah's Bakehouse** (26 Water St., 207/326-9510, www.bahsworld.com, 7 A.M.–3 P.M. daily) and, sharing the same location, **Stella's Jazz Nocturnal** (207/326-9710, 5:30–11 P.M. Tues.–Sun., food service 5:30–10 P.M. Tues.–Sun., $9–18). Upstairs is Bah's, a higgledy-piggledy eatery of three rooms and a deck at the end of an alleyway tucked between Main and Water Streets. Its slogan is "creative flour arrangements," and creative it is. Stop here for coffee, cold juices, pastries, interesting snacks and salads, homemade soups, wine or beer, good sandwiches, and if you're lucky, fish cakes. Be forewarned: If it's crowded, go elsewhere—the kitchen is quickly overwhelmed and service can be slow to frustrating. Underneath the deck is Stella's, an intimate dining room and lounge where live jazz is performed Thursday–Sunday.

On a warm summer day, it's hard to find a better place to while away a few hours than **Dennett's Wharf** (15 Sea St., 207/326-9045, www.dennettswharf.net, 11 A.M.–midnight daily May–mid Oct., entrées $10–25), and that's likely what you'll do here, as service can be slow. Next to the town dock, it's a colorful barn of a place with an outside deck and front-row windjammer-watching seats in summer. The best advice is to keep your order simple.

The Pine Cone Pub at the Manor Inn (76 Battle Ave., 207/326-4861, from 5 P.M. Tues.–Sat.) serves a light menu, with such choices as Caesar salad and fish-and-chips.

Fine Dining

Jazz music plays softly and dinner is by candlelight at the ◖ **Pentagöet** (26 Main St., 207/326-8616 or 800/845-1701, www.pentagoet.com, from 6 P.M. Tues.–Sat., entrées

© HILARY NANGLE

Dennett's Wharf at Castine's harbor is a good spot for a brew and a burger.

$18–29). In fine weather you can dine on the porch. Choices vary from roasted *loup de mer* to slow-cooked lamb shank, or simply make a meal of small plates, such as lamb lollipops and crab cakes and a salad. Don't miss the lobster bouillabaisse or the chocolate *budino,* a scrumptious warm Italian pudding that melts in your mouth (a must for chocoholics).

The bi-level Commodore Room at **The Manor Inn** (76 Battle Ave., 207/326-4861, 6–8:30 P.M. Tues.–Sat. summer, 6–8:30 P.M. Thurs.–Sat. off-season, entrées $16–27) overlooks the gardens and lawn. Dinner is served from an extensive menu accented with Asian tastes, Indian curries, and other worldly flavors, accompanied by home-baked breads, and always including vegetarian choices. Reservations are essential on weekends. It's open from Valentine's Day to late December.

INFORMATION AND SERVICES

Castine has no local information office, but all businesses and lodgings in town have copies of the Castine Merchants Association's visitors brochure-map. For additional information, go to the **Castine Town Office** (Emerson Hall, 67 Court St., 207/326-4502, www.castine.me.us, 8 A.M.–3:30 P.M. Mon.–Fri.).

Libraries

Check out **Witherle Memorial Library** (41 School St., 207/326-4375, www.witherle.lib. me.us). Also accessible to the public is the Nutting Memorial Library, in Platz Hall on the Maine Maritime Academy campus.

Public Restrooms

Castine has public restrooms on the town dock, at the foot of Main Street.

Deer Isle

"Deer Isle is like Avalon," wrote John Steinbeck in *Travels with Charley*—"it must disappear when you are not there." Deer Isle, the name of both the island and its midpoint town, has been romancing authors and artisans for decades, but it is unmistakably real to the quarrymen and fishermen who've been here for centuries. These long-timers are a sturdy lot, as even Steinbeck recognized: "I would hate to try to force them to do anything they didn't want to do."

Early-18th-century maps show no name for the island, but by the late 1800s nearly 100 families lived here, supporting themselves first by farming, then by fishing. In 1789, when Deer Isle was incorporated, 80 local sailing vessels were scouring the Gulf of Maine in pursuit of mackerel and cod, and Deer Isle men were circling the globe as yachting skippers and merchant seamen. At the same time, in the once-quiet village of Green's Landing (now called Stonington), the shipbuilding and granite industries boomed, spurring development, prosperity, and the kinds of rough high jinks typical of commercial ports the world over.

Green's Landing became the "big city" for an international crowd of quarrymen carving out the terrain on Deer Isle and nearby Crotch Island, source of high-quality granite for Boston's Museum of Fine Arts, the Smithsonian Institution, a humongous fountain for John D. Rockefeller's New York estate, and less showy projects all along the Eastern Seaboard. The heyday is long past, but the industry did extend into the 20th century (including a contract for the pink granite at President John F. Kennedy's Arlington National Cemetery gravesite). Today, Crotch Island is the site of Maine's only operating island granite quarry.

Measuring about nine miles north to south (plus another three miles for Little Deer Isle), the island of Deer Isle today has a handful of hamlets (including **Sunshine, Sunset, Mountainville,** and **Oceanville**) and two

towns—**Stonington** and **Deer Isle**—with a population of fewer than 3,000. Road access is via Route 15 on the Blue Hill Peninsula. A huge suspension bridge, built in 1939 over Eggemoggin Reach, links the Sargentville section of Sedgwick with Little Deer Isle; from there, a sinuous 0.4-mile causeway connects to the northern tip of Deer Isle.

Deer Isle remains an artisans' enclave, anchored by the Haystack Mountain School of Crafts. Studios and galleries are plentiful, although many require tooling along back roads to find them. Stonington, a rough-and-tumble fishing port with an idyllic setting, is slowly being gentrified, as each season more and more galleries and upscale shops open for the summer. Locals are holding their collective breaths, hoping that any improvements don't change the town too much (although most visitors could do without the car racing on Main Street

Lobster fishing is an economic mainstay on Deer Isle.

© TOM NANGLE

PUMPKIN ISLAND
LIGHT VIEW

To Blue Hill

15

Sargentville

Sedgwick

175

**DEER
ISLE**

175

EGGEMOGGIN RD

Billings
Cove

Benjamin R.

DEER ISLE
INFORMATION CENTER

**Little
Deer
Isle**

Stave
Island

THE INN AT
FERRY LANDING

175

Blastow
Cove

Carney
Island

Haven

Pickering
Island

Causeway
Beach

Eggemoggin

Reach

REACH   RD

North

15

Deer

Northwest Harbor

DOW RD

Isle

Torrey
Pond

Pressey
Cove

Lily
Pond

Oak
Point

Conary
Island

Deer Isle
Village

Campbell
Island

PILGRIM'S INN

Shore Acres
Preserve

White
Island

South

Mill
Pond

Greenlaw Cove

Sylvester
Cove

Sunset

Deer

Long Cove

SUNSHINE RD

Mountainville

Stinson Neck

SALOME
SELLERS
HOUSE

ISLAND
COUNTRY
CLUB

**Southeast
Harbor**

Edgar
Tennis
Preserve

Freese
Island

Sunshine

Sheephead
Island

Smalls Cove

SOUTH DEER ISLE CROSS RD

15

Isle

15A

GOOSE COVE RD

Crockett Cove

LILY'S CAFE AND
WINE BAR

Oceanville

HAYSTACK
MOUNTAIN SCHOOL
OF CRAFTS

Barred Island
Preserve

Crockett Cove Woods
Preserve

AIRPORT RD

Settlement
Quarry

OCEANVILLE

OLD QUARRY OCEAN
ADVENTURES

Sheep
Island

Goose Cove

Burnt Cove

Webb Cove

GUIDED ISLAND TOURS

MAIN
ST

Ames
Pond

Thorofare

PRES DU PORT
Stonington

BOYCES MOTEL
THE INN ON THE HARBOR

Camp
Island

Bold Island

DEER ISLE GRANITE MUSEUM

Moose
Island

Deer Island

Devil
Island

Saddleback
Island

Crotch
Island

Green
Island

Millet
Island

Bare
Island

Spruce
Island

0   1 mi

0   1 km

Ferry to Isle au Haut

© AVALON TRAVEL

THE MAINE ISLAND TRAIL

In the early 1980s, a "trail" of coastal Maine islands was only the germ of an idea. By 2000 the **Maine Island Trail Association** (MITA, 207/761-8225, www.mita.org) counted some 4,000 members dedicated to conscientious (low- or no-impact) recreational use of about 180 public and private islands along 375 miles of Maine coastline between Kennebunkport and Machias, and it continues to grow.

More than a dozen of these islands (each year new ones are added and others are subtracted) are in the Acadia region, between Isle au Haut and Schoodic Point. In fact, one of the best island clusters along the entire trail is in the waters off Stonington on Deer Isle.

Access to the trail is only by private boat, and the best choice is a sea kayak, to navigate shallow or rock-strewn coves. Sea kayak rentals are available in Bar Harbor, Southwest Harbor, Blue Hill, Castine, and Stonington, and several outfitters offer island tours. The best source of information is the Maine Association of Sea Kayaking Guides and Instructors (MASKGI), whose members agree to adhere to the "leave no trace" philosophy.

The trail's publicly owned islands – supervised by the state Bureau of Public Lands – are open to anyone; the private islands are restricted to MITA members, who pay $45 pp or $65 per family annually for the privilege (and, it's important to add, the responsibility). With the fee comes the *Maine Island Trail Guidebook*, providing directions and information for each of the islands. With membership comes the expectation of care and concern. "Low impact" means different things to different people, so MITA experienced acute growing pains when enthusiasm began leading to "tent sprawl."

To cope with and reverse the overuse, MITA has created an "adopt-an-island" program, in which volunteers become stewards for specific islands and keep track of their use and condition. MITA members are urged to pick up trash, use tent platforms where they exist, and move on if an island has already reached its assigned capacity (stipulated on a shoreline sign and in the guidebook).

A superb complement to the *Maine Island Trail Guidebook* is a copy of *Hot Showers!* by Lee Bumsted, a former MITA staff member. Recognizing the need for alternating island camping with warm beds and hot showers, Bumsted has almost single-handedly alleviated island stress and strain. Some of the bed-and-breakfasts and inns listed in her guide give discounts to MITA members.

---

at night). Already, real-estate prices and accompanying taxes have escalated way past the point where many a local fisherman can hope to buy, and in some cases maintain, a home.

SIGHTS

Sightseeing on Deer Isle means exploring back roads, browsing the galleries, walking the trails, hanging out on the docks, and soaking in the ambience.

◀ Haystack Mountain School of Crafts

The renowned Haystack Mountain School of Crafts (Sunshine Rd., Deer Isle, 207/348-2306, www.haystack-mtn.org) in Sunshine is open to the public on a limited basis, but if it fits in your schedule, go. Anyone can visit the school store or walk down the central stairs to the water; to see more of the campus, take a tour (1 P.M. Wed., $5), which includes a video, viewing works on display, and the opportunity to visit some studios. Beyond that, there are slide programs, lectures, demonstrations, and concerts presented by faculty and visiting artists starting at 8 P.M. on varying weeknights early June–late August. Perhaps the best opportunities are the End-of-Session auctions, held on Thursday nights every 2–3 weeks, when you can tour the studios for free 4–6 P.M. and view the works the teachers and students have produced, then return for the auction preview at 7:30 P.M., followed by the auction at 8 P.M. It's a great

© HILARY NANGLE

Architect Edward Larrabee Barnes designed the oceanfront Haystack Mountain School of Crafts on Deer Isle.

opportunity to buy craftwork at often very reasonable prices.

Historic Houses and Museums

There's more to the 1830 **Salome Sellers House** (416 Sunset Rd./Rte. 15A, Sunset Village, 207/348-2897, 1–4 P.M. Wed. and Fri. July–early Sept., donation) than first meets the eye. A repository of local memorabilia, archives, and intriguing artifacts, it's also the headquarters of the **Deer Isle-Stonington Historical Society.** Sellers, matriarch of an island family, was a direct descendant of Mayflower settlers. She lived to be 108, a lifetime spanning 1800–1908, earning the record for oldest recorded Maine resident. The house contains Sellers's furnishings, and in a small exhibit space in the rear is a fine exhibit of baskets made by Maine Native Americans. Behind the house are the archives, heritage gardens, and an exhibit hall filled with nautical artifacts. Bringing all this to life are enthusiastic volunteer guides, many of them island natives. They love to provide tidbits about various items; seafarers' logs and

ship models are particularly intriguing, and don't miss the 1920s peapod, the original lobster boat on the island. The house is just north of the Island Country Club and across from Eaton's Plumbing.

Close to the Stonington waterfront, the **Deer Isle Granite Museum** (51 Main St., Stonington, 207/367-6331) was established to commemorate the centennial of the quarrying business hereabouts. The best feature of the small museum is a 15-foot-long working model of Crotch Island, center of the industry, as it appeared at the turn of the 20th century. Flatcars roll, boats glide, and derricks move—it all looks very real. The museum is open in July–August, but it's best to call for current days and hours of operation. The recommended donation is $5 per family.

Another downtown Stonington attraction is a Lilliputian complex known as the **Miniature Village.** Some years ago, the late Everett Knowlton created a dozen and a half replicas of local buildings and displayed them on granite blocks in his yard. Since his death, they've

GETTING CRAFTY

Internationally famed artisans – sculptors and papermakers, weavers and jewelers, potters and printmakers – become the faculty each summer for the unique **Haystack Mountain School of Crafts.** Founded in 1950 by Mary Beasom Bishop (1885-1972) and a group of talented Maine artisans as a studio research and study program, Haystack has grown into one of the top craft schools in the country.

Under the direction of beloved former director Francis Merritt, the school opened its first campus near Haystack Mountain, in Montville, Maine, in 1951. Ten years later, when the state unveiled plans to build a new highway (Route 3) that would bisect that campus, the school moved to its present 40-acre oceanfront location at the end of the Sunshine Road in Deer Isle. It was a good move.

You would be hard-pressed to find a more artistically stimulating and architecturally stunning environment. Architect Edward Larrabee Barnes's award-winning campus perfectly complements its dramatic setting. The angular cedar-shingled buildings are connected via walkways and teaching decks and a central staircase that cascades like a waterfall down the wooded hillside to the rocky coast below. The visual impression is one of spruce and ledge, glass and wood, islands and water.

One thing that makes Haystack work is its diverse student body. Students of all abilities, from beginners through advanced professionals, come from around the globe for the 2-3-week summer sessions, taking weekday classes and enjoying round-the-clock studio access to follow their creative muses. In a recent year, students ranged in age 18-75, and in professions from a retired teacher to a physicist. What brings them all here, says current director Stuart Kestenbaum, is the "direct making experience." That experience draws not only those who make but also those who collect. For a collector of fine craft, he says, taking a class is a "great way to get insight into the making process; it gives a different relationship with the craft being collected." Each session also includes a range of crafts. These may include blacksmithing, drawing, metals, wood, beads, clay, fibers, printmaking, glass, weaving, mixed media, paper, and baskets.

been restored and put on display each summer in town—along with a donation box to support the upkeep. The village is set up on East Main Street (Rte. 15), below Hoy Gallery.

Pumpkin Island Light

A fine view of Pumpkin Island Light can be had from the cul-de-sac at the end of the Eggemoggin Road on Little Deer Isle. If heading south on Route 15, bear right at the information booth after crossing the bridge and continue to the end.

ENTERTAINMENT AND EVENTS

Stonington's National Historic Landmark, the 1912 **Opera House** (207/367-2788, www.operahousearts.org), is home to Opera House Arts, which hosts films, plays, lectures, concerts, family programs, and workshops year-round.

Mid-June, when lupines in various shades of pink and purple seem to be blooming everywhere, brings the **Lupine Festival** (207/348-2676 or 207/367-2420), a weekend event that includes art openings and shows, boat rides, a private garden tour, and entertainment ranging from a contra dance to movies.

Early July–early October is the season for **First Friday,** an open-house night held on the first Friday evening of each month, with demonstrations, music, and refreshments sponsored by the Stonington Galleries (www.stonington-galleries.com).

Seamark Community Arts (207/348-2333, www.seamarkcommunityarts.com) hosts arts workshops for children and adults in areas such as book arts, nature crafts, pottery, drawing and painting, film and video, printmaking, basketry, textile arts, and more. The summer highlight is the themed annual auction; in 2010 local artists embellished ornamental goose eggs with that year's theme, "Ovals and Eggs."

Mid-July brings the **Stonington Lobsterboat Races** (207/348-2804), very popular competitions held in the harbor, with lots of possible vantage points. Stonington is one of the major locales in the lobster-boat race circuit.

In mid September is **Peninsula Potters Studio Tour and Sale** (207/348-5681, www.peninsulapotters.com), during which more than a dozen potters from Blue Hill to Stonington welcome visitors.

Want to meet locals and learn more about the area? **Island Heritage Trust** sponsors a series of walks, talks, and tours late May–mid-September. For information and reservations, call 207/348-2455.

◖ ART AND CRAFT GALLERIES

Thanks to the presence and influence of Haystack Mountain School of Crafts, talented artists and artisans lurk in every corner of the island. Most galleries are tucked away on back roads, so watch for roadside signs. Many have studios open to the public where you can watch the artists at work. Here's just a sampling.

North End of Deer Isle

Although **Ronald Hayes Pearson** has died, his innovative and beautiful jewelry lives on in his eponymous studio and gallery (29 Old Ferry Rd., 207/348-2535), where artisans continue to create his designs under the watchful eye of his wife.

The nearby **Greene-Ziner Gallery** (73 Reach Rd., 207/348-2601, www.melissagreene.com) is a double treat. Melissa Greene turns out incredible painted and incised pottery (she's represented in the Smithsonian's Renwick Gallery) and Eric Ziner works magic in metal sculpture and furnishings. Your budget may not allow for one of Melissa's pots (in the four-figure range), but I guarantee you'll covet them. The gallery also displays the work of several other local artists.

Deer Isle Village Area

One of the island's premier galleries is Elena Kubler's **The Turtle Gallery** (61 N. Deer Isle Rd./Rte. 15, 207/348-9977, www.turtlegallery .com), in a handsome space formerly known as the Old Centennial House Barn (owned by the late Haystack director Francis Merritt) and the adjacent farmhouse. Group and solo shows of contemporary paintings, prints, and crafts are hung upstairs and down in the barn; works by gallery artists are in the farmhouse; and there's usually sculpture in the gardens both in front and in back. It's just north of Deer Isle Village, across from the Shakespeare School.

After the death of its founder, Mary Nyburg, the future of the famed **Blue Heron Gallery** (207/348-2267, www.blueherondeerisle.com) was uncertain. Supporters, Haystack alumni, and friends rose to the occasion, and now the gallery is secure, even if its location moves every season. It remains a retail outlet for the work of the school's internationally renowned faculty—printmakers, blacksmiths, potters, weavers, papermakers, glassworkers, and more; it is worth visiting.

The **Pearson Legacy Gallery** (13 Dow Rd., 207/348-6848) exhibits fine craft and contemporary art in rotating exhibitions and also hosts lectures and other events.

In the village, the **Red Dot Gallery** (3 Main St., 207/348-2733, www.reddotgallery.net) shows the works of 10 artists creating in varied media, and the **Deer Isle Artists Association** (5 Main St., Deer Isle, 207/348-2330, www .deerisleartists.com) features two-week exhibits of paintings, prints, drawings, and photos.

Sunshine Road

Now for a bit of whimsy. From Route 15 in Deer Isle Village, take the Sunshine Road east 2.9 miles to **Peter Beerits Sculpture** (600 Sunshine Rd., 800/777-6845, www.nervousnellies.com). The meadows and woods surrounding the studio teem with whimsical wood and metal sculptures, including dragons, Huns on horseback, moose, a blues joint, a western saloon, a general store, and more. The property is also home to Beerits's other enterprise,

© TOM NANGLE

Peter Beerits's whimsical sculptures accent the tea room at Nervous Nellie's.

Nervous Nellie's Jams and Jellies, known for outstandingly creative condiments; sampling is encouraged. The best time to come is 9 A.M.–5 P.M. daily May–early October, when the shop operates the ultra-casual **Mountainville Cafe,** serving tea, coffee, and delicious scones—with, of course, delicious Nervous Nellie's products. Stock up, because they're sold in only a few shops.

Stonington

Cabinetmaker Geoffrey Warner features his work as well as that of other local woodworkers in rotating shows at **Geoffrey Warner Studio** (431 N. Main St., 207/367-6555, www.geoffrey-warnerstudio.com). Warner mixes classic techniques with contemporary styles and Eastern, nature-based, and arts and crafts accents to create some unusual and rather striking pieces. He also crafts the budget-friendly ergonomic Owl stool as well as offering kits and workshops.

Bright and airy **Isalos Fine Art** (Main St., Stonington, 207/367-2700, www.isalosart.com) shows the work of local artists in rotating shows.

Debi Mortenson shows her paintings, photography, and sculptures at **D Mortenson Gallery** (10 W. Main St., 207/367-5875, www.debimortenson.com) year-round.

The **gWatson Gallery** (68 Main St., 207/367-2900) is a fine art gallery representing a number of top-notch artists working in varied media.

More paintings, many in bold, bright colors, can be found at Jill Hoy's **Hoy Gallery** (E. Main St., 207/367-2368, www.jillhoy.com).

A bit off the beaten path but worth seeking out is the **Siri Beckman Studio** (115 Airport Rd., 207/367-5037, www.siribeckman.com), Beckman's home studio-gallery featuring her woodcuts, prints, and watercolors.

SHOPPING

The greatest concentration of shops is in Stonington, where galleries, clothing boutiques, and eclectic shops line Main Street.

Antiques, Books, and Gifts

In "downtown" Deer Isle Village, you'll

find **The Periwinkle** (8 Main St., Deer Isle, 207/348-2256), where Neva Beck carries a fine inventory of Maine books as well as crafts, note cards, and gifts. Look for Neva's hand-braided rugs and chair pads along with her baby quilts.

The eclectic selection at **Bayside Antiques and Gifts** (131 Main St., Stonington, 207/367-8714) includes antiques, decorative accessories, and gifts, but the specialty is quality 18th–19th-century furniture and accessories from the Northeast.

In downtown Stonington, below the Opera House, **Dockside Books & Gifts** (62 W. Main St., Stonington, 207/367-2652) carries just what its name promises, with a specialty in marine and Maine books. The rustic two-room shop has spectacular harbor views.

Janice Glenn's emporium, **Old Schoolhouse Antiques at Burnt Cove** (194 Burnt Cove Rd., Stonington, 207/367-2849, no credit cards), is located across from the grocery store. It's a funky shop jam-packed with vintage clothing, kitchenware (organized by color), textiles, cookbooks, and other collectibles, with an especially nice collection of quilts, rugs, and samplers.

Eclectic Shops

If you're looking for Maine pottery, weaving, metalwork, pewter ware, imported tiles, or walking sticks, go directly to the **Harbor Farm Store** (Rte. 15, Little Deer Isle, 207/348-7755 or 800/342-8003, www.harborfarm.com), one of the state's best gift shops.

At the bottom of the island, **The Seasons of Stonington** (6 Thurlow's Hill Rd., Stonington, 207/367-6348) sells wine, fine foods, art, and other finds.

RECREATION
Parks and Preserves

Foresighted benefactors have managed to set aside precious acreage for respectful public use on Deer Isle. The Nature Conservancy (207/729-5181, www.nature.org) owns two properties, **Crockett Cove Woods Preserve** and **Barred Island Preserve**. The

conscientious steward of other local properties is the **Island Heritage Trust** (420 Sunset Rd., Sunset, 207/348-2455, www.islandheritagetrust.org). At the office, open daily in summer and 1–4 P.M. Wednesday and Friday in winter, you can pick up note cards, photos, T-shirts, and helpful maps and information on hiking trails and nature preserves. Proceeds benefit the Island Heritage Trust's efforts; donations are appreciated.

SETTLEMENT QUARRY

Here's one of the easiest, shortest walks in the area, leading to an impressive vista. From the parking lot on Oceanville Road (just under 1 mile off Rte. 15), marked by a carved granite sign, it's about five minutes to the top of the old quarry, where the viewing platform (a.k.a. the "throne room") takes in the panorama—all the way to the Camden Hills on a good day. In early August, wild raspberries are an additional enticement. Three short loop trails lead into the surrounding woods from here. A map is available in the trailhead box.

EDGAR TENNIS PRESERVE

The 145-acre Tennis Preserve, off the Sunshine Road, has very limited parking, so don't try to squeeze in if there isn't room; schedule your visit for another hour or day. But do go, and bring at least a snack if not a full picnic to enjoy on one of the convenient rocky outcroppings (be sure to carry out what you carry in). Allow at least 90 minutes to enjoy the walking trails, one of which skirts Pickering Cove, providing sigh-producing views. Another trail leads to an old cemetery. Parts of the trails can be wet, so wear appropriate footwear. Bring binoculars for bird-watching. The preserve is open sunrise–sunset. To find it, take the Sunshine Road 2.5 miles to Tennis Road, and follow it to the preserve.

SHORE ACRES PRESERVE

The 38-acre preserve, a gift in 2000 from Judy Hill to the Island Heritage Trust, comprises old farmland, woodlands, clam flats, a salt marsh, and granite shorefront. Three walking

TED AMES, GENIUS

Ted Ames, the man behind the Penobscot East Resource Center and the Lobster Hatchery in Stonington, is a genius. In 2005 he was awarded a $500,000 MacArthur Fellowship. These prestigious "genius grants" are awarded to "talented individuals who have shown extraordinary originality and dedication in their creative pursuits and a marked capacity for self-direction." The foundation credited Ames with fusing "the roles of fisherman and applied scientist in response to increasing threats to the fishery ecosystem resulting from decades of over-harvesting." Criteria for selection are: exceptional creativity, promise for important future advances based on a track record of significant accomplishment, and potential for the fellowship to facilitate subsequent creative work. No question that they found the right guy in Ted Ames.

A humble, soft-spoken man with dogged determination, Ames found little time to bask in the limelight from the award. While he certainly appreciated the money and the attention paid to his causes, the numerous interviews with TV, radio, and newspaper reporters took up valuable time that he would rather use researching fisheries, collecting data, and devising ways to develop community-based fisheries management.

Ames is a fascinating guy, a combination fisherman, lobsterman, and research scientist with deep Maine roots. "My family were some of the original settlers of Vinalhaven," he says. Ancestors on his father's side arrived in 1757 on the island off Rockland in Maine's Mid-Coast. "My mother's side came from Mount Desert," the original settlers on Bartlett's Island. When King George told the family to leave, they refused and stayed put. Ames grew up in a fishing family on Vinalhaven and went on to earn a master's degree in biochemistry from the University of Maine. But fishing was

in his blood, and he eventually returned to the sea as a lobsterman and ground fisherman.

His years on the water gave him firsthand experience watching the changes in Maine's fisheries. He watched Maine's coastal economy change as fishing ports became more gentrified: Commercial piers gave way to oceanfront homes, and marine-related businesses gave way to fancy boutiques. His education combined with his experiences gave him tools and the insight needed to work toward developing new fisheries management practices and supporting fishing communities. He studied fishing patterns in the Gulf of Maine, noting spawning and habitat, and he complemented his research by listening to the stories and experiences of aging fishermen. By doing so, he was able to establish a fishing timeline beginning with historical patterns and following their evolution to current ones.

The Penobscot East Resource Center, which he founded with his wife, Robin, a former marine resources commissioner, and the Lobster Hatchery both are designed as research facilities as well as places for community members and others to learn more about fishing, meet commercial fishermen and women, and learn about their lifestyles in order to help support them and preserve the tradition and the economy. Ames, a master at gaining community support (due perhaps to his impeccable Maine credentials), managed to raise $25,000 from local fishing families, businesses, and individuals in an area not known for wealth.

Ames is using the unrestricted MacArthur Fellows Program money to continue his fisheries research and to develop "community-based groundfishing management to make it sustainable, so coastal fishing communities can survive into the next century. That's a challenge, but we're in the midst of it." There's no better person to be at the forefront than Ted Ames.

trails connect in a 1.5-mile loop, with the Shore Trail section edging Greenlaw Cove. As you walk along the waterfront, look for the islands of Mount Desert rising in the distance and seals basking on offshore ledges. Do not walk across the salt marsh, and try to avoid stepping on beach plants. To find the preserve, take the Sunshine Road 1.2 miles and then bear left at the fork onto Greenlaw District Road. The preserve's parking area is just shy of one mile down the road. Park only in the parking area, not on the paved road.

CROCKETT COVE WOODS PRESERVE

Donated to the Nature Conservancy by benevolent eco-conscious local artist Emily Muir, 98-acre Crockett Cove Woods Preserve is Deer Isle's natural gem—a coastal fog forest laden with lichens and mosses. Four interlinked walking trails cover the whole preserve, starting with a short nature trail. Pick up the helpful map-brochure at the registration box. Wear rubberized shoes or boots, and respect adjacent private property. The preserve is open sunrise–sunset daily year-round. From Deer Isle Village, take Route 15A to Sunset Village. Go 2.5 miles to Whitman Road and then to Fire Lane 88. The local contact phone number is 207/367-2674.

BARRED ISLAND PRESERVE

Owned by the Nature Conservancy but managed by the Island Heritage Trust, Barred Island Preserve was donated by Carolyn Olmsted, grandniece of noted landscape architect Frederick Law Olmsted, who summered nearby. A former owner of Goose Cove Lodge donated an additional 48 acres of maritime boreal fog forest. A single walking trail, one mile long, leads from the parking lot to the point. At low tide, and when eagles aren't nesting, you can continue out to Barred Island. Another trail skirts the shoreline of Goose Cove, before retreating inland and rejoining with the main trail. From a high point on the main trail, you can see more than a dozen islands, many of which are protected from development, as well as Saddleback Ledge Light, 14 miles distant.

To get to the preserve, follow Route 15A to Goose Cove Road and then continue to the parking area on the right. If it's full, return another day.

HOLT MILL POND PRESERVE

The Stonington Conservation Commission administers this town-owned preserve, where more than 47 bird species have been identified (bring binoculars). It comprises four habitats: upland spruce forest, lowland spruce–mixed forest, freshwater marsh, and saltwater marsh. A self-guiding nature trail is accessible off the Airport Road (off Route 15 at the intersection with Lily's Café). Look for the Nature Trail sign just beyond the medical center. The detailed self-guiding trail brochure, available at the trailhead registration kiosk, is accented with drawings by noted artist Siri Beckman.

AMES POND

Ames Pond is neither park nor preserve, but it might as well be. On a back road close to Stonington, it's a mandatory stop in July–August, when the pond wears a blanket of pink and white water lilies. From downtown Stonington, take Indian Point Road just under a mile east to the pond.

CAUSEWAY BEACH AND SCOTT'S LANDING

If you're itching to dip your toes in the water, stop by Causeway Beach along the causeway linking Little Deer Isle to Deer Isle. It's popular for swimming and is also a significant habitat for birds and other wildlife. On the other side of Route 15 is Scott's Landing, with more than 20 acres of fields, trails, and shorefront.

ED WOODSUM PRESERVE AT MARSHALL ISLAND

The Maine Coast Heritage Trust (www.mcht.org) owns 985-acre Marshall Island, the largest undeveloped island on the Eastern Seaboard. Since acquiring it in 2003, the trust has added 10 miles of hiking trails. After exploring, picnic on Sand Cove beach on the southeastern shore. To get there, arrange a trip with Steve Johnson (207/460-8679), who will transport you on weekends for about $140 round trip for two people plus $35 pp per hour for each additional person or hour. Primitive camping is available by reservation (207/729-7366) at designated sites; fires require a permit (207/827-1800).

Sporting Outfitters and Guided Trips

The biggest operation is **Old Quarry Ocean Adventures** (Stonington, 207/367-8977 or 877/479-8977, mobile 207/266-7778, www.oldquarry.com), with a broad range of outdoor adventure choices. Bill Baker's ever-expanding enterprise rents canoes, kayaks, sailboats, bikes, moorings, platform tent sites, and cabins. Bicycle rentals are $22 per day or $110 per week. Sea kayak rentals are $58 per day for a single, $67 for a tandem. Half-day rates (based on a four-hour rental) are $42 and $52, respectively. Overnight 24-hour rental is available for a 10 percent surcharge. Other options include canoes, rowboats, and sailboats; check the website for details. For all boat rentals, you must demonstrate competency in the vessel. They'll deliver and pick up anywhere on the island for a fee of $22. All-day guided tours in single kayaks are $110; tandems are $195. Half-day tours are $60 and $120, respectively. Plenty of other options are available, including sunset tours, family trips, and gourmet picnic paddles.

Overnight kayaking camping trips on nearby islands are led by a Registered Maine Guide. Rates, including meals, begin around $300 per adult for one night, with a three-person minimum. If you're bringing your own kayak, you can park your car ($7 per night up to two nights, $6 per night for three or more nights) and launch from here ($5 per boat for launching); they'll take your trash and any trash you find. Old Quarry is off the Oceanville Road, less than a mile from Route 15, just before you reach the Settlement Quarry preserve. It's well signposted.

Guided Walks

The Island Heritage Trust (402 Sunset Rd., Sunset, 207/348-2455, www.islandheritagetrust.org), along with the Stonington and Deer Isle Conservation Commissions, sponsors a Walks and Talks series. Guided walks cover topics such as "Birds and Bird Calls for Beginners," "The Geology of Deer Isle," and "Migrating Shorebird Walk." Call for information and reservations.

Sea Kayaking

The waters around Deer Isle, with lots of islets and protected coves, are extremely popular for sea kayaking, especially off Stonington.

If you sign up with the **Maine Island Trail Association** (207/761-8225, www.mita.org, $45 per year), you'll receive a handy manual that steers you to more than a dozen islands in the Deer Isle archipelago where you can camp, hike, and picnic—eco-sensitively, please. Boat traffic can be a bit heavy at the height of summer, so to best appreciate the tranquility of this area, try this in September after the Labor Day

© HILARY NANGLE

Explore the islands around Deer Isle and Isle au Haut by sea kayak.

holiday. Nights can be cool, but days are likely to be brilliant. Remember that this is a working harbor.

The six-mile paddle from Stonington to Isle au Haut is best left to experienced paddlers, especially since fishing folks refer to kayakers as "speed bumps."

For equipment rentals or guided trips, **Old Quarry Ocean Adventures** (Stonington, 207/367-8977 or 877/479-8977, mobile 207/266-7778, www.oldquarry.com) is especially helpful and provides many services for kayakers. Old Quarry is off Oceanville Road, less than a mile from Route 15, just before you reach the Settlement Quarry preserve. It's well signposted.

Swimming

The island's only major freshwater swimming hole is the **Lily Pond,** northeast of Deer Isle Village. Just north of the Shakespeare School, turn into the Deer Run Apartments complex. Park and take the path to the pond, which has a shallow area for small children.

Golf and Tennis

About two miles south of Deer Isle Village, watch for the large sign (on the left) for the **Island Country Club** (Rte. 15A, Sunset, 207/348-2379, early June–late Sept.), a nine-hole public course that has been here since 1928. Also at the club are three Har-Tru tennis courts. The club's cheeseburgers and salads are among the island's best bargain lunches.

Excursion Boats
ISLE AU HAUT BOAT COMPANY

If you're not up for self-propulsion, board the *Miss Lizzie,* which departs at 2 P.M. Monday–Saturday mid-June–late August from the Isle au Haut Boat Company (Seabreeze Ave., Stonington, 207/367-5193 or 207/367-6516, www.isleauhaut.com) dock in Stonington for a narrated one-hour trip among the islands; on morning tours, the crew hauls a string of lobster traps. Cost is $18 adults, $9.50 under age 12. Another option is to cruise over and back to Isle au Haut, without stepping foot off the

boat ($19 adults). Reservations are advisable, especially in July–August. Day parking is available at the pier for $4, or find a spot in town and save the surcharge.

(GUIDED ISLAND TOURS

Captain Walter Reed's Guided Island Tours (207/348-6789, www.guidedislandtours.com) aboard the *Gael* are custom designed for a maximum of four passengers. Walt is a Registered Maine Guide and professional biologist who also is a steward for Mark Island Lighthouse and several uninhabited islands in the area. He provides in-depth perspective and the local scoop. The cost is $35 pp for the first hour plus $25 pp for each additional hour (no credit cards); kids under 12 are half price. Reservations are required; box lunches are available for an additional fee.

OLD QUARRY OCEAN ADVENTURES

Yet another aspect of the Old Quarry Ocean Adventures (Stonington, 207/367-8977 or 877/479-8977, mobile 207/266-7778, www.oldquarry.com) empire are sightseeing tours on the *Nigh Duck.* The three-hour trips, one in the morning (9 A.M.–noon) and one in the afternoon (1–4 P.M.), are $40 adults and $26 under age 12. Both highlight the natural history of the area as Captain Bill navigates the boat through the archipelago. Lobster traps are hauled on both trips (but not on Sunday); the morning trip visits Isle au Haut. The afternoon excursion features an island swimming break in a freshwater quarry. Also available is a 1.5-hour sunset cruise, departing half an hour before sunset, for $36 adults and $26 under age 12. And if that's not enough, Old Quarry also offers puffin, lighthouse, whale-watching, and island cruises, with rates beginning at $60 adults, $40 children. Of course, if none of this floats your boat, you can also arrange for a custom charter for $150 per hour.

Old Quarry also offers a number of special trips in conjunction with Island Heritage Trust. Most are noted on Old Quarry's website, but for reservations or more info, call 207/348-2455.

ACCOMMODATIONS
Inns and Bed-and-Breakfasts

Pilgrim's Inn (20 Main St., Deer Isle, 207/348-6615, www.pilgrimsinn.com, early May–mid-Oct., $149–259) is a beautifully restored colonial building and newer cottages overlooking the peaceful Mill Pond. The inn, on the National Register of Historic Places, began life in 1793 as a boardinghouse named The Ark; be sure to check out the fascinating guestbook, with names dating back to 1901. Rates include a full breakfast. The Whale's Rib Tavern serves dinner.

◖ The Inn on the Harbor (45 Main St., Stonington, 207/367-2420 or 800/942-2420, www.innontheharbor.com, $139–225) is exactly as its name proclaims—its expansive deck hangs right over the harbor. Although recently updated, the 1880s complex still has an air of unpretentiousness. Most of the 14 guest rooms and suites, each named after a windjammer, have fantastic harbor views and private or shared decks where you can keep an eye on lobster boats, small ferries, windjammers, and pleasure craft; binoculars are provided. Streetside rooms can be noisy at night. Rates include a continental buffet breakfast. An espresso bar is open 11 A.M.–4:30 P.M. daily. Nearby are antiques, gift, and craft shops; guest moorings are available. The inn is open all year, but call ahead in the off-season, when rates are lower.

In downtown Stonington, just up the hill from the Inn on the Harbor and convenient for walking to everything, even a small sandy beach a mile away, is **Pres du Port** (W. Main St. and Highland Ave., Stonington, 207/367-5007, www.presduport.com, $150, no credit cards), a bright bed-and-breakfast run by amiable innkeeper Charlotte Casgrain. After many summers at a Deer Isle French summer camp and a career as a Connecticut French teacher, she's settled here. Three guest rooms have detached baths, and one has a private bath; there are vanity sinks in the rooms. Children are welcome, and there's even a toy cupboard to entertain them. Adults can relax in the water-view hot tub or climb to Charlotte's Folly, a rooftop lookout, for the extensive views.

Eggemoggin Reach is almost on the doorstep at **The Inn at Ferry Landing** (77 Old Ferry Rd., Deer Isle, 207/348-7760, www.ferrylanding.com, $130–185), overlooking the abandoned Sargentville–Deer Isle ferry wharf. The view is wide open from the inn's great room, where guests gather to read, play games, talk, and watch passing windjammers. Professional musician Gerald Wheeler has installed two grand pianos in the room; it's a treat when he plays. His wife, Jean, is the hospitable innkeeper, managing three waterview guest rooms and a suite. A harpsichord and a great view are big pluses in the suite. The Mooring, an annex that sleeps five, is rented by the week ($1,700 without breakfast). The inn is open year-round except Thanksgiving and Christmas; Wi-Fi is available throughout.

Motels

Right in downtown Stonington, just across the street from the harbor, is **Boyce's Motel** (44 Main St., Stonington, 207/367-2421 or 800/224-2421, www.boycesmotel.com, year-round, $69–135). Eleven units all have TVs, phones, and refrigerators; some have kitchens and living rooms, and one has two bedrooms. Across the street, Boyce's has a private harborfront deck for its guests. Ask for rooms well back from Main Street to lessen the noise of locals cruising the street at night.

Hostels

In 2009 the rustic, bordering on primitive **Deer Isle Hostel** (65 Tennis Rd., Deer Isle, 207/348-2308, www.deerislehostel.com, $25 adults, $15 under age 12, no credit cards) opened near the Tennis Preserve. Owner Dennis Carter, a Surry, Maine, native and local stoneworker and carpenter, modeled it on The Hostel in the Forest in Brunswick, Georgia. It's completely off the grid, with a pump in the kitchen for water and an outhouse. Carter expects guests to work in the extensive organic gardens, using produce for shared meals prepared on a wood stove, the sole source of heat. The three-story timber-frame design is taken from a late-17th-century home in Massachusetts. Carter hand-cut the granite for the basement, and the timbers in the nail-free frame are hand-hewn from local blown-down spruce. The goal is sustainability, not profit.

Camping

Plan ahead if you want to camp at **Old Quarry Ocean Adventures Campground** (130 Settlement Rd., Stonington, 207/367-8977, www.oldquarry.com), with both oceanfront and secluded platform sites for tents and just three RV sites. Rates range $38–50 for two people, plus $17 for each additional adult, varying with location and hookups. Children under age 12 are $6, and under age 5 are free. Leashed pets are permitted ($2). Parking is designed so that vehicles are kept away from most campsites, but you can use a garden cart to transport your equipment between your car and your site. The campground is adjacent to Settlement Quarry Park.

FOOD

As always, hours are listed for peak season; call to verify days and hours of operation. Stonington restaurants suffer from a lack of consistency. One night the food and service might be fine, the next not so. Patience is more than a virtue here; it's a necessity.

Local Flavors

After browsing the shops, you just might need a double-dip cone from **Harbor Ice Cream,** across the street from the Periwinkle in Deer Isle Village, or **Stonington Cow Ice Cream,** on the main drag in Stonington.

Craving sweets? Head to **Susie Q's Sweets and Curiosities** (40 School St., Stonington, 207/367-2415, 8 A.M.–3 P.M. Wed.–Mon.). Susan Scott bakes a fine selection of cookies and pies, offers a limited selection of breakfast and lunch choices (including homemade doughnuts), and also carries antiques, books, quilts, toys, and other fun items. It's a Wi-Fi hotspot.

Burnt Cove Market (Rte. 15, Stonington, 207/367-2681, 6 A.M.–9 P.M. Mon.–Sat.,

9 A.M.–9 P.M. Sun.) sells pizza, fried chicken, and sandwiches, plus beer and wine.

Creativity defines the menu at ◖ **Lily's Cafe and Wine Bar** (450 Airport Rd. at Rte. 15, Stonington, 207/367-5936, 7 A.M.–5 P.M. Mon.–Thurs., 7 A.M.–8 P.M. Fri.), mercifully expanded in 2008. It's all very casual; order at the counter and find a table either inside, on the upstairs deck, or outside in the garden. Or assemble an haute gourmet picnic from veggie and meat sandwiches, Mediterranean salads, cheeses, and homemade soups and breads. Upstairs is the Chef's Attic, with a smattering of antiques as well as works by local artists. Alas, it's closed on weekends. Beer and wine are served. Most lunch entrées are about $9.

The Island Community Center (6 Memorial Lane, just off School St., Stonington) is the locale for the lively **Island Farmers Market** (10 A.M.–noon Fri. late May–late Sept.), selling smoked and organic meats, fresh herbs and flowers, produce, gelato and yogurt, maple syrup, jams and jellies, fabulous breads and baked goods, chocolates, ethnic foods, crafts, and so much more. Go early; items sell out quickly.

Family Favorites

Harbor Cafe (Main St., Stonington, 207/367-5099, 6 A.M.–8 P.M. Mon.–Thurs., 6 A.M.–9 P.M. Fri.–Sat., 6 A.M.–2 P.M. Sun., $5–20) is *the* place to go for breakfast (you can eavesdrop on the local fisherfolk if you're early enough), but it's also reliable for lunch and dinner (especially on Friday nights for the seafood fry, with free seconds).

The views are top-notch from the harbor-front **Fisherman's Friend Restaurant** (5 Atlantic Ave., Stonington, 207/367-2442, 11 A.M.–9 P.M. Sun.–Thurs., 11 A.M.–10 P.M. Fri.–Sat. early May–late Oct.). The restaurant gets turns out decent fried food, generous portions, ultrafresh seafood, and outstanding desserts, but it seems to have lost its soul when it moved from its old digs to this larger and more modern space. Still, where else can you get lobster prepared 30 different ways? Prices are reasonable—the Friday-night fish fry, with free seconds, is around $10.

Casual Dining

The **Whale's Rib Tavern** (20 Main St./Sunset Rd., Deer Isle Village, 207/348-5222, $18–25) is a comfy white-tablecloth tavern in the lower level of the Pilgrim's Inn. It's open for dinner, with nights varying in season; call for details.

You have a front-row seat—and a comfortable one at that—for all the harbor action at **The Seasons of Stonington Restaurant and Bakery** (27 Main St., Stonington, 207/367-2600, www.seasonsofstonington.com, 8 A.M.–8:30 P.M. daily, $18–25). Big windows frame the harbor from the dining room, and there's also lunch seating on the harbor-side deck. The menu emphasizes seafood (no surprise), but there are other choices and always a vegetarian selection. There's also seating on the harbor-hugging deck, although service tends to be slower there.

INFORMATION AND SERVICES

The **Deer Isle-Stonington Chamber of Commerce** (207/348-6124, www.deerisle-maine.com) has a summer information booth on a grassy triangle on Route 15 in Little Deer Isle, 0.25 miles after crossing the bridge from Sargentville (Sedgwick).

Across from the Pilgrim's Inn is the **Chase Emerson Memorial Library** (Main St., Deer Isle Village, 207/348-2899). At the tip of the island is the **Stonington Public Library** (Main St., Stonington, 207/367-5926).

Public Restrooms

Public restrooms are at the Atlantic Avenue Hardware pier and at the Stonington Town Hall on Main Street; at the Chase Emerson Library in Deer Isle Village; and behind the information booth on Little Deer Isle.

Isle au Haut

Eight miles off Stonington lies 4,700-acre Isle au Haut, roughly half of which belongs to Acadia National Park. Pronounced variously as "aisle-a-HO" or "AISLE-a-ho," the island has nearly 20 miles of hiking trails, excellent bird-watching, and a tiny village.

About 60 souls call 5,800-acre Isle au Haut home year-round, most of them eking out a living from the sea. Each summer, the population temporarily swells with day-trippers, campers, and cottagers—then settles back in fall to the measured pace of life on an offshore island.

Samuel de Champlain, threading his way through this archipelago in 1605 and noting the island's prominent central ridge, came up with the name of Isle au Haut—High Island. Appropriately, the tallest peak (543 feet) is now named Mount Champlain.

More recent fame has come to the island thanks to island-based author Linda Greenlaw, of *Perfect Storm* fame, who wrote *The Lobster Chronicles*. Although that book piqued interest,

Isle au Haut remains uncrowded and well off the beaten tourist track.

Most of the southern half of the six-mile-long island belongs to Acadia National Park, thanks to the wealthy summer visitors who began arriving in the 1880s. It was their heirs who, in the 1940s, donated valuable acreage to the federal government. Today, this offshore division of the national park has a well-managed 18-mile network of trails, a few lean-tos, several miles of unpaved road, and summertime passenger-ferry service to the park entrance.

In the island's northern half are the private residences of fisherfolk and summer folk, a minuscule village (including a market and a post office), a five-mile paved road, and a lighthouse. The only vehicles on the island are owned by residents.

If spending the night on Isle au Haut sounds appealing (it is), you'll need to plan well ahead; it's no place for spur-of-the-moment sleepovers (even spontaneous day trips aren't always possible). The best part about staying overnight

© HILARY NANGLE

Isle au Haut's lighthouse, built in 1907, is now listed on the National Historic Register.

on Isle au Haut is that you'll have so much more than seven hours to enjoy this idyllic island.

◖ ACADIA NATIONAL PARK

Mention Acadia National Park, and most people think of Bar Harbor and Mount Desert Island, where more than 3 million visitors arrive each year. The Isle au Haut section of the park sees maybe 5,000 visitors per year—partly because only 48 people per day (not counting campers) are allowed to land here. But the remoteness of the island and the scarcity of beds and campsites also contribute to the low count.

Near the town landing, where the year-round mail boat and another boat dock, is the **Park Ranger Station** (207/335-5551), where you can pick up trail maps and park information—and use the island's only public toilets. Do yourself a favor, though: Make your plans by downloading Isle au Haut maps and information from the Acadia National Park website, www.nps.gov/acad.

Hiking

Hiking on Acadia National Park trails is the major recreation on Isle au Haut, and even in the densest fog you'll see valiant hikers going for it. A loop road circles the whole island; an unpaved section goes through the park, connecting with the mostly paved nonpark section. Walking on that is easy. Beyond the road, none of the park's 18 miles of trails could be labeled "easy"; the footing is rocky, rooty, and often squishy. But the park trails are well marked, and the views—of islets, distant hills, and the ocean—make the effort worthwhile. Go prepared with proper footwear.

The most-used park trail is the four-mile one-way **Duck Harbor Trail,** connecting the town landing with Duck Harbor. You can either use this trail or follow the island road—mostly unpaved in this stretch—to get to the campground when the summer ferry ends its Duck Harbor runs.

Even though the summit is only 314 feet, **Duck Harbor Mountain** is the island's toughest trail. Still, it's worth the 1.2-mile one-way effort for the stunning 360-degree views from the summit. Option: Rather than return via the trail's steep, bouldery sections, cut off at the Goat Trail and return to the trailhead that way.

For terrific shoreline scenery, take **Western Head Trail** and **Cliff Trail** at the island's southwestern corner. They form a nice loop around Western Head. The route follows the coastline, ascending to ridges and cliffs and descending to rocky beaches, with some forested sections. Options: Close the loop by returning via the Western Head Road. If the tide is out (and only if it's out), you can walk across the tidal flats to the quaintly named Western Ear for views back toward the island. Western Ear is privately owned, so don't linger. The **Goat Trail** adds another four miles (round-trip) of moderate coastline hiking east of the Cliff Trail; views are fabulous and bird-watching is good, but if you're here only for a day, you'll need to decide whether there's time to do this and still catch the return mail boat. If you do have the time and the energy, you can connect from the Goat Trail to the **Duck Harbor Mountain Trail.**

Cycling is one way to get around Isle au Haut.

© HILARY NANGLE

OTHER RECREATION

Biking

Pedaling is limited to the 12 or so miles of mostly unpaved, hilly roads, and while it is a way to get around, frankly the terrain is neither exciting, fun, nor view-worthy. Mountain bikes are not allowed on the park's hiking trails, and rangers try to discourage park visitors from bringing them to the island. If you're staying at the Inn at Isle au Haut, you can borrow a bike, which is handy around the "village" and for going swimming in Long Pond. You can also rent a bike on the island from the Isle au Haut Ferry Service or Old Quarry Ocean Adventures. It costs $20 round-trip to bring your own bike aboard the Isle au Haut Ferry. Both boats carry bikes only to the town landing, not to Duck Harbor.

Swimming

For superb **freshwater swimming,** head for Long Pond, a skinny 1.5-mile-long swimming hole running north–south on the east side of the island, abutting national park land. You can bike over there, clockwise along the road, almost five miles, from the town landing. Or bum a ride from an island resident. There's a minuscule beach-like area on the southern end with a picnic table and a float. If you're here only for the day, though, there's not enough time to do this and get in a long hike. Opt for the hiking—or do a short hike and then go for a swim. The shallowest part is at the southern tip.

ACCOMMODATIONS AND FOOD

Options for food are extremely limited on Isle au Haut, so if you're coming for a day trip, bring sufficient food and water.

Inn

On the east side of the island is **The Inn at Isle au Haut** (Lighthouse Point, Isle au Haut, off-island 207/335-5141, www.innatisleauhaut.com, early June–late Sept., $300–375), a mansard-roofed waterfront Victorian home that Diana Santospago has turned into an inn.

An accomplished cook, Diana whips up fabulous breakfasts, lunches, and dinners for her guests; bring your own beer or wine. The inn is open to nonguests for dinner by reservation. The downstairs guest room with a private bath is the most spacious. Three rather small guest rooms on the second floor share one bath; all but one have water views. Single-speed bikes are provided for guests, and it's an easy pedal to Long Pond for swimming or to connect with park trails. Special early- and late-summer packages at the inn include cruises, tours, and cooking classes with Linda Greenlaw.

Camping

You'll need to get your bid in early to reserve one of the five six-person lean-tos at the national park's **Duck Harbor Campground,** the only camping on Isle au Haut, open May 15–October 15. Before April 1, contact the park (Acadia National Park, 207/288-3338, www.nps.gov/acad) for a reservation request form. From April 1 (not before, or the park people will send it back to you), return the completed form along with a check for $25 to reserve camping for up to six people for a maximum of five nights May 15–June 14, three nights June 15–September 15, and five nights September 16–October 15. Mark the envelope "Attn: Isle au Haut Reservations." Competition is stiff in the height of summer, so list alternate dates. The park refunds the check if there's no space; otherwise it's nonrefundable, and you'll receive a "special-use permit" (do not forget to bring it along). There's no additional fee for camping.

Unless you don't mind backpacking nearly five miles to reach the campground, try to plan your visit mid-June–Labor Day, when the mail boat makes a stop at Duck Harbor. It's wise to call the Isle au Haut Company for the current ferry schedule before choosing dates for a lean-to reservation.

The trash policy is carry-in, carry-out, so pack a trash bag or two with your gear. Also bring a container for carting water from the campground pump, since it's 0.3 miles from the lean-tos. It's a longish walk to the general store for food, when you could be better spending your time hiking the island's trails, so bring enough food to cover your stay.

The three-sided lean-tos are big enough (8 by 12 feet, 8 feet high) to hold a small (two-person) tent, so bring one along if you prefer being fully enclosed. A tarp will also do the trick. Also bring mosquito repellent—some years, the critters show up en masse. No camping is permitted outside of the lean-tos, and nothing can be attached to trees.

Food

Isle au Haut is pretty much a BYO place—and for the most part, that means BYO food. Although the Inn at Isle au Haut is open to nonguests for dinner by reservation, you need to get there and back, only possible if you're staying in a rental cottage with a car.

Thanks to the seasonal **Isle au Haut General Store** (207/335-5211, www.theisland-store.net), less than a five-minute walk from the town landing, you won't starve. The inventory isn't extensive, but it can be intriguing due to the store manager, who travels worldwide and stocks the shop with her finds. On the other hand, food probably won't be your prime interest here—the island itself is as good as it gets.

Even more intriguing is **Black Dinah Chocolatiers** (207/335-5010, www.blackdi-nahchocolatiers.com), just shy of a mile from the town landing. Steve and Kate Shaffer's little shop doubles as a café, serving pastries, organic coffees and teas, a few lunch-type offerings, and, of course, decadent handmade chocolates. It also has free Wi-Fi. If you can't get to Isle au Haut, look for Black Dinah chocolates at area farmers markets.

GETTING THERE
Isle au Haut Boat Company

The Isle au Haut Boat Company (Seabreeze Ave., Stonington, 207/367-5193, www.isleau-haut.com) generally operates five daily trips Monday–Saturday, plus two on Sunday, mid-June–early September. Other months, there are 2–3 trips Monday–Saturday.

Round-trips April–mid-October are $36 adults, $19 under age 12 (two bags per adult, one bag per child). Round-trip surcharges include bikes ($20), kayaks and canoes ($40 minimum), and pets ($8). If you're considering bringing a bike, be sure to inquire about on-island bike rentals ($25 per day). Weather seldom affects the schedule, but be aware that storms or very heavy seas could cancel a trip.

There is twice-daily ferry service mid-June–Labor Day from Stonington to Duck Harbor, at the edge of Isle au Haut's Acadia National Park campground. For a day trip, the schedule allows you 6.5 hours on the island Monday–Saturday and 4.5 hours on Sunday. No boats or bikes are allowed on this route, and no dogs are allowed in the campground. A ranger boards the boat at the town landing and goes along to Duck Harbor to answer questions and distribute maps. Before mid-June and after Labor Day, you'll be off-loaded at the Isle au Haut town landing, about five miles from Duck Harbor. The six-mile passage from Stonington

to the Isle au Haut town landing takes 45 minutes; the trip to Duck Harbor is 75 minutes.

Ferries depart from the Isle au Haut Boat Company dock (Seabreeze Ave., off E. Main St. in downtown Stonington). Parking ($9 per day outside, $11 indoors) is available next to the ferry landing.

Old Quarry Ocean Adventures

The new kid on the block offering seasonal service to Isle au Haut, Old Quarry Ocean Adventures (Stonington, 207/367-8977 or 877/479-8977, mobile 207/266-7778, www.oldquarry.com) transports passengers on the renovated *Nigh Duck*. The boat usually leaves Old Quarry at 9 A.M. and arrives at the island's town landing one hour later. It departs from the same point at 5 P.M., arriving back at Old Quarry around 6 P.M. The fare is $35 round-trip for adults, $18 under age 12. You can add an island bike rental for an additional $22. Old Quarry also offers a taxi service to Isle au Haut for $150 per hour for up to six people.

ACADIA REGION

Summer folk have been visiting Mount Desert Island (MDI) for millennia. The earliest Native Americans discovered fabulous fishing and clamming, good hunting and camping, and invigorating salt air. Today's arrivals find variations on the same theme: thousands of lodgings and campsites, hundreds of restaurant seats, dozens of shops, plus 40,000 acres of Acadia National Park.

It's no coincidence that artists were a large part of the 19th-century vanguard here: The dramatic landscape, with both bare and wooded mountains descending to the sea, still inspires everyone who sees it. Once the word got out, painterly images began confirming the reports, and the surge began. Even today, no saltwater locale on the entire Eastern Seaboard can compete with the variety of scenery on Mount Desert Island.

Those pioneering artists brilliantly portrayed this area, adding romantic touches to landscapes that really need no enhancement. From the 1,530-foot summit of Cadillac Mountain, preferably at an off hour, you'll sense the grandeur of it all—the slopes careening toward the bay and the handful of islands below looking like the last footholds between Bar Harbor and Bordeaux.

For nearly four centuries, controversy has raged about the pronunciation of the island's name, and we won't resolve it here. French explorer Samuel de Champlain apparently gets credit for naming it l'Ile des Monts Deserts, "island of bare mountains," when he sailed by in 1604. The accent in French would be on the second syllable, but today "De-SERT" and "DES-ert" both have their advocates,

© TOM NANGLE

HIGHLIGHTS

(Park Loop Road: If you do nothing else on Mount Desert, drive this magnificent road that takes in many of Acadia National Park's highlights (page 302).

(The Carriage Roads: Whether you walk, bike, or ride in a horse-drawn carriage, make it a point to see Mr. Rockefeller's roads and bridges (page 302).

(Jordan Pond House: For more than a century, afternoon tea and popovers on the lawn of the Jordan Pond House have been a tradition. Make reservations for an afternoon pick-me-up, perhaps after walking or biking the many carriage roads that lead here (page 307).

(Abbe Museum: The downtown Abbe Museum and its seasonal museum at Sieur de Monts Springs are fascinating places to while away a few hours and learn about Maine's Native American heritage (page 307).

(Oceanarium: A fabulous introduction to the coastal ecology is provided at this low-tech, kid-friendly site (page 310).

(Dive-In Theater Boat Cruise: Got kids? Don't miss this tour, where Diver Ed brings the undersea world aboard (page 315).

(Asticou Azalea Garden and Thuya Garden: Magical and enchanting best describes these two peaceful gardens. While Zen-like Asticou is best seen in spring, Thuya delivers color through summer and also has hiking paths (page 324).

(Wendell Gilley Museum: Gilley's intricately carved birds, from miniature shorebirds to life-size birds of prey, are a marvel to behold (page 330).

(Island Cruises: Kim Strauss shares his deep knowledge of island ways and waters on the lunchtime cruise that allows time to explore Frenchboro (page 333).

(Schoodic Loop: An ultra-scenic six-mile road, the loop edges the pink-granite shores of Acadia National Park's only mainland section and accesses hiking trails and picnic spots (page 346).

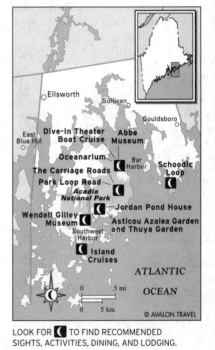

LOOK FOR (TO FIND RECOMMENDED SIGHTS, ACTIVITIES, DINING, AND LODGING.

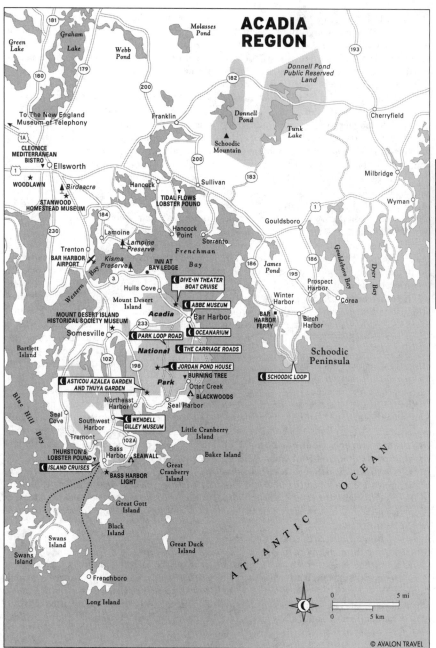

ACADIA REGION

Green Lake
Graham Lake
Webb Pond
Molasses Pond

Donnell Pond Public Reserved Land

Cherryfield

Franklin

Donnell Pond

Tunk Lake

Schoodic Mountain

Milbridge

To The New England Museum of Telephony

CLEONICE MEDITERRANEAN BISTRO
Ellsworth

WOODLAWN
Birdsacre
STANWOOD HOMESTEAD MUSEUM

Hancock
Sullivan

TIDAL FLOWS LOBSTER POUND

Wyman

Lamoine
Hancock Point
Sorrento
Frenchman
Bay

Gouldsboro

Lamoine Preserve

Trenton
Kisma Preserve
BAR HARBOR AIRPORT

INN AT BAY LEDGE

James Pond
Prospect Harbor
Corea

Hulls Cove

DIVE-IN THEATER BOAT CRUISE

Winter Harbor
Birch Harbor

Mount Desert Island

ABBE MUSEUM
Bar Harbor

MOUNT DESERT ISLAND HISTORICAL SOCIETY MUSEUM
Acadia

BAR HARBOR FERRY

Somesville
PARK LOOP ROAD
OCEANARIUM

Bartlett Island
National
THE CARRIAGE ROADS

Schoodic Peninsula

Park
JORDAN POND HOUSE

SCHOODIC LOOP

ASTICOU AZALEA GARDEN AND THUYA GARDEN
BURNING TREE
Otter Creek
BLACKWOODS

Blue Hill Bay
Northeast Harbor
Seal Harbor

Seal Cove
Southwest Harbor
WENDELL GILLEY MUSEUM
Little Cranberry Island

Tremont
Bass Harbor
SEAWALL
Great Cranberry Island
Baker Island

THURSTON'S LOBSTER POUND
ISLAND CRUISES
BASS HARBOR LIGHT

Great Gott Island

Black Island
Great Duck Island

ATLANTIC   OCEAN

Swans Island

Swans Island

Frenchboro

Long Island

ATLANTIC

0   5 mi
0   5 km

© AVALON TRAVEL

although the former gets the accuracy nod. In any case, the island is anything but deserted today. Even as you approach it, via the shire town of **Ellsworth** and especially in **Trenton,** you'll run the gauntlet of big box stores, amusements, and enough high-cholesterol eateries to stun the surgeon general. Don't panic: Acadia National Park lies ahead, and amidst the thick of consumer congestion there are glimpses of the prize. Even on the most crowded days, if you venture more than a few steps into the park, you'll find you have it nearly to yourself.

As you drive or bike around Mount Desert—vaguely shaped like a lobster claw and indented by Somes Sound (the only fjord on the U.S. East Coast)—you'll cross and recross the national-park boundaries, reminders that Acadia National Park, covering a third of the island, is indeed the major presence here. It affects traffic, indoor and outdoor pursuits, and, in a way, even the climate.

The other major presence is **Bar Harbor,** largest and best known of the island's communities. It's the source of just about anything you could want, from T-shirts to tacos, books to bike rentals. The contrast with Acadia is astonishing as the park struggles to maintain its image and character. And yet, even in Bar Harbor, the park's presence is felt.

Bar Harbor shares the island with **Southwest Harbor, Tremont,** and a number of small villages: **Bass Harbor, Bernard, Northeast Harbor, Seal Harbor, Otter Creek, Somesville,** and **Hall Quarry.** From Bass, Northeast, and Southwest Harbors, private and state ferries shuttle bike and foot traffic to offshore **Swans Island, Frenchboro** (Long Island), and the **Cranberry Isles** (and cars to Swans Island).

Stay on Route 1 instead of taking Route 3 to the island and the congestion disappears. The towns lining the eastern shore of Frenchman Bay—**Hancock, Sullivan, Winter Harbor,** and **Gouldsboro**—have some of the best views of all: front-row seats facing the peaks of Mount Desert Island. It's no wonder many artists and artisans make their homes here. And at the tip of the **Schoodic Peninsula,** a stunning pocket of Acadia National Park sees only a fraction of the visitors who descend on the main part of the park.

PLANNING YOUR TIME

So much to do, so little time—that's the lament of most visitors. While you can circumnavigate Mount Desert Island in a day, hitting the highlights along the Park Loop with just enough time to ooh and aah at each, to appreciate Acadia you need time to hike the trails, ride the carriage roads, get afloat on a whale-watching cruise or a sea kayak, visit museums, and explore an offshore island or two. A week or longer is best, but you can get a taste of Acadia in 3–4 days.

The region is very seasonal, with most restaurants, accommodations, and shops open mid-May–mid-October. May and June bring the new greens of spring and blooming rhododendrons and azaleas in Northeast Harbor's Asticou Garden, but mosquitoes and blackflies are at their worst and weather is temperamental—perhaps sunny and hot one day, damp and cold the next, a packing nightmare. July and August bring summer at its best, along with the biggest crowds. September is a gem of a time to visit: no bugs, fewer people, less fog, and the golden light of fall. Foliage usually begins turning in early October, making it an especially beautiful time to visit (the Columbus Day holiday weekend brings a spike in visitors). Winter is Acadia's silent season, best left for independent travelers who don't mind making do or perhaps making a meal of peanut-butter crackers if an open restaurant can't be found.

The only way onto Mount Desert Island is Route 3. Unless you're traveling in the wee hours of the morning or late at night, expect traffic. Avoid it during shift changes on-island, 8–9 A.M. and 3–4 P.M. weekdays, when traffic slows to a crawl. On the island, use the Island Explorer bus system to avoid parking hassles.

Ellsworth

The punch line to an old Maine joke is "Ya cahn't get they-ah from he-ah." The truth is, you can't get to Acadia without going through Ellsworth and Trenton. Indeed, when you're crawling along in bumper-to-bumper traffic, it might seem as if all roads lead to downtown Ellsworth. And the truth is that many do. Route 1, the main thoroughfare along the coast, and Route 1A, which connects to Bangor, meet in downtown Ellsworth. Route 172 leads to the Blue Hill Peninsula and on to Deer Isle, Stonington, and the mail boat to Isle au Haut. Route 1 continues north, providing access to the Schoodic Peninsula and a remote section of the park. And the Bar Harbor Road (Rte. 3) is something of an Achilles heel—often a summertime bottleneck as it funnels all traffic to Mount Desert Island.

While there are ways to skirt around a few of the worst bottlenecks, the region does have its calling cards. Ellsworth, Hancock County's shire town, has mushroomed with the popularity of Acadia National Park, but you can still find handsome architectural remnants of the city's 19th-century lumbering heyday (which began shortly after its incorporation in 1800). Brigs, barks, and full-rigged ships—built in Ellsworth and captained by local fellows—loaded lumber here and carried it around the globe. Despite a ruinous 1855 fire that swept through downtown, the lumber trade thrived until late in the 19th century, along with factories and mills turning out shoes, bricks, boxes, and butter.

These days, Ellsworth is the region's shopping mecca. Antiques shops and small stores line Main Street, which doubles as Route 1 in the downtown section; supermarkets, strip malls, and big-box stores line Routes 1 and 3 between Ellsworth and Trenton.

One more plus for the area is the Bar Harbor Chamber of Commerce Information Center, on Route 3 in Trenton. If you're day-tripping to Mount Desert Island, you can leave your car here and hop aboard the free Island Explorer bus, eliminating driving and parking hassles.

SIGHTS
Woodlawn

Very little has changed at the Woodlawn (Surry Rd./Rte. 172, 207/667-8671, www.woodlawnmuseum.com, 10 A.M.–5 P.M. Tues.–Sat., 1–4 P.M. Sun. June–Sept., 1–4 P.M. Tues.–Sun. May and Oct., $10 adults, $3 ages 5–12, grounds free) since George Nixon Black donated his home, also known as "the Black Mansion," to the town in 1928. Completed in 1828, the Georgian house is a marvel of preservation—one of Maine's best—filled with Black family antiques and artifacts. Enthusiastic docents lead hour-long tours, beginning on the hour, to point out the circular staircase, rare books and artifacts, canopied beds, a barrel organ, and lots more. Afterward, plan to picnic on the manicured grounds, then explore two sleigh-filled barns, the Memorial Garden, and the two miles of mostly level trails in the woods up beyond the house. Consider timing

ACADIA REGION

Ellsworth City Hall is a local landmark.

© TOM NANGLE

a visit to one of the frequent events: There's a farmers market on Sunday, golf croquet tournaments on Tuesday afternoon ($5), and on several Wednesday afternoons in July–August there are elegant teas in the garden (or in the carriage house if it's raining), with china, silver, linens, special-blend tea, sandwiches, pastries, and live music—all for $20 pp; reservations are required. On Route 172, a quarter mile southwest of Route 1, watch for the small sign and turn into the winding uphill driveway.

Birdsacre

En route to Bar Harbor, watch carefully on the right for the sign that marks Birdsacre (Rte. 3, Bar Harbor Rd., 207/667-8460, www.birdsacre .com), a 200-acre urban sanctuary. Wander the trails in this peaceful preserve, spotting wildflowers, birds, and well-labeled shrubs and trees, and you'll have trouble believing you're surrounded by prime tourist territory. One trail, a boardwalk loop through woods behind the nature center, is wheelchair- and stroller-accessible. The sanctuary is open sunrise–sunset daily. At the sanctuary entrance is the 1850 **Stanwood Homestead Museum,** with period furnishings and wildlife exhibits. Once owned by noted ornithologist Cordelia Stanwood, the volunteer-operated museum is open for tours by chance or by appointment mid-May–mid-October. Admission to the preserve and the homestead is free, but donations are needed and are greatly appreciated. Birdsacre is also a wildlife rehabilitation center, so expect to see all kinds of winged creatures, especially hawks and owls, in various stages of rescue. Some will be returned to the wild while others remain here for educational purposes. Stop by the Nature Center for even more exhibits.

Kisma Preserve

I can't stress this enough: Kisma Preserve (446 Bar Harbor Rd./Rte. 3, Trenton, 207/667-3244, www.kismapreserve.org, 9:30 A.M.–dusk daily mid-May–late fall, $16 adults, $13 children) is not a zoo; it's a nonprofit educational facility, and everything revolves around preserving and protecting the animals, most of

which are either rescues or retirees. Rules are strictly enforced—no running, loud voices, or disruptive behavior are permitted. The only way to view the animals is on a guided tour. Guides educate visitors about the biology of the animals, how they came to be here, and whether they'll be returned to the wild. For serious animal lovers, the preserve offers behind-the-scenes tours and close-ups for fees beginning around $20 pp; there are even options for staying in the preserve overnight. It truly is a special place, with more than 100 exotic and not-so-exotic creatures—reindeer, bison, wolves, moose, big cats, and more. Donations are essential to Kisma's survival, and yes, it's pricey, but so is feeding and caring for these animals.

The New England Museum of Telephony

What was life like before cell phones or touch-tone dialing? Find out at the New England Museum of Telephony (166 Winkumpaugh Rd., 207/667-9491, www.thetelephonemuseum .org, 1–4 P.M. Thurs.–Sun. July–late Sept., $5 adults, $2.50 children), a hands-on museum with the largest collection of old-fashioned switching systems in the East, including many from Maine. Place a call to see how these old systems work. To find the museum, head 10 miles north on Route 1A toward Bangor, then go left on Winkumpaugh Road for one mile.

Downeast Scenic Railroad

All Aboard! The all-volunteer **Downeast Rail Heritage Preservation Trust** (800/449-7245, www.downeastscenicrail.org) has restored a 1948 diesel engine and rehabilitated the tracks between Ellsworth–Washington Junction and Green Lake. On Saturday and Sunday you can board the passenger car or caboose for a 10-mile, 90-minute scenic excursion ($12–17 adults, $8–13 ages 4–12).

Flightseeing

Two businesses provide a variety of ways to get an eagle's-eye view of the area. Both are based on the Route 3 side of Hancock County/Bar Harbor

Airport, just north of Mount Desert Island, and 12 miles north of downtown Bar Harbor.

Scenic Flights of Acadia (Bar Harbor Rd./ Rte. 3, Trenton, 207/667-6527, www.scenic-flightsofacadia.com) offers low-level flightseeing services in the Mount Desert Island region. Flights range 22–60 minutes and begin around $50 pp with a two-passenger minimum.

Scenic Biplane and Glider Rides (968 Bar Harbor Rd./Rte. 3, Trenton, 207/667-7627, www.acadiaairtours.com) lets you soar in silence with daily glider flights. The one- or two-passenger gliders are towed to an altitude of at least 2,500 feet and then released. An FAA-certified pilot guides the glider. Rates begin at $219 for a 20-minute flight for two, $149 for one. Or ride in a biplane: A 20-minute ride in an open-cockpit plane is $225 for two, $175 for one. All flights are subject to an airport fee.

ENTERTAINMENT

Ellsworth has three free summer series. The **Ellsworth Concert Band** performs Wednesday evenings in the plaza outside Ellsworth City Hall. If it rains, it's held inside City Hall. Practice begins at 6:30 P.M., concerts start at 8 P.M., and the 50-member community band even welcomes visitors with talent and instruments—just show up at practice time. **Outdoor family movies** (www.ellswortharts.org) are shown at sunset Thursday on the lawn of the Knowlton School. **Concerts** (www.downtownellsworth.com) are staged at Harbor Parks at 6 P.M. on Friday.

Ace lumberjack "Timber" Tina Scheer has been competing around the world since she was seven, and she shows her prowess at **The Great Maine Lumberjack Show** (Rte. 3, 207/667-0067, www.mainelumberjack.com, 7 P.M. daily mid-June–early Sept., 4 P.M. Sat. and 2 P.M. Sun. early Sept.–mid Oct., $9.50 adults, $6.75 ages 4–11). During the 75-minute "Olympics of the Forest," you'll watch two teams compete in 14 events, including ax throwing, crosscut sawing, log rolling, speed climbing, and more. Some are open to participation. (Kids can learn some skills by appointment.) Performances are

held rain or shine. Seating is under a roof, but dress for the weather if it's inclement. The ticket office opens at 6 P.M.

The carefully restored art deco **Grand Auditorium** of Hancock County (100 Main St., 207/667-9500, www.grandonline.org) is the year-round site of films, concerts, plays, and art exhibits.

SHOPPING
Specialty Shops
You're unlikely to meet a single soul who has left the **Big Chicken Barn Books and Antiques** (1768 Bucksport Rd./Rte. 1, 207/667-7308) without buying something. You'll find every kind of collectible on the vast first floor, courtesy of more than four dozen dealers. Climb the stairs for books, magazines, old music, and more. With 21,000 square feet, this place is addictive, with free coffee, restrooms, and hassle-free browsing. The Big Chicken is 11 miles east of Bucksport, 8.5 miles west of Ellsworth.

Just south of downtown, in a property listed on the National Register of Historic Places, the 1838 courthouse at the corner of Court Street and Route 1 is **Courthouse Gallery Fine Art** (6 Court St., 207/667-6611, www.courthouse-gallery.com), showcasing works by some of Maine's top contemporary artists.

A fine collection of antiquarian and used books fills the shelves of **Apple Tree Books** (71 Main St., 207/667-7999).

The 40-plus-dealer **Old Creamery Antique Mall** (13 Hancock St., 207/667-0522) fills 6,000 square feet on two jam-packed floors.

Around the corner is **Atlantic Art Glass** (25 Pine St., 207/664-0222), where you can watch Linda and Ken Perrin demonstrate glass blowing and buy their contemporary creations.

Don't miss **Rooster Brother** (29 Main St./ Rte. 1, 207/667-8675 or 800/866-0054, www .roosterbrother.com) for gourmet cookware, cards, and books on the main floor; coffee, tea, candy, cheeses, a huge array of exotic condiments, fresh breads, and other gourmet items on the lower level; and discounted merchandise on the second floor, open seasonally. You can easily pick up all the fixings for a fancy picnic here.

It's hard to categorize **J&B Atlantic Company** (142 Main St./Rte. 1, 207/667-2082). It takes up a good part of the block, with room after room filled with furniture, home accessories, gifts, books, and antiques.

John Edwards Market (158 Main St., 207/667-9377) is a two-fold find: Upstairs is a natural-foods store; downstairs is the Wine Cellar Gallery, a terrific space showcasing Maine artists throughout the year.

Discount Shopping
You can certainly find bargains at the **L. L. Bean Factory Store** (150 High St./Rte. 1, 207/667-7753), but this is an outlet, so scrutinize the goods for flaws and blemishes before buying.

Across the road is **Reny's Department Store** (Ellsworth Shopping Center, 185 High St./Rte. 1, 207/667-5166, www.renys.com), a Maine-based discount operation with a "you never know what you'll find" philosophy. Trust me, you'll find something here.

Marden's (225 High St./Rte. 1A, 207/669-6036, www.mardenssurplus.com) is another Maine "bit of this, bit of that" enterprise with the catchy slogan "I shoulda bought it, when I saw it." Good advice.

ACCOMMODATIONS
Rates reflect peak season.

Motels and Inns
The year-round **Acadia Birches** (20 Thorsen Rd., facing Rte. 1, 207/667-3621 or 800/435-1287, www.acadiabirchesmotel.com, $99–199, under age 17 free) is a clean, generic, somewhat dated motel with 67 air-conditioned guest rooms, all with kitchenettes. It's popular with tour groups. Request a room overlooking the nine-hole course. Rooms have phones and cable TV; some have kitchenettes.

The family-owned **Open Hearth Inn** (Rte. 3, Trenton, 207/667-2930 or 800/655-0234, www.openhearthinn.com, year-round,

$75–150) is on the Island Explorer bus route, less than 0.25 miles from the bridge connecting Trenton to Mount Desert and within walking distance of four lobster restaurants. Although the property is dated, it's clean, cheap, and convenient. Choose an inn room or opt for a tourist court–style cottage or motel room (all with continental buffet breakfast), or an apartment with a kitchen. All have TVs, fridges, air-conditioning, and Wi-Fi. Also on the premises is an enclosed family hot tub. The only drawback might be traffic noise. Kids under 12 are free, and free pickup at Bar Harbor Airport is offered during business hours.

Camping
Equally convenient to the Schoodic Region and Mount Desert Island is the 55-acre **Lamoine State Park** (23 State Park Rd./Rte. 184, Lamoine, 207/667-4778, www.parksandlands.com). Park facilities include a pebble beach and a picnic area with a spectacular view, a boat-launch ramp, and a children's play area. Day-use admission is $4.50 nonresident adults, $3 Maine resident adults, $1 ages 5–11. Camping (62 sites, mid-May–mid-Sept.) is $25 per site per night for nonresidents, $15 for Maine residents, plus a $2-per-night fee for reservations. No hookups are available; minimum stay is two nights with a 14-night maximum. Reserve online at www.state.me.us/doc/parks/reservations using a credit card, or call 207/624-9950 or 800/332-1501 weekdays within Maine. Leashed pets are allowed, but not on the beach, and cleanup is required.

FOOD
Local Flavors
Order breakfast anytime at **The Riverside Café** (151 Main St., 207/667-7220, www.insideriversidecafe.com, 6 A.M.–2 P.M. Mon.–Thurs., 6 A.M.–8 P.M. Fri., 7 A.M.–8 P.M. Sat., 7 A.M.–2 P.M. Sun.). Lunch service begins at 11 A.M. On weekend nights there's often entertainment. And the café's name? It used to be down the street, overlooking the Union River.

Less creative but no less delicious are the home-style breakfasts at **Martha's Diner** (Reny's Plaza, 151 High St., 207/664-2495, 6 A.M.–2 P.M. Mon.–Sat., 7 A.M.–1 P.M. Sun.), where lunch is also served 11 A.M.–2 P.M. Monday–Friday. Almost everything on the menu is less than $5, booths are red leatherette and Formica, and the waitresses likely will call you "doll."

Jordan's Snack Bar (200 Down East Hwy./Rte. 1, 207/667-2174, 10:30 A.M.–9 P.M. daily) has almost a cult following for its crabmeat rolls and fried clams. Wednesday Cruise-Ins, beginning at 6 P.M., usually feature live entertainment and draw up to 50 vintage cars.

Breakfast and deli sandwiches, salads, wraps, smoothies, and sweets are served at **The Maine Grind** (192 Main St., 207/667-0011, www.mainegrind.com, 7:30 A.M.–5:30 P.M. Mon.–Sat.). There's free Wi-Fi service too.

Always reliable **Pectic Seafood** (367 Rte. 3, Bar Harbor Rd., Trenton, 207/667-7566, www.pecticseafood.com) has indoor and outdoor seating and a menu ranging from burgers and subs to fried seafood dinners and fresh lobster rolls. In addition, Pectic sells prepared heat-and-eat foods such as seafood Newberg, baked stuffed haddock, vegetable lasagna, and chicken soup, and it sells a wide array of fresh fish and specialty foods.

Casual Dining

◖ Cleonice Mediterranean Bistro (112 Main St., 207/664-7554, www.cleonice.com, 11:30 A.M.–8:30 P.M. daily summer, call for off-season hours) is named for chef-owner Richard Hanson's mother, Cleonice Renzetti. (It helps if you learn how to pronounce it: klee-oh-NEESE.) Gleaming woodwork and brass lighting fixtures combine for a golden glow in the long dining room, lined with wooden booths on one side and a 32-foot wooden bar, dating from 1938, on the other. The tapas and meze selection alone, served 2:30–5 P.M., is worth the trip—covering the Mediterranean circuit (spanakopita, hummus, manchego cheese with pear sauce, and even *brandade de morue*); most are around $5. Dinner runs $13–30.

Lobster

It's hard to say which is better—the serene views or the tasty lobster—at Brian and Jane Langley's **Union River Lobster Pot** (8 South St., 207/667-5077, www.lobsterpot.com, 4–9 P.M. daily June–mid-Sept.). It's tucked behind Rooster Brother, right on the banks of the Union River. Remember to save room for the pie—especially the blueberry.

Far more touristy is **Trenton Bridge Lobster Pound** (Bar Harbor Rd./Rte. 3, Trenton, 207/667-2977, www.trentonbridgelobster.com, 11 A.M.–7:30 P.M. Mon.–Sat. late May–mid-Oct.), on the right next to the bridge leading to Mount Desert Island. Watch for the "smoke signals"—steam billowing from the huge vats.

INFORMATION AND SERVICES

The **Ellsworth Area Chamber of Commerce** (163 High St., 207/667-5584, www.ellsworth-chamber.org) has information and an area guidebook.

En route from Ellsworth on Route 3, and shortly before you reach Mount Desert, you'll see (on your right) the **Bar Harbor Chamber of Commerce** (Rte. 3, Trenton, 207/288-5103 or 888/540-9990, www.barharbormaine.com). You'll find all sorts of info on the island and other locations, plus restrooms, phones, and helpful staff.

George Nixon Black, grandson of the builder of the Woodlawn Museum, donated the National Register of Historic Places–listed Federalist **Ellsworth Public Library** (46 State St., 207/667-6363, www.ellsworth.lib.me.us) to the city in 1897.

GETTING AROUND

Route No. 1 of the **Island Explorer** (www.exploreacadia.com) bus system, which primarily serves Mount Desert Island with its fleet of propane-fueled fare-free vehicles, connects the Hancock County/Bar Harbor Airport in Trenton with downtown Bar Harbor. Operated by Downeast Transportation, the Island Explorer runs late June–mid-October.

Acadia National Park on Mount Desert Island

Rather like an octopus, or perhaps an amoeba, Acadia National Park extends its reach here and there on Mount Desert Island. The first national park east of the Mississippi River and the only national park in the northeastern United States, it was created from donated parcels—a big chunk here, a tiny chunk there—and slowly but surely fused into its present-day size of more than 46,000 acres. Within the boundaries of this splendid space are mountains, lakes, ponds, trails, fabulous vistas, and several campgrounds. Each year more than 2 million visitors bike, hike, and drive into and through the park. Yet even at the height of summer, when the whole world seems to have arrived, it's possible to find peaceful niches and less-trodden paths.

Acadia's history is unique among national parks and is indeed fascinating. Several books have been written about some of the high-minded (in the positive sense) and high-profile personalities who provided the impetus and wherewithal for the park's inception and never flagged in their interest and support. Just to spotlight a few, we can thank George B. Dorr, Charles W. Eliot, and John D. Rockefeller Jr. for the park we have today.

The most comprehensive guide to the park and surrounding area is *Moon Acadia National Park*.

NATIONAL PARK INFORMATION

Anyone entering the park by any means should buy a pass. Entrance fees, covering pedestrians, bicyclists, and motorized vehicles, are $20 late June–early October, and $10 May 1–late June and most of October. That covers one vehicle for seven days. If you're traveling alone, an individual seven-day pass is $5. An annual pass to Acadia is $40, the America the Beautiful pass covering all federal recreation sites is $80, a lifetime senior pass is $10, and an access pass for disabled citizens is free. Passes are available at the visitors centers.

Hulls Cove Visitor Center

The modern Hulls Cove Visitor Center (Rte. 3, Hulls Cove, 207/288-3338, 8 A.M.–4:30 P.M. daily mid-Apr.–late Oct., 8 A.M.–6 P.M. daily June–Aug., 8 A.M.–5 P.M. daily Sept.) is eight miles southeast of the head of Mount Desert Island and well signposted. Here you can buy your park pass, make reservations for ranger-guided natural- and cultural-history programs, watch a 15-minute film about Acadia, study a relief map of the park, buy books, park souvenirs, and CD or cassette guides, and use the restrooms. Pick up a copy of the *Beaver Log,* the tabloid-format park newspaper, a monthly schedule of park activities plus tide calendars and the entire schedule for the excellent **Island Explorer** shuttle-bus system, which operates late June–Columbus Day. The Island Explorer is supported by entrance fees (park pass required), as well as by Friends of Acadia and L. L. Bean. If you have children, enroll them in the park's **Junior Ranger Program** (a nominal fee may be charged). They'll receive a booklet. To earn a Junior Ranger Patch, they must complete the activities and join one or two ranger-led programs or walks.

Thompson Island Visitor Center

As you cross the bridge from Trenton toward Mount Desert Island, you might not even notice that you arrive first on tiny Thompson Island, site of a visitors center (8 A.M.–6 P.M. daily mid-May–mid-Oct.) established jointly by the chambers of commerce of Mount Desert Island's towns and Acadia National Park. In season, a park ranger is usually posted here to answer questions and provide basic advice on hiking trails and other park activities, but consider this a stopgap—be sure to continue to the park's main visitors center.

Acadia National Park Headquarters

November–April, information is available at Acadia National Park Headquarters (Eagle

WITH A LITTLE HELP FROM OUR FRIENDS . . .

Every park in the country needs a safety net like **Friends of Acadia (FOA),** a dynamic organization headquartered in Bar Harbor. Propane-powered shuttle-bus service needs expanding? FOA finds a multimillion-dollar donor. Well-used trails need maintenance? FOA organizes volunteer work parties. New connector trails needed? FOA gets them done. No need seems to go unfilled.

FOA – one of Acadia National Park's greatest assets – is both reactive and proactive. It's an amazingly symbiotic relationship. When informed of a need, the Friends stand ready to help; when they themselves perceive a need, they propose solutions to park management and jointly figure out ways to make them happen. It's hard to avoid sounding like a media flack when describing this organization.

Friends of Acadia was founded in 1986 to preserve and protect the park for resource-sensitive tourism and myriad recreational uses. Since 1995, FOA has contributed more than $13.5 million to the park and surrounding communities for trail upkeep, carriage road maintenance, seasonal park staff funding, and conservation projects. Plus FOA co-founded the Island Explorer bus system and instigated the Acadia Trails Forever program, a joint park-FOA partnership for trail rehabilitation. In 2003, for instance, FOA and the park announced the reopening (after considerable planning and rebuilding) of the Homans Path, on the east side of Dorr Mountain. The trail, built around 1916 and named after Eliza Homans, a generous benefactor, fell into disuse in the 1940s. It ascends via a granite stairway to a ledge with a commanding view of the Great Meadow and Frenchman Bay. More recently, FOA reconstructed the East Cliffs Trail on Sargent Mountain and reopened the abandoned Penobscot Mountain Trail. As part of its Tranquility Project to reduce traffic congestion on the island, FOA purchased land in Trenton for an off-island transit and welcome center and has sold approximately 150 acres to the Maine Department of Transportation for the facility.

The Schoodic Committee of Friends of Acadia (www.friendsofschoodic.org) does much of the same type of work to preserve and protect the Schoodic section of the park. It conducts roadside and shoreline cleanups, helps maintain trails, and assists with advocacy.

You can join FOA and its 3,500-plus members and support this worthy cause for $35 per year; gifts of any amount are welcome (43 Cottage St., Bar Harbor, 207/288-3340 or 800/625-0321, www.friendsofacadia.org). You can also lend a hand while you're here. FOA and the park organize volunteer work parties for Acadia trail, carriage roads, and other outdoor maintenance three times weekly June–Columbus Day – 8:20 A.M.-12:30 P.M. Tuesday, Thursday, and Saturday. Call the recorded information line (207/288-3934) for the work locations, or 207/288-3340 or 800/625-0321 for answers to questions. The meeting point is Park Headquarters (Eagle Lake Rd./Rte. 233, Bar Harbor), about three miles west of town. This is a terrific way to give something back to the park, and the camaraderie is contagious. Be sure to take your own water, lunch, and bug repellent. Dress in layers and wear closed-toe shoes. More than 8,000 volunteer hours a year go toward this effort.

Each summer, Friends of Acadia also sponsors a handful of **Ridge Runners,** who work under park supervision and spend their days out and about on the trails repairing cairns, explaining the "leave no trace" philosophy to visitors, and assisting with research projects.

If you plan to be in the region on the first Saturday in November, call the FOA office in advance to register for the annual carriage road cleanup, which usually draws 250 or so volunteers. Bring water and gloves; there's a free hot lunch at midday for everyone who participates. It's dubbed Take Pride in Acadia Day – indeed an apt label.

Lake Rd./Rte. 233, 8 A.M.–4:30 P.M. daily), about 3.5 miles west of downtown Bar Harbor. During the summer it's open weekdays only.

SIGHTS
◖ Park Loop Road

The 27-mile Park Loop Road takes in most of the park's big-ticket sites. It begins at the visitors center, winds past several of the park's scenic highlights (with parking areas), ascends to the summit of **Cadillac Mountain,** and provides overlooks to magnificent vistas. Along the route are trailheads and overlooks as well as **Sieur de Monts Spring** (Acadia Nature Center, Wild Gardens of Acadia, Abbe Museum summer site, and the convergence of several spectacular trails), **Sand Beach, Thunder Hole, Otter Cliffs, Fabbri picnic area** (there's one wheelchair-accessible picnic table), **Jordan Pond House, Bubble Pond, Eagle Lake,** and the summit of **Cadillac Mountain.** Just before you get to Sand Beach, you'll see the Park Entrance Station, where you'll need to buy a pass if you haven't already done so. If you're here during nesting and fledging season—April–mid-August—be sure to stop in the Precipice Trailhead parking area.

Start at the parking lot below the Hulls Cove Visitor Center and follow the signs; part of the loop is one-way, so you'll be doing the loop clockwise. Traffic gets heavy at midday in midsummer, so aim for an early-morning start if you can. Maximum speed is 35 mph, but be alert for gawkers and photographers stopping without warning, and pedestrians dashing across the road from stopped cars or tour buses. If you're out here at midday in midsummer, don't be surprised to see cars and RVs parked in the right lane in the one-way sections; it's permitted.

Allow a couple of hours so you can stop along the way. You can rent an audio tour on cassette or CD for $13 (including directions, an instruction sheet, and a map) at the Hull's Cove Visitor Center. Another option is to pick up the drive-it-yourself tour booklet **Motorist Guide: Park Loop Road** ($1.50), available at the Thompson Island and Hulls Cove Visitor Centers.

◖ The Carriage Roads

In 1913, John D. Rockefeller Jr. began laying out what eventually became a 57-mile carriage-road system, and he oversaw the project through the 1940s. Motorized vehicles have never been allowed on these lovely graded byways, making them real escapes from the auto world. Devoted now to multiple uses, the "Rockefeller roads" see hikers, bikers, baby strollers, wheelchairs, and even horse-drawn carriages. Fortunately, a $6 million restoration campaign, undertaken during the 1990s, has done a remarkable job of upgrading surfaces, opening overgrown panoramas, and returning the roads to their original 16-foot width.

Pick up a free copy of the carriage-road map at any of the centers selling park passes. The busiest times are 10 A.M.–2 P.M.

The most crowded carriage roads are those closest to the visitors center—the Witch Hole Pond Loop, Duck Brook, and Eagle Lake. Avoid these, opting instead for roads west of Jordan Pond; or go early in the morning or late in the day. Better still, go off-season, when you can enjoy the fall foliage (late Sept.–mid-Oct.) or winter's cross-country skiing.

If you need a bicycle to explore the carriage roads, you can rent one in Bar Harbor or Southwest Harbor. Be forewarned that hikers are allowed on the carriage roads that spill over onto private property south of the Jordan Pond House, but they are off-limits to bicyclists. The no-biking areas are signaled with Green Rock Company markers. The carriage-road map clearly indicates the biking and no-biking areas. Bicyclists must be especially speed-sensitive on the carriage roads, keeping an eye out for hikers, horseback riders, small children, and the hearing impaired.

To recapture the early carriage-roads era, take one of the horse-drawn open-carriage tours run by **Carriages of Acadia,** based at Wildwood Stables (Park Loop Rd., Seal Harbor, 877/276-3622, www.carriagesofacadia .com), a mile south of the Jordan Pond House. Six one- and two-hour trips start at 9 A.M. daily

© TOM NANGLE

Seventeen unique bridges accent Acadia's famed carriage roads.

mid-June–mid October. Reservations are not required, but they're encouraged, especially in midsummer. The best outing is the two-hour **Day Mountain Summit** ($25 adults, $10 ages 6–12, $7 ages 2–5) sunset ride. Other routes are around $20 adults, $10 children, $6 little kids. If you take the two-hour carriage ride to Jordan Pond House departing at 1:15 P.M. daily ($20 adults, not including food and beverages), you're guaranteed a reserved lawn chair for tea and popovers.

Bass Harbor Light

At the southern end of Mount Desert's western "claw," follow Route 102A to the turn-off toward Bass Harbor Head. Drive or bike to the end of Lighthouse Road, walk down a steep wooden stairway, and look up and to the right. Voilà! Bass Harbor Head Light—its red glow automated since 1974—stands sentinel at the eastern entrance to Blue Hill Bay. Built in 1858, the 26-foot tower and light keeper's house are privately owned, but the dramatic setting is a photographer's dream.

Baker Island

The best way to get to—and to appreciate— history-rich Baker Island is on the ranger-narrated Acadia National Park Baker Island Tour aboard the *Miss Samantha*, booked through **Bar Harbor Whale Watch Co.** (1 West St., Bar Harbor, 207/288-2386 or 888/942-5374, www.barharborwhales.com, $43 adults, $20 ages 6–14, $5 under age 6). The half-day tours are offered mid June–mid-September and include access via skiff to the 130-acre island with a farmstead, a lighthouse, and intriguing rock formations. The return trip provides a view from the water of Otter Cliffs (bring binoculars and look for climbers), Thunder Hole, Sand Beach, and Great Head. Call for the current schedule.

RECREATION
Hikes

If you're spending more than a day on Mount Desert Island, plan to buy a copy of *A Walk in the Park: Acadia's Hiking Guide,* by Tom St. Germain, which details more than 60 hikes, including some outside the park. Remember that pets are allowed on park trails, but only on leashes no longer than six feet. Four of the Island Explorer bus routes are particularly useful for hikers, alleviating the problems of backtracking and car-jammed parking lots. Here's a handful of favorite Acadia hikes, from easy to rugged.

These three easy trails are ideal for young families. **Jordan Pond Nature Trail:** Start at the Jordan Pond parking area. This is an easy wheelchair-accessible one-mile wooded loop trail; pick up a brochure. Include Jordan Pond House (for tea and popovers) in your schedule. **Ship Harbor Nature Trail:** Start at Ship Harbor parking area, on Route 102A between Bass Harbor and Seawall Campground, in the southwestern corner of the island. The easy 1.3-mile loop trail leads to the shore; pick up a brochure at the trailhead. Ship Harbor is particularly popular among bird-watchers seeking warblers, and you just might spot an eagle while you picnic on the rocks. **Wonderland:** An even easier trail, with its parking area just east of the Ship Harbor parking area, Wonderland is 1.4 miles round-trip.

Great Head Trail: This moderately easy 1.4-mile loop trail starts at the eastern end of Sand Beach, off the Park Loop Road. Park in the Sand Beach parking area, and cross the beach to the trailhead. Or take Schooner Head Road from downtown Bar Harbor and park in the small area where the road dead-ends. There are actually two trail loops here, both of which have enough elevation to provide terrific views.

Gorham Mountain: Another moderate hike with great views is this 1.8-mile round-trip. It's a great family hike, as kids especially love the Cadillac Cliffs section. Access is off the Park Loop Road, just beyond Thunder Hole.

Beech Mountain: A moderate hike, Beech Mountain's summit has an abandoned fire tower, from which you can look out toward Long Pond and the Blue Hill Peninsula. A knob near the top is a prime viewing site for the migration of hawks and other raptors in September. Round-trip on the wooded route is

about 1.2 miles, although a couple of side trails can extend it. You'll have less competition here in a quieter part of the park. Take Route 102 south from Somesville, heading toward Pretty Marsh. Turn left onto Beech Hill Road and follow it to the parking area at the end.

Beehive Trail and **Precipice Trail:** These two are the park's toughest routes, with sheer faces and iron ladders; Precipice is often closed (usually mid-Apr.–late July) to protect nesting peregrine falcons. If challenges are your thing and these trails are open (check beforehand at the visitors center), go ahead. But a fine alternative in the difficult category is the **Beachcroft Trail** on Huguenot Head. Also called the Beachcroft Path, the trail is best known for its 1,500 beautifully engineered granite steps. Round-trip is about 2.2 miles, or you can continue a loop at the top, taking in the **Bear Brook Trail** on Champlain Mountain, for about 4.4 miles. The parking area is just north of Route 3, near Sieur de Monts Spring.

Rock Climbing

Acadia has a number of splendid sites prized by climbers: the sea cliffs at Otter Cliffs and Great Head; South Bubble Mountain; Canada Cliff (on the island's western side); and the South Wall and the Central Slabs on Champlain Mountain. If you haven't tried climbing, never do it yourself without instruction. **Acadia Mountain Guides Climbing School** (228 Main St., Bar Harbor, 207/288-8186 or 888/232-9559, www.acadiamountainguides .com) and **Atlantic Climbing School** (ACS, 24 Cottage St., 2nd fl., Bar Harbor, 207/288-2521, www.climbacadia.com) both provide instruction and guided climbs. Costs depend on the site, experience, session length, and number of climbers; call for details.

Swimming

Slightly below the Park Loop Road (take Island Explorer Route No. 3—Sand Beach), **Sand Beach** is the park's and the island's biggest sandy beach. Lifeguards are on duty during the summer, and even then, the biggest threat can be hypothermia. The salt water is

© HILARY NANGLE

Acadia's Sand Beach

Park Ranger Programs

When you stop at the Hulls Cove Visitor Center and pick up the current issue of the park's *Beaver Log* newspaper (or download it ahead of time at www.nps.gov/acad), you'll find a whole raft of possibilities for learning more about the park's natural and cultural history.

The park ranger programs, lasting 1–3 hours, are great—and most are free. During July–August there are about 100 programs each week, all listed in the *Beaver Log*. Included are early-morning (7 A.M.) bird-watching walks; moderate-level mountain hikes; tours of the historic Carroll Homestead, a 19th-century farm; Cadillac summit natural-history tours; children's expeditions to learn about tide pools and geology (an adult must accompany kids); trips for those in wheelchairs; and even a couple of tours a week in French. Some tours require reservations, most do not; a few, including boat tours, have fees.

Park rangers also give the evening lectures during the summer in the amphitheaters at Blackwoods and Seawall Campgrounds.

CAMPING

Mount Desert Island has at least a dozen commercial campgrounds, but there are only two—Blackwoods and Seawall—within park boundaries on the island; neither has hookups. Both have seasonal restrooms with no showers and have dumping stations. Both also have seasonal amphitheaters, where rangers present evening programs.

Blackwoods Campground

Year-round Blackwoods, just off Route 3, five miles south of Bar Harbor, has 306 sites. Because of its location on the east side of the island, it's also the more popular of the two campgrounds. Reservations (877/444-6777, www.recreation.gov, credit card required) are suggested May 1–October 31, when the fee is $20 per site per night. Reservations can be made up to six months ahead. In April and November, camping is $10; December–March it's free.

terminally glacial—in mid-July it still might not reach 60°F. The best solution is to walk to the far end of the beach, where a warmer shallow stream meets the ocean. On a hot August day, arrive early; the parking lot fills up.

The park's most popular freshwater swimming site, staffed with a lifeguard and inevitably crowded on hot days, is **Echo Lake,** south of Somesville on Route 102 and well signposted (take Island Explorer Route No. 7—Southwest Harbor).

If you have a canoe, kayak, or rowboat, you can reach swimming holes in **Seal Cove Pond** and **Round Pond,** both on the western side of Mount Desert. The eastern shore of **Hodgdon Pond** (also on the western side of the island) is accessible by car via Hodgdon Road and Long Pond Fire Road. **Lake Wood,** at the northern end of Mount Desert, has a tiny beach, restrooms, and auto access. To get to Lake Wood from Route 3, head west on Crooked Road to unpaved Park Road. Turn left and continue to the parking area, which will be crowded on a hot day, so arrive early.

ACADIA REGION

JORDAN POND HOUSE

© HILARY NANGLE

Tea and popovers on the lawn at Acadia National Park's Jordan Pond House are a long-standing island tradition.

In the late 19th century, when Bar Harbor was in the throes of becoming "the great new place" to escape the heat of Washington, New York, Philadelphia, and the Midwest, gentle ladies and men patronized an unassuming farmhouse-teahouse on the shores of Jordan Pond. By 1895 or 1896, under the stewardship of Thomas McIntire, it became Jordan Pond House – a determinedly rustic establishment with massive fieldstone fireplaces, serving afternoon tea and leisurely luncheons during the summer and fall.

And rustic it remained, well into the late 20th century – until it was leveled by a disastrous fire in the summer of 1979. At that point, it was owned by Acadia National Park – John D. Rockefeller Jr. had bought it in the 1930s and donated it to the park in the early 1940s. Since then, it has been managed on behalf of the park by concessionaires – at present the Acadia Corporation (which also operates gift shops in several locations).

Today, Jordan Pond House, the only restaurant within Acadia National Park, must rely on its framed antique photos to conjure a bit of nostalgia for the bygone era. The building is modern and open, the pace in summer is frenetic, and the food is average. But the view from the lawn over Jordan Pond and the astounding Bubbles is incredible. Surely *it* hasn't changed.

So...at least once, brave the crowds and have afternoon tea on the lawn at Jordan Pond House. Order tea or Oregon chai or even cappuccino and fresh popovers with extraordinary strawberry jam.

If you think you'll need a popover fix when you return home, you can always buy a package of the mix along with the jam in the gift shop, or make them from scratch. Here's the Jordan Pond House recipe:

JORDAN POND HOUSE POPOVERS

- 2 large eggs

- 1 cup whole milk

- 1 cup all-purpose flour (presifted)

- ½ teaspoon salt

- ⅛ teaspoon baking soda

Preheat oven to 425°F. Beat eggs with electric mixer at high speed 3 minutes. Reduce mixer speed to lowest setting and very gradually pour in half the milk. In separate bowl, combine sifted flour, salt, and baking soda and sift again.

With mixer still running at slowest speed, add dry ingredients to egg-and-milk mixture. Turn off mixer and use rubber spatula to blend mixture thoroughly.

Set mixer to medium speed and very gradually pour in remaining milk, blending 1 minute. Raise mixer speed to highest setting and beat 10 minutes.

Strain batter through fine-mesh strainer to remove lumps and then pour into well-buttered popover or custard cups. Bake 15 minutes. Without opening the oven, reduce heat to 350°F and bake 15 more minutes (20 minutes if the oven door has a window).

Serve immediately with fresh jam and room-temperature butter.

Hint: Popovers turn out significantly better if baked in ovenproof cups rather than in metal or glass.

The recipe makes two popovers. Increase as desired, but be sure to measure carefully.

Seawall Campground

Reservations are not accepted at Seawall Campground, on Route 102A in the Seawall district, four miles south of Southwest Harbor—it's first-come, first-served. In midsummer you'll need to arrive as early as 8:30 A.M. (when the ranger station opens) to secure one of the 200 or so sites. Seawall is open late May–September. The cost is $20 per night for drive-up sites and $14 per night for walk-in tent sites.

RV length at Seawall is limited to 35 feet, with the width limited to an awning extended no more than 12 feet. Generators are not allowed in the campground.

FOOD
◖ Jordan Pond House

The only restaurant within the park is the Jordan Pond House (Park Loop Rd., 207/276-3316, www.thejordanpondhouse.com, 11:30 A.M.–8 P.M. daily mid-May–late Oct., 11:30 A.M.–9 P.M. late June–early Sept.), a modern facility in a spectacular waterside setting. Jordan Pond House began life as a rustic 19th-century teahouse; wonderful old photos still line the walls of the current incarnation, which went up after a disastrous fire in 1979. Afternoon tea is still a tradition, with tea, popovers, and extraordinary strawberry jam served on the lawn until 5:30 P.M. daily in summer, weather permitting. It is not exactly a bargain at nearly $10, but it's worth it. However, Jordan Pond is far from a secret, so expect to wait for seats at the height of summer. Better yet, plan ahead and make reservations. Jordan Pond House is on the Island Explorer's Route No. 5. *A health note:* Perhaps because of all the sweet drinks and jam served outdoors, patrons at the lawn tables sometimes find themselves pestered by bees. They don't usually sting unless you pester them back, but be alert if anyone in your party is allergic to bee stings.

Bar Harbor and Vicinity

In 1996, Bar Harbor celebrated the bicentennial of its founding (as the town of Eden). In the late 19th century and well into the 20th, the town grew to become one of the East Coast's fanciest summer watering holes.

In those days, ferries and steam yachts arrived from points south, large and small resort hotels sprang up, and exclusive mansions (quaintly dubbed "cottages") were the venues of parties thrown by summer-resident Drexels, DuPonts, Vanderbilts, and prominent academics, journalists, and lawyers. The "rusticators" came for the season with huge entourages of servants, children, pets, and horses. The area's renown was such that by the 1890s, even the staffs of the British, Austrian, and Ottoman embassies retreated here for the summer from Washington, D.C.

The establishment of the national park in 1919 and the arrival of the automobile changed the character of Bar Harbor and Mount Desert Island; two World Wars and the Great Depression took an additional toll in myriad ways; but the coup de grâce for Bar Harbor's era of elegance came with the Great Fire of 1947, a wind-whipped conflagration that devastated more than 17,000 acres on the eastern half of the island and leveled gorgeous mansions, humble homes, and more trees than anyone could ever count. Only three people died, but property damage was estimated at $2 million. Whole books have been written about the October inferno; fascinating scrapbooks in Bar Harbor's Jesup Memorial Library dramatically relate the gripping details of the story. Even though some of the elegant cottages have survived, the fire altered life here forever.

SIGHTS
◖ Abbe Museum

The fabulous Abbe Museum is a superb place to introduce children (and adults) to prehistoric,

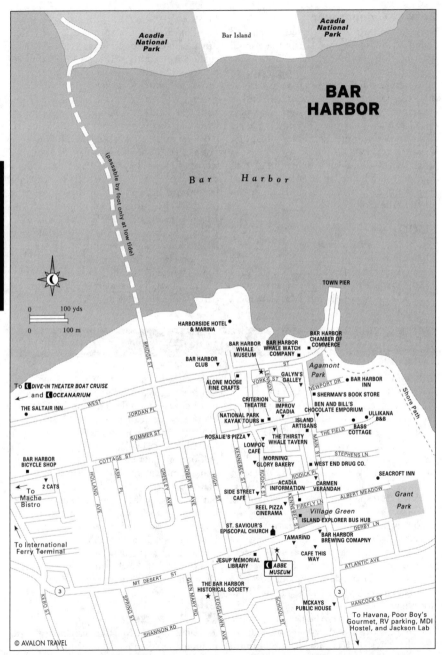

Acadia National Park

Bar Island

Acadia National Park

BAR HARBOR

Bar Harbor

(passable by foot only at low tide)

0   100 yds
0   100 m

TOWN PIER

HARBORSIDE HOTEL & MARINA

BAR HARBOR CHAMBER OF COMMERCE

BAR HARBOR WHALE MUSEUM

BAR HARBOR WHALE WATCH COMPANY

BAR HARBOR CLUB

Agamont Park

GALYN'S GALLEY

BAR HARBOR INN

To **DIVE-IN THEATER BOAT CRUISE** and **OCEANARIUM**

ALONE MOOSE FINE CRAFTS

NEWPORT DR.

SHERMAN'S BOOK STORE

THE SALTAIR INN

CRITERION THEATRE

IMPROV ACADIA

BEN AND BILL'S CHOCOLATE EMPORIUM

ULLIKANA B&B

NATIONAL PARK KAYAK TOURS

ISLAND ARTISANS

BASS COTTAGE

ROSALIE'S PIZZA

THE THIRSTY WHALE TAVERN

LOMPOC CAFÉ

STEPHENS LN.

MORNING GLORY BAKERY

WEST END DRUG CO.

BAR HARBOR BICYCLE SHOP

SEACROFT INN

ACADIA INFORMATION

CARMEN VERANDAH

2 CATS

SIDE STREET CAFÉ

ALBERT MEADOW

Grant Park

To Mache Bistro

REEL PIZZA CINERAMA

Village Green

ISLAND EXPLORER BUS HUB

ST. SAVIOUR'S EPISCOPAL CHURCH

To International Ferry Terminal

TAMARIND

BAR HARBOR BREWING COMAPNY

JESUP MEMORIAL LIBRARY

CAFE THIS WAY

ABBE MUSEUM

THE BAR HARBOR HISTORICAL SOCIETY

MCKAYS PUBLIC HOUSE

To Havana, Poor Boy's Gourmet, RV parking, MDI Hostel, and Jackson Lab

Shore Path

BRIDGE ST.

WEST

JORDAN PL.

SUMMER ST.

COTTAGE ST.

HOLLAND AVE.

ASH ST.

GREELEY AVE.

ROBERTS AVE.

HIGH ST.

KENNEBEC ST.

LENOX ST.

YORK ST.

MAIN ST.

THE FIELD

RODICK PL.

RODICK ST.

FIREFLY LN.

KENNEBEC ST.

DERBY LN.

MT. DESERT ST.

GLEN MARY RD.

LEDGELAWN AVE.

SCHOOL ST.

ATLANTIC AVE.

HANCOCK ST.

KEBO ST.

SPRING ST.

SHANNON RD.

3

3

© AVALON TRAVEL

ACADIA REGION

© TOM NANGLE

Bar Harbor's grassy waterfront park is a fine place to watch the harbor traffic.

historic, and contemporary Native American tools, crafts, and other cultural artifacts, with an emphasis on Maine's Micmac, Maliseet, Passamaquoddy, and Penobscot people. Everything about this privately funded museum, established in 1927, is tasteful. It has two campuses: The main campus (26 Mt. Desert St., Bar Harbor, 207/288-3519, www.abbemuseum.org, 10 A.M.–6 P.M. daily late May–early Nov., call for off-season hours, $6 adults, $2 ages 6–15) is home to a collection spanning nearly 12,000 years. Museum-sponsored events include craft workshops, hands-on children's programs, archaeological field schools, and the **Native American Festival** (held at the College of the Atlantic, usually the first Saturday after the Fourth of July). The museum's gift shop has an especially nice selection of Native American–made baskets.

Admission to the in-town Abbe also includes admission to the museum's original site in the park, about 2.5 miles south of Bar Harbor, at Sieur de Monts Spring, where Route 3 meets the Park Loop Road (9 A.M.–4 P.M. daily mid-May–mid-Oct.). Inside a small but handsome National Historic Register building are displays from a 50,000-item collection. Admission to only the Sieur de Monts Spring Abbe is $3 adults, $2 ages 6–15; admission here can be credited to main museum fees.

While you're at the original Abbe Museum site, take the time to wander the paths in the adjacent **Wild Gardens of Acadia,** a 0.75-acre microcosm of more than 400 plant species native to Mount Desert Island. Twelve separate display areas, carefully maintained and labeled by the Bar Harbor Garden Club, represent native plant habitats; pick up the map-brochure that explains each.

St. Saviour's Episcopal Church

St. Saviour's (41 Mt. Desert St., Bar Harbor, 207/288-4215, 7 A.M.–dusk daily), close to downtown Bar Harbor, boasts Maine's largest collection of Tiffany stained-glass windows. Ten originals are here; an 11th was stolen in 1988 and replaced by a locally made window. Of the 32 non-Tiffany windows, the most intriguing is a memorial to Clarence Little, founder of the Jackson Laboratory and a descendant of Paul Revere. Images in the window include the laboratory, DNA, and mice. In July–August, volunteers regularly conduct free tours of the Victorian-era church, completed in 1878; call for the schedule or make an appointment for an off-season tour. The church is open for self-guided tours 8 A.M.–8 P.M. daily—pick up a brochure in the back. If old cemeteries intrigue you, spend time wandering the 18th-century town graveyard next to the church.

Oceanarium

At the northern edge of Mount Desert Island, 8.5 miles northwest of downtown Bar Harbor, is this understated but fascinating spot, also called the **Maine Lobster Museum and Hatchery** (1351 Rte. 3, Bar Harbor, 207/288-5005, www.theoceanarium.com, 9 A.M.–5 P.M. Mon.–Sat. mid-May–late-Oct.). This low-tech, high-interest operation awes the kids, and it's pretty darn interesting for adults too. David and Audrey Mills have been at it since 1972 and are determined to educate visitors while showing them a good time. Visitors on tour view thousands of tiny lobster hatchlings, enjoy a museum, finger sea life in a touch tank, and meander along a salt marsh walk, where you can check out tidal creatures and vegetation. All tours begin on the hour and half hour. Allow 1–2 hours to see everything. Tickets are $12 adults, $7 ages 4–12, covering admission to the lobster hatchery, lobster museum, and touch tank; an expanded program includes a 45-minute Marsh Walk for $14 adults, $8 children.

College of the Atlantic

A museum, a gallery, and a pleasant campus for walking are reasons to visit the College of the Atlantic (COA, 105 Eden St./Rte. 3, Bar Harbor, 207/288-5015, www.coa.edu), which specializes in human ecology, or humans' inter-relationship with the environment. In a handsome renovated building, the **George B. Dorr Natural History Museum** (10 A.M.–5 P.M. Tues.–Sat., donation) showcases regional birds and mammals in realistic dioramas made by COA students. The biggest attraction for children is the please-touch philosophy, allowing kids to reach into a touch tank and to feel fur, skulls, and even whale baleen. The museum also sponsors six full-week programs of an excellent and very popular **Family Nature Camp** (800/597-9500, www.coa.edu/summer, late June–mid-Aug., $900 adults, $450 ages 5–15 covers almost everything). It's essential to register well in advance; ask about early-season discounts. Families are housed and fed on the campus. The museum gift shop has a particularly good collection of books and gifts for budding naturalists.

Across the way is the **Ethel H. Blum Gallery** (207/288-5015, ext. 254, 11 A.M.–4 P.M. Tues.–Sat. summer, 9 A.M.–5 P.M. Mon.–Fri. during the academic year), a small space that hosts some intriguing exhibits.

Also on campus is the **Beatrix Farrand Garden,** which is undergoing restoration. The garden, designed in 1928, contained more than 50 varieties of roses and was the prototype for the rose garden at Dumbarton Oaks in Washington, D.C. Both are known for Farrand's use of garden rooms, such as the terraces in this garden.

The first floor of **The Turrets,** a magnificent 1895 seaside cottage that's now an administration building, can be explored. Don't miss the gardens in front.

The college and its museum are 0.5 miles northwest of downtown Bar Harbor; take Island Explorer Route No. 2 (Eden Street).

Bar Harbor Whale Museum

For a whale of a good time, don't miss the small but jam-packed Bar Harbor Whale Museum (52 West St., Bar Harbor, 207/288-0288, www.barharborwhalemuseum.org, 10 A.M.–8 P.M. daily June and Sept.–Oct., 9 A.M.–9 P.M. daily July–Aug., hours may vary off-season), operated by research associates affiliated with College of the Atlantic's Allied Whale program. Features include a life-sized model of a prehistoric walking whale, a 29.5-foot humpback whale skeleton, seals, marine birds, a 22-foot-long minke porpoise, and interactive exhibits on whales and climate change. There's also a mesmerizing video of whales in their habitat. Admission is free, but donations support marine mammal research and conservation. While here, ask about COA's **Adopt a Finback or Humpback Whale** program. Biologists from Allied Whale have identified more than 1,000 finbacks and more than 6,000 humpbacks. Your $40–50 contribution supports research and nets you a color photo of your whale, a brief history of it, and a book as well as an adoption certificate and newsletter subscription. The museum's gift shop is green—lots of good choices here for budding naturalists—and the museum uses no plastic. Note that the museum may be moving in 2011; call for details.

The Bar Harbor Historical Society

The Bar Harbor Historical Society (33 Ledgelawn Ave., Bar Harbor, 207/288-0000, www.barharborhistorical.org, 1–4 P.M. Mon.–Sat. mid-June–mid-Oct., free), in its own building listed on the National Register of Historic Places, has fascinating displays, stereopticon images, and a scrapbook about the 1947 fire that devastated the island. The photographs alone are worth the visit. Also here are antique maps, Victorian-era hotel registers, and other local memorabilia. In winter it's open by appointment.

For a sample of Bar Harbor before the great fire, wander over to upper West Street, which is on the National Register of Historic Places thanks to the remaining grand cottages that line it.

Hulls Cove Tool Barn and Sculpture Garden

Part shop, part nature center, part art gallery, the Hulls Cove Tool Barn and Sculpture Garden (17 Breakneck Rd., behind Hulls Cove General Store, Hulls Cove, 207/288-5126, www.jonesport-wood.com, 9 A.M.–5 P.M. Wed.–Sat., noon–5 P.M. Sun.) is just one of creative Skip Brack's enterprises. Inside the barn is an extensive selection of old tools, with an emphasis on woodworking hand tools. Paths run through perennial gardens, woods, and fields at the Davistown Museum Sculpture Garden, which surrounds the barn and continues across the street. Throughout the garden are sculptures by noted Maine artists and found-object creations by Brack. Take the Island Explorer Route No. 1 (Campgrounds) and request a stop at the Hulls Cove General Store, then walk up the road.

Research Laboratories

Some of the world's top scientists live year-round or come to Bar Harbor in summer to work at two prominent scientific laboratories.

World-renowned in genetic research, scientists at **The Jackson Laboratory for Mammalian Research** (600 Main St./Rte. 3, Bar Harbor, 207/288-6000, www.jax.org) study cancer, diabetes, muscular dystrophy, heart disease, and Alzheimer's disease, among others—with considerable success. The nonprofit research institution, locally called JAX or just "the lab," is also renowned for its genetics databases and for producing genetically defined laboratory mice, which are shipped to research labs worldwide. Free scheduled public tours (limited to 15 people, call for details, preregistration required) begin in the lab's visitors lobby and visit the lab's three main research wings. These show the evolution of facilities over the decades, beginning with the 1980s, and the guide discusses the genetic research occurring in each. The lab is 1.5 miles south of downtown Bar Harbor.

No less impressive is the **Mount Desert Island Biological Laboratory** (MDIBL, 159 Old Bar Harbor Rd., Salisbury Cove, 207/288-3605, www.mdibl.org), one of the few scientific research institutions in the world dedicated to studying marine animals to learn more about human health and environmental health. It is the only comprehensive effort in the country to sequence genomes. Family-oriented public programs include **Splash!** (late June–late Aug., call for schedule). This hands-on program introduces genetics and marine life using MDIBL's MIT-designed LEGO sets to see how DNA divides and mutates, then progresses to the touch tanks and aquarium. To avoid crowds, go on a nice day. The lab also presents **Science Fridays** about once a month, a two-hour program that includes lunch with a scientist followed by lab time; it's limited to 15 participants, and the minimum age is 16. **Family Science Night,** held once or twice each summer, is an interactive program of performances, demonstrations, and hands-on science; reservations are recommended. The lab also presents a symposium and lectures by top scientists. The lab is six miles north of Bar Harbor off Route 3.

Bar Harbor and Park Tours

The veteran of the Bar Harbor–based bus tours is **Acadia National Park Tours** (tickets at Testa's Restaurant, Bayside Landing, 53 Main St., Bar Harbor, 207/288-3327, www.acadia-tours.com, $27.50 adults, $15 under age 13), operating May–October. A 2.5–3-hour naturalist-led tour of Bar Harbor and Acadia departs at 10 A.M. and 2 P.M. daily from downtown Bar Harbor (Testa's is across from Agamont Park, near the Bar Harbor Inn). Reservations are advised in midsummer and during fall-foliage season (late Sept.–early Oct.); pick up reserved tickets 30 minutes before departure.

If you have a time crunch, take the one-hour trolley-bus tour operated by **Oli's Trolley** (ticket office at 1 West St., Bar Harbor, 207/288-9899 or 866/987-6553, www.acadi-aislandtours.com), which departs downtown Bar Harbor four times daily 10 A.M.–3:30 P.M. in July–August, including Bar Harbor mansion drive-bys and the Cadillac summit. Purchase tickets at Harbor Place (1 West St.), next to the town pier on the waterfront. Dress warmly if the air is at all cool; it's an open-air trolley. Cost is $15 adults, $10 under age 12. Reservations are advisable. The trolley also does 2.5-hour park tours at 10 A.M. and 2 P.M. daily May–October. Tickets are $29 adults, $15 under age 12. The bus and trolley routes both include potty stops.

While the Island Explorer buses do reach a number of key park sights, they are not tour buses. There is no narration, the bus cuts off the Park Loop at Otter Cliffs, and it excludes the summit of Cadillac Mountain.

Bird-Watching and Nature Tours

For private tours of the park and other parts of the island, contact Michael Good at **Down East Nature Tours** (150 Knox Rd., Bar Harbor, 207/288-8128, www.downeastna-turetours.com). A biologist and Maine Guide, Good is simply batty about birds. He has spent more than 25 years studying the birds of North America, and he has even turned his home property on Mount Desert Island into a bird sanctuary. Good specializes in avian ecology in the Gulf of Maine, giving special attention to native and migrating birds. Whether you're a first-timer wanting to spot eagles, peregrine falcons, shorebirds, and warblers or a serious bird-watcher seeking to add to your life list, perhaps with a Nelson's sharp-tailed sparrow, Good's your man. Prices begin at $75 pp for four hours and include transportation from your lodging; kids are half price. Bring your own binoculars, but Good supplies a spotting scope. A two-hour wetland ecology tour is $40 adults, $20 kids.

ENTERTAINMENT

The **Bar Harbor Town Band** performs for free at 8 P.M. Monday and Thursday evenings July–mid-August on the Village Green (Main St. and Mt. Desert St., Bar Harbor).

Above Rupununi restaurant, **Carmen Verandah** (119 Main St., Bar Harbor, 207/288-2766) is the weekend place to be and be seen, with music, dancing, and more.

You never know quite what's going to happen at **Improv Acadia** (15 Cottage St., Bar Harbor, 207/288-2503, www.improvacadia.com, $15 adults, $10 under age 13). Every show is different, as actors use audience suggestions to create comedy sketches. Shows are staged once or twice a night late May–mid-October. Dessert, snacks, and drinks are available.

The **Bar Harbor Music Festival** (207/288-5744 in July–August, 212/222-1026 off-season, www.barharbormusicfestival.org), a summer tradition since 1967, emphasizes up-and-coming musical talent in a series of classical, jazz, and pop concerts and even an opera, usually Friday and Sunday early July–early August, at various island locations that include local inns and an annual outdoor concert in Acadia National Park. Tickets are $25–35 adults, $15 students and can be purchased at the festival office building (59 Cottage St., Bar Harbor). Reservations are advised.

Theaters

Built in 1932 and listed on the National Register of Historic Places, the beautifully refurbished **Criterion Theatre and Arts Center** (35 Cottage St., Bar Harbor, 207/288-3441 for films, 207/288-5829 for concerts, www.criteriontheatre.com) is a gem. In 2007 it gained nonprofit status, with a mission to make arts and theater more accessible through diverse programs. In addition to screening films, the Criterion puts on concerts, plays, and other special events. You'll soak up the nostalgia in this art deco classic with 877 seats, including an elegant floating balcony.

Combine pizza with your picture show at **Reel Pizza Cinerama** (33 Kennebec Pl., Bar Harbor, 207/288-3811 for films, 207/288-3828 for food, www.reelpizza.net). Two films are screened nightly on each of two screens. All tickets are $6; pizzas start at $9. Doors open at 4:30 P.M.; get there early for the best seats.

EVENTS

Bar Harbor is home to numerous special events; here's just a sampling. For more, call 207/288-5103 or visit www.barharbormaine.com.

In mid-June, the annual **Acadia Birding Festival** attracts bird-watchers with guided walks, boating excursions, tours, talks, and meals.

In late June, **Legacy of the Arts** is a week-long celebration of music, art, theater, dance, and history, with tours, exhibits, workshops, concerts, lectures, demonstrations, and more.

The **Fourth of July** is always a big deal in Bar Harbor, celebrated with a 6 A.M. blueberry-pancake breakfast, a 10 A.M. parade, an 11 A.M. seafood festival, a band concert, and fireworks. A highlight is the Lobster Race, a crustacean competition drawing contestants such as Lobzilla and Larry the Lobster in a four-lane saltwater tank on the Village Green. Independence Day celebrations in the island's smaller villages always evoke a bygone era.

The Abbe Museum, the College of the Atlantic, and the Maine Indian Basketmakers Alliance sponsor the annual **Native American Festival** (10 A.M.–4 P.M. first Sat. after July 4, free), featuring baskets, beadwork, and other handicrafts for sale as well as Indian drumming and dancing, held at College of the Atlantic.

In even-numbered years, the **Mount Desert Garden Club Tour** presents a rare chance to visit some of Maine's most spectacular private gardens on the second or third Saturday in July (confirm the date with the Bar Harbor Chamber of Commerce, 207/288-5103 or 888/540-9990, www.barharbormaine.com).

The **Directions Craft Show** fills a weekend in late July or early August with extraordinary displays and sales of crafts by members of the Maine Crafts Guild. You'll find it at Mount Desert Island High School (Rte. 233/Eagle Lake Rd., Bar Harbor).

SHOPPING

Bar Harbor's boutiques—running the gamut from attractive to kitschy—are indisputably visitor-oriented; many shut down for the winter.

Downtown Bar Harbor's best craft gallery is **Island Artisans** (99 Main St., Bar Harbor, 207/288-4214, www.islandartisans.com). More than 100 Maine artists are represented here, and the quality is outstanding. Don't miss it. You'll find basketwork, handmade paper, wood carvings, blown glass, jewelry, weaving, metalwork, ceramics, and more.

For more than three decades, **Alone Moose Fine Crafts** (78 West St., Bar Harbor, 207/288-4229, www.finemainecrafts.com) has lured collectors and browsers with its selection of sculpture, pottery, jewelry, and other works.

Toys, cards, and newspapers blend in with the new-book inventory at **Sherman's Book Store**

(56 Main St., Bar Harbor, 207/288-3161). It's just the place to pick up maps and trail guides for fine days and puzzles for foggy days.

RECREATION
Walks

A real treat is a stroll along downtown Bar Harbor's **Shore Path,** a well-trodden granite-edged byway built around 1880. Along the craggy shoreline are granite-and-wood benches, town-owned **Grant Park** (great for picnics), birch trees, and several handsome mansions that escaped the 1947 fire. Offshore are the four Porcupine Islands. The path is open 6:30 A.M.–dusk, and leashed pets are allowed. Allow about 30 minutes for the mile loop, beginning next to the town pier and the Bar Harbor Inn and returning via Wayman Lane.

Check local newspapers or the Bar Harbor Chamber of Commerce visitor booklet for the times of low tide, then walk across the gravel bar to wooded **Bar Island** (formerly Rodick's Island) from the foot of Bridge Street in downtown Bar Harbor. Shell heaps recorded on the eastern end of the island indicate that Native Americans enjoyed this turf in the distant past. You'll have the most time to explore the island during new-moon or full-moon low tides, but no more than four hours—about two hours before and two hours after low tide. Be sure to wear a watch so you don't get trapped (for up to 10 hours). The foot of Bridge Street is also an excellent kayak-launching site.

About a mile from downtown along Main Street (Rte. 3) is **Compass Harbor,** a section of the park where you can stroll through woods to the water's edge and explore the overgrown ruins of Acadia National Park cofounder George Dorr's home.

Bear right at the fork just after the Thompson Island Visitor Center on Route 102/198 to reach **Indian Point–Blagden Preserve,** a lovely preserve owned by the Nature Conservancy. Five trails wind through forested 110-acre Indian Point–Blagden Preserve, a rectangular parcel with island, hill, and bay vistas. Seal-watching and bird-watching are popular, and there are harbor seals on offshore rocks as well as

Bar Harbor's famed Shore Path edges the waterfront.

© HILARY NANGLE

woodpeckers and 130 other species in blow-down areas. To spot the seals, plan your hike around low tide, when they'll be sprawled on the rocks close to shore. Wear rubberized shoes. Bring binoculars or use the telescope installed here for the purpose. To keep from disturbing the seals, watch quietly and avoid jerky movements. Park near the preserve entrance and follow the Big Woods Trail, which runs the length of the preserve. A second parking area is further in, but then you'll miss much of the preserve. When you reach the second parking area, just past an old field, bear left along the Shore Trail to see the seals. Register at the caretaker's house (just beyond the first parking lot, where you can pick up bird and flora checklists), and respect private property on either side of the preserve. It's open dawn–6 P.M. daily year-round. From the junction of Routes 3 and 102/198, continue 1.8 miles to Indian Point Road and turn right. Go 1.7 miles to a fork and turn right. Watch for the preserve entrance on the right, marked by a Nature Conservancy oak leaf.

Bicycling

With all the great biking options, including 33 miles of carriage roads open to bicycles and some of the best roadside bike routes in Maine, you'll want to bring a bike or rent one here.

The Minutolo family's **Bar Harbor Bicycle Shop** (141 Cottage St., Bar Harbor, 207/288-3886, www.barharborbike.com), on the corner of Route 3, has been in business since 1977 and has earned an excellent reputation. If you have your own bike, stop here for advice on routes—the Minutolos have cycled everywhere on the island and can suggest the perfect mountain-bike or road-bike loop based on your ability and schedule. The shop organizes free Sunday-morning group road rides, usually 9 A.M.–noon, with a longer option for more experienced cyclists. The shop has rentals varying from standard mountain bikes to full-suspension models and even tandems as well as all the accessories and gear you might need; rates begin at about $22 per day. Hours in summer are 8 A.M.–6 P.M. daily, 9 A.M.–5:30 P.M. Tuesday–Saturday in other months.

Sea Kayaking

National Park Kayak Tours (39 Cottage St., Bar Harbor, 207/288-0342 or 800/347-0940, www.acadiakayak.com) limits its Registered Maine Guide–led tours to a maximum of six tandem kayaks per trip. Four-hour morning, midday, afternoon, or sunset paddles are offered, including shuttle service, a paddle and safety lesson, and a brief stop, for $48 pp in July–August, $44 off-season. Most trips cover about six miles. Multiday camping trips also are offered. Try to make reservations at least one day in advance.

Golf

Duffers first teed off in 1888 at **Kebo Valley Golf Club** (100 Eagle Lake Rd./Rte. 233, Bar Harbor, 207/288-5000, www.kebovalleyclub .com, May–Oct.), Maine's oldest club and the eighth-oldest in the nation. The 17th hole became legendary when it took President William Howard Taft 27 tries to sink a ball in 1911.

Excursion Boats

◖ DIVE-IN THEATER BOAT CRUISE

You don't have to go diving in these frigid waters; others will do it for you. When the kids are clamoring to touch slimy sea cucumbers and starfish at various touch tanks in the area, they're likely to be primed for Diver Ed's Dive-In Theater Boat Cruise (207/288-3483 or 800/979-3370, www.divered.com), departing from the College of the Atlantic pier (105 Eden St., Bar Harbor). Former Bar Harbor harbormaster and College of the Atlantic grad Ed Monat heads the crew aboard the 46-passenger *Starfish Enterprise,* which goes a mile or two offshore where Ed, a professional diver, goes overboard with a video camera and a mini-Ed, who helps put things in proportion. You and the kids stay on deck, all warm and dry, along with Captain Evil, who explains the action on a TV screen. There's communication back and forth, so the kids can ask questions as the divers pick up urchins, starfish, crabs, lobsters, and other sea life. When Ed resurfaces, he brings a bag of touchable specimens—another chance to pet some slimy creatures (which go back into the water after show-and-tell). It's a great concept.

Watch the kids' expressions—this is a big hit. The two-hour trips depart three times daily Monday–Friday, twice daily Saturday, and once on Sunday early July–early September; fewer trips are made in spring and fall. The cost is $35 adults, $30 seniors, $25 ages 5–12, $10 under age 5. Usually twice weekly there's a park ranger or naturalist on board and the tour lasts for three hours—check the park's *Beaver Log* newspaper or Diver Ed's website for the schedule and reservation information—these trips cost an additional $5. Advance reservations are strongly recommended.

WHALE-WATCHING AND PUFFIN-WATCHING

Whale-watching boats go as far as 20 miles offshore, so no matter what the weather in Bar Harbor, dress warmly and bring more clothing than you think you'll need—even gloves, if you're especially sensitive to cold. I've been out on days when it's close to 90°F on the island but feels more like 30°F in a moving boat on the open ocean. Motion-sensitive children and adults should plan in advance for appropriate medication, such as seasickness pills or patches. Adults are required to show a photo ID when boarding the boat.

Whale-watching, puffin-watching, and combo excursions are offered by **Bar Harbor Whale Watch Company** (1 West St., Bar Harbor, 207/288-2386 or 800/942-5374, www.barharborwhales.com), sailing from the town pier (1 West St.) in downtown Bar Harbor. The company operates under various names, including Acadian Whale Watcher, and has a number of boats. Most trips are accompanied by a naturalist (often from Allied Whale at the College of the Atlantic), who regales passengers with all sorts of interesting trivia about the whales, porpoises, seabirds, and other marine life spotted along the way. In season, some trips go out as far as the puffin colony on Petit Manan Light. Trips depart daily late May–late October, but with so many options it's impossible to list the schedule—call for the latest details. Tickets are $52–56 adults, $28 ages 6–14, $8 under age 6. A portion of the ticket price benefits Allied

Whale, which researches and protects marine animals in the Gulf of Maine.

Trips may extend longer than the time advertised, so don't plan anything else too tightly around the trip. However, do try to visit the Whale Museum either before or after.

Scenic Nature Cruises (1.5–2 hours) and kid-friendly Lobster and Seal Watch Cruises (1.5 hours) are also offered. Rates for these are around $26 adults, $17 children, $5 little kids.

SAILING

Captain Steve Pagels, under the umbrella of **Downeast Windjammer Cruises** (207/288-4585 or 207/288-2373, www.downeastwindjammer.com), offers 1.5–2-hour day sails on the 151-foot steel-hulled *Margaret Todd,* a gorgeous four-masted schooner with tanbark sails that he designed and launched in 1998. Trips depart at 10 A.M., 2 P.M., and around sunset daily mid-May–mid-October (weather permitting) from the Bar Harbor Inn pier, just east of the town pier in downtown Bar Harbor. You'll get the best wildlife sightings on the morning trip, but better sailing on the afternoon trip; there's live music on the sunset one. Some morning sails are narrated by a park ranger. Buy tickets either at the pier, at 27 Main Street, or online with a credit card; plan to arrive at least half an hour early. The cost is $35 adults, $33 seniors, $25 ages 6–11, $5 ages 2–5. Dogs are welcome on all sails.

SEA VENTURE

Captain Winston Shaw's custom boat tour by Sea Venture (207/288-3355, www.svboattours.com) lets you design the perfect trip aboard *Reflection,* a 20-foot motor launch. Captain Shaw, a Registered Maine Guide and committed environmentalist, specializes in nature-oriented tours. He's the founder and director of the Coastal Maine Bald Eagle Project, and he was involved in the inaugural Earth Day celebration in 1970. He's been studying coastal birds for more than 25 years. You can pick from 10 recommended cruises lasting 1–8 hours, or design your own. In any case, the boat is yours. The boat charter rate is $120 per hour

B&N RECOMMENDS

We think you'll like these great titles:

501 Things to Do If You Dare: Dangerous...
by Ben Malisow

Uncle John's Heavy Duty Bathroom Reader
by Bathroom Readers

Extraordinary Uses for Ordinary Things:...
by Reader's Digest Editors

445 Fascinating Word Origins
by Webb Garrison

Uncle John's Briefs: Quick Bits of...
by Bathroom Readers

audio may not be returned, but can be exchanged only for the same title if defective.

<u>After 14 days or without a sales receipt</u>, returns or exchanges will not be permitted.

Magazines, newspapers, and used books are not returnable. Product not carried by Barnes & Noble or Barnes & Noble.com will not be accepted for return.

Policy on receipt may appear in two sections.

Return Policy

<u>With a sales receipt</u>, a full refund in the original form of payment will be issued from any Barnes & Noble store for returns of new and unread books (except textbooks) and unopened music/DVDs/audio made within (i) 14 days of purchase from a Barnes & Noble retail store (except for purchases made by check less than 7 days prior to the date of return) or (ii) 14 days of delivery date for Barnes & Noble.com purchases (except for purchases made via PayPal). A store credit for the purchase price will be issued for (i) purchases made by check less than 7 days prior to the date of return, (ii) when a gift receipt is presented within 60 days of purchase, (iii) textbooks returned with a receipt

© HILARY NANGLE

A sail on the four-masted schooner *Margaret Todd* is a fine way to see Bar Harbor by sea.

for up to two people, $110 for 3–4, and $150 for 5–6. Captain Shaw can also arrange for picnic lunches. On longer trips, restroom stops are available. The boat departs from the Atlantic Oakes Motel pier, off Route 3 in Bar Harbor.

LOBSTER CRUISE

When you're ready to learn the truth about lobsters, sign up for a two-hour cruise aboard **Captain John Nicolai's** *Lulu* (56 West St., Bar Harbor, 207/963-2341 or 866/235-2341, www.lululobsterboat.com), a traditional Maine lobster boat that departs up to four times daily from the Harborside Hotel and Marina. Captain Nicolai provides an entertaining commentary on anything and everything, but especially about lobsters and lobstering. He hauls a lobster trap and explains intimate details of the hapless critters. (Lobstering is banned on Sunday June–August; the cruises operate, but there's no hauling that day.) Reservations are required. Cost is $30 adults, $27 seniors and military, $17 ages 2–12. Free parking is available in the hotel's lot.

ACCOMMODATIONS

Unless otherwise noted, these properties operate seasonally; most are open May–October. Rates listed are for peak season.

Hotels and Motels

One of the town's best-known and best-situated hotels is the **Bar Harbor Inn** (Newport Dr., Bar Harbor, 207/288-3351 or 800/248-3351, www.barharborinn.com, $199–379), a sprawling complex on eight acres with a spectacular location overlooking the harbor and Bar Island. The 153 guest rooms and suites vary considerably in style, from traditional inn to motel, and are in three different buildings. Continental breakfast is included. Frills aplenty including restaurants, a heated outdoor pool, and a full-service spa.

The appropriately named **Harborside Hotel & Marina** (55 West St., Bar Harbor, 207/288-5033 or 800/238-5033, www.theharborsidehotel.com, from $250) fronts the water in downtown Bar Harbor. Almost all of the 187 guest rooms and suites have a water view and semiprivate balconies. Some have whirlpool tubs; deluxe rooms have marble baths, and some have large outdoor hot tubs. A fine-dining restaurant and full-service spa are located in the beautifully restored Bar Harbor Club. An Italian restaurant is in the hotel. Facilities also include an outdoor heated pool, a hot tub, and a pier.

On the edge of downtown, across from College of the Atlantic, are two adjacent sister properties tiered up a hillside: **Wonder View Inn & Suites** (55 Eden St., Bar Harbor, 888/439-8439, www.wonderviewinn.com) and the **Bluenose Hotel** (90 Eden St., Bar Harbor, 207/288-3348 or 800/445-4077, www.barharborhotel.com). The pet-friendly (for $20 per night) Wonder View comprises four older motels on estate-like grounds with grassy lawns and mature shade trees. On the premises are an outdoor pool and a restaurant. Guest rooms vary, with rates beginning at $109 in season, including afternoon cookies and tea. The Bluenose, one of the island's top properties, comprises two buildings. Mizzentop is newest, and its guest rooms and suites are quite elegant, many with fireplaces, all with fabulous views and balconies. Also here is a spa, a fitness center, indoor and outdoor pools, and a lounge with live music every evening. Stenna Nordica guest rooms are more modest and have outdoor corridors, but still have views; rates range $179–529.

On the edge of town, the **Cromwell Harbor Motel** (359 Main St., Bar Harbor, 207/288-3201 or 800/544-3201, www.cromwellharbor.com, $129–145) is set back from the road on nicely landscaped grounds with an outdoor pool. All guest rooms have air-conditioning, phones, TVs, microwaves, and refrigerators. The location puts all of downtown's sights within walking distance.

On the lower end of the budgetary scale are two neighboring motels: **Edenbrook Motel** (96 Eden St./Rte. 3, Bar Harbor, 207/288-4975 or 800/323-7819, www.edenbrookmotelbh.com, $70–120), with panoramic views of Frenchman Bay from some rooms, and the wee bit fancier **Highbrook Motel** (94 Eden St./

Rte. 3, Bar Harbor, 207/288-3591 or 800/338-9688, www.highbrookmotel.com, $99–149). Both are about 1.5 miles from Acadia's main entrance, one mile from downtown.

If all you want is a room with a bed, **Robbins Motel** (396 Rte. 3, Bar Harbor, 207/288-4659 or 800/858-0769, $58), an older motel, has 30 small, unadorned (some might call them dismal) but clean queen-bed guest rooms (with air-conditioning, TVs, and Wi-Fi) and an outdoor pool. There is no charm, it's not quiet, but it's cheap.

Inns and Bed-and-Breakfasts

Few innkeepers have mastered the art of hospitality as well as Roy Kasindorf and Hélène Harton, owners of the ◖ **Ullikana Bed and Breakfast** (16 The Field, Bar Harbor, 207/288-9552, www.ullikana.com, $195–340), a 10-room Victorian Tudor inn built by Alpheus Hardy, Bar Harbor's first "cottager" in 1885. They genuinely enjoy their guests. Hélène is a whiz in the kitchen; after one of her multicourse breakfasts, usually served on the waterview patio, you won't be needing lunch. She's also a decorating genius, blending antiques and modern art, vibrant color with soothing hues, folk art and fine art, with a result like a finely tuned orchestra. Roy excels at helping guests select just the right hike, bike route, or other activity. Afternoon refreshments provide a time for guests to gather and share experiences. The comfortable rooms all have private baths; many have working fireplaces, and some have private terraces with water views. Hélène and Roy also own The Yellow House next door, with six lovely guest rooms decorated in old Bar Harbor style and a huge living room filled with antique wicker. They're in a quiet downtown location close to Bar Harbor's Shore Path; French is spoken.

Right next door is the gorgeously renovated and rejuvenated ◖ **Bass Cottage** (14 The Field, Bar Harbor, 207/288-1234 or 866/782-9224, www.basscottage.com, $230–370). Corporate refugees Teri and Jeff Anderholm purchased the 26-room 1885 cottage in 2003 and spent a year gutting it, salvaging the best

© HILARY NANGLE

The Ullikana Bed and Breakfast is tucked in a quiet downtown location, just steps from Main Street or the waterfront.

of the old and blending in new to turn it into a luxurious and stylish 10-room inn. It retains its Victorian bones, yet it is most un-Victorian in style. Guest rooms are soothingly decorated with cream- and pastel-colored walls and have phones, Wi-Fi, and TVs with DVD players (a DVD library is available—valuable on a stormy day); many rooms have fireplaces and whirlpool tubs. The spacious and elegant public rooms—expansive living rooms, a cozy library, porches—flow from one to another. Teri puts her culinary degree to use preparing baked goods, fruits, and savory and sweet entrées for breakfast and evening refreshments. A guest pantry is stocked with tea, coffee, and snacks. Plans call for dinner to be served too.

Situated on one oceanfront acre in the West Street Historical District, **The Saltair Inn** (121 West St., Bar Harbor, 207/288-2882, www.saltairinn.com, $240–355) was originally built in 1887 as a guesthouse. Innkeepers Kristi and Matt Losquadro and their young family now welcome guests in five spacious guest rooms, three of which face Frenchman Bay. Frills vary

by room but might include whirlpool tubs, fireplaces, and balconies. All have TVs and Wi-Fi. A full breakfast is served either in the dining room or on the water-view deck. It's steps from downtown, but really, with a location like this, why leave?

Outside of town, in a serene location with fabulous views of Frenchman Bay, is Jack and Jeani Ochtera's ◖ **Inn at Bay Ledge** (150 Sand Point Rd., Bar Harbor, summer 207/288-4204, winter 207/875-3262, www.innatbayledge.com, $150–475), an oasis of calm tucked under towering pines atop an 80-foot cliff. Terraced decks descend to a pool and hot tub and onto the lawn, which stretches to the cliff's edge. Stairs descend to a private stone beach below. It's an elegant, casual retreat. Almost all guest rooms have water views. Beds are topped with down comforters and feather beds; some rooms have whirlpool tubs, and second-floor rooms have private decks. A sauna and steam shower are available. Also available are cottages; hillside ones lack the view but have use of the inn's facilities; the Summer House at Bay

Ledge is a shingled cottage with a deck 25 feet from the edge of Frenchman Bay.

Much less pricey and a find for families is the **Seacroft Inn** (18 Albert Meadow, Bar Harbor, 207/288-4669 or 800/824-9694, www.seacroftinn.com, $99–139), well situated just off Main Street and near the Shore Path. All rooms in Bunny and Dave Brown's white multigabled cottage have air-conditioning, phones, TVs, refrigerators, and microwaves; a continental breakfast is available for $5 pp. Housekeeping is $10 per day. Some rooms can be joined as family suites.

Hostels

The **Bar Harbor/Mount Desert Island Hostel** (321 Main St., Bar Harbor, 207/288-5587, www.barharborhostel.com, $25 dorm bed, $80 private room, $15 tent platform), in a beautifully renovated building on the edge of town, has a well-equipped kitchen and a laundry. Linens are provided. There is no smoking and no liquor allowed, credit cards are not accepted, and the curfew is midnight. Reservations are essential, as this is a popular location.

FOOD

You won't go hungry in Bar Harbor, and you won't find chain fast-food places. The island's best collection of good inexpensive restaurants are along Rodick Street, from Reel Pizza down to Rosalie's, which actually fronts on Cottage Street. You'll find a good ethnic mix, including Mexican, Thai, and Italian. For sit-down restaurants, make reservations as far in advance as possible. Hours listed are for peak season; expect reduced operations during spring and fall; few places are open in winter, but the greatest concentration is on Rodick Street.

Local Flavors

Only a masochist could bypass **Ben and Bill's Chocolate Emporium** (66 Main St., Bar Harbor, 207/288-3281 or 800/806-3281), a long-running taste experience in downtown Bar Harbor. The homemade candies and more than 50 ice cream flavors (including a dubious lobster flavor) are nothing short of outrageous; the whole place smells like the inside of a chocolate truffle. It opens daily at 10 A.M., with closing dependent on the season and crowds, but usually late in the evening.

If ice cream is your passion, a must-stop is **Mt. Desert Ice Cream** (325 Main St. and 7 Firefly Lane, Bar Harbor, 207/460-5515) for wildly creative flavors.

Probably the least-expensive lunch or ice cream option in town is **West End Drug Co.** (105 Main St., Bar Harbor, 207/288-3318), where you can get grilled-cheese sandwiches, PBJ, and other white-bread basics as well as frappés (a Maine-ism—frappés are made with ice cream, milk shakes aren't) and sundaes at the fountain.

Between Mother's Day and late October, the **Eden Farmers Market** operates out of the YMCA parking lot off Lower Main Street in Bar Harbor, 9 A.M.–noon each Sunday. You'll find fresh meats and produce, local cheeses and maple syrup, yogurt and ice cream, bread, honey, preserves, and even prepared Asian foods.

Efficient, friendly cafeteria-style service makes **EPI's Pizza** (8 Cottage St., Bar Harbor, 207/288-5853, www.epispizza.com, 11 A.M.–8 P.M. daily Sept.–June, 11 A.M.–9 P.M. daily July–Aug.) an excellent choice for subs, salads, pizzas, and even spaghetti. If the weather closes in, there are always the pinball machines in the back room.

When it comes to pub-grub favorites, such as burgers and fish sandwiches, **The Thirsty Whale Tavern** (40 Cottage St., Bar Harbor, 207/288-9335, www.thirstywhaletavern.com, 11 A.M.–9:30 P.M. daily) does it right.

For breakfast or brunch, you can't beat **2 Cats** (130 Cottage St., Bar Harbor, 207/288-2808 or 800/355-2828, www.2catsbarharbor.com, 7 A.M.–1 P.M. daily). Fun, funky, and fresh best describe both the restaurant and the food ($8–12). Dine inside or on the patio. Dinner is also served at 2 Cats—call for nights and hours. Three upstairs guest rooms are available for $165–195, less in winter—with breakfast, of course.

Picnic Fare

Although a few of these places have some seating, most are for the grab-and-go crowd.

For a light inexpensive meal, you can't go wrong at **Morning Glory Bakery** (39 Rodick St., Bar Harbor, 207/288-3041, www.morningglorybakery.com, 7 A.M.–7 P.M. Mon.–Fri., 8 A.M.–7 P.M. Sat.–Sun.). Fresh-baked goodies, breakfast and regular sandwiches, soups, and salads are all made from scratch. Planning a day in the park? Call ahead for a boxed lunch.

If you happen to be on Route 102 in the Town Hill area around lunchtime, plan to pick up picnic fare at **Mother's Kitchen** (Rte. 102, Town Hill, Bar Harbor, 207/288-4403, www.motherskitchenfoods.com, 8 A.M.–2 P.M. Mon.–Fri.). The plain, minuscule building next to Salsbury's (look for the Real Good Food sign) is deceiving—it has been operating since 1995 and turns out 20 different sandwiches as well as deli salads, scones, breakfast sandwiches, great cookies, and pies.

Brewpubs and Microbreweries

Bar Harbor's longest-lived brewpub is the **Lompoc Cafe** (36 Rodick St., Bar Harbor, 207/288-9392, www.lompoccafe.com, 11:30 A.M.–9 P.M. daily late Apr.–mid-Dec.), with ales from Atlantic Brewing Co. on tap. Go for pizzas, salads, and entrées ($10–18), along with boccie in the beer garden and live entertainment on weekends. After 9 P.M. there's just beer and thin-crust pizza until about 1 A.M.

Lompoc's signature Bar Harbor Real Ale and 5–6 others are brewed by the **Atlantic Brewing Company** (15 Knox Rd., Town Hill, in the upper section of the island, 207/288-2337 or 800/475-5417, www.atlanticbrewing.com). Free brewery tours, including tastings, are given daily at 2, 3, and 4 P.M. late May–mid-October. Also operating here in summer is **Mainely Meat Bar-B-Q** (207/288-9200, 11:30 A.M.–8 P.M. daily, $8–16), offering pulled pork, chicken, ribs, and similar fare for lunch and dinner.

Bar Harbor Brewing Company (8 Mt. Desert St., Bar Harbor, 207/288-4592, www.barharborbrewing.com) is the island's oldest brewery. It offers free tastings daily.

Family Favorites

An unscientific but reliable local survey gives the best-pizza ribbon to **Rosalie's Pizza & Italian Restaurant** (46 Cottage St., Bar Harbor, 207/288-5666, www.rosaliespizza.com, 4–10 P.M. daily), where the Wurlitzer jukebox churns out tunes from the 1950s. Rosalie's earns high marks for consistency with its homemade pizza, in four sizes or by the slice, along with calzones and subs; there are lots of vegetarian options. If you need something a bit heartier, try the Italian dinners—spaghetti, eggplant parmigiana, and others—all less than $10, including a garlic roll. Beer and wine are available. Here's a hint: Avoid the downstairs lines by heading upstairs and ordering at that counter, or call in your order.

Route 66 Restaurant (21 Cottage St., Bar Harbor, 207/288-3708, www.bhroute66.com, 7 A.M.–about 8 P.M. daily, $9–24), filled with 1950s memorabilia and old toys, is a fun restaurant that's a real hit with kids (check out the train running around just below the ceiling). The wide-ranging menu includes sandwiches, burgers, pizza, steak, chicken, seafood, and kids choices. No raves here, just OK food in a fun atmosphere.

Casual Dining

You can't go wrong at **Galyn's Galley** (17 Main St., Bar Harbor, 207/288-9706, www.galynsbarharbor.com, 11:30 A.M.–10 P.M. daily Mar.–Nov., dinner entrées $15–31). Once a Victorian boardinghouse and later a 1920s speakeasy, Galyn's has been a popular restaurant since 1986. Lots of plants, modern decor, reliable service, a great downtown location, and several indoor and outdoor dining areas contribute to the loyalty of the clientele. The cuisine is consistently good if not outstandingly creative. Reservations are advisable in midsummer.

When you're craving fresh and delicious fare but not a heavy meal, the **Side Street Café** (49 Rodick St., Bar Harbor, 207/801-2581, www.sidestreetbarharbor.com, 11 A.M.–9:30 P.M.

daily, $8–16) delivers. It's a cheerful place with a relaxed demeanor combined with good service and a friendly attitude. The lobster roll and the crab melt earn high fives, as do the burgers.

Set back from the road behind a garden is the very popular **McKays Public House** (231 Main St., Bar Harbor, 207/288-2002, www.mckayspublichouse.com, 4:30–10 P.M. daily, $8–24), a comfortable pub with seating indoors in small dining rooms or at the bar, or outdoors in the garden. The best bet is the classic pub fare, which includes Reuben sandwiches, shepherd's pie, burgers, and fish-and-chips. Fancier entrées, such as seafood risotto, are also available.

Good food at a fair price reels them into **Poor Boy's Gourmet** (300 Main St., Bar Harbor, 207/288-4148, www.poorboysgourmet.com, from 4:30 P.M. daily). Until 6 P.M. it serves an early bird menu with a half-dozen entrées as well as another 10 all-you-can-eat pasta choices for about $10. The price jumps just a bit after that, with most entrées running $11–24. There's even a cheap lobster feast.

Casual, friendly, creative, and reliable defines **Cafe This Way** (14 Mt. Desert St., Bar Harbor, 207/288-4483, www.cafethisway.com, 7–11:30 A.M. Mon.–Sat., 8 A.M.–1 P.M. Sun., dinner 5:30–9:30 P.M. daily, $16–25), where it's easy to make a meal out of the appetizers alone. Vegetarians will be happy here, and there's a gluten-free menu too. It's not a choice for quiet dining.

Chef-owner Karl Yarborough is putting **◖ Mache Bistro** (135 Cottage St., Bar Harbor, 207/288-0447, www.machebistro.com, from 5:30 P.M. Mon.–Sat., $16–28) on the must-dine list. His interpretations of "French food with local flair" are creative without being over the top.

Savor the panoramic views over Bar Harbor, Frenchman Bay, and the Porcupine Islands along with breakfast or dinner ($11–36) at the **Looking Glass Restaurant** (Wonder View Inn, 50 Eden St., Bar Harbor, 207/288-5663, www.wonderviewinn.com, 7–10:30 A.M. and 5:30–9 P.M. daily). It's quite casual, with

choices ranging from sandwiches to rack of lamb; there's a children's menu too.

Ethnic and Vegetarian Fare

For natural flavors, head to **Tamarind** (16 Mt. Desert St., Bar Harbor, 207/288-2600, 7 A.M.–10 P.M. daily, $6–8), an ultracasual order-at-the-counter place specializing in tasty and healthful foods, with gluten-free, vegan, and vegetarian choices. You'll find breakfast bagels, paninis, soups and salads, and even pizzas.

For Thai food, **Siam Orchard** (30 Rodick St., Bar Harbor, 207/288-9669, 11 A.M.–11 P.M. daily year-round) gets the locals' nod. House specials run $14–18; curries and noodle dishes, such as pad thai, are $11–15. Lunch specials are around $8, and a sushi two-for-one happy hour runs 3–5 P.M. There are plenty of choices for vegetarians. Siam Orchard serves beer and wine only.

Sharing the same building is **Gringo's** (30 Rodick St., Bar Harbor, 207/288-2326, 11 A.M.–10 P.M. daily), a Mexican hole-in-the-wall specializing in takeout burritos, wraps, homemade salsas, and smoothies, with almost everything—margaritas and beer included—less than $8. For a real kick, don't miss the jalapeño brownies.

For "American fine dining with Latin flair," head to **◖ Havana** (318 Main St., Bar Harbor, 207/288-2822, www.havana-maine.com, 5–10 P.M. daily May–late Oct., 5–10 P.M. Wed.–Sat. late Oct.–Apr., entrées $19–35), where the innovative Cuban-esque menu changes frequently to take advantage of what's locally available. Inside, bright orange walls and white tablecloths set a tone that's equally festive and accomplished.

Italian with pizzazz is served in both half and full portions at **Guinness and Porcelli's** (191 Main St., Bar Harbor, 207/288-0300, www.guinnessporcellis.com, 4:30 P.M.–close daily). Pizzas, creative soups and salads, and entrées ($13–24) please all appetites and tastes.

Fine Dining

Five miles south of Bar Harbor, in the village of Otter Creek, which itself is in the town of Mount Desert, is the inauspicious-looking ♥ **Burning Tree** (Rte. 3, Otter Creek, 207/288-9331, 5–10 P.M. Wed.–Mon. late June–early Oct., closed Mon. after Labor Day, $19–25), which is anything but nondescript inside. Chef-owners Allison Martin and Elmer Beal Jr. have created one of Mount Desert Island's best restaurants. Bright and airy, with about 16 tables crowded in three areas, it serves a casually chic crowd. Reservations are essential in summer. Specialties are imaginative seafood entrées and vegetarian dishes. The homemade breads and desserts are delicious. At the height of summer, service can be a bit rushed and the kitchen runs out of popular entrées. Solution: Plan to eat early; it's worth it.

INFORMATION AND SERVICES

The **Bar Harbor Chamber of Commerce** (1201 Bar Harbor Rd./Rte. 3, Trenton, 207/288-5103 or 888/540-9990, www.barharbormaine.com) is open daily in summer, Monday–Friday off-season. Late May–mid-October, the chamber operates a downtown branch.

Once you're on Mount Desert, if you manage to bestir yourself early enough to catch sunrise on the Cadillac summit (you won't be alone—it's a popular activity), stop in at the Chamber of Commerce office later and request an official membership card for the **Cadillac Mountain Sunrise Club** (they'll take your word for it).

Libraries

Jesup Memorial Library (34 Mt. Desert St., Bar Harbor, 207/288-4245, www.jesup.lib. me.us) is open all year.

Public Restrooms

Downtown Bar Harbor has public restrooms in Agamont Park, in the Harbor Place complex at the town pier, in the municipal building (the fire and police station) across from the Village Green, and on the School Street side of the athletic field, where there is RV parking. Restrooms are also at the Mount Desert Island Hospital.

Parking

Make it easy on yourself, help improve the air quality, and reduce stress levels by leaving your car at your lodging (or if day-tripping at the Bar Harbor Chamber of Commerce on Route 3 in Trenton) and taking the Island Explorer bus.

RVs are not allowed to park near the town pier; designated RV parking is alongside the athletic field, on Lower Main and Park Streets, about eight blocks from the center of town.

Northeast Harbor

Ever since the late 19th century, the upper crust from Philadelphia has been summering in and around Northeast Harbor. Sure, they also show up in other parts of Maine, but it's hard not to notice the preponderance of Pennsylvania license plates surrounding Northeast Harbor's elegant "cottages" mid-July–mid-August.

Actually, even though Northeast Harbor is a well-known name with special cachet, it isn't even an official township; it's a zip-coded village within the town of Mount Desert, which collects the breathtaking property taxes and doles out the municipal services.

The attractive boutiques and eateries in Northeast Harbor's small downtown area cater to a casually posh clientele, while the well-protected harbor attracts a tony crowd of yachties. For their convenience, a palm-size annual directory, *The Redbook,* discreetly lists owners' summer residences and winter addresses—but no phone numbers.

SIGHTS
Somes Sound

As you head toward Northeast Harbor on Route 198 from the northern end of Mount

© HILARY NANGLE

Some of the best views of Somes Sound are along Sargent Drive.

Desert Island, you'll begin seeing cliff-lined Somes Sound on your right. Experts disagree as to whether Somes is a true fjord, but in any case it's a lovely chunk of real estate. The glacier-sculpted sound juts five miles into the interior of Mount Desert Island from its mouth, between Northeast and Southwest Harbors. Watch for the right-hand turn for Sargent Drive (no RVs allowed), and follow the lovely granite-lined route along the east side of the sound. Halfway along, a marker explains the geology of this spectacular natural inlet. There aren't many pullouts en route, and traffic can be fairly thick in midsummer, but don't miss it. An ideal way to appreciate Somes Sound is from the water—sign up for an excursion out of Northeast or Southwest Harbor.

Asticou Azalea Garden and Thuya Garden

If you have the slightest interest in gardens, allow time for Northeast Harbor's two marvelous public gardens. Both are operated by the nonprofit Mount Desert Land and Garden Preserve

(207/276-3727, www.gardenpreserve.org). If gardens are extra-high on your priority list, inquire locally about visiting the private Rockefeller garden (www.rockgardenmaine.wordpress.com), accessible on a very limited basis.

One of Maine's best spring showcases is the Asticou Azalea Garden, a 2.3-acre pocket where about 70 varieties of azaleas, rhododendrons, and laurels—many from the classic Reef Point garden of famed landscape designer Beatrix Farrand—burst into bloom. When Charles K. Savage, beloved former innkeeper of the Asticou Inn, learned the Reef Point garden was being undone in 1956, he went into high gear to find funding and managed to rescue the azaleas and provide them with the gorgeous setting they have today, across the road and around the corner from the inn. Serenity is the key—with a Japanese sand garden, stone lanterns, granite outcrops, pink gravel paths, and a tranquil pond. Try to visit early in the season and early in the morning to savor the effect. Blossoming occurs May–August, but the prime time for

THE MAINE SEA COAST MISSION

Remote islands and other isolated communities along Maine's rugged coastline may still have a church, but few have a full-time minister; fewer yet have a health-care provider. Yet these communities aren't entirely shut off from either preaching or medical assistance.

Since 1905, the Maine Sea Coast Mission (127 West St., Bar Harbor, 207/288-5097 or 888/824-7258, www.seacoastmission.org), a nondenominational, nonprofit organization rooted in a Christian ministry, has offered a lifeline to these communities. The mission serves nearly 2,800 people on eight different islands, including Frenchboro, the Cranberries, Swans, and Isle au Haut, as well as others living in remote coastal locations on the mainland. Its numerous much-needed services include a Christmas program, youth programs, emergency financial assistance, food and clothing assistance, ministers to island and coastal communities, scholarships, health services, even work on fisheries management.

Many of these services are delivered via the mission's *Sunbeam V*, a 75-foot diesel boat that has no limitation on when it can travel and few on where it can travel. In winter, it even serves as an icebreaker, clearing harbors and protecting boats from ice damage.

A nurse and a minister usually travel on the *Sunbeam*. The minister may conduct services on the island or on the boat, which also functions as a gathering place for fellowship, meals, and meetings. The minister also reaches out to those in need, marginalized, or ill, and often helps with island funerals. Onboard telemedicine equipment enables the nurse to provide much-needed health care, including screening clinics for diabetes, cholesterol, and prostate and skin cancer; and providing flu and pneumonia vaccines and tetanus shots.

During your travels in the Acadia region, you might see the *Sunbeam* homeported in Northeast Harbor or on its island rounds.

ACADIA REGION

azaleas is roughly mid-May–mid-June. The garden is on Route 198, at the northern edge of Northeast Harbor, immediately north of the junction with Peabody Drive (Rte. 3). Watch for a tiny sign on the left (if you're coming from the north), marking access to the parking area. A small box suggests a $1 donation, and another box contains a garden guide ($2). Pets are not allowed in the garden. Take Island Explorer Route No. 5 (Jordan Pond) or Route No. 6 (Brown Mountain) and request a stop.

Behind a carved wooden gate on a forested hillside not far from Asticou lies an enchanted garden also designed by Charles K. Savage and inspired by Beatrix Farrand. Special features of Thuya Garden are perennial borders and sculpted shrubbery. On a misty summer day, when few visitors appear, the colors are brilliant. Adjacent to the garden is **Thuya Lodge** (207/276-5130), former summer cottage of Joseph Curtis, donor of this awesome municipal park. The lodge, with an extensive botanical library and quiet rooms for reading, is open 10 A.M.–4:30 P.M. daily late June–Labor Day. The garden is open 7 A.M.–7 P.M. daily. A collection box next to the front gate requests a $5 donation per adult. To reach Thuya, continue on Route 3 beyond Asticou Azalea Garden and watch for the Asticou Terraces parking area (no RVs; two-hour limit) on the right. Cross the road and climb the Asticou Terraces Trail (0.4 miles) to the garden. Or drive 0.2 miles beyond the Route 3 parking area, watching for a minuscule Thuya Garden sign on the left. Go 0.5 miles up the steep, narrow, and curving driveway to the parking area. Or take Island Explorer Route No. 5 (Jordan Pond) and request a stop.

After you've visited Thuya Garden, open the back gate, where you'll see a sign for the **Eliot Mountain Trail,** a moderately difficult (lots of exposed roots) 1.4-mile round-trip trail. Near the summit, Northeast Harbor spreads out

Northeast Harbor's Asticou Azalea Garden is spectacular in spring, when the azaleas are in full bloom.

before you. If you're here in August, sample the wild blueberries. Much of the Eliot Mountain Trail is on private land, so stay on the path and be respectful of private property.

Petite Plaisance

On Northeast Harbor's quiet South Shore Road, Petite Plaisance is a special-interest museum commemorating noted Belgian-born author and college professor Marguerite Yourcenar (pen name of Marguerite de Crayencour), the first woman elected to the prestigious Académie Française. From the early 1950s to 1987, Petite Plaisance was her home, and it's hard to believe she's no longer here; her intriguing possessions and presence fill the two-story house, of particular interest to Yourcenar devotees. Free hour-long tours of the first floor are given in French or English, depending on visitors' preferences; French-speaking visitors often make pilgrimages here. The house is open for tours daily June 15–August 31. No children under 12 are allowed. Call 207/276-3940 at least a day ahead,

between 9 A.M.–4 P.M., for an appointment and directions, or write: Petite Plaisance Trust, P.O. Box 403, Northeast Harbor, ME 04662. Yourcenar admirers should request directions to Brookside Cemetery in Somesville, seven miles away, where she is buried.

Great Harbor Maritime Museum

Annual exhibits focusing on the maritime heritage of the Mount Desert Island area are held in the small, eclectic Great Harbor Maritime Museum (124 Main St., Northeast Harbor, 207/276-5262, 10 A.M.–5 P.M. Tues.–Sat. late June–Labor Day, $3), housed in the old village fire station and municipal building. ("Great Harbor" refers to the Somes Sound area—Northeast, Southwest, and Seal Harbors, as well as the Cranberry Isles.) Yachting, coastal trade, and fishing receive special emphasis. Look for the canvas rowing canoe, built in Veazie, Maine, between 1917 and 1920; it's the only one of its kind known to exist today. Special programs and exhibitions are held during the summer.

ENTERTAINMENT
Mount Desert Festival of Chamber Music

Since 1964 the Mount Desert Festival of Chamber Music (207/276-3988, www.mtdesertfestival.org) has presented concerts in the century-old Neighborhood House on Main Street at 8:15 P.M. Tuesday mid-July–mid-August. Tickets ($25 general admission, $10 students) are available at the Neighborhood House box office on Monday–Tuesday during the concert season or by phone reservation.

SHOPPING

Upscale shops, galleries, and boutiques with clothing, artworks, housewares, antiques, and antiquarian books line both sides of Main Street, making for intriguing browsing and expensive buying (but be sure to check the sale rooms of the clothing shops for bona fide bargains). The season is short, though, with some shops open only in July–August.

One must-visit is **Shaw Contemporary Jewelry** (100 Main St., 207/276-5000 or 877/276-5001, www.shawjewelry.com, year-round). Besides the spectacular silver and gold beachstone jewelry created by Rhode Island School of Design alumnus Sam Shaw, the work of more than 100 other jewelers is displayed exquisitely. Plus there are sculptures, Asian art, and rotating art exhibits. It all leads back toward a lovely light-filled garden. Prices are in the stratosphere, but appropriately so. As one well-dressed customer was overheard sighing to her companion: "If I had only one jewelry store to go to in my entire life, this would be it."

RECREATION
Excursion Boats

Northeast Harbor is the starting point for a couple of boat services headed for the **Cranberry Isles.** The vessels leave from the commercial floats at the end of the concrete municipal pier on Sea Street. (Other boats depart from Southwest Harbor, and there's also regular ferry and mail-boat service between Northeast Harbor and the Cranberries, both described later.)

The 75-foot *Sea Princess* (207/276-5352, www.barharborcruises.com) carries visitors as well as an Acadia National Park naturalist on a 2.5-hour morning trip around the mouth of Somes Sound and out to Little Cranberry Island (Islesford) for a 50-minute stopover. The boat leaves Northeast Harbor at 10 A.M. daily mid-May–mid-October. A narrated afternoon trip departs at 1 P.M. on the same route. A scenic 1.5-hour Somes Sound cruise departs at 3:45 P.M. daily late June–early September. The same months, two sunset cruises are offered. The three-hour sunset dinner cruise departs for the Islesford Dock Restaurant on Little Cranberry (Islesford) at 5:15 P.M. Dinner is on your own at the restaurant. A 1.5-hour sunset cruise of Somes Sound departs at 7 P.M. Cost for all tours is $20–25 adults, $15 ages 5–12, $5 under age 5. Reservations are advisable for all trips, although even that provides no guarantee, since the cruises require a 15-passenger minimum.

ACCOMMODATIONS

Rates are listed for peak season.

Inns

If money's no object and a classic yet haute ambience appeals, spring for the **Asticou Inn** (Rte. 3, Northeast Harbor, 207/276-3344 or 800/258-3373, www.asticou.com). Built in 1883, the harbor-view inn came under Kennebunk's White Barn Inn management in spring 2010, and updates and upgrades began immediately, with more planned. Because so much is up for change, it's wise to call to learn about its current status and details.

Bed-and-Breakfasts

The casual elegance of a bygone era still exists at **Grey Rock Inn** (Rte. 3/198, Northeast Harbor, summer 207/276-9360, winter 207/244-4437, www.greyrockinn.com, mid-May–late Oct., $185–375), an antiques-filled mansion with to-die-for views over Northeast Harbor to the outer islands. Guest rooms are comfortable and large; many have fireplaces. Common rooms, most with fireplaces, flow from one to another. Trails lace the property's seven acres, which are bordered by Acadia National Park on two sides. Head out for a hike, perhaps to the summit of Norumbega Mountain, or stroll down the street to downtown Northeast Harbor. Rates include a full breakfast.

In 1888, architect Fred Savage designed the two shingle-style buildings that make up the three-story **Harbourside Inn** (Main St., Northeast Harbor, 207/276-3272, www .harboursideinn.com, mid-June–mid-Sept., $125–295). The Sweet family has preserved the old-fashioned feel by decorating the 11 spacious guest rooms and three suites with antiques, yet modern amenities include some kitchenettes and phones. Most rooms have working fireplaces. A continental breakfast is served. Trails to Norumbega Mountain and Upper Hadlock Pond leave from the back of the property. Over the years the waterfront property has been sold off, so despite the inn's name, only glimpses of the harbor can be seen.

For those who prefer something more modern, the new in 2009 **Colonel's Suites** (143 Maine St., Northeast Harbor, 207/288-4775, www.colonelssuites.com, $199), above the restaurant of the same name, provide comfortable accommodations with modern amenities. Every suite has a separate seating area, refrigerator, and flat-screen TV. Rates include a full breakfast in the restaurant.

Three miles from Northeast Harbor, in equally tony Seal Harbor, is a true bargain, the **Lighthouse Inn and Restaurant** (12 Main St./Rte. 3, Seal Harbor, 207/276-3958, www.lighthouseinnandrestaurant.com, $75–125). Sure, the three guest rooms (one small, one very large with a kitchenette, one two-room suite with a kitchenette) are a bit dated and dowdy, but at these prices, who cares. All have private baths, and downstairs is a restaurant (8 A.M.–9 P.M. Mon.–Sat., 8 A.M.–4 P.M. Sun.), serving all meals at equally reasonable prices. It's a short walk to Seal Harbor Beach and the Seal Harbor entrance to the Park Loop Road.

Seal Harbor is a peaceful place in the evening.

© TOM NANGLE

Motels

Although it's overdue for an overhaul—every guest room has two double beds and the decor is uninspired—you can't beat the location of the **Kimball Terrace Inn** (10 Huntington Rd., Northeast Harbor, 207/276-3383 or 800/454-6225, www.kimballterraceinn.com, $175–205). The three-story motel faces the harbor, and every guest room has a patio or private balcony (ask for a harbor-facing room). Bring binoculars for yacht-spotting. The motel has a pool, a restaurant serving three meals daily, and a lounge, and it is a short walk to Northeast Harbor's downtown. It is a popular wedding venue, so if that's a concern, ask if there are any groups in-house before you book.

FOOD

Hours listed are for peak season, early July–early September. If you're visiting at other times, call, as most restaurants are open fewer days and hours during slower periods.

Local Flavors

In the **Pine Tree Market** (121 Main St., Northeast Harbor, 207/276-3335, 7 A.M.–7 P.M. Mon.–Sat., 8 A.M.–6 P.M. Sun.), you'll find gourmet goodies, a huge wine selection, a resident butcher, fresh fish, a deli, homemade breads, pastries, sandwiches, and salads. The market offers free delivery to homes and boats.

Pop into **Full Belli Deli** (5 Sea St., Northeast Harbor, 207/276-4299, 8 A.M.–8 P.M. daily) for soups, fat sandwiches, pizzas, and breakfast fare.

From June well into October, the **Northeast Harbor Farmers Market** is set up 9 A.M.–noon each Thursday across from the Kimball Terrace Inn on Huntington Road.

The homemade doughnuts are reason enough to visit **The Colonel's Restaurant and Bakery** (143 Maine St., Northeast Harbor, 207/288-4775, 7 A.M.–9 P.M. daily).

Casual Dining

Casual yet sophisticated, **Redbird Provisions** (11 Sea St., Northeast Harbor, 207/276-3006, www.redbirdprovisions.com, 11:30 A.M.–2 P.M. and 6–9 P.M. Tues.–Sun. July–Aug.) is the perfect neighborhood restaurant—if your neighbors are the yachting type. Inspired lunches and dinners ($22–35) reflecting seasonally available ingredients are served in a renovated house and on the weatherized patio. Call for June and September hours.

Fine Dining

The elegant mural-lined dining room at the **Asticou Inn** (Rte. 3, 207/276-3344 or 800/258-3373, 7–9 A.M., 11:30 A.M.–2 P.M., and 6–9 P.M. daily) is open to nonguests for breakfast, lunch, Sunday brunch, and dinner ($22–35). Lunch is served on the harbor-side deck, with serene views over Northeast Harbor. Jackets and ties are advised for dinner. The restaurant is under new management, so changes are likely; call for details.

INFORMATION AND SERVICES

The harbor-front Chamber Information Bureau (also called the Yachtsmen's Building) of the **Mount Desert Chamber of Commerce** (18 Harbor Rd., Northeast Harbor, 207/276-5040, 8 A.M.–5 P.M. daily mid-June–mid-Oct.) covers the villages of Somesville, Northeast Harbor, Seal Harbor, Otter Creek, Pretty Marsh, Hall Quarry, and Beech Hill.

Public Restrooms

Restrooms are at the end of the building housing the Great Harbor Maritime Museum, in the town office on Sea Street, and at the harbor.

GETTING AROUND

Northeast Harbor is served by Route No. 5 (Jordan Pond) and Route No. 6 (Brown Mountain) of the Island Explorer bus system.

The Quiet Side

Southwest Harbor considers itself the hub of Mount Desert Island's "quiet side." In summer, its tiny downtown district is probably the busiest spot on the whole western side of the island (west of Somes Sound), but that's not saying a great deal. "Southwest" has the feel of a settled community, a year-round flavor that Bar Harbor sometimes lacks. And it competes with the best in the scenery department. The Southwest Harbor area serves as a very convenient base for exploring Acadia National Park, as well as the island's less-crowded villages and offshore Swans Island, Frenchboro, and the Cranberry Isles.

The quirky nature of the island's four town boundaries creates complications in trying to categorize various island segments. Officially, the town of Southwest Harbor includes only the villages of **Manset** and **Seawall,** but nearby is the precious hamlet of **Somesville.** The Somesville National Historic District, with its distinctive arched white footbridge, is especially appealing, but traffic gets congested here along Route 102, so rather than just rubbernecking, plan to stop and walk around.

The "quiet side" of the island becomes even quieter as you round the southwestern edge into **Tremont,** which includes the villages of **Bernard; Bass Harbor,** home of Bass Harbor Head Light and ferry services to offshore islands; and **Seal Cove.** Tremont occupies the southwesternmost corner of Mount Desert Island. It's about as far as you can get from Bar Harbor, but the free Island Explorer bus service's Route No. 7 (Southwest Harbor) comes through here regularly.

Be sure to visit these small villages. Views are fabulous, the pace is slow, and you'll feel as if you've stumbled upon "the real Maine."

SIGHTS
◖ Wendell Gilley Museum
In the center of Southwest Harbor, the Wendell Gilley Museum (Herrick Rd. and Rte. 102, Southwest Harbor, 207/244-7555, www .wendellgilleymuseum.org, 10 A.M.–5 P.M. daily July–Aug., 10 A.M.–4 P.M. Tues.–Sun. June and Sept.–Oct., 10 A.M.–5 P.M. Fri.–Sun. May and Nov.–Dec., $5 adults, $2 ages 5–12) was established in 1981 to display the life work of local woodcarver Wendell Gilley (1904–1983), a onetime plumber who had gained a national reputation for his carvings by the time of his death. The modern, energy-efficient museum houses more than 200 of his astonishingly realistic bird specimens carved over more than 50 years. Summer exhibits also feature other wildlife artists. Many days, a local artist gives woodcarving demonstrations, and members of the local carving club often can be seen whittling away. The gift shop carries an ornithological potpourri, including books, binoculars, and carving tools. Kids over eight appreciate this more than younger ones. If you're bitten by the carving bug, workshops are available, ranging from 90-minute introductory lessons for adults and children ($25), offered most weekdays during the summer, to multiday classes on specific birds.

Mount Desert Island Historical Society Museum
This tiny museum (Rte. 102, Somesville, 207/276-9323, 1–4 P.M. Tues.–Sat., seasonal, donation) is adjacent to the gently curving white bridge in Somesville, so there's a good chance you're going to stop nearby, if just for a photo. In season, the heirloom garden, filled with flowering plants and herbs of the 19th and early 20th centuries, is worth a photo or two. The one-room museum has local artifacts and memorabilia displayed in a themed exhibit that changes annually. You can purchase a walking-tour guide to Somesville in the museum. If you're especially interested in history, ask about the museum's programs, which include speakers, demonstrations, and workshops.

Charlotte Rhoades Park and Butterfly Garden

It's easy to miss the Charlotte Rhoades Park and Butterfly Garden (Rte. 102, Southwest Harbor, 207/244-5405), but that would be a mistake. This tiny seaside park was donated to the town in 1973, and the butterfly garden was established and is maintained entirely by volunteers. The park is seldom busy, and it's a delightful place for a picnic. A kiosk is stocked with butterfly observation sheets. The park is located on the water side of Route 102 between the Causeway Golf Club and the Seal Cove Road.

Country Store Museum

Stepping inside the former general store that's now headquarters for the **Tremont Historical Society** (Shore Rd., Bass Harbor, 207/244-9753, www.tremontmainehistory.us, 1–4 P.M. Mon. and Wed. July–mid Oct.) is like stepping into the 1800s. Displays highlight the local heritage. If you're lucky, seventh-generation islander Muriel Davidson might be on duty and regale you with stories about her aunt, author Ruth Moore. You can buy copies of Moore's books here—good reads all. The museum is located across from the Seafood Ketch.

The Seal Cove Auto Museum

The late Richard C. Paine Jr.'s Brass Era (1905–1917) car collection, one of the largest in the country, is nicely displayed and identified in the Seal Cove Auto Museum (Pretty Marsh Rd./Rte. 102, Seal Cove, 207/244-9242, www.sealcoveautomuseum.org, 10 A.M.–5 P.M. daily late May–mid-Oct., $5 adults, $4.50 seniors, $2 under age 13). All vehicles are in as-found condition; this ranges from fresh-from-the-barn to meticulously restored. It's easy for kids of any age to spend an hour here, reminiscing or fantasizing. Among the highlights are a 1907 Chadwick Touring Car and a 1910 Chadwick Racer, two of only three Chadwicks still in existence; a 1915 F.R.P., the fifth of only nine built and the only one still in existence; an original 1903 Ford Model A, the

first car commercially produced by the Ford Motor Co., and a 1909 Ford Model T "Tin Lizzie," from the first year of production. The oldest car in the collection is an 1899 DeDion-Bouton, one of the earliest cars produced in the world. The museum is about six miles southwest of Somesville. Or, if you're coming from Southwest Harbor, take Route 102 north to Seal Cove Road (partly unpaved) west to the other side of Route 102 (it makes a giant loop) and go north about 1.5 miles. This is not on the Island Explorer route.

ENTERTAINMENT
Acadia Repertory Theatre

Somesville is home to the Acadia Repertory Theatre (Rte. 102, Somesville, 207/244-7260 or 888/362-7480, www.acadiarep.com, $23 adults, $18 seniors, students, and military, $10 under age 16), which has been providing first-rate professional summer stock on the stage of Somesville's antique Masonic Hall since the 1970s. Classic plays by Oscar Wilde, Neil Simon, and even Molière have been staples, as has the annual Agatha Christie mystery. Performances in the 144-seat hall run at 8:15 P.M. Tuesday–Sunday late June–late August, with 2 P.M. matinees on the last Sunday of each play's run. Special children's plays are performed at 10:30 A.M. Wednesday and Saturday in July–August. Tickets for children's theater programs are $8 adults, $5 children.

Lecture and Concert Series

During July–August, the Claremont Hotel (22 Claremont Rd., Southwest Harbor, 207/244-5036 or 800/244-5036, www.theclaremonthotel.com) sponsors a free weekly lecture series at 8 P.M. on Thursday evenings. Past topics have ranged from Arab-Israeli peace possibilities to wildlife on Mount Desert Island. It also offers a Saturday Evening Concert series ($8), with music ranging from blue grass to classical.

EVENTS

During July–August, the Wednesday **Pie Sale** at the Somesville Union Meeting House is always a sellout. Go early; the doors open at 10 A.M.

In early August, the annual **Claremont Croquet Classic,** held on the grounds of the classic Claremont Hotel, is open to all ages.

In September, Smuggler's Den Campground, on Route 102 in Southwest Harbor, is home to the annual **MDI Garlic Festival,** with entertainment and opportunities to savor the stinking rose, and in October the campground hosts the annual **Oktoberfest and Food Festival** (207/244-9264 or 800/423-9264, www.acadiachamber.com), a one-day celebration with crafts, food, games, music, and about two dozen Maine microbrewers presenting about 80 different brews.

SHOPPING
Southwest Harbor
Fine art of the 19th and early 20th centuries is the specialty at **Clark Point Gallery** (46 Clark Point Rd., Southwest Harbor, 207/244-0920, www.clarkpointgallery.com). Most works depict Maine and Mount Desert Island.

Jewelry approaches fine art at **Aylen & Son Jewelers** (332 Main St./Rte. 102, Southwest Harbor, 207/244-7369, www.peteraylen.com). For more than 25 years Peter and Judy Aylen have been crafting and selling jewelry in 18-karat gold and sterling silver and augmenting it with fine gemstones or intriguing beads.

More than 50 coastal Maine artisans sell their crafts at **Flying Mountain Artisans** (28 Main St./Rte. 102, Southwest Harbor, 207/244-0404), a cooperatively owned shop with a good range of creative goods, from quilts to blown glass. Also here is a gallery showing the works of more than 20 artists. Consider stopping in after a hike on Flying Mountain.

Bernard and Seal Cove
It's fun to poke around **Ravenswood** (McMullen Ave., Bass Harbor, 207/669-4287), a musty shop filled with old books, nautical gifts, model ship kits, and marvelous birds carved on site.

Stop in at **E. L. Higgins** (Bernard Rd., Bernard, 207/244-3983, www.antiquewicker

.com), where Edward Higgins has the state's best collection of antique wicker furniture, about 400 pieces at any given time, in two one-time classrooms in an 1890s schoolhouse.

Right next door is **Linda Fernandez Handknits** (Bernard Rd., Bernard, 207/244-7224), with beautiful hand-knit sweaters, mittens, hats, socks, Christmas stockings, and embroidered pillowcases all handcrafted by the talented and extended Fernandez family. The kids' lobster sweaters are especially cute.

When a psychic told A. Jones more than 30 years ago that she would move to an island, she thought, *Wrong.* But the psychic was right: Continue down Bernard Road, then hang a left on Columbia Avenue to find **A. Jones Gallery** (Columbia Ave., Bernard, 207/244-5634). Inside is a double find: artworks in a variety of media and styles as well as a working studio in the barn; country antiques and folk-art finds in the garage.

Potters Lisbeth Faulkner and Edwin Davis can often be seen working in their studio at **Seal Cove Pottery & Gallery** (Kelleytown Rd., Seal Cove, 207/244-3602, www.sealcovepottery.com). In addition to their functional hand-thrown or hand-built pottery, they exhibit Davis's paintings as well as crafts by other island artisans.

RECREATION
Hiking
At the Southwest Harbor/Tremont Chamber of Commerce office, or at any of the area's stores, lodgings, and restaurants, pick up a free copy of the *Trail Map/Hiking Guide,* a very handy foldout map showing more than 20 hikes on the west side of Mount Desert Island. Trail descriptions include distances, time required, and skill levels (easy to strenuous).

Bicycle Rentals
Southwest Cycle (370 Main St., Southwest Harbor, 207/244-5856 or 800/649-5856, www.southwestcycle.com) rents bikes by the day and week and is open year-round (the June–September hours are 8:30 A.M.–5:30 P.M. Mon.–Sat., 9:30 A.M.–4 P.M. Sun.). The staff

© HILARY NANGLE

Long Pond, Acadia National Park

will fix you up with maps and lots of good advice for three loops (10–30 miles) on the western side of Mount Desert. Rentals begin around $16 for a half day and $22 for a full day. The shop also rents every imaginable accessory, from baby seats to jogging strollers.

Golf

Play a quick nine at the **Causeway Club** (Fernald Point Rd., 207/244-3780), which edges the ocean. Be forewarned: It's more challenging than it looks.

Excursion Boats
⚓ ISLAND CRUISES

High praise goes to Captain Kim Strauss's Island Cruises (Little Island Marine, Shore Rd., Bass Harbor, 207/244-5785, www .bassharborcruises.com) for its narrated 3.5-hour **lunch cruise to Frenchboro.** The 49-passenger *R. L. Gott,* which Strauss built, departs at 11 A.M. daily during the summer. Kim has been navigating these waters for more than 55 years, and his experience shows not only in his boat handling but also in his narration. Expect to pick up lots of local heritage and lore about once-thriving and now abandoned granite-quarrying and fishing communities, the sardine industry, and lobstering; and to see seals, cormorants, guillemots, and often eagles. The trip allows enough time on Frenchboro for a picnic (or lunch at the summertime deli on the dock) and a short village stroll, then a return through the sprinkling of islands along the 8.3-mile route. Kim also hauls a few traps and explains lobstering. He also earns major points for maneuvering the boat so that passengers on both sides get an up-close view of key sights. It's an excellent, enthralling tour for all ages. Round-trip cost is $27 adults, $17 children 11 and younger. Be sure to make reservations, and if the weather looks iffy, call ahead to confirm. Most of the trip is in sheltered water, but rough seas can put the kibosh on it. Island Cruises also does a two-hour **afternoon nature cruise** among the islands that covers the same topics but spends a bit more time at seal ledges and other spots

($23 adults, $17 children). On either trip, don't forget to bring binoculars. Also offered is a 1.5-hour **sunset cruise** ($20 adults, $12 children). You'll find the Island Cruises dock by following signs to the Swans Island Ferry and turning right at the sign shortly before the state ferry dock.

FRIENDSHIP SLOOP CHARTERS
Charter a traditional Friendship sloop with **Downeast Friendship Sloop Charters** (Dysert's Great Harbor Marina, Apple Lane, Southwest Harbor, 207/266-5210, www .downeastfriendshipsloop.com). Private charters start at $125 per hour, including an appetizer; shared trips are $50 pp for two hours, $75 pp for three hours. A sunset sail is a lovely way to end a day. One of the boats used is the oldest known Friendship sloop still sailing.

DEEP-SEA FISHING
Go fishing with the **Masako Queen Fishing Company** (Beal's Wharf, Clark Point Rd., Southwest Harbor, 207/244-5385, www.masa-koqueen.com, $59 adults, $39 ages 5–12) aboard the 43-foot *Vagabond* and you might return with a lobster. The boat goes 8–20 miles offshore for mackerel, bluefish, codfish, and more. All equipment is included; dress warmly.

Boat Rentals and Lessons
Mansell Boat Rental Co. (135 Shore Rd., Manset, next to Hinckley, 207/244-5625, www.mansellboatrentals.com) rents sailboats and powerboats by the day or week, including a keel day-sailor for $195 per day and a 13.6-foot Boston Whaler for $175 per day. Also available are sailing lessons: $195 for a two-plus-hour sail lesson cruise for two, which includes rigging and unrigging the boat; $100 per hour for private lessons, minimum two hours.

Paddling
SEA KAYAKING
On the outskirts of Southwest Harbor's downtown is **Maine State Kayak** (254 Main St.,

Southwest Harbor, 207/244-9500 or 877/481-9500, www.mainestatekayak.com). Staffed with experienced, environmentally sensitive kayakers (several are Registered Maine Guides), the company offers four-hour guided trips departing at 8:30 and 10 A.M. and 2 P.M. along with a sunset tour, with a choice of half a dozen routes that depend on tides, visibility, and wind conditions. The rate is $48 pp, $44 in June and September. Most trips include island or beach breaks. Maximum group size is six tandems; minimum age is 12. Neophytes are welcome.

If you have your own boat, consider putting in at either the park's Pretty Marsh picnic area, off Route 102 in Pretty Marsh, or at the public boat launch at the end of Bartlett's Landing Road, off Indian Point Road near the Route 102 end.

CALM-WATER PADDLING
Just west of Somesville (take Pretty Marsh Rd.) and across the road from Long Pond, the largest lake on Mount Desert Island, **National Park Canoe & Kayak Rental** (145 Pretty Marsh Rd./Rte. 102, Mount Desert, 207/244-5854 or 877/378-6907, www.na-tionalparkcanoerental.com, mid-May–mid-Oct.) makes canoeing and kayaking a snap. Just rent the boat, carry it across the road to Pond's End, and launch it. Be sure to pack a picnic. Rates begin at $28 for a three-hour canoe or solo kayak rental, $31 for a tandem kayak. A do-it-yourself sunset canoe or kayak tour (5 P.M.–sunset) is $18 pp. The late fee is $10 per half hour. Reservations are essential in July–August.

If you've brought your own canoe or kayak, launch it here at Pond's End and head off. It's four miles to the southern end of the lake. If the wind kicks up, skirt the shore; if it really kicks up from the north, don't paddle too far down the lake, as you'll have a difficult time getting back.

Almost the entire west side of **Long Pond** is Acadia National Park property, so plan to picnic and swim along here; tuck into the sheltered area west of Southern Neck, a crooked finger of land that points northward from the western shore. Stay clear of private property on the east side of the lake.

ACCOMMODATIONS

Rates are listed for peak season.

Inn

When you're ready to splurge, **The Claremont** (22 Claremont Rd., Southwest Harbor, 207/244-5036 or 800/244-5036, www.theclaremonthotel.com) may well be your choice. The most popular time here is the first week in August, during the annual Claremont Croquet Classic. An elegant grande dame dressed in mustard-yellow clapboard, the Claremont dominates a six-acre hilltop with stupendous views over Somes Sound. Guests have access to croquet courts, a clay tennis court, bikes, rowboats, and a library. Dating from 1884, the main building has 24 guest rooms, most of them refurbished yet pleasantly old-fashioned and neither fussy nor fancy. Additional guest rooms are in the Phillips House and Cole Cottage.

Guest rooms in these buildings begin at $170 in summer, including buffet breakfast. Also on the premises are 14 cottages ($203–340). A hefty 15 percent service charge is added to all rates. Children are welcome. The hotel and dining room are open early June–mid-October; cottages are open late May–mid-October.

Bed-and-Breakfasts

Many of Southwest Harbor's bed-and-breakfasts are clustered downtown, along Main Street and the Clark Point Road.

Set on a corner, well back from Clark Point Road, is **(Harbour Cottage Inn** (9 Dirigo Rd., Southwest Harbor, 207/244-5738 or 888/843-3022, www.harbourcottageinn .com, $198–255), appealingly revamped in 2002 when Javier Montesinos and Don Jalbert took over the reins. Built in 1870, it was the annex for the island's first hotel and housed the increasing numbers of rusticators who patronized this part of the island. It has evolved into a lovely bed-and-breakfast with eight guest rooms and three suites decorated

© HILARY NANGLE

Watch boats sail by from The Claremont's wrap-around porch.

in a colorful and fun cottage style. Most guest rooms have whirlpool baths or steam-sauna showers, some have fireplaces, and all have TVs and Wi-Fi. Rates include a multicourse breakfast. Also part of Harbour Cottage is **Pier One,** which offers five truly waterfront suites ($1,484–1,798 weekly), including a studio cottage. All were renovated in 2009 in a comfortable cottage style; all have kitchens, TVs, and phones. Guests have private use of a 150-foot pier, and they can dock or launch canoes, kayaks, or other small boats from right outside their doors; dockage is available for larger boats. It's all within walking distance of downtown.

The linden-blossom fragrance can be intoxicating in summer at the **Lindenwood Inn** (118 Clark Point Rd., Southwest Harbor, 207/244-5335 or 800/307-5335, www.lindenwoodinn.com, $155–295). Jim King, the Australian owner, has imaginatively decorated the inn's nine guest rooms and poolside bungalow with artifacts from everywhere in a style that's sophisticated yet comfortable. After you hike Acadia's trails, the heated pool and hot tub are especially welcome, and after that, perhaps enjoy a drink while shooting pool or playing darts. Some guest rooms have harbor views.

In 2004, Ann and Charlie Bradford sold the family home that had housed their long-time bed-and-breakfast and reopened a petite version of the **Island House** (36 Freeman Ridge, Southwest Harbor, 207/244-5180, www.islandhousebb.com, year-round) in their new custom home, built atop a ridge in a quiet neighborhood about a mile from downtown. They've downsized the guest space to just two comfy guest rooms ($130) plus a guest living-dining room, all on one level (a great place for anyone with mobility problems, although it's not wheelchair-accessible). Anne's warm hospitality and delicious full breakfasts remain the same. The Bradfords also rent a separate two-bedroom apartment above the garage ($185), with a tiny deck offering glimpses of distant islands.

Even glimpsed through the trees from the road, **The Birches** (46 Fernald Point Rd., Southwest Harbor, 207/244-5182, www.thebirchesbnb.com, $135–170) is appealing. A wooded drive winds down to the large home fronting the ocean, near the mouth of Somes Sound. It's just 350 yards to the Causeway Golf Club and a short walk to the Flying Mountain trailhead. Built as a summer cottage in 1916, The Birches retains that casual summer ease, right down to the stone fireplace in the living room and the croquet court on the lawn. Guest rooms are large and minimally decorated. Hosts Dick and Rocky Homer serve a full breakfast.

In Manset, adjacent to the Hinckley Yacht complex and with jaw-dropping views down Somes Sound, is **The Moorings** (133 Shore Rd., Manset, 207/244-5523 or 800/596-5523, www.mooringsinn.com, $110–195), owned and operated by the King family since 1960. The oceanfront complex is part motel, part cottage rental, and part old-fashioned bed-and-breakfast. Rooms are named after locally built sailing vessels. The motel-style rooms in the Lighthouse View Wing have refrigerators, microwaves, waterfront decks, and incredible views (spend the afternoon counting the Hinckley yachts). Also on the property or nearby are cottage units ($125–245). Bikes, canoes, and kayaks are available for guests, so you can paddle around the harbor; Mansell Boat Rental Co. is also on the premises. Dogs are allowed.

When price is no object and you really want pampering, check into **Ann's Point Inn & Spa** (79 Anns Point Rd., Bass Harbor, 207/244-9595, www.annspointinn.com, $325–345), an oceanfront inn at the tip of Ann's Point. Each of four guest rooms has a king bed covered in luxurious linens, a gas fireplace, and all the amenities you might expect, including robes and slippers, in-room TVs and DVD players, phones, Wi-Fi, CD players, and air-conditioning. Rooms are huge, and all have ocean views. If that's not enough, there's an indoor pool, a hot tub, and a sauna, plus afternoon hors d'oeuvres and evening sweets. All this is on two acres with 690 feet of shorefront. The inn is open year-round.

Motels and Cottages

Right smack on the harbor and just a two-minute walk from downtown is the appropriately named **Harbor View Motel & Cottages** (11 Ocean Way, Southwest Harbor, 207/244-5031 or 800/538-6463, www.harborviewmotelandcottages.com). The family-owned complex comprises motel rooms ($86–128 per night, $540–815 per week) spread out in two older one-story buildings and a newer three-story structure that fronts the harbor. A continental breakfast is served to motel guests July 1–early September. Also on the premises are seven housekeeping cottages with kitchenettes (weekly rentals only, $740–1,225), ranging from studios to two-bedrooms. Pets are welcome in some units.

Right across from the famed seawall and adjacent to the park is the **Seawall Motel** (566 Seawall Rd./Rte. 102A, Southwest Harbor, 207/244-9250 or 800/248-9250, www.seawallmotel.com, $115). The no-surprises two-story motel (upstairs guest rooms have the best views) has free Wi-Fi, in-room phones, and cable TV. A continental breakfast is included mid-May–October. Kids 12 and younger stay free. The location is excellent for bird-watchers. Also on the premises is the **Common Good Cafe** (207/244-3007, www.commongoodsoupkitchen.org, 8:30 A.M.–3 P.M. Tues.–Sun.), operated by the Common Good Soup Kitchen Community and serving soups, sandwiches, salads, and specials; it's a cool place, check it out.

Camping

On the eastern edge of Somesville, just off Route 198 at the head of Somes Sound, the **Mount Desert Campground** (516 Somes Sound Dr./Rte. 198, Somesville, 207/244-3710, www.mountdesertcampground.com, $36–49) has 152 wooded tent sites, about 45 on the water, spread out on 58 acres. Reservations are essential in midsummer—there is a one-week minimum for waterfront sites and a three-day minimum for off-water sites in July–August. Campers book a year ahead for the waterfront sites. This deservedly popular and low-key campground gets high marks for maintenance, noise control, and convenient tent platforms. Electrical hookups are available for $2 per night. Pets are not allowed July–early September; trailers over 20 feet are not allowed. Kayak and canoe rentals are available.

Built on the site of an old quarry, on a hillside descending to rocky frontage on Somes Sound, **Somes Sound View Campground** (86 Hall Quarry Rd., Mount Desert, 207/244-3890, off-season 207/244-7452, www.ssvc.info, late May to mid-Oct., $29–55, no credit cards) is among the smallest campgrounds on the island, with fewer than 60 sites, all geared to tents and vans. Facilities include hot showers (if you're camping on the lowest levels, it's a good hike up to the bathhouse), a heated pool, a boat launch, kayak and paddleboat rentals, and a fishing dock. You can swim in the sound from a rocky beach. Leashed pets are allowed. It's two miles south and east of Somesville and a mile east of Route 102.

For RVs and big rigs, **Smuggler's Den Campground** (Rte. 102, Southwest Harbor, 207/244-3944, www.smugglersdencampground.com, $31–51) is a midsized campground between Echo Lake and downtown Southwest Harbor. Facilities include a heated pool and a kiddie pool, laundry, free hot showers, lobster and ice cream sales, and entertainment. Well-behaved pets are allowed.

FOOD
Local Flavors

Lots of goodies for picnics can be found at **Sawyer's Market** (Main St., Southwest Harbor, 207/244-7061, 5:30 A.M.–7:30 P.M. Mon.–Sat.); for wine and cheese head across the street to **Sawyer's Specialties** (Main St., Southwest Harbor, 207/244-3317, open daily).

The students at College of the Atlantic run **Beech Hill Farm** (Beech Hill Rd., Mount Desert, 207/244-5204, 8 A.M.–5 P.M. Tues.–Sat.), a five-acre farm certified organic by the Maine Organic Farmers and Gardeners Association that also has acres of heirloom apple trees and 65 acres of forestland. Visit the farm stand for fresh produce as well as other organic or natural foods such as cheeses and baked goods.

Ethnic Fare

Craving a taste of Mexico? **XYZ Restaurant** (80 Seawall Rd./Rte. 102A, Manset, 207/244-5221, 5:30–9 P.M. daily, entrées $24) specializes in the flavors of interior Mexico: Xalapa, Yucatán, and Zacatecas (hence "XYZ"). The most popular dish is *cochinitas*—citrus-marinated pork rubbed with achiote paste, worthy of its reputation. The margaritas are classic—requiring, allegedly, 1,100 pounds of fresh limes each year. For dessert, try the XYZ pie. Dine inside or on the porch. The food is great, but it's served with a dose of attitude.

From the outside, it doesn't look like much, but locals know you can count on **DeMuro's Top of the Hill** (Rte. 102, Southwest Harbor, 207/244-0033, www.topofthehilldining.com, 4:30 P.M.–close daily, $10–25) for a good meal at a fair price. The Italian-influenced menu has something in all price ranges. Early-bird specials are served 4:30–6:30 P.M.

Craving authentic Chinese, Thai, or Japanese fare with a few Italian accents? Chiaolin and Ken Korona's **Chow Maine Ciao Maine** (19 Clark Point Rd., Southwest Harbor, 207/699-4142, www.chow-maine.com, 11:30 A.M.–9 P.M. Mon.–Sat.) serves sushi, sashimi, teriyaki, curry, and even homemade meatballs and spaghetti in a minimalist, almost Zen-like dining space adjacent to the post office; BYOB. They also own and operate the adjacent **Corner Café** (from 7 A.M.) serving soups, salads, and sandwiches with indoor and outdoor seating.

Casual Dining

By day, ◖ **Eat-a-Pita** (326 Main St., Southwest Harbor, 207/244-4344, 8 A.M.–4 P.M. daily, dinner 5–9 P.M. Tues.–Sun.) is a casual, order-at-the-counter restaurant serving breakfast and lunch. At night it morphs into **Cafe 2,** a full-service restaurant.

The dining room, furnished with old oak tables and chairs, has a funky, artsy 'tude; there's also patio seating outside and an outdoor bar (think pink flamingos). Start the day with a Greek or Acapulco omelet. Lunch emphasizes pita sandwiches, burgers, paninis, and salads (delicious—call in advance for takeout); dinner choices ($9–26) include salads, light meals, a half-dozen pastas, and entrées.

Good food, good coffee, and good wine mix with a Mediterranean-influenced menu at **Sips** (4 Clark Point Rd., Southwest Harbor, 207/244-4550, 7 A.M.–9 P.M. daily), a congenial place. Small- and large-plate and tapas-style choices range $8–25; the risottos are especially good. Service can be iffy.

Earning high praise for its internationally accented fare, good service, fabulous views over the harbor, and incredible martinis is **Fiddlers' Green** (411 Main St., Southwest Harbor, 207/244-9416, www.fiddlersgreenrestaurant .com, 5:30 P.M.–close Tues.–Sun.). House specialties, such as Asian vegetable hot pot, tempura scallops, and steaks, range $16–32, but you can also make a meal of small plates, soups, and salads.

Fine Dining

The dreamy views from **Xanthus** (22 Claremont Rd., 207/244-5036 or 800/244-5036, 6–9 P.M. daily), at the Claremont hotel, descend over the lawns and croquet courts, boathouse, and dock to the water backed by mountains. It's truly a special place for an elegant meal complemented by an old-fashioned grace. Unfortunately the chefs seem to change annually, so it's hard to predict the quality; it's best to ask locally, but when it's on, it sings. Jackets are not required, but men won't feel out of place wearing one. Entrées range $24–30; a three-course prix fixe dinner is $29. Dining-room reservations are advised in midsummer. In July–August, informal lunches and cocktails are served in the shorefront Boat House, also open to nonguests.

Red sky at night, diners delight: Gold walls, artwork, wood floors, and a giant hearth set a chic tone for **Red Sky** (14 Clark Point Rd.,

207/244-0476, www.redskyrestaurant.com, 5:30–9 P.M. daily, entrées $19–30), one of the island's tonier restaurants. The creative fare emphasizes fresh seafood, hand-cut meats, and local organic produce; there's always a vegetarian choice. The restaurant is open Valentine's Day–New Year's Eve.

Seafood and Lobster in the Rough

If you have a penchant for puns—or can tune them out—head for the family-run **Seafood Ketch Restaurant** (McMullin Ave., Bass Harbor, 207/244-7463, 11 A.M.–9 P.M. daily). The corny humor begins with "Please, no fishing from dining room windows or the deck" and "What foods these morsels be," and goes up (or down, depending on your perspective) from there. But there's nothing corny about the seafood roll, an interesting change from the usual lobster or crab roll. There are a few "landlubber delights," but mostly the menu has fresh seafood dishes—including the baked lobster-seafood casserole, a recipe requested by *Gourmet* magazine. Most entrées run $19–24,

a bit pricey given the informality and service, but sandwiches and lighter fare are available. This is a prime family spot, with a kids menu, where the best tables are on the flagstone patio overlooking Bass Harbor (bring bug repellent). Follow signs for the Swans Island ferry terminal.

Few restaurants have as idyllic a setting as **Thurston's Lobster Pound** (Steamboat Wharf Rd., Bernard, 207/244-7600, www.thurstonslobster.com, 11 A.M.–8:30 P.M. daily, market rates), which overlooks lobster boat-filled Bass Harbor. The screened dining room practically sits in the water. Family-oriented Thurston's also has chowders, sandwiches, and terrific desserts. Beer and wine are available. Be sure to read the directions at the entrance and order before you find a table on one of two levels.

The appropriately named **Gilley's Head of the Harbor** (433 Main St., Southwest Harbor, 207/244-5222, 11 A.M.–9 P.M. daily, entrées $10–30) serves lobster and a whole lot more in a pleasant dining room with big windows

© HILARY NANGLE

Thurston's Lobster Pound hangs over Bass Harbor.

overlooking the harbor. There's often entertainment on weekends.

INFORMATION AND SERVICES
Information

Near the public parking lots and fire station (behind Sawyer's Market) is the **Southwest Harbor/ Tremont Chamber of Commerce** (Village Green Way, Southwest Harbor, 207/244-9264 or 800/423-9264, www.acadiachamber.com).

Check out **Southwest Harbor Public Library** (338 Main St., Southwest Harbor, 207/244-7065, www.swhplibrary.org).

Public Restrooms

In downtown Southwest Harbor, public restrooms are at the southern end of the parking lot behind the Main Street park and near the fire station. Across Main Street, Harbor House also has a restroom, and there are portable toilets at the town docks. There's also a public restroom at the Swans Island ferry terminal.

GETTING AROUND

Southwest Harbor, Tremont, and Bass Harbor are serviced by Route No. 7 (Southwest Harbor) of the Island Explorer bus system.

Islands near Mount Desert

Sure, Mount Desert is an island, but for a sampling of real island life, you'll want to make a day trip to one of the offshore islands. Most popular are the **Cranberry Isles** and **Swans Island,** but don't overlook **Frenchboro,** an off-the-radar gem.

CRANBERRY ISLES

The Cranberry Isles, south of Northeast and Seal Harbors, comprise Great Cranberry, Little Cranberry (called Islesford), Sutton, Baker, and Bear Islands. Islesford and Baker include property belonging to Acadia National Park. Bring a bike and explore the narrow, mostly level roads on the two largest islands, Great Cranberry and Islesford, but remember to respect private property. Unless you've asked permission, do not cut across private land to reach the shore.

The Cranberry name has been attributed to 18th-century loyalist governor Francis Bernard, who received these islands along with all of Mount Desert as a king's grant in 1762. Cranberry bogs (now long gone) on the two largest islands evidently caught his attention. Permanent European settlers arrived in the 1760s, and there was even steamboat service by the 1820s.

Lobstering and other fishing industries are the commercial mainstays, boosted in summer by the various visitor-related pursuits. Artists and writers come for a week, a month, or longer; day-trippers spend time on Great Cranberry and Islesford.

Largest of the islands is **Great Cranberry,** with a general store, a small historical museum with a café, and a gift shop, but not much else except pretty views.

The second-largest island is **Little Cranberry,** locally known as Islesford. It's easy to spend the better part of a day here exploring. Begin at **The Islesford Historical Museum** (207/288-3338, 10 A.M.–noon and 12:30–4:30 P.M. Mon.–Sat., 10:45 A.M.–noon and 12:30–4:30 P.M. Sun. mid-June–late Sept., free), operated by the National Park Service. The exhibits focus on local history, much of it maritime, so displays include ship models, household goods, fishing gear, and other memorabilia. Also on Islesford are public restrooms (across from the museum), a handful of galleries, and a general store. For lunch, bring a picnic or head to **The Islesford Dock** (207/244-7494, www.islesford.com, 11 A.M.–3 P.M. Tues.–Sat., 10 A.M.–2 P.M. Sun., dinner 5–9 P.M. daily late June–Labor Day), where prices are moderate, the food is home-cooked, and the views across to Acadia's mountains are incredible.

Osprey build their nests in high places, such as these rocky cliffs on one of Acadia's offshore islands.

Getting There

Decades-old family-run **Beal and Bunker** (207/244-3575) provides year-round mail and passenger boat service to the Cranberries from Northeast Harbor. The schedule makes it possible to do both islands in one day. The summer season, with more frequent trips, runs late June–Labor Day. The first boat departs Northeast Harbor's municipal pier at 7:30 A.M. Monday–Saturday; the first Sunday boat is 10 A.M. The last boat for Northeast Harbor leaves Islesford at 6:30 P.M. and leaves Great Cranberry at 6:45 P.M. The boats make a variety of stops on the three-island route (including Sutton in summer), so be patient as they make the circuit. It's a people-watching treat. If you just did a round-trip and stayed aboard, the loop would take about 1.5 hours. Round-trip tickets (covering the whole loop, including intraisland trips if you want to visit both Great Cranberry and Islesford) are $24 adults, $12 ages 3–11, free under age 3. Bicycles are $7 round-trip. The off-season schedule operates early May–mid-June and early September–mid-

October; the winter schedule runs mid-October–April. In winter, the boat company advises phoning ahead on what Mainers quaintly call "weather days."

The **Cranberry Cove Ferry** (upper town dock, Clark Point Rd., Southwest Harbor, 207/244-5882, cell 207/460-1981, www .downeastwindjammer.com) operates a summertime service to the Cranberries mid-May–mid-October aboard the 47-passenger *Island Queen*. The ferry route begins at the upper town dock (Clark Point Rd.) in Southwest Harbor, with stops in Manset and Great Cranberry before reaching Islesford an hour later. (Stops at Sutton can be arranged.) In summer (mid-June–mid-Sept.) there are six daily round-trips, with two additional evening trips Wednesday–Saturday. The first departure from Southwest Harbor is 7 A.M.; the last departure from Islesford is 6 P.M. Round-trip fares are $24 adults, $16 children, $6 bicycles.

The **MDI Water Taxi** (207/244-7312), a converted lobster boat, makes frequent on-demand trips to the Cranberries.

© HILARY NANGLE

FRENCHBORO, LONG ISLAND

Since Maine has more Long Islands than anyone cares to count, most of them have other labels for easy distinction. Here's a case in point – a Long Island known universally as Frenchboro, the name of the village that wraps around Lunts Harbor. With a year-round population hovering around 70, Frenchboro has had ferry service only since 1960. Since then, the island has acquired phone service, electricity, and satellite TV, but don't expect to notice much of that when you get here. It's a very quiet place where islanders live as islanders always have – making a living from the sea and proud of it. In 1999, when more than half the island (914 acres, including 5.5 miles of shorefront) went up for sale by a private owner, an incredible fund-raising effort collected nearly $3 million, allowing purchase of the land in January 2000 by the Maine Coast Heritage Trust. Some of the funding has been put toward restoration of the village's church and one-room schoolhouse; islanders and visitors will still have full access to all the acreage, and interested developers will have to look elsewhere.

Frenchboro is a delightful day trip. A good way to get a sense of the place is to take the 3.5-hour lunch cruise run by Captain Kim Strauss of **Island Cruises** (207/244-5785, www.bassharborcruises.com). For an even longer day trip to Frenchboro, plan to take the passenger ferry *R. L. Gott* during her weekly run for the Maine State Ferry Service. Each Friday early April–late October, the *Gott* departs Bass Harbor at 8 A.M., arriving in Frenchboro at 9 A.M. The return trip to Bass Harbor is at 6 P.M., allowing nine hours on the island. The Maine State Ferry Service uses the ferry *Captain Henry Lee* (the same one used on the Swans Island route) for service to Frenchboro on Wednesday, Thursday, and Sunday, but the service is only over-and-back (50 minutes each way), leaving no time to explore the island.

When you go, take a picnic with you, or stop at **Lunt's Dockside Deli** (207/334-2922), open in July–August only. It's a very casual

establishment – order at the window, grab a picnic table, and wait for your name to be called. Lobster rolls and fish chowder are the specialties, but there are plenty of other choices, including sandwiches, hot dogs, and even vegetable wraps. Of course, you can get lobster too. Prices are low, the view is wonderful, and you might even get to watch lobsters being unloaded from a boat. You can also purchase treats at the Frenchboro Bakery and Island Candy Shop (207/460-2099) and the Offshore Store (207/334-2943).

The **Frenchboro Historical Society Museum,** just up from the dock, has interesting old tools, other local artifacts, and a small gift shop. It's usually open afternoons Memorial Day–Labor Day. The island has a network of maintained trails through the woods and along the shore. Some are easy and others not-so-easy; some can be squishy, and some are along bouldery beachfront. The trails are rustic and most are unmarked, so proceed carefully. In the center of the island is a beaver pond. (You'll get a sketchy map on the boat, but you can also get one at the Historical Society.)

Frenchboro is the subject of *Hauling by Hand,* a fascinating, well-researched "biography" published in 1999 by eighth-generation islander Dean Lunt, now a journalist in Portland. His website (www.frenchboroonline.com) has helpful info for visiting the island; another good site is www.frenchboromaine.com.

There's a restroom above the Dockside Deli and two others near the museum. If you're captivated by the island, you can rent a harbor-front cottage on the property of the **Israel B. Lunt House** (207/334-2973 or 207/334-2991).

In August, Frenchboro hosts its annual **Lobster Festival** (Lunt & Lunt Lobster Company, 207/334-2922), a midday meal of lobster, chicken salad, hot dogs, coleslaw, homemade pies, and more, served rain or shine, with proceeds benefiting a local cause. Islanders and hundreds of visitors gather in the village for the occasion. The Maine State Ferry makes a special run that day.

Captain John Dwelley (207/244-5724) also operates a water-taxi service to the Cranberries. His six-passenger **Delight** makes the run from Northeast, Southwest, or Seal Harbor for $55–70 per trip, depending on the time of day, early June–late September. Reservations are required for trips 6–8 A.M. and 6–11 P.M. Custom cruises are available, including excursions to Baker's Island. Consider the sunset cruise to the Islesford Dock for dinner: $110 covers up to six people round-trip.

SWANS ISLAND

Six miles off Mount Desert Island lies scenic, roughly 7,000-acre Swans Island, named after Colonel James Swan, who bought it and two dozen other islands as an investment in 1786. Unfortunately the island's library, home to its historical society collection, burned to the ground in 2008. As with the Cranberries, fishing is the year-round way of life here, with lobstering being the primary occupation. In summer the population practically triples with the arrival of artists, writers, and other seasonal visitors. The island has no campsites, few public restrooms, and only a handful of guest rooms. Visitors who want to spend more than a day tend to rent cottages by the week.

You'll need either a bicycle or a car to get around on the island, as the ferry comes in on one side and the village center is on the other. Should you choose to bring a car, it's wise to make reservations for the ferry, especially for the return trip. Bicycling is a good way to get around, but be forewarned that the roads are narrow, lack shoulders, and are hilly in spots.

If you can be flexible, wait for a clear day, then pack a picnic and catch the first ferry (7:30 A.M.) from Bass Harbor. At the ferry office in Bass Harbor, request a Swans Island map. Keep an eye on your watch so you don't miss the last ferry (4:30 P.M.) back to Bass Harbor.

The ferry arrives in the northeast corner of the island. Head off down the main road toward Burnt Coat Harbor. The island has three villages—Atlantic, Minturn, and Swans Island. Pedal or drive around to the west side of the harbor and down the peninsula to **Hockamock Head Light** (officially called Burnt Coat Harbor Light). From the ferry landing, Hockamock Head is 4.5 miles. The distinctive square lighthouse, built in 1872 and now automated, sits on a rocky promontory overlooking Burnt Coat Harbor, Harbor Island, lobster-boat traffic, and crashing surf. The keeper's house is unoccupied; the grounds are great for picnics.

If it's hot, ask for directions to one of two prime island swimming spots: **Fine Sand Beach** (saltwater) or **Quarry Pond** (freshwater). Fine Sand Beach is on the west side of Toothacher Cove; you'll have to navigate about a mile of unpaved road to get there, but it's worth the trouble. Be prepared for chilly water, however. Quarry Pond is in Minturn, on the opposite side of Burnt Coat Harbor from the lighthouse. Follow the one-way loop around, and you'll see it on your right as you're rounding the far side of the loop.

Shopping options are few on Swans Island, but there is one worth noting. If you head left at the end of Ferry Terminal Road, you'll come to **Saturn Press** (463 Atlantic Rd., 207/526-4000), where designer Jane Goodrich and printer James Van Pernis create note cards and papers using antique letterpresses. The shop is usually open 9 A.M.–5 P.M. Monday–Friday, and the informal tours explain the letterpress process (you can usually see them in action) and visit the studios where the designs, based on the company's library of tens of thousands of graphic image ephemera, are created. Afterward, pick up some note cards or at least a catalog in the small shop. Saturn has few retail outlets, as most of its products are carried by museums and fine paper stores.

A Swans Island summer highlight is the **Sweet Chariot Music Festival,** a three-night midweek extravaganza in early August. Windjammers arrive from Camden and Rockland, enthusiasts show up on their private boats, and the island's Oddfellows Hall is standing-room-only for three evenings of folk singing, storytelling, and impromptu high jinks. In mid-afternoon of the first two days (about 3:30 P.M.), musicians go from boat to boat in Burnt Coat Harbor, entertaining with sea chanteys. Along the route from harbor to concert, enterprising local kids peddle lemonade, homemade brownies, and kitschy craft items. It's all very festive but definitely a "boat thing," not very convenient for anyone without water transport.

Overnight accommodations are available at **The Harbor Watch Motel** (111 Minturn Rd., 207/526-4563 or 800/532-7928, www.swansisland.com, $95–120). Swans has one small, struggling grocery store, **Carrying Place Market** (Minturn Rd., 207/526-4043), plus **Island Bake Shop** (73 Ferry Terminal Rd., 207/526-4123, 9 A.M.–2 P.M. Mon.–Sat.) and **Boathouse Take-Out** (207/526-4201), clinging to a cliff-side overlooking the harbor on the way to the lighthouse.

Getting There and Around

Swans Island is a six-mile, 40-minute trip on the state-operated car ferry *Captain Henry Lee*, operated by the **Maine State Ferry Service** (207/244-3254, daily recorded info 800/491-4883, www.exploremaine.org). The ferry makes up to six round-trips a day, the first from Bass Harbor at 7:30 A.M. Monday–Saturday, 9 A.M. Sunday, and the last from Swans Island at 4:30 P.M. Round-trip fares are around $17.50 adults, $8.50 ages 5–11; bikes are $16.50 adults, $9.50 children; vehicles are $49.50. Reservations are accepted only for vehicles; be in line at least 15 minutes before departure or you risk forfeiting your space.

© TOM NANGLE

Hop on a passenger ferry to the Cranberry Isles.

To reach the Bass Harbor ferry terminal on Mount Desert Island, follow the distinctive blue signs, marked "Swans Island Ferry," along Routes 102 and 102A.

Southwest Cycle (Main St., Southwest Harbor, 207/244-5856 or 800/649-5856) rents bikes by the day and week and is open year-round. It also has ferry schedules and Swans Island maps. For the early-morning ferry, you'll need to pick up bikes the day before; be sure to reserve them if you're doing this in July–August.

Schoodic Peninsula

Slightly more than 2,366 of Acadia National Park's acres are on the mainland Schoodic Peninsula; the rest are all on islands, including Mount Desert. World-class scenery and the relative lack of congestion, even at the height of summer, are just two reasons to sneak around to the eastern side of Frenchman Bay. Other reasons are abundant opportunities for outdoor recreation, two scenic byways, and dozens of artists' and artisans' studios tucked throughout this region.

Still, the biggest attractions in this area are the spectacular vignettes and vistas—of offshore lighthouses, distant mountains, and close-in islands—and the unchanged villages. **Winter Harbor,** known best as the gateway to Schoodic, shares the area with an old-money, low-profile Philadelphia-linked summer colony on exclusive Grindstone Neck.

Gouldsboro, including the not-to-be-missed villages of **Birch Harbor, Corea,** and **Prospect Harbor,** earned its own minor fame from Louise Dickinson Rich's 1958 book *The Peninsula,* a tribute to her summers on Corea's Cranberry Point, "a place that has stood still in time." Since 1958, change has crept into Corea, but not so as you'd notice. It's still the same quintessential lobster-fishing community, perfect for photo ops. A new section of the Maine Coastal Islands National Wildlife Reserve, the 431-acre **Corea Heath Unit,** has taken over former Navy lands along Route 195 in Corea. Plans call for developing trails, including one along the shorefront (call 207/546-2124 for updated information). In another initiative, the Frenchman Bay Conservancy acquired the 600-acre Northern Corea Heath, across the highway, home to Grand Marsh and Grand Marsh Bay.

Between Ellsworth and Gouldsboro are **Hancock, Sullivan,** and **Sorrento.** Venture down the ocean-side back roads and you'll discover an old-timey summer colony at Hancock Point, complete with a library, a post office, a yacht club, and tennis courts.

Meander inland to find the **Donnell Pond Public Reserved Lands,** a spectacular chunk of mostly undeveloped lakes for boating and fishing, peaks for hiking, and even a beach for camping.

SCHOODIC SECTION OF ACADIA NATIONAL PARK

The Schoodic section of Acadia is much smaller, less busy, and provides fewer recreational opportunities than that on Mount Desert Island, but it's still magnificent and well worth visiting.

As with so much of Acadia's acreage on Mount Desert Island, the Schoodic section became part of the park largely because of the deft diplomacy and perseverance of George B. Dorr. No obstacle ever seemed too daunting to Dorr. In 1928, when the owners objected to donating their land to a national park tagged with the Lafayette name (geopolitics being involved

Corea Harbor

© HILARY NANGLE

at the time), Dorr even managed to obtain congressional approval for the 1929 name change to Acadia National Park—and Schoodic was part of the deal.

To reach the park boundary from Route 1 in Gouldsboro, take Route 186 south to Winter Harbor. Continue through town, heading east, and then turn right and continue to the park entrance sign, just before the bridge over Mosquito Harbor.

You can also tour the park using the free Island Explorer bus, which circulates through Winter Harbor, around the Schoodic Loop, and on to Prospect Harbor, with stops along the way. It's an efficient and environmentally friendly way to go.

Perhaps one of the best ways to get to know the park is to become involved with the **Friends of Schoodic** (www.friendsofschoodic .org), which supports the park with cleanup projects, trail and building maintenance, and staffing the visitors information booth at the Gatehouse.

C Schoodic Loop

The major sights of Acadia's Schoodic section lie along the six-mile one-way road that meanders counterclockwise around the tip of the Schoodic Peninsula. You'll discover official and unofficial picnic areas, hiking trailheads, offshore lighthouses, and turnouts with scenic vistas. Also named the Park Loop Road, it's best referred to as the Schoodic Loop to distinguish it from the one on Mount Desert.

The first landmark is **Frazer Point Picnic Area,** with lovely vistas, picnic tables, and wheelchair-accessible restrooms. Other spots are fine for picnics, but this is the only official one. If you've brought bikes, leave your car here and do a counterclockwise 12.2-mile loop through the park and back to your car via Birch Harbor and Route 186. It's a fine day trip.

From the picnic area, the road becomes one-way. Unlike on the Park Loop Road on Mount Desert, no parking is allowed in the right lane. There are periodic pullouts, but not many cars can squeeze in. Despite the fact that this is far from the busiest section of Acadia, it can still be frustrating to be unable to find a space in the summer months. The best advice is to stay in the area and do this loop early in the morning or later in the afternoon, perhaps in May or June. (The late September–early October

SCENIC BYWAYS

This region boasts not one but two designated scenic byways: the **Schoodic National Scenic Byway,** which wraps around the peninsula, and the **Blackwoods Scenic Byway** (formerly the State Route 182 Scenic Byway), an inland blue highway cutting through the Donnell Pond Public Reserved Lands. If time permits, drive at least one of these two routes. Ideally, you'd do both, because the scenery differs greatly. Best idea yet: Connect the two via Route 1, creating a route that includes lakes and forests, mountains and fields, ocean and rocky coast. If you only have one day to explore this region, this takes in the best of it. In early-mid-October, when the foliage is at its peak, the vistas are especially stunning.

The 29-mile Schoodic National Scenic Byway stretches from Sullivan on Route 1 to Gouldsboro and then southward on Route 186 and around the Schoodic Peninsula, ending in Prospect Harbor. A detailed guide is available online at www.schoodicbyway.org. Other information is available at www.byways.org.

The 12.5-mile Blackwoods Scenic Byway meanders along State Route 182 inland of Route 1, from Franklin to Cherryfield, edging lakes and passing through small villages. You'll find access to trailheads and boat launches at Donnell Pond and Tunk Lake. Although Cherryfield is beyond the Schoodic region, it's a beautiful town to visit, filled with stately Victorian homes, and it's also the self-proclaimed wild blueberry capital of the world. Maps and information are available at www.blackwoodsbyway.org.

foliage is gorgeous, but traffic does increase then.) While you're driving, if you see a viewpoint you like (with room to pull off), stop; it's a long way around to return.

From this side of Frenchman Bay, the vistas of Mount Desert's summits are gorgeous behind islands sprinkled here and there.

Drive 1.6 miles from the picnic area to Raven's Head, a Thunder Hole–type cliff with sheer drops to the churning surf below and fabulous views (there are no fences, so it's not a good place for little ones). The trail is unmarked, but there's a small pullout on the left side of the road opposite it. Be extremely careful here—stay on the path (the environment is very fragile and erosion is a major problem), and stay well away from the cliff's edge.

At 2.2 miles past the picnic area, watch for a narrow unpaved road on the left, across from an open beach vista. It winds for a mile (keep left at the fork) up to a tiny parking circle, from which you can follow the trail (signposted "Schoodic Trails") to the open ledges on 440-foot Schoodic Head. From the circle, there's already a glimpse of the view, but it gets much better. If you bear right at the fork, you'll come to a grassy parking area with access to the Alder Trail and the Schoodic Head Trail.

Continue on the Schoodic Loop Road, and hang a right onto a short two-way spur to **Schoodic Point.** Just before it is a small info center, staffed by volunteers and park rangers. It's located on the site of a former top-secret U.S. Navy base that became part of the park in 2002. The campus is now the Schoodic Education and Research Center (locally called by its acronym, SERC); occasional lectures and programs are held here.

From Schoodic Point, return to the Loop Road. Look to your right and you'll see Little Moose Island, which can be accessed at low tide. Be careful not to get stranded here. Continue to the **Blueberry Hill** parking area (about one mile from the Schoodic Point–Loop Road intersection), a moor-like setting where the low growth allows almost 180-degree views of the bay and islands. There are a few trails in this area—all eventually converging

on **Schoodic Head,** the highest point on the peninsula. (Don't confuse this with Schoodic Mountain, which is well north of here.) Across the road and up the road a bit is the trailhead for the 180-foot-high **Anvil** headland.

As you continue along this stretch of road, keep your eyes peeled for eagles, which frequently soar here. There's a nest on the northern end of Rolling Island; you can see it with binoculars from some of the roadside pullouts.

From Blueberry Hill, continue 1.2 miles to a pullout for the East Trail, the shortest and most direct route to Schoodic Head. It's about another mile to the park exit, in Wonsqueak Harbor. It's another two miles to the intersection with Route 186 in Birch Harbor. (If you didn't bring a picnic lunch or dinner, Bunker's Wharf Restaurant is an excellent, if slightly pricey, stop, with views of a working wharf.)

Schoodic Education and Research Center

Acadia Partners for Science and Learning (207/288-1326, www.acadiapartners.org) is working with Acadia National Park to create a scientific research center at Schoodic Education and Research Center (www.nps.gov/acad/serc. htm) on the old Navy base on Schoodic Point, locally called SERC. In 2007 it launched a biennial international sculpture symposium with the aim of creating granite sculptures to place within coastal communities throughout the region. A lecture series, presented in Moore Auditorium every second Saturday evening year-round (and more often in summer), features speakers, usually researchers or nationally known experts, addressing environmental topics related to the park and its surroundings.

In 2009 local benefactor Edith Robb Dixon donated $1 million to Acadia Partners in the name of her late husband, Fritz Eugene Dixon Jr., to renovate the Rockefeller Building, the Norman Revival–style mansion near the SERC entrance. Initial plans call for a welcome center on the first floor and executive offices and accommodations for researchers and faculty on the upper floors.

the Rockefeller Building on SERC's campus

ENTERTAINMENT AND EVENTS

Winter Harbor's biggest wingding is the annual **Lobster Festival** (www.acadia-schoodic.org), the second Saturday in August. The gala daylong event includes a parade, live entertainment, lobster-boat races (a serious competition in these parts), crafts fair, games, and more crustaceans than you could ever consume.

Concerts, art classes, coffeehouses, workshops, and related activities are presented year-round by **Schoodic Arts for All** (207/963-2569, www.schoodicarts.org). Many are held at historic Hammond Hall in downtown Winter Harbor. A summer series presents monthly concerts on Friday evenings May–October. In early August the two-week **Schoodic Arts Festival** is jam-packed with daily workshops and nightly performances for all ages.

The **Pierre Monteux School for Conductors and Orchestra Musicians** (Rte. 1, Hancock, 207/422-3280, www.monteux school.org), a prestigious summer program founded in 1943, has achieved international renown for training dozens of national and international classical musicians. It presents two well-attended concert series starting in late June and running through July. The Wednesday series (7:30 P.M., $10 adults, $5 children) features chamber music; the Sunday concerts (5 P.M., $15 adults, $5 students) feature symphonies. An annual children's concert is usually held on a Monday (1 P.M.) in early–mid-July. All concerts are held in the school's Forest Studio.

Seeking to add more vibrancy and diversity to the peninsula's entertainment offerings and to indulge their own interests in music and the sciences, the owners of Oceanside Meadows Inn created the **Innstitute for the Arts and Sciences** (207/963-5557, www.oceaninn.com), which presents a series of Thursday-night events late June–late September, with a break during the Schoodic Arts Festival. The wide-ranging calendar includes lectures and concerts as well as art shows. Some are free; others are $10 in advance or $12 at the door.

During July, **Hancock County Friends of the Arts** (Rte. 1, East Sullivan, 207/422-3615) presents a free entertainment series for children in a barn that Ginia Davis Wexler, a former singer, and her husband, Morris, turned into a theater in the late 1960s for just this purpose. Two shows are presented. Admission is free, but donations are appreciated. The barn is three miles south of the Gouldsboro Post Office.

Late June–mid August, Frenchman Bay Conservancy presents **Monday Night Concerts** at its Tidal Falls preserve.

SHOPPING

You can find just about anything at the **Winter Harbor 5 and 10** (Main St., Winter Harbor, 207/963-7927, www.winterharbor5and10 .com). It's the genuine article, an old fashioned five-and-dime that's somehow still surviving in the age of Wal-Mart.

Art, Books, and Antiques

Winter Harbor Antiques and Works of Hand (424–426 Main St., Winter Harbor, 207/963-2547) is a double treat: Antiques fill one building, and works by local craftspeople and artists fill the other. It's across from Hammond Hall and set behind colorful well-tended gardens.

Barbara Noel makes most of the sea-glass jewelry, mobiles, and other creations at **Harbor Treasures** (358 and 368 Main St., Winter Harbor, 207/963-7086).

Works by contemporary Maine artists, including noted painters and sculptors associated with the Schoodic International Sculpture Symposium, are shown in rotating shows at **Littlefield Gallery** (145 Main St., Winter Harbor, 207/963-6005).

Here's a nifty place: **Chapter Two** (611 Corea Rd., Corea, 207/963-7269, www.chaptertwocorea.com) is home to the Corea Rug Hooking Company and Accumulated Books Gallery. Spread out in three buildings is a nice selection of used and antiquarian books, fine

crafts, and Rosemary's hand-hooked rugs. Sip on tea or coffee while browsing. Yarn, rug-hooking supplies, and lessons are available. Ask Garry for info on hiking local preserve trails, and don't miss the short trail behind the shop.

Ever seen a *palmara,* durian jack, *Pangium edule,* or *dompaum?* **Coastal Antiques** (Rte. 186, Prospect Harbor, 207/963-5546) has the original nut collection from Perry's Nut House in Belfast, which pulled in tourists from around the globe until its demise. Some specimens are amazing to see. The shop, which also sells antiques, shares a building with DeMarco Realty at the intersection with the Corea Road (Rte. 195).

Need a good read? Duck into **Scottie's Bookhouse** (209 Rte. 1, Hancock, 207/667-6834) and choose from a wide-ranging selection of about 35,000 used books.

Food and Wine

German and Italian presses, Portuguese corks, and Maine fruit all contribute to the creation of Bob and Kathe Bartlett's award-winning dinner and dessert wines. Not ones to rest on their many laurels, in 2008 the Bartletts introduced grape wines. Founded in 1982, **Bartlett Maine Estate Winery** (175 Chicken Mill Pond Rd., Gouldsboro, 207/546-2408, 10 A.M.–5 P.M. Mon.–Sat. late May–mid-Oct.) produces more than 20,000 gallons annually in a handsome wood-and-stone building designed by the Bartletts. There are no tours, but you're welcome to sample the wines. Reserve wines and others of limited vintage are sold only on-site. Bartlett's is 0.5 miles south of Route 1 in Gouldsboro.

Organic fruit and honey wines are produced at family-operated **Shalom Orchard Organic Farm and Winery** (158 Eastbrook Rd., Franklin, 207/565-2312, www.shalomorchard .com). The certified-organic farm is well off the beaten path but worth a visit not only for the wines but also for the views of Frenchman Bay from the hilltop orchard. To find the farm, take Route 182 to Route 200 (Eastbrook Rd.) and go 1.6 miles.

GALLERY HOPPING

Artist and artisan studios and galleries are numerous, and it's easy to while away a foggy day browsing and buying. Begin by picking up copies of the *Artist Studio Tour Map*, which details and provides directions to about a dozen galleries in Franklin, Sullivan, and Hancock, as well as the *Schoodic Peninsula* brochure, which notes galleries and shops on the peninsula. Both are widely available and free. Hours and days of operation vary; it's best to call first if you really want to visit a gallery. Here's a sampling to get you started.

HANCOCK AND SULLIVAN

Take the Point Road 2.5 miles to find Russell and Akemi Wray's **Raven Tree Gallery** (536 Point Rd., Hancock, 207/422-8273). Russell specializes in wood sculpture, bronzes, prints, and jewelry; Akemi crafts pottery. Out front is a small sculpture gallery.

Return to Route 1 and take Eastside Road, just before the Hancock–Sullivan Bridge, and drive 1.5 miles south to **Gull Rock Pottery** (103 Gull Rock Rd., off Eastside Rd., Hancock, 207/422-3990, www.gullrockpottery.com), where Torj and Kurt Wray (Russell's parents) have a magical waterfront setting and sculpture gallery. Inside is wheel-thrown, hand-painted dishwasher-safe pottery decorated with blue-and-white motifs representing local landscapes.

Cross the Hancock–Sullivan Bridge and then take the first left off Route 1 onto Taunton Drive to find the next three galleries. Drawing from her experiences as an oil painter and from her life in Japan, Peg McAloon creates masterful one-of-a-kind quilts at **Wildfire Run Quilt Boutique** (148 Taunton Dr., Sullivan, 207/422-3935, www.maineus. com/wildfirerun).

Nearby **Lunaform** (Cedar Lane, West Sullivan, 207/422-0923, www.lunaform.com) is in a class by itself. First there's the setting – the beautifully landscaped grounds surrounding an abandoned granite quarry. Then there's the realization that many of the wonderfully aesthetic garden ornaments created here look like hand-turned *pottery*, when in fact they're hand turned but made of steel-reinforced concrete. It takes a bit of zigging and zagging to get here. Go right onto Track Road; after 0.5 miles, go left onto Cedar Lane.

Bet you can't keep from smiling at the whimsical animal sculptures and fun furniture of talented sculptor-painter Philip Barter. His work is the cornerstone of the eclectic **Barter Family Gallery** (Shore Rd., Sullivan, 207/422-3190, www.barterfamilygallery.com). But there's more: Barter's wife and seven children have put their considerable skills to work producing hooked and braided rugs, jewelry, and other craft items. Follow Taunton Road 2.5 miles from Route 1.

Continue north on Taunton Road as it loops around Hog Bay and onto Route 200 for the next three stops. Charles and Susanne Grosjean's **Hog Bay Pottery** (245 Hog Bay Rd./Rte. 200, Franklin, 207/565-2282, www. hogbay.com) is another double treat. Inside the casual, laid-back showroom are Charles's functional nature-themed pottery and Susanne's stunning handwoven rugs.

Handwoven textiles are the specialty at **Moosetrack Studio** (388 Bert Gray Rd./

RECREATION
Preserves

The very active Frenchman Bay Conservancy (FBC, 207/422-2328, www.frenchmanbay.org) manages a number of small preserves dotting the region, and most have at least one trail providing access. The Conservancy publishes a free *Short Hikes* map, available locally, that provides directions to seven of these.

TIDAL FALLS PRESERVE

FBC's four-acre Tidal Falls Preserve (off Eastside Rd., Hancock) overlooks Frenchman Bay's only reversing falls (roiling water when the tide turns). There's no longer a lobster pound, but there are still picnic tables on the lawn overlooking the falls and ledges where seals often slumber. It's an idyllic spot.

Rte. 200, Sullivan, 207/422-9017, www .moosetrackhandweaving.com), where the selections vary from handwoven area rugs to shawls woven from merino wool and silk. Camilla Stege has been weaving since 1969, and her work reflects her experience and expertise.

Paul Breeden, best known for the remarkable illustrations, calligraphy, and maps he's done for *National Geographic*, Time-Life Books, and other national and international publications, displays and sells his paintings at the **Spring Woods Gallery and Willowbrook Garden** (40A Willowbrook Lane, Sullivan, 207/422-3007, www.springwoodsgallery.com, www.willowbrookgarden.com). Also filling the handsome modern gallery space are paintings by Ann Breeden and metal sculptures and silk scarves by the talented Breeden offspring. Be sure to allow time to meander through the sculpture garden, where there's even a playhouse for kids.

SCHOODIC PENINSULA

From Route 1, loop down to Winter Harbor and back up on Route 186 through Prospect Harbor to find these galleries.

Architectural stoneware, with a specialty in sinks, is the drawing card at **Maine Kiln Works** (115 S. Gouldsboro Rd./Rte. 186, Gouldsboro, 207/963-5819, www.waterstonesink.com), but you'll also find functional pottery in the shop. You might also see Dan Weaver at work on the wheel in the back room.

Every piece handcrafted at **Gypsy Moose Glass Studio** (20 Williamsbrook Rd., South Gouldsboro, 207/963-2674) is made from a single glass rod, which means no two are alike. You'll find glass beads, fused-glass earrings, swan weather predictors, and much more at this working studio just off Route 186.

If you're lucky, you might catch Susan Dickson-Smith throwing a pot at **Stave Island Gallery/ Proper Clay Stoneware** (Rte. 186, South Gouldsboro, 207/963-2040, www.properclay.com).

An old post office houses **Lee Art Glass** (679 S. Gouldsboro Rd./Rte. 186, Gouldsboro, 207/963-7280). Although Rod Lee has died, his works live on thanks to Wayne Tucker and Sheldon R. Bickford, who bought the business after training with Lee. The fused-glass tableware is created by taking two pieces of window glass and firing them on terra-cotta or bisque molds at 1,500°F. What makes the end result so appealing are the colors and the patterns – crocheted doilies or stencils – impressed into the glass. The almost magical results are beautiful and delicate looking yet functional.

Visiting the **U.S. Bells Foundry and Watering Cove Pottery** (56 W. Bay Rd./Rte. 186, Prospect Harbor, 207/963-7184, www. usbells.com) is a treat for the ears, as browsers try out the many varieties of cast-bronze bells made in the adjacent foundry by Richard Fisher. If you're lucky, he may have time to explain the process – particularly intriguing for children and a distraction from their instinctive urge to test every bell in the shop. The store also carries quilts by Dick's wife, Cindy, and wood-fired stoneware and porcelain by their daughter-in-law Liza Fisher. U.S. Bells is 0.25 miles up the hill from Prospect Harbor's post office.

COREA HEATH

In 2008 FBC purchased 600 acres of land known as the Corea Heath, and that summer volunteers began cutting trails. *Heath* is a local word for peat land or bog, and this one is a rare coastal plateau bog, distinguished because it rises above the surrounding landscape. It's a spectacular property, with divergent ecosystems including bogs, ledges, and mixed-wood forest. Natural features include pitcher plants, sphagnum mosses, rare vascular plants, and jack pines. It's a fabulous place for bird-watching too, and the preserve borders a section of the Maine Coastal Islands National Wildlife Refuge. Check with the Conservancy or stop into Chapter Two (611 Corea Rd., Corea, 207/963-7269, www.chaptertwocorea.com) for more info. Trail access is off the Corea Road, and parking is limited.

DONNELL POND
PUBLIC RESERVED LAND

More than 14,000 acres of remote forests, ponds, lakes, and mountains have been preserved for public access in Donnell Pond Public Reserved Land (Maine Bureau of Parks and Lands, 207/827-1818, www.parksandlands .com), north and east of Sullivan. Hikers can climb Schoodic, Black, and Caribou Mountains; paddlers and anglers have Donnell Pond, Tunk Lake, Spring River Lake, Long Pond, Round Pond, and Little Pond, among others. There are primitive campsites too. Route 182, an official Scenic Highway, cuts through the Donnell Pond preserve. Hunting is permitted, so take special care during hunting season.

The hiking isn't easy here, but it isn't technical, and the options are many. The interconnecting trail system takes in Schoodic Mountain, Black Mountain, and Caribou Mountain. Follow the Schoodic Mountain Loop clockwise, heading westward first. To make a day of it, pack a picnic and take a swimsuit (and don't forget a camera and binoculars for the summit views). On a brilliantly clear day, you'll see Baxter State Park's Katahdin, the peaks of Acadia National Park, and the ocean beyond. And in late July–early August, blueberries are abundant on the summit. For such rewards, this is a popular hike, so don't expect to be alone, especially on fall weekends, when the foliage colors are spectacular.

The Black Mountain ascent begins easily enough and then climbs steadily through the woods, easing off a bit before reaching bald ledges. Continue to the true summit by taking the trail past Wizard Pond. Views take in forested lands, nearby lakes and peaks, and out to Acadia's peaks. You can piggyback it with Schoodic Mountain, using that trailhead base for both climbs. Another possibility is to add Caribou Mountain. That loop exceeds seven miles, making a full day of hiking.

Trailheads are accessible by either boat or vehicle. To reach the vehicle-access trailhead for Schoodic Mountain from Route 1 in East Sullivan, drive just over four miles northeast

on Route 183 (Tunk Lake Rd.). Cross the Maine Central Railroad tracks and turn left at the Donnell Pond sign onto an unpaved road (marked as a jeep track on the USGS map). Go about 0.25 miles and then turn left for the parking area and trailhead for Schoodic Mountain, Black Mountain, Caribou Mountain, and a trail to Schoodic Beach. If you continue straight, you'll come to another trailhead for Black and Caribou Mountains. Water-access trailheads are at Schoodic Beach and Redman's Beach.

Bicycling

The best choices for cycling are the **Schoodic Loop** and the quiet roads of **Grindstone Neck** and **Corea.**

SeaScape Kayaking (18 E. Schoodic Dr., Birch Harbor, 207/963-5806, www.seascape-kayaking.com) rents bicycles for $15 per day.

Paddling

Experienced sea kayakers can explore the coastline throughout this region. Canoeists can paddle the placid waters of Jones Pond on the Schoodic Peninsula. In Donnell Pond Public Reserved Land, the major water bodies are **Donnell Pond** (big enough by most gauges to be called a lake) and **Tunk** and **Spring River Lakes;** all are accessible for boats (even, alas, powerboats).

To reach the boat-launching area for Donnell Pond from Route 1 in Sullivan, take Route 200 north to Route 182. Turn right and go about 1.5 miles to a right turn just before Swan Brook. Turn and go not quite two miles to the put-in; the road is poor in spots but adequate for a regular vehicle. The Narrows, where you'll put in, is lined with summer cottages ("camps" in the Maine vernacular); keep paddling eastward to the more open part of the lake. Continue on Route 182 to find the boat launches for Tunk Lake and Spring River Lake (hand-carry only). Canoeists and kayakers can access Tunk Stream from Spring River Lake.

Still within the preserve boundaries, but farther east, you can put in a canoe at the northern end of Long Pond and paddle southward into adjoining Round Pond. In early August, Round Mountain, rising a few hundred feet from Long Pond's eastern shore, is a great spot for gathering blueberries and huckleberries. The put-in for Long Pond is on the south side of Route 182 (park well off the road), about two miles east of Tunk Lake.

OUTFITTERS AND TRIPS

Paddle around the waters of Schoodic or Flanders Bay with **SeaScape Kayaking** (18 E. Schoodic Dr., Birch Harbor, 207/963-5806, www.seascapekayaking.com). Guided 3–4-hour tours are $50 pp, including fortification: homemade blueberry scones for morning trips and blueberry–white chocolate chip cookies in the afternoon. Canoe rental for lake usage is $45 per 24-hours; kayaks are $45 double, $35 single.

Master Maine Guides Darrin Kelly and Megan Gahl are committed to sustainability and education—they not only talk the talk, they walk the walk, living off the grid in a yurt surrounded by protected lands. Their enthusiasm and knowledge come through on their trips. **Ardea EcoExpeditions** (34 Hacmatack Rd., Gouldsboro, 207/460-9731, www.ardea-ecoexpeditions.com) offers a wide range of sea kayaking options, including half-day and full-day trips, camping, inn-to-inn overnights, and research expeditions. A half-day coastal exploration and introduction to sea kayaking is $65; a full day of island hopping is $105, including lunch. Family trips are available ($65 adults, $55 accompanying children), as are instructional trips, a first-light sunrise tour geared to bird-watchers, and a sunset tour that can be combined with a lobster bake. Custom overnights begin at $145 pp per day. Ask about "voluntourism" research expeditions, including island inventory and monitoring and seabird surveys. Ardea donates 1 percent of sales to local nonprofits—all the more reason to choose this outfitter.

Antonio Blasi, a Registered Maine Sea Kayak and Recreational Guide, leads guided tours of Frenchman or Taunton Bay and hiking and camping expeditions through **Hancock Point Kayak Tours** (58 Point Rd., Hancock, 207/422-6854, www.hancockpointkayak.com). A three-hour paddle, including all equipment, safety and paddling demonstrations, and usually an island break, is $45. Overnight kayak camping trips are $150 pp. Antonio also leads overnight backpacking trips for $125 pp, and cross-country skiing and snowshoe tours are available in winter.

Swimming

The best freshwater swimming in the area is at **Jones Beach,** a community-owned recreation area on Jones Pond in West Gouldsboro. Here you'll find restrooms, a nice playground, picnic facilities, a boat launch, a swim area with a float, and a small beach. It's at the end of Recreation Road, off Route 195, which is 0.3 miles south of Route 1.

Two beach areas on Donnell Pond are also popular for swimming—**Schoodic Beach** and **Redman's Beach**—and both have picnic tables, fire rings, and pit toilets. It's a 0.5-mile hike to Schoodic Beach from the parking lot. Redman's Beach is accessible only by boat. Other pocket beaches are also accessible by boat, and there's a rope swing (use at your own risk) by a roadside pullout for Fox Pond.

Golf

Play a nine-hole round at the **Grindstone Neck Golf Course** (Grindstone Ave., Winter Harbor, 207/963-7760, www.grindstonegolf.com), just for the dynamite scenery and for a glimpse of this exclusive late-19th-century summer enclave.

ACCOMMODATIONS

Rates noted are for peak season.

Country Inns

Le Domaine (1513 Rte. 1, Hancock, 207/422-3395 or 800/554-8498, www.ledomaine.com) has gained a five-star reputation for its restaurant, founded in 1946—long before fine dining had cachet here. But that's only part of the story. Above the restaurant is a charming five-room French country inn. The 80-acre inn property, nine miles east of Ellsworth, is like Provence, an oasis transplanted magically to Maine. On the garden-view balconies, or on the lawn out back, you're oblivious to the traffic whizzing by. Better yet, follow the lovely wooded trail to a quiet pond. Three guest rooms ($150) and two suites ($225) all are named after locales in Provence. Continental breakfast is included, and guests receive a 10 percent discount on dinners. Alert the inn if you'll be arriving after 5:30 P.M., when the staff has to focus on dinner.

Follow Hancock Point Road 4.8 miles south of Route 1 to the three-story gray-blue **Crocker House Country Inn** (967 Point Rd., Hancock, 207/422-6806, www.crockerhouse .com, $110–160), Rich and Liz Malaby's antidote to Bar Harbor's summer traffic. Built as a summer hotel in 1884, the inn underwent rehabbing a century later, but it retains a decidedly old-fashioned air despite now offering Wi-Fi. Breakfast is included. Guests can relax in the common room or reserve spa time in the carriage house. One kayak and a few bicycles are available; clay tennis courts are nearby. If you're arriving by boat, request a mooring. The inn's dining room is a draw in itself.

Bed-and-Breakfasts

Overlooking the Gouldsboro Peninsula's only sandy saltwater beach, **◖ Oceanside Meadows Inn** (Rte. 195, Corea Rd., Prospect Harbor, 207/963-5557, www.oceaninn.com, May–mid-Oct., $149–209) is a jewel of a place on 200 acres with organic gardens, wildlife habitat, and walking trails. The elegant 1860s captain's house has seven attractive guest rooms, and the 1820 Shaw farmhouse next door has another seven. Breakfast is an impressive four-course event, usually featuring herbs and flowers from the inn's gardens. Energetic husband-and-wife team Ben Walter and Sonja Sundaram seem to have thought of everything—hot drinks available all day, a guest fridge, beach toys, even detailed guides to the property's trails and habitats (great for entertaining kids). As if all that weren't enough, Sonja and Ben have totally restored the 1820

timber-frame barn out back—creating the **Oceanside Meadows Innstitute for the Arts and Sciences.** Local art hangs on the walls, and the 125-seat barn has a full schedule of concerts and lectures June–September on natural history, Native American traditions, and more, usually on Thursday nights. Some are free, some require tickets; all require reservations. The inn's website is also a phenomenal resource on area activities. Oceanside Meadows is six miles off Route 1.

Watch lobster boats unload their catch at the dock opposite **Elsa's Inn on the Harbor** (179 Main St., Prospect Harbor, 207/963-7571, www.elsasinn.com, $120–165). Jeffrey and Cynthia Alley; their daughter, Megan; her husband, Glenn Moshier; and grandsons Andrew and Emmett have turned the home of Jeff's mother, Elsa, into a warm and welcoming inn. The Alley family roots in the area go back more than 10 generations, so you're guaranteed to receive solid information on where to go and what to do. Every room has an ocean view, and Megan pampers guests with sumptuous linens, down duvets, terry robes, Wi-Fi, and a hearty hot breakfast. After a day exploring, settle into a rocker on the veranda and gaze over the boat-filled harbor out to Prospect Harbor Light. And afterward? Well, perhaps a lobster bake. Upon request, Megan's dad will bring over some fresh lobster, and Megan will prepare a complete lobster dinner—corn on the cob, coleslaw, homemade rolls, and a seasonal dessert, all for about $25 pp, depending on market rates.

Set well back from Route 1, **Acadia View Bed and Breakfast** (175 Rte. 1, Gouldsboro, 866/963-7457, www.acadiaview.com, $139–169) is built on a bluff with views across Frenchman Bay to the peaks of Mount Desert and a path down to the shorefront. Pat and Jim Close built the oceanfront house as a bed-and-breakfast that opened in 2005. It's filled with antique treasures from the Closes' former life in Connecticut. Each of the four guest rooms has a private deck. The Route 1 location is convenient to everything.

Off the beaten path is Bob Travers and

Barry Canner's **Black Duck Inn on Corea Harbor** (Crowley Island Rd., Corea, 207/963-2689, www.blackduck.com, $140–200, May–mid-Oct.), literally the end of the line on the Gouldsboro Peninsula. Set on 12 acres in this timeless fishing village, the bed-and-breakfast has four handsomely decorated guest rooms and plenty of common space. Across the way, perched on the harbor's edge, are two little seasonal cottages, one rented by the day with a three-night minimum and one by the week. The inn and Corea are geared to wanderers, readers, and anyone seeking serenity. Rocky outcrops dot the property, and a nature trail meanders to a millpond; in early August, the blueberries are ready. If the fog socks in the area, the large parlor has comfortable chairs and loads of books.

Something of a categorical anomaly, **The Bluff House Inn** (Rte. 186, Gouldsboro, 207/963-7805, www.bluffinn.com, year-round, $75–130) is part motel, part hotel, part bed-and-breakfast—a seemingly successful mix in a 1980s building overlooking Frenchman Bay on the west side of the Gouldsboro Peninsula. Verandas wrap around the first and second floors, so bring binoculars for sighting ospreys and bald eagles. Pine walls and flooring give a lodge feeling to the open first floor. Settle by the stone fireplace or grab a seat by the window. Breakfast is a generous continental. On Friday nights, a lobster bake is served (market rates, usually around $25). The eight second-floor rooms are decorated "country" fashion, with quilts on the very comfortable beds. (In hot weather, request a corner room.) Wi-Fi is available. Pet-friendly rooms are available for a $15 cleaning fee. Also available is a two-bedroom apartment over the garage ($150 per night or $850 per week).

Machias native Dottie Mace operated a bed-and-breakfast in Virginia before returning to Maine to open **Taunton River Bed & Breakfast** (19 Taunton Dr., Sullivan, 207/422-2070, www.tauntonriverbandb.com, $115–125) in a 19th-century farmhouse with river views. Rooms are carefully decorated; they're warm and inviting, formal without being stuffy.

Two of the three guest rooms share a bath. It would be easy to spend the day just sitting on the porch swing, but it's an easy pedal or drive to local art galleries. The inn is just a stone's throw off Route 1, so traffic noise might bother the noise-sensitive.

Sustainable living is the focus of Karen and Ed Curtis's peaceful **Three Pines Bed and Breakfast** (274 East Side Rd., Hancock, 207/460-7595, www.threepinesbandb.com, year-round, $100–125), fronting on Sullivan Harbor, just below the Reversing Falls. Their quiet off-the-grid 40-acre oceanfront organic farm faces Sullivan Harbor and is home to a llama, rare-breed chickens and sheep, ducks, and bees as well as a large organic garden, berry bushes, an orchard, and greenhouses. Photovoltaic cells provide electricity; appliances are primarily propane-powered; satellite technology operates the phone, TV, and Internet systems. Two inviting guest rooms have private entrances and water views. A full vegetarian breakfast (with fresh eggs from the farm) is served. Bicycles and a canoe are available. You can walk or pedal along an abandoned railway line down to the point, and you can launch a canoe or kayak from the back—or is it the front?—yard. Children are welcome; pets are allowed.

Innkeeper Carolyn Bucklin is determined to create the perfect bed-and-breakfast experience at **Cottage by the Sea** (38 Kilkenny Cove, Hancock, 207/422-6783, www.cottagebytheseamaine.com, June 1–mid-Oct., $145–165). Top-quality linens, fully equipped guest rooms (satellite TV, irons and ironing boards, hair dryers, phones), evening turndown service, and air-conditioning make it hard to tear yourself away from the oceanfront inn. Three guest rooms are available, one with a view of Kilkenny Cove. Breakfast is a multicourse affair; afternoon refreshments are served. Pets are not allowed as there is a resident dog.

Cottages

Roger and Pearl Barto, whose family roots in this region go back five generations, have four rental accommodations on their Henry's Cove

The rustic Albee's Shorehouse Cottages are waterfront accommodations.

oceanfront property, **Main Stay Cottages** (66 Sargent St., Winter Harbor, 207/963-2601, www.awa-web.com/stayinn, $80–115). Most unusual is the small one-bedroom Boat House, which has stood since the 1880s. It hangs over the harbor, with views to Mark Island Light, and you can hear the water gurgling below you at high tide. Other options include a very comfortable efficiency cottage, a one-bedroom cottage, a second-floor suite with a private entrance, and a four-bedroom house ($250 per night). All have big decks and fabulous views over the lobster boat–filled harbor; watch for the eagles that frequently soar overhead. Main Stay is on the Island Explorer bus route and just a short walk from where the Bar Harbor Ferry docks.

Simple and rustic, but charming in a sweet old-fashioned way, are **Albee's Shorehouse Cottages** (Rte. 186, Prospect Harbor, 207/963-2336 or 800/963-2336, www.theshorehouse .com, May–mid-Oct., $85–135), a cluster of 10 vintage cottages decorated with braided rugs, fresh flowers, and other homey touches.

Two things make this place special: the waterfront location—and it's truly waterfront; many of the cottages are just a couple of feet from the high-tide mark—and the management. Owner Richard Rieth goes out of his way to make guests feel welcome. Pick up lobsters and say what time you want dinner, and they'll be cooked and delivered to your cottage. He's slowly fixing up the cottages, but these will never be fancy; if you're fussy, go elsewhere. In peak season, preference is given to Saturday–Saturday rentals, but shorter stays are often available. Wi-Fi is available throughout, and dogs are welcome.

Camping
DONNELL POND PUBLIC RESERVED LAND
A handful of authorized primitive campsites can be found on Tunk Lake (southwestern corner) and Donnell Pond (at Schoodic Beach and Redman's Beach), all accessible on foot or by boat. Each has a table, a fire ring, and a nearby pit toilet. Many of the sites are on the

lakefront. All are first-come, first-served with no fees or permits required; they are snapped up quickly on midsummer weekends. You can camp elsewhere within this public land, except in day-use areas, but fires are not permitted at unofficial sites.

FOOD
Local Flavors
Make a point to attend one of the many **public suppers** held throughout the summer in this area and so many other rural corners of Maine. Typically benefiting a worthy cause, these usually feature beans, chowder, or spaghetti and the serendipity of plain potluck. Everyone saves room for the homemade pies. Notices of such suppers are usually posted on public bulletin boards in country stores and in libraries, on signs in front of churches, and at other places where people gather.

This area has two excellent smokehouses. Defying its name, **Sullivan Harbor Smokehouse** (Rte. 1, Hancock, 207/422-3735 or 800/422-4014, www.sullivanharborfarm.com) has moved to spacious modern new digs in Hancock. Big interior windows allow visitors to see into the production facility and watch the action. The newer **Grindstone Neck of Maine** (311 Newman St./Rte. 186, just north of downtown Winter Harbor, 207/963-7347 or 866/831-8734, www.grindstoneneck.com) also earns high marks for its smoked salmon, shellfish, spreads, and pâtés, all made without preservatives or artificial ingredients. Also available are fresh fish, wine, and frozen foods for campers. In summer you can purchase fresh lobster and crab rolls.

Eat while you shop or vice versa at **Harbor Girl Emporium & Cafe** (4 Duck Pond Rd., Winter Harbor, 207/963-5900, 11 A.M.–9 P.M. daily), a pleasant little spot near the beginning of the Schoodic Loop. Inside are Prospect Harbor Soap Co. products and works by local crafters, as well as a menu ranging from pizza to lobster.

Pick up veggies, meats, eggs, cheeses, and handcrafted fiber products as well as jams, preserves, and baked goods at the **Winter Harbor Farmers Market** (parking lot, Newman St. and Rte. 186, Winter Harbor, 9 A.M.–noon Tues. late June–early Sept.).

Once a true old-fashioned country store with a classic traditional soda fountain and penny candy, **J. M. Gerrish Provisions** (352 Main St., Winter Harbor, 207/963-6100, 8 A.M.–7 P.M. daily) has undergone many changes in recent years. Now it's under the steady hands of owners Brian Flanders, a Culinary Institute of America–trained chef, and his wife, pastry chef Maria Flanders. Stop in for the made-from-scratch pastries, soups, great sandwiches, ice cream and gelato, or some heftier fare.

Craving curry? Call in your order 24 hours in advance and **Tandoor Downeast** (119 Eastbrook Rd., Franklin, 207/565-3598, www.tandoordowneast.com, 5–8 P.M. Mon.–Fri., 1–8 P.M. Sat.–Sun.) will prepare authentic Indian cuisine for you to take out. Chef Gunjan Gilbert's menu is extensive, and prices are reasonable, with most choices $6–8. Or take your chances and simply stop by and choose from whatever's available. If you have a cottage, in-house preparation—they come and cook in your kitchen—is available. A selection is usually also available at the Winter Harbor Farmers Market. In 2009, Tandoor began offering sit-down dinners at the Franklin Veteran's Club once a week; call for details.

From India, step into Italy at Buzzy Gioia's **Maple Knoll Pizza** (132 Blackswoods Rd./Rte. 182, Franklin, 207/565-2068, 2–8 P.M. Wed.–Sun.), on the eastern edge of in-town Franklin. Buzzy draws on his Italian heritage—his parents came from the old country—to craft authentic pizzas, submarine sandwiches, and calzones.

Family Favorites
The best place for grub and gossip in Winter Harbor is **Chase's Restaurant** (193 Main St., Winter Harbor, 207/963-7171, 7 A.M.–8 P.M. daily, 7 A.M.–2 P.M. Sun.), a seasoned no-frills booth-and-counter operation that turns out decent fish chowder, fries, onion rings, wraps, home-style dinners, and downright cheap breakfasts.

Don't be put off by the lobster "sculpture" outside **Ruth & Wimpy's Kitchen** (792 Rte. 1, Hancock, 207/422-3723, www.ruthand-wimpys.com, 11 A.M.–9 P.M. Mon.–Sat.); you'll probably see a crowd as well. This family-fare standby serves hefty sandwiches, lobster prepared 30 ways, pizza, pasta, and steak. Prices begin at less than $3 for a cheeseburger and climb to about $25 for a twin lobster dinner. Locals praise the lobster roll as the cheapest and best around. Antique license plates and collections of miniature cars and trucks accent the interior. It's five miles east of Ellsworth, close to the Hancock Point turnoff.

Good food served by friendly folks is what pulls the locals into **❰ Chester Pike's Galley** (2336 Rte. 1, Sullivan, 207/422-8200, 6 A.M.–2 P.M. Tues.–Thurs. and Sat., 6 A.M.–2 P.M. and 4:30–8:30 P.M. Fri., 7 A.M.–2 P.M. Sun., $6–15). The prices are low, the portions big. If you're on a diet, don't even *look* at the glass case filled with fresh-baked pies, cakes, and cookies. Go early if you want to snag one of the homemade doughnuts (and order dessert first). It's also open Friday nights for a fish fry with free seconds.

Here's a surprise: You can't get much farther from Mexico than coastal Maine and still be in the United States, but **The Mexican Restaurant** (1166 Rte. 1, Hancock, 207/422-3723) has earned a reputation for being a hot spot for authentic Mexican and Central American fare. Originally in Harrington, where it catered to the region's migrant blueberry pickers, this multiple-generation family operation now shares a huge log building with a motorcycle shop. Everything's made on the premises, even the tortilla chips. The interior is bright and cheerful, and there are also tables on the porch and a few picnic tables on the lawn. Almost everything on the menu is $3–10, and the choices are plentiful. Call before making a special trip as the hours (allegedly 11:30 A.M.–8 P.M. daily) seem to change at whim.

Casual Dining

The Fisherman's Inn (7 Newman St./ Rte. 186, Winter Harbor, 207/963-5585,

11:30 A.M.–2 P.M. and 4:30–9 P.M. Mon.–Sat., 10 A.M.–2 P.M. and 4:30–9 P.M. Sun. late May–mid-Oct.) has been an institution in these parts since 1947; some years it's great, other years not. Kathy Johnson runs the front of the house; her husband, Carl, is the chef. He's also the brains behind Grindstone Neck of Maine, the smoked seafood operation just up the road, and diners are welcomed with a sample of smoked salmon spread and a cheese spread. That's followed up with Carl's focaccia bread and the house dipping sauce, a tasty blend of Romano cheese, fresh garlic, red pepper, and parsley with olive oil. And that all comes before any appetizers. Seafood is the specialty here, and there's a good chance that the guy at the neighboring booth caught your lobster or fish. Asian influences are evident too. Entrées range $17–28, and some dishes can top that given seasonal market rates, but early-dining specials, usually around $13, are available 4:30–5:30 P.M. A three-course Sunday brunch is $15.

Fine Dining

❰ Le Domaine (1513 Rte. 1, Hancock, 207/422-3395 or 800/554-8498, www.ledo-maine.com, 6–9 P.M. Tues.–Sun. mid-June–mid-Oct. and 10:30 A.M.–1:30 P.M. Sun. mid-June–early Oct., entrées $29–32) has gained a five-star reputation for *très* French fare, an excellent wine cellar, and lovely Provençal decor. Reservations are essential, especially in July–August. Opt for the four-course fixed-price menu for $40; otherwise the tab may dent your budget, but stack that up against airfare to France.

The unpretentious dining rooms at the **Crocker House Country Inn** (967 Point Rd., Hancock Point, 207/422-6806, www.crock-erhouse.com, 5:30–9 P.M. daily May 1–Oct. 31, 5:30–9 P.M. Fri.–Sun. Apr. and Nov.–Dec., entrées $22–32) provide a setting for well-prepared continental fare with flair, crafted from fresh and local ingredients; reservations are essential as this is one of the area's most consistent and popular dining spots.

One of the more dependable dining experiences in the area is **Chipper's** (Rte. 1,

Hancock, 207/422-8238, http://chippersrestaurant.com, 5–9 P.M. Tues.–Sun.). Owner Chipper Butterwick opened his popular restaurant in 1995 and expanded the simple cape-style building in 2010, adding a pub. The wide-ranging menu includes rack of lamb and even chateaubriand, but the emphasis is on seafood; the crab cakes earn rave reviews. Meals include a sampling of tasty haddock chowder and a salad, but save room for the homemade ice cream for dessert. Entrées are in the $17–32 range, but some appetizer-salad combos provide budget options, and lighter fare is available in the pub.

INFORMATION AND SERVICES

For advance information about eastern Hancock County, contact the **Schoodic Peninsula Chamber of Commerce** (207/963-7658, www.acadia-schoodic.org).

To plan ahead, see the Acadia website (www.nps.gov/acad), where you can download a Schoodic map.

Libraries

Check out **Dorcas Library** (Rte. 186, Prospect Harbor, 207/963-4027, www.dorcas.lib.me.us) or **Winter Harbor Public Library** (18 Chapel Lane, Winter Harbor, 207/963-7556, www.winterharbor.lib.me.us), in the 1888 beach stone and fieldstone Channing Chapel.

The inviting octagonal **Hancock Point Library** (Hancock Point Rd., Hancock Point, 207/422-6400, summer only, call for hours) was formed in 1899. More than a library, it's a center for village activities. Check the bulletin boards by the entrance to find out what's happening and when.

GETTING AROUND

The passenger-only **Bar Harbor Ferry** (207/288-2984, www.barharborferry.com, round-trip $29.50 adults, $19.50 children, $6 bicycle) operates five times daily late June–late August and coordinates with the free **Island Explorer** (www.exploreacadia.com) bus's summertime Schoodic route, making a super car-free excursion in either direction.

ACADIA REGION

THE DOWN EAST COAST

The term *Down East* is rooted in the direction the wind blows—the prevailing southwest wind that powered 19th-century sailing vessels along this rugged coastline. But to be truly Down East, in the minds of most Mainers, you have to be physically here in Washington County—a stunning landscape of waterways, forests, blueberry barrens, rocky shoreline dotted with islands and lighthouses, and independent pocket-size communities, many still dependent upon fishing or lobstering for their economies.

At one time, most of the Maine coast used to be as underdeveloped as this part of it. You can set your clock back a generation or two while you're here; you'll find no giant malls, only a couple of fast-food joints, and two—count 'em—traffic lights. While there are a handful of restaurants offering fine dining, for the most part your choices are limited to family-style restaurants specializing in home cooking with an emphasis on fresh (usually fried) seafood and lobster rolls. Nor will you find grand resorts or even not-so-grand hotels. Motels, tourist cabins, and small inns and bed-and-breakfasts dot the region. The upside is that prices too are a generation removed. If you're searching for the Maine of your memories or your imagination, this is it.

When eastern Hancock County flows into western Washington County, you're on the Down East Coast (sometimes called the Sunrise Coast). From Steuben eastward to Jonesport, Machias, and Lubec—then "around the corner" to Eastport, Calais, Princeton, and Grand Lake Stream—Washington County is

HIGHLIGHTS

◖ Maine Coastal Islands National Wildlife Refuge: More than 300 birds have been sighted at Petit Manan Point, but even if you're not a bird-watcher, come for the hiking and, in August, the blueberries (page 365).

◖ Great Wass Island Preserve: The finest natural treasure in this part of Maine is the Great Wass Archipelago, partly owned by the Nature Conservancy, with opportunities for hiking and bird-watching (page 370).

◖ Machias Seal Island Puffin Tour: Excursion boats depart from Jonesport and Cutler for Machias Seal Island, home to Atlantic puffins (the clowns of the sea), as well as razorbill auks, Arctic terns, and common murres (pages 370 and 379).

◖ West Quoddy Head State Park: This candy-striped lighthouse is a Maine Coast icon, and even a short hike along the paths edging the cliffs reaps big rewards (page 382).

◖ Roosevelt Campobello International Park: Make it an international vacation by venturing over to this New Brunswick park, home to the Roosevelt Cottage and miles of hiking trails, jointly managed by the United States and Canada (page 389).

◖ Whale-Watching: Cruise into Passamaquoddy Bay, pass the Old Sow Whirlpool, and ogle seabirds and whales (page 391).

◖ Shackford Head State Park: The rewards for this easy hike are panoramic views over Cobscook Bay from Eastport to Campobello (page 395).

LOOK FOR ◖ TO FIND RECOMMENDED SIGHTS, ACTIVITIES, DINING, AND LODGING.

twice the size of Rhode Island, covers 2,528 square miles, has about 35,000 residents, and stakes a claim as the first U.S. real estate to see the morning sun. The region also includes handfuls of offshore islands—some accessible by ferry, charter boat, or private vessels. (Some, with sensitive bird-nesting sites, are off-limits during the summer.) At the uppermost point of the coast, and conveniently linked to Lubec by a bridge, New Brunswick's Campobello Island is a popular day-trip destination—the locale of Franklin D. Roosevelt's summer retreat.

Other attractions in this area include festivals, concert series, art and antiques galleries, lighthouses, two Native American reservations, and the great outdoors for hiking, biking, birding, sea kayaking, whale-watching, camping, swimming, and fishing. Hook inland to Grand Lake Stream to find a remote, wild land of lakes famed for fishing and old-fashioned family-style summer vacations.

One of the Down East Coast's millennial buzzwords has been eco-tourism, and local conservation organizations and chambers of

THE DOWN EAST COAST

CANADA

0   10 mi

0   10 km

To Houlton

Forest City

Spednic Lake

Vanceboro

St. Croix

Baskahegan Lake

Sysladobsis Lake

West Grand Lake

Grand Falls Flowage

St. Croix River

Fourth Machias Lake

LITTLE MAYBERRY COVE TRAIL

Grand Lake Stream

Peter Dane Point

Princeton

Third Machias Lake

Big Lake

Pocomoonshine Lake

Woodland (Baileyville)

Meddybemps Lake

St. Stephen

Calais

Baring

WHITELOCK MILL LIGHTHOUSE

ST. CROIX ISLAND

Red Beach

Robbinston

Passamaquoddy Bay

WHALE-WATCHING

To I-295

MILL   RD.

STUD

Mooschorn National Wildlife Refuge

Meddybemps

Charlotte

Boyden Lake

Perry

214

Pennamaquan Lake

Pembroke

West Pembroke

ROOSEVELT CAMPOBELLO INT'L PARK

SHACKFORD HEAD STATE PARK

Wesley

192

Lake Cathance

Dennys River

191

Dennysville

Mooschorn National Wildlife Refuge

Cobscook Bay

Edmunds

North Lubec

Eastport

Campobello Island

Lubec

9

Beddington

To Bangor

193

Machias River

Hadley Lake

Cobscook Bay State Park

Whiting

South Trescott

WEST QUODDY HEAD STATE PARK

189

Gardner Lake

Bailey's Mistake

Deblois

Marshfield

East Machias

191

CUTLER COAST TRAILS

Narraguagus

Whitneyville

Machias

1A

Machiasport

Cutler Coast Public Preserve

Columbia Falls

Jonesboro

Bucks Harbor

Machias Bay

Cutler

RUGGLES HOUSE

Harrington

1

Addison

BLUEBERRY PATCH

Roque Bluffs

JASPER BEACH

Western Head

Cherryfield

187

Roque Bluffs State Park

Starboard

Cross Island

To Ellsworth

Indian River

PLEASANT BAY B&B LLAMA KEEP

1A

West Jonesport

Roque Island

Englishman Bay

Chandler Bay

Milbridge

River

Pleasant Bay

Cape Split

South Addison

Beals

Jonesport

MACHIAS SEAL ISLAND PUFFIN TOUR

Steuben

1

Narraguagus Bay

Western Bay

Great Wass Island

THE HUMBOLDT FIELD RESEARCH INSTITUTE

Dyer Bay

GREAT WASS ISLAND PRESERVE

MAINE COASTAL ISLANDS NATIONAL WILDLIFE REFUGE

ATLANTIC   OCEAN

© AVALON TRAVEL

commerce have targeted and welcomed visitors willing to be careful of the fragile ecosystems here—visitors who will contribute to the economy while respecting the natural resources and leaving them untrammeled, visitors who don't cross the fine line between light use and overuse. Low-impact tourism is essential for this area. However, outfitters and canoe, kayak, and bicycle rental outlets are few and far between.

One natural phenomenon no visitor can affect is the tide—the inexorable ebb and flow, predictably in and predictably out. If you're not used to it, even the 6–10-foot tidal ranges of southern Maine may surprise you. But along this coastline, the tides are astonishing—as much as 28 feet difference in water level within six hours. Old-timers tell stories of big money lost betting on horses racing the fast-moving tides.

Another surprise to visitors may be how early the sun rises—and sets—on the Sunrise Coast. Keep in mind that if you cross into Canada in either Lubec or Calais, you enter the Atlantic time zone, and you'll need to set your clock ahead one hour.

Yet another distinctive natural feature of Washington County is its blueberry barrens (fields). Depending on the time of year, the fields will be black (torched by growers to jump-start the crop), blue (ready for harvest), or maroon (fall foliage, fabulous for photography). In early summer, a million rented bees set to work pollinating the blossoms. By August,

when a blue haze forms over the knee-high shrubs, bent-over bodies use old-fashioned wooden rakes to harvest the ripe berries. It's backbreaking work, but the employment lines usually form quickly when newspaper ads announce the start of the annual harvest.

One bit of advice you might not receive from the tourism people is that warm clothing is essential in this corner of Maine. It may be nicknamed the Sunrise Coast, but it also gets plenty of fog, rain, and cool temperatures. Temperatures tend to be warmer, and the fog diminishes, as you head toward the inland parts of the county, but you can never count on that. Mother Nature is an accomplished curveball pitcher, and El Niño and La Niña periodically provide an assist.

PLANNING YOUR TIME

Down East Maine is not for those in a hurry. Traffic ambles along, and towns are few and far between. Nature is the biggest calling card here, and to appreciate it you'll need time to hike, bike, canoe, sea kayak, or take an excursion boat. Although Route 1 follows the coast in general, it's often miles from the water. You'll want to ramble down the peninsulas to explore the seaside villages, see lighthouses, or hike in parks and preserves, and perhaps wander inland to the unspoiled lakes. You'll need at least three days to begin to cover the territory, ideally five days or longer if you want to really explore it.

THE DOWN EAST COAST

Milbridge

The pace begins to slow a bit by the time you've left Hancock County and entered western Washington County, the beginning of the Down East Coast. In this little pocket are the towns of **Steuben, Milbridge, Cherryfield,** and **Harrington.**

Nowadays life can be tough here, where once great wooden ships slid down the ways and brought prosperity and trade to shippers, builders, and barons of the timber industry, of

which Cherryfield's stunning houses are evidence enough. The barons now control the blueberry fields, covering much of the inland area of western Washington County and annually shipping millions of pounds of blueberries out of headquarters in Milbridge and Cherryfield. The big names here are Jasper Wyman and Sons and Cherryfield Foods.

Milbridge straddles Route 1 and the Narraguagus River (Nar-ra-GWAY-gus, a

Native American name meaning "above the boggy place"), once the state's premier source of Atlantic salmon. Cherryfield is at the tidal limit of the Narraguagus. Even though Route 1A trims maybe three miles off the trip from Milbridge to Harrington, resist the urge to take it. Take Route 1 from Milbridge to Cherryfield—the Narraguagus Highway—and then continue to Harrington. You shouldn't miss Cherryfield.

Steuben's claim to fame is the Petit Manan section of the Maine Coastal Islands National Wildlife Refuge.

SIGHTS
Milbridge Historical Society Museum

A group of energetic residents worked tirelessly to establish the Milbridge Historical Society Museum (S. Main St., Milbridge, 207/546-4471, www.milbridgehistoricalsociety.org, 1–4 P.M. Sat.–Sun. June–Sept. and also Tues. July–Aug., donation). Displays in the large exhibit room focus on Milbridge's essential role in the shipbuilding trade, but kids will enjoy such oddities as an amputation knife used by a local doctor and a recreated country kitchen. The museum also sponsors a monthly lecture series March–October.

Scenic Fall Foliage Routes

In fall—roughly early September–early October in this part of Maine—the postharvest blueberry fields take on brilliant scarlet hues, then maroon. They're gorgeous. The best barren-viewing road is Route 193 between Cherryfield and Beddington, via Deblois, the link between Routes 1 and 9—a 21-mile stretch of granite outcrops, pine windscreens, and fiery-red fields.

Cherryfield Historic District

Imagine a little town this far Down East having a 75-acre National Register Historic District with 52 architecturally significant buildings. If architecture appeals, don't miss Cherryfield. The **Cherryfield-Narraguagus Historical Society** (88 River Rd., Cherryfield,

207/546-2076, www.cherryfieldhistorical.com, 1–4 P.M. Sat. summer) has produced a free brochure-map, *Walking Tour of the Cherryfield Historic District,* which you can download. Architectural styles included on the route are Greek Revival, Italianate, Queen Anne, Colonial Revival, Second Empire, Federal, and Gothic Revival—dating 1803–1940, with most from the late 19th century. Especially impressive for such a small town are the Second Empire–style homes.

ENTERTAINMENT AND EVENTS

The biggest event in this end of Washington County is **Milbridge Days,** the last weekend in July, drawing hundreds of visitors. The Saturday-afternoon highlight is the codfish relay race—hilarious enough to have been featured in *Sports Illustrated* magazine and on national television. The four-member teams, clad in slickers and hip boots, really do hand off a greased cod instead of the usual baton. Race rules specify that runners must be "reasonably sober" and not carry the codfish between their teeth or legs. Also on the schedule are blueberry pancake breakfasts, a fun parade, kids' games, an auction, a dance, beano and cribbage tournaments, craft booths, and a lobster bake. You have to be there. The relay race has been going since the mid-1980s; the festival has been going for a century and a half.

Check locally for the concert schedule of the **Cherryfield Band,** an impressive community group with about three dozen enthusiastic members. They're in demand May–December, but best of all are their concerts, usually Tuesday evenings, in the lovely downtown bandstand overlooking the Narraguagus River.

The Humboldt Field Research Institute (59 Eagle Hill Rd., Steuben, 207/546-2821, www.eaglehill.us, 7:30 P.M. Thurs. and Sat. early July–late Aug., $5–8) offers lectures, sometimes preceded by optional dinners (fee, advance reservation required), by guest lecturers, authors, and scholars on wide-ranging natural history and cultural history topics with a scientific focus. Call for the current schedule. The institute is four miles off Route 1. Take Dyer Bay Road off Route 1, bearing left at the fork onto Mogador Road for a total of 3.6 miles, then left on Schooner Point Road, and then right on Eagle Hill Road. Programs take place in the dining hall lecture room.

SHOPPING

Arthur Smith (Rogers Point Rd., Steuben, 207/546-3462) is the real thing when it comes to chainsaw carvings. He's an extremely talented folk artist who looks at a piece of wood and sees an animal in it. His carvings of great blue herons, eagles, wolves, porcupines, flamingoes, and other creatures are incredibly detailed, and his wife, Marie, paints them in lifelike colors. Don't expect a fancy studio; much of the work can be viewed roadside.

Also in Steuben, but on the other end of the spectrum, is **Ray Carbone** (460 Pigeon Hill Rd., Steuben, 207/546-2170), whose masterful wood, stone, and bronze sculptures and fine furniture are definitely worth stopping to see or buy. Don't miss the granite sculptures and birdbaths in the garden.

RECREATION
◖ Maine Coastal Islands National Wildlife Refuge

Occupying a 2,166-acre peninsula in Steuben with 10 miles of rocky shoreline and three offshore islands is the refuge's outstandingly scenic **Petit Manan Point Division** (Pigeon Hill Rd., Steuben, 207/546-2124, www.fws.gov/northeast/mainecoastal). The remote location means it sees only about 15,000 visitors a year, most of those likely bird-watchers, as more than 300 different birds have been sighted here. The refuge's primary focus is restoring colonies of nesting seabirds. Among the other natural highlights here are stands of jack pine, coastal raised peat lands, blueberry barrens, freshwater and salt marshes, granite shores, and cobble beaches. When asking directions locally, you might hear it called 'tit Manan.

The moderately easy four-mile round-trip Birch Point Trail and easy 1.5-mile round-trip

Hollingsworth or Shore Trail provide splendid views and opportunities to spot wildlife along the shore and in the fields, forests, and marshland. The Hollingsworth Trail, leading you to the shoreline, is the best. On clear days, you can see the 123-foot lighthouse on Petit Manan Island, 2.5 miles offshore. The Birch Point Trail heads through blueberry fields to Dyer Bay and loops by the waterfront, with much of the trail passing through woods.

From Route 1, on the east side of Steuben, take Pigeon Hill Road. Six miles down is the first parking lot, for the Birch Point Trail; another half mile takes you to the parking area for the Hollingsworth Trail; space is limited at both parking areas. If you arrive in August, help yourself to blueberries. The refuge is open sunrise–sunset daily all year; cross-country skiing is permitted in winter.

McClellan Park

You can picnic, hike, and camp at this 10-acre oceanfront park. Go tide-pooling, clamber over rocks, or just admire the views over the rugged islands offshore.

Excursion Boats

Captain Jaime Robertson's **Robertson Sea Tours and Adventures** (Milbridge Marina, Fickett's Point Rd., 207/546-3883 or 207/461-7439, www.robertsonseatours.com, May 15–Oct. 1) offers cruises from the Milbridge Marina aboard the *Mairi Leigh,* a classic Maine lobster boat. Options include puffins and seabirds, island lighthouses, and a lobstering cruise. Prices range $55–80 adults, $45–65 children for the 2–4-hour cruises. Boat minimums may apply. Captain Robertson also offers a **whale-watching cruise** aboard the six-passenger 33-foot *Elisabeth Rose* ($90 pp, $360 minimum).

Captain Harry "Buzzy" Shinn's **Downeast Coastal Cruises** (207/546-7720, cell 207/598-7740, www.downeastcoastalcruises.com) depart from the Milbridge Landing aboard the comfortable *Alyce K.* for island cruises, lighthouse cruises, puffin cruises, lobster cruises (complete with a meal), sunset cruises, and charters.

Cruises last 2–3.5 hours and cost $45–75 adults, $35–65 children; boat minimums apply.

ACCOMMODATIONS

One of Cherryfield's 52 buildings on the National Register of Historic Places, the 1793 Archibald-Adams House is now the **Englishman's Bed and Breakfast** (122 Main St., Cherryfield, 207/546-2337, www.english-mansbandb.com, $95–155). The magnificently restored Federal-style home borders the Narraguagus River and makes a superb base for exploring inland and Down East Maine. The lovely grounds have gardens and a screened-in gazebo. Owners Peter (the Englishman) and Kathy Winham are archaeologists and serious tea drinkers—they also sell fine teas online (www.teasofcherryfield.com) and in area specialty stores. Two guest rooms in the main house have river views. One has a private half bath but shares a full bath. A riverside guesthouse, built in the 1990s, melds beautifully with the inn's architecture and is self-catering; pets are allowed here for $7 per night.

Camping

Since 1958 the Ayr family has welcomed campers at its quiet, well-off-the-beaten-path property on Joy Cove. With a convenient location 15 minutes from Petit Manan National Wildlife Refuge and 20 minutes from Schoodic Point, **Mainayr Campground** (321 Village Rd., Steuben, 207/542-2690, www.mainayr.com, late May–mid-Oct., $27–32) has 35 tenting and RV sites (five with full hookups). Also on the premises are a playground, a laundry, a beach for tidal swimming, clamming flats, a grassy launch area for kayaks and canoes, a camp store, berries for picking, and fresh lobsters. If that's not enough, David Ayr enjoys regaling campers with stories.

FOOD

It's always wise to call ahead to verify days and hours of operation.

Local Flavors

You can easily pick up enough goodies for a picnic lunch or to stock a cottage kitchen at the Saturday-morning **Milbridge Farmers Market** (9 A.M.–noon Sat. early June–mid-Oct.), which sets up downtown, across from Kelco.

Family Favorites

In Milbridge, the best choice is **44 Degrees North** (17 Main St., Milbridge, 207/546-4440, www.44-degrees-north.com, 11 A.M.–9 P.M. Tues.–Sun., 11 A.M.–3 P.M. Mon.). The front room is family oriented, with booths, tables, and cheerful decor. The back room doubles as a bar and has a big-screen TV. Expect home cooking, with a few surprises, and as is usually the case in this part of Maine, mouthwatering desserts. Most heartier choices are less than $16.

More good home cooking, from shepherd's pie to fried fish, comes out of the kitchen at **Scovils Millside Dining** (1276 Main St./Rte. 1, Harrington, 207/483-6544, 7 A.M.–7 P.M. daily), a cheerful family-run restaurant near the intersections of Routes 1 and 1A. The Friday all-you-can-eat fish fry is $10.

INFORMATION

The best source for area info is the **Machias Bay Area Chamber of Commerce** (207/255-4402, www.machiaschamber.org).

Jonesport and Beals Area

Between western Washington County and the Machias Bay area is the molar-shaped Jonesport Peninsula, reached from the west via the attractive little town of **Columbia Falls,** bordering Route 1. Rounding the peninsula are the picturesque towns of **Addison, Jonesport,** and **Beals Island.** First settled around 1762, Columbia Falls still has a handful of houses dating from the late 18th century, but its best-known structure is the early-19th-century Ruggles House.

On the banks of the Pleasant River, just south of Columbia Falls, Addison once had four huge shipyards cranking out wooden cargo vessels that circled the world. Since that 19th-century heyday, little seems to have changed, and the town today may be best known as the haunt of painter John Marin, who first came to Maine in 1914.

Jonesport and Beals Island are traditional hardworking fishing communities—old-fashioned, friendly, and photogenic. Beals, connected to Jonesport via an arched bridge over Moosabec Reach, is named for Manwarren Beal Jr. and his wife, Lydia, who arrived around 1773 and quickly threw themselves into the Revolutionary War effort. But that's not all they did—the current phone book covering Jonesport and Beals Island lists dozens of Beal descendants (as well as dozens of Alleys and Carvers, other early names).

Even more memorable than Manwarren Beal was his six-foot, seven-inch descendant Barnabas, dubbed "Tall Barney" for obvious reasons. The larger-than-life fellow became the stuff of legend all along the Maine coast—and a popular Jonesport restaurant preserves his name.

Also legendary here is the lobster-boat design known as the Jonesport hull. People "from away" won't recognize its distinctive shape, but count on the fishing pros to know it. The harbor here is jam-packed with Jonesport lobster boats, and souped-up versions are consistent winners in the summertime lobster-boat race series.

SIGHTS
Ruggles House

Behind a picket fence on a quiet street in Columbia Falls stands the remarkable Ruggles House (Main St., Columbia Falls, 207/483-4637, www.ruggleshouse.org, 9:30 A.M.–4:30 P.M. Mon.–Sat., noon–4:30 P.M. Sun. June 1–Oct. 15, $5 adults, $2 ages 6–12). Built in 1818 for Judge Thomas Ruggles—lumber baron, militia captain, even postmaster—the tiny house on a grand scale boasts a famous flying (unsupported) staircase, intricately carved moldings, a Palladian window, and unusual period furnishings. Rescued in the mid-20th century and maintained by the Ruggles House Society, this gem has become a magnet for savvy preservationists. A quarter mile east of Route 1, it's open for hour-long guided tours.

At the house, pick up a copy of the Columbia Falls walking-tour brochure, which details the intriguing history of other houses in this hamlet.

Maine Coast Sardine History Museum

In the first half of the 20th century, sardine processing was big business in Maine, with more than 400 factories along the coast, and Jonesport was home to 15 of them. Ronnie Peabody, director of the Maine Coast Sardine History Museum (24 Mason Bay Rd., Jonesport, 207/497-2961, http://mainesardinemuseum.tripod.com, noon–4 P.M. Tues.–Fri. and Sun., $4 adults, $2 students) and his wife, Mary, began collecting sardine artifacts and memorabilia in 2001 and opened this museum in 2008. Ronnie is a passionate guide who brings life to the photos, equipment, and even the cans displayed. You can zip through on your own in about 20 minutes, but start asking Ronnie questions or ask him to guide you through, and you'll wonder where the hour went.

"Rita Willey The Mahammad Ali Of All Sardine Packers"

Ted Sylvester Bangor Daily News Aug. 4th 1983

The Maine Coast Sardine History Museum in Jonesport celebrates the region's herring heritage.

Downeast Institute for Applied Marine Research and Education

University of Maine at Machias professor Brian Beals founded the Beals Island Regional Shellfish Hatchery, now the Downeast Institute (Black Duck Cove, Great Wass Island, 207/497-5769, www.downeastinstitute.org), a marine field station for the University of Maine at Machias. Learn everything there is to know about shellfish, especially soft-shell clams, on this eight-acre property with two natural coves. Tours are by appointment.

Wild Salmon Research Center

Established in 1922, this center (Columbia Falls, 207/483-4336, www.mainesalmonrivers.org, 8 A.M.–4 P.M. Mon.–Fri., free) has a few educational displays and a library. In the basement is a volunteer-run fish hatchery that raises 50,000 Atlantic salmon fry annually. Staff welcome visitors and explain the efforts to save Maine's endangered salmon. You might also ask about the status of the East Machias Aquatic Research Center, a new facility under development by the Downeast Salmon Federation. Hatchery operations began in 2009. Also planned are laboratories, a resources center, and a small museum.

ENTERTAINMENT AND EVENTS

For a taste of real Maine, don't miss the early April **Fried Smelt Dinner.**

The biggest annual wingding hereabouts is the Jonesport **Fourth of July** celebration, with several days of special activities, including barbecues, beauty pageant, kids' games, fireworks, and the famed **Jonesport Lobster Boat Races** in Moosabec Reach.

Peabody Memorial Library presents bimonthly art shows and sponsors a summer music series.

SHOPPING

Flower-design majolica pottery and whimsical terra-cotta items are April Adams's specialties at **Columbia Falls Pottery** (150 Main St., Columbia Falls, 207/483-4075

MAINE CENTRAL MODEL RAILROAD

Inside the purpose-built garage-like building adjacent to Harold "Buz" and Helen Beal's home is what may be Maine's largest model railway. The Beal's Maine Central Model Railway covers 900 square feet and features 4,000 trees, 407 train cars, 3,000 feet of track, 11 bridges and trestles, and 200 switches. There may be a private one that's larger, but the Beals welcome visitors.

Tracks wind through towns modeled on real Maine places, passing mines and mills, lobster boats and lighthouses, cities and villages. Sharp eyes can spy Stephen King's house and Dysart's Truck Stop in Bangor, Champion Paper in Bucksport, seals basking on rocks, hikers in wooded mountains, lobstermen docking at Cape Split, Harbor House in Jonesport, lumberman rolling logs, a hunter surprised by a bear, even an accident scene complete with ambulance. "We hit about everything, there's even an outhouse; now, that's getting down to the nitty gritty," Buz says.

"I've got railroading in my blood," says Buz, a Jonesport native and 26-year Coast Guard veteran whose grandfather was a Canadian Pacific engineer. He began planning the model's layout as a boy, but it wasn't until he returned to Jonesport nearly 50 years later that he began building his dream. "You have to have the place, the opportunity, and the patience," he says. And the right partner. "Helen's family were railroad people. We've married 25 years and never had an argument; we're two peas in a pod."

Buz had a track plan, and he knew the model would fill the building before they started construction. They did everything themselves, by hand using tweezers, glue, and plaster of Paris. "We didn't know what the heck we were doing. We did it as we went along, six to eight feet at a time," Buz says. The model rests on a maze of tables with varying heights. "I didn't want it all the same; it gets humdrum if you do that," he says. The design allows visitors to walk through the layout.

Helen built the little houses and cut 600 windows by hand using an X-Acto knife. She also planted trees and painted all the small pieces. Buzz painted the houses and built and painted the larger structures. Some cars were built from scratch, some made from kits, others bought. The landscape – granite cliffs and wooded mountains – was created with two layers of plaster-soaked Bounty towels, layered with plaster. "I figured it out as I went along," he says. It took 12 years and thousands of hours to complete.

Buz needs two other individuals to operate the three divisions, and it takes years of training to understand all the intricacies of each. There are boxcars and grain cars, gondolas, and cars designed to carry gas, oil, or coal. "You have to know all the businesses, how many cars can fit on a siding by each business, and know what every car is and what it carries or is used for," he says. "There's a lot to it. People look and don't realize that. Me and the boys run it all every Sunday, if I can get them together."

Buz operates one train through the full layout for most visitors, and that takes nine minutes. When he flips the power switch, lights come on inside the building and the clang, whistles, and chug of trains fills the air. "I don't know what it is about a train that's so fascinating. It's just two engines pulling cars behind; it's not rocket science," he says, as his eyes follow the train through the Maine landscape. "It's just mesmerizing. I never tire of it."

Visitors are welcome most days, but it's best to call ahead (207/497-2255) to be sure someone's home. Look for the sign on Route 187, about four miles northeast of downtown Jonesport. (Route 187 makes a loop through the peninsula; the Beals are on the easternmost side of the loop – 7.7 miles south of Route 1.) There's no charge, but donations are welcome.

or 800/235-2512, www.columbiafallspottery.com), an appealing shop in a rehabbed country store next to the Ruggles House.

Allow time to browse **Gray Wolf Gift, Gallery & Frame Shop** (280 Water St., Addison, 207/483-6567). Owner and artist Beth Ferriero has filled it with work by more than 30 area artists and artisans, and the quality is top-notch.

Two adjacent antiques shops brighten Jonesport's waterfront. Maureen Hart sells antiques, paintings by Audrey Soule, and whimsies at **Harbor House on Sawyer Cove** (32 Sawyer Sq., 207/497-5417). Eclectic finds await browsers at **Moospecke Antiques** (Sawyer Sq., 207/497-2457). Seeking rock and roll memorabilia? **Crow Haven** (2140 Rte. 187, Jonesport) has that as well as other collectibles.

In downtown Jonesport, **Church's True Value** (Main St./Rte. 187, Jonesport, 207/497-2778) carries all the usual hardware items, plus gifts, souvenirs, and sportswear. Helpful owners John and Sharon Church can also answer any question about the area and solve most any problem.

Nelson Decoys Downeast Gallery (Cranberry Lane, Jonesport, 207/497-3488) is equal parts shop, gallery, and museum. Inside are not only hand-carved decoys but also creations by other area artists and artisans. It's in an old schoolhouse, just off Main Street downtown.

RECREATION
◀ Great Wass Island Preserve

Allow a whole day to explore 1,576-acre Great Wass Island, an extraordinary preserve, even when it's drenched in fog—a not-infrequent event. Owned by the Nature Conservancy (207/729-5181, www.nature.org), the preserve is at the tip of Jonesport's peninsula. Easiest hiking routes are the wooded two-mile Little Cape Point and 1.5-mile Mud Hole Trails, retracing your path for each. (Making a loop by connecting the two along the rocky shoreline adds considerably to the time and difficulty, but do it if you have time; allow about six hours and wear waterproof footwear.) Expect to see beach-head irises (like a blue flag) and orchids,

jack pines, a peat bog, seals, pink granite, pitcher plants, lots of warblers, and maybe some grouse. Carry water and a picnic; wear bug repellent. No camping, fires, or pets are allowed, and there are no toilet facilities; access is during daytime only. To reach the preserve from Route 1, take Route 187 to Jonesport (12 miles) and then cross the arched bridge to Beals Island. Continue across Beals to the Great Wass causeway (locally called "the Flying Place") and then go three miles on Black Duck Cove Road to the parking area (on the left). Watch for the Nature Conservancy oak-leaf symbol. At the parking area, pick up a trail map and a bird checklist.

Also owned by the Nature Conservancy is 21-acre **Mistake Island,** accessible only by boat. Low and shrubby, Mistake has a Coast Guard–built boardwalk from the landing at the northwest corner to **Moose Peak Light,** standing 72 feet above the water at the eastern end of the island. The only negative on this lovely island is rubble left behind when the government leveled the keeper's house.

Excursion Boats
◀ MACHIAS SEAL ISLAND PUFFIN TOUR

A great-grandson of legendary local "Tall Barney" Beal, Captain Barna Norton began offering puffin-watching trips to Machias Seal Island (MSI) in 1940 in a 33-foot boat incautiously named *If.* Now his descendants have taken over the helm of **Norton of Jonesport** (118 Main St., Jonesport, 207/497-5933 or 207/497-5933, www.machiassealisland.com, $100). The *Chief* heads 20 miles offshore to an island claimed by both the United States and Canada—a colorful saga. To preserve the fragile nesting sites of Atlantic puffins and arctic terns, access to the 15-acre island is restricted. Passengers are off-loaded into small boats, but sea swells sometimes prevent landing. (The captain supplies antiseasickness wristbands to queasy passengers.) The trip is not appropriate for small children or unsteady adults. The boat departs Jonesport around 7 A.M. and returns around noon. Wear waterproof hiking boots, take a hat, and pack some munchies.

PUFFINS

The chickadee is the Maine state bird, and the bald eagle is our national emblem, but probably the best-loved bird along the Maine coast is the Atlantic puffin *(Fratercula arctica)*, a member of the auk (Alcidae) family. Photographs show an imposing-looking creature with a quizzical mien; amazingly, this larger-than-life seabird is only about 12 inches long. Black-backed and white-chested, the puffin has bright orange legs, "clown-makeup" eyes, and a distinctive, rather outlandish red-and-yellow beak. Its diet is fish and shellfish.

Almost nonexistent in this part of the world as recently as the 1970s, the puffin (or "sea parrot") has recovered dramatically thanks to the unstinting efforts of Cornell University ornithologist Stephen Kress and his Project Puffin (www.projectpuffin.org). Starting with an orphan colony of two on remote Matinicus Rock, Kress painstakingly transferred nearly a thousand puffin chicks (also known fondly as "pufflings") from Newfoundland and used artificial nests and decoys to entice the birds to adapt to and reproduce on Eastern Egg Rock in Muscongus Bay.

In 1981, thanks to the assistance and persistence of hundreds of interns and volunteers, and despite the predations of great black-backed gulls, puffins finally were fledged on Eastern Egg, and the rest, as they say, is history. Within 20 years, more than three dozen puffin couples were nesting on Eastern Egg Rock, and still more had established nests on other islands in the area. Kress's methods have received international attention, and his proven techniques have been used to reintroduce bird populations in remote parts of the globe. In 2001, *Down East* magazine singled out Kress to receive its prestigious annual Environmental Award.

HOW AND WHERE TO SEE PUFFINS

Puffin-watching, like whale-watching, involves heading offshore, so be prepared with warm clothing, rubber-soled shoes, a hat, sunscreen, binoculars, and, if you're motion-sensitive, appropriate medication.

The Maine Audubon Society undertakes evening excursions from New Harbor to Eastern Egg Rock 2-3 times a summer, and Hardy Boat Cruises has puffin-watching trips from New Harbor daily early June–mid-August, but the best daily up-close-and-personal opportunities for puffin-watching along the Down East Coast – specifically, on Machias Seal Island – are aboard boats departing from Cutler and Jonesport. Both **Bold Coast Charters** (207/259-4484, www.boldcoast.com) and **Norton of Jonesport** (207/497-5933 www.machiassealisland.com) operate May–August and cost about $100 pp. Weather permitting, you'll be allowed to disembark on the 20-acre island.

ADOPT-A-PUFFIN PROGRAM

Stephen Kress's Project Puffin has devised a clever way to enlist supporters via the Adopt-a-Puffin program (www.projectpuffin.org). For a $100 donation, you'll receive a certificate of adoption, vital statistics on your adoptee, annual updates, and a color photo.

THE DOWN EAST COAST

SCENIC CRUISE

Operating as **Coastal Cruises** (Kelley Point Rd., Jonesport, 207/497-3064 or 207/497-2699, www.cruisedowneast.com), Captain Laura Fish and her brother Harry Fish, a certified dive master, offer three-hour Moosabec Reach cruises in the 23-foot powerboat *Aaron Thomas*. Among the sights are Great Wass Island and Mistake Island. Rates begin at $50 pp, varying with the number of passengers; six-person maximum. Dive trips begin at $75 pp for two or more. Reservations are required. Trips depart from Jonesport and operate May–mid-October.

ACCOMMODATIONS

Rates noted are for peak season.

Bed-and-Breakfasts

How about staying in a beautiful modern farmhouse overlooking the water—with llamas lolling outside? At ◖ **Pleasant Bay Bed**

© HILARY NANGLE

Harbor House on Sawyer Cove is both a bed-and-breakfast and an antique shop.

and Breakfast and Llama Keep (338 West Side Rd., Addison, 207/483-4490, www.pleasantbay.com, year-round, $50–150), Joan and Lee Yeaton manage to pamper more than 40 llamas and a herd of red deer as well as their two-legged guests. Three miles of trails wind through the 110 acres, and a canoe is available for guests. Three lovely guest rooms (private and shared baths) and one suite, with a microwave and a refrigerator, all have water views. Rates include a delicious breakfast. Arrange in advance for a llama walk ($15 per llama). The farm borders Pleasant Bay, 3.9 miles southwest of Route 1.

The fanciest digs in Jonesport are at **Harbor House on Sawyer Cove** (Sawyer Sq., Jonesport, 207/497-5417, www.harborhs.com, year-round, $125), hospitably run by Maureen and Gene Hart—she's a former nurse, he a former engineer. They've been sharing their passion for Jonesport with Harbor House guests for more than a dozen years. Two very comfortable and spacious second-floor rooms—named Beach Rose and Lupine and

decorated accordingly—have incredible views of Moosabec Reach. Binoculars are provided so you can watch the action. The rooms also have TV and Wi-Fi, and a guest phone, fridge, and microwave are provided. The Harts operate an antiques shop, selling what they call "curiosities," on the first floor of this fascinating old building, once Jonesport's telegraph office. Maureen serves a great breakfast—early enough for bird-watchers—on the harbor-view porch.

Cottages and Apartments

Proprietor Dorothy Higgins's **Cranberry Cove Cottages** (56 Kelley Point Rd., Jonesport, 207/497-2139, ddhiggi@hotmail.com, $135) comprise two second-story apartments, each distinctively furnished in cottage style and with TVs, phones, and harbor views. Both have kitchenettes provisioned with all sorts of goodies, from fresh eggs to wine and cheese. Pets are welcome. Rates decrease with the length of stay.

Abigail Oates-Alley has two carefully decorated, nicely appointed, and well-equipped two-bedroom units in a harbor-front duplex called **Moose-a-bec** (34 Old House Point, Jonesport, 207/497-2121, $135). Both have big views, full baths with laundry, dishwashers, and TV. Really, Abigail has thought of just about everything, right down to kitchen supplies such as foil, plastic wrap, and napkins. Outside are lovely gardens, a children's play set, and stairs leading to a small pebble beach. It's adjacent to a working wharf, so expect to see and hear the boats going out and returning each day. The downstairs unit is wheelchair-accessible. The second bedroom upstairs is more bed than room.

Camping

The town of Jonesport operates the low-key, no-frills **Jonesport Campground** (Henry Point, Kelley Point Rd., Jonesport, early May–Labor Day) on two acres with fabulous views over Sawyer Cove and Moosabec Reach. Basic facilities include outhouses, picnic tables, and fire rings; three power poles provide hookups. Showers and washing machines are available across the cove at Jonesport Shipyard (207/497-2701). The campground is exposed to wind off the water, so expect nights to be cool. Sites are allocated on a first-come, first-served basis for a small fee. Avoid the campground during Fourth of July festivities; it's jam-packed. From Route 187 at the northeastern edge of Jonesport, turn right onto Kelley Point Road and then right again to Henry Point.

FOOD

Call ahead to verify days and hours of operation.

For divine pastries along with submarine sandwiches and brick-oven pizza, stromboli, and calzones, head to **Bohemian Mama's**

Bakery (251 Ridge Rd., Addison, 207/483-6132). Another local bakery is **Purity Pastries** (315 East Side Rd., Addison, 207/483-2021). Both bakeries have quite limited days and hours of operation; call first.

For local color, start at **Tall Barney's** (52 Main St./Rte. 187, Jonesport, 207/497-2403, www.tallbarneys.com, no credit cards), where you'll find homemade baked beans and chowders, pizza, and more—and you won't break the bank. Sit back and watch the servers chat up the lobstermen regulars camped out at the big center table, known locally as the Liars' Table. Join them if you dare. Days and hours of operation change frequently; call ahead.

Locals praise **Smoky Toast Café** (1183 Rte. 1, Jonesboro, 207/434-5910, 5 A.M.–2 P.M. Mon.–Fri.) as a great spot to relax over breakfast or lunch, and they rave about the sticky buns. Service is friendly, the place is spotless, and the only drawback is that it isn't open on weekends.

Another possibility is **The Lighthouse Cafe** (138 Main St., Jonesport, 207/497-5650, 11 A.M.–4 P.M. Tues., 11 A.M.–8 P.M. Wed.–Fri., 11 A.M.–6 P.M. Sat.), a cheerful place serving inexpensive home-style fare.

INFORMATION AND SERVICES

The **Machias Bay Area Chamber of Commerce** (12 E. Main St., Machias, 207/255-4402, www.machiaschamber.org) handles inquires for the Machias area as well as Jonesport.

In downtown Jonesport, two reliable sources for local information are **Church's True Value** (Main St./Rte. 187, Jonesport, 207/497-2778), open Monday–Saturday, and Maureen Hart at **Antiques on the Harbor** (Sawyer Square, 207/497-5417).

THE DOWN EAST COAST

Machias Bay Area

The only negative thing about **Machias** (muh-CHAI-us) is its Micmac Indian name, meaning "bad little falls" (even though it's accurate—the midtown waterfall here is treacherous). A contagious local esprit pervades this shire town of Washington County thanks to antique homes, a splendid river-valley setting, Revolutionary War monuments, and a small but busy university campus.

If you regard crowds as fun, an ideal time to land here is during the renowned annual Machias Wild Blueberry Festival, the third weekend in August, when harvesting is under way in Washington County's blueberry fields and you can stuff your face with blueberry everything—muffins, jam, pancakes, ice cream, and pies. You can also collect blueberry-logo napkins, T-shirts, magnets, pottery, and jewelry. Biggest highlight: the annual summer musical parody.

Among the other summer draws are a chamber-music series, art shows, and semiprofessional theater performances. Within a few miles are day trips galore—options for hiking, biking, golfing, swimming, and sea kayaking.

Also included within the Machias sphere are the towns of **Roque Bluffs, Jonesboro, Whitneyville, Marshfield, East Machias,** and **Machiasport.** Just to the east, between Machias and Lubec, are the towns of **Whiting** and **Cutler.**

HISTORICAL SIGHTS

History is a big deal in this area, and since Machias was the first settled Maine town east of the Penobscot River, lots of enthusiastic amateur historians have helped rescue homes and sites dating from as far back as the Revolutionary War.

English settlers, uprooted from communities farther west on the Maine coast, put down permanent roots here in 1763, harvesting timber to ensure their survival. Stirrings of revolutionary discontent surfaced even at this remote outpost, and when British loyalists in Boston

began usurping some of the valuable harvest, Machias patriots plotted revenge. By 1775, when the armed British schooner *Margaretta* arrived as a cargo escort, local residents aboard the sloop *Unity,* in a real David-and-Goliath episode, chased and captured the *Margaretta.* On June 12, 1775, two months after the famed Battles of Lexington and Concord (and five days before the Battle of Bunker Hill), Machias Bay was the site of what author James Fenimore Cooper called "The Lexington of the Sea"—the first naval battle of the American Revolution. The name of patriot leader Jeremiah O'Brien today appears throughout Machias—on a school, a street, a cemetery, and a state park. In 1784, Machias was incorporated; it became the shire town in 1790.

Museums

One-hour guided tours vividly convey the atmosphere of the 1770 **Burnham Tavern** (Main St./Rte. 192, Machias, 207/255-6930, www.burnhamtavern.com, 9:30 A.M.–4 P.M. Mon.–Sat. mid-June–late Sept. or by appointment, $5 adults, $0.25 under age 12), one of 21 homes in the entire country designated as most significant to the American Revolution. Upstart local patriots met here in 1775 to plot revolution against the British. Job and Mary Burnham's tavern-home next served as an infirmary for casualties from the Revolution's first naval battle, just offshore. Lots of fascinating history lies in this National Historic Site, maintained by the Daughters of the American Revolution. Hanging outside is a sign reading "Drink for the thirsty, food for the hungry, lodging for the weary, and good keeping for horses, by Job Burnham."

Headquarters for the Machiasport Historical Society and one of the area's three oldest residences, the 1810 **Gates House** (344 Port Rd., Machiasport, 207/255-8461, call for hours, donation) was snatched from ruin and restored in 1966. The building, on the National Register of Historic Places, overlooks Machias Bay and contains fascinating period furnishings and

© TOM NANGLE

Discover the significant role Machias played in the American Revolution at the Burnham Tavern museum.

artifacts, many related to the lumbering and shipbuilding era. The museum, four miles southeast of Route 1, has limited parking on a hazardous curve.

O'Brien Cemetery

Old-cemetery buffs will want to stop at O'Brien Cemetery, resting place of the town's earliest settlers. It's next to Bad Little Falls Park, close to downtown, off Route 92 toward Machiasport. A big plus here is the view, especially in autumn, of blueberry barrens, the waterfall, and the bay.

Fort O'Brien State Historic Site

The American Revolution's first naval battle was fought just offshore from Fort O'Brien (207/942-4014, www.parksandlands.com, free) in June 1775. Now a State Historic Site, the fort was built and rebuilt several times—originally to guard Machias during the Revolutionary War. Only Civil War–era earthworks now remain, plus well-maintained lawns overlooking the Machias River. Steep banks lead down to

the water; keep small children well back from the edge. There are no restrooms or other facilities, but there's a playground at the Fort O'Brien School next door. Officially the park is open Memorial Day weekend–Labor Day, but it's accessible all year. Take Route 92 from Machias about five miles toward Machiasport; the parking area is on the left.

OTHER SIGHTS
Maine Sea Salt Company

Season your visit with a tour of the Maine Sea Salt Company (11 Church Lane, Marshfield, 207/255-3310, www.maineseasalt.com), which produces sea salt in its solar green houses and shallow pools using evaporation and reduction of seawater. Free tours (available most days 9 A.M.–5 P.M., call first) explain the process and include tastings of natural, seasoned, and smoked salts.

University of Maine at Machias

Founded in 1909 as Washington State Normal School, the University of Maine at Machias

(UMM, 9 O'Brien Ave., Machias, 207/255-1200, www.umm.maine.edu) is now part of the state university system. The **UMM Art Galleries** (Powers Hall, afternoon Mon.–Fri. during school terms or by appointment) feature works from the university's expanding permanent collection of Maine painters—including John Marin, William Zorach, Lyonel Feininger, and Reuben Tam. Rotating exhibits occur throughout the school year.

UMM's **Center for Lifelong Learning** has a state-of-the-art fitness center, six-lane heated pool, and the George Simpson Murdock Bookstore, which stocks more than textbooks. The pool and fitness room are open to the public ($7); call for schedule.

Also open to the public is **Merrill Library** (207/255-1284).

ENTERTAINMENT AND EVENTS

The University of Maine at Machias is the cultural focus in this area, particularly during the school year. **Stage Front: The Arts Downeast** puts on an annual series of concerts, plays, recitals, and other events in the Performing Arts Center at the university. The summer series, once a month, usually features classical and pops concerts, including at least one performance by the energetic Steuben-based Opera Maine organization. Contact UMM (207/255-1384) for schedule information.

If the UMM Ukulele Club is performing anywhere, don't miss them.

Machias Bay Chamber Concerts (207/255-3849, www.machiasbaychamberconcerts.com, $15 adults, $8 students, free under age 13) are held at 7:30 P.M. Tuesday evenings early July–mid-August at the Centre Street Congregational Church. Art exhibits accompany concerts.

The **Machias Wild Blueberry Festival** (www.machiasblueberry.com) is the summer highlight, running Friday–Sunday the third weekend in August and featuring a pancake breakfast, road races, concerts, a craft show, a baked-bean supper, a homegrown musical, and more. The blueberry motif is everywhere.

It's organized by Centre Street Congregational Church in downtown Machias.

A few times each summer, the **Little River Lighthouse** (Cutler, 207/259-3833, www.littleriverlight.org) is open for tours.

SHOPPING

Influenced by traditional Japanese designs, Connie Harter-Bagley markets her dramatic raku ceramics at **Connie's Clay of Fundy** (Rte. 1, East Machias, 207/255-4574, www.clayoffundy.com), on the East Machias River, four miles east of Machias. If she's at the wheel, you can also watch her work.

A number of regional artists and artisans show and sell their wares at **Unique Possibilities** (300 E. Main St./Rte. 1, Machias, 207/255-3337), in the Causeway Common building (in the same complex as Dunkin' Donuts). Out back is **Kandee's Bakery by the Bay** (207/263-5015, http://kandeesbakery.com), serving light lunches and homemade breads and pastries.

Need a read? **Jim's Books, Etc.** (8 Elm St., Machias, 207/255-9058), at the third house on the left on Route 32, just beyond the university campus, is open by chance or by appointment.

RECREATION
Parks and Preserves

Just as dedicated as the historical preservationists are the hikers, bird-watchers, and other eco-sensitive outdoors enthusiasts who've helped preserve thousands of acres in this part of Maine for public access and appreciation.

At **Bad Little Falls Park,** alongside the Machias River, stop to catch the view from the footbridge overlooking the roiling falls (especially in spring). Bring a picnic and enjoy this midtown oasis tucked between Routes 1 and 92.

Thanks to a handful of foresighted year-round and summer residents, spectacular crescent-shaped **Jasper Beach**—piled high with ocean-polished jasper and other rocks—has been preserved by the town of Machiasport. There is no sand here, just stones, in intriguing

TWO SCENIC ROUTES

The drives described below can also be bike routes (easy to moderately difficult), but be forewarned that the roads are narrow and shoulderless, so caution is essential. Heed biking etiquette.

ROUTE 191, THE CUTLER ROAD

Never mind that Route 191, between East Machias and West Lubec, is one of Maine's most stunning coastal drives – you can still follow the entire 27-mile stretch and meet only a handful of cars. **East Machias** even has its own historic district, with architectural gems dating from the late 18th century along High and Water Streets. Further along Route 191, you'll find fishing wharves, low moorlands, a hamlet or two, and islands popping over the horizon. The only peculiarly jarring note is the 26-tower forest of North Cutler's Naval Computer and Telecommunications Station, nearly 1,000 feet high – monitoring global communications – but you'll see this only briefly. (At night, the skyscraping red lights are really eerie, especially if you're offshore aboard a boat.) Off Route 191 are minor roads and hiking trails worth exploring, especially the coastal trails of the Cutler Coast Public Preserve. About three miles south of the Route 191 terminus, you can also check out **Bailey's Mistake,** a hamlet with a black-sand (volcanic) beach. The name? Allegedly it stems from one Captain Bailey who, misplotting his course and thinking he was in Lubec, drove his vessel ashore here one night in the late 19th century.

Unwilling to face the consequences of his lapse, he and his crew off-loaded their cargo of lumber and built themselves dwellings. Whether true or not, it makes a great saga. Even though it's in the town of **Trescott,** and the hamlet is really South Trescott, everyone knows this section as Bailey's Mistake.

ROUTE 92, STARBOARD PENINSULA

Pack a picnic and set out on Route 92 (beginning at Elm Street in downtown Machias) down the 10-mile length of the Starboard Peninsula to a stunning spot known as the Point of Maine. Along the way are the villages of Larrabee, Bucks Harbor, and Starboard, all part of the town of Machiasport. In Bucks Harbor is the turnoff (a short detour to the right) to **Yoho Head,** a controversial upscale development overlooking Little Kennebec Bay.

South of the Yoho Head turnoff is the sign for **Jasper Beach.** From the Jasper Beach sign, continue 1.4 miles to two red buildings (the old Starboard School House and the volunteer fire department). Turn left onto a dirt road and continue to a sign reading "Driveway." Go around the right side of a shed and park on the beach. (Keep track of the tide level, though.) You're at **Point of Maine,** a quintessential Down East panorama of sea and islands. On a clear day, you can see offshore **Libby Island Light,** the focus of Philmore Wass's entertaining narrative *Lighthouse in My Life: The Story of a Maine Lightkeeper's Family.*

shapes and colors. Resist the urge to fill your pockets with souvenirs. Parking is limited, and there are no facilities. From Route 1 in downtown Machias, take Route 92 (Machias Rd.) 9.5 miles southeast, past the village of Bucks Harbor. Watch for a large sign on your left. The beach is on Howard's Cove, 0.2 miles off the road and accessible year-round.

Southwest of Machias, six miles south of Route 1, is **Roque Bluffs State Park** (Roque Bluffs Rd., Roque Bluffs, 207/255-3475, www.parksandlands.com). Saltwater swimming this far north is for the young and brave, but this park also has a 60-acre freshwater pond warm and shallow enough for toddlers and the old and timid. Facilities include primitive changing rooms, outhouses, a play area, and picnic tables; there is no food and no lifeguards. Views go on forever from the wide-open mile-long sweep of sand beach. Admission is $4.50 nonresident adults, $3 Maine resident adults, $1 ages 5–11. The fee box relies on the honor system. The park is open daily May 15–September 15, but the beach is accessible year-round.

On Route 191, about 4.5 miles northeast of the center of Cutler, watch for the parking area (on the right) for the **Cutler Coast Public Preserve,** a 12,234-acre preserve with nearly a dozen miles of beautifully engineered hiking trails on the seaward side of Route 191. It's popular with wildlife watchers: Birding is great, and you might spot whales (humpback, finback, northern right, and minke), seals, and porpoises. Easiest is the 2.8-mile round-trip Coastal Trail through a cedar swamp and spruce-fir forest to an ocean promontory and back. Allow 5–6 hours to continue with the 5.5-mile Black Point Brook Loop, which progresses along a stretch of moderately rugged hiking southward along dramatic tree-fringed shoreline cliffs. Then head back via the Black Point Brook cutoff and connect with the Inland Trail to return to the parking area. Bring binoculars and a camera; the views from this wild coastline are fabulous. Also bring insect repellent—inland boggy stretches are buggy. Carry a picnic and commandeer a granite ledge overlooking the surf. Precipitous cliffs and narrow stretches can make the shoreline section of this trail perilous for small children or insecure adults, so use extreme caution and common sense. There are no facilities in the preserve. If you're here in August, you can stock up on blueberries and even some wild raspberries. Another option, the 9.1-mile Fairy Head Loop, starts the same way as the Black Point Brook Loop but continues southward along the coast, leading to three primitive campsites (stoves only, no fires), available on a first-come, first-served basis. There's no way to reserve these, so you take your chances. Unless you have gazelle genes, the longer loop almost demands an overnight trip. Information on the preserve, including a helpful map, is available from the **Maine Bureau of Parks and Lands** (207/287-3821, www.parksandlands.com). Originally about 2,100 acres, this preserve expanded fivefold in 1997 when several donors, primarily the Richard King Mellon Foundation, deeded to the state 10,055 acres of fields and forests across Route 191 from the trail area, creating a phenomenal tract that now runs from the ocean all the way back to Route 1. Mostly in Cutler but also in Whiting, it is Maine's second-largest public-land gift after Baxter State Park.

Adjacent to it is Maine Coast Heritage Trust's (www.mcht.org) new 1,500-acre **Bog Brook Cove Preserve.** Between the two preserves, this is the largest contiguous area of conservation land in the state outside of Acadia National Park. Bog Brook Cove's lands flow from Cutler into neighboring Trescott and include nearly three miles of ocean frontage, headlands, gravel beaches, coastal peat lands, and 10-acre Norse Pond. Trails are under construction.

Multiuse Trails

The 85-mile **Down East Sunrise Trail** (www.sunrisetrail.org), a rails-to-trails conversion, stretches from Washington Junction near Ellsworth to Ayers Junction in Charlotte, just west of Calais. The 30-miles-plus section between Whitneyville and Ayers Junction is open to pedestrians, snowmobiles, ATVs, cyclists, skiers, and equestrians; construction is proceeding on the rest. Check the website for updates and a downloadable map.

Golf

With lovely water views and tidal inlets serving as obstacles, the nine-hole **Great Cove Golf Course** (387 Great Cove Rd., off Roque Bluffs Rd., Jonesboro, 207/434-7200) is a good challenge. You can also play a quick nine at **Barren View Golf Course** (Rte. 1, Jonesboro, 207/434-6531, www.barrenview.com).

Water Sports

If you've brought your own sea kayak, there are public launching ramps in Bucks Harbor (east of the main Machias Road) and at Roque Bluffs State Park. You can also put in at Sanborn Cove, beyond the O'Brien School on Route 92, about five miles south of Machias, where there's a small parking area. Before setting out, be sure to check the tide calendar and plan your strategy so you don't have to slog through acres of muck when you return.

Sunrise Canoe and Kayak (100 feet off Rte. 1 on an unsigned road, behind Margaretta Motel, Machias, 207/255-3375 or 877/980-2300, www.sunrisecanoeandkayak.com) rents canoes and kayaks for $25–35 per day and offers half-day sea-kayak excursions on Machias Bay, including one to a petroglyph site ($48 pp). It also offers guided day trips and fully outfitted multiday canoeing and kayaking excursions on the Machias and St. Croix Rivers and along the Bold Coast.

The spectacular **Machias River,** one of Maine's most technically demanding canoeing rivers, is a dynamite trip mid-May–mid-June, but no beginner should attempt it. The best advice is to sign on with an outfitter or guide. The run lasts from four days up to six days if you start from Fifth Machias Lake. Expect to see wildlife such as ospreys, eagles, ducks, loons, moose, deer, beavers, and snapping turtles. Be aware, though, that the Machias is probably the buggiest river in the state, and blackflies will form a welcoming party. In addition to Sunrise Canoe and Kayak, Bangor-based **Sunrise Expeditions** (207/942-9300 or 800/748-3730, www.sunrise-exp.com) also offers fully outfitted trips.

Excursion Boats
◖ MACHIAS SEAL ISLAND PUFFIN TOUR

Andy Patterson, the skipper of the 40-foot *Barbara Frost,* operates the **Bold Coast Charter Company** (207/259-4484, www.bold-coast.com), homeported in Cutler Harbor. Andy provides knowledgeable narration, answers questions in depth, and shares his considerable enthusiasm for this pristine corner of Maine. He is best known for his five-hour puffin-sighting trips to Machias Seal Island (departing between 7 and 8 A.M. daily mid-May–Aug., $100, no credit cards); the trip is unsuitable for small children or adults who are susceptible to seasickness. Daily access to the island is restricted, and swells can roll in, so passengers occasionally cannot disembark, but the curious puffins often surround the boat, providing plenty of photo opportunities. A

seabird tour, without an island visit, is available for $100 adults, $60 under age 15. No matter what the air temperature on the mainland, be sure to dress warmly and wear sturdy shoes. The *Barbara Frost*'s wharf is on Cutler Harbor, just off Route 191. Look for the Little River Lobster Company sign; you'll depart from the boat-launching ramp. All trips are dependent on weather and tide conditions, and reservations are required.

Bicycling
Sunrise Canoe and Kayak (100 feet off Rte. 1 on an unsigned road, behind Margaretta Motel, Machias, 207/255-3375 or 877/980-2300, www.sunrisecanoeandkayak.com) rents hybrid mountain bikes for $20 per day. Pickup and delivery service is available.

ACCOMMODATIONS
Rates noted are for peak season.

Bed-and-Breakfasts and Inns
The beautifully restored 1797 **Chandler River Lodge** (654 Rte. 1, Jonesboro, 207/434-2540, www.chandlerriverlodge.com, $100–150) sits well off the highway and overlooks treed lawns that roll down to the Chandler River. It's an idyllic spot, with Adirondack-style chairs positioned just where you want to sit to take in the views. Rates include a continental breakfast, and the dining room is open to nonguests.

Victoriana rules at the **Riverside Inn** (Rte. 1, East Machias, 207/255-4134, www.riverside-inn-maine.com, $99–135), a meticulously restored early-19th-century sea captain's home with four guest rooms (one with a kitchenette). Relax on the deck overlooking the East Machias River or sit in the lovely terraced perennial gardens and you'll forget you're a few steps from a busy highway. The dining room is open to nonguests.

The barn-red **Inn at Schoppee Farm** (Rte. 1, Machias, 207/255-4648, www.schoppeefarm.com, $95) fronts on the tidal Machias River. The 19th-century farm operated as a dairy for three generations before Machias natives David and Julie Barker returned home to operate it as a bed-and-breakfast. They welcome guests with two guest rooms, each furnished with antiques and such niceties as air-conditioning, Wi-Fi, whirlpool baths, satellite TV, and soft down comforters in addition to river views and a full breakfast. Just east of the causeway, it's a healthy walk to downtown diversions.

The second generation of owners now operates **Micmac Farm Guesthouses** (Rte. 92, Machiasport, 207/255-3008, www.micmacfarm.com, $95 per night, $595 per week). Stay in one of Anthony and Bonnie Dunn's three rustic but comfortable and well-equipped cottages and you'll find yourself relaxing on the deck overlooking the tidal Machias River and watching for seabirds, seals, and eagles. No breakfast is provided, but each wood-paneled cottage has a kitchenette and dining area. Pets and children are welcome. There's also a river-view room in the restored 18th-century Gardner House, with a private bath with a whirlpool tub. Guests have use of the farmhouse, including a library. A light breakfast is provided for Gardner House guests.

Motels

The best feature of the two-story **Machias Motor Inn** (109 Main St./Rte. 1, Machias, 207/255-4861, www.machiasmotorinn.com, year-round, $89–109) is its location overlooking the tidal Machias River; sliding doors open onto decks with a view. Twenty-eight guest rooms and six efficiencies have extra-long beds as well as cable TV, air-conditioning, Wi-Fi, and phones. Next door is Helen's Restaurant—famed for seasonal fruit pies and an all-you-can-eat weekend breakfast buffet. Well-behaved dogs ($5 per dog per night) are welcome. The motel is within easy walking distance of downtown, which makes it perfect if you're here for the Blueberry Festival.

For inexpensive digs, you can't beat the **Blueberry Patch** (550 Rte. 1, Jonesboro, 207/434-5411, $55–75), a clean and bright motel and tourist cabins, with three efficiency units. Mark and Norma Lyons provide homespun hospitality with a few extras. All rooms have satellite TV, air-conditioning, Wi-Fi, and

phones, and there's even a pool and a small playground. If you're taller than six feet, choose a motel room rather than a cabin; the cabin bathrooms are tiny. A light continental breakfast is available.

Lighthouse

Yes, you can spend a night or more at **Little River Lighthouse** (Cutler, 207/259-3833, www.littleriverlight.org, $125–150), thanks to the Friends of Little River Lighthouse. Three guest rooms sharing two baths are available, but you have to bring food, bottled water, towels, bed linens or sleeping bags, and all personal items (soap, shampoo) and clean up after yourself. Guests have use of a kitchen. Transportation to the lighthouse is provided, but you have to coordinate your arrival with the tide.

FOOD

Watch the local papers for listings of **public suppers, spaghetti suppers,** or **baked bean suppers,** a terrific way to sample the culinary talents of local cooks. Most begin at 5 P.M., and it's wise to arrive early to get near the head of the line. The suppers often benefit needy individuals or struggling nonprofits, and where else can you eat nonstop for less than $10?

Call ahead to verify days and hours of operation for the venues listed.

Local Flavors

Ask locals where to get the best pizzas, sandwiches, and salads, and the answer is always **Fat Cat Deli** (291 Main St., Machias, 207/255-6777, 11 A.M.–8 P.M. Mon.–Sat., 4–8 P.M. Sun.).

Craving something healthful? The **Whole Life Natural Market** (4 Colonial Way, Machias, 207/255-8855, www.wholelifemarket.com, 9 A.M.–6 P.M. Mon.–Sat., 10 A.M.–2 P.M. Sun.) has a pleasant café serving salads, soups, sandwiches, and baked goods made from organic fruits, vegetables, and grains as well as hormone-free dairy products.

Another source for fresh, healthful foods is the **Machias Valley Farmers Market** (9 A.M.–1 P.M. Sat. May–Oct.). It's held on

Little River Lighthouse

"the dike," a low causeway next to the Machias River. It's usually a good source for blueberries in late July–August.

Family Favorites

Family-owned and very popular all day long is **The Blue Bird Ranch Family Restaurant** (78 Main St./Rte. 1, Machias, 207/255-3351, www .bluebirdranchrestaurant.com, 6 A.M.–8 P.M. daily, $8–22), named for the Prout family's other enterprise, the Blue Bird Ranch Trucking Company. Service is efficient, the food is hearty, the desserts are homemade, and the portions are ample in the three dining rooms.

Helen's (111 Main St./Rte. 1, Machias, 207/255-8423, 6 A.M.–8 P.M. Mon.–Sat., 7 A.M.–7:30 P.M. Sun., $7–18) is renowned for its blueberry pie. A new generation has spruced up the restaurant, an institution in these parts since 1950.

Fine Dining

When you want to splurge, reserve a table at one of these inns.

Oak furnishings and lacy white tablecloths set the tone at the **C Riverside Inn** (Rte. 1, East Machias, 207/255-4134, www.riversi-deinn-maine.com, 5–8 P.M. Tues.–Sun., $24–29), one of the region's most consistent and long-lasting fine-dining spots. The well-prepared fare ranges from trout meunière to beef Wellington. Reservations are required.

Gaze out at the river while dining fireside at the **Chandler River Lodge** (654 Rte. 1, Jonesboro, 207/434-2540, lunch 11:30 A.M.–2 P.M. Thurs.–Fri., dinner 5–8 P.M. Wed.–Sat., entrées $22–32), and be sure to stroll the grounds either before or afterward. At dinner, entrées might include seafood pasta or veal roulade.

INFORMATION AND SERVICES

The **Machias Bay Area Chamber of Commerce** (12 E. Main St., Machias, 207/255-4402, www.machiaschamber.org) stocks brochures, maps, and information on area hiking trails.

Lubec and Vicinity

As the nation's easternmost point, Lubec is literally the beginning of the United States. Lubec residents love to point out that the closest traffic light is 50 miles away.

Settled in 1780 as part of Eastport, it split off in 1811 and was named for the German port of Lübeck (for convoluted reasons still not totally clear). The town's most famous resident was Hopley Yeaton, first captain in the U.S. Revenue-Marine (now the U.S. Coast Guard), who retired here in 1809.

With appealing homes and more than 90 miles of meandering waterfront, Lubec conveys the aura of realness: a hardscrabble fishing community that extends a wary welcome to visitors. Along the main drag, Water Street, a number of shuttered buildings reflect the town's roller-coaster history. Once the world's sardine capital, Lubec no longer has a packing plant, but new businesses are slowly arriving, and each year the town looks a bit spiffier.

No longer a fishing town, these days the summer residents far outnumber year-rounders. In 2010 the community reluctantly closed its high school, which will likely accelerate the transition.

Arrive here on a fine summer day and it's easy to understand why so many visitors are smitten and, seduced by the views and the real estate prices, purchase a piece of a dream.

SIGHTS

◖ West Quoddy Head State Park

Beachcombing, bird-watching, hiking, picnicking, and an up-close look at Maine's only red-and-white-striped lighthouse are the big draws at 541-acre Quoddy Head State Park (West Quoddy Head Rd., Lubec, 207/733-0911, www.parksandlands.com, 9 A.M.–sunset May 15–Oct. 15, $3 nonresident adults, $2 Maine resident adults, $1 children), the easternmost point of U.S. land. Begin with a visit

© HILARY NANGLE

When you get as far down east as Lubec, the yachts and pleasure crafts disappear.

to the **Visitor Center** (207/733-2180, www .westquoddy.com, 10 A.M.–4 P.M. daily late May–mid-Oct., free), located in the 1858 keeper's house and operated by the enthusiastic all-volunteer West Quoddy Head Light Keepers Association. Inside are exhibits on lighthouse memorabilia, local flora and fauna, and area heritage; a gallery displaying local works; and a staffed information desk.

The current **West Quoddy Head Light,** towering 83 feet above mean high water, was built in 1857. (Its counterpart, East Quoddy Head Light, is on New Brunswick's Campobello Island.) Views from the lighthouse grounds are fabulous, and whale sightings are common in summer. The lighthouse tower is open annually for one day in June or early July, during Lighthouse Week, and other times when the Coast Guard is on-site.

The cliffs of Canada's Grand Manan Island are visible from the park's grounds. A 1.75-mile moderately difficult trail follows the 90-foot cliffs to Carrying Place Cove, and an easy mile-long boardwalk winds through a unique moss and heath bog; a second bog is designated as a National Natural Landmark. Be forewarned that the park gate is locked at sunset. In winter the park is accessible for snowshoeing. From Route 189 on the outskirts of Lubec, take South Lubec Road (well signposted) to West Quoddy Head Road. Turn left and continue to the parking area.

Mulholland Market and McCurdy's Smokehouse

Lubec Landmarks (207/733-2197, www .lubecbeclandmarks.org) is working to preserve these two local landmarks. The smokehouse complex, one of the last herring-smoking operations in the country (closed in 1991 and now a National Historic Landmark), can be seen on the water side of Water Street. In 2007, after years of effort, it finally reopened to the public ($3 donation). You can tour it on your own, or volunteer guides will explain the exhibits. Next door, Mulholland Market (50 Water St.), which now doubles as a community center, is the organization's headquarters. Inside

are displays about the smokehouses, exhibits of local art, and a small gift shop. It is volunteer-operated, so hours change frequently; call for the current schedule.

Lubec Historical Society

The society's small museum in the **Old Columbian Store** (135 Main St., 207/733-2274, 9 A.M.–3 P.M. Mon., Wed., and Fri., free) doubles as a visitors information center. Among the historical and genealogical displays is a working model of the machine used in the infamous Gold from Seawater swindle of 1898. Volunteers will gladly fill you in on that, or you can pick up a brochure. While here, also pick up the *Lubec Historic Walking Tour* brochure, which highlights about a dozen historical sites in downtown Lubec. The museum is on the left as you're entering town, just beyond Uncle Kippy's restaurant.

Robert S. Peacock Fire Museum

Worth a look-see for fans of old fire equipment, the small museum at the fire station (40 School St., Lubec, 207/733-4641) is usually open 10 A.M.–4 P.M. Monday–Friday, but it's wise to call first.

Lubec Breakwater

Even the humongous tides and dramatic sunsets over Johnson Bay can get your attention if you hang out at the breakwater. Across the channel on Campobello Island is red-capped **Mulholland Point Lighthouse,** an abandoned beacon built in 1885. As the tide goes out—18 or so feet—you'll also see hungry harbor seals dunking for dinner. And if you're lucky, you might spot the eagle pair that nests on an island in the channel (bring binoculars).

Quoddy Mist

The old RJ Peacock factory is now home to Quoddy Mist (72 Water St., Lubec, 207/733-4847, www.quoddymist.com), which produces all-natural sea salt in about a dozen flavors. Tastings are available, and free tours explain the process. It's tucked behind Dianne's Glass Gallery.

THE DOWN EAST COAST

ENTERTAINMENT AND EVENTS

Classical music is the focus (for the most part) at **SummerKeys** (207/733-2316, 973/316-6220 off-season, www.summerkeys.com), a music camp for adults, no prior experience required, with weeklong programs in piano, voice, oboe, flute, clarinet, guitar, violin, and cello. Free concerts by visiting artists, faculty, and students are held at 7:30 P.M. Wednesday evenings late June–early September in the Congregational Christian Church on Church Street.

Live music is usually on tap on weekends at Cohill's Inn and Annabell's Pub, both on Water Street.

During summer, concerts are usually held Thursday evenings at the town bandstand on Main Street, often accompanied by a chicken barbecue.

An ambitious grassroots group has launched **Cobscook Community Learning Center** (CCLC, Timber Cove Rd., Trescott, 207/733-2233, www.thecclc.org). Two timber-frame buildings house CCLC's year-round programs, an open pottery studio, a fiber-arts studio, and multipurpose classrooms. Festivals, adult education, indigenous education, sustainable and value-added eco-ventures, youth programs, and more are offered. Open-jam music nights, held on the second, fourth, and fifth Mondays of each month (7–10 P.M., donation), bring in as many as 20 musicians and a good crowd of listeners.

Bird-watching is big here, and spring brings **The Down East Spring Birding Festival** (207/733-2233) to the Cobscook Bay Area, held annually in late May. Guided and self-guided explorations, presentations, and tours fill the schedule, and participation is limited, so register early.

Downeast Coastal Conservancy (www.downeastcoastalconservancy.org) offers workshops, guided walks, boat trips, and other events throughout the summer.

SHOPPING

Two downtown shops are within strolling distance of each other. Dianne Larkin sells her handcrafted hot-fused glass jewelry, plates, and

Entrepreneurs are slowly sprucing up the buildings along Lubec's Water Street. Most of the restaurants here feature decks with views of Campobello Island.

other creations at **Dianne's Glass Gallery** (72 Water St., Lubec, 207/733-2458, www.diannesglass.com). **Northern Tides** (24 Water St., Lubec, 207/733-2500) carries intriguing works by local artisans such as sea-glass creations, pottery crafted with finds from the sea, felt work, and weaving.

En route to West Quoddy Head, stop at **Crow Town Gallery** (406 S. Lubec Rd., Lubec, 207/733-8860) to view a fine selection of locally inspired art.

Lighthouse buffs must stop at **West Quoddy Gifts** (Quoddy Head Rd., 1 mile before the lighthouse, 207/733-2457). It's stocked with souvenirs and gift items, most with a lighthouse theme.

RECREATION
Tours

Native Lubec residents, often with roots going back generations and with specialties as diverse as wildlife, bird-watching, photography, and diving, deliver insights and share their knowledge on **Tours of Lubec and Cobscook** (135 Main St., Lubec, 207/733-2997 or 888/347-9302, www.toursoflubecandcobscook.com). Credit enthusiastic Lubec resident Ruta Jordans for creating the nonprofit Association to Promote and Protect the Lubec Environment (APPLE) to help visitors learn more about Lubec. APPLE sponsors personalized interpretive tours covering area art, culture, the environment, history, and heritage. Tours ($20–45 pp) cover topics such as Art Odyssey, Tide Mill Organic Farm, Bogs and the Ice Age, and Lighthouses by the Sea. Call or visit the website to create an itinerary that works for you.

Excursion Boats

Explore Cobscook, Fundy, and Passamaquoddy Bay on a tour with **Downeast Charter Boat Tours** (207/733-2009, www.downeastcharterboattours.com) aboard the 25-foot lobster boat *Lorna Doone*. You'll pass lighthouses and likely also spy whales.

Jet-boat whale-watching tours are offered by **The Inn on the Wharf** (60 Johnson St., Lubec, 207/733-4400, www.wharfrentals.com). The 2.5–3-hour tours are $45 pp.

Hiking and Walking

Tag along with Lubec's **Pathfinders Walking Group,** enthusiastic area residents who go exploring every Sunday year-round, usually meeting at 2 P.M. for a two-hour ramble; check local papers for the schedule. Nonmembers are welcome, there's no fee, and you'll see a side of Lubec and more that most visitors never encounter.

Two preserves run by the Maine Coast Heritage Trust (www.mcht.org) are fine places for a walk. The 1,225-acre **Hamilton Cove Preserve**'s 1.5 miles of ocean frontage are highlighted by cobble beaches, rocky cliffs, and jaw-dropping views (on a clear day) of Grand Manan. To find it, take Route 189 to South Lubec Road toward Quoddy Head, but bear right at the fork on Boot Cove Road, and continue 2.4 miles to a small parking lot on the left. There's a kiosk with maps about 100 feet down the trail. It's about one mile to an observation platform and another 0.5 miles to the bench at the trail's end. Continue on Boot Cove Road another 1.5 miles to find 700-acre **Boot Head Preserve,** with dramatic cliffs and ravines that epitomize Maine's Bold Coast reputation. The trail passes through a rare coastal raised peat land before continuing to a viewing platform on the coast. From the parking lot to Boot Cove via the Coastal Trail, it's 1.25 miles; return via the Interior Trail for another 0.75 miles.

For information on other hikes in the area, pick up a copy of *Cobscook Trails,* a guidebook with maps and trail details. It's available for about $7 at local stores. Another resource available locally is *Self-Guided Birding Explorations, Washington County, Maine,* published in conjunction with the Down East Spring Birding Festival. It lists and maps walks and hikes and notes habitats and bird species.

In 2010, *Travel + Leisure* magazine named Lubec one of the best beach towns in the country. Where's the beach, you ask? **Mowry Beach,** managed by the Downeast Coastal

Conservancy (www.downeastcoastalconservancy.org), is at the end of Pleasant Street; continue past the wastewater treatment plant to a parking lot. Follow the path over the dunes to the beach. There's also a nice boardwalk designed for bird-watching.

Biking and Kayaking

The Wharf (60 Johnson St., Lubec, 207/733-4400, www.wharfrentals.com) rents bikes for $18 per day, $15 per half day as well as kayaks for $25–35.

ACCOMMODATIONS

Rates noted are for peak season.

Many visitors use Lubec as a base for day trips to Campobello Island, so it's essential to make reservations at the height of summer. Several lodgings are also available on Campobello.

Bed-and-Breakfasts and Inns

Built in 1860 by a British sea captain, **Peacock House Bed and Breakfast** (27 Summer St., Lubec, 207/733-2403 or 888/305-0036, www.peacockhouse.com, $95–135) has long been one of Lubec's most prestigious residences. Among the notables who have stayed here are Donald MacMillan, the famous Arctic explorer, as well as U.S. senators Margaret Chase Smith and Edmund Muskie. It has three guest rooms and four suites, which have TVs and sitting areas; one has a gas fireplace and a refrigerator. One guest room is wheelchair-accessible.

Unusual antiques fill the guest rooms and sitting room of the 19th-century **Home Port Inn** (45 Main St., Lubec, 207/733-2077 or 800/457-2077 outside Maine, www.homeportinn.com, $95–115), ensconced on a Lubec hilltop. Each of the seven guest rooms has a private bath, although some are detached; some have water views. Rates include a generous continental breakfast. The inn also serves dinner by reservation.

Piano students at SummerKeys often practice on the living room piano at **BayViews** (6 Monument St., Lubec, 207/733-2181, $60–100), providing impromptu concerts for other

guests. The 1824 Victorian house sits on two acres edging Johnson Bay. It's a relaxed bed-and-breakfast filled with eclectic antiques, art, and books (owner Kathryn Rubeor has a master's in English literature). It's an easy walk to town if you can tear yourself away from the back deck, lawn chairs, or hammock. Breakfast is a bountiful continental, with fresh fruit and juice, home-baked bread, and homemade granola and toppings. One huge suite, perfect for a family, and one twin room that has a piano have private baths; two double rooms and one single share a bath.

Ellen and Jack Gearrin extend a warm Irish welcome to guests at **Cohill's Inn** (7 Water St., 207/733-4300, www.cohillsinn.com, $95–135), which overlooks the Bay of Fundy on one side and the Narrows on the other. There are no frills or fuss in the simply but nicely furnished guest rooms; each has a fan and a TV, beds are covered with comforters and quilts, and a continental breakfast is included in the

© HILARY NANGLE

Guests at BayViews often get to hear impromptu concerts, as students from the SummerKeys program practice on the inn's pianos.

rates. Wi-Fi is available. Downstairs is a popular and reliable pub, but service ends at 8 P.M., so it's quiet at night.

Motel

The lackluster **Eastland Motel** (385 County Rd./Rte. 189, Lubec, 207/733-5501, www.eastlandmotel.com, $70–80) has 20 guest rooms with cable TV, Wi-Fi, and air-conditioning. Request one of the 12 guest rooms in the newer section. Continental breakfast is included in the rates, and small pets ($10) are allowed.

Apartments, Suites, and Houses

Bill Clark has rescued the former Coast Guard station at West Quoddy Head and restored, renovated, and reopened it as ◖ **West Quoddy Station** (S. Lubec Rd., Lubec, 207/733-4452 or 877/535-4714, www.quoddyvacation.com), with five one-bedroom units (four in the lodge and one separate cabin), plus the five-bedroom, 2.5-bath Station House. All have kitchens, Wi-Fi, and satellite TV. Views are stupendous and extend to East Quoddy Head on Campobello; West Quoddy Head is about 0.5 miles' walk. Rates begin at $95 per night, when available, but weekly rentals ($600–1,800) get first preference.

Another restoration project is taking place at the former Lubec Sardine Company's Factory B, where Judy and Victor Trafford are renovating the truly waterfront complex into ◖ **The Inn on the Wharf** (60 Johnson St., Lubec, 207/733-4400, www.wharfrentals.com), comprising lodging and a lobster shack restaurant, while preserving the working waterfront. Guest rooms ($100 per night, $550 per week) have use of a common kitchen and dining area. Two-bedroom, two-bathroom apartments ($150 per night, $850 per week) have full kitchens and laundry facilities. All have incredible views and Wi-Fi. Also on the premises are a yoga studio and bike and kayak rentals. A whale-watching boat and water taxi to Eastport departs from the wharf. That's all great, but what really distinguishes this property is that hidden on the basement level are huge tanks holding lobsters, crabs, and eels; an a area for processing the periwinkle harvest; and other intriguing spots where you might catch local fisheries folks brining in their catches.

Camping

A 3.5-mile network of nature trails, picnic spots, great bird-watching and berry picking, hot showers, a boat launch, and wooded shorefront campsites make **Cobscook Bay State Park** (Rte. 1, Edmunds Township, 207/726-4412, www.parksandlands.com), on the 888-acre Moosehorn Reserve, one of Maine's most spectacular state parks. It's even entertaining just to watch the 24-foot tides surging in and out of this area at five or so feet per hour; there's no swimming because of the undertow. Reserve well ahead to get a place on the shore. There are no hookups, but there's a dump station for RVs. To guarantee a site in July–August, using MasterCard or Visa, call 207/624-9950 (800/332-1501 in Maine) or visit www.campwithme.com; the reservation fee is $2 per site per night with a two-night minimum. The park is open daily mid-May–mid-October; trails are groomed in winter for cross-country skiing, and one section goes right along the shore. Summer day-use fees are $4.50 nonresident adults, $3 Maine resident adults, $1.50 nonresident seniors, free Maine resident seniors, $1 ages 5–11. The nonresident camping fee is $24 per site per night; the fee for Maine residents is $14.

FOOD
Local Flavors

You can't go wrong with a stop at **Bold Coast Smokehouse** (224 County Rd./Rte. 189, Lubec, 207/733-8912 or 888/733-0807, www.boldcoastsmokehouse.com). Vinny Gartmayer is a master of the smoking process, creating delectable hot and cold smoked salmon, smoked fish spreads, smoked salmon sticks (great for picnics; try the garlic-pepper), and other goodies. He also makes and sells lobster rolls and other good-to-go picnic fare.

Monica's (100 County Rd./Rte. 189., Lubec, 866/952-4500, www.monicaschocolates.com, 8 A.M.–8 P.M. daily) gives meaning to the term sinfully delicious. Monica Elliott creates sumptuous handmade gourmet chocolates using family recipes from her native Peru. Visitors can sample chocolates before buying; it's a smart policy, as you're guaranteed to buy after you taste them. Lunch also is served Wednesday–Friday.

Stave off a midday hunger attack with home-baked goodies with an organic twist from **Sun Porch Industries** (99 Johnson St., Lubec, 207/733-7587, 11 A.M.–5 P.M. Wed.–Sun.), a tiny natural and organic foods store.

Baked goods, pizzas, and other light fare is served at **Atlantic House Coffee & Deli** (52 Water St., Lubec, 207/733-0906, 7 A.M.–7 P.M. daily). Take it to one of two back decks overlooking the water.

It's a treat to visit the Bell family's 200-year-old organic saltwater farm, **Tide Mill Farms** (91 Tide Mill Rd., Edmunds, 2 miles north of Rte. 189, 207/733-2110, www.tidemillfarm.com, 10 A.M.–3 P.M. Sat.).

Family Favorites

Good burgers, chowders, and other choices from the daily chalkboard menu as well as Guinness, Smithwick's, and microbrews have earned ⟨ **Cohill's Inn** (7 Water St., Lubec, 207/733-4300, www.cohillsinn.com, 11:30 A.M.–8 P.M. daily, $8–22) an enthusiastic two thumbs up from locals and visitors alike. The dining room has fabulous water views, and there's often entertainment on Saturday afternoon.

Across the street from Cohill's Inn is **Frank's Dockside Deli** (Water St., Lubec, 11 A.M.–7 P.M. daily, $8–16), with both takeout and indoor seating. The fare leans to Italian.

Depending on your source, **Uncle Kippy's** (County Rd./Rte. 189, Lubec, 207/733-2400, www.unclekippys.com, 11 A.M.–8 P.M. Tues.–Thurs. and Sun., 11 A.M.–9 P.M. Fri.–Sat., $5–19) gets high marks in Lubec for wholesome cooking. A sign out front announces "Stop in or we'll both starve." Steak and seafood are specialties—at unfancy prices—and the pizza is the area's best. Don't be put off by the "For Sale" sign; it has been there for more than a decade.

Casual Dining

Hours noted here are a rough guideline, as schedules tend to vary frequently; call ahead before making a special trip.

The brightest spot on the waterfront is Jim and Judy Heyer's **Water Street Tavern** (12 Water St., Lubec, 207/733-2477, 11:30 A.M.–8 P.M. Wed.–Sun., $10–20). They spent two years renovating the building. The first-floor restaurant, which spills onto a back deck, serves seafood, lobster, pasta, savory pies, and a few red-meat offerings. A good bet is the haddock with crab stuffing.

The nicest dining room in the area is at the **Home Port Inn** (45 Main St., Lubec, 207/733-2077 or 800/457-2077 outside Maine, www.homeportinn.com, 5–8 P.M. daily, entrées $18–26). Reservations are advised for this very popular restaurant, which has a sunken dining room with table seating for 30. The specialty is seafood, but the food often doesn't match the setting.

Lobster

The Boiler Room at the Inn on the Wharf (60 Johnson St., Lubec, 207/733-4400, www.wharfrentals.com) was expected to open in 2011, serving lunch and dinner daily in season. Co-owner Victor Trafford plans a lobster shack–type experience, with tables inside a renovated sardine factory, on an outside deck, and on the working wharf with panoramic views over Cobscook Bay to Eastport's Shakford Head.

INFORMATION AND SERVICES

The **Cobscook Bay Area Chamber of Commerce** (www.cobscookbay.com) covers the Cobscook Bay region, including Lubec. Another good resource is the Tourist Information link on the Lubec town website (www.lubecme.govoffice2.com). Local sources of information include **The Puffin Pines** (240 Rte. 1, Whiting); the **Old Columbian Store** (Main St., Lubec, 207/733-4696, 9 A.M.–3 P.M. Mon., Wed., and Fri.); and the **Visitor Center at West Quoddy Head Lighthouse** (207/733-2180, www.westquoddy.com, 10 A.M.–4 P.M. daily late May–mid-Oct.).

Lubec Memorial Library (Water St. and School St., Lubec, 207/733-2491) has a public restroom.

GETTING AROUND

To & Fro Water Taxi, at The Wharf (69 Johnson St., 207/733-4400, $16 round-trip) operates between Lubec and Eastport; call for a current schedule.

Campobello Island

◖ ROOSEVELT CAMPOBELLO INTERNATIONAL PARK

Just over the Franklin D. Roosevelt Memorial Bridge from Lubec lies nine-mile-long Campobello Island, in Canada's New Brunswick province. Since 1964, Roosevelt Campobello International Park's 2,800 acres of the island have been under joint U.S. and Canadian jurisdiction, commemorating U.S. president Franklin D. Roosevelt. FDR summered here as a youth, and it was here that he came down with infantile paralysis (polio) in 1921. The park, covering most of the island's southern end, has well-maintained trails, picnic sites, and dramatic vistas, but its centerpiece is the imposing Roosevelt Cottage, one mile northeast of the bridge. It's interesting to note that before becoming a summer retreat for wealthy Americans, Campobello was the feudal fiefdom of a Welsh family. King George III awarded the grant to Captain William Owen in 1767, and he arrived in 1770.

Roosevelt Cottage and Visitor Centre

Little seems to have changed in the 34-room red-shingled Roosevelt "Cottage" overlooking Passamaquoddy Bay since President Roosevelt

THE DOWN EAST COAST

© HILARY NANGLE

Roosevelt Cottage and Visitor Centre

last visited in 1939. The Roosevelt Cottage (459 Rte. 774, Welshpool, Campobello, NB, Canada, 506/752-2922 in season, www.fdr .net) grounds are beautifully landscaped, and the many family mementos—especially those in the late president's den—bring history alive. It all feels very personal and far less stuffy than most presidential memorials.

Stop first at the park's Visitor Centre, where you can pick up brochures (including a trail map, bird-watching guide, and bog guide), use the restrooms, and see a short video setting the stage for the cottage visit. Then walk across to the house-museum (10 A.M.–6 P.M. Atlantic time, 9 A.M.–5 P.M. eastern time, last tour at 5:45 P.M., mid-May–mid-Oct., free). Guides are stationed in various rooms to explain and answer questions. Also be sure to visit the neighboring **Hubbard Cottage,** open July 1–early September whenever it isn't in use by conferences. Free outside walking tours of the estate and on-site presentations on local ecology are given, weather and staff permitting.

The Park by Car

If time is short or you're unable to hike, at least take some of the park's driving routes—**Cranberry Point Drive,** 5.4 miles round-trip from the Visitor Centre; **Liberty Point Drive,** 12.4 miles round-trip, via Glensevern Road, from the Visitor Centre; and **Fox Hill Drive,** a 2.2-mile link between the other two main routes. Even with a car, you'll have access to beaches, picnic sites, spruce and fir forests, and great views of lighthouses, islands, and the Bay of Fundy.

Just west of the main access road from the bridge is the **Mulholland Point picnic area,** where you can spread out your lunch next to the distinctive red-capped lighthouse overlooking Lubec Narrows.

Hiking and Picnicking

Within the international park are 8.5 miles of walking-hiking trails, varying from dead easy to moderately difficult. Easiest is the 1.2-mile (round-trip) walk from the Visitor Centre to **Friar's Head picnic area,** named for its distinctive promontory jutting into the bay. For the best angle, climb up to the observation deck on the "head." Grills and tables are here for picnickers. Pick up a brochure at the Visitor Centre detailing natural sights along the route.

The most difficult—and most dramatic—trail is a 2.4-mile stretch from **Liberty Point to Raccoon Beach,** along the southeastern shore of the island. Precipitous cliffs can make parts of this trail risky for small children or insecure adults, so use caution. Liberty Point is incredibly rugged, but observation platforms make it easy to see the tortured rocks and wide-open Bay of Fundy. Along the way is the SunSweep Sculpture, an international art project by David Barr. At broad Raccoon Beach, you can walk the sands, have a picnic, or watch for whales, porpoises, and ospreys. To avoid returning via the same route, park at Liberty Point and walk back along Liberty Point Drive from Raccoon Beach. If you're traveling with nonhikers, arrange for them to meet you with a vehicle at Con Robinson's Point.

A fascinating boardwalk, perfect for those in wheelchairs, is **Eagle Hill Bog,** 1.8 miles down the Glensevern Road. Interpretive signs explain the lichens, scrub pines, pitcher plants, and other flora and fauna within the bogs. A spur trail leads to a trail that climbs quickly to an observation deck.

You can also walk the park's perimeter, including just more than six miles of shoreline, but only if you're in good shape, have waterproof hiking boots, and can spend an entire day on the trails. Before attempting this, however, inquire at the Visitor Centre about trail conditions and tide levels.

CAMPOBELLO BEYOND THE INTERNATIONAL PARK

Take a day or two and explore Campobello beyond the park. You can also continue by ferry from here to New Brunswick's Deer Island and on to Eastport.

Herring Cove Provincial Park

New Brunswick's provincial government does a conscientious job of running 1,049-acre

Herring Cove Provincial Park (506/752-7010 or 800/561-0123), with picnic areas, 88 campsites (506/752-7010), a four-mile trail system, a mile-long sandy beach, freshwater Glensevern Lake, a restaurant with fabulous views, and the nine-hole championship-level **Herring Cove Golf Course** (506/752-2467). The park is open early June–September.

East Quoddy Head Light

Consult the tide calendar before planning your assault on East Quoddy Head Light (also known as Head Harbour Light), at Campobello's northernmost tip. The 51-foot-tall light, built in 1829, is on an islet accessible only at low tide. The distinctive white light tower bears a huge red cross. (You're likely to pass near it on whale-watching trips out of Eastport.) From the Roosevelt Cottage, follow Route 774 through the village of Wilson's Beach and continue to the parking area. A stern Canadian Coast Guard warning sign tells the story:

East Quoddy Head Light is easily recognized by its distinctive red cross marking.

Extreme Hazard. Beach exposed only at low tide. Incoming tide rises 5 feet per hour and may leave you stranded for 8 hours. Wading or swimming are extremely dangerous due to swift currents and cold water. Proceed at your own risk.

It's definitely worth the effort for the bay and island views from the lighthouse grounds, often including whales and eagles. Allow about an hour before and after dead low tide (be sure your watch coincides with the Atlantic-time tide calendar).

In 2005 the **Friends of the Head Harbour Lightstation** (916 Rte. 774, Welshpool, NB, Canada, www.campobello.com/lighthouse), a local group, took over maintenance of the station to preserve it. It now charges access fees to support the efforts. You can see the light from the nearby grounds at no charge, but if you want to hike out to the island or visit the light, the suggested donation is $5–10. The Friends are restoring the interior with period furnishings and plan to add an interpretive center highlighting the lighthouse's history, maritime ecosystems in the Bay of Fundy, and whale-rescue efforts. In the meantime, work parties provide an opportunity to peek inside. You can support the efforts with a membership, available for US$25 individual or US$35 family.

Whale-Watching

Island Cruises (506/752-1107 or 888/249-4400, www.bayoffundywhales.com, $49 adults, $39 children) depart three times daily from Head Harbour Wharf for scenic whale-watching cruises aboard the *Mister Matthew,* a 37-foot traditional Bay of Fundy fishing boat that carries 20 passengers. Captain Mac Greene is a member of the Fundy Whale Rescue Team, so he has great insights and stories to share.

ACCOMMODATIONS AND FOOD

In midsummer, if you'd like to overnight on the island, be sure to reserve lodgings well in advance; Campobello is a popular destination. The nearest backup beds are in Lubec, and those fill up too. Rates noted are for peak season.

❮ The Owen House (11 Welshpool St., Welshpool, 506/752-2977, www.owenhouse .ca, late May–mid-Oct., C$110–210) is the island's best address, a comfortably elegant early-19th-century inn on 10 acres on Deer Point overlooking Passamaquoddy Bay and Eastport in the distance. Nine guest rooms (two with shared baths) on three floors are decorated with antiques and family treasures along with owner Joyce Morrel's paintings (Joyce grew up in this house) and assorted handmade quilts. There's a first-floor guest room that's ideal for those with mobility problems. Joyce and innkeeper Jan Meiners are very active in the lighthouse preservation efforts. Just north of the inn is the Deer Island ferry landing.

Campsites and tent cabins are available at **Herring Cove Provincial Park** (506/752-7010, C$22–35).

Don't expect culinary creativity on Campobello, but you won't starve—at least during the summer season. The best choice is **Family Fisheries** (1977 Rte. 774, Wilson's Beach, 506/752-2470, 10:30 A.M.–8 or 9 P.M. daily, C$6–28), a seafood restaurant and fish market toward the northern end of the island. Portions are huge, service is OK, the fish is superfresh, and the homemade desserts are decent. BYOB. The only island restaurant with a liquor license is Lupine Lodge, which has more atmosphere.

INFORMATION AND SERVICES

To visit Campobello, you'll have to pass immigration checkpoints on the U.S. and Canadian ends of the Franklin D. Roosevelt Memorial Bridge (U.S. Customs, Lubec, 207/733-4331; Canada Border Services,

Campobello, 506/752-2091). Be sure to have the required identification: a passport or a passport card.

Be aware that there's a one-hour time difference between Lubec and Campobello. Lubec, like the rest of Maine, is on eastern time; Campobello, like the rest of New Brunswick, is on Atlantic time, an hour later. As soon as you reach the island, set your clock ahead an hour.

There is no need to convert U.S. currency to Canadian money for use on Campobello; U.S. dollars are accepted everywhere on the island, but prices tend to be quoted in Canadian dollars.

Off the bridge, stop at the **Tourist Information Centre** (44 Rte. 774, Welshpool, 506/752-7043, May–Oct.) on your right for an island map, trail maps of the international park, tide info for lighthouse visits, and New Brunswick visitor information.

For information on Campobello Island, contact **Campobello Island Tourism Association** (506/752-7010, www.campobelloislandtourism .com). More information is available at www .campobello.com.

Eastport Ferry

If your next stop on the Maine Coast is Eastport, you might consider taking the funky two-stage boat-and-barge **East Coast Ferries** (877/747-2159, www.eastcoastferries.nb.ca, no credit cards). It departs Campobello for Deer Island on the hour 9 A.M.–7 P.M. Atlantic time late June–early September; the fare is $18 per car plus $3 per passenger over age 11, $25 maximum per car. It connects with the ferry from Deer Island to Eastport, which departs on the hour 9 A.M.–6 P.M. Atlantic time, $15 per car and driver plus $3 per passenger over age 11, $20 maximum per car. Motorcycles on each ferry are $10.

Eastport and Vicinity

When you leave Whiting, the gateway to Lubec and Campobello, and continue north on Route 1 around Cobscook Bay, it's hard to believe that life could slow down any more than it already has, but it does. The landscape's raw beauty is occasionally punctuated by farmhouses or a convenience store, but little else.

Edmunds Township's claims to fame are its splendid public lands—Cobscook Bay State Park and a unit of Moosehorn National Wildlife Refuge. Just past the state park, loop along the scenic shoreline before returning to Route 1.

Pembroke, once part of adjoining **Dennysville,** is home to Reversing Falls Park, where you can watch and hear ebbing and flowing tides draining and filling Cobscook Bay.

If time allows a short scenic detour, especially in fall, turn left (northwest) on Route 214 and drive 10 miles to quaintly named **Meddybemps,** allegedly a Passamaquoddy word meaning "plenty of alewives [herring]." Views over Meddybemps Lake, on the north side of the road, are spectacular, and you can launch a canoe or kayak into the lake here, less than a mile beyond the junction with Route 191 (take the dead-end unpaved road toward the water).

Backtracking to Route 1, heading east from Pembroke, you'll come to **Perry,** best known for the **Sipayik Indian Reservation** at Pleasant Point, a Passamaquoddy settlement, two miles east of Route 1, that has been here since 1822. Route 191 cuts through the heart of the reservation.

The city (yes, it's officially a city) of **Eastport** is on Moose Island, connected by a causeway to the mainland at Sipayik (Pleasant Point). Views are terrific on both sides, especially at sunset, as you hopscotch from one blob of land to another and finally reach this mini city, where the sardine industry was introduced as long ago as 1875. Five sardine canneries once operated here, employing hundreds of local residents who snipped the heads off herring and stuffed them into cans.

Settled in 1772, Eastport has had its ups and downs, mostly mirroring the fishing industry. It's now on an upswing as people "from away" have arrived to soak up the vibe of a small town with a heavy Down East accent. Artists, artisans, and antiques shops are leading the town's rejuvenation as a tourist destination, with the Tides Institute at the forefront. A big push came in 2001 when the Fox Network reality-TV series *Murder in Small Town X* was filmed here; the city morphed into the village of Sunrise, Maine, and local residents eagerly filled in as extras. The huge waterfront statue of a fisherman is a remnant of the filming.

Until 1811 the town also included Lubec, which is about 2.5 miles across the water in a boat but over 40 miles in a car. A Lubec-based passenger ferry connects the two.

© TOM NANGLE

Commercial fishing drives Eastport's economy.

TIDES

Nowhere in Maine is the adage "Time and tide wait for no man" truer than along the Washington County coastline. The nation's most extreme tidal ranges occur in this area, so the hundreds of miles of tidal shore frontage between Steuben and Calais provide countless opportunities for observing tidal phenomena. Every six hours or so, the tide begins either ebbing or flowing. The farther Down East you go, the higher (and lower) the tides. Although tides in Canada's Bay of Fundy are far higher, the highest tides in New England occur along the St. Croix River at Calais.

Tides govern coastal life – particularly Down East, where average tidal ranges may be 10-20 feet and extremes approach 28 feet. Everyone is a slave to the tide calendar, which coastal-community newspapers diligently publish. Boats tie up with extra-long lines; clammers and wormdiggers schedule their days by the tides; hikers have to plan for shoreline exploring; and kayakers need to plan their routes to avoid getting stuck in the muck.

Tides, as we learned in school, are lunar phenomena, created by the gravitational pull of the moon; the tidal range depends on the lunar phase. Tides are most extreme at new and full moons – when the sun, moon, and Earth are aligned. These are spring tides, supposedly because the water springs upward (the term has nothing to do with the season). And tides are smallest during the moon's first and third quarters – when the sun, Earth, and moon have a right-angle configuration. These are neap tides ("neap" comes from an Old English word meaning "scanty"). Other lunar and solar phenomena, such as the equinoxes and solstices, can also affect tidal ranges.

The best time for shoreline exploration is on a new-moon or full-moon day, when low tide exposes mussels, sea urchins, sea cucumbers, starfish, periwinkles, hermit crabs, rockweed, and assorted nonbiodegradable trash. Rubber boots or waterproof, treaded shoes are essential on the wet, slippery terrain.

Caution is also essential in tidal areas. Unless you've carefully plotted tide times and heights, don't park a car, bike, or boat trailer on a beach; make sure your sea kayak is lashed securely to a tree or bollard; don't take a long nap on shoreline granite; and don't cross a low-tide land spit without an eye on your watch.

A perhaps apocryphal but almost believable story goes that one flatlander stormed up to a ranger at Cobscook Bay State Park one bright summer morning and demanded indignantly to know why they had had the nerve to drain the water from her shorefront campsite during the night. When it comes to tides...you have to go with the flow.

Tides in Eastport rise and fall as much as 28 feet. A huge breakwater helps protect the working fleet.

© TOM NANGLE

SIGHTS
Historic Walking Tour

The best way to appreciate Eastport's history is to pick up and follow the route in *A Walking Guide to Eastport,* available locally for $2.75. The handy map-brochure spotlights the city's 18th-, 19th-, and early-20th-century homes, businesses, and monuments, many now on the National Register of Historic Places. Among the highlights are historic homes converted to bed-and-breakfasts, two museums, and a large chunk of downtown Water Street, with many handsome brick buildings erected after a disastrous fire swept through in 1886. A free walking map, with far fewer details, is also available.

Raye's Mustard Mill Museum

How often do you have a chance to watch mustard being made in a turn-of-the-20th-century mustard mill? Drive by J. W. Raye and Co. (83 Washington St./Rte. 190, Eastport, 207/853-4451 or 800/853-1903, www.rayesmustard.com, 9 A.M.–5 P.M. Mon.–Fri., 10 A.M.–5 P.M. Sat.–Sun.) at the edge of Eastport and stop in for a free 15-minute tour (offered as schedules permit, call first). You'll get to see the granite millstones, the mustard seeds being winnowed, and enormous vats of future mustard. Raye's sells mustard under its own label and produces it for major customers under their labels. The shop stocks all of Raye's mustard varieties (samples available), other Maine-made food, and gift items, and it also has a small café where you can buy coffee, tea, and light fare. Both Martha Stewart and Rachael Ray have discovered Raye's, which took home both gold and bronze medals from the 2007 World-Wide Mustard Competition.

The Tides Institute and Museum of Art

One of the most promising additions to Eastport's downtown is the Tides Institute (43 Water St., 207/853-4047, www.tidesinstitute.org, 10 A.M.–4 P.M. Tues.–Sat., free), housed in a former bank that's being restored. The institute's impressive goals are to build significant cultural collections and to produce new culturally important works employing printmaking, letterpress, photography, bookmaking, oral history, and other media. For its collection, the institute is focusing on works by artists associated with the U.S.-Canada northeast coast but with an eye to the broader world. It already has significant works by artists such as Martin Johnson Heade and photographers such as Paul Caponigro, a fine selection of baskets by Native Americans, and two organs made by the local Pembroke organ company in the 1880s. A series of rotating shows during the summer highlights both the permanent collections and loaned works. The research and reference library has more than 4,000 volumes. The institute also offers programs on a range of topics and workshops by visiting artists. These are open to the public by reservation; definitely stop in for a visit.

Passamaquoddy Indian Reservation

To get to Eastport, you pass through the Passamaquoddy's Sipayik or Pleasant Point Reservation (www.wabanaki.com). Ask locally or check the website to find basket makers and other traditional artists who might sell from their homes. The decorative and work baskets are treasures that constantly escalate in price. It's a real treat to be able to buy one from the maker.

Downeast Observatory

The Downeast Amateur Astronomers' Downeast Observatory (356 Old County Rd., Pembroke, 207/214-5706, www.downeastaa.com), with an eight-inch DE8 reflector and 3–5-inch refractors, is open to the public for free by appointment, but donations are greatly appreciated. Contact Charlie Sawyer at the observatory for details.

PARKS AND PRESERVES
◖ Shackford Head State Park

Ninety-acre Shackford Head (off Deep Cove Rd., Eastport, www.parksandlands.com, free) is on a peninsula that juts into Cobscook Bay. The trailhead and parking area are just east of the Washington County Community College Marine Technology Center at the southern end of Eastport. The park has five miles of wooded trails, with the easiest being the 1.2-mile round-trip to Shackford Head Overlook and its continuation onto the steeper Ship Point Trail, which adds another 0.5 miles, rising gently to a 175-foot-high headland with wide-open views of Eastport and, depending on weather, Campobello Island, Lubec, Pembroke, and even Grand Manan. This state preserve is a particularly good family hike. There's a toilet near the parking area but no other facilities. Also here is a memorial with plaques detailing the history of five Civil War ships that were decommissioned and burned on Cony Beach by the U.S. government between 1901 and 1920. Eastport's huge tides allowed the ships to be brought in and beached and then taken apart as the tide receded. Fourteen Eastport men served on four of the ships.

Reversing Falls Park

There's plenty of room for adults to relax and kids to play at the 140-acre Reversing Falls Park in West Pembroke—plus shorefront ledges and a front-row seat overlooking a fascinating tidal phenomenon. It's connected via hiking trails to the Downeast Coastal Conservancy's Reversing Falls Conservation Area (www.downeastcoastalconservancy.org), a nearly 200-acre property with 1.5 miles of shorefront and 70 acres of coastal wetlands. Pack a picnic and then check newspapers or information offices for the tide times so that you can watch the saltwater surging through a 300-yard-wide passage at about 25 knots, creating a whirlpool and churning "falls." The park is at Mahar Point in West Pembroke, 7.2 miles south of Route 1. Coming from the south (Dennysville), leave Route 1 in West Pembroke when you see the Triangle Grocery Store. Turn right and go 0.3 miles to Leighton Point Road, where you'll see a sign saying "Shore Access 5.5 miles." Turn right and go 3.8 miles past gorgeous meadows, low shrubs, and views of Cobscook Bay. Turn right on Clarkside Road, at a very tiny "Reversing Falls" sign posted high on a telephone pole.

Go about 1.5 miles to the end and then turn left onto a gravel road and continue two miles to the park.

Gleason Cove

This quiet park and boat launch is a delightful place to walk along the shorefront or to grab a table and spread out a picnic while drinking in the dreamy views over fishing weirs and islands in Passamaquoddy Bay. To get here, take Shore Road (opposite the New Friendly Restaurant) and then take a right on Gleason Cove Road.

ENTERTAINMENT

The **Eastport Arts Center** (36 Washington St., Eastport, 207/853-4650, www.eastportartscenter.com) is an umbrella organization for local arts groups, with headquarters and performance space in a former church. You can pick up a brochure with a complete schedule, which usually includes concerts, workshops, films, puppet shows, productions by local theater group **Stage East,** and other cultural events. Also based here is the **Penobscot Bay Symphony Orchestra,** formed in 2007 by conductor Trond Saeverud, who doubles as concertmaster of the Bangor Symphony Orchestra. Some years, the center provides a ferry to the free **SummerKeys** concerts, held Wednesday nights late June–early September in Lubec.

FESTIVALS AND EVENTS

For a small community, Eastport manages to pull together and put on plenty of successful events during the year.

Eastport's annual four-day **Fourth of July–Old Home Week** extravaganza includes a parade, pancake breakfasts, barbecues, a flea market, an auction, races, live entertainment, and fireworks. This is one of Maine's best Fourth of July celebrations and attracts a crowd of more than 10,000. Lodgings are booked months in advance, so plan ahead.

Indian Ceremonial Days, a three-day Native American celebration, includes children's games, canoe races, craft demos, talking circles, fireworks, and traditional food and dancing at Sipayik, the Pleasant Point Reservation in Perry, the second weekend in August.

The **Eastport Salmon Festival** celebrates the area's aquaculture industry. If you like salmon, you'll love this event, which combines a salmon barbecue, craft booths, live entertainment, and boat trips at the Eastport breakwater the Sunday after Labor Day.

Also in September is the **Two Countries One Bay Art Studio Tour** (www.twocountriesart .com), a weekend of open galleries and studios in communities edging Passamaquoddy Bay.

A great resource for area happenings is **CulturePass** (www.culturepass.net), which covers the entire Passamaquoddy Bay region.

SHOPPING
Art, Crafts, and Antiques

Eastport has long been a magnet for artists and craftspeople yearning to work in a supportive environment, but the influx has increased in recent years. Proof of this is **The Eastport Gallery** (74 Water St., Eastport, 207/853-4166, www.eastportgallery.com, mid-June–Sept.), a cooperative whose works in varied media line the walls of a downtown building. The gallery also sponsors the annual **Paint Eastport Day,** usually held the second Saturday in September, when anyone is invited to paint a local scene; a reception and "wet paint" auction follow.

A gaggle of energetic women with local ties renovated a waterfront building, turning it into **The Commons** (51 Water St., Eastport, 207/853-4123), a fabulous gallery displaying works by nearly 100 area artists and artisans. The group has plans to renovate a nearby waterfront warehouse into more shops and a hotel.

Earth Forms (5 Dana St., Eastport, 207/853-2430, www.earthforms.biz) features potter Donald Sutherland's intriguing (and sometimes whimsical) wheel-thrown work—which he describes as "functional, nonfunctional, and dysfunctional" pottery. You can often see him at work on his wheel. It's tough to walk out without buying one of these special pieces.

Galleries and antiques shops are finding homes in the historical brick buildings that line Eastport's main thoroughfare.

© HILARY NANGLE

THE DOWN EAST COAST

Woodworker Roland LaVallee's gallery **Crow Tracks** (11 Water St., Eastport, 207/853-2336, www.crowtracks.com) is filled with his intricate carvings of birds and local fauna. The tiny garden entryway doubles the pleasure of a visit.

Art gallery, café, coffee shop: **Cappuccino Gallery and Gardens** (530 Rte. 1, Pembroke, 207/726-4761) is a bit of each. Photographer-owner Kathy McCabe mixes lattes with local art and light fare, and it works.

A number of very talented artists and artisans are tucked along the back roads of the area. You might get lucky and find them open, but it's wise to call before making a special trip. These include **Wrenovations** (84 Mill Stream Rd., Robbinston, 207/454-2382), with stained art creations by Mark Wren; **The Red Sleigh** (Rte. 1, Perry, 207/854-6688), filled with locally made treasures, from jewelry to pies; and **Susan Designs** (behind Loring's Body Shop, Gin Cove Rd., Perry, 207/853-4315), where gifted quilt artist Susan Plachy sells her creations.

Gifts and Home

Describing **45th Parallel: The Store** (Rte. 1, Perry, 207/853-9500) is a tough assignment. You really have to go and see for yourself; the aesthetic displays are worth the trip to this eclectic emporium. Housed in a one-story log building two miles (northeast, in the Calais direction) from the junction of Routes 190 and 1, the 45th Parallel is part antiques shop, part gift shop, part global marketplace—and entirely seductive.

Stop in, if only for a few minutes, at **S. W. Wadsworth and Son** (42 Water St., Eastport, 207/853-4343), the oldest ship chandlery in the country and the oldest retail business in Maine. In addition to hardware and marine gear, you'll find nautical gifts and souvenirs.

RECREATION
Excursion Boats
SYLVINA BEAL

Eastporter Butch Harris gave the waterfront a shot in the arm when he bought the sleek

© HILARY NANGLE

It's possible to board a windjammer for a sail through Passamaquoddy Bay.

Sylvina Beal, a historic 84-foot schooner built in 1911. His company, **Eastport Windjammers** (207/853-2500 or 207/853-4303, www.eastportwindjammers.com), offers a number of options to sail. The three-hour whale-watching cruise ($42 adults, $25 ages 5–12, $10 under age 5) departs at 1:30 P.M. daily and heads out into the prime whale-feeding grounds of Passamaquoddy Bay—passing the Old Sow whirlpool (the largest tidal whirlpool in the northern hemisphere), salmon aquaculture pens, and Campobello Island. En route you'll see bald eagles, porpoises, possibly puffins and ospreys, and more. The best months are July and August, when sightings are frequent, but Butch is a skilled spotter, so if they're there, he'll find them. A two-hour sunset cruise ($32 adults, $20 children) departs the Eastport Pier (call for times). Also available are lobstering cruises aboard the *Lady H;* call for details.

VONNIE AND FAL

Join Captain Skip Harris aboard the *Vonnie and Fal,* a 33-foot sportfishing boat, and test your skills at catching cod, pollack, haddock, shark, tuna, or striped bass ($125 pp full-day, $54 pp half-day, boat minimums apply). Captain Harris's **Fundy Breeze Charters** (109 Water St., Eastport, 207/853-4660, www.fundybreeze.com) also offers lighthouse, puffin, and whale-watching tours ($55–110 pp, boat minimums apply).

Sea Kayaking and Canoeing

Explore the region by sea kayak with **Cobscook Hikes and Paddles** (13 Woodcock Way, Robbinston, 207/726-4776 summer, 207/454-2130 winter, www.cobscookhikesandpaddles .com), which serves the area between Whiting and Calais. Registered Maine Guides Stephen and Tessa Ftorek lead three-hour ocean or lake paddles ($50 pp) designed to meet your interests and ability. Two-hour sunrise or sunset paddles are $40. On Friday nights you can watch luminescent organisms sparkle in the water on a two-hour Phosphorescent Paddle ($45). The Ftoreks also offer guided full-day ($80) and half-day ($40) hikes and snowshoeing adventures in winter.

ACCOMMODATIONS

Rates noted are for peak season.

Bed-and-Breakfasts

In 1833, renowned artist John James Audubon stayed at the elegant **Weston House** (26 Boynton St., Eastport, 207/853-2907 or 800/853-2907, www.westonhouse-maine.com, $85–95), so one of the three second-floor guest rooms bears his name—and the walls are lined with Audubon bird prints. All the guest rooms share two baths, but don't let that dissuade you from staying at this lovely home. Jett and John Peterson's family antiques and interesting art and crafts fill the beautifully decorated house on a quiet side street two blocks above the waterfront. Breakfast is outstanding (Jett is Eastport's favorite caterer), complete with a candelabra and classical music. Outside are croquet and badminton facilities, plus lovely gardens with a gazebo, chairs, and a table. Tea and sherry are available in the afternoon. With notice, Jett will prepare a private dinner and serve it in the formal dining room, a smart and delicious choice given Eastport's limited number of restaurants.

The old-shoe-comfortable **Milliken House Bed and Breakfast** (29 Washington St., Eastport, 207/853-2955 or 888/507-9370, www.eastport-inn.com, $75–85) is a good choice for families, but be forewarned that it's more homestay than inn, and you'll have to carry your luggage up at least one, and perhaps two, tall flights of stairs. Hosts Bill and Mary Williams welcome children and pets to their in-town home, an easy walk to shops and restaurants. Breakfasts are huge and served family-style in the very-Victorian dining room. There's a big TV in the double parlor downstairs, Wi-Fi throughout, and a phone is available. Call ahead in winter.

Pretty gardens surround the **Chadbourne House** (19 Shackford St., Eastport, 207/853-2727 or 888/853-2728, www.chadbournehouse.com, $135–175). Jill and David Westphal's antiques-filled Federal-style home has four guest rooms, two with fireplaces and one that fills most of the third floor. Two caveats: No shoes in the house, and prayers are said over breakfast. There is Wi-Fi throughout.

Motel

Guests at **The Motel East** (23A Water St., Eastport, 207/853-4747, year-round, $105–150) have front-row seats on Passamaquoddy Bay, overlooking Campobello Island. Get up early and catch the sunrise; later, watch boats unload their catches. Six good-size guest rooms and eight efficiency suites have Wi-Fi, phones, and cable TV, although all could use freshening. Guest rooms on the upper floors share balconies; avoid those on the basement level. There is free coffee in the lobby, and the pet fee is $20. The separate Friar Roads Cottage ($150 d) is also available.

Apartments

On the second floor of **The Commons** (51 Water St., Eastport, 207/853-4123, www.thecommonseastport.com), a newly renovated downtown building on the waterfront, are two nicely appointed two-bedroom apartments with decks and spectacular harbor views. Tide Watcher has two baths and rents for $950 per week; Water's Edge has one bath and rents for $900 per week; either is $150 per night with a three-night minimum, when available.

FOOD

Dining options have improved in Eastport in recent years, but as always in this region, ask locally about the current reputations. And always call before making a special trip, as hours and days of operation seem to change week to week, never mind season to season.

Local Flavors

Updated in 2010, **The Blue Iris Bistro** (31 Water St., Eastport, 207/853-2440, 8 A.M.–5 P.M. Wed.–Sun.) shares space with a floral shop. Well-spaced indoor tables and outdoor ones on a bi-level deck all have water views. Breakfast is served all day; lunch is available from 11 A.M. Service is cheerful but can be, um, leisurely. There's often an open-mike night on Saturday.

Here's something a bit different: **Blueberry Point Chefs** (Rte. 1, Perry, 207/853-4629, www.blueberrypointchefs.com) is a cooking school held on a 150-acre blueberry farm with panoramic views over Passamaquoddy Bay. Chef Audrey Patterson's classes (usually held 5–8:30 P.M. Mon. late May–late Sept., $55 pp) conclude with a meal. Check the website for the specifics of each class. Also on the premises is the **Ice House Wine and Cheese Shop** (10 A.M.–5 P.M. Tues.–Sat.).

Family Favorites

Casual, friendly, and inexpensive is **The Happy Crab** (35 Water St., Eastport, 207/853-9400, www.happycrabmaine.com, 11 A.M.–9 P.M. daily), a grill and sports bar. Pizza and finger food are usually available after 8 P.M. until the bar closes. Play pool while you wait. If the weather's fine, grab a seat on the deck.

A popular roadside eatery with a well-deserved reputation, the aptly named **New Friendly Restaurant** (1014 Rte. 1, Perry, 207/853-6610, 11 A.M.–8 P.M. daily, $6–20) lays on home-cooked offerings for "dinnah" (a Maine-ism meaning lunch), specializing in steak and seafood, including what many label the area's best lobster roll.

Time your meal right and you can watch the Deer Isle ferry arrive and depart or view the windjammer *Sylvina Beal* sail by from the bi-level **Eastport Chowder House** (167 Water St., Eastport, 207/853-4700, www.eastportchowderhouse.com, 11 A.M.–9 P.M. daily). Seafood, natch, is the specialty, with entrées in the $13–20 range. There's a bar downstairs and a harbor-front deck too.

Casual Dining

Breaking the norm of fried fish and lobster rolls for Eastport is **The Pickled Herring** (32 Water St., Eastport, 207/853-2323, www.thepickledherring.com, from 5 P.M. Wed.–Sun.). Decent pizzas come from the wood-fired oven, and fancier fare is served too. There's a nice wine list, and the bartender mixes a mean martini. Reservations are advised.

Lobster

When the weather's clear, there's nothing finer than lobster at **❰ Quoddy Bay Lobster** (7 Sea St., Eastport, 207/853-6640, 10 A.M.–6 P.M. Mon.–Sat., 11 A.M.–6 P.M. Sun.). Lobster is the headliner—watch boats unload their catch, it's that fresh—but there are other options. The only seating is at outside tables on the harbor's edge.

INFORMATION AND SERVICES
Information

Brochures are available at the **Quoddy Maritime Museum and Visitor Center** (70 Water St., Eastport, 10 A.M.–6 P.M. daily June–Sept.). In the museum section of the center is a huge model of the failed 1936 Passamaquoddy Tidal Power Project, an idea whose time hadn't come when it was proposed. A new tidal project is in the works today.

Information is also available from the **Eastport Chamber of Commerce** (207/853-3633, www.eastportchamber.net) and online at www.cobscookbay.com.

The handsome stone **Peavey Memorial Library** (26 Water St., Eastport, 207/853-4021), built in 1893, is named after the inventor of the Peavey grain elevator.

Deer Island-Lubec Ferry

If your next stop on the Maine Coast is Lubec, you might consider taking the funky two-stage boat-and-barge **East Coast Ferries** (877/747-2159, www.eastcoastferries.nb.ca, no credit cards) which connect through Deer Island to Campobello Island (passport required). It departs Eastport for Deer Island on the half hour 9:30 A.M.–6:30 P.M. Atlantic time late June–early September; fares are $18 per car plus $3 per passenger over age 11, $25 maximum per car. It connects with the ferry from Deer Island to Campobello, which departs on the half hour 8:30 A.M.–6:30 P.M. Atlantic time, $15 per car and driver plus $3 per passenger over age 11, $20 maximum per car. Motorcycles on each ferry are $10.

Public Restrooms

Restrooms are available at the library, and in summer there are portable toilets on Eastport's breakwater.

Calais and Vicinity

Calais (CAL-us) is as far as you'll get on the coast of Maine; from here on, you're headed inland. Europeans showed up in this area as early as 1604, when French adventurers established an ill-fated colony on St. Croix Island in the St. Croix River—16 whole years before the Pilgrims even thought about Massachusetts. After a winter-long debacle, all became relatively quiet until 1779, when the first permanent settler arrived.

Southeast of Calais is tiny Robbinston, a booming shipbuilding community in the 19th century but today little more than a 500-person blip on the map.

Calais is major border crossing into New Brunswick, Canada.

SIGHTS
Walking Tour
Pick up a copy of the *Walking Tour Guide to Calais Residential Historic District* at the Maine Tourism Information Center (39 Union St., Calais). The guide, produced by the St. Croix Historical Society, briefly covers the town's history and maps and describes the architecture and early owners of 23 historic houses, four of which are listed on the National Register of Historic Places.

St. Croix Island
Unless you have your own boat, you can't get over to 6.5-acre St. Croix Island, an International Historic Site under joint U.S. and Canadian jurisdiction (Rte. 1, Red Beach Cove, 8 miles south of Calais, www.nps.gov/sacr, free). But you can stop here, view exhibits in the visitors center, and enjoy the heritage trail, with bronze statues depicting various key personae or cultures in the development of the colony. It ends on the point with views of the island. Also here are picnic tables, restrooms, a gravel beach, and a boat launch.

The island is the site of the pioneering colony established by French explorers Samuel de Champlain and Pierre du Gua de Monts in 1604. Doomed by disease, mosquitoes, lack of food, and a grueling winter, 35 settlers died; in spring the emaciated survivors abandoned their effort and moved on to Nova Scotia. In 1969, archaeologists found the graves of 23 victims, but the only monument on the island is a commemorative plaque dating from 1904.

The current in the St. Croix River is strong, and tidal ranges can be as high as 28 feet, so neophyte boaters shouldn't even attempt a crossing, but local residents often picnic and swim off the island's sandy beach on the southern end.

Whitlock Mill Lighthouse
From the lovely Pikewoods Rest Area, beside Route 1 about four miles southeast of Calais, there's a prime view of 32-foot-high Whitlock Mill Lighthouse on the southern shore of the St. Croix River. Built in 1892, the green flashing light is accessible only over private land, so check it out from this vantage point. You can also have a picnic break here.

Calais-Robbinston Milestones
A quirky little local feature, the Calais-Robbinston milestones are a dozen red-granite chunks marking each of the 12 miles between Robbinston and Calais. Presaging today's highway mile markers, late-19th-century entrepreneur and journalist James S. Pike had the stones installed on the north side of Route 1 to keep track of the distance while training his pacing horses.

ENTERTAINMENT AND FESTIVALS
Music on the Green is a series of free concerts presented at 6:30 P.M. Wednesday at Triangle Park in downtown Calais.

Calais, Maine, and St. Stephen, New Brunswick, collaborate the first or second week of August for the nine-day **International Festival** of dinners, concerts, dances, a craft fair, ball games, and a cross-border parade and road race. Newspapers carry schedules (be sure

THE DOWN EAST COAST

to note which events are on eastern time and which are on Atlantic time).

SHOPPING

Downtown Calais has a few shops worthy of a look-see. **St. Croix Valley Antiques and Collectibles** (4 Monroe St., Calais, 866/420-1167) is a big shop with a wide range of furniture, quilts, baskets, and tableware. **The Dusty Rose** (22 North St., Calais, 207/454-7351) is chock-full of vintage finds for fans of old stuff. The **Urban Moose** (80 Main St., Calais, 207/454-8277) has an eclectic inventory that invites browsing. Perhaps most intriguing is Captain Craig Little's **Little Ships of the Maritimes,** tucked behind North Street downtown, which specializes in custom scale models. Nearly two dozen regional artists and artisans sell their works at **Cat's Eye Gallery** (272 North St., Calais, 207/454-2020). Books new, old, and rare are sold at the **Calais Book Shop** (405 Main St., Calais, 207/454-1110).

If you stop in at **Katie's on the Cove** (Rte. 1, Mill Cove, Robbinston, 207/454-3297 or 800/494-5283, 10 A.M.–5 P.M. Tues.–Sat. late May–mid-Oct.), do so at your own risk—chocoholics may need a restraining order. Joseph and Lea Sullivan's family operation, begun in 1982, has become a great success story. They now produce about four dozen varieties of homemade fudge, truffles, caramels, peanut brittle, and even marzipan. The shop, 12 miles southeast of Calais and about 15 miles west of Eastport, is no place for unruly or demanding kids—space is limited and the candy is pricey.

RECREATION
Parks and Preserves
MOOSEHORN NATIONAL WILDLIFE REFUGE

More than 50 miles of trails and gravel roads wind through the 17,257-acre Baring Unit of the Moosehorn National Wildlife Refuge (Charlotte Rd., Baring, 207/454-7161, http://moosehorn. fws.gov, sunrise–sunset daily, free), on the outskirts of Calais. Start with the 1.2-mile nature trail near the refuge headquarters and get ready for major-league wildlife-watching: 35 mammal

and 220 bird species have been spotted in the refuge's fields, forests, ponds, and marshes. Wear waterproof shoes and insect repellent. In August, help yourself to wild blueberries. During November deer-hunting season, either avoid the refuge Monday–Saturday or wear a hunter-orange hat and vest. Trails are accessible by snowshoe, snowmobile, or cross-country skis in winter. To reach refuge headquarters, take Route 1 north from downtown Calais about three miles. Turn left onto Charlotte Road, and go 2.4 miles to the headquarters sign. The office is open 8 A.M.–4 P.M. Monday–Friday all year, except major national holidays; you can pick up free trail maps, bird checklists, and other informative brochures. If you want to help support the conservation of wildlife in eastern Maine and educational programs, you can join Friends of Moosehorn National Wildlife Refuge (http://friendsofmoosehorn.org). A check for a mere $15 will do the trick.

By the way, if you don't have time to walk the trails, watch for the elevated artificial nesting platforms—avian high-rises for bald eagles—outside of Calais alongside Route 1 North, near the junction with Charlotte Road. Depending on the season, you may spot a nesting pair or even a fledgling. The chicks, usually twins but occasionally triplets, hatch around mid-May and try their wings by early August. A 400-square-foot observation deck across Route 1 is the best place for eagle-watching.

Continuing on Charlotte Road past the Moosehorn Refuge headquarters, you'll come to **Round Lake** (locally called Round Pond), a lovely spot where you can picnic, swim, or put in a kayak or canoe. Across the road, with a great lake view, is the interesting old Round Pond Cemetery, dating from the early 19th century. (Why do graveyards always have the best views?) Just after the cemetery, a left turn puts you on Pennamaquam Lake Road (or Charlotte Rd.) toward Perry; a right turn takes you to Route 214, near Pembroke.

DEVIL'S HEAD

About six miles south of Calais, watch for signs pointing to Devil's Head, and take the dirt road on the river side. The 315-acre site has a mile of frontage on the St. Croix River estuary and views to St. Croix Island. A road with two parking areas descends to the shoreline, and there are pit toilets and a marked hiking trail, approximately 1.5 miles looping from the road, leading to the highest point of coastal land north of Cadillac Mountain. According to locals, the headland was originally called d'Orville Head but it morphed into Devil's Head.

PIKE'S PARK
Calais has a lovely riverfront park at the foot of North Street. Pike's is the perfect place for a picnic. From here you have access to the **Calais Waterfront Walk,** which edges the river, running for 0.9 miles upriver and 0.6 miles downriver.

Golf
At the nine-hole **St. Croix Country Club** (River Rd./Rte. 1, Calais, 207/454-8875, late Apr.–late Oct.), the toughest and most scenic hole is the seventh, one of five holes on the river side of Route 1.

ACCOMMODATIONS
Rates noted are for peak season.

Bed-and-Breakfasts
Within easy walking distance of downtown is **Greystone Bed and Breakfast** (13 Calais Ave., Calais, 207/454-2848, www.greystonecalaisme.com, $89), Alan and Candace Dwelley's masterfully restored 1840 Greek Revival home. The property, listed on the National Register of Historic Places, is an architectural gem within, with Corinthian columns and black marble fireplace mantels. One of the two guest rooms can be paired with a third, smaller room. The Dwelleys serve a more-than-full breakfast and are eager to share their recommendations for local sights and shopping.

Motels
The Gothic-styled, gingerbread-trimmed **Redclyffe Shore Motel and Dining Room** (Rte. 1, Robbinston, 207/454-3270, www

.redclyffeshoremotorinn.com, $95) sits on a bluff jutting into the St. Croix River as it widens into Passamaquoddy Bay. The 16 motel units have cable TV, phones, and sunset-facing river views. Redclyffe is locally popular for its greenhouse-style dining room (just ignore the plastic flowers) with ocean views, serving dinner nightly ($11–26). It's 12 miles south of Calais.

The same family has owned and operated the **International Motel** (626 Main St., Calais, 207/454-7515 or 800/336-7515, www.theinternationalmotel.com, $75–85) since 1955. The nicest guest rooms are in the newer Riverview building. Some guest rooms have refrigerators; all have air-conditioning, TVs, and Wi-Fi. Pet-friendly rooms are available.

FOOD
Like the rest of Down East Maine, it's wise to call ahead as hours and days of operation change frequently. Hours noted are for peak season.

Local Flavors
If you're near downtown Calais, order picnic sandwiches to go at **Border Town Subz** (311 Main St., Calais, 207/454-8562, 11 A.M.–6 P.M. Mon.–Thurs., 11 A.M.–7 P.M. Fri.–Sat., 10 A.M.–6 P.M. Sun.), a reliable local favorite.

Another choice for picnic fixings, cottage staples, and other goodies is the **Sunrise County Farmers Market** (11 A.M.–3 P.M. Tues. late June–early Oct.). Look for it in the downtown park.

Casual Dining
White Christmas lights brighten the ceiling of **Bernardini's** (257 Main St., Calais, 207/454-2237, www.bernardinis.com, 11 A.M.–2 P.M. and 4–8 P.M. Mon.–Sat., entrées $11–22), a popular downtown restaurant that has earned its reputation with always-reliable Tuscany-inspired Italian cuisine. The pleasant dining room is accented by woodwork salvaged from a local church. Save room for the tiramisu.

Fabulous soups, fresh and fat sandwiches, bright salads, gluten-free options, and heartier choices, many with a Southwestern accent, make ◖ **Julianna's World Cafe** (North St., Calais, 207/454-2299, www.juliannasworld-cafe.com, 11 A.M.–9 P.M. Mon.–Sat., $5–20) an especially appealing downtown spot, despite the lackluster interior decor. There's a full bar and free Wi-Fi.

Here's a sleeper that's gained a top-notch reputation among locals for excellent food and service: **Nook and Cranny** (575 Airline Rd./Rte. 9, Baileyville, 207/454-3335, www.nookncrannyrestaurant.com, 11 A.M.–9 P.M. Tues.–Sun.). The wide-ranging menu has a bit of this and some of that, with most choices in the $8–18 range.

INFORMATION AND SERVICES
Information
The **Maine Visitor Information Center** (39 Union St., Calais, 207/454-2211) has free Wi-Fi, clean restrooms, and scads of brochures, including those produced by the **St. Croix Valley Chamber of Commerce** (207/454-2308 or 888/422-3112, www.visitcalais.com). The information center is open 8 A.M.–6 P.M. daily mid-May–mid-October, 9 A.M.–5:30 P.M. daily the rest of the year.

Check out **Calais Free Library** (Union St., Calais, 207/454-2758, www.calais.lib.me.us).

Public Restrooms
Restrooms are available at the Maine Visitor Information Center (39 Union St., Calais) and at the St. Croix International Heritage Site in Red Beach.

Crossing into Canada
If you plan to cross into Canada, you'll have to pass immigration checkpoints on both the U.S. (Calais, 207/454-3621) and Canadian (St. Stephen, 506/466-2363) ends of the bridges. Be sure to have the required identification (passport or passport card) and paperwork.

Pay attention to your watch too—Calais is on eastern time, while St. Stephen and the rest of New Brunswick is on Atlantic time, one hour later.

Grand Lake Stream

For a tiny community of about 200 year-rounders, Grand Lake Stream has a well-deserved larger-than-life reputation. It's the center of a vast area of rivers and lakes, ponds and streams—a recreational paradise, and more than 27,000 acres, including 62 miles of shore frontage, has been preserved by the **Downeast Lakes Land Trust** (www.downeastlakes.org). It's the literal town at the end of the world, remote in every sense of the word.

The famous stream is a narrow three-mile neck of prime scenic and sportfishing water connecting West Grand Lake and Big Lake. A dam spans the bottom of West Grand, and just downstream is a state-run salmon hatchery. Since the mid-19th century, the stream and its lakes have been drawing fishing fans to trout and landlocked-salmon spawning grounds, and fourth and fifth generations now return here each year.

Canoe building has contributed to the area's mystique. The distinctive Grand Lake canoe (or "Grand Laker"), a lightweight, square-sterned, motorized 20-footer, was developed in the 1920s specifically for sportfishing in these waters. In the off-season, several villagers still hunker down in their workshops and turn out these stable cedar beauties. (Interested? Call Bill Shamel, 207/796-8199.)

RECREATION
The region has the greatest concentration of Registered Maine Guides in the state, which gives you an indication of the fishing, hunting, and canoeing opportunities here. Truly the best way to experience Grand Lake Stream is with a member of the **Grand Lake Stream Guides Association** (www.grandlakestreamguides

The square-sterned Grand Laker canoe was designed specifically for fishing the Grand Lakes.

.com). The website lists members and specialties. You can arrange for one of these skilled guides to lead you on a fishing expedition, wildlife or photographic safari, or canoeing trip for a half day or longer.

Hiking

The 2.6-mile **Little Mayberry Cove Trail** edges the western shoreline of West Grand Lake. Pick up a trail map at the Pine Tree Store, and then park at the dam.

EVENTS

A great time to visit the village is the last full weekend in July for the annual **Grand Lake Stream Folk Art Festival** (207/796-8199, 10 A.M.–5 P.M. Sat.–Sun., $5 one day, $8 both days), held on the town's grassy ball field. Tents shelter approximately 50 top-notch juried artisans. Nonstop bluegrass and folk music is another attraction. There's an exhibit highlighting the region's canoe-building tradition and another displaying antique and contemporary quilts. Breakfast, lunch, and snacks are

available. Complementing the festival are lakeside barbecues by the guides, usually lobster on Friday evening, chicken on Saturday evening, with tickets available at the Pine Tree Store, across from the festival grounds. A contra dance takes place Saturday night, and a music jam, open to anyone, takes place Sunday morning. Leashed pets are welcome on festival grounds.

ACCOMMODATIONS

Cabin accommodations, with or without meals, are the lodgings of choice in Grand Lake Stream, and there's enough variety for every taste and budget. Few guests stay one night; most stay several days or a week. Rates quoted below are for two; many cabins can sleep more than that, and rates may be lower for extra people. Some housekeeping cabins require your own sheets and towels. Most camps have boat rentals for about $25 per day (a motor brings the total to about $50).

Mike and Jean Lombardo's **Shore Line Camps** (207/796-5539, www.shorelinecamps .com, no credit cards) has eight 1–3-bedroom housekeeping cabins, most fronting right on Big Lake. All have spotless pine interiors and full kitchens. The base rate is $45 pp, kids under age 2 are free, $20 kids under age 12, but all cabins have a minimum rate per night. Canoes, rowboats, and motorboats are available for rental.

Leen's Lodge (207/796-2929 or 800/995-3367, www.leenslodge.com, May–Oct.), on a spacious wooded shore and peninsula of West Grand Lake, has 10 small and large rustic cabins with baths. Rates, including breakfast, pack lunch, and dinner, are $110–165 pp. Children 12 and under pay $10 multiplied by their age, and kids age 5 and under are free. Housekeeping rates are also sometimes available. Leashed pets are welcome, and kennels are provided. BYOB. Canoe and motorboat rentals should be arranged in advance.

Grand Lake Lodge (207/796-5584, www .grandlakelodgemaine.com, $50 d, $42 s pp, no credit cards), on the shore of West Grand Lake and two blocks from the village center, is a particularly good choice for families, with a safe swimming area.

The Lakeside (14 Rolfe St., Princeton, 888/677-2874, www.thelakeside.org) is set well back from Route 1 on Lewy Lake, which flows through Long Lake into Big Lake. Gary and Jennifer Dubovick have five housekeeping cabins ($60–75) along the lakeshore plus eight housekeeping rooms (two with private baths) in the main house ($45 without breakfast, $70

with breakfast). Rooms are comfy, have TVs, and there's also Wi-Fi, a living room with a TV, and a billiards room. If you want breakfast, a box lunch, dinner, and maid service, its $65 pp per day. Guide services and boat rentals are available.

FOOD

If you opt for housekeeping arrangements, you'll want to provision before you get here, but you can pick up essentials at the **Pine Tree Store** (3 Water St., Grand Lake Stream, 207/796-5027), in the heart of the village.

Both **Leen's Lodge** and **Weatherby's** (207/796-5558) open their dining rooms to guests by reservation. Expect to pay $25–35 for a full meal.

INFORMATION AND SERVICES

The volunteer-run **Grand Lake Stream Chamber of Commerce** (www.grandlakestream.org) produces a brochure listing accommodations, shops, and services.

GETTING THERE

To get to Grand Lake Stream, head north on Route 1 from Calais through Princeton. About two miles north of Princeton, turn left (west) onto Grand Lake Stream Road (also called Princeton Rd.). Continue about 10 miles to the village.

AROOSTOOK COUNTY

Welcome to the Crown of Maine. When Mainers refer to "The County," they're referring to Aroostook, a Micmac Indian word meaning "bright" or "shining." At nearly 6,500 square miles, Maine's largest county is larger than Connecticut and Rhode Island combined, but it's population numbers fewer than 72,000 residents, and fully a quarter of them live in only two smallish cities, Presque Isle and Caribou.

Neat farmhouses and huge, half-buried potato-storage barns anchor vast undulating patches of potatoes, broccoli, and barley. The sky seems to go on forever. Potato fields define The County—bright green in spring, pink and white in summer, dirt-brown and gold just before the autumn harvest.

Aroostook County, like the rest of Maine, has its share of hills, forests, and waterways, but the most significant hills here—Quaggy Jo, Mars, Debouillie, Haystack, Number Nine—are startling. Almost accidental, they appear out of nowhere—chunks the glaciers seem to have overlooked. Thanks to them, you'll find authentic vertical hiking, although Aroostook's trails are more often horizontal, through marshlands and woodlands and along abandoned rail beds.

Winters are long, snowy, and cold. Snowmobiling is a big deal here. Legions of snowmobilers (often called "sledders" locally) crisscross The County every winter, exploring hundreds of miles of the incredible Interconnecting Trail System (ITS). More recently, Aroostook has embraced a return to its cross-country skiing heritage, thanks to the

Maine Winter Sports Center's mission and properties. It now is home to an Olympic biathlon training center and even hosts World Cup cross-country skiing events.

The County's agricultural preeminence sets it apart from the rest of Maine, but so do its immigrant cultures. Acadian culture permeates the northernmost **St. John Valley,** where the French dialect is unlike anything you'll ever hear in language classes (or in France). It leads to some wonderfully whimsical street and road names—for instance, Brise Culotte Road, roughly translated as "Torn Trousers Road." Islands of Acadian or French culture exist in other parts of Maine, but it's in "the Valley" that you'll be tempted to pile on the pounds with such regional specialties as *poutine* (French fries smothered with cheese and gravy), *tourtière* (pork pie), and *tarte au saumon* (salmon tart).

Swedish surnames are prevalent too, especially around New Sweden and environs, and more recently Amish families have moved here, drawn by The County's rural farming traditions.

As often occurs with remote rural areas, The County sometimes gets a bum rap (never from the snowmobiling crowd) among downstaters and others who've never been here. But it deserves notice—for the scenery if nothing else. Admittedly, it's a long haul—it's about as far as you can get from the rockbound coast—but you're guaranteed a totally different Maine experience. For many visitors, there's a sensation of traveling back 20 or 30 years to an era when life was simpler, communities were small, and everyone greeted each other by name.

PLANNING YOUR TIME

Covering such a large expanse of geography takes time. While you can loop around Aroostook's periphery in 2–3 days, you'll need 4–5 days to explore the region and tease out its many charms.

Snowmobilers and cross-country skiers come January–March, when The County measures its snow in feet, not inches.

In June, newly planted potato fields

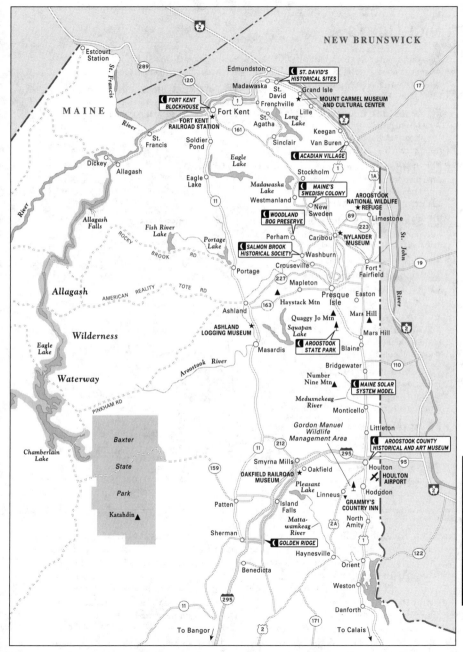

HIGHLIGHTS

◖ Maine Solar System Model: Stretching 40 miles between Houlton to Presque Isle is a three-dimensional scale model of the solar system (page 412).

◖ Aroostook County Historical and Art Museum: There are plenty of treasures for history buffs, including military artifacts dating from the Civil War (page 413).

◖ Golden Ridge: Route 2, between Sherman Mills and Houlton, passes along the ridge top, with panoramic views from Katahdin to distant lakes (page 414).

◖ Salmon Brook Historical Society: Learn about the traditional potato-farm lifestyle at this National Historic Register property and museum (page 418).

◖ Maine's Swedish Colony: It's an authentic touch of Sweden, and the best time to visit is during the annual June Midsommar Festival (page 420).

◖ Aroostook State Park: Maine's first state park has opportunities for hiking, swimming, and boating (page 421).

◖ Woodland Bog Preserve: In early summer, schedule a walk with Nature Conservancy steward Richard Clark to learn about the flora and fauna and see rare orchids (page 422).

◖ Acadian Village: Delve into Maine's Acadian history and heritage on a guided tour of 16 antique and replica buildings (page 429).

◖ St. David's Historical Sites: Learn about Acadian heroine Tante Blanche, visit a typical homestead and school, and see where the Acadians first landed (page 430).

◖ Fort Kent Blockhouse: A relic of the bloodless Aroostook War, the 1839 blockhouse is being restored to its original design (page 430).

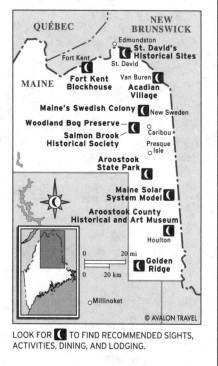

LOOK FOR ◖ TO FIND RECOMMENDED SIGHTS, ACTIVITIES, DINING, AND LODGING.

---

resemble Ireland in their vibrant greens, although the blackflies and mosquitoes can be annoying, and two major festivals, Midsommar in mid-June and the Acadian Festival toward the end of the month mean lodging can be nearly impossible to obtain without advance booking.

Most museums and historical sites are open during the summer, so that's the best time for history buffs to visit. Days are long and temperatures moderate, also making it ideal for hikers, cyclists, and paddlers. In mid-July, the potato fields blossom, a gorgeous sight.

Autumn comes early, with leaves beginning to turn color as early as late August in the northern parts of The County.

Be sure to get off Route 1 and Route 11 and mosey along some of the back roads that meander through the farmlands and by lakes and rivers. Doing so will let you experience Maine's Big Sky Country, a landscape where endless fields meet expansive sky. And do make time to loop through the St. John Valley for a taste of Maine unlike any other. From Caribou or Presque Isle, you can drive up to the crown, visit Valley sites, and return in a long day.

Southern Aroostook County

Driving north on I-95, you find the interstate petering out at Houlton, about 120 miles northeast of Bangor. That sometimes makes this feel like the end of the earth, but it's actually just the beginning of Aroostook County.

Southern Aroostook, centered on **Houlton,** is a narrow north-south corridor stretching from Sherman Mills on I-95 to the Canadian border, roughly straddling Route 1 from **Danforth** to **Presque Isle.** Among its communities are **Island Falls, Oakfield, Smyrna Mills, Monticello,** and **Bridgewater.** It's in this region that the forests and mountains of the Maine Highlands begin to give way to the rolling farmlands characteristic of The County.

Hard by the New Brunswick border, Houlton has carved out its own niche as the shire town, and, according to the local historical society, "history's hiding place." Incorporated in 1834, Houlton is quiet and not often considered a destination, but the county courts and other government offices are all here, so there's a fair amount of activity—at least during the week.

SIGHTS
Oakfield Railroad Museum
Housed in a 1910 Bangor and Aroostook Railroad station and run by the Oakfield Historical Society, the Oakfield Railroad Museum (Station St., Oakfield, 207/757-8575,

© TOM NANGLE

AROOSTOOK COUNTY

An impressive collection of iron-horse memorabilia fills the Oakfield Railroad Museum.

1–4 P.M. Sat.–Sun. late May–early Sept., free) contains an impressive collection of iron-horse memorabilia. Tour the station, the adjacent reading room library, and the outbuildings, including a restored caboose. If you're really lucky, a train might pass by on the tracks. Donations are welcome. The museum is 17 miles west of Houlton, off I-95 Exit 286.

Smyrna Amish Community

Many folks think they've stepped back in time when visiting The County, but that feeling intensifies in Smyrna, where horse-drawn carriages signal the presence of the Smyrna Amish community. Seeking a quiet place to work, raise their families, practice their faith, and interact with outsiders, five Midwestern families established a community in this rural farming town about 15 miles west of Houlton in 1996. Since then, the community has grown steadily. In addition to farming, the Smyrna Amish operate a number of businesses, open to the public, all of which are clustered along a short stretch of Route 2, one mile west of I-95 Exit 295. These include Sturdi-Bilt, which builds wooden sheds and outbuildings; Kauffman Metals, which fabricates metal roofing and building; Northeastern Rustic Furniture; and Pioneer Place, a wonderful little general store where you can purchase locally made goods and foods. Most of the businesses are closed on weekends. While the Amish welcome visitors to their businesses, remember they're not a tourist attraction. This is a living, breathing community that has opened a window to its lifestyle. Respect their personal and community property, and ask before taking photos of people.

◖ Maine Solar System Model

Space travel is possible in Aroostook County, where the three-dimensional Maine Solar System Model (207/764-6561 or 800/764-7420, www.umpi.maine.edu/info/nmms/solar) stretches 40 miles along Route 1. The model comprises the sun, the planets, and moons for earth, Saturn, Jupiter, and Pluto. All the planets, except demoted Pluto, which is only one

This store in Smyrna sells Amish-made furniture and preserves.

inch in diameter, are large enough to be seen while driving along Route 1, where one mile is equal to the distance between Earth and the sun.

The 93-million-to-one scale model was masterminded by Kevin McCartney, a geology professor at the University of Maine at Presque Isle, and implemented with the help of hundreds of local volunteers, including service and school groups, businesses, and individuals. Local students built the planets.

Pluto (still considered a planet in this neck of the woods) is found at the Visitor Information Center in Houlton, just off Route 1, north of the I-95 interchange. Other models are mounted on 10-foot-tall posts and dot parking lots and fields along the route. The project is detailed and mapped both in a brochure, available at the center, and on the Internet.

Market Square Historic District

A arced pedestrian bridge across the Meduxnekeag River links Gateway Park, on Route 1, with Market Square's 28 turn-of-the-20th-century buildings listed on the National Register of Historic Places (the architecture is lovely, but unfortunately more than a few storefronts are empty). Along the bridge and walkway (both wheelchair-accessible) are markers detailing Houlton's downtown history. A walking guide is available at the **Greater Houlton Area Chamber of Commerce** (109 Main St., Houlton), two blocks up Main Street.

◖ Aroostook County Historical and Art Museum

The 1903 White Memorial Building, the Colonial Revival residence that houses the chamber, is also home to the Aroostook County Historical and Art Museum (207/532-2519, 1–4 P.M. Tues.–Fri. late May–early Sept. or by appointment, donation), containing a fine collection of photos, books, vintage clothing, antique tools, and housewares. You can wander through on your own, but a guide will bring the collection to life. Of particular interest are military artifacts from the Hancock Barracks, the Civil War, and the Camp Houlton POW

internment camp. Also on view are the ventilator cowl from the battleship *Maine,* which sank in Havana Harbor, and a Confederate battle flag captured by a Houlton member of the First Calvary Maine. Donations are appreciated.

Museum staff can also provide information about and direct you to a number of local historical sites. Unfortunately most haven't been maintained. I've watched them deteriorate and all but disappear over the years. There is not much to see at either of these, but they are worth mentioning for their places in history.

Garrison Park, site of the **Hancock Barracks,** was established in 1828 to protect American border settlements and garrisoned troops during the 1838–1839 Aroostook War. It provided frontier training for West Point graduates, and General Robert E. Lee visited here. To find the overgrown, gated site, take Route 2 toward the airport and turn left onto Garrison Road, near the top of the hill.

The still functioning **Houlton Airport** dates from the early 1940s. Neutrality laws prevented U.S.-built planes from flying directly from the United States to Britain, so during the months before Pearl Harbor, planes were known to land in Houlton and then be towed across the border to Canada for takeoff. That all changed when the U.S. Army took over the airport during World War II and turned it into an airbase and Maine's largest **German POW camp.** About 4,000 prisoners lived here in barracks while laboring in lumber camps, canneries, potato farms, and paper mills. To find the site, take Route 2 east from downtown. At the T intersection, bear right and follow it to the end.

Watson Settlement Bridge

About six miles north of Houlton, amid typical Aroostook farmland in Littleton, stands Maine's northernmost (yes, and easternmost) covered bridge, built in the early 20th century and last used in 1985. The wood-truss bridge, straddling a branch of the Meduxnekeag River, feels quite forlorn, a remnant of the past just sitting here unused (except, unfortunately, by graffiti artists). Maine once had 120 or so

© TOM NANGLE

A short detour off Route 1, just north of Houlton, will bring you to the Watson Settlement Bridge.

covered bridges; only nine remain, and this is the only one using the Howe truss system. For the prettiest route to the bridge from Houlton, take Foxcroft Road from Route 2 and continue 6.1 miles; turn left onto Carson Road. From Route 1 in Littleton, go right on Carson Road, which winds its way down to the river (bear left at the fork). The quicker route is to head north on Route 1 four miles from the I-95 interchange and then go right on Carson Road for 2.9 miles.

Southern Aroostook Agricultural Museum

Farming memorabilia fills the Southern Aroostook Agricultural Museum (1664 Rte. 1, Littleton, 207/538-9300, www.oldplow .org, 1–4 P.M. Thurs.–Sat. June–late Sept., $5 adults, $3 under age 10), started as a retirement project for Cedric and Emily Shaw. The collection grew, and in 2001 the museum moved from the Shaws' farm to the former Littleton Elementary School. Local support has allowed it to continue growing, adding a tool collection

and a former one-room schoolhouse as well as building a model potato barn and most recently a new barn.

Scenic Routes
⟨ GOLDEN RIDGE

The interstate is the fastest route to Houlton, but Route 2, from Sherman Mills through Oakfield and Smyrna, is the best choice for moseyers, and it really isn't that much longer. The far-less-traveled route passes through gorgeous countryside dotted with farms, lakes, and small villages. The views from Golden Ridge, a section between Island Falls and Oakfield, reach to Katahdin and beyond. Be sure to watch for potato barns, a unique barn built into the ground for cold potato storage. Most have a gambrel roof topping the landscape.

MILLION-DOLLAR VIEW SCENIC BYWAY
South of Houlton and stretching eight miles along Route 1 between Danforth and Orient is an especially scenic drive that passes over Peekaboo Mountain and offers panoramic

views over the Chiputneticook chain of lakes and to Katahdin. It's also prime moose-watching country. There are two scenic pull-outs, but no services on the route.

ENTERTAINMENT AND EVENTS

For canoeists and kayakers, the year's biggest event is the eight-mile spring-runoff **Meduxnekeag River Race,** held on a Saturday in late April–early May. Beginning in New Limerick, west of town, the route includes a short stretch of Class III rapids. For more information, contact the Greater Houlton Chamber of Commerce (207/532-4216).

Check local listings and posters for the frequent outdoor **concerts** staged in local parks.

The annual **Soapbox Derby,** held in mid-June in Community Park, always attracts a big crowd.

The early July **Houlton Fair** (www.houltonfair.com) includes a carnival, a pig scramble, truck pulling, pageants, entertainment, baking contests, and craft and agricultural exhibits.

RECREATION
Parks and Preserves
PIERCE PARK

Near downtown Houlton, mystery surrounds the origins of Pierce Park's quaint fountain with a centerpiece statue usually called *The Boy with the Leaking Boot.* Donated to the town in 1916, it's one of two dozen or so similar statues in the United States and Europe. Legends have it coming from Germany or Belgium or Italy, but no record exists. Benches surround the fountain, and lower- and upper-level troughs provide fresh water for pets and their owners. The Houlton Garden Club maintains the flowers in the park—a popular local spot for photographs, picnics, and coffee breaks.

A. E. HOWELL WILDLIFE CONSERVATION CENTER AND SPRUCE ACRES REFUGE

Art and Dot Howell and their family have dedicated 64 acres of their land and their lives to conservation and wildlife rehabilitation, and their enthusiasm is contagious. Most creatures in the nonprofit refuge (Lycette Rd., North Amity, 207/532-6880, 10 A.M.–4 P.M. Tues.–Fri., 10 A.M.–3 P.M. Sat. mid-May–late Oct.) will be cared for and released, but permanent residents include a great horned owl, two bald eagles, and a bobcat. Frequent visitors include more than 65 species of birds, white-tailed deer, black bears, red foxes, woodchucks, turkey vultures, and various hares. All visitors are taken through on guided tours, and appointments are required. Minimum donation is $5 per adult; kids are free. If you have time, volunteer to lend a hand; there's always a need, and it's a rewarding experience. Usually there also are one-day open houses with admission by donation in July–August. Do not bring pets, but do bring binoculars. The refuge is just west of Route 1, on Lycette Road, 15 miles south of Houlton.

GORDON MANUEL WILDLIFE MANAGEMENT AREA

Just south of Houlton in Hodgdon, the Gordon Manuel Wildlife Management Area (no phone) covers 6,488 acres of fields, woods, and marshland along the Meduxnekeag River. From Route 1, turn right (west) onto Hodgdon Road and watch for a dairy bar (there's a water access point adjacent to it). Take the first left after it onto the unpaved Horseback Road. Continue 1.7 miles and turn left at a narrow dirt road. Wind through the trees about 0.2 miles to a small parking area on the Meduxnekeag River. Watch for ospreys, green herons, even bald eagles. You can launch a canoe or kayak (no motors allowed) and explore the area. The setting is particularly gorgeous during the fall foliage season, but be forewarned that hunting is allowed here, so wear a hunter-orange vest and hat mid-October–November.

If you don't have a canoe or kayak and just want to do some birding, this is a particularly relaxing bike ride, even from Houlton.

Golf
On a clear day, Baxter State Park's Katahdin is visible from **Va-Jo-Wa Golf Club** (142-A

AROOSTOOK COUNTY

Walker Settlement Rd., Island Falls, 207/463-2128, www.vajowa.com), a particularly scenic 18-hole, par-72 course named after Vaughn, John, and Warren Walker. Call for a starting time; this course is popular.

Southwest of Houlton is the nine-hole **Houlton Community Golf Club** (Drew's Lake Rd., New Limerick, 207/532-2662, www.houltongolf.com), built on onetime potato fields in 1921. The setting is lovely, on the shores of Nickerson Lake; the lakefront clubhouse has a snack bar. Bring a swimsuit; a dip in the lake feels great after a round of golf.

Winter Recreation

Houlton is at the fringe of prime **snowmobiling** country. The crowds tend to head up the road to Presque Isle, Caribou, and the St. John Valley, but there are plenty of trails here. For information on snowmobiling in the Houlton area, contact the chamber of commerce or the **Maine Snowmobile Association** (207/622-6983, www.mesnow.com), which can put you in touch with local snowmobile clubs. When snowmobiling in the Houlton area, you'll notice on trail maps that some routes cross into Canada. Be sure you are carrying a passport or passport card when you are near the border. The Houlton border crossing is open 24 hours.

Also lacing the region are **cross-country ski trails.**

ACCOMMODATIONS

Clean and well maintained, **Ivey's Motor Lodge** (Rte. 1, Houlton, 207/532-4206 or 800/244-4206 in Maine, www.houlton.net/iveys, $80–110) wins folks over with good-size guest rooms, friendly service, and amenities unexpected in a vintage small motel. All rooms have TVs, DVD players, fridges, and microwaves. Rates include continental breakfast. On the premises is an Irish pub with big-screen TV. It's on Route 1, on the north side of I-95 Exit 302.

The **Shiretown Motor Inn** (282 North Rd./Rte. 1, Houlton, 207/532-9421 or 800/441-9421, www.shiretownmotorinn.com, $90–140)

has an indoor pool, a fitness room, and Wi-Fi. Ask for a room in the new building. Rates include continental breakfast.

FOOD

Hours noted are for peak season but are subject to change. It's always wise to call ahead.

Local Flavors

Most of Maine's farmers markets operate one or maybe two days a week; the **Houlton Farmers Market** sets up shop daily early May–mid-October next to McDonald's on Route 1, just south of I-95 Exit 62.

Craving something natural? **Country Junction** (53 Main St., Houlton, 207/532-2218, 7 A.M.–4 P.M. Mon.–Fri., 7 A.M.–2 P.M. Sat.) is a good choice for terrific baked goods, coffees, teas, and a full range of natural foods and groceries. There's seating inside.

Zippy's (Courtyard Sq., 207/532-7678, 11 A.M.–3 P.M. Mon.–Tues., 11 A.M.–8 P.M. Wed.–Sat.), a takeout with seating on the square, in a good choice when the weather cooperates.

Maple syrup and honey are produced at **Spring Break** (3315 Rte. 2, Smyrna Mills, 207/757-7373), a sugarhouse and gift shop near the Amish colony.

Family Favorites

For humongous portions (even by County standards), home cooking, good service, and local color, **◖ Grammy's Country Inn** (1687 Bangor Rd., Linneus, 207/532-7808) is the choice. It's nothing fancy, mind you, but where else might you find deep-fried lobster on the menu? Save room for dessert, order conservatively, and even then, plan on having leftovers. And save room for dessert, which includes two-fisted whoopie pies. The best part though is that nearly everything on the menu is less than $12.

Another long-time fave for old-fashioned meals such as country-fried steak and liver and onions, a Friday night fish fry, and rave-worthy desserts is **Elm Tree Diner** (146 Bangor Rd., 207/532-3777, 5:30 A.M.–8 P.M. Sun.–Thurs.,

5:30 A.M.–9 P.M. Fri.–Sat., $3–18), which re-opened in bright new digs after a fire destroyed the original location.

It's easy to spot **The Blue Moose** (180 Rte. 1, Monticello, 207/538-0991, 7 A.M.–8 P.M. Sun. and Tues.–Thurs., 7 A.M.–9 P.M. Fri.–Sat.)—just look for the, um, blue moose. Rather nondescript on the exterior, inside it's warm, inviting, and lodge-like. The family-operated restaurant serves mighty fine home-style fare at better-than-reasonable prices, and there's a children's menu. As with most such restaurants in the region, the desserts are homemade and scrumptious.

Casual Dining

One of the region's most enduring popular restaurants is **Horn of Plenty** (382 North Rd., Houlton, 11 A.M.–2:30 P.M. and 5–8 P.M. Wed.–Sat., $7–19). Chef Bill Roderick's menu blends comfort foods with a bit of international flair.

Hidden in the back of the small downtown Fishman Mall and displaying the work of local artists, Joyce Transue's **The Courtyard Café** (61 Main St., Houlton, 207/532-0787, www .thecourtyardcafe.biz, 11 A.M.–2 P.M. Mon.–Fri., dinner 5–8 P.M. Mon.–Thurs., 5–9 P.M. Fri.–Sat.) is well worth finding. The menu changes daily, but dinner possibilities ($14–20)

might include chicken parmesan or bourbon-glazed Norwegian salmon. Reservations are recommended.

Across the street, occupying a former bank, is **The Vault** (64 Main St., Houlton, 207/532-2222, 5–10 P.M. Wed.–Sat., entrées $10–16). Less pricey than the Courtyard, it serves simple, home-style meals; BYOB.

INFORMATION AND SERVICES

The **Greater Houlton Chamber of Commerce** (109 Main St., Houlton, 207/532-4216, www .greaterhoulton.com) is in the same 1903 Colonial Revival building as the Aroostook Historical and Art Museum. Be sure to request the *Walking Guide to Market Square Historic District.*

Check out **Cary Memorial Library** (107 Main St., Houlton, 207/532-1302, www.carey .lib.me.us).

The **Maine Visitor Information Center** (28 Ludlow Rd., Houlton, 207/532-6346), with brochures and maps covering the entire state, is open 9 A.M.–5 P.M. weekdays year-round, with weekend and extended weekday hours in summer. Restrooms are also available.

Aroostook County Tourism (888/216-2463, www.visitaroostook.com) has information on and links for the entire county.

Central Aroostook County

Ahh. Sighs of contentment are common in a region where folks know their neighbors, crime is rare, and the only traffic jams are caused by slow-moving farm equipment. In addition to road signs urging drivers to be wary of moose, there are others encouraging sharing the road with roller-skiers and Amish horse-and-buggies.

Most of the 60,000 acres planted with spuds in Maine are found in the "Potato Triangle," the region framed by **Presque Isle** to the south, **Caribou** to the north, and **Fort Fairfield** on the Canadian border, tied together

by the zigzagging course of the Aroostook River. Farmhouses, potato barns, and rolling fields dominate the landscape—and when those fields bloom in mid-July, it's one of the prettiest sights around. Northeast of Caribou is **Limestone;** south of Presque Isle is **Mars Hill.** Each is a day's stage ride from the others, about 13 miles, making it easy to explore the region from one base.

The economic impact caused by the closing of Limestone's Loring Air Force Base in the late 1990s devastated the region, and although the population erosion continues, the base is becoming a success story with the establishment of the Loring Commerce Centre and the creation of Aroostook National Wildlife Refuge.

Outdoor enthusiasts, especially, will find plenty: 904-acre Aroostook State Park, miles of multiuse trails, two small alpine areas, and impressive cross-country facilities that have hosted World Cup events. Cross-country skiing was introduced to Maine by settlers of the Swedish Colony, the region northwest of Caribou anchored by New Sweden and Stockholm.

A handful of intriguing low-tech museums and heritage sites entertain history buffs. What you won't find here is much in the way of interesting shopping.

SIGHTS

Most historical sights in the area are run by volunteers, so hours change frequently. It's wise to call before making a special trip.

University of Maine at Presque Isle

Established in 1903 as the Aroostook State Normal School for training teachers, the University of Maine at Presque Isle (UMPI, 181 Main St./Rte. 1, Presque Isle, 207/768-9400, www.umpi.edu) has more than 1,500 two-year and four-year students on its 150-acre campus at the southern end of the city. The school is noted for its training in physical education and recreation.

In the Campus Center is the **Reed Art Gallery,** a one-room gallery that overflows into the hallway, where rotating exhibits spotlight Maine and Canadian artists. During the school year, the gallery is open 9 A.M.–4 P.M. Monday–Saturday; the summer schedule tends to be less predictable.

Science wunderkind Kevin McCartney, a geology professor and the powerhouse behind the Maine Solar System scale model, also gets credit for the **Northern Maine Museum of Science,** in Folsom Hall. Hallways in the three-story science building have been turned into a free teaching museum, where you can take a test to see if you're color blind, touch a real dinosaur bone, and take in all manner of

scientific and mathematical exhibits explaining such hard-to-grasp concepts as DNA and the Fibonacci sequence and displays varying from bottle-nosed dolphins to fluorescent minerals. Also here is the sun, the epicenter of the Route 1 solar system model, as well as another scale model that extends the length of the second floor. Nothing is high-tech, but it's enjoyable and well presented. Be sure to pick up a brochure that explains the exhibits—look for it on case tops. Also look for a guide to the **West Campus Woods Nature Trail,** protected by the museum. There are 10 interpretive stations that illustrate features of the northern forest.

◖ Salmon Brook Historical Society

Here's a worthwhile two-for-one deal, with lots of charm and character: In tiny downtown Washburn, across from the First Baptist Church, the Salmon Brook Historical Society (1267 Main St./Rte. 164, Washburn, 207/455-5339) operates the **Benjamin C. Wilder Homestead,** an 1852 farmhouse on the National Register of Historic Places, and the **Aroostook Agricultural Museum** in the adjacent red barn. The well-restored 10-room house has period furnishings and displays; the barn contains old tools and antique cookware and pottery. The museums, on 2.5 acres, are open 8–11 A.M. Wednesday and 1–4 P.M. Sunday mid-June–mid-September, other times by appointment. Admission is free, but donations are welcome. Washburn is 11 miles northwest of Presque Isle and 10 miles southwest of Caribou.

Nylander Museum

If you were an eccentric self-educated geologist and needed a place to display and store everything you'd accumulated, you'd create a place like the Nylander Museum (393 Main St., Caribou, 207/493-4209, www.nylander-museum.org, 9 A.M.–5 P.M. Fri.–Sat., donation). Swedish-born Olof Olssen Nylander traveled the world collecting specimens, settled in Caribou, and bequeathed his work, including 6,000 fossils and 40,000 shells, to the

ONE POTATO, TWO POTATO

Native to South America, the potato is king in Aroostook County, where 90 percent of Maine's spuds grow on more than 60,000 acres – Maine is the country's fifth- to eighth-largest producer (depending on the harvest).

Aroostook County's potato heritage dates back more than 150 years, says fourth-generation potato farmer Keith LaBrie of Labrie's Farms in St. Agatha. "It became a staple on family farms generations ago. Back 50, 60 years ago, there were thousands of small growers, with 15-20-acre farms. Those have consolidated into 300-500-acre farms, and the harvesting is mechanized now for efficiency."

In the past, he says, Maine predominantly grew the round, white table stock variety. Recently there's been more of a move toward russet types. While most of what Maine grows is used for processed French fries and potato chips, Maine potatoes are now being used to produce Cold River Vodka (www.coldriver-vodka.com), made and sold in Freeport.

Potato fields are in full blossom in mid-July. Different varieties produce differently colored flowers, so there will be white in one field, red in another.

Annual festivals in Fort Fairfield and Houlton celebrate the blossoms and the harvest; potatoes appear on every restaurant menu and family table; and countless roadside stands peddle them by the bag. Although high schools still close for 2-3 weeks in September so students (and teachers) can assist with the harvest, most of the work is done mechanically these days.

Now, if you don't get enough of this potato business while you're here in The County, there's always a membership in the **Maine Potato Sampler of the Month Club.** Eight months a year, Wood Prairie Farm (49 Kinney Rd., Bridgewater, 800/829-9765, www.wood-prairie.com), an organic farm in Bridgewater, sends its members a 10-pound gift box of three different kinds of organic potatoes. The package comes with postcards and recipes, so you're all set. The base price for the eight-month club is $299; one month is $39.95.

Information on the potato industry is available from the **Maine Potato Board** (207/764-4148, www.mainepotatoes.com).

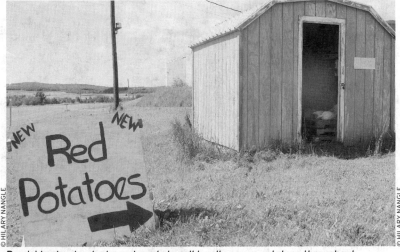

© HILARY NANGLE

© HILARY NANGLE

Roadside stands, sheds, and markets sell locally grown potatoes throughout Aroostook County.

city. Since his 1943 death, the museum has acquired other collections: butterflies, mounted birds, and additional geological specimens. It's all displayed in two small galleries.

◪ Maine's Swedish Colony

Maine's Swedish Colony (www.maineswedish colony.info) comprises New Sweden, Stockholm, and Woodland, and spills over into neighboring towns, including Perham, Westmanland, Madawaska Lake, and Caribou.

New Sweden is eight miles northwest of downtown Caribou via Route 161. At the **New Sweden Historical Museum** (Capitol Hill Rd. and Station Rd., New Sweden, 207/896-3018), three floors of memorabilia reflect the rugged life in this frontier community. An exact replica of the colony's "Kapitoleum" (capitol), the museum was built in 1971 after fire leveled the original structure. Check out the museum's guestbook: Visitors have come from all over Scandinavia to see this cultural enclave. The museum, 0.5 miles north and east of Route 161, is open 1–4 P.M. daily Memorial Day weekend–mid-September, Admission is free, but donations are welcome. Next door, in the **Capitol Hill School,** a gift shop carries Swedish items. Out back is a monument with the list of the original settlers.

Continuing east on Station Road, you'll pass **W. W. Thomas Memorial Park** on the left, a great spot for a picnic, with a play area for kids and a dramatic vista over the rolling countryside. Concerts occur periodically in the band shell. About 0.2 miles farther are the circa-1870 **Larsson/Ostlund Log Home,** one of the colony's oldest buildings, and the shingled **Lars Noak Blacksmith and Woodworking Shop,** another remnant of the early settlers.

More exhibits await at the **Stockholm Historical Society Museum,** but hours for it aren't formal. Ask at the post office across the street, nearby Anderson Store, or simply call one of the names listed on the front door for access.

A fun time to visit New Sweden is during the **Midsommar** festival, on the closest weekend to Midsummer Day (June 21), when most sites are open for tours and residents don traditional Swedish costumes and celebrate the year's longest day. Activities include decorating a maypole, Swedish dancing, a smorgasbord, concerts, and a prayer service. Non-Scandinavians are welcome to join in, but you'll need to plan way ahead; the smorgasbord's two seatings are usually sold out by mid-May.

Frontier Heritage Historical Society

Fort Fairfield's historical society maintains a number of local properties, but few are open except during the annual Potato Festival in July. The **Fort Fairfield Blockhouse Museum** (Main St.) is a 1976 replica of the original, and it's filled with local memorabilia. The **Friends Church Museum** (Rte. 1A), built in 1858 as a Quaker meetinghouse, served as a station on the Underground Railroad during the Civil

The artifacts, memorabilia, and exhibits at the New Sweden Historical Museum reflect the rugged life of the Swedish community here.

© HILARY NANGLE

War. The **Railroad Museum** (Depot St., off Brown St.) comprises locomotives and cars and an 1875 Canadian-Pacific Railroad station. Also on the railroad site is the restored **Black/McIntosh One-Room School House,** built in 1848.

Double Eagle Park

Just beyond the state park access road is a tiny park (Spragueville Rd., Presque Isle) commemorating the launch of the helium balloon *Double Eagle II.* A replica (which has seen better days) honors the first transatlantic balloon flight in August 1978, when a crew of three made the Presque Isle–France passage in approximately 137 hours. (The first solo transatlantic balloon flight, six years later, took off from Caribou.)

Scenic Routes

With so much open space in The County, particularly in the Potato Triangle, drivers and bicyclists can enjoy great long vistas. One route, a favorite of Senator Susan Collins, who ought to know, is **Route 164** between Caribou and Presque Isle, half of it along the Aroostook River. (Locals call it the Back Presque Isle Road; it's also the Washburn Road and the Caribou Road—just to make things totally confusing.) On the way, you can check out the museums in Washburn, detour on the multiuse trail, or loop out on Route 228 and visit the Woods Edge Gallery in Perham.

Another scenic drive is **Route 167,** between Presque Isle and Fort Fairfield; the 12-mile stretch is especially dramatic in mid-July when the rolling fields are draped with pink and white potato blossoms and Fort Fairfield puts on its annual Potato Blossom Festival.

RECREATION
◖ Aroostook State Park

Aroostook State Park (State Park Rd., Presque Isle, 207/768-8341, www.parksandlands.com, $3 nonresident adults, $2 Maine resident adults, $1 ages 5–11 and nonresident seniors) has the distinction of being Maine's first state park, created in 1939, when inspired citizens

of Presque Isle donated 100 acres of land to the state. The park has grown significantly since then; it now comprises 904 acres, encompassing Quaggy Jo Mountain and Echo Lake and providing plentiful opportunities for hiking, water sports, snow sports, camping, and more. Quaggy Jo comes from the Micmac word *quaquajo,* which translates as "twin-peaked." Allow 2–3 hours for the moderate (with steep sections) three-mile hike (clockwise) via the North Peak, North-South Peak Ridge, and South Peak Trails to take in both summits; the views, especially from North Peak, are superb. After hiking, have a lakeside picnic and then cool off with a swim or fish for brook trout. Public boat access is available, as are canoe and paddleboat rentals ($3 per hour). Call it a night at one of 30 campsites. The park is equally inviting in winter, when a selection of trails are open for cross-country skiing. These range from the one-mile Novice Trail to the four-mile Quaggy Jo Mountain Trail, which is best for advanced skiers. Groomed snowmobile trails also pass through the park. The park is open daily mid-May–mid-October. The gate is 1.5 miles west of Route 1, five miles south of downtown Presque Isle.

Goughan's Farm

Goughan's (872 Fort Fairfield Rd./Rte. 161, Caribou, 207/498-6565, 8 A.M.–5 P.M. daily Mar.–mid-Dec.) has a bit of everything, depending on when you show up. Goughan's (pronounced GAWNS) has maple syrup in spring; pick-your-own strawberries, raspberries, string beans, and peas in summer; buy apples and choose-your-own pumpkins in fall; and Christmas wreaths and trees in winter. Kids can feed and pet the farm animals, ride the carousel, and get delicious homemade ice cream and pie at the dairy bar.

Aroostook National Wildlife Refuge

Nearly 5,000 acres encompassing grasslands, forests, 10 ponds, two brooks, and one stream of the Cold War–era Loring Air Force Base have found new life as Aroostook National Wildlife Refuge (97 Refuge Rd., Limestone, 207/328-4634). Established in 1998, the refuge is still actively restoring habitat by removing buildings, railroad tracks, and fencing as well as restoring wetlands. Seven trails, ranging 0.12–1.9 miles, provide excellent wildlife viewing, especially early in the morning or late in the evening. According to the Friends of Aroostook National Wildlife Refuge (www.friendsofaroostooknwr.org), Aroostook County supports the largest density of moose and black bears in the Lower 48, and sightings of each are a daily occurrence on the refuge. Migratory songbirds nest here in spring and summer, and various ducks, Canada geese, woodcocks, and ruffled grouse are also frequently sighted. Stop at the visitors center on Refuge Road to pick up simple maps of the system. The refuge is off Route 89, eight miles east of Caribou, five miles west of Limestone. Trails are open sunrise–sunset daily; visitors center hours are limited, so call.

◀ Woodland Bog Preserve

About six miles west of Caribou, Woodland Bog Preserve, a 265-acre Nature Conservancy property, is home to several rare orchid species and dozens of bird species (nearly 90 have been banded here). Mid-May–mid-July, Perham resident Richard Clark—the Nature Conservancy's on-site steward—leads fascinating free walks through this bog (technically, a calcareous fen surrounded by a cedar swamp) as well as the 200-acre **Perham Bog Preserve.** Clark also leads walks in **Salmon Brook Lake Bog,** 1,850 acres bought by the state under the Land for Maine's Future program. To set up a time, call Clark (207/455-8359 days or 207/455-8060 evenings and Mon.). Wear waterproof shoes and insect repellent. Dedicated environmentalists, Richard and his wife, Susan, have donated an easement on a 135-acre parcel that connects two sections of the state's land. Note that these preserves have extremely fragile ecosystems, so don't even consider visiting them on your own.

Multiuse Trails

In downtown Caribou, a 1.23-mile loop circles around **Collins Pond,** an old millpond and waterfall downtown. Walk or bike the path through a town park, with a picnic area, beside ball fields, and along city sidewalks. It passes through wetlands populated by muskrat, moose, red-winged blackbirds, and other species; bring binoculars and head out in the early morning or before sunset for the best wildlife spotting.

BANGOR-AROOSTOOK VALLEY TRAILS

Led by the Caribou Recreation Department, several volunteer groups have worked to open up more than 80 miles of abandoned railroad beds for year-round use by bikers, hikers, snowmobilers, all-terrain vehicles, and cross-country skiers. The trails are mostly packed gravel, so you'll want a mountain bike. The prettiest and most rural section of this impressive network begins in Washburn and ends in Stockholm (40 miles one-way), including a short stretch through the Woodland Bog. Park in downtown Washburn, and be sure to carry plenty of water. From Caribou, you can go to Stockholm and on to Van Buren (29 miles one-way). Or begin in Carson (just west of Caribou) and go to New Sweden (9 miles one-way).

Biking and Roller-Skiing

Mojo (719 Main St., Presque Isle, 207/760-9500, www.melsmojo.com) rents bikes ($15 per day) and kayaks ($25 per day). It also organizes a series of organized rides, including women's rides, family rides, and trips for serious cyclists.

Twenty miles of marked world-class mountain-biking trails are available free at the **Maine Nordic Heritage Center** (Nordic Heritage Access Rd., off Rte. 167, Presque Isle, 207/492-1444, www.mainewsc.org), part of the Maine Winter Sports Center. Also here is a 0.6-mile paved roller-ski loop. Afterward, finish up with a sauna in the lodge.

Golf

Check out the 18-hole **Presque Isle Country Club** (Rte. 205/Parkhurst Siding Rd., Presque

Isle, 207/764-0430 or 207/769-7431, www.picountryclub.com). Another easy-on-the-budget choice is the 18-hole **Mars Hill Country Club** (75 Country Club Rd., Mars Hill, 207/425-4802, www.golfmhcc.com).

Water Sports

Swim, fish, hike, bike, boat, picnic, camp, and play at 85-acre **Trafton Lake Recreation Area** (Ward Rd., Limestone, 207/325-4025).

Paddle the Aroostook River from Washburn to Presque Isle, an easy-going 12-mile trip on calm water. **Perception of Aroostook** (9 Caribou Rd./Rte. 1, Presque Isle, 207/764-5506, www.perceptionofaroostook.com) rents canoes and kayaks and will provide shuttles. It also offers ecological paddling tours and fishing trips, with rates varying by adventure.

Fitness and Recreation Center

Weather not cooperating for outdoor fun? Inside **Caroline D. Gentile Hall** (University of Maine at Presque Isle campus, 207/768-9772, www.umpi.maine.edu) are a walking and running track, a gym, a 37-foot rock wall and bouldering wall, strength machines and free weights, cardio trainers, and a pool. A day pass is $7 adults, $4 under age 14.

Winter Sports

It's no surprise, given the Swedish ancestry prevalent in this area, that cross-country skiing is part of the region's heritage. Helping to keep it alive and grow is the **Maine Nordic Heritage Center** (Nordic Heritage Access Rd., off Rte. 167, Presque Isle, 207/492-1444, www.mainewsc.org), part of the Maine Winter Sports Center. The center is considered one of the world's best internationally licensed cross-country facilities, and it has hosted international biathlon and cross-country races. This is a full biathlon facility, with 30 shooting stations. Also on the premises is a lighted roller-ski loop and a sauna. Best of all, it's free.

If alpine skiing is your preference, the center also operates the adjacent **Quaggy Joe Ski Area** (Rte. 167, Presque Isle, 207/764-3016) and the **Big Rock Ski Area** (Graves Rd., Mars Hill, 207/328-0991, www.bigrockmaine.com). Quaggy Joe is tiny, with only a T-bar serving its 218-foot vertical range, but it's very inexpensive. Big Rock is a good-size community ski area with five lifts (a triple chair, a double chair, and three tows) and 28 trails and glades, a terrain park, and a tubing park on a 980-foot vertical range. Although the area averages 160 inches of snow, 80 percent of the terrain is covered by snowmaking. About 55 percent is open for night skiing. Big Rock has a ski school; a café serving grilled foods, homemade soups, and sandwiches; and a rental shop. Also on the premises are about six miles of cross-country trails and a snowshoe trail. The area is open Wednesday–Sunday as well as holidays and school vacation periods. An adult weekend ticket is $30, ages 65–74 and 6–17 are $25.

Snowmobile rentals are available at **The Sled Shop** (108 Main St., Presque Isle, 207/764-2900, www.thesledshopinc.com). Rates begin at $200 per day. Links to local snowmobile clubs are on its website.

ENTERTAINMENT AND EVENTS

One of The County's biggest wingdings is the **Maine Potato Blossom Festival** held in Fort Fairfield in mid-July. Pageantry, potatoes, crafts, potatoes, entertainment, potatoes, fireworks, and potatoes.

Agriculture exhibits, harness racing, live entertainment, and fireworks are all part of Presque Isle's **Northern Maine Fair,** the biggest country fair in this part of Maine, the first full week of August.

SHOPPING

About 11 miles west of Caribou, the **Woods Edge Gallery** (High Meadow Rd., Perham, 207/455-8359, 1–5 P.M. Tues.–Sat. year-round) devotes almost 1,000 feet of exhibit space to watercolor and acrylic landscapes, plus photography—mostly by Aroostook County artists. The gallery is 1.25 miles west of Route 228. Gallery owner Richard Clark, steward for the Nature Conservancy's nearby Woodland Bog, also leads seasonal nature tours there.

Monica's Scandinavian Imports (176 Sweden St., Caribou, 207/493-4600) is chock-full of imported goods, from linens to clothing, cheese, and jewelry.

ACCOMMODATIONS

Lodging choices are few in the area, so it's smart to have advance reservations.

Bed-and-Breakfasts

Art professor Clifton Boudman and his wife, Judith, put out an unforgettable spread—a Scottish breakfast—when you stay at the **Rum Rapids Inn** (Rte. 164/Rum Rapids Dr., Crouseville, 207/455-8096, www.rumrapidsinn.com, $89), a beautifully furnished 1839 house. By prior arrangement, an elegant multi-course candlelight dinner ($38–48, BYOB) is available, but the Boudmans now concentrate their culinary efforts on Café Sopresso, which they also own. In summer, relax on the deck overlooking Rum Rapids; in winter, cross-country ski on the Boudmans' 15 acres and afterward soak in the whirlpool spa. Guests have free use of bikes, cross-country skis, and tennis rackets. Two guest rooms have TVs and video players as well as Wi-Fi. The inn is five miles northwest of Presque Isle; watch for a tiny sign on the left.

Within walking distance of downtown Caribou sights and restaurants, the **Old Iron Inn B&B** (155 High St., Caribou, 207/492-4766, www.oldironinn.com, $79) comes by its name honestly. Hundreds of antique irons are displayed through the in-town 1913 arts and crafts–style house, and geology professor Kevin McCartney can recount the background of each one. Four guest rooms, two with private baths, are comfortably furnished with quilts and oak antiques. A small office has a fax machine, a fridge, a TV, and a video collection; Wi-Fi is available. Settle into the living room with a choice from the extensive magazine selections or choose a good read—plenty of mysteries, along with Lincoln and aviation libraries—from the well-stocked bookcases. Known for her culinary talent, Kate McCartney serves a delicious breakfast in the

Victorian dining room. Ask Kevin about the Maine Solar System or the Science Museum at UMPI, both of which he developed—a clever and industrious fellow he.

Motels

Patronized primarily for its convenient downtown site, **The Northeastland Hotel** (436 Main St., Presque Isle, 207/768-5321 or 800/244-5321 in Maine, www.mainerec.com/eastland.shtml, $97–103), dating from 1934, has 50 guest rooms with air-conditioning, TVs, Wi-Fi, and phones. Pets are not allowed; children 12 and under stay free.

The 148-room **Presque Isle Inn and Convention Center** (Rte. 1, Presque Isle, 207/764-3321 or 800/533-3971, www.presqueisleinn.com, $89–150) is a bit tired, but it's the area's best full-service lodging. Amenities include a restaurant, a health club, an indoor pool, an on-site coin laundry, Wi-Fi, and cable TV. The bar is a popular local rendezvous spot, and there's live entertainment on weekends in the lounge. Some rooms have kitchenettes. In winter, when the parking lot has more snowmobiles than cars, don't even think about arriving sans reservation. Pets are welcome.

Just south of town, the two-story **Caribou Inn and Convention Center** (Rte. 1, Caribou, 207/498-3733, www.caribouinn.com, $110–150), a sister property of the Presque Isle Inn, has 73 large, comfortable guest rooms and suites with air-conditioning, cable TV, Wi-Fi, and refrigerators (suites have kitchenettes). Facilities include an indoor pool, a health club, a restaurant, and a coin-op laundry. (Request a room away from the pool area.) Kids under age 13 stay free.

Russell's Motel (357 Main St., Caribou, 207/498-2567, www.connectmaine.com/russells, $61) is a vintage motel that provides a lot of bang for the buck. The paneled rooms have TVs, air-conditioning, fridges, microwaves, and Wi-Fi. Long distance calls are free, and kids under age 12 stay free.

Camping

Campsites at **Aroostook State Park** (State Park Rd., Presque Isle, 207/768-8341, www

.parksandlands.com) are $20 for nonresidents, $15 for Maine residents. Sites are wooded and close to Echo Lake. Campers have a new shower house with free hot showers and a new cookhouse with a cookstove, a sink for washing dishes, picnic tables, and a cabinet of games. To be sure of a campsite on summer weekends, make reservations online (www.campwithme .com) or by phone (207/624-9950 out of state or 800/332-1501 in Maine; MasterCard or Visa required) at least two weeks ahead; there is a two-night minimum for reservations.

The 24 lakefront campsites at **Trafton Lake Campground** (Ward Rd., Limestone, 207/325-4025, late May–mid-Sept.) have full hookups and are $20 per day, $110 per week. The 10 tent sites are $10 per day or $60 per week. The campground is 2.5 miles off Route 89.

FOOD

As with other parts of Maine, Aroostook County has frequent **public suppers** throughout the summer. Visitors are welcome, even encouraged (most suppers benefit a good cause), so check the papers, line up early, and enjoy the local food and color.

Restaurant hours noted are for peak season but are subject to change. It's always wise to call ahead.

Mars Hill

For a guaranteed dose of local color—and decent food besides—pull up at **Al's Diner** (87 Main St./Rte. 1, Mars Hill, 207/429-8186, 5 A.M.–8 P.M. Mon.–Thurs., 5 A.M.–9 P.M. Fri.–Sat., 6 A.M.–9 P.M. Sun., $6–14), a friendly village restaurant that started as an ice cream shop in 1937. The third generation is now running the place. For breakfast, try the Aroostook omelet, made with potatoes, of course.

Presque Isle

Here's a welcome change to the usual deep-fried and family fare: **☾ Café Sorpreso** (415 Main St., Presque Isle, 207/764-1854, dinner entrées $13–25) is an inviting, contemporary downtown restaurant with a menu that changes weekly and emphasizes fresh and,

when possible, local Maine foods. Expect full entrées as well as smaller bistro plates ($13–23). It's owned and operated by Clifton and Judy Boudman of the Rum Rapids Inn, who expanded their dining endeavors when demand exceeded dining capacity at their B&B.

Where can you get a bowl of gourmet lobster stew in February? At **Winnie's Restaurant and Dairy Bar** (79 Parsons St., Presque Isle, 207/769-4971, 10:30 A.M.–9 P.M. daily year-round, $3–17). The restaurant's delicious lobster stew became so famous for being "the real thing" (with no fillers) that then-owner Patty Leblanc made it into a business of its own in 1999 (Winnie was the first owner in the 1940s), but the stew is still served here. Also known for its Winnie's burgers, this is a supercasual, call-your-number kind of place, with food served in plastic containers and by carhops on summer evenings. It's always thronged with locals; in winter, snowmobilers arrive en masse, so be prepared to wait.

Despite its name, the **Riverside Inn Restaurant** (399 Main St., Presque Isle, 207/764-1447, 5 A.M.–3 P.M. Mon.–Wed., 5 A.M.–7 P.M. Thurs. and Sat., 5 A.M.–8 P.M. Fri., 6 A.M.–3 P.M. Sun., $5–12) doesn't have a river view. It's a cozy neighborhood place with perhaps a dozen booths, a four-stool counter, and a glass case filled with home-baked goodies, including doughnuts and cookies. Breakfast is served all day along with the usual home-style fare. It's in downtown Presque Isle close to Riverside Park and set back from the street.

Corned beef and cabbage, shepherd's pie, bangers and mash, and fish-and-chips are nightly dinner specials at the **Irish Setter Pub** (710 Main St., 207/764-5400, 11 A.M.–11 P.M. Mon.–Sat., $7–13), a congenial and popular spot just north of downtown.

Lunch in an arts center? Why not: The **Wintergreen Arts Center** (149 State St., 11 A.M.–2 P.M. Tues.–Fri.) serves lunch. While there, check out what's on exhibit; there might also be children's programs in progress. All profits support the center.

Stock up on picnic goodies at the **Presque Isle Farmers Market** (9 A.M.–1 P.M. Sat.

mid-May–mid-Oct.) held in the Sears parking area at the Aroostook Centre Mall. The market is The County's largest, with a good-size crowd of vendors setting up shop.

Caribou

An extremely loyal clientele makes unpretentious **Frederick's Southside** (217 S. Main St., Caribou, 207/498-3464, 11 A.M.–8 P.M. Tues.–Sat., noon–8 P.M. Sun.) busy most of the time. Inexpensive home cooking is the draw.

Craving Asian? **The Far East Kitchen** (159 Bennett Dr., Caribou, 207/493-7858, 11 A.M.–7 P.M. Mon.–Fri., noon–7 P.M. Sat.) does a creditable job with noodle dishes.

Fort Fairfield

Wander well off the beaten path for an enchanted evening at ◖ **Canterbury Royale** (182 Sam Everett Rd., 207/472-4910), a destination-dining experience. Guests are immersed in an Old World European setting for elegant seven-course diners Tuesday–Saturday featuring haute French cuisine served in a private dining room. You're provided a menu in advance, from which you choose the entrée from among nearly 20 choices, and then half-sisters and classically trained chefs Barbara Boucher and Renee O'Neill choose the other courses. The setting, presentation, and food are sublime. Tables are set with crystal, silver, elaborate candelabras, and marble accents. Some furnishings and the elaborate, decorative woodwork were hand-carved by Renee. Cost varies with menu choices, ranging $37–100 pp, plus tax, tip, and wine. Plan far in advance, as only two parties are seated each evening. Reservations are required, and jeans, T-shirts, shorts, or sneakers are not allowed. The restaurant also offers European-style five-course brunches for $25 pp.

Good food at a fair price keeps locals returning to **Boondock's Grille** (294 Main St., 207/472-6074, 11 A.M.–8 P.M. Tues.–Thurs., 11 A.M.–9 P.M. Fri.–Sat.), another home-style gem with prices in the $6–15 range.

Stockholm

Time a visit to the Swedish Colony to enjoy a meal at **Eureka Hall** (5 School St., Stockholm, 207/896-3196, 4:30–9 P.M. Thurs.–Sat., 8–11:30 A.M. Sun., $6–18), serving American fare in a sit-down setting upstairs and pizza and subs downstairs.

INFORMATION AND SERVICES

Local info is available from the **Presque Isle Area Chamber of Commerce** (3 Houlton Rd./Rte. 1, Presque Isle, 207/764-6561 or 800/764-7420, www.pichamber.com) and the **Caribou Chamber of Commerce** (24 Sweden St., Caribou, 207/498-6156 or 800/722-7648, www.caribouchamber.com). Also check out **Caribou Public Library** (30 High St., Caribou, 207/493-4214, www.caribou-public .lib.me.us).

Aroostook County Tourism (888/216-2463, www.visitaroostook.com) has information and Web links for the entire county.

GETTING THERE

US Airways operates daily nonstop flights between Boston's Logan Airport and Northern Maine Regional Airport in Presque Isle (PQI, 650 Airport Dr., 207/764-2550, www.flypresqueisle.com). While at the airport, check out the **Presque Isle Air Museum** (207/764-2542), which displays historical photos and memorabilia from Presque Isle's impressive aviation history in two corridors.

The St. John Valley

Settled by Acadians in 1785, the St. John Valley isn't quite sure whether it should be the 51st state or Canada's 11th province. Valley hallmarks are huge Roman Catholic churches, small riverside communities, unfancy but tidy homes, an eclectic French patois, and a handful of unique culinary specialties—all thanks to a twist of fate.

Henry Wadsworth Longfellow's immortal epic poem *Evangeline* relates a saga of *le grand dérangement,* when more than 10,000 French-speaking Acadians tragically lost their lease on Nova Scotia after the British expelled them for disloyalty in 1755—a date engraved ever since in the minds of their thousands of descendants now living on the American and Canadian sides of the St. John River. (Thousands more of their kin ended up in Louisiana, where Acadian-Cajun traditions also remain strong.)

In this part of Maine, Smiths and Joneses are few—countless residents bear such names as Cyr, Daigle, Gagnon, Michaud, Ouellette, Pelletier, Sirois, and Thibodeau. In Van Buren, Grand Isle, Madawaska, St. Agatha, and Frenchville, French is the mother tongue for 97 percent of the residents, who refer to the Upper St. John Valley as *chez nous* ("our place"), their homeland. Many roadside and shop signs are bilingual—even the name board for the University of Maine branch in Fort Kent.

Religion is as pervasive an influence as language. When a Madawaska beauty represented Maine in the Miss America contest in 1995, the local *St. John Valley Times* admonished its readers: "Keep your fingers crossed and your rosaries hot."

Since the 1970s, renewed local interest in and appreciation for Acadian culture has spurred cultural projects, celebrations, and genealogical research throughout the valley, with

© TOM NANGLE

AROOSTOOK COUNTY

This Acadian cross marks the reputed landing spot of the St. John Valley's pioneer Acadian families in 1785.

THE BLOODLESS AROOSTOOK WAR

© TOM NANGLE

The Fort Kent Blockhouse was built in 1839 during the U.S.-Canada border dispute known as the Aroostook War.

Aroostook County's major brush with historic notoriety occurred in 1839, with the skirmish known as the Aroostook War. Always described as "bloodless" – since there were no casualties (other than a farmer accidentally downed by friendly fire) – the war was essentially a boundary dispute between Maine and New Brunswick that had simmered since 1784, when New Brunswick was established.

The 1783 Treaty of Paris had set the St. Croix River as the Washington County line, but loopholes left the northernmost border ill-defined. Maine feared losing timber-rich real estate to Canada, and matters heated up when 200 burly militiamen descended on the region in early 1839 to defend the young state's territory. About 3,000 troops ended up supporting the Maine cause, and legendary war hero General Winfield ("Old Fuss and Feathers") Scott was sent to Augusta for three weeks in March 1839 to negotiate the successful truce.

After the "war," Aroostook was incorporated as a county, and by 1842 the Webster-Ashburton Treaty (sometimes also called the Treaty of Washington), negotiated by Daniel Webster and Lord Ashburton, brought a long-awaited peace that opened the area for stepped-up settlement.

Among the remnants of the Aroostook War are two wooden blockhouses, one an original and a National Historic Site, on the banks of the St. John River in Fort Kent, the other a replica on the Aroostook River in Fort Fairfield.

the eventual goal of a National Park Service Acadian culture center. "Valley French," a unique archaic patois long stigmatized in Maine schools, has undergone a revival. Since the 1970s, several valley schools have established bilingual programs, and a 1991 survey estimated that 40 percent of valley schoolchildren speak both English and French.

Controversy erupts periodically over whose lineage is "true" Acadian (as opposed to Québécois—although many Acadians also fled to Québec), but valley residents all turn out en masse for the summer highlight: Madawaska's multiday Acadian Festival, centered on Acadian Day, June 28. It's a local festival unlike any other in Maine. If you plan to visit then, make lodging plans far in advance. Thousands of far-flung descendants of whichever founding family is being honored each year book every room on both sides of the border. The valley is also beginning to gear up for hosting the 2014 Acadian World Congress.

Between Madawaska and Fort Kent, detour off Route 1, via Route 162, into the lovely lake district, locally known as the "back settlements," through the town of St. Agatha (usually pronounced the French way: "Saint a-GAHT") and the village of Sinclair. T-shaped **Long Lake** is the northernmost of the Fish River Chain of Lakes, extending southwest to Eagle Lake.

West of Fort Kent are the tiny and tinier riverside communities of St. John, St. Francis, Allagash, and Dickey, the latter two serving as endpoints for two of Maine's most popular long-distance canoe routes: the St. John River and the Allagash Wilderness Waterway. The town of Allagash, curiously enough, was settled by Irish and English immigrants, so it's not unusual to find lots of Irish surnames in this part of the valley. Contemporary author Cathie Pelletier grew up in Allagash, called "Mattagash" in her entertaining novels of life in northern Maine. Pack up a picnic, allow a couple of hours, and take a jaunt out here in a car or on a bike. In mid-September, one of the best times to be here, the hills on your left are a riot of color all the way to Allagash. On your right, the river usually dribbles along this time of year, exposing gravel bars much of the way. It's a far cry from late winter and spring, when ice jams and spring runoff are the rule.

An excellent companion when touring the St. John Valley is *Voici the Valley Cultureway,* an guidebook and CD that highlights the heritage and sights. It can be purchased locally ($15) or ordered in advance from the **Maine Acadian Heritage Council** (207/728-6826, www.voicithevalley.org).

SIGHTS
◖ Acadian Village

In the hamlet of Keegan, about two miles northwest of downtown Van Buren, is a prominent reminder of the heritage in this valley. Begun as a small-scale bicentennial project in 1976, the Acadian Village (Rte. 1, Van Buren, 207/868-5042, www.connectmaine.com/acadianvillage, $6 adults, $3 children, noon–5 P.M. daily June 15–Sept. 15) is a 2.5-acre open-air museum comprising 16 antique and replica

Maine's Acadian heritage is preserved at the Acadian Village in the St. John Valley.

buildings in an A-shaped layout. Included are a country store, a forge, a schoolhouse, a chapel, and several residences. Tours by attentive guides vividly convey the daily struggles of 18th–19th-century Acadians in the valley. Kids particularly enjoy the schoolhouse and the barbershop; outside, there's plenty of letting-off-steam room.

Mount Carmel Museum and Cultural Center

As with the other religion-dominated communities in the valley, the most prominent landmark in the Lille village of Grand Isle (population 569) is the Catholic church, a twin golden-domed building undergoing long-term restoration as a nonprofit bilingual museum and cultural center. Built in 1909, Our Lady of Mount Carmel Church had its first mass on New Year's Day 1910 and its last in 1978. Since historian, preservationist, and renaissance man Don Cyr took over the wooden church in 1984, he has organized concerts and other events under the aegis of the nonprofit Mount Carmel Cultural and Historic Association. He also shares his collection of Acadian antiques and artifacts. The church is usually open noon–4 P.M. Sunday–Friday early June–mid-September. For information, contact Cyr (207/895-3339). While here, walk 100 yards or so down Route 1 to Cyr's new gallery.

(St. David's Historical Sites

As you reach the eastern edge of Madawaska, you can't help but notice the bell tower of the imposing brick neo-Gothic **St. David Catholic Church,** established in 1871. The building, on the National Register of Historic Places, is usually open and has a high arched ceiling, a domed altar, and stained-glass windows.

Just to the right (east) of St. David's is the one-room **Tante Blanche Museum** (Rte. 1, St. David Parish, Madawaska, 207/728-4518, free), containing Acadian artifacts. Run by the Madawaska Historical Society (www.madawaskahistorical.org), the log museum commemorates Marguerite Blanche Thibodeau Cyr ("Tante Blanche"), an Acadian heroine during a 1797 famine. The museum is usually open 11 A.M.–4 P.M. Wednesday–Sunday mid-June–early September; on-site volunteers answer questions and provide guidance. The museum's campus also includes the 1870 **School House No. 1** and the circa 1840 **Albert House.**

Continue down the 0.5-mile gravel road to the riverfront, where a 14-foot-high marble **Acadian Cross** marks the reputed 1785 landing spot of Acadians expelled by the British from Nova Scotia and New Brunswick. During the annual Acadian Festival, the landing is reenacted.

(Fort Kent Blockhouse

Built in 1839 during the decades-long U.S.-Canada border dispute known as the Aroostook War, the Fort Kent Blockhouse (Blockhouse Rd., Fort Kent, 9 A.M.–5 P.M. daily late May–early Sept., free), on the National Register of Historic Places, is the only remnant of a complex that once included barracks, a hospital, and an ammunition hoard. On the second floor are historic artifacts plus information about the curious "bloodless" border skirmish over timber rights. Bring a picnic and commandeer a table in the pretty little riverside park just below the fort (tent camping is allowed, $4 pp or $10 per carload). Early in the summer, before the river dwindles, you can also launch a canoe or kayak here. The Fort Kent Boy Scouts maintain and staff the blockhouse and the nearby log-cabin gift shop.

Fort Kent Railroad Station

The station, on the National Register of Historic Places, was in service 1902–1979 and was part of the Bangor and Aroostook Railroad's Fish River division. It's now the home of the Fort Kent Historical Society and Gardens (207/834-5258). and is open 1–4 P.M. Tuesday–Friday late June–mid August.

The First Mile

Depending on the direction you travel, the bridge to Canada marks the northern end of Historic U.S. Route 1, with Key West, Florida, anchoring the southern end. You are 318 miles north of Portland, 368 miles north of the New Hampshire border at Kittery, and 2,209 miles north of Key West.

St. Agatha Historical House and Preservation Center

Wow! For a tiny town (population about 800), St. Agatha has one heck of a museum (433 Main St., St. Agatha, 207/543-6911, 1–4 P.M. Tues.–Sun. mid June–early Sept., donation). Volunteers assist guests touring both the oldest house in town and the museum, which is chock-full of interesting artifacts and exhibits (carvings, textiles, farm equipment, religious and school goods, and much more). It's easy to while away an hour or so here.

University of Maine at Fort Kent

Founded in 1878 as a teacher-training school, the University of Maine at Fort Kent (UMFK, 25 Pleasant St., Fort Kent, 207/834-7500, www.umfk.maine.edu) still prides itself on the quality of its teacher-education program. Because of its location in the Upper St. John Valley, UMFK also offers a BS degree in bilingual and bicultural studies, and the school's **Acadian Archives** (207/834-7535, www.umfk.maine.edu/archives) are the state's best resource on Maine's Acadian heritage.

RECREATION
Parks and Preserves
FISH RIVER FALLS

An idyllic setting for a picnic, Fish River Falls is a bit of a local secret, since finding it isn't easy. Take Route 162 south, and when you see Bouchard Family Farms (which grows acres of buckwheat for *ployes,* a traditional Acadian pancake), bear right on Strip Road; watch for Airport Road on the right. There's a small sign noting falls access. Once you get to the parking area, the falls are a 10-minute stroll slightly downhill. Carry a picnic and sit on the rocks, which have great wells formed by grinding boulders.

DEBOULLIE PUBLIC RESERVE LANDS

Wildlife-watchers, hikers, anglers, campers, snowmobilers, and pretty much anyone who enjoys the great outdoors will appreciate the 22,000-acre Deboullie Public Reserve Lands (207/435-7963, www.parksandlands.com). Wildlife-watching is excellent throughout the reserve thanks to varied habitats that include ponds, streams, marshes, and woodlands. Watch for deer and moose, beavers and snowshoe hares, loons and bald eagles. While the northern three-quarters of the preserve is gently rolling forested ridges, the southern quarter has mountains to climb and ponds for boating and fishing. Brook trout are abundant in most of the ponds; landlocked salmon can be hooked in Togue Pond. Hike Deboullie Mountain to the inactive fire station at the top for panoramic views of the region. Along the route, keep an eye out for ice caves, deep crevices in the rocks where ice can remain year-round. Allow at least four hours for the six-mile hike. Primitive waterfront campsites dot the preserve, but for those who prefer a roof over their heads, Red River Camps (www.redrivercamps.com) is a traditional sporting camp on Island Pond. Debouillie gives meaning to the word *remote.* It's about 30 rugged miles southwest of Fort Kent. Access is via the North Maine Woods (www.northmainewoods.org) checkpoint in St. Francis. The name Deboullie, by the way, is derived from a French term meaning "rock slides."

Multiuse Trail

The 17-mile crushed-stone **Saint John Valley Heritage Trail** edges the south bank of the St. John River between Fort Kent and St. Francis and connects with area ATV and snowmobile trails. It's also part of the National Park Service's Acadian interpretation efforts.

Canoeing the Allagash and St. John Rivers

Shuttles, pickups, food, and very basic lodgings are all available in Allagash and Dickey, the endpoints for many Allagash and St. John Rivers paddlers. A good resource is **Northern Forest Canoe Trail** (www.northernforestcanoetrail.org).

Canoeists paddle the St. John River, which divides Maine's St. John Valley from New Brunswick, Canada.

Golf

The Bangor and Aroostook Railroad line runs right through the first and ninth holes at the **Fort Kent Golf Club** (St. John Rd./Rte. 161, Fort Kent, 207/834-3149). The nine-hole hilly course has dynamite views of the St. John River. The attractive clubhouse has a bar and light meals.

The ninth hole at the nine-hole **Birch Point Country Club** (Birch Point Rd., St. David, 207/895-6957) has the distinction of being New England's northernmost golfing hole. The clubhouse has a bar and a basic food menu; cart rentals are available.

Swimming and Canoeing

Birch Point Beach (Chapel Rd., St. David, on the east side of Long Lake; turnoff to the beach at St. Michael's Chapel) has a small grassy area with picnic tables; the lake views are fantastic.

A lovely **picnic and recreation area** (Rte. 162, St. Agatha) on the western shore of Long Lake has a boat launch, a beach, grills, and restrooms.

Winter Sports

CROSS-COUNTRY SKIING

One of the top cross-country skiing facilities in the world, **The 10th Mountain Center** (Paradise Circle Rd., Fort Kent, 207/834-6203, www.10thmtskiclub.org, free) has hosted World Cup Biathlon events. Another of the successful Maine Winter Sports Center facilities, this one has a biathlon and cross-country facility, with 7.5 miles of biathlon trails, plus an additional 16 miles of cross-country trails, a lighted roller-ski loop, a wax building, a stadium, and a full biathlon range with 30 shooting stations. Snowshoes and pets are permitted on 1.4-mile Volunteer's Way, also known as the Pet Loop. The lodge, with a sauna and a fireplace, is a comfy place to relax after a day on the trails. The center's access road is 1.6 miles south of downtown Fort Kent off Route 1.

ALPINE SKIING

Just a couple of blocks off Main Street is **Lonesome Pine Trails** (Forest Ave., Fort Kent, 207/834-5202, www.lonesomepines.org), a volunteer-run community hill with a 500-foot vertical drop served by two tows; there is also night skiing. Adult tickets are $20 full-day, $15 half-day.

SNOWMOBILING

This is prime sledding country. The best resource for trail info is **Fort Kent SnoRiders** (www.fortkentsnoriders.com). At **Top of Maine Rentals** (379 Aroostook Rd./Rte. 11, Fort Kent, 207/834-3095) expect to pay around $175 for a one-day rental.

EVENTS

Spectators crowd the snowy streets to watch Fort Kent's five-day March **Can Am Crown International Sled Dog Races** (http://can-am.sjv.net). Special locations offer vantage points for watching teams competing in races for 30, 60, and 250 miles. A mushers' award ceremony is the finale.

Madawaska hosts the Franco-American **Acadian Festival,** with a historical reenactment, tournaments, a fishing derby, Acadian food, music and dancing, a parade, and a featured-family reunion late in June.

ACCOMMODATIONS

Lodging options are slim on this side of the border.

Van Buren

The circa 1969 **Aroostook Hospitality Inn** (95 Main St., Van Buren, 207/455-8567, www.aroostookhospitalityinn.com, from $75) was completely renovated in 2009 and now welcomes guests with new furnishings and fixtures. Manager Scott Cormier aims to please, and rates include a nice continental breakfast. Guests have access to a huge gathering room with a fireplace—nice for a winter's eve. Guest rooms have refrigerators, air-conditioning, and Wi-Fi. It's walking distance to downtown shops and restaurants.

Madawaska

The **Long Lake Motor Inn** (596 Main St./Rte. 162, St. Agatha, 207/543-5006, www.stagatha .com/longlake, $70) has 18 guest rooms with phones and cable TV, 11 with lake views (and great sunrises), two with kitchenettes. Continental breakfast is included. If you're here in winter, reserve well ahead or the snowmobilers will beat you to it.

The **Lakeview Camping Resort** (9 Lakeview Dr., St. Agatha, 207/543-6331, www.lakeviewrestaurant.biz) has 100 mostly wooded sites, with areas for RVs ($24–33 d) and tents ($19 d). Also on-site are a convenience store, a shower house, and a restaurant.

Fort Kent

Clean, comfortable, and inexpensive, the downtown ◖ **Northern Door Inn** (356 W. Main St., Fort Kent, 207/834-3133 or 866/834-3133, www.northerndoorinn.com, $76–82) has a nice gathering area in the lobby, where a continental breakfast is served. Rooms have air-conditioning, phones, TVs, and Wi-Fi. Pets are $5 each per night.

The fanciest lodging in the region is a the **Four Seasons Inn of Soldier Pond** (13 Church St., Wallagrass, 207/834-4722, www .fourseasonsinnofsoldierpond.com, $99–199), a renovated merchant's house overlooking the Fishkill River about 15 minutes south of Fort Kent. A lot of thought went into the renovations; every room has air conditioning, Wi-Fi, plush bedding, robes, and flat-screen TVs; some have jetted tubs and river views. Public spaces include a formal parlor, a comfy library, a guest pantry, and a gazebo by the river. The innkeeper doesn't live on the premises.

FOOD

Be sure to check local papers and bulletin boards for notices about **public suppers,** an inexpensive way to break bread with the locals.

The restaurant hours noted are for peak season but are subject to change. It's always wise to call ahead.

Van Buren

Here's a nice surprise: **Robin's Restaurant** (44 Main St., Van Buren, 207/868-3044, 10 A.M.–7 P.M. Mon.–Thurs., 10 A.M.–8 P.M.

AROOSTOOK COUNTY

Fri.–Sat., 8 A.M.–7 P.M. Sun., $3–14), a welcoming family-owned and operated downtown spot serving all meals daily, has a menu that ranges from burgers and pizzas to pork chops and lobster Alfredo.

Frenchville

Roughly 11 miles west of Madawaska, on Route 1 North, you'll find Frenchville. If you arrive in time for lunch or dinner, stop in at **Rosette's Restaurant** (240 Main St./Rte. 1, Frenchville, 207/543-7759, 10:30 A.M.–8 P.M. Tues.–Thurs., 7 A.M.–9 P.M. Fri.–Sat., 7 A.M.–8 P.M. Sun., $3–20), a valley favorite. Almost everything's homemade, prices are very reasonable, and the color is local; expect to hear a mix of French and English.

Ask anyone in the valley: When it comes to *ployes, creton* (a meat spread) and chicken stew, no one does it better than (**Dolly's** (Rte. 1, Frenchville, 207/728-7050, 7 A.M.–8 P.M. Wed.–Mon., 7 A.M.–8:30 P.M. Fri.–Sat., $4–18).

St. Agatha

When it's time for a meal, head up the hill for the best panorama in town at **The Lakeview Restaurant** (9 Lakeview Dr., St. Agatha, 207/543-6331, www.lakeviewrestaurant.biz, 11 A.M.–9 P.M. Mon.–Fri., 7 A.M.–9 P.M. Sat.–Sun., $3–20). An awning-covered deck has sweeping views over Long Lake; indoor booths and tables have plenty of visibility. The wide-ranging menu has a choice and price for every taste and budget. A big surge occurs after 5 P.M. mass lets out on Saturday, so don't plan to eat early. Lakeview doesn't take reservations.

The best view in the village of **Sinclair,** about six miles down the road from St. Agatha, is at the **Long Lake Sporting Club Resort** (Rte. 162, Sinclair, 207/543-7584 or 800/431-7584, 5–9 P.M. Mon.–Sat., noon–8 P.M. Sun. July–Aug., 5–9 P.M. Tues.–Sat., noon–8 P.M. Sun. the Sept.–June). In the middle of nowhere, this informal place is almost always crowded. In summer, guests come by boat or car, occasionally by floatplane; in winter, they arrive by snowmobile. The deck has a

fabulous view over Long Lake. Huge steaks and giant lobsters are specialties, and all meals come with *ployes,* Acadian buckwheat pancakes typically served with an artery-clogging pâté called *creton.* Settle in the lounge, choose from six entrées ($10–19, except lobster), and you'll be ushered to your table when it's all ready. If you're ready to party, there's live music Saturday night, but be prepared for plenty of noise.

Fort Kent

Rock's Family Diner (W. Main St., 207/834-2888, 6 A.M.–7 P.M. daily), a local favorite since 1945, serves inexpensive sandwiches, burgers, and fried foods for lunch and dinner and the usuals for breakfast.

Almost everything at **The Swamp Buck** (250 W. Main St./Rte. 1, Fort Kent, 207/834-3055, 11 A.M.–9 P.M. daily, $10–24) is made from scratch. Prime rib is the specialty, but the menu ranges from burgers to blackened haddock, and there's a kids menu too.

Walk into **Doris's Cafe** (345 Market St./Rte. 161, Fort Kent Mills, 207/834-6262, 5 A.M.–2 P.M. Mon.–Fri., 5 A.M.–noon Sat.), and conversation ceases as every head in the place turns to see the stranger. Not to worry; chatter quickly resumes—and you can catch all the local gossip. If you've never had *poutine* (French fries smothered with gravy and cheese), you can order it here.

INFORMATION AND SERVICES

For local information, check with the **Greater Madawaska Chamber of Commerce** (356 Main St./Rte. 1, Madawaska, 207/728-7000, www.greatermadawaskachamber.com) and the **Greater Fort Kent Area Chamber of Commerce** (76 W. Main St./Rte. 1, Fort Kent, 207/834-5354 or 800/733-3563, www.fortkentchamber.com), which serves as a clearinghouse for much of the Upper St. John Valley.

Aroostook County Tourism (888/216-2463, www.visitaroostook.com) has information and Web links for the entire county. It also publishes the annual **Northern Maine Snowmobile Trail Map,** a must-have for sledders in The County.

The 1994 National Park Service publication *Acadian Culture in Maine* is available online at http://acim.umfk.maine.edu.

GETTING AROUND

If you're planning to pass through one of the three U.S.-Canada border stations, be sure to have the proper identification and paperwork. For crossings into the United States, see www.cbp.gov. For crossings into Canada, see www.cbsa-asfc.gc.ca. Remember that New Brunswick is on Atlantic time, an hour later than eastern time.

The **U.S. Customs office** maintains offices in Van Buren (207/868-3391), Madawaska (207/728-4376), and Fort Kent (207/834-5255). All are open 24 hours daily.

South from the Peak of the Crown

The rolling farmlands of northern Aroostook give way to forests and mountains as you drive south on Route 11 from Fort Kent. If you took a poll among those who know, especially photographers, the stretch from Fort Kent through Eagle Lake to Portage would probably rank near the top as a favorite fall foliage drive. What's so appealing along this 37-mile Scenic Highway? Brilliant colors, rolling hills, open vistas, and a smattering of lakes and ponds are truly stunning, either by car or on a bike.

Through the years, **Eagle Lake** has benefited heavily from being the hometown of John Martin, one of Maine's most influential politicians, who served an unprecedented 10 terms as speaker of Maine's House of Representatives. The town really looks as though someone has been paying attention. The official rest area, overlooking the lake, has picnic tables and plenty of parking. Many a photo has been snapped here. If it's a typically bright fall day, you'll see why: It's a prime hilltop with a pristine lake surrounded by multicolored foliage. Eighteen-mile-long L-shaped Eagle Lake is a key link in the Fish River Chain of Lakes, starting at Long Lake in St. Agatha. In winter, the lake supports wall-to-wall ice-fishing shacks.

Portage is particularly popular as a summer playground, and many county residents have built or rented camps on the shores of Portage Lake.

Considered the "Gateway to the North Maine Woods," **Ashland** is the home of North Maine Woods (207/435-6213, www.northmainewoods.org), a private organization charged with managing recreational use of more than 3 million acres of northern Maine's working timberlands. Visit the website to download maps and a detailed brochure or for information on where to go, how to get there, what to do, and where to sleep.

Route 11 continues southward and out of Aroostook County to Patten, Medway, and Millinocket.

SIGHTS

There's not much to see at the open-air **Ashland Logging Museum** (Garfield Rd., Ashland, 207/435-6679, www.townofashland.com), which has six buildings containing a blacksmith shop, old woods rigs, and other gear, but it's worth a quick look-see. For a more in-depth look, make an appointment with curator Ed Chase (207/436-6679). Just before Ashland, when Route 11 takes a sharp left, turn right onto Garfield Road and go a little less than a mile.

RECREATION
Hiking

About eight miles south of Eagle Lake is the wooded **Hedgehog Mountain Rest Area,** trailhead for Hedgehog Mountain. It's not the most exciting climb, and the summit view is so-so, but it's easy exercise for an hour or so. The trail is just over one mile round-trip.

About 10 miles east of Ashland on Route 163 (Presque Isle Rd.) is the trailhead (on the left) for **Haystack Mountain,** a short, steep climb—easy to moderate—to a fairly bald summit. Pack a picnic so you can enjoy the almost 360-degree view.

Golf

Play a round at nine-hole **Portage Hills Country Club** (Portage, 207/435-8221), where the challenges come with the rolling terrain.

Water Sports

Eagle Lake's **town park,** down at lake level, has shorefront picnic tables and grills. The wind kicks up wildly at times, but on a calm day, this is a fine place to launch a canoe. From Route 11, turn at Old Main Street and go 0.6 miles; there's plenty of parking.

From Route 11, turn west at West Cottage Road and go 0.5 miles to reach the Portage **town beach.** The view is fabulous, and parking is ample; there are picnic tables, a grill, and a grassy "beach."

Roughly midway between Ashland and Masardis, in the town of Masardis, is an access road to the boat landing for **Squa Pan Lake,** probably the oddest-shaped lake in the state.

ACCOMMODATIONS

If you'd like to overnight along Route 11, opt for the immaculately maintained **Overlook Motel** (N. Main St./Rte. 11, Eagle Lake, 207/444-4535, www.overlookmotel.com, $72–138), with the same dramatic view as the official rest area. Opened in 1995, it has become one of Route 11's most popular lodgings. Rooms range from one queen bed to three-bedroom apartments. Also available are fully-equipped three-bedroom lakeside cabins ($170). Amenities include phones, air-conditioning, TVs, microwaves, fridges, a coin-op laundry, and use of a canoe, a paddleboat, and a kayak; lake cruises are available. Children 10 and under are free; pets are $5. In winter, snowmobilers pile in.

Route 11 in Portage provides access to **Moose Point Camps** (Fish River Lake, Portage, 207/435-6156, www.moosepoint camps.com), an idyllic spot out of another era with 10 rustic hewn-log cabins on the shore of five-mile-long Fish River Lake (a.k.a. Fish Lake). Rates are $395 per week pp or $85 per day on the American Plan (with all meals), and $80 per week for children under 12. BYOB. Motorboat rentals are $40 per day, including gas; canoes and kayaks are $12 per day. In the main lodge are games, books, and a huge fireplace. It's open for fishing and vacationers early May–late August. Watch for the sign on Route 11 and turn west; it's 17 miles over rugged logging roads to camp. About four miles from Portage, you'll reach the Fish River Checkpoint, the tollbooth for entering the logging area. Round-trip admission is $30 per week for nonresidents, $20 for Maine residents; seniors and kids under 15 are free.

Don't expect to be alone with the moose and other wildlife out here; logging trucks legally own the road, and they know it, so give them a wide berth.

FOOD

The dining room at **Dean's Motor Lodge** (Rte. 11, Portage, 207/435-3701 or 207/435-6840, www.deansmotorlodge.com, $5–18) is a favorite with sportsmen and women. Breakfast is served 5–11 A.M. Monday–Saturday, 7–11 A.M. Sunday, and then the menu changes over, with steak and seafood as the house specialties. Burgers, sandwiches, and pizza are available. Expect to watch NASCAR or sports on the big-screen TV.

MAINE HIGHLANDS

Home to Maine's highest mountain and largest lake, the Maine Highlands region, covering all of Piscataquis County and the northern two-thirds of Penobscot County, typifies Maine's rugged North Woods. Within Piscataquis County are 40-mile-long Moosehead Lake, the appealing frontier town of Greenville, the headwaters of the Allagash Wilderness Waterway, the mile-high Mount Katahdin, and the controlled wilds of Baxter State Park.

Sport hunters and anglers have always frequented the North Woods, and they still do. But hunters, sportfishers, and back-to-the-landers increasingly have to share their untamed turf with a new generation of visitor. Sporting camps originally built for rugged anglers and hunters now welcome photographers, birders, and families; white-water rafting,

canoeing, kayaking, and snowmobiling are all big business; and hikers have found nirvana in a vast network of trails—particularly the huge, carefully monitored trail system in Baxter State Park.

In the 1970s, paper companies were forced by environmental concerns to halt the perilous river-run log drives that took their products to market. This cessation not only cleaned up the rivers but also spared the lives of the hardy breed of men who once made a living unjamming the logs in roiling waters. The alternative now is roads, lots of them, mostly unpaved—a huge network that has opened up the area to more and more outdoors enthusiasts. For generations, paper companies allowed public recreation on their lands and access via their roads, but as they sell off large chunks of wilderness,

© HILARY NANGLE

HIGHLIGHTS

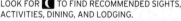 **Patten Lumbermen's Museum:** A visit to this replica of a lumber camp will cure any romantic notions about being a lumberjack (page 442).

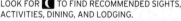 **Ambajejus Boom House:** Paddle or cruise to this artifact from the log-driving era (page 442).

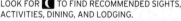 **Hiking in Baxter State Park:** Explore Maine's gem, choosing from more than 200 miles of trails crowned by Katahdin, Maine's tallest peak (page 455).

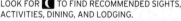 **Cruise on the *Kate*:** See Moosehead Lake from the water on a historic vessel (page 464).

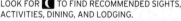 **Kineo:** It's worth the effort to get a close-up view of Kineo's icon cliffs and to hike to its summit (page 465).

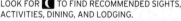 **Moose Safaris:** You can't go home without spotting at least one moose, so go with a guide who knows where they hang out (page 467).

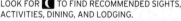 **Gulf Hagas Reserve:** Nicknamed the Grand Canyon of the East, the 3.5-mile-long gorge makes a spectacular hike (page 481).

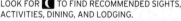 **University of Maine Museum of Art:** Bangor lured the university's collection away from the Orono campus (page 486).

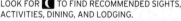 **University of Maine:** The Orono campus is home to a planetarium, gardens, museums, and a performing-arts venue (page 493).

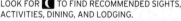 **Penobscot Nation Museum:** Cross the bridge to Indian Island to see this engaging collection of artifacts, videos, and artwork from Maine's Penobscot Native Americans (page 494).

LOOK FOR 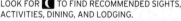 TO FIND RECOMMENDED SIGHTS, ACTIVITIES, DINING, AND LODGING.

the patterns are changing. Some new owners are discontinuing the open-road and open-land policies, and that's a cause for concern among many outdoor-oriented folks.

The area is rich in aquatic possibilities too. Maine's best-known classic canoe trips follow the Allagash and St. John Rivers northward, but no one can even begin to count the other lakes, rivers, and streams that have wonderful canoeing.

Stay at one of this region's primitive forest campsites and you'll really sense the wilderness—owls hoot, loons cry, frogs croak—and yes, insects annoy. No matter how much civilization intrudes, it's still remote and wild. As one writer put it, "Trees grow, die, fall, and rot, never having been seen by anyone. They litter the shores of lakes, form temporary islands, block streams, and quickly eradicate paths."

The air gateway to the region is Bangor, Maine's second-largest city and home to horror maven Stephen King. Between Bangor and nearby Orono, a university town, there's enough "cultcha" to balance the wilderness.

PLANNING YOUR TIME

If you merely want a taste of the wilderness, you can swoop from Bangor up to Millinocket on Route 11, segue over to Greenville on the Golden Road, and back down to Bangor via Monson, Guilford, and Dover-Foxcroft on Route 15 in two days, but if you want to experience it, you'll need time to paddle, hike, and explore—plan on at least a week. Greenville makes a fine base for exploring the region; it's on the edge of the wilderness, within striking distance of Baxter State Park and the Penobscot River, on the shore of Moosehead Lake, and surrounded by endless opportunities for outdoor recreation.

From mid-May–early July, the blackflies are more than annoying. When they begin to wane, the mosquitoes take up the charge. Arm yourself with bug repellent. While DEET is the strongest, I've had excellent results with Lewey's Eco-Blends, an all-natural repellent available widely in Maine. The key is applying it liberally and often. One Baxter Park ranger I spoke with swore by Bounce dryer sheets—place one under a cap and the other under your shirt around the waistline to create a "force field" that keeps the bugs from biting.

Bangor's annual American Folk Festival, in August, is worth planning a visit around, and spending a day or so in Bangor lets you ease into the woods.

Autumn foliage comes early to these parts, with leaves often beginning to turn by early September. While this can be a beautiful time to be in the woods—bugs are few, color is gorgeous—it's also the beginning of hunting season, and it's wise to take precautions.

Winter is cold and usually very snowy, a real plus for cross-country skiing, snowshoeing, and especially snowmobiling.

Most timber-company throughways remain there for all to use, but never forget that the logging trucks *own* them—in more ways than one. As they barrel along, give them room—and some slack as well; you may even be glad they're there, especially if you get lost. The *DeLorme Atlas* is essential for exploring the area, but every time the loggers begin working a new patch, they open new roads, so the cartographers can barely keep up.

Finally, never underestimate the North Woods: Bring versatile clothing (more than you think you'll need), don't strike out alone without telling anyone, stock up on insect repellent and water, use a decent vehicle (4WD if possible), and carry a flashlight, maps, and a compass. Perhaps most important, be a conscientious, eco-sensitive visitor.

Millinocket and Vicinity

Once crucial to the timber industry, Millinocket is fighting for its future. For generations, paper mills provided the major support for the local economy, but major downsizings have left them a shadow of their former selves and have resulted in shrinking populations in the area's towns. Half the locals hope for the resurgence of the local mills and woods-based work; the other half are gung-ho for a tourism-based economy. The latter are pushing to recreate area towns as recreation destinations, and with the seemingly endless sporting opportunities—canoeing, rafting, kayaking, fishing,

hunting, hiking, camping, and more—in the surrounding wilderness, that seems like a smart idea. Developers are circling—real estate here is a bargain—and plans are being filed for building major resorts that take advantage of the spectacular setting and the eco-vacation trend. Controversy is rampant, and local politics are hot.

Millinocket is the closest civilization to Baxter State Park's southern entrance, so most Baxter visitors find themselves here at some time or other. Food, lodging, books, auto fuel, and other essentials are all available. For

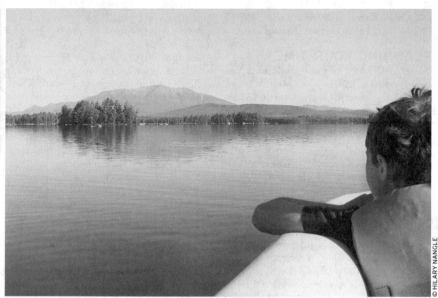

© HILARY NANGLE

Some of the finest views of Katahdin are from the lakes and rivers in its shadow.

a vision of the region's timbering past, wander into the Post Office to view John W. Beauchamp's 1942 oil-on-canvas *Logging in the Maine Woods,* a New Deal mural.

The town of Medway links I-95 with the two mill towns; just to the north on Route 11 are the communities of Sherman, Sherman Station, Patten, and Shin Pond, providing access to the less-used northeast entrance (Matagamon Gate) of Baxter State Park.

SIGHTS
◖ Patten Lumbermen's Museum
About 40 miles northeast of Millinocket, 0.5 miles west of downtown Patten and about 25 miles southeast of Baxter State Park's Matagamon Gate, is a family-oriented museum commemorating the lumberman's grueling life. The nine buildings at the open-air Patten Lumbermen's Museum (Waters Rd./ Rte. 159, Patten, 207/528-2650, www.lumbermensmuseum.org, 10 A.M.–4 P.M. Tues.–Sun. early July–mid-Oct., 10 A.M.–4 P.M. Fri.–Sun. in spring, $8 adults, $7 seniors, $3 ages 6–11)

tell the tale of timber in the 19th and early 20th centuries: cramped quarters, hazardous equipment, rugged terrain, and nasty weather. Lots of working gear and colorful dioramas appeal to children, and there are picnic tables, a snack bar, and room to roam. A summer highlight is the annual **beanhole bean dinner** (beans baked underground overnight), held the second Saturday in August.

◖ Ambajejus Boom House
The only access to the Ambajejus Boom House, a property on Ambajejus Lake that is listed on the National Register of Historic Places, is via boat or snowmobile. You can arrange a cruise with Katahdin Cruises or a canoe rental or guided trip with New England Outdoor Center or do it yourself. It's always open and filled with incredible lumbering-era artifacts. The boom house, erected here in 1906, was used as a rest stop for 65 years by rugged river drivers, lumbermen who "boomed out" (collected with immense chains) and actually rode logs downstream to the sawmills. The meticulous

restoration of the once-derelict house has been done as a personal project by Chuck Harris, a onetime river driver who is often on-site. If you go on your own, launch your boat in Spencer Cove, near Katahdin Air Service, on the west side of the Golden Road, and paddle or motor out and around to the right, to the head of the lake. Stay close to shore, as the wind can pick up unexpectedly. (If you need a canoe, you can rent one across the road at the Big Moose Inn.)

Flightseeing

Based at Ambajejus Lake, about eight miles northwest of Millinocket on the road to Baxter State Park, **Katahdin Air Service (KAS)** (Millinocket, 866/359-6246, www.katahdinair.com) provides access to wilderness locations in every direction, but even if you have no particular destination, the scenic floatplane flights are fabulous. Fall-foliage trips are beyond fabulous. Rates begin at $75 pp (two-person minimum). You'll fly over Katahdin and the Penobscot River's West Branch, perhaps spotting moose en route. The best flight, though, is an hour-long trip over Baxter State Park to the Allagash Wilderness Waterway and back along the West Branch. Flights operate daily late May–October, weather permitting.

Katahdin Air Service is also a major link in the sporting-camp network, flying guests into and out of the remote camps via floatplane. When you contact a sporting camp for rate information, be sure to request the rates for floatplane access. It won't be cheap, but it's safe and fun. For a token sporting-camp experience without an overnight, sign up for one of KAS's "fly 'n' dine" trips. For $110 pp (two-person minimum, covering meals and

MAINE'S BIG DIG: THE GOLDEN ROAD

The era of nimble lumberjacks driving logs downriver ended in the early 1970s when Maine's paper companies began building roads into the wilderness for access to their timberlands. The most famous of these, The Golden Road, runs from Millinocket around the top of Moosehead Lake to the Québec border. It took nearly 1,000 workers almost five years to build the private, 96-mile, mostly unpaved road. Completed in 1975 and originally called the West Branch Haul Road, Maine's version of the Big Dig reputedly earned its current name from the megacost ($3.2 million) of construction.

The Golden Road is the most scenic link between Millinocket and Greenville, a 71-mile trip, two-thirds unpaved, through the wilderness. Red-and-white mile markers tacked to trees tick off the distance – if you can spot them. Driving this route is a true adventure, but it's not for everybody. If you're not used to driving backwoods dirt roads, this might not be the place to start. If you choose to do so, it's vital to ask about the road's condition – if there has been a lot of cutting going on along the route or if it has been a while between gradings, it could be in uncomfortably rough shape. Remember, it's a private road built for trucks and logs, not cars and people.

When driving from Millinocket, you'll exit the Golden Road after about 48 miles. Watch for a fork in the road, with a crude sign denoting Greenville Road; if you make it to the North Woods checkpoint, you've overshot it. The Greenville Road then parallels Moosehead Lake's east shore to Greenville. Keep an eye peeled for moose, deer, and even black bears.

Remember that you are entering true wilderness. There are no gas stations, restaurants, lodgings or anything but water, trees, and wildlife, and cell phone service is spotty at best. Go prepared with a full tank of gas, bottles of water, energy bars, bug repellent, and a good spare tire. Bicycles, motorcycles, ATVs, and horses are not allowed on the road.

Should you meet a logging truck along the way, pull way, way over and let it pass. If it's loaded, it might be carrying as much as 100,000 pounds of logs (and unlike Harry Chapin's song about bananas, it's you, not the logs, that will be mashed).

© HILARY NANGLE

Keep an eye out for moose while traveling in the Maine Highlands region.

transport), it'll fly you into a sporting camp for dinner and take you back afterward. It's a delicious adventure.

If you prefer your plane to have wheels, book a sightseeing flight with **West Branch Aviation** (Millinocket Municipal Airport, 16 Medway Rd., Millinocket, 207/723-4375, www.katahdingateway.com/wba). The rate is $42 pp for a half hour, $68 pp for a full hour, with a two-person minimum on all flights.

Moose-Spotting

Want some assistance finding an elusive moose? Dale Stevens's **Maine-ly Moose and Photo Tour** (353 Penobscot Ave., Millinocket, 207/723-5465, www.mainelyphotos.com) provides van tours with guaranteed moose sightings. Tours are personalized and cost $50 pp for two, with a family rate of $45 pp.

New England Outdoor Center (800/766-7238, www.neoc.com) offers guided moose-spotting tours via canoe, touring kayaks, and pontoon boats for $49 adults, $39 under age 12. If you don't see a moose or if your tour

doesn't meet your every expectation, you can return free.

ENTERTAINMENT AND EVENTS

Family fun is the specialty at **Magic City Mini Golf** (237 Penobscot Ave., Millinocket, 207/723-4404), an indoor fun center with an 18-hole miniature golf course, golf simulator, video games, and a pool table.

Millinocket is widely known for its week-long **Fourth of July** celebration (the fireworks display is outstanding). Every fifth year, there's also a giant homecoming celebration, bringing several thousand former residents back to their roots.

In August, the **Wooden Canoe Festival** has demonstrations, a white-water race, a pig roast, music, and fireworks.

Patten's **Annual Beanhole Bean Dinner** is a great celebration featuring good food (and a fascinating culinary tradition) at the Patten Lumbermen's Museum the second Saturday in August.

SHOPPING

Unless you're looking for camping or sporting supplies, shopping choices are slim in the area, but **North Light Gallery** (256 Penobscot Ave., Millinocket, 207/723-4414 or 800/970-4278, www.artnorthlight.com) is well worth a stop. Owner Marsha Donahue specializes in art from the Katahdin-and-Lakes School, and she shows the works of numerous talented artists and artisans. You can't miss the building; Donahue has painted murals on the exterior.

If you can't leave without a photograph of a moose, Mark Picard's **Moose Prints Gallery** (58 Central St., Millinocket, 207/447-6906) is a must-stop. He also offers guided photographic tours; call for details.

SUMMER RECREATION
Mattawamkeag Wilderness Park

Talk about a well-kept secret that shouldn't be: Check out the 1,000-acre town-owned Mattawamkeag Wilderness Park (Rte. 2, Mattawamkeag, 207/736-4881 or 888/724-2465, www.mwpark.com), about an hour's drive southeast of Baxter State Park's southern gate. The park's well-managed facilities include 15 miles of trails, picnic tables, restrooms, free hot showers, a recreation hall, a playground, a sand beach (on the Mattawamkeag River), and fishing for bass, salmon, and trout. There's also access to fine canoeing, including flat water and Class V white water, on one of northern Maine's most underused rivers. And you can stay the night at one of the 56 wooded campsites and 11 lean-tos. The entrance is about eight miles east of Route 2 on an unpaved logging road locally called "the park road"; it's signposted on Route 2. Day use is $3 pp, maximum $7 per car. Camping fees are $20–32 per site per night; six sites have hookups. The park is open daily late May–October.

Excursion Boat

Katahdin Scenic Cruises (207/723-8391, www.katahdinsceniccruises.com), based at the Big Moose Inn, makes it easy to get out on the lakes to see the wildlife and Katahdin if you don't want to brave a canoe, kayak, or raft. Options include one-hour ($20 pp), two-hour ($45 pp), and three-hour trips ($55 pp); boat minimums may apply.

Water Sports
CANOEING AND KAYAKING

This part of Maine is a canoeist's paradise, well known as the springboard for Allagash Wilderness Waterway and St. John River trips.

Close to Millinocket, experienced canoeists and kayakers may want to attempt sections of the **East and West Branches of the Penobscot River,** but no neophyte should try them. We're talking Big Water. Refer to the *AMC River Guide* for details, or contact one of the local outfitters such as New England Outdoor Center or Maine Quest Adventures.

A relatively gentle, early-summer canoe trip ideal for less-experienced paddlers is on the **Seboeis River,** between the Shin Pond–Grand Lake Road and Whetstone Falls, about 24 miles. Even easier, and a good family trip, is the flat-water run putting in below Whetstone Falls (west of Stacyville) and taking out before Grindstone Falls.

If you launch your canoe early in the day on **Sawtelle Deadwater,** near Shin Pond, west of Patten, you're bound to see moose. From Shin Pond, head northwest, crossing the Seboeis River at about six miles, and then turn right onto the next unpaved road and continue less than two miles to the water. You can also reach the Deadwater off the parallel paved Huber Road. Canoe rentals are also available at Shin Pond Village.

White-Water Kayak School: If you're itching to master a roll or better your whitewater paddling techniques, **Maine Kayak** (866/624-6352, www.mainekayak.com) operates a whitewater kayaking school with courses costing about $240 for a two-day course.

Outfitters: Most accommodations have canoes available for their guests, but if you need to rent, stop at **Maine Quest Adventures** (Rte. 157, Medway, 207/746-9615 or 207/290-1733, www.mainequestadventures.com). Daily canoe and kayak rentals are $25, fishing boats begin

THE UNGAINLY, BELOVED MOOSE

Everyone loves Maine's state animal, *Alces alces americana*. The ungainly moose, bulbous-nosed and top-heavy, stops traffic and brings out the cameras. It also stops cars literally, usually a lose-lose situation. The moose's long legs put its head and shoulders about windshield level, and a crash can propel the animal headfirst through the glass. Human and animal fatalities are common.

State biologists estimate that Maine has nearly 30,000 moose, most in the North Woods, so it's pretty hard not to encounter one if you're driving the roads or hiking the trails in the Maine Highlands region.

Moose pay no heed to those yellow-and-black diamond-shaped moose-crossing signs, but officials post them near typical moose hangouts, so slow down when you see them. During daylight hours, especially early and late in the day, keep your binoculars and camera handy. In late spring and early summer, pesky flies and midges drive the moose from the deepest woods, so you're more likely to see them close to the roadside. At night, be even more careful, as moose don't tend to focus in

on headlights (as deer do), and their eyes don't reflect at an angle that drivers can see.

Moose are vegetarians, preferring new shoots and twigs in aquatic settings, so the best places to see them are wetlands and ponds fringed with grass and shrubs. These spots are likely to be buggy too, so slather yourself with insect repellent.

Moose hunting, officially sanctioned, is somewhat controversial, partly because the creatures seem to present little sporting challenge. But they are a challenge, not because of wile or speed but because of heft. Imagine dragging one of these fellows out of the woods to a waiting truck; it's no mean feat. In Maine's annual Moose Lottery — a herd-thinning scheme concocted by the Department of Inland Fisheries and Wildlife — hunters receive permits to shoot moose in specific zones in late September–mid-October. At official state weighing stations, the hapless moose are strung up, weighed, tested for parasites, and often butchered on the spot by freelance meat packagers. Moose meat is actually tasty.

at $70, and a pontoon boat rents for $200; weekly rates are available for all.

WHITE-WATER RAFTING
Maine's biggest white-water rafting area is around The Forks, where the Kennebec and Dead Rivers meet, in the Kennebec Valley Region, but the second-largest area is along the West Branch of the Penobscot River near Millinocket. One-day Penobscot River rafting trips pass through Ripogenous Gorge, a rip-roaring chasm of roiling Class IV and V white water, over nine-foot Nesoudnehunk Falls, through a few other Class IV rapids and a few ponds, all in the shadow of Katahdin. It's a fabulous adventure, and a riverside lunch is included.

The primary rafting outfitter here is the **New England Outdoor Center (NEOC)** (Old Medway Rd., Millinocket, 207/723-5438

or 800/766-7238, www.neoc.com), based in a huge complex on the eastern outskirts of Millinocket. NEOC's Rice Farm headquarters organizes West Branch rafting trips ($79–119 pp, depending on day and month). For lodging, NEOC has campsites ($10–12 pp) and cabin tents and bunkhouses ($20–56 d) at its Rice Farm location. NEOC also has contemporary sporting-camp log cabins at its Twin Pine Camps on Millinocket Lake, eight miles northwest of Millinocket; rates begin around $200 d per cabin, and pets are permitted for $20 per night. Lots of special packages are available, covering lodging, breakfasts, and dinners. To reach the Rice Farm from I-95, take Exit 56 and head west on Route 157 toward Millinocket for eight miles. After the causeway over Dolby Pond, turn left (south) and go 1.2 miles to the NEOC.

MOOSE TRIVIA

- Typical height for an adult bull moose is seven feet at the shoulders; typical weight is about 1,000 pounds, with 1,400-pounders also recorded. Cow moose run about 800 pounds.

- Moose usually lumber along, seemingly in no hurry, but they've been known to run as fast as 35 mph.

- The bull moose's rack of antlers can measure six feet across; the largest recorded was a hair under seven feet.

- Moose give birth in late May-early June, after a 35-week pregnancy; singles are normal, twins are less common, triplets are very rare. A newborn calf weighs 20-30 pounds, occasionally 35 pounds.

- Moose have extremely acute senses of hearing and smell, but their eyesight is pitiable. If you're utterly quiet and stay downwind of them, they probably won't spot you.

- Moose have no history of harming humans, but stay out of their way during "the rut," when they're charging around and out of the woods looking for females in heat. This usually occurs mid-September-mid-October, when the foliage is at its peak, hikers are out and about, and Moose Lottery winners are in hot pursuit.

MOOSE-WATCHING HOT SPOTS

- Sandy Stream Pond, Baxter State Park

- Grassy Pond, Baxter State Park

- Russell Pond, Baxter State Park

- Sawtelle Deadwater, off Shin Pond Road, about seven miles northwest of Shin Pond

- Lazy Tom Bog, off Lily Bay Road, about 19 miles north of Greenville

- Route 6/15, between Greenville Junction and Rockwood, on the west side of Moosehead Lake

- The Golden Road, between Ripogenus Dam and Pittston Farm

FISHING

Water, water everywhere. That means primo fishing, including streams, rivers, and walk-in and fly-in ponds for brook trout; ponds and lakes for splake and lake trout; rivers and lakes for landlocked salmon; brooks and streams for wild and native brook trout; lakes for brown trout; and streams and rivers for bass. The Maine Department of Inland Fisheries and Wildlife (www.mefishwildlife.com) produces *Fishing Opportunities in the Katahdin Region,* a brochure detailing where to fish for what. Fishing licenses and other info also are available on the website.

For local info and supplies visit **Two Rivers Canoe and Kayak** (Rte. 175, Medway, 207/746-8181, www.tworiverscanoe.com), conveniently situated just west of the I-95 interchange.

Guided and outfitted fishing trips for one or two anglers with **Maine Quest Adventures** (Rte. 157, Medway, 207/746-9615 or 207/290-1733, www.mainequestadventures.com) are $300 full-day with lunch, $175 half-day with a snack; multiday trips are also available.

Serious anglers should consider one of the sporting camps listed in *Accommodations.*

WINTER RECREATION

Winter can be magical in the North Country. Snow is usually measured in feet, not inches, so snowmobiling and cross-country skiing are big business; snowshoeing and ice fishing also draw winter sports fans. Motels in Millinocket fill up fast in snow season, so plan well ahead for winter adventures.

Snowmobiling

More than 350 miles of the Interconnecting Trail System (ITS) crisscross the Millinocket area, including some that run right through town. Local snowmobile clubs produce excellent trail maps available from the Katahdin Area Chamber of Commerce. Snowmobile enthusiasts might also want to visit the Northern Timber Cruisers Snowmobile Club's **Antique Snowmobile Museum** (Millinocket Lake Rd., Millinocket, 207/723-6203, www.northerntimbercruisers.com, weekends and by appointment), which contains about three dozen machines. The clubhouse also serves food.

Snowmobile rentals ($185–215), clothing rentals ($10–25), and guided trips are available from **The New England Outdoor Center's Twin Pine Snowmobile Rentals** (800/634-7238, www.neoc.com), based at Twin Pine Camps, near ITS 86 in Millinocket.

Cross-Country Skiing

The Northern Timber Cruisers also groom and track more than 20 miles of free wilderness cross-country trails. Begin at the clubhouse on Baxter State Park Road 1.6 miles

northeast of Millinocket. For trail conditions, call 207/723-4329.

ACCOMMODATIONS

Besides in-town and area lodgings, Millinocket is also the springboard for a number of wilderness sporting camps, some of which are inaccessible, or nearly so, by road. Small planes equipped with skis or pontoons ferry clients to the remote sites—not an inexpensive undertaking, but a great adventure that's well worth the splurge.

Bed-and-Breakfasts

Whoo-ee! Millinocket's getting some fancy with the addition of **(5 Lakes Lodge** (off Route 11, South Twin Lake, Millinocket, 207/723-5045, www.5lakeslodge.com, $175–275). Area natives Rick and Debbie LeVasseur built this eye-catching two-story log lodge on a spit of land extending into South Twin Lake. Soaring windows and a stone fireplace dominate the two-story living room, with stunning

© HILARY NANGLE

Thanks to its location on a peninsula, 5 Lakes Lodge is surrounded by water on three sides. It also faces Katahdin.

views of Katahdin over the chain of lakes out front. Every guest room has a handcrafted, quilt-covered king bed, a bath with a double whirlpool tub, satellite TV, a gas stove, air-conditioning, a fridge, a data port, and that view. The LeVasseurs provide canoes and kayaks for their guests on the pebble beach out front; small fishing boats are available for rental at the dock out back, and flight-seeing tours will pick up right here. Rates include a full breakfast. It's cushy, comfy, and a fine place for wildlife-watching: five pairs of eagles and 24 pairs of loons nest on the interconnecting lakes, and Rick has a few "guaranteed" moose-spotting sites. Rick and Debbie throw in a lot of extras for their guests. For example, when the weather cooperates and their schedule permits, the take guests for lake tours aboard their pontoon boat. Also available is a very private one-bedroom lakeside cabin that sleeps nine.

In downtown Millinocket, **The Young House Bed and Breakfast** (193 Central St., Millinocket, 207/723-5452, www.theyounghousebandb.com, $90). Each of the five small-ish guest rooms has air-conditioning, a TV and DVD player, and Wi-Fi. Public rooms include a parlor with a baby grand. A full country-style breakfast is included.

Motels

The two-story, 48-room **Baxter Park Inn** (935 Central St./Rte. 157, Millinocket, 207/723-9777, www.baxterparkinn.com, $79–89 d) received a facelift in 2005 with the addition of a small indoor pool and the updating of its rooms (unfortunately, most face the highway or a parking lot). Other pluses are air-conditioning, free Wi-Fi, and continental breakfast. It's also right on ITS 83. Kids 12 and younger stay free; pets are allowed with a signed waiver. Despite its name, it is in town and not near the park.

Close to I-95's Exit 56 is the **Gateway Inn** (Rte. 157, Medway, 207/746-3193, www.medwaygateway.com, $55–105), a motel with 38 rooms and suites opened in 1995. Rooms on the west side have decks, great views of Katahdin (weather permitting), and higher rates. Pets are welcome. Continental breakfast is included; air-conditioning, phones, satellite TV, and an indoor pool are all available. There's even a guest kitchen with a fridge and a microwave.

For a cheap sleep, check in to the roadside **Katahdin Shadows Motel** (2166 Medway Rd./Rte. 157, Medway, 800/593-2267, www.katahdinshadowsmotel.com, $59–79). Ten nicely decorated rooms have air-conditioning, TVs, and mini-fridges; some have kitchenettes. Guests have use of a river dock, an outdoor pool, a hot tub, and a community kitchen.

Eclectic Properties

Hardest to characterize is the **Big Moose Inn** (Baxter State Park Rd., Millinocket, 207/723-8391, www.bigmoosecabins.com) on Millinocket Lake, midway between Millinocket and Baxter State Park's southern boundary. It's part inn, part sporting camp, part campground. Two white-water rafting companies are based here. This is not the place to stay if you're seeking peace and quiet, but it is a great property steeped in Maine woods traditions. The main lodge is everything you'd expect: comfy antiques and country furniture, a big stone fireplace, a moose head and other woodsy accents, and a big screened-in porch. Traditional guest rooms ($53–56 pp) with shared baths are inviting but very small (if you're over six feet tall, don't even think about it, as some have short beds); rates include continental breakfast. Three suites with private baths are $140 d with breakfast. On the grounds are 36 tent sites ($10 pp) and six screened lean-tos ($13 pp), plus 14 cabins that sleep 2–16, all with screened porches ($45–49 pp; minimum varies by cabin; bring your own towels). Canoe or kayak rental is $5 per hour or $15 per day. The inn has a restaurant and pub, and next door is North Woods Trading Post, with pizza, sandwiches, and supplies. Smoking and pets are not allowed. The lodge, cabins, and campground are open May–Columbus Day.

Hikers take note: The **Appalachian Trail Lodge** (33 Penobscot Ave., Millinocket, 207/723-4321, www.appalachiantraillodge.com)

BE A SPORT

Although dozens of traditional sporting camps exist all over Maine, most of the veterans are in the Katahdin-Moosehead Region, with the Kennebec Valley and Western Mountains running a close second. Almost all are north of Bangor.

Sporting camps deliver an authentic wilderness experience without camping. Noise and light pollution are nonexistent; on a clear night, the stars are magnificent. They're so much more than a place to stay; they're an experience, often a throwback to the 19th century, or at least to the early 20th century.

They're so varied that it's impossible to paint them with one broad brush. All but a few are accessible by road, but the "road" might be a rutted, muddy tank trap, making passengers yearn for a floatplane. All are rustic no-frills operations, some much more so than others. (If you're a frill-seeker, forget it; seek elsewhere.) Some have electricity and flush toilets; others have kerosene lanterns and private or shared outhouses. All are on or close to freshwater, meant to be convenient for fishing. Some offer American Plan (AP) rates, serving three meals a day, usually family-style; others have housekeeping facilities, where you're on your own; some let you choose.

Most camps have on-site guides available for hire – take advantage. Guides know the woods and water, and whether you want to find the fish or simply take a long walk in the woods, they know the best places and will point out hidden sights and wildlife.

With all the logging roads crisscrossing the region, there are only a few sporting camps now inaccessible by road, but most guests opt to fly in and out. As one guide put it, "People prefer flying over dying; those logging trucks run up and over a couple of cars every year."

If all this sounds intriguing, the **Maine Sporting Camp Association** (www.mainesportingcamps.com), founded in 1987, has more info.

The easiest way to get to a remote sporting camp is via floatplane.

© TOM NANGLE

provides cheap sleeps ($25 bunk, $35–55 private room with shared bath, $95 family suite with kitchen) and caters to you with a hiking shuttle, laundry service, and a community kitchenette.

If you're approaching Baxter State Park from the North Gate, **Morning Glory Farm** (199 Happy Corner Rd., Patten, 800/219-7950, www.mountaingloryfarm.com, $100) has two apartments in a beautifully renovated 1864 farmhouse. Advance reservations are required; rates decrease with length of stay.

New England Outdoor Center

A full-service year-round outfitter, New England Outdoor Center (800/766-7238, www.neoc.com) has lakeside accommodations ranging from small cabins to green-built guesthouses on its Twin Pine campus. Accommodations sleep 2–14 and have full kitchens and access to a recreation hall with a hot tub and games as well as use of canoes and docking facilities. Rates begin about $235 d for a small cabin during peak season, but packages that include everything from activities to meals are available. Pets are accommodated ($20).

Sporting Camps

Eight miles off the access road to Baxter's northern gate is **Bowlin Camps** (Patten, 207/528-2022, www.bowlincamps.com), a traditional fishing and hunting camp on the shore of the Penobscot River's East Branch. It now also welcomes family groups, especially in July–August. Kids love the suspension bridge across the river, and there are trails to ponds and two waterfalls. An easy 16-mile canoe run starts here (rentals are available), and someone will meet you at the other end. Cabins are rustic, heated with woodstoves; two have private baths and six share the clean bathhouse. Summer rates in cabins are about $500 pp per week for adults or $85 per night, including family-style meals served in the main lodge. Children under 16 are half price. There are three good-size housekeeping cabins (no meals provided, $105–165 per night). Snowmobiling

is huge here, and there are 12 miles of cross-country trails; Bowlin is open all year.

Two excellent sporting camps with long-standing reputations off to the north are Libby Camps and Bradford Camps. Both require 60–90-minute drives on unpaved roads; it's worth the splurge to arrive by floatplane. July–August are the best times for families, as fishing is slow and hunting hasn't started.

About 150 miles north of Bangor, **Libby Camps** (Millinocket Lake, 207/435-8274, www.libbycamps.com), on the east shore of a different Millinocket Lake than the one near Millinocket, is flanked by Baxter State Park and the Allagash Wilderness Waterway. Matt and Ellen Libby are the third generation to run this fishing and hunting camp, built in 1890; their son Matt and his wife, Jess, are next in line, and daughter Alison and her husband help out too—it's a serious business. If you catch a trophy salmon or brook trout at this Orvis-endorsed fly-fishing lodge, they'll even ready it for the taxidermist. Eight comfortable cabins have flush toilets, propane lights, and quilt-topped beds. The basic daily rate, including three meals, a boat, and a cabin, is $175 pp d. Pets are allowed. Hearty meals are served close to an enormous stone fireplace in the handsome log-beam lodge. (Pray that Ellen will make her peanut-butter squares for dessert, and be sure to buy a copy of her cookbook.) Canoes, kayaks, and motorboats are available for guests, and there's a sandy beach. The Libbys also own 10 "outpost cabins" on wildly remote ponds. (Even more remote is their Riverkeep Lodge on the Atikonak River in Labrador.) Libby Camps is open May–November. Both Matts are licensed pilots, and they'll fly you in on a seaplane from the Presque Isle Airport or Matagamon Lake near Patten, or you can arrange transport with other flying services.

The only sporting camp on a pristine 1,500-acre lake, **The Bradford Camps** (Munsungan Lake, 207/746-7777, winter 207/439-6364, www.bradfordcamps.com) is owned by Igor and Karen Sikorsky. (If the name rings a bell, think helicopters.) The scenery and sunsets are magnificent, the loons are mystical, and moose sightings are frequent. This is a special place. Eight good-size log cabins (with bathrooms and propane lamps), lined up along the lakefront, are $148 pp per day or $944 per week; family rate for two adults and two kids under 17 is $2,495 per week. Rates include excellent meals served family-style in the lake-view lodge. Most fascinating is the antique ice house, containing brilliantly clear ice cut arduously from the lake the previous winter. Canoes and kayaks are free for guests, a boat with a motor and gas is $50 per day, and hiking trails await. A guide ($200–250 per day) is essential for fishing these waters—noted for rare blue-back trout—and helpful for canoeing a nearby stretch of the Allagash. The Bradford is open May–November; in October–November most guests are hunters seeking deer, moose, and grouse. If you're an aviation fan, ask about the Sikorsky Seminar weekend, usually in early July. Karen and Igor can arrange flights from Millinocket Lake ($150–300 pp round-trip depending on take-off point), or you can drive 60 miles over rough logging roads and pay $30 pp gate fees (trust me: fly).

Camping

Probably the closest you can get to Baxter's south gate with an RV is **Chewonki's Big Eddy Campground** (8027 Golden Rd., Greenville, 207/350-1599 Apr. 1–Oct. 15, 207/882-7323 Oct. 16–Mar. 31, www.bigeddy.org). Many of the 75-acre campground's primitive sites ($10 pp, $6 ages 13–17) edge the Penobscot River at the famed Big Eddy landlocked salmon pools. Chewonki also offers camping gear rental, canoe rentals, and shuttles. They'll even set up and break down your camp site ($40).

The closest campground to the north gate is the Christianson family's **Matagamon Wilderness** (Patten, 207/446-4635, www.matagamonwilderness.com), which is just a few miles from the Matagamon gate. On the premises and bordering the East Branch of the Penobscot River are 36 wilderness campsites that can accommodate up to a 42-foot RV ($18), housekeeping cabins ($30–40 pp per day), a general store with food service, and boat rentals. Pets are allowed in the campground for $10 per stay.

FOOD

While the local options are improving, this isn't a destination for foodies, not by a long shot. With few exceptions, most of what's available is good home cookin', and you're welcome anywhere in jeans.

Restaurant hours noted are for peak season, but are subject to change. It's always wise to call ahead.

Local Flavors

Sandwiches, salads, paninis, and daily specials, most with an Italian accent, are the specialties at **Orvieto** (67 Prospect St., Millinocket, 207/723-8399, www.dicensiinc.com, 7 A.M.–6 P.M. Mon.–Fri.).

For breakfast, lunch, or luscious baked goods, dip into **Effie's Bakery** (551 Central St., Millinocket, 207/723-4515, http://effiesbakeryandcatering.vpweb.com, 6:30 A.M.–3 P.M. Tues.–Fri., 7:30 A.M.–1 P.M. Sat.).

For pizza, locals equally recommend **Millinocket House of Pizza** (Northern Plaza, 782 Central St., Millinocket, 207/723-4528, breakfast from 5 A.M.) on the strip east of town and **Angelo's** (118 Penobscot Ave., 207/723-6767) downtown. Both have way more than pizza on their menus, free local delivery, and are open until at least 9 P.M. Monday–Saturday; Sunday hours vary.

The **Appalachian Trail Café** (210 Main St., Millinocket, 207/723-6720, 5 A.M.–8 P.M. daily June–Nov., 7 A.M.–6 P.M. Mon.–Fri., 7 A.M.–3 P.M. Sat.–Sun. Dec.–May) knows how to feed hungry hikers, rafters, anglers, and other outdoor adventurers. Breakfast is served all day. Lunch and dinner means burgers, fried foods, and other budget-friendly comfort foods.

Casual Dining

When locals want to celebrate, they head to one of these restaurants.

The nicest downtown restaurant is the **Scootic Inn** (70 Penobscot Ave., Millinocket, 207/723-4566, 11 A.M.–10 P.M. Mon.–Sat., 4–10 P.M. Sun., bar until 1 A.M., $6–15), Millinocket's long-standing "Sunday dinnah" restaurant. The dining areas are pleasant, there's a full bar, and kids are welcome. The menu varies from pizzas, calzones, sandwiches, burgers, and fried foods to entrées such as broiled chicken and scallops Michelle.

Dine inside on one of the antique oak tables in the airy, light-filled dining room or outdoors on the screened-in porch at **Fredericka's** in the Big Moose Inn (Baxter State Park Rd., Millinocket, 207/723-8391, www.bigmoose-cabins.com, 5–9 P.M. Wed.–Sat. Sept.–June, 5–9 P.M. Wed.–Sun. July–Aug., $16–24). The creative menu emphasizes fresh and local ingredients. Entrée choices may include almond-crusted halibut or Angus rib eye. Lighter fare is served at the inn's **Loose Moose Bar and Grill** (5–11 P.M. Wed.–Sat. Sept.–June, 5–11 P.M. Wed.–Sun. July–Aug., $7–11).

A tad more relaxed is **River Drivers Restaurant** at the New England Outdoor Center's Rice Farm campus (Old Medway Rd., Millinocket, 207/723-8475 or 800/766-7238, www.neoc.com, 5–9 P.M. Tues.–Sat., $18–33). The dining room and deck have glimpses of the Penobscot River through the trees, and the fare, which emphasizes fresh and local, is well prepared.

INFORMATION AND SERVICES
Information
The **Katahdin Area Chamber of Commerce** (1029 Central St./Rte. 157, Millinocket, 207/723-4443, www.katahdinmaine.com) is based in a small prefab building at the eastern edge of Millinocket.

Check out **Millinocket Memorial Library** (5 Maine Ave., Millinocket, 207/723-7020, www.millinocket.lib.me.us).

Public Restrooms
Just east of Northern Plaza in Millinocket, Baxter State Park Headquarters, open weekdays, has public restrooms, as does Millinocket's municipal building (197 Penobscot Ave.) and the chamber of commerce.

Kennels
If you're headed for Baxter State Park with your pet, you'll need a kennel, as pets are not allowed in the park. **Just for Dogs Daycare & Boarding** (2211 Medway Rd., Medway, 207/746-9800, www.justfordogsdaycare.com) offers day care and overnight boarding. They run a free doggie shuttle in Medway and East Millinocket, and to Millinocket for a fee.

GETTING AROUND
Katahdin Air Service (KAS) (Millinocket, 866/359-6246, www.katahdinair.com) has an excellent half-century reputation offering charter floatplane flights to remote campsites and sporting camps May–November.

A full-service shuttle provider, **Maine Quest Adventures** (Rte. 157, Medway, 207/746-9615, www.mainequestadventures.com) shuttles adventurers throughout the region. It also offers airport pickup.

Baxter State Park

Consider the foresight of Maine Governor Percival Proctor Baxter. After years of battling the state legislature to protect the area around Katahdin, Maine's highest mountain, he bade good-bye to state government in 1925 and proceeded to make his dream happen on his own. Determined to preserve this chunk of real estate for Maine residents and posterity, he pleaded the cause with landowners and managed to accumulate an initial 5,960-acre parcel—the nucleus of today's 209,501-acre Baxter State Park—and donated it to the state in 1931. From then on, he acquired and donated more and more bits and pieces, adding his last 7,764-acre parcel in 1962, just seven years before his death at the age of 90. The governor's prescience went far beyond mere purchases of land; his gift carried stiff restrictions that have been little altered since then. And thanks to interest accrued on his final bequest, as well as small and large donations from park users and supporters, park authorities have been able to add even more acreage—including a splendid 4,119-acre parcel donated in 2006.

Today this fantastic recreational wilderness has 46 mountain peaks and about 200 miles of trails. One rough unpaved road (limited to 20 mph) circles the park; no pets or radios are allowed; cell phones may be carried but used only for emergencies. No gasoline, drinking water, or food is available; camping is carry-in, carry-out.

Camping, in fact, is the only way to sleep in Baxter—at tent sites, lean-tos, bunkhouses, or rustic log cabins. Competition for sleeping space can be fierce on midsummer weekends; it's pure luck to find an opening, so you need to plan well ahead. Guaranteeing a spot, particularly one of the coveted 22 cabins, means reserving well in advance (no refunds). The rewards are rare alpine flowers, unique rock formations, pristine ponds, waterfalls, wildlife sightings (especially moose), dramatic vistas, and in late September, spectacular fall foliage.

The hiking here is incomparable. Peakbaggers accustomed to 8,000-footers (or more) may be unimpressed by the altitudes, but no one should underestimate the ruggedness of Baxter's terrain or the vagaries of the weather in this unique microclimate.

Percival Baxter was by no means the first to discover this wilderness. His best-known predecessor was author Henry David Thoreau, who climbed Katahdin in 1846 from what's now Abol Campground but who never reached the summit. He didn't even reach Thoreau Spring (4,636 feet), named in his honor, but he did wax eloquent about the experience:

This was that Earth of which we have heard, made out of Chaos and Old Night.... It was the fresh and natural surface of the planet Earth, as it was made forever and ever ...so Nature made it, and man may use it if he can.

Locked in what he called "a cloud factory," Thoreau declined to approach the summit: "Pomola [the Penobscot Indians' malevolent spirit of Katahdin] is always angry with those who climb to the summit of Ktaadn." And Native Americans traditionally stayed below the tree line, fearing the resident evil spirits. They all had a point. The current trail system didn't exist in the Native Americans' or Thoreau's days, of course (the first recorded summiteer was Charles Turner Jr. in 1804), so fatalities were probably more frequent, but even in the 21st century, climbers have died on Katahdin, and difficult rescues occur every year.

Regulations

The list of rules (www.baxterstateparkauthority .com/miscPages/rules.html) is long at Baxter, and park rangers make the rounds to ensure enforcement. In the end, the rules are what make Baxter so splendid.

No motorcycles, motorbikes, or ATVs are allowed in the park; **bicycles** are allowed only on maintained roads, not on trails, but the narrow, rough Perimeter Road is not particularly bike friendly. When weather has been especially dry, bicyclists end up with mouthfuls of dust. **Snowmobiles** are restricted to certain areas; check with park rangers.

The park bans the use of **cell phones, TVs, radios,** and **CD or cassette players.** Noise levels in the park are strictly monitored by the rangers. There are no pay phones in the park, but all park rangers have radiophones.

No domestic animals are allowed in the park.

Baxter in Winter

The roads aren't plowed, campgrounds are closed, and the lakes and ponds are frozen solid, but Baxter authorities allow winter use of the park—with a multipage list of rigid restrictions. If this sounds appealing, contact the Baxter State Park Authority for winter information.

DAY USE

Most day-use visitors are here to hike; on summer and fall weekends, you'll need to arrive early—even if you're not climbing Katahdin—because the day-use parking areas fill up. (There are only 284 day-use parking spots in the park.) On weekends, a long line forms before dawn at the Togue Pond Gate. A notice board at each gatehouse specifies which day-use parking areas are closed and which are open; there's almost always some place to park (although never alongside the Perimeter Road or campground access roads), and zillions of trails to hike, even if it may not be what you had in mind. So plan to arrive early (no later than 7 A.M. to hike Katahdin) or be prepared to be totally flexible about your hiking choice.

Maine residents can take advantage of a special parking privilege by calling well in advance for free reservations (one site per month Apr.–Oct.) for one of 16 daily parking spaces at three Katahdin trailheads. Call park headquarters, provide your Maine license-plate number, and be sure to show up at Togue Pond Gate to claim your reservation no later than 9 A.M.

The northern end of the park is much less used than the southern end, so consider entering via the northern Matagamon Gate and hiking the wonderful trails in that part of Baxter. Take I-95 Exit 264 (Sherman) and then drive another 33 miles west, via Patten and Shin Pond, to Matagamon Gate.

Picnicking

Picnic areas, some with only a single table, are spotted throughout the park; most of the vehicle-accessible campgrounds also have picnic areas where noncampers are welcome. At the campgrounds, park in the day-use parking area, not the campers' lots.

◖ HIKING

Baxter's 200 or so miles of trails could occupy hikers for their entire lives. There's no such thing as "best" hikes, but some are indeed better (for various reasons) than others. Below is a range of options; consult the most recent edition of Stephen Clark's *Katahdin: A Guide to Baxter State Park and Katahdin* for details and more suggestions.

Trails originating at campgrounds all have registration clipboards; sign-in is required for Katahdin hikes and encouraged for all other hikes. All trails are blue-blazed, except for white-blazed ones that are part of the Appalachian Trail. Carved brown signs appear at all major trail junctions. All hikers are required to carry a flashlight.

Wear Polartec, polypropylene, Gore-Tex, or wool clothing, not cotton. Jeans can be a real drag (literally) if you get soaked in a stream, waterfall, or rainstorm. If you're planning to hike Katahdin, bring more layers than you think you'll need. Bring plenty of insect repellent, especially in June, when the blackflies are on the rampage. In June, you'll probably be best off with 100 percent DEET bug repellent, although the eco-friendly Lewey's Eco-Blends insect repellent is very effective, and some outfitters (such as L. L. Bean) now feature clothing impregnated with it. Wear light-colored long pants and a long-sleeved shirt and sweater with tight-fitting wrists and a snug collar.

Nature Trails and Family Hikes

Baxter has three easy nature trails that make ideal hikes for families with a range of age and skill levels. Nature-trail maps are available at park headquarters, the park entrance gates, and the nearest ranger stations to the trailheads. The 1.8-mile **Daicey Pond Nature Trail,** beginning at Daicey Pond Campground, circumnavigates the pond counterclockwise, taking about an hour. In August, help yourself to the raspberries near the end of the circuit. Best of all, you can extend the hike at the end by renting a canoe ($1 per hour or $8 per day) at the campground's ranger station, in the shadow of Katahdin's west flank. After that, take the easy 1.2-mile round-trip hike from the campground access road to Big Niagara Falls.

The other nature trails are **South Branch Nature Trail,** a 0.7-mile walk starting at South Branch Campground in the northern part of the park, and **Roaring Brook Nature Trail,** a 0.75-mile walk starting near Roaring Brook Campground, in the southeastern corner of the park, with dramatic views of Katahdin's east flank.

Other easy to moderate good family hikes are Trout Brook Mountain, Burnt Mountain, and Howe Brook Trail—all in the northern section of the park. Burnt Mountain has a fire tower at the top, and you'll need to climb the tower to see the view; the summit itself is quite overgrown. In the southern end of the park, a short easy trail leads from Upper Togue Pond to **Cranberry Pond.** An easy 5.2-mile round-trip from Daicey Pond Campground goes to **Lily Pad Pond** and then via canoe to **Windy Pitch Ponds.** Plan to picnic en route alongside Big Niagara Falls. (Before departing, stop at the Daicey Pond office and pick up the keys for the canoe locks at Lily Pad Pond.)

Howe Brook Trail, departing from South Branch Campground, requires fording the brook several times in summer, so wear waterproof footgear. The reward, higher up, is a series of waterfalls and little pools where the kids can swim (the water is frigid)—and flat boulders where you can picnic and sunbathe. In the fall, the foliage on this hike is especially gorgeous. For this six-mile hike, allow about four hours round-trip for lunch, a swim, and dawdling. Afterward, rent a canoe at the campground ($1 per hour or $8 per day) and paddle around scenic Lower South Branch Pond, in the shadow of North Traveler Mountain.

In 2006, after a multimillion-dollar fund-raising campaign, the Trust for Public Land donated 4,119 acres on the park's eastern flank to the Baxter State Park Authority. Centerpiece of the parcel is spectacular Katahdin Lake—long coveted by Percival Baxter for inclusion in the park. The six-mile (round-trip) hike is relatively easy—via the trailhead at Avalanche Field in the southeastern corner of the park. If you're inclined to linger longer at the lake, year-round accommodations in the form of housekeeping and American Plan (with all meals) options are available in the 10 lakeside log cabins managed by Holly and Bryce Hamilton at Katahdin Lake Wilderness Camps (www.katahdinlakewildernesscamps.com).

Moderate Hikes

Good hikes generally classified as moderate are Doubletop Mountain, Sentinel Mountain, and the Owl. If you decide to hike **Doubletop Mountain,** start at the Nesowadnehunk (Ne-SOWD-na-hunk) Field trailhead and go south to Kidney Pond Campground, an eight-mile one-way trek, up and over and down. It's much less strenuous this way. Allow about six hours.

Allow about six hours also for the **Sentinel Mountain Trail** from Daicey Pond Campground (6.6 miles round-trip) or Kidney Pond Campground (4 miles round-trip). It's not difficult; the only moderate part involves a boulder field about midway up. Take a picnic and hang out at the top; the view across to Katahdin, the Owl, and Mount O-J-I is splendid. With binoculars, you'll probably spot moose in the ponds below. Keep one eye on your lunch, however; a resident Canada jay at the summit has an acquisitive streak.

If the weather has been rainy, do not hike the Owl. It verges on being strenuous even under normal conditions.

Katahdin

Mile-high Katahdin, northern terminus of the Appalachian Trail, is the Holy Grail for most Baxter State Park hikers—and certainly for Appalachian Trail through-hikers, who have walked 2,158 miles from Springer Mountain, Georgia, to get here. Thousands of hikers scale Katahdin annually via several different routes. The climb is strenuous, requires a full day, and is not suitable for small children; kids under age six are banned above the tree line. You'll be a lot happier and a lot less exhausted if you plan to camp in the park before and after the Katahdin hike.

Katahdin, by the way, is a Native American word meaning "greatest mountain"—hence there's no need to refer to it as "Mount" Katahdin. The Katahdin massif actually comprises a single high point (Baxter Peak, 5,267 feet) and several neighboring peaks (Pamola Peak, 4,902 feet; Hamlin Peak, 4,756 feet; and the three Howe Peaks, 4,612–4,734 feet).

Even though Thoreau never made it to Katahdin's summit (Baxter Peak), countless others have, and the mountain sees a virtual traffic jam in summer and fall, particularly late in the season, when most of the through-hikers are nearing the end of their odyssey. Some hikers make the summit an annual ritual; others consider it a onetime rite of passage and then opt for less-trodden paths and less-strenuous climbs.

Rangers post weather reports at 7 A.M. daily at all the campgrounds. Heed them. Katahdin has its own biome, and weather on the summit can be dramatically different from that down below. At times, especially in high-wind and blowing-snow conditions, park officials close trails to the summit. They don't do it frivolously; Katahdin is literally a killer.

Besides the requisite photo next to the Baxter Peak summit sign, Katahdin's other "been there, done that" experience is a traverse of the aptly named **Knife Edge,** a treacherous 1.1-mile-long granite spine (minimum width three feet) between Baxter and Pamola Peaks.

If you can stand the experience, hanging on for all you're worth next to a 1,500-foot drop, go for it; the views are incredible. But don't push beyond your personal limits; you're hours from the nearest hospital.

The most-used route to Baxter Peak is the **Hunt Trail,** a 10-mile round-trip that coincides with the Appalachian Trail from Katahdin Stream Campground; allow at least eight hours round-trip. Other routes start from Russell Pond, Chimney Pond, Roaring Brook, and Abol Campgrounds. See Stephen Clark's *Katahdin* guide for specific route information.

CAMPING

Facilities at 10 campgrounds vary from cabins to tent sites, lean-tos, and bunkhouses; there also are several backcountry campsites supervised by the nearest campground rangers.

All the campgrounds close October 15; they open on various dates beginning May 15. One hike-in campground (Chimney Pond) opens June 1. Fees are $30 per night for a lean-to

© HILARY NANGLE

Immerse yourself in Baxter State Park by booking a cabin at Daicey Pond Campground.

or tent site, $11 pp per night in a bunkhouse, and $55 per night for a two-person cabin. Fees must be prepaid and are not refundable.

The park's only cabins are in the southwest corner—at **Daicey Pond Campground** (10 cabins) and **Kidney Pond Campground** (12 cabins). Daicey Pond has the best views— Katahdin from every cabin, and the sunrises are unmatched. With two exceptions, Kidney Pond cabins overlook the pond and surrounding woods, but not the mountains; Doubletop Mountain is in back of the campground. All cabins have woodstoves (for heating only), gas lanterns, outhouses, outside fireplaces, and beds; bring your own linens, water, food, and whatever else you think you might need.

Chimney Pond and **Russell Pond Campgrounds** are hike-in; the distance from the Roaring Brook parking area to Chimney Pond is 3.3 miles, and to Russell Pond is seven miles. Chimney Pond has a bunkhouse and nine four-person lean-tos. Russell Pond has a bunkhouse, four lean-tos, and three tent sites—all arranged around the pond, where you can also rent canoes ($1 per hour or $8 per day).

South Branch Pond Campground, close to Matagamon Gate, has an eight-person bunkhouse, 12 lean-tos, and 21 tent sites in an especially idyllic setting; seven of the lean-tos are right next to the pond.

June–August, bring fabric screening if you're staying in a lean-to; a tarp may foil the blackflies, mosquitoes, and no-see-ums, but you don't want to suffocate.

Getting Reservations

Camping reservations must be made by mail or in person; no phone reservations (except within 14 days). July gets booked up first, then August; weekends are more crowded than weekdays.

In 2005, Baxter officials established a new reservation system in hopes of providing a more equitable allocation of space in the park's cabins, bunkhouses, tent sites, and lean-tos. Under this rather eccentric "rolling reservation system," campers can make reservations any time beginning four months before the desired

camping start date. For instance, to request a site or sites for July 14, you'll need to mail your reservation to arrive no earlier than March 14 (see www.baxterstateparkauthority.com/camping/chart.htm for the reservation schedule). Maximum length of stay is seven nights per campground, 14 nights total in the park.

Download the application form from the park website and mail it—along with payment and a self-addressed stamped legal-size envelope—to Baxter State Park Reservations (64 Balsam Dr., Millinocket, ME 04462). (If you'd prefer to hand-deliver it, the office is open 8 A.M.–4 P.M. weekdays in spring and daily Memorial Day–Columbus Day. Do not try to send the reservation via email, as the website is not secure. Reservations are processed each day the office is open—applications from Maine residents are handled first.

If you can't plan four months ahead but can be fairly flexible, send in your request close to when you want to camp, or even take a chance on showing up at the last minute. Phone requests (207/723-5140; have your Visa or MasterCard handy) are accepted within 14 days of your visit—but there are no guarantees. Except on weekends July–mid-August, however, a tent site can usually be found. But be sure to have a fallback plan (it might have to be in Millinocket, 18 miles beyond the Togue Pond Gate).

If you make a reservation and can't keep it, be considerate and call or email the park headquarters to cancel, even though you won't receive a refund. It will give someone else a chance to enjoy the beauty of Baxter.

PARK ACCESS, INFORMATION, AND SERVICES

Unless you're hiking the Appalachian Trail (AT), the only way to enter the park is via one of two gates. **Togue Pond Gate** (6 A.M.–10 P.M. Mon.–Fri., 5 A.M.–10 P.M. Sat.–Sun. May 15–Oct. 15) at the southern end of the park is the choice for visitors from Greenville or Millinocket and is the most-used gate. At the northeast corner of the park is **Matagamon Gate** (6 A.M.–9 P.M. Mon.–Fri., 5 A.M.–9 P.M.

Sat.–Sun. May 15–Oct. 15), accessible via I-95, Patten, and Shin Pond Road.

Before you enter the park, check your fuel gauge and fill up your tank; there are no fuel facilities in the park.

If you have camping reservations, be sure that you do not arrive at the park with more people than your receipt indicates; the rangers at the gate check this, and the campground rangers even do body counts to be sure you haven't stuffed extra people into cabins or lean-tos.

Appalachian Trail through-hikers are required to register at the Abol Stream kiosk at the edge of the park as well as at Katahdin Stream Campground, before ascending Katahdin.

Maine residents have free daytime use of the park—one of Governor Baxter's stipulations. At the gates, **nonresidents** pay $14 per vehicle for a day pass; a nonresident season pass is $39. (A rental car with Maine plates no longer qualifies in the resident category.) Everyone must pay for camping.

There is no public transportation to or within Baxter State Park, so you'll need a car, truck, or bicycle. The park's website lists a couple of enterprises that offer shuttle services. RVs are also allowed, but maximum size is nine feet high, seven feet wide, and 22 feet long (or 44 feet for a car and trailer). Baxter is not a drive-through park. The park's 43-mile unpaved **Perimeter Road,** connecting Togue Pond and Matagamon Gates, is narrow and corrugated, evidently deliberately so; it's designed for access, not joyriding.

A few trail loops include the Perimeter Road, but avoid walking on it if possible. In wet weather, you'll be splashed by cars navigating the potholes; in hot weather, the gritty dust gets in your teeth. Hitchhiking is discouraged, but you can usually get a ride if you need it.

Information

Books, maps, and information are available at **Baxter State Park Headquarters** (64 Balsam Dr., Millinocket, 207/723-5140, www.baxterstateparkauthority.com, 8 A.M.–5 P.M. Mon.–Fri. year-round), at campground ranger stations, and at the Togue Pond Visitor Center.

Pick up a *Day Use Hiking Guide* at the visitors center or at park headquarters. The fold-out map, quite sketchy, also has basic info on major park trails.

The Allagash and St. John Rivers

ALLAGASH WILDERNESS WATERWAY

In 1966, the state established a 92-mile stretch of the Allagash River as the Allagash Wilderness Waterway (AWW), a collection of lakes, ponds, and streams starting at Telos Lake and ending at East Twin Brook, about six miles before the Allagash meets the St. John River. Also recognized as a National Wild and Scenic River, the waterway's habitats shelter rare plants, 30 or so mammal species, and more than 120 bird species. You'll spot plenty of wildlife along the way.

Arranging a flexible schedule to do the Allagash gives you enough slack to wait out strong winds on the three largest lakes. Such a schedule also allows time for a leisurely pace, side trips, and fishing along the way.

Highlights

Allagash Lake, one of the state's most pristine lakes, feeds into Chamberlain Lake from the west via Allagash Stream. No motors are allowed on Allagash Lake, making it especially tranquil. The side trip is six miles one-way, and water levels (too high or too low) can make it a rough go. At Lock Dam, ask about conditions. Between Chamberlain and Eagle Lakes, on a narrow spit of land seemingly in the middle of nowhere, stand two of the waterway's oddities—two old **steam engines,** relics rusted out and long abandoned. Once linked to the Eagle

Lake and Umbazooksus Railroad, the short-run Lombard Hauler locomotives operated around the clock six days a week 1927–1933, hauling 125,000 cords of pulpwood annually for the timber industry.

An exhilarating white-water run is the reward for tackling **Chase Rapids,** a nine-mile stretch starting just below Churchill Dam. You can usually expect Class II white water—sometimes Class III—if you launch with the dam's water release schedule. Two hours after the dam has been closed, the route can get pretty "bony," so you're likely to be hung up temporarily several times along the way. In the afternoon, wear well-secured sunglasses to protect yourself from glare. For a fee, the Churchill rangers will portage your gear to the end of the rapids, so you have to get only yourselves and your canoes to the end of the run. If you're at all hesitant about making the run, or the water is too low, the rangers will also carry passengers to the end of the run.

Allagash Falls, eight miles before the end of the waterway and 13 miles before the river meets the St. John, is a dramatic 40-foot drop. Needless to say, you'll need to portage here (on the right)—but only 0.3 miles.

When to Go
Canoeing season on the AWW usually runs from late May (after "ice-out") to early October. Water and insect levels are high and water temperature is low in May–June; July–August are most crowded but have better weather; September can be chilly, but the foliage is fabulous. The average annual temperature in this area is 40°F; winter temperatures average 20°F. The AWW is accessible in winter for snowmobiling and ice fishing. Winter camping is permitted at the Chamberlain Thoroughfare Bridge parking lot on a first-come, first-served basis.

Camping
There are 80 signposted campsites along the waterway; all are first-come, first served. July–August, when canoe traffic is fairly heavy, don't wait too late in the day to set up camp. Sites are $10 per night (including tax) for nonresidents, $8 per night for Maine residents. Children under age 15 are free. Fees are payable in advance at the ranger station where you enter the waterway. Theoretically, you're expected to stay only one night at any site, but an extension usually isn't a big problem.

Sporting Camps
Close to one of the major waterway access points, and roughly 50 miles north of Millinocket, **Nugent's Camps** (Chamberlain Lake, 207/944-5991, www.nugent-mcnallycamps.com) is reachable only by boat, floatplane, or snowmobile. Built in 1936, the 12 clean cabins are determinedly rustic, all have privies, and there's a common shower. Although housekeeping rates are available (bring your own sleeping bags and towels; no meals; $38 pp per night), opt for the American Plan ($110 pp per day includes linens and all meals) to save lugging victuals and to take advantage of the hearty family-style meals in the character-full main lodge. Cabin and dinner only are $65 pp. Boat rentals are $55 per day (plus gas).

Also on the paddling route are **McNally's Ross Stream Camps** (207/944-9995 or 254/241-1704, www.mcnallysrossstreamcamps.com), on Chemquasabamticook Stream. The six circa 1940 camps have woodstoves, running water, showers, and flush toilets. Rates, including all meals, are $100 pp per day, kids under age 12 are $60.

Information
The **Maine Bureau of Parks and Lands,** in the Department of Conservation (Northern Region, 106 Hogan Rd., Bangor, 207/941-4014, www.parksandlands.com), manages operations on the Allagash Wilderness Waterway. During the season, rangers are stationed at key sites all along the route. Call or write the office for a useful free map and a list of outfitters. For seasonal water-level information, call the Forest Service (207/435-7963, 8 A.M.–5 P.M. daily late Apr.–mid-Dec.).

Information also is available from **North Maine Woods** (207/435-6213, www

.northmainewoods.org) and the **Northern Forest Canoe Trail** (802/496-2285, www .northernforestcanoetrail.org).

A particularly lovely pictorial overview of the waterway is naturalist Dean Bennett's excellent book *Allagash: Maine's Wild and Scenic River.*

Getting There

The Allagash Wilderness Waterway is accessible by private logging roads at specified points. You'll need to pay the North Maine Woods gate fees when you cross onto timber-company land ($6 per day Maine residents, $10 nonresidents). You can get here from Greenville or Millinocket, or from the Aroostook County community of Ashland. Official access points with parking areas are Chamberlain Thoroughfare Bridge, Churchill Dam, Umsaskis Thoroughfare, and Michaud Farm. Winter access sites are different.

THE ST. JOHN RIVER

Like the Allagash, the St. John has long been associated with the timber industry—and the spring log drives when huge loads of giant logs were driven *upstream* and eventually to the mills. The history of the late-19th and early-20th-century lumbering era is especially colorful, loaded with tales of unbelievably rugged conditions and equally rugged characters. It's only a memory since the log drives ended, but you'll see remnants of the industry along the way.

When to Go

The prime season for canoeing the St. John River is May–early June, although many years there's enough water until late June. North Maine Woods (NMW) monitors daily water levels on the river, so you'll need to call a day in advance (207/435-6213) to confirm that water flow is adequate, especially after mid-June. NMW suggests that 3,000 cfs (cubic feet per second) is the minimum for enjoyable canoeing—to avoid grounding out or extensive portaging—but experienced canoeists recommend a minimum of 2,000 cfs.

June brings out the blackflies at campsites, so be sure you are well prepared to combat them with high-powered (100 percent DEET) bug repellent and tight-fitting, light-colored clothing.

Camping

Between Baker Lake and Allagash village, there are 28 riverside camping areas with a total of more than 60 sites. All are signposted. Most are on the left (west) side of the St. John; some require climbing the bank to reach level ground. Campsites are first-come, first-served. If a site is filled, you'll have to move on, anywhere from 2–5 more miles. Camping is allowed only at designated sites. About half of the sites have at least one sheltered picnic table, a real plus that saves rigging tarps for meals in rainy weather. Other facilities are outhouses and fire rings.

Even though the St. John has no dams, a heavy rainstorm can swell the water level, causing the river to rise as much as three feet overnight. Keep this in mind when lashing your canoe for the night; secure it well and as high as possible.

Information

Download a St. John River brochure from **North Maine Woods** (207/435-6213, www .northmainewoods.org), the nonprofit recreational manager for this area. The Northwoods Maine Gate fee is $6 pp per day for Maine residents, and $10 for nonresidents, plus a nightly camping fee ($8 Maine residents pp per night, $10 nonresidents). People over age 70 have free day use, and camping is $4; under age 15 have free day use and camping.

Getting There

There are five main access points for the St. John River, plus the final takeout point downriver at the top of Maine. From the southernmost point, **5th St. John Pond,** it's 143 miles to the town of Allagash. The easiest way to get here is via one of Greenville's two flying services. Downstream are **Baker Lake, St. Juste Road Bridge,** and **Moody Bridge,** the latter being best for low-water conditions; drive in via

Ashland (about 3.5 hours on American Realty Rd.). By the time you get to **Priestly Bridge,** you're more than halfway downriver—almost not worth the trip. Opt instead for starting at Baker Lake or Moody Bridge—or, if you're going with a guiding service, wherever your guides prefer to start. Shuttle arrangements can be complicated for St. John trips. Be sure all details are worked out in advance, and include access and camping fees in your budget.

GUIDES

Neophyte canoeists should think twice before setting out without a guide on multi-day canoe trips. You should have experience with Class II white water before attempting either of these rivers. Even experienced paddlers who are unfamiliar with Maine's rivers ought to assess the pluses and minuses of a do-it-yourself expedition versus a guided trip. It's rare to find a deserted campsite. The costs of provisioning, arranging shuttles, camping fees, and gear rental can add up—and guides spare you from cooking and cleanup. It's not a bad tradeoff.

Most guide services have their specialties, but few specialize in only one river. Some arrange trips all over the state; others go to Canada, Alaska, and beyond. Veteran guide services that offer trips on both the St. John and the Allagash Rivers include Mike Patterson's **Wilds of Maine Guide Service** (207/338-3932, www.wildsofmaine.com), the Cochrane family's **Allagash Canoe Trips** (207/237-3077, www.allagashcanoetrips.com), and Blaine Miller's **Allagash Guide Inc.** (207/634-3748, www.allagashguide.com).

If you're planning to visit a sporting camp within reasonable distance of the Allagash River, check to see whether it arranges Allagash trips; a number of them do.

Costs vary for guided trips, usually including everything except transportation to Maine; figure around $175 pp per day.

Greenville and Vicinity

Greenville is the jumping-off point for the North Woods—ground zero for floatplanes and ski-planes maintaining contact with remote hamlets and sporting camps. Although barely larger than a small town, it's the big city for tinier communities in every direction. The truth is, it's a bit like a frontier town itself. Greenville looks out over **Moosehead Lake**—Maine's largest—from its southern end. Moosehead is 40 miles long and covers 117 square miles, but counting all the niches and notches, its shoreline runs to more than 400 miles.

The origin of the lake's name has to be from the large number of antlered critters hereabouts, especially along the shore toward **Rockwood** or **Kokadjo**. In addition to moose-watching, you can wear yourself out with all the recreational choices: swimming, boating, fishing, camping, hiking, white-water rafting, golfing, picnicking, birding, skiing, snowshoeing, and snowmobiling. In spring, summer, and fall, you can also cruise the lake aboard an antique steamer.

Moosehead has been attracting outdoors enthusiasts, primarily hunters and anglers, since the 1880s. The long haul from lower New England, ending with the passenger train from Bangor, apparently was worth it for the clean air, prime angling, and chance to rough it. That era has long passed, and the clientele has changed noticeably, but Greenville's downtown still has a rustic air, the outlying hamlets even more so.

Greenville was incorporated in 1836, just before the timber industry began to take off. Steamboats hauled huge corrals ("booms") of logs down the lake to the East Outlet of the Kennebec River (East and West Outlets are both on the west side of Moosehead Lake), where river drivers took over. All that ended fairly recently, in the 1970s. The steamer *Katahdin* is a relic of that colorful era.

Greenville's lakeshore twin, **Greenville Junction,** once a busy rail crossroads, has now become one of those blink-and-you'll-miss-it places, but you can still eat and sleep here. Twenty miles northwest of Greenville on Route 6/15 is the small and somewhat crowded hamlet of Rockwood, the closest spot to Kineo, a lake icon marked by cliffs that plunge to the water. One of the best Kineo views is from the public boat landing, on a loop road just off Route 6/15. Route 6/15 then continues west, along Brassua Lake and the aptly named Moose River, to **Jackman**—a lovely 30-mile drive popular with moose-watchers.

When you make inquiries about the Moosehead area, you'll hear lots of references to "ice-out." It's almost a season—the time when winter's ice releases its grip on the lake and spring and summer activities can begin. Depending on the severity of the winter, ice-out occurs anywhere in early–late May. Fisherfolk arrive, plumbing begins to work,

A sign just outside the village of Kokadjo says it all.

and a few weeks later the blackfly larvae start to hatch. Spring is under way.

SIGHTS
◖ Cruise on the *Kate*

A turn-of-the-20th-century wooden vessel once used in the lumber industry, the steamboat *Katahdin,* locally called the *Kate,* has been converted to diesel and now runs cruises on 40-mile-long Moosehead Lake from its base at the bottom of the lake next to the **Moosehead Marine Museum** (12 Lily Bay Rd., Greenville, 207/695-2716, www.katahdincruises.com). The best trip for children is the regular three-hour midday run (the schedule changes annually, call for details). Tickets are $32 adults, $28 seniors, $17 ages 11–16; kids under age 11 are free. A 4.5-hour **Mount Kineo cruise** ($37 adults, $33 seniors, $20 children), three hours if passenger minimum isn't met, is offered occasionally July–early October. An all-day head-of-lake trip (call for rates) operates the last Saturday of September, when it's chilly, but the fall foliage is fantastic. There is indoor

and outdoor seating, and dinner is available on board. Smoking and high-heeled shoes are not allowed; the boat is wheelchair-accessible. Cruises operate on a regular schedule July–early September, but only on weekends late May–June and on a limited schedule through September. A full schedule resumes for foliage season, through early October. Reservations are advisable for the longer cruises.

Moosehead Historical Museum

The **Moosehead Historical Society** (207/695-2909, www.mooseheadhistory.org) operates two properties in Greenville. Most impressive is the artifact-filled and exhibit-packed 1899 **Eveleth-Crafts-Sheridan Historical House, Carriage House, and Lumberman's Museum** (444 Pritham Ave., Greenville, 1–4 P.M. Wed.–Fri. June–Sept., $5 adults, $2 children). Guided tours of the main house and adjacent carriage house provide a personalized glimpse into town life, leisure activities, and the roll of the logging industry; the last tour is at 3:30 P.M. The **Center for Moosehead History** (6 Lakeview

LITTLE FARM IN THE BIG WILDERNESS

Trust me: If you continue up Route 6/15 from Greenville 20 miles to Rockwood, and then another 20 miles on an unpaved road, you're guaranteed to have an adventure at **Pittston Farm** (207/280-0000, www.pittstonfarm.com).

The South and North Branches of the Penobscot River wrap around Pittston Farm, which is truly an oasis in the wilderness. Once a working logging camp where teamsters were based, its two impressive barns and a three-story farmhouse remain relatively intact. Current owners Bob and Jenny Mills, along with their son, grandkids, and parents, are investing in updating this property, on the National Register of Historic Places, without losing its come-as-you-are hospitality. Although the frills are few, the welcome is warm, the price is right, and the experience is priceless. You'll likely spot a moose or two on the way; drive defensively.

A few miles before the farm, you'll need to stop at the timber-company checkpoint; there is no fee for those visiting Pittston Farm.

This unincorporated territory, officially called the Pittston Academy Grant, once was a major center for timber operations along the Penobscot River. Now the 100-acre riverside farm is known as *the* place to go by car, flying service, or snowmobile for meals fit for lumberjacks. Dress down (suspenders will fit right in). All-you-can-eat breakfasts are served beginning at 7 A.M., lunch from a menu is available 11 A.M.-3 P.M., and the huge dinner buffet is served 5-7 P.M.; BYOB. It's hearty home cooking, definitely meat-oriented, and you won't eat alone. The homemade pies and cookies alone are worth the trip. Reservations are advisable. No credit cards are accepted.

After eating, spend some time in the museum, blacksmith shop, and chapel (a former potato barn), stroll the grounds, and visit the horses, goats, and cattle. Canoe and kayak rentals are available, and there are plenty of hiking trails in the area.

The main lodge is comfy, with a big wraparound porch and – surprise! – wireless Internet. Basic accommodations in the lodge (many guest rooms share few baths) go for $109 pp; renovated carriage house rooms (the name sounds fancy, but the rooms are extremely modest) have private baths, air-conditioning, and satellite TV and go for $114 pp. Also available are seven no-frills cabins, with newly added private baths ($114 pp). All lodging rates include the all-you-can-eat home-style meals, bedding, and towels. RV sites in the field are $28, including electric hookups; water and dump station are nearby. Tent sites are $18 for two adults and three kids younger than 18.

If you're tentative about making the trip, call the Millses to see if they're offering any programs that include transportation from Greenville.

St., Greenville, 10 A.M.–4 P.M. Thurs.–Sat.) has a nice display of Native American artifacts.

Flightseeing

Moosehead Lake from the air during fall-foliage season is incomparable—you'll bank over Mount Kineo, survey a palette of autumn colors, and very possibly see a moose or two. (They're easiest to spot in the sad-looking tracts clear-cut by the timber companies.) Most fun is the lakefront takeoff and landing. **Currier's Flying Service** (Pritham Ave./Rte. 6/15, Greenville Junction, 207/695-2778, www.curriersflyingservice.com) flies a whole slew of on-demand trips over Mount Kineo, Squaw Mountain, and Katahdin. Costs range $35–140 pp with a two-person minimum. Moose-watching trips, depending on their length, are $70–140 pp. Call to arrange a flight schedule; planes depart from Greenville Junction, where the Currier family also operates a small gift shop, selling Sue Currier's handsewn wall hangings.

Kineo

Moosehead Lake's most distinctive landmark, at the lake's "waistline," is Mount Kineo, a

763-foot-high chunk of green-tinged rhyolite or felsite that erupted from the bowels of the earth about 425 million years ago. Smoothed by glacial activity on the west side, Kineo has sharp cliffs on its east side. The chert-like volcanic stone (not flint; Maine has no native flint) was a major reason Native Americans glommed on to the Moosehead area thousands of years ago; its hardness served them well for weapons and fishing and hunting tools. The surrounding woodlands yielded prime birch bark, supplying raw material for canoes, carryalls, and even shelters. Stone tools and arrowheads still turn up occasionally, especially along the shore when the water level is low, but most have been carted off by amateur collectors. Resist the urge to take home samples. Once the site of a monumental summer resort hotel, Kineo is rather sleepy these days, with only a small B&B and no other services. But if your schedule permits, go; a hike up Mount Kineo is a must.

Kineo is accessible via rough roads on the east side of the lake, but just barely. It's far easier and better to rent a boat on the west side of the lake in Rockwood (but beware of fluky lake winds), or take the Rockwood Village–Kineo shuttle service, which departs regularly from the village dock ($10 adults, $5 ages 6–11). Each Wednesday during the season, the steamboat *Katahdin* makes a 1.5-hour stop at the base of Mount Kineo—not enough time for a major hike but ample to get a sense of the site. For a more in-depth experience, join Northwoods Outfitters on its Moosehead Lake Boat Cruise and Kineo Hike ($325 for two people). The six-hour trip includes time to hike and explore as well lunch on the summit.

From the dock, the Indian and Bridle Trails lead to the top, but signposting is a bit lax; keep an eye out for blue blazes. The Bridle Trail is easier. Allow about three hours round-trip for the hike; carry a picnic. In winter, when Moosehead Lake freezes solid, you can get to the Kineo peninsula by snowmobile (weather and common sense determine the schedule), but the trails are too full of snow for hiking.

© HILARY NANGLE

The distinctive cliffs of Kineo make it a landmark on Moosehead Lake.

ENTERTAINMENT AND EVENTS

Moosemainea, an annual monthlong moose-oriented festival sponsored by the Moosehead Lake Region Chamber of Commerce, combines canoe, rowboat, and mountain-bike races; a family fun day; moose safaris; and even a "best moose photo" contest. Register your own moose sightings on a huge map at the chamber of commerce. Events take place in Greenville and Rockwood mid-May–mid-June.

The first full weekend in September, the **International Seaplane Fly-In Weekend** is a four-day event at Greenville and Greenville Junction drawing seaplanes from all over New England for public breakfasts, a two-day craft fair, flightseeing, and more. Beds are very scarce during the Fly-In, so either book well ahead to be part of it or wait for another time to visit.

The **Natural Resource Education Center at Moosehead Lake** (207/695-3705, www.naturalresourceeducationcenter.org) presents a summer series of lectures and field trips.

In February, the **100-Mile Wilderness Sled Dog Race** attracts dog teams from throughout the Northeast.

SHOPPING

The Greenville area, and especially downtown Greenville, is filled with shops selling moose-related merchandise and other goods with a woodsy theme.

If you're entering Greenville from the south, cresting the last hill you'll see on your right the **Indian Hill Trading Post** (Rte. 15, Greenville, 207/695-2104 or 800/675-4487, www.indian hill.com), one-stop shopping with camping gear, clothing, footwear, an ATM, fishing and hunting licenses, souvenirs, and a supermarket that sells ice, liquor, groceries, and even live lobsters. In short, if it doesn't have it, you don't need it.

On the main drag downtown is **Kamp Kamp** (Pritham Ave., Greenville, 207/695-0789), located in the historic Indian Store building. It's filled with woods-related merchandise from moose and bear doodads to antiques. There is plenty of cool stuff here that is definitely worth a visit.

Just beyond the town offices, **Joe Bolf** (Minden St., Greenville, 207/695-3002, www .joebolf.com) works magic with a chainsaw; don't miss the "band."

Peter Templeton is keeping a family tradition of boatbuilding alive at **Ship Shape** (296 Pritham Ave., Greenville, 207/695-2402). Templeton specializes in building replica models of the steamships that used to ply Moosehead Lake, but he builds other models too and takes commissions.

For reading material, **Gabriel's Studio** (Rte. 6/15, Greenville, 207/695-3968) has a good selection of inexpensive used books, while **From Away Books** (38 Main St., Greenville, 207/695-0266) has three rooms stocked with used and antiquarian books as well as a few other treasures, all at excellent prices.

Just north of downtown, the **Artisan Barn** (241 Pritham Ave., Greenville, 207/695-3522) is a multi-find: It's an artisans co-op filled with handcrafted items such as baskets, rugs, pottery, and clothing; also here is an Internet café

serving baked goods and coffee most mornings in season.

RECREATION
Multisport Outfitters

The biggest and best outfitter in this neck of the woods is **Northwoods Outfitters** (Main St., Greenville, 866/223-1380 or 207/695-3288, www.maineoutfitter.com), in downtown Greenville right across from the *Katahdin*. Northwoods should be your first stop no matter what your choice of activity. These folks are the region's outdoor pros. Even if you have your own equipment and have no need of a guide, stop in for advice and information, maps, and perhaps a cup of java and final posting from the civilized world from its **Internet Café.** Northwoods does it all, offering rental equipment, shuttles, and guided trips: Moose safaris, lake cruises, mountain biking, hiking, sailing, canoeing, white-water rafting, fishing, dog-sledding, snowmobiling, snowshoeing, and so on. Even better, it uses guides who are passionate about their individual sports. It's open 9 A.M.–5 P.M. daily with extended hours during peak seasons.

Lily Bay State Park

Lining the eastern shore of Moosehead Lake, 925-acre Lily Bay State Park (Lily Bay Rd., Greenville, 207/695-2700, www.parksand-lands.com, $3 Maine resident adults, $4.50 nonresident adults, $1.50 nonresident seniors, $1 ages 5–11, free over age 65 and under age 5) is the place to go for moose-watching, fishing, picnicking, hiking, canoeing, swimming, birding, and camping at some of Maine's most desirable waterfront sites. The park is open 7 A.M.–11 P.M. daily May 1–October 15, but it's accessible in winter for cross-country skiing and snowmobiling. From Greenville, head north on Lily Bay Road for eight miles; the park is on the left.

◖ Moose Safaris

Ed Mathieu is the chief honcho of **Moose Country Safaris** (191 N. Dexter Rd., Sangerville, 207/876-4907, www.moose countrysafaris.com), usually operating in the

Greenville area. Reservations are essential. Moose safaris, lasting about four hours, go out at 5:45 A.M. and 2 P.M. mid-May–mid-October by 4WD and canoe or kayak; there's a two-person minimum, and the cost is $135–140 for two. Opt for the morning trip, which includes breakfast at West Branch Pond Camps.

Northwoods Outfitters also offers three-hour moose safaris by land or water ($40 pp); Currier's does its moose-watching from the air.

If you go on your own, swampy **Lazy Tom Bog** is one of the region's best moose-watching haunts. Plan to go soon after sunrise or just before sunset. From Greenville, take Lily Bay Road north to Kokadjo, 18 miles. A mile later, when the road forks, take the left fork (signposted "Spencer Pond Camps"). Continue 0.5 miles to a small bridge. Park on either side of the bridge and have your camera ready, preferably with a long lens. If you want to emerge from your car, or even stick your lens through the open window, you may need to douse yourself with insect repellent. And try to keep the kids quiet.

Hiking

Except for early June, when blackflies torment woodland hikers as well as moose, the Greenville area is sublime for hiking. The chamber of commerce has a list that includes hiking directions for **Number Four Mountain, Big and Little Squaw Mountains, Big and Little Spencer Mountains,** and **Elephant Mountain** (a B-52 crash site). Also ask at the chamber for directions to **Moose Mountain,** off Route 6/16, topped with the first fire tower in the United States. It's a bit rickety but still there. The hike is moderate to difficult and takes about four hours round-trip.

Northwoods Outfitters offers **guided hikes** with Registered Maine Guides ($275 for 8 hours) including Christopher Keene, author of *North Woods Walks: A Collection of Hikes in Northern Maine.*

Mountain Biking

Given all the backwoods trails, mountain biking is very popular. You can bring a bike and strike out on your own, rent a bike, or go with a guide or group. Remember, however, that bicycles are *not* allowed on logging roads; the huge lumber trucks are intimidating enough for passenger vehicles, never mind bicycles.

Mountain bike rentals are available from **Northwoods Outfitters** for $25 per day. Also available are kids' bikes, child seats, and Trail-a-Bikes.

Twenty miles north of Greenville, **The Birches Resort** (Rockwood, 207/534-7305, www.birches.com) rents mountain bikes ($40 per day) and sends you off on its network of mountain-bike trails. It also offers a four-hour group trail ride ($60 pp includes lunch).

Water Sports

In addition to Lily Bay State Park, there's fine swimming at **Red Cross Beach** in downtown Greenville. The parking area is near the Masonic Temple on Pritham Avenue, and a short path through the woods leads to the beach. You'll find lifeguards, picnic tables, and even floats.

CANOEING AND KAYAKING

If you're not an experienced paddler, be cautious about canoeing or kayaking on Moosehead Lake. The sheltered bays and coves are usually safe, but you can have serious trouble in the open areas—especially the stretch between Rockwood and Kineo. Do not attempt it; even pros have been swamped by rogue winds on that route. At Lily Bay State Park, you can launch a canoe from the waterfront campsites and easily make it to Sugar Island.

At **Northwoods Outfitters,** canoe or kayak rentals begin at $25 per day; weekly rentals and deliveries are available, as is shuttle service.

BOAT RENTALS

If you want to explore Moosehead Lake's numerous nooks and crannies, the best way is with a powerboat. **Beaver Cove Marina** (16 Coveside Rd., Beaver Cove, 207/695-3526, www.beavercovemarina.com) rents 18–23-footers for $275–310 per day. Careful: The lake is shallow.

WHITE-WATER RAFTING

From Greenville, you're well positioned to raft either the Kennebec or the Penobscot Rivers. Check with Northwoods Outfitters, which also provides transportation.

FLY-FISHING

The best local resource for fly-fishing, hands down, is the **Maine Guide Fly Shop and Guide Service** (34 Greenville Rd., Greenville, 207/695-2266, www.maineguideflyshop.com). This veteran operation, owned by Dan Legere, will set you up with a guide and all the equipment you need to do it right. Rates for a guided drift-boat experience, including lunch and gear, are $350 for one person, $400 for two.

Golf

The most popular, scenic, and windswept course in the area is the nine-hole **Kineo Golf Club** (207/534-9012, www.mooseheadlakegolf.com), built for the 500 or so guests at the turn-of-the-20th-century Mount Kineo House. At every turn you'll see Mount Kineo, or Moosehead Lake, or both. There are dynamite views. The course is open June–mid-October, and you'll need to get there by boat.

Built in the 1920s, nine-hole **Squaw Mountain Village Golf Course** (Rte. 6/15, Greenville Junction, 207/695-3609) is now part of a modern condo complex. Greens fees are low, and the pace is unhurried.

Winter Sports
DOGSLEDDING AND SNOWSHOEING

Former Outward Bound instructor, Certified Wilderness Responder, and Registered Maine Guide Stephen Madera is the ideal guy to head into the Maine woods with via dogsled. His company, **Song in the Woods** (207/876-4736, www.songinthewoods.com), offers trips of all lengths into the wilderness around Gulf Hagas and the Roach Ponds. You can even mush your own team. Rates for dogsledding begin at $350 for two people for a short day trip, $400 for two for a full day with lunch. Snowshoeing adventures begin at $35 for a two-hour tour. Multiday trips are available. In

summer, Madera also offers customized hiking and paddling trips into the region, beginning at $85 pp for a half-day.

SNOWMOBILING

The biggest winter pursuit hereabouts is snowmobiling, thanks to an average 102-inch annual snowfall and 300 miles of Greenville-area trails connecting to the entire state network. It's pretty competitive trying to get a bed in winter if you don't plan well ahead; be forewarned. Incidentally, if you're curious about how people get around northern Maine in winter, check out the parking lot at the Greenville school complex (Pritham Ave.); the vehicle of choice is the snowmobile.

A particularly popular loop is the 160-mile **Moosehead Trail**, which circumnavigates Moosehead Lake: Greenville to Rockwood to Pittston Farm, Seboomook, Northeast Carry, Kokadjo, and back to Greenville. You can start at any access point along the route and go in either direction.

The chamber of commerce has snowmobile trail maps and can put you in touch with local snowmobile clubs. Thanks to these energetic clubs, trails are well maintained and signposted.

For snowmobile rentals or guided tours, contact Northwoods Outfitters. Rates begin around $180 for a rental sled. An introductory guided tour is $99.

CROSS-COUNTRY SKIING

The Birches Resort (Rockwood, 207/534-7305, www.birches.com) has 40 miles of groomed cross-country ski trails winding through an 11,000-acre nature preserve. A trail pass is $14 full-day, $11 half-day for adults; kids are $10 or $8. Full-day rates include use of the hot tub and sauna. Equipment rentals are available at the Birches Ski Touring Center. For lodging at the Birches, escape to one of its remote woodstove-heated trailside yurts for $40 pp.

For a real adventure, ski between the **Appalachian Mountain Club**'s (www.outdoors .org) three wilderness lodges—Medawisla,

Little Lyford, and Gorman Chairback—and privately owned West Branch Pond Camps. Groomed wilderness trails connect the properties, which all welcome adventurers with woodstove-heated cabins and hot family-style meals. Both guided and self-guided adventures are available, as is gear shuttle.

ACCOMMODATIONS

Lodging in the area varies from just a few grades above camping to exquisite country inns and lodges.

Country Inns

Wow! Combine a magnificent Victorian hillside manse with eye-popping views of Moosehead Lake with an English manor house decor and ambience, and the result is the ◖ **Blair Hill Inn** (Lily Bay Rd., Greenville, 207/695-0224, www.blairhill.com, $350–495), where Dan and Ruth McLaughlin (escapees from the software industry) have created a relaxing, elegant retreat. Eight spacious second- and third-floor guest rooms in the magnificent 1891 home are furnished with comfy antiques and accented with ornate woodwork, fabulous lighting, and fine paintings. Some have working fireplaces; Room 6 has views down to Kineo from the window seat, and many of the bathrooms have separate soaking tubs and large showers. A truly gourmet breakfast is included, and a five-course dinner ($59 pp) is available Thursday–Saturday in peak season. Take in the expansive views from the dining room, living room, or comfy lounge; even better, score a seat on the front porch. The grounds include lovely gardens, greenhouses, a huge barn, and rolling lawns edged with stone walls. During summer, the inn hosts a concert series on the lawn. Service is top-notch, yet unobtrusive; the innkeepers will arrange activities and make recommendations on request.

Elegance and comfort are also bywords at Linda and Dennis Bortis's **The Lodge at Moosehead Lake** (Lily Bay Rd., Greenville, 207/695-4400, www.lodgeatmooseheadlake .com, $250–595 summer–fall, $195–495 off-season), which immerses guests in a chic version

of a cabin in the woods. Perhaps the most astonishing feature is the furniture. Each of the five guest rooms in the main building has a theme—Trout, Loon, Moose, Totem, and Bear—and each has beds and mirrors hand-carved by local woodworking master Joe Bolf, plus lots of accessories, to carry it out. All but the Trout have dramatic views of Moosehead Lake. Whirlpool tubs, fireplaces, and camouflaged video players are in each room as well as in the three bi-level water-view carriage-house suites—named Allagash, Baxter, and Katahdin. In Allagash and Baxter, lumber-era boom chains hold swaying queen-size beds with incredible lake views; Katahdin has a fireplace in the *bathroom*. In the guest pantry is a small gift shop with clever moose-themed items, snacks, and dozens of videos for guests to borrow. There is Wi-Fi throughout. Upstairs is the two-bedroom Kineo suite, with a kitchen, a living-dining room, a big deck, and jaw-dropping views. Breakfast is included all year. On Friday–Sunday evenings during peak season, the lodge's dining room serves a Maine woods version of comfort foods, with entrées ($18–26) such as buffalo meatloaf or lobster mac and cheese; in winter, supper is available for guests on Friday–Saturday nights. Note: Meals are for guests, with limited availability to nonguests; call first.

Tucked on a side street in Greenville and just "300 steps" from the lake is **Pleasant Street Inn** (26 Pleasant St., Greenville, 207/695-3400, www.pleasantstreetinn.com, $110–260), a lovely Victorian dating from 1889, with tiger oak woodwork throughout that has been burnished and polished to a soft glow. Guest rooms are spread on three floors, and most have private baths (although some are detached; robes are provided). Be sure to check out the tower room, with views to the lake. Two other parlors and a wraparound porch mean there's plenty of room to spread out. Rates include a full breakfast and afternoon snacks. Kids over age 14 are welcome.

Motels

The **Kineo View Motor Lodge** (Rte. 15, Greenville, 207/695-4470 or 800/659-8439, www.kineoview.com), three miles south of Greenville, sits on a prime hilltop with a dead-on view of Mount Kineo and gorgeous sunsets. Opened in 1993, the chalet-style three-story motel has 12 good-size guest rooms with phones, TVs, fridges, microwaves, and balconies) for $79–109, including continental breakfast late May–mid-October; rates are $69–99 d (no breakfast) in other months. Two suites, one with a full kitchen, are $179 each. This is a great place to bring kids—there's lots of acreage to run around, including nature trails. Outside are picnic tables and a grill. Some rooms accommodate pets, $10 by reservation.

Two miles closer to Greenville than Kineo View and with a hilltop view delivering elevated views down Moosehead Lake, the **Indian Hill Motel** (127 Moosehead Lake Rd./ Rte. 15, Greenville Junction, 207/695-2623 or 800/771-4620, www.indianhillmotel.biz, $68 summer, $53–73 other months) is a vintage motel with 15 good-size guest rooms that have air-conditioning, phones, cable TV, and tiny baths. Ask for a room far off the highway to lessen the traffic noise. In the commercial complex across Route 15 are a supermarket and the chamber of commerce.

You're practically *in* the lake at **Chalet Moosehead** (Birch St., Greenville Junction, 207/695-2950 or 800/290-3645, www .mooseheadlodging.com). The newer two-story building is where you want to stay; first-and second-floor guest rooms have whirlpool tubs, fridges, TVs, phones, air-conditioning, and private balconies with dynamite views for $125–145 in season (higher rates during the Sept. Fly-in event). The older two-story section has seven basic guest rooms for $98 in season, $102 with a kitchenette. Kids age five and under stay free; pets ($10 per dog) are allowed in the older units. Dock space is free if you bring your own boat, and guests have free use of canoes, paddleboats, gas grills, and a private swimming area.

For a room with vroom, consider the **Moose Mountain Inn** (314 Rockwood Rd., Greenville, 800/792-1858, www.moosemountaininn .com, $69–99), a vintage few-frills motel at the base of Little Moose Mountain. It's owned by Northwoods Outfitters, which operates a snowmobile and ATV rental outpost here. All guest rooms have TVs, air-conditioning, microwaves, refrigerators, and Wi-Fi. There's also a pool on the premises. Rates include a continental breakfast.

Small Cottage Colonies

What a location! Smack-dab on Moosehead Lake adjacent to the East Outlet of the Kennebec River's dam is **Wilsons on Moosehead Lake** (Greenville Junction, 207/695-2549 or 800/817-2549, www.wilsonsonmooseheadlake.com). The 1–5-bedroom housekeeping cottages are spotless, and all have screened porches as well as kitchens and fireplaces. Rates are $95–425 per night or $610–2,400 per week in July–August, less off-season. Canoe, motorboat, and paddleboat rentals are available. Pets are $10 per day or $50 per week with prior approval.

Fifty acres of woods etched with trails surround the new, nicely appointed **Moosehead Hills Cabins** (418 Lily Bay Rd., Greenville, 207/695-2514, www.mooseheadhills.com). Three hillside cabins have nice Moosehead views. A path and a road lead to the shoreline, where guests have use of a dock and kayaks. Also available are two cabins on seven-mile-long Loon Pond, also known as Wilson Pond, each with a private dock and water frontage. Peak rates are $200–375 per night, $1,375–2,600 per week with a one-week minimum in July–August and a 2–3-night minimum the rest of the year. Dogs are allowed in some cabins for $15 per pooch per day.

Sporting Camps

Ease into sporting camp life at **Maynard's in Maine** (Rockwood, 207/534-7703 or 888/518-2055, www.maynardsinmaine.com), operated by Gail and William Maynard. Cross the Rockwood bridge, take a left, and you're on tarred road right to the property. Although it's not remote by most sporting camp standards, it's a rural gem. Meals are served in the central lodge; guests stay in the cabins, all with

© TOM NANGLE

The Appalachian Mountain Club operates Medawisla, a sporting camp on the Roach River.

full baths and most with views over the Moose River to the Blue Ridge (a blaze of color during foliage season). The food is great—freshly made and home-baked. Guests choose from two entrées each night. At first glance it may seem more run-down than rustic, but the cabins are comfy, the mattresses firm, and the plumbing is inside. Rates, including breakfast, dinner, and a packed lunch, are $65 adults, $32 ages 3–12; without meals, it's $40 adults. Cabins have 1–3 bedrooms. Pets are allowed for $20 per stay. Motorboat rental is $55 per day; canoes are $10.

Eric Stirling is the fourth-generation host at **West Branch Pond Camps** (Kokadjo, 207/695-2561, www.westbranchpondcamps .com). Lining the shore of First West Branch Pond, overlooking White Cap Mountain, are eight classically rustic cabins with indoor plumbing and evening electricity. Eric is slowly fixing them up, replacing mattresses, fixing screens, and repairing broken boards. For wilderness lovers who prefer a tad of comfort, this is the real thing. The camps are set upon 30

private acres surrounded by conservation lands, and the authenticity and peacefulness are all-encompassing. Fly-fishing, hiking, and canoeing are the major pursuits here. Cross-country skiers and snowshoers come in winter. If you're hoping to spot a moose, well, the gangly mammals often stroll right through the property, even peeking in the kitchen window. Speaking of the kitchen: When the bell rings for meals, guests head to the 1890 lakeside lodge and vacuum up the hearty cuisine described in one upscale national magazine as "simple, soulful Yankee cooking." Thursday nights, the prime-rib dinner ($14–25 pp, including dessert) is open to nonguests by reservation. BYOB. Most guests stay for a week, and the many repeats make it tough to book space, but the daily rate is $98 pp adults, $50 ages 5–11, which includes meals, lodging, a boat, firewood, and linens. Well-behaved pets are $20 per stay. Take Lily Bay Road from Greenville 17 miles; turn right onto an unpaved road (signposted "West Branch Ponds") and go 10 more miles. It's open May–September and late January–late March.

The **Appalachian Mountain Club** (603/466-2727, www.outdoors.org) operates three trail-connected traditional sporting camps in the 100-Mile-Wilderness Region. All are primitive to rustic, with woodstoves providing the only cabin heat in winter. **Medawisla,** sited where the Roach River flows into Second Roach Pond, has seven private pet-friendly cabins and offers both self-service lodging and full-service with family-style meals and trail lunches. It's open year-round except April and December, with indoor showers and toilets in each cabin during the warmer months, outhouses and a central shower during winter. **Little Lyford,** dating from 1874, near Gulf Hagas and the Appalachian Trail, Little Lyford Pond, and the Pleasant River, is the most primitive of the three. Guests share a central bathhouse with hot showers, a winter sauna, and composting toilets. It's a full-service lodge with three daily meals provided. **Gorman Chairback** on the shores of Long Pond is the newest and nicest of the three, with renovated log cabins, a central bathhouse with showers and a sauna, and a new environmentally friendly lodge. Packages that include gear shuttle for lodge-to-lodge skiing are available. Rates vary by season, and you'll get the best price if you join the AMC. Nonmember rates, including meals, begin at $119 pp.

Forty-three miles northeast of Greenville is **Nahmakanta Lake Camps** (207/731-8888, www.nahmakanta.com), Don and Angel Hibbs's oasis in the wilderness on Nahmakanta Lake. Nine restored cabins right on the lake have screened porches, full kitchens, and woodstoves. There is no electricity. Guests share six common bathhouses with showers and flush toilets, but each cabin also has a private privy. Choose from the full American Plan, including all meals ($140 pp per day adults, plus $7 multiplied by age for ages 1–17); the Modified American Plan, including supper ($110 pp per day adults, $5 multiplied by age for children), or housekeeping ($80 pp per day adults, $4 multiplied by age for kids). All rates are based on two-adult minimum and three-night stay, five-night stay mid-July–August 30. Canoes and kayaks are provided; boats and motors are

$60 per day; guides are available. Summer access is via 25 miles of gravel roads or floatplane. Dogs are welcome with advance notice. Now, here's the really cool (OK, cold) part: Nahmakanta is open in winter. Access is by cross-country ski, snowmobile shuttle ($50 per load), or dog team. Relax in a wood-fired cedar sauna upon arrival, and yes, there are hot showers. Housekeeping rates are $50 per adult. The best deal is the three-day dogsledding package (www.mainedogsledding.com) for $1,175 pp, which includes meals, lodging, shuttle, and guide service.

Camping

The **Maine Forest Service** supervises and maintains free campsites with fireplaces and outhouses, many on the shores of Moosehead Lake. Most are accessible only by boat on a first come, first served basis. For information, contact the Maine Forest Service office (downtown Greenville, 207/695-3721).

At the northern end of Moosehead Lake, about 5.5 miles south of the Golden Road, **Seboomook Wilderness Campground** (Seboomook Village, 207/280-0555, www.seboomookwildernesscampground.us), has 84 wooded and open tent and RV sites, Adirondack shelters, and housekeeping cabins (no linens), many right on the water. Everything is very rustic, although there is a central bathhouse with flush toilets and free hot showers. Request a site on the eastern side, away from the long-term RV area. Facilities include a small, shallow beach and a grocery store with a lunch counter. History buffs take note: This is the site of a World War II German POW camp. Camping sites are $18–30 per day; shelters are $30 d; cabins are $50–100 per day. Weekly rates are also available. Seboomook's store is open all winter for snowmobilers and cross-country skiers; campsites are open mid-May–November. Canoes, kayaks, and motorboat rentals are available. The campground is about 28 unpaved miles north of Rockwood; you'll need to pay a user fee ($8 for nonresidents, $5 for Maine residents over age 14) at the Twenty-Mile Checkpoint just before Pittston Farm.

You can't get much closer to the water than some of the primitive sites at **South Inlet Wilderness Campground** (Frenchville Rd., Kokadjo, 207/695-2474 evenings, 207/695-3954 winter, $12–15). Although near a dirt road, many of the sites front on First Roach Pond. There's also a field for bigger RVs but no hookups. Facilities include a beach, a boat launch, privies, fire rings, and picnic tables.

Plan well in advance to snag one of the primo waterfront sites at **Lily Bay State Park** (Lily Bay Rd., Greenville, 207/695-2700); on weekends July–August, campsite reservations are essential, with a two-night minimum (call 207/287-3824 and have a MasterCard, Visa, or Discover card ready, or visit www.campwithme .com). Only the lucky will find a last-minute space, even though there are 93 sites in two clusters; none have hookups. Camping fees are $24 nonresidents, $14 Maine residents, plus the reservation fee of $2 per site per night.

FOOD

The range of dining experiences in and near Greenville is amazingly broad. One caveat: While choices are plentiful in summer, they're scanty at best in the off-season.

Restaurant hours noted are for peak season but are subject to change. It's always wise to call ahead.

Local Flavors

The gossip is as good as the grub at the **Kokadjo Trading Post** (3424 Lily Bay Rd., Greenville, 207/695-3993, www.kokadjo.com), right across the road from First Roach Pond. There might not be a sign out front; it's kind of quirky that way. Inside are a small shop, a takeout counter, and restaurant seating. Fred and Marie Candeloro also rent cabins, from run-down to ultra fancy.

Extremely popular among local residents for breakfast and lunch is **Flatlanders** (38 Pritham Ave., Greenville, 207/695-3373). The best choice is the broasted chicken, which one waitress described as "kinda like fried chicken but cooked in a pressure cooker so it's more healthy." Whatever; everyone agrees it's tasty.

Buy pizza and subs, beer and wine coolers, and worms and crawlers at **Jamo's** (Pritham Ave., Greenville, 207/695-2201). OK, skip the latter pairing, but the pizza's decent, and the Dagwood sandwiches, made on fresh-baked pita bread, earn raves.

The riverside **Moose River Country Store** (Rte. 6/15, Rockwood, 207/534-7352, 6 A.M.–8 P.M. Sun.–Thurs., 6 A.M.–9 P.M. Fri.–Sat.) sells huge sandwiches (one large easily feeds two normal-size appetites) as well as burgers and pizza and, in the morning, breakfast fare. Eat in or take out.

Casual Dining

A dining bright spot in downtown Greenville, **Rod-N-Reel Cafe** (44 Pritham Ave., Greenville, 207/695-0388, www.rodnreelcafe .com, 4–9 P.M. Wed.–Sun.) reels them in for reliable home-style food with flair. Fish is the dominant theme, from the name to the decor to the menu, but you can get steaks, chicken, and pasta as well. Dinner entrées are $12–24, but lighter fare is available. Friday and Saturday are prime rib nights. In peak summer it usually opens for lunch too.

For upscale pub food, such as wraps and salads, as well as burgers and chili, detour into the **Stress-free Moose** (65 Pritham Ave., Greenville, 207/695-3100, 11 A.M.–10 P.M., 11 A.M.–11 P.M. Fri.–Sat). While you can sit inside, the big wraparound porch is the place to while away an afternoon or evening.

In Greenville Junction, with fantastic lake views, is **Kelly's Landing** (Rte. 6/15, Greenville Junction, 207/695-4438, http:// kellysatmoosehead.com, 7 A.M.–9 P.M. daily year-round, $8–21). The food is hit or miss, but you can't beat the location. If the weather's fine, dine on the deck; if not, the dining rooms have big windows on the lake. A kids' menu is available. The Sunday breakfast buffet is a megabargain at $11. There's always a crowd, and boaters can tie up at the dock.

Experience sporting-camp life and meals without getting too far into the woods at **Maynard's in Maine** (207/534-7703 or 888/518-2055, www.maynardsinmaine.com),

© HILARY NANGLE

Maynard's in Maine, in Rockwood, provides a gentle introduction to sporting camp life. Even if you don't stay, go for breakfast or dinner.

an authentic main lodge and cabins overlooking the Moose River in Rockwood. Maynard's is open to nonguests (breakfast 7–9 A.M. daily, dinner 5:30–7:30 P.M. daily, reservations required). There's a full menu for breakfast and a set menu with a choice of two entrées at dinner ($22), including soup or juice, salad, sides, dessert, and a nonalcoholic beverage. Everything is homemade or baked and served family-style in the pleasant dining room.

Another good choice for a fine meal in a great setting is **Northern Pride Lodge** (3405 Lily Bay Rd., Frenchtown Township, 207/695-2890, www.northernpridelodge.com, 5–8 P.M. daily, by advance reservation only), 18 miles north of Greenville overlooking First Roach Pond in Kokadjo. Entrées, such as pork tenderloin medallions, baked salmon, and roast duckling, are around $20. Reservations are required by noon. If you don't want to drive the moose slalom back to Greenville, rooms ($59 s, $98 d) are available with shared baths and include breakfast.

If you're willing to drive a good 10 miles

into the woods to dine, book a table at **West Branch Pond Camps** (Kokadjo 207/695-2561, www.westbranchpondcamps.com). This is the real deal, with a set menu offered at 6 P.M. Monday–Saturday and at noon Sunday; prices range $14–25, depending on the meal. Dining here is an adventure, and the food never disappoints. Advance reservations are required.

Fine Dining

The elegant **⟨ Blair Hill Inn** (Lily Bay Rd., 207/695-0224) serves a fixed-price five-course menu ($59) 5:30–8:30 P.M. Thursday–Saturday evenings in the elegant dining room and adjacent glassed-in porch high on a hill with sweeping sunset views over Moosehead Lake. The inn has an indoor wood-burning grill, so meats and fish are grilled, and much of the produce comes from the inn's greenhouses and gardens. And almost everything is made from scratch—from sorbet and ice cream to breads and soups; special diets can be accommodated, including vegan with notice. It's open mid-June–mid-October and Saturday nights in January–February. Arrive early to enjoy a sunset cocktail in the lounge or on the porch.

INFORMATION AND SERVICES

The **Moosehead Lake Region Chamber of Commerce** (156 Rte. 15, Greenville, 888/876-2778, www.mooseheadlake.org) has information about member businesses and area activities.

DeLorme Mapping produces a widely available foldout *Map and Guide of Moosehead Lake,* with excellent detail and information on sightseeing and recreational pursuits.

The **Shaw Public Library** (N. Main St., Greenville, 207/695-3579, www.greenvilleme.com/library) has archives loaded with North Woods lore.

State agencies with offices in Greenville are the **Maine Warden Service** (MWS, 207/695-3756) and the **Maine Forest Service** (MFS, Lakeview St., Greenville, 207/695-3721). The Greenville MWS office, with jurisdiction for all search-and-rescue missions of Maine's acreage, undertakes at least one search-and-rescue mission per week. The MFS, besides fire-spotting duty, is also responsible for a number of public campsites in the region.

Public Restrooms

In Greenville, the Indian Hill Trading Post has restrooms, as do the chamber of commerce office and the Moosehead Marine Museum, next to the *Katahdin* wharf. In Greenville Junction, there are restrooms at Junction Wharf; in Rockwood, there are restrooms at the public boat landing.

GETTING AROUND

Greenville flying services operating small pontoon- or ski-equipped planes act as the lifelines to remote North Woods sporting camps, campsites, rivers, lakes, and ponds inaccessible overland. In some cases, road access exists, but you'll jeopardize your vehicle, your innards, and maybe your life along the way. **Currier's Flying Service** (Pritham Ave./Rte. 6/15, Greenville Junction, 207/695-2778, www.curriersflyingservice.com) and **Jack's Air Service** (Pritham Ave., Greenville, 207/695-3020), based in downtown Greenville, provide on-demand charter service to remote locales. Both firms have flat hourly rates if you want to create your own itinerary.

You don't need a plane to get to Kineo, but you will need a boat. First, drive the 20 miles along Route 6/15 to Rockwood, where the lake is narrowest—about 4,000 feet across. The *Kineo Shuttle,* a pontoon boat, runs on a set schedule, departing hourly in July–August, less frequently spring and fall, from the Rockwood public landing (on the village loop just off the highway). Just show up and climb aboard. The fare is $10 pp round-trip.

Many of the **roads** in the Greenville area are unpaved; paper-company roads tend to be the best maintained, because access is essential for their huge log trucks and machinery. But others, especially roads leading to sporting camps, can become tank traps in spring—April–May—and after a heavy downpour. Before setting out during those times—especially if you don't have a 4WD vehicle—be sure to check on road conditions. Ask the chamber of commerce, the Maine Forest Service, the county sheriff, or the sporting camp owners.

Dover-Foxcroft Area

At the bottom of Piscataquis (piss-CAT-uh-kwiss) County, Dover-Foxcroft is the county seat, hub for the surrounding towns of **Milo, Brownville Junction, Sangerville, Guilford, Abbot,** and **Monson.** Here's an area that's often overlooked, probably because Greenville, Moosehead Lake, and Baxter State Park are just up the road. But it's easy to spend a couple of days exploring here—notably for dramatic Gulf Hagas Reserve and Borestone Mountain Sanctuary, but also for a handful of out-of-the-way towns few visitors get to appreciate.

One town growing steadily in renown is Monson, 20 miles northwest of Dover-Foxcroft and 15 miles south of Greenville. Incorporated in 1822, Monson has an old reputation and a new one. The old one comes from its slate quarries, first mined in the 1870s, which shipped slate around the nation for sinks, roof tiles, blackboards, and even urinals. A considerable Finnish community grew up here to work the quarries; their descendants still celebrate traditional holidays. Although the industry has declined, and only two companies still operate, Monson slate monuments adorn the gravesites of John F. Kennedy and Jacqueline Kennedy Onassis. You can still see an abandoned quarry pit on Pleasant Street, near Lake Hebron, on the western side of town.

Monson's current fame comes from Appalachian Trail (AT) through-hikers, whose energetic grapevine carries the word about the town's hospitality to the rugged outdoors folk nearing the end of their arduous trek from Springer Mountain, Georgia. The Monson stopover comes just before the AT leg known as the 100-Mile Wilderness, so it's a place to regroup, clean up, and rev up for the isolated week or 10 days ahead. It's also home to a handful of shops selling quality work by local artists and artisans and hodgepodge antiques.

Sangerville, incorporated in 1813, is the birthplace of the infamous Sir Harry Oakes, a colorful adventurer who acquired a fortune in Canadian gold mining. Murdered in bed in his Nassau (Bahamas) mansion in 1943, gazillionaire Oakes was interred in Dover-Foxcroft. His killer was never found. Also born in Sangerville was Sir Hiram Maxim, inventor of the Maxim gun. These days, it's the East Sangerville Grange that gets the attention, especially in winter, when there's entertainment accompanied by fantastic desserts.

Dexter and Corinna are actually in the Sebasticook Valley area, but since many visitors pass through them on Route 7, they're included here.

SIGHTS
Monson

Most folks zip through this pretty little lakeside village, but Monson is worth a linger. A handful of antiques and artisans' shops lining Main Street and a good barbecue joint are reason enough to visit, but Monson is also a major stop on the Appalachian Trail, the last vestige of civilization before northbound hikers enter the infamous 100-Mile Wilderness on the way to Katahdin.

Low's Covered Bridge

In 1987, the raging Piscataquis River, swollen by spring rains, wiped out 130-foot-long Low's Covered Bridge, near Sangerville. Named after settler Robert Low, the original bridge was built in 1830 and replaced in 1843 and 1857. The current incarnation, a well-made replica, reopened in 1990 at a cost of $650,000. It's one of only nine covered bridges now in Maine. Close to Route 16/6/15, the bridge is 3.7 miles east of Guilford and 4.5 miles west of Dover-Foxcroft.

Katahdin Iron Works

Only a lonely stone blast furnace and a charcoal kiln remain at Katahdin Iron Works, the site of a once-thriving 19th-century community where iron mining produced 2,000 tons of ore a year and steam trains brought tourists to the three-story Silver Lake House to "take the

© HILARY NANGLE

The Katahdin Iron Works blast furnace is one of the few remnants left from a once-thriving 19th-century community.

waters" at Katahdin Mineral Springs. Today most visitors drive down the unpaved 6.5 miles from Route 11 and stop just across the road, at the North Maine Woods **KI Checkpoint,** for hiking in Gulf Hagas Reserve. Entrance to the KI site (as it's known locally) is free.

Lake Onawa
Four-mile-long Lake Onawa is the mountain-ringed setting for the charming hamlet of **Onawa,** once linked to civilization only by train. Then came the road, and passenger service ceased, leaving Onawa as a summer colony with a year-round population of three. A prime attraction is an incredible 126-foot-high wooden railroad trestle (featured in one of Stephen King's films) that challenges even brave-hearted souls. Acrophobes, forget it. There's a walkway alongside, but it's still scary; don't attempt it on a windy day, and keep in mind that the tracks are still active. During World War II, the trestle was protected by African American security guards,

among them Edward Brooke, the late U.S. senator from Massachusetts. The 1,400-foot-long trestle, officially the Ship Pond Stream Viaduct, soars over Ship Pond Stream at the southern end of the lake, about 0.5 miles beyond the cluster of cottages. To reach Onawa, from Route 6/16/15 at the northern edge of Monson, take the partly unpaved Elliotsville Road northeast; turn right at the Big Wilson Stream bridge, and then take the next left onto Onawa Road. Continue about three miles to the settlement.

Historical Society Museums
Locals are proud of their history, and a handful of small museums are worthy of visits if you're a history buff.

The **Dexter Historical Society** (207/924-5721, www.dexterhistoricalsociety.com) operates three museums on its downtown Grist Mill campus (off Rte. 23, 10 A.M.–4 P.M. Mon.–Fri., 1–4 P.M. Sat. mid-June–early Sept., 1–4 P.M. Mon.–Sat. Sept.): the one-room Carr Schoolhouse, the 1825 Miller's house, and the water-powered Grist Mill. The society's Abbott Museum headquarters (Rte. 7/23, 10 A.M.–4 P.M. Mon.–Sat. late May–mid-Oct., noon–4 P.M. Wed.–Fri., 10 A.M.–4 P.M. Sat. winter) now doubles as a shop with works by local artisans. Admission is free, but donations are encouraged.

In downtown Monson, the old town hall has been reborn as the home of the **Monson Historical Society** (Main St., 207/876-3073, call for hours), with a Scandinavian gift shop downstairs and exhibits upstairs (check out the birch shoes).

ENTERTAINMENT AND EVENTS
October–May, the East Sangerville Grange Hall hosts its monthly Saturday night **Winter Coffee House Series** where the entertainment is fab and the desserts are beyond amazing as local cooks vie to outdo each other.

Live music, community theater, movies, and other entertainment are regularly scheduled at the **Center Theatre for the Performing Arts**

(20 E. Main St., Dover-Foxcroft, 207/564-8943, www.centertheatre.org), which opened in 2006 in a nicely renovated 300-seat movie theater. The Saturday Night Concert Series is presented on the third Saturday of the month June–December. Ask about the local doctor who was married on stage during a presentation by the Maine Hysterical Society, complete with reception line during intermission.

The last Saturday in April, the early-season **Piscataquis River Canoe Race** covers eight miles of mostly flat water between Guilford and Dover-Foxcroft. An hour-long family-oriented race goes under Low's Covered Bridge. Starting time is 11 A.M., next to the Guilford Industries factory.

The one-day **Maine Whoopie Pie Festival** is held in June, with tastings, tours, crafts, and entertainment.

The **Piscataquis Valley Fair** (www.piscataquisvalleyfair.com) takes place the fourth weekend in August. A family-oriented traditional county fair, it features agricultural exhibits, a pig scramble, a homemade ice cream parlor, fireworks, and a carnival. It's at the Piscataquis Valley Fairgrounds (Fairview Ave., just south of Rte. 6/15, east side of Dover-Foxcroft).

Throughout the summer, Finn dances take place on Saturday nights at the **Finnish Farmers Club.** Look for the small sign hanging in front of the white frame building just south of Monson village on the west side of Route 6/15. Expect dancing, perhaps traditional costumes, coffee, and bulla bread. Finnish music is performed by Woodsong.

The Belvin family's **The Junction General Store and Entertainment Park** (197 Davis St./Rte. 11, Brownville Junction, 207/965-8876, www.thejunctiongeneral.com) is entertainment central in these parts. It sponsors a summer concert series with tribute concerts to bands such as Aerosmith, the Eagles, and others; has a drive-in theater; and operates a café serving big breakfasts, lunches, and ice cream.

Leaping Lipizzaners! **Isaac Royal Farm** (849 Range Rd., Dover-Foxcroft, 207/564-3499, www.isaacroyalfarm.com) operates a renowned equestrian school with world-class instructors, holds dressage shows, and stages don't-miss themed equestrian theatrical presentations complete with music, choreography, and costumes. Check the website to see what's scheduled during your visit or to find out about lessons and camps.

SHOPPING
Shopping isn't a big deal here, but you'll find a handful of arts-and-crafts shops in Monson and Abbott.

Buy wonderful maple syrup, great dressings, and bison meat at **Breakneck Ridge Farm** (160 Mountain Rd., Blanchard Township, 207/997-3922, www.breakneckridgefarm.com). The farm has a few open houses each year; private tours are available year-round by reservation.

Fans of antiques, fine arts, and handmade goods will find plenty in the shops along Monson's Main Street; most are open seasonally. **Lake Hebron Artisans** has an excellent selection of fine and folk crafts. Across the street, the **Hebron Gallery** (207/997-3950) is a small gallery showing fine art by local artists. **Violet's Everything Shop** (207/997-3945) delivers on its name with an eclectic selection of antiques and collectibles.

Bob Moore is the king of maple in these parts. At **Bob's Sugar House** (252 E. Main St./Rte. 15, Dover-Foxcroft, 207/564-2145, www.mainemaplesyrup.com), you'll find pure Maine maple syrup, maple butter, maple cream, maple popcorn, maple barbecue seasoning, and the list goes on.

RECREATION
Peaks-Kenny State Park
Get organized to arrive at Peaks-Kenny State Park (Sebec Lake Rd., Dover-Foxcroft, 207/564-2003, www.parksandlands.com, $6 nonresident adults, $4 Maine resident adults, $2 nonresident seniors, $1 ages 5–11, free under age 5) well before 11 A.M. on weekends in June–August—after that, you may be turned away or have to wait. This particularly

CONSERVING FOR THE FUTURE

Anyone who has visited Maine's North Woods knows that this landscape of woods, water, and mountains is a treasure. While the state and federal government had protected bits and pieces, most notably Baxter State Park, Nahmakanta, and Gulf Hagas, it was a hop-scotch pattern that left the connecting areas, including those sheltering the famed 100-Mile Wilderness section of the Appalachian Trail, vulnerable.

Enter the Appalachian Mountain Club (AMC), which in 2003 launched the Maine Woods Initiative, a strategy for land conservation that combines outdoor recreation, resource protection, sustainable forestry, and community partnerships in the 100-Mile Wilderness region. Through its work on the initiative, AMC is protection land from development, maintaining public access in perpetuity.

In 2003, the AMC acquired the Katahdin Iron Works tract, a spectacular 37,000-acre parcel of wilderness that includes the headwaters of the West Branch of the Pleasant River and abuts federally protected Gulf Hagas. Within this tract, the AMC created a 10,000-acre ecological reserve to protect the West Branch watershed as well as a few other special zones to protect other vital ecological resources. The remaining acreage remains a working forest, maintained with sustainable techniques, and open to hunters, anglers, paddlers, mountain bikers, wildlife-watchers, skiers, snowshoers, snowmobilers, campers, and hikers.

In 2009, the AMC acquired the Roach Ponds Tract, which abuts not only the Katahdin Iron Works Tract but also the state's Nahmakanta Public Reserved Land. The purchase of the 29,500-acre Roach Ponds tract was an historic transaction that marked the creation of a 63-mile-long corridor of conservation land stretching from the AMC's Katahdin Iron Works property near Greenville north to Baxter State Park. The holdings comprise nearly 650,000 acres of conservation land that's a playground for outdoor enthusiasts. Within the AMC's 66,500-acre Maine Woods Property alone are 23 ponds, more than 70 miles of managed recreational trails, and more than 200 miles of dirt roads.

Even better, it's possible to immerse oneself in this chunk of heaven without sacrificing all creature comforts. Within the Maine Woods Property are three AMC-managed sporting camps: Medawisla Wilderness Lodge and Cabins, Little Lyford Lodge and Cabins, and Gorman Chairback Lodge and Cabins; the privately owned West Branch Pond Camps; and a mix of drive-in, hike-in, and paddle-in campsites.

---

scenic park on 14-mile-long Sebec Lake has 50 picnic sites, a playground, a lifeguard-staffed sand beach, nine miles of hiking trails, and 56 campsites. Canoe rentals are $3 per hour.

Hiking

For details on these or other hikes, consult *North Woods Walks* by Christopher Keene (a guide for Northwoods Outfitters) or AMC's *Maine Mountain Guide*, available in local bookstores.

BORESTONE MOUNTAIN SANCTUARY

Owned and maintained by the Maine Audubon Society (www.maineaudubon.org), Borestone Mountain Sanctuary (Elliotsville Rd., Elliotsville Plantation, 207/631-4050, Oct.–May 207/781-2330, 8 A.M.–sunset May–Oct., $4 adults, $2 ages 6–18 and over age 60) is a 1,600-acre preserve that provides a wonderful hiking experience for all ages. The two-mile (each way) moderately difficult trail to the rocky open summit delivers ample rewards at the top: full-circle views that include Lake Onawa below and the mountains of the 100-Mile Wilderness. Foliage season is especially dramatic here. Allow 4–5 hours for the four-mile round-trip, including a halfway-up stop at the Sunrise Pond visitors center, with displays on local flora and fauna; don't miss it. Pets are not allowed. From Route 6/16/15 at the northern edge of Monson, take the partly unpaved Elliotsville Road northeast 8.5 miles to the trailhead.

APPALACHIAN TRAIL
Sample the country's eastern footpath from the trailhead north of Monson on Route 6/15, just south of Spectacle Ponds. Unless you're a serious hiker, you won't want to venture too far, as this is one of the most difficult sections of the trail.

◖ GULF HAGAS RESERVE
Hiking in and around Gulf Hagas Reserve, a spectacular 400-foot-high, 3.5-mile-long wooded and rocky gorge along the West Branch of the Pleasant River, requires registering first at the **KI Checkpoint** (207/965-8135) operated by North Maine Woods, the forest recreation-management association. (KI is short for Katahdin Ironworks.) The checkpoint is one of the entrances into the **KI Jo-Mary Multiple Use Forest,** a working forest of more than 200,000 acres. (Jo-Mary is the name of a legendary Indian chief.) The checkpoint is open 6 A.M.–9 P.M. (sometimes later on midsummer weekends) early May–Columbus Day. The staffers have maps of the reserve ($2) and KI Jo-Mary ($3); do not hike Gulf Hagas without the map. Access is $10 for nonresidents, $6 for Maine residents. No bicycles, motorcycles, or ATVs can go beyond this point. Camping at one of the 60 scenic primitive sites in this area costs an extra $10 pp per night, $5 for seniors. It's wise to call the checkpoint ahead of time to reserve one of the sites, which have outhouses, picnic tables, and fire rings. The policy is carry-in, carry-out. There's also a commercial campground here.

You'll need to drive about seven miles from the checkpoint to one of the two parking areas; remember that logging trucks have the right-of-way on this road. As you walk from your vehicle toward the gulf, you'll go through **The Hermitage,** a 35-acre preserve of old-growth pines. Gulf Hagas Reserve, a National Natural Landmark that's part of the Appalachian Trail corridor, is no cakewalk. Almost weekly, rangers have to rescue injured

or lost hikers who underestimate the terrain. Ledges are narrow, with 100-foot drop-offs, and rain can make them perilous. Leave rambunctious children at home; the section beyond **Screw Auger Falls** is particularly dangerous for kids under 12. Wear waterproof hiking boots—you have to cross a stream to gain access to the reserve.

Caveats aside, the hike is fantastic—especially mid-September–early October, when the leaves are gorgeous and the bugs have retreated. Carry a compass and a flashlight and allow 6–8 hours for the 8.3-mile canyon circuit (although there are shortcuts if you tucker out before the end). Most hikers do the loop clockwise. North Maine Woods trails are blue-blazed; a spur of the Appalachian Trail is white-blazed. The trails are open mid-May–late October, but atypical weather can affect the schedule. The checkpoint is 11.5 miles northwest of Brownville Junction (6.5 miles northwest of Rte. 11).

The Appalachian Mountain Club's Little Lyford Camps is a convenient base for hiking Gulf Hagas.

Multiuse Trails
Stretching 27 miles, the **Newport/Dover-Foxcroft Rail Trail** is extremely popular, especially among horseback riders. From its Newport base on the north side of Route 7 to its end near Fairview Street in Dover-Foxcroft, the trail passes through towns and rural countryside, including farms, woods, and wetlands, and edges Sebasticook and Corundel Lakes, the east branch of the Sebasticook River, and the Piscataquis River.

The 10-mile Guilford Memorial River Walk edges the Piscataquis River from Guilford to Abbot. The trailheads are off Route 15 in Guilford, east of the athletic fields, and at the Sangerville Station bridge on Route 23.

Water Sports
Lakes and rivers color much of the map blue in this region. If you have your own boat, quiet-water paddling options include the Sebec River above Milo, the Piscataquis River above the

dam in Guilford, Lake Hebron in Monson, and Branns Mill Pond in Dover-Foxcroft.

Kayak rentals for three-mile-long Lake Hebron are available from **Lakeshore House** (9 Tenney Hill Rd./Rte. 5/15, Monson, 207/997-7069, www.lakeshore-house.com) for a donation to the local food pantry.

ACCOMMODATIONS
Bed-and-Breakfasts
On a prominent hilltop and surrounded by gardens, the dark-red-painted **Guilford Bed and Breakfast** (Elm St./Rte. 6/15/16, Guilford, 207/876-3477, www.guilfordbandb.com, $105–135), built by a woolen mill owner as a wedding gift for his daughter, exudes history, wealth, and prominence of a bygone era. Innkeepers Isobel and Harland Young, from Ohio, were longtime guests before buying the inn in 2006 and then undertaking a historical restoration, completed in 2009. A big screened porch wraps around the Queen Anne–style Victorian's front, leading into the formal hall and spacious public rooms, all filled with comfortable furnishings.

Just beyond the Dover-Foxcroft area, but close enough, the ⟨ **Brewster Inn** (37 Zion's Hill Rd., Dexter, 207/924-3130, www.brewsterinn.com, $69–139) is an attractive 19-room mansion, on the National Register of Historic Places, designed by John Calvin Stevens and once owned by Maine governor Ralph Brewster. The nine guest rooms all have phones, air-conditioning, TVs, and stories to tell. The knotty-pine Game Room was the governor's private hideout, and guess who once slept in the Truman Room? Breakfast is a generous buffet with one hot dish. English innkeepers Mark and Judith Stephens, who arrived in 2007, have been remodeling the rooms and bringing back the lovely gardens to their mid-20th-century splendor. The Stephens also serve dinner to guests by advance reservation.

Neither hostel nor B&B, Rebekah Santagata's **Lakeshore House** (9 Tenney Hill Rd./Rte. 5/15, Monson, 207/997-7069, www.lakeshore-house.com) is a continually evolving lakeside business housing a launderette,

guest rooms, a pub, and canoe and kayak rentals on Lake Hebron. Options vary from a bunk in a shared room ($25) to a private double ($55). All guests share two baths, a living room with a TV, and a kitchenette. There is Wi-Fi on the premises with one laptop available to guests.

Hostel
Headquarters for Appalachian Trail through-hikers, a home-away-from-home since 1977 is the legendary **Shaw's Boarding Home** (Pleasant St., Monson, 207/997-3597, www.shawslodging.com). To weary hikers, this welcoming no-frills operation feels like the Hyatt Regency. Short-haul hikers are also welcome, as are snowmobilers in winter; couch potatoes will feel totally out of place. The home can accommodate nearly three dozen guests in varied arrangements—private rooms in the main house ($35 s, $56 d), bunkhouse beds ($23 pp), and tent sites ($12). A lumberjack-quality breakfast is $7, and dinner is $12. For small fees, shuttle and mail-drop service and laundry facilities are available; parking for short-haulers is $1 per day.

Camping
Within the boundaries of the KI Jo-Mary Multiple Use Forest is a single commercial campground, the **Jo-Mary Lake Campground** (Upper Jo-Mary Lake, Millinocket, 207/723-8117 or 800/494-0031, www.northmainewoods.org, mid-May–late Sept.), on the southern shore of five-mile-long Upper Jo-Mary Lake. Despite being remote, the campground has 70 sites, flush toilets, hot showers, laundry facilities, a snack bar, plenty of play space for kids, and a sandy beach. Sites are about $16–20 pp, two-person minimum (includes access fee). There's a Wednesday night beanhole bean supper (beans baked underground) July–August. The campground is 15 miles southwest of Millinocket and 20 miles north of Brownville. From Brownville Junction, take Route 11 northwest about 15 miles, turn left onto an unpaved road, and stop at the Jo-Mary Checkpoint (access fee $10 per

day nonresidents, $8 Maine residents, free for seniors and kids under age 15), and then continue six miles northwest to the campground.

Peaks-Kenny State Park (Sebec Lake Rd., Dover-Foxcroft, 207/564-2003) has 56 campsites. On weekends July–August, reservations are essential (two-night minimum; call 207/287-3824 using MasterCard or Visa). Nonresident camping fees are $25 per site per night, Maine residents $15 per site per night, plus the reservation fee of $2 per site per night; no hookups. Leashed pets are allowed.

FOOD
Restaurant hours noted are for peak season but are subject to change. It's always wise to call ahead.

Abbott Village
The claim to fame at the **Abbott Bakery** (Rte. 6/15, 207/876-4243, 4:30 A.M.–9 P.M. daily) is the nine-inch Skidder Tire Doughnut (available by request, call). It's a homely li'l spot, but it's a good choice for homemade doughnuts, breads, sweets, and sandwiches on homemade bread.

Dover-Foxcroft
Good home cooking with a few surprises packs **The Nor'easter Restaurant** (44 North St., 207/564-2122, 11 A.M.–8 P.M. Sat.–Thurs., 11 A.M.–9 P.M. Fri., $4–16), a congenial place with country-style decor and seating both at the counter and tables. The service is warm and attentive.

Named after Dover-Foxcroft's first settler, **Abel Blood's** (100 Main St., 207/564-3177, 4–9 P.M. Wed.–Sat., $8–17) serves the region's best steaks as well as plenty of other choices, including quesadillas, burgers, and grilled pizzas.

The favorite local farm market is **Stutzman's** (891 Doughty Hill Rd., 207/564-8596), on the back road between Sangerville and Dover-Foxcroft. Stock up on fresh produce and baked goodies and pick your own berries, peas, and more in season.

Some of the most popular flavors at **Butterfield's Ice Cream** (946 W. Main St., 207/564-2513) are vanilla peanut butter and chocolate peanut butter, but there are plenty of other options available.

Monson
This barbecue oasis is no secret: Even celebrity chef Anthony Bourdain has discovered Mike and Kim Witham's **C Spring Creek Bar-B-Q** (26 Greenville Rd./Rte. 15, 207/997-7025, 10 A.M.–8 P.M. Thurs.–Sat., 9 A.M.–5 P.M. Sun.), although he visited the winter snowmobile-trail location. Prices and portions are geared to Appalachian Trail hikers, so you won't go hungry or poor. There are tables inside and outside; they have no liquor license and don't take credit cards. About the hours: They stay open until the food's gone.

Reasonably priced pub fare is served at the **Lakeshore House** (9 Tenney Hill Rd./Rte. 5/15, 207/997-7069, www.lakeshore-house.com, 4–11 P.M. or so Tues.–Thurs., noon–midnight Fri.–Sat., noon–8 P.M. Sun., kitchen closes at 9 P.M., $6–11), a casual spot overlooking Lake Hebron with seating indoors and out. Salads, sandwiches, pizza, tacos, and daily specials provide plenty of choices.

INFORMATION AND SERVICES
Local information is available from the **Southern Piscataquis County Chamber of Commerce** (100 South St./Rte. 7, Dover-Foxcroft, 207/564-7533, www.spccc.org).

For information about Gulf Hagas Reserve and the KI Jo-Mary Multiple Use Forest, contact **North Maine Woods** (207/435-6213, www.northmainewoods.org).

The Town of Monson has local information posted at www.monsonmaine.org.

Bangor Area

Maine's Queen City is best identified by a trio of kings, but its appeal extends to those on a pauper's budget. Home to king of horror Stephen King, Bangor was folksinger Roger Miller's destination in "King of the Road" and is home to a gigantic statue of king of the woods Paul Bunyan. One would think with so many kingly claims, Bangor (BANG-gore) would be nicknamed the King City, but for reasons now unknown, it's been promoted as the Queen City since the late 19th century.

Lumber capital of the world in the 19th century, Bangor is still northern Maine's magnet for commerce and culture—the big city for the northern three-quarters of the state. The county seat for Penobscot County, downtown Bangor is awakening from a slump dating to the 1960s, typical of many urban areas. The 2002–2004 waterfront National Folk Festivals brought excitement and major crowds to the city and dusted off its sense of possibility, and Bangor has continued the three-day late-August event as the American Folk Festival. Now you can stroll alongside Kenduskeag Stream, duck into shops and an increasing number of restaurants, and end the evening with music, a show, or perhaps trying your luck at the state's first (and so far only) slots.

Bangor incorporated in 1791, but when explorer Samuel de Champlain landed here in 1604 (an event commemorated by a plaque downtown, next to Kenduskeag Stream), the Queen City bore the Native American name of Kenduskeag, meaning "eel-catching place."

In the late 19th century, when the lumber trade moved westward, smaller industries moved into greater Bangor to take up the slack, but a disastrous fire on April 30, 1911, leveled 55 acres of Bangor's commercial and residential neighborhoods, retarding progress for several decades.

Bangor highlights fine specimens of Victorian, Italianate, Queen Anne, and Greek Revival architecture—and who knows, you might see legendary author Stephen King in your travels. Part of what King enjoys about Bangor is that locals are used to him and accord him "normal person" treatment.

SIGHTS

Downtown Bangor lends itself to walking, especially if hills don't intimidate you. About twice monthly July–October, the Bangor Museum offers **Ghost Lamp Tours** (www.bangormuseum.com, $5, free under age 13) of the downtown.

The Standpipe

A distinctive west-side landmark is the Thomas Hill Standpipe. The 1.75-million-gallon riveted-steel water tower and observatory, built in 1897, is a National Historic and American Water Landmark. Some say it's the queen city's crown, and a case can be made that it resembles one when viewed from afar. The Standpipe is open four days each year for tours, usually once per season, which allows visitors to climb the interior staircase circling to the top and access the great view from the observation platform. For

tour information, call the Bangor Water District (207/947-4516, www.bangorwater.org).

Paul Bunyan Statue

Bangor's Victorian-era fortunes were built on the millions of trees felled in the North Woods and driven down the Penobscot River, then milled and shipped from its busy port. One local tall tale paints super-logger Paul Bunyan as a native son, allegedly born in Bangor on February 12, 1834. That might explain the 31-foot-tall statue of him in Bass Park downtown. Weighing 3,200 pounds, the colorful statue was erected in 1959 during the city's 125th anniversary. Inside the base is a time capsule due to be opened in 2084. While Bunyan's status as a local might be questionable, the tool he holds is genuine Maine-made: After observing the difficulties river drivers were having shepherding logs down the Penobscot River with the traditional cant dog, local blacksmith Joseph Peavey invented the tool that bears his name.

© HILARY NANGLE

Legendary lumberjack Paul Bunyan is allegedly a Bangor native.

Stephen King-dom

Maine native and naturalized hometown boy, horror honcho Stephen King is anything but a myth. Born in Portland, he has lived in Bangor since 1980, and you may spot him around town (especially at baseball and basketball games). His turreted mansion on West Broadway looks like a set from one of the movies based on his novels and stories—complete with a wrought-iron front gate and fence festooned with iron bats and cobwebs. Heed the "No Trespassing" sign; the best-selling author has had his share of odd encounters with off-the-wall devotees, not to mention his 1999 encounter with an out-of-control minivan. These days, even though he's back at work, it's best to keep up with him via his website (www.stephenking.com).

The Greater Bangor Convention and Visitors Bureau offers **Tommyknockers and More** bus tours (800/916-6673, www.bangorcvb.org, $20) about once a month. Advance registration and payment is required, and space is limited.

Thomas A. Hill House

Built by a wealthy attorney in 1836 and listed on the National Register of Historic Places, the handsome brick Thomas A. Hill House (159 Union St., Bangor, 207/942-1900, www.bangormuseum.com, 10 A.M.–4 P.M. Tues.–Fri. June 1–Oct. 1, $3 over age 11), on the corner of High Street, has been restored to Victorian elegance, with period furnishings, Maine paintings, and special exhibits.

◖ University of Maine Museum of Art (UMMA)

Bangor scored a coup when it lured UMMA (Norumbega Hall, 40 Harlow St., Bangor, 207/561-3350, www.umma.umaine.edu, 10 A.M.–5 P.M. Mon.–Sat.) downtown. The museum's primary strengths are photography and contemporary works on paper, and its focus is on modern and contemporary art. Among the significant items in the museum's collection of more than 6,500 original works are pieces by John Marin, Roy Lichenstein,

The best way to see how the Bangor-area sights have influenced local author Stephen King's work is on a Tommyknockers and More bus tour.

Willem de Kooning, and Alex Katz. Exhibits are displayed in one permanent and three changing galleries. Admission is usually free, thanks to an annual gift.

Kenduskeag Stream Trail
Pick up a copy of the Kenduskeag Stream map at the visitors bureau and follow it to 13 marked sites, including where Portuguese navigator Esteban Gómez landed in 1525, followed by French geographer Samuel de Champlain in 1604. Also on the trail is Lovers Leap, a 150-foot-tall cliff where a Native American couple plunged to their deaths after being denied permission to marry.

Maine Discovery Museum
Here's a major kid magnet with a wide range of interactive exhibits that encourage creative play. The Maine Discovery Museum (74 Main St., Bangor, 207/262-7200, www.mainediscoverymuseum.org, 9:30 A.M.–5 P.M. Tues.–Sat., noon–5 P.M. Sun., $7.50) occupies more than 22,000 square feet on three floors of the former Freese's Department Store. Seven permanent exhibit areas feature nature, geography, art, science, anatomy, Maine children's literature, and music. Special programs are scheduled for children and families throughout the year.

Air and Fire Museums
On the grounds of Bangor International Airport, the **Maine Air Museum** (98 Maine Ave., Bangor, 877/280-6247 in Maine or 207/941-6757, www.maineairmuseum.org, 10 A.M.–4 P.M. Sat., noon–4 P.M. Sun. late May–early Sept., $2) is a fledgling museum operated by the Maine Aviation Historical Society and dedicated to the history of Maine aviation.

Kids get a kick out of the fire-fighting artifacts and fire trucks at the **Hose 5 Fire Museum** (247 State St., Bangor, 207/945-3229, call for hours, free), in an 1897 fire station.

Cole Land Transportation Museum
Children love the Cole Land Transportation Museum (405 Perry Rd., Bangor, 207/990-

3600, www.colemuseum.org, 9 A.M.–5 P.M. daily May–mid-Nov., $6 adults, $4 seniors, free under age 20), a sprawling facility founded by Bangor trucking magnate Galen Cole. More than 200 19th- and 20th-century vehicles—just about anything that has ever rolled across Maine's landscape—fill the museum. Besides vintage cars, there are fire engines, tractors, logging vehicles, baby carriages, even a replica railroad station. And this being Maine, the museum believes it owns the largest collection of snow-removal equipment in the country. A gift shop stocks transportation-related items. Outside are picnic tables and a covered bridge to walk over and under. The museum is near the junction of I-95 and I-395.

Winterport
In Waldo County, 12 miles downriver from Bangor, is Winterport, a pretty little sleeper of a town tucked along the Penobscot River. It earned its name as the limit of winter navigation for Bangor's lumber trade; ice blocked shipping traffic from proceeding farther upriver. The National Register **Winterport Historic District** includes splendid 19th-century Greek Revival homes and commercial buildings on Route 1A and the short side streets descending to the river. The **Winterport Winery** (279 S. Main St., Winterport, 207/223-4500, www.winterportwinery.com) has a tasting room for its fruit wines and a gallery for exhibiting local artists.

Mount Hope Cemetery
In a state where burial grounds usually command views to die for, the standout is Mount Hope (207/945-6589, www.mthopebgr.com, 7:30 A.M.–7:30 P.M. daily Apr. 1–Nov. 1, 7:30 A.M.–4 P.M. daily Nov. 1–Apr. 1), established in 1834, consecrated in 1836, and easily the state's loveliest. Here you can hobnob with some of Maine's dearly departed. Among the sights are unusual grave markers, including one elevated sarcophagus, and the graves of Hannibal Hamlin, Abe Lincoln's vice president during the Civil War, and gangster Al Brady, listed as Public Enemy Number 1 and killed in a firestorm of bullets in downtown Bangor

in 1937. Also of note is 20-foot-tall Soldier's Monument, erected in 1864 and among the oldest Civil War monuments in the country. Inspired by the design of Mount Auburn Cemetery in Cambridge, Massachusetts, 264-acre Mount Hope is more park than cemetery—with gardens, ponds, bridges, paved paths, lots of greenery, a few picnic tables, and wandering deer. The entrance to the green-fenced cemetery is at 1048 State Street (Rte. 2), about 0.25 miles east of Hogan Road. Cemetery tours are offered by the Bangor Historical Society (207/942-1900, www.bangormuseum.com, $5, free under age 12). Call or check the website for the schedule.

ENTERTAINMENT

More than a century ago, when cabin-feverish lumberjacks roared into Bangor for R&R, they were apt to patronize Fan Jones's "establishment" on Harlow Street. Adult entertainment is still available in the city, but so is higher-brow stuff. That said, nights in Bangor are pretty quiet for a city.

Bangor Symphony Orchestra (BSO)

Founded in 1896, Maine's BSO (207/942-5555 or 800/639-3221, www.bangorsymphony.com) has an enviable reputation as one of the country's oldest and best community orchestras. During the regular season, September–May, monthly concerts are presented weekends at the Maine Center for the Arts in Orono. The orchestra occasionally performs in summer too.

Penobscot Theatre Company

Bangor's professional theater company, Penobscot Theatre (131 Main St., Bangor, 207/942-3333, www.penobscottheatre.org) performs classic and contemporary comedies and dramas September–early June, along with an annual New Play Festival in late June, in the 1920 Bangor Opera House.

Summer Concerts

On Tuesday evenings late spring–summer, the **Bangor Band** performs free concerts in the Paul Bunyan Park grandstand on Main Street, near the Bangor Auditorium.

Every Thursday evening in June–July, the **Cool Sounds of Summer** free outdoor concerts are held in Pickering Square. Bangor Library also sponsors a summer concert series on its lawn.

FESTIVALS AND EVENTS

In April (usually the third Saturday), the **Kenduskeag Stream Canoe Race** is an annual 16.5-mile spring-runoff race sponsored by Bangor Parks and Recreation (207/992-4490). It draws upward of 700 canoes and thousands of spectators and finishes in downtown Bangor. The best location for spotting action is Six Mile Falls—take Broadway (Rte. 15) about six miles northwest of downtown.

Late July–early August, the **Bangor State Fair,** held in Bass Park, is a huge 10-day affair with agricultural and crafts exhibits, a carnival, fireworks, sinful food, and big-name live music. This is a big deal and attracts thousands from all over northern Maine.

Multiple stages of continuous music and dance by more than two dozen performing groups representing various cultures along with dozens of artisans, many demonstrating their crafts, bring in tens of thousands for the annual and free (so far) **American Folk Festival** (207/992-2630, www.americanfolkfestival.com), held on the Bangor waterfront. It's a fabulous event and one worth making an extra effort to attend.

SHOPPING
Antiques and More

Browse, eat, sip, and buy at the **Antique Marketplace and Cafe** (65 Maine St., Bangor, 207/941-2111 or 877/941-2111, www.antiquemarketplacecafe.com). Filling two floors are a wide range of antiques, along with used books and a café serving breakfast and lunch daily.

Books

If you need a good read, Bangor has plenty of sources.

If you can't decide between new or used, head to **BookMarc's Bookstore and Cafe** (78 Harlow St., Bangor, 207/942-3206), where you can peruse both and grab a cuppa joe.

Also in downtown Bangor is **Pro Libris** (10 3rd St., Bangor, 207/942-3019), billing itself as a "readers' paradise." With 30,000 used paperbacks and hardcovers, that's just about right.

Gifts and Clothing

Believe it when **The Grasshopper Shop** (1 W. Market Sq., Bangor, 207/945-3132) claims to be the state's largest boutique—it sprawls over two floors in downtown Bangor.

Outdoor Market

Nearly 40 vendors, including artisans, farmers, and bakers, sell their products along the Kenduskeg Stream, behind Pickering Square Garage, on Thursday evenings mid-June–early August. It complements the Cool Sounds concert series in Pickering Square (www.downtownbangor.com).

RECREATION
Fields Pond Audubon Center

South of Bangor-Brewer (although it feels as if you're heading east) is the Maine Audubon Society's Fields Pond Audubon Center (216 Fields Pond Rd., Holden, 207/989-2591). About four miles of footpaths wind through 192 acres of woods, fields, marshes, and lakeshore, all open sunrise–sunset daily year-round. (Wear waterproof shoes or boots; parts of the trail can be wet.) Canoe rentals are available to explore the pond. The headquarters is the L. Robert Rolde Nature Center (10 A.M.–5 P.M. Thurs.–Sat.), where you can pick up brochures and maps. A full schedule of programs occurs here throughout the year, including lectures, nature walks, slide talks, even a nature-book discussion group. Cost averages $5–10 pp. A nature store carries books, cards, and gifts.

Bangor City Forest and Orono Bog

Here's a double treat that's rich in flora and fauna. About nine miles of trails and more than four miles of roads meander through the 650-acre working Bangor City Forest (http://cityforest.bangorinfo.com). It's a great place for a walk or bike ride and for wildlife-spotting.

Accessible through the Bangor City Forest, the mile-long **Orono Bog Boardwalk** (Tripp Dr., Bangor, 207/581-2850, www.oronobogwalk.org), a National Natural Landmark, is wheelchair-accessible, has a restroom, benches every 200 feet, and interpretive signage. A series of guided nature walks are offered 9–11 A.M. Saturday early June–late September. Most are free; reservations are recommended (207/989-2591).

The forest and bog parking area are on Tripp Road, off Stillwater Avenue, about midway between the Bangor Mall and Kelly Road. Leashed pets are allowed in the forest, but not the bog.

Golf

Considered a standout among public courses, the **Bangor Municipal Golf Course** (280 Webster Ave., Bangor, 207/941-0232) has 18 holes dating from 1964 and a newer (and tougher) nine holes. Stretching over both sides of Webster Avenue, the course is also on the Bangor Airport flight path; don't flinch when a jet screams overhead. Tee times are needed for the newer nine and on weekends for the 18, but plan to arrive early in midsummer (the course opens at 7 A.M.). Also on-site are a driving range and two practice greens.

Twelve miles southeast of Bangor, across from the Lucerne Inn, the nine-hole **Lucerne-in-Maine Golf Course** (Rte. 1A, Dedham, 207/843-6282), is worth a visit just for the spectacular view.

Hiking

In Dedham, 12 miles southeast of Bangor, a favorite hike climbs **Bald Mountain** (sometimes called Dedham Bald Mountain) to the disused fire tower on the bald summit. On a clear day, climb the tower for panoramic views to both Katahdin and Cadillac Mountain. Allow about two hours round-trip if you plan to picnic and climb the tower. To reach the trailhead from downtown Bangor, take Rte. 1A (Wilson St.) about 8.5 miles from the Penobscot River bridge to the Route 46 junction. Just beyond the junction, turn right onto Upper Dedham Road. Go about 2.5 miles, and just after a stream, bear left onto Dedham Road. Continue about 3.5 miles to the parking area, on the left. The trail leads up from here, over a few steep ledgy spots. It's well worth the climb, especially during fall foliage season.

ACCOMMODATIONS

Rates noted are for peak season.

Just over the bridge but within walking distance of downtown Bangor, **The Fiddlehead Inn** (5 E. Summer St., Brewer, 888/983-4466, www.fiddleheadinn.com, $95) is a meticulously renovated and decorated early-20th-century home with two guest rooms sharing one bathroom. Innkeeper Saundra Haley serves a hearty vegetarian breakfast.

Many of the guests at the **Riverside Inn** (495 State St., Bangor, 207/973-4100 or 800/252-4044, www.riversidebangor.org, $78–149) have business at Eastern Maine Medical Center next door, but the inn is open to everyone (as is the hospital's 24-hour cafeteria). The inn's guest rooms—56 total, including 15 suites—are several notches above generic motel decor. Request one overlooking the Penobscot River; avoid rooms overlooking the hospital parking lot. Phones, air-conditioning, cable TV, and continental breakfast are all included; a coin-op laundry is available. Some pets are allowed ($5).

Six miles north of downtown is **Nonesuch Farm Bed and Breakfast** (59 Hudson Rd., Bangor, 207/942-3631, www.bangorsfirstbedandbreakfast.com, $120–145), Jim and Mary Louis Davitt's 1865 farmhouse and working farm. Although much restoration and renovation has occurred, many of the original fixtures remain. Some of the welcome additions are an enclosed sun porch and an outdoor hot tub, as well as Wi-Fi and air-conditioning. Trails lace the property, and Six Mile Falls, a Class IV drop, is a lure for expert paddlers. Laundry is available with notice. Children are welcome.

Rates include full breakfast June–November, continental breakfast off-season. Rates drop with the number of nights booked. Pets are not allowed because of the farm animals on-site.

Route 1A runs between Winterport and Bangor, then turns southeast and returns to the coast at Ellsworth. Twelve miles southeast of Bangor (and 25 miles northwest of Ellsworth) is **The Lucerne Inn** (Bar Harbor Rd./Rte. 1A, Dedham, 207/843-5123 or 800/325-5123, www.lucerneinn.com, $109–219), a retrofitted early-19th-century stagecoach hostelry on a 10-acre hilltop overlooking Phillips Lake and the hills beyond. Despite the highway out front, noise is no problem in the antiques-filled, rear-facing guest rooms, which have air-conditioning, phones, TVs, and fireplaces. Rates include continental breakfast, and an on-site dining room serves dinner and a popular Sunday brunch. Outside there's a pool; Pets are not allowed.

FOOD

Restaurant hours noted are for peak season but are subject to change. It's always wise to call ahead.

Local Flavors

A downtown landmark since 1978, **Bagel Central** (33 Central St., Bangor, 207/947-1654, 6 A.M.–6 P.M. Mon.–Thurs., 6 A.M.–5:30 P.M. Fri., 6 A.M.–2 P.M. Sun.) is a cheerful spot to meet, greet, and grab some handmade bagels (try the blueberry), great deli sandwiches, soups, and more. It's operated under Orthodox rabbinical supervision.

A few doors down at **Friars Bakehouse** (21 Central St., Bangor, 207/947-3770), Brother Kent and Brother Donald bake divine breads along with sinful whoopie pies and other treats and a very limited selection of soups and sandwiches. Tables are communal; prayers are free. Days and hours of operation change frequently, and it often sells out early; call or follow the advice on the door: If the light's on, it's open.

The menu changes daily at **Montes International Catering** (72 Columbia St.,

Bangor, 207/945-3990, www.montesinternational.com, 9 A.M.–5:30 P.M. Mon.–Fri.), but you can count on a mouthwatering selection of soups, salads, sandwiches, and perhaps quesadillas, fajitas, and pizza. After 3:30 P.M., you can even pick up gourmet dinners to go. The daily menu is posted online.

Just east of Bangor is the **Stonehouse Café** (1492 State St., Veazie, 207/942-9552, 7 A.M.–7 P.M. Tues.–Thurs., 7 A.M.–8 P.M. Fri., 7 A.M.–3 P.M. Sat.–Sun., $4–18), a cozy hole-in-the-wall where breakfast is served all day and the fried fish is a big draw.

I scream, you scream, everyone screams for **Pete's Pretty Good Ice Cream and Café** (858 Main Rd./Rte. 1A, Holden, 207/943-0444, www.petesicecream.com, 11 A.M.–9 P.M. daily), which in addition to some amazingly creative flavors of super creamy ice cream also serves a noteworthy hand-picked lobster roll as well as fried seafood and grilled fare.

Family Favorites

On the Brewer side of the river with fine views of Bangor's waterfront is the **Muddy Rudder** (5 S. Main St., Brewer, 207/989-5389, www.muddyrudder.com, 11 A.M.–10 P.M. Sun.–Thurs., 11 A.M.–midnight Fri.–Sat., $9–21). Seafood's the specialty, but there are chicken, steak, sandwiches, and salads as well as a kids' menu.

Convenient to I-95 Exit 180, **Dysart's** (Coldbrook Rd., Hermon, 207/942-4878, www.dysarts.com) is a truckers' destination resort—you can grab some grub, shower, shop, phone home, play video games, fuel up, and even sneak a bit of shut-eye. For real flavor, opt for the truckers' dining room, where the music is country and dozens of bleary-eyed drivers have reached the end of their transcontinental treks. If you're here with a carload, order an 18-Wheeler—18 scoops of ice cream with a collection of toppings. No question, Dysart's is unique, and it's open 24 hours daily year-round.

Famed for its lobster roll and all-you-can-eat fish fry, **Eagles Nest** (1016 Main St., Brewer, 207/989-7635, 7 A.M.–7:45 P.M. Sun.–Wed., 7 A.M.–8:45 P.M. Thurs.–Sat.) isn't fancy (some

might call it a dive), but it's a local family favorite. The tiny diner, wedged between the roadside and the river about two miles east of downtown on Route 9, is staffed by one cook and one waitress, so be patient and enjoy the Penobscot River views.

Ethnic Fare

Everything is prepared to order at **Bahaar Pakistani Restaurant** (23 Hammond St., Bangor, 207/945-5979, 11 A.M.–2:30 P.M. and 5–9 P.M. Tues.–Fri., noon–9 P.M. Sat.). Vegetarians find lots of options among the 70-plus appetizers, *biryanis,* and curries, which you can order hot, hotter, and hottest. Most choices are around $10. Takeout is available, and they have a full liquor license. Reservations are advisable on weekend nights. Be advised that the restaurant doesn't stick to its promised hours.

Insiders give the nod to **Yoshi Japanese Restaurant** (373 Wilson St., Brewer, 207/989-9688, www.yoshi09brewerme.com, 11 A.M.–2:30 P.M. and 4:30–9 P.M. Mon.–Wed., 11 A.M.–2:30 P.M. and 4:30–10 P.M. Thurs.–Sat., noon–9 P.M. Sun., entrées from $10), which opened in 2009, for the region's best sushi. The dining room is minimalist in decor. Choose from regular tables, cushions on the floor around sunken tables, or the sushi bar, where you can watch the maestros at work. With a 12-page menu, the choices seem endless.

Rome-born Massimo Ranni creates authentic Italian fare (his grandmother ran a bakery in the old country) at **Massimo's Cucina Italiana** (96 Hammond St., Bangor, 207/945-5600, www.massimoscucinaitaliana.com, 5–9 P.M. Mon.–Sat., $13–25). Hint: skip the pasta in favor of the small plates or meat dishes. Be forewarned, the chef doesn't take kindly to requests to alter ingredients.

The Smith family's **Market/Bistro** (735 Main St., 207/941-9594, www.market-bistrobangor.com, 5–9 p.m. Wed.–Sat., 9 a.m.–2 a.m.p.m. Sun., $12–30) serves a French-inspired menu that emphasizes rustic, farm-to-table fare. Options range from pizza to steak frites.

Casual Dining

Seasonally appropriate comfort foods with pizzazz are served at ❰ **Fiddlehead** (84 Hammond St., Bangor, 207/942-3336, www.thefiddleheadrestaurant.com, 4–9 P.M. Tues.– Fri., 5–10 P.M. Sat., 5–9 P.M. Sun.), a downtown restaurant with a cozy, neighborhood feel; it can be a bit loud, given the wood floors and brick walls, and everybody seems to know everybody else. Owners Laura Albin, who runs the front of the house, and Melissa Chaiken, the chef, are especially accommodating of vegetarians and the glucose intolerant, but the menu, which changes quarterly, ranges from burgers to seafood.

Thistle's (175 Exchange St., Bangor, 207/945-5480, www.thistlesrestaurant.com, 11 A.M.–2:30 P.M., 4:30–9 P.M. Tues.–Sat., entrées $16–28) is a longtime reliable place. Creative, moderately priced continental entrées with a Latin flair, plus excellent homemade breads and desserts, still draw the crowds, especially at lunchtime. Paella is a specialty. A pianist plays quietly in the background Thursday and Saturday evenings and often during lunch.

INFORMATION AND SERVICES

The best sources for local information are **The Bangor Region Chamber of Commerce** (519 Main St., Bangor, 207/947-0307, www.bangorregion.com) and **The Greater Bangor Convention and Visitors Bureau** (40 Harlow St., Bangor, 207/947-5205 or 800/916-6673, www.bangorcvb.org).

Two **Maine Visitor Information Centers** (8 A.M.–6 P.M. daily) are just south of Bangor on I-95, one on each side of the highway. The modern gray-clapboard buildings have racks of statewide information, agreeable staffers, clean restrooms, vending machines, and covered picnic tables. Northbound, the center is at mile 175 (207/862-6628); southbound, it's at mile 179 (207/862-6638).

Check out **Bangor Public Library** (145 Harlow St., Bangor, 207/947-8336, www.bpl.lib.me.us).

GETTING THERE AND GETTING AROUND

Bangor International Airport (BIA, 287 Godfrey Blvd., Bangor, 207/992-4600, www.flybangor.com) is served by major U.S. carriers.

Both **Concord Coachlines** (1039 Union St./Rte. 222, Bangor, 207/945-4000 or 800/639-3317, www.concordcoachlines.com) and **Greyhound Bus** (158 Main St., Bangor, 207/945-3000, www.greyhound.com) serve Bangor, connecting with Portland and points south.

Cyr Bus Line (207/827-2335 or 800/244-2335, www.cyrbustours.com) operates one round-trip daily between Aroostook County and Bangor, stopping in Bangor at the Greyhound and Concord bus terminals.

Operating once daily between Bangor and Calais is **West's Coastal Connection** (207/546-2823 or 800/596-2823, www.westbusservice.com), stopping in Bangor at the Greyhound and Concord terminals as well as at the airport.

Serving Bangor, Brewer, Old Town, Veazie, Orono, and Hampden is **BAT Community Connector** (207/992-4670, www.bangormaine.gov/cs_publictransit.php). The service operates 6:15 A.M.–6:15 P.M. Monday–Saturday, with no Hamden service on Saturday. The fare is $1.25, exact change required.

Orono and Vicinity

Home of the University of Maine's flagship campus, Orono is part college town, part generic Maine village, and a fine example of the tail wagging the dog. More than 11,000 university students converge on this Bangor suburb every year, fairly overwhelming the year-round population.

Called Stillwater when it was settled by Europeans in the 1770s, the town adopted the name of Penobscot Indian chief Joseph Orono and incorporated in 1806. By 1840, along with Bangor, eight miles to the southwest, prosperity descended, thanks to the huge Penobscot River log drives spurring the lumber industry's heyday. A stroll along Orono's Main Street Historic District, especially between Maplewood Avenue and Pine Street, attests to the timber magnates' success; the gorgeous homes are a veritable catalog of au courant architectural styles: Italianate, Greek Revival, Queen Anne, Federal, and Colonial Revival. Contact Orono's municipal office for a free copy of *Orono Tree Walk,* describing the trees of the town.

Old Town gained its own identity in 1840 after separating from Orono. ("Old Town" is the English translation of the settlement's Wabanaki name.) In those days, sawmills lined the shores of the town's Marsh Island between the Stillwater and Penobscot Rivers—the end of the line for the log drives and the backbone of Old Town's economy. That all crumbled in 1856, though, when a devastating fire swept through the area. Occurring as residents exited from memorial services for Abraham Lincoln, it was called the "Lincoln Fire." Several decades later, Old Town finally regained its economic footing, thanks to factories making shoes, canoes, and paper products.

Under separate tribal administration and linked to Old Town by a bridge built in 1951, Indian Island Reservation is home to about 400 Penobscot Indians.

SIGHTS
◖ University of Maine
Orono's major sights are on the 660-acre campus of the University of Maine (UMO), a venerable institution founded in 1868 as the State College of Agriculture and Mechanical Arts. It received its current designation in 1897 and now awards bachelor's, master's, and doctoral degrees. The oldest building on campus is North Hall, an updated version of the original Frost family farmhouse.

Information about the campus, including guided tours, is available from the **visitors center** (Buchanan Alumni House, University of Maine, Orono, 207/581-3740, www.umaine.edu, 8 A.M.–4 P.M. Mon.–Fri. and also 10 A.M.–2 P.M. Sat. during the academic year). Guided campus tours are offered daily.

One of the newest buildings, built in 1986 and renovated in 2009, is the **Collins Center for the Arts,** scene of year-round activity. Located on the second floor is the expanded **Hudson Museum** (207/581-1901, 9 A.M.–4 P.M. Mon.–Fri., 11 A.M.–4 P.M. Sat. and before selected performances, free), spotlighting traditional and contemporary world cultures in three contiguous galleries. The World Cultures Gallery comprises eight display areas, organized by theme, including one devoted to the museums' superlative Palmer collection of pre-Columbian artifacts. The Maine Indian Gallery highlights the museum's impressive Maliseet, Micmac, Passamaquoddy, and Penobscot holdings. Temporary exhibitions fill the Merritt Gallery.

The Maine sky takes center stage at the **Maynard F. Jordan Planetarium** (5781 Wingate Hall, Munson Rd., University of Maine, Orono, 207/581-1341, www.galaxymaine.com), on the second floor of Wingate Hall. Multimedia presentations help explain the workings of our universe and bring astronomy to life. Comet collisions and rocketing asteroids keep the kids transfixed. Program scheduling is variable, so you'll need to call ahead to confirm the schedule and reserve space in the 45-seat auditorium. Admission to scheduled events is $3 across the board. The public is invited to view the sky though a telescope at the **Jordan Observatory** on many clear Friday–Saturday evenings.

At the eastern edge of the campus, the seven-acre **Lyle E. Littlefield Ornamental Trial Garden** (Rangeley Rd., 207/594-2948) contains more than 2,500 plant species, many being tested for winter durability. The best time to come is early June, when crabapples and lilacs put on their perennial show. The garden is open daily; bring a picnic. Horticulture fans will also enjoy the 10-acre riverside **Fay Hyland Arboretum,** on the western edge of campus.

In the last agricultural building on campus (the barn predates UMO), the **Page Farm and Home Museum** (207/581-4100, 9 A.M.–4 P.M. Tues.–Sat.) houses a collection of farm implements and home items; on-site are a one-room schoolhouse, a blacksmith's shop, heritage gardens, and a general store stocked with goods made by local artisans. The museum presents an annual community picnic lunch at the end of July. Blacksmithing, old-fashioned games, and ice cream–making are part of the festivities.

Campus **parking** is a major sticking point at UMO, so you'll need a parking permit for most areas except the Maine Center for the Arts and the sports complex when events are taking place. For other times and lots, you can obtain a free one-day permit either from campus security or the parking office. For more information call 207/581-4053.

Old Town Museum

In the former St. Mary's Catholic Church, the Old Town Museum (353 S. Main St., Old Town, 207/827-7256, www.oldtownmuseum .org, 1–5 P.M. Wed.–Sun. early June–mid-Oct., donation) has well-organized exhibit areas focusing primarily on Old Town's pivotal role in the 19th-century lumbering industry. Other displays feature woodcarvings by sculptor Bernard Langlais, an Old Town native, and an excellent collection of Native American sweetgrass baskets. Each year, temporary exhibits add to the mix. Ask about the

2 P.M. Sunday afternoon programs—they can include anything from carving, weaving, beadwork, and quilting demonstrations to hand-bell concerts and historical lectures.

◖ Penobscot Nation Museum

Don't be put off by the humble exterior of Indian Island's Penobscot Nation Museum (12 Downstreet St., Indian Island, 207/827-4153, www.penobscotculture.com, 9 A.M.–2 P.M. Mon.–Thurs., 10 A.M.–3 P.M. Sat., free, donation appreciated); inside it's jam-packed with Native American historical artifacts and artwork, including exhibits of baskets, beadwork, dress, antique tools, and birch-bark canoes. Curator James Nepture brings the collection to life and will show videos of Penobscot life, including *Penobscot: The People and Their River.* Jewelry, dream catchers, and other handcrafted items are for sale in the small store. Be sure to call ahead, as posted hours aren't always maintained.

In the island's Protestant cemetery is the grave of **Louis Sockalexis,** the best Native American baseball player at the turn of the 20th century. Allegedly, his acceptance onto Cleveland's baseball team spurred management to dub the team the Indians—a name that has stuck.

Leonard's Mills

Officially known as the **Maine Forest and Logging Museum** (off Rte. 9, Bradley, 207/581-2871, www.leonardsmills.com), 400-acre Leonard's Mills recreates a 1790s logging village, with a sawmill, a blacksmith shop, a covered bridge, a log cabin, and other buildings. The site is accessible sunrise–sunset late April–October, but the best times to visit are during the museum's special-events days (the schedule varies) when dozens of museum volunteers don period dress and bring the village to life. Demonstrations, beanhole bean suppers, hayrides, antique games, and kids dipping candles or making cider are all part of the mix. The season's biggest events are **Living History Days,** a two-day festival held in mid-July and the first weekend in October. Admission varies by event, but is usually about $5–8 adults, $3–4 children. An ongoing museum project is the restoration to working condition of one of the old Lombard Haulers, an important part of the North Woods story. The museum is on Penobscot Experimental Forest Road in Bradley, 1.3 miles southeast of Route 178. It's directly across the river from Orono, but the only bridges are north (Old Town–Milford) and south (Bangor-Brewer).

ENTERTAINMENT AND EVENTS

In early December, at the Hudson Museum on the Orono campus of the University of Maine, the **Maine Indian Basketmakers Sale and Demonstration** includes Maine Indian baskets, carvings, jewelry, and traditional arts. Demonstrations, drumming, and singing are all on the agenda. For more information, contact the Hudson Museum (207/581-1904).

On the UMO campus, the **Collins Center for the Arts** (207/581-1755, www.collinscenterforthearts.com) is the year-round site of concerts, dramas, and other events with big-name performers. The box office (800/622-8499 for ticket orders) is open 9 A.M.–4 P.M. weekdays and 90 minutes prior to each event.

Orono Parks and Recreation presents a **Summer Concerts in the Park** series on Wednesday evenings.

SHOPPING

The world's oldest continuously operating canoe manufacturer, **Old Town Canoe Company** (125 Gilman Falls Rd./Rte. 43, Old Town, 207/827-1530, www.oldtowncanoe.com), incorporated in 1904, was turning out as many as 400 boats a month two years later. In 1915 the list of dealers included Harrod's in London and the Hudson's Bay Company in far northern Canada, and Old Town had supplied canoes to expeditions in Egypt and the Arctic. Quality is high at Old Town, so its boats are pricey, but you can visit the **Old Town Canoe Factory Outlet Store** and look over the supply of "factory-blemished" canoe and kayak models. You may end up with a real bargain.

There's also a full line of paddles, jackets, compasses, and other accessories. While here, inquire about factory tours. To find it, follow Main Street (Rte. 43) north.

RECREATION
Sunkhaze Meadows National Wildlife Refuge

The best time to visit Sunkhaze Meadows National Wildlife Refuge (off Rte. 2, Milford, 207/827-6138, ww.sunkhaze.org) is during the fall waterfowl migration, but hunting is allowed then, so wear a hunter-orange hat or vest. More than 200 bird species have been spotted here; moose and beavers are common. The best way to see them is to paddle the five-mile stretch of Sunkhaze Stream that bisects the refuge. Allow about six hours for this expedition, putting in on Stud Mill Road (park in the lot at the Ash Landing trailhead; do not park on Stud Mill Road) and taking out on Route 2 (you'll need two vehicles for this). Don't forget insect repellent. Access is via the unpaved Stud Mill Road or County Road, north of Milford. No staff or facilities are available at the 11,672-acre refuge, but you can download maps from the website. In winter, the refuge trails are open for cross-country skiing.

University of Maine

Recreation resources are abundant at UMO. Campus Recreation (207/581-1082, www.umaine.edu/campusrecreation) oversees facilities including **Wallace Pool, Alfond Arena, Latti Fitness Center, Memorial Gym,** and the **Student Recreation and Fitness Center.** Hours vary at each, and a small access fee may be required.

Ask at the campus recreation center or visitors center for a map of **University Forest,** with trails for biking, walking, snowshoeing, and cross-country skiing.

ACCOMMODATIONS

Less than a mile from the university campus is **University Inn Academic Suites** (5 College Ave., Orono, 207/866-4921 or 800/321-4921, www.universityinnorono.com, $90–182), a somewhat dated but updated and well-maintained motel overlooking the Stillwater River. All guest rooms have balconies and Wi-Fi; suites have refrigerators and microwaves. Rates include a hot breakfast buffet. Also on-site are an outdoor heated pool with bar service and a family recreation center with foosball, a pool table, and a big-screen TV. There's a dock for boat launching; canoe and kayak rentals are available.

Even closer to the university and just off I-95 is the three-story **Black Bear Inn** (4 Godfrey Dr., Orono, 207/866-7120 or 800/528-1234, www.blackbearinnorono.com, $90–275), decorated with a black bear theme, right down to the welcoming teddy bear on the bed. Opened in 1990, it has 68 motel-style rooms, a coin-op laundry, Wi-Fi, an exercise room, and a sauna. The priciest guest rooms are the hot-tub suites. Rates include continental breakfast with a waffle station. At night, the breakfast room morphs into a small but casual café. Pets are accepted for $10.

In Milford is a real bargain for families. The **Milford Motel on the River** (154 Rte. 2, Milford, 800/282-3330, www.milfordmotelontheriver.com, from $85) is an older but well-maintained property with accommodations ranging from guest rooms with kitchenettes to two-bedroom suites with living areas and full kitchens. There's a coin-op laundry on the premises.

FOOD
Local Flavors
After visiting Leonard's Mills, head over to **Spencer's Ice Cream,** which has been dishing out homemade ice cream since 1930.

Burritos, quesadillas, smoothies, and bagels constitute the menu at **Verve** (2 Mill St., Orono, 207/866-4004, www.verveburritos.com, 8 A.M.–4 P.M. Mon.–Sat., 8 A.M.–2 P.M. Sun.), an order-at-the-counter joint, with both table and lounge-style seating.

Orono's veteran restaurant is **Pat's Pizza** (11 Mill St., Orono, 207/866-2111, 7 A.M.–midnight Sun.–Thurs., 7 A.M.–1 A.M. Fri.–Sat.), a statewide family-owned chain founded in Orono in July 1931 by C. D. "Pat" Farnsworth. Then known as Farnsworth's Cafe, it became Pat's Pizza in 1953. Pizza toppings are endless and even include pineapple, sauerkraut, and capers. Subs, calzones, burgers, and "tomato Italian" entrées are also on the menu.

For natural foods as well as baked goods and premade sandwiches at lunch and cappuccino anytime, head to **The Store-Ampersand** (22 Mill St., Orono, 207/866-4110), just off Main Street.

Casual Dining
Every college town needs a **Woodman's** (31 Main St., Orono, 207/866-4040, 4–10 P.M. daily, $9–22), a casual restaurant with a menu ranging from burgers and sandwiches to chicken marsala and New York strip. Don't go looking for culinary wonders here, just good food and service.

The Mediterranean-inspired choices at the casual **Market Cafe** (827 Stillwater Ave., Old Town, 207/827-3663, 11 A.M.–9:30 P.M. daily, $8–12) include pizzas, salads, strombolis, sandwiches, and a few entrées.

INFORMATION AND SERVICES
The best source of information on Orono and Old Town is the **Bangor Region Chamber of Commerce** (519 Main St., Bangor, 207/947-0307, www.bangorregion.com). Also helpful is the **Orono Town Office** (59 Main St., Orono, 207/866-2556, www.orono.org).

KENNEBEC AND MOOSE RIVER REGION

For more than 3,000 years, the Kennebec and Québec's Chaudière Rivers have been the primary routes for trade and migration between Canada's St. Lawrence River and the Gulf of Maine, between Québec City and the sea. People and goods have moved through history along this corridor: farmers migrating north, hoping to profit from the Québec market; French, Irish, and British families moving south in search of opportunity; escaping slaves following the Underground Railroad north; economic opportunists smuggling alcohol south during prohibition. The most famous traveler was Benedict Arnold, who followed the route on foot and in bateaux with a band of Colonial militia in 1775 in his ill-fated attempt to capture Québec City from the British.

The river wends its way through Somerset and Kennebec Counties from Indian Pond through The Forks, Bingham, Skowhegan, Waterville, Augusta, and Richmond, and then on toward the sea at Bath. Augusta, the state's capital, is rich in historical sights and balanced by the shops and restaurants in Hallowell. Waterville is home to Colby College, alone worth a visit for its Museum of Art. The region's lovely lakes districts—Belgrade Lakes, China Lakes, and Winthrop Lakes—have been favorite summer destinations for as long as anyone can remember. On the outskirts are rural farming communities such as Unity, home to an annual organic-foods fair that's a draw for urbanites and back-to-the-landers alike.

Many towns along the Kennebec had wood

© TOM NANGLE

HIGHLIGHTS

Maine State Museum: Spend a few hours immersed in Maine's history and pick up all kinds of "Well, what do you know?" trivia (page 502).

Old Fort Western: The nation's oldest stockaded fort hosted Benedict Arnold on his march to Québec (page 503).

Great Pond Mail Boat: Remember the movie *On Golden Pond?* Take a ride on the mail boat that inspired it (page 513).

Colby College: Stroll the lovely grounds, visit the arboretum, and don't miss the Museum of Art (page 519).

L. C. Bates Museum: View all sorts of eccentric natural-history relics and then walk the trails in the forest (page 526).

South Solon Meetinghouse: From the exterior it looks like just another New England meetinghouse – inside, however, wow! (page 526).

Moxie Falls: It's a short hike into one of New England's tallest waterfalls (page 531).

Old Canada Road National Scenic Byway: Benedict Arnold marched his troops along a good stretch of this National Scenic Byway along the Kennebec River (page 531).

White-Water Rafting: For thrills, take a wild guided ride down the Kennebec River (page 532).

LOOK FOR ◖ TO FIND RECOMMENDED SIGHTS, ACTIVITIES, DINING, AND LODGING.

---

or textile mills. Locals called the rotten-egg stench emitted from the papermaking smokestacks "the smell of money." The region's mill-driven economy is dying, and dependent communities take a big hit with each closure or cutback. Many are finding new hope for the future in renovating old mills into new housing and business complexes or in eco-tourism, especially from Skowhegan north, where the wilderness lakes, forests, and mountains provide endless opportunities for outdoors-oriented folks.

Traditional outdoor sports such as hunting, fishing, hiking, camping, and boating were joined by white-water rafting in 1976. That's the year timber companies stopped floating logs down the Kennebec to their lumber mills and gutsy outdoorsman Wayne Hockmeyer decided to take a rubber raft through the Kennebec Gorge. He survived, and since then, white-water rafting has mushroomed, focusing long-overdue attention on the beautiful Upper Kennebec Valley and creating a whole new crowd of enthusiasts for this region. Now more than a dozen outfitters have bases in the region, and most are multisport outfitters with canoeing and kayaking, sometimes hiking, and snowmobiling in winter.

KENNEBEC AND MOOSE RIVER REGION

QUÉBEC

Moosehead
Lake

Moose River
Jackman
Big Wood Lake
Attean Pond
ATTEAN
LAKE LODGE

Long Pond

Brassua
Lake

Moose River

Lake Parlin

Enchanted
Pond

WHITE-WATER
RAFTING

Greenville

MOXIE FALLS

West
Forks

The
Forks

Lake
Moxie

Appalachian

Flagstaff
Mtn

Pierce
Pond

Pleasant
Pond Mtn

Pleasant
Pond

Caratunk

OLD CANADA
ROAD NATIONAL
SCENIC BYWAY

Guilford

Dover-
Foxcroft

Flagstaff
Lake

Wyman
Lake

Moscow
Bingham

Rangeley
Lakes

Appalachian Trail

Embden
Pond

North
New Portland

Solon

SOUTH SOLON
MEETINGHOUSE

Athens

Hartland

Newport

New
Portland

Embden

North Anson

Lake Wesserunsett

Anson

Madison

Skowhegan

Pittsfield

Starks

Norridgewock

L. C. BATES MUSEUM

Farmington

North Pond

Mt Phillips

Smithfield
East
Pond

Fairfield

Hinckley

Unity

Rome Corner
Rome

Belgrade Lakes
Mt Vernon

GREAT POND
MAIL BOAT

Oakland

Waterville

COLBY COLLEGE

Winslow

Vassalboro

China

China Lake

Belfast

Belgrade

Readfield

Kents Hill

Sidney

Wayne

MAINE STATE
MUSEUM

AUGUSTA

Windsor

Winthrop
Manchester

Hallowell

OLD FORT WESTERN

Monmouth

Gardiner

Randolph

Litchfield

Pittston

Lewiston
Auburn

Peacock Beach
State Park

To Portland

Richmond

Waldoboro

Rockland

© AVALON TRAVEL

PLANNING YOUR TIME

Depending on your interests, you can swim, canoe, raft, hike, snowmobile, or cross-country ski; tour museums and historic sites; take walking tours; shop; or blend it all into one rich excursion of history, heritage, culture, and adventure.

Getting around the region is easy: Route 201 parallels the Kennebec River from one end to the other. The downside is that Route 201 is also the major highway from Québec to the U.S. coast, and it may seem as if everyone else but you is simply trying to get from point A to point B in record time. Traffic generally isn't heavy, but it can be disconcerting to have a big rig on your bumper on the narrow and winding stretches of the road. Once you're above Skowhegan, moose also become a danger. Be wary, especially around dawn and dusk or in early spring, when moose often lick salt residue on roadsides.

Think of Route 201 as the region's spine, and Routes 2, 3, 16, 17, and 27 as crucial vertebrae linking it to Maine's Western Lakes and Mountains, Highlands, and Mid-Coast regions. There's a good chance you're going to pass through the region if you're gallivanting around the state. From Norridgewock, Route 201A parallels the river on its western banks, passing through Madison and the Ansons and pretty farm country before rejoining Route 201 in Bingham.

Unless you're a snowmobiler, May–October is the best time to appreciate this part of Maine. In May–June, blackflies are notorious and can make outdoor pleasures—with the exception of fishing—true misery. July–September, when both the air and water are warm, is the best time for white-water rafting, for recreation on the lakes, and for hiking. In late September–early October, when the foliage is at its peak, driving the northern stretch of Route 201, a National Scenic Byway, is glorious.

Outdoor enthusiasts will want to spend at least 2–3 days in and around The Forks or Jackman region, where rafting, canoeing, and hiking opportunities are plentiful. Plan on another 2–3 days to visit the cultural diversions clustered in Augusta and Waterville. If you want to loop out to Unity and Thorndike, add another half day or so (but don't even consider doing so during the third weekend in September, unless you're ready to brave the crowds headed to the Maine Organic Farmers and Gardeners Association's annual Common Ground Fair). Of course, generations of folk spend a week or longer every summer in the lakes regions surrounding Augusta, but you can dip your toes in for a sample in a day or two.

If you're history-minded—or just interested in "heritage touring"—consider following the **Kennebec-Chaudière International Corridor,** a historic route that stretches from Bath, Maine, to Québec City. Native Americans used it on foot and by canoe; Benedict Arnold used it; and enterprising 19th-century traders found it invaluable for moving their wares between the United States and Canada. Along the route are museums, churches, dramatic scenery, and French and American cultural centers. The heritage, people, and landscape are brought to life on a CD, *Deep Woods and River Roads,* narrated by Nick Spitzer, folklorist and host of Public Radio International's *American Routes.* It can be purchased at museums and visitors centers along the route.

Augusta and Vicinity

As the state capital, Augusta is where everything is supposed to happen. A lot does happen here, but don't be surprised to find the imposing State House and lovely governor's mansion the centerpieces of a relatively sleepy city. Augusta is the seventh-largest city in Maine and no megalopolis, but it *is* the heart of state government and central Maine.

Pilgrims first settled here on the banks of the Kennebec River in the 17th century, and Boston merchants established Fort Western in the mid-18th century. Augusta was named state capital in 1827.

The three best-known communities south of Augusta—Hallowell, Gardiner, and Richmond—all scale down hillsides to the river, making their settings especially attractive. In **Hallowell,** settled in 1762, the main thoroughfare still retains the air of its former days as a prosperous port and source of granite and ice. The entire downtown, with brick sidewalks and attractive shops and restaurants, is a National Historic District.

Six miles south of Augusta, **Gardiner,** the "Tilbury Town" of noted author Edwin Arlington Robinson, claims more buildings on the National Register of Historic Places than any of its neighbors. The Gardiner Historic District includes more than 45 downtown buildings. Main Street is a gem, and although still too many storefronts are empty, there's a bit of a buzz here. Besides Robinson, another prominent Gardiner resident was Laura Howe Richards, author of *Captain January* and daughter of Julia Ward Howe, who wrote "The Battle Hymn of the Republic." (The yellow Federal-style home where Richards and her husband raised seven children, at 3 Dennis Street, is not open to the public.) Most outstanding of Gardiner's mansions (also not open to the public) is Oaklands, a Gothic Revival home built in 1836 by the grandson of founding father Dr. Sylvester Gardiner, a wealthy land speculator.

Just over the border in Sagadahoc County,

Richmond, also flush with handsome buildings, was the site of a Russian émigré community in the 1950s. Here's a town that awaits rediscovery.

West of Augusta, amidst the Winthrop Lakes region, the town of Monmouth is the site of Cumston Hall, a dramatic turn-of-the-20th-century structure that now houses the Theater at Monmouth as well as the municipal offices and public library.

SIGHTS
Maine State House

From almost every vantage point in Augusta, your eye catches the prominent dome of the Maine State House, centerpiece of the government complex on the west side of the Kennebec River. Occupying the corner of State and Capitol Streets, the State House dates originally from 1832, when it was completed to the design of famed Boston architect Charles Bulfinch, who modeled it on his Massachusetts State House design. Only a dozen years had passed since Maine had separated from Massachusetts; Augusta had become the state capital in 1827. Granite for the building came from quarries in nearby Hallowell; the total construction cost was $145,000. Atop the oxidized copper dome stands a gold-gilded sculpture, *Lady Wisdom.* In the early 20th century, space needs forced a major expansion of the building, leaving only the eight-columned front portico as the Bulfinch legacy.

Visitors are welcome to wander around the State House, but check first to see whether the legislature is in session. If so, parking becomes scarce, the hallways become congested, and access may be restricted. The best place to enter the building is on the west side, facing the more modern state office building; the entrance is marked "Maine State House." Pick up the useful brochure for a self-guided tour, or better still, take a free guided tour, usually available 9 A.M.–1 P.M. weekdays. Call ahead (207/287-2301; tours are organized by

The Maine State House was originally designed by noted Boston architect Charles Bulfinch.

© HILARY NANGLE

the Maine State Museum) to arrange it, or ask at the kiosk.

On the Blaine House side of the State House is a replica of the **Liberty Bell,** with the same dimensions, weight, aged-oak yoke, iron straps, hand-forged bolts, and inscription. Only the crack is indicated, so this one can ring true. The bell was crafted in 1950, when the U.S. Department of the Treasury donated one to each state to promote the Savings Bond Independence Drive.

Maine State Museum

If the Smithsonian is the nation's attic, welcome to Maine's attic—and a well-organized one at that. At the Maine State Museum (State House Complex, Augusta, 207/287-2301, mainestatemuseum.org, 9 A.M.–5 P.M. Tues.– Fri., 10 A.M.–4 P.M. Sat., $2 adults, $1 ages 6–18 and seniors, $6 family), gears and tools spin and whir in the intriguing *Made in Maine* industrial exhibits, focusing on quarrying, ice harvesting, fishing, agriculture, lumbering, and shipbuilding. A spiraled archaeological exhibit

covers the past 12 millennia of Maine's history. Some displays are interactive, and all exhibits are wheelchair-accessible. Gallery guides are available in French, German, Spanish, Japanese, and Russian. During the winter, the museum sponsors a free lecture series, and special programs occur throughout the year. A small gift shop stocks historical publications and Maine-related gifts and toys. The museum is part of the state government complex that includes the State House and the Maine State Library. The museum and library share a building, separated by a parking lot from the State House.

The Blaine House

In 1833, a year after the State House was ready for business, retired sea captain James Hall finished his elegant new home across the street. But it was not until 29 years later, when prominent politico James G. Blaine assumed ownership, that the house became the hotbed of state and national political ferment. No underachiever, Blaine was a Maine congressman and senator, Speaker of the U.S. House, U.S.

THE RUSSIANS WERE COMING

In the 1950s, the sleepy Kennebec River town of Richmond, 12 miles south of Maine's state capital, became the center of a unique and unlikely colony as several hundred Russian-speaking refugee families settled among the area's villages and rolling farmland. The Kennebec Valley, economically depressed and remote from other Russian immigrant centers in the United States, seems an improbable choice for a Slavic enclave. Yet Richmond soon boasted a Russian restaurant, a Russian boot-maker's shop, and even onion domes – on St. Alexander Nevsky, Maine's first Russian Orthodox church. For the first time, Russian was heard on Richmond's streets, and Russian-speaking children enrolled in local schools.

The settlement was the brainchild of Baron Vladimir von Poushental, a swashbuckling veteran of the czar's World War I air force. Fleeing the Bolshevik Revolution, he landed in New York, where his personality and family connections gained him entry to a series of managerial jobs, if not to the wealth he had enjoyed as a Russian noble. An expert marksman and dedicated hunter, von Poushental in 1947 decided to retire to a modest cabin in the Kennebec Valley, where he had hunted and fished for many years. There he began buying up abandoned farms and promoting the valley's attractions to fellow Russian émigrés. The climate and countryside resembled Russia's, he said, and land was cheap. For a few thousand dollars, a refugee could buy a house and 30 acres. To create a nucleus for the settlers, the baron donated a 400-acre farm to the aging veterans of Russia's White armies, and he helped them establish a retirement home and an Orthodox chapel.

And so they came: Ukrainians, Russians, Belorussians, and Cossacks; professors, farmers, artists, and carpenters. Some came directly from Europe's displaced-persons camps, others from homes and jobs in U.S. cities where they had lived for years. The settlers shared a common language, their Orthodox faith, a zest for life, and a hatred of the Soviet regime. The younger émigrés worked, raised families, and became part of the larger American community around them. Their elderly parents felt more comfortable associating with other Russian-speakers.

Today the boot-maker and restaurant are gone. Most of the elderly – the old émigrés from pre-Communist Russia – are dead, their Cyrillic gravestones dotting the Richmond cemetery. A few old-timers, still hardy, stand each Sunday through the long Orthodox service, and they bake piroshki or sweets for church sales on special occasions, like the town's late-July celebration of Richmond Days.

Their grandchildren, Russian Americans, have merged successfully into the mainstream United States. Most have married outside their ethnic group, and many have taken jobs outside the Kennebec Valley, not necessarily by choice. Yet a fair number still live and work in the area. In a way that might have surprised even von Poushental, who died in 1978, the colony he sponsored took root and flourished in a part of the country he loved.

Secretary of State under two presidents, and Republican candidate for the presidency. Two decades after his death, Blaine's widow donated the family home to the state of Maine; it has been the governor's mansion ever since.

Free half-hour guided tours of the ground-floor public areas of the Blaine House (State St. and Capitol St., Augusta, 207/287-2121, www.blainehouse.org) are given 2–4 P.M. Tuesday–Thursday year-round. A special event occasionally cancels the tour schedule, so it's wise to call ahead. Self-guided tours of the New England Garden are available during the same hours by appointment.

◖ Old Fort Western

Built in 1754 for the French and Indian Wars and restored as recently as 1988, Old Fort Western (16 Cony St., Augusta, 207/626-2385, www.oldfortwestern.org, 1–4 P.M. daily late May–early Sept., 1–4 P.M. Sat.–Sun. early Sept.–mid Oct., $6 adults, $4 ages

6–16), reputedly the nation's oldest remaining stockaded fort, has witnessed British, French, and Native Americans squabbling over this Kennebec riverfront site. Benedict Arnold and his troops camped here during their 1775 march on Québec. Today, costumed interpreters help visitors travel through time to the 18th century; hands-on demonstrations—butter churning, musket drill, barrel building, weaving, even vinegar making—occur daily Fourth of July–Labor Day. The fort is also open 1–3 P.M. on the first Sunday of the month November–January, and 1–3 P.M. on Maple Syrup Day, the fourth Sunday in March. The museum is on the east bank of the Kennebec River in downtown Augusta, next to Augusta City Hall.

Walking and Driving Tours

Many of Hallowell's distinctive homes have stories to tell. Stop by Hallowell City Hall (1 Winthrop St., 207/623-4021, http://hallowell.govoffice.com) to buy a copy of *Historic Old Hallowell Walking Tour* or visit www .historichallowell.org and see the "Museum in the Streets" link.

Fans of poet Edgar Arlington Robinson will find a map of Gardiner-area ("Tilbury Town") sites at www.earobinson.com.

ENTERTAINMENT

The **Gaslight Theater,** a talented community-theater group, performs periodically throughout the year at the **Hallowell City Hall Auditorium** (Winthrop St., Hallowell, 207/626-3698, www.gaslighttheater.org).

Six miles south of Augusta, the 1864 **Johnson Hall Performing Arts Center** (280 Water St., Gardiner, 207/582-7144, www.johnsonhall.org) is the year-round site of just about anything anyone wants to present—plays, lectures, art camps, after-school programs, classes, concerts, and more.

Maine's enduring Shakespearean theater is the **Theater at Monmouth** (Main St./Rte. 132, Monmouth, box office 207/933-9999 or 800/769-9698 in Maine, www.theaterat

Don't miss an opportunity to catch a performance at the architecturally astonishing Cumston Hall, home to the Theater at Monmouth.

© HILARY NANGLE

monmouth.org, $10–26), based in Monmouth's architecturally astonishing **Cumston Hall**. Completed in 1900, the Romanesque Victorian structure has columns, cutout shingles, stained glass, and a huge square tower. The interior is equally stunning, with frescoes and a vaulted ceiling. The theater's summer season, performed by professionals in rotating repertory, runs early July–August. Shakespeare gets the nod for at least two of the four plays. Tickets range $20–26, with $10 rush tickets at the door five minutes before curtain when available.

Late June–mid-August, free concerts by students and faculty are offered at the **New England Music Camp** (Lake Messalonskee, Sidney, 207/465-3025, www.nemusiccamp.com). Call or check the website for current schedule. Weekend concerts are at the outdoor "Bowl-in-the-Pines" (bring a blanket or folding chair); midweek performances take place in Alumni Hall.

During the school year, the **University of Maine at Augusta** campus schedules lectures, concerts, and other performances. Check with the school (student activities 207/621-3000, ext. 3442, or information center 877/862-1234, www.uma.edu) for current information.

Hallowell presents a free series of **concerts** in the Hallowell Bandstand beginning at 7 P.M. on Tuesday evenings.

FESTIVALS AND EVENTS

The Augusta area seems to claim more country fairs than any other part of the state; don't miss an opportunity to attend at least one. Each has a different flavor, but there are always lots of animals, games, and junk food, often a carnival, and sometimes harness racing.

In June, the Maine Alpaca Association sponsors the **Maine Fiber Frolic** (www.fiberfrolic .com), a celebration of fiber, fiber animals, and fiber arts at the Windsor Fairgrounds. Expect llamas, alpacas, angora rabbits, sheep, goats, and other livestock as well as demonstrations, workshops, and exhibits.

In mid-June, the annual **Blistered Fingers Family Bluegrass Music Festival** (www.blisteredfingers.com) takes place at the Litchfield Fairgrounds in Litchfield.

The small four-day **Pittston Fair** (www .pittstonfair.com) features agricultural exhibits, a carnival, and even a woodsman contest at the Pittston Fairgrounds, East Pittston, in mid-July. The third Saturday in July, **Old Hallowell Day** (oldhallowellday.org) includes a craft fair, a parade, food booths, and a road race in downtown Hallowell. The **Monmouth Fair** fills four days with agricultural exhibits, a carnival, and crafts in early August.

The last week of August, the Windsor Fairgrounds come alive with the weeklong **Windsor Fair,** with agricultural exhibits, harness racing, a demolition derby, a beauty pageant, and a carnival.

The three-day **Litchfield Fair** has farm exhibits, animal pulling, a carnival, and more the second weekend in September.

SHOPPING

One mile south of Augusta is **Hallowell,** where boutiques, restaurants, and nearly a dozen antiques shops line historic Water Street.

Art, Crafts, and Antiques

Brahms Mount Textiles (19 Central St., Hallowell, 207/623-5277 or 800/545-9347, www.brahmsmount.com) is an honest-to-goodness factory outlet, delivering significant savings on the luxurious linen and cotton blankets and throws woven on the premises. **Kennebec River Artisans** (130 Water St., 207/623-2345) shows and sells the wares of more than three dozen craftspeople. The **Harlow Gallery** (160 Water St., Hallowell, 207/622-3813), headquarters for the Kennebec Valley Art Association, serves as a magnet not only for its member artists but also for friends of art. One of Maine's best sources for vintage lighting is **Brass and Friends Antiques** (154 Water St., 207/626-3287). Goods varying from antique china to felted bowls fill the appropriately named **Potluck Shop** (109 Water St., 207/622-8992).

Books

The apt slogan at **Merrill's Bookshop** (134 Water St., 2nd Fl., Hallowell, 207/623-2055) is "Good literature from Edward Abbey to Leane

© HILARY NANGLE

If they don't have it at Hussey's General Store, you probably don't need it.

Zugsmith." John Merrill has an eye for unusual rare and used books, so you may walk out with a personal treasure.

General Store

"Guns. Wedding Gowns. Cold Beer." The sign outside **Hussey's General Store** (510 Ridge Rd./Rte. 32 at Rte. 105, Windsor, 207/445-2511, www.husseysgeneralstore.com) says it all. With merchandise spread out on three floors, there isn't much that Hussey's doesn't have, and that bridal department does a steady business. Its slogan: "If we don't have it, you don't need it." From Augusta, take Route 105 about 11 miles east to Route 32; Hussey's is on the corner. If you're at the Windsor Fairgrounds, the store is only about two miles farther north on Route 32.

RECREATION
Parks and Preserves

On the east side of State Street, between the State House and the river, is 10-acre **Capitol Park,** a great place for a picnic after visiting the Maine State Museum, the State House, and the

Blaine House. In the park is the **Maine Vietnam Veterans Memorial,** a dramatic "you are there" walk-through monument erected in 1985.

VILES ARBORETUM

On the east side of the Kennebec River, the **Viles Arboretum** (153 Hospital St./Rte. 9, Augusta, 207/621-0031, www.vilesarboretum .org, dawn–dusk daily) devotes 224 acres to more than 300 varieties of trees and shrubs. Bring a picnic (carry-in, carry-out) and wander the nearly six-mile trail network. If you're a birder, bring binoculars; more than 150 species have been spotted here. Well-designed planting clusters include hosta and rhododendron collections, a rock garden, an antique apple orchard, and the Governors Grove, with a white pine dedicated to each Maine governor. Stop first at the Viles Visitor Center (8 A.M.–4 P.M. Mon.–Fri.) to pick up a trail map. Leashed pets are allowed; smoking is not allowed on the grounds. During the winter, the trails are groomed for cross-country skiing. Admission is free; donations are appreciated.

Next to the arboretum parking lot is **Cony Cemetery** (also known as Knight Cemetery), one of Augusta's oldest, with gravestones dating from the late 18th century. Old-cemetery buffs will want to check it out, but rubbings are not permitted.

KENNEBEC VALLEY GARDEN CLUB PARK

Escape the shopping hubbub in this pocket of tranquility at the Augusta Civic Center. Designed in 1974 by Lyle Littlefield, a professor of horticulture at the University of Maine, it's now maintained by club members. Within the two-acre park's borders are a water-lily pond rimmed with cattails, two formal gardens, and trails edged by perennials. Nearby are children's butterfly and hummingbird gardens and woodlands with wildflowers.

JAMIES POND WILDLIFE MANAGEMENT AREA

Maine's Department of Inland Fisheries and Wildlife manages this 840-acre preserve with a 107-acre pond. The pond, stocked with brook trout and splake, appeals equally to anglers, birders, wildlife-watchers, and paddlers. Mapped trails weave through the surrounding woodlands. Access is from Outlet Road, just west of the Maple Hill Farm Inn in Hallowell.

Swan Island

The Maine Department of Inland Fisheries and Wildlife (IF&W) has established a byzantine reservation system to limit visitors to its **Steve Powell Wildlife Management Area** (207/547-5322, www.state.me.us/ifw/education/swanisland) on 1,755-acre, four-mile-long Swan Island in the middle of the Kennebec River. Don't be daunted; it's worth the effort. The entire island is on the National Register of Historic Places. Well-marked trails are everywhere; one trail takes 30 minutes, another takes three hours and goes the length of the lovely wooded island. Plan to take the free hour-long ranger-guided tour. No license is needed for fishing, but even private boats

need permission to land here (near the campground); small boats are not recommended because of 10-foot tidal variations. Bikes are permitted on the center main road only, and cars and pets are not allowed.

Getting here requires taking a small ferry the very short distance from a dock in Richmond, next to the town-owned Waterfront Park on Route 24. The boat operates May 1–Labor Day. Call for reservations. Day-use admission is $8 over age 3. Pack a picnic lunch; fireplaces at the campground are available for day use if no campers are using them, but bring tinfoil for cooking. Alcohol is not allowed on the island.

The island, settled in the early 1700s, once had as many as 95 resident farmers, fishermen, ice cutters, and shipbuilders. Now there are derelict antique houses, a herd of white-tailed deer, wild turkeys, nesting bald eagles, plenty of waterfowl and other birds, and the primitive campground.

Swan Island's campground has 10 well-spaced lean-tos, each sleeping six, with picnic tables, fireplaces, and outhouses; firewood and potable water are provided. Cost is $14 over age 3, plus the state's 7 percent lodging tax. There's a two-night maximum. The policy is carry-in, carry-out, so bring trash bags. A rickety flatbed truck with benches meets campers at the island dock and transports them the 1.5 miles to the campground. The same truck does the island tour.

Bicycling

You can walk, bike, ski, or run the **Kennebec River Rail Trail** (KRRT), keeping an eye peeled for bald eagles, salmon, and just the general flow of the Kennebec. The Friends of KRRT (www.KRRT.org) maintains the 6.5-mile riverside trail connecting Augusta's Waterfront Park to Gardiner.

Golf

Ten miles north of Augusta and 12 miles south of Waterville, the **Natanis Golf Club** (Webber Pond Rd., Vassalboro, 207/622-3561, www.natanisgc.com) has been the site of many a Maine golf tournament. Named after a trusted Indian guide, the Natanis club has two separate 18-hole courses.

Water Sports

Take a look at a map of the region and you'll find plenty of blue indicating lakes, ponds, rivers, and streams. **Farmingdale Kayak and Canoe** (27 Northern Ave., Farmingdale, 207/582-1916, www.farmingdalekayakrentals .com) rents Old Town canoes and double kayaks for $30 and single kayaks for $25 per 24-hour period, with the daily rate decreasing with longer rentals; call for reservations. Guided trips are also possible.

For swimming, head 12 miles south of Augusta to **Peacock Beach** (Rte. 201, Richmond, 207/737-4305), a quiet 100-acre park on long, narrow Pleasant Pond.

Fish for stripers and blue fish on the Kennebec River with Gardiner-based **Maine Experience Guide Service** (207/215-3828, www.maineexperienceguideservice.com) with Master Maine Guide Jay Farris. Rates begin at $200 for four hours and cover up to three people. In autumn, Farris also offers a five-hour foliage tour down the Kennebec, including a shore lunch, for $175, covering up to two people.

Richmond Corner Sauna

Meriting a recreational category of its own—or maybe it should qualify as entertainment—the clothing-optional Richmond Corner Sauna (81 Dingley Rd., Richmond, 207/737-4752 or 800/400-5751, www.richmondsauna.com, $25 pp) is one of those funky places you either like or you don't. But it has been here since 1976, and maybe you'll like it. Finnish-American owner Richard Jarvi has built a loyal clientele for his authentic wood-heated sauna house with six private rooms and a group one. In between and afterward, there's a pool and a hot tub. If nudity bothers you, don't come. If you're too relaxed to drive after the sauna, the casual, clothing-optional main house, built in 1831, has five B&B guest rooms ($85 d) with shared baths; room rates include sauna, pool, and hot

tub access as well as a continental breakfast. The sauna is open 5–9 P.M. Tuesday–Sunday in winter, 6–10 P.M. Tuesday–Sunday in summer. From downtown Richmond, take Route 197 west about five miles and turn left (south) onto Route 138. Take an immediate left onto Dingley Road, where you'll see the sign.

ACCOMMODATIONS

On the western side of the city, close to I-95 but convenient to downtown and the Capitol complex, is the **Senator Inn and Spa** (284 Western Ave., Augusta, 207/622-5804 or 877/772-2224, www.senatorinn.com, $130–280 d). Recent upgrades—including a good restaurant with a great Sunday brunch, a full-service spa, and indoor and outdoor heated pools—have made this the area's most upscale lodging; some rooms have fireplaces or whirlpool tubs. A full cooked breakfast is included in the rates. Pets are allowed in certain rooms with a security deposit and a pet fee.

Bed-and-Breakfasts

On a back road only 10 minutes from the State House, 130-acre **C Maple Hill Farm Bed and Breakfast Inn and Conference Center** (11 Inn Rd., off Outlet Rd., Hallowell, 207/622-2708 or 800/622-2708, www.maplebb.com, $100–205) provides an ultra-green rural respite. Eight guest rooms (all with Wi-Fi, phones, cable TV, video players, air-conditioning, and individual heat control) in the informal renovated 1890s farmhouse overlook woods, fields, gardens, and even the Camden Hills. Some guest rooms have double whirlpool tubs, gas fireplaces, and private decks. Public areas include a living room, a hot tub, and a sauna. Breakfast is a custom-cooked affair from a menu and features the inn's own fresh eggs as an option. Coffee, tea, and baked goodies are available any time in the inn's common guest kitchen. No pets are permitted because of the delightful farm animals, including llamas, cows, and goats. The eco-aware inn is a leader in the green movement. It has a wind-generating turbine, extensive solar panels, and other green initiatives.

© HILARY NANGLE

Maple Hill Farm Bed and Breakfast Inn and Conference Center is an especially eco-friendly lodging.

Maple Hill Farm is three miles west of downtown Hallowell, next to an 800-acre wildlife preserve with an extensive trail network and a wonderful pond.

About 10 miles southwest of Augusta but a world removed is **A Rise and Shine B&B** (19 Moose Run Dr./Rte. 135, Monmouth, 207/933-9876, www.riseandshinebb.com, $150–200), the former Woolworth family estate overlooking Lake Cobbosseeconte in Monmouth. Restoring the main house after it had been empty for five years has been ongoing for partners Lorette Comeau and Tom Crocker, but they're turning it into a real gem, with Lorette's hand-painted murals in a few of the eight guest rooms. The overall atmosphere is very inviting, with plenty of shared public rooms—a great room, a living room, a dining room, a huge patio, and a TV room—to spread out and relax. They welcome families and have even created a children's garden as well as a giant checkerboard court (OK, adults love it too). Rates include a full breakfast; Wi-Fi and computer access

are provided. Two first-floor rooms connect through a bath for a family suite. In the evenings, Tom, a professional singer, often entertains guests—a real treat. Also on the premises is a small rental cottage with two bedrooms and a full kitchen ($300). Here's a twist on pets: The property previously was a racehorse farm, so horses can be accommodated by arrangement.

The **Benjamin Wales House Bed And Breakfast** (49 Middle St., Hallowell, 207/512-2461, www.benjaminwales.com, $129–169), an 1820 Federal listed on the National Register of Historic Places and surrounded by well-tended gardens, has four Maine-inspired air-conditioned guest rooms with TVs and Wi-Fi. In the parlor are both a player grand piano and a regulation pool table. Rates include a full breakfast.

FOOD

Restaurant hours noted are for peak season but are subject to change. It's always wise to call ahead.

Local Flavors

The yummy aromas of Old World–style baking are reason enough to venture off the beaten path to find **Black Crow Bakery** (232 Plains Rd., Litchfield, 207/268-9927, blackcrowbread.com, 7 A.M.–7 P.M. Tues.–Sat.), where the specialty, a Tuscan loaf, is as pretty as it is tasty. Almost all the breads baked in the brick oven are sourdough-based, and every day features a different loaf, perhaps Sicilian, olive herb, focaccia, the fantastic apricot almond, or Greek cheese. A modern mixer is Mark and Tinker Mickalide's only high-tech tool; they operate a very traditional bakery in their 1810 farmhouse's former summer kitchen, even grinding their own grains on Maine granite. The shop, which operates on the honor system, is across from the Legion Hall, between I-495 and the Litchfield Fairgrounds.

Great sandwiches, soups, salads, breads, delish cookies, and other treats come from **Slates Bakery** (169 Water St., Hallowell, 207/622-4104, 7 A.M.–6 P.M. daily, 7 A.M.–4 P.M. Sun.).

Yet another source of fabulous baked goods is **Blue Sky Bakery** (339 Water St., Gardiner, 207/582-5450, www.blueskybakery.net, 6 A.M.–5 P.M. Wed.–Fri., 7 A.M.–4 P.M. Sat.), an artisanal bakery using ultrafresh and ultragood ingredients and making pastries and other goodies from scratch. On Saturday, you can pick up beans and brown bread.

On a fine summer day, grab a seat outside on **Joyce's** (192 Water St., Hallowell, 207/512-8433, 11 A.M.–9 P.M. Mon.–Sat.) for light fare and heavy-duty cocktails.

Expanding from its original Belfast store to a location near the State House, **Bay Wrap** (1 Hitchborn St., Augusta, 207/620-9727, www.thebaywrap.com, 7 am.–5:30 P.M. Mon.–Fri.) fills tortillas with all kinds of concoctions. The Samurai Salmon is divine.

If you're wandering around the back roads and make it as far as Readfield Center, duck into **Emporium Pizza** (Rte. 41 and Rte. 17, 207/685-7348, 5–9 P.M. Tues.–Sun. summer only, $7–10) for an ultracasual dinner. Pizza is the big draw, but with options such as pizza spanakopita or pizza piccata, it's no ordinary pie shop. And here's a cool piece of trivia:

Noted contemporary designer Alexis Bittar used to own the place, and you still might be able to see examples of his work here.

Put your lights on for service at **Fast Eddies** (Rte. 202, Winthrop, 207/377-5550, 11 A.M.–9 P.M. daily mid-Apr.–late Sept.), but even if you opt for car-hop service, make it a point to visit the dining room, where James Dean, Elvis, Marilyn Monroe, and Betty Boop preside over a cool collection of 1950s memorabilia. Burgers, shakes, fried foods, and homemade ice cream are the draws.

This region is blessed with excellent homemade ice cream. Worth the trip are: **Webber's** (Rte. 201, Farmingdale); **Hamilton's** (Water St./Rte. 201, downtown Hallowell); **Tubby's** (Main St., Wayne, 207/685-8181), which makes outrageous flavors from scratch and has a lovely lakeside deck out back; and **Old Colony Ice Cream** (28 Bowdoin St., Winthrop, 207/377-7788), just a couple of blocks from a lakeside park.

The **Augusta Farmers Market** operates 10 A.M.–1 P.M. Wednesday and Saturday at the Turnpike Mall on Western Avenue. There's also **Farmers Market at Mill Park** at the old Edwards Mill site on the north end of Water Street, operating 2–6 P.M. Tuesday. West of Augusta, the **Winthrop Farmers Market** is set up in the municipal building parking lot (Main St. in Winthrop) 9 A.M.–1 P.M. Tuesday and Saturday.

Family Favorites

When you have a hankering for finger-lickin' Memphis-style barbecue, **Riverfront Barbeque and Grill** (300 Water St., 207/622-8899, www.riverfrontbbq.com, 11 A.M.–9 P.M. Mon.–Wed., 11 A.M.–10 P.M. Thurs.–Sat., noon–9 P.M. Sun., $9–24) delivers, serving big portions of slow-smoked goodness—and a few surprises, such as veggie risotto—at affordable prices. Everything's prepared from scratch using local ingredients, whenever possible.

Chowders and seafood are the specialties at **Hattie's Chowder House** (103 Water St., Hallowell, 207/621-4114, 11 A.M.–9 P.M. Mon.–Sat., 11 A.M.–8 P.M. Sun., $7–24), but the menu has a bit of everything.

KENNEBEC

The A1-Diner serves far more than classic diner fare.

Downriver from Augusta, the **Railway Café** (64 Main St., Richmond, 207/737-2277, dinner entrées $6–14) has been the favorite local gathering spot since 1984. Looking at the original 19th-century woodwork and tin ceiling, who'd guess it had once been a funeral parlor? Dinner entrées include steak, seafood, grilled chicken, and pizza. The café is open year-round for breakfast, lunch, and dinner.

Casual Dining

It's the 20-ounce pint glass, not politics, that helped christen **The Liberal Cup** (115 Water St., Hallowell, 207/623-2739, 11:30 A.M.–10 P.M. daily, $6–14), a brewpub and restaurant where owner Geoffrey Houghton, who studied in Britain, brews great beers. Homemade is true of the food too; the place is packed with diners sampling the salads, salmon, steak, fish-and-chips, and shepherd's pie. Even the salad dressings are made on the premises.

The first-rate **A-1 Diner** (3 Bridge St., Gardiner, 207/582-4804, www.a1diner.com, 7 A.M.–8 P.M. Mon.–Sat., 8 A.M.–1 P.M. Sun.) is

the real thing, a genuine classic diner with moderate prices and some added attractions, such as air-conditioning. The menu, however, goes well beyond diner fare. How about tilapia with pesto, Transylvania eggplant casserole, or wild mushroom ragout? Board specials are $9–15. The soups are great too. There's also a regular diner menu, and Sunday brunch draws a big crowd.

Ask anyone where to eat in the Augusta area and chances are high that the answer will be **Slates** (167 Water St., Hallowell, 207/622-9575, 7:30–11 A.M. Mon.–Fri., lunch 11 A.M.–2:30 P.M. Tues.–Fri., 10 A.M.–2 P.M. Sat.–Sun., dinner 5:30–8 P.M. Mon., 5:30–9 P.M. Tues.–Sat.), the Energizer bunny of local restaurants. Founded in 1979, it just keeps improving. Destroyed by fire in early 2007, it rose from the ashes revitalized. Dinner entrées—mostly creative seafood and chicken, and a few token tournedos—are in the $10–20 range. The weekend brunches are fabulous: grilled fish and meats, unique omelets and Benedicts, huevos rancheros, stuffed croissants, homemade granola, and salads.

Don't let the location inside a hotel deter you from **Cloud 9** (Senator Inn and Spa, 284 Western Ave., Augusta, 207/622-5804, 6:30 A.M.–9 P.M. daily, $10–25). The chefs are committed to using local ingredients and take great care in preparing the fare. Choices vary from wood-oven pizzas to handmade pastas, burgers and fries to filet mignon. The brunch buffet, served 11 A.M.–2 P.M. Sunday, brings them in from points far and wide.

Ethnic Fare

Café de Bangkok (272 Water St., 207/622-2638, 11 A.M.–9:30 P.M. Mon.–Sat., 11 A.M.–10 P.M. Fri.–Sat., 4–9 P.M. Sun., $11–23) deserves its rep as one of Maine's best Thai restaurants. Not only is the food excellent—with great sushi—but the setting on the Kennebec River is lovely.

If you're feeding bottomless-stomach teens, **Lucky Garden** (222 Water St., Hallowell, 207/622-3465, 11 A.M.–9 P.M. daily) is a great choice. The all-you-can-eat buffet is $8 for lunch, served daily, or $11 for dinner on Friday–Saturday. The restaurant, with a nice dining room overlooking the river, is locally known for its sesame chicken.

INFORMATION AND SERVICES

Local information is available from the **Kennebec Valley Chamber of Commerce**

(207/623-4559, www.augustamaine.com), the **Hallowell Board of Trade** (207/620-7477, www.hallowell.org), and the **Kennebec Valley Tourism Council** (207/623-4884, www.kennebecvalley.org).

The Romanesque Revival **Lithgow Public Library** (Winthrop St. and State St., Augusta, 207/626-2415, www.lithgow.lib.me.us), one of Maine's handsomest libraries, was built in 1896 of Maine granite. Do not miss the gorgeous reading room, with a Tiffany clock, stained-glass windows, and French-inspired decor.

The **Maine State Library** (Maine State Cultural Building, Augusta, 207/287-5600, www.maine.gov/msl), in the State House complex, includes the Maine State Museum and the State Archives (207/287-5790) within its walls.

GETTING THERE AND AROUND

US Airways Express (800/428-4322, www.usairways.com) operates flights year-round between Boston's Logan Airport and the Augusta State Airport (AUG, 75 Airport Rd., Augusta, 207/626-2306).

Concord Coachlines (Augusta Transportation Center, 9 Industrial Dr., Augusta, 800/639-3317, www.concordcoachlines.com) operates bus service among Portland, Augusta, and Bangor, connecting with the Maine Coast, Boston, and points south.

Belgrade Lakes Area

The Belgrade Lakes area is one of those Proustian memories-of-childhood places where multigenerational family groups return year after year for idyllic summer visits full of nothing but playing, going for hikes or swims, fishing, listening for the loons, watching sunsets, and dreading the return to civilization. Today's parents, recalling carefree days at one of the many Belgrade-area summer camps, now send their own kids to camp here, or they rent lakefront cottages and devote their energies to recreating those youthful days.

Water, water everywhere: Mosey along the back roads and it seems as if there's yet another body of water around every other bend. Belgrade's chain of lakes is seven major lakes and ponds: Long Pond, North Pond, Great Pond, East Pond, Salmon Pond, McGrath Pond, and Messalonskee Lake (also known as Snow Pond), as well as numerous smaller ones; as you continue south, so do the lakes and ponds. Camps and cottages are sprinkled around their shores—you might even spot Elizabeth Arden's once-famed Maine Chance

Farm. Roadside put-ins and boat-launch ramps, from which you can put in a canoe, kayak, or powerboat, can be found on every lake. This is a great area just to strap a canoe or kayak on the car and wander, stopping wherever seems interesting for a paddle. Incidentally, the village of Belgrade Lakes, heart of the region, has its own post office but is part of the towns of Belgrade and Rome.

Since the Belgrade Lakes area is tucked in between Waterville and Augusta, those cities serve as the easily accessible commercial and cultural hubs for Belgrade visitors.

Directly west of Belgrade Lakes village is the charming, out-of-the-way hamlet of **Mount Vernon,** founded in 1792 and worth a visit by car or bike. North of that is **Vienna** (VI-enna); south is lovely **Kents Hill,** home to a prep school, and just beyond that is **Readfield.**

SIGHTS

◖ Great Pond Mail Boat

Remember the movie *On Golden Pond?* Author Ernest Thompson found his inspiration summering on the shore of Great Pond. (He's still here, although Hollywood's version was filmed in New Hampshire.) You can join the real-life postman on his rounds, feeding the 100-plus lakefront mailboxes—but you'll be in a pontoon boat instead of a Chris-Craft. Bring binoculars, a camera, a jacket, and a sandwich, and settle in aboard the stable boat. Reservations are essential—it takes only four passengers per trip, so call well ahead, especially in July–August. If your kids can behave for the duration of the up to four-hour excursion, by all means try this one. But leave them ashore if they're restless types (there's only an emergency Porta-Potty on board). Operated by Great Pond Mail Boat (207/215-7520, $20), the mail boat departs at 10 A.M. Monday–Saturday mid-June–mid-September from Great Pond Marina, off Route 27 just south of Belgrade Lakes village.

D. E. W. Animal Kingdom

Lions and tigers and bears, oh, my! And monkeys, camels, wallabies, ostriches, a binturong, a hyena, and, well, the list goes on. Allow at least an hour to visit the 42-acre D. E. W. (domestic, exotic, wild) Animal Kingdom (9918 Pond Rd./Rte. 41, Mount Vernon, 207/293-2837, www.dewanimalkingdom.com, 10 A.M.–5 P.M. Tues.–Sun. Apr.–mid-Sept., $10 over age 3), west of Belgrade Lakes village. Kids love the hands-on stuff at Julie and Bob Miner's innovative nonprofit zoo, where they raise and rehabilitate exotic and other animals, enhancing rare and endangered breeds, and educate visitors about them. Bob, a disabled Vietnam vet, has rescued animals from zoos and shows and even New York City apartments. Julie and Bob have hand-raised and bottle-fed many of these animals from infancy, and they enter every cage. Bob kisses the bears and the lions, and Julie nuzzles the panther, but visitors watch from behind a double fence; trust me, it's plenty close enough, especially when you learn such facts as that the hyena has the strongest jaw pressure of any land mammal. The zoo, on Route 41, is in West Mount

Lions and other exotic animals reside at the D. E. W. Animal Kingdom.

© HILARY NANGLE

KENNEBEC

Vernon, midway between Mount Vernon village and Kents Hill. Note: Whining children are strongly discouraged.

Flightseeing

Take off from the water and cruise by air over the lakes with **Airlink** (Great Pond Marina, 207/859-0109, www.airlinkconnection .com), with flights starting at $55 pp for 20 minutes.

ENTERTAINMENT AND EVENTS

The big entertainment here is shared family time on the lakes, but there are a few nearby venues worth exploring.

The **New England Music Camp** (207/465-3025, www.nemusiccamp.com) in Sidney stages faculty and student performances during camp sessions.

SHOPPING

Mosey and poke around the back roads and you'll be rewarded with a handful of galleries and what-not shops.

Multipurpose Store

Cars and canoes are about the only things you can't buy at **Day's Store** (Main St./Rte. 27, Belgrade Lakes, 207/495-2205 or 800/993-9500, www.go2days.com), a legendary institution since 1960. From firewater to fishing tackle, sandwiches (including the Long Pond Grinder) to souvenirs, and more than a dozen kinds of homemade fudge, it's a general store par excellence. Don't expect fancy; the local flavor provides its character. Long Pond is at its back door, providing access by boat or car. Day's is in the center of the village; you can't miss it.

Gifts and Crafts

A few doors south of the Village Inn in Belgrade Lakes is the seasonal branch of Waterville's **Maine Made and More Shop** (Main St./Rte. 27, Belgrade Lakes, 207/495-2274), a summer landmark since 1980. Here's the place to stock up on tasteful gifts and crafts: jams and maple

syrup, cards and guidebooks, T-shirts and sweatshirts, stuffed moose, and even shoes.

Delivering what its name promises, **Maine Bone Carving** (Rte. 41, Mt. Vernon, 877/562-6637, www.mainebonecarving.com) sells hand-carved moose bone and also sells the works of Maine and New Zealand artisans. Open by chance or by appointment.

The ultra-talented duo of potter Mark Hutton and weaver Hillary Hutton sell their gorgeous handcrafted works from their home-based **Huttonstudios** (277 Tower Rd., Vienna, 207/293-3686, www.huttonstudios.com), open by chance or by appointment.

RECREATION
Parks and Views

Just north of Day's Store in Belgrade Lakes village is a cute little picnic area on Long Pond, **Belgrade Peninsula Park** (5:30 A.M.–10:30 P.M.), next to an old dam. Late in the day it's a great spot for sunset-watching and fishing; no camping or fires are permitted. The Belgrade Lakes Conservation Corps restored it in 1996, and there is space for five carefully parked cars.

Another scenic standout, with a super photo op of Long Pond and Belgrade Lakes village, is the state-maintained overlook at **Blueberry Hill** on the west side of Long Pond. From Route 27, just south of Belgrade Lakes village, take Castle Island Road west about three miles to Watson Pond Road. Turn right (north) and continue about 1.5 miles. (Another 2.8 miles north of Blueberry Hill is the trailhead for French's Mountain.)

Golf

Golf has taken center stage here ever since the opening of the splendid **Belgrade Lakes Golf Club** (West Rd., Belgrade Lakes, 207/495-4653, www.belgradelakesgolf.com) in 1998. Designed by noted British expert Clive Clark, the course is an 18-hole standout, and the view from the elegant clubhouse is dazzling.

Hiking

Proactive in protecting much of the region's beautiful land for hiking and responsible enjoyment, the **Belgrade Regional Conservation Alliance (BRCA)** (207/495-6039, www.belgradelakes.org) has a terrific trail map and hiking guide to the Kennebec Highlands—although it doesn't show every protected acre, since the alliance is managing to protect land faster than it can print maps.

The two good hikes listed here are included on the map, which can also be obtained at local general stores such as Day's. Both hikes are just north of Belgrade Lakes village in the town of Rome. Neither is particularly high, but their summits are isolated enough to provide panoramic vistas.

For lots of gain, little pain, and a good family hike, head for **French's Mountain,** on the west side of Long Pond. To reach the trailhead from Route 27, go about 4.2 miles north of Belgrade Lakes village and turn left onto Watson Pond Road. Go less than a mile; the trail (signposted) begins on the left. Allow about 20 minutes to reach the summit, with fantastic views of Long Pond, the village, and Great Pond. Take a picnic (and a litter bag) and stretch out on the ledges.

A marginally tougher yet still-easy hike is **Mount Phillips,** a 755-footer with summit views of Great Pond. Allow about 20 minutes to reach the top from the Route 225 trailhead. From Route 27, north of Belgrade Lakes village, turn right onto Route 225 at Rome Corner (Logan's Country Antiques is at the fork). Continue another 1.5 miles to the trailhead (on the left), across from a "Hemlock Trail" sign. Park as far off the road as possible. Head on up the blue-blazed trail to the summit.

Water Sports

Good places for swimming are **Long Pond Public Beach** on Lakeshore Drive in Belgrade Lakes village (near Sunset Grille) and at the Belgrade Community Center, on Route 27 just south of the village. In addition to the lakefront, the center also has a pool open to nonresidents for $2 during community swim hours.

© TOM NANGLE

Pontoon boats, motor boats, pleasure crafts, and kayaks are all great ways to explore the Belgrade Lakes.

FISHING

Fishing is a big deal here, particularly in May–June and September (the season runs Apr. 1–Oct. 1). Among the 20 species in the seven major lakes and ponds are landlocked salmon, brown trout, black bass, pickerel, white perch, and eastern brook trout. You'll have to stick to bag, weight, and length limits. Pick up tackle and nonresident fishing licenses at Day's Store (Main St., Belgrade Lakes, 207/495-2205 or 800/993-9500).

Cast a line for northern pike with **Maine Wilderness Tours** (207/465-4333, www.main-ewildernesstours.com). Trips include rod, reel, tackle, and bait, with rates beginning at $175 for four hours for up to two anglers.

BOATING

About five miles south of Belgrade Lakes village, across from the turn to Oakland, Ralph Ardito's **Belgrade Canoe and Kayak** (Rte. 27, Belgrade, 207/495-2005 or 888/226-6311, www.kayakandcanoe.com) has a hefty inventory of Old Town kayaks, canoes, and accessories for sale, and also rents canoes and kayaks. You can try them outside in the store's demo pond or on a local streams tour.

Great Pond Marina (25 Marina Dr., Belgrade Lakes, 207/495-2213, www.great-pondmarina.com) rents fishing boats ($62 per day), runabouts (from $155 per day), pontoon boats (from $224 per day), and kayaks ($30 per day s, $50 d), and a security deposit is required.

Cruise the Great Pond aboard a pontoon boat with Jim Kaiser's **Selak Boat Tours** (161 Main St., Belgrade Lakes, 207/495-8826), which offers afternoon and evening cruises ($20 pp) on weekdays.

Roller Skating

Here's a throwback: When the windows are open, it feels as if you could dive out into the water at **Sunbeam Roller Rink** (Rte. 8, Smithfield, 207/362-4951), an old-fashioned roller-skating rink that's right on North Pond. It's open evenings in summer; call for the schedule.

Belgrade Community Center

Belgrade's spiffy recreation center (Rte. 27, Belgrade, 207/495-3481, www.belgrademaine.com) fronts on Great Pond and has a beach as well as an outdoor pool. Inside are the town library and a full-size basketball court. Everything's open to visitors, although if you want to borrow a book or two, you'll have to join the library as a nonresident for $10 (well worth it if the weather isn't cooperating and you're in a camp or cottage for the week). The center offers a full range of programs, from pickup basketball and volleyball to a summer kids' camp to a knitting and crafts club.

ACCOMMODATIONS

Rates reflect peak summer season.

Inns, Guesthouses, and Bed-and-Breakfasts

Practically hidden on a hillside just steps from downtown Belgrade Lakes is the **【 Wings Hill Inn and Restaurant** (Rte. 27, Belgrade Lakes, 866/495-2400, www.wingshillinn.com, $155–195). Built around the turn of the 18th century, the rambling farmhouse-turned-inn houses six guest rooms and the area's best fine-dining restaurant, thanks to hands-on chef-owners Christopher and Tracey Anderson. The downstairs Sage Suite sleeps three and has a private entrance, a TV with a DVD player, and a small fridge. All of the second-floor rooms have balconies, some shared. The best guest room is Moonlight, a spacious room with a large private deck and lake views. Relax on the screened wraparound porch or snag an Adirondack-style chair on the lawn or a patio seat or, in winter, a place inside by the fire. A TV and a guest phone are in the living room; Wi-Fi is available throughout. Rates include a sumptuous full breakfast and fresh-baked treats with afternoon tea.

On the eastern side of Great Pond is the aptly named **Among the Lakes Bed and Breakfast** (58 Smithfield Rd., Belgrade, 207/465-5900, www.amongthelakes.com, $125–145). Although it doesn't have a lake view, Great Pond is about a one-mile stroll down a private lane. Each of the five guest rooms has air-conditioning; some share baths. Rates include a full breakfast.

Just west of Waterville on the eastern edge of the Belgrade Lakes region is **The Pressey House Lakeside Bed and Breakfast** (32 Belgrade Rd., Oakland, 207/465-3500, www.presseyhouse.com), Lorne and Lorie McMillan's mid-19th-century octagonal house with an ell and a barn at the head of nine-mile-long Messalonskee Lake (also known as Snow Pond). There are five good-size suites, most with kitchens; one has a balcony overlooking the lake, another has a fireplace. Rates are $130–225 d mid-May–mid-October, $115–185 d other months, including a full breakfast; the inn is family-friendly, and suites sleep as many as five. Smoking and pets are not allowed. Relax in the Gallery great room, which has a huge brick fireplace dividing it in two, or on the patio. You can borrow the canoe, a paddleboat, or a motorboat to explore the lake. The Pressey House, a five-minute drive from I-95 Exit 127, is open year-round.

You can almost dive into Lake Minnehonk from the back porch of the **Lakeside Loft** (386 Pond Rd./Rte. 41, Mt. Vernon, 207/293-4855, www.thelakesideloft.com, $80–172). Three self-catering units with cooking facilities face the lake, and guests have access to the living room as well as a kayak, canoes, backpacks, and in winter, snowshoes. There's also Wi-Fi and a video library.

Sporting Camps

Distant from most of Maine's sporting camps, these classic Belgrade-area operations nonetheless retain the flavor of those much farther north. And it's a heck of a lot easier to reach when driving from the south.

Established in 1910 and still operated by the same family, **Bear Spring Camps** (60 Jamaica Point Rd., Rome, www.bearspring-camps.com, mid-May–early Oct.) is one of the state's largest sporting camps, with 32 rustic cottages on 400 wooded acres. All have baths and Franklin stoves and overlook the North Bay of nine-mile-long Great Pond.

Each cottage has its own dock; rental motorboats, kayaks, canoes, and even a pontoon boat are available. Other facilities include a sandy beach, a tennis court, and hiking trails. Cottages have 1–4 bedrooms with rates from $965 d per week, including all meals, served in the main lodge. In traditional style, lunch (called "dinner") is the main meal of the day, while supper is lighter fare. The staff will cook the fish you catch. Cabins are available only by the week mid-June–Labor Day, and reservations are tough to come by; off-season, when they're available, daily rates are available. Some guests stay for a month, and they book a year ahead. Pets are not allowed. Bear Spring Camps is 0.25 miles off Route 225, four miles east of Route 27.

Founded in 1909, **Alden Camps** (3 Alden Camps Cove, Oakland, 207/465-7703, www.aldencamps.com, mid-May–late Sept.) has an incredibly loyal following that includes fourth-generation guests, which makes getting reservations tough but not impossible. The 18 rustic cottages face great sunrises across three-mile-long East Pond (a.k.a. East Lake). Most guests spend a week. Each no-frills cottage has a screened porch, electricity, a bath, a fridge, and daily maid service. The crew of college kids aims to please, and former staffers now show up as guests. Meals are hearty and surprisingly creative with about a dozen or so entrée choices nightly (limited reservations for nonguests, entrées $20, including a salad course). The Friday-night lobster bake or clam bake—open to nonguests, call for reservations—is a longstanding tradition. BYOB. The 40-acre spread on Route 137 has a clay tennis court, a sand beach, a waterskiing boat, boat rentals, and a kids' play area. Rates, which include all meals, vary with cottage size and occupancy, beginning around $118 pp per night or $710 pp per week d for a one-room cottage. Children under age 13 are $18–75 per day or $110–453 per week, depending on age. Spring and late summer rates are lower. After the Labor Day–late September season, cottages are available without meals for $84–168 per day or $502–1,010 per week. Rates do not include gratuities. Low-season midweek specials are a

Castle Island Camps occupies all of the tiny Castle Island.

real steal. Pets are grudgingly allowed for $25 per day. Boat rentals are $20 per day or $120 per week; canoes and kayaks are free. Alden Camps is seven miles off I-95 Exit 127.

Occupying all of tiny Castle Island, a blip on the causeway-bridge dividing Long Lake, is **Castle Island Camps** (Castle Island Rd., Belgrade Lakes, 207/495-3312 or winter 207/293-2266, www.castleislandcamps.com, May 1–Sept. 30, no credit cards). What a location! The 12 rustic cabins are geared to anglers, but they're popular with families in summer who want a simple old-fashioned lake-based holiday. Each cabin fronts on the lake, and homestyle meals, served in the lodge, are included in the rates ($85 s, $160 d per night; $570 s, $1,075 d per week; kids' rates begin at $25 under age 3 and increase with age). Rental boats ($55 per day with gas) and kayaks ($30 per day, $20 halfday) are available. Other amenities are Wi-Fi, a swimming dock, and a games room.

Seasonal Rentals

Seasonal rentals are the preferred lodging in the Belgrade Lakes area. For possibilities, call **Belgrade Reservation Center** (207/495-2104, www.belgraderental.com).

FOOD

Restaurant hours noted are for peak season but are subject to change. It's always wise to call ahead.

Local Flavors

If you're looking for picnic fare or a quick bite, stop in at **Day's Store** (Main St./Rte. 27, Belgrade Lakes, 207/495-2205 or 800/993-9500, www.go2days.com) and pick up pizza, sandwiches, and baked goodies.

Detour down by the old millstream to **The Olde Post Office Café** (366 Pond Rd., Village Center, Mt. Vernon, 207/293-4978). The café overlooks Minnehonk Lake and is open 7 A.M.–2 P.M. Monday–Friday, 8 A.M.–2 P.M. Saturday–Sunday and occasionally for Saturday night dinners with music. Sandwiches, salads, paninis, and wraps fill the menu along with baked goodies. Grab a seat inside or on the screened porch overlooking the stream. Don't miss the old wheel-driven mill across the street.

Reliability is the biggest selling point for the **Sunset Grille** (4 West Rd., Belgrade Lakes, 207/495-2439, 7 A.M.–10 P.M. Sun.–Thurs., 7 A.M.–midnight Fri.–Sat.). The local grub and gossip spot is open daily for breakfast, lunch, and dinner, and it has a full bar. Stick to the basics and the chili.

Casual Dining

Who'd a thunk a sporting camp would serve fare such as beef *chimichurri* or Thai sizzling snapper? You'll have to call in advance to book one of the few seats on the porch available to nonguests at **Alden Camps** (3 Alden Camps Cove, Oakland, 207/465-7703, www.alden-camps.com, dinner daily late May–early Sept.). Even though you'll hear the passing whiz of traffic, the experience is worth it. The menu, posted nightly on the blackboard, lists more than a dozen choices, from rack of lamb to smoked mozzarella ravioli. The chef obviously knows his way around the kitchen. Entrées are $20, and that includes a loaf of fresh baked bread and a salad with homemade dressing choice. BYOB. On Friday nights, it's an outdoor lobster and seafood bake—a very popular choice.

Fine Dining

Fortunately for diners at the inn, innkeepers Tracey and Christopher Anderson of the **Wings Hill Inn and Restaurant** (Rte. 27, Belgrade Lakes, 866/495-2400, www.wingshillinn.com) met while attending culinary school. The five courses on their fixed-price menu (seatings at 6 and 8 P.M. Thurs.–Sun. Sept.–June, 6 and 8 P.M. Wed.–Sun. July–Aug., $57), change weekly and provide appetizers, choices of soup, a salad, and main courses such as grilled pork or slow-roasted Cornish hen. In the off-season, a three-course menu may be available for $35. BYOB. Reservations are strongly recommended.

INFORMATION

Local information is available from **The Belgrade Lakes Region Business Group** (www.belgradelakesmaine.com) and **Kennebec Valley Tourism Council** (207/623-4884, www.kennebecvalley.org).

Summertime in the Lakes, a free tabloid with ads, features, and calendar listings, is an especially helpful local publication that appears weekly during the summer. Copies are available at the information center and at most of the restaurants and shops in the region.

Check out the **Belgrade Public Library** (Belgrade Community Center, Rte. 27, Belgrade, 207/495-3481, www.belgrademaine.com).

Waterville and Vicinity

Most visitors come to Waterville drawn by Colby College, an elite liberal arts institution whose students and faculty give a college-town flavor to this mill town, incorporated in 1802. The school's Museum of Art is reason enough to visit this small city. Other draws include a fabulous film festival and the oldest blockhouse in the nation, in nearby **Winslow.**

As early as 1653, Europeans set up a trading entrepôt here, calling it Teconnet—the earlier version of today's Ticonic Falls, on the Kennebec River—and commerce with Native Americans thrived until the onset of the Indian Wars two decades later. In the late 19th century a contingent of Lebanese immigrants arrived, finding employment in the town's mills, and many of their descendants have become prominent community members. Best known of these is favorite son and former U.S. Senate Majority Leader George J. Mitchell, who still returns to spend time with his many relatives here.

SIGHTS
Colby College

Crowning Mayflower Hill, two miles from downtown Waterville, Colby College (Mayflower Hill, Waterville, 207/872-3000, www.colby.edu)

is a must-see. Colby's 1,800 students attend a huge variety of liberal-arts programs on a 713-acre campus noted for its handsome Georgian buildings. Founded by Baptists in 1813 as the all-male Maine Literary and Theological Institution, Colby received its current name in 1867 and went coed in 1871. Campus tours are available through the Admissions Office (207/859-4828 or 800/723-3032, 8 A.M.–5 P.M. Mon.–Fri., 8 A.M.–noon Sat.).

The **Colby College Museum of Art** (207/859-5600, 10 A.M.–4:30 P.M. Tues.–Sat., noon–4:30 P.M. Sun., free), in the Bixler Art and Music Center, has earned an especially distinguished reputation for its remarkable permanent collection of 18th–20th-century American art. Colby's museum is a stop on the Maine Art Museum Trail, which highlights the state's seven major art museums. In 1996 the museum opened its $1.5 million Paul J. Schupf Wing to house 415 paintings and sculptures created by artist Alex Katz during a 50-year period. In July 1999, the architecturally stunning $1.3 million Lunder Wing opened, expanding the museum's exhibit space to 28,000 square feet. Other significant holdings include works by Gilbert Stuart, Winslow Homer, and John Marin; special solo and group shows are mounted throughout the year. And don't miss the tasteful gift shop. The museum is on the east side of the campus's main quadrangle, just north of Mayflower Hill Drive.

Also on the campus is the 128-acre **Perkins Arboretum and Bird Sanctuary,** with three nature trails. Bring a picnic and blanket and stretch out next to Johnson Pond. In winter there's ice-skating on the pond.

Fort Halifax

Left over from a fort built in 1754, the two-story Fort Halifax (Bay St., Winslow) stands sentinel where the Sebasticook River meets the Kennebec River. The oldest blockhouse in the nation, it was built of doweled logs during the French and Indian Wars. In 1984, after rampaging Kennebec floodwaters swept the building away, more than three dozen of the giant timbers were retrieved downstream.

Fort Halifax, the nation's oldest blockhouse, was rebuilt from original timbers after floodwaters carried it away.

© TOM NANGLE

Energetic fund-raising allowed the blockhouse to be meticulously restored. The surrounding park is a great place for a picnic, with tables dotting shaded grassy lawns rolling to the river's edge.

Two-Cent Bridge

Spanning the Kennebec from Benton Avenue in Winslow to Front Street in Waterville (walk down Temple St. in Waterville), the 700-foot-long Two-Cent Bridge (officially the Ticonic Footbridge) was built in 1903 for pedestrian commuters to the Scott Paper mill in Winslow, who paid $0.02 to cross. Closed in 1973, the bridge was recently reopened and is the forerunner of a Head of Falls waterfront redevelopment effort. Possibly the only toll pedestrian bridge left in the United States, its replica tollbooth is a "stand still" museum. A stroll over the bridge gives a good view of "Empire Falls."

Redington Museum

Home of the Waterville Historical Society, the Redington Museum and Apothecary (62 Silver St., Waterville, 207/872-9439, www.redingtonmuseum.org, 10 A.M.–3 P.M. Tues.–Sat. Memorial Day week–Labor Day, closed holidays, tours 10 and 11 A.M., 1 and 2 P.M., $3 adults, $2 under age 12) has a particularly intriguing 19th-century pharmacy as well as Native American artifacts. The Federal-style Redington House was built in 1814 by early settler Asa Redington for his son, Silas.

ENTERTAINMENT

One of Maine's premier art-film houses is in downtown Waterville. The two-screen **Railroad Square Cinema** (17 Railroad Sq., Waterville, 207/873-6526, www.railroadsquarecinema.com) is the home of the Maine International Film Festival (MIFF, www.miff.org), which has brought such luminaries as Sissy Spacek and Peter Fonda to town to receive Mid-Life Achievement Awards. For festival passes, call 207/873-7000. The 10-day summer festival screens about 100 films representing about 50 filmmakers.

Above City Hall is the refurbished turn-of-the-20th-century **Waterville Opera House** (93 Main St., 207/873-5381, tickets 207/873-7000, www.operahouse.com). Once the haunt of vaudevillians, the Opera House is now the site of plays, dance performances, and concerts throughout the year.

About 20 minutes northeast in rural Unity is **Unity Centre for the Performing Arts** (42 Depot St., Unity, 207/948-7469, www.unity-maine.org/theater), a 200-seat theater built by Bert and Coral Clifford and donated to Unity College in 2007.

The downtown **Midnight Blues Club and Restaurant** (2 Silver St., Waterville, 207/877-8300, www.midnightbluesclub.net, 11 A.M.–1 A.M. daily) frequently has entertainment.

EVENTS

During the academic year, and less often in summer, Colby College (207/859-4353, www.colby.edu/news) is the venue for exhibits, lectures, concerts, performances, and other events.

A gathering of New England's best fiddlers, the **East Benton Fiddlers' Convention** (207/453-2017, www.eastbentonfiddlers.com) draws close to 2,000 enthusiasts to open-air performances at the Littlefield farm in East Benton. The convention happens noon–dusk the last Sunday in July.

Downtown Waterville is the site of mid-summer **Taste of Greater Waterville.** The food-focused one-day festival is usually held on a Wednesday. There's alfresco dining along with music for kids and adults.

During the third weekend in September, sleepy Unity comes alive with the **Common Ground Fair,** a celebration of organic foods and country life sponsored by the Maine Organic Farmers and Gardeners Association.

SHOPPING

Unlike so many former mill towns, Waterville's downtown has life, with shops and restaurants and plenty of free parking in The Concourse, the triangle framed by Elm, Main, and Spring Streets.

KENNEBEC

New, Used, and Children's Books

Conveniently situated downtown and facing the square, **Re-Books** (25 E. Concourse, Waterville, 207/877-2484) is a basement-level shop with a fairly extensive selection of hardcovers and paperbacks. Directly above it, despite the name, and facing Main Street is the **Children's Book Cellar** (207/872-4543), a very kid-friendly space with a great selection of books and toys.

Crafts and Gifts

Paula and George Gordon's **Maine Made and More Shop** (93 Main St., Waterville, 207/872-7378) spotlights the work of Maine individuals and companies, but you'll find far more than crafts, and everything is of high quality.

Stained Glass Express (10 Railroad Sq., Waterville, 207/872-9305) is a working glass studio selling supplies as well as finished goods. It also offers classes.

Johnny's Selected Seeds

If you're a gardener, farmer, horticulturalist, or just plain curious, take a 15-minute drive east of Waterville to visit the research farm of Johnny's Selected Seeds (Foss Hill Rd., Albion). Pick up a map and then take a self-guided tour of the 40 acres of trial gardens 9 A.M.–4 P.M. Monday–Friday July–August. Or visit the store (207/861-3999) and headquarters (955 Benton Ave., Winslow, 207/861-3900, www.johnny-seeds.com). The eponymous seed source has a national reputation. More than 2,000 varieties of herbs, veggies, and flowers are grown in the trial gardens, which were started in 1973. Known for high-quality seeds and service, the company makes good on anything that doesn't sprout.

RECREATION

Kennebec Messalonskee Trails (207/873-6443, www.kmtrails.org) has constructed a number of trails in the region, which are mapped and detailed on its website.

ACCOMMODATIONS

Chains dominate the lodging in this region, but The Pressey House, in the Belgrade Lakes area, is convenient to Waterville.

Guests at **84 The Pleasant Street Inn** (84 Pleasant St., Waterville, 207/680-2515, www.84pleasantstreet.com, $60–95) have access to a full kitchen, a dining area, and a living room, making it easy to feel at home. Five guest rooms have full baths, one has a half bath, and one has a shared bath; all have Wi-Fi and air-conditioning. It's clean and cozy, and rates include a self-serve continental breakfast.

About 20 minutes northeast of Waterville is **The Copper Heron** (130 Main St., Unity, 207/948-9003, www.copperheron.com, $95), with four guest rooms in an in-town Greek Revival house built in 1842. Common areas include a library with a TV and video player as well as a dining room where full breakfasts (and dinners by arrangement) are served. You can walk to the Unity Centre for the Performing Arts, Unity College, and lovely Unity Pond (there's a boat put-in, but you'll want to drive to that). Unity is also home to the Maine Organic Farmers and Gardeners Association and its annual Common Ground Fair in September. Children are welcome.

FOOD

Restaurant hours noted are for peak season but are subject to change. It's always wise to call ahead.

Local Flavors

In a local twist on the traditional Maine public suppers—thanks to Waterville's substantial Lebanese community—**St. Joseph Maronite Church** (3 Appleton St., Waterville, 207/872-8515) puts on a Lebanese supper at least once a year (the second Sunday after Easter). If you enjoy Eastern Mediterranean home cooking, be there. Call the church for details.

Nothing's finer on a hot summer day than a banana or peanut butter–chocolate chip ice cream from **North Street Dairy Cone** (127 North St., Waterville, 207/873-0977).

Jorgensen's Café (103 Main St., Waterville, 207/872-8711, 7 A.M.–6 P.M. Mon.–Sat., 7 A.M.–4 P.M. Sun.) is a downtown institution where you might hear French spoken. Bagels, muffins, breakfast sandwiches, and more than

25 varieties of coffee brewed daily attract morning crowds; lunch comprises specialty sandwiches, with every kind of deli meat available, plus quiche, salads, and soups. There's also an unusually interesting selection of gourmet gifts, implements, wine, and sweets.

Much newer on the scene but quickly earning community kudos is **Barrels Community Market** (74 Main St., Waterville, 207/660-4844, www.barrelsmarket.com, 10 A.M.–7 P.M. Mon.–Fri., 10 A.M.–5 P.M. Sat.). It sells locally produced foods and goods and doubles as an educational center. You can easily assemble a picnic here.

An extremely popular hangout, **Big G's Deli** (Benton Ave., Winslow, 207/873-7808, www.big-g-s-deli.com, 6 A.M.–7 P.M. daily, no credit cards) began as a sandwich shop in 1986 and now seats 200. It's renowned for enormous "name" sandwiches such as the Miles Standwich (nearly a whole turkey dinner), all on thick slices of homemade bread (half sandwiches are available). In fact, all breads and pastries are house-made. You can enjoy breakfast until 1 P.M. Order at the counter and try for a seat; or get it to go for the mother of all picnics. On the east side of the Kennebec River, Big G's is about a mile north of the Route 201 bridge to Waterville.

The **Grand Central Café** (10 Railroad Sq., 207/872-9135, 11 A.M.–8 P.M. Mon.–Wed., 5–8 P.M. Thurs., 11 A.M.–9 P.M. Fri.–Sat., 11 A.M.–2 P.M. Sun.) is a local favorite for fancy brick-oven pizza.

The **Downtown Waterville Farmers Market** (2–6 P.M. Thurs.) sets up in the concourse along Appleton Street downtown.

Casual Dining

Locals have been patronizing **George's Restaurant** (4 Union St., Waterville, 207/872-2629, 11 A.M.–9 P.M. Wed.–Sat., $11–24) for more than 30 years. No wonder: Tucked in a blue house, the cozy paneled dining room is a neighborhood favorite serving good steak, Italian classics, and Lebanese specialties. It's nothing fancy, just good cooking.

Fresh, flavorful cuisine with varied ethnic inspirations makes dining at **The Last Unicorn** (98 Silver St./Rte. 201, Waterville, 207/873-6378, 11 A.M.–10 P.M. daily, dinner entrées $20–25) a delicious adventure. Creative appetizers, an extensive wine and cocktail list, and weekend brunch are other pluses of this friendly place, which has patio dining in summer. Soups, salads, spreads, and desserts are made are made on the premises.

The ⬛ **Riverside Farm Market** (291 Fairfield St., Oakland, 207/465-4439, www.riversidefarmmarket.com, 10 A.M.–6 P.M. Mon.–Sat., 9 A.M.–1 P.M. Sun.) doubles as a casual café (11 A.M.–3 P.M. Tues.–Sat., 9 A.M.–1 P.M. Sun., dinner 5:30–8:30 P.M. Thurs.–Sat., $18–22) serves fabulous sandwiches, soups, and salads with a Mediterranean bent, scrumptious baked goods, and designer coffees for breakfast, lunch, and Sunday brunch. You also can pick up baked goods or lunch—soups, salads, quiche, and sandwiches—at the deli and baked goods counter. The dinner menu changes weekly but might include saltimbocca or grilled New York strip.

Up a steep flight of stairs, on the second floor of a Victorian home that also houses a spa, is **Apollo's Bistro** (91 Silver St., Waterville, 207/872-2242, www.apollosalonspa.com, 5:30–10 P.M. Fri.–Sat., $18–24), an elegant choice for a creative meal. Given that it's connected to the spa, it's no surprise that the emphasis is on fresh, local, and organic foods. Expect a leisurely meal, as all meals are prepared to order.

Ethnic Fare

Linked like a conjoined twin to the Railroad Square Cinema, **Buen Apetito** (4 Chaplin St., Railroad Sq., Waterville, 207/861-4649, www.buenapetitorestaurant.com, 5–8 P.M. Sun.–Mon., 4–8 P.M. Tues.–Thurs., 11 A.M.–9 P.M. Fri.–Sat., $8–13) serves popular Tex-Mex fare accented by fresh salsas and homemade tortillas.

A rising star in Waterville is the downtown **Cancun Mexican Restaurant** (14 Silver St., 207/872-7400, www.cancunwaterville.com, 11 A.M.–9 P.M. Mon.–Sat., noon–9 P.M. Sun.,

$8–13), owned by Mexican immigrant Hector Fuentes. It's a festive spot where mariachi bands play on weekend evenings; patio dining in summer.

It doesn't look like much from the outside—or on the inside, for that matter—but the little **Lebanese Cuisine** (34 Temple St., Waterville, 207/873-7813, 9 A.M.–4 P.M. Mon.–Fri., 9 A.M.–1 P.M. Sat.) serves very inexpensive, authentic, and delicious homemade spinach and meat pies, hummus, tabbouleh, and kibbe. The baklava is heavenly—not the sticky, overly sweet stuff that masquerades as baklava, but a flavorful treat. Eat here, or get it to go.

The area has numerous Asian restaurants, and one that has stood the test of time is **Asian Café** (53 Bay St., Winslow, 207/877-6688, 11 A.M.–9:30 P.M. daily, $5–15), serving Japanese, Korean, Thai, and Vietnamese cuisine. Portions are generous, and service is friendly and efficient.

INFORMATION AND SERVICES

The best sources of local information are the **Mid-Maine Chamber of Commerce** (207/873-3315, www.midmainechamber.com), **Waterville Main Street** (207/680-2055, www.watervillemainstreet.org), and **Kennebec Valley Tourism Council** (207/623-4884, www.kennebecvalley.org).

Check out **Waterville Public Library** (73 Elm St., Waterville, 207/872-5433, www.waterville.lib.me.us). **Miller Library** (Colby College, Waterville, 207/859-5100) has a huge Irish literature collection and a room dedicated to poet Edwin Arlington Robinson.

Skowhegan Area

The Wabanaki named Skowhegan (skow-HE-gun), meaning "the place to watch for fish," because that's just what the early Native Americans did at the Kennebec River's twin waterfalls. Their spears were ready when lunch came leaping up the river. The island between the falls later formed the core for European settlement of Skowhegan, the largest town and county seat of Somerset County. Named for England's Somerset, the county was incorporated in 1823 and covers 3,633 square miles.

Favorite daughter Margaret Chase Smith, one of Maine's preeminent politicians, put Skowhegan on the map, and even since her 1995 death, admirers and historians have made pilgrimages to her former home. During her years in the U.S. House and Senate, "The Lady from Maine" would return to her constituents—and she was never too busy to autograph placemats at her favorite local restaurant or to wave from her chair in her house's street-side solarium. Older local residents still recall the day President Dwight D. Eisenhower and his entourage visited Mrs. Smith in 1955, when "Ike" spoke to an enthusiastic crowd at the Skowhegan Fairgrounds.

Another local institution is the nationally and internationally renowned Skowhegan School of Painting and Sculpture, founded in 1946 as a summer residency program. One of the few art schools in the United States offering workshops in fresco painting, Skowhegan provides 65 artists with a bucolic 300-acre lakeside setting for honing their skills and interacting with peers and prominent visiting artists. Gaining admission is highly competitive for the nine-week program. Skowhegan's annual summer lecture series, featuring big names in the art world, is open to the public.

In the early 18th century, the town of **Norridgewock** (NORE-ridge-wok) was a French and Indian stronghold against the British. A century earlier, French Jesuit missionaries had moved in among the Norridgewock Indians at their settlement here and converted them to Catholicism. Best known of these was Father Sébastien Râle, beloved of his Indian parishioners. In 1724, taking revenge for Indian forays against them, a British militia detachment marched in and massacred the priest and his followers, a major milestone during what was known as Dummer's War. Today, a granite monument to Father Râle stands at the scene, Old Point, along the Kennebec River about two miles south of downtown Madison, close to the Madison-Norridgewock town boundary.

Meaning "smooth water between rapids," Norridgewock was the last bit of civilization for Benedict Arnold and his men before they headed into the Upper Kennebec wilderness on their March to Québec in 1775. Stopping for almost a week, they spent most of their time caulking their leaky bateaux. Today the town has a slew of handsome 18th- and 19th-century homes.

More recently, some of the scenes in the 2005 movie *Empire Falls* were shot in Skowhegan. That was one of the bright spots in a town that's fighting for its economic survival. It recently received grants to spruce up its architecturally rich main street, which unfortunately doubles as Route 201, the major thoroughfare between Québec and the U.S. coast. Take care crossing the street.

SIGHTS
Margaret Chase Smith Library
Beautifully sited on Neil Hill, high above the Kennebec River, the Margaret Chase Smith Library (56 Norridgewock Ave., Skowhegan, 207/474-7133, www.mcslibrary.org, 10 A.M.–4 P.M. Mon.–Fri., donation) bulges with fascinating memorabilia from the life and times of one of Maine's best-known politicians, who spent 32 years in the U.S. House and Senate and died in 1995. Over the entrance door is her signature red rose; inside is a 20-minute video describing her career. In 2000, the library held a special commemoration of the 50th anniversary of Senator Smith's "declaration of conscience" speech, in which she courageously castigated

Senator Joseph McCarthy for his "Red Scare" witch-hunting tactics. Ask if a staff member is available to show you Senator Smith's house, connected to the library on the 15-acre estate. (She was born at 81 North Ave. in Skowhegan.) The library is closed the week between Christmas and New Year's Day. The complex is 0.5 miles west of Route 201 (Madison Ave.).

Skowhegan History House
When you enter the handsome red-brick Skowhegan History House (40 Elm St., Skowhegan, 207/474-6632, www.skowhegan-historyhouse.org, 1–5 P.M. Tues.–Fri. early June–late Sept., $2 adults, $1 children and seniors), with only half a dozen rooms, you'll find it hard to believe that blacksmith Aaron Spear built it in 1839 for his family of 10 children. It must have been mighty cozy sleeping. Skowhegan treasures—antique clocks, china, and other furnishings—now fill the two-story structure, which has a commanding view over the Kennebec River and lovely gardens. The house is just west of Route 201, at the junction of Elm and Pleasant Streets.

The Skowhegan Indian Monument
Rising 62 feet above its pedestal and weighing 24,000 pounds, the giant wooden Skowhegan Indian statue was carved in 1969 by Maine sculptor Bernard Langlais, a Skowhegan School of Painting alum who died in 1977. Known nationally for his work, Langlais dedicated the monument to the Native Americans who first settled this area. One hand holds a spear, the other holds a stylized fishing weir. Unfortunately, the sculpture is in need of some repair work, but it's still a standout. It's just off Route 201, tucked in the back corner of a parking lot behind a Cumberland Farms at the intersection with High Street.

Skowhegan Historic District
Bounded roughly by Water and Russell Streets and Madison Avenue, the Skowhegan Historic

© TOM NANGLE

Sculptor Bernard Langlais carved the Skowhegan Indian statue in 1969.

District, close to the Kennebec River, contains 38 turn-of-the-20th-century buildings from the town's heyday as a commercial center. After trains arrived in 1856, the wireless telegraph in 1862, and telephones in 1883, Skowhegan saw incredible prosperity. It's worth a walkabout to admire the architectural details of a bygone era, although sad to say, many of the buildings need maintenance.

❰ L. C. Bates Museum

Offbeat doesn't begin to describe this treasure chest. In a Romanesque building, listed on the National Register of Historic Places, on the Good Will–Hinckley School campus, which was established in 1889 as a school for disadvantaged children, the L. C. Bates Museum (Rte. 201, Hinckley, 207/238-4250, www.gwh.org, 10 A.M.–4:30 P.M. Wed.–Sat., 1–4:30 P.M. Sun. Apr. 1–mid-Nov., 9 A.M.–4:30 P.M. Wed.–Sat. mid-Nov.–Mar. or by appointment, $2.50 adults, $1 under age 17) is a way-cool, way-retro museum, with a broadly eclectic collection focusing on natural history.

Among the treasures in the dozen or so rooms are hundreds of mounted rare birds, priceless Native American artifacts, and a trophy marlin caught by Ernest Hemingway.

Behind the museum, visit the arboretum and nature trails, open dawn–dusk. *Forest Walking Trails* maps are available in the museum. Alongside the trails are monuments to prominent conservationists. For a small fee, kids can attend natural-history workshops on Saturday mornings May–November. The turreted brick-and-granite building is five miles north of I-95 Exit 133, between Fairfield and Skowhegan, and is visible from Route 201 at the southern end of the campus.

❰ South Solon Meetinghouse

This place is nothing short of amazing. As you drive out on East Madison Road from Skowhegan, headed north, you'll pass Lake Wesserunsett and soon come to the hamlet of South Solon, which is little more than a crossroads. Here you'll find a serene white clapboard building, a traditional circa-1842 New England meetinghouse now listed on the National Register of Historic Places. Inside, it is completely frescoed with interdenominational religious scenes. One of the founders of the Skowhegan School of Painting and Sculpture rescued the church from ruin in the 1930s; in the 1950s fresco artists selected in a stiff competition were given a free hand to paint the place. The riot of color followed until every square inch of wall and ceiling was covered. (A fresco program still continues at the Skowhegan School.) The local caretaker is Andy Davis (207/643-2555). The meetinghouse is on the corner of South Solon Road and Meetinghouse Road, north of Route 43 and east of Route 201.

Pedestrian Bridges

Spanning the South Channel of the Kennebec River, the **Swinging Bridge** connects Skowhegan Island (from behind the ice cream stand) to Alder Street, off West Front Street. First built in 1883, floods in 1888, 1901, 1936, and 1987 damaged or destroyed the wire footbridge. Its latest incarnation was unveiled in 2006, when the town completely renovated it. The views are terrific, and the island park is a jewel.

The **Skowhegan Walking Bridge** spans the river about a block below the dam, opposite where Route 201 North and Route 2 split downtown. This one traces its history back to 1856, when it was constructed for the Somerset and Kennebec Railroad. The following year it was carried away by floodwaters. A wooden bridge followed, and then a steel one, also destroyed by floodwaters. The current bridge was built in 1988. Like the Swinging Bridge, it's worth a stroll just for the views.

ENTERTAINMENT
Theaters

For a dose of nostalgia, plan to catch a flick at the 350-car **Skowhegan Drive-In** (Waterville Rd./Rte. 201, Skowhegan, 207/474-9277, www .skowhegandrivein.com), a landmark since 1954. Nightly double features start at dusk or whenever the sun disappears. Gates open at 7:30 P.M.

Built in 1901, the **Lakewood Theater** (Rte. 201, Madison, 207/474-7176, www.lakewood-theater.org), on the shores of Lake Wesserunsett six miles north of Skowhegan, has had a roller-coaster history, but it's now in a decidedly "up" phase. Maine's oldest summer theater presents nine musicals, comedies, and light dramas each season. Performances are at 8 P.M. Thursday–Saturday and at 4 P.M. every other Sunday, plus matinees at 2 P.M. every other Wednesday late May–mid-September. On matinee Wednesdays, there is also a 7 P.M. evening performance. Tickets are $20–25 adults and about $15 ages 4–17. For about $15 more, you can have cabaret seating on the side balconies.

Lectures and Concerts

Performing-arts events are sometimes scheduled in Skowhegan's **Opera House** inside the circa-1909 City Hall, where Booker T. Washington spoke in 1912.

Mid-June–early August, the evening **Barbara Fish Lee Lecture Series** draws nationally and internationally noted artists to participate in its lecture and presentation series at the Old Dominion Fresco Barn at the Skowhegan School of Painting and Sculpture. Contact the school (207/474-9345) for dates and times.

A **concert series** is held at **Skowhegan's Coburn Park** at 5 P.M. Sunday during July–August.

EVENTS

Megaomelets made in the world's largest omelet pan, a parade, a craft fair, live entertainment, a carnival, and fireworks are among the features of the **Central Maine Egg Festival.** The biggest day is Saturday. It's held at Manson Park in Pittsfield mid–late July.

Billed as the oldest country fair in the United States, dating back more than 175 years, and also Maine's largest outdoor event, the **Skowhegan State Fair** is a 10-day extravaganza with agricultural exhibits galore, live entertainment, harness racing, food booths, a carnival, and a demolition derby at the Skowhegan Fairgrounds (Rte. 201, Skowhegan) early–mid-August.

On the Fourth of July, the **In Spite of Life Players** stage a performance at the gravel pit in West Athens.

SHOPPING
Factory Outlet

Discounts of up to 50 percent are typical for athletic-shoe seconds at the **New Balance Factory Store** (12 Walnut St., Skowhegan, 207/474-6231). The store also carries sportswear, socks, sports bags, and such. The outlet is just off Route 201 (W. Front St.) south of the Kennebec. The turn is next to Skowhegan Savings Bank.

Antiques

The **Fairfield Antiques Mall** (382 Rte. 201, Fairfield, 207/453-4100) boasts that it's the state's largest antiques group shop. Judge for yourself; it's 2.5 miles north of the I-95 interchange.

In downtown Skowhegan, **Hilltop Antiques** (48 Water St., 207/474-0055) has 27 rooms brimming with finds spread out on three floors.

Crafts

About 20 talented area artists show their works at the cooperatively owned **River Roads Artisans Gallery** (75 Water St., Skowhegan).

RECREATION
Coburn Park

Donated to the town by Abner Coburn, 13-acre Coburn Park, a wonderful riverside oasis, has a lily pond, memorial gardens (including a hospice garden and a Margaret Chase Smith rose garden), a summer concert series at the gazebo, pagodas, and more than 100 species of trees and shrubs. Bring a picnic, grab a table, and enjoy. The park is on Water Street (Rte. 2) at the eastern edge of town.

Arnold's Way Rest Area

About three miles north of Solon, close to the Solon-Bingham town line and just north of the area known as Arnold's Landing, is this state rest area, with covered picnic tables, grills, and an outhouse. Interpretive panels here mark the first of two dozen panels along the Old Canada Road Scenic Byway at Moscow, The Forks, Parlin Pond, and Attean, helping motorists get a feel for area history and activities such as logging.

Golf

The 18-hole **Lakewood Golf Course** (Rte. 201, Madison, 207/474-5955, www.lakewoodgolf-maine.com), five miles north of Skowhegan, dates from 1925.

ACCOMMODATIONS
Bed-and-Breakfasts

Helen Lamphere and her daughter Charlene run **Helen's Bed and Breakfast** (165 Madison Ave./Rte. 201, Skowhegan, 207/474-0066, www.helensbandb.com, Apr.–Dec., $65–95 d), a handsome 19th-century brick Victorian with four air-conditioned rooms. Antiques, country pieces, and Helen's hand-braided rugs create a comfy retreat. Helen also sells her rugs. Guests share the large deck and yard.

Sleep where the stars slept at **The Colony House Inn Bed and Breakfast** (Madison, 207/474-6599 or 888/268-2853, $40 pp), a lovely—if a bit tired—lakefront historical B&B adjacent to the Lakeside Theater. The shingle-style inn is wrapped in old-style elegance, with comfy public rooms, a nice screened porch, and a many-windowed dining room where a full breakfast is served. The prices reflect the old-fashioned baths: One guest room has a private bath, two lake-facing guest rooms are connected by a bath, and two other guest rooms share a bath. Also on the premises are two cottages ($550–650 per week or $60–100 d per night), one lakefront, the other facing the lake. Within walking distance are the theater, golf course, and a spiritualist camp that has been running for more than 125 years. Rent a boat, or simply settle into one of the Adirondack chairs on the lawn and gaze out at Lake Wesserunsett; it's heaven.

Motels

Convenient to downtown, the **Towne Motel** (172 Madison Ave./Rte. 201 N., Skowhegan, 207/474-5151 or 800/843-4405, www.townemotel.com, $92–114 July–mid-Oct., $73–87 mid-Oct.–June) has 33 guest rooms, all with phones, air-conditioning, cable TV, and high-speed Internet access; some have kitchenettes. Continental breakfast is included. The large outdoor pool is great for kids. Pets are welcome in some guest rooms.

For a cheap sleep, check in to the quaint but vintage **Breezy Acres Motel** (315 Waterville Rd./Rte. 201, Skowhegan, 207/474-2703, $58–80), owned by Dennis and Nancy Willete since 1979. One the grounds are a picnic area, a trout pond with paddleboating, an outdoor pool, and even a nine-hole bell-golf course.

Camping

How often do you find a campground on the National Register of Historic Places? That's the case at **The Evergreens Campground and Restaurant** (Rte. 201A, Solon, 207/643-2324, www.evergreenscampground.com), on a prehistoric site used by Native Americans about 4,000 years ago. Many stone tools and weapons excavated here are now in the Maine State Museum in Augusta; a small collection is displayed at the campground. The campground has mostly wooded sites (tent sites $7.50 pp, RV sites $24 d, free under age 8), some right on the Kennebec River. Cottages are $30 pp. Pets are allowed; rental canoes, kayaks, and tubes are available by the day; and shuttle service is available. There is a small launch fee for people bringing their own boats, and a guest fee. The restaurant, open 5–8:30 P.M. Friday–Saturday for dinner and 7–11 A.M. Saturday–Sunday for breakfast, has a bar and a riverfront deck. Directly across the river (technically in Embden) is a huge outcrop covered with ancient Indian petroglyphs; eagles can often be seen on this shore. The campground, a mile south of the center of Solon, is open all year, except mud season, and caters to snowmobilers in winter.

FOOD

Restaurant hours noted are for peak season but are subject to change. It's always wise to call ahead.

Local Flavors

Just south of downtown, the **Snack Shack** (100 Waterville Rd./Rte. 201, Skowhegan, 207/474-0550, 11 A.M.–8 P.M. Tues.–Wed., 11 A.M.–10 P.M. Thurs.–Sat., noon–8 P.M. Sun.) never disappoints for fried foods or sandwiches. It has a few tables, but most folks get takeout.

An 1864 bank now houses **The Bankery** (87 Water St., Skowhegan, 207/474-2253, 7:30 A.M.–5:30 P.M. Tues.–Sat.), a fine source for made-from-scratch baked goods that include breads, cookies, cakes, pies, and other treats. You can even watch the bakers at work.

More than two dozen fat sandwiches, as well as good salads and a soup of the day, draw locals into **Kel-Matt Café** (112 Madison Ave./Rte. 201, Skowhegan, 207/474-0200, www.kelmatcafe.com, 11 A.M.–3 P.M. Mon.–Sat.), in a Victorian house just north of downtown across from Bangor Savings Bank. Order at the counter and then grab a table in one of the small dining rooms, both spotless, or out on the front porch. Service is friendly and efficient. Be careful to park only in the restaurant's designated lot and not in that of the insurance agency next door.

I scream, you scream, and in Maine everyone screams for **Gifford's Ice Cream** (307 Madison Ave./Rte 1, Skowhegan, no phone). At this roadside institution, you can lick whoopie pie, Maine tracks, Denali peanut butter Iditarod, or Maine wild blueberry flavors while playing a game of miniature golf.

One doesn't expect much from a place that promises "Eat Here and Get Gas," but **Griswold's Country Store & Diner** (112B S. Main St, Solon, 207/643-2771, 6 A.M.–9 P.M. daily) is a welcome stop for unfussy food, with prices on most items well below $6.

The **Skowhegan Farmers Market** sets up at Court and High Streets 9 A.M.–1 P.M. Saturday early July–October.

Family Favorite

The parking lot's always busy at **Ken's Family Restaurant** (414 Madison Ave./Rte. 201, Skowhegan, 207/474-3120, www.kens familyrestaurant.com, 10:30 A.M.–8 P.M. Mon.–Thurs., 7 A.M.–9 P.M. Fri.–Sat., 7 A.M.–8 P.M. Sun.), in its second generation of Dionne family ownership. Seafood is the specialty, and seconds are on the house when you order the jumbo fish fry ($11). The Italian menu is equally popular; select a pasta and pair it with a sauce for $7. Families know they can count on good home cooking, and there's always the all-you-care-to-eat breakfast, served weekends. The children's menu lists about a dozen choices for less than $4, and of course there's the kid-pleasing dirt pudding.

Casual Dining

Two doors from the Towne Motel, in a renovated 19th-century home, the **Heritage House Restaurant** (182 Madison Ave., Skowhegan, 207/474-5100, lunch buffet 11:30 A.M.–2 P.M. Tues.–Fri., dinner 5–9 P.M. Sun.–Thurs., 5–10 P.M. Fri.–Sat. year-round, dinner entrées $10–20) is Skowhegan's best dining choice. Apricot mustard chicken breast is a specialty. Reservations are advisable on weekends.

INFORMATION AND SERVICES

The **Skowhegan Area Chamber of Commerce** (23 Commercial St., Skowhegan, 207/474-3621 or 888/772-4392, www.skowheganchamber .com) has info, as does the town's website (www .skowhegan.org). More information is available from **Kennebec Valley Tourism Council** (207/623-4884, www.kennebecvalley.org).

Check out **Skowhegan Free Public Library** (9 Elm St., Skowhegan, 207/474-9072, www .skowhegan.lib.me.us).

Bingham to Jackman

Route 201, from **Solon** north to **Jackman,** is a National Scenic Byway threading through the rural towns of **Bingham, Moscow,** and **The Forks.** Until the arrival of white-water rafting in the late 1970s, the Upper Kennebec Valley was best known to anglers, hunters, timber truckers, and families who'd been summering here for generations. And long before that, before dams changed the river's flow patterns, Native Americans used the Kennebec as a convenient chute from the interior's dense forests to summer encampments on the coast. In 1775, Colonel Benedict Arnold led more than 1,000 men up this river in a futile campaign to storm the ramparts of Québec City.

Midway between Skowhegan and The Forks, 23 miles in each direction, Bingham is also right on the 45th parallel and thus equidistant between the North Pole and the equator (3,107 miles in each direction). This quiet valley town is a low-key commercial center with attractive, manicured homes and is a stopping point for many white-water rafters en route to Caratunk and The Forks. The town was named for William Bingham, an influential Colonial-era banker and land speculator who made a fortune in privateering. Roscoe Vernon ("Gadabout") Gaddis, TV's pioneering Flying Fisherman, built Bingham's funky grass airfield, the Gadabout Gaddis Airport, site of an annual September fly-in with plane rides and aerobatics.

Just north of Bingham is Moscow, home of the 155-foot-high Wyman Dam, harnessing the Kennebec River for hydroelectric power. Backed up behind the dam is gorgeous Wyman Lake, lined with birches, evergreens, frequent pullouts (great for shutterbugs), and a small lakeside picnic area on the west side of Route 201.

Appropriately named, The Forks stands at the confluence of the Kennebec and Dead Rivers, making it obvious why rafting companies have set up shop here. The tiny year-round population supports an ever-expanding transient population for the white-water rafting trade late April–mid-October.

Surrounded by mountains, Jackman is the valley's frontier town, the last outpost before the Québec border, 16 miles northward. In the middle of town, the Moose River links Jackman to the town of Moose River, just to the north. Wander into local businesses and you'll likely hear a French lilt to conversation.

From Bingham to Jackman, Route 201 is better known as "Moose Alley." Even though state transportation officials have built rumble strips into the road and littered the roadsides with flashing yellow lights and cautionary "Moose Crossing" signs, drivers still barrel along, and every year fatalities occur. Those who drive carefully, though, have a treat in store: Moose sightings are relatively frequent,

THE BENEDICT ARNOLD TRAIL

"A tragic masterpiece of bad timing, bad maps, and bad luck" is author Ogden Tanner's summation of Colonel Benedict Arnold's March on Québec. Even though Arnold's expedition has been little more than a footnote to history, it's an incredible story, and one best appreciated during a visit to this region.

Arnold marched his troops up the Kennebec River Valley before crossing it and veering inland and up along the Carrabassett River. From Pittston to the Carrying Place (10 miles north of Bingham) and along Route 27, between Kingfield and the border, Arnold Trail historical markers note the expedition's rest stops, obstacles, and other details.

When you see the terrain, you'll begin to understand some of the awful rigors endured by Arnold (before his change of heart and alliance) and his men when they chose a route through the Kennebec Valley to attack the British in Québec City in 1775. Although he later betrayed the Revolutionary cause, Ar-

nold was in good graces when he set out that fall with 1,100 adventurers to remove the English from their Québec stronghold.

In Pittston, six miles south of Augusta, the expedition assembled 220 locally made bateaux and then continued up the Kennebec River to Augusta, camping at Old Fort Western, Skowhegan, and Norridgewock – cutting a swath through the Kennebec River Valley before portaging westward at Carrying Place Township to the Western Lakes and Mountains region and on into Canada. Afflicted by disease, hunger, cold, insects, and unforgiving terrain, the group was devastated before dragging into Québec City in December 1775.

If you're interested in Arnold, pick up a copy of *Following Their Footsteps: A Travel Guide and History of the 1775 Secret Expedition to Capture Quebec* by Stephen Clark. The book includes history, maps, canoe routes, and an appendix of places to visit along the way.

KENNEBEC

especially early and late in the day. If you notice a car or two pulled off the road, it's likely someone has spotted a moose. (Another Moose Alley in this area—a pretty sure bet for spotting one of the behemoths—is Route 6/15 from Jackman east to Rockwood.)

SIGHTS
◖ Moxie Falls
Here's a big reward for little effort: One of New England's highest waterfalls, Moxie Falls, with drops of as much as 100 feet, is one of the easiest to reach. From Route 201, just south of the Kennebec River bridge in The Forks, drive 1.8 miles east on Lake Moxie Road to the signposted parking area. From here, via an easy wide trail, plus steps and a boardwalk, it's 0.6 miles to the falls in Moxie Stream. Allow a relaxed hour for the round-trip; if it's hot, cool off in the stepped pools. Avoid the falls in June, when blackflies will have you for lunch.

◖ Old Canada Road National Scenic Byway
High on everyone's list of the best roads to drive in fall is **Route 201,** the 78-mile officially designated Old Canada Road Scenic Byway between Lakewood and the Canadian border (www.byways.org/explore/byways/11510). Every curve in the winding two-lane road reveals a red, gold, and green palette any artist would die for. But truly, it's gorgeous in any season.

It's also a historic route. Benedict Arnold marched his troops along the Kennebec River to the north of Moscow before crossing the river and turning inland. Rest stops along the route have interpretive signage and picnic tables. Two of the prettiest are **Wyman Lake Rest Area,** about midway between Bingham and The Forks, and **Attean View Rest Area,** just south of Jackman (climb the Owl's Head Trail for an even more spectacular view). The rest area in The Forks, just before the bridge, is a great place to watch rafts float by at the end of their thrilling trip down the Kennebec River. Detour into the neat little hamlet of **Caratunk,** a smidgen east of Route 201 on the way to Pleasant Pond.

In 2010, the **Old Canada Road Historical Society** (16 Sidney St., Bingham, www.old-canadaroad.org, check website for hours) opened a headquarters with exhibits. It expects to play a role in the 2012 bicentennial events in Bingham.

RECREATION

Recreation is the big focus in this part of Maine. Among the opportunities in the Upper Kennebec Valley are hiking, canoeing, kayaking, bicycling, fishing, and snowmobiling—just for a start—but the big business is white-water rafting, based in and around The Forks.

Water Sports

◖ WHITE-WATER RAFTING

Carefully regulated by the state, the rafting companies have come a long way since the sport really took off in the early 1980s. Most have sprawling base-camp complexes and have diversified year-round into other adventure sports such as mountain biking, canoeing, kayaking, camping, rock climbing, horseback riding, snowmobiling, and cross-country skiing. The state strictly monitors the number of rafts allowed on the rivers; on midsummer weekends there's a near-capacity crowd.

The focus of white-water rafting in this region is the **East Branch of the Kennebec River,** a 12-mile run from the Hydro Harris Station hydroelectric dam, below Indian Pond, to The Forks. The dam's controlled water releases produce waves of up to eight feet, and the trip begins with a bang in the Alleyway. The highlight is Magic Falls, a Class IV drop that appears as nothing more than a horizon line when approaching it but that has the punch to flip rafts. The excitement is concentrated in the first half of the trip; by the end of it you're just floating along, but that provides opportunities for swimming, water fights between rafts, and perhaps kayaking. Some companies also break

White-water rafting on the Kennebec River is the big attraction in The Forks.

for a riverside lunch. Kennebec trips operate early May–mid-October.

Most of the rafting companies also organize trips on the more challenging and oddly named **Dead River,** but serious water releases occur only half a dozen times during the season, mostly on spring weekends. Competition is stiff for space on the infrequent Dead River trips, an exhilarating 16-mile run through Class III–V white water from below Grand Falls to The Forks. The biggest thrill is Poplar Hill Falls. In July–August, the Dead River lives up to its placid name, and outfitters organize moderately priced Sport-Yak and family rafting trips.

The cost of a one-day Kennebec River trip ranges $80–130 pp, depending on whether it's a weekday, weekend, or midsummer. Prices include a hearty cookout or lunch either along the river or back at base camp. The cost of the one-day Dead River trip ranges $90–140 pp. Scads of economical package rates are available—covering lodging, meals, and other activities—especially early and late in the season. Be forewarned that all outfitters have age minimums, usually 10 on the upper Kennebec and 15 on the Dead. Some also impose a weight minimum.

If you want to make more than a day of it—definitely a good plan, since trips start early in the morning and you'll be exhilarated but dog-tired at the end of the day—spend a night or two, maybe one night before and one night afterward. Most of the outfitters have accommodations and dining for every budget. The camaraderie is contagious when everyone around you is about to go rafting or has just done it.

About a dozen outfitters operate on the Kennebec and Dead Rivers. The oldest and biggest is **Northern Outdoors** (1771 Route 201, The Forks, 800/765-7238, www.northernoutdoors.com), with extensive base facilities including lodging, dining, rentals, and more. About a half-dozen companies operate under the umbrella of **Raft Maine** (800/723-8633, www.raftmaine.com), which provides info, sends out brochures, and fields reservation requests. The toll-free number rotates like Russian roulette, connecting you to the next in-line rafting outfitter. If you prefer, contact individual outfitters directly—check the website for individual listings.

CANOEING AND KAYAKING

If you're a neophyte canoeist, if you have never done a multiday trip, or if you want to go en famille, your baptismal expedition probably ought to be the three-day **Moose River Bow Trip,** an easy 45-mile loop (ergo "bow") with mostly flat water. Of course, you can do this yourself, and you don't even need to arrange a shuttle, but a guided trip has its advantages—not the least of which is that the guides provide the know-how for the beginners, they do the cooking and cleanup, and they're a big help for portaging.

Experienced guides Andy and Leslie McKendry operate **Cry of the Loon Kayak Adventures** (207/668-7808, www.cryoftheloon.net), which does a three-day Moose River Bow ($325 pp, with only one portage). Maximum group size is eight and minimum four. Leslie's gourmet meals are included in the cost. Andy and Leslie will also do one-day guided trips ($60 pp with lunch), or they'll customize a multisport trip for you, with kayaking, rafting, rock climbing, and hiking. If you want to be on your own, they rent Old Town kayaks for $25 per day and Old Town canoes for $20 per day. Avoid June, when the blackflies descend; the water level can be a problem in August for the bow trip. Cry of the Loon's base is 6.5 miles east of Jackman on Route 15.

Maine Huts and Trails

The nonmotorized multiuse Maine Huts and Trails (www.mainehuts.org) network, which extends from Carrabassett Valley to The Forks, has a full-service hut sited about two miles below Grand Falls on the Dead River, making it easy to hike or bike the trail or even hike in, then paddle out.

Hiking

The **Appalachian Trail** (AT), extending 2,158 miles from Springer Mountain, Georgia, to the summit of Maine's Katahdin, crosses the Upper Kennebec Valley near Caratunk, just south of The Forks. The *Appalachian Trail Guide to Maine* provides details for reaching several sections of the white-blazed trail accessible to short-haul hikers. Crossing the 70-yard-wide Kennebec at this point would be a major obstacle were it not for the seasonal free ferry service operated for AT hikers by the Maine Appalachian Trail Club (www .matc.org/Ferry.htm). Check the website for the current schedule.

Other hikes abound, but access is often through a maze of logging roads or through territory where active logging may change landmarks. Ask locally for directions to the trailheads to **Sally Mountain, Number 5** (topped with a fire tower), **Coburn Falls,** and **Kibby Mountain** (with an observation deck).

If you're spending any time in the woods mid-October–November, do not go out without at least a hunter-orange cap to signal your presence to hunters; a hunter-orange vest is even better. Even though some properties are posted "No Hunting," don't take a chance; one scofflaw can make a life-and-death difference. If you're skittish or don't have the proper clothing, you can hike on Sunday, when hunting is banned.

Mountain Biking

Mountain biking is growing in popularity here, but be forewarned that this is logging country, and on the woods roads, logging trucks and equipment have the right of way; don't mess with them.

The **Kennebec Valley Trail** is an easy 12-mile multiuse loop trail that follows an old railroad bed (with no tracks) from between the Williams Dam public landing, alongside the Kennebec River in Solon, and Gaddis Airport, on the southern outskirts of Bingham. The route roughly parallels the river and Route 201.

In the Jackman area, an easy-to-moderate 10-mile trip is the **Sandy Bay Loop,** beginning seven miles north of downtown Jackman. Jackman's chamber office has a recreational map detailing this route and others in the area.

Snowmobiling and ATVing

The region is a snowmobiling hotbed, with hundreds of miles of groomed snowmobile trails that connect east to the Moosehead Lake area, west to the Sugarloaf area, and north into Canada. Most double as ATV trails.

Escape into the winter wilderness with **Northern Outdoors** (1771 Rte. 201, The Forks, 800/765-7238, www.northernoutdoors .com). If you're comfortable exploring the backwoods on your own, rental sleds begin at $190 per single sled. Better yet, go with a guide; 6–8 hour tours begin at $260.

Maxx's ATV Rentals (490 Main St., 207/668-4210, www.maxxsatvrentals.com) offers half-day and full-day rides with rates beginning at $135. A $1,000 credit card deposit is required.

ACCOMMODATIONS

Most of the white-water rafting companies have lodging, and it's convenient to stay where you play. But if you aren't rafting, staying at these places can be a bit overwhelming, especially with the après-raft party atmosphere. If you're planning to be in this area during snowmobiling season, especially in Jackman, be sure to book well in advance; the lodgings get chockablock full of sledders.

◖ **Attean Lake Lodge** (Birch Island, Jackman, 207/668-3792, www.atteanlodge .com, Memorial Day–Sept.) has certain trappings of a traditional sporting camp, but it's more like an upscale rustic cottage colony geared to families. Owned by the Holden family since 1900, it's on Birch Island in the center of island- and rock-sprinkled Attean Lake (also called Attean Pond). Brad and Andrea Holden now make it all work—flawlessly. Fourteen well-maintained log cabins (some old, some new, 2–6 beds) have baths, fireplaces, gas or kerosene lamps, and porches with fantastic views of the lake and surrounding mountains. Guests tend to collect in the new main lodge, with its cathedral ceiling, stone fireplaces, and window-walled dining room. Kids love the sandy beach. Meals have plenty of creativity (swordfish with ginger sauce, for instance). Motorboats are $30 per day; canoes, kayaks, paddleboats, and a sailboat are free. July–Labor Day, rates for two adults are $325 per day, including three meals (wine and beer are available), but nobody stays just one night. Early and late in the season, rates are $260 d per day; children's rates are much lower. Book well ahead; this is a popular getaway, and many families have been coming for years. Some guests barely leave the island the whole time they're here, but be sure to paddle across the pond and climb **Sally Mountain** (about 1.5 miles round-trip) for views that stretch as far as Katahdin; in fall, the foliage vistas are fabulous. Access to the island is via the lodge launch, a five-minute run.

The nicest motel in town is **Bishop's Country Inn Motel** (461 Main St., Jackman, 207/668-3231 or 888/991-7669, www.bishopsmotel.com, $85–130 d), a newish two-story building with free Wi-Fi and HBO, air-conditioning, and continental breakfast. All rooms also have a fridge, a microwave, and a coffeemaker, and there's a coin-op laundry on the premises. It's directly across Route 201 from Bishop's Store, where you can get everything else you might possibly want or need.

Here's a different twist on a B&B: **Big Wood Lake Bed and Breakfast** (19 Forest St., Jackman, 207/668-4461, www.bigwoodlakebedandbreakfast.com, $45 pp s or d) is a private house just a two-minute walk from its namesake lake. The kitchen is stocked with breakfast fixings, including bagels, muffins, OJ, fruit, and cereals. Also available are kayaks, a washer and dryer, an outdoor hot tub, and an outdoor grill.

Just south of downtown is **Mountainview Resort** (263 Main St., 207/668-7700, $99–279), a somewhat dated timeshare resort with guest rooms and 1–3-bedroom cabins, all with woodsy decor and full kitchens. It's sited on 40 acres with seemingly endless wilderness mountain views. The resort has indoor and outdoor pools, an exercise room, a sauna, and laundry facilities. The best lodging is the cabins. Rates vary by season and accommodation.

Camping

Indian Pond Campground (The Forks, 800/371-7774, mid-Apr.–mid-Oct.), next to Harris Station on the East Branch of the Kennebec, where Upper Kennebec rafting trips begin, has 27 tent and RV sites ($14 for two adults, kids under age 10 stay free) that have picnic tables and fire rings but no hookups. There also are 21 water-access primitive sites ($5 pp over age 14). Other facilities include showers, restrooms, RV dump station, laundry machines, and a boat launch. Leashed pets are allowed. You can hike from here to Magic Rock and watch Kennebec River rafters surging through Magic Falls. If hydroelectric plants pique your interest, ask at the gatehouse about a tour of Harris Station. To reach the campground from Route 201 in The Forks, take Lake Moxie Road (also called Moxie Pond Rd.) about five miles east; turn left (north) onto Harris Station Road and continue eight miles to the campground gatehouse.

On Heald Stream in Moose River, a mile east of downtown Jackman, the 24-acre **Moose River Campground and Cabins** (207/668-3341, www.mooserivercampground.net, mid-May–mid-Oct.) has 51 tent and RV sites close to a picturesque old dam site. Now crumbling from disuse, the dam was once part of a thriving turn-of-the-20th-century lumber mill that employed more than 700 workers to turn out 35 million board feet annually. Open and wooded campsites are $24–30 per family. Housekeeping cabins are $30 pp, kids 5–12 are half price, and dogs are welcome. Canoe rentals are available. Facilities include a snack bar, a swimming pool, a trout pond, a laundry room, and a children's play area. Also on-site are three year-round cabins.

FOOD

Fine dining simply doesn't exist in this region, but you'll find good home cooking. It's always wise to ask locally about current reputations, as they do seem to change with the wind as cooks blow in and out of town or head downriver. Most of the rafting companies also operate restaurants. Restaurant hours noted are for peak season but are subject to change. It's always wise to call ahead.

You've got two choices in Bingham, both serving inexpensive no-nonsense fare, both with full bars: **Thompson's Restaurant** (348 Main St./Rte. 201, Bingham, 207/672-3330, 11 A.M.–10 P.M. daily) has been around forever. Newer on the scene and with a recent facelift is **Maplewood** (418 Main St., Bingham, 207/672-3021, 11 A.M.–9 P.M. Tues.–Sat., 8 A.M.–9 P.M. Sun.), serving a Saturday-night buffet and a Sunday brunch.

Gas, food, clothing: You can get it at **Berry's Store** (Rte. 201, The Forks, 207/663-4461), an institution in these parts. Gordon Berry provides everything the sports-minded person might want or need. Or you might just want to sit down a spell in one of the rockers by the register and catch up on the local gossip.

When Jim and Karen Hewke's kids left home, the Hewkes turned their house into **Bigwood Steakhouse** (1 Forest St., Jackman, 207/668-5572, www.bigwoodsteakhouse .com, 5–9 P.M. Wed.–Mon.). The decor is purely functional, but the portions are big, and the food—home-style steak and seafood preparations—is good. Most choices are $10–25.

Home cookin' is also the specialty at **Mama Bear's** (420 Main St., Jackman, 207/668-4222, 4 A.M.–8 P.M. Mon.–Thurs., 4 A.M.–9 P.M. Fri.–Sat.). You can't miss it: It's pinkish purple with teal trim.

INFORMATION AND SERVICES

Local information is available from the **Upper Kennebec Valley Chamber of Commerce** (207/672-4100), **The Forks Area Chamber of Commerce** (The Forks, 207/663-4430, www .forksarea.com), the **Jackman/Moose River Region Chamber of Commerce** (207/668-4171 or 888/633-5225, www.jackmanmaine .org), and **Kennebec Valley Tourism Council** (207/623-4884, www.kennebecvalley.org).

WESTERN LAKES AND MOUNTAINS

When I tire of the summertime coastal crowds or I'm ready to hit the slopes, I head for Maine's Western Lakes and Mountains—about 4,500 outstandingly scenic square miles of Franklin, Oxford, Androscoggin, and Cumberland Counties. The recreational variety is astonishing. In winter, the state's two alpine powerhouses—Sunday River and Sugarloaf—entice skiers and riders from throughout the Northeast and even abroad. Six smaller, family-oriented ski areas—Saddleback, Shawnee Peak, Mount Abram, Black Mountain, Titcomb, and Lost Valley—deliver fewer on-mountain amenities but offer more wallet-friendly prices. Cross-country and snowshoeing trails also lace the region, dogsledding is increasingly popular, and snowmobiling is big business. There are trails for winter hiking and ponds for skating.

Still, winter is the off-season in much of this region. The multitude of lakes, ponds, rivers, and streams satisfy recreational boaters and anglers, while the mountains attract hikers. One of the most rugged stretches of the 2,158-mile Appalachian Trail, which runs from Georgia to Maine, passes through this area.

Of Maine's nine covered bridges (seven originals and two carefully built replicas), five are in the Western Lakes and Mountains—including the picturesque "Artist's Covered Bridge," near Sunday River, my favorite because you can ski through the forest and suddenly come upon it.

Sprawling, mountainous Oxford County, with its back to New Hampshire, has fabulous trails for hiking and rivers for canoeing. There's gold—and all kinds of other minerals—in the Oxford Hills; the official state gemstone,

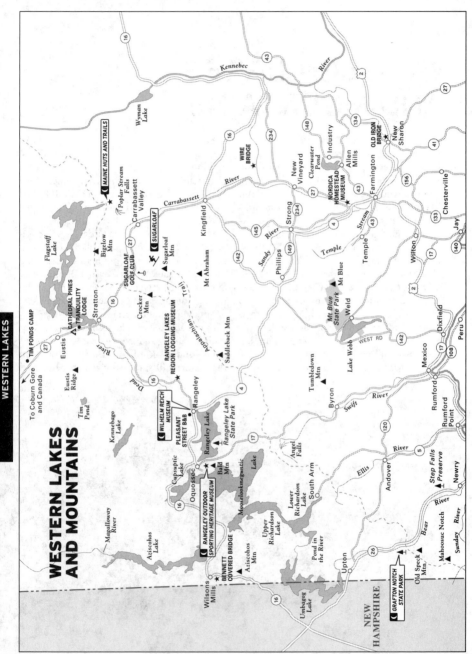

WESTERN LAKES

WESTERN LAKES
AND MOUNTAINS

© AVALON TRAVEL

HIGHLIGHTS

◖ **Sugarloaf:** The summit snowfields are the only lift-accessible skiing and riding above the tree line in the East (page 548).

◖ **Maine Huts and Trails:** Hike, bike, paddle, ski, or snowshoe from hut to hut on this spectacular wilderness trail (page 550).

◖ **Rangeley Outdoor Sporting Heritage Museum:** Learn about the sporting legends who made Rangeley famous (page 556).

◖ **Wilhelm Reich Museum:** You don't have to agree with the controversial scientist to enjoy the views from the estate (page 556).

◖ **Grafton Notch State Park:** This is a spectacular chunk of real estate, with hiking trails, waterfalls, and picnic areas (page 573).

◖ **Paris Hill:** Take a walk around this hidden hilltop National Historic District (page 585).

◖ **Willowbrook Museum Village:** A village preserved in time with 25 buildings on the National Register of Historic Places (page 597).

◖ *Songo River Queen II:* Take in views to Mount Washington on a cruise across Long Lake (page 601).

◖ **Poland Spring:** Tour through the history of famed Poland Spring Water and Hiram Ricker's family empire (page 611).

◖ **Shaker Museum:** Visit the world's last inhabited Shaker community (page 612).

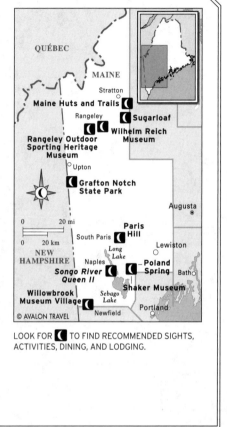

LOOK FOR ◖ TO FIND RECOMMENDED SIGHTS, ACTIVITIES, DINING, AND LODGING.

tourmaline, an intriguing stone that turns up in green, blue, or pink, is most prevalent in western Maine. Grab a digging tool or gold pan and try your hand at amateur prospecting. You're unlikely to find more than a few flakes or some pretty specimens of sparkly pyrite (fool's gold), but the fun is in the adventure.

East of Oxford County, Franklin County comprises Sugarloaf and the lovely Rangeley Lakes recreational area. Farmington is the county seat and a university town. Mostly rural Androscoggin, fourth-smallest of the state's

16 counties, takes its commercial and political cues from Lewiston and Auburn, the state's second-largest population center.

Directly west of Portland, and partly in Cumberland County, are Sebago and Long Lakes, surrounded by towns and villages that swell with visitors throughout the summer. Also here are most of the state's youth summer camps—some many generations old. During the annual summer-camp parents' weekend in July, Bridgton's tiny besieged downtown feels like Times Square at rush hour.

PLANNING YOUR TIME

If you're coming for warm-weather recreation—boating, swimming, hiking, and simply playing in the great outdoors—you'll find it here in abundance. And in July–August, you won't be alone on the Route 302 corridor stretching from Windham through Bridgton. Skip north to the Oxford Hills, Bethel, and the Kingfield region, and the crowds diminish. Bethel, home to Sunday River, and Kingfield, the nearest big town to Sugarloaf, come to life during the ski season, but otherwise are quiet places to escape, recreate, and especially to enjoy fall's foliage. If winter sports are your priority, late February–mid-March usually brings the best combination of snow and temperatures.

While you can loop through this region in 3–4 days, to get the most out of the summer recreational opportunities, pick one spot and explore from there. Good hubs are Rangeley, Bethel, Bridgton, and Naples.

If you're interested in Franco American culture, plan on spending the better part of a day in the Lewiston-Auburn area. For antiquing, be sure to slip over to Cornish. For fishing, make Rangeley your base. No matter where you stay, don't overplan. The region's riches demand that you get off the highways and byways and onto the back roads. Wander around and you'll stumble on spectacular views, great hikes, country stores, and swimming holes.

GLOBAL MAINE

Posted almost casually on an undistinguished corner in western Maine is a roadside landmark that inevitably appears in any travel book or slide show with a sense of the whimsical. Nine markers direct bikers, hikers, or drivers to Maine communities bearing the names of international locales: **Norway, Paris, Denmark, Naples, Sweden, Poland, Mexico, Peru,** and **China.** All are within 94 miles of the sign, which stands at the junction of Routes 5 and 35 in the burg of Lynchville (part of Albany Township), about 14 miles west of Norway. If you approach the sign from the south on Route 35, you're likely to miss it; it's most noticeable when coming from the north on Route 35 or the west on Route 5.

For tackling the many miles of trails in this region, you may find several guidebooks helpful—especially *AMC Maine Mountain Guide, 50 Hikes in the Maine Mountains, Guide to the Appalachian Trail in Maine,* and *Hikes in and Around Maine's Lake Region.* If you can afford only one, pick up the *Hikes* booklet, a handy, inexpensive publication written by a local resident and available locally or through REI (http://rei.com).

WESTERN LAKES

Farmington Area

Farmington is a sleeper of a town—home to a respected University of Maine campus, an easily walkable downtown, and an unusual opera museum. What's more, mountain towns and scenery stretch out and beyond in every direction. Less than an hour's drive north of town is the Carrabassett Valley, a recreation stronghold made famous by the year-round Sugarloaf alpine resort. Off to the northwest are the fabled Rangeley Lakes, and a drive southwest leads to Bethel, home of Sunday River Ski Resort, mineral quarries, and the White Mountain National Forest.

Farmington was incorporated in 1794 and became the county seat for Franklin County 44 years later. It remains the judicial hub but also is the commercial center for the nearby towns of **Wilton, Weld, New Sharon, Temple,** and **Industry.** To the south and west are **Jay, Livermore Falls, Livermore, Dixfield, Mexico,** and **Rumford.**

In Rumford and Jay, your nose will tell you it's paper-mill territory, part of Maine's economic lifeline; locals call the sulfuric odor "the smell of money." Residents have become inured to the aroma, but visitors may need a chance to adjust. Livermore is the site of the Norlands Living History Center, a unique participatory museum that rewards you with a real "feel" for the past.

And, lest we forget, Farmington's leading candidate for favorite son is Chester Greenwood, who, in 1873, rigged beaver fur, velvet, and a bit of wire to create "Champion ear protectors"—called earmuffs these days—when he was only 15. The clever fellow patented his invention and then went on to earn 100 more patents for such things as doughnut hooks and shock absorbers. His early-December birthday inspires the quirky annual Chester Greenwood Day celebration in downtown Farmington.

SIGHTS
Nordica Homestead Museum
Gem-encrusted gowns, opera librettos, lavish gifts from royalty, and family treasures fill the handful of rooms in the Nordica Homestead Museum (116 Nordica Lane, Farmington, 207/778-2042, www.lilliannordica.com, 10 A.M.–noon and 1–5 P.M. Tues.–Sat., 1–5 P.M. Sun. June 15–Sept. 15, by appointment Sept. 15–Oct. 15, $2 adults, $1 children over age 5), birthplace of Lillian Norton (1857–1914), better known as Madame Lillian Nordica, the legendary turn-of-the-20th-century Wagnerian opera diva. Her influence still pervades the house, where scratchy recordings play in the background and newspaper clippings line the walls. No opera buff should miss this. A caretaker is on hand to answer questions. Even the kids get a kick out of the costumed mannequins, and there's lots of space on the grounds for letting off steam. Take Route 4/27 north from Farmington and turn right (east) onto Holley Road; the farm is half a mile down the road.

Maine's Paper and Heritage Museum
The fledgling Maine's Paper and Heritage Museum (22 Church St., Livermore Falls, 207/592-1807, www.papermuseumof-maine.org) aims to grow into an interactive experience where visitors can experience life in a papermaking community. Currently it's primarily an online photography collection, but check to see if it's opened its doors.

PARKS AND RECREATION
Mount Blue State Park
Mount Blue State Park (299 Center Hill Rd., Weld, 207/585-2261, www.parksandlands.com, campground 207/585-2261, www.campwithme.com), covering 5,021 acres, is one of Maine's best-kept secrets. Yes, it's crowded in summer, but mostly with Mainers. It offers multilevel hiking, superb swimming, wooded campsites, mountain scenery, and daily interpretive natural-history programs in summer. There are movies on weekends, guided hikes, weekly guest speakers, even gold-panning expeditions—you'll never be bored. The park is split into two sections: Swimming and camping are on Lake Webb's west side; the Center Hill section, including the trail to Mount Blue itself, is on the lake's east side. The main entrance, with a two-mile access road, is eight miles from Weld, on the lake's west side. Day-use admission is $6 nonresident adults, $4 Maine resident adults, $1 ages 5–11. Canoe rentals are $3 per hour. Winter activities include snowshoeing, snowmobiling, and more than a dozen miles of groomed cross-country ski trails.

Swimming and Paddling
Five miles northeast of downtown Farmington is the hamlet of Allens Mills (officially the town of Industry), where you can swim or paddle in aptly named **Clearwater Lake.** To get there from Farmington, follow Broadway (Rte. 43) until you reach the T junction and boat landing at the lake.

Another local swimming hole is at the Route 4 bridge in Fairbanks, just north of Farmington.

Hiking
You're getting into western Maine's serious mountains here, so there are plenty of great hiking opportunities, running the gamut from a cakewalk to a workout.

In Weld, a deservedly popular hiking route goes up 3,187-foot **Mount Blue,** in the eastern section of Mount Blue State Park. From Route 142 in Weld village, follow signs and take Maxwell Road and then Center Hill Road about 2.5 miles to the parking area for Center Hill itself. (There's no fee in this part of the park.) You can stop for a picnic (sweeping views even at this level, plus picnic tables and outhouses), follow the mile-long self-guided nature-trail loop (pick up a brochure here), and then go on. It's also a great spot for sunset-watching. Continue up the unpaved road 3.5 miles to the parking lot for the Mount Blue trailhead. Allow about three hours for the steepish three-mile round-trip (easy, then moderately difficult). In midsummer, carry plenty of water. Hope for clear air on the summit; vistas of the Longfellows and beyond are awesome.

Other good hikes around Weld, on the west side of Lake Webb, are **Tumbledown Mountain** (3,068 feet via several route options; nesting peregrines can restrict access in early summer) and **Little Jackson Mountain** (3,434 feet). Tumbledown, moderately strenuous, attracts the "been there, done that" set. A much easier hike, but likely to be more crowded, is 2,386-foot **Bald Mountain,** with a scoured summit fine for picnics if it's not too blustery. Allow about two hours for the three-mile round-trip, including a lunch break. To reach the trailhead from Weld, take Route 156 southeast about 5.5 miles. There's limited parking on the right; watch for the sign.

Multiuse Trail

The trailhead and parking for the 14-mile **Whistlestop Trail,** between Jay and Farmington, is on Oak Street (off Rte. 2/4), adjacent to a CN Brown station.

Fitness Center

A rainy-day godsend is the $4.5 million University of Maine at Farmington **Health and Fitness Center** (152 Québec St. at Lincoln St., Farmington, 207/778-7495, www.umf.maine. edu). It's open to the public for weight training, indoor jogging, tennis, and swimming in

a six-lane heated pool. Call for current hours and fees.

ENTERTAINMENT

Throughout the year, something is always happening at the **University of Maine at Farmington** (207/778-7000, www.umf.maine. edu): lectures, concerts, plays, you name it. Contact the college for schedule and details.

At Meetinghouse Park on Main Street in downtown Farmington, **band concerts** are held at 7:30 P.M. periodically during the summer; take a folding chair or a blanket. The Old Crow Band holds forth in a green and white octagonal bandstand. Check locally for the schedule.

One certainly doesn't expect to find a venue like **Skye Theatre Performing Arts Center** (2 Highland Dr. S., Carthage, 207/562-4445, www.necelticarts.com) in what's aptly described as the middle of nowhere. Emphasis is on Celtic music, but a wide range of talent finds its way to this offbeat venue.

FESTIVALS AND EVENTS

The two-day **Wilton Blueberry Festival,** in early August, is an always-crowded blueberry-oriented celebration that includes a parade, road races, games, craft booths, a book sale, a museum open house, live entertainment, a lobster-roll lunch, a chicken barbecue, and a pig roast in downtown Wilton.

The third week of September is given over to the **Farmington Fair,** a weeklong country fair—one of the last of the season—with agricultural exhibits, a parade, harness racing, and live entertainment at the Farmington Fairgrounds.

The first Saturday in December, Farmington honors a native son on **Chester Greenwood Day.** Festivities commemorating the inventor of earmuffs include a road race, an oddball earmuff parade, a polar-bear swim, and other activities.

SHOPPING

Downtown Farmington has just enough options to entertain shoppers of all budgets.

Fans of fine craft simply must visit **SugarWood Gallery** (248 Broadway, Farmington, 207/778-9105), which features the work of western Maine artisans. Furniture, pottery, weaving, art quilts, handmade teddy bears, and more fill this cooperative gallery.

It's hard to resist the cheerful, welcoming ambience at **Devaney Doak and Garrett Booksellers** (193 Broadway, Farmington, 207/778-3454, www.ddgbooks.com), not to mention the children's corner piled high with books, toys, and games. Owner Kenny Brechner does the ordering and the website's book reviews; his eclectic taste is evident. And how many independent bookshops have a website with hilarious parodic reviews?

Around the corner, **Twice-Sold Tales** (155 Main St., Farmington, 207/778-4411) has a well-chosen and well-organized selection; Maine titles are a specialty, and prices are reasonable (paperback mysteries are only $1). Ask owner Jim Logan, an avid outdoorsman, about hiking options in Farmington and beyond.

I always introduce visiting friends to **Reny's** (24 Broadway, Farmington, 207/778-4641), and they always leave with at least a bag or two. From clothing to cleaning supplies to electronics to food, Reny's has it all. Part of a small statewide chain, this one is spread out on three floors—be sure to wander everywhere; even the back corners have finds.

ACCOMMODATIONS

Surprisingly for a county seat that doubles as a college town, there are few lodgings in Farmington itself.

The **Farmington Motel** (489 Farmington Falls Rd., Farmington, 207/778-4680 or 800/654-1133 outside Maine, www.farmingtonmotel.com, $70–129), an older property that could use a facelift, gets the nod for inexpensive, clean lodging, but don't expect lots of amenities. All 38 guest rooms and one two-bedroom suite have phones, air-conditioning, free Wi-Fi, and cable TV. Pets are not allowed. The biggest plus is behind the motel: a nature trail leading down to the Sandy River, where you can launch a canoe or just sit on the shore. The motel is amidst farmland about 1.5 miles southeast of downtown Farmington.

Just west of Farmington on Wilson Lake, **Wilson Lake Inn** (183 Lake Rd., Wilton, 207/645-3721 or 800/626-7463, www.wilsonlakeinn.com, $79–179), previously called Whispering Pines Motel, is a well-maintained family-owned property that's been expanded over the years to include extended-stay two-bedroom suites in addition to basic guest rooms. The grounds are lovely, with gardens and a lawn leading to the lakefront. All rooms have free HBO, air-conditioning, mini-fridges, free Wi-Fi, data ports, and phones, and there's a laundry on the premises. Guests have free use of a canoe, paddleboat, and kayaks as well as outdoor grills. A floatplane shuttle from Portland and sightseeing flights leave from the inn's dock. Hint: For the best rates, call; don't book online.

Here's a real gem: a lakefront lodge-style inn and cabins tucked under the shelter of towering pines. Since purchasing the **Kawanhee Inn** (12 Ann's Way/Rte. 142, Weld, 207/585-2000, www.maineinn.net, late May–mid-Oct.) in 2004, owners Chris and Jodi Huntington have been renovating the cabins and updating the rooms, all while preserving the classic 1920s style. Sunsets in this mountain-and-lake setting on Lake Webb are spectacular; loons' cries add to the magic. Eleven second-floor guest rooms with shared and private baths in the large main lodge are $110–165 per day with a two-night minimum stay on weekends. Cabins (rates begin at $1,150 per week) vary in age, size, and facilities; all have lake views, fieldstone fireplaces, and screened-in porches. Pets are welcome for $35 per dog per night plus a $200 security deposit. There's free Wi-Fi. The sandy beach is great for kids, and superb hiking is close by. The lodge's lake-view dining room is open to nonguests for dinner ($18–40) nightly late May–early September. Devotees keep returning here, so book well ahead for midsummer. In mid-September, nights are coolish and it's pretty quiet, but the foliage is incredible.

Camping

Mount Blue State Park (299 Center Hill Rd., Weld, 207/585-2261, www.parksand-lands.com; campground 207/585-2261, www.campwithme.com) has 136 wooded sites but no hookups. Camping fees are $25 per site for nonresidents, $15 for Maine residents. Reservations are handled through the state-park reservation system; from out of state call 207/287-3824 at least two weeks ahead or book reservations online from February 1 at www.campwithme.com. The reservation fee is $2 per site per night, two-night minimum.

FOOD

Restaurant hours noted are for peak season but are subject to change. It's always wise to call ahead.

Local Flavors

In downtown Farmington, **Up Front and Pleasant Gourmet** (157 Front St., Farmington, 207/778-5671, no credit cards) has all kinds of condiments, cheeses, homemade pasta, plus a decent wine selection.

The **Sandy River Farmers Market** sets up its tables in the parking lot of the Better Living Center (Front St., Farmington, 9 A.M.–2 P.M. Fri. May–Oct.). You'll find herbs, home-made bread, cheeses, and organic meats and produce.

If you'll be camping or staying in a condo or cottage with cooking facilities, swing by **Whitewater Farm** (28 Mercer Rd./Rte. 2, Mercer, 207/778-4748) for local naturally raised beef, lamb, chicken, turkey, rabbit, pork, cheeses, eggs, and produce.

There's always a line at **Gifford's Ice Cream** (Rte. 4/27, Farmington, 207/778-3617, 11 A.M.–10 P.M. daily summer, 11 A.M.–9 P.M. daily spring and fall), a longtime takeout spot. Besides about four-dozen terrific ice cream flavors, it also has foot-long hot dogs. It's open mid-March–early November.

My favorite stop in Farmington is the or-der-at-the-counter **Soup for You! Cafe** (222 Broadway, Farmington, 207/779-0799, 10 A.M.–7 P.M. Mon.–Sat., 11 A.M.–5 P.M. Sun.), which oozes college-town funk and concocts some of the best soups you'll ever taste; usually about six are made daily, with vegan, vegetarian, and gluten-free options. Also available are sandwiches, both named and create-your-own varieties. Smoothies and coffee drinks are very popular here too. Vegetarians will find plenty of choices, and kids can get PB&J. Nothing on the menu is more than $6.

In Weld village, west of Farmington and northwest of Wilton, you'll find the seasonal **Morning Glory Bake Shop** (207/585-2479), with breakfast items, sandwiches, and goodies.

Casual Dining

Tucked away on a side street, with a deck overlooking the Sandy River, **The Granary** (147 Pleasant St., Farmington, 207/779-0710, www.thegranarybrewpub.com, 11 A.M.–10 P.M. daily) packs them in, especially when the university is in session. The extensive menu includes burgers, salads, and fresh-dough brick-oven pizzas as well as entrées ($10–30) ranging from pasta to lobster. Lunch, vegetarian, and kids' menus are available, as is inexpensive pub food. Most weekends there's live music; Tuesday is open-mike night. Dine inside, on the deck, or on the screened porch. Next to the bar is a games room.

Breakfast, lunch, dinner, even tapas— **The Homestead Bakery Restaurant** (186 Broadway, Farmington, 207/778-6162, www.homesteadbakery.com, 8 A.M.–2 P.M. Tues.–Sat., 11 A.M.–2 P.M. Sun.–Mon., dinner 5–9 P.M. Mon.–Sat., dinner $9–23), serves it all. There's plenty of ethnic variety—Mediterranean, Mexican, Thai, fancy pizzas, even vegetarian. A martini and wine bar, with couches by a fireplace, provides cozier seating.

One of the area's best restaurants is the dining room at the **Kawanhee Inn** (12 Ann's Way/Rte. 142, Weld, 207/585-2000, www.maineinn.net, lunch Fri.–Sun., dinner daily mid-June–early Sept., hours vary spring and fall, $10–28). The lakefront setting is spectacular, especially at sunset, and Chef Brian Anderson's creative cuisine takes advantage of what's fresh and locally available, in addition to some standards. Menu items might include bistro steak, seafood stew, and duck. Reservations are recommended.

The former Bass Shoe factory now houses **Calzolaio Pasta Co.** (284 Main St., Wilton, 207/645-9500, www.calzolaiopasta.com, 11 A.M.–9 P.M. daily), which prepares decent Italian fare from pizzas and pastas to specialty entrées such a veal saltimbocca and Sicilian chicken. Opt for a terrace table if the weather's fine.

INFORMATION AND SERVICES

The Franklin County Chamber of Commerce (248 Wilton Rd., Farmington, 207/778-4215, www.farmingtonchamber.org) publishes a visitors guide. The website **Downtown Farmington** (www.downtownfarmington.com) is another resource.

Check out **Cutler Memorial Library** (117 Academy St., Farmington, 207/778-4312, www.farmington.lib.me.us).

Sugarloaf Area

The thread tying together the Sugarloaf area is the lovely Carrabassett River, which winds its way through the smashingly scenic **Carrabassett Valley** from the area more or less around **Sugarloaf** through **Kingfield** to North Anson, where it tumbles over treacherous falls and flows into the mighty Kennebec River. On both sides of the valley, the Longfellow and Bigelow Ranges boast six of Maine's ten 4,000-footers—a hiker's paradise.

Flanking the west side of the valley is the huge Sugarloaf resort. In 1951, Kingfield businessman Amos Winter and some of his pals, known locally as the "Bigelow Boys," cut the first ski trail from the snowfields above the tree line atop Sugarloaf Mountain, dubbing it "Winter's Way." A downhill run required skiing three miles to the base of the trail and then strapping on animal skins for the uphill trek. Three runs on wooden skis would be about the daily max in those days. By 1954 the prophetically named Winter and some foresighted investors had established the Sugarloaf Mountain Ski Club; and the rest, as they say, is history.

Sugarloaf is the megataxpayer in the relatively new town of Carrabassett Valley. It bills itself as a year-round resort, which is true, but winter is definitely the peak season, when the head count is highest and so are the prices. Everything's open and humming

November–late April; spring skiing has been known to extend even into June.

Before Amos Winter brought fame and fortune to his hometown and the valley, Kingfield was best known as a timber center and the birthplace of the Stanley twins (designers of the Stanley Steamer). Today it's an appealing slice-of-life rural town, with handsome old homes and off-mountain beds and restaurants.

In **Stratton,** old-timers reminisce over the towns of Flagstaff and Dead River—already historic two centuries before they were consigned to the history books in the 1950s. That's when the Long Falls Dam, built on the Dead River, backed up the water behind it, inundated the towns, and created 20,000-acre Flagstaff Lake. The hydroelectric dam now controls the water flow for spring white-water rafting on the Dead River.

Flagstaff owes its name to Colonel Benedict Arnold, whose troops en route to Québec in 1775 flew their flag at the site of today's Cathedral Pines Campground. After struggling up the Kennebec River to the spot known as the Carrying Place, the disheartened soldiers turned northwest along the Dead River's North Branch at Flagstaff and then on through the Chain of Ponds to Canada.

Route 27, from Kingfield to the Canadian border at Coburn Gore, is an officially designated Scenic Highway, a 54-mile stretch that's most spectacular in mid–late September. But there's no pot of gold at the end; there's not much to Coburn Gore except a Customs outpost, a convenience store (with fuel), and a few unimpressive dwellings.

SIGHTS
Stanley Museum

Here's a reason to go back to school: The small but captivating Stanley Museum (40 School St., Kingfield, 207/265-2729, www.stanley-museum.org, 1–4 P.M. Tues.–Sun. June–Oct., 1–4 P.M. Tues.–Fri. Nov.–May or by appointment, $4 adults, $3 seniors, $2 under age 12), located in the town's old schoolhouse, is dedicated to educating visitors about Kingfield's most famous native sons, twin brothers Francis Edgar (F. E.) and Freelan Oscar (F. O.) Stanley. Although best known for the Stanley Steamer, the identical twin legacy of invention and innovation extends far beyond either the automobile or Kingfield. These versatile overachievers also invented the photographic dry plate, eventually selling out to George Eastman. Freelan Stanley, the first to climb Mount Washington by car, later became a noted violinmaker. He was also a talented portrait artist—one of his subjects was poet Henry Wadsworth Longfellow—and he's credited with inventing the first airbrush. Also in the museum are hundreds of superb photographs (and glass-plate negatives) by the twins' clever sister, Chansonetta Stanley Emmons, and work by Chansonetta's artist-daughter, Dorothy. The museum gift shop contains auto-related books, pamphlets, and other specialty items.

Ski Museum of Maine

Established in 1995, the Ski Museum (Main St., Kingfield, 207/265-2023, www.skimuse-umofmaine.org, 9 A.M.–5 P.M. Thurs.–Mon., free) began exhibiting its collection of Maine-related ski artifacts and memorabilia in 2006 and moved to its current location above the Sugarloaf Sports Outlet shop in 2010. Exhibits document Maine's role in the growth and development of the sport, from immigrant Swedes to manufacturing to resorts.

Nowetah's American Indian Museum

A bold, in-your-face sign announces the driveway to Nowetah's American Indian Museum (Rte. 27, New Portland, 207/628-4981, www.nowetahs.webs.com, 10 A.M.–5 P.M. daily, free), an astonishing repository of hundreds of Maine Indian baskets and bark objects—plus porcupine-quill embroidery, trade beads, musical instruments, soapstone carvings, and other Native American esoterica. Susquehanna-Cherokee owner and übercollector Nowetah Cyr loves explaining unique details about the artifacts she's displayed here since 1969; but be forewarned: She's a talker. In the museum's gift shop are many Native American craft pieces as well as books. It's 16 miles north of Farmington.

Wire Bridge

Now here's a most unusual landmark, about seven miles south of Kingfield and not far from Nowetah's museum: Twenty-five-foot-tall

The Wire Bridge spanning the Carrabassett River is listed on the National Register of Historic Places.

© HILARY NANGLE

shingled towers announce the entrance to the Wire Bridge suspended over the Carrabassett River in New Portland. Built in 1841–1842 at a cost of $2,000, with steel supports imported from England, the bridge is on the National Register of Historic Places. Locals often refer to it as "rustproof" for its stainless-steel construction, or "flood-proof" for its longtime survival despite nasty spring floods. To find the bridge from Route 146 in New Portland, turn north onto Wire Bridge Road and follow signs for less than a mile.

Dead River Historical Society Museum

Unless you're a rabid history fan or have an area connection, many local historical society museums can be a bit of a snore. Not so the Dead River Historical Society (11 A.M.–3 P.M. Sat.–Sun. July–early Sept., donation), which contains fascinating memorabilia from the two villages submerged when the Dead River was dammed and Flagstaff Lake created.

Benedict Arnold Trail

In the fall of 1775, Benedict Arnold marched north from Augusta with the goal of capturing Québec. He followed the Kennebec River, then portaged to the Dead River, following it to Chain of Ponds near the Québec border. While there are dirt woods roads that ramble through this region, Route 27 roughly follows the route north from Kingfield, and there are roadside historical markers from Stratton north. It's a gorgeous drive, especially in autumn, when leaves are turning and snow might fringe the peaks.

PICNIC AND REST AREAS

Several riverside and viewpoint rest areas on or near Route 27 make picnicking almost mandatory in the Carrabassett Valley—especially in September, when the leaf colors are fabulous. The mountains, the foliage parade, the rock-clogged river—all really splendid. On Route 27, roughly halfway between Kingfield and the Sugarloaf access road, a lovely picnic area is sandwiched between the highway and the

Carrabassett River, just north of Hammond Field Brook.

About 12 miles north of the Sugarloaf access road, turn left (west) onto Eustis Ridge Road and go two miles to the **Eustis Ridge picnic area,** a tiny park with an expansive view of the Bigelow Range.

Finally, on Route 27, about 23 miles north of Sugarloaf, there's another scenic picnic area, this one alongside the Dead River on the east side of the highway.

Sugarloaf

Best known as the king of alpine resorts in Maine, Sugarloaf (Carrabassett, 207/237-2000 or 800/843-5623, www.sugarloaf.com) is a four-season destination resort with alpine skiing and snowboarding, snowshoeing, cross-country skiing, and ice-skating December–late April; golf, hiking, and mountain biking during warmer months; and zip-lining during both seasons. A compact base village has a hotel, an inn, and gazillions of condos as well as restaurants, a chapel, a handful of shops, and a base

Sugarloaf is Maine's largest alpine resort.

lodge housing a snow school and rental operations. The separate Outdoor Center, linked via shuttle and trails, houses cross-country skiing operations and has an ice-skating rink and an excellent, but very casual, café.

ALPINE SKIING AND RIDING

At 4,237 feet, Sugarloaf is not only Maine's highest skiing mountain, it also has the only lift-serviced terrain above the tree line in the East. Well over 100 named trails and glades, served by 15 lifts that range from a T-bar to detachable high-speed quads, ribbon its 2,820 vertical feet. Even beginners can ski from the summit, a 3.5-mile descent via the longest run. Although the resort has produced national and international ski and snowboard champions (2006 and 2010 Olympic gold snowboard cross medalist Seth Wescott calls it home), Sugarloaf has always been especially family-friendly, with day care and all kinds of children's ski and entertainment programs. Adult full-day lift tickets are about $78 adults, $66 teens, and $53 ages 6–12 and 65–80; age 5 and younger as well as age 80 and older ski free. Most lodging packages include lift tickets; multiday tickets are less expensive, as are those purchased online.

SUGARLOAF OUTDOOR CENTER

On Route 27 about a mile south of the Sugarloaf access road is the entrance to the Sugarloaf Outdoor Center (207/237-6830), geared in winter toward cross-country skiing, snowshoeing, and ice-skating. Some sections of the 63-mile cross-country skiing trail network are on Maine Public Reserve Land, and some are on Penobscot Indian Nation land. Also at the Outdoor Center is an Olympic-size outdoor ice-skating rink, lighted on weekend nights and holiday weeks. The renovated glass-walled lodge looking out on Sugarloaf Mountain has ski, snowshoe, and skate rentals, plus a casual café. Cross-country lessons are available. Call for current hours and fees for all programs, and ask about special events such as guided moonlight tours and snowshoe tours.

GOLF

Designed by Robert Trent Jones Jr., and regularly ranked in national golf magazines as Maine's top course, the 18-hole, par-72 **Sugarloaf Golf Club and Golf School** meanders through woods and alongside the Carrabassett River in the shadow of the Longfellow Range. It's actually a town-owned course but is managed by Sugarloaf. You get what you pay for; greens fees are steep. Tee times are essential; book a week or two in advance for weekends. Sugarloaf's golf school offers multiday programs all summer, with special weeks designed for Women's Golf School and Junior Golf Camp. Club rentals and private lessons are available; carts are mandatory. A driving range, a pro shop, and a café round out the facilities.

OTHER ACTIVITIES

Summer activities at Sugarloaf include guided hikes, boat trips, moose-spotting tours, mountain biking, fly-fishing, scenic chair rides, and wilderness cookouts. **Zip-line tours** ($39 pp) on six lines varying 140–240 feet in length are offered year round.

ANTIGRAVITY CENTER

A partnership between Sugarloaf, the town, and CVA (Carrabassett Valley Academy, a ski preparatory school at the mountain's base that has produced many Olympians), the Antigravity Center (207/237-5566, www.carrabassettvalley .org), locally called the AGC, is the answer to a parent's frustration when the weather doesn't cooperate. It houses a gym, a climbing wall, a skate park, trampolines, a weight room, and more, and fitness classes are offered. Call for current hours and programs.

ENTERTAINMENT AND EVENTS

Sugarloaf is entertainment central in these parts. Every night in winter there's live music somewhere here, so you can hopscotch from The Bag to Gepetto's to The Rack (owned by double Olympic snowboard-cross gold medalist Seth Wescott) and back again.

The last full week in January is **White White World Week,** Sugarloaf's winter carnival, with discount lift tickets, reduced lodging rates, ski races, fireworks, a torchlight parade, and other special events.

Sugarloaf meets the Caribbean during **Reggae Fest** with spring skiing, reggae bands day and night, and lots of boisterous fun over a mid–late-April weekend.

In early July, the annual **Kingfield POPS** concert features the Bangor Symphony Orchestra, an arts-and-crafts festival, a garden tour, and more.

RECREATION
Multisport Trails

The town-owned **Narrow Gauge Trail** begins at Campbell Field on the east side of Route 27 near the foot of the Sugarloaf access road and continues seven miles, gradually downhill, to the Carrabassett Valley Town Park. The trail follows the abandoned narrow-gauge railway bed along the river. Pack a picnic and wear a bathing suit under your biking duds; you'll be passing swimming holes along the way. In winter, it's groomed weekly for cross-country skiing. From the trail, you can connect to the Maine Huts and Trails network. You can download a map from www.carrabassettvalley.org.

Maine Huts and Trails

Inch by inch, mile by mile: Imagine a 180-mile-long highway through the wilderness. When finished, the easygoing 12-foot-wide corridor through the wilderness will stretch from Newry in the Mahoosuc Mountains to Rockwood on Moosehead Lake, with offshoot dedicated hiking trails. It's not a trail for motorized vehicles, but rather for hikers, mountain bikers, snowshoers, cross-country skiers (it's groomed in winter), even paddlers.

Larry Warren, a former Sugarloaf manager, town founder, and preservation advocate, had the vision, and in 2008, after years of arm-twisting, persuasion, and major fund-raising, the first section of the Maine Huts and Trails

© HILARY NANGLE

The popular stream hut, in the first section of the Maine Huts and Trails system, is an oasis of hot food, hot showers, and warm bunks in the Maine wilderness.

WESTERN LAKES

system (office 375 N. Main St., Kingfield, 207/265-2400, www.mainehuts.org) opened in Carrabassett Valley. By 2011, this 36-mile section had grown to include three full-service huts spaced roughly 10–12 miles—or a day's hike—apart, connecting the valley to The Forks.

Ultracomfy (practically luxe) off-the-grid backwoods lodges provide beds (including a pillow and fleece blanket, but not sheets) in dorms (private and family rooms available) and hot meals. The main lodges have composting toilets, hot showers, and gathering rooms furnished with leather sofas and chairs, braided rugs, and other nice touches.

Huts are located at **Poplar Falls,** in the shadow of Little Bigelow Mountain, accessed from the Carrabassett Valley trailhead near the town recreation center off Route 27; on the shores of **Flagstaff Lake,** also accessed via a trailhead on the Long Falls Dam Road north of North New Portland or by boat across the lake; and at **Grand Falls** on the Dead River near The Forks, from which you can arrange a white-water paddle or raft trip. This is absolutely gorgeous territory, and the trail's design makes it welcoming to beginning hikers and mountain bikers and especially families. Pricing varies by season and choice of accommodations. Trust me: This is an experience that should be incorporated into every vacation in this region.

Hiking

The Sugarloaf summer website (www.sugarloaf.com) has an excellent listing of area hikes under "Events & Activities."

An easy family hike, combining a picnic and swim, goes to the twin cascades of **Poplar Stream Falls.** Off Route 27 in Carrabassett Valley, leave your car at the Maine Huts parking lot and walk northeast 1.5 miles to the falls, veering off the Maine Huts trail. Pack a picnic and let the kids have a swim.

Just east of Stratton (eight miles northwest of Sugarloaf) is the dedicated hiker's dream: 35,000-acre **Bigelow Preserve** is all public land thanks to conservationists who organized a statewide referendum and yanked it

from developers' hands in 1976. Within the preserve are the multiple peaks of the **Bigelow Range**—the Horns Peaks (3,810 and 3,831 feet), West Peak (4,150 feet), Avery Peak (4,088 feet), and Little Bigelow (3,040 feet), as well as 3,213-foot Cranberry Peak. In the fall when the hardwoods all change colors, the vistas are incomparable. In winter, snowmobilers crisscross the preserve, and cross-country skiers often take advantage of their trails, especially along the East Flagstaff Road, where you might be able to stop for hot chocolate at volunteer-staffed Bigelow Lodge. The trailhead for Cranberry Peak (6.6 miles round-trip, moderate to strenuous) is next to Route 27 at the southern end of Stratton village.

About five miles southeast of Stratton, the **Appalachian Trail** (AT) crosses Route 27 and continues north and then east across the Bigelow Peaks, the spine of the Bigelow Range. You can get to the AT here, or drive back northwest 0.5 miles on Route 27 and go 0.9 miles on rugged unpaved Stratton Brook Road to another AT trailhead. In any case, if you do the whole AT traverse, 16.5 miles from Route 27 to East Flagstaff Road, you'll probably want to arrange a shuttle at East Flagstaff Road (via Long Falls Dam Rd. from North New Portland). The white-blazed AT route is strenuous; four free campsites with lean-tos are sited along the way. (The most-used campsite is Horns Pond, where space can be tight.) You can detour to the Maine Huts' Flagstaff hut too.

Depending on your enthusiasm, your stamina level, and your time frame (and maybe the weather), there are lots of options for short hikes along the AT or on a number of side trails. Preserve maps are usually available at the Sugarloaf Area Chamber of Commerce, but for planning your hikes, request or download a copy of the Bigelow Preserve map-brochure from the Maine Bureau of Parks and Lands (22 State House Station, Augusta, 207/287-3821, www.parksandlands.com). Also helpful is the *Appalachian Trail Guide to Maine.*

Water Sports

Along the Carrabassett River between Kingfield

and the Sugarloaf access road are half a dozen swimming holes used by generations of local residents. Several spots have natural waterslides and room for shallow dives. Not all are easy to find, and parking is limited, but a refreshing river dip on a hot day is worth the bother. Look for roadside pullouts with parked cars.

On mountain-rimmed Flagstaff Lake in Eustis, about 11 miles north of Sugarloaf, the town-owned beach next to the Cathedral Pines Campground has a playground and changing rooms. There are no lifeguards, but there's also no admission fee. (Do not use the campground's beach unless you're staying there.)

BOATING
If you want to paddle across Flagstaff Lake, rent a canoe or kayak from **Arnold Trail Sports Center** (108 Main St., Stratton, 207/246-2244). The Old Town boats rent in the $25–30 range per day, and free local delivery is available to area boat landings on a set schedule. If you want a guide, that can be arranged too.

The Original Bigelow-Flagstaff Canoe & Kayak Rental (Bog Rd., Dead River Township, 207/678-2171 Sun.–Wed. or 207/678-2010 Thurs.–Sat.) rents canoes and kayaks for $40 per day, $25 half-day. Also on the premises is a rustic five-bed bunkhouse ($15 pp) with a cookstove and an outhouse.

Master Maine Guide Jeff Hinman's **Flagstaff Scenic Boat Tours** (Eustis, 207/246-2277) provides pontoon boat tours on the lake, detailing the story of the flooded villages below the surface and pointing out wildlife en route. Options include a 2.5-hour historic tour ($40 pp) and a 4.5-hour luncheon cruise to the Maine Huts and Trails Flagstaff Hut ($55 pp) that includes lunch. Boat minimum is four people.

Moose-Watching
Head up Route 27 to Route 16 and go west. Early or late in the day, perhaps en route to dinner in Rangeley, you're almost guaranteed to see a moose in the boggy areas or near the sand and salt piles stored for winter use. Just remember to drive slowly and watchfully. No

one wins when you hit a moose. Sugarloaf resort offers guided moose-spotting tours.

ACCOMMODATIONS
When you've had a long day on the slopes, a bed close by can be mighty tempting—plus you can be upward bound quickly in the morning. But such convenience doesn't come cheaply, so your budget may dictate where you decide to stay. Basically, the choices are on the mountain at Sugarloaf, in Carrabassett Valley near the Sugarloaf access road, or farther afield in Kingfield, Stratton, Eustis, and beyond. On weekends and holiday periods, on-mountain beds are scarce to nonexistent, so reservations well in advance are necessary.

Many of the lodgings in the region around Sugarloaf provide discount passes for cross-country skiing out of the Sugarloaf Outdoor Center. It's a nice little perk, so if you're planning any cross-country skiing, be sure to ask when you're inquiring about a room.

Sugarloaf
Accommodations are available all year at the resort (800/843-5623), and prices vary widely depending on the property and the dates. Possibilities include condominiums and two hotels. The winter-only **Sugarloaf Inn** (207/237-6837), conveniently situated adjacent to the Sawduster double chairlift, has 42 guest rooms (some in need of a facelift) with rates in the same ranges as the condos. It's home to the Shipyard Brew Haus, open for breakfast, lunch, and dinner daily. The imposing **Grand Summit Resort Hotel** (207/237-2222 or 800/527-9879), with 119 guest rooms and suites and two penthouses, is in the village center. Amenities include microwaves, refrigerators, and video players. Guests have use of a small health club. Pets and smoking are not allowed. All reservations booked by Sugarloaf include use of the **Sugarloaf Sports and Fitness Club** (207/237-6946), in the Sugartree condo complex on Mountainside Road, and both properties have free Wi-Fi. Packages with lift tickets are the way to go.

Just south of the mountain access road but on the shuttle route is **Nestlewood Inn** (3004

Town Line, Carrabassett Valley, 207/237-2077, www.nestlewoodinn.com), a purpose-built log structure with seven guest rooms and spacious living rooms. Peak season rates range $125–210 and include a full breakfast and afternoon snacks. Wi-Fi is available.

Kingfield

Slumber in history at the renovated 1918 **Herbert Grand Hotel** (246 Main St., Kingfield, 207/265-2000 or 800/843-4372, www.herbert grandhotel.com, $89–159), an antiques-filled, three-story, 26-room Victorian hotel in downtown Kingfield. Rooms vary widely, some are a bit quirky, and there are a few two-bedroom, bathroom-connected suites. Rates include a light continental breakfast and Wi-Fi access. Dogs are welcome for $10 each per night.

Next door to One Stanley Avenue restaurant and under the same ownership, **Three Stanley Avenue** (3 Stanley Ave., Kingfield, 207/265-5541, www.stanleyavenue.com, $70–80 d) has been a B&B since the early 1980s. The antiques-filled yellow Victorian (built by Bayard

Stanley, younger brother of the famed Stanley Steamer twins) has three first-floor guest rooms with private baths and three second-floor guest rooms sharing two baths. It's all very welcoming, with comfortable wicker chairs on the front porch and a traditional gazebo, formerly a bandstand, in the backyard. Rates include a full breakfast served at the adjacent restaurant.

Stratton and Eustis

You can launch a canoe or kayak into Flagstaff Lake from the backyard of **Tranquility Lodge** (Rte. 27, Stratton, 207/246-2122, www.tranquillitylodgebandb.com, $76–105), an especially peaceful bed-and-breakfast in a converted 19th-century post-and-beam barn just north of Stratton village. Old farming tools decorate the walls, and there's a carriage, which keeps the feeling rural and rustic. Most rates include a continental breakfast. Free Wi-Fi is available.

A wonderful traditional sporting camp, **Tim Pond Camps** (Eustis, 207/243-2947 or 207/897-4056 winter, www.timpondcamps.com)

© HILARY NANGLE

the 1918 Herbert Grand Hotel, downtown Kingfield

has been operating since 1877, when guests took so long to get here that they stayed the whole summer. Harvey and Betty Calden have owned this idyllic lakeside retreat since 1980. Eleven rustic log cabins, all with full baths and maid service, are nestled in the woods on either side of a modern-rustic lodge (the original lodge burned down), where everyone gathers three times a day for great comfort food; the dinner bell rings promptly at 5:30 P.M. BYOB. Daily rates are $180 pp, including all meals and use of a classic Rangeley boat with a motor and gas, and a canoe; half price for children 5–12. The pet fee is $10 per visit. Be forewarned, though, that it's worth your life to get a reservation here—about 90 percent of the guests are repeats, and most stay at least a week. Fly-fishing for brook trout is the prime pursuit (every spring a fly-fishing school is offered), but it's a fine place just to relax and listen to the loons. Here's how one avid fisherman describes the schedule: "Fish, eat breakfast, fish, eat lunch, fish, eat supper, fish, sleep." A family discount is available in July–August. Cabins have baths, electricity until 10 P.M., daily maid service, and fascinating guest journals. Tim Pond Camps is at the northern end of mile-long Tim Pond, on a dirt road about 10 miles west of Route 27 in Eustis. It's open mid-May–mid-October, then again in November. The dining room is open to nonguests July–September by reservation.

Camping

With 115 wooded sites (most with hookups) on 300 acres, nonprofit **Cathedral Pines Campground** (Rte. 27, Eustis, 207/246-3491, www.gopinescamping.com, $22–30) has one of Maine's most scenic locations. It's set amid gigantic red pines and surrounded by mountains on the shore of Flagstaff Lake. Look for the marker that designates this site as one of Benedict Arnold's stops during his march to Québec City in 1775. Facilities include a recreation hall, a bathhouse, laundry, a swimming beach, basketball, a playground, canoe rentals, and paddleboat rentals. Pets are allowed. The campground is 26 miles south of the Québec border.

FOOD

You can bounce around to different Sugarloaf-area restaurants in the winter season and even catch a twofer night here and there. You certainly won't starve if you stick with the food at one of the resort-based restaurants, and the range of choices means you won't bust your budget, but do yourself a favor and explore the dining options in the surrounding communities. During holidays and winter weekends, be sure to make advance dinner reservations. Hours noted are for peak winter season; call in advance during spring, summer, and autumn.

Sugarloaf Resort

Bullwinkle's Grill (207/237-2000), off Tote Road on the mountain's western side, is the resort's only on-mountain restaurant. In 2007 it was mercifully expanded with a spacious restaurant in addition to the cafeteria fare. On Saturday nights, and sometimes on midweek nights during peak periods, it morphs into a rustically elegant restaurant, accessed via snowcat. The adventure includes the snowcat transportation and a five-course meal; expect to pay around $100 pp for the package.

In the base village are two extremely popular sit-down restaurants, **Gepetto's** (207/237-2192, 11 A.M.–9 P.M. daily late Nov.–mid April, $8–30) and **The Bag** (207/237-2451, 11 A.M.–9 P.M. daily late Nov.–mid April, $8–30). It's hard to say which is better. The Bag, which doubles as a brewpub, is famous for its burgers, soups, and wood-fired-oven pizzas, although the menu is much broader than that; Blues Monday features live music. Gepetto's, a bit fancier and known for its ultrafresh seafood, has seating areas that include a plant-filled atrium warmed by a gas stove, and it's open during the summer season for dinner; Tuesday is twofer night. Truly, you can't go wrong with either one.

For ample sandwiches, homemade soups, salads, and hearty breakfasts, **D'Ellies** (207/237-2490) is one of Sugarloaf Village's most popular eateries. It's open for breakfast and lunch daily during summer and ski seasons. Seating is extremely limited—this is more of a to-go kind of place. To avoid the swarming noontime rush, call in your sandwich order in the morning before heading for the lift line. Name a time, and it'll be ready for pick up at the express register, where you can also grab drinks, soups, and baked goods.

Carrabassett Valley

Reservations are a good idea at **Hug's** (Rte. 27, Carrabassett Valley, 207/237-2392, 5–9:30 P.M. Tues.–Sun., entrées $12–24), a northern Italian restaurant that's always jam-packed. Be forewarned: Tables are tight and there's little place to wait for a table. But who cares—the food is good, the atmosphere festive, the pesto breadsticks are addictive, and the family-style salad is delicious. Kids' portions are available. Hug's is a mile south of the Sugarloaf access road.

Six miles south of the Sugarloaf access road is **Tufulio's** (Rte. 27, Valley Crossing, Carrabassett Valley, 207/235-2010, 4–9:30 P.M. daily summer, 5–9:30 P.M. daily other seasons, $10–30), another Italian-accented family favorite and producers of the valley's best pizza. The shrimp-and-artichoke pesto pie is tops. Also on the menu are seafood, chicken, and plenty of pasta dishes. Go on Sunday for the two-for-one specials. In summer you can eat on the deck, when it opens at 4 P.M. for a popular happy hour.

Kingfield

The Orange Cat Cafe (329 Main St., Kingfield, 207/265-2860, www.orangecatcafe .com), in the "brick castle" and open for breakfast and lunch, is a favorite for breakfast sandwiches and pastries, homemade soups, creative sandwiches, salads, and other goodies.

Everyone eventually shows up at the **Kingfield Woodsman** (Rte. 27, Kingfield, 207/265-2561, 5 A.M.–2 P.M. Mon.–Fri., 7 A.M.–2 P.M. Sat., 7 A.M.–1 P.M. Sun.), usually just referred to as "the Woodsman." It's the best choice in the area for local color, especially at breakfast, which starts early. The rustic eatery has been a local landmark since the mid-1970s. Don't be surprised if the staff gives you the once-over and proclaims that you shouldn't order the tall stack of pancakes 'cause it's too big.

The area's top fine dining restaurant is **One Stanley Avenue** (1 Stanley Ave., Kingfield, 207/265-5541, www.stanleyavenue.com, 5–9:30 P.M. Tues.–Sun. Jan.–Mar., entrées $21–35), a Kingfield magnet since 1972 with a menu that never changes (entrées are noted with the year they were added to the menu). Cocktails in the Victorian lounge precede a dining experience: unobtrusive service, understated decor, and entrées such as roast duck with rhubarb glaze, chicken with fiddleheads, and saged rabbit. Reservations are essential on winter weekends; the restaurant attracts Sugarloaf's higher-end ski crowd.

INFORMATION AND SERVICES

The **Sugarloaf Area Chamber of Commerce** (Rte. 27, Carrabassett Valley, www.sugarloaf-chamber.org) has information for the whole valley, including Sugarloaf. The office, across the road from Ayotte's Country Store, has an info kiosk, portable toilets, and free Wi-Fi.

Sugarloaf (5092 Access Rd., Carrabassett Valley, 207/237-2000, www.sugarloaf.com) provides information on anything and everything on the mountain. During the ski season, the free tabloid *Sugarloaf This Week,* published biweekly, carries comprehensive information about on-mountain activities. It's available everywhere on the mountain and throughout the valley and beyond.

If you're staying on the mountain or in the valley and have cable TV, tune to channel 17 (WSKI) for weather, snow, trail, and lift updates, plus an entertainment rundown.

The **Flagstaff Area Business Association** (207/246-4221, www.eustismaine.com) has information about the Stratton-Eustis region.

GETTING AROUND

The free **Sugarloaf Explorer** shuttle service (207/237-6853, www.sugarloafexplorer.com) operates 8 A.M.–approximately midnight daily during the winter season; it's on an on-call basis midweek and on a set schedule on weekends and during holiday periods. Various routes serve the condos, outdoor center, and valley.

Rangeley Lakes Area

Rangeley, incorporated in 1855, is the centerpiece of a vast system of lakes and streams surrounded by forested mountains. Rangeley is a catchall name. First applied to the town (formerly known as the Lake Settlement), it now also refers to the lake and the entire region. "I'm going to Rangeley" could indicate a destination anywhere in the extensive network of interconnecting lakes, rivers, and streams backing up to New Hampshire. The Rangeley Lakes make up the headwaters of the Androscoggin River, which technically begins at Umbagog Lake and flows seaward for 167 miles to meet the Kennebec River in Merrymeeting Bay, near Brunswick and Topsham.

Excavations have revealed evidence of human habitation in this area as long ago as 9000 B.C. More than 8,000 stone tools and other artifacts were uncovered at the Vail site, on the edge of Aziscohos Lake. Native Americans certainly left their linguistic mark here too with tongue-twisting names applied to the lakes and other natural features. Mooselookmeguntic means "where hunters watch moose at night"; Umbagog means "shallow water"; Mollychunkamunk (a.k.a. Upper Richardson Lake) means "crooked water"; Oquossoc means "landing place"; and Kennebago means "land of sweet water." The town's more prosaic name comes from 19th-century landowner Squire James Rangeley.

The region has been a vacation magnet since the late 1800s, drawing sports who came first by stagecoach and later by rail and steamer to breathe in the unspoiled air, paddle and fish the clear waters, hike mountain trails, and hunt in vast wild lands. Folks still come today for many of the same reasons, but to these add golf, tennis, and winter sports that include skiing, snowshoeing, ice fishing, and especially snowmobiling. Recreation is the primary attraction, but there are also cultural events, old-fashioned annual festivals and fairs, the unique Wilhelm Reich Museum, and shops that carry antiques, books, sportswear, and crafts.

Southeast of Rangeley, the town of **Phillips** was the birthplace of fly-fishing legend Cornelia T. "Fly Rod" Crosby (1854–1946), recipient of the first Registered Maine Guide license issued by the state—the imprimatur for outdoors professionals. Crosby, who wrote columns for the local paper, was a fanatic angler and hunter who always kept a china tea set neatly stowed in her gear.

Along Route 17 about 23 miles south of Oquossoc is Coos Canyon, in the town of **Byron,** where gold was found in the early 1800s on the East Branch of the Swift River. Amateur prospectors still flock to the area, but don't get your hopes up—it's more play than profits.

SIGHTS

◖ Rangeley Outdoor Sporting Heritage Museum

Don and Stephanie Palmer began collecting artifacts relating to the region's rich sporting heritage back in the mid-1990s, and as the collection grew they realized they needed a museum to house it. Opened in 2010 after a major fund-raising effort, the Rangeley Outdoor Sporting Heritage Museum (Rte. 17, Oquossoc Village, 207/864-5647, www.rangeleyoutdoormuseum.org, $5 over age 11) has engaging exhibits that tell the stories of Rangeley's many sporting luminaries, including Fly-Rod Crosby; fly-tier Carrie Stevens; taxidermist, painter, and angler Herb Welch; and boatbuilder Herbie Ellis. You enter through a reconstructed 1890 log cabin, which sets the tone. This museum is a community treasure, and locals and summer residents are helping it grow its collections with finds from their attics. Don't miss it. As a five-year-old remarked when I visited, "This museum is so cool."

◖ Wilhelm Reich Museum

Controversial Austrian-born psychoanalyst and natural scientist Wilhelm Reich (1897–1957), noted expert on sexual energy, chose

Rangeley for his residence and research. Hour-long guided tours of the Wilhelm Reich Museum (Dodge Pond Rd., Rangeley, 207/864-3443, www.wilhelmreichmuseum .org, 1–5 P.M. Wed.–Sun. July–Aug., 1–5 P.M. Sun. Sept., $6 adults, free under age 13), his handsome fieldstone mansion, include a slide presentation covering Reich's life, eccentric philosophy, experiments, and inventions such as the orgone accumulator and the cloud-buster. Reich is buried on the estate grounds. Views are spectacular from the roof of the museum, also known as Orgonon, so bring binoculars and a camera. A nature-trail system, including a bird blind, winds through the wooded acreage. The museum hosts free outdoor-oriented natural-science programs 2–4 P.M. Sunday.

Rangley Lakes Scenic Byway

While most visitors reach Rangeley via Route 4 from the Farmington area, another popular route is Route 17 from the Rumford-Mexico area. When you reach Byron on the Swift River, you enter the 35-mile Rangeley Lakes Scenic Byway (www.byways.org/explore/byways/13830), stretching from Byron north to Oquossoc and then southward down Route 4 through Rangeley to Madrid. The label is unquestionably deserved, especially in autumn when the vibrant colors are unforgettable. The two-lane road winds through the rural woods of western Maine, opening up periodically to reveal stunning views of lakes, streams, forested hillsides, and the Swift River. You might even see a moose. Highlights are two signposted viewpoints—Height of Land and the Rangeley Scenic Overlook—surveying Mooselookmeguntic and Rangeley Lakes, respectively. Height of Land, 11 miles south of Oquossoc, adjoins the Appalachian Trail.

Rangeley Lakes Region Logging Museum

On the grounds of the three-story Rangeley Lakes Region Logging Museum (Rte. 16, Rangeley, 207/864-5595, 11 A.M.–2 P.M.

Sat.–Sun. July–early Sept. or by appointment) are an eclectic assortment of lumberjack paraphernalia, artifacts, and samples of traditional artwork created in the camps. Call first; I've found it closed even during posted open hours.

Every year on the last Friday–Saturday in July, the museum sponsors Logging Festival Days, complete with beanhole beans, music, and a woodsmen's competition.

Bennett Covered Bridge

Spanning the Magalloway River beneath Aziscohos Mountain, the 93-foot-long Bennett Covered Bridge, built in 1901 and closed to traffic in 1985, sees far fewer visitors than most of Maine's eight other covered bridges. The setting, in the hamlet of Wilsons Mills, makes for great photos, so it's worth detouring on the unpaved road next to the Aziscohos Valley Camping Area, 0.3 miles west of Route 16 and 28 miles west of Rangeley.

Narrow Gauge Railroad

The **Sandy River and Rangeley Lakes Railroad** (Mill Hill Rd., Phillips, 207/788-3621, www.srrl-rr.org) dates to 1879, when the first section was constructed to connect northern Franklin County with Farmington, the terminus of the Maine Central Railroad. Since 1969, volunteers have been working to restore and reopen a section of the original two-foot narrow gauge track. Visit the small shop and station, then board a restored 1884 passenger car for the quick ride to the museum and roundhouse. The round-trip excursion takes about 50 minutes. The train operates June–mid-October on an erratic schedule. Fares are $6 adults, $1 ages 6–12. Call or check the website for current season info and schedule; even then, it's dependent on the availability of equipment and operators.

Moose-Spotting

Do-it-yourself moose-spotting is a favorite pastime in this area. The likelihood of spotting one of these gangly critters can be quite high, if conditions are ripe. Route 16 between

© TOM NANGLE

WESTERN LAKES

Take a ride along Maine's narrow gauge track aboard the Sandy River and Rangeley Lakes Railroad.

Rangeley and Stratton is well known as "moose alley," especially in the boggy areas close to the road. Sunrise and sunset are the best times for sighting moose. Keep your camera handy, and drive slowly; no one wins in a moose-car collision, and fatal accidents are not uncommon on this unlighted stretch.

Flightseeing

The best way to put the region in perspective is from the air. **Acadian Seaplanes** (207/252-6630, www.acadianseaplanes.com) offers tours of the Rangeley region via floatplane (beginning at $56 pp for 15 minutes). Also available are moose-spotting tours ($174 pp) and Fly & Dine trips ($250 per couple plus meal costs) to a remote sporting camp for dinner.

ENTERTAINMENT

The great outdoors is the Rangeley region's biggest source of entertainment, but there are some options for rainy days and evening fun. **Rangeley Friends of the Arts (RFA)** (207/864-2958, www.rangeleyarts.com) is a

local cultural organization that promotes the arts in the region through concerts, events, scholarships, and school programs. Call for event information.

Once a week, avid readers gather for a book discussion hosted by **Books, Line and Thinkers** (Main St., Rangeley, 207/864-4355, bltbooks@rangeley.org). Call the shop for details.

Lakeside Theater (2493 Main St., Rangeley, 207/864-5000, www.rangeley-movies.com) screens major films year-round (weekends only off-season). On Sunday nights during summer, independent films are shown. The theater also presents **Celtic Concerts** ($12.50 advance, $15 at the door, reservations recommended), a live music series that runs mid-May–mid-September.

The Club House (Main St., Rangeley, 207/864-9955) draws a crowd starting at 9 p.m. Friday–Saturday, when there's live music or a deejay. On winter weekends, there's frequently après-ski entertainment at **Saddleback.**

FESTIVALS AND EVENTS

Hardly a day goes by in July–August without something scheduled. At other times, events are less frequent.

Avid snowmobilers shouldn't miss the annual January **Snodeo.** Events at the family-oriented festival include competitions, food, games, an auction, raffles, live entertainment, radar runs, children's events, a snowmobile parade, antique snowmobile displays, fireworks, and more.

The third Sunday in July, the **Old-Time Fiddlers' Contest** draws great musicians and includes a barbecue. Bring your own chair or blanket and expect lots of foot-stomping fun. The last weekend in July, **Logging Museum Festival Days** includes a parade, a beanhole bean supper, lumberjack events, and the Little Miss Woodchip contest. It's held on the Rangeley Logging Museum grounds on Route 16.

On the first Thursday in August, the **Sidewalk Art Show** is an all-day street festival featuring dozens of artists displaying a wide range of talents along Rangeley's Main Street. Downtown Rangeley comes alive the third Thursday in August for the **Annual Blueberry Festival,** a daylong celebration of the blueberry harvest, with sales of everything blueberry.

In even-numbered years, **Quilts in the Garden** is an outdoor quilt show in the colorful gardens behind Threads Galore Quilt Shop.

Held the first Saturday in October, the **Logging Museum Apple Festival** is a daylong apple-themed celebration that includes cider pressing. It's held on the Rangeley Logging Museum grounds on Route 16.

SHOPPING

The new-book selection is distinguished at **Books, Lines, and Thinkers** (Main St., Rangeley, 207/864-4355, bltbooks@rangeley.org) thanks to owner Wess Connally, a former high-school English teacher in Rangeley. The small user-friendly shop has lots of great reading; trust me, you won't leave empty-handed. Wess organizes and leads a book-discussion group year-round, and visitors are welcome.

Ecopelagicon: A Nature Store (3 Pond St., Rangeley, 207/864-2771) is a kind of miniaturized (and less expensive) Nature Company, emphasizing eco-oriented gifts, books, toys, games, and cosmetics.

The flavors of the lakes and woods are captured at **The Gallery at Stony Batter** (Rte. 4, Oquossoc, 207/864-3373), which sells regionally themed artwork, furnishings, and antiques, from moose merchandise to fine art.

RECREATION
Parks
RANGELEY LAKE STATE PARK

With 1.2 miles of lake frontage and panoramic views toward the mountains, 869-acre Rangeley Lake State Park (S. Shore Dr., Rangeley, 207/864-3858, www.parksandlands.com, $4.50 nonresident adults, $3.50 Maine resident adults, $1.50 ages 5–11 and nonresident seniors, free for Maine seniors) gets high marks for picnicking, swimming, fishing, birding, boating, and camping. The swimming "beach" is a large patch of grass. None of the 50 campsites is at water's edge, but a dozen have easy shore access. (For camping reservations, visit www.campwithme.com; from out of state call 207/287-3824 at least two business days in advance—MasterCard and Visa only. Maine residents call 800/332-1501.) If you're doing any boating, stay close to shore until you're comfortable with the wind conditions; the wind picks up very quickly on Rangeley Lake, especially in the south and southeast coves near the park. Camping is $25 per site nonresidents, $15 for Maine residents, plus $2 per site per night for a reservation; there are no hookups, but there are hot showers. The park, four miles off Route 17, is open mid-May–September, but it's accessible in the winter for cross-country skiing and snowmobiling.

LAKESIDE PARK

In downtown Rangeley, overlooking both lake and mountains, is this lovely grassy town park with a tiny beach and a safe swim area, grills and covered picnic tables, tennis courts, a playground with plenty of swings, lots of

© HILARY NANGLE

One of the more pleasant ways to tour Rangeley Lake is by boat.

lawn for running, and a busy boat-launching ramp. Restrooms are open when a lifeguard is on duty. Access is from Main Street (Rte. 4) near the Parkside and Main Restaurant and the chamber of commerce office.

SMALLS' FALLS REST AREA

One of Maine's most accessible cascades, Smalls' Falls is right next to Route 4 at a state rest area 12 miles south of Rangeley. Pull into the parking area and walk a few steps to the overlook. Bring a picnic. Locals love to swim in the pools between the falls. For more of a challenge, ascend a bit farther to Chandler's Mill Stream Falls. The rest area is officially open mid-May–October, but it's easy to park alongside the highway early and late in the season.

Preserves

Since its founding in 1991, Rangeley Lakes Heritage Trust (RLHT, Rte. 4, Oquossoc, 207/864-7311, www.rlht.org) has preserved more than 12,500 acres, including 45 miles of water frontage, 15 islands, and Bald Mountain. Trail maps can be printed from the website.

HUNTER COVE WILDLIFE SANCTUARY

Loons, ducks, and other waterfowl are the principal residents of RLHT's Hunter Cove Wildlife Sanctuary. While walking the three miles of easy blazed trails, best covered in a clockwise direction, keep an eye out for the blue-flag iris, which blossoms throughout the summer. You may even spot a moose. If you launch a canoe into Hunter Cove and paddle under the Mingo Loop Road bridge early in the season, you'll come face-to-face with nesting cliff swallows. To reach the sanctuary, take Route 4 west of downtown Rangeley for about 2.5 miles, turning left into the preserve across the road from Dodge Pond. It's signposted. The preserve is open sunrise–sunset daily, and admission is free.

Hiking

Hiking opportunities in this region are plentiful, and indeed there are numerous hiking guidebooks that provide details on more serious endeavors. Here's a sampling of a few hikes that reap big rewards for basic efforts. Be sure to wear appropriate footwear and carry water, snacks or lunch, and bug repellent.

BALD MOUNTAIN

Centerpiece of a 1,953-acre parcel of Maine Public Reserve Land, Bald Mountain is a relatively easy two-hour round-trip hike that ascends less than 1,000 feet, yet the minimal effort leads to stunning views of Mooselookmeguntic and Upper Richardson Lakes—not to mention the surrounding mountains. Even three-year-olds can tackle this without terrifying their parents. Pack a picnic. The trailhead is on Bald Mountain Road in Oquossoc, about a mile south of Route 4 and roughly across from the entrance to Bald Mountain Camps. Park well off the road.

ANGEL FALLS

Dropping 90 feet straight down, dramatic Angel Falls is one of New England's highest cascades, reached after a fairly short easy-to-moderate hike. Even in midsummer, you'll be fording running water, so wear rubberized or waterproof shoes or boots. The best time to come is autumn, when most of the rivulets have dried up and the woods are brilliantly colorful. Allow 1–1.5 hours for the 1.5-mile round-trip hike. The trail is mostly red-blazed, with the addition of orange strips tied at crucial points. From Oquossoc, take Route 17 South 17.9 miles to the unpaved Bemis Track, on the right. Follow the road along Berdeen Stream about 3.6 miles until you see a steep road descending to a gravel pit on the left. Park alongside the Bemis Track, then walk down the hill. This is a popular hike, so you should see other cars. The trail leads off to the left.

PIAZZA ROCK AND SADDLEBACK MOUNTAIN

A distinctive landmark on the western slope of Saddleback Mountain, Piazza Rock is a giant cantilevered boulder 600 feet off the

Appalachian Trail (AT). The hike up is easy to moderate, not a cakewalk but fine for families, along the white-blazed AT from Route 4. From downtown Rangeley, go seven miles southeast on Route 4 and park in the new lot on the south side of the highway. Piazza Rock is 1.2 miles northeast of the highway.

If you continue on the AT from Piazza Rock, it's another four miles to the summit of 4,116-foot Saddleback Mountain, but most hikers take the shorter route up the mountain from the ski area's Base Lodge. To get there from Rangeley, go south on Route 4 to Dallas Hill Road and then go 2.5 miles to Saddleback Mountain Road. From the lodge, follow the orange trail markers. Expect a stiff breeze and 360-degree vistas. A trail map is available at the lodge.

CASCADE STREAM GORGE

A 16-foot cascade, a 2,000-foot gorge, and well-placed picnic tables are the rewards for this short but sometimes steep trail. Allow about 30 minutes for the one-mile round trip without stops. From downtown Rangeley, head south 3.5 miles on Route 4, turning east Town Hall Road. Take the second left, then watch for the trail sign.

Other excellent hikes west and north of Rangeley are **Aziscohos Mountain** and **West Kennebago Mountain.** Both are easy to moderate, have terrific views from their summits, and require 3–4 hours round-trip from their trailheads. West Kennebago has a fire tower.

Excursion Boat

Cruise the waters of Rangeley, Mooselookmeguntic, or Cupsuptic Lakes aboard the 1947 antique launch *Oquossoc Lady* with **Rangeley Region Lake Cruises** (207/864-2038, www.rangeleylakecruises .com). Most cruises last one hour and cost $25 adults, $10 under age 11. Rangeley Lake cruises depart from Saddleback Marina in Oquossoc. During some summer weeks, the boat is relocated to Haines Landing on Mooselookmeguntic Lake for cruises there and on Cupsuptic Lake.

PADDLE ACROSS MAINE

You can paddle an ancient Native American route through the mountains and wilderness of northern New England and Québec. The 740-mile **Northern Forest Canoe Trail** (802/496-2285, www.northernforestcanoetrail.org) begins in Old Forge, New York, and passes through 35 communities in Vermont, Québec, New Hampshire, and Maine, following lakes, rivers, and streams, both flat water and white water, before finishing in Fort Kent. While some dedicated paddlers have completed the trek from start to finish, most folks dabble in various areas.

More than 350 miles of the waterway are in Maine. The trail enters the state via Lake Umbagog in section 8 and then progresses through the Rangeley Lakes and across Flagstaff Lake to Spencer Stream before crossing into the Kennebec River Valley region, following the Moose River, and finishing section 10 in Moosehead Lake. Sections 11 through 13 pass from the lake to the West Branch of the Penobscot and on to Chesuncook Lake. From here, it follows the Allagash Wilderness Waterway to its confluence with the St. John River at the tip of Maine.

If you get serious about paddling it, the trail is mapped in 13 sections (sections 8-13 are in Maine, maps are $10 each, available online or in local shops; the full set is $59.70). The maps detail the waterways, portages, dams, communities en route, and natural sights. Also beneficial is the *Northern Forest Canoe Trail Guidebook* ($25). Much information is available online, with even more available to those who join Northern Forest Canoe Trail; membership is $35.

Water Sports

FISHING

The Rangeley Lakes area earned its vaunted reputation for world-class fishing. Diehard anglers will always show up in May–early June, lured by landlocked salmon and brook trout. The region boasts of being the birthplace of contemporary fly-fishing, and indeed many famous flies originated here. The best fly-fishing correlates with the waves of fly hatches late May–early July. Both the **Kennebago River** and **Upper Dam** on Mooselookmeguntic Lake are hot spots for fly-fishing. If you're very serious about fishing, arrange to be flown into a wilderness pond.

The best local source of information on fly-fishing is **Rangeley Region Sport Shop** (2529 Main St., Rangeley, 207/864-5615, www.rangeleyregionsportshop.com), where the enthusiastic owners will get you outfitted, point you in the right direction, or help you find a guide.

Note that many waters are restricted to fly-fishing and catch-and-release is mandated on some bodies of water at certain times of the year. For the best advice, hire a local guide. Registered Maine Guide Larry Guile's **Westwind Charters and Guide Service** (207/864-5437, www.westwind-charters.com) has been fishing these waters for more than 35 years. He provides the tackle for half-day and full-day salmon or trout fishing expeditions aboard his 17.5-foot Sea Nymph Sportfisher.

Combine fly-fishing with literary heritage. Maine Guide Aldro French's **Rapid River Fly Fishing** (cell 207/650-3890, www.rapidriverflyfishing.com) is based at Forest Lodge, made famous by noted author Louise Dickinson Rich in *We Took to the Woods*. Aldro knew Rich, which makes the experience all the more authentic. You can even stay in Rich's Winter House ($250 d), a magical setting on the Rapid River. Aldro works closely with conservation groups and supports Project Healing Waters, which serves disabled veterans. Spend the day wading into the Rapid's pools with Aldro ($250 s, $350 d includes lunch). Buy any necessary gear, including proven flies, along with Rich's book at Aldro's Bare Bones Fly Shop, a shed in the woods. Be sure to ask Aldro how his efforts to preserve the property as a historical site are progressing.

CANOEING AND KAYAKING

Canoeing and kayaking are splendid throughout this region. Be forewarned, though, that Rangeley and Mooselookmeguntic Lakes are much larger than they look, and they have wide-open expanses where fluky winds can kick up suddenly and mightily and swamp boats. Fatalities have occurred in just such circumstances. Check on wind conditions before you head out. Do not take chances.

If you're looking for pristine waters where motorboats are banned, opt for **Saddleback Lake, Loon Lake, Little Kennebago Lake,** or **Quimby Pond,** all fairly close to Rangeley.

Choices for canoeing near Rangeley are Rangeley Lake (especially around Hunter Cove), the Cupsuptic River, the lower Kennebago River, and Mooselookmeguntic Lake. Slightly farther afield are Upper and Lower Richardson Lakes, both wonderfully scenic, as is Umbagog Lake (um-BAY-gog), straddling the Maine–New Hampshire border. The Cupsuptic, Kennebago, and Magalloway Rivers are all easy Class I waters. The Rangeley Lakes Area Chamber of Commerce has produced a suggested canoeing itinerary for the Rangeley Lakes chain, including information about wilderness campsites en route. Some of the campsites require reservations and fire permits.

Besides being a fishing-gear supplier and a place that has camping and hunting gear as well as water toys, outdoor clothing, and unique gifts, **River's Edge Sports** (Rte. 4, Oquossoc, 207/864-5582, www.riversedgesports.com) also rents canoes and kayaks. Rates start at $25 per day or $125 per week for a canoe or single kayak. Double kayaks are $40 per day and $200 per week. For $45, including canoe rental, River's Edge will shuttle you and the canoe up the Kennebago River to the start of an idyllic 2–3-hour downstream paddle to Route 16 and your car; go at sunrise for the best chance of spotting a moose.

Ecopelagicon (7 Pond St., Rangeley, 207/864-2771, www.ecopelagicon.com) rents kayaks for use on Haley Pond for a short paddle or to take to your camp. Single kayaks rent for $32 per day, $25 half-day, or $12 per hour; doubles are $36, $28, and $15. Long-term rates are available. Delivery and pickup are available for a fee.

Mookwa at Ecopelagicon offers guided kayak tours beginning at 8 A.M. on most Thursdays. Each week's trip visits a different waterway. The four-hour, half-day tours are $65 pp with a snack; full-day tours are $75 pp with lunch. Minimum age is 12. By the way, *mookwa* is a Cree word for loon.

MOTORBOATING

Of course, the easiest way to explore these massive lakes is by motorboat. Most lakes have public access points, but these may be busy. Put-ins for Rangeley Lake include the state park, Lakeside park, and off Route 4 in Oquossoc. The best one for Mooselookmeguntic is Haines Landing, at the end of Route 4. There's another ramp off Route 16 west, approximately four miles from the intersection with Route 4. Also off Route 16 is the Mill Brook access for Lake Richardson and the Black Cove Campground access for Aziscohos (be careful, as it's extremely shallow in places). Maine has strict rules about boating. For information, contact the Maine Department of Inland fisheries and Wildlife (www.maine.gov/ifw) or a local outfitter.

The best place to rent a sturdy motorboat is **Saddleback Marina** (Rte. 4, Oquossoc, 207/864-3463, www.oquossocmarine.com). Prices begin at $100 per day; half-day rates begin at $60; hourly rental is $35; gas and oil are extra. Restroom and picnic facilities are available.

Biking

In downtown Rangeley, the multiuse **Railroad Trail Loop** begins on Depot Street (not far from Seasonal Cycles). The 12.5-mile circuit travels over mixed terrain, including paved and unpaved roads and an abandoned railroad bed, and has some steep sections.

The Rangeley Lakes Trails Center (524 Saddleback Mountain Rd., 207/864-4309) has seven miles of trails on lower Saddleback

WESTERN LAKES

Mountain; two are easy, and the rest cater to advanced cyclists.

Golf

Noted golfers have been teeing off at **Mingo Springs Golf Course** (Country Club Rd., Rangeley, 207/864-5021) since 1925, when the course started with nine holes. Today's 18-hole, par-70 course boasts panoramic vistas of lakes and mountains—and sometimes an annoying breeze. Golf-and-lodging packages are available at the adjacent Country Club Inn.

Gold Panning

"Gold bought, sold, and lied about here" proclaims the sign outside **Coos Canyon Rock and Gift Shop** (472 Swift River Rd., Byron, 207/364-4900, www.cooscanyonrockandgift .com), a family operation since 1956. Check out the exhibits of some of the nuggets found in the Swift River and then rent equipment and try it yourself. A pan and trowel for use on-site are free, with a $5 deposit. Offsite use is $2 per day for a pan and screen, $1 for a trowel, or $15

for a fancier sluice box ($85 deposit). It's a relatively inexpensive lesson in patience.

Winter Sports

ALPINE SKIING AND SNOWBOARDING

Saddleback (207/864-5671 or 866/918-2225, www.saddlebackmaine.com) is the yin to nearby Sugarloaf's yang. Although it deserves its reputation as a low-key, wallet-friendly, family-oriented area, it's beginning to be discovered. This is big-mountain skiing, with a 2,000-foot vertical drop off a 4,116-foot summit laced with classic New England narrow and winding trails and some of the East's best gladed terrain. In 2003 the resort expanded the base lodge, added a beginner area with its own quad, replaced the summit T-bar with a quad, invested heavily in snowmaking and grooming, and cut new trails. In 2010 it unveiled Casablanca, a massive 44-acre glade expected to expand to more than 60 acres, complemented by mid-mountain yurt with food service and toilets. More expansion is planned.

Saddleback resort is an uncrowded gem, with narrow New England–style trails that feature panoramic views of the Rangeley Lakes.

CROSS-COUNTRY SKIING AND SNOWSHOEING

The volunteer-operated nonprofit Rangeley Lakes Cross Country Ski Club (524 Saddleback Mountain Rd., 207/864-4309, www.xc-skirangeley.com) operates the **Rangeley Lakes Trails Center,** with 34 miles of groomed trails lacing through the Saddleback preserve on lower Saddleback Mountain. Maps are available at the center, where a yurt serves as the lodge. Trails are open 8:30 A.M.–4:30 P.M. daily. Full-day trail passes are $12–17 adults, $8–9 ages 7–18; half day tickets are $9–13 and $6–7.

The summer nature trails at **Orgonon, the Wilhelm Reich Museum** (207/864-3443), west of downtown Rangeley, are accessible for free cross-country skiing or snowshoeing 9 A.M.–4 P.M. weekdays.

For cross-country ski or snowshoe rentals, visit **The Alpine Shop** (2504 Main St., Rangeley, 207/864-3741).

ICE-SKATING

A local skating club maintains a skating rink on **Haley Pond.** Free skate rentals are available from **Ecopelagicon** (3 Pond St., Rangeley, 207/864-2771). Haley Pond is also home to a winter pond hockey tournament in February.

SNOWMOBILING

Snowmobiling is big business in Rangeley, and in winter most accommodations and lodgings cater to it. The Rangeley area, linked to the state's Interconnected Trail System (ITS) via ITS 84, 89, and 117, has its own well-marked 150-mile groomed network thanks to the diligent efforts of the local Rangeley Lakes Snowmobile Club (www.rangeleysnowmobile .com). A family club membership is $42; individual membership is $27. Club gatherings and events are a good way to get the local scoop. The club also operates a conditions hotline (207/864-7336). Popular rides include a 65-mile lake loop; all or part of the 300-mile Black Fly Loop, which circles through Franklin and Somerset Counties; Kennebago Mountain; and even into Canada on the 12,500-mile

international circuit. There are no local trail fees, but support at local fund-raisers is appreciated.

For advice, rentals, or a midweek and non-holiday guided tour, check with **River's Edge Sports** (Rte. 4, Oquossoc, 207/864-5582, www.riversedgesports.com). Rental rates begin around $120 for a half-day; tours start at $170 for four hours, including clothing, equipment, and a guide.

ACCOMMODATIONS

Rates are for peak season, July–August.

Inns and Motels

Next to the stunning Mingo Springs Golf Course, the **Country Club Inn** (56 Country Club Rd., Rangeley, 207/864-3831, www .countryclubinnrangeley.com, mid-May–mid-Oct. and late Dec.–Mar.) claims the same fabulous lake-and-mountain panorama as the golf course. Nineteen 1960s-style lake-view guest rooms are $132 d with breakfast, $196 d with breakfast and dinner, or $112 d room only; ask about golf packages. Decor is classic lodge: two huge fireplaces in the living room accented by wildlife trophies, lots of pine paneling everywhere. There are no TVs or phones. The inn is superbly maintained and run, and there's an outdoor pool. Pets are $10 per night. The inn is 2.2 miles west of downtown Rangeley.

Completely renovated in 2007, the **Rangeley Saddleback Inn** (2303 Main St., Rangeley, 207/864-3434, www.rangeleysaddlebackinn .com, $125–160) is a family pleaser thanks to an indoor pool and jetted tub, onsite restaurant and pub, in-room TVs, microwaves, and mini-fridges, and four pet-friendly guest rooms.

The sunset views over Rangeley Lake are to die for from **Loon Lodge** (16 Pickford Rd., Rangeley, 207/864-5666, www.loonlodgeme .com, $110–150), which also houses a popular restaurant and pub. Beyond the back deck, the lawn rolls down to the lake, so you can wake with a morning swim. Some guest rooms are small with shared baths; the nicest are huge, have private baths, and have access to the back lawns.

Bed-and-Breakfasts

On a quiet hillside less than half a mile from downtown, Rob Welch, a retired principal, and his wife, Jan, a schoolteacher, are the enthusiastic hosts at (**Pleasant Street Inn B&B** (104 Pleasant St., Rangeley, 207/864-5916, www.pleasantstreetinnbb.com, $135–155 d). The Welches have completely renovated and expanded a traditional Maine farmhouse to include five good-size guest rooms, all with Wi-Fi and satellite TV, two with whirlpool tubs. It's bright, airy, and comfy. Guests have plenty of room to spread out in the guest parlor with a TV, spacious living room, and dining area, where a full breakfast is served. Guests also have access to a pantry stocked with afternoon refreshments as well as a guest computer. The inn is on the in-town snowmobile route, and there's plenty of parking for snowmobile trailers. Children younger than 12 and pets are not allowed.

Right downtown, with views over Rangeley Lake, is the **North Country Inn B&B** (2541 Main St., Rangeley, 800/295-4968, www .northcountrybb.com, $99–139). The two front guest rooms have the best views, but the two in back are quieter. All have queen beds and cable TV. The front porch is an inviting place to relax and watch the parade and fireworks during special events. Rates include Wi-Fi and a full breakfast; a gluten-free breakfast is available.

Cabin Colonies

On a quiet cove about four miles west of town, **Hunter Cove on Rangeley Lake** (office 334 Mingo Loop Rd., cabins Hunter Cove Rd., Rangeley, 207/864-3383, www .huntercove.com) has eight rustically modern well-equipped waterfront cabins on six acres. Each has 1–2 bedrooms, a screened porch, a woodstove, a phone, and a TV. Rates are $150–210 with a two-night minimum, but in July–August cabins are rented only by the week ($900–1,200). Rates cover up to four people; pets are $10 per day. It's open year-round, with lower rates off-season and midweek. From here, it's an easy paddle to the western edge of the

Hunter Cove Wildlife Sanctuary, and Mingo Springs Golf Course is nearby.

Far more remote is **Nioban Camps** (South Shore Dr., Rangeley, 207/864-2549, www.ni- boban.com). Although the sporting camp is historical, the original cottages were replaced in 2001 with nice two-bedroom lakefront cabins, each with a screened porch and a well-equipped kitchen. A Ping-Pong table, a phone, a TV, and games are available in the main lodge. Moose and deer sightings are frequent; beavers and ducks swim along the shore; and eagles fly overhead. The camps are open year-round for snowmobiling, snowshoeing, and skiing. Rates are $900 per week June–August. In May and September–March, cabins are available with a two-night minimum stay for $145–185 per night. Pets are $10 per day. A one-bedroom honeymoon cabin is $145 per night or $635 per week.

Sporting Camps

Stephen Philbrick is the third-generation owner of (**Bald Mountain Camps** (Bald Mountain Rd., Oquossoc, 207/864-3671, www.baldmountaincamps.com), a family-oriented traditional sporting camp on the shore of Mooselookmeguntic Lake. Established in 1897 and now run by Steve and his wife, Fernlyn, the superb operation has more than 90 percent repeat guests, some of whom have been returning since the 1930s. It's tough to get a reservation, especially in peak summer. Fifteen recently winterized, rustic waterfront log cabins can accommodate 2–8 people. Cabins are furnished, each offering a private porch, a fireplace, a living room, individual bedrooms, full housekeeping services, a mini-fridge, a microwave, and porter service. Three meals a day are served daily during peak season in the lake-view lodge. A highlight is the Friday-night cookout, with lobster, ribs, corn, steamed clams, and blueberry pancakes for dessert. The informal dining room is open to nonguests for dinner year-round (book well ahead) by reservation only. Among the activities are swimming at the sandy beach, fishing, tennis, canoeing, motorboating, sailing, and waterskiing. There's a playground for kids. Rates range $145–185 pp per day, depending on the season. Rates for kids vary by their ages and the month. Pets are $15 per day. It's open year-round, however meals are not included during the off seasons.

Grant's Kennebago Camps (Kennebago Rd., Rangeley, 207/864-3608 or 800/633-4815, www.grantscamps.com, mid-May–mid-Oct.) is a classic sporting camp built in 1905 on remote five-mile-long Kennebago Lake. Expect to hear lots of loons and see plenty of moose—if you can get a reservation. Seriously dedicated fly-fishers fill up the beds in May and September; families take their places July–August (check the family packages). Daily rates for the 18 rustic cabins, with private baths and hot showers, are $170–190 pp, including three meals daily in the water-view dining room. Children ages 4–12 are $60 per night; children under 4 are free. Pets are $15 per night per pet. The main lodge's lake-view dining room is open to nonguests for all meals by reservation (breakfast $12, lunch $15, dinner $30; BYOB), but the hearty cuisine makes it a popular place, so call well ahead. Canoe, kayak, and motorboat rentals range $30–60 per day. Grant's arranges a daily moose run ($30 pp) on the Kennebago River July–August. (Nonguests can also go on the moose run for a higher fee; call for details.) Access to Grant's is via a gated nine-mile road from Route 16, west of Rangeley. The gate is open 7 A.M.–6 P.M. only; if you're coming just for dinner, Grant's will arrange for access.

Avid fly fishers have been heading to **Lakewood Camps** (207/243-2959, www.lakewoodcamps.com, no credit cards) for more than 150 years. The camps are by Middle Dam, which separates Lower Richardson Lake from the famed Rapid River, and are accessible only by boat. The cold and wild Rapid River, which falls nearly 1,100 feet in less than eight miles, is restricted to fly-fishing. Landlocked salmon and brook trout are found in both the lake and river, but the lake is also home to togue (lake trout). Much of this area is protected Maine Public Reserve Land. Walk the Carry Road,

which parallels the river, and you'll pass the home where Louise Dickinson Rich lived when she wrote *We Took to the Woods*. The daily rate ($160 pp d, $120 ages 12–16, $70 ages 6–11) includes all meals and boat transportation as well as use of canoes and kayaks; row boats are $25; a motor boat with gas is $95. Guests stay in simple lakeside cabins that have Franklin fireplaces, generator-powered electricity, and full baths. Pets are $22 per night.

Camping

In addition to the nonprofit and commercial campgrounds described here, the Rangeley Lakes Region Chamber of Commerce maintains a list of no-fee and low-fee **remote wilderness campsites** throughout the Rangeley Lakes.

The **Maine Forest Service** (Rte. 16, Oquossoc, 207/864-5545), responsible for more than a dozen no-fee primitive campsites, will provide a copy of its list on request. The office also issues fire permits.

The **Stephen Phillips Memorial Preserve Trust** (Oquossoc, 207/864-2003) oversees 60 primitive tent sites on both the east and west shores of Mooselookmeguntic Lake and on Students, Toothaker, and other islands, all part of a 400-acre charitable preserve that includes more than four miles of lakefront. Many sites are on the lakefront; island sites and those on the west shore are accessible only by boat. Nightly cost is $16 per site for two people, teens or extra adults are $8, ages 6–12 are $5, dogs are $5 each. Two nature trails cross and circle Students Island.

At the southeast corner of Aziscohos Lake, **Black Brook Cove Campground** (Lincoln Pond Rd., Lincoln Plantation, 207/486-3828, www.blackbrookcove.com) provides three different kinds of camping experiences. The main campground has 30 tent and RV sites with hookups; the secluded east shore area has 26 wooded waterfront sites for small, self-contained units and tents. These wooded waterfront sites are 3.5 miles from the main campground and 100 feet from the water. Twenty-acre boat-accessible Beaver Island, out in the lake, has nine wilderness sites, and there are another seven wilderness sites around the lake. The remote sites include outhouses. Rates are $21 per family per site plus a hookup fee. The main campground facilities include coin-operated hot showers, a private beach, a convenience store, and rental boats and canoes.

Hardy folks can camp year-round at **Cupsuptic Family Campground** (Rte. 16, Oquossoc, 207/864-5249, www.cupsupticampground.com). The lakefront campground has a full range of sites in summer, with rates beginning at $18 for a wilderness site. Site fees cover two adults and two children. Rental boats are available, and dogs are permitted ($3 per day). Also on-site are a recreation hall, a sandwich shop, a bakery, a bandstand, a playground, and a sandy beach.

Seasonal Rentals

The **Morton and Furbish Agency** (207/864-5777 or 888/218-4882, www.rangeleyrentals .com) has a wide selection of daily, weekly, and monthly rental cottages, camps, houses, and condos for winter and summer use. The chamber of commerce can also assist with seasonal rentals.

FOOD

Check the local newspaper for announcements of **public suppers,** featuring chicken, beans, spaghetti, or just potluck. Most suppers benefit charitable causes, cost under $10 pp, and provide an ample supply of local color.

Hours are for peak season (July–August) but are only a guideline as they change frequently.

Local Flavors

While bagels are the specialty at **Moosely Bagels** (2588 Main St., Rangeley, 207/864-5955, 5:30 A.M.–2:30 P.M. Mon.–Sat., 6–11:30 A.M. Sun.), there's plenty more on the menu. For breakfast, choose from a full range of baked goods and simple to fanciful egg concoctions; lunch options include sandwiches, wraps, soups, and hot specials. There's seating inside or on the back, lake-view deck.

"Meet me at the Frosty" is Rangeley's summertime one-liner, a ritual for locals and visitors alike. **Pine Tree Frosty** (Main St., Rangeley, 207/864-5894, noon–10 P.M. daily in season), a tiny takeout near Haley Pond and the Rangeley Inn, serves ever-popular Gifford's ice cream in dozens of flavors along with good-size lobster rolls and superb onion rings.

Far more than the usual produce is available at **The Farmer's Wife** (Rte. 17 and Rangeley Ave., Oquossoc, 207/863-2492), a farm stand that also sells gourmet foods, fresh-baked breads and pies, salads, and wine. Nearby **Oquossoc Grocery** (Rte. 4, Oquossoc, 207/864-3662) has fresh-baked doughnuts, hot and cold sandwiches, and pizza.

Watch the game while chowing good burgers, nachos, hand-cut fries, and similar fare at ever-popular **Sarge's Sports Pub and Grub** (Main St., Rangeley, 207/864-5616). More substantial entrées ($10–17) are served after 5 P.M., and there's even a kids' menu. Weekends there's often live entertainment.

Ethnic Fare

Sam Sriweawnetr, the owner of Rangeley's fabulous Thai restaurant, is a real-life hero. A former chef at the U.S. embassy in Iran, he was instrumental in helping lead five hostages to freedom in 1979. He spent years in hiding and then eventually escaped to the United States. He opened an acclaimed restaurant in Boston, later relocating to Maine's Western Mountains. **Thai Blossom Express** (2473 Main St., Rangeley, 207/864-9035, 11 A.M.–8 P.M. Thurs.–Tues., $8–20) serves some of the state's best Thai food. There's some seating, but it's more of a to-go place, and has no restrooms.

Family Favorites

Several sporting camps in the Rangeley area open their dining rooms to nonguests, primarily for dinner, during the summer. Grab the opportunity to sample the sporting-camp ambience and the retro comfort food that brings guests back from one generation to the next.

A notable exception to the retro comfort-food theme is the lakefront restaurant at

Bald Mountain Camps (Bald Mountain Rd., Oquossoc, 207/864-3671, www.baldmountaincamps.com). Choose from an à la carte menu (entrées $16–35) or the regular house menu, which includes a full meal for $24–30. Especially popular is the Friday-night cookout, with lobster, spare ribs, chicken, burgers, dogs, and all the go-withs). Make reservations well in advance, and aim for sunset.

The Red Onion (Main St./Rte. 4, Rangeley, 207/864-5022, $6–20) is a barn of a place where you can also get award-winning chili and pizza made on homemade dough. Portions are large. The Onion is open 11 A.M.–9:30 P.M. daily year-round, unless, as the staff say, "High winds, low humidity, and plain laziness" inspire them to close the doors.

Try to snag a table on the deck overlooking the park and lake at **Parkside and Main** (2520 Main St./Rte. 4, Rangeley, 207/864-3774, 11:30 A.M.–11 P.M. daily, $8–22). The menu varies from burgers to steak; stick with the homemade soups and salads or simpler preparations. In summer there's often entertainment on the deck.

Casual Dining

Huge windows frame dramatic views of Rangeley Lake from the dining room of the hilltop 【 **Country Club Inn** (56 Country Club Rd., Rangeley, www.countryclubinnrangeley.com, dinner 6–8 P.M. Wed.–Sun., $10–30). White tablecloths drape the well-spaced tables, and the food complements the view. Entrées range from the casual to the classic. If the weather's fine, begin with cocktails on the deck overlooking the lake. The restaurant is open to nonguests by reservation for dinner, but tables for nonguests can be scarce when the inn is fully booked. Call well ahead, especially for summer weekends.

Setting a new tone for Rangeley is **The Corner Side Bistro** (2485 Main St., Rangeley, 207/864-2883, www.atthecornerside.com, $17–36), which opened in 2010. The restaurant, previously a general store, has been painstakingly renovated and meticulously decorated. In true bistro style, it's equally comforting, elegant, welcoming, and cozy. The food matches the setting, with a mix of options ranging from tapas to entrées and an emphasis on fresh and organic. It opened serving breakfast, lunch, and dinner daily, but expectations are that those hours will change as the restaurant matures and finds it niche. Call for the current schedule.

The sunset view over Rangeley Lake with the White Mountains as a backdrop is reason alone to reserve a table at **Loon Lodge** (16 Pickford Rd., Rangeley, 207/864-5666, www.loonlodgeme.com, 5–9 P.M. Tues.–Sat., $11–32), where pub and restaurant menus range from fish-and-chips to duck breast.

INFORMATION AND SERVICES

The **Rangeley Lakes Region Chamber of Commerce** (Lakeside Park, Rangeley, 207/864-5364 or 800/685-2537, www.rangeleymaine.com) produces annual guides to lodgings and services; the useful *Maine's Rangeley Lakes Map* costs $4. **Public restrooms** are located in a building adjacent to the chamber.

The **Rangeley Public Library** (7 Lake St., Rangeley, 207/864-5529, www.rangeleylibrary.com) is housed in a wonderful old stone building just off Main Street.

Bethel and Vicinity

Bethel is a sleeper. It's a classic New England village tucked in the folds of the White Mountains. White-steepled churches, an ivy-covered brick prep school (Gould Academy), lovely antique homes, a main street dotted with shops and restaurants, and a sprawling inn on the common are all easily explored on foot. Six miles away, Sunday River, one of New England's hottest alpine resorts, draws skiers and snowboarders to its modern slopes and lodges. The Ellis, Bear, and Androscoggin Rivers wind through the region, and in the river valleys are two covered bridges, a handful of ponds, and many working farms. Framing the region on two sides are two spectacular notches, Evans Notch, part of the White Mountain National Forest, and Grafton Notch, a state park, as well as the city of **Rumford,** with a paper mill that emits the "smell of money," as locals like to say. **Rumford Point, Center Rumford,** and **Hanover** are don't-blink villages between Rumford and Bethel, and each has its calling cards.

Thanks to Sunday River, winter is peak season here. In addition to skiing and riding, there's snowshoeing, snowmobiling, dogsledding, skijoring, ice-skating, ice fishing, even ice climbing. Spring brings canoeists and anglers. Summer is lovely, with hiking for all abilities, biking, boating, fishing, rockhounding in local quarries, golfing, even llama trekking.

Autumn is still surprisingly undiscovered. It's perhaps the region's prettiest season, when visitors can take advantage of all the summer activities and do so under a canopy of blazing crimson, gold, and orange backed by deep evergreen.

But let's back up a bit. Bethel's "modern" history dates from 1774, when settlers from Sudbury, Massachusetts, called it Sudbury Canada, a name reflected in the annual August Sudbury Canada Days festival. Another present-day festival, Mollyockett Day, commemorates one of the area's most intriguing historical figures, a Pequawket Indian woman named Mollyockett. She practiced herbal medicine among turn-of-the-19th-century settlers, including a baby named Hannibal Hamlin. Her remedies proved effective in snatching Abraham Lincoln's future vice president from death in 1809. (The incident actually occurred in the Hamlin home on Paris Hill, southeast of Bethel.) Mollyockett died August 2, 1816, and is buried in the Woodlawn Cemetery on Route 5 in Andover.

Meanwhile, the name Bethel surfaced in 1796, when the town was incorporated. Agriculture sustained the community for another half-century, until the Atlantic and St. Lawrence Railroad in 1851 connected Bethel to Portland (and later to Montreal) and access to major markets shifted the economic focus toward timber and wood products, which remain significant even today.

North of Bethel, **Andover** has become a word-of-mouth favorite among through-hikers and section hikers on the Appalachian Trail (AT), which snakes by about eight miles to the west. It's Maine's southernmost town near the AT, and the hikers pile into Andover for a break in August–September after negotiating the Mahoosuc Range, one of the AT's toughest sections.

East of Bethel are the tiny communities of **Locke Mills** (officially in the town of Greenwood) and **Bryant Pond** (in the town of Woodstock), both with summer and winter recreational attractions. Northeast of Bethel is Rumford, a paper-manufacturing center whose favorite son was former Secretary of State Edmund Muskie.

SIGHTS
Covered Bridges
Often called the **Artist's Covered Bridge** because so many artists have committed it to canvas, an 1872 wooden structure stands alongside a quiet country road north of the Sunday River Ski Resort. Kids love running back and forth across the disused bridge, and in summer they

can swim below it in the Sunday River. The bridge is 5.7 miles northwest of Bethel; take Route 2 toward Newry, turn left at the Sunday River Road, and then bear right at the fork. The bridge is well signposted, just beyond a small cemetery.

About 20 miles north of Bethel in South Andover, the **Lovejoy Bridge,** built in 1867, is one of the lesser-visited of Maine's nine covered bridges. It's also the shortest. Spanning the Ellis River, a tributary of the Androscoggin, the 70-foot-long bridge is 0.25 miles east of Route 5 but not visible from the highway; it's about 7.5 miles north of Rumford Point. In summer, local kids use the swimming hole just below the bridge.

Historical Houses and Tours

The **Bethel Historical Society** (Bethel Common, 14 Broad St., Bethel, 207/824-2908, www.bethelhistorical.org) maintains two downtown properties. Listed on the National Register of Historic Places, the 1813 Federal-style **Dr. Moses Mason House** (guided tours 1–4 P.M. Tues.–Sun. July–Aug. or by appointment, $3 adults, $1.50 ages 6–12, $7 per family) is a beautifully restored eight-room museum. Particularly significant in the museum are the hall murals painted by noted itinerant muralist Rufus Porter or his nephew Jonathan Poor. Dr. Moses Mason, a local physician, was elected to Congress a dozen years after Maine achieved statehood and served two terms as a Maine congressman. The Mason House is adjacent to the 1821 **O'Neil Robinson House** (10 A.M.–4 P.M. Tues.–Fri. Sept.–June, 10 A.M.–4 P.M. Tues.–Fri., 1–4 P.M. Sat.–Sun. July–Aug., donation), which has exhibit galleries and a small museum shop.

Bethel Historical Society interns and volunteers lead **Guided One-Hour Walking Tours of Bethel Hill** at 10 A.M. Saturday early July–early September. The tour departs from the bell tower on the north end of the common. Or do it yourself, armed with the society's free *Walking Tour of Bethel Hill Village* brochure, available from the society or chamber of commerce. It provides detailed information on 29 buildings and

monuments in the downtown area's Historic District. Officially, more than 60 structures are included in the district. Allow an hour to appreciate the 19th- and 20th-century architecture that gives real cachet to Bethel's heart.

ENTERTAINMENT

The **Mahoosuc Arts Council (MAC)** (207/824-3575, www.mahoosucarts.org) sponsors more than a dozen performances throughout the year, plus about a dozen art residencies and other cultural events in local schools.

At **Sunday River Ski Resort** there's live entertainment in several locations weekends and during school vacations. The resort also runs the Black Diamond Family Entertainment series, with performances such as vaudeville, marionettes, storytelling, and circus acts.

When the weather doesn't cooperate—and even if it does—and the kids need to let off steam, **BIG Adventure Center** (12 North Rd., Bethel, 207/824-0929, www.thebigadventurecenter.com) is just the ticket. Outdoor activities include two giant waterslides and an 18-hole miniature golf course; indoor possibilities include rock climbing and laser tag.

The hot spots for après-ski into the night are the **Foggy Goggle** at Sunday River; **The Matterhorn** (Sunday River Access Rd., 207/824-6836, www.matterhornskibar.com), a classic ski bar accented with cool alpine memorabilia and featuring live weekend entertainment; **Suds Pub** at the Sudbury Inn (207/824-6558, www.sudburyinn.com), where Hoot Night has been an open-mike tradition on Thursday since 1987; and **The Jolly Drayman** (Rte. 2, 207/824-4717, www.briarleainn.com), which attracts an older clientele who appreciate its English pub style.

EVENTS

On the nearest Saturday to April 1 in March or April, Bethel's **April Fools' Pole, Paddle, and Paw Race** pits two-person triathlon teams against one another in cross-country skiing, canoeing, and snowshoeing. Events begin at the Sunday River Cross-Country Ski Center.

In mid-June the annual three-day **Trek**

Across Maine: Sunday River to the Sea draws nearly 2,000 cyclists for the 180-mile bike expedition from Bethel to Rockland, proceeds from which benefit the Maine Lung Association. Registrations are accepted on a first-come, first-served basis, and the trek is usually fully booked by April. Pledges are required, and there's a registration fee. Call 800/458-6472 for details.

Don't like cycling? Perhaps the **Androscoggin River Source to the Sea Canoe Trek** is more your style. The annual 20-day paddle (spread over four-day weekends in midsummer) from the New Hampshire headwaters to Fort Popham near Bath—about 170 miles—is open to all canoeists, who can participate on any leg of the journey. A contribution is requested to benefit the Androscoggin Land Trust (207/583-2723, www.androscogginwatershed.org).

Bethel's **Annual Gem, Mineral, and Jewelry Show** is a long-running mid-July event with exhibits, demonstrations, and sales of almost everything imaginable in the rock and gem line—even guided field trips to nearby quarries.

The third Saturday in July, on Bethel Common in downtown Bethel, **Mollyockett Day** commemorates a legendary turn-of-the-19th-century Native American healer with a parade, children's activities, a craft fair, food booths, and fireworks. There's also usually an oddball race—a couple of years it was wheeled beds; another year it was spouse-carrying.

Andover presents a parade, live entertainment, children's games, art and flower shows, antique cars, a barbecue, and a beanhole bean supper the first weekend in August as part of **Andover Old Home Days.** The second weekend that month at the Moses Mason House in Bethel, **Sudbury Canada Days** commemorates Bethel's earliest settlers with traditional crafts, an art show, a parade, croquet, a bean supper, and a contra dance.

Maine artisans take center stage in the annual display and sale at the **Blue Mountains Arts and Crafts Festival,** held the second weekend in October at the Sunday River Ski Resort in Newry.

During winter, Sunday River's calendar is chock-full of events.

SHOPPING

While Bethel doesn't have tons of shops, the ones it does have are not the run-of-the-mill variety.

Check out the strikingly unusual designs and glazes at **Bonnema Potters** (146 Main St., 207/824-2821), in a handsomely restored studio across the street from the Sudbury Inn. Best of all are the earth colors used on tiles, dishes, vases, and lamps.

If something a bit more offbeat appeals, stop in for Moose-Drop earrings, allegedly the genuine article, at **Maine Line Products** (23 Main St., 207/824-2522), a source of whimsical souvenirs for your whimsical friends, as well as serious gifts such as jams, syrup, fudge, and wind chimes.

At **Mount Mann Jewelers** (57 Main St., 207/824-3030, www.mtmann.com), Jim Mann wears the hats of owner, miner, gem cutter, and jeweler, and he's full of information in every category. It's the Bethel area's best place to see Maine's special gems: tourmaline (the official state mineral), aquamarine, amethyst, and morganite. The shop also has a basement "crystal cave" where kids can "discover" minerals and learn to identify them. Jim also has maps to area mines and quarries open to the public. Inquire about guided quarry tours.

Shoppers entering **Linda Clifford–Scottish and Irish Merchant** (91 Main St., 207/824-6560, www.lindaclifford.com) are almost always overwhelmed by the quality and selection. Pottery, crystal, clothing, jewelry, tartans, and more are all elegantly displayed. Be prepared to drool or part with some serious bucks.

Shaker-reproduction furniture and a home store filled with decorative items and accessories and wood ware can be found at **Timberlake Home Store** (158 Rte. 2, Bethel, 207/824-6545 or 800/780-6681, www.stimberlake.com). Ask about lectures, demonstrations, and workshops.

Handcrafted wood products fill **Maine**

Artisans Wood Gallery (1180 Rte. 2, Rumford, 207/364-7500), which sells hardwood goods, including furniture and accent pieces.

A section of the store at **Pooh Corner Farm** (Bog Rd., off Rte. 2, West Bethel, 207/836-3276, www.poohfarm.com), western Maine's largest greenhouse and florist, is dedicated to Pooh-related merchandise; Pooh, Piglet, Rabbit, Roo, and Eeyore are in residence on the farm. You'll find fun garden items too.

RECREATION
Parks and Preserves
STEP FALLS PRESERVE
The Nature Conservancy's first Maine acquisition, in 1962, the 24-acre Step Falls Preserve is ideal for family hiking—an easy one-hour round-trip through the woods alongside an impressive series of cascades and pools. Pick up a trail map at the box in the parking area. Bring a picnic and have lunch on the rocks along the way. The waterfalls are most dramatic in late spring; the foliage is most spectacular in fall; the footing can be dicey in winter. The trailhead for the preserve is on Route 26, eight miles northwest of Route 2 and 10 miles southeast of the New Hampshire border. Watch for The Nature Conservancy oak-leaf sign on the right, next to Wight Brook.

GRAFTON NOTCH STATE PARK
Nestled in the mountains of western Maine, 3,192-acre Grafton Notch State Park (Rte. 26, Grafton Township, 207/824-2912 or 207/624-6080 off-season, www.parksandlands.com, $3 nonresident adults, $2 Maine resident adults, $1 ages 5–11 and nonresidents over age 64; payment is on the honor system) boasts splendid hiking trails, spectacular geological formations, and plenty of space for peace and quiet. It's hard to say enough about this lovely park, a must-visit. Bring a picnic. Highlights include **Screw Auger Falls, Mother Walker Falls,** and **Moose Gorge Cave.**

The best (but not easiest) hike is the **Table Rock Loop,** a 2.4-mile moderate-to-strenuous two-hour circuit from the main trailhead (signposted "Hiking Trails") at the edge of Route 26. The trailhead parking area is four miles inside the park's southern boundary and 0.8 miles beyond the Moose Cave parking area. Part of the route follows the white-blazed Appalachian Trail; otherwise the trail is orange- and blue-blazed. Some really steep sections are indeed a challenge, but it's well worth the climb for the dramatic mountain views from aptly named Table Rock.

Another favorite moderate-to-strenuous hike goes up **Old Speck Mountain** (4,180 feet), third highest of Maine's ten 4,000-footers and part of the Mahoosuc Range. The 28-foot-high viewing platform on the recently restored fire tower gets you above the wooded summit for incredible 360-degree views of the White Mountains, the Mahoosuc Range, and other mountains and lakes. Allow a solid seven hours for the 7.8-mile round-trip from the trailhead on the west side of Route 26 in Grafton Notch. The route follows the white-blazed Appalachian Trail (AT) most of the way; the tower is about 0.25 miles off the AT. Although there's a route map at the trailhead (at the same location as for the Table Rock hike), the best trail guide for this hike is in John Gibson's *50 Hikes in Southern and Coastal Maine.*

If you're driving along Route 26 early or late in the day, keep a lookout for moose; have your camera ready and exercise extreme caution. You'll usually spot them in boggy areas munching on aquatic plants, but when they decide to cross a highway, watch out—unlike us, they don't look both ways. And their eyes don't reflect headlights, so be vigilant after dark. Moose-car collisions are too often fatal for both moose and motorists.

THE MAHOOSUC RANGE
South and east of Grafton Notch State Park is a 27,253-acre chunk of Maine Public Reserve Land (Bureau of Parks and Lands, 207/287-3821, www.parksandlands.com) known as The Mahoosucs, or the Mahoosuc Range, where the hiking is rugged and strenuous but the scenic rewards are inestimable. The

Appalachian Trail traverses much of the reserve, and its hikers insist that the mile-long Mahoosuc Notch section, between Old Speck and Goose Eye Mountains, is one of their biggest challenges on the 2,158-mile Georgia-to-Maine route, requiring steep ascents and descents with insecure footing, gigantic boulders, and narrow passages. If you're an experienced hiker, go for it, and use reliable guidebooks and maps, preferably USGS maps. The best overview of the reserve is *Spectacular Scenic Touring Loop in the Mahoosucs* (www .mahoosuctouringmap.org). The helpful map and brochure provides info on trails, culture, campgrounds, outfitters, guides, and information sources.

WHITE MOUNTAIN NATIONAL FOREST

About 49,800 acres of the 770,000-acre White Mountain National Forest (www.fs.fed.us/r9/ white) lie on the Maine side of the border with New Hampshire. Route 113, roughly paralleling the border, bisects the **Caribou-Speckled Mountain Wilderness,** the designated name for this part of the national forest. It's all dramatically scenic, with terrific opportunities for hiking, camping, picnicking, swimming, and fishing.

A drive along Route 113, north to south between Gilead and Stow, is worth a detour. It takes about 30 minutes without stops, but bring a picnic and enjoy the mountain views from the tables at the Cold River Overlook, about a mile south of the Evans Notch highpoint. Route 113 is too narrow for bikes in midsummer, when logging trucks and visitor traffic can be fairly dense. Save this bike tour for a fall weekday, and take it south to north for a good downhill run from Evans Notch. The road is closed in winter. If you plan on stopping or hiking, Evans Notch requires a parking permit ($5 for 7 days). Some locations have an "iron ranger" allowing payment of $3 per parking place per day.

An easy family hike is the **Albany Brook Trail,** one mile each way between the Crocker Pond Campground (at the end of Crocker Pond Rd.) and the northern shore of Round Pond.

Outfitters and Guide Services

These companies provide rentals, guide services, and support for many of the sports detailed below. They're also great resources if you've brought your own equipment.

The Maine Guides at **Bethel Outdoor Adventures (BOA)** (121 Mayville Rd./Rte. 2, Bethel, 207/824-4224 or 800/533-3607, www .betheloutdooradventure.com) are pros at canoeing, kayaking, and bicycling. They also offer snowmobiling tours and rent machines. On the riverside premises are a campground and café.

Sun Valley Sports and Guide Service (129 Sunday River Rd., Bethel, 207/824-7533 or 877/851-7533, www.sunvalleysports.com) provides Orvis-endorsed wading and drift-boat trips, fly-fishing instruction, wildlife safaris, canoe and kayak rentals, and guided snowmobile and ATV tours in addition to equipment. It also provides shuttle services for those with their own boats and operates a full-service fly shop.

Veteran professional guides Polly Mahoney and Kevin Slater of **Mahoosuc Guide Service** (1513 Bear River Rd., Newry, 207/824-2073, www.mahoosuc.com) lead wilderness canoe trips not in the Bethel area but on the Allagash, Penobscot, and St. John Rivers as well as in Québec. With extensive wilderness backgrounds in such locales as Labrador and the Yukon Territory, management experience with Outward Bound, a flair for camp cooking, and a commitment to Native American traditions, Polly and Kevin are ideal trip leaders.

Hiking and Walking

Much of the hiking in this area is within the various parks and preserves, but a fun family hike not in that category is the easy-to-moderate ascent of **Mount Will** in Newry, on the outskirts of Bethel. The Bethel Conservation Commission has developed a 3.2-mile loop trail that provides mountain and river views; allow about 2.5 hours to do the loop. At the chamber of commerce information center, pick up a Mount Will trail-map brochure, which explains three different hiking options. There also may be maps at the trailhead, which is on the west side of Route 2/26, 1.9 miles north of the Riverside Rest Area—a terrific spot, incidentally, for a posthike picnic next to the Androscoggin River.

The wheelchair-accessible **Bethel Recreational Path** is about a mile long and parallels the Androscoggin River. It begins at Davis Park (Rte. 26 and Intervale Rd.), where there's also a skateboard park, picnic tables, a boat launch, and a playground, and ends near Bethel Outdoor Adventure on Route 2. Expect to share it with joggers, in-line skaters, and cyclists. The **Androscoggin River Recreational Walking Trail** covers 1.5 miles, beginning at the lovely Riverside Rest Area on Route 2, just east of the Sunday River access road, and continuing to the River View Resort.

Water Sports
ANDROSCOGGIN RIVER

The rivers in the Bethel area are a paddler's dream, varying from beginner and family stretches to white-water sections for intermediate and advanced canoeists. Fortunately, the major artery, the Androscoggin River, seldom has low-water problems, and you'll see lots of islands as well as eagles, moose, and a beaver dam. West of Bethel there's an old cable from a onetime ferry crossing.

The **Androscoggin River Canoe Trail,** created in 2001 by the Mahoosuc Land Trust (207/824-3806, www.mahoosuc.org), provides access points to the river spaced about five miles apart, from the Shelburne Dam in New Hampshire to Rumford. The *Map and Guide to the Androscoggin Canoe Trail* is available from the trust for $4.95 plus $1 postage.

The annual Androscoggin River Source to the Sea Canoe Trek is a celebration of the river's revival from years of unbridled pollution caused primarily by paper-mill runoff.

The best source of information on the Androscoggin is **Bethel Outdoor Adventures (BOA)** (121 Mayville Rd./Rte. 2, Bethel, 207/824-4224 or 800/533-3607, www.betheloutdooradventure.com). It offers canoe rentals, maps, shuttle service, and trip-planning advice. In addition, the BOA staff can advise on canoeing the Ellis, Little Androscoggin, and Sunday Rivers.

POND PADDLING

Just east of Locke Mills, before the Littlefield Beaches Campground (207/875-3290, www.littlefieldbeaches.com), you can put in at **Round Pond,** on the south side of Route 26, and continue into North and South Ponds. Bring a picnic, and before you head out, enjoy it across the road at the lovely state rest area, which has grills and covered picnic tables in a wooded setting.

FISHING

The 26-mile stretch of the Upper Androscoggin River between the New Hampshire border and Rumford Point, its tributaries, the Wild, Pleasant, Sunday, and Bear Rivers, and local brooks are popular with anglers seeking rainbows, brookies, browns, and landlocked salmon. Even during the peak of summer, it's possible to catch smallmouth bass on the Andro.

Pick up a copy of *A Guide to Local Fishing* at the Bethel Area Chamber of Commerce and also check the resources of the **Upper Andro Anglers Alliance** (www. upperandro.com).

Master Maine Guide **Sandy MacGregor** (1094 Rte. 2, Rumford, 207/364-2506, www.mountainranger.com) grew up fishing the Androscoggin River. He knows where to find rainbows, browns, and smallmouth bass, and fly-fishing is his passion. A half-day float trip is $250, and a full day is $375.

Wildlife, Scenic, and Recreational Safaris

Explore the Androscoggin River with Maine Guide Sandy MacGregor on a late-afternoon **Wine and Dine Naturalist Float Trip** (207/364-2506, www.mountainranger.com). MacGregor guides a maximum of four guests in the *Molly Alexis,* a 17-foot handcrafted wooden drift boat with swivel bucket seats. You bring the wine, but he'll customize a menu for you. Bring a camera and binoculars: You'll see all types of waterfowl, maybe river otters, muskrat, or beavers, perhaps even ospreys, eagles, or a moose. Sandy also offers other recreational tours, including gold panning in the Swift River, a moose safari-hike, boating on Richardson Lake and Aziscohos Lake, one of the Rangeley Lakes where, he believes, God lives. The basic fee for a daylong float trip is $375, excluding meals; a 15 percent discount applies for additional days.

Biking

The Bethel Area Chamber of Commerce has sheets detailing about a dozen rides in the region, with lengths varying from a five-mile Village Restaurant Ride (don't be deceived; it takes in Paradise Hill, a killer for Sunday cyclists) to the 53-mile covered bridge cruise. For an easy pedal, follow the Sunday River Road as it continues out past Artist's Covered Bridge. It's mostly level and winding, paralleling the river and providing beautiful mountain views. No matter where you ride, do follow the rules of the road, keeping right and riding single file.

Hybrid-bike rentals are available from **Bethel Bicycle** (53 Mayville Rd., 207/824-0100, www.bethelbicycle.com) and **Bethel Outdoor Adventures** (121 Mayville Rd./Rte. 2, Bethel, 207/824-4224 or 800/533-3607, www.betheloutdooradventure.com), a full-service shop. Expect to pay $25–30 per day.

SUNDAY RIVER BIKE PARK

Looking for a real mountain biking adventure? Sunday River's bike park (800/543-2-SKI—800/543-2754, www.sundayriver.com, 10 A.M.–5 P.M. Fri.–Sun., $29 adults, $18 under age 13; trail only $25) has 25 miles of lift-serviced mountain biking on 30 trails, accessed from its South Ridge Lodge. Terrain ranges from dirt roads to single tracks with jumps, features, and even a log ride. Rental bikes are $40 with front suspension, $80 with full suspension.

Golf

Thanks to its spectacular setting, the 18-hole championship course at the **Bethel Inn and**

The 18-hole championship course at the Bethel Inn and Country Club is especially scenic.

© HILARY NANGLE

Country Club (Bethel Common, Bethel, 207/824-2175, www.bethelinn.com) wows every golfer who plays here. Starting times are definitely required, and caddies are available. Also based here is the **Guaranteed Performance School of Golf** (800/654-0125, www.gpgolfschool.com). It includes five hours of on-course instruction and video analysis with PGA professionals, with a maximum of three students per instructor.

The newest course in the area is the spectacular Robert Trent Jones Jr.–designed 18-hole course at **Sunday River Ski Resort** (207/824-3000, www.sundayriver.com), which opened in 2005.

Rockhounding

Here's a great family experience: Maine's Western Mountains are filled with gems and minerals. Take a one-hour guided digging tour of the Bumpus Quarry in Albany with **Maine Mineralogy Expeditions,** which operates from Bethel Outdoor Adventures (121 Mayville Rd./Rte. 2, Bethel, 207/824-4224 or 800/533-3607, www.rocksme.biz or www.betheloutdooradventure.com). You'll learn about the mine's history of producing feldspar, mica, and beryl and have the opportunity to search for rose quartz or beryl in mine dump areas. The cost is $25 adults, $9 under age 13, $65 family maximum, with a minimum of eight people per trip.

Winter Sports
SUNDAY RIVER SKI RESORT

Sprawling octopus-like over eight connected mountains, Sunday River (Sunday River Rd., Newry, 207/824-3000 or 800/543-2754, snow phone 207/824-6400, www.sundayriver.com) defines the winter sports scene in this area, with downhill skiing and snowboarding, ice-skating, cross-country skiing, phenomenal snowmaking capability, slope-side lodging, and plentiful amenities that include a spa, night skiing, entertainment, restaurants, and lodging. Its 671 acres are laced with 132 designated trails and glades, four terrain parks, one superpipe, one minipipe, a snow-tubing park, and three base lodges (South Ridge is the

main one). Serving it all are 16 lifts, including a chondula (combination gondola and chairlift) and four high-speed quads. Don't even consider leaving the base without a trail map, and make sure everyone in your party knows exactly where to meet for lunch or at day's end.

Sunday River is also home to **Maine Handicapped Skiing** (800/639-7770, www.skimhs.org), which provides free lessons and tickets for alpine and cross-country skiing and snowboarding for people with physical disabilities. Reservations are required.

Sunday River has day-care facilities in three locations (reservations are advised), a ski school, rental equipment, a free on-mountain trolley-bus service, and plenty of places to grab a snack or a meal at a wide range of prices. Call or check the website for current ticket prices; one-day tickets purchased at the window can approach $80, so be smart and buy online in advance for the best price.

The ski season usually runs mid-October–early May, weather permitting; the average annual snowfall is 167 inches. There's only one road on and off the mountain, so expect delays early and late in the day during weekends and holidays.

Sunday River also has a **zip-line park** open both summer and winter.

CROSS-COUNTRY SKIING

Right in downtown Bethel, the **Bethel Inn Touring Center** (Bethel Common, 207/824-6276, www.caribourecreation.com, $18 adult day pass, $15 ages 5–15) has about 25 trails groomed for classic and skate skiing and five miles of snowshoe trails on the inn's scenic golf course. The ski shop has a wax room and a snack bar with seating areas. Ski and snowshoe rentals and half-day tickets are available.

About 30 miles of trails wind through 1,000 acres along the Androscoggin River at **Carter's Cross-Country Ski Center** (Middle Intervale Rd., Bethel, 207/539-4848, www.cartersxcski.com, $14 adults, $10 children), owned and managed by Carter's Cross-Country Ski Center in Oxford (207/539-4848). In winter, the Bethel location operates a lodge and ski shop with a snack bar and rents skis and snowshoes.

ICE-SKATING
Picture an old-fashioned Currier and Ives winter landscape with skaters skimming a snow-circled pond and you'll come close to the scene on Bethel Common in winter. Bring a camera. The groomed ice-skating area, in the downtown Historic District, is usually ready for skaters by Christmas vacation. Sunday River Ski Resort also has rink; skating is free, and rental skates are available.

DOGSLEDDING
When they're not off leading multiday dogsledding trips in the Mahoosucs or on Umbagog Lake (rates begin around $560 pp), or even with the Inuit in Canada's Nunavut Territory ($5,500 pp) or the Cree in Québec ($2,900 pp), Kevin Slater and Polly Mahoney of **Mahoosuc Guide Service** (1513 Bear River Rd., Newry,

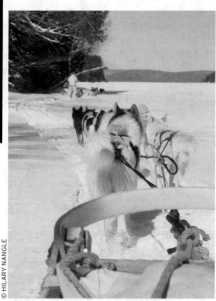

© HILARY NANGLE

The Mahoosuc Guide Service offers winter dogsledding trips across frozen Umbagog Lake.

207/824-2073, www.mahoosuc.com) will bundle you in a deerskin blanket and take you on a one-day dogsled trip on Umbagog Lake, beyond Grafton Notch State Park. Wear goggles or sunglasses; the dogs kick up the snow. Insulted parkas and footwear, a campfire lunch, and warm drinks are included in the $265 pp fee. Trips are limited, and they're very popular; book well in advance. Also on the premises are Mahoosuc's **Mahoosuc Mountain Lodge** and **Farmhouse Bed & Breakfast** (207/824-2073, www.mahoosucmountainlodge.com). Bunk rates range $35–50 pp. For more privacy, opt for one of the three shared-bath guest rooms ($90 d, $50 s, with breakfast) in the nicely renovated 1903 farmhouse.

In winter, there is a three-day Learn-to-Mush package at **Telemark Inn Wilderness Lodge** (591 King's Hwy., Mason Township, 207/836-2703, www.telemarkinn.com, $925 pp, d, $1,150 s, plus 10 percent gratuity) that includes three half-day guided mushing experiences, three nights lodging, and all meals.

SNOWMOBILING
Half-day guided snowmobile tours are available from **Sun Valley Sports** (129 Sunday River Rd., Bethel, 207/824-7533, www.sunvalleysports.com, $150 s, $175 d).

ACCOMMODATIONS
Conveniently, the **Bethel Area Chamber of Commerce Reservations Service** (800/442-5826, www.bethelmaine.com) provides toll-free lodging assistance for more than 1,000 beds in member B&Bs, motels, condos, and inns in Bethel, at Sunday River Ski Resort, and farther afield. If you're planning a winter visit, however, particularly during Thanksgiving and Christmas holidays, February school vacation, or the month of March, don't wait until the last minute. Procrastination will put you in a bed 40 miles from the slopes.

Keep in mind that peak season (ergo the highest room rates) in this part of Maine is in winter, not summer. Some lodgings also have higher rates for fall foliage in September–October.

Sunday River Lodging

On-mountain lodging options at Sunday River Ski Resort (207/824-3000, reservations 800/543-2754, www.sundayriver.com) include 425 guest rooms and suites in two full-service hotels—the **Grand Summit** and the **Jordan Grand Hotel**—as well as hundreds of slopeside condos and town houses in seven different clusters. Both hotels have restaurants and cafés, indoor and outdoor heated pools, tennis courts, video game rooms, and lots of extra amenities; the Jordan Grand is in an isolated location. Most guest rooms have full kitchen facilities. Except for the dorm rooms, lodging packages include lift tickets. Prices for accommodations and activity packages vary widely.

Country Inns

Bethel's grande dame, **The Bethel Inn and Country Club** (Bethel Common, Bethel, 207/824-2175 or 800/654-0125, www.bethelinn.com), is the centerpiece of a classic New England village scene. It faces the Bethel Common in the historical district; out the back door is the golf course backed by the White Mountains. Rooms are spread out between the traditional main inn and outbuildings. Also on the premises are 1–3-bedroom condominiums, but the inn is the better choice. Inn guest rooms vary widely in decor and quality; be forewarned that some are tired, to put it kindly. The best choices are in the new wing of the main inn. This is a full-service resort, and amenities include golf, tennis, a health club with a saltwater pool and a sauna, a game room, a lakeside outpost for swimming and boating, and a summer children's program. Inn rates, including breakfast, begin at around $80 pp d midweek and $100 pp d weekends and holidays. Children under age 12 stay free in the same room. Rates with dinner are available, but do check packages, which provide the best bang for the buck. A 15 percent service charge, covering dining and housekeeping gratuities, is added to all rates. Some accommodations permit dogs for $20 per night. It's open year-round, but the restaurant may be closed some nights during the off-season, although the tavern remains open.

Bethel's other longtime country inn, **The Sudbury Inn** (Main St., Bethel, 207/824-2174 or 800/395-7837, www.sudburyinn.com), is best known for its dining room and pub, but it's a classic B&B too. Guest rooms and suites (and even a three-bedroom apartment with a full kitchen and a fireplace) are spread between the main house and the dog-friendly carriage house ($15 per dog per day, including bed and bowls). The two-bedroom suites are especially good for families. All are comfortably furnished and have cable TV, air-conditioning, and phones. A full breakfast is included in the rates, which begin at $89–109 for a standard.

Bed-and-Breakfasts

The **Briar Lea B&B** (150 Mayville Rd./Rte. 2/26, Bethel, 207/824-4717 or 877/311-1299, $99–160) is a mid-19th-century Georgian Colonial farmhouse with a very popular authentic English pub. Rooms are comfortably decorated with floral wallpaper and antique furnishings updated with fancier linens. All have TVs and DVD players, Wi-Fi, and air-conditioning. A full breakfast is included. In summer, request a back-facing room if highway noise bothers you. It's just east of downtown Bethel.

Architect Stuart Crocker designed the lovely Shingle-style **Crocker Pond House** (917 North Rd., Bethel, 207/836-2027, www.crockerpond.com, $125–150) so that it fits naturally into its setting on 50 mostly wooded acres. It's a lovely environmentally designed inn that blends contemporary amenities, such as Wi-Fi, with traditional cottage design, Norwegian antiques, and Native American art in a restorative atmosphere (there is no TV). Crocker and his wife Ellen welcome guests in seven guest rooms, all south-facing with mountain views; one is wheelchair-accessible with a roll-in shower. Begin the morning with Stuart's blueberry pancakes, and after hiking or snowshoeing the trail behind the inn, relaxing by the pond, or exploring, return for afternoon tea and cookies. Pets are not allowed; two cats are in residence. Norwegian, French, and German are spoken at the inn. Children are welcome, and

WESTERN LAKES

After a day skiing at Sunday River or hiking in the Grafton Notch, retire to the Crocker Pond House, an especially peaceful and private bed-and-breakfast in Bethel.

© HILARY NANGLE

WESTERN LAKES

the loft rooms are especially good for families. Children under age 14 sharing a room are $15 each; older children are $25 each.

Traveling with your pooch? **Paws Inn** (372 Walkers Mill Rd./Rte. 26, Bethel, 207/824-6678, www.pawsinn.net, $75–85 d, $65–76 s) takes dog-friendly to the extreme. Carolyn Bailey and her sidekick, Sampson, provide two guest rooms, dog beds or crates, fenced-yard and barn play areas, doggie snacks, and plenty of love. You only need bring food for your dog; Carolyn prepares a generous continental breakfast. It's two miles south of Bethel.

Motels

The **Inn at the Rostay** (186 Mayville Rd./Rte. 2, Bethel, 207/824-3111 or 888/754-0072, www.rostay.com) is a motel that acts like an inn. The guest rooms are decorated with homey touches, and many have themes such as duck, goose, or cat. Note that sound carries between the rooms, so if you're noise sensitive, look elsewhere. Most rooms have refrigerators and microwaves, all have phones, cable TV and

video players with a video library available, and air-conditioning or ceiling fans. Wi-Fi is provided, and there's a quilt shop on the premises. Guests can have a full breakfast ($8), served in a dining room adjacent to a guest parlor; afternoon snacks are provided. Rates begin at $68 d midweek and vary greatly. Winter holiday weeks are priciest at $112–120.

For clean, cheap, and convenient digs, check into Ruthie's **Bethel Village Motel** (800/882-0293, www.bethelvillagemotel.com, from $60), smack downtown in a walk-to-everything location behind Ruthie's boutique. Guest rooms are pleasantly decorated, and all have air-conditioning, TVs, fridges, and Wi-Fi.

Lodge

Here's a property with a twist: In 1988 Steve Crone introduced llama trekking to Maine, and he's still at it, even more enthusiastically, offering half-day and multiday trips in the White Mountain National Forest from his casually rustic **Telemark Inn Wilderness Lodge** (591 King's Hwy., Mason Township, 207/836-

2703, www.telemarkinn.com, $125 d includes breakfast), open spring, summer, and fall. Be forewarned, though: You'll be hiking *with* the llamas, not *on* them; they tote the gear. A half-day llama trek, lasting about three hours, is $75 adults, $65 under age 14, including a stop for swimming and snacks. Better yet, book a lodging and trekking package that incorporates nature hikes, mountain biking, canoeing, or llama treks. Two–five-day activity packages are $390–875 pp adults, $300–675 pp children, including breakfasts, lunches, and guided day activities; five-day packages include family-style dinners. In winter, dogsledding replaces llama trekking, with a three-day Learn-to-Mush package priced at $925 pp d, $1,150 s, plus a 10 percent gratuity, which includes three half-day guided mushing experiences, three nights' lodging, all meals, and "all the dogs you can pet."

Camping

To really escape, **South Arm Campground** (62 Kennett Dr., Andover, 207/364-5155, www.southarm.com) has 38 lakeside wilderness sites ($15 per family), including island sites accessible only by boat, with transportation available. A bit less remote on a peninsula is the full-service main campground with 65 wooded sites ($24–32), all with water and 30-amp electricity; it has a marina, modern bathhouses, and a bakery and general store. From here, you can fly-fish the Rapid River, canoe the lake, fish, paddle (rentals available), take a sunset moose cruise, walk a section of the Appalachian Trail, bike logging roads, or just relax in this little slice of heaven.

Just south of it namesake, **Grafton Notch Campground** (1471 Bear River Rd./Rte. 26, Newry, 207/824-2292, www.campgrafton.com, $25) is a small, no-frills campground with 14 wooded sites with fire rings and picnic tables, a modern bathhouse, and a dump station ($10), but no hookups. Leashed dogs are permitted. Don't expect real quiet, though; you can hear the trucks on Route 26, but you can't beat the location if you want to hike in the state park.

Thirteen miles west of Bethel is the seven-acre **Hastings Campground** (800/280-2267 for credit-card reservations, www.campsnh.com/hastings.htm, $16), one of four campgrounds along Route 113 in the White Mountain National Forest. The 24-site campground is primitive, with no hookups or showers, but it does have vault toilets, a hand pump for water, fishing and hiking, and it is wheelchair-accessible. Route 113 is especially scenic, so this is a prime location for extensive hiking in the national forest. Trail information and maps are available from the Evans Notch Ranger District office. The campground is in Gilead, three miles south of Route 2.

Seasonal Rentals

For weekly, monthly, or seasonal rentals, contact **Maine Street Realty and Rentals** (20 Railroad St., Bethel, 207/824-2114, www.mainestreetrealty.com).

FOOD

Restaurant hours noted are for peak season but are subject to change. It's always wise to call ahead.

Local Flavors

You can feel good when eating at the **Good Food Store** (Rte. 2, Bethel, 207/824-3754 or 800/879-8926, www.goodfoodbethel.com, 9 A.M.–8 P.M. daily, $6–8). The combination store and takeout sells both good food and food that's good for you, and it stocks a huge array of natural foods. Create an instant picnic with sandwiches, salads, and soups, even beer and wine. If you're renting a condo and don't feel like cooking or eating out, you can pick up homemade soups, stews, and casseroles to go.

Also on the premises is **Smokin' Good BBQ** (Rte. 2, Bethel, 207/824-4744, www.therealbbqbob.com, 11:30 A.M.–7 P.M. Thurs.–Tues., 6–25), operating from Graceland, an orange trailer. A local transplanted Texan turned me onto this gem. Choices include pulled pork, beef brisket, ribs, chicken, and sides such as barbecue beans, slaw, and corn bread. Dress for the elements: There are only picnic tables for seating.

Baked goods made daily from scratch from all-natural ingredients have earned **DiCocoa's Bakery and Marketplace** (119 Main St.,

The baked goods, sandwiches, and soups that come from Cafe DiCocoa's kitchen are fabulous.

© HILARY NANGLE

Bethel, 207/824-5282, www.cafedicocoa.com) a solid following. Go for the fabulous baked goods, but don't miss the lunch specials, including panini and soup. The bakery doubles as a market selling fancy foods and take-home meals. It also makes scrumptious gelato, and I think the chocolate chip cookies are among the best I've ever had. It opens at 7 A.M. daily for breakfast and lunch.

For cheap eats at any meal, snag a table at the **Crossroads Diner & Deli** (24 Mayville Rd./Rte. 2, Bethel, 207/824-3673, www.crossroadsdiner.net, 5:30 A.M.–8 P.M. daily).

The **Bethel Farmers Market** sells good-for-you produce and other items 9 A.M.–noon Saturday mid-June–mid-October, on Route 26 (Railroad St.) next to Bethel Family Health Care at the southern edge of town.

You can see the aptly named **Front Porch Cafe** (6 Hall Hill Rd., Dixfield, 207/562-4646, 7 A.M.–3 P.M. Wed.–Mon.) from Route 2, and if you're hungry, stop in for homemade breakfasts and Maine classics such as baked beans. The dining room is small, the service is friendly, and the portions are generous. Dinner might be available.

On-Mountain Dining

The best choice at Sunday River is the independently owned **Phoenix House and Well** (Skiway Rd., across from the South Ridge base complex, Newry, 207/824-2222, www.phoenixhouseandwell.com, 11 A.M.–midnight daily during ski season, summer hours vary, $9–28), which has a split personality: Downstairs is a pub; upstairs is a fancier dining room. Choices range from burgers to filet mignon. It's also the best choice for Sunday brunch.

Pubs and Pizzas

Also open only in winter but farther down the access road is **Great Grizzly/Matterhorn** (292 Sunday River Rd., Newry, 207/824-6271, www.matterhornskibar.com, $9–20), an immensely popular barn-style restaurant that's *the* aprés-ski spot in Bethel, with entertainment on weekends. It's filled with co-owner Roger Beaudoin's finds, many from his travels and climbing expeditions in Switzerland (to the Matterhorn, of course). Antique mountain-climbing gear is in one room; a village motif complete with a real-estate office and old Sunoco pumps is in another; classic skis are everywhere. Be sure to check out the bar, made from 120 skis. The wide-ranging menu includes the best pizzas in the region, cooked in a wood-burning oven, as well as steaks, seafood, pastas, salads, and sandwiches. There's even a kids' menu. On weekend nights, there's usually entertainment in the early evening. Reservations are not accepted, so it's wise to dine early on weekends or expect to wait. Live entertainment, usually rock bands, begins at 9:30 P.M. on Friday–Saturday; a cover is charged unless you're already seated and have had dinner.

On the lower level of the Sudbury Inn is **Suds Pub** (151 Main St., Bethel, 207/824-2174 or 800/395-7837, www.sudburyinn .com), a very relaxing hangout. The moderately priced menu includes appetizers, burgers, soups, salads, pizza, and a few entrées, most in the $7–15 range. The full bar has 29 beers on tap. Thursday night is Hoot Night, an open-mike tradition since 1987 and a great chance to mingle with locals. There's also live music on Friday and Saturday nights.

For an authentic English pub experience, head to **The Jolly Drayman English Pub and Restaurant** (Briar Lea Inn, 150 Mayville Rd./ Rte. 2, Bethel, 207/824-4717 or 877/311-1299, www.briarleainn.com, 4–9 P.M. Mon.–Thurs., 5–9 P.M. Fri.–Sun., $8–18). Former owners remodeled the space based on a 15th-century English pub and named it for the drayman, the driver of the beer wagon. How good is it? Well, it was noticed by *Bon Appétit* magazine. It's a treat, with fine ales and stouts, and an internationally flavored menu that includes pub-style favorites such as Thatcher's shepherd's pie and bangers-and-mash along with a few surprises, such as Mrs. Balbir Singh's Indian korma and beef Vindaloo. There are sandwiches, salads, soups, and a children's menu too. On Mondays, its serves a burger with fries for $5; Wednesdays are trivia nights, with great prizes; and Thursdays feature all-you-can-eat fish-and-chips with live music.

Ethnic Fare

Cafe DiCocoa (125 Main St., Bethel, 207/824-5282, www.cafedicocoa.com, entrées $45) is open from 6:45 P.M. Saturday evenings during winter for "Gentle Dining," a candlelight-dinner experience during ski season. The five-course fixed-price dinner (BYOB) is by reservation only and features an internationally inspired menu. About once a month during winter, the restaurant also hosts Tasting Workshops or cooking classes ($29). The 2.5-hour evening workshops include an overview of the history and culture of the featured region, explanations of ingredients, cooking demonstrations, and plentiful samples. The restaurant's name is cleverly derived from that of co-owner Cathy diCocco.

It's hard to believe, but you can even get authentic—and truly delicious—Japanese and Korean food in Bethel. **Cho Sun** (141 Main St., Bethel, 207/824-7370, www.chosunrestaurant.com, 5 P.M.–close daily, entrées $18–25) is in a lovely New England Victorian house decorated with Asian art and antiques. Sushi is a specialty, but owner Pok Sun Lane's South Korean fare draws on her heritage.

Classic Italian fare is served at **22 Broad Street** (22 Broad St., Bethel, 207/824-3496, www.gideonhastingshouse.com, 5 P.M.–close daily, $16–25), located in the Greek Revival–style 1848 Gideon Hastings House across from the Bethel Inn. Choices include *gnocchi con prosciutto e funghi, lasagne di mia madre,* and *bistecca di tonno con eperone rosso salsa.*

Casual and Fine Dining

For an upscale dining experience, head to **The Sudbury Inn** (151 Main St., Bethel, 207/824-2174 or 800/395-7837, www.sudbury-inn.com, 5:30–9 P.M. Tues.–Sun.), a warmly retrofitted 1873 Victorian inn with several separate dining areas. Entrées range $18–32 (more if you order lobster), but there's no surcharge for sharing; the rack of lamb and the seafood stew are superb. Reservations are essential, especially on weekends and holidays.

The dining room at **The Bethel Inn** (on the common, Bethel, 207/824-2175, www.bethelinn.com) is open to nonguests for breakfast (7:30–9:30 A.M. Mon.–Fri. and 7–10 A.M. Sat.–Sun. holidays) and dinner (5:30–8:45 P.M. daily). The dining rooms overlook the golf course to the mountains beyond. The continental menu includes duck, tenderloin, and lobster, with entrées ranging $19–26. Ask about the early-seating dinner-for-two special, which includes four courses and a bottle of wine for about $30; reservations are required.

INFORMATION AND SERVICES

The **Bethel Area Chamber of Commerce** (Cross St., Bethel, 207/824-2282 or 800/442-5826, www.bethelmaine.com) has public restrooms. An excellent online planning tool for the region is www.westernmaine.org.

GETTING AROUND

The free **Bethel Explorer** (www.rostay.com/mountainexplorerbus.htm)bus service operates between Bethel and Sunday River. It runs 6:30–1 A.M. weekends Thanksgiving–mid-December and then daily mid-December–early April (but check the schedule).

At Sunday River, the free **Sunday River Trolley** (207/824-3000) circulates throughout the resort, operating weekends Thanksgiving–Christmas and then daily Christmas–early April. It runs on a 30-minute cycle, 8 A.M.–1 A.M. weekdays and 7 A.M.–1 A.M. weekends and holidays.

Oxford Hills

WESTERN LAKES

Sandwiched between the Lewiston-Auburn area and the Bethel area, with Sebago and Long Lakes off to the south, the Oxford Hills region centers on **Norway** and **South Paris.** The town of Norway shares the banks of the Little Androscoggin River with the community of South Paris, the major commercial center for the town of Paris.

From here it gets really complicated, although it's unlikely to affect a visitor. Oxford County's official seat is Paris, but all the relevant county offices are in South Paris. Next, throw into the mix the town of West Paris, which is in fact mostly *north* of Paris and South Paris. Within the boundaries of West Paris is the hamlet of North Paris. Fortunately, there's no East Paris, but there is the tiny enclave of **Paris Hill,** a pocket paradise many people never discover.

West Paris gained its own identity when it separated from Paris in 1957, but its traditions go way back. The Pequawket Indian princess Mollyockett, celebrated hereabouts as a healer, supposedly buried a golden treasure under a suspended animal trap, hence the name of Trap Corner for the junction of Routes 26 and 219 in West Paris. No such cache has been uncovered.

More recent traditions in West Paris come from Finland, home of many 19th- and early-20th-century immigrants who gravitated to a new life in this area.

Norway, fortunately, is far less complicated. The name, incidentally, comes not from Europe or Norwegian settlers but rather from a variation on a Native American word for waterfalls—cascades on the town's Pennesseewassee (PEN-a-see-WAH-see) Lake (called Norway Lake locally), which powered 19th-century mills. European settlement began in 1786. Norway's downtown National Historic District is slowly being revitalized.

Norway was the birthplace of C. A. Stephens (1844–1931), who wrote weekly stories for a 19th-century boys' magazine, *Youth's Companion,* for 55 years. Colorfully reflective of rural Maine life, the entertaining tales were collected in *Stories from the Old Squire's Farm,* published in 1995. Norway was known as the "Snowshoe Capital of the World" during the early 20th-century, when snowshoes made locally by Mellie Dunham were used on the 1909 Peary expedition to the North Pole. The multitalented Dunham also earned fame as one of the nation's top fiddlers.

Waterford is a must-see, especially the National Historic District known as Waterford Flat or Flats, with classic homes and tree-lined streets alongside Keoka Lake in the shadow of Mount Tire'm. It's a 19th-century village frozen in time. Visit during foliage season, and you may never leave.

SIGHTS
◖ Paris Hill

On Route 26, just beyond the northern edge of South Paris, a sign on the right marks one end of Paris Hill Road, a four-mile loop that reconnects farther along with Route 26. As you head uphill, past an old cemetery, you'll arrive at a Brigadoon-like enclave of elegant 18th- and 19th-century homes—a National Historic District with dramatic views off to the White Mountains and the lakes below. The centerpiece of the road is Paris Hill Common, a pristine park in front of the birthplace of former Vice President Hannibal Hamlin (1809–1891), which is not open to the public. South of the green stands the **Hamlin Memorial Library** (207/743-2980, www.hamlin.lib.me.us), the only Paris Hill building open to the public, where you can bone up on the history of this pocket paradise. Visit the library's website to download a copy of the Paris Hill walking tour.

Most children (and adults) get a kick out of entering a public library that was once a town jail. This one, built in 1822, held as many as 30 prisoners until 1896. Three prisoners somehow escaped in the 1830s, abandoning one of their pals stuck in the wall opening they had created. In 1902, the jail became the library, retaining the telltale signs of jail-bar hinges in the granite walls. Admission is free to the library's upper-level museum section, but donations are welcome. The library has no heat, so be sure to dress warmly if you're here early or late in the season. Hours vary with the seasons.

If you're in the area on the first December weekend in an even-numbered year, inquire about the **Biennial Holiday House Tour**, when a dozen of these elegant homes, decorated exquisitely for Christmas, are open to the public, all to benefit the Paris Hill Community Club.

Finnish-American Heritage Center

In the early 20th century, hundreds of Finnish immigrants moved to Maine's Oxford Hills, and the center (8 Maple St., West Paris, ww.mainefinns.org) relates their story. The building, which began life as a hotel before being converted to a boarding house for immigrant Finnish men, then later an American Legion Post, is open to visitors 2–4 P.M. Sunday July–August. Inside are displays, a library, and a gift shop. The center also presents occasional cultural events, which are promoted in local papers.

McLaughlin Garden

In 1997, a little miracle happened in South Paris. For more than 60 years, Bernard McLaughlin had lovingly tended his two-acre perennial garden alongside Route 26, eventually surrounded by commercial development, and he'd always welcomed the public into his floral oasis. In 1995, at the age of 98, McLaughlin died, stipulating in his will that the property be sold. Eager developers eyed it, but loyal flower fans dug in their heels, captured media attention, created a nonprofit foundation, and managed to buy the property—the beginning of the little miracle. The McLaughlin Garden (97 Main St., South Paris, 207/743-8820, www.mclaughlingarden.org, 10 A.M.–5 P.M. daily May–late Oct., free) lives on, with its 98 varieties of lilacs along with lilies and irises and so much more. The garden's main paths are wheelchair-accessible. Check the website for special events and programs. A gift shop in the house carries gardening items and high-end crafts and gifts, mostly Maine-made. A café may be operating on the premises.

Snow Falls

A 300-foot gorge on the Little Androscoggin River is the eye-catching centerpiece of Snow Falls rest area, an easy-off, easy-on roadside park where you can commandeer a table alongside the waterfall. What better place for a relaxing picnic? There are no grills but some sheltered tables. Trucks whiz by on the highway, but the noise of the water usually drowns them out. The rest area is on Route 26, about six miles north of the center of South Paris.

Downtown Norway

After most of downtown Norway burned during the Great Fire of 1894, it was rebuilt in brick and wood, reflecting the Victorian era's considerable embellishments. The Maine Historic Preservation Commission considers the downtown, now a National Historic District, one of the state's best examples of period architecture. It's currently undergoing a two-steps-forward, one-step-back Renaissance, with artists and entrepreneurs breathing new life into vacant storefronts and empty buildings. A walking tour guide ($2) detailing the history of many buildings is available from

The Maine Historic Preservation Commission considers downtown Norway one of the state's best examples of period architecture.

Books N' Things on Main Street; for a sampling, visit www.norwaydowntown.org.

RECREATION

The most popular Oxford Hills hikes are particularly family-friendly—no killer climbs or even major ascents, no bushwhacking, just darned good exercise and some worthwhile views. July–mid-August, don't be surprised to encounter clusters of summer campers, since camp counselors all over this region regularly gather up their kids and take them out on the trail or paddling the ponds. If you're spending more than a day hiking in this area, pick up a copy at bookstores and gift shops of *Hikes in and around Maine's Lake Region* by Marita Wiser; it's the best available advice on this area.

Hiking

It's hard to resist a hike up **Mount Tire'm** (1,104 feet)—if only to disprove its name. Actually, it's supposedly a convolution of a Native American name. The only steep section is at the beginning, after the memorial marker dedicated to 19th-century Waterfordite Daniel Brown, for whom the unblazed trail is named. Allow an hour or so for the 1.5-mile round-trip, especially if you're carrying a picnic. Allow time on the summit ledges to take in the views—all the way to Sebago on a clear day. From downtown Waterford (Rte. 35), take Plummer Hill Road about 300 feet beyond the community center. The trailhead is on the west side of the road; watch for the marker.

Straddling the Paris-Buckfield-Hebron town boundaries, the half-mile **Streaked Mountain** trail (pronounced STREAK-ed) climbs 800 feet, often steeply, to an expansive 1,770-foot summit with communications towers and vistas as far as Mount Washington. Pack a picnic. If you're here in early August, take along a small pail to collect wild blueberries. Late September–early October, it's indescribable, but remember to wear a hunter-orange hat or vest once hunting season has started—or tackle the trail on a Sunday, when there's no hunting. Allow about 1.5 hours for the one-mile round-trip, especially

WESTERN LAKES

if you're picnicking and blueberry-picking. To reach the trailhead from South Paris, take Route 117 west to Streaked Mountain Road, on the right (south); turn and go about 0.5 miles. Park well off the road. (You can also climb Streaked from the east, but it's a much longer hike that requires waterproof footwear.)

Golf

At nine-hole **Paris Hill Country Club** (355 Paris Hill Rd., Paris, 207/743-2371), founded in 1899, you'll find a low-key atmosphere, reasonable greens fees, cart rentals, and a snack bar. No tee times are needed. The rectangular course has all straight shots; the challenges come from slopes and unexpected traps.

It's not just golfers who patronize the nine-hole **Norway Country Club** (Lake Rd./Rte. 118, Norway, 207/743-9840); this is a popular spot to have lunch or kick back on the club porch. The mountain-lake scenery, especially in the fall, is awesome. Starting times are not required; it's first-come, first-served. Established in 1929, the club is a mile west of Route 117.

Spectator Sports

If you're partial to guerrilla warfare on wheels, the place to be is **Oxford Plains Speedway** (Rte. 26, Oxford, 207/539-8865, www.oxfordplains.com), Maine's center for stock-car racing. Late April–mid-September, souped-up high-performance vehicles careen around the track in pursuit of substantial monetary prizes. Almost all races begin at 6:30 P.M.

Sleigh Rides

Put on your winter warmies, then snuggle under a lap blanked on a 40-minute sleigh ride with **High View Farm** (4 Leander Harmon Rd., Harrison, 207/596-1601, www.high-view-farm.com, $50 per sleigh plus $5 pp, $70 minimum). Add a stop in the woods for a bonfire with roast marshmallows and hot chocolate for $35. Rides are offered 11 A.M.–7 P.M., are private, and are by reservation only. A small shop sells works by local artisans and farm-made products.

ENTERTAINMENT

Marcel Marceau wannabes come to study at the nationally famed **Celebration Barn Theater** (190 Stock Farm Rd., South Paris, 207/743-8452, www.celebrationbarn.com), established in 1972 by the late mime master Tony Montanaro. Mime, juggling, dance, clowning, storytelling, and improv comedy performances are open to the public in the 125-seat barn at 8 P.M. most Saturdays June–August. Reservations are required. Ticket prices range $10–20. Pack a picnic supper and arrive early. The theater also offers residential workshops for aspiring mimes, storytellers, comedians, and the like. Check the website for details. The theater (signposted) is just off Route 117.

Another place to catch a wide variety of shows is Michael Miclon's **Oddfellow Theater** (Rte. 117, Buckfield, 207/336-3306, www.oddfellow.com).

FESTIVALS AND EVENTS

Wall-to-wall paintings are for sale along Main Street in downtown Norway for the **Norway Arts Festival** (www.norwayartsfestival.org), the second Saturday in July, in which more than 100 artists participate. There's also street entertainment, a triathlon, and other events.

Founders' Day (www.hamlin.lib.me.us) brings craft and antiques exhibits, music, and an antique-car open house on Paris Hill Common in Paris Hill the third Saturday in July. A special highlight is a one-day showing of Robert and Sandra Bahre's collection of more than 60 vehicles, including Packards, Duesenbergs, Stutz Bearcats, and more.

The name of North Waterford's **World's Fair** (www.waterfordworldsfair.org) seems sort of cheeky for this three-day country medley of agricultural events, egg-throwing contests, talent show, live music, dancing, and more in mid July.

The family-oriented four-day agricultural **Oxford County Fair,** "The Horse-Powered Fair," held in mid-September, features 4-H exhibits, a beauty pageant, a pig scramble, live entertainment, an apple-pie contest, and plenty of crafts and food booths at the Oxford County Fairgrounds (www.oxfordcountyfair.com).

SHOPPING
Books
Books-N-Things (430 Main St., Norway, 207/743-7197, www.bntnorway.com) is one of those full-service bookstores that inspires you to buy more than you ever planned. There's an excellent children's section, plentiful toys, and even some specialty foods.

Peruse through more than 13,000 new, used, and out-of-print books as well as artwork at **The Maine Bookhouse** (1545 Main St./Rte. 26, Oxford, 207/743-9300, www.themaine-bookhouse.com).

Galleries and Gifts
A number of area galleries participate in a First Friday art tour. A gallery guide can be downloaded from www.frostfarmgallery.com/local-galleryguide.html.

The Western Maine Art Group sponsors the seasonal **Lajos Matolcsy Arts Center** (480 Main St., Norway, 207/739-6161, www.thewmag.org), which shows the work of member artists. Check the group's website for info on classes and other events.

Frost Farm Gallery (27 Pikes Hill, Norway, 207/743-8041, www.frostfarmgallery.com) hosts rotating exhibits.

MerMan Metal Sculpture and **Painted Mermaid** (6 Briggs Ave., South Paris, 207/515-1089, www.mermanmetal.com, www.painted-mermaid.com) is a dual find, with paintings and sculptures.

Just beyond the Celebration Barn Theater, **Christian Ridge Pottery** (210 Stock Farm Rd., South Paris, 207/743-8419, www.applebaker.com) produces functional ceramic designs and objets d'art, including a trademarked apple baker and a bagel cutter. You can see the work in progress at the shop.

It's hard to resist inhaling deeply upon entering **Maine Balsam Fir Products** (16 Morse Hill Rd., West Paris, 800/522-5726, www.mainebalsam.com), filled with balsam pillows, neck rolls, draft stoppers, trivets, and sachets along with

oil, soap, clothing, quilts, and more, all jammed in a one-room shop adjacent to where the balsam products are made. Tours are offered when the schedule permits; just ask.

ACCOMMODATIONS
Sumner
For a complete change of pace, back in time and back of beyond **Morrill Farm Bed and Breakfast** (85 Morrill Farm Rd., Sumner, 207/388-2059, www.morrillfarmbnb.com, $75 d, $65 s) is a late-18th-century farm with three unfussy second-floor guest rooms sharing one bath. On the 217-acre working farm are nature and cross-country skiing trails, river fishing, and a menagerie of domestic farm animals. Pets are kenneled on-site for $15 per day. The farm is north and east of Norway–South Paris, a mile from Route 219 (West Sumner Rd.). French is spoken.

South Paris
The 200-year-old expanded Cape that now houses the **King's Hill Inn** (56 King Hill Rd., South Paris, 207/744-0204, www.kingshillinn.com, $95–165) was the birthplace of Horatio King, who served as postmaster general under President Buchanan. Inside are three guest rooms and three suites, all with a range of comfortable touches, some with a gas stove, a microwave, and a dining area, a deck entrance, a whirlpool tub, or antiques. The quiet, rural location is convenient to hiking trails and the Celebration Barn Theatre. Rates include an especially bountiful breakfast.

Waterford
Waterford—that lovely little enclave flanked by Norway–South Paris, Bridgton-Naples, and the Lovells—has a couple of fine places to put your head.

Barbara Vanderzanden's traditionally elegant **Waterford Inne** (258 Chadbourne Rd., Waterford, 207/583-4037, www.waterfordinne.com, $120–195), an antiques-filled 19th-century farmhouse on 25 open and wooded acres, is a real treasure. Rooms are bright and airy; some have woodstoves and porches. A delicious breakfast is included; a four-course dinner is available for $40. Children are welcome, and pets are allowed for $15 extra. The inn is close to East Waterford, 0.5 miles west of Route 37. It's open year-round.

Jim and Christie Kerrigan's **((Bear Mountain Inn** (Rte. 35, South Waterford, 207/583-4404, www.bearmtninn.com), a beautifully updated 1820s B&B overlooking Bear Pond (it's really a lake), is one of those places that's hard to leave, especially after you settle in on the pond-view terrace or the beach. On the premises are boats, docks, hammocks, a lake-view hot tub, picnic tables and a barbecue, even trails up Bear and Hawk Mountains. Five bear-themed guest rooms with private and shared baths as well as Wi-Fi, go for $120–195 d; luxury and family suites are $240–325, including breakfast. The self-contained Sugar Bear cottage, with fireplace and kitchenette, is pet-friendly. A rental house that sleeps eight is $600. Also included are a stocked guest fridge, a TV with a video player and a video library, and, well, just about anything you might desire, within reason.

Quilt lovers will think they've arrived in heaven at the **Kedarburn Inn** (Rte. 35, Waterford, 207/583-6182 or 866/583-6182, www.kedarburn.com, $80–135), in an 1858 streamside home where Margaret Gibson also has Kedar Craft, a quilt and fabric shop filled with her handmade quilts and stocked with quilters' supplies. Of course, the house is filled with quilts, and Margaret also offers quilters' retreat weekends. Walk down the road to town and Lake Keoka. There are seven guest rooms, two of which share a bath. Rates include a continental breakfast.

FOOD

Restaurant hours noted are for peak season but are subject to change. It's always wise to call ahead.

Local Flavors

Many people flock to **The Lake Store** (14 Waterford Rd./Rte. 118 at Rte. 117, Norway Lake, Norway, 207/743-6562, 6 A.M.–9 P.M.

daily) just to check out the crazy collection of Coca-Cola memorabilia, but you can also load up with picnic fixings, pizza, liquor, groceries, and videos.

Homemade soups, salads, and daily specials, occasional concerts and wine tastings, free Wi-Fi, and the area's best coffee make **Café Nomad** (450 Main St., Norway, 207/739-2249, www.cafenomad.com, 7 A.M.–4 P.M. Mon.–Fri., 9 A.M.–3 P.M. Sat.) an especially popular local spot.

A bright spot in the lackluster hubbub on the fast-food strip is **Rising Sun Cafe and Bakery** (130 Main St./Rte. 26, South Paris, 207/743-7046, 6 A.M.–4 P.M. Tues.–Fri., 6 A.M.–2 P.M. Sat.), a local fave for baked goods, soups, salads, and sandwiches.

"Everything Shirley makes is good," a regular told me as I debated between the scones, cookies, muffins, soups, pies, beans, and other homemade treats at **Hungry Hollow Country Store** (28 Bethel Rd./Rte. 26, West Paris, 207/674-3012, 7 A.M.–5:30 P.M. Mon.–Sat., 10 A.M.–5:30 P.M. Sun.).

Local produce, honey, organic meat, perennials, preserves, syrup, cheese, and baked goods are all part of the stock at **Norway Farmers Market,** which sets up downtown at 15 Whiteman Street in the Fare Share parking lot, 2–6 P.M. Thursday late May–October.

If you're a fan of homemade doughnuts, seek out **Beep's Bakery** (1122 Main St./Rte. 219, Sumner, 207/388-2741, www.beepsbakery.com, 7:30 A.M.–5 P.M. Mon.–Fri., 7:30 A.M.–2 P.M. Sat.), where Glenn Hinckley makes not only doughnuts but muffins, pies, breads, and other goodies from scratch using primarily natural and locally sourced ingredients.

For exquisite pastries, cakes, tarts, and pies, slip into **Marta's Bakery** (684 Vallen Rd./Rte. 35, North Waterford, 207/583-2250, www.martasbakery.com), where Prague-born Marta Cistecky opened her bakery-café after a career as a baker in Boston.

Casual Dining

An unassuming exterior on a busy in-town thoroughfare camouflages the pleasant, if

WESTERN LAKES

dated, interior at **Maurice Restaurant** (109 Main St./Rte. 26, South Paris, 207/743-2532, www.mauricerestaurant.com, 11 A.M.–1:30 P.M. Tues.–Fri., 11 A.M.–2 P.M. Sun., dinner 4:30–8:30 P.M. daily, $14–24). A veteran in this area, the popular restaurant serves creditable French cuisine. Reservations are a good idea, especially on weekends.

By reservation, Barbara Vanderzanden will prepare a four-course dinner for guests and nonguests at the peaceful ◀ **Waterford Inne** (258 Chadbourne Rd., Waterford, 207/583-4037, www.waterfordinne.com, no credit cards). The leisurely meal is $40

pp; spring for it, as she does a wonderful job. BYOB.

INFORMATION AND SERVICES

The **Oxford Hills Chamber of Commerce** (4 Western Ave., South Paris, 207/743-2281, www.oxfordhillsmaine.com) produces an annual magazine that's actually an interesting read and far less promotional than the usual CC material.

Check out **Norway Memorial Library** (258 Main St., Norway, 207/743-5309, www.norway.lib.me.us).

Fryeburg Area

Fryeburg, a crossroads community on busy Route 302, is best known as the funnel to and from the factory outlets, hiking trails, and ski slopes of New Hampshire's North Conway and the White Mountains. Except during early October's annual extravaganza, the giant Fryeburg Fair, Fryeburg seldom ends up on anyone's itinerary. Too bad: The mountain-ringed community has lots of charm, historic homes, the flavor of rural life, and access to miles of Saco River canoeing waters.

Incorporated in 1763, Fryeburg is Oxford County's oldest town; even earlier it was known as Pequawket, an Indian settlement and trading post—until skirmishes with white settlers routed the Native Americans in 1725 during Dummer's War (also known as Lovewell's War). Casualties were heavy on both sides; Lovewell and the Pequawket chief were among the fatalities.

In 1792, Fryeburg Academy, a private school on Main Street, was chartered; the school's Webster Hall is named after famed statesman Daniel Webster, whose undistinguished teaching career at the school began and ended in 1802. Among the students at the time was Rufus Porter, who later gained renown as a muralist, inventor, and founder of *Scientific American* magazine. Today the school is one of

a handful of private academies in Maine that provide public secondary education, a uniquely successful private-public partnership.

Just north of Fryeburg is the town of **Lovell,** with three hamlets—known collectively as the Lovells—strung along Route 5, on the east side of gorgeous Kezar Lake. Anyone who has discovered Kezar Lake yearns to keep it a secret, but the word is out. The mountain-rimmed lake is too beautiful.

SIGHTS
Hemlock Covered Bridge

The 116-foot-long **Hemlock Bridge,** built in 1857 over the "Old Saco," or "Old Course," a former channel of the Saco River, is in the hamlet of East Fryeburg, just west of Kezar Pond. The best time to visit is July–October; mud or snow can prevent car access in other months, and June is buggy. From the Route 5/302 junction in Fryeburg, take Route 302 east 5.5 miles to Hemlock Bridge Road. Turn left (north) and go about three miles on a paved and then unpaved road to the bridge. Or paddle under the bridge on a detour from canoeing on the Saco River.

Hopalong Cassidy Memorabilia

When he died in 1956, longtime Fryeburg resident Clarence Mulford, author of the Hopalong

Cassidy books, left his extensive collection of Western Americana, including models, copies of his books, research materials, and more, along with enough money to display them, to the **Fryeburg Public Library** (98 Main St., Fryeburg, 207/935-2731, www.fryeburgmaine.org/library.html, 8 A.M.–5 P.M. Mon.–Thurs., 9 A.M.–noon Sat.).

ENTERTAINMENT

Anything happening in Bethel and vicinity, Oxford Hills, or Sebago and Long Lakes is also within easy reach of the Fryeburg area, especially in the daytime.

The **Leura Hill Eastman Performing Arts Center** (Fryeburg Academy, Fryeburg, 207/935-9232, www.fryeburgacademy.org) is a year-round venue that attracts regional and national entertainers. It's also the site of Monday Night at the Movies and Wednesday Night at the Opera series.

Singer-songwriter Carol Noonan has created a phenomenal 200-seat performing arts center on her hilltop farm. **Stone Mountain Arts Center** (695 Dug Way Rd., Brownfield, 866/227-6523, www.stonemountainartscenter.com) brings in nationally renowned performers such as Leo Kottke, The Capitol Steps, Livingston Taylor, Richie Havens, and Paula Poundstone, to name a few. The calendar is jam-packed. All events take place in the barn, and preshow dinners, pizzas, and salads ($13–18) are available by reservation. On the third Tuesday of most months, Stone Mountain offers a Rooster Revue, a luncheon variety show ($40, including lunch, the show, tip, and tax). Credit cards are taken for reservations, but cash or checks are required for actual payment. Be sure to print out a copy of the directions—this place is in the boonies.

The Lovell Brick Church for the Performing Arts (www.lovellbrickchurch.org) is the site of a summer entertainment series, with monthly performances May–September.

In summer, **outdoor concerts** are held Tuesday nights at the gazebo (or in the fire barn, if it's raining). During July, The **International Musical Arts Institute** (http:// imaifestival.org) presents concerts in Fryeburg Academy's Bion Cram Library.

EVENTS

The big event in these parts is the **Fryeburg Fair,** the last country fair of the season held the first week of October, sometimes including a few days in September. It's Maine's largest agricultural fair and an annual event since 1851. A parade, a carnival, craft demonstrations and exhibits, harness racing, pig scrambles, children's activities, ox pulling, and live entertainment are all here, as are plenty of food booths (it's sometimes called the "Fried-burg" Fair). More than 300,000 turn out for eight days of festivities, so expect traffic congestion. The fair runs Sunday–Sunday, and the busiest day is Saturday. No dogs are allowed on the 180-acre site. Spectacular fall foliage and mountain scenery just add to the appeal. Find it at the Fryeburg Fairgrounds (officially the West Oxford Agricultural Society Fairgrounds) on Route 5 in Fryeburg.

SHOPPING

It's hard to believe that the jewelry and crafts inside the **Harvest Gold Gallery** (Rte. 5, Center Lovell, 207/925-6502, www.harvest-goldgallery.com) are more stunning than the setting overlooking Kezar Lake. Magnificent gold jewelry, much of it accented with Maine gemstones, is made on the premises. Also here is a very well-chosen selection of high-end crafts, with an emphasis on fine glasswork. It's definitely not a place to bring young kids.

Less high-end but no lower in quality are the crafts at **Weston's** (48 River St./Rte. 113 N., Fryeburg, 207/935-2567, www.westons-farm.com). The mostly locally made selection includes baskets, bears, pillows, candles, and more.

RECREATION
Hiking

The easiest and therefore busiest trail in the area is the 20-minute stroll up **Jockey Cap,** named for a cantilevered ledge that has long since disappeared. At the summit, with a

WESTERN LAKES

360-degree view of lakes and mountains, is a monument to Admiral Robert Peary, the Arctic explorer who once lived in Fryeburg. The metal edge of the monument is a handy cheat sheet with profiles and names of all the mountains you're looking at—more than four dozen of them. The trail is fine for kids, but keep a close eye on the littlest ones; the drop-off is perilous on the south side. Jockey Cap is also popular with rock climbers and boulder mavens. The trailhead is on Route 302, about a mile east of downtown Fryeburg, on the left between the Jockey Cap Country Store and the Jockey Cap Motel. And here's a bit of trivia: Jockey Cap was the site of Maine's first ski tow.

Allow about half an hour to reach the summit of **Sabattus Mountain** in Lovell, north of Fryeburg. This is an especially good family hike, easy and short enough for small children. Carry a picnic and enjoy the views at the top—on the ledges of the more open second summit. You'll see the White Mountains,

Pleasant Mountain, and skinny Kezar Lake; in fall it's fabulous. To reach the trailhead from Fryeburg, take Route 5 North to Center Lovell. About 0.8 miles after the junction of Routes 5 and 5A, turn right onto Sabattus Road. Go about 1.6 miles, bearing right at the fork onto an unpaved road. Continue another 0.5 miles to a parking area on the left; the trailhead is across the road. The round-trip hike is about 1.5 miles.

Other good hikes in this area are **Mount Tom** (easy, about 2.5 hours round-trip), just east of Fryeburg; **Burnt Meadow Mountain** (moderately difficult, about four hours round-trip to the north peak, with good views of the Presidential Range), near Brownfield; and **Mount Cutler** (moderately difficult, about two hours round-trip), near Hiram.

Water Sports

Fryeburg has two public beaches that double as canoe put-ins. **Weston's Beach** (River St./ Rte. 5 N., just off Rte. 302) is a swath of sand

© TOM NANGLE

Weston's Beach, on the Saco River in Fryeburg, is a local favorite for sunning, sand castle building, and canoe launching.

extending into the Saco River that gets wider as the summer progresses and the river level drops. Another sand beach is adjacent to **Canal Bridge Campground,** just off Route 5 heading toward Lovell.

CANOEING

The **Saco River,** whose headwaters are in Crawford Notch, New Hampshire, meanders 84 miles from the Maine border at Fryeburg to the ocean at Saco and Biddeford. Its many miles of flat water, with intermittent sandbars and a few portages, make it wonderful for canoeing, camping, and swimming, but there's the rub: The summer weekend scene on the 35-mile western Maine stretch sometimes looks like bumper boats at Disneyland, especially weekends and holidays, and it can be quite raucous—with large parties towing canoes filled with beer. Aim for midweek or late September–early October, when the foliage is spectacular, the current is slower, noise levels are lower, and the crowds are busy elsewhere. For a relaxing trip, figure about two mph and you can do the Fryeburg-to-Hiram segment with two overnight stops, including a couple of interesting side-trip paddles to Hemlock Bridge, Pleasant Pond, and Lovewell's Pond. If you put in at Swan's Falls in Fryeburg (www .sacorivercouncil.org, parking $8–10 per day), you won't have to deal with portages between there and Hiram. For multiday trips, you'll need to get a **fire permit** (free; available at some local stores), or stay at one of the commercial campgrounds.

Saco River Canoe and Kayak (Rte. 5, Fryeburg, 207/935-2369, www.sacorivercanoe .com), close to the convenient put-in at Swan's Falls, rents canoes and tandem kayaks ($45 per day Fri.–Sun. July–Aug., $30 midweek and off-season) and provides delivery and pickup service along a 50-mile stretch of the Saco River. Shuttle costs range $6–16 for two canoes (depending on location). Safety-conscious owners Fred and Prudy Westerberg know their turf—they've been in the biz since the 1970s—and provide helpful advice for planning short and extended canoe trips.

If crowds on the Saco become a bit much, head east or north with your canoe or kayak to the area's lakes and ponds, even to **Brownfield Bog.** Prime canoeing spots are **Lovewell Pond** and **Kezar Pond** in Fryeburg; **Kezar Lake** in Lovell; and **Virginia Lake** in Stoneham. A north wind kicks up on Kezar Lake, so stay close to shore. The most spectacular is mile-long Virginia Lake, nudged up against the White Mountain National Forest. To see a house on the wooded shoreline is a rarity. The rough access road (off Rte. 5 between North Lovell and East Stoneham) is a mechanic's delight, but persevere; tranquility lies ahead.

The best way to see beautiful Kezar Lake is by renting a boat from **Kezar Lake Marina** (219 W. Lovell Rd., Lovell, 207/925-3000, www.kezarlake.com). Canoes and kayaks rent for $10 per hour or $25 per day. A 13-foot Boston Whaler is $50 per half-day, $90 for a full day.

Winter Sports
SNOWMOBILING
More than 600 miles of groomed trails are accessible from Fryeburg. For information and sled rental, try **Fryeburg Snowmobile Rentals** (103 Main St./Rte. 302, Fryeburg, 207/935-1220 or 800/458-1838, www.sledandbed.com), which rents environmentally friendly snow machines. Rates begin around $130 for a half-day. Full clothing, including boots, pants, jacket, and gloves, is $25. A two-hour guided tour up Black Cap Mountain is $95 s, $125 d.

ACCOMMODATIONS
If you're planning to be in the area during the Fryeburg Fair, you'll need to reserve beds or campsites months ahead, in some cases a year in advance; don't procrastinate.

Bed-and-Breakfasts
⬛ The Oxford House Inn (548 Main St./Rte. 302, Fryeburg, 207/935-3442 or 800/261-7206, www.oxfordhouseinn.com, $119–199 d) is better known for its dining, but upstairs are four spacious and inviting guest rooms, each

The Oxford House Inn, in downtown Fryeburg, is renowned for its dining room.

© TOM NANGLE

WESTERN LAKES

with a TV, air-conditioning, and Wi-Fi. Rear rooms have bucolic views over the Saco River Valley farmlands to the White Mountains. Breakfasts, served in the mountain-view porch–dining room, are every bit as creative as the inn's dinner menus.

The comments in one of the in-room guest books say everything you need to know about **Peace With-Inn** (254 W. Fryeburg Rd./Rte. 113 N., Fryeburg, 207/935-7363 or 877/935-7322, www.peacewithinn.com, $115–185): "peaceful," "cozy," "restorative." The truly rambling circa-1750 farmhouse on the winding road that climbs from the Saco River Valley farmlands up through Evans Notch is an ideal base for exploring the notch or other parts of the White Mountain National Forest or to retreat to after a shopping foray into nearby North Conway, New Hampshire. Each of the five guest rooms has air-conditioning and a TV, and a few have big whirlpool tubs. There's Wi-Fi, and for true bliss, a massage room with sauna. A living room, a den, a book nook, a games room, a porch, and a patio provide

plenty of room to spread out. A full breakfast is served family-style. The inn's owners live out of state but employ daytime innkeepers and resident caretakers. Guests who do not arrive by a specified time are instructed how to find their room.

Cottage Colony

The *New York Times* once headlined a story on **Quisisana** (42 Quisisana Dr., Center Lovell, 207/925-3500, www.quisisanaresort .com, no credit cards) as "Where Mozart Goes on Vacation." Amen. By day, the staff at this elegantly rustic 47-acre retreat masquerade as waiters and waitresses, chambermaids, boat crew, and kitchen help; each night, presto, they're the stars of musical performances worthy of Broadway and concert-hall ticket prices. Since 1947 it has been like this at "Quisi"—with staff recruited from the nation's best conservatories. Veteran managers literally attuned to guests' needs keep it all working smoothly.

The frosting on all this culture is the

setting—a beautifully landscaped pine grove on the shores of sandy-bottomed Kezar Lake, looking off to the White Mountains and dramatic sunsets. No wonder that reservations for the 38 neat white cottages are hard to come by. The New York–heavy clientele knows to book well ahead, often for the same week, and new generations have followed their parents here. In July–August, lodge rooms are $195–200 pp per night and cottages are $235–245 pp per night, all requiring one week minimum Saturday–Saturday only; rates include meals, musical entertainment, tennis, and nonmotorized boats. Mid-June–July, lower rates and occasionally shorter stays are available. Beer and wine only are available. Quisisana's season begins in mid-June and ends in late August.

Camping

Canoeing is the major focus at **Woodland Acres Campground** (Rte. 160, Brownfield, 207/935-2529, www.woodlandacres.com), with a 100-canoe fleet available for rent ($55 per day includes shuttle service to one location; reduced rates for additional days). The staff makes it all very convenient, even suggesting more than half a dozen daylong and multiday canoe trips for skill levels from beginner to expert. This well-maintained campground on the Saco River has 109 wooded tent and RV sites ($32–40 per family; two-night minimum on weekends). Riverfront sites are the best, but you'll need to stay a week in July–August unless you luck out with a cancellation. Facilities include a rec hall, a beach, a camp store, and free hot showers. Leashed pets are allowed ($2.50 per day). From Fryeburg, take Route 5/13 southeast to Route 160; turn left (north) and go a mile to the campground.

Also in Brownfield, and also geared toward canoeists, is **River Run** (Rte. 160, Brownfield, 207/452-2500, www.riverruncanoe.com), with 22 large primitive tent sites ($10 pp, no hookups) on 100-plus acres next to the Saco River's Brownfield Bridge. Canoe rentals and shuttle service are available—canoes run about $21 a day Monday–Thursday, $40 on

weekends and holidays, with the shuttle price about $9–20.

The Saco River Recreational Council maintains rustic **Swans Falls Campground** (198 Swans Falls Rd., Fryeburg, 207/935-3395, www.sacorivercouncil.org, $10 pp) on the Saco River just north of Fryeburg. The wooded grounds have 18 campsites with picnic tables and fire rings. Also here are a small educational facility and a store. Reservation requests, including numbers of people and equipment in your party, dates, and arrival time, are processed starting May 15, and need to be mailed attention of the campground manager. This is a very busy canoe and kayak access point on the Saco River.

FOOD

Restaurant hours noted are for peak season but are subject to change. It's always wise to call ahead.

Local Flavors

Two general stores serve the Lovell area, providing staples and more. The upscale-ish **Center Lovell Store** (Rte. 5, Center Lovell, 207/925-1051, 6 A.M.–7 P.M. Mon.–Thurs., 6 A.M.–8 P.M. Fri.–Sat., 8 A.M.–7 P.M. Sun.) serves pizza and sandwiches and has premade items as well as a full deli and even seating. Simpler is the **Lovell Village Store and Restaurant** (Rte. 5, Lovell, 207/925-1235, 5 A.M.–8 P.M. Mon.–Sat., 6 A.M.–7 P.M. Sun.), which serves breakfast all day.

Weston's Farm, established by the Weston family in 1799 and now operated by the sixth generation, edges the Saco River and is across from Weston's Beach. Stop at **Weston's Farm Stand** (48 River St./Rte. 113 N., Fryeburg, 207/935-2567, www.westonsfarm.com, 9 A.M.–6 P.M. daily mid-Apr.–Dec. 24) for all kinds of picnic and cottage fixings, from fresh produce and local meats to cheese and maple syrup.

Casual Dining

Here's a sleeper: Chef–co-owner and Culinary Institute of America grad Jonathan Spak crafts contemporary American fare with international (especially Asian) accents at **❰ The Oxford House Inn** (548 Main St., Fryeburg, 207/935-3442, www.oxfordhouseinn.com, 5:30–9 P.M. Wed.–Mon. July–mid-Oct., 5:30–9 P.M. Thurs.–Sun. mid-Oct.–June, $10–32). He offers half- and full-plate pastas, bistro plates, and full entrées, making it easy to assemble a meal that fits both your budget and cravings. The four dining rooms appear formal, but this is a casual place; request a table on the glassed-in back porch to watch the sun set behind the White Mountains. Lighter fare is served in the cozy downstairs pub. Dinner reservations are wise, especially July–August and during the Fryeburg Fair.

Fronting on the golf course yet hidden on a back road is a local secret with a big reputation—**Ebenezer's Restaurant and Pub** (44 Allen Rd., off W. Lovell Rd., Lovell, 207/925-3200, www.ebenezerspub.net, noon–9 P.M. daily summer, shorter hours off-season). Most folks come for the Belgian beer selection—easily the best in New England, perhaps in the entire country. And if you're not a fan of Belgian brews, there are dozens of other beer choices. Complementing that is good pub fare, burgers, sandwiches, salads, pizzas ($6–12) as well as heartier entrées ($15–20). Dine on the screened-in porch or inside the tavern and bar. Every August, Ebenezer's puts on an extravagant multicourse Belgian dinner with beer pairings as part of its weeklong Belgian Beer Festival.

Innkeeper Janice Sage won the **Center Lovell Inn and Restaurant** (1107 Main St., Center Lovell, 207/925-1575 or 800/777-2698, www.centerlovellinn.com, 6–9 P.M. daily, entrées $25–30) in an essay contest and become a cover story in the *New York Times Magazine.* She has been here since 1993, serving an enthusiastic clientele drawn to the wide-ranging continental menu, which changes weekly. The best tables are on the glassed-in porch, where you can watch the sun slip behind the mountains. Reservations are advised, especially in midsummer. Prefer to tumble into bed after dining? The inn has five second-floor guest rooms with private and shared baths in the 1805 main building, plus five more with private and shared baths in the adjacent Harmon House. Room rates are $119–159 d. The inn and the restaurant are open May–October and December–March.

If you have a hankering for barbecue and good times, the **302 West Smokehouse & Tavern** (636 Main St., Fryeburg, 207/935-3021, 11:30 A.M.–10 P.M. Mon.–Sat., 10 A.M.–10 P.M. Sun., bar until midnight Thurs.–Sat.) delivers on both counts. Big portions of ribs and barbecued entrées run $10–18; burgers, quesadillas, and the like begin around $8. If there's entertainment, plan on a crowd; this place is crazy popular with locals. If the weather's nice, grab a seat on the back deck.

INFORMATION

The **Greater Bridgton Lakes Region Chamber of Commerce** (207/647-3472, www.mainelakeschamber.com) covers Fryeburg.

Cornish

Folded in the foothills of the White Mountains and well off the radar screen of most tourists, Cornish, neighboring Limerick, and Newfield are charming rural towns filled with architectural gems and dotted with antiques shops. Lovely to visit spring through fall, they're especially treasured during foliage season, not only for the leaves but also for the apple harvest. Local historians boast that in the 1850s many of Cornish's splendid homes were moved by oxen from other parts of town to the main drag to be close to the stagecoach route. **Limerick,** which edges Lake Sokokis, provides easy access to **Newfield,** home to an amazing country museum. The Cornish area is convenient to Sebago, Portland, and the Southern Coast.

SIGHTS
Porter Covered Bridge

Just west of Cornish, this lovely bridge linking Oxford and York Counties and the towns of Porter and Parsonsfield spans the Ossipee River. Officially known as the **Parsonsfield-Porter Historical Bridge,** the current 152-foot double span dates from 1859.

Willowbrook Museum Village

Plan a day trip to tiny Newfield, home to the fascinating 19th-century Willowbrook Museum Village (Main St., just north of Rte. 11, Newfield, 207/793-2784, www.willowbrookmuseum.org, 10 a.m.–5 p.m. Thurs.–Mon. late May–mid Oct., $9 adults, $4 ages 6–18, $7.50 over age 64, free under age 6). The museum, created by Don King (not the music guy) and his wife, Pan, comprises 25 buildings listed on the National Register of Historic Places in a country village setting. While you can breeze through in an hour or so, you'll want to linger for half a day. What's to see? Two historical homes, a carriage house, a country store,

© HILARY NANGLE

The old-fashioned general store at Willowbrook Museum Village is stocked with all kinds of fun finds.

a schoolhouse, a magnificently restored carousel, and incredible collections of carriages and sleighs, farm tools, toys, and other curious antiquities. Occasionally there are demonstrations, but for the most part Willowbrook is yours to discover, a snapshot in time. Bring a picnic (or visit the café and ice cream shop) and a camera and soak up the rural history on this incredibly peaceful site.

ENTERTAINMENT AND EVENTS

The **Ossipee Valley Fair** is an old-fashioned four-day agricultural fair with tractor pulling, animal exhibits, live entertainment, food booths, games, and a carnival. It's in South Hiram the second weekend in July.

Every summer, the **Saco River Festival Association** (Parsonfield, 207/625-7116, www.sacoriverfestival.org) sponsors a concert series at the Old Cornish Fairgrounds.

The **Ossipee Valley Music Festival,** a long weekend of bluegrass, fiddling, and acoustical music, takes place in mid-July.

Apple Acres Farm (www.appleacresfarm.com) hosts a **bluegrass festival** in late September.

A great time to visit Cornish is the last Saturday in September, when the annual **Apple Festival** (207/625-7447, www.cornish-maine.org), held in downtown Cornish, celebrates the area's major crop with music, a crafts fair, and even an apple-pie contest. You can overdose all day on apples and stock up for winter, and do it just as fall foliage is starting to appear. For a spectacular panorama of fall colors along the Ossipee and Saco River Valleys, drive up Towles Hill Road (left turn, just west of town).

SHOPPING

Antiques and artisans' shops dominate Cornish's genuinely quaint and walkable downtown. Here's a sampling. **Cornish Trading Company** (19 Main St./Rte. 25, 207/625-8387) is a terrific group antiques shop in the handsome three-story Masonic building. Across the street is **Full Circle Artisan's Gallery** (22 Main St., 207/625-7725), carrying fine craft by Maine artists. For vintage commercial signage and memorabilia, visit **The Smith Co.** (Main St., 207/625-6030). **Village Jewelers** (Main St., 207/625-8958) has a drool-worthy selection of Maine gems. **Evie's Eclectic Collections** (Main St., 207/625-8916) delivers on its name, with merchandise displayed in a beautifully restored mansion. After exhausting the Main Street shops, head up High Street. If you're seeing quilting supplies, don't miss **Barking Rose Quilt Barn** (High St., 207/625-8856). **Cottage Treasures** (47 High Rd., 207/625-2301) specializes in porcelain, glass, and vintage linens. Antiques jumble with junktiques at **Red House Antiques** (53 High Rd., 207/625-8322).

RECREATION

Back Country Excursions (43 Woodward Rd., Parsonfield, 207/625-8189, www.bike-backcountry.com) has 23 miles of dedicated mountain-biking trails for all abilities as well as a technical terrain park for thrill-seekers on an 8,800-acre private recreational and logging preserve. Instruction and guided rides are available. Rates are $60 for a full day with lunch, $50 without lunch, or $30 half-day, which includes access to shower facilities and maps. Bikes rent for $30–45, and a helmet is $5. You also can rent a canoe for paddling local waterways for $20. Camping and lodging are available.

ACCOMMODATIONS

Smack-dab downtown is the delightfully old-fashioned **Cornish Inn** (2 High St., Cornish, 207/625-8501, www.cornishinn.com, $85–145), a three-story gently updated classic with a wraparound porch and an on-site dining room serving dinner. The 16 guest rooms are simple yet comfortable; most have air-conditioning. Rates include a self-serve continental breakfast (available outside your door) that borders on meager; opt for Krista's down the street if you're around on a weekend.

The barn-red **Midway Country Lodging** (712 S. Hiram Rd., Cornish, 207/625-8835, www.mainemidwaylodging.com, $65–99) is a motel-like inn, or maybe an inn-like motel.

Cornish Inn

Country is the theme, and all rooms have air-conditioning, TVs, Wi-Fi, fridges, microwaves, and phones; some have a whirlpool bath, a video player, or a balcony. The outdoor pool has a nice mountain view, and the landscaped grounds even have a fountain.

Here's a budget find: The handsome brick Greek Revival–style **Jeremiah Mason Bed & Breakfast** (40 Main St., Limerick, 207/793-4858, www.jeremiahmasonhouse.com, $50–70), built by a wealthy banker in 1859, retains the elegance of a bygone era. Spacious antiques-accented guest rooms have chandeliers, marble fireplaces, and floor-to-ceiling windows. Rates include a full breakfast; less expensive rooms have half-baths.

FOOD

Restaurant hours noted are for peak season but are subject to change. It's always wise to call ahead.

Fresh and seasonal are the hallmarks at the **Cornish Inn** (2 High St., Cornish, 207/625-8501, www.cornishinn.com, 11:30 A.M.–2 P.M. Sat.–Sun., dinner 4:30–9 P.M. Wed.–Sun., $13–22). The menu changes weekly to reflect what's locally available, with an emphasis on seafood.

◖ Krista's Restaurant (2 Main St., Cornish, 207/625-3600, www.kristasrestaurant.com, 11:30 A.M.–8 P.M. Thurs., 11:30 A.M.–9 P.M. Fri., 7 A.M.–9 P.M. Sat., 7 A.M.–8 P.M. Sun., $8–24) serves fabulous fresh fare in huge portions in its cheery air-conditioned dining rooms and on a screened deck overhanging a gurgling stream. Dinner options range from burgers and salads to entrées such as Tuscan baked haddock and herb-crusted prime rib.

Ultrafresh seafood is served at **Bay Haven Lobster Pound Two** (Maple St., Cornish, 207/625-7303, 11 A.M.–8 P.M. daily), operated by a fishing family. Portions are very generous; prices are reasonable. Dress down and order the humongous fisherman's platter (and plan on sharing).

Good food at a good price served in a pleasant country-style dining room across from

Lake Sokokis have made **The Peppermill Restaurant** (171 Washington St., Limerick, 207/793-2500, 7 A.M.–8 P.M. Sun.–Thurs., 7 A.M.–9 P.M. Fri.–Sat., dinner $8–15) a local favorite for breakfast, lunch, and dinner. Dinner choices range from comfort foods to surf and turf, with prime rib a specialty on Friday and Saturday nights.

Heather and Gary Labbe have turned four antiques- and treasure-filled rooms in their lovely Carpenter-Gothic home into the **Clipper Merchant Tea House** (58 Main St., Limerick, 207/793-3500, www.clippermerchant.com, 11 A.M.–4 P.M. Wed.–Sun. Apr.–early Sept., 11 A.M.–4 P.M. Wed.–Sat. early Sept.–Mar.). Begin with the lavender lemonade, then opt either for lunch ($9–13) or, even better, the indulgent high tea ($29 for 2).

INFORMATION

Area info is available from **The Cornish Association of Businesses** (207/625-8856, www.cornish-maine.org) and www.limerick-maine.com.

Sebago and Long Lakes

Maine's Lakes region, the area along the shores of Sebago and Long Lakes, includes the two major hubs of **Bridgton** and **Naples** as well as the smaller communities of **East Sebago** and **Harrison** and the larger communities of **Raymond, Casco,** and **Windham.** All are in Cumberland County.

Settled in 1768, Bridgton was incorporated in 1794; Naples was not incorporated until 1834. When the summer-vacation boom began in the mid-19th century and then erupted after the Civil War, visitors flowed into this area via stagecoach, the Cumberland and Oxford Canal, and later the Bridgton and Saco Railroad.

The 28-lock canal, opened in 1830 and shut down in 1870, connected the Fore River in Portland with Sebago and Long Lakes. Its only working remnant is the Songo Lock in Naples, on the Songo River between Brandy Pond and Sebago Lake.

Sebago is an apt Native American word meaning "large, open water"; it's the state's second-largest lake (after Moosehead), and fluky winds can kick up suddenly and toss around little boats, so be prudent. Now a major water source for Greater Portland, the lake reportedly served as the crossroads for major Native American trading routes, and artifacts still occasionally surface in the Sebago Basin area.

Engage in a heart-to-heart with an adult vacationing in this area and you're likely to find someone trying to recapture the past—the carefree days at summer camp in the Sebago and Long Lakes region. The shores of Sebago, Long, and Highland Lakes shelter dozens of children's camps that have created several generations of Maine enthusiasts—"people from away" who still can't resist an annual visit. Unless your own kids are in camp, however, or you're terminally masochistic, do not appear in Bridgton, Naples, or surrounding communities on the last weekend in July. Parents, grandparents, and surrogate parents all show up then for the midseason summer-camp break, and there isn't a bed or restaurant seat to be had in the entire county and maybe beyond. Gridlock is the rule.

Aside from that, this mountain-lake setting has incredible locales for canoeing, swimming, hiking, fishing, golfing, camping, biking, ice-skating, snowshoeing, and skiing. Maine's first ski lift opened in 1938 on Pleasant Mountain, now the Shawnee Peak ski area.

These lakes are quite convenient to Portland—Sebago is the large body of water you'll see to the west as you descend into the Portland Jetport.

SIGHTS
Narramissic, the Peabody-Fitch Farm

Built in 1797 and converted to Federal style in 1828, the Peabody-Fitch Farm is the crown jewel of the **Bridgton Historical Society** (207/647-3699, www.bridgtonhistory .org). Still undergoing restoration—now to the pre-Civil War era—the homestead includes a carriage house, an ell, a barn, a blacksmith shop, and historic gardens. The barn has its own story: It's known as the Temperance Barn because the landowners were avowed teetotalers, so the volunteer barn-raisers earned only water for their efforts. Narramissic is a relatively recent name, given to it by the 20th-century owner who donated it to the historical society in 1986. The name is a Native American word meaning "hard to find," reflecting her lengthy search for a family summer home. But it also suits the circuitous route, fortunately signposted, to the South Bridgton farm from downtown Bridgton: take Main Street to Route 117 south and turn left on Route 107, then right on Ingalls Road. A season highlight is the Woodworkers' Show in July. The farm is open July–August; call ahead for hours and admission prices.

❮ *Songo River Queen II*

Berthed in downtown Naples is a 90-foot Mississippi stern-wheeler replica that operates narrated cruises throughout the summer: the *Songo River Queen II* (Bay of Naples Causeway/ Rte. 302, Naples, 207/693-6861, www.songoriverqueen .net). For a quick excursion, book the one-hour Long Lake cruise ($12 adults, $6 children). Onboard are restrooms

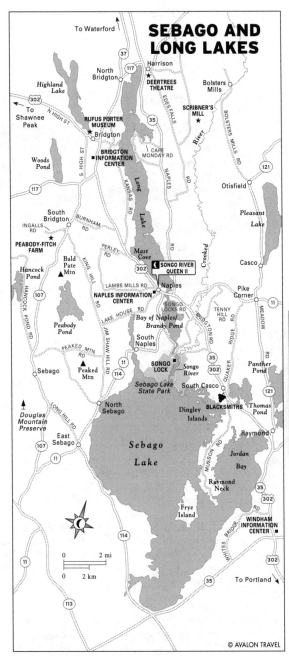

SEBAGO AND LONG LAKES

WESTERN LAKES

© AVALON TRAVEL

© HILARY NANGLE

The 90-foot Mississippi stern-wheeler replica *Songo River Queen II* cruises Long Lake.

and a snack bar. Cruises operate daily, rain or shine, July–Labor Day. Call ahead for May, June, and September dates. With the construction of the new bridge in Naples, the *Songo River Queen II* will no longer offer its 2.5-hour Songo River cruise, but until it is actually canceled, opt for it.

Presidential Maine

Inspired by a famous western Maine signpost giving directions to nine Maine towns named for foreign cities and countries, Boy Scouts in Casco decided to create some competition—a directional sign for 10 Maine towns named for U.S. presidents. The marker stands next to the village green in **Casco,** at the corner of Route 121 and Leach Hill Road, pointing to towns such as Washington (76 miles), Lincoln (175 miles), Madison, and Monroe. There's even a Clinton (84 miles).

If you're here in the fall, take time to detour briefly to Casco's "million-dollar view." Continue south from the signpost less than two miles on Route 121 to Route 11 (Pike Corner),

turn right (west) and go about 0.5 miles to Quaker Ridge Road and turn left (south). Views are spectacular along here, especially from the Quaker Hill area.

Rufus Porter Museum

The early 19th-century itinerant artist's murals and paintings are the focus at the Rufus Porter Museum and Cultural Heritage Center (67 N. High St., Bridgton, 207/647-2828, www.rufusportermuseum.org, $5 adults, $4 seniors and students, free under age 13, 10 A.M.–4 P.M. Wed.–Sat. late June–early Sept., 10 A.M.–4 P.M. Thurs.–Sat. early Sept.–mid-Oct., $8 adults, $7 seniors and students, free under age 16). Porter, the founder of *Scientific American* magazine, painted landscapes on the walls of homes throughout New England. Most were unsigned, and some of Porter's murals are displayed in the front hall of the house. During one week in July, the museum hosts a **Cultural Heritage Series** with classes, workshops, and lectures concentrating on the arts and sciences of the 19th and 20th

FAMILY-SIZE ALPINE AREAS

Maine's big resorts get most of the attention, but for young families or anyone on a budget, the smaller resorts provide not only a fun experience but also a good value. Perhaps the vertical range isn't as grand, but really, how often do you ski 2,000 feet without stopping? All of these little guys have night skiing, most have tubing parks, and some have cross-country trails too. If you're searching for areas with soul, for friendly faces, and places where kids matter, head to these slopes.

Lost Valley (200 Lost Valley Rd., off Young's Corner Rd., Auburn, 207/784-1561, www.lostvalleyski.com) is a vest-pocket ski area secreted in the barely rolling countryside outside Auburn. Don't be deceived by the hill's diminutive size. Although the vertical drop is only 240 feet, it was enough to produce four Olympians: Karl Anderson and Anna, Julie, and Rob Parisien. This is an especially family-friendly area; the base lodge doubles as the local baby-sitting service – parents just naturally watch out for one another's kids. According to Julie Parisien, who has coached local youth, you may be able to make only 10 turns from top to bottom, but that's 10 good turns. And that's what matters.

Maine's oldest ski area is **Shawnee Peak** (Rte. 302, Bridgton, 207/647-8444, www. shawneepeak.com), an increasingly popular destination given its proximity to Portland (45 miles). I have a soft spot for the area where I spent my youth – bring your family, and you'll likely understand why. The setting is rural and undeveloped, and Pleasant Mountain appears to rise out of Moose Pond. The views, which take in Mount Washington and the Presidential Range of the White Mountains, are calming, almost inspirational. It's one of the largest night-skiing facilities, acreage-wise, in New England. Arrive at night, and you'll notice that the trails spell out the word LOV in 1960s-block-style lettering. The mountain skis bigger than its

1,300-foot vertical range indicates, as it has two faces, with open slopes on one and squiggly trails ribboning the other.

For anyone weak in the wallet or overawed by megaresorts, **Mount Abram** (Howe Hill Rd., off Rte. 26, Locke Mills, 207/875-5002, www. skimtabram.com) is the solution. This long-time family favorite is something of a sleeper. Most folks drive right by on their way to glitzy Sunday River, just up the road. A savvy few turn off Route 26 in Locke Mills, drawn by this resort's commitment to family skiing and a decent 1,150-foot vertical range. The segregated learning area, tubing park, night lights, cross-country loop, low-key atmosphere, and lack of crowds make it a real gem.

A real success story is **Black Mountain of Maine** (39 Glover Rd., Rumford, 207/364-8977, www.skiblackmountain.org), where prices are low and spirit is high. It is owned and operated by the Maine Winter Sports Center (MWSC), which is committed to reestablishing skiing as part of the local lifestyle. MWSC has invested heavily in the 1,150-vertical-foot hill, putting in new lifts, cutting new trails, adding snowmaking, and making it smoke-free. Another plus is the cross-country trail system, designed by two-time Olympian Chummy Broomhall.

The Farmington Ski Club operates **Titcomb Mountain Ski Area** (Morrison Hill Rd., West Farmington, 207/778-9031, www.titcombmountain.com), an all-volunteer operation with a modest 340-foot vertical range. It's the hill where two-time Olympic gold medalist Seth Wescott played as a youth. In addition to the alpine terrain, there are nine miles of groomed trails for cross-country skiing and snowboarding (a potential solution for mixed marriages or partnerships). The operating schedule coincides with school hours, so it's open late afternoon and evenings, weekends, and daily during vacation weeks. Yes, it's a club, but nonmembers are welcome.

centuries. Other programs and classes are also offered. The museum is in a barn-red house on the northern edge of downtown Bridgton. Note that the museum is volunteer staffed, so it's wise to verify hours.

Scribner's Mill

In use by three generations of the Scribner family between 1847 and 1962, Scribner's Saw Mill and Homestead (207/585-6455, Scribner's Mill Rd., Harrison) is undergoing restoration as a working sawmill museum and is occasionally open for tours. The best time to visit is during the annual Back to the Past weekend in August, with tours, demonstrations, children's activities, and a pig roast and baked bean supper.

Flightseeing

The best way to figure out the lay of the lakes and land is on a scenic plane ride with **North Country Scenic Rides** (Causeway, Naples, 207/356-9924, www.northcountryscenicrides.com). Rates begin around $60 pp with a two-person minimum and a three-person maximum for a 15-minute flight.

ENTERTAINMENT

Tucked away on a back road in Harrison, east of Long Lake, dramatic-looking 278-seat **Deertrees Theatre and Cultural Center** (156 Deertrees Rd., Harrison, 207/583-6747, www.deertreestheatre.org) is a must-see even if you don't attend a performance. The acoustically superior building, constructed of rose hemlock in 1936, is on the National Register of Historic Places and has seen the likes of Rudy Vallée, Ethel Barrymore, Tallulah Bankhead, and Henry Winkler; restoration of the rustic building in the 1990s has given it an exciting new life. During the summer season, there's something going on nearly every night—musicals, plays, comedy, folk, jazz, blues, and weekly children's performances. The theater is signposted off Route 117 in the Harrison woods. Also here is the **BackStage Gallery** (10 A.M.–5 P.M. Tues.–Sat. and 1 hour before performances).

Mid-July–early August, the **Sebago-Long Lake Chamber Music Festival** (207/583-6747, www.sebagomusicfestival.org, $20 adults) brings Tuesday evening chamber-music concerts to Harrison's Deertrees Theatre. Advance booking is essential for this popular series, founded in 1975.

Sunday evening **band concerts** around the gazebo behind the Naples Information Center are free mid-July–mid-August. Bring a chair or blanket to the Village Green (Rte. 302, Naples).

Live entertainment is scheduled most weekends at **Bray's Brewpub and Eatery** (Rte. 302 and Rte. 35, Naples, 207/693-6806, www.braysbrewpub.com).

One of a dying species, **Bridgton Drive-In** (Rte. 302, Bridgton, 207/647-8666) screens a double feature beginning at dusk each night July–August. Sound comes via the FM radio in your car. The drive-in is 2.5 miles south of downtown Bridgton.

FESTIVALS AND EVENTS

The **Shawnee Peak** ski area (207/647-8444, www.shawneepeak.com) has a full schedule of family-oriented special events, including races, throughout the winter; call or check the website for information.

Nearly 100 teams compete in the **Mushers Bowl Winter Carnival** (www.mushersbowl.com), two days of dogsled and skijoring races on Highland Lake, a great spectator event along with activities, in West Bridgton in late January or early February. Be sure to leave your own pets at home.

The third Saturday in July, Bridgton is the scene of the **Annual Art in the Park** exhibition and sale, a mad success since its inception. Also in July is Bridgton's annual **Chickadee Quilters Show** (www.quiltguilds.com/maine.htm), with exhibits and sales of magnificent quilts and wall hangings at the Bridgton Town Hall.

In late September, the **Brewers Festival** (www.lakesbrewfest.com) brings meisters from all over Maine to the Point Sebago Resort in Casco to display their art.

SHOPPING

Anchored by **Reny's** (Main St., 207/647-3711), where you can buy just about anything portable at great prices, Bridgton offers the best collection of interesting shops, with most housed in historic buildings along the town's main drag. But there are other stores worth seeking in the area.

Art, Crafts, Gifts, and Antiques

More than 60 member artists exhibit their work at **Gallery 302** (112 Main St., Bridgton, 207/647-2787), home of the nonprofit Bridgton Art Guild. The co-op sponsors the town's annual Art in the Park, and the gallery hosts exhibits, receptions, classes, and workshops.

About a dozen vendors sell antiques and other finds at **Harry Barker's Emporium** (142 Main St., 207/647-4500). And the name? The shop is a fund-raising effort by the Harvest Hills animal shelter.

A onetime Unitarian church is the setting for the carefully chosen and superbly eclectic inventory at **Craftworks** (53 Main St., Bridgton, 207/647-5436), a Bridgton landmark since the early 1970s.

Cry of the Loon (Rte. 302, South Casco, 207/655-5060, www.cryoftheloon.com) has gifts and a tasteful, eclectic mix of gourmet condiments, Maine crafts, antiques, furniture, and much more spread out in three buildings on both sides of the road.

Since the 1970s, **Hole in the Wall Studioworks** (1544 Roosevelt Trail/Rte. 302, Raymond, 207/655-4592, www.holeinthewallstudioworks.com) has been selling an especially fine selection of American-made art and crafts. Don't miss the sculpture garden.

Maine-made crafts and a luscious selection of yarns are at **Rosemary's Gift Shop** (39 Roosevelt Trail/Rte. 302, Windham, 207/894-5770).

Books

Bridgton Books (140 Main St., Bridgton, 207/647-2122), an independent bookstore, carries an excellent selection of books (20,000 titles include new, selected used, and a large bargain-book section), cards, puzzles, and more.

Winery

Yes, there's even a winery in the region. **Blacksmiths** (Rte. 302, South Casco, 207/655-3292, www.blacksmithswinery.com) produces more than a dozen wines on the premises and offers tastings.

RECREATION

Sebago Lake State Park

Fourth-largest of Maine's state parks, 1,400-acre Sebago Lake State Park (11 Park Access Rd., Naples, 207/693-6613 late June–Labor Day, 207/693-6231 off-season, www.parksandlands.com, $6.50 nonresident adults, $4.50 Maine resident adults, $1.50 nonresident seniors, $1 ages 5–11) is one of the most popular—so don't anticipate peace and quiet here in July–August. Swimming and picnicking are superb, fishing is so-so, and personal watercraft are an increasing hazard. During the summer, park officials organize lectures, hikes, and other activities; the schedule is posted at the gate. The park is open mid-May–October, but there's winter access to 4.5 miles of groomed cross-country skiing trails—mostly beginner terrain. It's also ideal for snowshoeing.

You can reach the park's separate picnicking and camping areas from Route 302 in Casco. Take State Park Road to the fork, where you go left to the picnic area or right to Songo Lock and the camping area. Both sections have sandy beaches, now slightly diminished after major storms in 1996. Or, from downtown Naples, take Route 11/114 to Thompson Point Road and follow the signs.

Walks and Hikes

The **Lakes Environmental Association** (207/647-8580, www.mainelakes.org) hosts guided hikes, birding programs, talks, and other events throughout the year; check the website for current listings.

DOUGLAS MOUNTAIN PRESERVE

Douglas Mountain (also called Douglas Hill) is one of southern Maine's most popular hikes, so you probably won't be alone. Park ($3) in the lot on the left. Walk farther up, take a brochure from the registration box, and follow the easy Woods Trail to the 1,415-foot summit, a 30-minute walk at most. At the top is a 0.75-mile nature-trail loop, plus a 16-foot stone tower with a head-spinning view. In the fall, the vistas are incomparable. Be eco-sensitive and stick to the trails in this 169-acre preserve. Pets are not allowed. The trails are accessible dawn–dusk.

HOLT POND AND BALD PATE MOUNTAIN

The Holt Pond Preserve comprises more than 400 mostly wetland acres in Naples and is owned by the Lakes Environmental Association (207/647-8580, www.mainelakes.org). A trail with boardwalks makes it easy to spot the flora and fauna in the wetlands and bogs. The Town Farm Brook Trail connects to twin-peaked Bald Pate Mountain, part of a 486-acre preserve in South Bridgton maintained by the Loon Echo Land Trust (207/647-4352, www.loonecholandtrust.org). Bald Pate's trail network is open year-round, and there's a kiosk with trail maps at the parking lot (signposted off Rte. 107). The first peak has views to Pleasant Mountain, and the summit peak is bald, with panoramic views. Pack a lunch and plan for a full day if you decide to connect the two preserves. If you come in winter, some of Bald Pate's trails are groomed for cross-country skiing.

PLEASANT MOUNTAIN

Loon Echo Land Trust (207/647-4352, www.loonecholandtrust.org) also manages this preserve on the eastern sides of the Shawnee Peak alpine resort on Pleasant Mountain in Bridgton. Six interconnecting trails provide access to the main summit—at 2,000 feet it's the highest mountain in southern Maine and a landmark for pilots. The most popular—and relatively easiest for kids—is the Ledges (or Moose) Trail. In late July, allow four hours for the 3.5-mile round-trip so you can pick blueberries on the open ledges midway up. At the top is a disused fire tower and plenty of space for spreading out a picnic overlooking panoramic vistas of woods, lakes, and mountains. The mountain

straddles the Denmark-Bridgton town line as well as the Cumberland-Oxford County line. From Bridgton, drive 5.75 miles west on Route 302 to Mountain Road (just after the causeway over Moose Pond). Turn left (south) at signs for Shawnee Peak ski area and go 3.3 miles to the trailhead for the Ledges (or Moose) Trail; parking is limited. An alternate access route, from the west side of the mountain, is via the Wilton Warren Road, also south of Route 302.

Swimming

Besides two sandy beaches at Sebago Lake State Park, other swimming locations are the **Naples Town Beach; Crystal Lake Beach** in Harrison; **Salmon Point** and the **Town Beach on Highland Lake** in Bridgton; and **Tassel Top Beach** in Raymond, where the local Boy Scout troop maintains a nature trail through the woods bordering the beach.

You can also take a dip while picnicking at an unmarked picnic area on the island midway across Bridgton's Route 302 Moose Pond causeway. Look for a gated dirt road into the woods on the north side. There are lakeside picnic tables, a small playground, and a portable toilet.

Golf

The 18-hole **Bridgton Highlands Country Club** (Highland Ridge Rd., Bridgton, 207/647-3491, www.bridgtonhighlands.com) course is outstandingly scenic and very popular, especially at the height of summer. Starting times are required. Also here are a handsome clubhouse, tennis courts, a pro shop, and a snack bar.

Less expensive but also scenic is the **Naples Golf and Country Club** (Rte. 114, Naples, 207/693-6424, www.naplesgolfcourse.com), established in 1922. Light meals are available at the clubhouse, and there's a pro shop. On midsummer weekends, call for a starting time.

The championship-level **Point Sebago Golf Club** (Rte. 302, Casco, 207/655-2747, www.pointsebago.com, May–mid-Oct.) is part of a onetime low-key campground transformed into the 800-acre family-oriented Club Med–style

Point Sebago Resort. Call for starting times at the 18-hole course, which is open to the public. Golf-and-lodging packages are available.

Water Sports

You can rent a pontoon boat, a powerboat, or if you must, a water scooter (officially, a personal watercraft or PWC, often referred to by the trademark name Jet Ski). Water scooters have become a major itch on huge Sebago Lake as well as many other Maine lakes, and there's no gray area in the opinion department. The biggest objections are noise pollution and excessive speed. The state requires PWCs to be licensed as powerboats, but regulations are weak, the state legislature has taken little action, and inadequate funding has led to inadequate enforcement. Each year fatalities occur, spurring towns to try, usually unsuccessfully, to ban or limit PWCs. If you do rent one, play by the rules, exercise caution, and operate at sensible speeds.

Both **Naples Marina** (Rte. 302 and Rte.

© HILARY NANGLE

Daily waterskiing sessions are included in the rate for guests at Migis Lodge.

114, Naples, 207/693-6254, www.naplesmarinamaine.com) and **Causeway Marina** (Rte. 302, Naples, 207/693-6832, www.causewaymarina.com) rent powerboats, including pontoon boats, runabouts, and fishing boats.

The **Sports Haus** (103 Main St., Bridgton, 207/647-5100) rents canoes ($30 per day, $150 per week) and will deliver canoes, kayaks ($25–35 per day, $125–180 per week), sunfish sailboats (from $125 for 3 days), and more within 10 miles for $30 with a three-day minimum rental.

If you've brought a **canoe or kayak,** don't launch it into Sebago Lake; save it for the smaller lakes and ponds, where the winds are more predictable and the boat traffic is less congested. Long Lake is also a possibility if you put in at Harrison on the east side.

ACCOMMODATIONS

Rates reflect peak season.

Bed-and-Breakfasts

On a busy corner in downtown Bridgton, convenient to all the shops, **The Bridgton House Bed and Breakfast** (6 Main St., Bridgton, 866/779-3335, www.bridgtonhouse.com, $100–150), built in 1815, has been tastefully updated with five guest rooms, all with air-conditioning and Wi-Fi, three with private baths. If you're highly noise-sensitive, request a back-facing room. Rates include full breakfast and afternoon tea or snacks.

Just around the corner from the Bridgton House and off the main road, **The Noble House** (81 Highland Rd., Bridgton, 207/647-3733, www.noblehousebb.com, year-round) is a grand turn-of-the-20th-century Victorian with nine warmly decorated guest rooms, all with air-conditioning and Wi-Fi, some with screened porches or jetted tubs. Guests have use of a comfortable sitting room with a TV and a video player, a living room with a grand piano and an organ, and a great veranda. A short walk brings you to Bridgton's Highland Park on the lake, with swimming, picnicking, and boating access. Peak rates are $160–260 d (the latter rate for the honeymoon suite), including a full breakfast and access to a guest pantry with a bottomless cookie jar.

Innkeeper and talented chef Keith Neubert makes his guests feel as important as the Hollywood stars whose names grace the 16 meticulously decorated guest rooms at **The Inn at Long Lake** (15 Lake House Rd., Naples, 207/693-6226 or 800/437-0328, www.innatlonglake.com, year-round, $160–200 d). Built in the early 1900s, the inn is decorated with Victorian Revival flair. All rooms have Wi-Fi; some have lake views. The lovely grounds include a veranda, a gazebo, and a garden. Rates include a multicourse breakfast and afternoon refreshments. Packages with dinner may be available.

Wake up with a morning swim at the lakefront **Pleasant Lake House Bed and Breakfast** (1024 Meadow Rd., Casco, 207/627-6975, www.pleasantlakehouse.com, year-round, $135–225), an especially family friendly spot. Choose from four guest rooms and a suite in the main house, built in 1836, or a cottage with a full kitchen. Guests have use of the private beach and dock.

Motel

Alyssa's Motel on Thomas Pond (1 Roosevelt Tr., Casco, 207/655-2223, www.alyssasmotel.com, $135–250) has seven rooms and two suites decorated with a light country touch. All face the pond and have TVs, air-conditioning, and Wi-Fi; some have microwaves and fridges. Guests have use of a canoe, a paddleboat, and the dock; there's a public boat launch across the street.

Cottage Colonies and Resorts

Generations upon generations of families summer at the traditional lakeside cottage colonies so prevalent in this region. Many return to find the next generation of ownership running the resort but with little else changed. Some are housekeeping cottages; others provide all meals and more.

Ray and Cheryl Nelson are third-generation owners of **Sebago Lake Cottages** (774 Sebago Rd., Sebago, 207/787-3211, www

.sebagolakecottages.net), a colony of 16 cottages ringing a grassy recreation lawn just across the street from Nason's Beach. The cottages have 1–3 bedrooms, and all have knotty pine interiors and screened porches. A grocery store is just steps away, and boat, canoe, and kayak rentals and boat moorings are available. The cottages, which rent for $525–1,075 per week, or when available $85–175 per night, are on Routes 114 and 11 in North Sebago. No dogs are allowed in July–August.

Another multigenerational operation is **Sebago Lake Lodge and Cottages** (White's Bridge Rd., Windham, 207/892-2698, www .sebagolakelodge.com), which sits on a point of land with 700 feet of lake frontage adjacent to White's Bridge. Swimming, picnic and cookout facilities, free canoes, kayaks, and rowboats, rental motorboats, boat slips and moorings, and an adults-only fitness room are just a few of the amenities that make this spot special. Guest rooms in the main lodge, with its wonderful wraparound porch, have kitchenettes or kitchen privileges and nice screened porches. A continental breakfast is served in the gathering room, which also has a fireplace and a TV. The lake-view cottages have 1–2 bedrooms (guests provide their own linen and paper products); most have screened porches. Pets are allowed in the cottages by arrangement for $15 per day, but not in the lodge. Lodge rooms ($165–185) rent by the night; cottages are available Saturday–Saturday ($1,050–1,795 weekly). Discounts apply early and late in the season.

Welcome to heaven: At **Migis Lodge** (Migis Lodge Rd., South Casco, 207/655-4524, www.migis.com, no credit cards), on the east side of Sebago Lake, guests often confirm their next year's July or August booking before they depart for home. Don't let that dissuade you; there often are openings. The rustic elegance of 100-acre Migis, along with attentive service and a fabulous lakeside setting, have drawn big-name guests through the years—ever since the resort was established in the early 20th century as lodging for the parents of summer campers. Guests stay in spacious cabins within steps of the lake; each

© HILARY NANGLE

Guests at the Migis Lodge can cruise aboard the beautifully restored 1936 ChrisCraft Cruiser *Tykona.*

has a wood-burning fieldstone fireplace and is decorated in inviting Polo Ralph Lauren–meets–L. L. Bean style. Men wear jackets for dinner, and there is a supervised meal and playtime for children during dinner hours. All this comes at a price, which includes almost everything, from sailboats, canoes, and kayaks to island cookouts, waterskiing, tennis courts, and even a weekly lobster bake; exclusions include boats with motors and alcohol. Maine sales tax plus a 15 percent service charge is added on to lodging, food, and beverages. Rates for the 35 lake-view 1–6-bedroom cottages and six lodge rooms begin around $180 pp, with rates varying with the season and the accommodation. This is a fabulous place for an autumn foliage retreat. Pets are not allowed.

Camping

Camping is especially popular in this part of Maine, and many campgrounds have long-term RV or "immobile" home rentals (also known as "seasonal sites"), so you'll need to plan ahead and reserve sites well in advance.

Be forewarned, though, that if you're looking for a wilderness camping experience, especially in midsummer, you probably ought to head for the hills. Many of the campgrounds in this area feature nonstop organized fun, which is fine for enthusiastic families, but the intense activity can be overwhelming for those seeking a quiet respite.

It's crucial to book well ahead to land one of the 250 sites at **Sebago Lake State Park** (11 Park Access Rd., Naples, 207/693-6613 late June–Labor Day, www.parksandlands .com, reservations in Maine 800/332-1501, out of state 207/624-9950 or www.campwithme .com). Despite its popularity, well-spaced sites provide some privacy. Rates are $26 nonresidents, $15 Maine residents with a $2 per night reservation fee. Some sites have water and electric hookups ($37.45 nonresidents, $26.75 Maine residents).

Seasonal Rentals

Krainin Real Estate (800/639-2321, www .krainin.com) handles weekly and monthly rentals for cottages on Sebago and Long Lakes as well as many of the surrounding smaller lakes and ponds. Krainin also arranges rentals on **Frye Island,** a 1,000-acre summer community in the middle of Sebago Lake that's accessible only by car ferry.

FOOD

Restaurant hours noted are for peak season but are subject to change. It's always wise to call ahead.

Local Flavors

For **public suppers,** see listings in *The Bridgton News* (www.bridgtonnews.com) for details on chicken barbecues, potluck buffets, baked-bean suppers, and public breakfasts—all to benefit good local causes and usually well under $10 pp (less for kids).

Stock the pantry or prepare a picnic form local produce, breads, cheeses, baked goods, condiments, meats, shellfish, and more available at two local farmers markets. The **Naples Farmers Market** sets up on the Naples village green, off Route 302, 8 A.M.–1 P.M. Thursday early May–mid-September. The **Bridgton Farmers Market** is held 8 A.M.–1 P.M. Saturday mid-May–early October on Depot Street, behind Reny's.

Conveniently situated across from a lakeside picnic area at the intersection of Routes 302 and 85, **The Good Life Market** (1297 Roosevelt Tr., Raymond, 207/655-1196, www.thegoodlifemarket.com, 7 A.M.–7 P.M. daily) is a great place to pick up sandwiches, salads, fresh baked treats, wine, and specialty foods. There's even a very inexpensive kids' menu.

Just south of downtown Bridgton at the Route 117 intersection is a terrific natural-foods store and café, **Morning Dew** (19 Sandy Creek Rd., Bridgton, 207/647-4003, www.morningdewnatural.com, 9 A.M.–6 P.M. Mon.–Fri., 9 A.M.–5:30 P.M. Sat., 10 A.M.–5 P.M. Sun.). The menu goes far beyond usual natural-foods fare, with sandwiches, grilled items, burritos, salads, soups, and bagels.

Breakfast is an all-day affair at **Chute's Cafe and Bakery** (Rte. 302, South Casco, 207/655-

7111, 6 A.M.–2 P.M. Mon.–Sat., 6 A.M.–1 P.M. Sun., dinner 5–9 P.M. Fri.–Sat.), an always-popular local choice for good home cooking. Prices are low and portions ample. Lunch is served beginning at 11 A.M. On weekends, dinner choices run $9–19.

Beth's Kitchen Cafe (82 Main St., Bridgton, 207/647-5211, 7 A.M.–3 P.M. daily) is a pleasant spot for breakfast, create-your-own sandwiches, soups, pizzas, and baked goods. Grab it to go, and take it to the public park on Highland Lake.

Casual Dining

Café by day, bistro by night is the slogan at the **Black Bear Café** (215-Roosevelt Tr., Naples, 207/693-4770, www.theblackbearcafe.com, 7 A.M.–9 P.M. Mon.–Fri., 7 A.M.–10 P.M. Sat.–Sun., $8–18). The pleasant dining area is accented with a tin ceiling and local artwork. Dinner choices—burgers, salads, pizzas, and entrées such as lasagna and chicken saltimbocca as well as a kids' menu, make it easy to please everyone. On Sunday evenings there's a traditional Irish music session with local musicians.

For brews, burgers, and bands, head to **Bray's Brewpub and Eatery** (Rte. 302 and Rte. 35, Naples, 207/693-6806, www.braysbrewpub.com, 11:30 A.M.–10 P.M. daily, 11:30 A.M.–midnight Fri.–Sat., $7–20). Bray's, located in a Victorian farmhouse, is the pioneer brewpub in this part of Maine. A pub menu with lighter fare is served all day; heftier entrées are available in the evening. Stick with the simpler fare. Brewery tours are offered Thursdays at 2 P.M. Live bands play on weekends.

Although it doesn't look like much from the outside, family-friendly **Sydney's Restaurant and Pub** (Rte. 302, Naples, 207/693-3333, www.sydneysofnaples.com, 4–9 P.M. Tues.–Sat., 10 A.M.–2 P.M. Sun. Mar.–Oct., entrées $16–22) is widely regarded as one of the region's most dependable and best restaurants. The menu has a bit of everything, from salads and sandwiches to seafood and steak. An early-bird menu is served 4–6 P.M. with a choice of six entrées each night ($10–13 includes salad

POLAND SPRING **611**

and dessert). Lighter fare ($7–13) is served in the pub, where weekly specials may include $1 tacos on Wednesday. It's also a local fave for Sunday brunch.

North of downtown Bridgton, **Venezia Ristorante** (corner Rte. 302 and Rte. 93, Bridgton, 207/647-5333, 5–9 P.M. Tues.–Sun. summer, 5–9 P.M. Thurs.–Sat. winter, $15–20) is a funky little spot that has been dishing out OK Italian fare since the late 1980s.

Nonguests can dine at **Migis Lodge** (Migis Lodge Rd., South Casco, 207/655-4524, www.migis.com) on Sebago Lake by advance reservation. A five-course dinner is served in the dining room Monday–Thursday, there's a waterside lobster bake on Friday nights, and a buffet dinner is available in the dining room on Saturday nights. Each is $35; dining room meals require a jacket.

INFORMATION AND SERVICES

The **Greater Bridgton Lakes Region Chamber of Commerce** (207/647-3472, www.mainelakeschamber.com) has an attractive information center (with public restrooms) 0.5 miles south of downtown Bridgton on Route 302.

The **Sebago Lakes Region Chamber of Commerce** (Windham 207/892-8265, Naples 207/693-3285, www.sebagolakeschamber.com) operates two information centers, one on Route 302 in Windham, and a seasonal one on the Naples village green.

Poland Spring

The section of Route 26 between the Maine Turnpike (I-95) exit in Gray and Poland is rich in historical sites and worthwhile attractions, including a wildlife park, the last inhabited Shaker village, the remains of the Poland Spring House, and the source of famed Poland Spring water.

It was the water's fame that helped the Ricker family grow a small hotel into the Poland Spring House, a 300-room hotel that was an architectural and technological marvel. Also on their 5,000-acre property was the world's first resort golf course and one of the first courses designed by Donald Ross. During the resort's heyday in the early 20th century, the richest and most powerful people in the country gathered in Poland Spring to play golf and discuss world policy. Almost every U.S. president from Ulysses S. Grant to Theodore Roosevelt stayed here. Other guests and visitors of note include Babe Ruth, Alexander Graham Bell, Mae West, Betty Grable, and Judy Garland; Charles Lindberg flew over the hotel on July 25, 1927, but was unable to land because of the crowds.

The Poland Spring House was destroyed by fire in 1975, but the Maine State Building and the All Souls Chapel remain open to visitors, and the original spring that started it all can be viewed.

SIGHTS
◖ Poland Spring

Take a tour through the history of one of the world's most famous waters. It was Poland Spring Water that built Hiram Ricker's family empire, and a visit to Poland Spring should include **Poland Spring Preservation Park** (207/998-7143, www.polandspring.com/WeCare/PreservationPark.aspx, late May–mid Oct., call for hours, free), home to the Poland Spring Museum and Spring House, to learn about the legendary healing power of the water. The Maine State Building and All Souls Chapel are also both maintained by the **Poland Spring Preservation Society** (207/998-4142, www.polandspringps.org, 9 A.M.–4 P.M. Tues.–Sat. late May–mid Oct., $3 donation requested).

Begin at the **Poland Spring Museum,** where exhibits detail the history of the famed water and explain its origins. The water won the Medal of Excellence at the 1893 Chicago World's Fair, and the Grand Prize at the 1904 St. Louis

WESTERN LAKES

World's Fair. After touring the exhibits, be sure to visit the Spring House. Nature trails lace the grounds and connect to the other sites.

The three-story octagonal **Maine State Building** was built as the state pavilion for the 1893 Chicago World's Fair. Afterward, Ricker bought it for $30,000 and moved it to Maine aboard a special freight train and then via horse-drawn wagon to Ricker Hill, where it was reassembled piece by piece. One year later, it reopened as a library and art museum as part of the Ricker family's centennial celebration of their settlement at Poland Spring. Although it suffered years of neglect in the mid-20th century, it has been restored and is now operated by the Poland Spring Preservation Society as a museum and art gallery.

The adjacent **All Souls Chapel** was built in 1912 by the Ricker Family with donations from guests and staff of the Poland Spring House. The 1926 Skinner pipe organ and a set of Westminster chimes are still in working order. The chapel is home to a summer concert series (7 P.M. Mon., $7.50).

◖ Shaker Museum

Only a handful of Shakers remain in the world's last inhabited Shaker community, located three miles south of Poland Spring Resort. Nonetheless, the members of the United Society of Shakers, an 18th-century religious sect, keep a relatively high profile with a living-history museum, craft workshops, a store, publications, a mail-order herb and gift business, and even a music CD released in 1995. (See their website for the wonderful herb and herbal tea catalog.) Each year more than 8,000 visitors arrive at the 1,800-acre **Sabbathday Lake Shaker Community** (707 Shaker Rd./Rte. 26, New Gloucester, 207/926-4597, www.shaker.lib.me.us) to glimpse an endangered lifestyle, and the Shakers welcome the public to their 10 A.M. Sunday religious service, where men and women enter through separate doors and sit separately. The 75-minute basic guided tour ($6.50 adults, $2 ages 2–12) begin at 10:30 and are given every hour on the half hour, with the exception of the last tour of the day, given at 3:15 P.M. The village is open

Maine's Sabbathday Lake Shaker Community is the last living Shaker community in the world.

Monday–Saturday late May–mid-October. Check the special events calendar for workshops, demonstrations, and the annual **Maine Festival of American Music: Its Roots and Traditions** concert weekend.

Twice each year on Saturdays in late May and mid-October, the Friends of the Shakers at Sabbathday Lake (www.maineshakers.com/friends.html), a nonprofit group (annual membership $25 individual, $35 family), organizes **Friends' Work Day,** when 3–4 dozen volunteers show up at 10 A.M. to do spring and fall cleanup chores. The all-day work party includes a communal dinner.

Maine Wildlife Park

If you want to see where Maine's wild things are, visit the Maine Wildlife Park (56 Game Farm Rd., Gray, 207/657-4977, www.mainewildlifepark.com, 9:30 A.M.–6 P.M. daily mid-Apr.–early Nov., gate closes 4:30 P.M., $7 ages 13–60, $5 ages 4–12 and over age 60), located four miles south of the Shaker Village. Approximately 30 native species of wildlife can be seen at this state-operated wildlife refuge, including such ever-popular species as moose, black bears, white-tailed deer, and bald eagles. The park began in 1931 as a state-run game farm. For more than 50 years, the Department of Inland Fish and Game reared pheasants here for release during bird-hunting season. At the same time, wildlife biologists and game wardens with the state's Department of Inland Fisheries and Wildlife needed a place to care for orphaned or injured animals.

In 1982 the farm's mission was changed to that of a wildlife and conservation education facility. Today the park is a temporary haven for wildlife, although those who cannot survive in the wild live here permanently.

Among the wildlife that have been in residence at the park are lynx, deer, opossums, black bears, bobcats, porcupines, raccoon, red-tailed hawks, barred and great horned owls, mountain lions, bald eagles, ravens, skunks, woodchucks, and coyotes. Other frequent guests include wild turkeys, fishers, gray foxes, kestrels, turkey vultures, wood turtles, and box turtles. Most are here for protection and healing, and visitors are able to view them at close range.

In addition to the wildlife, there are numerous interactive exhibits and displays to view, nature trails to explore, a nature store, a snack shack, and even picnic facilities. Special programs and exhibits are often offered on weekends mid-May–mid-September. A self-guided audio tour is available for cell phones; call 207/288-1700 to access it. The park offers a Photographer's Pass, which provides special access to wildlife enclosures, for $50 per hour by advance reservation only.

The park is 3.5 miles north of Maine Turnpike (I-95) Exit 63. From the coast, take Route 115 from Main Street in downtown Yarmouth to Gray, and then head north on Route 26 for 3.5 miles.

ENTERTAINMENT

Each summer, **Poland Spring Preservation Society** hosts a series of weekly concerts in the All Souls Chapel. The music varies from acoustic guitar to jazz.

RECREATION
Range Ponds State Park

Brimming with swimmers when the temperature skyrockets, 777-acre Range (pronounced rang) Ponds State Park (Empire Rd., Poland, 207/998-4104) has facilities for swimming, including a lifeguard and a bathhouse, and picnicking as well as a playground and two miles of nature trails. (Part of the trail verges on a marsh; be prepared with bug repellent.) The beach, parking, restrooms, and picnic tables are wheelchair-accessible. Most of the park's acreage was once the estate of Hiram Ricker, owner of Poland Spring Water (it's now owned by Perrier). Bring a canoe or kayak and launch it into Lower Range Pond. Admission is $6.50 nonresident adults, $4.50 Maine resident adults, $1.50 nonresident seniors, $1 ages 5–11; the park is open mid-May–mid-October. From Lewiston-Auburn, take Route 202/11/100 South to Route 122. Turn right (east) and continue to Empire Road in Poland Spring; the turnoff to the park is well signposted.

WESTERN LAKES

Golf

The 18-hole **Poland Spring Country Club** (41 Ricker Rd., off Rte. 26, Poland Spring, 207/998-6002) was first laid out in 1893 on the grounds of the long-gone Poland Spring House, a health spa. In 1912, Donald Ross added the second nine. Call for tee times.

Rockhounding

Serious pegmatite collectors should consider **Poland Spring Mining Camps** (207/998-2350, www.polandminingcamps.com), which offers a variety of packages with access to private quarries.

ACCOMMODATIONS

Rates reflect peak season.

On the shores of Tripp Lake, the **Wolf Cove Inn Bed and Breakfast** (5 Jordan Shore Dr., Poland, 207/998-4976, www.wolfcoveinn.com, $120–250) is a delightful spot to recoup. Ten guest rooms and suites (eight with private baths, three with fireplaces, all with air-conditioning and Wi-Fi) are named after flowers. Paddle around in one of the inn's canoes, go for a swim in the lake, or hang out in the gazebo. Sunsets are magnificent here.

For dirt-cheap digs with few services and bring-your-own everything, from sheets to shampoo, check out the **Poland Spring Resort** (Rte. 26, Poland Spring, 207/998-4351, www.polandspringresort.com). A five-night package including buffet-style meals, lodging (bring your own sheets, towels, water glasses, and soap), golf, and other activities goes for about $180–429 pp for the whole shebang, but be sure to read the details on what's not included. It's not for everyone, but it's a reliable cheap sleep for if you're not fussy.

Camping

On the shore of Lower Range Pond, 40-acre **Poland Spring Campground** (Rte. 26, Poland Spring, 207/998-2151, www.polandspringcamp.com) has 130 wooded sites ($26–38 for 2 adults, 2 children, and 1 dog). Facilities include an outdoor pool, coin-operated showers, a general store, laundry, play areas, and rental canoes, kayaks, and rowboats. There's plenty of organized fun; be prepared for campfires, ice cream parties, hay rides, barbecues, and other activities, although noise rules are monitored. The campground is about 10 miles west of Auburn.

FOOD

Restaurant hours noted are for peak season but are subject to change. It's always wise to call ahead.

Pair a paddle with a meal at **Cyndi's Dockside** (Rte. 26 causeway, Poland Spring, 207/998-5008, www.dockside.me, 11:30 A.M.–8 P.M. Sun.–Thurs., 11:30 A.M.–10 P.M. Fri., 11:30 A.M.–9 P.M. Sat.), a lakeside restaurant with a boat-rental facility on Middle Range Pond. Burgers, sandwiches, fried seafood, and lobster ($6–19) provide something for everyone, and there's a kids' menu too. Kayak, canoe, and paddleboat rentals are $8 for one hour, $25 for four hours.

Farm, farm market, bakery, and pizza and sandwich shop: **Harvest Hill Farms** (Rte. 26, Mechanic Falls, 207/998-3467, www.harvesthillfarms.com, 6 A.M.–9 P.M. Mon.–Thurs., 6 A.M.–10 P.M. Fri., 7 A.M.–10 P.M. Sat., 7 A.M.–9 P.M. Sun.) is all that plus there's a slew of kid-friendly fun, including a pumpkin park and corn maze in autumn. With the exception of 14-inch pizzas, food is under $10, often far less.

INFORMATION AND SERVICES

Pick up a copy of the brochure or visit online for more information about the **Gems of Route 26** (www.gemsof26.com).

Lewiston and Auburn

A river runs through the heart of Lewiston and Auburn—the Androscoggin River, whose headwaters are in the Rangeley Lakes, courses southeastward until it joins the Kennebec River in Merrymeeting Bay near Brunswick. Surging over Great Falls, the mighty Androscoggin spurred 19th-century industrial development of the twin cities, where giant textile mills drew their power from the river and their hardworking employees from the local community of Yankees, then Irish, French Canadian, and other immigrants. The Québécois and Acadian French, who flocked to mills in Lewiston, Biddeford, Sanford, Augusta, and Brunswick, today constitute Maine's largest ethnic minority. In Lewiston and Auburn, the French-accented voting registers reveal long lists of Plourdes and Pomerleaus, Carons and Cloutiers, and the spires of Catholic churches still dominate the skyline.

Long before the falls of the Androscoggin were harnessed, Native Americans recognized the area for its prime salmon fishing and set up seasonal campsites and year-round settlements. Nowadays, their artifacts occasionally turn up along the riverbanks.

European settlers began putting down roots around 1770, earning their keep from small water-powered mills. Quakers established a community as early as 1773. By 1852 the giant Bates Mill (of bedspread fame) began manufacturing cotton, expanding to an annual output of more than 10 million yards by 1900. During the Civil War, Bates was a prime supplier of fabric for soldiers' tents. In 1861, Lewiston was incorporated as a city; Auburn was incorporated in 1869.

By the early 20th century, with a dozen more mills online, taking advantage of the convenient hydropower, the lower reaches of the Androscoggin became polluted, a stinky eyesore until the 1980s when environmental activists took up the cause. Now you can stroll the banks, fish the waters, paddle a canoe, and get up close on the walkways, bridges, and plazas linking the two cities.

Lewiston and Auburn also have quite a sporting heritage in boxing and, believe it or not, skiing. World-class boxer Joey Gamache emerged from the local clubs, and the controversial world title fight between Sonny Liston and Muhammad Ali took place here. Olympic skiers Karl Anderson and Julie Parisien (and her Olympian siblings Anna and Rob) are also local products.

Natural gems are found in the region. Auburn's Mount Apatite has produced record-setting tourmalines, Maine's state gemstone, as well as quartz and feldspar. Now owned by the city, the mountain is open to the prospecting public.

Lewiston and Auburn, known locally as "the other LA," are still not typical vacation destinations, but they deserve more than a drive-through glance. Lewiston is the state's second-largest city and home to Bates College, a highly selective private liberal-arts school and a magnet for visiting performers, artists, and lecturers.

Auburn, the Androscoggin County seat, began its industrial career with a single shoe factory in 1836, expanding swiftly in those heady days. By the turn of the 20th century, Auburn's shoe factories were turning out 6 million pairs a year.

Lewiston and Auburn occupy a pivotal location in southern Maine, with easy access to Portland (35 miles away) and Freeport (28 miles), the western mountains, and the state capital at Augusta (30 miles).

SIGHTS
Bates College
Founded in 1855 on foresighted egalitarian principles, Bates College (2 Andrews Rd., Lewiston, 207/786-6255, www.bates.edu) received its current name after major financial input from Benjamin Bates of the Bates Mill. On a lovely wooded 109-acre campus in the

WESTERN LAKES

To Lake Auburn,
Turner, and
Livermore Falls

To Augusta

LEWISTON AND AUBURN

MT AUBURN AVE

MONTELLO

11

202

100

To Lost
Valley

4

SUMMER ST

CENTER ST

WARE ST

WARE STREET
INN

CENTRAL AVE

RUSSELL ST

THORNCRAG BIRD
SANCTUARY

HIGHLAND SPRINGS RD

ST

BATES
COLLEGE

CAMPUS AVE

ST

126

Auburn

LAKE ST

UNION ST

TURNER ST

CENTRAL MAINE
MEDICAL CENTER

MAIN ST

COLLEGE ST

SABATTUS ST

PINE ST

EAST AVE

Heritage
Park

BATES ST

ASH ST

SAINTS PETER AND
PAUL BASILICA

COURT ST

ST

To Auburn-
Lewiston Airport

11

136

MUSEUM L-A

BATES MILL

CHESTNUT ST

CANAL ST

Kennedy Park

PARK ST

MAPLE ST

ST

Lewiston

BARTLETT ST

WEBSTER ST

202

100

CEDAR ST

PUBLIC
THEATRE

WEBBER AVE

PLEASANT ST

MITCHELL ST

MINOT AVE

11

121

Little Androscoggin River

MILL ST

MAIN ST

Androscoggin River

RIVERSIDE DR

River

136

ANDROSCOGGIN AVE

LINCOLN ST

LISBON ST

ST

PLEASANT ST

196

4

0   0.5 mi

0   0.5 km

To Freeport

To I-95 and
Portland

SOUTH AVE

FOCH ST

To Lisbon

© AVALON TRAVEL

heart of Lewiston, the college earns high marks for small class sizes, a stellar faculty, a rigorous academic program, and a low faculty-to-student ratio. The student body of 1,700 comes from almost every state and about four dozen foreign countries; diversity has always been evident and a point of honor. The oldest campus building is redbrick **Hathorn Hall,** built in 1856 and listed on the National Register of Historic Places; one of the newest buildings, the Olin Arts Center, built in 1986, is an award-winning complex overlooking artificial Lake Andrews.

Within the **Olin Arts Center** (Russell St. and Bardwell St., 207/786-6135) are the **Bates College Museum of Art** (75 Russell St., 207/786-6158) and the 300-seat **Olin Concert Hall.** Most college-sponsored exhibits, lectures, and concerts at the Arts Center are free and open to the public (other organizations also use the concert hall). At 6 P.M. each Thursday mid-July–mid-August, free **lakeside concerts** are presented outside the Arts Center; bring a picnic and a blanket or chair. The **Bates College Museum of Art** (10 A.M.–5 P.M. Tues.–Sat., free), with rotating exhibits, is open all year. A significant stop on the Maine Art Museum Trail, the Bates museum is best known for its holdings of prints, drawings, and paintings by Lewiston-born Marsden Hartley.

The college has won national and international acclaim for the summertime (mid-July–mid-Aug.) **Bates Dance Festival** (207/786-6161, www.batesdancefestival.org), featuring modern-dance workshops, lectures, and performances. Sellout student and faculty programs, most presented in 300-seat Schaeffer Theater, are open to the public.

Bates is the repository of the **Edmund S. Muskie Archives** (70 Campus Ave., 207/786-6354, 8:30 A.M.–noon and 1–5 P.M. Mon.–Fri.), containing the papers of the 1936 Bates graduate and former Maine governor, U.S. senator, and U.S. Secretary of State who died in 1996.

At the western edge of the campus, at the corner of Mountain Avenue and College Street, walk up **Mount David,** actually a grandly named hill, for a surprisingly good view of the Lewiston-Auburn skyline.

Bates Mill

Thanks to a progressive public-private partnership, the 19th-century Bates Mill complex, on Canal Street in downtown Lewiston, is being revitalized for a variety of new uses. Occupying 1.2 million square feet in 12 buildings spread over six acres, the mill once produced nearly a third of the nation's textiles. Since 1992, much of the hulking brick complex has been undergoing a long-term makeover—offices, studios, shops, restaurants, and even a museum have moved in, ever so slowly, helping the mill to reinvent itself.

MUSEUM L-A

If you want to understand Lewiston and Auburn, visit the fledgling Museum L-A (35 Canal St., Lewiston, 207/333-3881, www.museumla.org, 10 A.M.–4 P.M. Mon.–Sat., $5 adults, $4 seniors, $3 students). Appropriately situated inside the Bates Mill Complex, a visit immerses you into the region's industrial heyday; it's almost as if you can hear the machines and chatter as you tour the mill space. Exhibits tell the stories of LA's immigrant communities and document the region's textile-, brick-, and shoe-manufacturing industries.

Saints Peter and Paul Basilica

Most distinctive of Lewiston-Auburn's churches is the Gothic Revival Roman Catholic Saints Peter and Paul Basilica (27 Bartlett St. at Ash St., Lewiston, 207/777-1200, www.saintspeterandpaul.us), listed on the National Register of Historic Places. Noteworthy is a rose window replica of one in the Chartres Cathedral. It's the second-largest church in New England and capable of seating more than 2,000 for its separate services in English and French. Dedicated in 1938, the recently designated basilica is the only one in New England. Noonday and evening concerts, many featuring the Casavant organ, are scheduled during the summer.

ENTERTAINMENT

Throughout the year, **Bates College** (207/786-6255 weekdays, www.bates.edu) presents a full schedule of concerts, lectures, exhibits, sporting events, and other activities.

The former St. Mary's Church, considered one of the finest examples of Renaissance architecture in the country, has found new life as the **Franco-American Heritage Center** (46 Cedar St., Lewiston, 207/783-1585, box office 207/689-2000, www.francoamericanheritage.org), a performing arts center that presents symphonic, chamber, and choral music concerts as well as other events.

Since 1973, **L/A Arts** (221 Lisbon St., Lewiston, 207/782-7228 or 800/639-2919, www.laarts.org), a respected nonprofit arts-sponsorship organization, has been bringing a whole range of cultural events to the area, including films, concerts, family events, and more. The group sponsors **Music in the Parks,** with free concerts on Thursdays in Lewiston's Fountain Park and Auburn's Festival Plaza. It also operates **Gallery 5 at Lyceum Hall** (49

Lisbon St., Lewiston), with rotating shows. A fabulous resource is the Arts and Cultural Calendar link on its website.

Lewiston-Auburn's professional theater company, **The Public Theatre** (31 Maple St., Lewiston, box office 207/782-3200, www.thepublictheatre.org) has been presenting musicals and dramas for more than a decade, leading the way in the twin cities' cultural scene and receiving recognition for the quality of its performances. Ticket prices are about $18 adults, less for students and seniors.

The Maine Music Society (207/782-1403, www.mainemusicsociety.org) is the overseer of the 40-voice Androscoggin Chorale and the Maine Chamber Ensemble, which usually accompanies the chorale but also performs on its own. Concerts by both groups are held in various locations September–May.

Auburn's Festival Plaza is the venue for **Auburn Community Band Concerts** at 7 P.M. Wednesday July–August.

FESTIVALS AND EVENTS

Festival Franco Fun takes place in June at the Franco-American Heritage Center.

The second weekend in July brings the **Moxie Festival** (www.moxiefestival.com), a certifiably eccentric annual celebration of the obscure soft drink Moxie, invented in 1884 and still not consigned to the dustbin of history. Among the activities: a huge offbeat parade, food booths, a Moxie recipe contest, Chief Worumbo's Androscoggin Fun Race, and collectibles exhibits and sales. The biggest day is Saturday; it all happens in downtown Lisbon.

The acclaimed annual **Bates Dance Festival** at Bates College in Lewiston mid-July–mid-August features behind-the-scenes classes and workshops as well as performances, which are open to the public.

August brings the **Great Falls Balloon Festival,** with food, entertainment, a carnival, fireworks, and, of course, balloon launches.

The **Dempsey Challenge** run, walk, and cycle fund-raiser in October provides an opportunity to see Dr. McDreamy (actor Patrick Dempsey, who grew up in these parts).

RECREATION

Two organizations provide details on outdoor recreation, including hiking, biking, paddling, and fishing. Check the websites for **LA Trails** (www.latrails.org) and **Androscoggin Land Trust** (www.androscogginlandtrust.org) for places, maps, and opportunities such as guided walks or paddles.

Thorncrag Bird Sanctuary

Imagine being able to bird-watch, hike, cross-country ski, and snowshoe on 357 acres within the city limits of Lewiston in one of New England's largest bird sanctuaries. At the Thorncrag Bird Sanctuary (Montello St., Lewiston, 207/782-5238, www.stantonbird-club.org/thorncrg.htm, dawn–dusk daily year-round, free), pick up a trail map at the gate and head out on the three miles of well-maintained, color-coded, easy-to-moderate trails— past ponds, an old cellar hole, stone memorials and benches and through stands of beeches, hemlocks, white pines, and mixed hardwoods; bring a picnic. Bicycles are banned in the preserve. A 32-page guide to the sanctuary's flora and fauna is available for $1 at the customer service desk at Hannaford Supermarket on Sabbatus Street or the Lewiston or Auburn public libraries. Throughout the year the **Stanton Bird Club** sponsors close to three dozen lectures and free, open-to-the-public field trips; call or see its website for the schedule. The club also sponsors an excellent junior naturalist program. From downtown Lewiston, take Sabbatus Street (Rte. 126) east about three miles to Highland Springs Road. Turn left (north) and continue to the end at Montello Street. You'll be facing the entrance to the sanctuary.

Rockhounding

For sheer fun, spend a few hours searching for apatite, tourmaline, and quartz at **Mount Apatite Park** (dawn–dusk), a 325-acre park that's been popular with rock hounds for more than 150 years. For a detailed map, contact the Auburn Parks and Recreation Department (48 Pettingill Park, Auburn, 207/784-0191).

ACCOMMODATIONS

Rates reflect peak season.

At the popular **Ware Street Inn** (52 Ware St., Lewiston, 207/783-8171 or 877/783-8171, www.warestreetinn.com, $150–210), guests have the best of both worlds: an in-city accommodation right across the street from Bates College but surrounded by more than an acre of gardens and trees. Innkeeper Jan Barrett pampers guests, providing concierge services, afternoon snacks, and evening turndown. Guest rooms have Wi-Fi, TVs and video players, and comfortable seating; common areas include a library, a terrace, and a living room. Jan's husband, Mike, is an avid cyclist who can help you plan routes. Breakfast is a hot buffet. Two dogs are in residence.

Charmingly retro and spotless, the six-room **Sleepy Time Motel** (46 Danville Corner Rd., Auburn, 207/783-1435, www.sleepytimemotel .com, $85–95) offer a lot of bang for the buck. Perks in the pine-paneled guest rooms include air-conditioning, microwaves, refrigerators, recliners, Wi-Fi, and dining areas. The five-acre property is laced with three miles of trails for hiking and snowshoeing. Owners Lynn and Mark Klinger are hands-on and helpful. Pets are welcome for $10 per night.

FOOD

Restaurant hours noted are for peak season but are subject to change. It's always wise to call ahead.

Local Flavors

Look for the **Auburn Great Falls Center Farmers Market** at Great Falls Art Center, 2–6 P.M. Friday July–October.

Named for the river running through town, ◖ **Nezinscot Farm Store** (284 Turner Center Rd./Rte. 117, Turner, 207/225-3231, www .nezinscotfarm.com, 6 A.M.–6 P.M. Tues.–Fri., 7 A.M.–2 P.M. Sat., 8 A.M.–2 P.M. Sun.) is worth the detour. Besides organically grown produce,

the farm makes its own organic baked goods, cheeses, and cream products and sells plenty of other local goods. There's a café that makes meals to order and a tea shop serving both light and full teas. The shop sells all-natural wool yarns from the farm's sheep, llamas, alpacas, and goats. The farm is five miles east and north of the junction of Routes 4 and 117 (about 16 miles north of downtown Auburn). Call ahead to confirm hours if you're making a special trip.

The **Italian Bakery Products Co.** (225 Bartlett St., Lewiston, 207/782-8312, 6 A.M.– 5:30 P.M. Tues.–Fri., 6 A.M.–3 P.M. Sat., 6 A.M.– noon Sun.) is always bustling. It's a great little place to pick up baked goods such as cannoli or Bismarck doughnuts, sandwiches, soups, and pizzas for lunch, and daily specials such as Saturday beans. There is no seating.

Hipsters take note: **She Doesn't Like Guthries** (115 Middle St., Lewiston, 207/376-3344, www.guthriesplace.com, 9 A.M.–9 P.M. Mon.–Thurs., 9 A.M.–11 P.M. Fri.–Sat., $6–8) has you dialed. Begin with eclectic music, add local art, live entertainment on weekends, and an eco-friendly mission; top it off with inexpensive, well-prepared healthful fare that includes veggie, vegan, and wheat-free choices and even a kids' menu. Expect burritos, quesadillas, soups made from scratch, salads, and similar fare. And don't worry, even if you're not hip, you'll like this place.

Bates students love the '60s ambiance at the **Pop Shoppe Diner** (413 Main St., Lewiston, 207/777-7467), a classic diner serving breakfast and lunch, including $5 weekday specials.

For artisanal breads and excellent sandwiches, salads, and soups, duck into **The Bread Shack** (1056 Center St., Auburn, 207/376-3090, www.thebreadshack.com, 7 A.M.–6 P.M. Mon.–Fri., 8 A.M.–4 P.M. Sat., 8 A.M.–2 P.M. Sun.).

Breakfast, lunch, and tapas selections are available at **Holly's Own Deli & Restaurant** (84 Court St., Auburn, 207/333-3041, www .hollysown.com, 7:30 A.M.–4 P.M. Mon.– Tues., 7:30 A.M.–10 P.M. Wed.–Fri., 11 A.M.– 10 P.M. Sat.), a casual spot with an upstairs

WESTERN LAKES

wine and martini bar. The deli serves salads, soups, and sandwiches ranging from build-your-own to paninis, along with a few house specialties such as burgers and lasagna. The evening menu has tapas and full dinner options ($6–14). There's often entertainment Thursday–Saturday.

Family Favorites

In the retrofitted Bates Mill, **DaVinci's Eatery** (150 Mill St., Lewiston, 207/782-2088, www.davinciseatery.com, 11 A.M.–9 P.M. Mon.–Thurs., 11 A.M.–10 P.M. Fri.–Sat., 10 A.M.–10 P.M. Sun.) specializes in pasta and brick-oven pizza but has a variety of other regional American and Italian entrées in the $10–17 range. Weekdays and Tuesday evenings features a pizza buffet with a soup and salad bar for about $10.

The area's favorite steakhouse is **Mac's Grill** (1052 Minot Ave., Auburn, 207/783-6885, www.macsgrill.com, 11:30 A.M.–9 P.M. Tues.–Thurs., 11:30 A.M.–9:30 P.M. Fri.–Sat., 11:30 A.M.–8 P.M. Sun., $10–19).

Casual Dining

Fish Bones American Grill (70 Lincoln St., Lewiston, 207/333-3663, www.fishbonesag.com, 11:30 A.M.–9 P.M. Tues.–Sat., 11:30 A.M.–9:30 P.M. Fri., 4–9:30 P.M. Sat., $8–28), in a renovated mill with handsome brick-accented decor, serves both light and regular menus with an emphasis on seafood. It also offers a three-course theater menu, monthly wine dinners, and a killer Sunday brunch September–June.

Warm up on a cool evening at jazzy **Fuel** (49 Lisbon St., Lewiston, 207/333-3835, www.fuelmaine.com, 5–9 P.M. Tues.–Thurs., 5–10 P.M. Fri.–Sat., $10–30), a country French–inspired bistro and wine bar that opened in 2007 in historic Lyceum Hall. Owner Eric Agren calls the decor "urban cozy," and that seems about right. Expect dead-on service, well-prepared creative fare, an excellent wine list, and chic yet casual surroundings.

You might begin with fondue and then move on to chicken chasseur, steak frites, or perhaps the vegetarian choice of the day. Lighter fare ($10–12) is served in the bar. If you're feeling adventuresome, Chef Justin Oliver offers a four-course degustation menu for the table or a custom tasting menu (reservations required) at a chef's table in the kitchen.

And then there's a country inn standby: Dining is by reservation only at **The Sedgley Place** (54 Sedgley Rd., Greene, 207/946-5990 or 800/924-7778, www.sedgleyplace.com, seatings on the hour from 5 P.M. Tues.–Sun.), in a lovely Federal-style homestead a mile southwest of Route 202 (six miles north of Lewiston). The five-course menu ($29) changes weekly but always includes prime rib, fresh fish, and poultry; request vegetarian and children's portions ahead of time. The restaurant makes it a point to support local growers. Occasionally there are wine tastings.

INFORMATION AND SERVICES

The **Androscoggin County Chamber of Commerce** (207/783-2249, www.androscoggincounty.com, www.laitshappeninghere.com) serves as the tourism information center for the entire county. The website includes details on an exceptional historical walking tour, with photos of local landmarks.

Housed in a handsome granite 1903 Romanesque Revival building, the **Lewiston Public Library** (105 Park St., Lewiston, 207/784-0135, www.lplonline.org) is one of the sponsors of the Great Falls Forum, presenting monthly lunches with expert speakers on various thought-provoking topics. It's also home to the Marsden Hartley Cultural Center, a meeting and performance venue.

Equally worth a visit is the **Auburn Library** (49 Spring St., Auburn, 207/784-2300), which also has a café serving breakfast and lunch, including specials such as lobster bisque or white bean and chicken chili, Monday–Saturday.

BACKGROUND

The Land

Maine is an outdoor classroom for Geology 101, a living lesson in what the glaciers did and how they did it. Geologically, Maine is something of a youngster; the oldest rocks, found in the Chain of Ponds area in the western part of the state, are only 1.6 billion years old—more than 2 billion years younger than the world's oldest rocks.

But most significant is the great ice sheet that began to spread over Maine about 25,000 years ago, during the late Wisconsin Ice Age. As it moved southward from Canada, this continental glacier scraped, gouged, pulverized, and depressed the bedrock in its path. On it continued, charging up the north faces of mountains, clipping off their tops and moving southward, leaving behind jagged cliffs on the mountains' southern faces and odd deposits of stone and clay. By about 21,000 years ago, glacial ice extended well over the Gulf of Maine, perhaps as far as the Georges Bank fishing grounds.

But all that began to change with meltdown, beginning about 18,000 years ago. As the glacier melted and receded, ocean water moved in, covering much of the coastal plain and working its way inland up the rivers. By 11,000 years ago, glaciation had pulled back from all but a few minor corners at the top of Maine, revealing the Southern Coast's beaches and the

© HILARY NANGLE

unusual geologic traits—eskers and erratics, kettle holes and moraines, even a fjord—that make the rest of the state such a fascinating natural laboratory.

Today's Landscape

Seven distinct looks make up the contemporary Maine landscape.

Along the **Southern Coast,** from Kittery to Portland, are fine-sand beaches, marshlands, and only the occasional rocky headland. The **Mid-Coast** and **Penobscot Bay,** from Portland to the Penobscot River, feature one finger of rocky land after another, all jutting into the Gulf of Maine and all incredibly scenic. **Acadia** and the **Down East Coast,** from the Penobscot River to Eastport and including fantastic Acadia National Park, have many similarities to the Mid-Coast (gorgeous rocky peninsulas, offshore islands, granite everywhere), but, except on Mount Desert Island, takes on a different look and feel by virtue of its slower pace, higher tides, and quieter villages.

Turn inland toward the **Maine Highlands,** and the landscape changes again. The Down East mountains, roughly straddling "the Airline" (Route 9 from Bangor to Calais), are marked by open blueberry fields, serious woodlands, and mountains that seem to appear out of nowhere. The central upland—essentially a huge S-shape extending from the Portland area up to the **Kennebec River Valley,** through Augusta, Waterville, and Skowhegan, then on up into **Aroostook County** at the top of the state—is characterized by lakes, ponds, rolling fields, and occasional woodlands interspersed with river valleys. Aroostook County is the state's agricultural jackpot. The northern region—essentially the valleys of the north-flowing St. John and Allagash Rivers—was the last part of Maine to lose the glacier and is today dense forest crisscrossed with logging roads (you can count the settlements on two hands). The mountain upland, taking in all the state's major elevations and extending from inland York County to Baxter State Park and west through the **Western Lakes and Mountains** is rugged, beautiful, and the premier region for skiing, hiking, camping, and white-water rafting. Here too are seemingly endless lakes for swimming, boating, and birding.

GEOGRAPHY

Bounded by the Gulf of Maine (Atlantic Ocean), the St. Croix River, the province of New Brunswick, the St. John River, the province of Québec, and the state of New Hampshire (and the only state in the Union bordered by only one other state), Maine is the largest of the six New England states, roughly equivalent in size to the five others combined—offering plenty of space to hike, bike, camp, sail, swim, or just hang out. The state—and the coastline—extend from 43° 05' to 47° 28' north latitude and 66° 56' to 80° 50' west longitude. (Technically, Maine dips even farther southeast to take in five islands in the offshore Isles of Shoals archipelago.) It's all stitched together by 22,574 miles of highways and 3,561 bridges.

Maine's more than 5,000 rivers and streams provide nearly half of the watershed for the Gulf of Maine. The major rivers are the Penobscot (350 miles), the St. John (211 miles), the Androscoggin (175 miles), the Kennebec (150 miles), the Saco (104 miles), and the St. Croix (75 miles). The St. John and its tributaries flow northeast; all the others flow more or less south or southeast.

The Pine Tree State has more than 17 million acres of forest covering 89 percent of the state, 5,900 lakes and ponds, 4,617 saltwater islands, 10 mountains over 4,000 feet, and nearly 100 mountains higher than 3,000 feet. The highest peak in the state is Katahdin, at 5,267 feet. (Katahdin is a Penobscot Indian word meaning "greatest mountain," making "Mount Katahdin" redundant.)

Maine's largest lake is Moosehead, in Greenville, 32 miles long and 20 miles across at its widest point, with a maximum depth of 246 feet.

CLIMATE

Whoever invented the state's oldest cliché—"If you don't like the weather, wait a minute"—must have spent at least several minutes in Maine. The good news, though, is that if the weather is lousy, it's bound to change before too long. And when it does, it's intoxicating. Brilliant, cloud-free Maine weather has lured many a visitor to put down roots, buy a retirement home, or at least invest in a summer retreat.

The serendipity of it all necessitates two caveats: Always pack warmer clothing than you think you'll need, and never arrive without a sweater or jacket—even at the height of summer.

The National Weather Service assigns Maine's coastline a climatological category distinct from climatic types found in the interior.

The **coastal category,** which includes Portland, runs from Kittery northeast to Eastport and about 20 miles inland. Here, the ocean moderates the climate, making coastal winters warmer and summers cooler than in the interior (relatively speaking, of course). Early June–August, the Portland area—fairly typical of coastal weather—may have 3–8 days of temperatures over 90°F, 25–40 days over 80°F, 14–24 days of fog, and 5–10 inches of rain. Normal annual precipitation for the Portland area is 44 inches of rain and 71 inches of snow. The snow total is misleading, though, since intermittent thaws clear away much of the base.

The **southern interior** division, covering the bottom third of the state, sees the warmest weather in summer, the most clear days each year, and an average snowfall of 60–90 inches. The **northern interior** part of the state, with the highest mountains, covers the upper two-thirds of Maine and boasts a mixed bag of snowy winters, warm summers, and the state's lowest rainfall.

The Seasons

Maine has four distinct seasons: summer, fall, winter, and mud. Lovers of spring need to look elsewhere in March, the lowest month on the popularity scale with its mud-caked vehicles, soggy everything, irritable temperaments, tank-trap roads, and often the worst snowstorm of the year.

Summer can be idyllic—with moderate temperatures, clear air, and wispy breezes—but it can also close in with fog, rain, and chills. Prevailing winds are from the southwest. Officially, summer runs June 20 or 21–September 20 or 21, but June, July, and August is more like it, with temperatures in the Portland area averaging 70°F during the day and in the 50s at night. The normal growing season is 148 days.

A poll of Mainers might well show autumn as the favorite season—days are still warmish, nights are cool, winds are optimum for sailors, and the foliage is brilliant. Fall colors usually begin appearing far to the north about mid-September, reaching their peak in that region by the end of the month. The last of the color begins in late September in the southernmost part of the state and fades by mid-October. Early autumn, however, is also the height of hurricane season, the only potential flaw this time of year.

Winter, officially December 20 or 21–March 20 or 21, means deep snow and cold inland and an unpredictable potpourri along the coastline. When the cold and snow hit the coast, it's time for cross-country skiing, ice fishing, snowshoeing, ice-skating, ice climbing, and winter trekking and camping.

Spring, officially March 20 or 21–June 20 or 21, is the frequent butt of jokes. It's an ill-defined season that arrives much too late and departs all too quickly. Ice floes dot inland lakes and ponds until "ice-out" in early–mid-May; spring planting can't occur until well into May; lilacs explode in late May and disappear by mid-June. And just when you finally can enjoy being outside, blackflies stretch their wings and satisfy their hunger pangs. Along the coast, onshore breezes often keep the pesky creatures to a minimum.

Northeasters and Hurricanes

A northeaster is a counterclockwise, swirling storm that brings wild winds out of—you guessed it—the northeast. These storms can occur any time of year, whenever the conditions brew them up. Depending on the season, the winds are accompanied by rain, sleet, snow, or all of them together.

Hurricane season officially runs June–November but is most prevalent late August–September. Some years, the Maine coast remains out of harm's way; other years, head-on hurricanes and even glancing blows have eroded beaches, flooded roads, splintered boats, downed trees, knocked out power, and inflicted major residential and commercial damage.

Sea Smoke and Fog

Sea smoke and fog, two atmospheric phenomena resulting from opposing conditions, are only distantly related, but both can radically affect visibility and therefore be hazardous. In winter, when the ocean is at least 40°F warmer than the air, billowy sea smoke rises from the water, creating great photo ops for camera buffs but especially dangerous conditions for mariners.

In any season, when the ocean (or lake or land) is colder than the air, fog sets in, creating perilous conditions for drivers, mariners, and pilots. Romantics, however, see it otherwise, reveling in the womblike ambience and the muffled moans of foghorns. Portland averages about 31 days with heavy fog April–October, when visibility may be a quarter mile or less.

Storm Warnings

The National Weather Service's official daytime signal system for wind velocity consists of a series of flags representing specific wind speeds and sea conditions. Beachgoers and anyone planning to venture out in a kayak, canoe, sailboat, or powerboat should heed these signals. The flags are posted on all public beaches, and warnings are announced on TV and radio weather broadcasts, as well as on cable TV's Weather Channel and the NOAA broadcast network.

Fog frequently shrouds the coast of Maine.

© HILARY NANGLE

Flora and Fauna

From this elevation, just on the skirts of the clouds, we could overlook the country, west and south, for a hundred miles. There it was, the State of Maine, which we had seen on the map, but not much like that. Immeasurable forest for the sun to shine on.... No clearing, no house. It did not look as if a solitary traveler had cut so much as a walking stick there. Countless lakes.... and mountains. The forest looked like a firm grass sward, and the effect of these lakes in its midst has been well compared.... to that of a mirror broken into a thousand fragments, and widely scattered over the grass, reflecting the full blaze of the sun.

– Henry David Thoreau, *The Maine Woods*

Looking out over Maine from Katahdin today, as Thoreau did in 1857, you get a view that is still a mass of green stretching to the sea, broken by blue lakes and rivers. Although the forest has been cut several times since Thoreau saw it, Maine is proportionally still the most forested state in the nation.

It also is clearly one of the best watered. Receiving an average of more than 40 inches of precipitation a year, Maine is abundantly endowed with swamps, bogs, ponds, lakes, streams, and rivers. These in turn drain from a coast deeply indented by coves, estuaries, and bays.

In this state of trees and water, nature dominates more than most—Maine is the least densely populated state east of the Mississippi River. Here, where boreal and temperate ecosystems meet and mix, lives a rich diversity of plants and animals.

THE ALPINE TUNDRA

Three continental storm tracks converge on Maine, and the state's western mountains bear the brunt of the weather they bring. Stretching from Katahdin in the north along most of Maine's border with Québec and New Hampshire, these mountains have a far colder climate than their temperate latitude might suggest.

Timberline here occurs at only about 4,000 feet, and where the mountaintops reach above that, the environment is truly arctic—an alpine-tundra habitat where only the hardiest species can live. Beautiful pale-green "map" lichens cover many of the exposed rocks like shapes cut from an atlas, and sedges and rushes take root in the patches of thin topsoil. As many as 30 alpine plant species, typically found hundreds of miles to the north, grow in crevices or hollows in the lee of the blasting winds. Small and low-growing to conserve energy in this harsh climate, such plants as **bearberry willow, Lapland rosebay, alpine azalea, *Diapensia*, mountain cranberry,** and **black crowberry** reward the observant hiker with white, yellow, pink, and magenta flowers in late June–July.

Areas above the tree line are generally inhospitable to most animals other than secretive **voles, mice,** and **lemmings.** Even so, summer or winter, a hiker is likely to be aware of at least one other species: the **northern raven.** More than any of the 300 or so other bird species that regularly occur in Maine, the raven is the bird of the state's wild places, its mountain ridges, rocky coasts, and remote forests. Solid black like a crow but larger and stockier and with a wedge-shaped tail and broad wings, the northern raven is a magnificent flyer—soaring, hovering, diving, and often turning loops and rolls as though playing in the wind. Known to be among the most intelligent of all animals, ravens are quite social, actively communicating with one another in throaty croaks as they range over the landscape in search of carrion and other available plant and animal foods.

At the tree line and below, where conditions are moderate enough to allow black spruce and balsam fir to take hold, fauna becomes far more diverse. Among the wind- and ice-stunted trees, called *krummholz* (crooked wood), **northern**

© HILARY NANGLE

Keep an eye out for moose while traveling in Maine's remote areas.

juncos and **white-throated sparrows** forage. The latter's plaintive whistle (often mnemonically rendered as "Old Sam Peabody, Peabody, Peabody") is one of the most evocative sounds of the Maine woods.

THE BOREAL OR NORTHERN FOREST

Mention the Maine woods and the image that is likely to come to mind is the boreal forests of **spruce** and **fir.** In 1857, Thoreau captured the character of these woods when he wrote,

It is all mossy and moosey. In some of those dense fir and spruce woods there is hardly room for the smoke to go up. The trees are a standing night, and every fir and spruce which you fell is a plume plucked from night's raven wing. Then at night the general stillness is more impressive than any sound, but occasionally you hear the note of an owl farther or nearer in the woods, and if near a lake, the semi-human cry of the loons at their unearthly revels.

Well adapted to a short growing season, low temperatures, and rocky, nutrient-poor soils, spruce and fir do dominate the woods on mountainsides, in low-lying areas beside watercourses, and along the coast. By not having to produce new foliage every year, these evergreens conserve scarce nutrients and also retain their needles, which capture sunlight for photosynthesis during all but the coldest months. The needles also wick moisture from the low clouds and fog that frequently bathe their preferred habitat, bringing annual precipitation to more than 80 inches a year in some areas.

In the lush boreal forest environment grows a diverse ground cover of herbaceous plants, including **bearberry, bunchberry, clintonia, starflower,** and **wood sorrel.** In older spruce-fir stands, mosses and lichens often carpet much of the forest floor in a soft tapestry of greens and gray-blues. Maine is extraordinarily rich in **lichens,** with more than 700 species identified so far—20 percent of the total found in all of North America. **Usnea** is a familiar one; its common name, old man's beard,

FALLING FOR FOLIAGE

The timing of Maine's fall foliage owes much to the summer weather that precedes it, and so does the quality (although the annual spectacle never disappoints). In early September, as deciduous trees ready themselves for winter, they stop producing chlorophyll, and the green begins to disappear from their leaves. Taking its place are the spectacular pigments – brilliant reds, yellows, oranges, and purples – that paint the leaves and warm the hearts of every "leaf-peeper," shopkeeper, innkeeper, and restaurateur in the region.

The colorful display begins slowly, reaches a peak, and then fades – starting in the north in early-mid-September and working down to the southwest corner by mid-October. Peak foliage in far-north Aroostook County usually occurs in late September, about three weeks after the colors have begun to appear. Along the South Coast and Mid-Coast, the peak can occur as late as the middle of October, with the last bits of color hanging on even beyond that.

Trees put on their most magnificent show after a summer of moderate heat and rainfall; a summer of excessive heat and scant rainfall means colors will be less brilliant and disappear more quickly. Throw a September or October northeaster or hurricane into the mix, and estimates are up for grabs.

So predictions are imprecise, and you'll need to allow some schedule flexibility to take advantage of the changes in different parts of the state. Mid-September-mid-October, check the state's Department of Conservation website (www.mainefoliage.com) for frequently updated maps, panoramic photographs, and reports on the foliage status (this is gauged by the percentage of dropped leaf in every region of the state). Or call the Foliage Hotline (888/MAINE-45 – 888/624-6345). Another resource for info on driving tours during foliage season is the website of the Maine Office of Tourism (www.visitmaine.com).

A reminder: Fall-foliage trips are extremely popular and have become more so in recent years, so lodging can be scarce in some areas (although you'll often find beds in adjacent towns). Plan well ahead and make reservations, especially if you're headed for the Kennebunks, Boothbay Harbor, Camden, Bar Harbor, Greenville, Rangeley, and Bethel.

---

comes from its wispy strands that drip from the branches of spruce trees. The **northern parula,** a small blue, green, and yellow bird of the wood warbler family, weaves its ball-shaped pendulum nest from usnea.

The spruce-fir forest is prime habitat for many other species that are among the most sought-after by birders: **black-backed** and **three-toed woodpeckers,** the audaciously bold **gray jay** (or camp robber), **boreal chickadees, yellow-throated flycatchers, white-winged crossbills, Swainson's thrushes,** and a half-dozen other gem-like wood warblers.

Among the more unusual birds of this forest type is the **spruce grouse.** Sometimes hard to spot because it does not flush, a spruce grouse is so tame that a careful person can actually touch one. Not surprisingly, the spruce grouse earned the nickname "fool hen" early in the 19th century, and no doubt it would have become extinct long ago but for its menu preference of spruce and fir needles, which render its meat bitter and inedible (you can get an idea by tasting a few needles yourself).

Few of Maine's 56 mammal species are restricted to the boreal forest, but several are very characteristic of it. Most obvious from its trilling, far-carrying chatter is the **red squirrel.** Piles of cone remnants on the forest floor mark a red squirrel's recent banquet. The red squirrel itself is the favored prey of another coniferous forest inhabitant, the **pine marten.** An arboreal member of the mustelid family—which in Maine also includes **skunks, weasels, fishers,** and **otters**—the pine marten is a sleek, low-slung predator with blond to brown fur, an orange throat patch, and a long bushy tail. Its beautiful pelt nearly led to the animal's obliteration from Maine through overtrapping, but with protection, the marten population has rebounded.

Nearly half a century of protection also allowed the population recovery of Maine's most prominent mammal, the **moose**. Standing 6–7 feet tall at the shoulder and weighing as much as 1,200 pounds, the moose is the largest member of the Cervidae or deer family. A bull's massive antlers, which it sheds and regrows each year, may span five or more feet and weigh 75 pounds. The animal's long legs and bulbous nose give it an ungainly appearance, but the moose is ideally adapted to a life spent wading through deep snow, dense thickets, and swamps.

Usually the best place to observe a moose is at the edge of a body of water on a summer afternoon or evening. Wading out into the water, the animal may submerge its entire head to browse on the succulent aquatic plants below the surface. The water also offers a respite from the swarms of biting insects that plague moose (and people who venture into these woods without bug repellent). Except for a limited hunting season, moose have little to fear from humans and often will allow close approach. Be careful, however, and give them the respect their imposing size suggests; cows can be very protective of their calves, and bulls can be unpredictable, particularly during the fall rutting (mating) season.

Another word of caution about moose: When driving, especially in spring and early summer, be alert for moose wandering out of the woods and onto roadways to escape the flies. Moose are dark brown, their eyes do not reflect headlights in the way that most other animals' do, and they do not get out of the way of cars or anything else. Colliding with a half-ton animal can be a tragedy for all involved. Pay particular attention while driving in Oxford, Franklin, Somerset (especially Rte. 201), Piscataquis, and Aroostook Counties, but with an estimated 25,000–30,000 moose statewide, they can and do turn up anywhere and everywhere—even in downtown Portland and on offshore islands.

Protection from unlimited hunting was not the only reason for the dramatic increase in Maine's moose population; the invention of the chain saw and the skidder have played parts too. In a few days, one or two workers can now cut and yard a tract of forest that a whole crew with saws and horses formerly took weeks to harvest. With the increase in logging, particularly the clear-cutting of spruce and fir, whose long fibers are favored for papermaking, vast areas have been opened up for regeneration by fast-growing, sun-loving hardwoods. The leaves of these young **white birch, poplar, pin cherry,** and **striped maple** are a veritable moose salad bar.

THE TRANSITION ZONE: NORTHERN HARDWOOD FOREST

Although hardwoods have replaced spruce and fir in many areas, mixed woods of **sugar maple, American beech, yellow birch, red oak, red spruce, eastern hemlock,** and **white pine** have always been a major part of Maine's natural and social histories. This northern hardwood forest, as it is termed by ecologists, is a transitional zone between northern and southern ecosystems and is rich in species diversity.

Dominated by deciduous trees, this forest community is highly seasonal. Spring snowmelt brings a pulse of life to the newly exposed forest floor as herbaceous plants race to develop and flower before the trees overhead leaf out and limit the available sunlight. (Blink and you can practically miss a Maine spring.) **Trout lily, goldthread, trillium, violets, gaywing,** and **pink lady's slipper** are among the many woodland wildflowers whose blooms make a walk in the forest so rewarding at this time of year. Deciduous trees, shrubs, and a dozen species of ferns also must make the most of their short four-month growing season. In the Maine woods, the buds of mid-May unfurl into a full canopy of leaves by the first week of June.

Late spring and early summer in the northern hardwood forest is also a time of intense animal activity. Runoff from the melting snowpack has filled countless low-lying depressions throughout the woods. These ephemeral swamps and vernal pools are a haven for an enormous variety of aquatic invertebrates, insects, amphibians, and reptiles. Choruses of spring **peepers,** Maine's smallest but seemingly loudest frog, alert everyone with their high-pitched calls that the ice is going out and breeding season is at hand. Measuring only about an inch in length, these tiny frogs with X-shaped patterns on their backs can be surprisingly difficult to see without some determined effort. Look on the branches of shrubs overhanging the water; males often use them as perches from which to call prospective mates. But then why stop with peepers? There are eight other frog and toad species in Maine to search for too.

Spring is also the best time to look for **salamanders.** Driving a country road on a rainy night in mid-April provides an opportunity to witness one of nature's great mass migrations as salamanders and frogs of several species emerge from their wintering sites and make their way across roads to breeding pools and streams. Once breeding is completed, most salamanders return to the terrestrial environment, where they burrow into crevices or the moist litter of the forest floor. The movement of amphibians from wetlands to uplands has an important ecological function, providing a mechanism for the return of nutrients that runoff washes into low-lying areas. This may seem hard to believe until one considers the numbers of individuals involved in this movement. To illustrate, the total biomass of Maine's **redback salamander** population—just one of the eight salamander species found here—is heavier than the combined weight of all the state's moose.

The many bird species characteristic of the northern hardwood forest are also most in evidence during the late spring and early summer, when the males are engaged in holding breeding territory and attracting mates. For most passerines—perching birds—this means singing. Especially during the early-morning and evening hours, the woods are alive with choruses of song from such birds as the **purple finch, white-throated sparrow, solitary vireo, black-throated blue warbler, Canada warbler, mourning warbler, northern waterthrush,** and the most beautiful singer of them all, the **hermit thrush.**

Providing abundant browse as well as tubers, berries, and nuts, the northern hardwood forest supports many of Maine's mammal species. The **red-backed vole, snowshoe hare, porcupine,** and **white-tailed deer** are relatively abundant and in turn are prey for **foxes, bobcats, fishers,** and **eastern coyotes.** Now well established since its expansion into Maine in the 1950s and 1960s, the eastern coyote has filled the niche at the top of the food chain once held by wolves and mountain lions before their extermination in the state in the late 19th century. **Black bears,** of which Maine has an estimated 25,000, are technically classified as carnivores and will take a moose calf or deer on occasion, but most of their diet consists of vegetation, insects, and fish. In the fall, bears feast on beechnuts and acorns, putting on extra fat for the coming winter, which they spend sleeping (not hibernating, as is often presumed) in a sheltered spot dug out beneath a rock or log.

Autumn is a time of spectacular beauty in Maine's northern hardwood forest. With the shortening days and cooler temperatures of September, the dominant green chlorophyll molecules in deciduous leaves start breaking down. As they do, the yellow, orange, and red pigments (which are always present in the leaves and serve to capture light in parts of the spectrum not captured by the chlorophyll) are revealed. Sugar maples put on the most dazzling display, but beeches, birches, red maples, and poplars add their colors to make up an autumn landscape famous the world over.

Ecologically, one of the most significant mammals in the Maine woods is the **beaver.** After being trapped almost to extinction in the 1800s, this large swimming rodent has recolonized streams, rivers, and ponds throughout the state. Well known for its ability as a dam builder, the beaver can change low-lying woodland into a complex aquatic ecosystem. The impounded water behind the dam often kills the trees it inundates, but these provide ideal nest cavities for **mergansers, wood ducks, owls, woodpeckers,** and **swallows.** The still water is also a nursery for a rich diversity of invertebrates, fish, amphibians, and Maine's seven aquatic turtle species, most common of which is the beautiful but very shy **eastern painted turtle.**

THE AQUATIC ENVIRONMENT

Small woodland pools and streams are, of course, only a part of Maine's aquatic environment. The state's nearly 6,000 lakes and ponds provide open-water and deep-water habitats for many additional species. A favorite among them is the **common loon,** symbol of north country lakes across the continent. Loons impart a sense of wildness and mystery with their haunting calls and yodels resonating off the surrounding pines on still summer nights. Adding to their popular appeal are their striking black-and-white plumage, accented with red eyes, and their ability to vanish below the surface and then reappear in another part of the lake moments later. The annual census of Maine's common loons since the 1970s indicates a relatively stable population of about 3,200 breeding pairs.

Below the surface of Maine's lakes, ponds, rivers, and streams, 69 freshwater fish species live in the state, of which 17 were introduced. Among these exotic transplants are some of the most sought-after game fish, including **smallmouth** and **largemouth bass, rainbow trout,** and **northern pike.** These introductions may have benefited anglers, but they have displaced native species in many watersheds.

Several of Maine's native fish have interesting histories in that they became landlocked during the retreat of the glacier. At that time, Maine was climatically much like northern Canada is today, and **arctic char** ran up its rivers to spawn at the edges of the ice. As the ice continued to recede, some of these fish became trapped but nevertheless managed to survive and establish themselves in their new landlocked environments. Two remnant subspecies now exist: the **blue-back char,** which lives in the cold, deep water of 10 northern Maine lakes, and the **Sunapee char,** now found only in three lakes in Maine and two in Idaho. A similar history belongs to the **landlocked salmon,** a form of Atlantic salmon that many regard as the state's premier game fish and now widely stocked throughout the state and around the country.

Atlantic salmon still run up some Maine rivers every year to spawn, but dams and heavy commercial fishing at sea have depleted their numbers and distribution to a fraction of what they once were. Unlike salmon species on the Pacific coast, adult Atlantic salmon survive the fall spawning period and make their way back out to sea again. The young, or parr, hatch the following spring and live in streams and rivers for the next 2–3 years before migrating to the waters off Greenland. Active efforts are now under way to restore this species, including capturing and trucking the fish around dams. Salmon is just one of the species whose life cycle starts in fresh water and requires migrations to and from the sea. Called anadromous fish, others include **striped bass, sturgeon, shad, alewives, smelt,** and **eels.** All were once far more numerous in Maine, but fortunately pollution control and management efforts in the past three decades have helped their populations rebound slightly from their historic low numbers.

ESTUARIES AND MUDFLATS

Maine's estuaries, where freshwater and saltwater meet, are ecosystems of outstanding biological importance. South of Cape Elizabeth, where the Maine coast is low and sandy, estuaries harbor large salt marshes with **spartina** grasses that can tolerate the frequent variations in salinity as runoff and tides fluctuate. Producing an estimated four times more plant material than an equivalent area of wheat, these spartina marshes provide abundant nutrients and shelter for a host of marine organisms that ultimately account for as much as 60 percent of the value of the state's commercial fisheries.

The tidal range along the Maine coast varies 9–26 vertical feet, southwest to northeast.

Where the tide inundates sheltered estuaries for more than a few hours at a time, spartina grasses cannot take hold, and mudflats dominate. Although it may look like a barren wasteland at low tide, a mudflat is also a highly productive environment and home to abundant marine life. Several species of tiny primitive worms called **nematodes** can inhabit the mud in densities of 2,000 or more per square inch. Larger worm species are also very common. One, the **bloodworm,** grows up to a foot in length and is harvested in quantity for use as sportfishing bait.

More highly savored among the mudflat residents is the **soft-shelled clam,** famous for its outstanding flavor and an essential ingredient of an authentic Maine lobster bake. But because clams are suspension feeders, filtering phytoplankton through their long siphon, or "neck," they can accumulate pollutants that cause illness, including hepatitis. Many Maine mudflats are closed to clam harvesting because of leaking septic systems, so it's best to check with the state's Department of Marine Resources or the local municipal office before digging a mess of clams yourself.

For birds and birders, salt marshes and mudflats are an unparalleled attraction. Long-legged wading birds such as the **glossy ibis, snowy egret, little blue heron, great blue heron, tricolored heron, green heron,** and **black-crowned night heron** frequent the marshes in great numbers throughout the summer months, hunting the shallow waters for mummichogs and other small salt-marsh fish, crustaceans, and invertebrates. Mid-May–early June and then again mid-July–mid-September, migrating shorebirds pass through Maine to and from their subarctic breeding grounds. On a good day, a discerning birder can find 17 or more species of shorebirds probing the mudflats and marshes with pointed bills in search of their preferred foods. In turn, the large flocks of shorebirds don't escape the notice of their own predators: **merlins** and **peregrine falcons** dash in to catch a meal.

THE ROCKY SHORELINE AND THE MARINE ENVIRONMENT

On the more exposed rocky shores—the dominant shoreline from Cape Elizabeth all the way Down East to Lubec—where currents and waves keep mud and sand from accumulating, the plant and animal communities are entirely different from those in the inland aquatic areas. The most important requirement for life in this impenetrable rockbound environment is probably the ability to hang on tight. **Barnacles,** the calcium-armored crustaceans that attach themselves to the rocks immediately below the high-tide line, have developed a fascinating battery of adaptations to survive not only pounding waves but also prolonged exposure to air, solar heat, and extreme winter cold. Glued in place, however, they cannot escape being eaten by **dog whelks,** the predatory snails that also inhabit this intertidal zone. Whelks are larger and more elongate than the more numerous and ubiquitous **periwinkle,** accidentally transplanted from Europe in the mid-19th century.

Also hanging onto these rocks but at a lower level are the brown algae seaweeds. Like a marine forest, the four species of **rockweed** provide shelter for a wide variety of life beneath their fronds. A world of discovery awaits those who make the effort to go out onto the rocks at low tide and look under the clumps of seaweed and into the tidal pools they shelter. Venture into these chilly waters with a mask, fins, and a wetsuit and still another world opens for natural-history exploration. Beds of **blue mussels, sea urchins, sea stars,** and **sea cucumbers** dot the bottom close to shore. In crevices between and beneath the rocks lurk **rock crabs** and **lobsters.** Now a symbol of the Maine coast and the delicious seafood it provides, the lobster was once considered "poor man's food"—so plentiful that it was spread on fields as fertilizer. Although lobsters are far less common than they once were, they are one of Maine's most closely monitored species, and their population continues to support a large and thriving commercial fishing industry.

Sadly, the same cannot be said for most of

Maine's other commercially harvested marine fish. When Europeans first came to these shores four centuries ago, **cod, haddock, halibut, hake, flounder, herring,** and **tuna** were abundant, but no longer: Overharvested, their seabed habitat torn up by relentless dragging, these groundfish have all but disappeared. It will be decades before these species can recover, and then only if effective regulations can be put in place soon.

The familiar doglike face of the **harbor seal,** often seen peering alertly from the surface just offshore, provides a reminder that wildlife populations are resilient if given a chance. A century ago, there was a bounty on harbor seals because it was thought they ate too many lobsters and fish. Needless to say, neither fish nor lobsters increased when the seals all but disappeared. With the bounty's repeal and the advent of legal protection, Maine's harbor seal population has bounced back to an estimated 15,000–20,000. Scores of them can regularly be seen basking on offshore ledges, drying their tan, brown, black, silver, or reddish coats in the sun. Though it's tempting to approach for a closer look, avoid bringing a boat too near these haul-out ledges, as it causes the seals to flush into the water and imposes an unnecessary stress on the pups, which already face a first-year mortality rate of 30 percent.

Positive changes in our relationships with wildlife are even more apparent with the return of birds to the Maine coast. Watching the numerous **herring gulls** and **great black-backed gulls** soaring on a fresh ocean breeze today, it's hard to imagine that a century ago, egg collecting had so reduced their numbers that they were a rare sight. In 1903, there were just three pairs of **common eiders** left in Maine; today, 25,000 pairs nest along the coast. With creative help from dedicated researchers using sound recordings, decoys, and prepared burrows, **Atlantic puffins** are recolonizing historic offshore nesting islands. **Ospreys** and **bald eagles,** almost free of the lingering vestiges of damage from DDT and other pesticides, now range the length of the coast and up Maine's major rivers.

LOOKING INTO THE FUTURE

Many Maine plants and animals, however, remain subjects of concern. Listed or proposed for listing as endangered or threatened species in the state are 178 vascular plants and 54 vertebrates. Too little is known about most of the lesser plants and animals to determine what their status is, but as natural habitats continue to decline in size or become degraded, it is likely that many of these species will disappear from the state. It is impossible to say exactly what will be lost when any of these species cease to exist here, but to quote conservationist Aldo Leopold, "To keep every cog and wheel is the first precaution of intelligent tinkering."

It is clear, however, that life in Maine has been enriched by the recovery of populations of pine marten, moose, harbor seals, eiders, and others. The natural persistence and tenacity of wildlife suggests that such species as the Atlantic salmon, wolf, and mountain

Osprey build their nests on high platforms, such as this signal between the Little and Great Cranberry Isles.

© HILARY NANGLE

lion will someday return to Maine—provided we give them the chance and the space to survive.

This *Flora and Fauna* section was written by William P. Hancock, director of the Environmental Centers Department at the Maine Audubon Society and former editor of *Habitat Magazine.*

History

Prehistoric Mainers: The Paleo-Indians

As the great continental glacier receded north-westward out of Maine about 11,000 years ago, some prehistoric grapevine must have alerted small bands of hunter-gatherers—fur-clad Paleo-Indians—to the scrub sprouting in the tundra, burgeoning mammal populations, and the ocean's bountiful food supply. Because come they did, at first seasonally and then year-round. Anyone who thinks tourism is a recent Maine phenomenon needs only to explore the shoreline in Damariscotta, Boothbay Harbor, and Bar Harbor, where heaps of cast-off oyster shells and clamshells document the migration of early Native Americans from woodlands to waterfront. "The shore" has been a summer-time magnet for millennia.

Archaeological evidence from the Archaic period in Maine—roughly 8000–1000 B.C.—is fairly scant, but paleontologists have unearthed stone tools and weapons as well as small camp-sites attesting to a nomadic lifestyle supported by fishing and hunting, with fishing becoming more extensive as time went on. Toward the end of the tradition, during the late Archaic pe-riod, emerged a rather anomalous Indian cul-ture known officially as the Moorehead phase but informally called the Red Paint People; the name is due to their curious trait of using a distinctive red ocher (pulverized hematite) in burials. Dark red puddles and stone artifacts have led excavators to burial pits as far north as the St. John River. Just as mysteriously as they had arrived, the Red Paint People disappeared abruptly and inexplicably around 1800 B.C.

Following them almost immediately—and almost as suddenly—hunter-gatherers of the Susquehanna Tradition arrived from well to the south, moved across Maine's interior as far as the St. John River, and remained until about 1600 B.C., when they too enigmatically van-ished. Excavations have turned up relatively sophisticated stone tools and evidence that they cremated their dead. It was nearly 1,000 years before a major new cultural phase appeared.

The next great leap forward was marked by the advent of pottery making, introduced about 700 B.C. The Ceramic period stretched to the 16th century A.D., and cone-shaped pots (initially stamped, later incised with coiled-rope motifs) survived until the introduction of metals from Europe. Houses—seasonal wigwam-style dwellings for fishers and their families—appeared along the coast and on off-shore islands.

The Europeans Arrive

The identity of the first Europeans to set foot in Maine is a matter of debate. Historians dis-pute the romantically popular notion that Norse explorers checked out this part of the New World as early as A.D. 1000. Even an 11th-century Norse coin found in 1961 in Brooklin (on the Blue Hill Peninsula) probably was car-ried there from farther north.

Not until the late 15th century, the onset of the great Age of Discovery, did credible reports of the New World (including what's now Maine) filter back to Europe's courts and universities. Thanks to innovations in naval architecture, shipbuilding, and navigation, astonishingly courageous fellows crossed the Atlantic in search of rumored treasure and new routes for reaching it.

John Cabot, sailing from England aboard the ship *Mathew,* may have been the first European to reach Maine, in 1498, but historians have never confirmed a landing site. No question remains, however, about the account of Giovanni da Verrazzano, an Italian explorer commanding *La Dauphine* under the French flag, who reached the Maine coast in May 1524, probably at the tip of the Phippsburg Peninsula. Encountering less-than-friendly Indians, Verrazzano did a minimum of business and sailed onward. His brother's map of the site labels it "The Land of Bad People." Esteban Gómez and John Rut followed in Verrazzano's wake, but nothing came of their exploits.

Nearly half a century passed before the Maine coast turned up again on European explorers' itineraries. This time, interest was fueled by reports of a Brigadoon-like area called Norumbega (or Oranbega, as one map had it), a myth that arose, gathered steam, and took on a life of its own in the decades after Verrazzano's voyage.

By the early 17th century, when Europeans began arriving in more than twos and threes and getting serious about colonization, Native American agriculture was already under way at the mouths of the Saco and Kennebec Rivers, the cod fishery was thriving on offshore islands, Indians far to the north were hot to trade furs for European goodies, and the birch-bark canoe was the transport of choice on inland waterways.

In mid-May 1602, Bartholomew Gosnold, en route to a settlement off Cape Cod aboard the *Concord,* landed along Maine's southern coast. The following year, merchant trader Martin Pring and his boats *Speedwell* and *Discoverer* explored farther Down East, backtracked to Cape Cod, and returned to England with tales that inflamed royal curiosity and enough sassafras to satisfy royal appetites. Pring produced a detailed survey of the Maine coast from Kittery to Bucksport, including offshore islands.

On May 18, 1605, George Waymouth, skippering the *Archangel,* reached Monhegan Island, 11 miles off the Maine coast, and moored for the night in Monhegan Harbor (still treacherous even today, exposed to the weather from the southwest and northeast and subject to meteorological beatings and heaving swells; yachting guides urge sailors not to expect to anchor, moor, or tie up there). The next day, Waymouth crossed the bay and scouted the mainland. He took five Indians hostage and sailed up the St. George River, near present-day Thomaston. As maritime historian Roger Duncan has put it, "The Plimoth Pilgrims were little boys in short pants when George Waymouth was exploring this coastline."

Waymouth returned to England and awarded his hostages to officials Sir John Popham and Sir Ferdinando Gorges, who, their curiosity piqued, quickly agreed to subsidize the colonization effort. In 1607, the *Gift of God* and the *Mary and John* sailed for the New World carrying two of Waymouth's captives. After returning them to their native Pemaquid area, Captains George Popham and Raleigh Gilbert continued westward, establishing a colony called St. George or Fort George at the tip of the Phippsburg Peninsula in mid-August 1607 and exploring the shoreline between Portland and Pemaquid. Frigid weather, untimely deaths (including Popham's), and a storehouse fire doomed what's called the Popham Colony, but not before the 100 or so settlers built the 30-ton pinnace *Virginia,* the New World's first such vessel. When Gilbert received word of an inheritance waiting in England, he and the remaining colonists returned to the Old World.

In 1614, swashbuckling Captain John Smith, exploring from the Penobscot River westward to Cape Cod, reached Monhegan Island nine years after Waymouth's visit. Smith's meticulous map of the region was the first to use the "New England" appellation, and the 1616 publication of his *Description of New-England* became the catalyst for permanent settlements.

The French and the English Square Off

English dominance of exploration west of the Penobscot River in the early 17th century coincided roughly with French activity east of the river.

In 1604, French nobleman Pierre du Gua de Monts set out with cartographer Samuel de

Champlain to map the coastline, first reaching Nova Scotia's Bay of Fundy and then sailing up the St. Croix River. In mid-river, just west of present-day Calais, a crew planted gardens and erected buildings on today's St. Croix Island while de Monts and Champlain went off exploring. The two men reached the island Champlain named l'Isle des Monts Deserts (Mount Desert Island) and present-day Bangor before returning to face the winter with their ill-fated compatriots. Scurvy, lack of fuel and water, and a ferocious winter wiped out nearly half of the 79 men. In spring 1605, de Monts, Champlain, and other survivors headed southwest, exploring the coastline all the way to Cape Cod before heading northeast again and settling permanently at Nova Scotia's Port Royal (now Annapolis Royal).

Eight years later, French Jesuit missionaries en route to the Kennebec River ended up on Mount Desert Island and, with a band of French laymen, set about establishing the St. Sauveur settlement. But leadership squabbles led to building delays, and English marauder Samuel Argall—assigned to reclaim English territory—arrived to find them easy prey. The colony was leveled, the settlers were set adrift in small boats, the priests were carted off to Virginia, and Argall moved on to destroy Port Royal.

By the 1620s, more than four dozen English fishing vessels were combing New England waters in search of cod, and year-round fishing depots had sprung up along the coast between Pemaquid and Portland. At the same time, English trappers and dealers began usurping the Indians' fur trade—a valuable source of income.

The Massachusetts Bay Colony was established in 1630, and England's Council of New England, headed by Sir Ferdinando Gorges, began making vast land grants throughout Maine, giving rise to permanent coastal settlements, many dependent on agriculture. Among the earliest communities were Kittery, York, Wells, Saco, Scarborough, Falmouth, and Pemaquid—places where they tilled the acidic soil, fished the coast, eked out a living barely above subsistence, coped with predators and endless winters, bartered goods and services, and set up local governments and courts.

By the late 17th century, as these communities expanded, so did their requirements and responsibilities. Roads and bridges were built, preachers and teachers were hired, and militias were organized to deal with internecine and Indian skirmishes.

Even though England yearned to control the entire Maine coastline, its turf, realistically, was primarily south and west of the Penobscot River. The French had expanded from their Canadian colony of Acadia, for the most part north and east of the Penobscot. Unlike the absentee bosses who controlled the English territory, French merchants actually showed up, forming good relationships with the Indians and cornering the market in fishing, lumbering, and fur trading. And French Jesuit priests converted many Native Americans to Catholicism. Intermittently, overlapping Anglo-French land claims sparked locally messy conflicts.

In the mid-17th century, the strategic heart of French administration and activity in Maine was Fort Pentagouet, a sturdy stone outpost built in 1635 in what is now Castine. From here, the French controlled coastal trade between the St. George River and Mount Desert Island and well up the Penobscot River. In 1654, England captured and occupied the fort and much of French Acadia, but thanks to the 1667 Treaty of Breda, title returned to the French in 1670, and Pentagouet briefly became Acadia's capital.

A short but nasty Dutch foray against Acadia in 1674 resulted in Pentagouet's destruction ("levell'd with ye ground," by one account) and the raising of a third national flag over Castine.

The Indian Wars (1675-1760)

Caught in the middle of 17th- and 18th-century Anglo-French disputes throughout Maine were the Wabanaki (People of the Dawn), the collective name for the state's major Native American groups, all of whom spoke Algonquian languages. Modern ethnographers label these groups the Micmacs, Maliseets, Passamaquoddies, and Penobscots.

In the early 17th century, exposure to European diseases took its toll, wiping out three-quarters of the Wabanaki in 1616–1619. Opportunistic English and French traders quickly moved into the breach, and the Indians struggled to survive and regroup.

But regroup they did. Less than three generations later, a series of six Indian wars began, lasting nearly a century and pitting the Wabanaki most often against the English but occasionally against other Wabanaki. The conflicts, largely provoked by Anglo-French tensions in Europe, were King Philip's War (1675–1678), King William's War (1688–1699), Queen Anne's War (1703–1713), Dummer's War (1721–1726), King George's War (1744–1748), and the French and Indian War (1754–1760). Not until a get-together in 1762 at Fort Pownall (now Stockton Springs) did peace effectively return to the region—just in time for the heating up of the revolutionary movement.

Comes the Revolution

Near the end of the last Indian War, just beyond Maine's eastern border, a watershed event led to more than a century of cultural and political fallout. During the so-called Acadian Dispersal in 1755, the English expelled from Nova Scotia 10,000 French-speaking Acadians who refused to pledge allegiance to the British Crown. Scattered as far south as Louisiana and west toward New Brunswick and Québec, the Acadians lost farms, homes, and possessions in this *grand dérangement*. Not until 1785 was land allocated for resettlement of Acadians along both sides of the Upper St. John River, where thousands of their descendants remain today. Henry Wadsworth Longfellow's epic poem *Evangeline* dramatically relates the sorry Acadian saga.

In the District of Maine, on the other hand, with relative peace following a century of intermittent warfare, settlement again exploded, particularly in the southernmost counties. The 1764 census tallied Maine's population at just under 25,000; a decade later, the number had

Three national flags fly over the ramparts of the reconstructed Fort William Henry in the Pemaquid region.

© HILARY NANGLE

doubled. New towns emerged almost overnight, often heavily subsidized by wealthy investors from the parent Massachusetts Bay Colony. With almost 4,000 residents, the largest town in the district was Falmouth (later renamed Portland).

In 1770, based on population, 27 Maine towns became eligible to send representatives to the Massachusetts General Court, the colony's legislative body. But only six coastal towns could actually afford to send anyone, sowing seeds of resentment among settlers who were thus saddled with taxes without representation. Sporadic mob action accompanied unrest in southern Maine, but the flashpoint occurred in the Boston area.

On April 18, 1775, Paul Revere set out on the country's most famous horseback ride—from Lexington to Concord, Massachusetts—to announce the onset of what became the American Revolution. Most of the Revolution's action occurred south of Maine, but not all of it.

In June, the Down East outpost of Machias was the site of the war's first naval engagement. The well-armed but unsuspecting British vessel HMS *Margaretta* sailed into the bay and was besieged by local residents angry about a Machias merchant's sweetheart deal with the British. Before celebrating their David-and-Goliath victory, the rebels captured the *Margaretta,* killed her captain, and then captured two more British ships sent to the rescue.

In the fall of 1775, Colonel Benedict Arnold—better known to history as a notorious turncoat—assembled 1,100 sturdy men for a flawed and futile "March on Québec" to dislodge the English. From Newburyport, Massachusetts, they sailed to the mouth of the Kennebec River, near Bath, and then headed inland with the tide. In Pittston, six miles south of Augusta and close to the head of navigation, they transferred to a fleet of 220 locally made bateaux and laid over three nights at Fort Western in Augusta. Then they set off, poling, paddling, and portaging their way upriver. Skowhegan, Norridgewock, and Chain of Ponds were among the landmarks along the grueling route. The men endured cold, hunger, swamps, disease, dense underbrush, and the loss of nearly 600 of their comrades before reaching Québec in late 1775. In the Kennebec River Valley, Arnold Trail historical signposts today mark highlights (or, more aptly, lowlights) of the expedition.

Four years later, another futile attempt to dislodge the British, this time in the District of Maine, resulted in the worst U.S. naval defeat until World War II—a little-publicized debacle called the Penobscot Expedition. On August 14, 1779, as more than 40 American warships and transports carrying more than 2,000 Massachusetts men blockaded Castine to flush out a relatively small enclave of leftover Brits, a seven-vessel Royal Navy fleet appeared. Despite their own greater numbers, about 30 of the American ships turned tail up the Penobscot River. The captains torched their vessels, exploding the ammunition and leaving the survivors to walk in disgrace to Augusta or even Boston. Each side took close to 100 casualties, three commanders—including Paul Revere—were court-martialed, and Massachusetts was about $7 million poorer.

The American Revolution officially came to a close on September 3, 1783, with the signing of the Treaty of Paris between the United States and Great Britain. The U.S.-Canada border was set at the St. Croix River, but in a massive oversight, boundary lines were left unresolved for thousands of square miles in the northern District of Maine.

Trade Troubles and the War of 1812

In 1807, President Thomas Jefferson imposed the Embargo Act, banning trade with foreign entities—specifically France and Britain. With thousands of miles of coastline and harbor villages dependent on trade for revenue and basic necessities, Maine reeled. By the time the act was repealed, under President James Madison in 1809, France and Britain were almost unscathed, but the bottom had dropped out of New England's economy.

An active smuggling operation based in Eastport kept Mainers from utter despair, but the economy still had continued its downside. In 1812, the fledgling United States declared war on Great Britain, again disrupting coastal trade. In the fall of 1814, the situation reached its nadir when the British invaded the Maine coast and occupied all of the shoreline between the St. Croix and Penobscot Rivers. Later that same year, the Treaty of Ghent finally halted the squabble, forced the British to withdraw from Maine, and allowed the locals to get on with economic recovery.

Statehood

In October 1819, Mainers held a constitutional convention at the First Parish Church on Congress Street in Portland. (Known affectionately as "Old Jerusalem," the church was later replaced by the present-day structure.) The convention crafted a constitution modeled on that of Massachusetts, with two notable differences: Maine would have no official church (Massachusetts had the Puritans' Congregational Church), and Maine would place no religious requirements or restrictions on its gubernatorial candidates. When votes came in from 241 Maine towns, only nine voted against ratification.

For Maine, March 15, 1820, was one of those good news–bad news days: After 35 years of separatist agitation, the District of Maine broke from Massachusetts (signing the separation allegedly, and disputedly, at the Jameson Tavern in Freeport) and became the 23rd state in the Union. However, the Missouri Compromise, enacted by Congress only 12 days earlier to balance admission of slave and free states, mandated that the slave state of Missouri be admitted on the same day. Maine had abolished slavery in 1788, and there was deep resentment over the linkage.

Portland became the new state's capital (albeit only briefly; it switched to Augusta in 1832), and William King, one of statehood's most outspoken advocates, became the first governor.

Trouble in the North Country

Without an official boundary established on Maine's far northern frontier, turf battles were always simmering just under the surface. Timber was the sticking point—everyone wanted the vast wooded acreage. Finally in early 1839, militia reinforcements descended on the disputed area, heating up what has come to be known as the Aroostook War, a border confrontation with no battles and no casualties (except a farmer who was shot by friendly militia). It's a blip in the historical timeline, but remnants of fortifications in Houlton, Fort Fairfield, and Fort Kent keep the story alive today. By March 1839, a truce was negotiated, and the 1842 Webster-Ashburton Treaty established the modern border.

Maine in the Civil War

In the 1860s, with the state's population slightly more than 600,000, more than 70,000 Mainers suited up and went off to fight in the Civil War—the greatest per-capita show of force of any northern state. About 18,000 of them died in the conflict. Thirty-one Mainers were Union Army generals, the best-known being Joshua L. Chamberlain, a Bowdoin College professor who commanded the 20th Maine regiment and later became president of the college and governor of Maine.

During the war, young battlefield artist Winslow Homer, who later settled in Prouts Neck, south of Portland, created wartime sketches regularly for such publications as *Harper's Weekly*. In Washington, Maine senator Hannibal Hamlin was elected vice president under Abraham Lincoln in 1860 (he was removed from the ticket in favor of Andrew Johnson when Lincoln came up for reelection in 1864).

Maine Comes into Its Own

After the Civil War, Maine's influence in Republican-dominated Washington far outweighed the size of its population. In the late 1880s, Mainers held the federal offices of acting vice president, Speaker of the House, Secretary of State, Senate majority leader, Supreme Court justice, and several important committee chairmanships. Best-known of the notables were James G. Blaine (journalist, presidential aspirant, and Secretary of State) and Portland native Thomas Brackett Reed, presidential aspirant and Speaker of the House.

In Maine itself, traditional industries fell into decline after the Civil War, dealing the economy a body blow. Steel ships began replacing Maine's wooden clippers, refrigeration techniques made the block-ice industry obsolete, concrete threatened the granite-quarrying trade, and the output from Southern textile mills began to supplant that from Maine's mills.

Despite Maine's economic difficulties, however, wealthy urbanites began turning their sights toward the state, accumulating land (including islands) and building enormous summer "cottages" for their families, servants, and hangers-on. Bar Harbor was a prime example of the elegant summer colonies that sprang up, but others include Grindstone Neck in Winter Harbor, Prouts Neck in Scarborough, and Dark Harbor on Islesboro in Penobscot Bay. Vacationers who preferred fancy hotel-type digs reserved rooms for the summer at such sprawling complexes as Kineo House on Moosehead Lake; Poland Spring House, west of Portland; or the Samoset Hotel in Rockland. Built of wood and catering to long-term visitors, these and many others all eventually succumbed to altered vacation patterns and the ravages of fire.

As the 19th century spilled into the 20th, the state broadened its appeal beyond the well-to-do who had snared prime turf in the Victorian era. It launched an active promotion of Maine as "The Nation's Playground," successfully spurring an influx of visitors from all economic levels. By steamboat, train, and soon by car, people came to enjoy the ocean beaches, the woods, the mountains, the lakes, and the quaintness of it all. (Not that these features didn't really exist, but the state's aggressive public relations campaign at the turn of the 20th century stacks up against anything Madison Avenue puts out today.) The only major hiatus in the tourism explosion in the century's first two decades was 1914–1918, when 35,062 Mainers joined many thousands of other Americans in Europe to fight in World War I. Two years after the war ended, in 1920 (the centennial of its statehood), Maine women were the first in the nation to troop to the polls after ratification of the 19th Amendment granted universal suffrage.

Maine was slow to feel the repercussions of the Great Depression, but eventually they came, with bank failures all over the state. Federally subsidized programs such as the Civilian Conservation Corps (CCC) and the Works Progress Administration (WPA) left lasting legacies in Maine.

Politically, the state has contributed notables on both sides of the aisle. In 1954, Maine elected as its governor Edmund S. Muskie, only the fifth Democrat in the job since 1854. In 1958, Muskie ran for and won a seat in the Senate, and in 1980 he became secretary of state under President Jimmy Carter. Muskie died in 1996.

Elected in 1980, Waterville's George J. Mitchell made a respected name for himself as a Democratic senator and Senate majority leader before retiring in 1996, when Maine became only the second state in the union to have two women senators (Olympia Snowe and Susan Collins, both Republicans). After his 1996 reelection, President Bill Clinton appointed Mitchell's distinguished congressional colleague and three-term senator, Republican William Cohen of Bangor, as Secretary of Defense, a position he held through the rest of the Clinton administration. Mitchell spent considerable time during the Clinton years as the U.S. mediator for Northern Ireland's "troubles" and subsequently became the U.S. Special Envoy for Middle East Peace under President Barack Obama.

Government and Economy

STATE GOVERNMENT

Politics in Maine isn't quite as variable and unpredictable as the weather, but pundits are almost as wary as weather forecasters about making predictions. Despite a long tradition of Republicanism dating from the late 19th century, Maine's voters and politicians have a national reputation for being independent-minded—electing Democrats, Republicans, or independents more for their character than their political persuasions.

Four of the most notable recent examples are Margaret Chase Smith, Edmund S. Muskie, George J. Mitchell, and William Cohen—two Republicans and two Democrats, all Maine natives. Republican senator Margaret Chase Smith proved her flintiness when she spoke out against McCarthyism in the 1950s. Ed Muskie, the first prominent Democrat to come out of Maine, won every race he entered except an aborted bid for the presidency in 1972. George Mitchell, as mentioned, has gained a stellar reputation, as has William Cohen. In a manifestation of Maine's strong tradition of bipartisanship, Mitchell and Cohen worked together closely on many issues to benefit the state and the nation (they even wrote a book together).

In the 1970s, Maine elected an independent governor, James Longley, whose memory is still respected; Longley's son was later elected to Congress as a Republican, and his daughter to the state senate as a Democrat. In 1994, Maine voted in another independent, Angus King, and since then a Democrat and a Republican have been elected governor, including the incumbent, Paul LePage, a controversial Tea Party conservative who won the office with only 38 percent of the vote since the moderate Independent and liberal Democrat candidates split the majority of the vote. The governor serves a term of four years, limited to two terms.

The state's Supreme Judicial Court has a chief justice and six associate justices.

Maine is ruled by a bicameral, biennial citizen legislature comprising 151 members in the House of Representatives and 35 members in the state Senate, including a relatively high percentage of women and a fairly high proportion of retirees. Members of both houses serve two-year terms. In 1993, voters passed a statewide term-limits referendum restricting legislators to four terms.

Whereas nearly two dozen Maine cities are ruled by city councils, about 450 smaller towns and plantations retain the traditional form of rule: annual town meetings. Town meetings are generally held in March, when newspaper pages bulge with reports containing classic quotes from citizens exercising their rights to vote and vent. A few examples: "I believe in the pursuit of happiness until that pursuit infringes on the happiness of others"; "I don't know of anyone's dog running loose except my own, and I've arrested her several times"; and "Don't listen to him; he's from New Jersey."

ECONOMY

Governor after governor of Maine has tried to shorten the economic gap between the "three Maines." Southern Maine is prosperous, with good jobs (although never enough), lots of small businesses, and a highly competitive real-estate market. Northern Maine struggles along, suffering as much from its immensity and lack of infrastructure as its low population density. The central region lies between the two in every respect; there are a few more population centers and a little more industry. Efforts to stimulate economic development in the less developed areas have experienced fluctuating degrees of success that largely mirror the state of the U.S. economy. In recent years, Maine has suffered as manufacturing has moved overseas and military bases such as Loring Air Force Base in Aroostook County and Brunswick Naval Air Station have closed.

According to state economists, Maine currently faces three challenges. First, slow job growth: Over the past two decades, Maine's has been about half of the national average. Second, changing employment patterns: Once famed for producing textiles and shoes and for its woods-based industries, now health care and tourism provide the most jobs. Third, an aging population: Economic forecasters predict that more than one in five residents will be older than 65 by 2020, which poses a challenge for finding workers in the future.

Tourism

One in 10 Mainers is employed in tourism, and in 2009 leisure- and hospitality-related jobs generated approximately $1.5 billion in wages.

Paper and Other Forest Products

A combination of spruce and fir, the best woods for making paper, comprise 35 percent of the Pine Tree State's forests. Maine also boasts one of the finest white birch resources in the world. Nearly 89 percent of the state is covered by 17 million acres of woods, making Maine the most heavily forested state in the country. But that's changing as timber companies sell off holdings and conservationists and developers battle over the future of the lands.

Since 1990, paper-industry employment plummeted 50 percent, driven in part by lower production costs elsewhere in the world. The future lies in modernizing mills and in practicing sustainable forestry.

Heath Care

Approximately 16 percent of Maine's labor force is employed in health care, and it's currently the fastest growing job sector, with more than 10,000 new jobs predicted to be created by 2013. As the population ages, that growth will continue, although finding workers will be a challenge.

Fishing

Commercial fishing throughout New England has suffered ups and downs in the past decade because of downtrends in traditional stocks such as cod, haddock, and scallops, followed by stringent federal regulations. Maine coastal communities have depended on fishing for hundreds of years, and although the fleet has been reduced, anglers still harvest groundfish, shrimp, clams, mussels, and other seafood in mostly seasonal fisheries.

Lobster, for years Maine's most valuable seafood product, has also proven to be the state's most enduring fisheries resource, thanks to savvy conservation policies. Eighty percent of the nation's lobster catch comes from Maine. Nearly 1,200 lobstermen (although women are employed, they scoff at the term lobsterwomen) are considered full-time, dependent on their lobstering income for their livelihood. In 2010, lobstermen harvested a record 93.4 million pounds, valued at $308 million. The overall 2010 seafood harvest was 245.3 pounds, valued at $448.7 million.

Aquaculture

Maine's growing aquaculture comprises farms growing finfish (Atlantic salmon and steelhead

Lobster is Maine's most valuable seafood product.

© TOM NANGLE

Fields of wheat, barley, broccoli, and potatoes define the landscape in Aroostook County.

trout), shellfish (Eastern oysters, soft- and hard-shell clams, bay scallops, surf clams, and mussels), and sea vegetables (seaweed). In the early years the industry was plagued by problems, but investment in aquaculture research and facilities has reversed that trend. The estimated value of the 2008 harvest was $35 million.

Agriculture

In Maine, farming is s $1.2 billion industry. Maine is the world's largest producer of brown eggs and wild blueberries. Nationwide it ranks eighth for potato production and second for maple syrup. And in New England, it's second in milk and livestock production.

Increasingly, small farms are turning to organic techniques or specialty products such as cheese. And in recent years, wineries have popped up along the coast, perhaps an indicator of global climate change. The farm-to-table movement is especially strong in Maine.

Creative Economy

More and more attention is being paid to what has been termed the creative economy—the creators at the intersection of arts, technology, and entrepreneurship. To name just a few, this wide-ranging group includes: artists, chefs, software developers, scientists, dancers, graphic designers, craftspeople, carpenters, engineers, furniture makers, writers, photographers, and so on. They live in abundance in Maine, and efforts are now under way to foster growth in this sector.

People and Culture

THE PEOPLE

Maine's population didn't top the 1 million mark until 1970. Forty years later, according to Census Bureau estimates, the state had 1,318,301 residents. Along the coast, Cumberland County, comprising the Greater Portland area, has the largest head count.

Despite the longstanding presence of several substantial minority ethnic groups, plus four Native American groups that make up about 1 percent of the population, diversity is a relatively recent phenomenon in Maine, and the population is about 95 percent Caucasian. A steady influx of refugees, beginning after the Vietnam War, forced the state to address diversity issues, and it continues to do so today.

Natives Mainers and People from Away

People who weren't born in Maine aren't natives. Even people who *were* born here may experience close scrutiny of their credentials. In Maine, there are natives, and then there are *natives*. Every day, the obituary pages describe Mainers who have barely left the houses in which they were born—even in which their grandparents were born; we're talking roots. Along with this kind of heritage comes a whole vocabulary all its own—lingo distinctive to Maine, or at least to New England.

Part of the native picture is the matter of native produce. Hand-lettered signs sprout everywhere during the summer advertising native corn, native peas, even—believe it or not—native ice. In Maine, homegrown is well grown.

"People from away," on the other hand, are those whose families haven't lived here year-round for a generation or more. But people from away (also called flatlanders) exist all over Maine, and they have come to stay, putting down roots of their own and altering the way the state is run, looks, and will look.

Senators Snowe and Collins are natives, but past governors and cabinet members have been from away. You'll find other flatlanders as teachers, corporate executives, artists, retirees, writers, town selectmen, and even lobstermen.

In the 19th century, arriving flatlanders were mostly "rusticators" or "summer complaints"—summer residents who lived well, often in enclaves, and never set foot in the state off-season. They did, however, pay property taxes, contribute to causes, and provide employment for local residents. Another 19th-century wave of people from away came from the bottom of the economic ladder: Irish escaping the potato famine and French Canadians fleeing poverty in Québec. Both groups experienced subtle and overt anti-Catholicism but rather quickly assimilated into the mainstream, taking jobs in mills and factories and becoming staunch American patriots.

The late 1960s and early 1970s brought bunches of "back-to-the-landers," who scorned plumbing and electricity and adopted retro ways of life. Although a few pockets of diehards still exist, most have changed with the times and have adopted contemporary mores (and conveniences).

Today, technocrats arrive from away with computers, cell phones, and other high-tech gear and "commute" via the Internet and modern electronics.

Native Americans

In Maine, the real natives are the Wabanaki (People of the Dawn)—the Micmac, Maliseet, Penobscot, and Passamaquoddy tribes of the eastern woodlands. Many live in or near three reservations, near the headquarters for their tribes' governors. The Passamaquoddies are at Pleasant Point in Perry, near Eastport, and at Indian Township in Princeton, near Calais. The Penobscots are based on Indian Island in Old Town, near Bangor. Other Native American population clusters—known as

MAINE FOOD SPECIALTIES

Everyone knows Maine is *the* place for lobster, but there are quite a few other foods that you should sample before you leave.

For a few weeks in May, right around Mother's Day (the second Sunday in May), a wonderful delicacy starts sprouting along Maine woodland streams: **fiddleheads,** the still-furled tops of the ostrich fern *(Matteuccia struthiopteris)*. Tasting vaguely like asparagus, fiddleheads have been on May menus ever since Native Americans taught the colonists to forage for the tasty vegetable. Don't go fiddleheading unless you're with a pro, though; the lookalikes are best left to the woods critters. If you find them on a restaurant menu, indulge.

As with fiddleheads, we owe thanks to Native Americans for introducing us to **maple syrup,** one of Maine's major agricultural exports. The annual crop averages 110,000 gallons. The syrup comes in four different colors and flavors, from light amber to extra dark amber, and inspectors strictly monitor syrup quality. The best syrup comes from the sugar or rock maple, *Acer saccharum*. On Maine Maple Sunday, usually the fourth Sunday in March, several dozen syrup producers open their rustic sugarhouses to the public for "sugaring-off" parties – to celebrate the sap harvest and share the final phase in the

Never pass up an opportunity to indulge at a public supper.

production process. Wood smoke billows from the sugarhouse chimney while everyone inside gathers around huge kettles used to boil down the watery sap. (A single gallon of syrup starts with 30-40 gallons of sap.) Finally, it's time to sample the syrup every which way – on pancakes and waffles, in tea, on ice cream, in puddings, in muffins, even just drizzled over snow. Most producers also have containers of syrup for sale.

The best place for Maine maple syrup is atop pancakes made with Maine **wild blueberries.** Packed with antioxidants and all kinds of good-for-you stuff, these flavorful berries are prized by bakers because they retain their

---

"off-reservation Indians"—are the Aroostook Band of Micmacs, based in Presque Isle, and the Houlton Band of Maliseets in Littleton, near Houlton.

In 1965, Maine became the first state to establish a Department of Indian Affairs, but just five years later the Passamaquoddy and Penobscot tribes initiated a 10-year-long land-claims case involving 12.5 million acres (about two-thirds of the state) weaseled from the Indians by Massachusetts in 1794. In 1980 a landmark agreement, signed by president Jimmy Carter, awarded the tribes $80.6 million in reparations. Despite this, the tribes still struggle to provide jobs on the reservations and to increase the overall standard of

living. A 2003 referendum on whether to allow the tribes to build a casino was defeated. The latest attempt to increase jobs and income is a controversial plan to bring a liquefied natural gas port to Native American lands in Perry.

One of the true success stories of the tribes is the revival of traditional arts as businesses. The Maine Indian Basketmakers Association has an active apprenticeship program, and two renowned basket makers—Mary Gabriel and Clara Keezer—have achieved National Heritage Fellowships. Several well-attended annual festivals—in Bar Harbor, Unity, and Bangor—highlight Indian traditions and heighten awareness of Native American form and flavor when cooked. Much smaller than the cultivated versions, wild blueberries are also raked, not picked. Although most of the Down East barren barons harvest their crops for the lucrative wholesale market, a few growers let you pick your own blueberries in mid-August. Contact the Wild Blueberry Commission (207/581-1475, www.wildblueberries.maine.edu) or the state Department of Agriculture (207/287-3491, www.getrealmaine.com) for locations, recipes, and other wild-blueberry information, or log on to the website of the Wild Blueberry Association of North America (207/570-3535, www.wildblueberries.com).

The best place to simply appreciate blueberries is Machias, site of the renowned annual Wild Blueberry Festival, held the third weekend in August. While harvesting is under way in the surrounding fields, you can stuff your face with blueberry everything – muffins, jam, pancakes, ice cream, and pies. Plus you can collect blueberry-logo napkins, T-shirts, fridge magnets, pottery, and jewelry.

Another don't-miss while in Maine is Maine-made **ice cream.** Skip the overpriced Ben and Jerry's outlets. Locally made ice cream and gelato are fresher and better and often come in an astounding range of flavors. The big name in the state is Gifford's, with regional companies being Shain's and Round Top. All beat the out-of-state competition by a long shot. Even better are some of the one-of-a-kind dairy bars and farm stands. Good bets are John's in Liberty, Morton's in Ellsworth, and Mt. Desert Ice Cream and Ben and Bill's, both in Bar Harbor.

If you make it up to the St. John Valley in Aroostook County, be sure to try *ployes,* Acadian buckwheat pancakes, usually served with *creton,* a meat spread. Another don't-miss Maine food is the **whoopie pie** (two small flat cakes with a sweet-cream frosting filling). Wash one down with **Moxie,** a soft drink that is an acquired taste and that retains a cult-like following here.

Finally, whenever you get a chance, shop at a **farmers market.** Their biggest asset is serendipity – you never know what you'll find. Everything is locally grown and often organic. Herbs, unusual vegetables, seedlings, baked goods, meat, free-range chicken, goat cheese, herb vinegars, berries, exotic condiments, smoked salmon, maple syrup, honey, and jams are just a few of the possibilities. The Maine Department of Agriculture (207/287-3491, www.getrealmaine.com) provides info on markets.

---

culture. Basket making, canoe building, and traditional dancing are all parts of the scene.

Acadians and Franco-Americans

Within about three decades of their 1755 expulsion from Nova Scotia in *le grand dérangement,* Acadians had established new communities and new lives in northern Maine's St. John Valley. Gradually, they explored farther into central and southern coastal Maine and west into New Hampshire. The Acadian diaspora has profoundly influenced Maine and its culture, and it continues to do so today. Along the coast, French is spoken on the streets of Biddeford, where there's an annual Franco-American festival and an extensive Franco-American research collection.

African Americans

Although Maine's African American population is small, the state has had an African American community since the 17th century; by the 1764 census, there were 322 slaves and free blacks in the District of Maine. Segregation remained the rule, however, so in the 19th century, blacks established their own parish, the Abyssinian Church, in Portland. Efforts are under way to restore the long-closed church as an African American cultural center and gathering place for Greater Portland's black community. For researchers delving into

"Maine's black experience," the University of Southern Maine in Portland houses the African American Archive of Maine, a significant collection of historic books, letters, and artifacts donated by Gerald Talbot, the first African American to serve in the Maine legislature.

Finns, Swedes, and Lebanese

Finns came to Maine in several 19th-century waves, primarily to work the granite quarries on the coast and on offshore islands and the slate quarries in Monson, near Greenville. Finnish families clustered near the quarries in St. George and on Vinalhaven and Hurricane Islands—all with landscapes similar to those of their homeland. Today, names such as Laukka, Lehtinen, Hamalainen, and Harjula are interspersed among the Yankee names in the Mid-Coast region.

In 1870, an idealistic American diplomat named William Widgery Thomas established a model agricultural community with 50 brave Swedes in the heart of Aroostook County. Their enclave, New Sweden, remains today, as does the town of Stockholm, and descendants of the pioneers have spread throughout Maine.

At the turn of the 20th century, Lebanese (and some Syrians) began descending on Waterville, where they found work in the textile mills and eventually established St. Joseph's Maronite Church in 1927. One of these immigrants was the mother of former senator George Mitchell.

Russians, Ukrainians, and Belarusans

Arriving after World War II, Slavic immigrants established a unique community in Richmond, just inland from Bath. Only a tiny nucleus remains today, along with an onion-domed church, but a stroll through the local cemetery hints at the extent of the original colony.

The Newest Arrivals

War has been the impetus for the more recent arrival of Asians, Africans, Central Americans, and Eastern Europeans. Most have settled in the Portland area, making that city the state's center of diversity, although many Somalis now call Lewiston-Auburn home. Vietnamese and Cambodians began settling in Maine in the mid-1970s. A handful of Afghanis who fled the Soviet-Afghan conflict also ended up in Portland. Somalis, Ethiopians, and Sudanese fled their war-torn countries in the early–mid-1990s, and Bosnians and Kosovars arrived in the last half of the 1990s. With every new conflict comes a new stream of immigrants— world citizens are becoming Mainers, and Mainers are becoming world citizens.

The Amish

Although Aroostook County has the dubious distinction of having negative population growth, Amish families are increasingly taking refuge there, buying farms and starting new businesses.

CONDUCT AND CUSTOMS

Mainers are an independent lot, many exhibiting the classic Yankee characteristics of dry humor,

© HILARY NANGLE

Bicycles and horse-and-buggies are the means of transportation for the Amish in Aroostook County.

thrift, and ingenuity. Those who can trace their roots back at least a generation or two in the state and have lived here through the duration can call themselves natives; everyone else, no matter how long they've lived here, is "from away."

Mainers react to outsiders depending on how those outsiders treat them. Treat a Mainer with a condescending attitude, and you'll receive a cold shoulder at best. Treat a Mainer with respect, and you'll be welcome, perhaps even invited in to share a mug of coffee. Mainers are wary of outsiders and often with good reason. Many outsiders move to Maine because they fall in love with its independence and rural simplicity, and then they demand that the farmer stop spreading that stinky manure on his farmlands, or they insist that the town initiate garbage pickup, or they build a glass-and-timber McMansion in the midst of white clapboard historical homes. In most of Maine, money doesn't impress folks. The truth is, that lobsterman in the old truck and the well-worn work clothes might be sitting on a small fortune, or living on it. Perhaps nothing has caused more troubles between natives and newcomers than the rapidly increasing value of land and the taxes that go with that. For many visitors, Maine real estate is a bargain they can't resist.

If you want real insight into Maine character, listen to a CD or watch a video by Maine master humorist Tim Sample. As he often says, "Wait a minute; it'll sneak up on you."

THE ARTS
Fine Art

In 1850, in a watershed moment for Maine landscape painting, Hudson River School artist par excellence Frederic Edwin Church (1826–1900) vacationed on Mount Desert Island. Influenced by the luminist tradition of such contemporaries as Fitz Hugh Lane (1804–1865), who summered in nearby Castine, Church accurately but romantically depicted the dramatic tableaux of Maine's coast and woodlands that even today attract slews of admirers.

By the 1880s, however, impressionism had become the style du jour and was being practiced by a coterie of artists who collected around Charles Herbert Woodbury (1864–1940) in Ogunquit. His program made Ogunquit the best-known summer art school in New England. After Hamilton Easter Field established another art school in town, modernism soon asserted itself. Among the artists who took up summertime Ogunquit residence was Walt Kuhn (1877–1949), a key organizer of New York's 1913 landmark Armory Show of modern art.

Meanwhile, a bit farther south, impressionist Childe Hassam (1859–1935), part of writer Celia Thaxter's circle, produced several hundred works on Maine's remote Appledore Island, in the Isles of Shoals off Kittery, and illustrated Thaxter's *An Island Garden*.

Another artistic summer colony found its niche in 1903, when Robert Henri (born Robert Henry Cozad, 1865–1929), charismatic leader of the Ashcan School of realists and modernists, visited Monhegan Island, about 11 miles offshore. Artists who followed him there included Rockwell Kent (1882–1971), Edward Hopper (1882–1967), George Bellows (1882–1925), and Randall Davey (1887–1964). Among the many other artists associated with Monhegan images were William Kienbusch (1914–1980), Reuben Tam (1916–1991), and printmakers Leo Meissner (1895–1977) and Stow Wengenroth (1906–1978).

But colonies were of scant interest to other notables, who chose to derive their inspiration from Maine's stark natural beauty and work mostly in their own orbits. Among these are genre painter Eastman Johnson (1824–1906); romantic realist Winslow Homer (1836–1910), who lived in Maine for 27 years and whose studio in Prouts Neck, Scarborough, still overlooks the surf-tossed scenery he so often depicted; pointillist watercolorist Maurice Prendergast (1858–1924); John Marin (1870–1953), a cubist who painted Down East subjects, mostly around Deer Isle and Addison, on Cape Split; Lewiston native Marsden Hartley (1877–1943), who first showed his abstractionist work in New York in 1909 and later worked in Berlin; Fairfield Porter (1907–1975), whose family summered on Great Spruce Head Island, in East Penobscot

THE LOBSTER EXPERIENCE

No Maine visit can be considered complete without the "real Maine" experience of a "lobsta dinnah" at a lobster wharf, pound, or shack. Keep an eye on the weather, pick a sunny day, and head out.

If you spot a lobster place with "restaurant" in its name and no outside dining, keep going. What you're looking for is the genuine article. You want to eat outdoors at a wooden picnic table with a knockout view of boats and the sea. Whatever place you choose, the drill is much the same, and the "dinners" are served anytime from about noon (some places close as early as 7 P.M.).

First of all, dress very casually so you can manhandle the lobster without messing up your good clothes. If you want beer or wine, call ahead and ask if the place serves it; you may need to bring your own, since many such operations don't have a beer and wine license, much less a liquor license. In the evening, carry some insect repellent in case mosquitoes crash the party.

A basic one-pound lobster and go-withs (coleslaw or potato salad, potato chips, perhaps corn on the cob, and butter or fake butter for dipping) should run $15 or less, but of course that depends on the current market prices. Depending on your hunger, though, you may want to indulge in a shore dinner (lobster, steamed clams, potato chips, and maybe chowder, coleslaw, or corn), for which you may have to part with $18-24. Don't skip dessert; many lobster pounds are known for their homemade pies.

It's not unusual either to see lobster-wharf devotees carting picnic baskets with hors d'oeuvres, salads, and baguettes. I've even seen candles and champagne. Creativity abounds, but don't stray too far from the main attraction – the crustaceans.

Typically, you'll need to survey a chalkboard or whiteboard menu and step up to a window to order. You'll either give the person your name or get a number. A few places have staff to take your order or deliver your meal, but usually you head back to the window when your name or number is called. Don your plastic lobster bib and begin the attack. If you're a neophyte, watch a pro at a nearby table. Some pounds have "how-to" info on printed paper placemats. If you're really worried (you needn't be), contact the Maine Lobster Promotion Council (382 Harlow St., Bangor, www.mainelobster-promotion.com). It publishes a brochure with detailed instructions. Don't worry about doing it "wrong"; you'll eventually get what you came for, and it'll be an experience to remember.

For the ultimate lobster feeding frenzy, plan to be in Rockland the first weekend in August, when volunteers at the annual Maine Lobster Festival stoke up the world's largest lobster cooker and serve thousands of pounds of lobsters nonstop to more than 50,000 enthusiastic diners.

By region, in alphabetical order, here are great places to experience lobster. All are described in more detail in the regional chapters.

SOUTHERN COAST

- **Kittery Point:** Chauncey Creek Lobster Pier, 207/439-1030

- **Ogunquit:** Barnacle Billy's Lobster Pound, 207/646-5575

GREATER PORTLAND

- **Cape Elizabeth (near Portland):** The Lobster Shack, 207/799-1677

- **Portland:** Portland Lobster Company, 207/775-2112

- **South Freeport:** Harraseeket Lunch and Lobster Company, 207/865-3535

MID-COAST

- **Boothbay Harbor:** The Lobster Dock, 207/635-7120

- **Cundy's Harbor:** Holbrook's Wharf, 207/729-0848

Locals know to bring all the fixings, from tableclothes to wine, when dining at a harborfront lobster shack.

- **Damariscotta and Pemaquid Peninsula:** Broad Cove Marine Services, Medomak, 207/529-5186; Shaw's Fish and Lobster Wharf, New Harbor, 207/677-2200; Pemaquid Fishermen's Co-op, Pemaquid Harbor, 207/677-2801; Muscongus Bay Lobster, Round Pond, 207/529-5528; Round Pond Lobster Co-op, Round Pond, 207/529-5725; South Bristol Fishermen's Co-op, South Bristol, 207/644-8224

- **Georgetown:** Five Islands Lobster Company, 207/371-2990

- **Small Point:** The Lobster House, 207/389-1596

PENOBSCOT BAY

- **Lincolnville Beach:** The Lobster Pound, 207/789-5550

- **South Thomaston (near Rockland):** Waterman's Beach Lobster, 207/596-7819

- **Spruce Head (near Rockland):** Miller's Lobster Company, 207/594-7406

BLUE HILL AND DEER ISLE

- **Castine:** Dennett's Wharf, 207/326-9045

ACADIA

- **Bernard (Mount Desert Island):** Thurston's Lobster Pound, 207/244-7600

- **Southwest Harbor:** Beal's Lobster Pier, 207/244-3202

- **Trenton:** Trenton Bridge Lobster Pound, 207/667-2977

DOWN EAST

- **Eastport:** Eastport Chowder House, 207/853-4700; Quoddy Bay Lobster, 207/853-6640

Bay; and Andrew Wyeth (1917–2009), whose reputation as a romantic realist in the late 20th century surpassed that of his illustrator father, N. C. Wyeth (1882–1945).

On a parallel track was sculptor Louise Nevelson (1899–1988), raised in a poor Russian-immigrant family in Rockland and far better known outside her home state for her monumental wood sculptures slathered in black or gold. Two other noted sculptors with Maine connections were William Zorach (1887–1966) and Gaston Lachaise (1882–1935), both of whom lived in Georgetown, near Bath.

Contemporary year-round or seasonal Maine residents with national (and international) reputations include Vinalhaven's Robert Indiana, Lincolnville's Alex Katz, North Haven's Eric Hopkins, Deer Isle's Karl Schrag, Tenants Harbor's Jamie Wyeth (third generation of the famous family), Kennebunk's Edward Betts, and Cushing's Lois Dodd and Alan Magee.

The two best collections of Maine art are at the **Portland Museum of Art** (7 Congress Sq., Portland, 207/775-6148) and the **Farnsworth Art Museum** (16 Museum St., Rockland, 207/596-6457). The Farnsworth, in fact, focuses only on Maine art, primarily from the 20th century. The Farnsworth is the home of the Wyeth Center, featuring the works of three generations of Wyeths.

The **Ogunquit Museum of American Art,** appropriately, also has a very respectable Maine collection (in a spectacular setting), as does the Monhegan Museum. Other Maine paintings, not always on exhibit, are at the Bowdoin College Museum of Art in Brunswick; Bates College Museum of Art in Lewiston; and Colby College Museum of Art in Waterville. Colby has a huge collection of works by painter Alex Katz.

Crafts

Any survey of Maine art, however brief, must include the significant role of crafts in the state's artistic tradition. As with painters, sculptors, and writers, craftspeople have gravitated to Maine—most notably since the establishment in 1950 of the Haystack Mountain School of Crafts. Started in the Belfast area, the school put down roots on Deer Isle in 1960. Craft studios are abundant in Maine, and many festivals include craft displays.

Literature

Maine's first big-name writer was probably the early 17th-century French explorer Samuel de Champlain (1570–1635), who scouted the Maine coast, established a colony in 1604 near present-day Calais, and lived to describe in detail his experiences. Several decades after Champlain's forays, English naturalist John Josselyn visited Scarborough and in the 1670s published the first two books accurately describing Maine's flora and fauna, aptly describing, for example, blackflies as "not only a pesterment but a plague to the country."

Today, Maine's best-known author is Bangor resident Stephen King (born 1947), wizard of the weird. Many of his dozens of horror novels and stories are set in Maine, and several have been filmed for the big screen here. King and his author wife, Tabitha, are avid fans of both education and team sports and have generously distributed their largesse among schools and teams in their hometown as well as other parts of the state.

Other best-selling contemporary authors writing in or about Maine include Carolyn Chute (born 1948), resident of Parsonsfield and author of the raw novels *The Beans of Egypt, Maine* and *Letourneau's Used Auto Parts;* Cathie Pelletier (born 1953), raised in tiny Allagash and author of such humor-filled novels as *The Funeral Makers* and *The Bubble Reputation;* and coastal-Maine resident Richard Russo (born 1949), author of *Empire Falls,* winner of the 2002 Pulitzer Prize in Fiction and named the year's best novel by *Time* magazine.

CHRONICLERS OF THE GREAT OUTDOORS

John Josselyn was perhaps the first practitioner of Maine's strong naturalist tradition in American letters, but the Pine Tree State's rugged scenic beauty and largely unspoiled environment have given rise to many ecologically and environmentally concerned writers.

The 20th century saw the arrival in Maine

of crusader Rachel Carson (1907–1964), whose 1962 wake-up call, *Silent Spring,* was based partly on observations and research in Maine. The Rachel Carson National Wildlife Refuge, headquartered in Wells and comprising 10 chunks of environmentally sensitive coastal real estate, covers nearly 3,500 acres between Kittery Point and the Mid-Coast region.

The tiny town of Nobleboro, near Damariscotta, drew nature writer Henry Beston (1888–1968); his *Northern Farm* lyrically chronicles a year in Maine. Beston's wife, Elizabeth Coatsworth (1893–1986), wrote more than 90 books—including *Chimney Farm,* about their life in Nobleboro.

Fannie Hardy Eckstorm (1865–1946), born in Brewer to Maine's most prosperous fur trader, graduated from Smith College and became a noted expert on Maine and Native American folklore. Among her extensive writings, *Indian Place-Names of the Penobscot Valley and the Maine Coast,* published in 1941, remains a sine qua non for researchers.

The out-of-doors and inner spirits shaped Cape Rosier adoptees Helen and Scott Nearing, whose 1954 *Living the Good Life* became the bible of Maine's back-to-the-landers.

CLASSIC WRITINGS ON THE STATE

Historical novels, such as *Arundel,* were the specialty of Kennebunk native Kenneth Roberts (1885–1957), but Roberts also wrote *Trending into Maine,* a potpourri of Maine observations and experiences (the original edition was illustrated by N. C. Wyeth). Kennebunkport's Booth Tarkington (1869–1946), author of the *Penrod* novels and *The Magnificent Ambersons,* described 1920s Kennebunkport in *Mary's Neck,* published in 1932.

A little subgenre of sociological literary classics comprises astute observations (mostly by women) of daily life in various parts of the state. Some are fiction, some nonfiction, some barely disguised romans à clef. Probably the best-known chronicler of such observations is Sarah Orne Jewett (1849–1909), author of *The Country of the Pointed Firs,* a fictional 1896 account of "Dunnet's Landing" (actually Tenants Harbor);

her ties, however, were in the South Berwick area, where she spent most of her life. Also in South Berwick, Gladys Hasty Carroll (1904–1999) scrutinized everyday life in her hamlet, Dunnybrook, in *As the Earth Turns* (a title later "borrowed" and tweaked by a soap-opera producer). Lura Beam (1887–1978) focused on her childhood in the Washington County village of Marshfield in *A Maine Hamlet,* published in 1957, while Louise Dickinson Rich (1903–1972) entertainingly described her coastal Corea experiences in *The Peninsula* after first having chronicled her rugged wilderness existence in *We Took to the Woods.* Ruth Moore (1903–1989), born on Gott's Island, near Acadia National Park, published her first book at the age of 40. Her tales, recently brought back into print, have earned her a whole new appreciative audience. Elisabeth Ogilvie (1917–2006) came to Maine in 1944 and lived for many years on remote Ragged Island, transformed into "Bennett's Island" in her fascinating "tide trilogy": *High Tide at Noon, Storm Tide,* and *The Ebbing Tide.* Ben Ames Williams (1887–1953), the token male in this roundup of perceptive observers, in 1940 produced *Come Spring,* an epic tale of hardy pioneers founding the town of Union, just inland from Rockland.

In the mid-19th century, antislavery crusader Harriet Beecher Stowe (1811–1896), seldom recognized for her Maine connection, lived in Brunswick, where she wrote *The Pearl of Orr's Island,* a folkloric novel about a tiny nearby fishing community.

Mary Ellen Chase was a Maine native, born in Blue Hill in 1887. She became an English professor at Smith College in 1926 and wrote about 30 books, including some about the Bible as literature. She died in 1973.

Two books do a creditable job of excerpting literature from throughout Maine—something of a daunting task. The most comprehensive is *Maine Speaks: An Anthology of Maine Literature,* published in 1989 by the Maine Writers and Publishers Alliance. *The Quotable Moose: A Contemporary Maine Reader,* edited by Wesley McNair and published in 1994 by the University Press of New England, focuses on 20th-century authors.

A WORLD OF HER OWN

For Marguerite Yourcenar (1903–1987), Maine provided solitude and inspiration for subjects ranging far beyond the state's borders. Yourcenar was a longtime Northeast Harbor resident and the first woman elected to the prestigious Académie Française. Her house, now a shrine to her work, is open to the public by appointment in summer.

ESSAYISTS, CRITICS, AND HUMORISTS NATIVE AND TRANSPLANTED

Maine's best-known essayist is and was E. B. White (1899–1985), who bought a farm in tiny Brooklin in 1933 and continued writing for *The New Yorker*. *One Man's Meat*, published in 1944, is one of the best collections of his wry, perceptive writings. His legions of admirers also include two generations raised on his classic children's stories *Stuart Little*, *Charlotte's Web*, and *The Trumpet of the Swan*.

Writer and critic Doris Grumbach (born 1918), who settled in Sargentville, not far from Brooklin but far from her New York ties, wrote two particularly wise works from the perspective of a Maine transplant: *Fifty Days of Solitude* and *Coming into the End Zone*.

Maine's best contemporary exemplar of humorous writing is the late John Gould (1908–2003), whose life in rural Friendship has provided grist for many a tale. Gould's hilarious columns in the *Christian Science Monitor* and his steady book output made him an icon of Maine humor.

PINE TREE POETS

Born in Portland, Henry Wadsworth Longfellow (1807–1882) is Maine's most famous poet; his marine themes clearly stem from his seashore childhood (in "My Lost Youth," he wistfully rhapsodized, "Often I think of the beautiful town / That is seated by the sea . . . ").

Widely recognized in her own era, poet Celia Thaxter (1835–1894) held court on Appledore Island in the Isles of Shoals, welcoming artists, authors, and musicians to her summer salon. Today, she's best known for *An Island Garden*, published in 1894 and detailing her attempts at horticultural TLC in a hostile environment.

Edna St. Vincent Millay (1892–1950) had connections to Camden, Rockland, and Union and described a stunning Camden panorama in "Renascence."

Whitehead Island, near Rockland, was the birthplace of Wilbert Snow (1883–1977), who went on to become president of Connecticut's Wesleyan University. His 1968 memoir, *Codline's Child*, makes fascinating reading.

A longtime resident of York, May Sarton (1912–1995) approached cult status as a guru of feminist poetry and prose—and as an articulate analyst of death and dying during her terminal illness.

Among respected Maine poets today are William Carpenter (born 1940) of Stockton Springs; Wesley McNair (born 1941) of Mercer; and Appleton's Kate Barnes (born 1932), named Maine's Poet Laureate 1996–1999. Although she comes by her acclaim legitimately, Barnes is also genetically disposed, being the daughter of writers Henry Beston and Elizabeth Coatsworth.

MAINE LIT FOR LITTLE ONES

Besides E. B. White's children's classics, *Stuart Little*, *Charlotte's Web*, and *The Trumpet of the Swan*, American kids were also weaned on books written and illustrated by Maine island summer resident Robert McCloskey (1914–2003)—notably *Time of Wonder*, *One Morning in Maine*, and *Blueberries for Sal*. Neck-and-neck in popularity is prolific Walpole illustrator-writer Barbara Cooney (1917–1999), whose award-winning titles included *Miss Rumphius*, *Island Boy*, and *Hattie and the Wild Waves*. Cooney produced more than 100 books, and it seems as if everyone has a different favorite.

C. A. (Charles Asbury) Stephens (1844–1931) for 60 years wrote for the magazine *Youth's Companion*. In 1995, a collection of his vivid children's stories was reissued as *Stories from the Old Squire's Farm*.

Maine can also lay partial claim to Kate Douglas Wiggin (1856–1923), author of the eternally popular *Rebecca of Sunnybrook Farm*; she spent summers at Quillcote in Hollis, west of Portland.

ESSENTIALS

Getting There

Coastal Maine has two major airports, two major bus networks, a toll highway, limited Amtrak service, and some ad hoc local transportation systems that fill in the gaps.

BY AIR

Maine's major airline gateway is **Portland International Jetport** (PWM, 207/774-7301, www.portlandjetport.org), although visitors headed farther north sometimes prefer **Bangor International Airport** (BGR, 207/947-0384, www.flybangor.com). The "international" in their names is a bit misleading. Charter flights from Europe often stop at Bangor for refueling and customs clearance, and sometimes bad weather also diverts flights there. Portland has a few flights connecting to eastern Canada. But Boston's Logan Airport is the nearest airport with direct flights from Europe and other worldwide destinations.

Airlines serving Portland and Bangor are **AirTran** (800/433-7300), **Continental** (800/523-3273), **Delta** (800/221-1212), **JetBlue** (800/538-2583), **United Express** (800/864-8331), and **US Airways** (800/428-4322). All increase their flight frequency during the summer to accommodate stepped-up demand.

Portland Jetport Facilities

Portland's airport is small and easy to navigate.

© HILARY NANGLE

Food options are few, but you won't starve. A business center in the gate area has Internet access. Visitor information is dispensed from a desk (unfortunately not always staffed) between the gates and the baggage-claim area. Since Portland is the terminus of most flights, baggage service isn't a priority; expect to have to wait for a while. If you have an emergency, contact the airport manager (207/773-8462).

Ground transportation options include the Greater Portland Transportation District's **Metro** (207/774-0351, www.gpmetrobus.com) bus route 1, which connects the airport with the Portland Transportation Center and in-town Portland Monday–Saturday. **Taxis** are available outside baggage claim.

Car-rental agencies at the airport include **Alamo** (207/775-0855 or 877/222-9075, www.alamo.com), **Avis** (207/874-7500 or 800/230-4898, www.avis.com), **Budget** (207/772-6789 or 800/527-0700, www.drivebudget.com), **Hertz** (207/774-4544 or 800/654-3131, www.hertz.com), and **National** (207/773-0036 or 877/222-9058, www.nationalcar.com).

Bangor Airport Facilities

Bangor's airport has scaled-down versions of Portland's facilities but all the necessary amenities. If you need help, contact the airport manager (207/947-0384).

Ground transportation options include the **Bangor Area Transportation** (BAT, 207/882-4670, www.bgrme.org) buses, which connect the airport to downtown Bangor Monday–Saturday. **West's Coastal Connection** (207/546-2823 or 800/596-2823, www.westbusservice.com) has scheduled service along Route 1 to Calais, with stops en route. **Taxis** are available outside baggage claim.

Car-rental agencies at the airport include **Alamo** (207/947-0158 or 800/462-5266, www.goalamo.com), **Avis** (207/947-8383 or 800/230-4898, www.avis.com), **Budget** (207/945-9429 or 800/527-0700, www.drivebudget.com), **Hertz** (207/942-5519 or 800/654-3131, www.hertz.com), and **National** (207/947-0158 or 800/227-7368, www.nationalcar.com).

Flying to a remote destination via a floatplane can be far faster and less bumpy than driving.

Regional Airports

Airports accessible via US Airways/Business Express from Boston are **Hancock County Airport** (BHB, 207/667-7329, www.bhbairport .com) near Bar Harbor; **Knox County Regional Airport** (RKD, 207/594-4131, www.knoxcounty .midcoast.com) at Owls Head, near Rockland and Camden (also served from Boston by Cape Air); **Augusta State Airport** (AUG, 207/626-2306, www.augustaairport.org); and **Northern Maine Regional Airport** (PQI, 207/764-2550, www.flypresqueisle.com), in Presque Isle.

Boston Logan Airport

If you fly into Boston Logan Airport (BOS), you easily can get to Maine via rental car (all major rental companies are at the airport, but it's not pleasant to navigate Logan in a rental car) or Concord Coachlines bus (the easiest and least expensive option). You'll need to connect to North Station if you want to take Amtrak's *Downeaster* train.

BY CAR

The major highway access to Maine from the south is **I-95**, which roughly parallels the coast until Bangor before shooting up to Houlton. Other busy access points are **Route 1,** also from New Hampshire, departing the coast in Calais at the New Brunswick border; **Route 302,** from North Conway, New Hampshire, entering Maine at Fryeburg; **Route 2,** from Gorham, New Hampshire, to Bethel; **Route 201,** entering from Québec just north of Jackman; and a couple of crossing points from New Brunswick into Aroostook and Washington Counties in northeastern Maine.

BY BUS

Concord Coachlines (800/639-3317, www .concordcoachlines.com) departs downtown Boston (South Station Transportation Center) and Logan Airport for Portland almost hourly from the wee hours of the morning until late at night, making pickups at all Logan airline terminals (on the lower level). Most of the buses continue directly to Bangor; three daily nonexpress buses continue along the coast to Searsport before turning inland to Bangor. The Portland bus terminal is the Portland Transportation Center, Thompson Point Road, just west of I-295. If you're headed for downtown Portland from the bus terminal, board the Metro city bus at the terminal and show your bus ticket to receive a free trip.

Also serving Maine but with far less frequent service is **Greyhound** (www.greyhound.com).

BY RAIL

Amtrak's *Downeaster* (800/872-7245, www .thedowneaster.com) makes five daily round-trip runs between Boston's North Station and Portland Transportation Center, with stops in Wells, Saco, and seasonally in Old Orchard Beach (May 1–Oct. 31). From the Portland station, Portland's Metro municipal bus service will take you gratis to downtown Portland; just show your Amtrak ticket stub. Plans call for service to be extended to Brunswick in 2012; from there, it connects with **Maine Eastern Railway** (866/637-2457, www.maineeastern-railroad.com), an excursion train with service to Rockland.

Getting Around

The Maine Department of Transportation (800/877-9171) operates the Explore Maine site (www.exploremaine.org), which has information on all forms of transportation in Maine.

BY BUS

Concord Coachlines (800/639-3317, www.concordcoachlines.com) has the most extensive bus network, with routes designed to assist students, island ferry passengers, and day-trippers. Buses from Boston's Logan Airport stop in downtown Portland and follow a mostly coastal route through Brunswick, Bath, Wiscasset, Damariscotta, Waldoboro, Rockland, Camden, Belfast, and Searsport, ending in Bangor, and then follow the same route in reverse. An inland route operates to Bangor, with some buses stopping in Augusta.

Once-a-day buses to and from Calais coordinate with the Bangor bus schedules. The Calais line, stopping in Ellsworth, Gouldsboro, Machias, and Perry (near Eastport), is operated by **West's Coastal Connection** (207/546-2823 or 800/596-2823, www.westbusservice.com). Flag stops along the route are permitted.

Portland, South Portland, Lewiston-Auburn, Waterville, and Bangor have **city bus service,** with some wheelchair-accessible vehicles. A number of smaller communities have established **local shuttle vans** or **trolley-buses,** but most of the latter are seasonal. Trolley-buses operate (for a fee) in Ogunquit, Wells, the Kennebunks, Portland, Bath, and Boothbay. Mount Desert Island and the Schoodic Peninsula have the **Island Explorer,** an excellent free summer bus service starting in late June.

BY CAR

No matter how much time and resourcefulness you summon, you'll never really be able to appreciate Maine without a car.

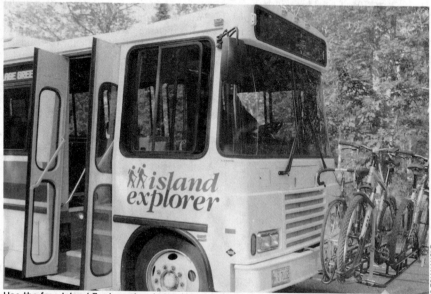

© TOM NANGLE

Use the free Island Explorer bus to explore Acadia National Park.

PRONUNCIATION 101: HOW TO SAY IT LIKE A LOCAL

Countless names for Maine cities, towns, villages, rivers, lakes, and streams have Native American origins; some are variations on French; and a few have German derivations. Here are some pronunciations to give you a leg up when requesting directions along the Maine coast:

- **Arundel** – uh-RUN-d'l

- **Bangor** – BANG-gore

- **Bremen** – BREE-m'n

- **Calais** – CAL-us

- **Castine** – kass-TEEN

- **Damariscotta** – dam-uh-riss-COTT-uh

- **Harraseeket** – hare-uh-SEEK-it

- **Isle au Haut** – aisle-a-HO, AISLE-a-ho (subject to plenty of dispute, depending on whether or not you live in the vicinity)

- **Katahdin** – kuh-TA-din

- **Lubec** – loo-BECK

- **Machias** – muh-CHAI-us

- **Matinicus** – muh-TIN-i-cuss

- **Medomak** – muh-DOM-ick

- **Megunticook** – muh-GUN-tuh-cook

- **Monhegan** – mun-HEE-gun

- **Mount Desert** – Mount Duh-ZERT

- **Narraguagus** – nare-uh-GWAY-gus

- **Naskeag** – NASS-keg

- **Passagassawakeag** – puh-sag-gus-uh-WAH-keg

- **Passamaquoddy** – pass-uh-muh-QUAD-dee

- **Pemaquid** – PEM-a-kwid

- **Saco** – SOCK-oh

- **Schoodic** – SKOO-dick

- **Steuben** – stew-BEN

- **Topsham** – TOPS-'m

- **Wiscasset** – wiss-CASS-it

- **Woolwich** – WOOL-itch

Two lanes wide from Kittery in the south to Fort Kent at the top, U.S. Route 1 is the state's most congested road, particularly in July–August. Mileage distances can be extremely deceptive, since it will take you much longer than anticipated to get from point A to point B. If you ask anyone about distances, chances are good that you'll receive an answer in hours rather than miles. If you're trying to make time, it's best to take the Maine Turnpike or I-95; if you want to see Coastal Maine, take U.S. 1 and lots of little offshoots. That said, bear in mind that even I-95 becomes very congested on summer weekends, and especially summer holiday weekends.

Note that the expressways can be a bit confusing to motorists. Between York and Augusta, I-95 is the same as the Maine Turnpike, regulated by the Maine Turnpike Authority (877/682-9433, travel conditions 800/675-7453, www.maineturnpike.com). All exit numbers along I-95 reflect the distance in miles from the New Hampshire border. I-295 splits from I-95 in Portland and follows the coast to Brunswick before veering inland and rejoining I-95 in Gardiner. Exits on I-295 reflect the distance from where it splits from I-95 just south of Portland at Exit 44.

Road Conditions

For real-time information on road conditions, weather, construction, and major delays, dial 511 in Maine, 866/282-7578 from out of state, or visit www.511maine.gov. Information is available in both English and French.

Driving Regulations

Seat belts are mandatory in Maine. Unless posted otherwise, Maine allows right turns at red lights after you stop and check for oncoming traffic. Never pass a stopped school bus in either direction. Maine law also requires drivers to turn on their car's headlights any time the windshield wipers are operating.

Roadside Assistance

Since Maine is enslaved to the automobile, it's not a bad idea for vacationers to carry membership in AAA in case of breakdowns, flat tires, and other car crises. Contact your nearest AAA office or AAA Northern New England (207/780-6800 or 800/482-7497, www.aaanne.com). The emergency road service number is 800/222-4357.

HITCHHIKING

Even though Maine's public transportation network is woefully inadequate and the crime rate is one of the lowest in the nation, it's still risky to hitchhike or pick up hitchhikers.

Tips for Travelers

VISAS AND OFFICIALDOM

Since 9/11, security has been excruciatingly tight for foreign visitors, with customs procedures in flux. For current rules, visit www.usa.gov/visitors/arriving.shtml. It's wise to make two sets of copies of all paperwork, one to carry separately on your trip and another left with a trusted friend or relative at home.

SMOKING

Maine now has laws banning smoking in restaurants, bars, and lounges as well as enclosed areas of public places, such as shopping malls. Only a handful of bed-and-breakfasts and country inns permit smoking, and increasingly motels, hotels, and resorts are limiting the number of rooms where smoking is permitted. Some accommodations ban smoking anywhere on the property, and many have instituted high fines for smoking in a non-smoking room. If you're a smoker, motels with direct outdoor access make it easiest to satisfy a craving.

ACCOMMODATIONS, FOOD, AND ALCOHOL

Accommodations

For all accommodation listings, rates are quoted for peak season, which is usually July–August but may extend through foliage season (mid-October); for winter sports destinations, peak rates occur during Christmas and school vacation periods. Rates drop, often dramatically, in the shoulder and off-season at accommodations that remain open. Especially during peak season, many accommodations require a 2–3-night minimum.

For the best rates, be sure to check Internet specials and to ask about packages. Many accommodations also provide discounts for members of travel clubs such as AAA, to seniors and members of the military, and other such groups.

Unless otherwise noted, accommodations listed have private baths.

Food

Days and hours of operation listed for places serving food are for peak season. These do change often, sometimes even within a season, and it's not uncommon for a restaurant to close early on a quiet night. To avoid disappointment, call before making a special trip.

Alcohol

As in the rest of the country, Maine's minimum drinking age is 21 years—and bar owners, bartenders, and serving staff can be held legally accountable for serving underage imbibers. If your blood alcohol level is 0.08 percent or higher, you are legally considered to be operating under the influence.

WHAT TO TAKE

Weather can be unpredictable anywhere in Maine, but especially along the coast, with fog, rain, and temperatures ranging from the low 30s on a cold spring day to the 90s on a hot summer one. But even summer sees days when a **fleece pullover** or jacket and a **lightweight, weatherproof jacket** are quite welcome. A hat and mittens are a plus when venturing far off shore on a windjammer or whale-watching boat or when paddling northern rivers on inclement days. Other handy items are **binoculars** for sighting boats, offshore lighthouses, birds, and wildlife; a small **backpack** for day trips or light hiking; and a small or collapsible **cooler** for picnics or storing food.

Unless you're dining at the White Barn Inn or Arrows, you won't need fancy clothing. Resort casual is the dress code in most good restaurants and in downtown Portland, with nice T-shirts and shorts being acceptable almost everywhere in beach communities.

In winter and spring, add warm **waterproof insulted boots, gloves,** a **hat,** and **winter-weight clothing** to your list. During hunting season, add **hunter-orange accessories** (a hat, gloves, and a vest), especially if you'll be in the woods anywhere in the state.

TIME ZONE

All of Maine is in the eastern time zone—the same as New York, Washington, D.C., Philadelphia, and Orlando. Eastern standard time (EST) runs from the first Sunday in November to the second Sunday in March; eastern daylight time (EDT), one hour later, prevails otherwise. Surprising to many first-time visitors, especially when visiting coastal areas, is how early the sun rises in the morning and how early it sets at night.

If your itinerary also includes Canada, remember that the provinces of New Brunswick and Nova Scotia are on Atlantic time—one hour later than eastern time—so if it's noon in Maine, it's 1 P.M. in these provinces.

Health and Safety

There's too much to do in Maine, and too much to see, to spend even a few hours laid low by illness or mishap. Be sensible—be sure to get enough sleep, wear sunscreen and appropriate clothing, know your limits and don't take foolhardy risks, heed weather and warning signs, carry water and snacks while hiking, don't overindulge in food or alcohol, always tell someone where you're going, and watch your step. If you're traveling with children, you should quadruple your caution.

MEDICAL CARE

In the event of any emergency, dial 911.

Southern Coast

York Hospital (15 Hospital Dr., York, emergency 207/351-2157); **Wells Urgent Care** (109 Sanford Rd., Wells, 207/646-5211, 8 A.M.–7 P.M. daily); **Kennebunk Walk-In Clinic** (24 Portland Rd./Rte. 1, Kennebunk, 207/985-6027); **Southern Maine Medical Center** (Rte. 111, Biddeford, 207/283-7000, emergency 207/294-5000).

Greater Portland

Maine Medical Center (22 Bramhall St., Portland, emergency 207/871-2381); **Mercy Hospital** (144 State St., Portland, emergency 207/879-3265).

Mid-Coast

Mid-Coast Hospital (Bath Rd., Cooks Corner, Brunswick, 207/729-0181); **Parkview Hospital** (329 Maine St., 1 mile south of Bowdoin

College, Brunswick, 207/373-2000); **St. Andrews Hospital and Healthcare Center** (3 St. Andrews Lane, Boothbay Harbor, 207/633-2121); **Miles Memorial Hospital** (Bristol Rd./Rte. 130, Damariscotta, 207/563-1234).

Penobscot Bay
Penobscot Bay Medical Center (Rte. 1, Rockport, 207/596-8000); **Waldo County General Hospital** (118 Northport Ave., Belfast, 207/338-2500 or 800/649-2536).

Blue Hill and Deer Isle
Blue Hill Memorial Hospital (57 Water St., Blue Hill, 207/374-3400, emergency 207/374-2836).

Acadia Region
Maine Coast Memorial Hospital (50 Union St., Ellsworth, 207/664-5311 or 888/645-8829, emergency 207/664-5340); **Mount Desert Island Hospital** (10 Wayman Lane, Bar Harbor, 207/288-5081).

Down East
Down East Community Hospital (Upper Court St./Rte. 1A, Machias, 207/255-3356); **Regional Medical Center at Lubec** (43 S. Lubec Rd., Lubec, 207/733-1090); **Eastport Health Care** (Boynton St., Eastport, 207/853-6001); **Calais Regional Hospital** (50 Franklin St., Calais, 207/454-7521).

Aroostook
Houlton Regional Hospital (20 Hartford St., Houlton, 207/532-2900); **Aroostook Medical Center/A. R. Gould Memorial Hospital** (140 Academy St./Rte. 10, Presque Isle, emergency room 207/768-4100); **Cary Medical Center** (163 Van Buren Rd., Caribou, 207/498-3111); **Northern Maine Medical Center** (94 E. Main St./Rte. 1, Fort Kent, 207/834-3155).

Maine Highlands
Millinocket Regional Hospital (200 Somerset St., Millinocket, 207/723-5161); **Charles A. Dean Memorial Hospital** (Pritham Ave., Greenville, 207/695-5200); **Mayo Regional Hospital** (75 W. Main St., Dover-Foxcroft, 207/564-8401); **Eastern Maine Medical Center** (489 State St., Bangor, 207/973-7000, emergency room 207/973-8000); **St. Joseph Hospital** (360 Broadway, Bangor, 207/907-1000).

Kennebec River Valley
MaineGeneral Medical Center (6 E. Chestnut St., Augusta, 207/626-1000); **MaineGeneral Medical Center** (149 North St., Waterville, 207/872-1000); **Redington-Fairview General Hospital** (Fairview Ave./Rte. 104, Skowhegan, 207/474-5121); **Jackman Region Health Center** (Main St./Rte. 201, Jackman, 207/668-2691).

Western Lakes and Mountains
Franklin Memorial Hospital (111 Franklin Health Commons, Farmington, 207/778-6031); **Rangeley Region Health Center** (Dallas Hill Rd., Rangeley, 207/864-3303); **The Bethel Family Health Center** (32 Railroad St., Bethel, 207/824-2193); **Rumford Hospital** (420 Franklin St., Rumford, 207/369-1000, emergency room 207/364-4581); **Western Maine Mountain Clinic** (South Ridge Base Area, Sunday River, 207/824-4900); **Stephens Memorial Hospital** (181 Main St., Norway, 207/743-5933); **Bridgton Hospital** (S. High St., Bridgton, 207/647-6000); **Central Maine Medical Center** (300 Main St., Lewiston, 207/795-0111); **St. Mary's Regional Medical Center** (Campus Ave., Lewiston, emergency room 207/777-8100).

AFFLICTIONS
Lyme Disease
A bacterial infection that causes severe arthritis-like symptoms, Lyme disease is spread by bites from tiny deer ticks (not the larger dog ticks; they don't carry it). The best advice is to take precautions, especially when hiking: Wear a long-sleeved shirt and long pants, and tuck pant legs into your socks. Light-colored clothing makes the ticks easier to spot. Buy tick repellent at a supermarket or convenience store and use it liberally. After any hike, check for ticks—especially behind the knees, and in the armpits, navel, and groin.

If you're traveling with a pet, be sure to check for ticks.

© HILARY NANGLE

Rabies

If you're bitten by any animal, especially one acting suspiciously, head for the nearest hospital emergency room. For statewide information about rabies, contact the Maine Disease Control Administration in Augusta (207/287-3591).

Allergies

If your medical history includes extreme allergies to shellfish or bee sting, you know the risks of eating a lobster or wandering around a wildflower meadow. However, if you come from a landlocked area and are new to crustaceans, you might not be aware of the potential hazard. Statistics indicate that less than 2 percent of adults have a severe shellfish allergy, but for those who do, the reaction can set in quickly. Immediate treatment is needed to keep the airways open. If you have a history of severe allergic reactions to anything, be prepared when you come to the Maine coast dreaming of lobster feasts. Ask your doctor for a prescription for an EpiPen (epinephrine), a preloaded, single-

use syringe containing 0.3 mg of the drug—enough to tide you over until you can get to a hospital.

Seasickness

If you're planning to do any boating in Maine—particularly sailing—you'll want to be prepared. (Being prepared may in fact keep you from succumbing, since fear of seasickness just about guarantees you'll get it.) Talk to a pharmacist or doctor about your options.

Hypothermia and Frostbite

Wind and weather can shift dramatically in Maine, especially at higher elevations, creating prime conditions for contracting hypothermia and frostbite. At risk are hikers, swimmers, canoeists, kayakers, sailors, skiers, and even cyclists.

To prevent hypothermia and frostbite, dress in layers and remove or add them as needed. Wool, waterproof nylon (such as Gore-Tex), and synthetic fleece (such as Polartec) are the best fabrics for repelling dampness. Polyester fleece lining wicks excess moisture away from your body. Especially in winter, always cover your head, since body heat escapes quickly through the head; a ski mask will protect ears and nose. Wear wool- or fleece-lined gloves and wool socks.

Special Considerations During Hunting Season

During Maine's fall hunting season (October–Thanksgiving weekend)—and especially during the November deer season—walk or hike only in wooded areas marked "No Hunting," "No Trespassing," or "Posted." And even if an area is closed to hunters, don't decide to explore the woods during deer or moose season without wearing a hunter-orange (eye-poppingly fluorescent) jacket or vest. If you take your dog along, be sure it wears an orange vest too. Hunting is illegal on Sunday.

During hunting season, moose and deer are on the move and made understandably skittish by the hunters invading their turf. Moose are primarily found inland, but deer are everywhere, and even the occasional moose strays into coastal areas of Maine. At night, particularly in wooded areas, these huge creatures often end up alongside or on the roads, so ratchet up your defensive-driving skills. Reduce your normal speed, use high beams when there's no oncoming traffic, and remain extra-alert. In a moose-versus-car encounter, no one wins, and human fatalities are common. An encounter between a deer and a car may be less dangerous to the humans (although the deer usually dies), but some damage is inevitable.

Information and Services

MONEY

If you need to exchange foreign currency—other than Canadian dollars—do it at or near border crossings or in Portland. In small communities, such transactions are more complicated; you may end up spending more time and money than necessary.

Typical banking hours are 9 A.M.–3 P.M. weekdays, occasionally with later hours on Friday. Drive-up windows at many banks tend to open as much as an hour earlier and stay open an hour or so after lobbies close. Some banks also maintain Saturday-morning hours. Automated teller machines (ATMs) are found throughout Maine.

Credit Cards and Traveler's Checks

Bank credit cards have become so preferred and so prevalent that it's nearly impossible to rent a car or check into a hotel without one. MasterCard and Visa are the most widely accepted in Maine, and Discover and American Express are the next most popular; Carte Blanche and Diners Club lag far behind. Be aware, however, that small restaurants (including lobster pounds), shops, and bed-and-breakfasts off the beaten track might not accept credit cards or nonlocal personal checks; you may need to settle your account with cash or traveler's checks.

Taxes

Maine charges a 5 percent sales tax on general purchases and services; 7 percent on prepared foods, candy, and lodging or camping; and 10 percent on auto rentals.

Tipping

Tip 15–20 percent of the pretax bill in restaurants.

Taxi drivers expect a 15 percent tip; airport porters expect at least $1 per bag, depending on the difficulty of the job.

The usual tip for housekeeping services in accommodations is $1–5 per person per night, depending upon the level of service. It's not necessary to tip at bed-and-breakfasts if the owners do the housekeeping.

Some accommodations add a 10–15-percent service fee to rates.

TIPS FOR THE BUDGET-CONSCIOUS

At first glance, Maine might seem pricey, but take another look. It is possible to keep a vacation within a reasonable budget, and here are a few tips for doing so.

For starters, avoid the big-name towns and seek out accommodations in smaller nearby ones instead. For example, instead of Damariscotta, consider Waldoboro; instead of Camden, try Belfast or Searsport; in place of Bar Harbor, check Trenton or Southwest Harbor. Or simply explore the Down East Coast or inland Maine, where rates are generally far lower than in other regions.

Small family-owned motels tend to have the lowest rates. Better yet, book a cabin or a cottage for a week rather than a room by the night. Not only can you find reasonable weekly rentals — especially if you plan well in advance — but also you'll have cooking facilities, which allow you to avoid eating all meals out.

Speaking of food, buy or bring a small cooler so you can stock up at supermarkets and farmers markets for picnic meals. Most Hannaford and Shaw's supermarkets have large selections of prepared foods and big salad bars and bakeries, and many local groceries have pizza and sandwich counters.

Check local papers and bulletin boards for Public Supper notices. Most are very inexpensive, raise money for a good cause, and provide an opportunity not only for a good meal but also to meet locals and gain a few insider tips.

Of course, sometimes you want to have a nice meal in a nice place. Consider going out for lunch, which is usually far less expensive than dinner, or take advantage of early-bird specials or the Friday-night all-you-can-eat fish fries offered at quite a few home-cooking restaurants.

Take advantage of Maine's vast outdoor-recreation opportunities; many are free. Even Acadia, with its miles and miles of trails and carriage roads, and its Explorer bus service, is a bargain; buy a park pass and it's all yours to use and explore.

Take advantage of free events: concerts, lectures, farmers markets, art shows and openings, and family events. Most are usually listed in local papers.

Avoid parking hassles and fees and save gas by using local transportation services when available, such as the trolley network on the Southern Coast and the Explorer bus system on Mount Desert Island.

Finally, before making reservations for anything, check to see if there's a special Internet rate or ask about any discounts that might apply to you: AAA, senior, military, government, family rate, and so forth. If you don't ask, you won't get.

TOURISM INFORMATION AND MAPS
Maine Tourism Association
The Maine Tourism Association (207/623-0363, www.mainetourism.com) publishes both an annual map and the magazine-style guidebook *Maine Invites You*, which details sights throughout the state and provides listings of chambers of commerce and other info helpful for travelers. Both are free.

State Visitors Information Centers
The Maine Tourism Association operates state visitors information centers in Calais, Fryeburg (May–October), Hampden, Houlton, Kittery, and Yarmouth. These are excellent places to visit to stock up on brochures, pick up a map, ask advice, and use restrooms.

Maine Online
The Maine Office of Tourism has established an excellent website: www.visitmaine .com. You'll find chamber of commerce addresses, articles, photos, information on lodgings, and access to a variety of Maine tourism businesses. Hundreds of other Maine pages are also up and running, so surf away. You can use the website to request a free state map and a copy of *Maine Invites You*. The state's

ADVENTURES IN LEARNING

A surprising number of educational programs operate in Maine. Here's a sampling.

HOME, SWEET HOME

In 1974, enterprising entrepreneurs Pat and Patsy Hennin jumped on the do-it-yourself bandwagon and established the **Shelter Institute** (873 Rte. 1, Woolwich, 207/442-7938, www.shelterinstitute.com) to train neophytes in energy-efficient home design and construction techniques. Since then, thousands of students have taken courses here, and enthusiastic alumni and their building projects span the globe. Students range in age from late teens to early 80s. Courses take place on the school's 68-acre campus in Woolwich, five miles north of Bath. Visitors are welcome any time, and anyone who appreciates fine woodworking tools has to visit the institute's **Woodbutcher Tools** retail shop and bookstore, open 9 A.M.-4:30 P.M. Monday-Friday, 9 A.M.-3 P.M. Saturday.

CONTEMPLATIVE SKIFF BUILDING

Word of mouth seems to be the best marketing tool for **The Carpenter's Boatshop** (440 Old County Rd., Pemaquid, 207/677-3768, www.carpentersboatshop.org). Founded in 1979 by Bobby Ives, an engaging Congregational minister, and his late wife, Ruth, the boat shop accepts interested applicants of any denomination to join a community dedicated to both spirituality and boatbuilding. This is no laid-back contemplative religious retreat; serious boatbuilding supports the community. Apprenticeships run mid-September-mid-June, and there's no tuition. Room and board are provided. The diverse group of 6-8 students all become part of the boatbuilding crew, working at least 40 hours a week in the huge shingled barn-boat shop. Each student builds a 9.5-foot Monhegan skiff, contributes to the construction of three types of stock wooden boats, helps with all the daily chores, and spends Saturday morning doing valuable community service on the Pemaquid Peninsula. During daily prayer gatherings, students can participate or use the time for reading or other reflective pursuits. Marine author Peter Spectre, an admitted skeptic, admiringly describes this unique program: "Just consider what all these people have done for themselves and the community." A summer program offers one-week courses in basic boat building, woodworking, furniture making, and related skills, with fees varying by course.

CREATING A SMALLER WORLD

Begun in 1986 to provide language classes for adults, **Penobscot School** (28 Gay St., Rockland, 207/594-1084, www.languagelearning.org) has become a multicultural clearinghouse with ties around the globe. In fall, winter, and spring, the school offers day and evening courses in nearly a dozen languages, sponsors ethnic dinners and festivals, organizes language-immersion weekends, and puts on international study programs in local schools. July-September, international students ages 18-65 arrive at the school for intensive three-week English-language courses. On summer weekdays, visitors are often invited for lunch at the school to interact with students practicing their English.

SAILING, SAILING

The best way to explore Maine's coast is aboard a boat. **Bay Island Sailing School** (207/596-7550 or 800/421-2492, www.bay-sailing.com), based in Rockland, is an American Sailing Association-approved summer program that has weekday, weekend, and live-aboard learn-to-sail classes – and special courses for teenagers and women. Contact the school for details.

FURNISH YOUR FUTURE

Alumni of the one-, two-, and 12-week workshops at the **Center for Furniture Craftsmanship** (25 Mill St., Rockport, 207/594-5611, www.woodschool.org), established in 1993, can't say enough about their experiences. One-week to nine-month courses are given for various skill levels, from beginner to pro. The center can help arrange for lodging and meals. It's open all year.

MUSICAL INTERLUDE

You're never too old to learn how to play a musical instrument or to sing. **SummerKeys** (207/733-2316 June 15–Oct. 15, 973/316-6220 Oct. 15–June 15, www.summerkeys.com) is a music school without admission requirements. Its premise is the inviting: "Come as you are to enjoy the study, the work, and the beauty of the Maine Coast." The school, in Lubec, offers instruction in a number of musical instruments, including piano, violin, flute, guitar, cello, and clarinet as well as in voice. Beginners are welcome.

BUILD, BUILD, BUILD YOUR BOAT

Build a boat, a canoe, a classic sea chest, or a remote-control pond yacht. Those are just a sampling from the dozens of boatbuilding and related craft courses offered each summer at the 60-acre waterfront campus of **The WoodenBoat School** (41 WoodenBoat Lane, Brooklin, 207/359-4651, www.thewoodenboat-school.com). There's even a popular family-week program. Lodging and meals packages are available.

BA IN FAMILY FUN

Explore tide pools, learn about animal tracks, discover the diversity of bats, go whale-watching, and take a hike to learn about the natural world in the process at College of the Atlantic's **Family Nature Camp** (105 Eden St., Bar Harbor, 800/597-9500, www.coa.edu/summer). This hands-on, participatory, naturalist-led program provides plenty of fodder for those "What I Did on My Summer Vacation" essays. The minimum age is five; extended families are welcome. Camp includes campus lodging, meals, field trips, and some boat tours.

TO EVERYTHING, TURN, TURN, TURN

Founded in 2004 by Ken Keoughan, the **Woodturning School** (10 Cappelletti Dr., Damariscotta, 207/380-8076, www.wood-turningschool.org) introduces students to woodturning, a woodworking skill that produces hollow vessels. All tools are provided.

FIDDLING AROUND

Learn to play the fiddle by ear at the **Maine Fiddle Camp** (207/443-5411, www.mainefiddle.org), held on the grounds of Camp NEOFA in Montville. Campers stay in rustic cabins or tents, enjoy communal meals outdoors, and there's plenty of time to swim or hang out in the afternoon before the evening concerts, dances, and jams. A weekend camp is usually held in June, with weeklong sessions offered in August.

DOES THE NAME SIKORSKY RING A BELL?

Here's a must for aviation buffs: **Bradford Camps' Sikorsky Seminar** (207/433-0660, www.bradfordcamps.com). Bradford Camps is a traditional Maine sporting camp comprising lakefront log cabins on the shores of undeveloped Munsungan Lake and a central lodge, where all meals are served. Every July, one special weekend is dedicated to the grandfather of Igor I. Sikorsky III, who operates the camps with his wife, Karen. Igor's grandfather is best known for his work in developing the helicopter, but he also built the world's first multiengine aircraft, designed and built the largest aircraft used in World War I, and later worked with large amphibians, which paved the way for commercial aviation. The Sikorsky Weekend is an opportunity to learn more about the aviation pioneer and talk shop with flight buffs while perusing books, artifacts, videos, and photos.

SURFBOARD CAMP

York's Grain Surfboards is renowned for its handcrafted wooden surfboards, but it also offers **surfboard-building classes** and a **Surfboard Builder's Fantasy Camp** (207/457-5313, www.grainsurfboards.com). The former are group programs; the latter is a one-on-one week-long program where you work with a personal board builder to craft your own perfect board.

toll-free information hotline is 888/MAINE-45—888/624-6345.

Maps

Peek in any Mainer's car and you're likely to see a copy of *The Maine Atlas and Gazetteer,* published by DeLorme Mapping Company in Yarmouth. Despite an oversize format inconvenient for hiking and kayaking, this 96-page paperbound book just about guarantees that you won't get lost (and if you're good at map reading, it can get you out of a lot of traffic jams). Scaled at 0.5 inches to the mile, it's meticulously compiled from aerial photographs, satellite images, U.S. Geological Survey maps, GPS readings, and timber-company maps, and it is revised annually. It details back roads and dirt roads and shows elevation, boat ramps, public lands, campgrounds, picnic areas, and trailheads. DeLorme products are available nationwide in book and map stores, but you can also order direct (800/452-5931, www .delorme.com). The atlas is $19.95 and shipping is $4 (Maine residents need to add 5 percent sales tax).

The Maine Tourism Association also publishes a less detailed but free state map.

MEDIA AND COMMUNICATIONS

Area Code

Maine still has only one telephone area code, 207. To call long distance in state and out of state, dial 1 plus the area code before the number. For directory assistance, dial 411.

Toll-Free Calling

Any number with an area code of 800, 888, 877, 866, 855, 844, 833, or 822 is toll-free.

Cell Phones

Transmission towers are now sprinkled pretty much throughout Maine; only a few pockets—mostly down peninsulas and in remote valleys and hollows—are out of cell-phone range. Of course, reception also varies by carrier. Still, getting reception often requires doing the cell-phone hokey-pokey—putting your left arm out, your right leg in, and so on to find the strongest signal.

Internet Access

Internet access is widely available at libraries and coffeehouses. Most hotels and many inns and bed-and-breakfasts also offer Internet access; many provide data ports or Wi-Fi.

RESOURCES

Glossary

To help you translate some of the lingo used off the beaten track at places like country stores and county fairs, farm stands, and flea markets, here's a sampling of local terms and expressions:

alewives herring

ayuh yes

barrens as in "blueberry barrens"; fields where wild blueberries grow

beamy wide (as in a boat or a person)

beans shorthand for the traditional Saturday-night meal, which always includes baked beans

blowdown a forest area leveled by wind

blowing a gale very windy

camp a vacation house (small or large), usually on freshwater and in the woods

chance serendipity or luck, as in "open by appointment or by chance"

chicken dressing chicken manure

chowder (pronounced "chowdah") soup made with lobster, clams, or fish, or a combination thereof; lobster version sometimes called lobster stew

chowderhead mischief- or troublemakers, usually interchangeable with "idiot"

coneheads tourists (because of their presumed penchant for ice cream)

cottage a vacation house (anything from a bungalow to a mansion), usually on saltwater

culch (also cultch) stuff; the contents of attics, basements, and some flea markets

cull a discount lobster, usually minus a claw

cunnin' cute, usually describing a baby or small child

dinner (pronounced "dinnah") the noon meal

dinner pail lunch box

dite a very small amount

dooryard the yard near a house's main entrance

downcellar in the basement

Down East with the prevailing wind; the old coastal sailing route from Boston to Nova Scotia

dry-ki driftwood, usually remnants from the logging industry

ell a residential structural section that links a house and a barn; formerly a popular location for the "summer kitchen," to spare the house from woodstove heat

exercised upset; angry

fiddleheads unopened ostrich-fern fronds, a spring delicacy

finest kind top quality; good news; an expression of general approval; also a term of appreciation

flatlander a person not from Maine, often but not exclusively someone from the Midwest

floatplane a small plane equipped with pontoons for landing on water; the same aircraft often becomes a ski-plane in winter

flowage a body of water created by damming, usually beaver handiwork (also called "beaver flowage")

FR Fire Road, used in mailing addresses

frappé a thick drink containing milk, ice cream, and flavored syrup, as opposed to a milkshake, which does not include ice cream (but beware: a frappé offered in other parts of the United States is an ice cream sundae topped with whipped cream)

from away not native to Maine

galamander a wheeled contraption formerly used to transport quarry granite to building sites or to boats for onward shipment

gore a sliver of land left over from inaccurate boundary surveys. Maine has several gores; Hibberts Gore, for instance, has a population of one.

got done quit a job; was let go

harbormaster local official who monitors water traffic and assigns moorings; often a very political job

hardshell lobster that hasn't molted yet (scarcer, thus more pricey in summer)

HC Home Carrier, used in mailing addresses

hod wooden "basket" used for carrying clams

ice-out the departure of winter ice from ponds, lakes, rivers, and streams; many communities have ice-out contests, awarding prizes for guessing the exact time of ice-out, in April or May

Italian long soft bread roll sliced on top and filled with peppers, onions, tomatoes, sliced meat, black olives, and sprinkled with olive oil, salt, and pepper; veggie versions available

jimmies chocolate sprinkles, like those on an ice cream cone

lobster car a large floating crate for storing lobsters

Maine Guide a member of the Maine Professional Guides Association, trained and tested for outdoor and survival skills; also called Registered Maine Guide

market price restaurant menu term for "the going rate," usually referring to the price of lobster or clams

molt what a lobster does when it sheds its shell for a larger one; the act of molting is called ecdysis (as a stripper is an ecdysiast)

money tree a collection device for a monetary gift

mud season mid-March–mid-April, when back roads and unpaved driveways become virtual tank traps

nasty neat extremely meticulous

near stingy

notional stubborn, determined

off island the mainland, to an islander

place another word for a house (as in "Herb Pendleton's place")

ployes Acadian buckwheat pancakes

pot trap, as in "lobster pot"

public landing see "town landing"

rake hand tool used for harvesting blueberries

RFD Rural Free Delivery, used in mailing addresses

roller-skiing cross-country skiing on wheels; popular among cross-country skiers, triathletes, and others as a training technique

rusticator a summer visitor, particularly in bygone days

scooch (or scootch) to squat; to move sideways

sea smoke heavy mist rising off the water when the air temperature suddenly becomes much colder than the ocean temperature

select a lobster with claws intact

Selectmen the elected men and women who handle local affairs in small communities; the First Selectman chairs meetings. In some towns, "people from away" have tried to propose substituting a gender-neutral term, but in most cases the effort has failed.

shedder a lobster with a new (soft) shell; generally occurs in July–August (more common then, thus less expensive than hardshells)

shire town county seat

shore dinner the works: chowder, clams, lobster, and sometimes corn on the cob too; usually the most expensive item on a menu

short a small, illegal-size lobster

slumgullion tasteless food; a mess

slut a poor housekeeper

slut's wool dust balls found under beds, couches, and so on

snapper an undersize, illegal lobster

soda cola, root beer, and so on (referred to as "pop" in some other parts of the country)

softshell see "shedder"

some very (as in "some hot")

spleeny overly sensitive

steamers clams, before or after they are steamed

sternman a lobsterman's helper (male or female)

summer complaint a tourist

supper (pronounced "suppah") evening meal, eaten by Mainers around 5 or 6 P.M. (as opposed to flatlanders and summer people, who eat dinner 7–9 P.M.)

tad slightly; a little bit
thick-o'-fog zero-visibility fog
to home at home
tomalley a lobster's green insides; considered a delicacy by some
town landing shore access; often a park or a parking lot, next to a wharf or boat-launch ramp

upattic in the attic
Whoopie! Pie the trademarked name for a high-fat, calorie-laden, cakelike snack that only kids and dentists could love
wicked cold frigid
wicked good excellent
williwaws uncomfortable feeling

Suggested Reading

MAPS
The Maine Atlas and Gazetteer. Yarmouth, ME: DeLorme, updated annually. You'll be hard put to get lost if you're carrying this essential volume; 70 full-page, oversize-format topographical maps with GPS grids.

LITERATURE, ART, AND PHOTOGRAPHY
Bennett, D. *Allagash: Maine's Wild and Scenic River.* Camden, ME: Down East Books, 1994. Elegant portrait of the Allagash Wilderness Waterway by a veteran Maine naturalist.

Curtis, J., W. Curtis, and F. Lieberman. *Monhegan: The Artists' Island.* Camden, ME: Down East Books, 1995. Fascinating island history interspersed with landscape and seascape paintings and drawings by more than 150 artists, including Bellows, Henri, Hopper, Kent, Porter, Tam, and Wyeth.

Maine Speaks: An Anthology of Maine Literature. Brunswick, ME: Maine Writers and Publishers Alliance, 1989.

McNair, W., ed. *The Maine Poets: An Anthology of Verse.* Camden, ME: Down East Books, 2003. McNair's selection of best works by Maine's finest poets.

Spectre, P. H. *Passage in Time.* New York: W. W. Norton, 1991. A noted marine writer cruises the coast aboard traditional windjammers; gorgeous photos complement the colorful text.

Thoreau, H. D. *The Maine Woods.* New Haven, CT: Yale University Press, 2009 [annotated edition of the 1864 original]. A Maine classic, first published two years after the author's death; mid-19th-century exploration of Maine's wilderness around Greenville, Chesuncook, Katahdin, and more.

Tobyne, D. *Thoreau's Maine Woods.* Camden, ME: Down East Books, 2010. Photographer Dan Tobyne follows in Thoreau's path, pairing book excerpts with stunning images.

Van Riper, F. *Down East Maine: A World Apart.* Camden, ME: Down East Books, 1998. Maine's Washington County, captured with incredible insight and compassion by a master photographer and insightful wordsmith.

HISTORY
Acadian Culture in Maine. Washington, DC: National Park Service, North Atlantic Region, 1994. A project report on Acadians and their traditions in the Upper St. John Valley.

Clark, Stephen. *Following Their Footsteps: A Travel Guide and History of the 1775 Secret Expedition to Capture Quebec.* Shapleigh, ME: Clark Books, 2003.

Duncan, R. F., E. G. Barlow, K. Bray, and C. Hanks. *Coastal Maine: A Maritime History.* Woodstock, VT: Countrymen Press, 2002. Updated version of the classic work.

Isaacson, D., ed. *Maine: A Guide "Down East,"* 2nd ed. Maine League of Historical Societies and Museums, 1970. Revised version of the Depression-era Works Progress Administration guidebook, still interesting for background reading.

Jaster, R. S. *Russian Voices on the Kennebec: The Story of Maine's Unlikely Colony.* Orono, ME: University of Maine Press, 1999. A riveting account of the founding of a Russian-speaking colony in Richmond, Maine, in the 1950s. Superb historical photographs.

Judd, R. W., E. A. Churchill, and J. W. Eastman, eds. *Maine: The Pine Tree State from Prehistory to the Present.* Orono, ME: University of Maine Press, 1995. The best available Maine history, with excellent historical maps.

Paine, L. P. *Down East: A Maritime History of Maine.* Gardiner, ME: Tilbury House, 2000. A noted maritime historian provides an enlightening introduction to the state's seafaring tradition.

LOBSTERS AND LIGHTHOUSES

Bachelder, Peter Dow, and P. M. Mason. *Maine Lighthouse Map and Guide.* Glendale, CO: Bella Terra Publishing, 2009. An illustrated map and guide providing directions on how to find all Maine beacons as well as brief histories.

Caldwell, W. *Lighthouses of Maine.* Camden, ME: Down East Books, 2002. A historical tour of Maine's lighthouses, with the emphasis on history, legends, and lore.

Corson, T. *The Secret Life of Lobsters.* New York: HarperCollins, 2004. Everything you wanted—or perhaps didn't want—to know about lobster.

Woodward, C. *The Lobster Coast: Rebels, Rusticators, and the Struggle for a Forgotten Frontier.* New York: Viking, 2004. A veteran journalist's take on the history of the Maine Coast.

MEMOIRS

Dawson, L. B. *Saltwater Farm.* Westford, ME: Impatiens Press, 1993. Witty, charming stories of growing up on the Cushing peninsula.

Greenlaw, L. *The Lobster Chronicles: Life on a Very Small Island.* New York: Hyperion, 2002. Swordfishing boat captain Linda Greenlaw's account of returning to life on Isle au Haut after weathering *The Perfect Storm.*

Hamlin, H. *Nine Mile Bridge: Three Years in the Maine Woods.* Yarmouth and Frenchboro, ME: Islandport Press, 2006 [orig. pub. 1945]. Hamlin's experiences as a teacher at a remote lumber camp near the headwaters of the Allagash River, where her husband was a game warden.

Lunt, D. L. *Hauling by Hand: The Life and Times of a Maine Island,* 2nd ed. Frenchboro, ME: Islandport Press, 2007. A sensitive history of Frenchboro (a.k.a. Long Island), eight miles offshore, written by an eighth-generation islander and journalist.

Szelog, T. M. *Our Point of View: Fourteen Years at a Maine Lighthouse.* Camden, ME: Down East Books, 2007. A professional photographer documents in words and photos 14 years at Marsha Point Lighthouse.

NATURAL HISTORY

Bennett, D. *Maine's Natural Heritage: Rare Species and Unique Natural Features.* Camden, ME: Down East Books, 1988. A dated book that examines both the special ecology of the state and how it's threatened.

Conkling, P. W. *Islands in Time: A Natural and Cultural History of the Islands of the Gulf of Maine,* 2nd ed. Camden, ME: Down East Books, and Rockland, ME: Island Institute, 1999. A thoughtful overview by the president of Maine's Island Institute.

Dwelley, M. J. *Spring Wildflowers of New England,* 2nd ed. Camden, ME: Down East Books, 2000. Back in print after several years, this beautifully illustrated gem is an essential guide for exploring spring woodlands.

Dwelley, M. J. *Summer and Fall Wildflowers of New England,* 2nd ed. Camden, ME: Down East Books, 2004. Flowers are grouped by color; more than 700 lovely colored-pencil drawings simplify identification.

Kendall, D. L. *Glaciers and Granite: A Guide to Maine's Landscape and Geology.* Unity, ME: North Country Press, 1993. Explains why Maine looks the way it does.

Maine's Ice Age Trail Down East Map and Guide. Orono, ME: University of Maine Press, 2007. Information on 46 glacial sites, also available online at http://iceagetrail.umaine.edu.

RECREATION
Acadia National Park and Mount Desert Island

Monkman, J., and M. Monkman. *Discover Acadia National Park: A Guide to the Best Hiking, Biking, and Paddling,* 2nd ed. Boston: Appalachian Mountain Club Books, 2005. A comprehensive guide to well-chosen hikes, bike trips, and paddling routes, accompanied by an excellent pullout map.

Nangle, H. *Moon Acadia National Park,* 3rd ed. Berkeley, CA: Avalon Travel, 2009. A Mainer since childhood and veteran travel writer is the ideal escort for exploring this region in depth.

Roberts, A. R. *Mr. Rockefeller's Roads.* Camden, ME: Down East Books, 1990. The story behind Acadia's scenic carriage roads, written by the granddaughter of John D. Rockefeller, who created them.

St. Germain, T. A. Jr. *A Walk in the Park: Acadia's Hiking Guide,* 10th ed. Bar Harbor, ME: Parkman Publications, 2004. The best Acadia National Park hiking guide, in a handy

Michelin-type vertical format. Part of the proceeds go to Friends of Acadia's Acadia Trails Forever campaign.

Bicycling

Stone, H. *25 Bicycle Tours in Maine: Coastal and Inland Rides from Kittery to Caribou,* 3d ed. Woodstock, VT: Countryman Press/ Backcountry Guides, 1998.

Birding

Duchesne, B. *Maine Birding Trail: The Official Guide to more than 260 Accessible Sites.* Camden, ME: Down East Books, 2009. Authorized guide to the Maine Birding Trail.

Pierson, E. C., J. E. Pierson, and P. D. Vickery. *A Birder's Guide to Maine.* Camden, ME: Down East Books, 1996. An expanded version of *A Birder's Guide to the Coast of Maine.* No ornithologist, novice or expert, should explore Maine without this valuable guide.

Boating

AMC River Guide: Maine, 4th ed. Boston: Appalachian Mountain Club Books, 2008. Detailed guide to canoeing or kayaking Maine's large and small rivers.

The Maine Island Trail: Stewardship Handbook and Guidebook. Rockland, ME: Maine Island Trail Association, updated annually. Available only with MITA membership (annual dues $45), providing access to dozens of islands along the watery trail.

Miller, D. *Kayaking the Maine Coast: A Paddler's Guide to Day Trips from Kittery to Cobscook,* 2nd ed. Woodstock, VT: Countryman Press/Backcountry Guides, 2006. A well-researched volume by a veteran kayaker.

The Northern Forest Canoe Trail: Enjoy 740 Miles of Canoe and Kayak Destinations in New York, Vermont, Quebec, New Hampshire, and

Maine. Seattle, WA: Mountaineers Books, 2010. Details and maps the waterway, including highlights en route.

Taft, H., J. Taft, and C. Rindlaub. *A Cruising Guide to the Maine Coast,* 5th ed. Peaks Island, ME: Diamond Pass Publishing, 2008. Don't even consider cruising the coast without this volume.

Wilson, A., and J. Hayes. *Quiet Water Maine: Canoe Guides,* 2nd ed. Boston: Appalachian Mountain Club Books, 2005. Comprehensive handbook with helpful maps for inland paddling.

Hiking and Walking

AMC Maine Mountain Guide, 9th ed. Boston: Appalachian Mountain Club Books, 2005. The definitive statewide resource for going vertical, in a handy small format.

Clark, Stephen. *Katahdin: A Guide to Baxter State Park and Katahdin,* 6th ed. Shapleigh, ME: Clark Books, 2009. The most comprehensive guide to Katahdin and Baxter State Park.

Collins, Jan M. *Nature Walks in Southern Maine.* Boston: Appalachian Mountain Club Books, 1996. Easy walks, mostly horizontal, and good natural-history commentary. Maps are primitive but do the job.

Collins, J., and J. E. McCarthy. *Cobscook Trails: A Guide to Walking Opportunities around Cobscook Bay and the Bold Coast,* 2d ed. Whiting, ME: Quoddy Regional Land Trust, 2000. Essential handbook for exploring this part of the Down East Coast, with excellent maps.

Gibson, J. *50 Hikes in Coastal and Inland Maine,* 4th ed. Woodstock, VT: Countryman Press/ Backcountry Guides, 2001. Well-researched, detailed resource by a veteran hiker.

Keene, C. *North Woods Walks: A Collection of Hikes in Northern Maine,* 2nd ed. Greenville Junction, ME: Tahdin Books, 2010.

Roberts, P. *On the Trail in Lincoln County.* Newcastle and Damariscotta, ME: Lincoln County Publishing, 2003. A great guide to more than 60 walks in preserves from Wiscasset through Waldoboro, with detailed directions to trailheads.

Ronan, Ray, ed. *Appalachian Trail Guide to Maine,* 15th ed. Maine Appalachian Trail Club, 2000. The official guide to Maine's 281 miles of the trail.

Wiser, Marita. *Hikes in and around Maine's Lake Region.* Williston, VT: Peregrine Outfitters, 2004.

Internet Resources

GENERAL INFORMATION
State of Maine
www.maine.gov
Everything you wanted to know about Maine and then some, with links to all government departments and Maine-related sites. Buy a fishing license online, reserve a campsite at Lamoine State Park (near Acadia), or check the fall foliage conditions via the site's Leaf Cam. (You can also access foliage info at www.

mainefoliage.com, where you can sign up for weekly email foliage reports in September and early October.) Also listed is information on accessible arts and recreation.

Maine Office of Tourism
www.visitmaine.com
The biggest and most useful of all Maine-related tourism sites, with sections for where to visit, where to stay, things to do, trip planning,

packages, and search capabilities as well lodging specials and a comprehensive calendar of events.

Maine Tourism Association
www.mainetourism.com
Find lodging, camping, restaurants, attractions, services, and more as well as links for weather, foliage, transportation planning, and chambers of commerce.

Maine Emergency
Management Association
www.state.me.us/mema/weather/weather.htm
Five-day weather forecasts broken down by 32 zones.

Maine Campground
Owners Association
www.campmaine.com
Find private campgrounds statewide.

Portland Papers
www.mainetoday.com
Home site for Maine's largest newspapers has current news as well as extensive information on travel, outdoor activities, entertainment, and sports.

Maine Travel Maven
www.mainetravelmaven.com
Moon Maine author Hilary Nangle's site for keeping readers updated on what's happening throughout the state.

TRANSPORTATION
Explore Maine
www.exploremaine.org
An invaluable site for trip planning, with information on and links to airports, rail service, bus service, automobile travel, and ferries as well as links to other key travel-planning sites.

Maine Department of Transportation
www.511maine.gov
Provides real-time information about major delays, accidents, road construction, and weather conditions. You can get the same info and more by dialing 511 in-state.

PARKS AND RECREATION
Department of Conservation, Maine Bureau of Parks and Lands
www.parksandlands.com
Information on state parks, public reserved lands, and state historic sites as well as details on facilities such as campsites, picnic areas, and boat launches. Make state campground reservations online.

Acadia National Park
www.nps.gov/acad
Information on all sections of Acadia National Park. Make ANP campground reservations online.

Baxter State Park
www.baxterstateparkauthority.com
Everything you need for planning a trip to Baxter.

Maine Audubon
www.maineaudubon.org
Information about Maine Audubon's eco-sensitive headquarters in Falmouth and all of the organization's environmental centers statewide. Activity and program schedules are included.

North Maine Woods
www.northmainewoods.org
Essential information for venturing into the privately owned North Woods.

The Nature Conservancy
www.nature.org/wherewework/northamerica/states/maine
Information about Maine preserves, field trips, and events.

Maine Land Trust Network
www.mltn.org
Maine has dozens of land trusts statewide, managing lands that provide opportunities

for hiking, walking, canoeing, kayaking, and other such activities.

Maine Department of Inland Fisheries and Wildlife
www.state.me.us/ifw
Info on wildlife, hunting, fishing, snowmobiling, and boating.

Healthy Maine Walks
www.healthymainewalks.com
Lists places for walking statewide.

Bicycle Coalition of Maine
www.bikemaine.org
Tons of information for bicyclists, including routes, shops, events, organized rides, and much more.

Maine Birding
www.mainebirding.net
A must-visit site for anyone interested in learning more about bird-watching in Maine, including news, checklists, events, forums, trips, and more.

Maine Windjammer Association
www.sailmainecoast.com
Windjammer schooners homeported in Rockland, Camden, and Rockport belong to this umbrella organization; there are links to the websites of all the vessels for online and phone information and reservations.

Ski Maine
www.skimaine.com
The go-to source for information on alpine skiing in Maine.

ARTS, ANTIQUES, AND MUSEUMS
Maine Archives and Museums
www.mainemuseums.org
Information on and links to museums, archives, historical societies, and historic sites in Maine.

Maine Art Museum Trail
www.maineartmuseums.org
Information on art museums with significant collections statewide, including the Ogunquit Museum of Art in Ogunquit, the Portland Museum of Art in Portland, Bowdoin College Museum of Art in Brunswick, and Farnsworth Art Museum in Rockland.

Maine Antiques Dealers Association
www.maineantiques.org
Lists member dealers statewide by location and specialty and provides information on upcoming antiques events.

FOOD AND DRINK
Maine Department of Agriculture
www.getrealmaine.com
Information on all things agricultural, including fairs, farmers markets, farm vacations, places to buy Maine foods, berry- and apple-picking sites, and more.

Portland Food Map
www.portlandfoodmap.com
A must for culinary travel in Maine's largest city. Information on anything and everything food- and drink-related, including openings and closings and links to reviews.

Index

List of Maps

www.moon.com

DESTINATIONS | ACTIVITIES | BLOGS | MAPS | BOOKS

MOON.COM is ready to help plan your next trip! Filled with fresh trip ideas and strategies, author interviews, informative travel blogs, a detailed map library, and descriptions of all the Moon guidebooks, Moon.com is all you need to get out and explore the world—or even places in your own backyard. While at Moon.com, sign up for our monthly e-newsletter for updates on new releases, travel tips, and expert advice from our on-the-go Moon authors. As always, when you travel with Moon, expect an experience that is uncommon and truly unique.

MOON IS ON FACEBOOK—BECOME A FAN!
JOIN THE MOON PHOTO GROUP ON FLICKR

MAP SYMBOLS

▭▭	Expressway	【	Highlight	✗	Airfield	⚲	Golf Course
▭▭	Primary Road	○	City/Town	✈	Airport	P	Parking Area
▭▭	Secondary Road	◉	State Capital	▲	Mountain	▰	Archaeological Site
▭▭	Unpaved Road	⊛	National Capital	✛	Unique Natural Feature	♠	Church
------	Trail	★	Point of Interest			♎	Gas Station
·········	Ferry	•	Accommodation	⟋	Waterfall	◯	Glacier
▭▭	Railroad	▼	Restaurant/Bar	▲	Park	◻	Mangrove
▭▭	Pedestrian Walkway	▪	Other Location	⬛	Trailhead	◻	Reef
▭▭	Stairs	ᴧ	Campground	✖	Skiing Area	◻	Swamp

CONVERSION TABLES

$°C = (°F - 32) / 1.8$
$°F = (°C \times 1.8) + 32$
1 inch = 2.54 centimeters (cm)
1 foot = 0.304 meters (m)
1 yard = 0.914 meters
1 mile = 1.6093 kilometers (km)
1 km = 0.6214 miles
1 fathom = 1.8288 m
1 chain = 20.1168 m
1 furlong = 201.168 m
1 acre = 0.4047 hectares
1 sq km = 100 hectares
1 sq mile = 2.59 square km
1 ounce = 28.35 grams
1 pound = 0.4536 kilograms
1 short ton = 0.90718 metric ton
1 short ton = 2,000 pounds
1 long ton = 1.016 metric tons
1 long ton = 2,240 pounds
1 metric ton = 1,000 kilograms
1 quart = 0.94635 liters
1 US gallon = 3.7854 liters
1 Imperial gallon = 4.5459 liters
1 nautical mile = 1.852 km

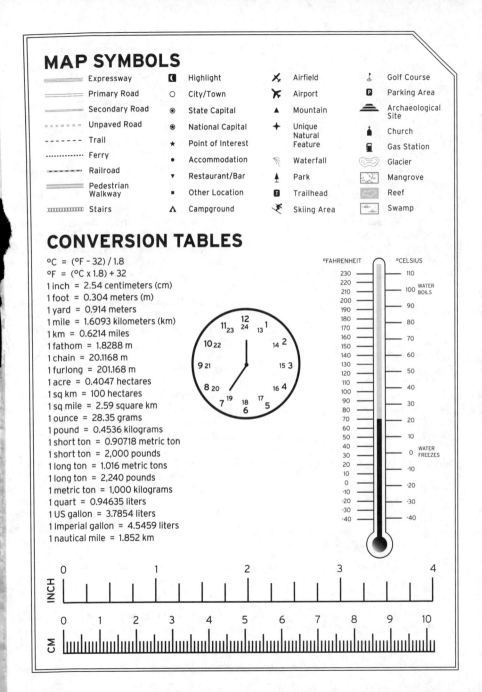

MOON MAINE
Avalon Travel
a member of the Perseus Books Group
1700 Fourth Street
Berkeley, CA 94710, USA
www.moon.com

Editor: Erin Raber
Series Manager: Kathryn Ettinger
Copy Editor: Christopher Church
Graphics Coordinator: Kathryn Osgood
Production Coordinators: Lucie Ericksen,
   Sean Bellows
Cover Designer: Lucie Ericksen
Map Editor: Brice Ticen
Cartographers: Kat Bennett, Albert Angulo,
   Chris Henrick
Indexer: Greg Jewett

ISBN: 978-1-59880-746-2
ISSN: 1531-5606

Printing History
1st Edition – 1998
5th Edition – July 2011
5 4 3 2 1

Front cover photo: *Margaret Todd* Windjammer Boat
   Tour at Bar Harbor © Laurie Chamberlain/Corbis
Title page photo: Maine's Western Mountains ©
   Hilary Nangle
Other front matter photos: pages 6, 7 left, 8, 9
   bottom, 10-13, 16-18, 20 top, 22-24: © Hilary Nangle;
   pages 7 middle and right, 9 top, 20 bottom, 21: ©
   Tom Nangle; page 19: © Greater Portland CVB

Printed in Canada by Friesens

KEEPING CURRENT

If you have a favorite gem you'd like to see included in the next edition, or see anything
that needs updating, clarification, or correction, please drop us a line. Send your
comments via email to feedback@moon.com, or use the address above.